The Oxford Spanish Language Program

The Oxford Spanish Language Program marks the start of a new age of Spanish Dictionaries. The Program has produced, with unrivaled clarity and authority, the only dictionaries to present the full wealth of Spanish from both sides of the Atlantic and across 24 different Spanish-speaking countries and regions.

The Bank of Spanish

Drawing on The Bank of Spanish, electronic databases of up-to-date, authentic language in use, these dictionaries provide a more accurate and complete picture of real language than has been possible before. The Bank shapes every dictionary entry and translation to meet the needs of today's users, highlighting important constructions, illustrating difficult meanings, and focusing attention on common usage.

The richest choice of words

Rich coverage of over 24 different regional varieties of Spanish with special emphasis on modern idioms and colloquial usage are distinctive elements of the Oxford Spanish Language Program. Words and phrases restricted to particular areas of the Spanish-speaking world are precisely labeled for country or wider region, from Spain to Chile to Mexico, from Central America to the River Plate. In addition, variant pronunciations and the degree of formality of words, from formal right through to taboo, are signaled wherever necessary.

The Spanish Literary Heritage

A wide range of vocabulary and usage found in the literary heritage of the Spanish-speaking world has been analyzed and described by the editors of the Program to assist readers and students of Spanish literature.

Total Language Accessibility

For over 150 years Oxford's hallmarks of integrity and authority have been adapted to meet the changing needs of dictionary users. Oxford's range of Spanish dictionaries are an integral part of this tradition and offer an unequalled range of carefully designed benefits to ensure maximum language accessibility.

Rapid access design

Oxford's new quick-access page designs and typography have been specially created to ensure exceptional clarity and accessibility. Paper and binding styles are carefully selected for their durability. Entries are written in clear, jargon-free language without confusing abbreviations.

Unrivalled practical help

Unrivalled practical grammatical help has been built into every dictionary within the range. Concise in-text notes and special Language Usage Panels address complex points of grammar and sets of words which behave in the same way. Generous numbers of examples, drawn from the evidence of the Bank of Spanish, are carefully selected to illustrate the many different nuances of meaning and context.

Supplementary Information

All the dictionaries in the Oxford range offer valuable additional help and information, which can include regular and irregular verbs tables, thematic vocabulary boxes, political and cultural information, guides to effective communication (how to write letters, CVs, book holidays, or take minutes), two colour texts, and pronunciation guidance.

The best range in the World

Oxford provides Spanish dictionaries for all levels of user, from advanced to beginner. In addition Oxford also publishes a wealth of Spanish reference titles, including guides to Spanish grammar, usage, verbs, correspondence and core vocabulary. Whatever type of dictionary — whether for children, native speakers, university students or learners; on paper or CD-ROM; in English, French, Spanish, German, Italian, Russian, Japanese, Latin, Greek, Arabic, Turkish, Portuguese, Hungarian, Hindi, Gujarati or Chinese — Oxford offers the most trusted range available anywhere in the world today.

The Oxford

Color

Spanish
Dictionary

Revised Edition

Spanish–English
English–Spanish

Español–Inglés
Inglés–Español

Christine Lea

*Word games
prepared by
Michael Britton*

Oxford   New York

OXFORD UNIVERSITY PRESS

1998

Oxford University Press, Great Clarendon Street, Oxford, OX2 6DP

Oxford New York

Athens Auckland Bangkok Bogota Bombay Buenos Aires
Calcutta Cape Town Dar es Salaam Delhi
Florence Hong Kong Istanbul Karachi
Kuala Lumpur Madras Madrid Melbourne
Mexico City Nairobi Paris Singapore
Taipei Tokyo Toronto Warsaw
and associated companies in
Berlin Ibadan

Oxford is a trade mark of Oxford University Press

© Oxford University Press 1995, 1998
First published 1993 as The Oxford Spanish Minidictionary
First issued as an Oxford University Press Paperback 1994
Two-colour edition first published 1995

This edition first published 1998

British Library Cataloguing in Publication Data
Data available

Library of Congress Cataloging in Publication Data
Data available

ISBN 0-19-8602146

10 9 8 7 6 5 4 3 2

Typeset by Pentacor PLC
Printed in Spain by
Mateu Cromo Artes Graficas S.A.
Madrid

Contents • Índice

Preface to the revised edition

The Oxford Color Spanish Dictionary is a dictionary designed for beginners of Spanish. The clear presentation and color headwords make it easily accessible. This new edition includes word games which are specifically designed to build key skills in using your dictionary more effectively, and to improve knowledge of Spanish vocabulary and usage in a fun and entertaining way. You will find answers to all puzzles and games at the end of the section.

Preface

This dictionary has been written with speakers of both English and Spanish in mind and contains the most useful words and expressions of the English and Spanish languages of today. Wide coverage of culinary and motoring terms has been included to help the tourist.

Common abbreviations, names of countries, and other useful geographical names are included.

English pronunciation is given by means of the International Phonetic Alphabet. It is shown for all headwords and for those derived words whose pronunciation is not easily deduced from that of a headword. The rules for pronunciation of Spanish are given on page x.

I should like to thank particularly Mary-Carmen Beaven, whose comments have been invaluable. I would also like to acknowledge the help given to me unwittingly by Dr M. Janes and Mrs J. Andrews, whose French and Italian Minidictionaries have served as models for the present work.

C. A. L

Prefacio

Este diccionario de Oxford se escribió tanto para los hablantes de español como para los hablantes de inglés y contiene las palabras y frases más corrientes de ambas lenguas de hoy. Se incluyen muchos términos culinarios y de automovilismo que pueden servir al turista.

Las abreviaturas más corrientes, los nombres de países, y otros términos geográficos figuran en este diccionario.

La pronunciación inglesa sigue el Alfabeto Fonético Internacional. Se incluye para cada palabra clave y todas las derivadas cuya pronunciación no es fácil de deducir a partir de la palabra clave. Las reglas de la pronunciación española se encuentran en la página x.

Quisiera agradecer la ayuda de Mary-Carmen Beaven, cuyas observaciones me han sido muy valiosas. También quiero expresar mi agradecimiento al Dr. M. Janes y a la Sra. J. Andrews, cuyos minidiccionarios de francés y de italiano me han servido de modelo para el presente.

C. A. L

Introduction

As an aid to easy reference in this dictionary all main headwords, compounds and derivatives appear in blue. The swung dash (~) is used to replace a headword or that part of a headword preceding the vertical bar (|). In both English and Spanish only irregular plurals are given. Normally Spanish nouns and adjectives ending in an unstressed vowel form the plural by adding *s* (e.g. *libro, libros*). Nouns and adjectives ending in a stressed vowel or a consonant add *es* (e.g. *rubí, rubíes, pared, paredes*). An accent on the final syllable is not required when *es* is added (e.g. *nación, naciones*). Final *z* becomes *ces* (e.g. *vez, veces*). Spanish nouns and adjectives ending in *o* form the feminine by changing the final *o* to *a* (e.g. *hermano, hermana*). Most Spanish nouns and adjectives ending in anything other than final *o* do not have a separate feminine form with the exception of those denoting nationality etc.; these add *a* to the masculine singular form (e.g. *español, española*). An accent on the final syllable is then not required (e.g. *inglés, inglesa*). Adjectives ending in *án, ón,* or *or* behave like those denoting nationality with the following exceptions: *inferior, mayor, mejor, menor, peor, superior*, where the feminine has the same form as the masculine. Spanish verb tables will be found in the appendix.

The Spanish alphabet

In Spanish *ch, ll* and *ñ* are considered separate letters and in the Spanish–English section, therefore, they will be found after *cu, lu'* and *ny* respectively.

Introducción

Con el propósito de facilitar la consulta, las cabezas de artículo, los compuestos y los derivados aparecen en azul. La tilde (∼) se emplea para sustituir la palabra cabeza de artículo o aquella parte de tal palabra que precede a la barra vertical (|). Tanto en inglés como en español se dan los plurales solamente si son irregulares. Para formar el plural regular en inglés se añade la letra *s* al sustantivo singular, pero se añade *es* cuando se trata de una palabra que termina en *ch, sh, s, ss, us, x, o, z* (p.ej. *sash, sashes*). En el caso de una palabra que termine en *y* precedida por una consonante, la *y* se transforma en *ies* (p.ej. *baby, babies*). Para formar el tiempo pasado y el participio pasado se añade *ed* al infinitivo de los verbos regulares ingleses (p.ej. *last, lasted*). En el caso de los verbos ingleses que terminan en *e* muda se añade sólo la *d* (p.ej. *move, moved*). En el caso de los verbos ingleses que terminan en *y*-hay que cambiar la *y* por *ied* (p.ej. *carry, carried*). Los verbos irregulares se encuentran en el diccionario por orden alfabético remitidos al infinitivo, y también en la lista del apéndice.

Pronunciation of Spanish

Vowels:

a   between pronunciation of *a* in English *cat* and *arm*

e   like *e* in English *bed*

i   like *ee* in English *see* but a little shorter

o   like *o* in English *hot* but a little longer

u   like *oo* in English *too*

y   when a vowel is as Spanish **i**

Consonants

b   (1) in initial position or after nasal consonant is like English *b*

     (2) in other positions is between English *b* and English *v*

c   (1) before **e** or **i** is like *th* in English *thin*

     (2) in other positions is like *c* in English *cat*

ch like *ch* in English *chip*

d   (1) in initial position, after nasal consonants and after **l** is like English **d**

     (2) in other positions is like *th* in English *this*

f   like English *f*

g   (1) before **e** or **i** is like *ch* in Scottish *loch*

     (2) in initial position is like *g* in English *get*

     (3) in other positions is like (2) but a little softer

h   silent in Spanish but see also **ch**

j   like *ch* in Scottish *loch*

k   like English *k*

l   like English *l* but see also **ll**

ll   like *lli* in English *million*

m   like English *m*

n	like English *n*
ñ	like *ni* in English *opinion*
p	like English *p*
q	like English *k*
r	rolled or trilled
s	like *s* in English *sit*
t	like English *t*
v	(1) in initial position or after nasal consonant is like English *b*
	(2) in other positions is between English *b* and English *v*
w	like Spanish **b** or **v**
x	like English *x*
y	like English *y*
z	like *th* in English *thin*

Pronunciación Inglesa

Símbolos fonéticos

Vocales y diptongos

iː	*see*	ɔː	*saw*	eɪ	p*a*ge	ɔɪ	j*oi*n
ɪ	s*i*t	ʊ	p*u*t	əʊ	h*o*me	ɪə	n*ea*r
e	t*e*n	uː	t*oo*	aɪ	f*i*ve	eə	h*ai*r
æ	h*a*t	ʌ	c*u*p	aɪə	f*i*re	ʊə	p*oo*r
ɑ	*ar*m	ɔː	f*u*r	aʊ	n*ow*		
ɒ	g*o*t	ə	*a*go	aʊə	fl*our*		

Consonantes

p	*p*en	tʃ	*ch*in	s	*s*o	n	*n*o
b	*b*ad	dʒ	*J*une	z	*z*oo	ŋ	si*ng*
t	*t*ea	f	*f*all	ʃ	*sh*e	l	*l*eg
d	*d*ip	v	*v*oice	ʒ	mea*s*ure	r	*r*ed
k	*c*at	θ	*th*in	h	*h*ow	j	*y*es
g	*g*ot	ð	*th*en	m	*m*an	w	*w*et

Abbreviations / Abreviaturas

adjective	*a*	adjetivo
abbreviation	*abbr /abrev*	abreviatura
administration	*admin*	administración
adverb	*adv*	adverbio
American	*Amer*	americano
anatomy	*anat*	anatomía
architecture	*archit /arquit*	arquitectura
definite article	*art def*	artículo definido
indefinite article	*art indef*	artículo indefinido
astrology	*astr*	astrología
motoring	*auto*	automóvil
auxiliary	*aux*	auxiliar
aviation	*aviat /aviac*	aviación
biology	*biol*	biología
botany	*bot*	botánica
commerce	*com*	comercio
conjunction	*conj*	conjunción
cookery	*culin*	cocina
electricity	*elec*	electricidad
school	*escol*	enseñanza
Spain	*Esp*	España
feminine	*f*	femenino
familiar	*fam*	familiar
figurative	*fig*	figurado
philosophy	*fil*	filosofía
photography	*foto*	fotografía
geography	*geog*	geografía
geology	*geol*	geología
grammar	*gram*	gramática
humorous	*hum*	humorístico
interjection	*int*	interjección
interrogative	*inter*	interrogativo
invariable	*invar*	invariable
legal, law	*jurid*	jurídico
Latin American	*LAm*	latinoamericano
language	*lang*	lengua(je)
masculine	*m*	masculino
mathematics	*mat(h)*	matemáticas

mechanics	*mec*	mecánica
medicine	*med*	medicina
military	*mil*	militar
music	*mus*	música
mythology	*myth*	mitología
noun	*n*	nombre
nautical	*naut*	náutica
oneself	*o. s.*	uno mismo, se
proprietary term	*P*	marca registrada
pejorative	*pej*	peyorativo
philosophy	*phil*	filosofía
photography	*photo*	fotografía
plural	*pl*	plural
politics	*pol*	política
possessive	*poss*	posesivo
past participle	*pp*	participio pasado
prefix	*pref*	prefijo
preposition	*prep*	preposición
present participle	*pres p*	participio de presente
pronoun	*pron*	pronombre
psychology	*psych*	psicología
past tense	*pt*	tiempo pasado
railroad	*rail*	ferrocarril
relative	*rel*	relativo
religion	*relig*	religión
school	*schol*	enseñanza
singular	*sing*	singular
slang	*sl*	argot
someone	*s. o.*	alguien
something	*sth*	algo
technical	*tec*	técnico
television	*TV*	televisión
university	*univ*	universidad
auxiliary verb	*v aux*	verbo auxiliar
verb	*vb*	verbo
intransitive verb	*vi*	verbo intransitivo
pronominal verb	*vpr*	verbo pronominal
transitive verb	*vt*	verbo transitivo
transitive & intransitive verb	*vti*	verbo transitivo e intransitivo

Proprietary terms

A

a *prep* in, at; (*dirección*) to; (*tiempo*) at; (*hasta*) to, until; (*fecha*) on; (*más tarde*) later; (*medio*) by; (*precio*) for, at. ~ **5 km** 5 km away. ¿~ **cuántos estamos?** what's the date? ~**l día siguiente** the next day. ~ **la francesa** in the French fashion. ~ **las 2** at 2 o'clock. ~ **los 25 años** (*edad*) at the age of 25; (*después de*) after 25 years. ~ **no ser por** but for. ~ **que** I bet. ~ **28 de febrero** on the 28th of February

ábaco *m* abacus

abad *m* abbot

abadejo *m* (*pez*) cod

abad|esa *f* abbess. ~**ía** *f* abbey

abajo *adv* (down) below; (*dirección*) down(wards); (*en casa*) downstairs. ● *int* down with. **calle** ~ down the street. **el** ~ **firmante** the undersigned. **escaleras** ~ downstairs. **la parte de** ~ the bottom part. **los de** ~ those at the bottom. **más** ~ below.

abalanzarse [10] *vpr* rush towards

abalorio *m* glass bead

abanderado *m* standard-bearer

abandon|ado *adj* abandoned; (*descuidado*) neglected; (*personas*) untidy. ~**ar** *vt* leave (*un lugar*); abandon (*personas, cosas*). ● *vi* give up. ~**arse** *vpr* give in; (*descuidarse*) let o.s. go. ~**o** *m* abandonment; (*estado*) abandon

abani|car [7] *vt* fan. ~**co** *m* fan. ~**queo** *m* fanning

abarata|miento *m* reduction in price. ~**r** *vt* reduce. ~**rse** *vpr* (*precios*) come down

abarca *f* sandal

abarcar [7] *vt* put one's arms around, embrace; (*comprender*) embrace; (*LAm, acaparar*) monopolize

abarquillar *vt* warp. ~**se** *vpr* warp

abarrotar *vt* overfill, pack full

abarrotes *mpl* (*LAm*) groceries

abast|ecer [11] *vt* supply. ~**ecimiento** *m* supply; (*acción*) supplying. ~**o** *m* supply. **dar** ~**o a** supply

abati|do *a* depressed. ~**miento** *m* depression. ~**r** *vt* knock down, demolish; (*fig, humillar*) humiliate. ~**rse** *vpr* swoop (**sobre** on); (*ponerse abatido*) get depressed

abdica|ción *f* abdication. ~**r** [7] *vt* give up. ● *vi* abdicate

abdom|en *m* abdomen. ~**inal** *a* abdominal

abec|é *m* (*fam*) alphabet, ABC. ~**edario** *m* alphabet

abedul *m* birch (tree)

abej|a *f* bee. ~**arrón** *m* bumble-bee. ~**ón** *m* drone. ~**orro** *m* bumble-bee; (*insecto coleóptero*) cockchafer

aberración *f* aberration

abertura *f* opening

abet|al *m* fir wood. ~**o** *m* fir (tree)

abierto *pp véase* **abrir**. ● *a* open

abigarra|do *a* multi-coloured; (*fig, mezclado*) mixed. ~**miento** *m* variegation

abigeato *m* (*Mex*) rustling

abism|al *a* abysmal; (*profundo*) deep. ~**ar** *vt* throw into an abyss; (*fig, abatir*) humble. ~**arse** *vpr* be absorbed (**en** in), be lost (**en** in). ~**o** *m* abyss; (*fig, diferencia*) world of difference

abizcochado *a* spongy

abjura|ción *f* abjuration. ~**r** *vt* forswear. ● *vi*. ~**r de** forswear

abland|a|miento *m* softening. ~**r** *vt* soften. ~**rse** *vpr* soften

ablución *f* ablution

abnega|ción *f* self-sacrifice. ~**do** *a* self-sacrificing

abob|a|do *a* silly. ~**miento** *m* silliness

aboca|do *a* (*vino*) medium. ~**r** [7] *vt* pour out

abocetar *vt* sketch

abocinado *a* trumpet-shaped

abochornar *vt* suffocate; *(fig, avergonzar)* embarrass. **~se** *vpr* feel embarrassed; *(plantas)* wilt

abofetear *vt* slap

aboga|cía *f* legal profession. **~do** *m* lawyer; *(notario)* solicitor; *(en el tribunal)* barrister, attorney *(Amer)*. **~r** [12] *vi* plead

abolengo *m* ancestry

aboli|ción *f* abolition. **~cionismo** *m* abolitionism. **~cionista** *m & f* abolitionist. **~r** [24] *vt* abolish

abolsado *a* baggy

abolla|dura *f* dent. **~r** *vt* dent

abomba|do *a* convex; *(Arg, borracho)* drunk. **~r** *vt* make convex. **~rse** *vpr* *(LAm, corromperse)* start to rot, go bad

abomina|ble *a* abominable. **~ción** *f* abomination. **~r** *vt* detest. ● *vi.* **~ de** detest

abona|ble *a* payable. **~do** *a* paid. ● *m* subscriber

abonanzar *vi* *(tormenta)* abate; *(tiempo)* improve

abon|ar *vt* pay; *(en agricultura)* fertilize. **~aré** [24] *m* promissory note. **~arse** *vpr* subscribe. **~o** *m* payment; *(estiércol)* fertilizer; *(a un periódico)* subscription

aborda|ble *a* reasonable; *(persona)* approachable. **~je** *m* boarding. **~r** *vt* tackle *(un asunto)*; approach *(una persona)*; *(naut)* come alongside

aborigen *a & m* native

aborrascarse [7] *vpr* get stormy

aborrec|er [11] *vt* hate; *(exasperar)* annoy. **~ible** *a* loathsome. **~ido** *a* hated. **~imiento** *m* hatred

aborregado *a* *(cielo)* mackerel

abort|ar *vi* have a miscarriage. **~ivo** *a* abortive. **~o** *m* miscarriage; *(voluntario)* abortion; *(fig, monstruo)* abortion. **hacerse ~ar** have an abortion

abotaga|miento *m* swelling. **~rse** [12] *vpr* swell up

abotonar *vt* button (up)

aboveda|do *a* vaulted. **~r** *vt* vault

abra *f* cove

abracadabra *m* abracadabra

abrasa|dor *a* burning. **~r** *vt* burn; *(fig, consumir)* consume. **~rse** *vpr* burn

abrasi|ón *f* abrasion; *(geología)* erosion. **~vo** *a* abrasive

abraz|adera *f* bracket. **~ar** *vt* [10] embrace; *(encerrar)* enclose. **~arse**

vpr embrace. **~o** *m* hug. **un fuerte ~o de** *(en una carta)* with best wishes from

abrecartas *m* paper-knife

ábrego *m* south wind

abrelatas *m* invar tin opener *(Brit)*, can opener

abreva|dero *m* watering place. **~r** *vt* water *(animales)*. **~rse** *vpr* *(animales)* drink

abrevia|ción *f* abbreviation; *(texto abreviado)* abridged text. **~do** *a* brief; *(texto)* abridged. **~r** *vt* abbreviate; abridge *(texto)*; cut short *(viaje etc)*. ● *vi* be brief. **~tura** *f* abbreviation

abrig|ada *f* shelter. **~adero** *m* shelter. **~ado** *a* *(lugar)* sheltered; *(personas)* well wrapped up. **~ar** [12] *vt* shelter; cherish *(esperanza)*; harbour *(duda, sospecha)*. **~arse** *vpr* (take) shelter; *(con ropa)* wrap up. **~o** *m* (over)coat; *(lugar)* shelter

abril *m* April. **~eño** *a* April

abrillantar *vt* polish

abrir [*pp* **abierto**] *vt/i* open. **~se** *vpr* open; *(extenderse)* open out; *(el tiempo)* clear

abrocha|dor *m* buttonhook. **~r** *vt* do up; *(con botones)* button up

abrojo *m* thistle

abronc|ar [7] *vt* *(fam)* tell off; *(abuchear)* boo; *(avergonzar)* shame. **~se** *vpr* be ashamed; *(enfadarse)* get annoyed

abroquelarse *vpr* shield o.s.

abruma|dor *a* overwhelming. **~r** *vt* overwhelm

abrupto *a* steep; *(áspero)* harsh

abrutado *a* brutish

absceso *m* abscess

absentismo *m* absenteeism

ábside *m* apse

absintio *m* absinthe

absolución *f* *(relig)* absolution; *(jurid)* acquittal

absolut|amente *adv* absolutely, completely. **~ismo** *m* absolutism. **~ista** *a & m & f* absolutist. **~o** *a* absolute. **~orio** *a* of acquittal. **en ~o** *(de manera absoluta)* absolutely; *(con sentido negativo)* (not) at all

absolver [2, *pp* **absuelto**] *vt* *(relig)* absolve; *(jurid)* acquit

absor|bente *a* absorbent; *(fig, interesante)* absorbing. **~ber** *vt* absorb. **~ción** *f* absorption. **~to** *a* absorbed

abstemio *a* teetotal. ● *m* teetotaller

absten|ción *f* abstention. **~erse** [40] *vpr* abstain, refrain (**de** from)

abstinen|cia *f* abstinence. **~te** *a* abstinent

abstra|cción *f* abstraction. **~cto** *a* abstract. **~er** [41] *vt* abstract. **~erse** *vpr* be lost in thought. **~ído** *a* absent-minded

abstruso *a* abstruse

absuelto *a* (*relig*) absolved; (*jurid*) acquitted

absurdo *a* absurd. ● *m* absurd thing

abuchea|r *vt* boo. **~o** *m* booing

abuel|la *f* grandmother. **~o** *m* grandfather. **~os** *mpl* grandparents

ab|ulia *f* lack of willpower. **~úlico** *a* weak-willed

abulta|do *a* bulky. **~miento** *m* bulkiness. **~r** *vt* enlarge; (*hinchar*) swell; (*fig, exagerar*) exaggerate. ● *vi* be bulky

abunda|ncia *f* abundance. **~nte** *a* abundant, plentiful. **~r** *vi* be plentiful. **nadar en la ~ncia** be rolling in money

aburguesa|miento *m* conversion to a middle-class way of life. **~rse** *vpr* become middle-class

aburri|do *a* (*con estar*) bored; (*con ser*) boring. **~miento** *m* boredom; (*cosa pesada*) bore. **~r** *vt* bore. **~rse** *vpr* be bored, get bored

abus|ar *vi* take advantage. **~ar de la bebida** drink too much. **~ivo** *a* excessive. **~o** *m* abuse. **~ón** *a* (*fam*) selfish

abyec|ción *f* wretchedness. **~to** *a* abject

acá *adv* here; (*hasta ahora*) until now. **~ y allá** here and there. **de ~ para allá** to and fro. **de ayer ~** since yesterday

acaba|do *a* finished; (*perfecto*) perfect; (*agotado*) worn out. ● *m* finish. **~miento** *m* finishing; (*fin*) end. **~r** *vt/i* finish. **~rse** *vpr* finish; (*agotarse*) run out; (*morirse*) die. **~r con** put an end to. **~r de** (+ *infinitivo*) have just (+ *pp*). **~ de llegar** he has just arrived. **~r por** (+ *infinitivo*) end up (+ *gerundio*). **¡se acabó!** that's it!

acabóse *m*. **ser el ~** be the end, be the limit

acacia *f* acacia

acad|emia *f* academy. **~émico** *a* academic

acaec|er [11] *vi* happen. **~imiento** *m* occurrence

acalora|damente *adv* heatedly. **~do** *a* heated. **~miento** *m* heat. **~r** *vt* warm up; (*fig, excitar*) excite. **~rse** *vpr* get hot; (*fig, excitarse*) get excited

acallar *vt* silence

acampanado *a* bell-shaped

acampar *vi* camp

acanala|do *a* grooved. **~dura** *f* groove. **~r** *vt* groove

acantilado *a* steep. ● *m* cliff

acanto *m* acanthus

acapara|r *vt* hoard; (*monopolizar*) monopolize. **~miento** *m* hoarding; (*monopolio*) monopolizing

acaracolado *a* spiral

acaricia|dor *a* caressing. **~r** *vt* caress; (*rozar*) brush; (*proyectos etc*) have in mind

ácaro *m* mite

acarre|ar *vt* transport; (*desgracias etc*) cause. **~o** *m* transport

acartona|do *a* (*persona*) wizened. **~rse** *vpr* (*ponerse rígido*) go stiff; (*persona*) become wizened

acaso *adv* maybe, perhaps. ● *m* chance. **~ llueva mañana** perhaps it will rain tomorrow. **al ~** at random. **por si ~** in case

acata|miento *m* respect (**a** for). **~r** *vt* respect

acatarrarse *vpr* catch a cold, get a cold

acaudalado *a* well off

acaudillar *vt* lead

acceder *vi* agree; (*tener acceso*) have access

acces|ibilidad *f* accessibility. **~ible** *a* accessible; (*persona*) approachable. **~o** *m* access, entry; (*med, ataque*) attack; (*llegada*) approach

accesorio *a & m* accessory

accidentado *a* (*terreno*) uneven; (*agitado*) troubled; (*persona*) injured

accident|al *a* accidental. **~arse** *vpr* have an accident. **~e** *m* accident

acci|ón *f* (*incl jurid*) action; (*hecho*) deed. **~onar** *vt* work. ● *vi* gesticulate. **~onista** *m & f* shareholder

acebo *m* holly (tree)

acebuche *m* wild olive tree

acecina|r *vt* cure (*carne*). **~se** *vpr* become wizened

acech|ar *vt* spy on; (*aguardar*) lie in wait for. **~o** *m* spying. **al ~o** on the look-out

acedera f sorrel

acedía f (*pez*) plaice; (*acidez*) heartburn

aceit|ar vt oil; (*culin*) add oil to. ∼e m oil; (*de oliva*) olive oil. ∼era f oil bottle; (*para engrasar*) oilcan. ∼ero a oil. ∼oso a oily

aceitun|a f olive. ∼ado a olive. ∼o m olive tree

acelera|ción f acceleration. ∼damente adv quickly. ∼dor m accelerator. ∼r vt accelerate; (*fig*) speed up, quicken

acelga f chard

ac|émila f mule; (*como insulto*) ass (*fam*). ∼emilero m muleteer

acendra|do a pure. ∼r vt purify; refine (*metales*)

acensuar vt tax

acent|o m accent; (*énfasis*) stress. ∼uación f accentuation. ∼uar [21] vt stress; (*fig*) emphasize. ∼uarse vpr become noticeable

aceña f water-mill

acepción f meaning, sense

acepta|ble a acceptable. ∼ción f acceptance; (*aprobación*) approval. ∼r vt accept

acequia f irrigation channel

acera f pavement (*Brit*), sidewalk (*Amer*)

acerado a steel; (*fig, mordaz*) sharp

acerca de prep about

acerca|miento m approach; (*fig*) reconciliation. ∼r [7] vt bring near. ∼rse vpr approach

acería f steelworks

acerico m pincushion

acero m steel. ∼ inoxidable stainless steel

acérrimo a (*fig*) staunch

acert|ado a right, correct; (*apropiado*) appropriate. ∼ar [1] vt hit (*el blanco*); (*adivinar*) get right, guess. ● vi get right. ∼ar a happen to. ∼ar con hit on. ∼ijo m riddle

acervo m pile; (*bienes*) common property

acetato m acetate

acético a acetic

acetileno m acetylene

acetona f acetone

aciago a unlucky

aciano m cornflower

ac|íbar m aloes; (*planta*) aloe; (*fig, amargura*) bitterness. ∼ibarar vt add aloes to; (*fig, amargar*) embitter

acicala|do a dressed up, overdressed. ∼r vt dress up. ∼rse vpr get dressed up

acicate m spur

acid|ez f acidity. ∼ificar [7] vt acidify. ∼ificarse vpr acidify

ácido a sour. ● m acid

acierto m success; (*idea*) good idea; (*habilidad*) skill

aclama|ción f acclaim; (*aplausos*) applause. ∼r vt acclaim; (*aplaudir*) applaud

aclara|ción f explanation. ∼r vt lighten (*colores*); (*explicar*) clarify; (*enjuagar*) rinse. ● vi (*el tiempo*) brighten up. ∼rse vpr become clear. ∼torio a explanatory

aclimata|ción f acclimatization, acclimation (*Amer*). ∼r vt acclimatize, acclimate (*Amer*). ∼rse vpr become acclimatized, become acclimated (*Amer*)

acné m acne

acobardar vt intimidate. ∼se vpr get frightened

acocil m (*Mex*) freshwater shrimp

acod|ado a bent. ∼ar vt (*doblar*) bend; (*agricultura*) layer. ∼arse vpr lean on (*en* on). ∼o m layer

acog|edor a welcoming; (*ambiente*) friendly. ∼er [14] vt welcome; (*proteger*) shelter; (*recibir*) receive. ∼erse vpr take refuge. ∼ida f welcome; (*refugio*) refuge

acogollar vi bud. ∼se vpr bud

acolchado a quilted. ∼r vt quilt, pad

acólito m acolyte; (*monaguillo*) altar boy

acomet|edor a aggressive; (*emprendedor*) enterprising. ∼er vt attack; (*emprender*) undertake; (*llenar*) fill. ∼ida f attack. ∼ividad f aggression; (*iniciativa*) enterprise

acomod|able a adaptable. ∼adizo a accommodating. ∼ado a well off. ∼ador m usher. ∼adora f usherette. ∼amiento m suitability. ∼ar vt arrange; (*adaptar*) adjust. ● vi be suitable. ∼arse vpr settle down; (*adaptarse*) conform. ∼aticio a accommodating. ∼o m position

acompaña|do a accompanied; (*concurrido*) busy. ∼miento m accompaniment. ∼nta f companion. ∼nte m companion; (*mus*) accompanist. ∼r vt accompany; (*adjuntar*) enclose. ~**se** *vpr* (*mus*) accompany o.s.

acompasa|do *a* rhythmic. ~**r** *vt* keep in time; (*fig, ajustar*) adjust

acondiciona|do *a* equipped. ~**miento** *m* conditioning. ~**r** *vt* fit out; (*preparar*) prepare

acongojar *vt* distress. ~**se** *vpr* get upset

acónito *m* aconite

aconseja|ble *a* advisable. ~**do** *a* advised. ~**r** *vt* advise. ~**rse** *vpr* take advice. ~**rse con** consult

aconsonantar *vt/i* rhyme

acontec|er [11] *vi* happen. ~**imiento** *m* event

acopi|ar *vt* collect. ~**o** *m* store

acopla|do *a* coordinated. ~**miento** *m* coupling; (*elec*) connection. ~**r** *vt* fit; (*elec*) connect; (*rail*) couple

acoquina|miento *m* intimidation. ~**r** *vt* intimidate. ~**rse** *vpr* be intimidated

acoraza|do *a* armour-plated. ● *m* battleship. ~**r** [10] *vt* armour

acorazonado *a* heart-shaped

acorcha|do *a* spongy. ~**rse** *vpr* go spongy; (*parte del cuerpo*) go to sleep

acord|ado *a* agreed. ~**ar** [2] *vt* agree (upon); (*decidir*) decide; (*recordar*) remind. ~**e** *a* in agreement; (*mus*) harmonious. ● *m* chord

acorde|ón *m* accordion. ~**onista** *m* & *f* accordionist

acordona|do *a* (*lugar*) cordoned off. ~**miento** *m* cordoning off. ~**r** *vt* tie, lace; (*rodear*) surround, cordon off

acorrala|miento *m* (*de animales*) rounding up; (*de personas*) cornering. ~**r** *vt* round up (*animales*); corner (*personas*)

acorta|miento *m* shortening. ~**r** *vt* shorten; (*fig*) cut down

acos|ar *vt* hound; (*fig*) pester. ~**o** *m* pursuit; (*fig*) pestering

acostar [2] *vt* put to bed; (*naut*) bring alongside. ● *vi* (*naut*) reach land. ~**se** *vpr* go to bed; (*echarse*) lie down; (*Mex, parir*) give birth

acostumbra|do *a* (*habitual*) usual. ~**do a** used to, accustomed to. ~**r** *vt* get used. **me ha acostumbrado a levantarme por la noche** he's got me used to getting up at night. ● *vi*. ~**r** (**a**) be accustomed to. **acostumbro comer a la una** I usually have lunch at one o'clock. ~**rse** *vpr* become accustomed, get used

acota|ción *f* (*nota*) marginal note; (*en el teatro*) stage direction; (*cota*) elevation mark. ~**do** *a* enclosed. ~**r** *vt* mark out (*terreno*); (*anotar*) annotate

ácrata *a* anarchistic. ● *m* & *f* anarchist

acre *m* acre. ● *a* (*olor*) pungent; (*sabor*) sharp, bitter

acrecenta|miento *m* increase. ~**r** [1] *vt* increase. ~**rse** *vpr* increase

acrec|er [11] *vt* increase. ~**imiento** *m* increase

acredita|do *a* reputable; (*pol*) accredited. ~**r** *vt* prove; accredit (*representante diplomático*); (*garantizar*) guarantee; (*autorizar*) authorize. ~**rse** *vpr* make one's name

acreedor *a* worthy (**a** of). ● *m* creditor

acribillar *vt* (*a balazos*) riddle (**a** with); (*a picotazos*) cover (**a** with); (*fig, a preguntas etc*) pester (**a** with)

acrimonia *f* (*de sabor*) sharpness; (*de olor*) pungency; (*fig*) bitterness

acrisola|do *a* pure; (*fig*) proven. ~**r** *vt* purify; (*confirmar*) prove

acritud *f* (*de sabor*) sharpness; (*de olor*) pungency; (*fig*) bitterness

acr|obacia *f* acrobatics. ~**obacias aéreas** aerobatics. ~**óbata** *m* & *f* acrobat. ~**obático** *a* acrobatic. ~**obatismo** *m* acrobatics

acrónimo *m* acronym

acróstico *a* & *m* acrostic

acta *f* minutes; (*certificado*) certificate

actinia *f* sea anemone

actitud *f* posture, position; (*fig*) attitude, position

activ|ación *f* speed-up. ~**amente** *adv* actively. ~**ar** *vt* activate; (*acelerar*) speed up. ~**idad** *f* activity. ~**o** *a* active. ● *m* assets

acto *m* act; (*ceremonia*) ceremony. **en el** ~ immediately

act|or *m* actor. ~**riz** *f* actress

actuación *f* action; (*conducta*) behaviour; (*theat*) performance

actual *a* present; (*asunto*) topical. ~**idad** *f* present. ~**idades** *fpl* current affairs. ~**ización** *f* modernization. ~**izar** [10] *vt* modernize. ~**mente** *adv* now, at the present time. **en la** ~**idad** nowadays

actuar [21] *vt* work. ● *vi* act. ~ **como**, ~ **de** act as

actuario *m* clerk of the court. ∼ **(de seguros)** actuary

acuarel|a *f* watercolour. ∼**ista** *m* & *f* watercolourist

acuario *m* aquarium. **A**∼ Aquarius

acuartela|do *a* quartered. ∼**miento** *m* quartering. ∼**r** *vt* quarter, billet; *(mantener en cuartel)* confine to barracks

acuático *a* aquatic

acuci|ador pressing. ∼**ar** *vt* urge on; *(dar prisa a)* hasten. ∼**oso** *a* keen

acuclillarse *vpr* crouch down, squat down

acuchilla|do *a* slashed; *(persona)* stabbed. ∼**r** *vt* slash; stab *(persona)*; *(alisar)* smooth

acudir *vi.* ∼ **a** go to, attend; keep *(una cita)*; *(en auxilio)* go to help

acueducto *m* aqueduct

acuerdo *m* agreement. ● *vb véase* **acordar.** ¡**de** ∼! OK! **de** ∼ **con** in accordance with. **estar de** ∼ agree. **ponerse de** ∼ agree

acuesto *vb véase* **acostar**

acuidad *f* acuity, sharpness

acumula|ción *f* accumulation. ∼**dor** *a* accumulative. ● *m* accumulator. ∼**r** *vt* accumulate.∼**rse** *vpr* accumulate

acunar *vt* rock

acuña|ción *f* minting, coining. ∼**r** *vt* mint, coin

acuos|idad *f* wateriness. ∼**o** *a* watery

acupuntura *f* acupuncture

acurrucarse [7] *vpr* curl up

acusa|ción *f* accusation. ∼**do** *a* accused; *(destacado)* marked. ● *m* accused. ∼**dor** *a* accusing. ● *m* accuser. ∼**r** *vt* accuse; *(mostrar)* show; *(denunciar)* denounce. ∼**rse** *vpr* confess; *(notarse)* become marked. ∼**torio** *a* accusatory

acuse *m.* ∼ **de recibo** acknowledgement of receipt

acus|ica *m* & *f (fam)* telltale.∼**ón** *a* & *m* telltale

acústic|a *f* acoustics. ∼**o** *a* acoustic

achacar [7] *vt* attribute

achacoso *a* sickly

achaflanar *vt* bevel

achantar *vt (fam)* intimidate. ∼**se** *vpr* hide; *(fig)* back down

achaparrado *a* stocky

achaque *m* ailment

achares *mpl (fam).* **dar** ∼ make jealous

achata|miento *m* flattening. ∼**r** *vt* flatten

achica|do *a* childish. ∼**r** [7] *vt* make smaller; *(fig, empequeñecer, fam)* belittle; *(naut)* bale out. ∼**rse** *vpr* become smaller; *(humillarse)* be humiliated

achicopalado *a (Mex)* depressed

achicoria *f* chicory

achicharra|dero *m* inferno. ∼**nte** *a* sweltering. ∼**r** *vt* burn; *(fig)* pester. ∼**rse** *vpr* burn

achispa|do *a* tipsy. ∼**rse** *vpr* get tipsy

achocolatado *a* (chocolate-)brown

achuch|ado *a (fam)* hard. ∼**ar** *vt* jostle, push.∼**ón** *m* shove, push

achulado *a* cocky

adagio *m* adage, proverb; *(mus)* adagio

adalid *m* leader

adamascado *a* damask

adapta|ble *a* adaptable. ∼**ción** *f* adaptation. ∼**dor** *m* adapter. ∼**r** *vt* adapt; *(ajustar)* fit. ∼**rse** *vpr* adapt o.s.

adecentar *vt* clean up. ∼**se** *vpr* tidy o.s. up

adecua|ción *f* suitability. ∼**damente** *adv* suitably. ∼**do** *a* suitable. ∼**r** *vt* adapt, make suitable

adelant|ado *a* advanced; *(niño)* precocious; *(reloj)* fast. ∼**amiento** *m* advance(ment); *(auto)* overtaking. ∼**ar** *vt* advance, move forward; *(acelerar)* speed up; put forward *(reloj)*; *(auto)* overtake. ● *vi* advance, go forward; *(reloj)* gain, be fast. ∼**arse** *vpr* advance, move forward; *(reloj)* gain; *(auto)* overtake. ∼**e** *adv* forward. ● *int* come in!; *(¡siga!)* carry on! ∼**o** *m* advance; *(progreso)* progress. **más** ∼**e** *(lugar)* further on; *(tiempo)* later on. **pagar por** ∼**ado** pay in advance.

adelfa *f* oleander

adelgaza|dor *a* slimming. ∼**miento** *m* slimming. ∼**r** [10] *vt* make thin. ● *vi* lose weight; *(adrede)* slim. ∼**rse** *vpr* lose weight; *(adrede)* slim

ademán *m* gesture. **ademanes** *mpl (modales)* manners. **en** ∼ **de** as if to

además *adv* besides; *(también)* also. ∼ **de** besides

adentr|arse *vpr.* ∼ **en** penetrate into; study thoroughly *(tema etc)*. ∼**o** *adv* in(side). **mar** ∼**o** out at sea. **tierra** ∼**o** inland

adepto *m* supporter

aderez|ar [10] *vt* flavour ⟨*bebidas*⟩; ⟨*condimentar*⟩ season; dress ⟨*ensalada*⟩. **~o** *m* flavouring; ⟨*con condimentos*⟩ seasoning; ⟨*para ensalada*⟩ dressing
adeud|ar *vt* owe. **~o** *m* debit
adhe|rencia *f* adhesion; ⟨*fig*⟩ adherence. **~rente** *a* adherent. **~rir** [4] *vt* stick on. ● *vi* stick. **~rirse** *vpr* stick; ⟨*fig*⟩ follow. **~sión** *f* adhesion; ⟨*fig*⟩ support. **~sivo** *a* & *m* adhesive
adici|ón *f* addition. **~onal** *a* additional. **~onar** *vt* add
adicto *a* devoted. ● *m* follower
adiestra|do *a* trained. **~miento** *m* training. **~r** *vt* train. **~rse** *vpr* practise
adinerado *a* wealthy
adiós *int* goodbye!; ⟨*al cruzarse con alguien*⟩ hello!
adit|amento *m* addition; ⟨*accesorio*⟩ accessory. **~ivo** *m* additive
adivina|ción *f* divination; ⟨*por conjeturas*⟩ guessing. **~dor** *m* fortune-teller. **~anza** *f* riddle. **~ar** *vt* foretell; ⟨*acertar*⟩ guess. **~o** *m* fortune-teller
adjetivo *a* adjectival. ● *m* adjective
adjudica|ción *f* award. **~r** [7] *vt* award. **~rse** *vpr* appropriate. **~tario** *m* winner of an award
adjunt|ar *vt* enclose. **~o** *a* enclosed; ⟨*auxiliar*⟩ assistant. ● *m* assistant
adminículo *m* thing, gadget
administra|ción *f* administration; ⟨*gestión*⟩ management. **~dor** *m* administrator; ⟨*gerente*⟩ manager. **~dora** *f* administrator; manageress. **~r** *vt* administer. **~tivo** *a* administrative
admira|ble *a* admirable. **~ción** *f* admiration. **~dor** *m* admirer. **~r** *vt* admire; ⟨*asombrar*⟩ astonish. **~rse** *vpr* be astonished. **~tivo** *a* admiring
admi|sibilidad *f* admissibility. **~sible** *a* acceptable. **~sión** *f* admission; ⟨*aceptación*⟩ acceptance. **~tir** *vt* admit; ⟨*aceptar*⟩ accept
adobar *vt* ⟨*culin*⟩ pickle; ⟨*fig*⟩ twist
adobe *m* sun-dried brick. **~ra** *f* mould for making (sun-dried) bricks
adobo *m* pickle
adocena|do *a* common. **~rse** *vpr* become common
adoctrinamiento *m* indoctrination
adolecer [11] *vi* be ill. **~ de** suffer with

adolescen|cia *f* adolescent. **~te** *a* & *m* & *f* adolescent
adonde *conj* where
adónde *adv* where?
adop|ción *f* adoption. **~tar** *vt* adopt. **~tivo** *a* adoptive; ⟨*patria*⟩ of adoption
adoqu|ín *m* paving stone; ⟨*imbécil*⟩ idiot. **~inado** *m* paving. **~inar** *vt* pave
adora|ble *a* adorable. **~ción** *f* adoration. **~dor** *a* adoring. ● *n* worshipper. **~r** *vt* adore
adormec|edor *a* soporific; ⟨*droga*⟩ sedative. **~er** [11] *vt* send to sleep; ⟨*fig, calmar*⟩ calm, soothe. **~erse** *vpr* fall asleep; ⟨*un miembro*⟩ go to sleep. **~ido** *a* sleepy; ⟨*un miembro*⟩ numb. **~imiento** *m* sleepiness; ⟨*de un miembro*⟩ numbness
adormidera *f* opium poppy
adormilarse *vpr* doze
adorn|ar *vt* adorn (**con, de** with). **~o** *m* decoration
adosar *vt* lean (**a** against)
adqui|rido *a* acquired. **~rir** [4] *vt* acquire; ⟨*comprar*⟩ buy. **~sición** *f* acquisition; ⟨*compra*⟩ purchase. **~sitivo** *a* acquisitive. **poder** *m* **~sitivo** purchasing power
adrede *adv* on purpose
adrenalina *f* adrenalin
adscribir [*pp* **adscrito**] *vt* appoint
aduan|a *f* customs. **~ero** *a* customs. ● *m* customs officer
aducir [47] *vt* allege
adueñarse *vpr* take possession
adul|ación *f* flattery. **~ador** *a* flattering. ● *m* flatterer. **~ar** *vt* flatter
ad|ulteración *f* adulteration. **~ulterar** *vt* adulterate. ● *vi* commit adultery. **~ulterino** *a* adulterous. **~ulterio** *m* adultery. **~últera** *f* adulteress. **~último** *a* adulterous. ● *m* adulterer
adulto *a* & *m* adult, grown-up
adusto *a* severe, harsh
advenedizo *a* & *m* upstart
advenimiento *m* advent, arrival; ⟨*subida al trono*⟩ accession
adventicio *a* accidental
adverbi|al *a* adverbial. **~o** *m* adverb
advers|ario *m* adversary. **~idad** *f* adversity. **~o** *a* adverse, unfavourable
advert|encia *f* warning; ⟨*prólogo*⟩ foreword. **~ido** *a* informed. **~ir** [4] *vt* warn; ⟨*notar*⟩ notice

adviento m Advent

advocación f dedication

adyacente a adjacent

aéreo a air; (photo) aerial; (ferrocarril) overhead; (fig) flimsy

aeróbica f aerobics

aerodeslizador m hovercraft

aerodinámic|a f aerodynamics. ~o a aerodynamic

aeródromo m aerodrome, airdrome (Amer)

aero|espacial a aerospace. ~faro m beacon. ~lito m meteorite. ~nauta m & f aeronaut. ~náutica f aeronautics. ~náutico a aeronautical. ~nave f airship. ~puerto m airport. ~sol m aerosol

afab|ilidad f affability. ~le a affable

afamado a famous

af|án m hard work; (deseo) desire. ~anar vt (fam) pinch. ~anarse vpr strive (en, por to). ~anoso a laborious

afea|miento m disfigurement. ~r vt disfigure, make ugly; (censurar) censure

afección f disease

afecta|ción f affectation. ~do a affected. ~r vt affect

afect|ísimo a affectionate. ~ísimo amigo (en cartas) my dear friend. ~ividad f emotional nature. ~ivo a sensitive. ~o m (cariño) affection. ● a. ~o a attached to. ~uosidad f affection. ~uoso a affectionate. con un ~uoso saludo (en cartas) with kind regards. suyo ~ísimo (en cartas) yours sincerely

afeita|do m shave. ~dora f electric razor. ~r vt shave. ~rse vpr (have a) shave

afelpado a velvety

afemina|do a effeminate. ● m effeminate person. ~miento m effeminacy. ~rse vpr become effeminate

aferrar [1] vt grasp

afgano a & m Afghan

afianza|miento m (reforzar) strengthening; (garantía) guarantee. ~rse [10] vpr become established

afici|ón f liking; (conjunto de aficionados) fans. ~onado a keen (a on), fond (a of). ● m fan. ~onar vt make fond. ~onarse vpr take a liking to. por ~ón as a hobby

afila|do a sharp. ~dor m knife-grinder. ~dura f sharpening. ~r vt sharpen. ~rse vpr get sharp; (ponerse flaco) grow thin

afilia|ción f affiliation. ~do a affiliated. ~rse vpr become a member (a of)

afiligranado a filigreed; (fig) delicate

afín a similar; (próximo) adjacent; ⟨personas⟩ related

afina|ción f refining; (auto, mus) tuning. ~do a finished; (mus) in tune. ~r vt refine; (afilar) sharpen; (acabar) finish; (auto, mus) tune. ● vi be in tune. ~rse vpr become more refined

afincarse [7] vpr settle

afinidad f affinity; (parentesco) relationship

afirma|ción f affirmation. ~r vt make firm; (asentir) affirm. ~rse vpr steady o.s.; (confirmar) confirm. ~tivo a affirmative

aflic|ción f affliction. ~tivo a distressing

afligi|do a distressed. ~r [14] vt distress. ~rse vpr grieve

afloja|miento m loosening. ~r vt loosen; (relajar) ease. ● vi let up

aflora|miento m outcrop. ~r vi appear on the surface

aflu|encia f flow. ~ente a flowing. ● m tributary. ~ir [17] vi flow (a into)

af|onía f hoarseness. ~ónico a hoarse

aforismo m aphorism

aforo m capacity

afortunado a fortunate, lucky

afrancesado a francophile

afrent|a f insult; (vergüenza) disgrace. ~ar vt insult. ~oso a insulting

África f Africa. ~ del Sur South Africa

africano a & m African

afrodisíaco a & m, **afrodisiaco** a & m aphrodisiac

afrontar vt bring face to face; (enfrentar) face, confront

afuera adv out(side). ¡~! out of the way! ~s fpl outskirts

agachar vt lower. ~se vpr bend over

agalla f (de los peces) gill. ~s fpl (fig) guts

agarrada f row

agarrader|a f (LAm) handle. ~o m handle. **tener ~as** (LAm), **tener ~os** have influence

agarr|ado a (fig, fam) mean. **~ador** a (Arg) ⟨bebida⟩ strong. **~ar** vt grasp; (esp LAm) take, catch. ● vi ⟨plantas⟩ take root. **~arse** vpr hold on; (reñirse, fam) fight. **~ón** m tug; (LAm, riña) row

agarrota|miento m tightening; ⟨auto⟩ seizing up. **~r** vt tie tightly; ⟨el frío⟩ stiffen; garotte ⟨un reo⟩. **~rse** vpr go stiff; ⟨auto⟩ seize up

agasaj|ado m guest of honour. **~ar** vt look after well. **~o** m good treatment

ágata f agate

agavilla|dora f ⟨máquina⟩ binder. **~r** vt bind

agazaparse vpr hide

agencia f agency. **~ de viajes** travel agency. **~ inmobiliaria** estate agency (Brit), real estate agency (Amer). **~r** vt find. **~rse** vpr find (out) for o.s.

agenda f notebook

agente m agent; ⟨de policía⟩ policeman. **~ de aduanas** customs officer. **~ de bolsa** stockbroker

ágil a agile

agilidad f agility

agita|ción f waving; ⟨de un líquido⟩ stirring; ⟨intranquilidad⟩ agitation. **~do** a ⟨el mar⟩ rough; (fig) agitated. **~dor** m (pol) agitator

agitanado a gypsy-like

agitar vt wave; shake ⟨botellas etc⟩; stir ⟨líquidos⟩; (fig) stir up. **~se** vpr wave; ⟨el mar⟩ get rough; (fig) get excited

aglomera|ción f agglomeration; ⟨de tráfico⟩ traffic jam. **~r** vt amass. **~rse** vpr form a crowd

agn|osticismo m agnosticism. **~óstico** a & m agnostic

agobi|ador a ⟨trabajo⟩ exhausting; ⟨calor⟩ oppressive. **~ante** a ⟨trabajo⟩ exhausting; ⟨calor⟩ oppressive. **~ar** vt weigh down; (fig, abrumar) overwhelm. **~o** m weight; ⟨cansancio⟩ exhaustion; ⟨opresión⟩ oppression

agolpa|miento m ⟨de gente⟩ crowd; ⟨de cosas⟩ pile. **~rse** vpr crowd together

agon|ía f death throes; (fig) agony. **~izante** a dying; ⟨luz⟩ failing. **~izar** [10] vi be dying

agor|ar [16] vt prophesy. **~ero** a of ill omen. ● m soothsayer

agostar vt wither

agosto m August. **hacer su ~** feather one's nest

agota|do a exhausted; ⟨libro⟩ out of print. **~dor** a exhausting. **~miento** m exhaustion. **~r** vt exhaust. **~rse** vpr be exhausted; ⟨libro⟩ go out of print

agracia|do a attractive; ⟨que tiene suerte⟩ lucky. **~r** make attractive

agrada|ble a pleasant, nice. **~r** vi please. **esto me ~** I like this

agradec|er [11] vt thank ⟨persona⟩; be grateful for ⟨cosa⟩. **~ido** a grateful. **~imiento** m gratitude. **¡muy ~ido!** thanks a lot!

agrado m pleasure; ⟨amabilidad⟩ friendliness

agrandar vt enlarge; (fig) exaggerate. **~se** vpr get bigger

agrario a agrarian, land; ⟨política⟩ agricultural

agrava|miento m worsening. **~nte** a aggravating. **~r** vt aggravate; ⟨aumentar el peso⟩ make heavier. **~rse** vpr get worse

agravi|ar vt offend; ⟨perjudicar⟩ wrong. **~arse** vpr be offended. **~o** m offence

agraz m. **en ~** prematurely

agredir [24] vt attack. **~ de palabra** insult

agrega|do m aggregate; ⟨funcionario diplomático⟩ attaché. **~r** [12] vt add; ⟨unir⟩ join; appoint ⟨persona⟩

agremiar vt form into a union. **~se** vpr form a union

agres|ión f aggression; ⟨ataque⟩ attack. **~ividad** f aggressiveness. **~ivo** a aggressive. **~or** m aggressor

agreste a country

agria|do a (fig) embittered. **~r** [regular, o raramente 20] vt sour. **~rse** vpr turn sour; (fig) become embittered

agr|ícola a agricultural. **~icultor** a agricultural. ● m farmer. **~icultura** f agriculture, farming

agridulce a bitter-sweet; ⟨culin⟩ sweet-and-sour

agriera f (LAm) heartburn

agrietar vt crack. **~se** vpr crack; ⟨piel⟩ chap

agrimens|or m surveyor. **~ura** f surveying

agrio a sour; (fig) sharp. **~s** mpl citrus fruits

agronomía f agronomy

agropecuario a farming

agrupa|ción f group; (acción) grouping. **~r** vt group. **~rse** vpr form a group

agua f water; (lluvia) rain; (marea) tide; (vertiente del tejado) slope. **~ abajo** downstream. **~ arriba** upstream. **~ bendita** holy water. **~ caliente** hot water. **estar entre dos ~s** sit on the fence. **hacer ~** (naut) leak. **nadar entre dos ~s** sit on the fence

aguacate m avocado pear; (árbol) avocado pear tree

aguacero m downpour, heavy shower

agua f **corriente** running water

aguachinarse vpr (Mex) (cultivos) be flooded

aguada f watering place; (naut) drinking water; (acuarela) watercolour

agua f **de colonia** eau-de-Cologne

aguad|o a watery. **~ucho** m refreshment kiosk

agua: ~ dulce fresh water. **~fiestas** m & f invar spoil-sport, wet blanket. **~ fría** cold water. **~fuerte** m etching

aguaje m spring tide

agua: ~mala f, **~mar** m jellyfish

aguamarina f aquamarine

agua: ~miel f mead. **~ mineral con gas** fizzy mineral water. **~ mineral sin gas** still mineral water. **~nieve** f sleet

aguanoso a watery; (tierra) waterlogged

aguant|able a bearable. **~aderas** fpl patience. **~ar** vt put up with, bear; (sostener) support. ● vi hold out. **~arse** vpr restrain o.s. **~e** m patience; (resistencia) endurance

agua: ~pié m watery wine. **~ potable** drinking water. **~r** [15] vt water down. **~ salada** salt water.

aguardar vt wait for. ● vi wait

agua: ~rdiente m (cheap) brandy. **~rrás** m turpentine, turps (fam). **~turma** f Jerusalem artichoke. **~zal** m puddle

agud|eza f sharpness; (fig, perspicacia) insight; (fig, ingenio) wit. **~izar** [10] vt sharpen. **~izarse** vpr (enfermedad) get worse. **~o** a sharp; (ángulo, enfermedad) acute; (voz) high-pitched

agüero m omen. **ser de buen ~** augur well

aguij|ada f goad. **~ar** vt (incl fig) goad. **~ón** m point of a goad. **~onazo** m prick. **~onear** vt goad

águila f eagle; (persona perspicaz) astute person

aguileña f columbine

aguil|eño a aquiline. **~ucho** m eaglet

aguinaldo m Christmas box

aguja f needle; (del reloj) hand; (arquit) steeple. **~s** fpl (rail) points

aguje|ar vt make holes in. **~o** m hole

agujetas fpl stiffness. **tener ~** be stiff

agujón m hairpin

agusanado a full of maggots

agutí m (LAm) guinea pig

aguza|do a sharp. **~miento** m sharpening. **~r** [10] vt sharpen

ah int ah!, oh!

aherrojar vt (fig) oppress

ahí adv there. **de ~ que** so that. **por ~** over there; (aproximadamente) thereabouts

ahija|da f god-daughter, godchild. **~do** m godson, godchild. **~r** vt adopt

ahínco m enthusiasm; (empeño) insistence

ahíto a full up

ahog|ado a (en el agua) drowned; (asfixiado) suffocated. **~ar** [12] vt (en el agua) drown; (asfixiar) suffocate; put out (fuego). **~arse** vpr (en el agua) drown; (asfixiarse) suffocate. **~o** m breathlessness; (fig, angustia) distress; (apuro) financial trouble

ahondar vt deepen. ● vi go deep. **~ en** (fig) examine in depth. **~se** vpr get deeper

ahora adv now; (hace muy poco) just now; (dentro de poco) very soon. **~ bien** but. **~ mismo** right now. **de ~ en adelante** from now on, in future. **por ~** for the time being

ahorca|dura f hanging. **~r** [7] vt hang. **~rse** vpr hang o.s.

ahorita adv (fam) now. **~ mismo** right now

ahorquillar vt shape like a fork

ahorr|ador a thrifty. **~ar** vt save. **~arse** vpr save o.s. **~o** m saving; (cantidad ahorrada) savings. **~os** mpl savings

ahuecar [7] vt hollow; fluff up (colchón); deepen (la voz); (marcharse, fam) clear off (fam)

ahuizote m (Mex) bore

ahulado *m* (*LAm*) oilskin

ahuma|do *a* (*culin*) smoked; (*de colores*) smoky. **~r** *vt* (*culin*) smoke; (*llenar de humo*) fill with smoke. ● *vi* smoke. **~rse** *vpr* become smoky; (*comida*) acquire a smoky taste; (*emborracharse, fam*) get drunk

ahusa|do *a* tapering. **~rse** *vpr* taper

ahuyentar *vt* drive away; banish (*pensamientos etc*)

airado *a* annoyed

aire *m* air; (*viento*) breeze; (*corriente*) draught; (*aspecto*) appearance; (*mus*) tune, air. **~ación** *f* ventilation. **~ acondicionado** air-conditioned. **~ar** *vt* air; (*ventilar*) ventilate; (*fig, publicar*) make public. **~arse** *vpr*. **salir para ~arse** go out for some fresh air. **al ~ libre** in the open air. **darse ~s** give o.s. airs

airón *m* heron

airos|amente *adv* gracefully. **~o** *a* draughty; (*fig*) elegant

aisla|do *a* isolated; (*elec*) insulated. **~dor** *a* (*elec*) insulating. ● *m* (*elec*) insulator. **~miento** *m* isolation; (*elec*) insulation. **~nte** *a* insulating. **~r** [23] *vt* isolate; (*elec*) insulate

ajajá *int* good! splendid!

ajar *vt* crumple; (*estropear*) spoil

ajedre|cista *m* & *f* chess-player. **~z** *m* chess. **~zado** *a* chequered, checked

ajenjo *m* absinthe

ajeno *a* (*de otro*) someone else's; (*de otros*) other people's; (*extraño*) alien

ajetre|arse *vpr* be busy. **~o** *m* bustle

ají *m* (*LAm*) chilli; (*salsa*) chilli sauce

aj|iaceite *m* garlic sauce. **~ilimójili** *m* piquant garlic sauce. **~illo** *m* garlic. **al ~illo** cooked with garlic. **~o** *m* garlic. **~o-a-rriero** *m* cod in garlic sauce

ajorca *f* bracelet

ajuar *m* furnishings; (*de novia*) trousseau

ajuma|do *a* (*fam*) drunk. **~rse** *vpr* (*fam*) get drunk

ajust|ado *a* right; (*vestido*) tight. **~ador** *m* fitter. **~amiento** *m* fitting; (*adaptación*) adjustment; (*acuerdo*) agreement; (*de una cuenta*) settlement. **~ar** *vt* fit; (*adaptar*) adapt; (*acordar*) agree; settle (*una cuenta*); (*apretar*) tighten. ● *vi* fit. **~arse** *vpr* fit; (*adaptarse*) adapt o.s.; (*acordarse*) come to an agreement. **~e** *m* fitting; (*adaptación*) adjustment; (*acuerdo*)

agreement; (*de una cuenta*) settlement

ajusticiar *vt* execute

al = **a** + **el**

ala *f* wing; (*de sombrero*) brim; (*deportes*) winger

alaba|ncioso *a* boastful. **~nza** *f* praise. **~r** *vt* praise. **~rse** *vpr* boast

alabastro *m* alabaster

álabe *m* (*paleta*) paddle; (*diente*) cog

alabe|ar *vt* warp. **~arse** *vpr* warp. **~o** *m* warping

alacena *f* cupboard (*Brit*), closet (*Amer*)

alacrán *m* scorpion

alacridad *f* alacrity

alado *a* winged

alambi|cado *a* distilled; (*fig*) subtle. **~camiento** *m* distillation; (*fig*) subtlety. **~car** [7] *vt* distil. **~que** *m* still

alambr|ada *f* wire fence; (*de alambre de espinas*) barbed wire fence. **~ar** *vt* fence. **~e** *m* wire. **~e de espinas** barbed wire. **~era** *f* fireguard

alameda *f* avenue; (*plantío de álamos*) poplar grove

álamo *m* poplar. **~ temblón** aspen

alano *m* mastiff

alarde *m* show. **~ar** *vi* boast

alarga|dera *f* extension. **~do** *a* long. **~dor** *m* extension. **~miento** *m* lengthening. **~r** [12] *vt* lengthen; stretch out (*mano etc*); (*dar*) give, pass. **~rse** *vpr* lengthen, get longer

alarido *m* shriek

alarm|a *f* alarm. **~ante** *a* alarming. **~ar** *vt* alarm, frighten. **~arse** *vpr* be alarmed. **~ista** *m* & *f* alarmist

alba *f* dawn

albacea *m* executor. ● *f* executrix

albacora (*culin*) tuna(-fish)

albahaca *f* basil

albanés *a* & *m* Albanian

Albania *f* Albania

albañal *m* sewer, drain

albañil *m* bricklayer. **~ería** *f* (*arte*) bricklaying

albarán *m* delivery note

albarda *f* packsaddle; (*Mex*) saddle. **~r** *vt* saddle

albaricoque *m* apricot. **~ro** *m* apricot tree

albatros *m* albatross

albedrío *m* will. **libre ~** free will

albéitar *m* veterinary surgeon (*Brit*), veterinarian (*Amer*), vet (*fam*)

alberca *f* tank, reservoir

alberg|ar [12] *vt* (*alojar*) put up; (*viviendas*) house; (*dar asilo*) shelter. ~**arse** *vpr* stay; (*refugiarse*) shelter. ~**ue** *m* accommodation; (*refugio*) shelter. ~**ue de juventud** youth hostel

albóndiga *f* meatball, rissole

albor *m* dawn. ~**ada** *f* dawn; (*mus*) dawn song. ~**ear** *vi* dawn

albornoz *m* (*de los moros*) burnous; (*para el baño*) bathrobe

alborot|adizo *a* excitable. ~**ado** *a* excited; (*aturdido*) hasty. ~**ador** *a* rowdy. ● *m* trouble-maker. ~**ar** *vt* disturb, upset. ● *vi* make a racket. ~**arse** *vpr* get excited; (*el mar*) get rough. ~**o** *m* row, uproar

alboroz|ado *a* overjoyed. ~**ar** [10] *vt* make laugh; (*regocijar*) make happy. ~**arse** *vpr* be overjoyed. ~**o** *m* joy

albufera *f* lagoon

álbum *m* (*pl* ~**es** o ~**s**) album

alcachofa *f* artichoke

alcald|e *m* mayor. ~**esa** *f* mayoress. ~**ía** *f* mayoralty; (*oficina*) mayor's office

álcali *m* alkali

alcalino *a* alkaline

alcance *m* reach; (*de arma, telescopio etc*) range; (*déficit*) deficit

alcancía *f* money-box

alcantarilla *f* sewer; (*boca*) drain

alcanzar [10] *vt* (*llegar a*) catch up; (*coger*) reach; catch (*un autobús*); (*bala etc*) strike, hit. ● *vi* reach; (*ser suficiente*) be enough. ~**a** manage

alcaparra *f* caper

alcaucil *m* artichoke

alcayata *f* hook

alcazaba *f* fortress

alcázar *m* fortress

alcoba *f* bedroom

alcoh|ol *m* alcohol. ~**ol desnaturalizado** methylated spirits, meths (*fam*). ~**ólico** *a* & *m* alcoholic. ~**olímetro** *m* breathalyser (*Brit*). ~**olismo** *m* alcoholism. ~**olizarse** [10] *vpr* become an alcoholic

Alcorán *m* Koran

alcornoque *m* cork-oak; (*persona torpe*) idiot

alcuza *f* (*olive*) oil bottle

aldaba *f* door-knocker. ~**da** *f* knock at the door

alde|a *f* village. ~**ano** *a* village; (*campesino*) rustic, country. ~**huela** *f* hamlet

alea|ción *f* alloy. ~**r** *vt* alloy

aleatorio *a* uncertain

alecciona|dor *a* instructive. ~**miento** *m* instruction. ~**r** *vt* instruct

aledaños *mpl* outskirts

alega|ción *f* allegation; (*Arg, Mex, disputa*) argument. ~**r** [12] *vt* claim; (*jurid*) allege. ● *vi* (*LAm*) argue. ~**to** *m* plea

aleg|oría *f* allegory. ~**órico** *a* allegorical

alegr|ar *vt* make happy; (*avivar*) brighten up. ~**arse** *vpr* be happy; (*emborracharse*) get merry. ~**e** *a* happy; (*achispado*) merry, tight. ~**emente** *adv* happily. ~**ía** *f* happiness. ~**ón** *m* sudden joy, great happiness

aleja|do *a* distant. ~**miento** *m* removal; (*entre personas*) estrangement; (*distancia*) distance. ~**r** *vt* remove; (*ahuyentar*) get rid of; (*fig, apartar*) separate. ~**rse** *vpr* move away

alela|do *a* stupid. ~**r** *vt* stupefy. ~**rse** *vpr* be stupefied

aleluya *m* & *f* alleluia

alemán *a* & *m* German

Alemania *f* Germany. ~ **Occidental** (*historia*) West Germany. ~ **Oriental** (*historia*) East Germany

alenta|dor *a* encouraging. ~**r** [1] *vt* encourage. ● *vi* breathe

alerce *m* larch

al|ergia *f* allergy. ~**érgico** *a* allergic

alero *m* (*del tejado*) eaves

alerón *m* aileron

alerta *adv* alert, on the alert. ¡~! look out! ~**r** *vt* alert

aleta *f* wing; (*de pez*) fin

aletarga|do *a* lethargic. ~**miento** *m* lethargy. ~**r** [12] *vt* make lethargic. ~**rse** *vpr* become lethargic

alet|azo *m* (*de un ave*) flap of the wings; (*de un pez*) flick of the fin. ~**ear** *vi* flap its wings, flutter. ~**eo** *m* flapping (of the wings)

aleve *a* treacherous

alevín *m* young fish

alevos|ía *f* treachery. ~**o** *a* treacherous

alfab|ético *a* alphabetical. ~**etizar** [10] *vt* alphabetize; teach to read and write (*a uno*). ~**eto** *m* alphabet. ~**eto Morse** Morse code

alfalfa *f* lucerne (*Brit*), alfalfa (*Amer*)

alfar *m* pottery. ~**ería** *f* pottery. ~**ero** *m* potter

alféizar *m* window-sill

alferecía f epilepsy

alférez m second lieutenant

alfil m (en ajedrez) bishop

alfile|r m pin. ~razo m pinprick. ~tero m pin-case

alfombr|a f (grande) carpet; (pequeña) rug, mat. ~ar vt carpet. ~illa f rug, mat; (med) German measles

alforja f saddle-bag

algas fpl seaweed

algarabía f (fig, fam) gibberish, non-sense

algarada f uproar

algarrob|a f carob bean. ~o m carob tree

algazara f uproar

álgebra f algebra

algebraico a algebraic

álgido a (fig) decisive

algo pron something; (en frases interrogativas) anything. • adv rather. ¿~ más? is there anything else? ¿quieres tomar ~? (de beber) would you like a drink?; (de comer) would you like something to eat?

algod|ón m cotton. ~ón de azúcar candy floss (Brit), cotton candy (Amer). ~onero a cotton. • m cotton plant. ~ón hidrófilo cotton wool

alguacil m bailiff

alguien pron someone, somebody; (en frases interrogativas) anyone, anybody

alguno a (delante de nombres masculinos en singular algún) some; (en frases interrogativas) any; (pospuesto al nombre en frases negativas) at all. no tiene idea alguna he hasn't any idea at all. • pron one; (en plural) some; (alguien) someone. alguna que otra vez from time to time. algunas veces, alguna vez sometimes

alhaja f piece of jewellery; (fig) treasure. ~r vt deck with jewels; (amueblar) furnish

alharaca f fuss

alhelí m wallflower

alheña f privet

alhucema f lavender

alia|do a allied. • m ally. ~nza f alliance; (anillo) wedding ring. ~r [20] vt combine. ~rse vpr be combined; (formar una alianza) form an alliance

alias adv & m alias

alicaído a (fig, débil) weak; (fig, abatido) depressed

alicates mpl pliers

aliciente m incentive; (de un lugar) attraction

alien|ado a mentally ill. ~ista m & f psychiatrist

aliento m breath; (ánimo) courage

aligera|miento m lightening; (alivio) alleviation. ~r vt make lighter; (aliviar) alleviate, ease; (apresurar) quicken

alij|ar vt (descargar) unload; smuggle (contrabando). ~o m unloading; (contrabando) contraband

alimaña f vicious animal

aliment|ación f (acción) feeding. ~ar vt feed; (nutrir) nourish. • vi be nourishing. ~arse vpr feed (con, de on). ~icio a nourishing. ~o m food. ~os mpl (jurid) alimony. productos mpl ~icios foodstuffs

alimón. al ~ adv jointly

aline|ación f alignment; (en deportes) line-up. ~r vt align, line up

aliñ|ar vt (culin) season. ~o m seasoning

alioli m garlic sauce

alisar vt smooth

alisios apl. vientos mpl ~ trade winds

aliso m alder (tree)

alista|miento m enrolment. ~r vt put on a list; (mil) enlist. ~rse vpr enrol; (mil) enlist

aliteración f alliteration

alivi|ador a comforting. ~ar vt lighten; relieve (dolor, etc); (hurtar, fam) steal, pinch (fam). ~arse vpr (dolor) diminish; (persona) get better. ~o m relief

aljibe m tank

alma f soul; (habitante) inhabitant

almac|én m warehouse; (LAm, tienda) grocer's shop; (de un arma) magazine. ~enes mpl department store. ~enaje m storage; (derechos) storage charges. ~enamiento m storage; (mercancías almacenadas) stock. ~enar vt store; stock up with (provisiones). ~enero m (Arg) shopkeeper. ~enista m & f shopkeeper

almádena f sledge-hammer

almanaque m almanac

almeja f clam

almendr|a f almond. ~ado a almond-shaped. ~o m almond tree

almiar m haystack

alm|íbar m syrup. ~ibarado a syrupy. ~ibarar vt cover in syrup

almid|ón *m* starch. **~onado** *a* starched; (*fig, estirado*) starchy

alminar *m* minaret

almirant|azgo *m* admiralty. **~e** *m* admiral

almirez *m* mortar

almizcle *m* musk

almohad|a *f* cushion; (*de la cama*) pillow; (*funda*) pillowcase. **~illa** *f* small cushion; (*acerico*) pincushion. **~ón** *m* large pillow, bolster. **consultar con la ~a** sleep on it

almorranas *fpl* haemorrhoids, piles

alm|orzar [2 & 10] *vt* (*a mediodía*) have for lunch; (*desayunar*) have for breakfast. ● *vi* (*a mediodía*) have lunch; (*desayunar*) have breakfast. **~uerzo** *m* (*a mediodía*) lunch; (*desayuno*) breakfast

alocado *a* scatter-brained

alocución *f* address, speech

aloja|do *m* (Mex) lodger, guest. **~miento** *m* accommodation. **~r** *vt* put up. **~rse** *vpr* stay

alondra *f* lark

alpaca *f* alpaca

alpargat|a *f* canvas shoe, espadrille. **~ería** *f* shoe shop

Alpes *mpl* Alps

alpin|ismo *m* mountaineering, climbing. **~ista** *m & f* mountaineer, climber. **~o** *a* Alpine

alpiste *m* birdseed

alquil|ar *vt* (*tomar en alquiler*) hire (*vehículo*), rent (*piso, casa*); (*dar en alquiler*) hire (out) (*vehículo*), rent (out) (*piso, casa*). **~arse** *vpr* (*casa*) be let; (*vehículo*) be on hire. **se alquila** to let (*Brit*), for rent (*Amer*). **~er** *m* (*acción de alquilar un piso etc*) renting; (*acción de alquilar un vehículo*) hiring; (*precio por el que se alquila un piso etc*) rent; (*precio por el que se alquila un vehículo*) hire charge. **de ~er** for hire

alquimi|a *f* alchemy. **~sta** *m* alchemist

alquitara *f* still. **~r** *vt* distil

alquitr|án *m* tar. **~anar** *vt* tar

alrededor *adv* around. **~ de** around; (*con números*) about. **~es** *mpl* surroundings; (*de una ciudad*) outskirts

alta *f* discharge

altamente *adv* highly

altaner|ía *f* (*orgullo*) pride. **~o** *a* proud, haughty

altar *m* altar

altavoz *m* loudspeaker

altera|bilidad *f* changeability. **~ble** *a* changeable. **~ción** *f* change, alteration. **~do** *a* changed, altered; (*perturbado*) disturbed. **~r** *vt* change, alter; (*perturbar*) disturb; (*enfadar*) anger, irritate. **~rse** *vpr* change, alter; (*agitarse*) get upset; (*enfadarse*) get angry; (*comida*) go off

alterca|do *m* argument. **~r** [7] *vi* argue

altern|ado *a* alternate. **~ador** *m* alternator. **~ante** *a* alternating. **~ar** *vt/i* alternate. **~arse** *vpr* take turns. **~ativa** *f* alternative. **~ativo** *a* alternating. **~o** *a* alternate

alteza *f* height. **A~** (*título*) Highness

altibajos *mpl* (*de terreno*) unevenness; (*fig*) ups and downs

altiplanicie *f* high plateau

altísimo *a* very high. ● *m*. **el A~** the Almighty

altisonante *a*, **altísono** *a* pompous

altitud *f* height; (*aviat, geog*) altitude

altiv|ez *f* arrogance. **~o** *a* arrogant

alto *a* high; (*persona*) tall; (*voz*) loud; (*fig, elevado*) lofty; (*mus*) (*nota*) high(-pitched); (*mus*) (*voz, instrumento*) alto; (*horas*) early. **tiene 3 metros de ~** it is 3 metres high. ● *adv* high; (*de sonidos*) loud(ly). ● *m* height; (*de un edificio*) high floor; (*viola*) viola; (*voz*) alto; (*parada*) stop. ● *int* halt!, stop! **en lo ~ de** on the top of

altoparlante *m* (*esp LAm*) loudspeaker

altruis|mo *m* altruism. **~ta** *a* altruistic. ● *m & f* altruist

altura *f* height; (*altitud*) altitude; (*de agua*) depth; (*fig, cielo*) sky. **a estas ~s** at this stage. **tiene 3 metros de ~** it is 3 metres high

alubia *f* French bean

alucinación *f* hallucination

alud *m* avalanche

aludi|do *a* in question. **darse por ~do** take it personally. **no darse por ~do** turn a deaf ear. **~r** *vi* mention

alumbra|do *a* lit; (*achispado, fam*) tipsy. ● *m* lighting. **~miento** *m* lighting; (*parto*) childbirth. **~r** *vt* light. ● *vi* give birth. **~rse** *vpr* (*emborracharse*) get tipsy

aluminio *m* aluminium (*Brit*), aluminum (*Amer*)

alumno *m* pupil; (*univ*) student

aluniza|je *m* landing on the moon. **~r** [10] *vi* land on the moon

alusi|ón *f* allusion. **~vo** *a* allusive

alverja *f* vetch; (*LAm, guisante*) pea

alza *f* rise. **~cuello** *m* clerical collar, dog-collar (*fam*). **~da** *f* (*de caballo*) height; (*jurid*) appeal. **~do** *a* raised; (*persona*) fraudulently bankrupt; (*Mex, soberbio*) vain; (*precio*) fixed. **~miento** *m* raising; (*aumento*) rise, increase; (*pol*) revolt. **~r** [10] *vt* raise, lift (up); raise (*precios*). **~rse** *vpr* rise; (*ponerse en pie*) stand up; (*pol*) revolt; (*quebrar*) go fraudulently bankrupt; (*apelar*) appeal

allá *adv* there. **i~ él!** that's his business. **~ fuera** out there. **~ por el 1970** around about 1970. **el más ~** the beyond. **más ~** further on. **más ~ de** beyond. **por ~** over there

allana|miento *m* levelling; (*de obstáculos*) removal. **~miento de morada** burglary. **~r** *vt* level; remove (*obstáculos*); (*fig*) iron out (*dificultades etc*); burgle (*una casa*). **~rse** *vpr* level off; (*hundirse*) fall down; (*ceder*) submit (**a** to)

allega|do *a* close. **●** *m* relation. **~r** [12] *vt* collect

allí *adv* there; (*tiempo*) then. **~ donde** wherever. **~ fuera** out there. **por ~** over there

ama *f* lady of the house. **~ de casa** housewife. **~ de cría** wet-nurse. **~ de llaves** housekeeper

amab|ilidad *f* kindness. **~le** *a* kind; (*simpático*) nice

amado *a* dear. **~r** *m* lover

amaestra|do *a* trained; (*en circo*) performing. **~miento** *m* training. **~r** *vt* train

amag|ar [12] *vt* (*amenazar*) threaten; (*mostrar intención de*) show signs of. **●** *vi* threaten; (*algo bueno*) be in the offing. **~o** *m* threat; (*señal*) sign; (*med*) sympton

amalgama *f* amalgam. **~r** *vt* amalgamate

amamantar *vt* breast-feed

amancebarse *vpr* live together

amanecer *m* dawn. **●** *vi* dawn; (*persona*) wake up. **al ~** at dawn, at daybreak

amanera|do *a* affected. **~miento** *m* affectation. **~rse** *vpr* become affected

amanezca *f* (*Mex*) dawn

amansa|dor *m* tamer. **~miento** *m* taming. **~r** *vt* tame; break in (*un caballo*); soothe (*dolor etc*). **~rse** *vpr* calm down

amante *a* fond. **●** *m & f* lover

amañ|ar *vt* arrange. **~o** *m* scheme

amapola *f* poppy

amar *vt* love

amara|je *m* landing on the sea; (*de astronave*) splash-down. **~r** *vt* land on the sea; (*astronave*) splash down

amarg|ado *a* embittered. **~ar** [12] *vt* make bitter; embitter (*persona*). **~arse** *vpr* get bitter. **~o** *a* bitter. **●** *m* bitterness. **~ura** *f* bitterness

amariconado *a* effeminate

amarill|ear *vi* go yellow. **~ento** *a* yellowish; (*tez*) sallow. **~ez** *f* yellow; (*de una persona*) paleness. **~o** *a & m* yellow

amarra *f* mooring rope. **~s** *fpl* (*fig, fam*) influence. **~do** *a* (*LAm*) mean. **~r** *vt* moor; (*atar*) tie. **●** *vi* (*empollar, fam*) study hard, swot (*fam*)

amartillar *vt* cock (*arma de fuego*)

amas|ar *vt* knead; (*fig, tramar, fam*) concoct, cook up (*fam*). **~ijo** *m* dough; (*acción*) kneading; (*fig, mezcla, fam*) hotchpotch

amate *m* (*Mex*) fig tree

amateur *a & m & f* amateur

amatista *f* amethyst

amazona *f* Amazon; (*mujer varonil*) mannish woman; (*que monta a caballo*) horsewoman

Amazonas *m*. **el río ~** the Amazon

ambages *mpl* circumlocutions. **sin ~** in plain language

ámbar *m* amber

ambarino *a* amber

ambici|ón *f* ambition. **~onar** *vt* strive after. **~onar ser** have an ambition to be. **~oso** *a* ambitious. **●** *m* ambitious person

ambidextro *a* ambidextrous. **●** *m* ambidextrous person

ambient|ar *vt* give an atmosphere to. **~arse** *vpr* adapt o.s. **~e** *m* atmosphere; (*medio*) environment

ambig|uamente *adv* ambiguously. **~üedad** *f* ambiguity. **~uo** *a* ambiguous; (*fig, afeminado, fam*) effeminate

ámbito *m* ambit

ambos *a & pron* both. **~ a dos** both (of them)

ambulancia *f* ambulance; (*hospital móvil*) field hospital ambulante *a* travelling

ambulatorio *m* out-patients' department

amedrentar *vt* frighten, scare. ~se *vpr* be frightened

amén *m* amen. ● *int* amen! en un decir ~ in an instant

amenaza *f* threat. ~dor *a*, ~nte *a* threatening. ~r [10] *vt* threaten

amen|idad *f* pleasantness. ~izar [10] *vt* brighten up. ~o *a* pleasant

América *f* America. ~ Central Central America. ~ del Norte North America. ~ del Sur South America. ~ Latina Latin America

american|a *f* jacket. ~ismo *m* Americanism. ~ista *m & f* Americanist. ~o *a* American

amerindio *a & m & f* Amerindian, American Indian

ameriza|je *m* landing on the sea; *(de astronave)* splash-down. ~r [10] *vt* land on the sea; *(astronave)* splash down

ametralla|dora *f* machine-gun. ~r *vt* machine-gun

amianto *m* asbestos

amig|a *f* friend; *(novia)* girl-friend; *(amante)* lover. ~able *a* friendly. ~ablemente *adv* amicably. ~rse [12] *vpr* live together

am|ígdala *f* tonsil. ~igdalitis *f* tonsillitis

amigo *a* friendly. ● *m* friend; *(novio)* boy-friend; *(amante)* lover. ser ~ de be fond of. ser muy ~s be good friends

amilanar *vt* frighten, scare. ~se *vpr* be frightened

aminorar *vt* lessen; slow down *(velocidad)*

amist|ad *f* friendship. ~ades *mpl* friends. ~osamente *adv* amicably. ~oso *a* friendly

amnesia *f* amnesia

amnist|ía *f* amnesty. ~iar [20] *vt* grant an amnesty to

amo *m* master; *(dueño)* owner; *(jefe)* boss; *(cabeza de familia)* head of the family

amodorra|miento *m* sleepiness. ~rse *vpr* get sleepy

amojonar *vt* mark out

amola|dor *m* knife-grinder. ~r [2] *vt* sharpen; *(molestar, fam)* annoy

amoldar *vt* mould; *(acomodar)* fit

amonedar *vt* coin, mint

amonesta|ción *f* rebuke, reprimand; *(de una boda)* banns. ~r *vt* rebuke, reprimand; *(anunciar la boda)* publish the banns

amoníaco *m*, amoniaco *m* ammonia

amontillado *m* Amontillado, pale dry sherry

amontona|damente *adv* in a heap. ~miento *m* piling up. ~r *vt* pile up; *(fig, acumular)* accumulate. ~rse *vpr* pile up; *(gente)* crowd together; *(amancebarse, fam)* live together

amor *m* love. ~es *mpl* *(relaciones amorosas)* love affairs. con mil ~es, de mil ~es with (the greatest of) pleasure. hacer el ~ make love. por (el) ~ de Dios for God's sake

amorata|do *a* purple; *(de frío)* blue. ~rse *vpr* go black and blue

amorcillo *m* Cupid

amordazar [10] *vt* gag; *(fig)* silence

amorfo *a* amorphous, shapeless

amor: ~ío *m* affair. ~oso *a* loving; *(cartas)* love

amortajar *vt* shroud

amortigua|dor *a* deadening. ● *m* *(auto)* shock absorber. ~miento *m* deadening; *(de la luz)* dimming. ~r [15] *vt* deaden *(ruido)*; dim *(luz)*; cushion *(golpe)*; tone down *(color)*

amortiza|ble *a* redeemable. ~ción *f* *(de una deuda)* repayment; *(recuperación)* redemption. ~r [10] *vt* repay *(una deuda)*

amoscarse [7] *vpr* *(fam)* get cross, get irritated

amostazarse [10] *vpr* get cross

amotina|do *a & m* insurgent, rebellious. ~miento *m* riot; *(mil)* mutiny. ~r *vt* incite to riot. ~rse *vpr* rebel; *(mil)* mutiny

ampar|ar *vt* help; *(proteger)* protect. ~arse *vpr* seek protection; *(de la lluvia)* shelter. ~o *m* protection; *(de la lluvia)* shelter. al ~o de under the protection of

amperio *m* ampere, amp *(fam)*

amplia|ción *f* extension; *(photo)* enlargement. ~r [20] *vt* enlarge, extend; *(photo)* enlarge

amplifica|ción *f* amplification. ~dor *m* amplifier. ~r [7] *vt* amplify

ampli|o *a* wide; *(espacioso)* spacious; *(ropa)* loose-fitting. ~tud *f* extent; *(espaciosidad)* spaciousness; *(espacio)* space

ampolla *f* *(med)* blister; *(frasco)* flask; *(de medicamento)* ampoule, phial

ampuloso *a* pompous

amputa|ción *f* amputation; (*fig*) deletion. ~r *vt* amputate; (*fig*) delete

amueblar *vt* furnish

amuinar *vt* (*Mex*) annoy

amuralla|do *a* walled. ~r *vt* build a wall around

anacardo *m* (*fruto*) cashew nut

anaconda *f* anaconda

anacr|ónico *a* anachronistic. ~onismo *m* anachronism

ánade *m & f* duck

anagrama *m* anagram

anales *mpl* annals

analfabet|ismo *m* illiteracy. ~o *a & m* illiterate

analgésico *a & m* analgesic, painkiller

an|álisis *m invar* analysis. ~álisis de sangre blood test. ~alista *m & f* analyst. ~alítico *a* analytical. ~alizar [10] *vt* analyze

an|alogía *f* analogy. ~álogo *a* analogous

ananás *m* pineapple

anaquel *m* shelf

anaranjado *a* orange

an|arquía *f* anarchy. ~árquico *a* anarchic. ~arquismo *m* anarchism. ~arquista *a* anarchistic. ● *m & f* anarchist

anatema *m* anathema

anat|omía *f* anatomy. ~ómico *a* anatomical

anca *f* haunch; (*parte superior*) rump; (*nalgas, fam*) bottom. ~s *fpl* de rana frogs' legs

ancestral *a* ancestral

anciano *a* elderly, old. ● *m* elderly man, old man; (*relig*) elder. los ~s old people

ancla *f* anchor. ~dero *m* anchorage. ~r *vi* anchor, drop anchor. echar ~s anchor. levar ~s weigh anchor

áncora *f* anchor; (*fig*) refuge

ancho *a* wide; (*ropa*) loose-fitting; (*fig*) relieved; (*demasiado grande*) too big; (*ufano*) smug. ● *m* width; (*rail*) gauge. a mis anchas, a sus anchas etc comfortable, relaxed. quedarse tan ~ behave as if nothing has happened. tiene 3 metros de ~ it is 3 metres wide

anchoa *f* anchovy

anchura *f* width; (*medida*) measurement

andaderas *fpl* baby-walker

andad|or *a* good at walking. ● *m* baby-walker. ~ura *f* walking; (*manera de andar*) walk

Andalucía *f* Andalusia

andaluz *a & m* Andalusian

andamio *m* platform. ~s *mpl* scaffolding

andar [25] *vt* (*recorrer*) cover, go. ● *vi* walk; (*máquina*) go, work; (*estar*) be; (*moverse*) move. ● *m* walk. ¡anda! go on! come on! ~iego *a* fond of walking; (*itinerante*) wandering. ~ por be about. ~se *vpr* (*marcharse*) go away

andén *m* platform; (*de un muelle*) quayside; (*LAm, acera*) pavement (*Brit*), sidewalk (*Amer*)

Andes *mpl* Andes

andino *a* Andean

Andorra *f* Andorra

andrajo *m* rag. ~so *a* ragged

andurriales *mpl* (*fam*) out-of-the-way place

anduve *vb véase* **andar**

anécdota *f* anecdote

anega|dizo *a* subject to flooding. ~r [12] *vt* flood. ~rse *vpr* be flooded, flood

anejo *a* attached. ● *m* annexe; (*de libro etc*) appendix

an|emia *f* anaemia. ~émico *a* anaemic

anest|esia *f* anaesthesia. ~ésico *a & m* anaesthetic. ~esista *m & f* anaesthetist

anex|ión *f* annexation. ~ionar *vt* annex. ~o *a* attached. ● *m* annexe

anfibio *a* amphibious. ● *m* amphibian

anfiteatro *m* amphitheatre; (*en un teatro*) upper circle

anfitri|ón *m* host. ~ona *f* hostess

ángel *m* angel; (*encanto*) charm

angelical *a*, **angélico** *a* angelic

angina *f*. ~ de pecho angina (pectoris). tener ~s have tonsillitis

anglicano *a & m* Anglican

anglicismo *m* Anglicism

anglófilo *a & m* Anglophile

anglo|hispánico *a* Anglo-Spanish. ~sajón *a & m* Anglo-Saxon

angosto *a* narrow

anguila *f* eel

angula *f* elver, baby eel

angular *a* angular

ángulo *m* angle; (*rincón, esquina*) corner; (*curva*) bend

anguloso *a* angular

angusti|a *f* anguish. **~ar** *vt* distress; (*inquietar*) worry. **~arse** *vpr* get distressed; (*inquietarse*) get worried. **~oso** *a* anguished; (*que causa angustia*) distressing

anhel|ante *a* panting; (*deseoso*) longing. **~ar** *vt* (+ *nombre*) long for; (+ *verbo*) long to. ● *vi* pant. **~o** *m* (*fig*) yearning. **~oso** *a* panting; (*fig*) eager

anidar *vi* nest

anill|a *f* ring. **~o** *m* ring. **~o de boda** wedding ring

ánima *f* soul

anima|ción *f* (*de personas*) life; (*de cosas*) liveliness; (*bullicio*) bustle; (*en el cine*) animation. **~do** *a* lively; (*sitio etc*) busy. **~dor** *m* compère, host

animadversión *f* ill will

animal *a* animal; (*fig, torpe, fam*) stupid. ● *m* animal; (*fig, idiota, fam*) idiot; (*fig, bruto, fam*) brute

animar *vt* give life to; (*dar ánimo*) encourage; (*dar vivacidad*) liven up. **~se** *vpr* (*decidirse*) decide; (*ponerse alegre*) cheer up. **¿te animas a venir al cine?** do you fancy coming to the cinema?

ánimo *m* soul; (*mente*) mind; (*valor*) courage; (*intención*) intention. **¡~!** come on!, cheer up! **dar ~s** encourage

animosidad *f* animosity

animoso *a* brave; (*resuelto*) determined

aniquila|ción *f* annihilation. **~miento** *m* annihilation. **~r** *vt* annihilate; (*acabar con*) ruin. **~rse** *vpr* deteriorate

anís *m* aniseed; (*licor*) anisette

aniversario *m* anniversary

ano *m* anus

anoche *adv* last night, yesterday evening

anochecer [11] *vi* get dark; ⟨*persona*⟩ be at dusk. **anochecí en Madrid** I was in Madrid at dusk. ● *m* nightfall, dusk. **al ~** at nightfall

anodino *a* indifferent

an|omalía *f* anomaly. **~ómalo** *a* anomalous

an|onimato *m* anonymity. **~ónimo** *a* anonymous; ⟨*sociedad*⟩ limited. ● *m* anonymity; (*carta*) anonymous letter

anormal *a* abnormal; (*fam*) stupid, silly. **~idad** *f* abnormality

anota|ción *f* noting; (*acción de poner notas*) annotation; (*nota*) note. **~r** *vt* (*poner nota*) annotate; (*apuntar*) make a note of

anquilosa|miento *m* paralysis. **~r** *vt* paralyze. **~rse** *vpr* become paralyzed

ansi|a *f* anxiety, worry; (*anhelo*) yearning. **~ar** [20 *o regular*] *vt* long for. **~edad** *f* anxiety. **~oso** *a* anxious; (*deseoso*) eager

antag|ónico *a* antagonistic. **~onismo** *m* antagonism. **~onista** *m & f* antagonist

antaño *adv* in days gone by

antártico *a & m* Antarctic

ante *prep* in front of, before; (*en comparación con*) compared with; (*frente a peligro, enemigo*) in the face of; (*en vista de*) in view of. ● *m* (*piel*) suede. **~anoche** *adv* the night before last. **~ayer** *adv* the day before yesterday. **~brazo** *m* forearm

ante... *pref* ante...

antece|dente *a* previous. ● *m* antecedent. **~dentes** *mpl* history, background. **~dentes penales** criminal record. **~der** *vt* precede. **~sor** *m* predecessor; (*antepasado*) ancestor

antedicho *a* aforesaid

antelación *f* advance. **con ~** in advance

antemano *adv*. **de ~** beforehand

antena *f* antenna; (*radio, TV*) aerial

anteojeras *fpl* blinkers

anteojo *m* telescope. **~s** *mpl* (*gemelos*) opera glasses; (*prismáticos*) binoculars; (*LAm, gafas*) glasses, spectacles

ante: ~pasados *mpl* forebears, ancestors. **~pecho** *m* rail; (*de ventana*) sill. **~poner** [34] *vt* put in front (**a** of); (*fig*) put before, prefer. **~proyecto** *m* preliminary sketch; (*fig*) blueprint. **~puesto** *a* put before

anterior *a* previous; (*delantero*) front, fore. **~idad** *f*. **con ~idad** previously. **~mente** *adv* previously

antes *adv* before; (*antiguamente*) in days gone by; (*mejor*) rather; (*primero*) first. **~ de** before. **~ de ayer** the day before yesterday. **~ de que** + *subj* before. **~ de que llegue** before he arrives. **cuanto ~, lo ~ posible** as soon as possible

antesala *f* anteroom; (*sala de espera*) waiting-room. **hacer ~** wait (to be received)

anti... *pref* anti...

anti: ~aéreo *a* anti-aircraft. ~bió- tico *a* & *m* antibiotic. ~ciclón *m* anticyclone

anticip|ación *f* anticipation. con ~ación in advance. con media hora de ~ación half an hour early. ~adamente *adv* in advance. ~ado *a*. por ~ado in advance. ~ar *vt* bring forward; advance ⟨*dinero*⟩. ~arse *vpr* be early. ~o *m* ⟨*dinero*⟩ advance; *(fig)* foretaste

anti: ~concepcional *a* & *m* contraceptive. ~conceptivo *a* & *m* contraceptive. ~congelante *m* antifreeze

anticua|do *a* old-fashioned. ~rio *m* antique dealer. ~rse *vpr* go out of date

anticuerpo *m* antibody

antídoto *m* antidote

anti: ~estético *a* ugly. ~faz *m* mask. ~gás *a invar*. careta ~gás gas mask

antig|ualla *f* old relic. ~uamente *adv* formerly; *(hace mucho tiempo)* long ago. ~üedad *f* antiquity; *(objeto)* antique; *(en un empleo)* length of service. ~uo *a* old, ancient. chapado a la ~ua old-fashioned

antílope *m* antelope

Antillas *fpl* West Indies

antinatural *a* unnatural

antip|atía *f* dislike; *(cualidad de antipático)* unpleasantness. ~ático *a* unpleasant, unfriendly

anti: ~semita *m* & *f* anti-Semite. ~semítico *a* anti-Semitic. ~semitismo *m* anti-Semitism. ~séptico *a* & *m* antiseptic. ~social *a* antisocial

antítesis *f invar* antithesis

antoj|adizo *a* capricious. ~arse *vpr* fancy. se le ~a un caramelo he fancies a sweet. ~o *m* whim; *(de embarazada)* crav ng

antología *f* anth⟨l⟩gy

antorcha *f* torch

antro *m* cavern; *(fig)* dump, hole. ~ de perversión den of iniquity

antropófago *m* cannibal

antrop|ología *f* anthropology. ~ólogo *m* & *f* anthropologist

anua|l *a* annual. ~lidad *f* annuity. ~lmente *adv* yearly. ~rio *m* yearbook

anudar *vt* tie, knot; *(fig, iniciar)* begin; *(fig, continuar)* resume. ~se

vpr get into knots. ~se la voz get a lump in one's throat

anula|ción *f* annulment, cancellation. ~r *vt* annul, cancel. ● *a* ⟨*dedo*⟩ ring. ● *m* ring finger

Anunciación *f* Annunciation

anunci|ante *m* & *f* advertiser. ~ar *vt* announce; advertise ⟨*producto comercial*⟩; *(presagiar)* be a sign of. ~arse *vpr* promise to be. ~o *m* announcement; *(para vender algo)* advertisement, advert *(fam)*; *(cartel)* poster

anzuelo *m* (fish)hook; *(fig)* bait. tragar el ~ be taken in, fall for it

añadi|do *a* added. ~dura *f* addition. ~r *vt* add. por ~dura besides

añejo *a* ⟨*vino*⟩ mature; ⟨*jamón etc*⟩ cured

añicos *mpl* bits. hacer ~ *(romper)* smash (to pieces); *(dejar cansado)* wear out

añil *m* indigo

año *m* year. ~ bisiesto leap year. ~ nuevo new year. al ~ per year, a year. ¿cuántos ~s tiene? tiene 5 ~s how old is he? he's 5 (years old). el ~ pasado last year. el ~ que viene next year. entrado en ~s elderly. los ~s 60 the sixties

añora|nza *f* nostalgia. ~r *vt* miss. ● *vi* pine

apabullar *vt* crush; *(fig)* intimidate

apacentar [1] *vt* graze. ~se *vpr* graze

apacib|ilidad *f* gentleness; *(calma)* peacefulness. ~le *a* gentle; ⟨*tiempo*⟩ mild

apacigua|dor *a* pacifying. ~miento *m* appeasement. ~r [15] *vt* pacify; *(calmar)* calm; relieve ⟨*dolor etc*⟩. ~rse *vpr* calm down

apadrina|miento *m* sponsorship. ~r *vt* sponsor; be godfather to ⟨*a un niño*⟩; *(en una boda)* be best man for

apaga|dizo *a* slow to burn. ~do *a* extinguished; ⟨*color*⟩ dull; ⟨*aparato eléctrico*⟩ off; ⟨*persona*⟩ lifeless; ⟨*sonido*⟩ muffled. ~r [12] *vt* put out ⟨*fuego, incendio*⟩; turn off, switch off ⟨*aparato eléctrico*⟩; quench ⟨*sed*⟩; muffle ⟨*sonido*⟩. ~rse *vpr* ⟨*fuego*⟩ go out; ⟨*luz*⟩ go out; ⟨*sonido*⟩ die away; *(fig)* pass away

apagón *m* blackout

apalabrar *vt* make a verbal agreement; *(contratar)* engage. ~se *vpr* come to a verbal agreement

apalanca|miento *m* leverage. **~r** [7] *vt* (*levantar*) lever up; (*abrir*) lever open

apalea|miento *m* (*de grano*) winnowing; (*de alfombras, frutos, personas*) beating. **~r** *vt* winnow (*grano*); beat (*alfombras, frutos, personas*); (*fig*) be rolling in (*dinero*)

apantallado *a* (*Mex*) stupid

apañ|ado *a* handy. **~ar** *vt* (*arreglar*) fix; (*remendar*) mend; (*agarrar*) grasp, take hold of. **~arse** *vpr* get along, manage. ¡**estoy ~ado!** that's all I need!

aparador *m* sideboard

aparato *m* apparatus; (*máquina*) machine; (*teléfono*) telephone; (*radio, TV*) set; (*ostentación*) show, pomp. **~samente** *adv* ostentatiously; (*impresionante*) spectacularly. **~sidad** *f* ostentation. **~so** *a* showy, ostentatious; (*caída*) spectacular

aparca|miento *m* car park (*Brit*), parking lot (*Amer*). **~r** [7] *vt/i* park

aparea|miento *m* pairing off. **~r** *vt* pair off; mate (*animales*). **~rse** *vpr* match; (*animales*) mate

aparecer [11] *vi* appear. **~se** *vpr* appear

aparej|ado *a* ready; (*adecuado*) fitting. **llevar ~ado, traer ~ado** mean, entail. **~o** *m* preparation; (*avíos*) equipment

aparent|ar *vt* (*afectar*) feign; (*parecer*) look. ● *vi* show off. **~a 20 años** she looks like she's 20. **~e** *a* apparent; (*adecuado, fam*) suitable

apari|ción *f* appearance; (*visión*) apparition. **~encia** *f* appearance; (*fig*) show. **cubrir las ~encias** keep up appearances

apartad|ero *m* lay-by; (*rail*) siding. **~o** *a* separated; (*aislado*) isolated. ● *m* (*de un texto*) section. **~o** (*de correos*) post-office box, PO box

apartamento *m* flat (*Brit*), apartment

apart|amiento *m* separation; (*LAm, piso*) flat (*Brit*), apartment; (*aislamiento*) seclusion. **~ar** *vt* separate; (*quitar*) remove. **~arse** *vpr* leave; abandon (*creencia*); (*quitarse de en medio*) get out of the way; (*aislarse*) cut o.s. off. **~e** *adv* apart; (*por separado*) separately; (*además*) besides. ● *m* aside; (*párrafo*) new paragraph. **~e de** apart from. **dejar**

~e leave aside. **eso ~e** apart from that

apasiona|do *a* passionate; (*entusiasta*) enthusiastic; (*falto de objetividad*) biassed. ● *m* lover (**de** of). **~miento** *m* passion. **~r** *vt* excite. **~rse** *vpr* get excited (**de, por** about), be mad (**de, por** about); (*ser parcial*) become biassed

apatía *f* apathy. **~ático** *a* apathetic

apea|dero *m* (*rail*) halt. **~r** *vt* fell (*árbol*); (*disuadir*) dissuade; overcome (*dificultad*); sort out (*problema*). **~rse** *vpr* (*de un vehículo*) get off

apechugar [12] *vi* push (with one's chest). **~ con** put up with

apedrear *vt* stone

apeg|ado *a* attached. **~o** *m* (*fam*) affection. **tener ~o a** be fond of

apela|ción *f* appeal. **~r** appeal; (*recurrir*) resort (**a** to)

apelmazar [10] *vt* compress

apellid|ar *vt* call. **~arse** *vpr* be called. ¿**cómo te apellidas?** what's your surname? **~o** *m* surname

apenar *vt* pain. **~se** *vpr* grieve

apenas *adv* hardly, scarcely; (*enseguida que*) as soon as. **~ si** (*fam*) hardly

ap|éndice *m* (*med*) appendix; (*fig*) appendage; (*de un libro*) appendix. **~endicitis** *f* appendicitis

apercibi|miento *m* warning. **~r** *vt* warn (**de** of, about); (*amenazar*) threaten. **~rse** *vpr* prepare; (*percatarse*) provide o.s. (**de** with)

apergaminado *a* (*piel*) wrinkled

aperitivo *m* (*bebida*) aperitif; (*comida*) appetizer

aperos *mpl* agricultural equipment

apertura *f* opening

apesadumbrar *vt* upset. **~se** *vpr* be upset

apestar *vt* stink out; (*fastidiar*) pester. ● *vi* stink (**a** of)

apet|ecer [11] *vt* long for; (*interesar*) appeal to. ¿**te ~ece una copa?** do you fancy a drink? do you feel like a drink?. ● *vi* be welcome. **~ecible** *a* attractive. **~ito** *m* appetite; (*fig*) desire. **~itoso** *a* tempting

apiadarse *vpr* feel sorry (**de** for)

ápice *m* (*nada, en frases negativas*) anything. **no ceder un ~** not give an inch

apicult|or *m* bee-keeper. **~ura** *f* bee-keeping

apilar *vt* pile up

apiñar *vt* pack in. ~se *vpr* ⟨*personas*⟩ crowd together; ⟨*cosas*⟩ be packed tight

apio *m* celery

apisonadora *f* steamroller

aplacar [7] *vt* placate; relieve ⟨*dolor*⟩

aplanar *vt* smooth. ~se *vpr* become smooth; ⟨*persona*⟩ lose heart

aplasta|nte *a* overwhelming. ~r *vt* crush. ~rse *vpr* flatten o.s.

aplatanarse *vpr* become lethargic

aplau|dir *vt* clap, applaud; (*fig*) applaud. ~so *m* applause; (*fig*) praise

aplaza|miento *m* postponement. ~r [10] *vt* postpone; defer ⟨*pago*⟩

aplebeyarse *vpr* lower o.s.

aplica|ble *a* applicable. ~ción *f* application. ~do *a* ⟨*persona*⟩ diligent. ~r [7] *vt* apply; (*fijar*) attach. ~rse *vpr* apply o.s.

aplom|ado *a* self-confident; (*vertical*) vertical. ~o *m* (self-) confidence, aplomb; (*verticalidad*) verticality

apocado *a* timid

Apocalipsis *f* Apocalypse

apocalíptico *a* apocalyptic

apoca|miento *m* diffidence. ~r [7] *vt* belittle ⟨*persona*⟩. ~rse *vpr* feel small

apodar *vt* nickname

apodera|do *m* representative. ~r *vt* authorize. ~rse *vpr* seize

apodo *m* nickname

apogeo *m* (*fig*) height

apolilla|do *a* moth-eaten. ~rse *vpr* get moth-eaten

apolítico *a* non-political

apología *f* defence

apoltronarse *vpr* get lazy

apoplejía *f* stroke

apoquinar *vt/i* (*fam*) fork out

aporrear *vt* hit, thump; beat up ⟨*persona*⟩

aporta|ción *f* contribution. ~r *vt* contribute

aposent|ar *vt* put up, lodge. ~o *m* room, lodgings

apósito *m* dressing

aposta *adv* on purpose

apostar[1] [2] *vt/i* bet

apostar[2] *vt* station. ~se *vpr* station o.s.

apostilla *f* note. ~r *vt* add notes to

apóstol *m* apostle

apóstrofo *m* apostrophe

apoy|ar *vt* lean (**en** against); (*descansar*) rest; (*asentar*) base; (*reforzar*) support. ~arse *vpr* lean, rest. ~o *m* support

apreci|able *a* appreciable; (*digno de estima*) worthy. ~ación *f* appreciation; (*valoración*) appraisal. ~ar *vt* value; (*estimar*) appreciate. ~ativo *a* appreciative. ~o *m* appraisal; (*fig*) esteem

aprehensión *f* capture

apremi|ante *a* urgent, pressing. ~ar *vt* urge; (*obligar*) compel; (*dar prisa a*) hurry up. • *vi* be urgent. ~o *m* urgency; (*obligación*) obligation

aprender *vt/i* learn. ~se *vpr* learn (by heart)

aprendiz *m* apprentice. ~aje *m* apprenticeship

aprensi|ón *f* apprehension; (*miedo*) fear. ~vo *a* apprehensive, fearful

apresa|dor *m* captor. ~miento *m* capture. ~r *vt* seize; (*prender*) capture

aprestar *vt* prepare. ~se *vpr* prepare

apresura|damente *adv* hurriedly, in a hurry. ~do *a* in a hurry; (*hecho con prisa*) hurried. ~miento *m* hurry. ~r *vt* hurry. ~rse *vpr* hurry

apret|ado *a* tight; (*difícil*) difficult; (*tacaño*) stingy, mean. ~ar [1] *vt* tighten; press ⟨*botón*⟩; squeeze ⟨*persona*⟩; (*comprimir*) press down. • *vi* be too tight. ~arse *vpr* crowd together. ~ón *m* squeeze. ~ón de manos handshake

aprieto *m* difficulty. **verse en un** ~ be in a tight spot

aprisa *adv* quickly

aprisionar *vt* imprison

aproba|ción *f* approval. ~r [2] *vt* approve (of); pass ⟨*examen*⟩. • *vi* pass

apropia|do *a* appropriate. ~rse *vpr*. ~rse de appropriate, take

aprovecha|ble *a* usable. ~do *a* (*aplicado*) diligent; (*ingenioso*) resourceful; (*egoísta*) selfish; (*económico*) thrifty. ~miento *m* advantage; (*uso*) use. ~r *vt* take advantage of; (*utilizar*) make use of. • *vi* be useful. ~rse *vpr* make the most of it. ~rse de take advantage of. **¡que aproveche!** enjoy your meal!

aprovisionar *vt* supply (**con, de** with)

aproxima|ción f approximation; (*proximidad*) closeness; (*en la lotería*) consolation prize. ~**damente** adv roughly, approximately. ~**do** a approximate, rough. ~**r** vt bring near; (*fig*) bring together (*personas*). ~**rse** vpr come closer, approach

apt|itud f suitability; (*capacidad*) ability. ~**o** a (*capaz*) capable; (*adecuado*) suitable

apuesta f bet

apuesto m smart. ●vb véase **apostar**[1]

apunta|ción f note. ~**do** a sharp. ~**dor** m prompter

apuntalar vt shore up

apunt|amiento m aiming; (*nota*) note. ~**ar** vt aim (*arma*); (*señalar*) point at; (*anotar*) make a note of, note down; (*sacar punta*) sharpen; (*en el teatro*) prompt. ~**arse** vpr put one's name down; score (*triunfo, tanto etc*). ~**e** m note; (*bosquejo*) sketch. **tomar** ~**s** take notes

apuñalar vt stab

apur|adamente adv with difficulty. ~**ado** a difficult; (*sin dinero*) hard up; (*agotado*) exhausted; (*exacto*) precise, carefully done. ~**ar** vt exhaust; (*acabar*) finish; drain (*vaso etc*); (*fastidiar*) annoy; (*causar vergüenza*) embarrass. ~**arse** vpr worry; (*esp LAm, apresurarse*) hurry up. ~**o** m tight spot, difficult situation; (*vergüenza*) embarrassment; (*estrechez*) hardship, want; (*esp LAm, prisa*) hurry

aquejar vt trouble

aquel a (f **aquella**, mpl **aquellos**, fpl **aquellas**) that; (*en plural*) those; (*primero de dos*) former

aquél pron (f **aquélla**, mpl **aquéllos**, fpl **aquéllas**) that one; (*en plural*) those; (*primero de dos*) the former

aquello pron that; (*asunto*) that business

aquí adv here. **de** ~ from here. **de** ~ **a 15 días** in a fortnight's time. **de** ~ **para allí** to and fro. **de** ~ **que** so that. **hasta** ~ until now. **por** ~ around here

aquiescencia f acquiescence

aquietar vt calm (down)

aquí: ~ **fuera** out here. ~ **mismo** right here

árabe a & m & f Arab; (*lengua*) Arabic

Arabia f Arabia. ~ **saudita**, ~ **saudí** Saudi Arabia

arábigo a Arabic

arado m plough. ~**r** m ploughman

Aragón m Aragon

aragonés a & m Aragonese

arancel m tariff. ~**ario** a tariff

arandela f washer

araña f spider; (*lámpara*) chandelier

arañar vt scratch

arar vt plough

arbitra|je m arbitration; (*en deportes*) refereeing. ~**r** vt/i arbitrate; (*en fútbol etc*) referee; (*en tenis etc*) umpire

arbitr|ariedad f arbitrariness. ~**ario** a arbitrary. ~**io** m (free) will; (*jurid*) decision, judgement

árbitro m arbitrator; (*en fútbol etc*) referee; (*en tenis etc*) umpire

árbol m tree; (*eje*) axle; (*palo*) mast

arbol|ado m trees. ~**adura** f rigging. ~**eda** f wood

árbol: ~ **genealógico** family tree. ~ **de navidad** Christmas tree

arbusto m bush

arca f (*caja*) chest. ~ **de Noé** Noah's ark

arcada f arcade; (*de un puente*) arches; (*náuseas*) retching

arca|ico a archaic. ~**ísmo** m archaism

arcángel m archangel

arcano m mystery. ●a mysterious, secret

arce m maple (tree)

arcén m (*de autopista*) hard shoulder; (*de carretera*) verge

arcilla f clay

arco m arch; (*de curva*) arc; (*arma, mus*) bow. ~ **iris** m rainbow

archipiélago m archipelago

archiv|ador m filing cabinet. ~**ar** vt file (away). ~**o** m file; (*de documentos históricos*) archives

arder vt/i burn; (*fig, de ira*) seethe. ~**se** vpr burn (up). **estar que arde** be very tense. **y va que arde** and that's enough

ardid m trick, scheme

ardiente a burning. ~**mente** adv passionately

ardilla f squirrel

ardor m heat; (*fig*) ardour. ~ **de estómago** m heartburn. ~**oso** a burning

arduo a arduous

área f area

arena f sand; (*en deportes*) arena; (*en los toros*) (bull)ring. ∼l m sandy area

arenga f harangue. ∼r [12] vt harangue

aren|isca f sandstone. ∼isco a, ∼oso a sandy

arenque m herring. ∼ **ahumado** kipper

argamasa f mortar

Argel m Algiers. ∼ia f Algeria

argelino a & m Algerian

argentado a silver-plated

Argentina f. la ∼ Argentina

argentin|ismo m Argentinism. ∼o a silvery; (*de la Argentina*) Argentinian, Argentine. ● m Argentinian

argolla f ring

argot m slang

argucia f sophism

argüir [19] vt (*deducir*) deduce; (*probar*) prove, show; (*argumentar*) argue; (*echar en cara*) reproach. ● vi argue

argument|ación f argument. ∼ador a argumentative. ∼ar vt/i argue. ∼o m argument; (*de libro, película etc*) story, plot; (*resumen*) synopsis

aria f aria

aridez f aridity, dryness

árido a arid, dry. ● m. ∼s mpl dry goods

Aries m Aries

arisco a (*persona*) unsociable; (*animal*) vicious

arist|ocracia f aristocracy. ∼ócrata m & f aristocrat. ∼ocrático a aristocratic

aritmética f arithmetic

arma f arm, weapon; (*sección*) section. ∼da f navy; (*flota*) fleet. ∼ **de fuego** firearm. ∼do a armed (**de** with). ∼dura f armour; (*de gafas etc*) frame; (*tec*) framework. ∼mento m arms, armaments; (*acción de armar*) armament. ∼r vt arm (**de** with); (*montar*) put together. ∼r un lío kick up a fuss. La A∼da Invencible the Armada

armario m cupboard; (*para ropa*) wardrobe. ∼ **ropero** wardrobe

armatoste m monstrosity, hulk (*fam*)

armazón m & f frame(work)

armer|ía f gunsmith's shop; (*museo*) war museum. ∼o m gunsmith

armiño m ermine

armisticio m armistice

armonía f harmony

armónica f harmonica, mouth organ

armoni|oso harmonious. ∼zación f harmonizing. ∼zar [10] vt harmonize. ● vi harmonize; (*personas*) get on well (**con** with); (*colores*) go well (**con** with)

arnés m armour. **arneses** mpl harness

aro m ring, hoop; (*Arg, pendiente*) earring

arom|a m aroma; (*de vino*) bouquet. ∼ático a aromatic. ∼atizar [10] vt perfume; (*culin*) flavour

arpa f harp

arpado a serrated

arpía f harpy; (*fig*) hag

arpillera f sackcloth, sacking

arpista m & f harpist

arp|ón m harpoon. ∼onar vt, ∼onear vt harpoon

arque|ar vt arch, bend. ∼arse vpr arch, bend. ∼o m arching, bending

arque|ología f archaeology. ∼ológico a archaeological. ∼ólogo m archaeologist

arquería f arcade

arquero m archer; (*com*) cashier

arqueta f chest

arquetipo m archetype; (*prototipo*) prototype

arquitect|o m architect. ∼ónico a architectural. ∼ura f architecture

arrabal m suburb; (*LAm, tugurio*) slum. ∼es mpl outskirts. ∼ero a suburban; (*de modales groseros*) common

arracima|do a in a bunch; (*apiñado*) bunched together. ∼rse vpr bunch together

arraiga|damente adv firmly. ∼r [12] vi take root. ∼rse vpr take root; (*fig*) settle

arran|cada f sudden start. ∼car [7] vt pull up (*planta*); extract (*diente*); (*arrebatar*) snatch; (*auto*) start. ● vi start. ∼carse vpr start. ∼que m sudden start; (*auto*) start; (*de emoción*) outburst

arras fpl security

arrasa|dor a overwhelming, devastating. ∼r vt level, smooth; raze to the ground (*edificio etc*); (*llenar*) fill to the brim. ● vi (*el cielo*) clear. ∼rse vpr (*el cielo*) clear; (*los ojos*) fill with tears; (*triunfar*) triumph

arrastr|ado a (penoso) wretched. ~**ar** vt pull; (rozar contra el suelo) drag (along); give rise to (consecuencias). • vi trail on the ground. ~**arse** vpr crawl; (humillarse) grovel. ~**e** m dragging; (transporte) haulage. **estar para el** ~**e** (fam) have had it, be worn out. **ir** ~**ado** be hard up

arrayán m myrtle

arre int gee up! ~**ar** vt urge on; give (golpe)

arrebañar vt scrape together; scrape clean (plato etc)

arrebat|ado a enraged; (irreflexivo) impetuous; (cara) flushed. ~**ar** vt snatch (away); (el viento) blow away; (fig) win (over); captivate (corazón etc). ~**arse** vpr get carried away. ~**o** m (de cólera etc) fit; (éxtasis) extasy

arrebol m red glow

arreciar vi get worse, increase

arrecife m reef

arregl|ado a neat; (bien vestido) well-dressed; (moderado) moderate. ~**ar** vt arrange; (poner en orden) tidy up; sort out (asunto, problema etc); (reparar) mend. ~**arse** vpr (ponerse bien) improve; (prepararse) get ready; (apañarse) manage, make do; (ponerse de acuerdo) come to an agreement. ~**árselas** manage, get by. ~**o** m (incl mus) arrangement; (acción de reparar) repair; (acuerdo) agreement; (orden) order. **con** ~**o a** according to

arrellanarse vpr lounge, sit back

arremangar [12] vt roll up (mangas); tuck up (falda). ~**se** vpr roll up one's sleeves

arremet|er vt/i attack. ~**ida** f attack

arremolinarse vpr mill about

arrenda|dor m (que da en alquiler) landlord; (que toma en alquiler) tenant. ~**miento** m renting; (contrato) lease; (precio) rent. ~**r** [1] vt (dar casa en alquiler) let; (dar cosa en alquiler) hire out; (tomar en alquiler) rent. ~**tario** m tenant

arreos mpl harness

arrepenti|miento m repentance, regret. ~**rse** [4] vpr. ~**rse de** be sorry, regret; repent (pecados)

arrest|ar vt arrest, detain; (encarcelar) imprison. ~**o** m arrest; (encarcelamiento) imprisonment

arriar [20] vt lower (bandera, vela); (aflojar) loosen; (inundar) flood. ~**se** vpr be flooded

arriba adv (up) above; (dirección) up(wards); (en casa) upstairs. • int up with; (¡levántate!) up you get!; (¡ánimo!) come on! ¡~ España! long live Spain! ~ **mencionado** aforementioned. **calle** ~ up the street. **de** ~ **abajo** from top to bottom. **de 100 pesetas para** ~ more than 100 pesetas. **escaleras** ~ upstairs. **la parte de** ~ the top part. **los de** ~ those at the top. **más** ~ above

arribar vi (barco) reach port; (esp LAm, llegar) arrive

arribista m & f self-seeking person, arriviste

arribo m (esp LAm) arrival

arriero m muleteer

arriesga|do a risky. ~**r** [12] vt risk; (aventurar) venture. ~**rse** vpr take a risk

arrim|ar vt bring close(r); (apartar) move out of the way (cosa); (apartar) push aside (persona). ~**arse** vpr come closer, approach; (apoyarse) lean (a on). ~**o** m support. **al** ~**o de** with the support of

arrincona|do a forgotten. ~**rse** vt put in a corner; (perseguir) corner; (arrumbar) put aside; (apartar a uno) leave out, ignore. ~**rse** vpr become a recluse

arriscado a (terreno) uneven

arrobar vt entrance. ~**se** vpr be enraptured

arrocero a rice

arrodillarse vpr kneel (down)

arrogan|cia f arrogance; (orgullo) pride. ~**te** a arrogant; (orgulloso) proud

arrogarse [12] vpr assume

arroj|ado a brave. ~**ar** vt throw; (dejar caer) drop; (emitir) give off, throw out; (producir) produce. • vi (esp LAm, vomitar) be sick. ~**arse** vpr throw o.s. ~**o** m courage

arrolla|dor a overwhelming. ~**r** vt roll (up); (atropellar) run over; (ejército) crush; (agua) sweep away; (tratar sin respeto) have no respect for

arropar vt wrap up; (en la cama) tuck up; (fig, amparar) protect. ~**se** vpr wrap (o.s.) up

arroyo m stream; (de una calle) gutter; (fig, de lágrimas) flood; (fig, de sangre) pool. **poner en el** ~**o** throw into the street. ~**uelo** m small stream

arroz m rice. ~**al** m rice field. ~ **con leche** rice pudding

arruga f (en la piel) wrinkle, line; (en tela) crease. ~**r** [12] vt wrinkle; crumple ⟨papel⟩; crease ⟨tela⟩. ~**rse** vpr ⟨la piel⟩ wrinkle, get wrinkled; ⟨tela⟩ crease, get creased

arruinar vt ruin; (destruir) destroy. ~**se** vpr ⟨persona⟩ be ruined; ⟨edificio⟩ fall into ruins

arrullar vt lull to sleep. ● vi ⟨palomas⟩ coo. ~**se** vpr bill and coo

arrumaco m caress; (zalamería) flattery

arrumbar vt put aside

arsenal m (astillero) shipyard; (de armas) arsenal; (fig) store

arsénico m arsenic

arte m en singular, f en plural art; (habilidad) skill; (astucia) cunning. **bellas** ~**s** fine arts. **con** ~ skilfully. **malas** ~**s** trickery. **por amor al** ~ for nothing, for love

artefacto m device

arter|amente adv artfully. ~**ía** f cunning

arteria f artery; (fig, calle) main road

artero a cunning

artesan|al a craft. ~**ía** f handicrafts. ~**o** m artisan, craftsman. **objeto** m **de** ~**ía** hand-made article

ártico a & m Arctic

articula|ción f joint; (pronunciación) articulation. ~**damente** adv articulately. ~**do** a articulated; ⟨lenguaje⟩ articulate. ~**r** vt articulate

articulista m & f columnist

artículo m article. ~**s** mpl (géneros) goods. ~ **de exportación** export commodity. ~ **de fondo** editorial, leader

artificial a artificial

artificiero m bomb-disposal expert

artificio m (habilidad) skill; (dispositivo) device; (engaño) trick. ~**so** a clever; (astuto) artful

artilugio m gadget

artiller|ía f artillery. ~**o** m artilleryman, gunner

artimaña f trap

art|ista m & f artist; (en espectáculos) artiste. ~**ísticamente** adv artistically. ~**ístico** a artistic

artr|ítico a arthritic. ~**itis** f arthritis

arveja f vetch; (LAm, guisante) pea

arzobispo m archbishop

as m ace

asa f handle

asad|o a roast(ed). ● m roast (meat), joint. ~**o a la parrilla** grilled. ~**o al horno** (sin grasa) baked; (con grasa) roast. ~**or** m spit. ~**ura** f offal

asalariado a salaried. ● m employee

asalt|ante m attacker; (de un banco) robber. ~**ar** vt storm ⟨fortaleza⟩; attack ⟨persona⟩; raid ⟨banco etc⟩; (fig) ⟨duda⟩ assail; (fig) ⟨idea etc⟩ cross one's mind. ~**o** m attack; (en boxeo) round

asamble|a f assembly; (reunión) meeting; (congreso) conference. ~**ísta** m & f member of an assembly

asapán m (Mex) flying squirrel

asar vt roast; (fig, acosar) pester (**a** with). ~**se** vpr be very hot. ~ **a la parrilla** grill. ~**al horno** (sin grasa) bake; (con grasa) roast

asbesto m asbestos

ascendencia f descent

ascend|ente a ascending. ~**er** [1] vt promote. ● vi go up, ascend; ⟨cuenta etc⟩ come to, amount to; (ser ascendido) be promoted. ~**iente** m & f ancestor; (influencia) influence

ascens|ión f ascent; (de grado) promotion. ~**ional** a upward. ~**o** m ascent; (de grado) promotion. **día** m **de la A**~**ión** Ascension Day

ascensor m lift (Brit), elevator (Amer). ~**ista** m & f lift attendant (Brit), elevator operator (Amer)

asc|eta m & f ascetic. ~**ético** a ascetic

asco m disgust. **dar** ~ be disgusting; (fig, causar enfado) be infuriating. **estar hecho un** ~ be disgusting. **hacer** ~**s de algo** turn up one's nose at sth. **me da** ~ **el ajo** I can't stand garlic. **¡qué** ~! how disgusting! **ser un** ~ be a disgrace

ascua f ember. **estar en** ~**s** be on tenterhooks

asea|damente adv cleanly. ~**do** a clean; (arreglado) neat. ~**r** vt (lavar) wash; (limpiar) clean; (arreglar) tidy up

asedi|ar vt besiege; (fig) pester. ~**o** m siege

asegura|do a & m insured. ~**dor** m insurer. ~**r** vt secure, make safe; (decir) assure; (concertar un seguro) insure; (preservar) safeguard. ~**rse** vpr make sure

asemejarse vpr be alike

asenta|da f. **de una** ~**da** at a sitting. ~**do** a situated; (arraigado) established. ~**r** [1] vt place; (asegurar) settle; (*anotar*) note down. ● *vi* be suitable. ∼**rse** *vpr* settle; (*estar situado*) be situated

asenti|miento *m* consent. ∼**r** [4] *vi* agree (**a** to). ∼**r con la cabeza** nod

aseo *m* cleanliness. ∼**s** *mpl* toilets

asequible *a* obtainable; (*precio*) reasonable; (*persona*) approachable

asesin|ar *vt* murder; (*pol*) assassinate. ∼**ato** *m* murder; (*pol*) assassination. ∼**o** *m* murderer; (*pol*) assassin

asesor *m* adviser, consultant. ∼**amiento** *m* advice. ∼**ar** *vt* advise. ∼**arse** *vpr*. ∼**arse con/de** consult. ∼**ía** *f* consultancy; (*oficina*) consultant's office

asestar *vt* aim (*arma*); strike (*golpe etc*); (*disparar*) fire

asevera|ción *f* assertion. ∼**r** *vt* assert

asfalt|ado *a* asphalt. ∼**ar** *vt* asphalt. ∼**o** *m* asphalt

asfixia *f* suffocation. ∼**nte** *a* suffocating. ∼**r** *vt* suffocate. ∼**rse** *vpr* suffocate

así *adv* so; (*de esta manera*) like this, like that. ● *a* such. ∼ ∼, ∼ **asá**, ∼ **asado** so-so. ∼ **como** just as. ∼.... **como** both... and. ∼ **pues** so. ∼ **que** so; (*enseguida*) as soon as. ∼ **sea** so be it. ∼ **y todo** even so. **aun** ∼ even so. **¿no es** ∼**?** isn't that right? **y** ∼ **(sucesivamente)** and so on

Asia *f* Asia

asiático *a & m* Asian

asidero *m* handle; (*fig, pretexto*) excuse

asidu|amente *adv* regularly. ∼**idad** *f* regularity. ∼**o** *a & m* regular

asiento *m* seat; (*situación*) site. ∼ **delantero** front seat. ∼ **trasero** back seat. **tome Vd** ∼ please take a seat

asigna|ción *f* assignment; (*sueldo*) salary. ∼**r** *vt* assign; allot (*porción, tiempo etc*)

asignatura *f* subject. ∼ **pendiente** (*escol*) failed subject; (*fig*) matter still to be resolved

asil|ado *m* inmate. ∼**ado político** refugee. ∼**o** *m* asylum; (*fig*) shelter; (*de ancianos etc*) home. ∼**o de huérfanos** orphanage. **pedir** ∼**o político** ask for political asylum

asimétrico *a* asymmetrical

asimila|ción *f* assimilation. ∼**r** *vt* assimilate. ∼**rse** *vpr* be assimilated. ∼**rse a** resemble

asimismo *adv* in the same way, likewise

asir [45] *vt* grasp. ∼**se** *vpr* grab hold (**a, de** of)

asist|encia *f* attendance; (*gente*) people (present); (*en un teatro etc*) audience; (*ayuda*) assistance. ∼**encia médica** medical care. ∼**enta** *f* assistant; (*mujer de la limpieza*) charwoman. ∼**ente** *m* assistant. ∼**ente social** social worker. ∼**ido** *a* assisted. ∼**ir** *vt* assist, help; (*un médico*) treat. ● *vi*. ∼**ir a** attend, be present at

asma *f* asthma. ∼**ático** *a & m* asthmatic

asn|ada *f* (*fig*) silly thing. ∼**o** *m* donkey; (*fig*) ass

asocia|ción *f* association; (*com*) partnership. ∼**do** *a* associated; (*miembro etc*) associate. ● *m* associate. ∼**r** *vt* associate; (*com*) take into partnership. ∼**rse** *vpr* associate; (*com*) become a partner

asolador *a* destructive

asolar[1] *vt* destroy. ∼**se** *vpr* be destroyed

asolar *vt* dry up (*plantas*)

asoma|da *f* brief appearance. ∼**r** *vt* show. ● *vi* appear, show. ∼**rse** *vpr* (*persona*) lean out (**a, por** of); (*cosa*) appear

asombr|adizo *a* easily frightened. ∼**ar** *vt* (*pasmar*) amaze; (*sorprender*) surprise. ∼**arse** *vpr* be amazed; (*sorprenderse*) be surprised. ∼**o** *m* amazement, surprise. ∼**osamente** *adv* amazingly. ∼**oso** *a* amazing, astonishing

asomo *m* sign. **ni por** ∼ by no means

asonada *f* mob; (*motín*) riot

aspa *f* cross, X-shape; (*de molino*) (windmill) sail. ∼**do** *a* X-shaped

aspaviento *m* show, fuss. ∼**s** *mpl* gestures. **hacer** ∼**s** make a big fuss

aspecto *m* look, appearance; (*fig*) aspect

aspereza *f* roughness; (*de sabor etc*) sourness

áspero *a* rough; (*sabor etc*) bitter

aspersión *f* sprinkling

aspiración *f* breath; (*deseo*) ambition

aspirador *a* suction. ∼**a** *f* vacuum cleaner

aspira|nte *m* candidate. ∼**r** *vt* breathe in; (*máquina*) suck up. ● *vi* breathe in; (*máquina*) suck. ∼**r a** aspire to

aspirina f aspirin

asquear vt sicken. • vi be sickening. ～se vpr be disgusted

asqueros|amente adv disgustingly. ～idad f filthiness. ～o a disgusting

asta f spear; (de la bandera) flagpole; (mango) handle; (cuerno) horn. a media ～ at half-mast. ～do a horned

asterisco m asterisk

astilla f splinter. ～s fpl firewood. ～r vt splinter. hacer ～s smash. hacerse ～s shatter

astillero m shipyard

astringente a & m astringent

astro m star

astr|ología f astrology. ～ólogo m astrologer

astrona|uta m & f astronaut. ～ve f spaceship

astr|onomía f astronomy. ～onómico a astronomical. ～ónomo m astronomer

astu|cia f cleverness; (ardid) cunning. ～to a astute; (taimado) cunning

asturiano a & m Asturian

Asturias fpl Asturias

asueto m time off, holiday

asumir vt assume

asunción f assumption. A～ Assumption

asunto m subject; (cuestión) matter; (de una novela) plot; (negocio) business. ～s mpl exteriores foreign affairs. el ～ es que the fact is that

asusta|dizo a easily frightened. ～r vt frighten. ～rse vpr be frightened

ataca|nte m & f attacker. ～r [7] vt attack

atad|ero m rope; (cierre) fastening; (gancho) hook. ～ijo m bundle. ～o a tied; (fig) timid. • m bundle. ～ura f tying; (cuerda) string

ataj|ar vi take a short cut. ～o m short cut; (grupo) bunch. echar por el ～o take the easy way out

atalaya f watch-tower; (fig) vantage point

atañer [22] vt concern

ataque m attack; (med) fit, attack. ～ al corazón heart attack. ～ de nervios hysterics

atar vt tie (up). ～se vpr get tied up

atardecer [11] vi get dark. • m dusk. al ～ at dusk

atarea|do a busy. ～rse vpr work hard

atasc|adero m (fig) stumbling block. ～ar [7] vt block; (fig) hinder. ～arse vpr get stuck; (tubo etc) block. ～o m obstruction; (auto) traffic jam

ataúd m coffin

atav|iar [20] vt dress up. ～iarse vpr dress up, get dressed up. ～ío m dress, attire

atemorizar [10] vt frighten. ～se vpr be frightened

Atenas fpl Athens

atenazar [10] vt (fig) torture; (duda, miedo) grip

atención f attention; (cortesía) courtesy, kindness; (interés) interest. ¡～! look out! ～ a beware of. llamar la ～ attract attention, catch the eye. prestar ～ pay attention

atender [1] vt attend to; heed (consejo etc); (cuidar) look after. • vi pay attention

atenerse [40] vpr abide (a by)

atentado m offence; (ataque) attack. ～ contra la vida de uno attempt on s.o.'s life

atentamente adv attentively; (con cortesía) politely; (con amabilidad) kindly. le saluda ～ (en cartas) yours faithfully

atentar vi commit an offence. ～ contra la vida de uno make an attempt on s.o.'s life

atento a attentive; (cortés) polite; (amable) kind

atenua|nte a extenuating. • f extenuating circumstance. ～r [21] vt attenuate; (hacer menor) diminish, lessen. ～rse vpr weaken

ateo a atheistic. • m atheist

aterciopelado a velvety

aterido a frozen (stiff), numb (with cold)

aterra|dor a terrifying. ～r vt terrify. ～rse vpr be terrified

aterriza|je m landing. ～je forzoso emergency landing. ～r [10] vt land

aterrorizar [10] vt terrify

atesorar vt hoard

atesta|do a packed, full up. • m sworn statement. ～r vt fill up, pack; (jurid) testify

atestiguar [15] vt testify to; (fig) prove

atiborrar vt fill, stuff. ～se vpr stuff o.s.

ático m attic

atilda|do a elegant, neat. ～r vt put a tilde over; (arreglar) tidy up. ～rse vpr smarten o.s. up

atina|damente adv rightly. ~**do** a right; (juicioso) wise, sensible. ~**r** vt/i hit upon; (acertar) guess right

atípico a exceptional

atiplado a high-pitched

atirantar vt tighten

atisb|ar vt spy on; (vislumbrar) make out. ~**o** m spying; (indicio) hint, sign

atizar [10] vt poke; give (golpe); (fig) stir up; arouse, excite (pasión etc)

atlántico a Atlantic. **el (océano) A~** the Atlantic (Ocean)

atlas m atlas

atl|eta m & f athlete. ~**ético** a athletic. ~**etismo** m athletics

atm|ósfera f atmosphere. ~**osférico** a atmospheric

atolondra|do a scatter-brained; (aturdido) bewildered. ~**miento** m bewilderment; (irreflexión) thoughtlessness. ~**r** vt bewilder; (pasmar) stun. ~**rse** vpr be bewildered

atolladero m bog; (fig) tight corner

at|ómico a atomic. ~**omizador** m atomizer. ~**omizar** [10] vt atomize

átomo m atom

atónito m amazed

atonta|do a bewildered; (tonto) stupid. ~**r** vt stun. ~**rse** vpr get confused

atormenta|dor a tormenting. ● m tormentor. ~**r** vt torture. ~**rse** vpr worry, torment o.s.

atornillar vt screw on

atosigar [12] vt pester

atracadero m quay

atracador m bandit

atracar [7] vt (amarrar) tie up; (arrimar) bring alongside; rob (banco, persona). ● vi (barco) tie up; (astronave) dock. ~**se** vpr stuff o.s. (de with)

atracci|ón f attraction. ~**ones** fpl entertainment, amusements

atrac|o m hold-up, robbery. ~**ón** m. **darse un** ~**ón** stuff o.s.

atractivo a attractive. ● m attraction; (encanto) charm

atraer [41] vt attract

atragantarse vpr choke (con on). **la historia se me atraganta** I can't stand history

atranc|ar [7] vt bolt (puerta); block up (tubo etc). ~**arse** vpr get stuck; (tubo) get blocked. ~**o** m difficulty

atrapar vt trap; (fig) land (empleo etc); catch (resfriado)

atrás adv behind; (dirección) backwards); (tiempo) previously, before. ● int back! **dar un paso** ~ step backwards. **hacia** ~, **para** ~ backwards

atras|ado a behind; (reloj) slow; (con deudas) in arrears; (país) backward. **llegar** ~**ado** arrive late. ~**ar** vt slow down; (retrasar) put back; (demorar) delay, postpone. ● vi (reloj) be slow. ~**arse** vpr be late; (reloj) be slow; (quedarse atrás) be behind. ~**o** m delay; (de un reloj) slowness; (de un país) backwardness. ~**os** mpl arrears

atravesa|do a lying across; (bizco) cross-eyed; (fig, malo) wicked. ~**r** [1] vt cross; (traspasar) go through; (poner transversalmente) lay across. ~**rse** vpr lie across; (en la garganta) get stuck, stick; (entrometerse) interfere

atrayente a attractive

atrev|erse vpr dare. ~**erse con** tackle. ~**ido** a daring, bold; (insolente) insolent. ~**imiento** m daring, boldness; (descaro) insolence

atribución f attribution. **atribuciones** fpl authority

atribuir [17] vt attribute; confer (función). ~**se** vpr take the credit for

atribular vt afflict. ~**se** vpr be distressed

atribut|ivo a attributive. ~**o** m attribute; (símbolo) symbol

atril m lectern; (mus) music stand

atrincherar vt fortify with trenches. ~**se** vpr entrench (o.s.)

atrocidad f atrocity; (fam) huge. **¡qué** ~! how terrible!

atrochar vi take a short cut

atrojarse vpr (Mex) be cornered

atrona|dor a deafening. ~**r** [2] vt deafen

atropell|adamente adv hurriedly. ~**ado** a hasty. ~**ar** vt knock down, run over; (empujar) push aside; (maltratar) bully; (fig) outrage, insult. ~**arse** vpr rush. ~**o** m (auto) accident; (fig) outrage

atroz a atrocious; (fam) huge. ~**mente** adv atrociously, awfully

atuendo m dress, attire

atufar vt choke; (fig) irritate. ~**se** vpr be overcome; (enfadarse) get cross

atún m tuna (fish)

aturdi|do a bewildered; (irreflexivo) thoughtless. ~**r** vt bewilder, stun;

⟨ruido⟩ deafen. ∼**rse** vpr be stunned; ⟨intentar olvidar⟩ try to forget

atur(r)ullar vt bewilder

atusar vt smooth; trim ⟨pelo⟩

auda|cia f boldness, audacity. ∼**z** a bold

audib|ilidad f audibility. ∼**le** a audible

audición f hearing; ⟨concierto⟩ concert

audiencia f audience; ⟨tribunal⟩ court

auditor m judge-advocate; ⟨de cuentas⟩ auditor

auditorio m audience; ⟨sala⟩ auditorium

auge m peak; ⟨com⟩ boom

augur|ar vt predict; ⟨cosas⟩ augur. ∼**io** m omen. ∼**ios** mpl. **con nuestros** ∼**ios para** with our best wishes for

augusto a august

aula f class-room; ⟨univ⟩ lecture room

aulaga f gorse

aull|ar [23] vi howl. ∼**ido** m howl

aument|ar vt increase; put up ⟨precios⟩; magnify ⟨imagen⟩; step up ⟨producción, voltaje⟩. ● vi increase. ∼**arse** vpr increase. ∼**ativo** a & m augmentative. ∼**o** m increase; ⟨de sueldo⟩ rise

aun adv even. ∼ **así** even so. ∼ **cuando** although. **más** ∼ even more. **ni** ∼ not even

aún adv still, yet. ∼ **no ha llegado** it still hasn't arrived, it hasn't arrived yet

aunar [23] vt join. ∼**se** vpr join together

aunque conj although, (even) though

aúpa int up! **de** ∼ wonderful

aureola f halo

auricular m ⟨de teléfono⟩ receiver. ∼**es** mpl headphones

aurora f dawn

ausen|cia f absence. ∼**tarse** vpr leave. ∼**te** a absent. ● m & f absentee; ⟨jurid⟩ missing person. **en** ∼ **de** in the absence of

auspicio m omen. **bajo los** ∼**s de** sponsored by

auster|idad f austerity. ∼**o** a austere

austral a southern. ● m ⟨unidad monetaria argentina⟩ austral

Australia m Australia

australiano a & m Australian

Austria f Austria

austriaco, austríaco a & m Austrian

aut|enticar [7] authenticate. ∼**enticidad** f authenticity. ∼**éntico** a authentic

auto m sentence; ⟨auto, fam⟩ car. ∼**s** mpl proceedings

auto... pref auto...

auto|ayuda f self-help. ∼**biografía** f autobiography. ∼**biográfico** a autobiographical. ∼**bombo** m self-glorification

autobús m bus. **en** ∼ by bus

autocar m coach ⟨Brit⟩, (long-distance) bus ⟨Amer⟩

aut|ocracia f autocracy. ∼**ócrata** m & f autocrat. ∼**ocrático** a autocratic

autóctono a autochthonous

auto: ∼**determinación** f self-determination. ∼**defensa** f self-defence. ∼**didacto** a self-taught. ● m autodidact. ∼**escuela** f driving school. ∼**giro** m autogiro

autógrafo m autograph

automación f automation

autómata m robot

autom|ático a automatic. ● m press-stud. ∼**atización** f automation. ∼**atizar** [10] vt automate

automotor a ⟨f **automotriz**⟩ self-propelled. ● m diesel train

autom|óvil a self-propelled. ● m car. ∼**ovilismo** m motoring. ∼**ovilista** m & f driver, motorist

aut|onomía f autonomy. ∼**onómico** a, ∼**ónomo** a autonomous

autopista f motorway ⟨Brit⟩, freeway ⟨Amer⟩

autopsia f autopsy

autor m author. ∼**a** f author(ess)

autori|dad f authority. ∼**tario** a authoritarian. ∼**tarismo** m authoritarianism

autoriza|ción f authorization. ∼**damente** adv officially. ∼**do** a authorized, offical; ⟨opinión etc⟩ authoritative. ∼**r** [10] vt authorize

auto: ∼**rretrato** m self-portrait. ∼**servicio** m self-service restaurant. ∼**stop** m hitch-hiking. **hacer** ∼**stop** hitch-hike

autosuficien|cia f self-sufficiency. ∼**te** a self-sufficient

autovía f dual carriageway

auxili|ar a assistant; ⟨servicios⟩ auxiliary. ● m assistant. ● vt help. ∼**o** m help. ¡∼**o!** help! ∼**os espirituales** last rites. **en** ∼**o de** in aid of. **pedir**

~o shout for help. **primeros** ~os first aid

Av. *abrev* (*Avenida*) Ave, Avenue

aval *m* guarantee

avalancha *f* avalanche

avalar *vt* guarantee

avalorar *vt* enhance; (*fig*) encourage

avance *m* advance; (*en el cine*) trailer; (*balance*) balance; (*de noticias*) early news bulletin. ● **informativo** publicity hand-out

avante *adv* (*esp LAm*) forward

avanza|do *a* advanced. ~r [10] *vt* move forward. ● *vi* advance

avar|icia *f* avarice. ~**icioso** *a*, ~**iento** *a* greedy; (*tacaño*) miserly. ~**o** *a* miserly. ● *m* miser

avasalla|dor *a* overwhelming. ~r *vt* dominate

Avda. *abrev* (*Avenida*) Ave, Avenue

ave *f* bird. ~ **de paso** (*incl fig*) bird of passage. ~ **de presa**, ~ **de rapiña** bird of prey

avecinarse *vpr* approach

avecindarse *vpr* settle

avejentarse *vpr* age

avellan|a *f* hazel-nut. ~**o** *m* hazel (tree)

avemaría *f* Hail Mary. **al** ~ at dusk

avena *f* oats

avenar *vt* drain

avenida *f* (*calle*) avenue; (*de río*) flood

avenir [53] *vt* reconcile. ~**se** *vpr* come to an agreement

aventaja|do *a* outstanding. ~r *vt* surpass

aventar [1] *vt* fan; winnow ‹*grano etc*›; (*viento*) blow away

aventur|a *f* adventure; (*riesgo*) risk. ~**a amorosa** love affair. ~**ado** *a* risky. ~**ar** *vt* risk. ~**arse** *vpr* dare. ~**a sentimental** love affair. ~**ero** *a* adventurous. ● *m* adventurer

avergonza|do *a* ashamed; (*embarazado*) embarrassed. ~r [10 & 16] *vt* shame; (*embarazar*) embarrass. ~**rse** *vpr* be ashamed; (*embarazarse*) be embarrassed

aver|ía *f* (*auto*) breakdown; (*daño*) damage. ~**iado** *a* broken down; (*fruta*) damaged, spoilt. ~**iar** [20] *vt* damage. ~**iarse** *vpr* get damaged; (*coche*) break down

averigua|ble *a* verifiable. ~**ción** *f* verification; (*investigación*) investigation; (*Mex, disputa*) argument. ~**dor** *m* investigator. ~**r**

[15] *vt* verify; (*enterarse de*) find out; (*investigar*) investigate. ● *vi* (*Mex*) quarrel

aversión *f* aversion (**a, hacia, por** for)

avestruz *m* ostrich

aviación *f* aviation; (*mil*) air force

aviado *a* (*Arg*) well off. **estar** ~ be in a mess

aviador *m* (*aviat*) member of the crew; (*piloto*) pilot; (*Arg, prestamista*) money-lender; (*Arg, de minas*) mining speculator

aviar [20] *vt* get ready, prepare; (*arreglar*) tidy; (*reparar*) repair; (*LAm, prestar dinero*) lend money; (*dar prisa*) hurry up. ~**se** *vpr* get ready. **¡avíate!** hurry up!

avícola *a* poultry. ~**icultor** *m* poultry farmer. ~**icultura** *f* poultry farming

avidez *f* eagerness, greed

ávido *a* eager, greedy

avieso *a* (*maligno*) wicked

avinagra|do *a* sour. ~r *vt* sour; (*fig*) embitter. ~**rse** *vpr* go sour; (*fig*) become embittered

avío *m* preparation. ~**s** *mpl* provisions; (*utensilios*) equipment

avi|ón *m* aeroplane (*Brit*), airplane (*Amer*). ~**oneta** *f* light aircraft

avis|ado *a* wise. ~**ar** *vt* warn; (*informar*) notify, inform; call ‹*médico etc*›. ~**o** *m* warning; (*anuncio*) notice. **estar sobre** ~**o** be on the alert. **mal** ~**ado** ill-advised. **sin previo** ~**o** without notice

avisp|a *f* wasp. ~**ado** *a* sharp. ~**ero** *m* wasps' nest; (*fig*) mess. ~**ón** *m* hornet

avistar *vt* catch sight of

avitualla|miento *m* supplying. ~r *vt* provision

avivar *vt* stoke up ‹*fuego*›; brighten up ‹*color*›; arouse ‹*interés, pasión*›; intensify ‹*dolor*›. ~**se** *vpr* revive; (*animarse*) cheer up

axila *f* axilla, armpit

axioma *m* axiom. ~**ático** *a* axiomatic

ay *int* (*de dolor*) ouch!; (*de susto*) oh!; (*de pena*) oh dear! ● **de poor.** ¡~ **de ti!** poor you!

aya *f* governess, child's nurse

ayer *adv* yesterday. ● *m* past. **antes de** ~ the day before yesterday. ~ **por la mañana** yesterday morning. ~ **(por la) noche** last night

ayo *m* tutor

ayote *m* (*Mex*) pumpkin

ayuda *f* help, aid. ~ **de cámara** valet. ~**nta** *f*, ~**nte** *m* assistant; (*mil*) adjutant. ~**nte técnico sanitario (ATS)** nurse. ~**r** *vt* help

ayun|ar *vi* fast. ~**as** *fpl*. **estar en ~as** have had no breakfast; (*fig, fam*) be in the dark. ~**o** *m* fasting

ayuntamiento *m* town council, city council; (*edificio*) town hall

azabache *m* jet

azad|a *f* hoe. ~**ón** *m* (large) hoe

azafata *f* air hostess

azafrán *m* saffron

azahar *m* orange blossom

azar *m* chance; (*desgracia*) misfortune. **al ~** at random. **por ~** by chance

azararse *vpr* go wrong; (*fig*) get flustered

azaros|amente *adv* hazardously. ~**o** *a* hazardous, risky; (*persona*) unlucky

azoga|do *a* restless. ~**rse** [12] *vpr* be restless

azolve *m* (*Mex*) obstruction

azora|do *a* flustered, excited, alarmed. ~**miento** *m* confusion, embarrassment. ~**r** *vt* embarrass; (*aturdir*) alarm. ~**rse** *vpr* get flustered, be alarmed

Azores *fpl* Azores

azot|aina *f* beating. ~**ar** *vt* whip, beat. ~**e** *m* whip; (*golpe*) smack; (*fig, calamidad*) calamity

azotea *f* flat roof. **estar mal de la ~** be mad

azteca *a & m & f* Aztec

az|úcar *m & f* sugar. ~**ucarado** *a* sweet. ~**ucarar** *vt* sweeten. ~**ucarero** *m* sugar bowl

azucena *f* (white) lily

azufre *m* sulphur

azul *a & m* blue. ~**ado** *a* bluish. ~ **de lavar** (washing) blue. ~ **marino** navy blue

azulejo *m* tile

azuzar *vt* urge on, incite

B

bab|a *f* spittle. ~**ear** *vi* drool, slobber; (*niño*) dribble. **caerse la ~a** be delighted

babel *f* bedlam

babe|o *m* drooling; (*de un niño*) dribbling. ~**ro** *m* bib

Babia *f*. **estar en ~** have one's head in the clouds

babieca *a* stupid. ● *m & f* simpleton

babor *m* port. **a ~** to port, on the port side

babosa *f* slug

babosada *f* (*Mex*) silly remark

babos|ear *vt* slobber over; (*niño*) dribble over. ~**eo** *m* drooling; (*de niño*) dribbling. ~**o** *a* slimy; (*LAm, tonto*) silly

babucha *f* slipper

babuino *m* baboon

baca *f* luggage rack

bacaladilla *f* small cod

bacalao *m* cod

bacon *m* bacon

bacteria *f* bacterium

bache *m* hole; (*fig*) bad patch

bachillerato *m* school-leaving examination

badaj|azo *m* stroke (of a bell). ~**o** *m* clapper; (*persona*) chatterbox

bagaje *m* baggage; (*animal*) beast of burden; (*fig*) knowledge

bagatela *f* trifle

Bahamas *fpl* Bahamas

bahía *f* bay

bail|able *a* dance. ~**ador** *a* dancing. ● *m* dancer. ~**aor** *m* Flamenco dancer. ~**ar** *vt/i* dance. ~**arín** *m* dancer. ~**arina** *f* dancer; (*de baile clásico*) ballerina. ~**e** *m* dance. ~**e de etiqueta** ball. **ir a ~ar** go dancing

baja *f* drop, fall; (*mil*) casualty. ~ **por maternidad** maternity leave. ~**da** *f* slope; (*acto de bajar*) descent. ~**mar** *m* low tide. ~**r** *vt* lower; (*llevar abajo*) get down; bow (*la cabeza*). ~ **la escalera** go downstairs. ● *vi* go down; (*temperatura, precio*) fall. ~**rse** *vpr* bend down. ~**r(se) de** get out of (*coche*); get off (*autobús, caballo, tren, bicicleta*). **dar(se) de ~** take sick leave

bajeza *f* vile deed

bajío *m* sandbank

bajo *a* low; (*de estatura*) short, small; (*cabeza, ojos*) lowered; (*humilde*) humble, low; (*vil*) vile, low; (*color*) pale; (*voz*) low; (*mus*) deep. ● *m* lowland; (*bajío*) sandbank; (*mus*) bass. ● *adv* quietly; (*volar*) low. ● *prep* under; (*temperatura*) below. ~ **la lluvia** in the rain. **los ~s fondos** the low district. **por lo ~** under one's breath; (*fig*) in secret

bajón *m* drop; (*de salud*) decline; (*com*) slump

bala *f* bullet; (*de algodón etc*) bale. ~ **perdida** stray bullet. **como una ~** like a shot

balada *f* ballad

baladí *a* trivial

baladrón *a* boastful

baladron|ada *f* boast. ~**ear** *vi* boast

balan|ce *m* swinging; (*de una cuenta*) balance; (*documento*) balance sheet. ~**cear** *vt* balance. ● *vi* hesitate. ~**cearse** *vpr* swing; (*vacilar*) hesitate. ~**ceo** *m* swinging. ~**za** *f* scales; (*com*) balance

balar *vi* bleat

balaustrada *f* balustrade, railing(s); (*de escalera*) banisters

balay *m* (*LAm*) wicker basket

balazo *m* (*disparo*) shot; (*herida*) bullet wound

balboa *f* (*unidad monetaria panameña*) balboa

balbuc|ear *vt/i* stammer; ⟨*niño*⟩ babble. ~**eo** *m* stammering; (*de niño*) babbling. ~**iente** *a* stammering; ⟨*niño*⟩ babbling. ~**ir** [24] *vt/i* stammer; ⟨*niño*⟩ babble

balcón *m* balcony. ~**onada** *f* row of balconies. ~**onaje** *m* row of balconies

balda *f* shelf

baldado *a* disabled, crippled; (*rendido*) shattered. ● *m* disabled person, cripple

baldaquín *m*, **baldaquino** *m* canopy

baldar *vt* cripple

balde *m* bucket. **de ~** free (of charge). **en ~** in vain. ~**ar** *vt* wash down

baldío *a* ⟨*terreno*⟩ waste; (*fig*) useless

baldosa *f* (*floor*) tile; (*losa*) flagstone

balduque *m* (*incl fig*) red tape

balear *a* Balearic. ● *m* native of the Balearic Islands. **las Islas** *fpl* **B~es** the Balearics, the Balearic Islands

baleo *m* (*LAm, tiroteo*) shooting; (*Mex, abanico*) fan

balido *m* bleat; (*varios sonidos*) bleating

ballín *m* small bullet. ~**ines** *mpl* shot

balística *f* ballistics

baliza *f* (*naut*) buoy; (*aviac*) beacon

balneario *m* spa; (*con playa*) seaside resort. ● *a*. **estación** *f* **balnearia** spa; (*con playa*) seaside resort

balompié *m* football (*Brit*), soccer

ball|ón *m* ball, football. ~**oncesto** *m* basketball. ~**onmano** *m* handball. ~**onvolea** *m* volleyball

balotaje *m* (*LAm*) voting

balsa *f* (*de agua*) pool; (*plataforma flotante*) raft

bálsamo *m* balsam; (*fig*) balm

balsón *m* (*Mex*) stagnant water

baluarte *m* (*incl fig*) bastion

balumba *f* mass, mountain

ballena *f* whale

ballesta *f* crossbow

ballet /ba'le/ (*pl* **ballets** /ba'le/) *m* ballet

bambole|ar *vi* sway; ⟨*mesa etc*⟩ wobble. ~**arse** *vpr* sway; ⟨*mesa etc*⟩ wobble. ~**o** *m* swaying; (*de mesa etc*) wobbling

bambú *m* (*pl* **bambúes**) bamboo

banal *a* banal. ~**idad** *f* banality

banan|a *f* (*esp LAm*) banana. ~**o** *m* (*LAm*) banana tree

banasta *f* large basket. ~**o** *m* large round basket

banc|a *f* banking; (*en juegos*) bank; (*LAm, asiento*) bench. ~**ario** *a* bank, banking. ~**arrota** *f* bankruptcy. ~**o** *m* (*asiento*) bench; (*com*) bank; (*bajío*) sandbank. **hacer ~arrota, ir a la ~arrota** go bankrupt

banda *f* (*incl mus, radio*) band; (*grupo*) gang, group; (*lado*) side. ~**da** *f* (*de aves*) flock; (*de peces*) shoal. ~ **de sonido, ~ sonora** sound-track

bandeja *f* tray; (*LAm, plato*) serving dish. **servir algo en ~ a uno** hand sth to s.o. on a plate

bandera *f* flag; (*estandarte*) banner, standard

banderill|a *f* banderilla. ~**ear** *vt* stick the banderillas in. ~**ero** *m* banderillero

banderín *m* pennant, small flag, banner

bandido *m* bandit

bando *m* edict, proclamation; (*partido*) faction. ~**s** *mpl* banns. **pasarse al otro ~** go over to the other side

bandolero *m* bandit

bandolina *f* mandolin

bandoneón *m* large accordion

banjo *m* banjo

banquero *m* banker

banqueta *f* stool; (*LAm, acera*) pavement (*Brit*), sidewalk (*Amer*)

banquete *m* banquet; (*de boda*) wedding reception. ~**ar** *vt/i* banquet

banquillo m bench; (jurid) dock; (taburete) footstool

bañ|ado m (LAm) swamp. **~ador** m (de mujer) swimming costume; (de hombre) swimming trunks. **~ar** vt bathe, immerse; bath (niño); (culin, recubrir) coat. **~arse** upr go swimming, have a swim; (en casa) have a bath. **~era** f bath, bath-tub. **~ero** m life-guard. **~ista** m & f bather. **~o** m bath; (en piscina, mar etc) swim; (bañera) bath, bath-tub; (capa) coating)

baptisterio m baptistery; (pila) font

baquet|a f (de fusil) ramrod; (de tambor) drumstick. **~ear** vt bother. **~eo** m nuisance, bore

bar m bar

barahúnda f uproar

baraja f pack of cards. **~r** vt shuffle; juggle, massage (cifras etc). ● vi argue (con with); (enemistarse) fall out (con with). **~s** fpl argument. **jugar a la ~** play cards. **jugar a dos ~s, jugar con dos ~s** be deceitful, indulge in double-dealing

baranda f, **barandal** m, **barandilla** f handrail; (de escalera) banisters

barat|a f (Mex) sale. **~ija** f trinket. **~illo** m junk shop; (géneros) cheap goods. **~o** a cheap. ● m sale. ● adv cheap(ly). **~ura** f cheapness

baraúnda f uproar

barba f chin; (pelo) beard. **~do** a bearded

barbacoa f barbecue; (Mex, carne) barbecued meat

bárbaramente adv savagely; (fig) tremendously

barbari|dad f barbarity; (fig) outrage; (mucho, fam) awful lot (fam). **¡qué ~dad!** how awful! **~e** f barbarity; (fig) ignorance. **~smo** m barbarism

bárbaro a barbaric, cruel; (bruto) uncouth; (estupendo, fam) terrific (fam). ● m barbarian. **¡qué ~!** how marvellous!

barbear vt (afeitar) shave; (Mex, lisonjear) fawn on

barbecho m fallow

barber|ía f barber's (shop). **~o** m barber; (Mex, adulador) flatterer

barbi|lampiño a beardless; (fig) inexperienced, green. **~lindo** m dandy

barbilla f chin

barbitúrico m barbiturate

barbo m barbel. **~ de mar** red mullet

barbot|ar vt/i mumble. **~ear** vt/i mumble. **~eo** m mumbling

barbudo a bearded

barbullar vi jabber

barca f (small) boat. **~ de pasaje** ferry. **~je** m fare. **~za** f barge

Barcelona f Barcelona

barcelonés a of Barcelona, from Barcelona. ● m native of Barcelona

barco m boat; (navío) ship. **~ cisterna** tanker. **~ de vapor** steamer. **~ de vela** sailing boat. **ir en ~** go by boat

bario m barium

barítono m baritone

barman m (pl barmans) barman

barniz m varnish; (para loza etc) glaze; (fig) veneer. **~ar** [10] vt varnish; glaze (loza etc)

bar|ométrico a barometric. **~ómetro** m barometer

bar|ón m baron. **~onesa** f baroness

barquero m boatman

barra f bar; (pan) French bread; (de oro o plata) ingot; (palanca) lever. **~ de labios** lipstick. **no pararse en ~s** stop at nothing

barrabasada f mischief, prank

barraca f hut; (vivienda pobre) shack, shanty

barranco m ravine, gully; (despeñadero) cliff, precipice

barre|dera f road-sweeper. **~dura** f rubbish. **~minas** m invar minesweeper

barren|a f drill, bit. **~ar** vt drill. **~o** m large (mechanical) drill. **entrar en ~a** (avión) go into a spin

barrer vt sweep; (quitar) sweep aside

barrera f barrier. **~ del sonido** sound barrier

barriada f district

barrica f barrel

barricada f barricade

barrido m sweeping

barrig|a f (pot-)belly. **~ón** a, **~udo** a pot-bellied

barril m barrel. **~ete** m keg, small barrel

barrio m district, area. **~bajero** a vulgar, common. **~s bajos** poor quarter, poor area. **el otro ~** (fig, fam) the other world

barro m mud; (arcilla) clay; (arcilla cocida) earthenware

barroco a Baroque. ● m Baroque style

barrote m heavy bar

barrunt|ar vt sense, have a feeling. ~e m, ~o m sign; (presentimiento) feeling

bartola f. tenderse a la ~, tumbarse a la ~ take it easy

bártulos mpl things. liar los ~ pack one's bags

barullo m uproar; (confusión) confusion. a ~ galore

basa f, **basamento** m base; (fig) basis

basar vt base. ~se vpr. ~se en be based on

basc|a f crowd. ~as fpl nausea. ~osidad f filth. la ~a the gang

báscula f scales

bascular vi tilt

base f base; (fig) basis, foundation. a ~ de thanks to; (mediante) by means of; (en una receta) as the basic ingredient(s). a ~ de bien very well. partiendo de la ~ de, tomando como ~ on the basis of

básico a basic

basílica f basilica

basilisco m basilisk. hecho un ~ furious

basta f tack, tacking stitch

bastante a enough; (varios) quite a few, quite a lot of. ● adv rather, fairly; (mucho tiempo) long enough; (suficiente) enough; (Mex, muy) very

bastar vi be enough. ¡basta! that's enough! basta decir que suffice it to say that. basta y sobra that's more than enough

bastardilla f italics. poner en ~ italicize

bastardo m bastard; (fig, vil) mean, base

bastidor m frame; (auto) chassis. ~es mpl (en el teatro) wings. entre ~es behind the scenes

bastión f (incl fig) bastion

basto a coarse. ~s mpl (naipes) clubs

bast|ón m walking stick. empuñar el ~ón take command. ~onazo m blow with a stick

basur|a f rubbish, garbage (Amer); (en la calle) litter. ~ero m dustman (Brit), garbage collector (Amer); (sitio) rubbish dump; (recipiente) dustbin (Brit), garbage can (Amer). cubo m de la ~a dustbin (Brit), garbage can (Amer)

bata f dressing-gown; (de médico etc) white coat. ~ de cola Flamenco dress

batall|a f battle. ~a campal pitched battle. ~ador a fighting. ● m fighter. ~ar vi battle, fight. ~ón m battalion. ● a. cuestión f batallona vexed question. de ~a everyday

batata f sweet potato

bate m bat. ~ador m batter; (cricket) batsman

batería f battery; (mus) percussion. ~ de cocina kitchen utensils, pots and pans

batido a beaten; (nata) whipped. ● m batter; (bebida) milk shake. ~ra f beater. ~ra eléctrica mixer

batín m dressing-gown

batir vt beat; (martillar) hammer; mint (monedas); whip (nata); (derribar) knock down. ~ el récord break the record. ~ palmas clap. ~se vpr fight

batuta f baton. llevar la ~ be in command, be the boss

baúl m trunk; (LAm, auto) boot (Brit), trunk (Amer)

bauti|smal a baptismal. ~smo m baptism, christening. ~sta a & m & f Baptist. ~zar [10] vt baptize, christen

baya f berry

bayeta f (floor-)cloth

bayoneta f bayonet. ~zo m (golpe) bayonet thrust; (herida) bayonet wound

baza f (naipes) trick; (fig) advantage. meter ~ interfere

bazar m bazaar

bazofia f leftovers; (basura) rubbish

beat|itud f (fig) bliss. ~o a blessed; (de religiosidad afectada) sanctimonious

bebé m baby

beb|edero m drinking trough; (sitio) watering place. ~edizo a drinkable. ● m potion; (veneno) poison. ~edor a drinking. ● m heavy drinker. ~er vt/i drink. dar de ~er a uno give s.o. a drink. ~ida f drink. ~ido a tipsy, drunk

beca f grant, scholarship. ~rio m scholarship holder, scholar

becerro m calf

befa f jeer, taunt. ~r vt scoff at. ~rse vpr. ~rse de scoff at. hacer ~ de scoff at

beige /beis, bes/ a & m beige

béisbol m baseball

beldad f beauty

belén *m* crib, nativity scene; *(barullo)* confusion

belga *a & m & f* Belgian

Bélgica *f* Belgium

bélico *a*, **belicoso** *a* warlike

beligerante *a* belligerent

bella|co *a* wicked. ● *m* rogue. ~**quear** *vi* cheat. ~**quería** *f* dirty trick

bell|eza *f* beauty. ~**o** *a* beautiful. ~**as artes** *fpl* fine arts

bellota *f* acorn

bemol *m* flat. **tener (muchos)** ~**es** be difficult

bencina *f* *(Arg, gasolina)* petrol *(Brit)*, gasoline *(Amer)*

bend|ecir [46 *pero imperativo* **bendice,** *futuro, condicional y pp regulares*] *vt* bless. ~**ición** *f* blessing. ~**ito** *a* blessed, holy; *(que tiene suerte)* lucky; *(feliz)* happy

benefactor *m* benefactor. ~**a** *f* benefactress

benefic|encia *f* *(organización pública)* charity. ~**iar** *vt* benefit. ~**iarse** *vpr* benefit. ~**iario** *m* beneficiary; *(de un cheque etc)* payee. ~**io** *m* benefit; *(ventaja)* advantage; *(ganancia)* profit, gain. ~**ioso** *a* beneficial, advantageous

benéfico *a* beneficial; *(de beneficencia)* charitable

benemérito *a* worthy

beneplácito *m* approval

ben|evolencia *f* benevolence. ~**évolo** *a* benevolent

bengala *f* flare. **luz** *f* **de B**~ flare

benign|idad *f* kindness; *(falta de gravedad)* mildness. ~**o** *a* kind; *(moderado)* gentle, mild; *(tumor)* benign

beodo *a* drunk

berberecho *m* cockle

berenjena *f* aubergine *(Brit)*, eggplant. ~**l** *m* *(fig)* mess

bermejo *a* red

berr|ear *vi* *(animales)* low, bellow; *(niño)* howl; *(cantar mal)* screech. ~**ido** *m* bellow; *(de niño)* howl; *(de cantante)* screech

berrinche *m* temper; *(de un niño)* tantrum

berro *m* watercress

berza *f* cabbage

besamel(a) *f* white sauce

bes|ar *vt* kiss; *(rozar)* brush against. ~**arse** *vpr* kiss (each other); *(tocarse)* touch each other. ~**o** *m* kiss

bestia *f* beast; *(bruto)* brute; *(idiota)* idiot. ~**de carga** beast of burden. ~**l** *a* bestial, animal; *(fig, fam)* terrific. ~**lidad** *f* bestiality; *(acción brutal)* horrid thing

besugo *m* sea-bream. **ser un** ~ be stupid

besuquear *vt* cover with kisses

betún *m* bitumen; *(para el calzado)* shoe polish

biberón *m* feeding-bottle

Biblia *f* Bible

bíblico *a* biblical

bibliografía *f* bibliography

biblioteca *f* library; *(librería)* bookcase. ~**de consulta** reference library. ~**de préstamo** lending library. ~**rio** *m* librarian

bicarbonato *m* bicarbonate. ~**sódico** bicarbonate of soda

bici *f* *(fam)* bicycle, bike *(fam)*. ~**cleta** *f* bicycle. **ir en** ~**cleta** go by bicycle, cycle. **montar en** ~**cleta** ride a bicycle

bicolor *a* two-colour

bicultural *a* bicultural

bicho *m* *(animal)* small animal, creature; *(insecto)* insect. ~**raro** odd sort. **cualquier** ~ **viviente, todo** ~ **viviente** everyone

bidé *m*, **bidet** *m* bidet

bidón *m* drum, can

bien *adv* *(mejor)* well; *(muy)* very, quite; *(correctamente)* right; *(de buena gana)* willingly. ● *m* good; *(efectos)* property; *(provecho)* advantage, benefit. **¡**~**!** fine!, OK!, good! ~**...** **(o)** ~ either... or. ~ **que** although. **¡está** ~**!** fine! alright! **más** ~ rather. **¡muy** ~**!** good! **no** ~ as soon as. **¡qué** ~**!** marvellous!, great! *(fam)*. **si** ~ although

bienal *a* biennial

bien: ~**aventurado** *a* fortunate. ~**estar** *m* well-being. ~**hablado** *a* well-spoken. ~**hechor** *m* benefactor. ~**hechora** *f* benefactress. ~**intencionado** *a* well-meaning

bienio *m* two years, two year-period

bien: ~**quistar** *vt* reconcile. ~**quistarse** *vpr* become reconciled. ~**quisto** *a* well-liked

bienvenid|a *f* welcome. ~**o** *a* welcome. **¡**~**o!** welcome! **dar la** ~**a a** uno welcome s.o.

bife *m* *(Arg)*, **biftek** *m* steak

bifurca|ción *f* fork, junction. ~**rse** [7] *vpr* fork

b|igamia f bigamy. **∼ígamo** a bigamous. ● m & f bigamist

bigot|e m moustache. **∼udo** a with a big moustache

bikini m bikini; (culin) toasted cheese and ham sandwich

bilingüe a bilingual

billar m billiards

billete m ticket; (de banco) note (Brit), bill (Amer). **∼ de banco** banknote. **∼ de ida y vuelta** return ticket (Brit), round-trip ticket (Amer). **∼ sencillo** single ticket (Brit), one-way ticket (Amer). **∼ro** m, **∼ra** f wallet, billfold (Amer)

billón m billion (Brit), trillion (Amer)

bimbalete m (Mex) swing

bi|mensual a fortnightly, twice-monthly. **∼mestral** a two-monthly. **∼motor** a twin-engined. ● m twin-engined plane

binocular a binocular. **∼es** mpl binoculars

biodegradable a biodegradable

bi|ografía f biography. **∼ográfico** a biographical. **∼ógrafo** m biographer

bi|ología f biology. **∼ológico** a biological. **∼ólogo** m biologist

biombo m folding screen

biopsia f biopsy

bioquímic|a f biochemistry; (persona) biochemist. **∼o** m biochemist

bípedo m biped

biplano m biplane

biquini m bikini

birlar vt (fam) steal, pinch (fam)

birlibirloque m. **por arte de ∼** (as if) by magic

Birmania f Burma

birmano a & m Burmese

biromen m (Arg) ball-point pen

bis m encore. ● adv twice. **¡∼!** encore! **vivo en el 3 ∼** I live at 3A

bisabuel|a f great-grandmother. **∼o** m great-grandfather. **∼os** mpl great-grandparents

bisagra f hinge

bisar vt encore

bisbise|ar vt whisper. **∼o** m whisper(ing)

bisemanal a twice-weekly

bisiesto a leap. **año** m **∼** leap year

bisniet|a f great-granddaughter. **∼o** m great-grandson. **∼os** mpl great-grandchildren

bisonte m bison

bisté m, **bistec** m steak

bisturí m scalpel

bisutería f imitation jewellery, costume jewellery

bizco a cross-eyed. **quedarse ∼** be dumbfounded

bizcocho m sponge (cake); (Mex, galleta) biscuit

bizquear vi squint

blanc|a f white woman; (mus) minim. **∼o** a white; (tez) fair. ● m white; (persona) white man; (intervalo) interval; (espacio) blank; (objetivo) target. **∼o de huevo** white of egg, egg-white. **dar en el ∼o** hit the mark. **dejar en ∼o** leave blank. **pasar la noche en ∼o** have a sleepless night. **∼o y negro** black and white. **∼ura** f whiteness. **∼uzco** a whitish

blandir [24] vt brandish

bland|o a soft; (carácter) weak; (cobarde) cowardly; (palabras) gentle, tender. **∼ura** f softness. **∼uzco** a softish

blanque|ar vt whiten; white-wash (paredes); bleach (tela). ● vi turn white; (presentarse blanco) look white. **∼cino** a whitish. **∼o** m whitening

blasfem|ador a blasphemous. ● m blasphemer. **∼ar** vi blaspheme. **∼ia** f blasphemy. **∼o** a blasphemous. ● m blasphemer

blas|ón m coat of arms; (fig,) honour, glory. **∼onar** vt emblazon. ● vi boast (de of, about)

bledo m nothing. **me importa un ∼, no se me da un ∼** I couldn't care less

blinda|je m armour. **∼r** vt armour

bloc m (pl blocs) pad

bloque m block; (pol) bloc. **∼ar** vt block; (mil) blockade; (com) freeze. **∼o** m blockade; (com) freezing. **en bloc** en bloc

blusa f blouse

boato m show, ostentation

bob|ada f silly thing. **∼alicón** a stupid. **∼ería** f silly thing. **decir ∼adas** talk nonsense

bobina f bobbin, reel; (foto) spool; (elec) coil

bobo a silly, stupid. ● m idiot, fool

boca f mouth; (fig, entrada) entrance; (de cañón) muzzle; (agujero) hole. **∼ abajo** face down. **∼ arriba** face up. **a ∼ de jarro** point-blank. **con la ∼ abierta** dumbfounded

bocacalle f junction. **la primera ~ a la derecha** the first turning on the right

bocad|illo m sandwich; (*comida ligera, fam*) snack. **~o** m mouthful; (*mordisco*) bite; (*de caballo*) bit

boca: ~jarro. a ~jarro point-blank. **~manga** f cuff

bocanada f puff; (*de vino etc*) mouthful

bocaza f invar, **bocazas** f invar bigmouth

boceto m outline, sketch

bocina f horn. **~zo** m toot, blast. **tocar la ~** sound one's horn

bock m beer mug

bocha f bowl. **~s** fpl bowls

bochinche m uproar

bochorno m sultry weather; (*fig, vergüenza*) embarrassment. **~so** a oppressive; (*fig*) embarrassing. **¡qué ~!** how embarrassing!

boda f marriage; (*ceremonia*) wedding

bodeg|a f cellar; (*de vino*) wine cellar; (*almacén*) warehouse; (*de un barco*) hold. **~ón** m cheap restaurant; (*pintura*) still life

bodoque m pellet; (*tonto, fam*) thickhead

bofes mpl lights. **echar los ~** slog away

bofet|ada f slap; (*fig*) blow. **dar una ~ada a uno** slap s.o. in the face. **darse de ~adas** clash. **~ón** m punch

boga m & f rower; (*hombre*) oarsman; (*mujer*) oarswoman; (*moda*) fashion. **estar en ~** be in fashion, be in vogue. **~da** f stroke (of the oar). **~dor** rower, oarsman. **~r** [12] vt row. **~vante** m (*crustáceo*) lobster

Bogotá f Bogotá

bogotano a from Bogotá. ● m native of Bogotá

bohemio a & m Bohemian

bohío m (*LAm*) hut

boicot m (pl **boicots**) boycott. **~ear** vt boycott. **~eo** m boycott. **hacer el ~** boycott

boina f beret

boîte /bwat/ m night-club

bola f ball; (*canica*) marble; (*naipes*) slam; (*betún*) shoe polish; (*mentira*) fib; (*Mex, reunión desordenada*) rowdy party. **~ del mundo** (*fam*) globe. **contar ~s** tell fibs. **dejar que**

ruede la ~ let things take their course. **meter ~s** tell fibs

bolas fpl (*LAm*) bolas

boleada f (*Mex*) polishing of shoes

boleadoras (*LAm*) fpl bolas

bolera f bowling alley

bolero m (*baile, chaquetilla*) bolero; (*fig, mentiroso, fam*) liar; (*Mex, limpiabotas*) bootblack

boletín m bulletin; (*publicación periódica*) journal; (*escolar*) report. **~ de noticias** news bulletin. **~ de precios** price list. **~ informativo** news bulletin. **~ meteorológico** weather forecast

boleto m (*esp LAm*) ticket

boli m (*fam*) Biro (P), ball-point pen

boliche m (*juego*) bowls; (*bolera*) bowling alley

bolígrafo m Biro (P), ball-point pen

bolillo m bobbin; (*Mex, panecillo*) (bread) roll

bolívar m (*unidad monetaria venezolana*) bolívar

Bolivia f Bolivia

boliviano a Bolivian. ● m Bolivian; (*unidad monetaria de Bolivia*) boliviano

bolo m skittle

bolsa f bag; (*monedero*) purse; (*LAm, bolsillo*) pocket; (*com*) stock exchange; (*cavidad*) cavity. **~ de agua caliente** hot-water bottle

bolsillo m pocket; (*monedero*) purse. **de ~** pocket

bolsista m & f stockbroker

bolso m (*de mujer*) handbag

boll|ería f baker's shop. **~ero** m baker. **~o** m roll; (*con azúcar*) bun; (*abolladura*) dent; (*chichón*) lump; (*fig, jaleo, fam*) fuss

bomba f bomb; (*máquina*) pump; (*noticia*) bombshell. **~ de aceite** (*auto*) oil pump. **~ de agua** (*auto*) water pump. **~ de incendios** fire-engine. **pasarlo ~** have a marvellous time

bombach|as fpl (*LAm*) knickers, pants. **~o** m (*esp Mex*) baggy trousers, baggy pants (*Amer*)

bombarde|ar vt bombard; (*mil*) bomb. **~o** m bombardment; (*mil*) bombing. **~ro** m (*avión*) bomber

bombazo m explosion

bombear vt pump; (*mil*) bomb

bombero m fireman. **cuerpo** m **de ~s** fire brigade (*Brit*), fire department (*Amer*)

bombilla f (light) bulb; (*LAm, para mate*) pipe for drinking maté; (*Mex, cucharón*) ladle

bombín m pump; (*sombrero, fam*) bowler (hat) (*Brit*), derby (*Amer*)

bombo m (*tambor*) bass drum. **a ~ y platillos** with a lot of fuss

bomb|ón m chocolate. **ser un ~ón** be a peach. **~ona** f container. **~onera** f chocolate box

bonachón a easygoing; (*bueno*) good-natured

bonaerense a from Buenos Aires. ● m native of Buenos Aires

bonanza f (*naut*) fair weather; (*prosperidad*) prosperity. **ir en ~** (*naut*) have fair weather; (*fig*) go well

bondad f goodness; (*amabilidad*) kindness. **tenga la ~** de would you be kind enough to. **~osamente** adv kindly. **~oso** a kind

bongo m (*LAm*) canoe

boniato m sweet potato

bonito a nice; (*mono*) pretty. ¡muy **~!**, ¡qué **~!** that's nice!, very nice!. ● m bonito

bono m voucher; (*título*) bond. **~ del Tesoro** government bond

boñiga f dung

boqueada f gasp. **dar las ~s** be dying

boquerón m anchovy

boquete m hole; (*brecha*) breach

boquiabierto a open-mouthed; (*fig*) amazed, dumbfounded. **quedarse ~** be amazed

boquilla f mouthpiece; (*para cigarillos*) cigarette-holder; (*filtro de cigarillo*) tip

borboll|ar vi bubble. **~ón** m bubble. **hablar a ~ones** gabble. **salir a ~ones** gush out

borbot|ar vt bubble. **~ón** m bubble. **hablar a ~ones** gabble. **salir a ~ones** gush out

bordado a embroidered. ● m embroidery. **quedar ~**, **salir ~** come out very well

bordante m (*Mex*) lodger

bordar vt embroider; (*fig, fam*) do very well

bord|e m edge; (*de carretera*) side; (*de plato etc*) rim; (*de un vestido*) hem. **~ear** vt go round the edge of; (*fig*) border on. **~illo** m kerb. **al ~e de** on the edge of; (*fig*) on the brink of

bordo m board. **a ~** on board

borinqueño a & m Puerto Rican

borla f tassel

borra f flock; (*pelusa*) fluff; (*sedimento*) sediment

borrach|era f drunkenness. **~ín** m drunkard. **~o** a drunk. ● m drunkard; (*temporalmente*) drunk. **estar ~o** be drunk. **ni ~o** never in a million years. **ser ~o** be a drunkard

borrador m rough copy; (*libro*) rough notebook

borradura f crossing-out

borrajear vt/i scribble

borrar vt rub out; (*tachar*) cross out

borrasc|a f storm. **~oso** a stormy

borreg|o m year-old lamb; (*fig*) simpleton; (*Mex, noticia falsa*) hoax. **~uil** a meek

borric|ada f silly thing. **~o** m donkey; (*fig, fam*) ass

borrón m smudge; (*fig, imperfección*) blemish; (*de una pintura*) sketch. **~ y cuenta nueva** let's forget about it!

borroso a blurred; (*fig*) vague

bos|caje m thicket. **~coso** a wooded. **~que** m wood, forest. **~quecillo** m copse

bosquej|ar vt sketch. **~o** m sketch

bosta f dung

bostez|ar [10] vi yawn. **~o** m yawn

bota f boot; (*recipiente*) leather wine bottle

botadero m (*Mex*) ford

botánic|a f botany. **~o** a botanical. ● m botanist

botar vt launch. ● vi bounce. **estar que bota** be hopping mad

botarat|ada f silly thing. **~e** m idiot

bote m bounce; (*golpe*) blow; (*salto*) jump; (*sacudida*) jolt; (*lata*) tin, can; (*vasija*) jar; (*en un bar*) jar for tips; (*barca*) boat. **~ salvavidas** lifeboat. **de ~ en ~** packed

botell|a f bottle. **~ita** f small bottle

botica f chemist's (shop) (*Brit*), drugstore (*Amer*). **~rio** m chemist (*Brit*), druggist (*Amer*)

botija f, **botijo** m earthenware jug

botín m half boot; (*despojos*) booty; (*LAm, calcetín*) sock

botiquín m medicine chest; (*de primeros auxilios*) first aid kit

bot|ón m button; (*yema*) bud. **~onadura** f buttons. **~ón de oro** buttercup. **~ones** m invar bellboy (*Brit*), bellhop (*Amer*)

botulismo m botulism

boutique /bu'tik/ m boutique

bóveda f vault

boxe|ador m boxer. **~ar** vi box. **~o** m boxing

boya f buoy; (*corcho*) float. **~nte** a buoyant

bozal m (*de perro etc*) muzzle; (*de caballo*) halter

bracear vi wave one's arms; (*nadar*) swim, crawl

bracero m labourer. **de ~** (*fam*) arm in arm

braga f underpants, knickers; (*cuerda*) rope. **~dura** f crotch. **~s** fpl knickers, pants. **~zas** m invar (*fam*) henpecked man

bragueta f flies

braille /breil/ m Braille

bram|ar vi roar; (*vaca*) moo; (*viento*) howl. **~ido** m roar

branquia f gill

bras|a f hot coal. **a la ~a** grilled. **~ero** m brazier; (*LAm, hogar*) hearth

Brasil m. **el ~** Brazil

brasile|ño a & m Brazilian. **~ro** a & m (*LAm*) Brazilian

bravata f boast

bravío a wild; (*persona*) coarse, uncouth

brav|o a brave; (*animales*) wild; (*mar*) rough. **¡~!** int well done! bravo! **~ura** f ferocity; (*valor*) courage

braz|a f fathom. **nadar a ~a** do the breast-stroke. **~ada** f waving of the arms; (*en natación*) stroke; (*cantidad*) armful. **~ado** m armful. **~al** m arm-band. **~alete** m bracelet; (*brazal*) arm-band. **~o** m arm; (*de animales*) foreleg; (*rama*) branch. **~o derecho** right-hand man. **a ~o** by hand. **del ~o** arm in arm

brea f tar, pitch

brear vt ill-treat

brécol m broccoli

brecha f gap; (*mil*) breach; (*med*) gash. **estar en la ~** be in the thick of it

brega f struggle. **~r** [12] vi struggle; (*trabajar mucho*) work hard, slog away. **andar a la ~** work hard

breña f, **breñal** m scrub

Bretaña f Brittany. **Gran ~** Great Britain

breve a short. **~dad** f shortness. **en ~** soon, shortly. **en ~s momentos** soon

brez|al m moor. **~o** m heather

brib|ón m rogue, rascal. **~onada** f, **~onería** f dirty trick

brida f bridle. **a toda ~** at full speed

bridge /britʃ/ m bridge

brigada f squad; (*mil*) brigade. **general de ~** brigadier (*Brit*), brigadier-general (*Amer*)

brill|ante a brilliant. ● m diamond. **~antez** f brilliance. **~ar** vi shine; (*centellear*) sparkle. **~o** m shine; (*brillantez*) brilliance; (*centelleo*) sparkle. **dar ~o, sacar ~o** polish

brinc|ar [7] vi jump up and down. **~o** m jump. **dar un ~o** jump. **estar que brinca** be hopping mad. **pegar un ~o** jump

brind|ar vt offer. ● vi. **~ar por** toast, drink a toast to. **~is** m toast

br|ío m energy; (*decisión*) determination. **~ioso** a spirited; (*garboso*) elegant

brisa f breeze

británico a British. ● m Briton, British person

brocado m brocade

bróculi m broccoli

brocha f paintbrush; (*para afeitarse*) shaving-brush

broche m clasp, fastener; (*joya*) brooch; (*Arg, sujetapapeles*) paperclip

brocheta f skewer

brom|a f joke. **~a pesada** practical joke. **~ear** vi joke. **~ista** a fun-loving. ● m & f joker. **de ~a, en ~a** in fun. **ni de ~a** never in a million years

bronca f row; (*represión*) telling-off

bronce m bronze. **~ado** a bronze; (*por el sol*) tanned, sunburnt. **~ar** vt tan (*piel*). **~arse** vpr get a suntan

bronco a rough

bronquitis f bronchitis

broqueta f skewer

brot|ar vi (*plantas*) bud, sprout; (*med*) break out; (*líquido*) gush forth; (*lágrimas*) well up. **~e** m bud, shoot; (*med*) outbreak; (*de líquido*) gushing; (*de lágrimas*) welling-up

bruces mpl. **de ~** face down(wards). **caer de ~** fall flat on one's face

bruj|a f witch. ● a (*Mex*) penniless. **~ear** vi practise witchcraft. **~ería** f witchcraft. **~o** m wizard, magician; (*LAm*) medicine man

brújula f compass

brum|a f mist; (*fig*) confusion. **~oso** a misty, foggy

bruñi|do m polish. **~r** [22] vt polish

brusco a (repentino) sudden; ⟨persona⟩ brusque

Bruselas fpl Brussels

brusquedad f abruptness

brut|**al** a brutal. ~**alidad** f brutality; (estupidez) stupidity. ~**o** a (estúpido) stupid; (tosco) rough, uncouth; ⟨peso, sueldo⟩ gross

bucal a oral

buce|**ar** vi dive; (fig) explore. ~**o** m diving

bucle m curl

budín m pudding

budis|**mo** m Buddhism. ~**ta** m & f Buddhist

buen véase **bueno**

buenamente adv easily; (voluntariamente) willingly

buenaventura f good luck; (adivinación) fortune. **decir la** ~ **a uno, echar la** ~ **a uno** tell s.o.'s fortune

bueno a (delante de nombre masculino en singular **buen**) good; (apropiado) fit; (amable) kind; ⟨tiempo⟩ fine. ● int well!; (de acuerdo) OK!, very well! **¡buena la has hecho!** you've gone and done it now! **¡buenas noches!** good night! **¡buenas tardes!** (antes del atardecer) good afternoon!; (después del atardecer) good evening! **¡** ~ **s días!** good morning! **estar de buenas** be in a good mood. **por las buenas** willingly

Buenos Aires m Buenos Aires

buey m ox

búfalo m buffalo

bufanda f scarf

bufar vi snort. **estar que bufa** be hopping mad

bufete m (mesa) writing-desk; (despacho) lawyer's office

bufido m snort; (de ira) outburst

buf|**o** a comic. ~**ón** a comical. ● m buffoon. ~**onada** f joke

bugle m bugle

buharda f, **buhardilla** f attic; (ventana) dormer window

búho m owl

buhoner|**ía** f pedlar's wares. ~**o** m pedlar

buitre m vulture

bujía f candle; (auto) spark(ing) plug

bula f bull

bulbo m bulb

bulevar m avenue, boulevard

Bulgaria f Bulgaria

búlgaro a & m Bulgarian

bulo m hoax

bulto m (volumen) volume; (tamaño) size; (forma) shape; (paquete) package; (protuberancia) lump. **a** ~ roughly

bulla f uproar; (muchedumbre) crowd

bullicio m hubbub; (movimiento) bustle. ~**so** a bustling; (ruidoso) noisy

bullir [22] vt stir, move. ● vi boil; (burbujear) bubble; (fig) bustle

buñuelo m doughnut; (fig) mess

BUP abrev (Bachillerato Unificado Polivalente) secondary school education

buque m ship, boat

burbuj|**a** f bubble. ~**ear** vi bubble; ⟨vino⟩ sparkle. ~**eo** m bubbling

burdel m brothel

burdo a rough, coarse; (excusa) clumsy

burgu|**és** a middle-class, bourgeois. ● m middle-class person. ~**esía** f middle class, bourgeoisie

burla f taunt; (broma) joke; (engaño) trick. ~**dor** a mocking. ● m seducer. ~**r** vt trick, deceive; (seducir) seduce. ~**rse** vpr. ~**rse de** mock, make fun of

burlesco a funny

burlón a mocking

bur|**ocracia** f civil service. ~**ócrata** m & f civil servant. ~**ocrático** a bureaucratic

burro m donkey; (fig) ass

bursátil a stock-exchange

bus m (fam) bus

busca f search. **a la** ~ **de** in search of. **en** ~ **de** in search of

busca: ~**pié** m feeler. ~**pleitos** m invar (LAm) trouble-maker

buscar [7] vt look for. ● vi look. **buscársela** ask for it. **ir a** ~ **a uno** fetch s.o.

buscarruidos m invar trouble-maker

buscona f prostitute

busilis m snag

búsqueda f search

busto m bust

butaca f armchair; (en el teatro etc) seat

butano m butane

buzo m diver

buzón m postbox (Brit), mailbox (Amer)

C

C/ abrev (Calle) St, Street, Rd, Road

cabal a exact; (completo) complete. **no estar en sus ~es** not be in one's right mind

cabalga|dura f mount, horse. **~r** [12] vt ride. ● vi ride, go riding. **~ta** f ride; (desfile) procession

cabalmente adv completely; (exactamente) exactly

caballa f mackerel

caballada f (LAm) stupid thing

caballeresco a gentlemanly. **literatura** f **caballeresca** books of chivalry

caballer|ía f mount, horse. **~iza** f stable. **~izo** m groom

caballero m gentleman; (de orden de caballería) knight; (tratamiento) sir. **~samente** adv like a gentleman. **~so** a gentlemanly

caballete m (del tejado) ridge; (de la nariz) bridge; (de pintor) easel

caballito m pony. **~ del diablo** dragonfly. **~ de mar** sea-horse. **los ~s** (tiovivo) merry-go-round

caballo m horse; (del ajedrez) knight; (de la baraja española) queen. **~ de vapor** horsepower. **a ~** on horseback

cabaña f hut

cabaret /kaba're/ m (pl **cabarets** /kaba're/) night-club

cabece|ar vi nod; (para negar) shake one's head. **~o** m nodding, nod; (acción de negar) shake of the head

cabecera f (de la cama, de la mesa) head; (en un impreso) heading

cabecilla m leader

cabell|o m hair. **~os** mpl hair. **~udo** a hairy

caber [28] vi fit (**en** into). **los libros no caben en la caja** the books won't fit into the box. **no cabe duda** there's no doubt

cabestr|illo m sling. **~o** m halter

cabeza f head; (fig, inteligencia) intelligence. **~da** f butt; (golpe recibido) blow; (saludo, al dormirse) nod. **~zo** m butt; (en fútbol) header. **andar de ~** have a lot to do. **dar una ~da** nod off

cabida f capacity; (extensión) area. **dar ~ a** leave room for, leave space for

cabina f (de avión) cabin, cockpit; (electoral) booth; (de camión) cab. **~ telefónica** telephone box (Brit), telephone booth (Amer)

cabizbajo a crestfallen

cable m cable

cabo m end; (trozo) bit; (mil) corporal; (mango) handle; (geog) cape; (naut) rope. **al ~** eventually. **al ~ de una hora** after an hour. **de ~ a rabo** from beginning to end. **llevar(se) a ~** carry out

cabr|a f goat. **~a montesa** f mountain goat. **~iola** f jump, skip. **~itilla** f kid. **~ito** m kid

cabrón m cuckold

cabuya f (LAm) pita, agave

cacahuate m (Mex), **cacahuete** m peanut

cacao m (planta y semillas) cacao; (polvo) cocoa; (fig) confusion

cacare|ar vt boast about. ● vi (gallo) crow; (gallina) cluck. **~o** m (incl fig) crowing; (de gallina) clucking

cacería f hunt

cacerola f casserole, saucepan

cacique m cacique, Indian chief; (pol) cacique, local political boss. **~il** a despotic. **~ismo** m caciquism, despotism

caco m pickpocket, thief

cacof|onía f cacophony. **~ónico** a cacophonous

cacto m cactus

cacumen m acumen

cacharro m earthenware pot; (para flores) vase; (coche estropeado) wreck; (cosa inútil) piece of junk; (chisme) thing. **~s** mpl pots and pans

cachear vt frisk

cachemir m, **cachemira** f cashmere

cacheo m frisking

cachetada f (LAm), **cachete** m slap

cachimba f pipe

cachiporra f club, truncheon. **~zo** m blow with a club

cachivache m thing, piece of junk

cacho m bit, piece; (LAm, cuerno) horn; (miga) crumb

cachondeo m (fam) joking, joke

cachorro m (perrito) puppy; (de otros animales) young

cada a invar each, every. **~ uno** each one, everyone. **uno de ~ cinco** one in five

cadalso m scaffold

cadáver m corpse. **ingresar ~** be dead on arrival

cadena f chain; (TV) channel. **~ de fabricación** production line. **~ de montañas** mountain range. **~ perpetua** life imprisonment

cadencia f cadence, rhythm

cadera *f* hip

cadete *m* cadet

caduc|ar [7] *vi* expire. ~**idad** *f*. **fecha** *f* **de** ~**idad** sell-by date. ~**o** *a* decrepit

cae|dizo *a* unsteady. ~**r** [29] *vi* fall. ~**rse** *vpr* fall (over). **dejar** ~**r** drop. **estar al** ~**r** be about to happen. **este vestido no me** ~ **bien** this dress doesn't suit me. **hacer** ~**r** knock over. **Juan me** ~ **bien** I get on well with Juan. **su cumpleaños cayó en martes** his birthday fell on a Tuesday

café *m* coffee; (*cafetería*) café. ● *a*. **color** ~ coffee-coloured. ~ **con leche** white coffee. ~ **cortado** coffee with a little milk. ~ **(solo)** black coffee

cafe|ína *f* caffeine. ~**tal** *m* coffee plantation. ~**tera** *f* coffee-pot. ~**tería** *f* café. ~**tero** *a* coffee

caíd|a *f* fall; (*disminución*) drop; (*pendiente*) slope. ~**o** *a* fallen; (*abatido*) dejected. ● *m* fallen

caigo *vb véase* **caer**

caimán *m* cayman, alligator

caj|a *f* box; (*grande*) case; (*de caudales*) safe; (*donde se efectúan los pagos*) cash desk; (*en supermercado*) check-out. ~**a de ahorros** savings bank. ~**a de caudales**, ~**a fuerte** safe. ~**a postal de ahorros** post office savings bank. ~**a registradora** till. ~**ero** *m* cashier. ~**etilla** *f* packet. ~**ita** *f* small box. ~**ón** *m* large box; (*de mueble*) drawer; (*puesto de mercado*) stall. **ser de** ~**ón** be a matter of course

cal *m* lime

cala *f* cove

calaba|cín *m* marrow; (*fig, idiota, fam*) idiot. ~**za** *f* pumpkin; (*fig, idiota, fam*) idiot

calabozo *m* prison; (*celda*) cell

calado *a* soaked. ● *m* (*naut*) draught. **estar** ~ **hasta los huesos** be soaked to the skin

calamar *m* squid

calambre *m* cramp

calami|dad *f* calamity, disaster. ~**toso** *a* calamitous, disastrous

calar *vt* soak; (*penetrar*) pierce; (*fig, penetrar*) see through; sample (*fruta*). ~**se** *vpr* get soaked; (*zapatos*) leak; (*auto*) stall

calavera *f* skull

calcar [7] *vt* trace; (*fig*) copy

calceta *f*. **hacer** ~ knit

calcetín *m* sock

calcinar *vt* burn

calcio *m* calcium

calco *m* tracing. ~**manía** *f* transfer. **papel** *m* **de** ~ tracing-paper

calcula|dor *a* calculating. ~**dora** *f* calculator. ~**dora de bolsillo** pocket calculator. ~**r** *vt* calculate; (*suponer*) reckon, think

cálculo *m* calculation; (*fig*) reckoning

caldea|miento *m* heating. ~**r** *vt* heat, warm. ~**rse** *vpr* get hot

calder|a *f* boiler; (*Arg, para café*) coffee-pot; (*Arg, para té*) teapot. ~**eta** *f* small boiler

calderilla *f* small change, coppers

calder|o *m* small boiler. ~**ón** *m* large boiler

caldo *m* stock; (*sopa*) soup, broth. **poner a** ~ **a uno** give s.o. a dressing-down

calefacción *f* heating. ~ **central** central heating

caleidoscopio *m* kaleidoscope

calendario *m* calendar

caléndula *f* marigold

calenta|dor *m* heater. ~**miento** *m* heating; (*en deportes*) warm-up. ~**r** [1] *vt* heat, warm. ~**rse** *vpr* get hot, warm up

calentur|a *f* fever, (high) temperature. ~**iento** *a* feverish

calibr|ar *vt* calibrate; (*fig*) measure. ~**e** *m* calibre; (*diámetro*) diameter; (*fig*) importance

calidad *f* quality; (*función*) capacity. **en** ~ **de** as

cálido *a* warm

calidoscopio *m* kaleidoscope

caliente *a* hot, warm; (*fig, enfadado*) angry

califica|ción *f* qualification; (*evaluación*) assessment; (*nota*) mark. ~**r** [7] *vt* qualify; (*evaluar*) assess; mark ‹*examen etc*›. ~**r de** describe as, label. ~**tivo** *a* qualifying. ● *m* epithet

caliz|a *f* limestone. ~**o** *a* lime

calm|a *f* calm. ¡~**a!** calm down! ~**ante** *a* & *m* sedative. ~**ar** *vt* calm, soothe. ● *vi* ‹*viento*› abate. ~**arse** *vpr* calm down; (*viento*) abate. ~**oso** *a* calm; (*flemático, fam*) phlegmatic. **en** ~**a** calm. **perder la** ~**a** lose one's composure

calor m heat, warmth. **hace** ∼ it's hot. **tener** ∼ be hot

caloría f calorie

calorífero m heater

calumni|a f calumny; (oral) slander; (escrita) libel. ∼**ar** vt slander; (por escrito) libel. ∼**oso** a slanderous; (cosa escrita) libellous

caluros|amente adv warmly. ∼**o** a warm

calv|a f bald patch. ∼**ero** m clearing. ∼**icie** f baldness. ∼**o** a bald; (terreno) barren

calza f (fam) stocking; (cuña) wedge

calzada f road

calza|do a wearing shoes. ● m footwear, shoe. ∼**dor** m shoehorn. ∼**r** [10] vt put shoes on; (llevar) wear. ● vi wear shoes. ∼**rse** vpr put on. ¿**qué número calza Vd?** what size shoe do you take?

calz|ón m shorts; (ropa interior) knickers, pants. ∼**ones** mpl shorts. ∼**oncillos** mpl underpants

calla|do a quiet. ∼**r** vt keep quiet; ⟨secreto⟩; hush up ⟨asunto⟩. ● vi be quiet, keep quiet, shut up (fam). ∼**rse** vpr be quiet, keep quiet, shut up (fam). ¡**cállate!** be quiet! shut up! (fam)

calle f street, road; (en deportes, en autopista) lane. ∼ **de dirección única** one-way street. ∼ **mayor** high street, main street. **abrir** ∼ make way

calleja f narrow street. ∼**ear** vi wander about the streets. ∼**ero** a street. ● m street plan. ∼**ón** m alley. ∼**uela** f back street, side street. ∼**ón sin salida** cul-de-sac

call|ista m & f chiropodist. ∼**o** m corn, callus. ∼**os** mpl tripe. ∼**oso** a hard, rough

cama f bed. ∼ **de matrimonio** double bed. ∼ **individual** single bed. **caer en la** ∼ fall ill. **guardar** ∼ be confined to bed

camada f litter; (fig, de ladrones) gang

camafeo m cameo

camaleón m chameleon

cámara f room; (de reyes) royal chamber; (fotográfica) camera; (de armas, pol) chamber. ∼ **fotográfica** camera. **a** ∼ **lenta** in slow motion

camarada f colleague; (amigo) companion

camarer|a f chambermaid; (de restaurante etc) waitress; (en casa) maid. ∼**o** m waiter

camarín m dressing-room; (naut) cabin

camarón m shrimp

camarote m cabin

cambi|able a changeable; (com etc) exchangeable. ∼**ante** a variable. ∼**ar** vt change; (trocar) exchange. ● vi change. ∼**ar de idea** change one's mind. ∼**arse** vpr change. ∼**o** m change; (com) exchange rate; (moneda menuda) (small) change. ∼**sta** m & f money-changer. **en** ∼**o** on the other hand

camelia f camellia

camello m camel

camilla f stretcher; (sofá) couch

camina|nte m traveller. ∼**r** vt cover. ● vi travel; (andar) walk; ⟨río, astros etc⟩ move. ∼**ta** f long walk

camino m road; (sendero) path, track; (dirección, medio) way. ∼ **de** towards, on the way to. **abrir** ∼ make way. **a medio** ∼, **a la mitad del** ∼ half-way. **de** ∼ on the way. **ponerse en** ∼ set out

cami|ón m lorry; (Mex, autobús) bus. ∼**onero** m lorry-driver. ∼**oneta** f van

camis|a f shirt; (de un fruto) skin. ∼**a de dormir** nightdress. ∼**a de fuerza** strait-jacket. ∼**ería** f shirt shop. ∼**eta** f T-shirt; (ropa interior) vest. ∼**ón** m nightdress

camorra f (fam) row. **buscar** ∼ look for trouble, pick a quarrel

camote m (LAm) sweet potato

campamento m camp

campan|a f bell. ∼**ada** f stroke of a bell; (de reloj) striking. ∼**ario** m bell tower, belfry. ∼**eo** m peal of bells. ∼**illa** f bell. ∼**udo** a bell-shaped; (estilo) bombastic

campaña f countryside; (mil, pol) campaign. **de** ∼ (mil) field

campe|ón a & m champion. ∼**onato** m championship

campes|ino a country. ● m peasant. ∼**tre** a country

camping /'kampin/ m (pl **campings** /'kampin/) camping; (lugar) campsite. **hacer** ∼ go camping

campiña f countryside

campo m country; (agricultura, fig) field; (de tenis) court; (de fútbol) pitch; (de golf) course. ~santo m cemetery

camufla|do a camouflaged. ~je m camouflage. ~r vt camouflage

cana f grey hair, white hair. echar una ~ al aire have a fling. peinar ~s be getting old

Canadá m. el ~ Canada

canadiense a & m Canadian

canal m (incl TV) channel; (artificial) canal; (del tejado) gutter. ~ de la Mancha English Channel. ~ de Panamá Panama Canal. ~ón m (horizontal) gutter; (vertical) drain-pipe

canalla f rabble. ● m (fig, fam) swine. ~da f dirty trick

canapé m sofa, couch; (culin) canapé

Canarias fpl. (las islas) ~ the Canary Islands, the Canaries

canario a of the Canary Islands. ● m native of the Canary Islands; (pájaro) canary

canast|a f (large) basket. ~illa f small basket; (para un bebé) layette. ~illo m small basket. ~o m (large) basket

cancela f gate

cancela|ción f cancellation. ~r vt cancel; write off (deuda); (fig) forget

cáncer m cancer. C~ Cancer

canciller m chancellor; (LAm, ministro de asuntos exteriores) Minister of Foreign Affairs

canci|ón f song. ~ón de cuna lullaby. ~onero m song-book. ¡siempre la misma ~ón! always the same old story!

cancha f (de fútbol) pitch, ground; (de tenis) court

candado m padlock

candel|a f candle. ~ero m candlestick. ~illa f candle

candente a (rojo) red-hot; (blanco) white-hot; (fig) burning

candidato m candidate

candidez f innocence; (ingenuidad) naïvety

cándido a naïve

candil m oil-lamp; (Mex, araña) chandelier. ~ejas fpl footlights

candinga m (Mex) devil

candor m innocence; (ingenuidad) naïvety. ~oso a innocent; (ingenuo) naïve

canela f cinnamon. ser ~ be beautiful

cangrejo m crab. ~ de río crayfish

canguro m kangaroo; (persona) baby-sitter

can|íbal a & m cannibal. ~ibalismo m cannibalism

canica f marble

canijo m weak

canino a canine. ● m canine (tooth)

canje m exchange. ~ar vt exchange

cano a grey-haired

canoa f canoe; (con motor) motor boat

canon m canon

can|ónigo m canon. ~onizar [10] vt canonize

canoso a grey-haired

cansa|do a tired. ~ncio m tiredness. ~r vt tire; (aburrir) bore. ● vi be tiring; (aburrir) get boring. ~rse vpr get tired

cantábrico a Cantabrian. el mar ~ the Bay of Biscay

canta|nte a singing. ● m singer; (en óperas) opera singer. ~or m Flamenco singer. ~r vt/i sing. ● m singing; (canción) song; (poema) poem. ~rlas claras speak frankly

cántar|a f pitcher. ~o m pitcher. llover a ~os pour down

cante m folk song. ~ flamenco, ~ jondo Flamenco singing

cantera f quarry

cantidad f quantity; (número) number; (de dinero) sum. una ~ de lots of

cantilena f, cantinela f song

cantimplora f water-bottle

cantina f canteen; (rail) buffet

canto m singing; (canción) song; (borde) edge; (de un cuchillo) blunt edge; (esquina) corner; (piedra) pebble. ~ rodado boulder. de ~ on edge

cantonés a Cantonese

cantor a singing. ● m singer

canturre|ar vt/i hum. ~o m humming

canuto m tube

caña f stalk, stem; (planta) reed; (vaso) glass; (de la pierna) shin. ~ de azúcar sugar-cane. ~ de pescar fishing-rod

cañada f ravine; (camino) track

cáñamo m hemp. ~ índio cannabis

cañ|ería f pipe; (tubería) piping. ~o m pipe, tube; (de fuente) jet. ~ón m pipe, tube; (de órgano) pipe; (de chimenea) flue; (arma de fuego) cannon; (desfiladero) canyon. ~onazo m gunshot. ~onera f gunboat

caoba f mahogany

ca|os m chaos. **~ótico** a chaotic

capa f cloak; (de pintura) coat; (culin) coating; (geol) stratum, layer

capacidad f capacity; (fig) ability

capacitar vt qualify, enable; (instruir) train

caparazón m shell

capataz m foreman

capaz a capable, able; (espacioso) roomy. **~ para** which holds, with a capacity of

capazo m large basket

capcioso a sly, insidious

capellán m chaplain

caperuza f hood; (de pluma) cap

capilla f chapel; (mus) choir

capita f small cloak, cape

capital a capital, very important. ● m (dinero) capital. ● f (ciudad) capital; (LAm, letra) capital (letter). **~ de provincia** county town

capitali|smo m capitalism. **~sta** a & m & f capitalist. **~zar** [10] vt capitalize

capit|án m captain. **~anear** vt lead, command; (un equipo) captain

capitel m (arquit) capital

capitulaci|ón f surrender; (acuerdo) agreement. **~ones** fpl marriage contract

capítulo m chapter. **~s matrimoniales** marriage contract

capó m bonnet (Brit), hood (Amer)

capón m (pollo) capon

caporal m chief, leader

capota f (de mujer) bonnet; (auto) folding top, sliding roof

capote m cape

Capricornio m Capricorn

capricho m whim. **~so** a capricious, whimsical. **a ~** capriciously

cápsula f capsule

captar vt harness (agua); grasp (sentido); hold (atención); win (confianza); (radio) pick up

captura f capture. **~r** vt capture

capucha f hood

capullo m bud; (de insecto) cocoon

caqui m khaki

cara f face; (de una moneda) obverse; (de un objeto) side; (aspecto) look, appearance; (descaro) cheek. **~ a** towards; (frente a) facing. **~ a ~** face to face. **~ o cruz** heads or tails. **dar la ~** face up to. **hacer ~ a** face. **no volver la ~ atrás** not look back. **tener ~ de** look, seem to be. **tener ~ para** have the face to. **tener mala ~** look ill. **volver la ~** look the other way

carabela f caravel, small light ship

carabina f rifle; (fig, señora, fam) chaperone

Caracas m Caracas

caracol m snail; (de pelo) curl. **¡~es!** Good Heavens! **escalera** f **de ~** spiral staircase

carácter m (pl caracteres) character. **con ~ de, por su ~ de** as

característic|a f characteristic; (LAm, teléfonos) dialling code. **~o** a characteristic, typical

caracteriza|do a characterized; (prestigioso) distinguished. **~r** [10] vt characterize

cara: ~ dura cheek, nerve. **~dura** m & f cheeky person, rotter (fam)

caramba int good heavens!, goodness me!

carámbano m icicle

caramelo m sweet (Brit), candy (Amer); (azúcar fundido) caramel

carancho m (Arg) vulture

carapacho m shell

caraqueño a from Caracas. ● m native of Caracas

carátula f mask; (fig, teatro) theatre; (Mex, esfera del reloj) face

caravana f caravan; (fig, grupo) group; (auto) long line, traffic jam

caray int (fam) good heavens!, goodness me!

carb|ón m coal; (papel) carbon (paper); (para dibujar) charcoal. **~oncillo** m charcoal. **~onero** a coal. ● m coal-merchant. **~onizar** [10] vt (fig) burn (to a cinder). **~ono** m carbon

carburador m carburettor

carcajada f burst of laughter. **reírse a ~s** roar with laughter. **soltar una ~** burst out laughing

cárcel m prison, jail; (en carpintería) clamp

carcel|ario a prison. **~ero** a prison. ● m prison officer

carcom|a f woodworm. **~er** vt eat away; (fig) undermine. **~erse** vpr be eaten away; (fig) waste away

cardenal m cardinal; (contusión) bruise

cárdeno a purple

cardiaco, cardíaco, a cardiac, heart. ● m heart patient

cardinal a cardinal

cardiólogo *m* cardiologist, heart specialist

cardo *m* thistle

carear *vt* bring face to face ‹*personas*›; compare ‹*cosas*›

carecer [11] *vi*. ~ **de** lack. ~ **de sentido** not to make sense

caren|cia *f* lack. **~te** *a* lacking

carero *a* expensive

carestía *f* (*precio elevado*) high price; (*escasez*) shortage

careta *f* mask

carey *m* tortoiseshell

carga *f* load; (*fig*) burden; (*acción*) loading; (*de barco*) cargo; (*obligación*) obligation. **~do** *a* loaded; (*fig*) burdened; (*tiempo*) heavy; ‹*hilo*› live; ‹*pila*› charged. **~mento** *m* load; (*acción*) loading; (*de un barco*) cargo. **~nte** *a* demanding. **~r** [12] *vt* load; (*fig*) burden; (*mil, elec*) charge; fill ‹*pluma etc*›; (*fig, molestar, fam*) annoy. ● *vi* load. **~r con** pick up. **~rse** *vpr* (*llenarse*) fill; ‹*cielo*› become overcast; (*enfadarse, fam*) get cross. **llevar la ~ de algo** be responsible for sth

cargo *m* load; (*fig*) burden; (*puesto*) post; (*acusación*) accusation, charge; (*responsabilidad*) charge. **a ~ de** in the charge of. **hacerse ~ de** take responsibility for. **tener a su ~** be in charge of

carguero *m* (*Arg*) beast of burden; (*naut*) cargo ship

cari *m* (*LAm*) grey

cariacontecido *a* crestfallen

caria|do *a* decayed. **~rse** *vpr* decay

caribe *a* Caribbean. **el mar** *m* **C~** the Caribbean (Sea)

caricatura *f* caricature

caricia *f* caress

caridad *f* charity. **¡por ~!** for goodness sake!

caries *f invar* (*dental*) decay

carilampiño *a* clean-shaven

cariño *m* affection; (*caricia*) caress. **~ mío** my darling. **~samente** *adv* tenderly, lovingly; (*en carta*) with love from. **~so** *a* affectionate. **con mucho ~** (*en carta*) with love from. **tener ~ a** be fond of. **tomar ~ a** take a liking to. **un ~** (*en carta*) with love from

carism|a *m* charisma. **~ático** *a* charismatic

caritativo *a* charitable

cariz *m* look

carlinga *f* cockpit

carmesí *a & m* crimson

carmín *m* (*de labios*) lipstick; (*color*) red

carnal *a* carnal; ‹*pariente*› blood, full. **primo ~** first cousin

carnaval *m* carnival. **~esco** *a* carnival. **martes** *m* **de ~** Shrove Tuesday

carne *f* (*incl de frutos*) flesh; (*para comer*) meat. **~ de cerdo** pork. **~ de cordero** lamb. **~ de gallina** gooseflesh. **~ picada** mince. **~ de ternera** veal. **~ de vaca** beef. **me pone la ~ de ~ y hueso** be only human

carné *m* card; (*cuaderno*) notebook. **~ de conducir** driving licence (*Brit*), driver's license (*Amer*). **~ de identidad** identity card.

carnero *m* sheep; (*culin*) lamb

carnet /kar'ne/ *m* card; (*cuaderno*) notebook. **~ de conducir** driving licence (*Brit*), driver's license (*Amer*). **~ de identidad** identity card

carnicer|ía *f* butcher's (shop); (*fig*) massacre. **~o** *a* carnivorous; (*fig, cruel*) cruel, savage. ● *m* butcher; (*animal*) carnivore

carnívoro *a* carnivorous. ● *m* carnivore

carnoso *a* fleshy

caro *a* dear. ● *adv* dear, dearly. **costar ~ a uno** cost s.o. dear

carpa *f* carp; (*tienda*) tent

carpeta *f* file, folder. **~zo** *m*. **dar ~zo a** shelve, put on one side

carpinter|ía *f* carpentry. **~o** *m* carpenter, joiner

carraspe|ar *vi* clear one's throat. **~ra** *f*. **tener ~ra** have a frog in one's throat

carrera *f* run; (*prisa*) rush; (*concurso*) race; (*recorrido, estudios*) course; (*profesión*) profession, career

carreta *f* cart. **~da** *f* cart-load

carrete *m* reel; (*película*) 35mm film

carretera *f* road. **~ de circunvalación** bypass, ring road. **~ nacional** A road (*Brit*), highway (*Amer*). **~ secundaria** B road (*Brit*), secondary road (*Amer*)

carret|illa *f* trolley; (*de una rueda*) wheelbarrow; (*de bebé*) baby-walker. **~ón** *m* small cart

carril *m* rut; (*rail*) rail; (*de autopista etc*) lane

carrillo m cheek; (polea) pulley

carrizo m reed

carro m cart; (LAm, coche) car. ~ **de asalto**, ~ **de combate** tank

carrocería f (auto) bodywork; (taller) car repairer's

carroña f carrion

carroza f coach, carriage; (en desfile de fiesta) float

carruaje m carriage

carrusel m merry-go-round

carta f letter; (documento) document; (lista de platos) menu; (lista de vinos) list; (geog) map; (naipe) card. ~ **blanca** free hand. ~ **de crédito** credit card

cartearse vpr correspond

cartel m poster; (de escuela etc) wallchart. ~**era** f hoarding; (en periódico) entertainments. ~**ito** m notice. **de** ~ celebrated. **tener** ~ be a hit, be successful

cartera f wallet; (de colegial) satchel; (para documentos) briefcase

cartería f sorting office

carterista m & f pickpocket

cartero m postman, mailman (Amer)

cartílago m cartilage

cartilla f first reading book. ~ **de ahorros** savings book. **leerle la** ~ **a uno** tell s.o. off

cartón m cardboard

cartucho m cartridge

cartulina f thin cardboard

casa f house; (hogar) home; (empresa) firm; (edificio) building. ~ **de correos** post office. ~ **de huéspedes** boarding-house. ~ **de socorro** first aid post. **amigo** m **de la** ~ family friend. **ir a** ~ go home. **salir de** ~ go out

casad|a f married woman. ~**o** a married. ● m married man. **los recién** ~**os** the newly-weds

casamentero m matchmaker

casa|miento m marriage; (ceremonia) wedding. ~**r** vt marry. ● vi get married. ~**rse** vpr get married

cascabel m small bell. ~**eo** m jingling

cascada f waterfall

cascado a broken; (voz) harsh

cascanueces m invar nutcrackers

cascar [7] vt break; crack (frutos secos); (pegar) beat. ● vi (fig, fam) chatter, natter (fam). ~**se** vpr crack

cáscara f (de huevo, frutos secos) shell; (de naranja) peel; (de plátano) skin

casco m helmet; (de cerámica etc) piece, fragment; (cabeza) head; (de barco) hull; (envase) empty bottle; (de caballo) hoof; (de una ciudad) part, area

cascote m rubble

caserío m country house; (conjunto de casas) hamlet

casero a home-made; (doméstico) domestic, household; (amante del hogar) home-loving; (reunión) family. ● m owner; (vigilante) caretaker

caseta f small house, cottage. ~ **de baño** bathing hut

caset(t)e m & f cassette

casi adv almost, nearly; (en frases negativas) hardly. ~ ~ very nearly. ~ **nada** hardly any. ¡~ **nada!** is that all! ~ **nunca** hardly ever

casilla f small house; (cabaña) hut; (de mercado) stall; (en ajedrez etc) square; (departamento de casillero) pigeon-hole

casillero m pigeon-holes

casimir m cashmere

casino m casino; (sociedad) club

caso m case; (atención) notice. ~ **perdido** hopeless case. ~ **urgente** emergency. **darse el** ~ **(de) que** happen. **el** ~ **es que** the fact is that. **en** ~ **de** in the event of. **en cualquier** ~ in any case, whatever happens. **en ese** ~ in that case. **en todo** ~ in any case. **en último** ~ as a last resort. **hacer** ~ **de** take notice of. **poner por** ~ suppose

caspa f dandruff

cáspita int good heavens!, goodness me!

casquivano a scatter-brained

cassette m & f cassette

casta f (de animal) breed; (de persona) descent

castaña f chestnut

castañet|a f click of the fingers. ~**ear** vi (dientes) chatter

castaño a chestnut, brown. ● m chestnut (tree)

castañuela f castanet

castellano a Castilian. ● m (persona) Castilian; (lengua) Castilian, Spanish. ~**parlante** a Castilian-speaking, Spanish-speaking. ¿**habla Vd** ~? do you speak Spanish?

castidad f chastity

castig|ar [12] vt punish; (en deportes) penalize. ~**o** m punishment; (en deportes) penalty

Castilla f Castille. ~ **la Nueva** New Castille. ~ **la Vieja** Old Castille

castillo m castle

cast|izo a true; ‹lengua› pure. ~**o** a pure

castor m beaver

castra|ción f castration. ~**r** vt castrate

castrense m military

casual a chance, accidental. ~**idad** f chance, coincidence. ~**mente** adv by chance. **dar la** ~**idad** happen. **de** ~**idad, por** ~**idad** by chance. **¡qué** ~**idad!** what a coincidence!

cataclismo m cataclysm

catador m taster; (fig) connoisseur

catalán a & m Catalan

catalejo m telescope

catalizador m catalyst

cat|alogar [12] vt catalogue; (fig) classify. ~**álogo** m catalogue

Cataluña f Catalonia

catamarán m catamaran

cataplúm int crash! bang!

catapulta f catapult

catar vt taste, try

catarata f waterfall, falls; (med) cataract

catarro m cold

cat|ástrofe m catastrophe. ~**astrófico** a catastrophic

catecismo m catechism

catedral f cathedral

catedrático m professor; (de instituto) teacher, head of department

categor|ía f category; (clase) class. ~**órico** a categorical. **de** ~**oría** important. **de primera** ~**oría** first-class

catinga f (LAm) bad smell

catita f (Arg) parrot

catoche m (Mex) bad mood

cat|olicismo m catholicism. ~**ólico** a (Roman) Catholic. ● m (Roman) Catholic

catorce a & m fourteen

cauce m river bed; (fig, artificial) channel

caución f caution; (jurid) guarantee

caucho m rubber

caudal m (de río) flow; (riqueza) wealth. ~**oso** a (río) large

caudillo m leader, caudillo

causa f cause; (motivo) reason; (jurid) lawsuit. ~**r** vt cause. **a** ~ **de, por** ~ **de** because of

cáustico a caustic

cautel|a f caution. ~**arse** vpr guard against. ~**osamente** adv warily, cautiously. ~**oso** a cautious, wary

cauterizar [10] vt cauterize; (fig) apply drastic measures to

cautiv|ar vt capture; (fig, fascinar) captivate. ~**erio** m, ~**idad** f captivity. ~**o** a & m captive

cauto a cautious

cavar vt/i dig

caverna f cave, cavern

caviar m caviare

cavidad f cavity

cavil|ar vi ponder, consider. ~**oso** a worried

cayado m (de pastor) crook; (de obispo) crozier

caza f hunting; (una expedición) hunt; (animales) game. ● m fighter. ~**dor** m hunter. ~**dora** f jacket. ~ **mayor** big game hunting. ~ **menor** small game hunting. ~**r** [10] vt hunt; (fig) track down; (obtener) catch, get. **andar a (la)** ~ **de** be in search of. **dar a** ~ chase, go after

cazo m saucepan; (cucharón) ladle. ~**leta** f (small) saucepan

cazuela f casserole

cebada f barley

ceb|ar vt fatten (up); (con trampa) bait; prime ‹arma de fuego›. ~**o** m bait; (de arma de fuego) charge

ceboll|a f onion. ~**ana** f chive. ~**eta** f spring onion. ~**ino** m chive

cebra f zebra

cece|ar vi lisp. ~**o** m lisp

cedazo m sieve

ceder vt give up. ● vi give in; (disminuir) ease off; (fallar) give way, collapse. **ceda el paso** give way

cedilla f cedilla

cedro m cedar

cédula f document; (ficha) index card

CE(E) abrev (Comunidad (Económica) Europea) E(E)C, European (Economic) Community

cefalea f severe headache

cefalea f eyebrow

cejar vi move back; (fig) give way

celada f ambush; (fig) trap

cela|dor m (de niños) monitor; (de cárcel) prison warder; (de museo etc) attendant. ~**r** vt watch

celda f cell

ceg|ador a blinding. ~**ar** [1 & 12] vt blind; (tapar) block up. ~**arse** vpr be blinded (**de** by). ~**ato** a short-sighted. ~**uera** f blindness

celebra|ción f celebration. **~r** vt celebrate; (alabar) praise. **~rse** vpr take place

célebre a famous; (fig, gracioso) funny

celebridad f fame; (persona) celebrity

celeridad f speed

celest|e a heavenly. **~ial** a heavenly. **azul ~** sky-blue

celibato m celibacy

célibe a celibate

celo m zeal. **~s** mpl jealousy. **dar ~s** make jealous. **papel** m **~** adhesive tape, Sellotape (P). **tener ~s** be jealous

celofán m cellophane

celoso a enthusiastic; (que tiene celos) jealous

celta a Celtic. ● m & f Celt

céltico a Celtic

célula f cell

celular a cellular

celuloide m celluloid

celulosa f cellulose

cellisca f sleetstorm

cementerio m cemetery

cemento m cement; (hormigón) concrete; (LAm, cola) glue

cena f dinner; (comida ligera) supper. **~duría** f(Mex) restaurant

cenag|al m marsh, bog; (fig) tight spot. **~oso** a muddy

cenar vt have for dinner; (en cena ligera) have for supper. ● vi have dinner; (tomar cena ligera) have supper

cenicero m ashtray

cenit m zenith

ceniz|a f ash. **~o** a ashen. ● m jinx

censo m census. **~ electoral** electoral roll

censura f censure; (de prensa etc) censorship. **~r** vt censure; censor (prensa etc)

centavo a & m hundredth; (moneda) centavo

centell|a f flash; (chispa) spark. **~ar** vi, **~ear** vi sparkle. **~eo** m sparkle, sparkling

centena f hundred. **~r** m hundred. **a ~res** by the hundred

centenario a centenary; (persona) centenarian. ● m centenary; (persona) centenarian

centeno m rye

centésim|a f hundredth. **~o** a hundredth; (moneda) centésimo

cent|ígrado a centigrade, Celsius. **~ígramo** m centigram. **~ilitro** m centilitre. **~ímetro** m centimetre

céntimo a hundredth. ● m cent

centinela f sentry

centolla f, **centollo** m spider crab

central a central. ● f head office. **~ de correos** general post office. **~ eléctrica** power station. **~ nuclear** nuclear power station. **~ telefónica** telephone exchange. **~ismo** m centralism. **~ita** f switchboard

centraliza|ción f centralization. **~r** [10] vt centralize

centrar vt centre

céntrico a central

centrífugo a centrifugal

centro m centre. **~ comercial** shopping centre

Centroamérica f Central America

centroamericano a & m Central American

centuplicar [7] vt increase a hundredfold

ceñi|do a tight. **~r** [5 & 22] vt surround, encircle; (vestido) be a tight fit. **~rse** vpr limit o.s. (a to)

ceñ|o m frown. **~udo** a frowning. **fruncir el ~o** frown

cepill|ar vt brush; (en carpintería) plane. **~o** m brush; (en carpintería) plane. **~o de dientes** toothbrush

cera f wax

cerámic|a f ceramics; (materia) pottery; (objeto) piece of pottery. **~o** a ceramic

cerca f fence. ● adv near, close. **~s** mpl foreground. **~ de** prep near; (con números, con tiempo) nearly. **de ~** from close up, closely

cercado m enclosure

cercan|ía f nearness, proximity. **~ías** fpl outskirts. **tren** m **de ~ías** local train. **~o** a near, close. **C~o Oriente** m Near East

cercar [7] vt fence in, enclose; (gente) surround, crowd round; (asediar) besiege

cerciorar vt convince. **~se** vpr make sure, find out

cerco m (grupo) circle; (cercado) enclosure; (asedio) siege

Cerdeña f Sardinia

cerdo m pig; (carne) pork

cereal m cereal

cerebr|al a cerebral. **~o** m brain; (fig, inteligencia) intelligence, brains

ceremoni|a f ceremony. ~**al** a ceremonial. ~**oso** a ceremonious, stiff

céreo a wax

cerez|a f cherry. ~**o** cherry tree

cerill|a f match. ~**o** m (Mex) match

cern|er [1] vt sieve. ~**erse** vpr hover; (fig, amenazar) hang over. ~**idor** m sieve

cero m nought, zero; (fútbol) nil (Brit), zero (Amer); (tenis) love; (persona) nonentity. **partir de** ~ start from scratch

cerquillo m (LAm, flequillo) fringe

cerquita adv very near

cerra|do a shut, closed; (espacio) shut in, enclosed; (cielo) overcast; (curva) sharp. ~**dura** f lock; (acción de cerrar) shutting, closing. ~**jero** m locksmith. ~**r** [1] vt shut, close; (con llave) lock; (con cerrojo) bolt; (cercar) enclose; turn off (grifo); block up (agujero etc). ● vi shut, close. ~**rse** vpr shut, close; (herida) heal. ~**r con llave** lock

cerro m hill. **irse por los** ~**s de Úbeda** ramble on

cerrojo m bolt. **echar el** ~ bolt

certamen m competition, contest

certero a accurate

certeza f, **certidumbre** f certainty

certifica|do a (carta etc) registered. ● m certificate; (carta) registered letter. ~**r** [7] vt certify; register (carta etc)

certitud f certainty

cervato m fawn

cerve|cería f beerhouse, bar; (fábrica) brewery. ~**za** f beer. ~**za de barril** draught beer. ~**za de botella** bottled beer

cesa|ción f cessation, suspension. ~**nte** a out of work. ~**r** vt stop. ● vi stop, cease; (dejar un empleo) give up. **sin** ~**r** incessantly

cesáreo a Caesarian. **operación** f **cesárea** Caesarian section

cese m cessation; (de un empleo) dismissal

césped m grass, lawn

cest|a f basket. ~**ada** f basketful. ~**o** m basket. ~**o de los papeles** wastepaper basket

cetro m sceptre; (fig) power

cianuro m cyanide

ciática f sciatica

cibernética f cybernetics

cicatriz f scar. ~**ación** f healing. ~**ar** [10] vt/i heal. ~**arse** vpr heal

ciclamino m cyclamen

cíclico a cyclic(al)

ciclis|mo m cycling. ~**ta** m & f cyclist

ciclo m cycle; (LAm, curso) course

ciclomotor m moped

ciclón m cyclone

ciclostilo m cyclostyle, duplicating machine

ciego a blind. ● m blind man, blind person. **a ciegas** in the dark

cielo m sky; (relig) heaven; (persona) darling. **i~s!** good heavens!, goodness me!

ciempiés m invar centipede

cien a a hundred. ~ **por** ~ (fam) completely, one hundred per cent. **me pone a** ~ it drives me mad

ciénaga f bog, swamp

ciencia f science; (fig) knowledge. ~**s** fpl (univ etc) science. ~**s empresariales** business studies. **saber a** ~ **cierta** know for a fact, know for certain

cieno m mud

científico a scientific. ● m scientist

ciento a & m (delante de nombres, y numerales a los que multiplica **cien**) a hundred, one hundred. **por** ~ per cent

cierne m blossoming. **en** ~ in blossom; (fig) in its infancy

cierre m fastener; (acción de cerrar) shutting, closing. ~ **de cremallera** zip, zipper (Amer)

cierro vb véase **cerrar**

cierto a certain; (verdad) true. **estar en lo** ~ be right. **lo** ~ **es que** the fact is that. **no es** ~ that's not true. **¿no es** ~? right? **por** ~ certainly, by the way. **si bien es** ~ **que** although

ciervo m deer

cifra f figure, number; (cantidad) sum. ~**do** a coded. ~**r** vt code; (resumir) summarize. **en** ~ code, in code

cigala f (Norway) lobster

cigarra f cicada

cigarr|illo m cigarette. ~**o** m (cigarillo) cigarette; (puro) cigar

cigüeña f stork

cil|índrico a cylindrical. ~**indro** m cylinder; (Mex, organillo) barrel organ

cima f top; (fig) summit

címbalo m cymbal

cimbrear vt shake. ~**se** vpr sway

cimentar [1] *vt* lay the foundations of; (*fig, reforzar*) strengthen

cimer|a *f* crest. **~o** *a* highest

cimiento *m* foundations; (*fig*) source. **desde los ~s** from the very beginning

cinc *m* zinc

cincel *m* chisel. **~ar** *vt* chisel

cinco *a* & *m* five

cincuent|a *a* & *m* fifty; (*quincuagésimo*) fiftieth. **~ón** *a* about fifty

cine *m* cinema. **~matografiar** [20] *vt* film

cinético *a* kinetic

cínico *a* cynical; (*desvergonzado*) shameless. • *m* cynic

cinismo *m* cynicism; (*desvergüenza*) shamelessness

cinta *f* band; (*adorno de pelo etc*) ribbon; (*película*) film; (*magnética*) tape; (*de máquina de escribir etc*) ribbon. **~ aisladora, ~ aislante** insulating tape. **~ magnetofónica** magnetic tape. **~ métrica** tape measure

cintur|a *f* waist. **~ón** *m* belt. **~ón de seguridad** safety belt. **~ón salvavidas** lifebelt

ciprés *m* cypress (tree)

circo *m* circus

circuito *m* circuit; (*viaje*) tour. **~ cerrado** closed circuit. **corto ~** short circuit

circula|ción *f* circulation; (*vehículos*) traffic. **~r** *a* circular. • *vt* circulate. • *vi* circulate; (*líquidos*) flow; (*conducir*) drive; (*autobús etc*) run

círculo *m* circle. **~ vicioso** vicious circle. **en ~** in a circle

circunci|dar *vt* circumcise. **~sión** *f* circumcision

circunda|nte *a* surrounding. **~r** *vt* surround

circunferencia *f* circumference

circunflejo *m* circumflex

circunscri|bir [*pp* circunscrito] *vt* confine. **~pción** *f* (*distrito*) district. **~pción electoral** constituency

circunspecto *a* wary, circumspect

circunstan|cia *f* circumstance. **~te** *a* surrounding. • *m* bystander. **los ~tes** those present

circunvalación *f*. **carretera** *f* **de ~** bypass, ring road

cirio *m* candle

ciruela *f* plum. **~ claudia** greengage. **~ damascena** damson

ciru|gía *f* surgery. **~jano** *m* surgeon

cisne *m* swan

cisterna *f* tank, cistern

cita *f* appointment; (*entre chico y chica*) date; (*referencia*) quotation. **~ción** *f* quotation; (*jurid*) summons. **~do** *a* aforementioned. **~r** *vt* make an appointment with; (*mencionar*) quote; (*jurid*) summons. **~rse** *vpr* arrange to meet

cítara *f* zither

ciudad *f* town; (*grande*) city. **~anía** *f* citizenship; (*habitantes*) citizens. **~ano** *a* civic. • *m* citizen, inhabitant; (*habitante de ciudad*) city dweller

cívico *a* civic

civil *a* civil. • *m* civil guard. **~idad** *f* politeness

civiliza|ción *f* civilization. **~r** [10] *vt* civilize. **~rse** *vpr* become civilized

civismo *m* community spirit

cizaña *f* (*fig*) discord

clam|ar *vi* cry out, clamour. **~or** *m* cry; (*griterío*) noise, clamour; (*protesta*) outcry. **~oroso** *a* noisy

clandestin|idad *f* secrecy. **~o** *a* clandestine, secret

clara *f* (*de huevo*) egg white

claraboya *f* skylight

clarear *vi* dawn; (*aclarar*) brighten up. **~se** *vpr* be transparent

clarete *m* rosé

claridad *f* clarity; (*luz*) light

clarifica|ción *f* clarification. **~r** [7] *vt* clarify

clarín *m* bugle

clarinet|e *m* clarinet; (*músico*) clarinettist. **~ista** *m* & *f* clarinettist

clarividen|cia *f* clairvoyance; (*fig*) far-sightedness. **~te** *a* clairvoyant; (*fig*) far-sighted

claro *a* (*con mucha luz*) bright; (*transparente, evidente*) clear; (*colores*) light; (*líquido*) thin. • *m* (*en bosque etc*) clearing; (*espacio*) gap. • *adv* clearly. • *int* of course! **~ de luna** moonlight. **¡~ que sí!** yes of course! **¡~ que no!** of course not!

clase *f* class; (*aula*) classroom. **~ media** middle class. **~ obrera** working class. **~ social** social class. **dar ~s** teach. **toda ~ de** all sorts of

clásico *a* classical; (*fig*) classic. • *m* classic

clasifica|ción *f* classification; (*deportes*) league. **~r** [7] *vt* classify; (*seleccionar*) sort

claudia *f* greengage

claudicar [7] (*ceder*) give in; (*cojear*) limp

claustro *m* cloister; (*univ*) staff

claustrof|obia *f* claustrophobia. ~**óbico** *a* claustrophobic

cláusula *f* clause

clausura *f* closure; (*ceremonia*) closing ceremony. ~**r** *vt* close

clava|do *a* fixed; (*con clavo*) nailed. ~**r** *vt* knock in (*clavo*); (*introducir a mano*) stick; (*fijar*) fix; (*juntar*) nail together. **es** ~**do a su padre** he's the spitting image of his father

clave *f* key; (*mus*) clef; (*clavicémbalo*) harpsichord

clavel *m* carnation

clavicémbalo *m* harpsichord

clavícula *f* collar bone, clavicle

clavija *f* peg; (*elec*) plug

clavo *m* nail; (*culin*) clove

claxon *m* (*pl* **claxons** /'klakson/) horn

clemen|cia *f* clemency, mercy. ~**te** *a* clement, merciful

clementina *f* tangerine

cleptómano *m* kleptomaniac

cler|ecía *f* priesthood. ~**ical** *a* clerical

clérigo *m* priest

clero *m* clergy

cliché *m* cliché; (*foto*) negative

cliente *m & f* client, customer; (*de médico*) patient. ~**la** *f* clientele, customers; (*de médico*) patients, practice

clim|a *m* climate. ~**ático** *a* climatic. ~**atizado** *a* air-conditioned. ~**atológico** *a* climatological

clínic|a *f* clinic. ~**o** *a* clinical. ● *m* clinician

clip *m* (*pl* **clips**) clip

clo *m* cluck. **hacer** ~ ~ cluck

cloaca *f* drain, sewer

cloque|ar *vi* cluck. ~**o** *m* clucking

cloro *m* chlorine

club *m* (*pl* **clubs** o **clubes**) club

coacci|ón *f* coercion, compulsion. ~**onar** *vt* coerce, compel

coagular *vt* coagulate; clot (*sangre*); curdle (*leche*). ~**se** *vpr* coagulate; (*sangre*) clot; (*leche*) curdle

coalición *f* coalition

coartada *f* alibi

coartar *vt* hinder; restrict (*libertad etc*)

cobard|e *a* cowardly. ● *m* coward. ~**ía** *f* cowardice

cobaya *f*, **cobayo** *m* guinea pig

cobert|era *f* (*tapadera*) lid. ~**izo** *m* lean-to, shelter. ~**or** *m* bedspread; (*manta*) blanket. ~**ura** *f* covering

cobij|a *f* (*LAm, ropa de cama*) bedclothes; (*Mex, manta*) blanket. ~**ar** *vt* shelter. ~**arse** *vpr* shelter, take shelter. ~**o** *m* shelter

cobra *f* cobra

cobra|dor *m* conductor. ~**dora** *f* conductress. ~**r** *vt* collect; (*ganar*) earn; charge (*precio*); cash (*cheque*); (*recuperar*) recover. ● *vi* be paid. ~**rse** *vpr* recover

cobre *m* copper; (*mus*) brass (instruments)

cobro *m* collection; (*de cheque*) cashing; (*pago*) payment. **ponerse en** ~ go into hiding. **presentar al** ~ cash

cocada *f* (*LAm*) sweet coconut

cocaína *f* cocaine

cocción *f* cooking; (*tec*) baking, firing

cocear *vt/i* kick

coc|er [2 & 9] *vt/i* cook; (*hervir*) boil; (*en horno*) bake. ~**ido** *a* cooked. ● *m* stew

cociente *m* quotient. ~ **intelectual** intelligence quotient, IQ

cocin|a *f* kitchen; (*arte de cocinar*) cookery, cuisine; (*aparato*) cooker. ~**a de gas** gas cooker. ~**a eléctrica** electric cooker. ~**ar** *vt/i* cook. ~**ero** *m* cook

coco *m* coconut; (*árbol*) coconut palm; (*cabeza*) head; (*duende*) bogeyman. **comerse el** ~ think hard

cocodrilo *m* crocodile

cocotero *m* coconut palm

cóctel *m* (*pl* **cóctels** o **cócteles**) cocktail; (*reunión*) cocktail party

coche *m* car (*Brit*), motor car (*Brit*), automobile (*Amer*); (*de tren*) coach, carriage. ~**-cama** sleeper. ~ **fúnebre** hearse. ~**ra** *f* garage; (*de autobuses*) depot. ~ **restaurante** dining-car. ~**s de choque** dodgems

cochin|ada *f* dirty thing. ~**o** *a* dirty, filthy. ● *m* pig

cod|azo *m* nudge (with one's elbow); (*Mex, aviso secreto*) tip-off. ~**ear** *vt/i* elbow, nudge

codici|a *f* greed. ~**ado** *a* coveted, sought after. ~**ar** *vt* covet. ~**oso** *a* greedy (**de** for)

código *m* code. ~ **de la circulación** Highway Code

codo *m* elbow; (*dobladura*) bend. **hablar por los** ~**s** talk too much. **hasta los** ~**s** up to one's neck

codorniz *m* quail

coeducación *f* coeducation

coerción *f* coercion

coetáneo *a* & *m* contemporary

coexist|encia *f* coexistence. ~**ir** *vi* coexist

cofradía *f* brotherhood

cofre *m* chest

coger [14] *vt* (*España*) take; catch ⟨*tren, autobús, pelota, catarro*⟩; (*agarrar*) take hold of; (*del suelo*) pick up; pick ⟨*frutos etc*⟩. ● *vi* (*caber*) fit. ~**se** *vpr* trap, catch

cogollo *m* (*de lechuga etc*) heart; (*fig, lo mejor*) cream; (*fig, núcleo*) centre

cogote *m* back of the neck

cohech|ar *vt* bribe. ~**o** *m* bribery

coherente *a* coherent

cohesión *f* cohesion

cohete *m* rocket; (*Mex, pistola*) pistol

cohibi|ción *f* inhibition. ~**r** *vt* restrict; inhibit ⟨*persona*⟩. ~**rse** *vpr* feel inhibited; (*contenerse*) restrain o.s.

coincid|encia *f* coincidence. ~**ente** *a* coincidental. ~**ir** *vt* coincide. **dar la** ~**encia** happen

coje|ar *vt* limp; ⟨*mueble*⟩ wobble. ~**ra** *f* lameness

coj|ín *m* cushion. ~**inete** *m* small cushion. ~**inete de bolas** ball bearing

cojo *a* lame; ⟨*mueble*⟩ wobbly. ● *m* lame person

col *f* cabbage. ~**es de Bruselas** Brussel sprouts

cola *f* tail; (*fila*) queue; (*para pegar*) glue. **a la** ~ at the end. **hacer** ~ queue (up). **tener** ~, **traer** ~ have serious consequences

colabora|ción *f* collaboration. ~**dor** *m* collaborator. ~**r** *vi* collaborate

colada *f* washing. **hacer la** ~ do the washing

colador *m* strainer

colapso *m* collapse; (*fig*) stoppage

colar [2] *vt* strain ⟨*líquidos*⟩; (*lavar*) wash; pass ⟨*moneda falsa etc*⟩. ● *vi* ⟨*líquido*⟩ seep through; (*fig*) be believed, wash (*fam*). ~**se** *vpr* slip; (*no hacer caso de la cola*) jump the queue; (*en fiesta*) gatecrash; (*meter la pata*) put one's foot in it

colch|a *f* bedspread. ~**ón** *m* mattress. ~**oneta** *f* mattress

colear *vi* wag its tail; ⟨*asunto*⟩ not be resolved. **vivito y coleando** alive and kicking

colecci|ón *f* collection; (*fig, gran número de*) a lot of. ~**onar** *vt* collect. ~**onista** *m* & *f* collector

colecta *f* collection

colectiv|idad *f* community. ~**o** *a* collective. ● *m* (*Arg*) minibus

colector *m* (*en las alcantarillas*) main sewer

colega *m* & *f* colleague

colegi|al *m* schoolboy. ~**ala** *f* schoolgirl. ~**o** *m* private school; (*de ciertas profesiones*) college. ~**o mayor** hall of residence

colegir [5 & 14] *vt* gather

cólera *f* cholera; (*ira*) anger, fury. **descargar su** ~ vent one's anger. **montar en** ~ fly into a rage

colérico *a* furious, irate

colesterol *m* cholesterol

coleta *f* pigtail

colga|nte *a* hanging. ● *m* pendant. ~**r** [2 & 12] *vt* hang; hang out ⟨*colada*⟩; hang up ⟨*abrigo etc*⟩. ● *vi* hang; (*teléfono*) hang up, ring off. ~**rse** *vpr* hang o.s. **dejar a uno** ~**do** let s.o. down

cólico *m* colic

coliflor *m* cauliflower

colilla *f* cigarette end

colina *f* hill

colinda|nte *a* adjacent. ~**r** *vt* border (con on)

colisión *f* collision, crash; (*fig*) clash

colmar *vt* fill to overflowing; (*fig*) fulfill. ~ **a uno de amabilidad** overwhelm s.o. with kindness

colmena *f* beehive, hive

colmillo *m* eye tooth, canine (tooth); (*de elefante*) tusk; (*de otros animales*) fang

colmo *m* height. **ser el** ~ be the limit, be the last straw

coloca|ción *f* positioning; (*empleo*) job, position. ~**r** [7] *vt* put, place; (*buscar empleo*) find work for. ~**rse** *vpr* find a job

Colombia *f* Colombia

colombiano *a* & *m* Colombian

colon *m* colon

colón *m* (*unidad monetaria de Costa Rica y El Salvador*) colón

Colonia *f* Cologne

coloni|a *f* colony; (*agua de colonia*) eau-de-Cologne; (*LAm, barrio*) suburb. ~**a de verano** holiday camp. ~**al** *a* colonial. ~**ales** *mpl* imported foodstuffs; (*comestibles en general*) groceries. ~**alista** *m* & *f* colonialist.

~zación f colonization. ~zar [10] colonize

coloqui|al a colloquial. ~o m conversation; (congreso) conference

color m colour. ~ado a (rojo) red. ~ante m colouring. ~ar vt colour. ~ear vt/i colour. ~ete m rouge. ~ido m colour. de ~ colour. en ~ (fotos, película) colour

colosal a colossal; (fig, magnífico, fam) terrific

columna f column; (fig, apoyo) support

columpi|ar vt swing. ~arse vpr swing. ~o m swing

collar m necklace; (de perro etc) collar

coma f comma. ● m (med) coma

comadre f midwife; (madrina) godmother; (vecina) neighbour. ~ar vi gossip

comadreja f weasel

comadrona f midwife

comand|ancia f command. ~ante m commander. ~o m command; (soldado) commando

comarca f area, region

comba f bend; (juguete) skipping-rope. ~r vt bend. ~rse vpr bend. saltar a la ~ skip

combat|e m fight; (fig) struggle. ~iente m fighter. ~ir vt/i fight

combina|ción f combination; (bebida) cocktail; (arreglo) plan, scheme; (prenda) slip. ~r vt combine; (arreglar) arrange; (armonizar) match, go well with. ~rse vpr combine; (ponerse de acuerdo) agree (para to)

combustible m fuel

comedia f comedy; (cualquier obra de teatro) play. hacer la ~ pretend

comedi|do a reserved. ~rse [5] vpr be restrained

comedor m dining-room; (restaurante) restaurant; (persona) glutton. ser buen ~ have a good appetite

comensal m companion at table, fellow diner

comentar vt comment on; (anotar) annotate. ~io m commentary; (observación) comment; (fam) gossip. ~ista m & f commentator

comenzar [1 & 10] vt/i begin, start

comer vt eat; (a mediodía) have for lunch; (corroer) eat away; (en ajedrez) take. ● vi eat; (a mediodía) have lunch. ~se vpr eat (up). dar de ~ a feed

comerci|al a commercial. ~ante m trader; (de tienda) shopkeeper. ~ar vt trade (con, en in); (con otra persona) do business. ~o m commerce; (actividad) trade; (tienda) shop; (negocio) business

comestible a edible. ~s mpl food. tienda de ~s grocer's (shop) (Brit), grocery (Amer)

cometa m comet. ● f kite

comet|er vt commit; make (falta). ~ido m task

comezón m itch

comicastro m poor actor, ham (fam)

comicios mpl elections

cómico a comic(al). ● m comic actor; (cualquier actor) actor

comida f food; (a mediodía) lunch. hacer la ~ prepare the meals

comidilla f topic of conversation. ser la ~ del pueblo be the talk of the town

comienzo m beginning, start. a ~s de at the beginning of

comil|ón a greedy. ~ona f feast

comillas fpl inverted commas

comino m cumin. (no) me importa un ~ I couldn't care less

comisar|ía f police station. ~io m commissioner; (deportes) steward. ~io de policía police superintendent

comisi|ón f assignment; (comité) commission, committee; (com) commission

comisura f corner. ~ de los labios corner of the mouth

comité m committee

como prep like, as. ● conj as; (en cuanto) as soon as. ~ quieras as you like. ~ sabes as you know. ~ si as if

cómo adv how? ¿~? I beg your pardon? ¿~ está Vd? how are you? ¡~ no! (esp LAm) of course! ¿~ son? what are they like? ¿~ te llamas? what's your name? ¡y ~! and how!

cómoda f chest of drawers

comodidad f comfort. a su ~ at your convenience

cómodo a comfortable; (útil) handy

comoquiera conj. ~ que since. ~ que sea however it may be

compacto a compact; (denso) dense; (líneas etc) close

compadecer [11] vt feel sorry for. ~se vpr. ~se de feel sorry for

compadre m godfather; (amigo) friend

compañ|ero m companion; (de trabajo) colleague; (amigo) friend. **~ía** f company. **en ~ía de** with

compara|ble a comparable. **~ción** f comparison. **~r** vt compare. **~tivo** a & m comparative. **en ~ción con** in comparison with, compared with

comparecer [11] vi appear

comparsa f group; (en el teatro) extra

compartimiento m compartment

compartir vt share

compás m (instrumento) (pair of) compasses; (ritmo) rhythm; (división) bar (Brit), measure (Amer); (naut) compass. **a ~** in time

compasi|ón f compassion, pity. **tener ~ón de** feel sorry for. **~vo** a compassionate

compatib|ilidad f compatibility. **~le** a compatible

compatriota m & f compatriot

compeler vt compel, force

compendi|ar vt summarize. **~o** m summary

compenetración f mutual understanding

compensa|ción f compensation. **~ción por despido** redundancy payment. **~r** vt compensate

competen|cia f competition; (capacidad) competence; (terreno) field, scope. **~te** a competent; (apropiado) appropriate, suitable

competi|ción f competition. **~dor** m competitor. **~r** [5] vi compete

compilar vt compile

compinche m accomplice; (amigo, fam) friend, mate (fam)

complac|encia f pleasure; (indulgencia) indulgence. **~er** [32] vt please; (prestar servicio) help. **~erse** vpr have pleasure, be pleased. **~iente** a helpful; (marido) complaisant

complej|idad f complexity. **~o** a & m complex

complement|ario a complementary. **~o** m complement; (gram) object, complement

complet|ar vt complete. **~o** a complete; (lleno) full; (perfecto) perfect

complexión f disposition; (constitución) constitution

complica|ción f complication. **~r** [7] vt complicate; involve (persona). **~rse** vpr become complicated

cómplice m accomplice

complot m (pl complots) plot

compon|ente a component. ● m component; (culin) ingredient; (miembro) member. **~er** [34] vt make up; (mus, literatura etc) write, compose; (reparar) mend; (culin) prepare; (arreglar) restore; settle (estómago); reconcile (diferencias). **~erse** vpr be made up; (arreglarse) get ready. **~érselas** manage

comporta|miento m behaviour. **~r** vt involve. **~rse** vpr behave. **~rse como es debido** behave properly. **~rse mal** misbehave

composi|ción f composition. **~tor** m composer

compostelano a from Santiago de Compostela. ● m native of Santiago de Compostela

compostura f composition; (arreglo) repair; (culin) condiment; (comedimiento) composure

compota f stewed fruit

compra f purchase. **~ a plazos** hire purchase. **~dor** m buyer; (en una tienda) customer. **~r** vt buy. **~venta** f dealing. **hacer la ~, ir a la ~, ir de ~s** do the shopping, go shopping. **negocio** m **de ~venta** second-hand shop

compren|der vt understand; (incluir) include. **~sible** a understandable. **~sión** f understanding. **~sivo** a understanding; (que incluye) comprehensive

compresa f compress; (de mujer) sanitary towel

compr|esión f compression. **~imido** a compressed. ● m pill, tablet. **~imir** vt compress; keep back (lágrimas); (fig) restrain

comproba|nte m (recibo) receipt. **~r** vt check; (confirmar) confirm

comprometer vt compromise; (arriesgar) endanger. **~erse** vpr compromise o.s.; (obligarse) agree to. **~ido** a (situación) awkward, embarrassing

compromiso m obligation; (apuro) predicament; (cita) appointment; (acuerdo) agreement. **sin ~** without obligation

compuesto a compound; (persona) smart. ● m compound

compungido a sad, sorry

computador m, **computadora** f computer

computar vt calculate

cómputo m calculation

comulgar [12] *vi* take Communion
común *a* common. ● *m* community.
en ~ in common. por lo ~ generally
comunal *a* municipal, communal
comunica|ción *f* communication.
~do *m* communiqué. ~do a la
prensa press release. ~r [7] *vt/i* com-
municate; pass on ⟨*enfermedad,
información*⟩. ~rse *vpr* com-
municate; ⟨*enfermedad*⟩ spread.
~tivo *a* communicative. está ~ndo
(*al teléfono*) it's engaged, the line's
engaged
comunidad *f* community. ~ de vecinos residents' association. C~
(Económica) Europea European
(Economic) Community. en ~ together
comunión *f* communion; (*relig*)
(Holy) Communion
comunis|mo *m* communism. ~ta *a*
& *m* & *f* communist
comúnmente *adv* generally,
usually
con *prep* with; (*a pesar de*) in spite of;
(+ *infinitivo*) by. ~ decir la verdad
by telling the truth. ~ que so. ~ tal
que as long as
conato *m* attempt
concatenación *f* chain, linking
cóncavo *a* concave
concebir [5] *vt/i* conceive
conceder *vt* concede, grant; award
⟨*premio*⟩; (*admitir*) admit
concej|al *m* councillor. ~o *m* town
council
concentra|ción *f* concentration.
~do *m* concentrated. ~r *vt* concentrate. ~rse *vpr* concentrate
concep|ción *f* conception. ~to *m*
concept; (*opinión*) opinion. bajo
ningún ~to in no way. en mi ~to in
my view. por ningún ~to in no way
concerniente *a* concerning. en lo ~
a with regard to
concertar [1] *vt* (*mus*) harmonize;
(*coordinar*) coordinate; (*poner de
acuerdo*) agree. ● *vi* be in tune; (*fig*)
agree. ~se *vpr* agree
concertina *f* concertina
concesión *f* concession
conciencia *f* conscience; (*conocimiento*) consciousness. ~ción *f*
awareness. ~ limpia clear conscience. ~ sucia guilty conscience.
a ~ de que fully aware that. en ~
honestly. tener ~ de be aware of. tomar ~ de become aware of

concienzudo *a* conscientious
concierto *m* concert; (*acuerdo*)
agreement; (*mus, composición*) concerto
concilia|ble *a* reconcilable. ~ción *f*
reconciliation. ~r *vt* reconcile. ~r el
sueño get to sleep. ~rse *vpr* gain
concilio *m* council
conciso *m* concise
conciudadano *m* fellow citizen
conclu|ir [17] *vt* finish; (*deducir*) con-
clude. ● *vi* finish, end. ~irse *vpr*
finish, end. ~sión *f* conclusion.
~yente *a* conclusive
concord|ancia *f* agreement. ~ar [2]
vt reconcile. ● *vi* agree. ~e *a* in
agreement. ~ia *f* harmony
concret|amente *adv* specifically, to
be exact. ~ar *vt* make specific. ~ar-
se *vpr* become definite; (*limitarse*)
confine o.s. ~o *a* concrete; (*determinado*) specific, particular. ● *m*
(*LAm, hormigón*) concrete. en ~o
definite; (*concretamente*) to be exact;
(*en resumen*) in short
concurr|encia *f* coincidence; (*reu-
nión*) crowd, audience. ~ido *a*
crowded, busy. ~ir *vi* meet; (*asistir*)
attend; (*coincidir*) coincide; (*contribuir*) contribute; (*en concurso*)
compete
concurs|ante *m* & *f* competitor, con-
testant. ~ar *vi* compete, take part.
~o *m* competition; (*concurrencia*)
crowd; (*ayuda*) help
concha *f* shell; (*carey*) tortoiseshell
condado *m* county
conde *m* earl, count
condena *f* sentence. ~ción *f* con-
demnation. ~do *m* convict. ~r *vt*
condemn; (*jurid*) convict
condensa|ción *f* condensation. ~r
vt condense. ~rse *vpr* condense
condesa *f* countess
condescende|ncia *f* condescension;
(*tolerancia*) indulgence. ~r [1] *vi*
agree; (*dignarse*) condescend
condici|ón *f* condition; (*naturaleza*)
nature. ~onado *a*, ~onal *a* con-
ditional. ~onar *vt* condition. a ~ón
de (que) on the condition that
condiment|ar *vt* season. ~o *m* con-
diment
condolencia *f* condolence
condominio *m* joint ownership
condón *m* condom
condonar *vt* (*perdonar*) reprieve;
cancel ⟨*deuda*⟩

conducir [47] *vt* drive ⟨*vehículo*⟩; carry ⟨*electricidad, gas, agua etc*⟩. ● *vi* drive; (*fig, llevar*) lead. ~**se** *vpr* behave. ¿**a qué conduce?** what's the point?

conducta *f* behaviour

conducto *m* pipe, tube; (*anat*) duct. **por** ~ **de** through

conductor *m* driver; (*jefe*) leader; (*elec*) conductor

conduzco *vb véase* **conducir**

conectar *vt/i* connect; (*enchufar*) plug in

conejo *m* rabbit

conexión *f* connection

confabularse *vpr* plot

confección *f* making; (*prenda*) ready-made garment. ~**ones** *fpl* clothing, clothes. ~**onado** *a* ready-made. ~**onar** *vt* make

confederación *f* confederation

conferencia *f* conference; (*al teléfono*) long-distance call; (*univ etc*) lecture. ~ **cumbre**, ~ **en la cima**, ~ **en la cumbre** summit conference. ~**nte** *m & f* lecturer

conferir [4] *vt* confer; award ⟨*premio*⟩

confesar [1] *vt/i* confess. ~**arse** *vpr* confess. ~**ión** *f* confession. ~**ional** *a* confessional. ~**ionario** *m* confessional. ~**or** *m* confessor

confeti *m* confetti

confiado *a* trusting; (*seguro de sí mismo*) confident. ~**nza** *f* trust; (*en sí mismo*) confidence; (*intimidad*) familiarity. ~**r** [20] *vt* entrust. ● *vi* trust. ~**rse** *vpr* put one's trust in

confidencia *f* confidence, secret. ~**cial** *a* confidential. ~**te** *m & f* close friend; (*de policía*) informer

configuración *f* configuration, shape

confín *m* border. ~**inar** *vt* confine; (*desterrar*) banish. ● *vi* border (**con** on). ~**ines** *mpl* outermost parts

confirmación *f* confirmation. ~**r** *vt* confirm

confiscar [7] *vt* confiscate

confitería *f* sweet-shop (*Brit*), candy store (*Amer*). ~**ura** *f* jam

conflagración *f* conflagration

conflicto *m* conflict

confluencia *f* confluence

conformación *f* conformation, shape. ~**r** *vt* (*acomodar*) adjust. ● *vi* agree. ~**rse** *vpr* conform

conforme *a* in agreement; (*contento*) happy, satisfied; (*según*) according (**con** to). ● *conj* as. ● *int* OK!

~**e a** in accordance with, according to. ~**idad** *f* agreement; (*tolerancia*) resignation. ~**ista** *m & f* conformist

confortable *a* comfortable. ~**nte** *a* comforting. ~**r** *vt* comfort

confrontación *f* confrontation; (*comparación*) comparison. ~**r** *vt* confront; (*comparar*) compare

confundir *vt* blur; (*equivocar*) mistake, confuse; (*perder*) lose; (*mezclar*) mix up, confuse. ~**ndirse** *vpr* become confused; (*equivocarse*) make a mistake. ~**sión** *f* confusion; (*vergüenza*) embarrassment. ~**so** *a* confused; (*avergonzado*) embarrassed

congelado *a* frozen. ~**dor** *m* freezer. ~**r** *vt* freeze

congeniar *vi* get on

congestión *f* congestion. ~**onado** *a* congested. ~**onar** *vt* congest. ~**onarse** *vpr* become congested

congoja *f* distress

congraciar *vt* win over. ~**se** *vpr* ingratiate o.s.

congratular *vt* congratulate

congregación *f* gathering; (*relig*) congregation. ~**rse** [12] *vpr* gather, assemble

congresista *m & f* delegate, member of a congress. ~**o** *m* congress, conference. **C~o de los Diputados** House of Commons

cónico *a* conical

conífera *f* conifer. ~**o** *a* coniferous

conjetura *f* conjecture, guess. ~**r** *vt* conjecture, guess

conjugación *f* conjugation. ~**r** [12] *vt* conjugate

conjunción *f* conjunction

conjunto *a* joint. ● *m* collection; (*mus*) band; (*ropa*) suit, outfit. **en** ~ altogether

conjura *f*, **conjuración** *f* conspiracy

conjurar *vt* plot, conspire

conmemoración *f* commemoration. ~**r** *vt* commemorate. ~**tivo** *a* commemorative

conmigo *pron* with me

conminar *vt* threaten; (*avisar*) warn

conmiseración *f* commiseration

conmoción *f* shock; (*tumulto*) upheaval; (*terremoto*) earthquake. ~**cionar** *vt* shock. ~ **cerebral** concussion. ~**ver** [2] *vt* shake; (*emocionar*) move

conmutador *m* switch. ~**r** *vt* exchange

connivencia *f* connivance

connota|ción f connotation. **~r** vt connote

cono m cone

conoc|edor a & m expert. **~er** [11] vt know; (por primera vez) meet; (reconocer) recognize, know. **~erse** vpr know o.s.; (dos personas) know each other; (notarse) be obvious. **dar a ~er** make known. **darse a ~er** make o.s. known. **~ido** a well-known. ● m acquaintance. **~imiento** m knowledge; (sentido) consciousness; (conocido) acquaintance. **perder el ~imiento** faint. **se ~e que** apparently. **tener ~imiento de** know about

conozco vb véase **conocer**

conque conj so

conquense a from Cuenca. ● m native of Cuenca

conquista f conquest. **~dor** a conquering. ● m conqueror; (de América) conquistador; (fig) lady-killer. **~r** vt conquer, win

consabido a well-known

consagra|ción f consecration. **~r** vt consecrate; (fig) devote. **~rse** vpr devote o.s.

consanguíneo m blood relation

consciente a conscious

consecución f acquisition; (de un deseo) realization

consecuen|cia f consequence; (firmeza) consistency. **~te** a consistent. **a ~cia de** as a result of. **en ~cia, por ~cia** consequently

consecutivo a consecutive

conseguir [5 & 13] vt get, obtain; (lograr) manage; achieve (objetivo)

conseja f story, fable

consej|ero m adviser; (miembro de consejo) member. **~o** m advice; (pol) council. **~o de ministros** cabinet

consenso m assent, consent

consenti|do a (niño) spoilt. **~miento** m consent. **~r** [4] vt allow. ● vi consent. **~rse** vpr break

conserje m porter, caretaker. **~ría** f porter's office

conserva f preserves; (mermelada) jam, preserve; (en lata) tinned food. **~ción** f conservation; (de alimentos) preservation; (de edificio) maintenance. **en ~** preserved

conservador a & m (pol) conservative

conservar vt keep; preserve (alimentos). **~se** vpr keep; (costumbre etc) survive

conservatorio m conservatory

considera|ble a considerable. **~ción** f consideration; (respeto) respect. **~do** a considered; (amable) considerate; (respetado) respected. **~r** vt consider; (respetar) respect. **de ~ción** considerable. **de su ~ción** (en cartas) yours faithfully. **tomar en ~ción** take into consideration

consigna f order; (rail) left luggage office (Brit), baggage room (Amer); (eslogan) slogan

consigo pron (él) with him; (ella) with her; (Ud, Uds) with you; (uno mismo) with o.s.

consiguiente a consequent. **por ~** consequently

consist|encia f consistency. **~ente** a consisting (en of); (firme) solid. **~ir** vi consist (en of); (deberse) be due (en to)

consola|ción f consolation. **~r** [2] vt console, comfort

consolidar vt consolidate. **~se** vpr consolidate

consomé m clear soup, consommé

consonan|cia f consonance. **~te** a consonant. ● f consonant

consorcio m consortium

consorte m & f consort

conspicuo a eminent; (visible) visible

conspira|ción f conspiracy. **~dor** m conspirator. **~r** vi conspire

constan|cia f constancy. **~te** a constant

constar vi be clear; (figurar) appear, figure; (componerse) consist. **hacer ~** point out. **me consta que** I'm sure that. **que conste que** believe me

constatar vt check; (confirmar) confirm

constelación f constellation

consternación f consternation

constipa|do m cold. ● a. **estar ~do** have a cold. **~rse** vpr catch a cold

constitu|ción f constitution; (establecimiento) setting up. **~cional** a constitutional. **~ir** [17] vt constitute; (formar) form; (crear) set up, establish. **~irse** vpr set o.s. up (en as); (presentarse) appear. **~tivo** a, **~yente** a constituent

constreñir [5 & 22] vt force, oblige; (restringir) restrain

constricción f constriction

constru|cción f construction. **~ctor** m builder. **~ir** [17] vt construct; build (edificio)

consuelo m consolation, comfort

consuetudinario a customary

cónsul m consul

consula|do m consulate. ~r a consular

consult|a f consultation. ~ar vt consult. ~orio m surgery. ~orio sentimental problem page. horas fpl de ~a surgery hours. obra f de ~a reference book

consumar vt complete; commit ⟨crimen⟩; consummate ⟨matrimonio⟩

consum|ición f consumption; ⟨bebida⟩ drink; ⟨comida⟩ food. ~ido a ⟨persona⟩ skinny, wasted; ⟨frutas⟩ shrivelled. ~idor m consumer. ~ir vt consume. ~irse vpr ⟨persona⟩ waste away; ⟨cosa⟩ wear out; ⟨quedarse seco⟩ dry up. ~ismo m consumerism. ~o m consumption

contab|ilidad f book-keeping; ⟨profesión⟩ accountancy. ~le m & f accountant

contacto m contact. ponerse en ~ con get in touch with

contado a counted. ~s apl few. ~r m meter; ⟨LAm, contable⟩ accountant. al ~ cash

contagi|ar vt infect ⟨persona⟩; pass on ⟨enfermedd⟩; ⟨fig⟩ contaminate. ~o m infection. ~oso a infectious

contamina|ción f contamination, pollution. ~r vt contaminate, pollute

contante a. dinero m ~ cash

contar [2] vt count; tell ⟨relato⟩. ● vi count. ~ con rely on, count on. ~se vpr be included ⟨entre among⟩; ⟨decirse⟩ be said

contempla|ción f contemplation. ~r vt look at; ⟨fig⟩ contemplate. sin ~ciones unceremoniously

contemporáneo a & m contemporary

contend|er [1] vi compete. ~iente m & f competitor

conten|er [40] vt contain; ⟨restringir⟩ restrain. ~erse vpr restrain o.s. ~ido a contained. ● m contents

content|ar vt please. ~arse vpr. ~arse de be satisfied with, be pleased with. ~o a ⟨alegre⟩ happy; ⟨satisfecho⟩ pleased

contesta|ción f answer. ~dor m. ~ automático answering machine. ~r vt/i answer; ⟨replicar⟩ answer back

contexto m context

contienda f struggle

contigo pron with you

contiguo a adjacent

continen|cia f continence. ~tal a continental. ~te m continent

contingen|cia f contingency. ~te a contingent. ● m contingent; ⟨cuota⟩ quota

continu|ación f continuation. ~ar [21] vt continue, resume. ● vi continue. ~ará ⟨en revista, TV etc⟩ to be continued. ~idad f continuity. ~o a continuous; ⟨muy frecuente⟩ continual. a ~ación immediately after.

corriente f ~a direct current

contorno m outline; ⟨geog⟩ contour. ~s mpl surrounding area

contorsión f contortion

contra adv & prep against. ● m cons. en ~ against

contraalmirante m rear-admiral

contraata|car [7] vt/i counterattack. ~que m counter-attack

contrabajo m double-bass; ⟨persona⟩ double-bass player

contrabalancear vt counterbalance

contraband|ista m & f smuggler. ~o m contraband

contracción f contraction

contrachapado m plywood

contrad|ecir [46] vt contradict. ~icción f contradiction. ~ictorio a contradictory

contraer [41] vt contract. ~ matrimonio marry. ~se vpr contract; ⟨limitarse⟩ limit o.s.

contrafuerte m buttress

contragolpe m backlash

contrahecho a fake; ⟨moneda⟩ counterfeit; ⟨persona⟩ hunchbacked

contraindicación f contraindication

contralto m alto. ● f contralto

contramano. a ~ in the wrong direction

contrapartida f compensation

contrapelo. a ~ the wrong way

contrapes|ar vt counterbalance. ~o m counterbalance

contraponer [34] oppose; ⟨comparar⟩ compare

contraproducente a counter-productive

contrari|ar [20] vt oppose; ⟨molestar⟩ annoy. ~edad f obstacle; ⟨disgusto⟩ annoyance. ~o a contrary; ⟨dirección⟩ opposite; ⟨persona⟩ opposed. al ~o on the contrary. al ~o de contrary to. de lo ~o otherwise. en ~o against. **llevar la** ～**a** contradict. **por el** ～**o** on the contrary

contrarrestar vt counteract

contrasentido m contradiction

contraseña f secret mark; (palabra) password

contrast|ar vt check, verify. ● vi contrast. ～**e** m contrast; (en oro, plata etc) hallmark

contratar vt sign a contract for; engage (empleados)

contratiempo m setback; (accidente) accident

contrat|ista m & f contractor. ～**o** m contract

contraven|ción f contravention. ～**ir** [53] vi. ～**ira** contravene

contraventana f shutter

contribu|ción f contribution; (tributo) tax. ～**ir** [17] vt/i contribute. ～**yente** m & f contributor; (que paga impuestos) taxpayer

contrincante m rival, opponent

contrito a contrite

control m control; (inspección) check. ～**ar** vt control; (examinar) check

controversia f controversy

contundente a (arma) blunt; (argumento etc) convincing

conturbar vt perturb

contusión f bruise

convalec|encia f convalescence. ～**er** [11] vi convalesce. ～**iente** a & m & f convalescent

convalidar vt confirm; recognize (título)

convenc|er [9] vt convince. ～**imiento** m conviction

convenci|ón f convention. ～**onal** a conventional

conveni|encia f convenience; (aptitud) suitability. ～**encias** (sociales) conventions. ～**ente** a suitable; (aconsejable) advisable; (provechoso) useful, advantageous. ～**o** m agreement. ～**r** [53] vt agree. ● vi agree; (ser conveniente) be convenient for, suit; (ser aconsejable) be advisable

convento m (de monjes) monastery; (de monjas) convent

convergente a converging

converger [14] vi, **convergir** [14] vi converge

conversa|ción f conversation. ～**r** vi converse, talk

conver|sión f conversion. ～**so** a converted. ● m convert. ～**tible** a convertible. ～**tir** [4] vt convert. ～**tirse** vpr be converted

convexo a convex

convic|ción f conviction. ～**to** a convicted

convida|do m guest. ～**r** vt invite. **te convido a un helado** I'll treat you to an ice-cream

convincente a convincing

convite m invitation; (banquete) banquet

conviv|encia f coexistence. ～**ir** vi live together

convocar [7] vt convene (reunión); summon (personas)

convoy m convoy; (rail) train; (vinagrera) cruet

convulsión f convulsion; (fig) upheaval

conyugal a conjugal; (vida) married

cónyuge m spouse. ～**s** mpl (married) couple

coñac m (pl coñacs) brandy

coopera|ción f co-operation. ～**r** vi co-operate. ～**tiva** f co-operative. ～**tivo** a co-operative

coord|enada f coordinate. ～**inación** f co-ordination. ～**inar** vt co-ordinate

copa f glass; (deportes, fig) cup. ～**s** fpl (naipes) hearts. **tomar una** ～ have a drink

copia f copy. ～ **en limpio** fair copy. ～**r** vt copy. **sacar una** ～ make a copy

copioso a copious; (lluvia, nevada etc) heavy

copla f verse; (canción) song

copo m flake. ～ **de nieve** snowflake. ～**s de maíz** cornflakes

coquet|a f flirt; (mueble) dressing-table. ～**ear** vi flirt. ～**eo** m flirtation. ～**o** a flirtatious

coraje m courage; (rabia) anger. **dar** ～ make mad, make furious

coral a choral. ● m (materia, animal) coral

Corán m Koran

coraza f (naut) armour-plating; (de tortuga) shell

coraz|ón m heart; (persona) darling. ～**onada** f hunch; (impulso) impulse. **sin** ～**ón** heartless. **tener buen** ～**ón** be good-hearted

corbata f tie, necktie (esp Amer). ～ **de lazo** bow tie

corcova *f* hump. **~do** *a* hunchbacked

corchea *f* quaver

corchete *m* fastener, hook and eye; *(gancho)* hook; *(paréntesis)* square bracket

corcho *m* cork

cordel *m* cord, thin rope

cordero *m* lamb

cordial *a* cordial, friendly. ● *m* tonic. **~idad** *f* cordiality, warmth

cordillera *f* mountain range

córdoba *m* *(unidad monetaria de Nicaragua)* córdoba

Córdoba *f* Cordova

cordón *m* string; *(de zapatos)* lace; *(cable)* flex; *(fig)* cordon. **~ umbilical** umbilical cord

corear *vt* chant

coreografía *f* choreography

corista *m & f* member of the chorus. ● *f (bailarina)* chorus girl

cornet|a *f* bugle. **~ín** *m* cornet

Cornualles *m* Cornwall

cornucopia *f* cornucopia

cornudo *a* horned. ● *m* cuckold

coro *m* chorus; *(relig)* choir

corona *f* crown; *(de flores)* wreath, garland. **~ción** *f* coronation. **~r** *vt* crown

coronel *m* colonel

coronilla *f* crown. **estar hasta la ~** be fed up

corporación *f* corporation

corporal *a* corporal

corpulento *a* stout

corpúsculo *m* corpuscle

corral *m* pen. **aves** *fpl* **de ~** poultry

correa *f* strap; *(de perro)* lead; *(cinturón)* belt

correc|ción *f* correction; *(reprensión)* rebuke; *(cortesía)* good manners. **~to** *a* correct; *(cortés)* polite

corre|dizo *a* running. **nudo ~dizo** slip knot. **puerta** *f* **~diza** sliding door. **~dor** *m* runner; *(pasillo)* corridor; *(agente)* agent, broker. **~dor automovilista** racing driver

corregir [5 & 14] *vt* correct; *(reprender)* rebuke

correlaci|ón *f* correlation. **~onar** *vt* correlate

correo *m* courier; *(correos)* post, mail; *(tren)* mail train. **~s** *mpl* post office. **echar un ~** post

correr *vt* run; *(viajar)* travel; draw *(cortinas)*. ● *vi* run; *(agua, electricidad etc)* flow; *(tiempo)* pass. **~se** *vpr (apartarse)* move along; *(pasarse)* go too far; *(colores)* run. **~se una juerga** have a ball

correspond|encia *f* correspondence. **~er** *vi* correspond; *(ser adecuado)* be fitting; *(contestar)* reply; *(pertenecer)* belong; *(incumbir)* fall to. **~erse** *vpr (amarse)* love one another. **~iente** *a* corresponding

corresponsal *m* correspondent

corrid|a *f* run. **~a de toros** bullfight. **~o** *a (peso)* good; *(continuo)* continuous; *(avergonzado)* embarrassed. **de ~a** from memory

corriente *a (agua)* running *(monedas, publicación, cuenta, año etc)* current; *(ordinario)* ordinary. ● *f* current; *(de aire)* draught; *(fig)* tendency. ● *m* current month. **al ~** *(al día)* up-to-date; *(enterado)* aware

corr|illo *m* small group, circle. **~o** *m* circle

corroborar *vt* corroborate

corroer [24 & 37] *vt* corrode; *(geol)* erode; *(fig)* eat away. **~se** *vpr* corrode

corromper *vt* rot *(madera)*; turn bad *(alimentos)*; *(fig)* corrupt. ● *vi (fam)* stink. **~se** *vpr (madera)* rot; *(alimentos)* go bad; *(fig)* be corrupted

corrosi|ón *f* corrosion. **~vo** *a* corrosive

corrupción *f (de madera etc)* rot; *(soborno)* bribery; *(fig)* corruption

corsé *m* corset

cortacésped *m invar* lawn-mower

cortad|o *a* cut; *(leche)* sour; *(avergonzado)* embarrassed; *(confuso)* confused. ● *m* coffee with a little milk. **~ura** *f* cut

corta|nte *a* sharp; *(viento)* biting; *(frío)* bitter. **~r** *vt* cut; *(recortar)* cut out; *(aislar, detener)* cut off; *(interrumpir)* cut in. ● *vi* cut. **~rse** *vpr* cut o.s.; *(leche etc)* curdle; *(al teléfono)* be cut off; *(fig)* be embarrassed, become tongue-tied. **~rse el pelo** have one's hair cut. **~rse las uñas** cut one's nails

cortauñas *m invar* nail-clippers

corte *m* cutting; *(de instrumento cortante)* cutting edge; *(de corriente)* cut; *(de prendas de vestir)* cut; *(de tela)* length. ● *f* court. **~ de luz** power cut. **~ y confección** dressmaking. **hacer la ~** court. **las C~s** the Spanish parliament

cortej|ar vt court. ~o m (de rey etc) entourage. ~o fúnebre cortège, funeral procession. ~o nupcial wedding procession

cortés a polite

cortesan|a f courtesan. ~o m courtier

cortesía f courtesy

corteza f bark; (de naranja etc) peel, rind; (de pan) crust

cortijo m farm; (casa) farmhouse

cortina f curtain

corto a short; (escaso) scanty; (apocado) shy. ~circuito m short circuit. ~ de alcances dim, thick. ~ de oído hard of hearing. ~ de vista shortsighted. a la corta o a la larga sooner or later. quedarse ~ fall short; (miscalcular) under-estimate

Coruña f. La ~ Corunna

corvo a bent

cosa f thing; (asunto) business; (idea) idea. ~ de about. como si tal ~ just like that; (como si no hubiera pasado nada) as if nothing had happened. decirle a uno cuatro ~s tell s.o. a thing or two. lo que son las ~s much to my surprise

cosaco a & m Cossack

cosech|a f harvest; (de vino) vintage. ~ar vt harvest. ~ero m harvester

coser vt/i sew. ~se vpr stick to s.o. eso es ~ y cantar it's as easy as pie

cosmético a & m cosmetic

cósmico a cosmic

cosmonauta m & f cosmonaut

cosmopolita a & m & f cosmopolitan

cosmos m cosmos

cosquillas fpl ticklishness. buscar a uno las ~ provoke s.o. hacer ~ tickle. tener ~ be ticklish

costa f coast. a ~ de at the expense of. a toda ~ at any cost

costado m side

costal m sack

costar [2] vt/i cost. ~ caro be expensive. cueste lo que cueste at any cost

Costa Rica f Costa Rica

costarricense a & m, costarriqueño a & m Costa Rican

coste m cost. ~ar vt pay for; (naut) sail along the coast

costero a coastal

costilla f rib; (chuleta) chop

costo m cost. ~so a expensive

costumbre f custom, habit. de ~ a usual. ● adv usually

costur|a f sewing; (línea) seam; (confección) dressmaking. ~era f dressmaker. ~ero m sewing box

cotejar vt compare

cotidiano a daily

cotill|a f gossip. ~o m gossip

cotiza|ción f quotation, price. ~r [10] vt (en la bolsa) quote. ● vi pay one's subscription. ~rse vpr fetch; (en la bolsa) stand at; (fig) be valued

coto m enclosure; (de caza) preserve. ~ de caza game preserve

cotorr|a f parrot; (urraca) magpie; (fig) chatterbox. ~ear vi chatter

coyuntura f joint; (oportunidad) opportunity; (situación) situation; (circunstancia) occasion, juncture

coz f kick

cráneo m skull

cráter m crater

crea|ción f creation. ~dor a creative. ● m creator. ~r vt create

crec|er [11] vi grow; (aumentar) increase. ~ida f (de río) flood. ~ido a (persona) grown-up; (número) large, considerable; (plantas) fully-grown. ~iente a growing; (luna) crescent. ~imiento m growth

credencial a credential. ~es fpl credentials

credibilidad f credibility

crédito m credit. digno de ~ reliable, trustworthy

credo m creed. en un ~ in a flash

crédulo a credulous

cre|encia f belief. ~er [18] believe; (pensar) think. ~o que no I don't think so, I think not. ~o que sí I think so. ● vi believe. ~erse vpr consider o.s. no me lo ~o I don't believe it. ~íble a credible. ¡ya lo ~o! I should think so!

crema f cream; (culin) custard. ~ bronceadora sun-tan cream

cremación f cremation; (de basura) incineration

cremallera f zip, zipper (Amer)

crematorio m crematorium; (de basura) incinerator

crepitar vi crackle

crepúsculo m twilight

crescendo m crescendo

cresp|o a frizzy. ~ón m crêpe

cresta f crest; (tupé) toupee; (geog) ridge

Creta f Crete

cretino m cretin

creyente *m* believer

cría *f* breeding; *(animal)* baby animal

criada *f* maid, servant. **~dero** *m* nursery. **~do** *a* brought up. ● *m* servant. **~dor** *m* breeder. **~nza** *f* breeding. **~r** [20] *vt* suckle; grow *(plantas)*; breed *(animales)*; *(educar)* bring up. **~rse** *vpr* grow up

criatura *f* creature; *(niño)* baby

crim|en *m* crime. **~inal** *a* & *m* & *f* criminal

crin *m* mane; *(relleno)* horsehair

crinolina *f* crinoline

crío *m* child

criollo *a* & *m* Creole

cripta *f* crypt

crisantemo *m* chrysanthemum

crisis *f* crisis

crisol *m* melting-pot

crispar *vt* twitch; *(irritar, fam)* annoy. **~ los nervios a uno** get on s.o.'s nerves

cristal *m* crystal; *(vidrio)* glass; *(de una ventana)* pane of glass. **~ de aumento** magnifying glass. **~ino** *a* crystalline; *(fig)* crystal-clear. **~izar** [10] crystallize. **limpiar los ~es** clean the windows

cristian|amente *adv* in a Christian way. **~dad** *f* Christianity. **~ismo** *m* Christianity. **~o** *a* & *m* Christian

Cristo *m* Christ

cristo *m* crucifix

criterio *m* criterion; *(opinión)* opinion

cr|ítica *f* criticism; *(reseña)* review. **~iticar** [7] *vt* criticize. **~ítico** *a* critical. ● *m* critic

croar *vi* croak

crom|ado *a* chromium-plated. **~o** *m* chromium, chrome

cromosoma *m* chromosome

crónic|a *f* chronicle; *(de periódico)* news. **~o** *a* chronic

cronista *m* & *f* reporter

cronol|ogía *f* chronology. **~ógico** *a* chronological

cron|ometraje *m* timing. **~ometrar** *vt* time. **~ómetro** *m* chronometer; *(en deportes)* stopwatch

croquet /'kroket/ *m* croquet

croqueta *f* croquette

cruce *m* crossing; *(de calles, de carreteras)* crossroads; *(de peatones)* (pedestrian) crossing

crucial *a* cross-shaped; *(fig)* crucial

crucifi|car [7] *vt* crucify. **~jo** *m* crucifix. **~xión** *f* crucifixion

crucigrama *m* crossword (puzzle)

crudo *a* raw; *(fig)* crude. **petróleo ~** crude oil

cruel *a* cruel. **~dad** *f* cruelty

cruji|do *m* *(de seda, de hojas secas etc)* rustle; *(de muebles etc)* creak. **~r** *vi* *(seda, hojas secas etc)* rustle; *(muebles etc)* creak

cruz *f* cross; *(de moneda)* tails. **~ gamada** swastika. **la C~ Roja** the Red Cross

cruzada *f* crusade

cruzar [10] *vt* cross; *(poner de un lado a otro)* lay across. **~se** *vpr* cross; *(pasar en la calle)* pass

cuaderno *m* exercise book; *(para apuntes)* notebook

cuadra *f* *(caballeriza)* stable; *(LAm, manzana)* block

cuadrado *a* & *m* square

cuadragésimo *a* fortieth

cuadr|ar *vt* square. ● *vi* suit; *(estar de acuerdo)* agree. **~arse** *vpr* *(mil)* stand to attention; *(fig)* dig one's heels in. **~ilátero** *a* quadrilateral. ● *m* quadrilateral; *(boxeo)* ring

cuadrilla *f* group; *(pandilla)* gang

cuadro *m* square; *(pintura)* painting; *(de obra de teatro, escena)* scene; *(de jardín)* bed; *(de números)* table; *(de mando etc)* panel; *(conjunto del personal)* staff. **~ de distribución** switchboard. **a ~s, de ~s** check. **en ~** in a square. **¡qué ~!, ¡vaya un ~!** what a sight!

cuadrúpedo *m* quadruped

cuádruple *a* & *m* quadruple

cuajar *vt* thicken; clot *(sangre)*; curdle *(leche)*; *(llenar)* fill up. ● *vi* *(nieve)* settle; *(fig, fam)* work out. **cuajado de** full of. **~se** *vpr* coagulate; *(sangre)* clot; *(leche)* curdle. **~ón** *m* clot

cual *pron* **el ~, la ~** etc *(animales y cosas)* that, which; *(personas, sujeto)* who, that; *(personas, objeto)* whom. ● *adv* as, like. ● *a* such as. **~ si** as if. **~... tal** like... the. **cada ~** everyone. **por lo ~** because of which

cuál *pron* which

cualidad *f* quality; *(propiedad)* property

cualquiera *a* *(delante de nombres cualquier, pl cualesquiera)* any. ● *pron* *(pl cualesquiera)* anyone, anybody; (*cosas*) whatever, whichever. **un** ~ a nobody

cuando *adv* when. ● *conj* when; (*aunque*) even if. ~ **más** at the most. ~ **menos** at the least. ~ **no** if not. **aun** ~ even if. **de** ~ **en** ~ from time to time

cuándo *adv & conj* when. ¿**de** ~ **acá?**, ¿**desde** ~? since when?

cuant|ía *f* quantity; (*extensión*) extent. ~**ioso** *a* abundant

cuanto *a* as much... as, as many... as. ● *pron* as much as, as many as. ● *adv* as much as. ~ **más, mejor** the more the merrier. **en** ~ as soon as. **en** ~ **a** as for. **por** ~ since. **unos** ~s a few, some

cuánto *a* (*interrogativo*) how much?; (*interrogativo en plural*) how many?; (*exclamativo*) what a lot of! ● *pron* how much?; (*en plural*) how many? ● *adv* how much. ¿~ **tiempo?** how long? ¡~ **tiempo sin verte!** it's been a long time! ¡**a** ~? how much? ¿**a** ~**s estamos?** what's the date today? **un Sr. no sé** ~s Mr So-and-So

cuáquero *m* Quaker

cuarent|a *a & m* forty; (*cuadragésimo*) fortieth. ~**ena** *f* (about) forty; (*med*) quarantine. ~**ón** *a* about forty

cuaresma *f* Lent

cuarta *f* (*palmo*) span

cuartear *vt* quarter, divide into four; (*zigzaguear*) zigzag. ~**se** *vpr* crack

cuartel *m* (*mil*) barracks. ~ **general** headquarters. **no dar** ~ show no mercy

cuarteto *m* quartet

cuarto *a* fourth. ● *m* quarter; (*habitación*) room. ~ **de baño** bathroom. ~ **de estar** living room. ~ **de hora** quarter of an hour. **estar sin un** ~ be broke. **menos** ~ (a) quarter to. **y** ~ (a) quarter past

cuarzo *m* quartz

cuatro *a & m* four. ~**cientos** *a & m* four hundred

Cuba *f* Cuba

cuba: ~**libre** *m* rum and Coke (P). ~**no** *a & m* Cuban

cúbico *a* cubic

cubículo *m* cubicle

cubiert|a *f* cover, covering; (*de la cama*) bedspread; (*techo*) roof; (*neumático*) tyre; (*naut*) deck. ~**o** *a* covered; (*cielo*) overcast. ● *m* place

setting, cutlery; (*comida*) meal. **a** ~**o** under cover. **a** ~**o de** safe from

cubis|mo *m* cubism. ~**ta** *a & m & f* cubist

cubil *m* den, lair. ~**ete** *m* bowl; (*molde*) mould; (*para echar los dados*) cup

cubo *m* bucket; (*en geometría y matemáticas*) cube

cubrecama *m* bedspread

cubrir *vt* [*pp* **cubierto**] cover; (*sonido*) drown; fill (*vacante*). ~**se** *vpr* cover o.s.; (*ponerse el sombrero*) put on one's hat; (*el cielo*) cloud over, become overcast

cucaracha *f* cockroach

cuclillas. en ~ *adv* squatting

cuclillo *m* cuckoo

cuco *a* shrewd; (*mono*) pretty, nice. ● *m* cuckoo; (*insecto*) grub

cucurucho *m* cornet

cuchar|a *f* spoon. ~**ada** *f* spoonful. ~**adita** *f* teaspoonful. ~**illa** *f*, ~**ita** *f* teaspoon. ~**ón** *m* ladle

cuchiche|ar *vi* whisper. ~**o** *m* whispering

cuchill|a *f* large knife; (*de carnicero*) cleaver; (*hoja de afeitar*) razor blade. ~**ada** *f* slash; (*herida*) knife wound. ~**o** *m* knife

cuchitril *m* pigsty; (*fig*) hovel

cuello *m* neck; (*de camisa*) collar. **cortar el** ~ **a uno** cut s.o.'s throat

cuenc|a *f* hollow; (*del ojo*) (eye) socket; (*geog*) basin. ~**o** *m* hollow; (*vasija*) bowl

cuenta *f* count; (*acción de contar*) counting; (*factura*) bill; (*en banco, relato*) account; (*asunto*) affair; (*de collar etc*) bead. ~ **corriente** current account, checking account (*Amer*). **ajustar las** ~s settle accounts. **caer en la** ~ **de que** realize that. **darse** ~ **de** realize. **en resumidas** ~s in short. **por mi** ~ for myself. **tener en** ~, **tomar en** ~ bear in mind

cuentakilómetros *m invar* milometer

cuent|ista *m & f* story-writer; (*de mentiras*) fibber. ~**o** *m* story; (*mentira*) fib, tall story. ● *vb véase* **contar**

cuerda *f* rope; (*más fina*) string; (*mus*) string. ~ **floja** tightrope. **dar** ~ **a** wind up (*un reloj*)

cuerdo *a* (*persona*) sane; (*acción*) sensible

cuern|a *f* horns. ~**o** *m* horn

cuero m leather; (*piel*) skin; (*del grifo*) washer. ~ **cabelludo** scalp. **en** ~**s (vivos)** stark naked

cuerpo m body

cuervo m crow

cuesta f slope, hill. ~ **abajo** downhill. ~ **arriba** uphill. **a** ~**s** on one's back

cuesti|ón f matter; (*altercado*) quarrel; (*dificultad*) trouble. ~**onario** m questionnaire

cueva f cave; (*sótano*) cellar

cuida|do m care; (*preocupación*) worry; (*asunto*) affair. ¡~**do!** (be) careful! ~**doso** a careful. ~**dosamente** adv carefully. ~**r** vt look after. ● vi. ~**r de** look after. ~**rse** vpr look after o.s. ~**rse de** be careful to. **tener** ~**do** be careful

culata f (*de arma de fuego*) butt; (*auto*) cylinder head. ~**zo** m recoil

culebra f snake

culebrón m (*LAm*) soap opera

culinario a culinary

culmina|ción f culmination. ~**r** vi culminate

culo m (*fam*) bottom. **ir de** ~ go downhill

culpa f fault; (*jurid*) guilt. ~**bilidad** f guilt. ~**ble** a guilty. ● m culprit. ~**r** vt blame (**de** for). **echar la** ~ blame. **por** ~ **de** because of. **tener la** ~ **de** be to blame for

cultiv|ar vt farm; grow (*plantas*); (*fig*) cultivate. ~**o** m farming; (*de plantas*) growing

cult|o a (*tierra etc*) cultivated; (*persona*) educated. ● m cult; (*homenaje*) worship. ~**ura** f culture. ~**ural** a cultural

culturismo m body-building

cumbre f summit; (*fig*) height

cumpleaños m invar birthday

cumplido a perfect; (*grande*) large; (*cortés*) polite. ● m compliment. ~**r** a reliable. **de** ~ courtesy. **por** ~ out of politeness

cumplim|entar vt carry out; (*saludar*) pay a courtesy call to; (*felicitar*) congratulate. ~**iento** m carrying out, execution

cumplir vt carry out; observe (*ley*); serve (*condena*); reach (*años*); keep (*promesa*). ● vi do one's duty. ~**se** vpr expire; (*realizarse*) be fulfilled. **hoy cumple 3 años** he's 3 (years old) today. **por** ~ as a mere formality

cumulativo a cumulative

cúmulo m pile, heap

cuna f cradle; (*fig, nacimiento*) birthplace

cundir vi spread; (*rendir*) go a long way

cuneta f gutter

cuña f wedge

cuñad|a f sister-in-law. ~**o** m brother-in-law

cuño m stamp. **de nuevo** ~ new

cuota f quota; (*de sociedad etc*) subscription, fees

cupe vb véase **caber**

cupé m coupé

Cupido m Cupid

cupo m cuota

cupón m coupon

cúpula f dome

cura f cure; (*tratamiento*) treatment. ● m priest. ~**ble** a curable. ~**ción** f healing. ~**ndero** m faith-healer. ~**r** vt (*incl culin*) cure; dress (*herida*); (*tratar*) treat; (*fig*) remedy; tan (*pieles*). ● vi (*persona*) get better; (*herida*) heal; (*fig*) be cured. ~**rse** vpr get better

curios|ear vi pry; (*mirar*) browse. ~**idad** f curiosity; (*limpieza*) cleanliness. ~**o** a curious; (*raro*) odd, unusual; (*limpio*) clean

curriculum vitae m curriculum vitae

cursar vt send; (*estudiar*) study

cursi a pretentious, showy. ● m affected person

cursillo m short course

cursiva f italics

curso m course; (*univ etc*) year. **en** ~ under way; (*año etc*) current

curtir vt tan; (*fig*) harden. ~**se** vpr become tanned; (*fig*) become hardened

curv|a f curve; (*de carretera*) bend. ~**o** a curved

cúspide f peak

custodi|a f care, safe-keeping. ~**ar** vt take care of. ~**o** a & m guardian

cutáneo a skin. **enfermedad** f **cutánea** skin disease

cutícula f cuticle

cutis m skin, complexion

cuyo pron (*de persona*) whose, of whom; (*de cosa*) whose, of which. **en** ~ **caso** in which case

CH

chabacano a common; (*chiste etc*) vulgar. ● m (*Mex, albaricoque*) apricot

chabola f shack. ~s fpl shanty town
chacal m jackal
chacota f fun. echar a ~ make fun of
chacra f (LAm) farm
cháchara f chatter
chacharear vt (Mex) sell. • vi chatter
chafar vt crush. quedar chafado be
nonplussed
chal m shawl
chalado a (fam) crazy
chalé m house (with a garden), villa
chaleco m waistcoat, vest (Amer). ~
salvavidas life-jacket
chalequear vt (Arg, Mex) trick
chalet m (pl chalets) house (with a
garden), villa
chalón m (LAm) shawl
chalote m shallot
chalupa f boat
chamac|a f (esp Mex) girl. ~o m (esp
Mex) boy
chamagoso a (Mex) filthy
chamarr|a f sheepskin jacket. ~o m
(LAm) coarse blanket
chamba f (fam) fluke; (Mex, empleo)
job. por ~ by fluke
champán m, champaña m champagne
champiñón m mushroom
champú m (pl champúes o
champús) shampoo
chamuscar [7] vt scorch; (Mex,
vender) sell cheaply
chance m (esp LAm) chance
chanclo m clog; (de caucho) rubber
overshoe
chancho m (LAm) pig
chanchullo m swindle, fiddle (fam)
chandal m tracksuit
chanquete m whitebait
chantaj|e m blackmail. ~ista m & f
blackmailer
chanza f joke
chapa f plate, sheet; (de madera) plywood; (de botella) metal top. ~do a
plated. ~do a la antigua old-
fashioned. ~do de oro gold-plated
chaparrón m downpour. llover a
chaparrones pour (down), rain cats
and dogs
chapotear vi splash
chapuce|ar vt botch; (Mex, engañar)
deceive. ~ro a (persona) careless;
(cosas) shoddy. • m careless worker
chapurrar vt, chapurrear vt speak
badly, speak a little; mix (licores)
chapuza f botched job, mess; (de poca
importancia) odd job

chaqueta f jacket. cambiar la ~
change sides
chaquetero m turncoat
charada f charade
charc|a f pond, pool. ~o m puddle,
pool. cruzar el ~o cross the water;
(ir a América) cross the Atlantic
charla f chat; (conferencia) talk.
~dor a talkative. ~r vi (fam) chat
charlatán a talkative. • m chatterbox; (curandero) charlatan
charol m varnish; (cuero) patent
leather
chárter a charter
chascar [7] vt crack ⟨látigo⟩; click
⟨lengua⟩; snap ⟨dedos⟩. • vi ⟨látigo⟩
crack; (con la lengua) click one's
tongue; ⟨los dedos⟩ snap
chascarrillo m joke, funny story
chasco m disappointment; (broma)
joke; (engaño) trick
chasis m (auto) chassis
chasqu|ear vt crack ⟨látigo⟩; click
⟨lengua⟩; snap ⟨dedos⟩. • vi ⟨látigo⟩
crack; (con la lengua) click one's
tongue; ⟨los dedos⟩ snap. ~ido m
crack; (de la lengua) click; (de los
dedos) snap
chatarra f scrap iron; (fig) scrap
chato a ⟨nariz⟩ snub; ⟨persona⟩ snub-
nosed; ⟨objetos⟩ flat. • m wine glass;
(niño, mujer, fam) dear, darling;
(hombre, fam) mate (fam)
chaval m (fam) boy, lad. ~a f girl,
lass
che int (Arg) listen!, hey!
checo a & m Czech. la república f
Checa the Czech Republic
checoslovaco a & m (history)
Czechoslovak
Checoslovaquia f (history) Czecho-
slovakia
chelín m shilling
chelo a (Mex, rubio) fair
cheque m cheque. ~ de viaje traveller's cheque. ~ra f cheque-book
chica f girl; (criada) maid, servant
chicano a & m Chicano, Mexican-
American
chicle m chewing-gum
chico a (fam) small. • m boy. ~s mpl
children
chicoleo m compliment
chicoria f chicory
chicharra f cicada; (fig) chatterbox
chicharrón m (de cerdo) crackling;
(fig) sunburnt person
chichón m bump, lump

chifla|do a (fam) crazy, daft. ~r vt (fam) drive crazy. ~rse vpr be mad (por algo). **le chifla el chocolate** he's mad about chocolate. **le tiene chiflado esa chica** he's crazy about that girl

Chile m Chile

chile m chilli

chileno a & m Chilean

chill|ar vi scream, shriek; ⟨gato⟩ howl; ⟨ratón⟩ squeak; ⟨cerdo⟩ squeal. ~ido m scream, screech; (de gato etc) howl. ~ón a noisy; ⟨colores⟩ loud; ⟨sonido⟩ shrill

chimenea f chimney; (hogar) fireplace

chimpancé m chimpanzee

China f China

chinch|ar vt (fam) annoy, pester. ~e m drawing-pin (Brit), thumbtack (Amer); ⟨insecto⟩ bedbug; (fig) nuisance. ~eta f drawing-pin (Brit), thumbtack (Amer)

chinela f slipper

chino a & m Chinese

Chipre m Cyprus

chipriota a & m & f Cypriot

chiquillo a childish. ● m child, kid (fam)

chiquito a small, tiny. ● m child, kid (fam)

chiribita f spark. **estar que echa ~s** be furious

chirimoya f custard apple

chiripa f fluke. **por ~** by fluke

chirivía f parsnip

chirri|ar vi creak; ⟨pájaro⟩ chirp. ~do m creaking; (al freír) sizzling; (de pájaros) chirping

chis int sh!, hush!; (para llamar a uno, fam) hey!, psst!

chism|e m gadget, thingumajig (fam); (chismorreo) piece of gossip. ~es mpl things, bits and pieces. ~orreo m gossip. ~oso a gossipy. ● m gossip

chispa f spark; (gota) drop; (gracia) wit; (fig) sparkle. **estar que echa ~(s)** be furious

chispea|nte a sparkling. ~r vi spark; (lloviznar) drizzle; (fig) sparkle

chisporrotear vt throw out sparks; ⟨fuego⟩ crackle; ⟨aceite⟩ sizzle

chistar vi speak. **sin ~** without saying a word

chiste m joke, funny story. **hacer ~ de** make fun of. **tener ~** be funny

chistera f (fam) top hat, topper (fam)

chistoso a funny

chiva|r vi inform ⟨policía⟩; ⟨niño⟩ tell. ~tazo m tip-off. ~to m informer; ⟨niño⟩ telltale

chivo m kid, young goat

choca|nte a surprising; ⟨persona⟩ odd. ~r [7] vt clink ⟨vasos⟩; shake ⟨la mano⟩. ● vi collide, hit. ~r con, ~r contra crash into. **lo ~nte es que** the surprising thing is that

chocolate m chocolate. **tableta f de ~** bar of chocolate

choch|ear vi be senile. ~o a senile; (fig) soft

chófer m chauffeur; (conductor) driver

cholo a & m (LAm) half-breed

chopo m poplar

choque m collision; (fig) clash; (eléctrico) shock; (auto, rail etc) crash, accident; (sacudida) jolt

chorizo m salami

chorr|ear vi gush forth; (fig) be dripping. ~o m jet, stream; (caudal pequeño) trickle; (fig) stream. **a ~os** (fig) in abundance. **hablar a ~os** jabber

chovinis|mo m chauvinism. ~ta a chauvinistic. ● m & f chauvinist

choza f hut

chubas|co m squall, heavy shower; (fig) bad patch. ~quero m raincoat, anorak

chuchería f trinket; (culin) sweet

chufa f tiger nut

chuleta f chop

chulo a insolent; (vistoso) showy. ● m ruffian; (rufián) pimp

chumbo m prickly pear; (fam) bump. **higo m ~** prickly pear

chup|ada f suck; (al cigarro etc) puff. ~ado a skinny; (fácil, fam) very easy. ~ar vt suck; lick; puff at ⟨cigarro etc⟩; (absorber) absorb. ~arse vpr lose weight. ~ete m dummy (Brit), pacifier (Amer)

churro m fritter; (fam) mess. **me salió un ~** I made a mess of it

chusco a funny

chusma f riff-raff

chutar vi shoot. **¡va que chuta!** it's going well!

D

dactilógrafo m typist

dado m dice. ● a given; ⟨hora⟩ gone. **~ que** since, given that

dalia *f* dahlia

daltoniano *a* colour-blind

dama *f* lady; (*en la corte*) lady-in-waiting. **~s** *fpl* draughts (*Brit*), checkers (*Amer*)

damasco *m* damask

danés *a* Danish. ● *m* Dane; (*idioma*) Danish

danza *f* dance; (*acción*) dancing; (*enredo*) affair. **~r** [10] *vt/i* dance

dañ|ado *a* damaged. **~ar** *vt* damage; harm (*persona*). **~ino** *a* harmful. **~o** *m* damage; (*a una persona*) harm. **~oso** *a* harmful. **~os y perjuicios** damages. **hacer ~o a** harm; hurt (*persona*). **hacerse ~o** hurt o.s.

dar [26] *vt* give; (*producir*) yield; strike (*la hora*). ● *vi* give. **da igual** it doesn't matter. **¡dale!** go on! **da lo mismo** it doesn't matter. **~ a** (*ventana*) look on to; (*edificio*) face. **~ a luz** give birth. **~ con** meet (*persona*); find (*cosa*); **~ de cabeza** fall flat on one's face. **~ por** assume; (+ *infinitivo*) decide. **~se** *vpr* give o.s. up; (*suceder*) happen. **dárselas de** make o.s. out to be. **~se por** consider o.s. **¿qué más da?** it doesn't matter!

dardo *m* dart

dársena *f* dock

datar *vt* date. ● *vi*. **~ de** date from

dátil *m* date

dato *m* fact. **~s** *mpl* data, information

de *prep* of; (*procedencia*) from; (*suposición*) if. **~ día** by day. **~ dos en dos** two by two. **~ haberlo sabido** if I (you, he etc) had known. **~ niño** as a child. **el libro ~ mi amigo** my friend's book. **las 2 ~ la madrugada** 2 (o'clock) in the morning. **un puente ~ hierro** an iron bridge. **soy ~ Loughborough** I'm from Loughborough

deambular *vi* stroll

debajo *adv* underneath. **~ de** underneath, under. **el de ~** the one underneath. **por ~** underneath. **por ~ de** below

debat|e *m* debate. **~ir** *vt* debate

deber *vt* owe. ● *vi* have to, must. ● *m* duty. **~es** *mpl* homework. **~se** *vpr*. **~se a** be due to. **debo marcharme** I must go, I have to go

debido *a* due; (*correcto*) proper. **~ a** due to. **como es ~** as is proper. **con el respeto ~** with due respect

débil *a* weak; (*ruido*) faint; (*luz*) dim

debili|dad *f* weakness. **~tar** *vt* weaken. **~tarse** *vpr* weaken, get weak

débito *m* debit; (*deuda*) debt

debutar *vi* make one's debut

década *f* decade

deca|dencia *f* decline. **~dente** *a* decadent. **~er** [29] *vi* decline; (*debilitarse*) weaken. **~ído** *a* depressed. **~imiento** *m* decline, weakening

decano *m* dean; (*miembro más antiguo*) senior member

decantar *vt* decant (*vino etc*)

decapitar *vt* behead

decena *f* ten; (*aproximadamente*) about ten

decencia *f* decency, honesty

decenio *m* decade

decente *a* (*persona*) respectable, honest; (*cosas*) modest; (*limpio*) clean, tidy

decepci|ón *f* disappointment. **~onar** *vt* disappoint

decibelio *m* decibel

decidi|do *a* decided; (*persona*) determined, resolute. **~r** *vt* decide; settle (*cuestión etc*). ● *vi* decide. **~rse** *vpr* make up one's mind

decimal *a & m* decimal

décimo *a & m* tenth. ● *m* (*de lotería*) tenth part of a lottery ticket

decimo: **~ctavo** *a & m* eighteenth. **~cuarto** *a & m* fourteenth. **~nono** *a & m*, **~noveno** *a & m* nineteenth. **~quinto** *a & m* fifteenth. **~séptimo** *a & m* seventeenth. **~sexto** *a & m* sixteenth. **~tercero** *a & m*, **~tercio** *a & m* thirteenth

decir [46] *vt* say; (*contar*) tell. ● *m* saying. **~se** *vpr* be said. **~ que no** say no. **~ que sí** say yes. **dicho de otro modo** in other words. **dicho y hecho** no sooner said than done. **¿dígame?** can I help you? **¡dígame!** (*al teléfono*) hello! **digamos** let's say. **es ~** that is to say. **mejor dicho** rather. **¡no me digas!** you don't say!, really! **por así ~, por ~lo así** so to speak, as it were. **querer ~** mean. **se dice que** it is said that, they say that

decisi|ón *f* decision. **~vo** *a* decisive

declamar *vt* declaim

declara|ción *f* statement. **~ción de renta** income tax return. **~r** *vt/i* declare. **~rse** *vpr* declare o.s.; (*epidemia etc*) break out

declina|ción *f* (*gram*) declension. **~r** *vt/i* decline; (*salud*) deteriorate

declive *m* slope; (*fig*) decline. **en ~** sloping

decolorar *vt* discolour, fade. **~se** *vpr* become discoloured, fade

decora|ción *f* decoration. **~do** *m* (*en el teatro*) set. **~dor** *m* decorator. **~r** *vt* decorate. **~tivo** *a* decorative

decoro *m* decorum; (*respeto*) respect. **~so** *a* proper; (*modesto*) modest; ⟨*profesión*⟩ honourable

decrecer [11] *vi* decrease, diminish; ⟨*aguas*⟩ subside

decrépito *a* decrepit

decret|ar *vt* decree. **~o** *m* decree

dedal *m* thimble

dedica|ción *f* dedication. **~r** [7] *vt* dedicate; devote ⟨*tiempo*⟩. **~toria** *f* dedication, inscription

ded|il *m* finger-stall. **~illo** *m.* **al ~illo** at one's fingertips. **~o** *m* finger; (*del pie*) toe. **~o anular** ring finger. **~ corazón** middle finger. **~o gordo** thumb. **~o índice** index finger. **~o meñique** little finger. **~o pulgar** thumb

deduc|ción *f* deduction. **~ir** [47] *vt* deduce; (*descontar*) deduct

defect|o *m* fault, defect. **~uoso** *a* defective

defen|der [1] *vt* defend. **~sa** *f* defence. **~sivo** *a* defensive. **~sor** *m* defender. **abogado** *m* **~sor** defence counsel

deferen|cia *f* deference. **~te** *a* deferential

deficien|cia *f* deficiency. **~cia mental** mental handicap. **~te** *a* deficient; (*imperfecto*) defective. **~te mental** mentally handicapped

déficit *m invar* deficit

defini|ción *f* definition. **~do** *a* defined. **~r** *vt* define; (*aclarar*) clarify. **~tivo** *a* definitive. **en ~tiva** (*en resumen*) in short

deflación *f* deflation

deform|ación *f* deformation; (*TV etc*) distortion. **~ar** *vt* deform; (*TV etc*) distort. **~arse** *vpr* go out of shape. **~e** *a* deformed; (*feo*) ugly

defraudar *vt* cheat; (*decepcionar*) disappoint; evade ⟨*impuestos etc*⟩

defunción *f* death

degenera|ción *f* degeneration; (*moral*) degeneracy. **~do** *a* degenerate. **~r** *vi* degenerate

deglutir *vt/i* swallow

degollar [16] *vt* cut s.o.'s throat; (*fig, arruinar*) ruin

degradar *vt* degrade. **~se** *vpr* lower o.s.

degusta|ción *f* tasting. **~r** *vt* taste

dehesa *f* pasture

dei|dad *f* deity. **~ficar** [7] *vt* deify

deja|ción *f* surrender. **~dez** *f* abandon; (*pereza*) laziness. **~do** *a* negligent. **~r** *vt* leave; (*abandonar*) abandon; (*prestar*) lend; (*permitir*) let. **~r aparte**, **~r a un lado** leave aside. **~r de** stop. **no ~r de** not fail to

dejo *m* aftertaste; (*tonillo*) accent

del = de + el

delantal *m* apron

delante *adv* in front; (*enfrente*) opposite. **~ de** in front of. **de ~** front

delanter|a *f* front; (*de teatro etc*) front row; (*ventaja*) advantage. **coger la ~a** get ahead. **~o** *a* front. ● *m* forward. **llevar la ~a** be ahead

delat|ar *vt* denounce. **~or** *m* informer

delega|ción *f* delegation; (*sucursal*) branch. **~do** *m* delegate; (*com*) agent, representative. **~r** [12] *vt* delegate

deleit|ar *vt* delight. **~e** *m* delight

deletéreo *a* deleterious

deletre|ar *vt* spell (out). **~o** *m* spelling

deleznable *a* brittle, crumbly; ⟨*argumento etc*⟩ weak

delfín *m* dolphin

delgad|ez *f* thinness. **~o** *a* thin; (*esbelto*) slim. **~ucho** *a* skinny

delibera|ción *f* deliberation. **~r** *vt* discuss, decide. ● *vi* deliberate

delicad|eza *f* delicacy; (*fragilidad*) frailty; (*tacto*) tact. **~o** *a* delicate; (*sensible*) sensitive; (*discreto*) discreet. **falta de ~eza** tactlessness

delici|a *f* delight. **~oso** *a* delightful; ⟨*sabor etc*⟩ delicious; (*gracioso, fam*) funny

delimitar *vt* delimit

delincuen|cia *f* delinquency. **~te** *a & m* delinquent

delinea|nte *m* draughtsman. **~r** *vt* outline; (*dibujar*) draw

delinquir [8] *vi* commit an offence

delir|ante *a* delirious. **~ar** *vi* be delirious; (*fig*) talk nonsense. **~io** *m* delirium; (*fig*) frenzy

delito *m* crime, offence

delta *f* delta

demacrado *a* emaciated

demagogo *m* demagogue

demanda f. **en** ~ **de** asking for; (*en busca de*) in search of. ~**nte** m & f (*jurid*) plaintiff. ~**r** vt (*jurid*) bring an action against

demarca|ción f demarcation. ~**r** [7] vt demarcate

demás a rest of the, other. • *pron* rest, others. **lo** ~ the rest. **por** ~ useless; (*muy*) very. **por lo** ~ otherwise

demasía f excess; (*abuso*) outrage; (*atrevimiento*) insolence. **en** ~ too much

demasiado a too much; (*en plural*) too many. • *adv* too much; (*con adjetivo*) too

demen|cia f madness. ~**te** a demented, mad

dem|ocracia f democracy. ~**ócrata** m & f democrat. ~**ocrático** a democratic

demol|er [2] vt demolish. ~**ición** f demolition

demonio m devil, demon. ¡~**s**! hell! ¿**cómo** ~**s**? how the hell? ¡**qué** ~**s**! what the hell!

demora f delay. ~**r** vt delay. • vi stay on. ~**rse** vpr be a long time

demostra|ción f demonstration, show. ~**r** [2] vt demonstrate; (*mostrar*) show; (*probar*) prove. ~**tivo** a demonstrative

denegar [1 & 12] vt refuse

deng|oso a affected, finicky. ~**ue** m affectation

denigrar vt denigrate

denomina|ción f denomination. ~**do** a called. ~**dor** m denominator. ~**r** vt name

denotar vt denote

dens|idad f density. ~**o** a dense, thick

denta|dura f teeth. ~**dura postiza** denture, false teeth. ~**l** a dental

dentera f. **dar** ~ **a uno** set s.o.'s teeth on edge; (*dar envidia*) make s.o. green with envy

dentífrico m toothpaste

dentista m & f dentist

dentro *adv* inside; (*de un edificio*) indoors. ~ **de** in. ~ **de poco** soon. **por** ~ inside

denuncia f report; (*acusación*) accusation. ~**r** vt report (a crime); (*periódico etc*) denounce; (*indicar*) indicate

departamento m department; (*Arg, piso*) flat (*Brit*), apartment (*Amer*)

dependencia f dependence; (*sección*) section; (*sucursal*) branch

depender vi depend (**de** on)

dependient|a f shop assistant. ~**e** a dependent (**de** on). • m employee; (*de oficina*) clerk; (*de tienda*) shop assistant

depila|ción f depilation. ~**r** vt depilate. ~**torio** a depilatory

deplora|ble a deplorable. ~**r** vt deplore, regret

deponer [34] vt remove from office. • vi give evidence

deporta|ción f deportation. ~**r** vt deport

deport|e m sport. ~**ista** m sportsman. • f sportswoman. ~**ivo** a sports. • m sports car. **hacer** ~**e** take part in sports

deposición f deposition; (*de un empleo*) removal from office

dep|ositador m depositor. ~**ositante** m & f depositor. ~**ositar** vt deposit; (*poner*) put, place. ~**ósito** m deposit; (*conjunto de cosas*) store; (*almacén*) warehouse; (*mil*) depot; (*de líquidos*) tank

deprava|ción f depravity. ~**do** a depraved. ~**r** vt deprave. ~**rse** vpr become depraved

deprecia|ción f depreciation. ~**r** vt depreciate. ~**rse** vpr depreciate

depresión f depression

deprim|ente a depressing. ~**ido** a depressed. ~**ir** vt depress. ~**irse** vpr get depressed

depura|ción f purification; (*pol*) purging. ~**r** vt purify; (*pol*) purge

derech|a f (*mano*) right hand; (*lado*) right. ~**ista** a right-wing. • m & f right-winger. ~**o** a right; (*vertical*) upright; (*recto*) straight. • *adv* straight. • m right; (*ley*) law; (*lado*) right side. ~**os** *mpl* dues. ~**os de autor** royalties. **a la** ~**a** on the right; (*hacia el lado derecho*) to the right. **todo** ~**o** straight on

deriva f drift. **a la** ~ drifting, adrift

deriva|ción f derivation; (*cambio*) diversion. ~**do** a derived. • m derivative, by-product. ~**r** vt derive; (*cambiar la dirección de*) divert. • vi. ~**r de** derive from, be derived from. ~**rse** vpr be derived

derram|amiento m spilling. ~**amiento de sangre** bloodshed. ~**ar**

vt spill; (*verter*) pour; shed (*lágrimas*). ~**arse** *vpr* spill. ~**e** *m* spilling; (*pérdida*) leakage; (*cantidad perdida*) spillage; (*med*) discharge; (*med, de sangre*) haemorrhage

derretir [5] *vt* melt. ~**se** *vpr* melt; (*enamorarse*) fall in love (**por** with)

derriba|do *a* fallen down. ~**r** *vt* knock down; bring down, overthrow (*gobierno etc*). ~**rse** *vpr* fall down

derrocar [7] *vt* bring down, overthrow (*gobierno etc*)

derroch|ar *vt* squander. ~**e** *m* waste

derrot|a *f* defeat; (*rumbo*) course. ~**ar** *vt* defeat. ~**ado** *a* defeated; (*vestido*) shabby. ~**ero** *m* course

derrumba|miento *m* collapse. ~**r** *vt* (*derribar*) knock down. ~**rse** *vpr* collapse

desaborido *a* tasteless; (*persona*) dull

desabotonar *vt* unbutton, undo. ● *vi* bloom. ~**se** *vpr* come undone

desabrido *a* tasteless; (*tiempo*) unpleasant; (*persona*) surly

desabrochar *vt* undo. ~**se** *vpr* come undone

desacat|ar *vt* have no respect for. ~**o** *m* disrespect

desac|ertado *a* ill-advised; (*erróneo*) wrong. ~**ertar** [1] *vt* be wrong. ~**ierto** *m* mistake

desaconseja|ble *a* inadvisable. ~**do** *a* unwise, ill-advised. ~**r** *vt* advise against, dissuade

desacorde *a* discordant

desacostumbra|do *a* unusual. ~**r** *vt* give up

desacreditar *vt* discredit

desactivar *vt* defuse

desacuerdo *m* disagreement

desafiar [20] *vt* challenge; (*afrontar*) defy

desafilado *a* blunt

desafina|do *a* out of tune. ~**r** *vi* be out of tune. ~**rse** *vpr* go out of tune

desafío *m* challenge; (*combate*) duel

desaforado *a* (*comportamiento*) outrageous; (*desmedido*) excessive; (*sonido*) loud; (*enorme*) huge

desafortunad|amente *adv* unfortunately. ~**o** *a* unfortunate

desagrada|ble *a* unpleasant. ~**r** *vt* displease. ● *vi* be unpleasant. **me** ~ **el sabor** I don't like the taste

desagradecido *a* ungrateful

desagrado *m* displeasure. **con** ~ unwillingly

desagravi|ar *vt* make amends to. ~**o** *m* amends; (*expiación*) atonement

desagregar [12] *vt* break up. ~**se** *vpr* disintegrate

desagüe *m* drain; (*acción*) drainage. **tubo** *m* **de** ~ drain-pipe

desaguisado *a* illegal. ● *m* offence; (*fam*) disaster

desahog|ado *a* roomy; (*adinerado*) well-off; (*fig, descarado, fam*) impudent. ~**ar** [12] *vt* relieve; vent (*ira*). ~**arse** *vpr* (*desfogarse*) let off steam. ~**o** *m* comfort; (*alivio*) relief

desahuci|ar *vt* deprive of hope; give up hope for (*enfermo*); evict (*inquilino*). ~**o** *m* eviction

desair|ado *a* humiliating; (*persona*) humiliated, spurned. ~**ar** *vt* snub (*persona*); disregard (*cosa*). ~**e** *m* rebuff

desajuste *m* maladjustment; (*avería*) breakdown

desal|entador *a* disheartening. ~**entar** [1] *vt* (*fig*) discourage. ~**iento** *m* discouragement

desaliño *m* untidiness, scruffiness

desalmado *a* wicked

desalojar *vt* eject (*persona*); evacuate (*sitio*). ● *vi* move (house)

desampar|ado *a* helpless; (*abandonado*) abandoned. ~**ar** *vt* abandon. ~**o** *m* helplessness; (*abandono*) abandonment

desangelado *a* insipid, dull

desangrar *vt* bleed. ~**se** *vpr* bleed

desanima|do *a* down-hearted. ~**r** *vt* discourage. ~**rse** *vpr* lose heart

desánimo *m* discouragement

desanudar *vt* untie

desapacible *a* unpleasant; (*sonido*) harsh

desapar|ecer [11] *vi* disappear; (*efecto*) wear off. ~**ecido** *a* disappeared. ● *m* missing person. ~**ecidos** *mpl* missing. ~**ición** *f* disappearance

desapasionado *a* dispassionate

desapego *m* indifference

desapercibido *a* unnoticed

desaplicado *a* lazy

desaprensi|ón *f* unscrupulousness. ~**vo** *a* unscrupulous

desaproba|ción *f* disapproval. ~**r** [2] *vt* disapprove of; (*rechazar*) reject.

desaprovecha|do *a* wasted; (*alumno*) lazy. ~**r** *vt* waste

desarm|ar *vt* disarm; *(desmontar)* take to pieces. **~e** *m* disarmament

desarraig|ado *a* rootless. **~ar** [12] *vt* uproot; *(fig, erradicar)* wipe out. **~o** *m* uprooting; *(fig)* eradication

desarregl|ado *a* untidy; *(desordenado)* disorderly. **~ar** *vt* mess up; *(deshacer el orden)* make untidy. **~o** *m* disorder; *(de persona)* untidiness

desarroll|ado *a* (well-) developed. **~ar** *vt* develop; *(desenrollar)* unroll, unfold. **~arse** *vpr (incl foto)* develop; *(desenrollarse)* unroll; *(suceso)* take place. **~o** *m* development

desarrugar [12] *vt* smooth out

desarticular *vt* dislocate *(hueso)*; *(fig)* break up

desaseado *a* dirty; *(desordenado)* untidy

desasirse [45] *vpr* let go (**de** of)

desasos|egar [1 & 12] *vt* disturb. **~egarse** *vpr* get uneasy. **~iego** *m* anxiety; *(intranquilidad)* restlessness

desastr|ado *a* scruffy. **~e** *m* disaster. **~oso** *a* disastrous

desata|do *a* untied; *(fig)* wild. **~r** *vt* untie; *(fig, soltar)* unleash. **~rse** *vpr* come undone

desatascar [7] *vt* pull out of the mud; unblock *(tubo etc)*

desaten|ción *f* inattention; *(descortesía)* discourtesy. **~der** [1] *vt* not pay attention to; neglect *(deber etc)*. **~to** *a* inattentive; *(descortés)* discourteous

desatin|ado *a* silly. **~o** *m* silliness; *(error)* mistake

desatornillar *vt* unscrew

desatracar [7] *vt/i* disperse

desautorizar [10] *vt* declare unauthorized; *(desmentir)* deny

desavenencia *f* disagreement

desayun|ar *vt* have for breakfast. ● *vi* have breakfast. **~o** *m* breakfast

desazón *m* *(fig)* anxiety

desbandarse *vpr (mil)* disband; *(dispersarse)* disperse

desbarajust|ar *vt* throw into confusion. **~e** *m* confusion

desbaratar *vt* spoil

desbloquear *vt* unfreeze

desbocado *a* *(vasija etc)* chipped; *(caballo)* runaway; *(persona)* foul-mouthed

desborda|nte *a* overflowing. **~r** *vt* go beyond; *(exceder)* exceed. ● *vi* overflow. **~rse** *vpr* overflow

descabalgar [12] *vi* dismount

descabellado *a* crazy

descabezar [10] *vt* behead

descafeinado *a* decaffeinated. ● *m* decaffeinated coffee

descalabr|ar *vt* injure in the head; *(fig)* damage. **~o** *m* disaster

descalificar [7] *vt* disqualify; *(desacreditar)* discredit

descalz|ar [10] *vt* take off *(zapato)*. **~o** *a* barefoot

descaminar *vt* misdirect; *(fig)* lead astray

descamisado *a* shirtless; *(fig)* shabby

descampado *a* open. ● *m* open ground

descans|ado *a* rested; *(trabajo)* easy. **~apiés** *m* footrest. **~ar** *vt/i* rest. **~illo** *m* landing. **~o** *m* rest; *(descansillo)* landing; *(en deportes)* half-time; *(en el teatro etc)* interval

descapotable *a* convertible

descarado *a* insolent, cheeky; *(sin vergüenza)* shameless

descarg|a *f* unloading; *(mil, elec)* discharge. **~ar** [12] *vt* unload; *(mil, elec)* discharge, shock; deal *(golpe etc)*. ● *vi* flow into. **~o** *m* unloading; *(recibo)* receipt; *(jurid)* evidence

descarnado *a* scrawny, lean; *(fig)* bare

descaro *m* insolence, cheek; *(cinismo)* nerve, effrontery

descarriar [20] *vt* misdirect; *(fig)* lead astray. **~se** *vpr* go the wrong way; *(res)* stray; *(fig)* go astray

descarrila|miento *m* derailment. **~r** *vi* be derailed. **~se** *vpr* be derailed

descartar *vt* discard; *(rechazar)* reject. **~se** *vpr* discard

descascarar *vt* shell

descen|dencia *f* descent; *(personas)* descendants. **~dente** *a* descending. **~der** [1] *vt* lower, get down; go down *(escalera etc)*. ● *vi* go down; *(provenir)* be descended (**de** from). **~diente** *m & f* descendant. **~so** *m* descent; *(de temperatura, fiebre etc)* fall, drop

descentralizar [10] *vt* decentralize

descifrar *vt* decipher; decode *(clave)*

descolgar [2 & 12] *vt* take down; pick up *(el teléfono)*. **~se** *vpr* let o.s. down; *(fig, fam)* turn up

descolorar *vt* discolour, fade

descolori|do *a* discoloured, faded; ‹*persona*› pale. ~**r** *vt* discolour, fade

descomedido *a* rude; (*excesivo*) excessive, extreme

descomp|ás *m* disproportion. ~**a-sado** *a* disproportionate

descomp|oner [34] *vt* break down; decompose ‹*substancia*›; distort ‹*rasgos*›; (*estropear*) break; (*desarreglar*) disturb, spoil. ~**onerse** *vpr* decompose; ‹*persona*› lose one's temper. ~**osición** *f* decomposition; (*med*) diarrhoea. ~**ostura** *f* breaking; (*de un motor*) breakdown; (*desorden*) disorder. ~**uesto** *a* broken; (*podrido*) decomposed; (*encolerizado*) angry. **estar** ~**uesto** have diarrhoea

descomunal *a* (*fam*) enormous

desconc|ertante *a* disconcerting. ~**ertar** [1] *vt* disconcert; (*dejar perplejo*) puzzle. ~**ertarse** *vpr* be put out, be disconcerted; ‹*mecanismo*› break down. ~**ierto** *m* confusion

desconectar *vt* disconnect

desconfia|do *a* distrustful. ~**nza** *f* distrust, suspicion. ~**r** [20] *vi*. ~**r de** not trust; (*no creer*) doubt

descongelar *vt* defrost; (*com*) unfreeze

desconoc|er [11] *vt* not know, not recognize. ~**ido** *a* unknown; (*cambiado*) unrecognizable. ● *m* stranger. ~**imiento** *m* ignorance

desconsidera|ción *f* lack of consideration. ~**do** *a* inconsiderate

descons|olado *a* distressed. ~**olar** [2] *vt* distress. ~**olarse** *vpr* despair. ~**uelo** *m* distress; (*tristeza*) sadness

desconta|do *a*. **dar por** ~**do** take for granted. **por** ~**do** of course. ~**r** [2] *vt* discount

descontent|adizo *a* hard to please. ~**ar** *vt* displease. ~**o** *a* unhappy (**de** about), discontented (**de** with). ● *m* discontent

descontrolado *a* uncontrolled

descorazonar *vt* discourage. ~**se** *vpr* lose heart

descorchar *vt* uncork

descorrer *vt* draw ‹*cortina*›. ~ **el cerrojo** unbolt the door

descort|és *a* rude, discourteous. ~**esía** *f* rudeness

descos|er *vt* unpick. ~**erse** *vpr* come undone. ~**ido** *a* unstitched; (*fig*) disjointed. **como un** ~**ido** a lot

descoyuntar *vt* dislocate

descrédito *m* disrepute. **ir en** ~ **de** damage the reputation of

descreído *a* unbelieving

descremar *vt* skim

descri|bir [*pp* **descrito**] *vt* describe. ~**pción** *f* description. ~**ptivo** *a* descriptive

descuartizar [10] *vt* cut up

descubierto *a* discovered; (*no cubierto*) uncovered; (*expuesto*) exposed; ‹*cielo*› clear; (*sin sombrero*) bareheaded. ● *m* overdraft; (*déficit*) deficit. **poner al** ~ expose

descubri|miento *m* discovery. ~**r** [*pp* **descubierto**] *vt* discover; (*quitar lo que cubre*) uncover; (*revelar*) reveal; unveil ‹*estatua*›. ~**rse** *vpr* be discovered; ‹*cielo*› clear; (*quitarse el sombrero*) take off one's hat

descuento *m* discount

descuid|ado *a* careless; ‹*aspecto etc*› untidy; (*desprevenido*) unprepared. ~**ar** *vt* neglect. ● *vi* not worry. ~**arse** *vpr* be careless; (*no preocuparse*) not worry. ¡~**a!** don't worry! ~**o** *m* carelessness; (*negligencia*) negligence. **al** ~**o** nonchalantly. **estar** ~**ado** not worry, rest assured

desde *prep* (*lugar etc*) from; (*tiempo*) since, from. ~ **hace poco** for a short time. ~ **hace un mes** for a month. ~ **luego** of course. ~ **Madrid hasta Barcelona** from Madrid to Barcelona. ~ **niño** since childhood

desdecir [46, *pero imperativo* **desdice**, *futuro y condicional regulares*] *vi*. ~ **de** be unworthy of; (*no armonizar*) not match. ~**se** *vpr*. ~ **de** take back ‹*palabras etc*›; go back on ‹*promesa*›

desd|én *m* scorn. ~**eñable** *a* contemptible. ~**eñar** *vt* scorn. ~**eñoso** *a* scornful

desdicha *f* misfortune. ~**do** *a* unfortunate. **por** ~ unfortunately

desdoblar *vt* straighten; (*desplegar*) unfold

desea|ble *a* desirable. ~**r** *vt* want; wish ‹*algo a uno*›. **de** ~ desirable. **le deseo un buen viaje** I hope you have a good journey. **¿qué desea Vd?** can I help you?

desecar [7] *vt* dry up

desech|ar *vt* throw out. ~**o** *m* rubbish

desembalar *vt* unpack

desembarazar [10] *vt* clear. ~**se** *vpr* free o.s.

desembarca|dero *m* landing stage. ~**r** [7] *vt* unload. ● *vi* disembark

desemboca|dura *f* (*de río*) mouth; (*de calle*) opening. ~**r** [7] *vi*. ~**r en** ‹*río*› flow into; ‹*calle*› join; (*fig*) lead to, end in

desembols|ar *vt* pay. ~**o** *m* payment

desembragar [12] *vi* declutch

desembrollar *vt* unravel

desembuchar *vi* tell, reveal a secret

desemejan|te *a* unlike, dissimilar. ~**za** *f* dissimilarity

desempapelar *vt* unwrap

desempaquetar *vt* unpack, unwrap

desempat|ar *vi* break a tie. ~**e** *m* tie-breaker

desempeñ|ar *vt* redeem; play ‹*papel*›; hold ‹*cargo*›; perform, carry out ‹*deber etc*›. ~**arse** *vpr* get out of debt. ~**o** *m* redemption; (*de un papel, de un cargo*) performance

desemple|ado *a* unemployed. ● *m* unemployed person. ~**o** *m* unemployment. **los ~ados** *mpl* the unemployed

desempolvar *vt* dust; (*fig*) unearth

desencadenar *vt* unchain; (*fig*) unleash. ~**se** *vpr* break loose; ‹*guerra etc*› break out

desencajar *vt* dislocate; (*desconectar*) disconnect. ~**se** *vpr* become distorted

desencant|ar *vt* disillusion. ~**o** *m* disillusionment

desenchufar *vt* unplug

desenfad|ado *a* uninhibited. ~**ar** *vt* calm down. ~**arse** *vpr* calm down. ~**o** *m* openness; (*desenvoltura*) assurance

desenfocado *a* out of focus

desenfren|ado *a* unrestrained. ~**arse** *vpr* rage. ~**o** *m* licentiousness

desenganchar *vt* unhook

desengañ|ar *vt* disillusion. ~**arse** *vpr* be disillusioned; (*darse cuenta*) realize. ~**o** *m* disillusionment, disappointment

desengrasar *vt* remove the grease from. ● *vi* lose weight

desenla|ce *m* outcome. ~**zar** [10] *vt* undo; solve ‹*problema*›

desenmarañar *vt* unravel

desenmascarar *vt* unmask

desenojar *vt* calm down. ~**se** *vpr* calm down

desenred|ar *vt* unravel. ~**arse** *vpr* extricate o.s. ~**o** *m* denouement

desenrollar *vt* unroll, unwind

desenroscar [7] *vt* unscrew

desentenderse [1] *vpr* want nothing to do with; (*afectar ignorancia*) pretend not to know. **hacerse el desentendido** (*fingir no oír*) pretend not to hear

desenterrar [1] *vt* exhume; (*fig*) unearth

desenton|ar *vi* be out of tune; ‹*colores*› clash. ~**o** *m* rudeness

desentrañar *vt* work out

desenvoltura *f* ease; (*falta de timidez*) confidence; (*descaro*) insolence

desenvolver [2, *pp* desenvuelto] *vt* unwrap; expound ‹*idea etc*›. ~**se** *vpr* act with confidence

deseo *m* wish, desire. ~**so** *a* desirous. **arder en ~s de** long for. **buen ~** good intentions. **estar ~so de** be eager to

desequilibr|ado *a* unbalanced. ~**io** *m* imbalance

des|erción *f* desertion; (*pol*) defection. ~**ertar** *vt* desert. ~**értico** *a* desert-like. ~**ertor** *m* deserter

desespera|ción *f* despair. ~**do** *a* desperate. ~**nte** *a* infuriating. ~**r** *vt* drive to despair. ● *vi* despair (**de** of). ~**rse** *vpr* despair

desestimar *vt* (*rechazar*) reject

desfachat|ado *a* brazen, impudent. ~**ez** *f* impudence

desfalc|ar [7] *vt* embezzle. ~**o** *m* embezzlement

desfallec|er [11] *vt* weaken. ● *vi* get weak; (*desmayarse*) faint. ~**imiento** *m* weakness

desfas|ado *a* ‹*persona*› out of place, out of step; (*máquina etc*) out of phase. ~**e** *m* jet-lag. **estar ~ado** have jet-lag

desfavor|able *a* unfavourable. ~**ecer** [11] *vt* ‹*ropa*› not suit

desfigurar *vt* disfigure; (*desdibujar*) blur; (*fig*) distort

desfiladero *m* pass

desfil|ar *vi* march (past). ~**e** *m* procession, parade. ~**e de modelos** fashion show

desfogar [12] *vt* vent (**en, con** on). ~**se** *vpr* let off steam

desgajar *vt* tear off; (*fig*) uproot ‹*persona*›. ~**se** *vpr* come off

desgana f (falta de apetito) lack of appetite; (med) weakness, faintness; (fig) unwillingness

desgarr|ador a heart-rending. ~**ar** vt tear; (fig) break ⟨corazón⟩. ~**o** m tear, rip; (descaro) insolence. ~**ón** m tear

desgast|ar vt wear away; wear out ⟨ropa⟩. ~**arse** vpr wear away; ⟨ropa⟩ be worn out; ⟨persona⟩ wear o.s. out. ~**e** m wear

desgracia f misfortune; (accidente) accident; (mala suerte) bad luck. ~**damente** adv unfortunately. ~**do** a unlucky; (pobre) poor; (desagradable) unpleasant. ● m unfortunate person, poor devil (fam). ~**r** vt spoil. **caer en** ~ fall from favour. **estar en** ~ be unfortunate. **por** ~ unfortunately. **¡qué** ~! what a shame!

desgranar vt shell ⟨guisantes etc⟩

desgreñado a ruffled, dishevelled

desgua|ce m scrapyard. ~**zar** [10] vt scrap

deshabitado a uninhabited

deshabituarse [21] vpr get out of the habit

deshacer [31] vt undo; strip ⟨cama⟩; unpack ⟨maleta⟩; (desmontar) take to pieces; break ⟨trato⟩; (derretir) melt; (en agua) dissolve; (destruir) destroy; (estropear) spoil; (derrotar) defeat. ~**se** vpr come undone; (descomponerse) fall to pieces; (derretirse) melt. ~**se de algo** get rid of sth. ~**se en lágrimas** burst into tears. ~**se por hacer algo** go out of one's way to do sth

deshelar [1] vt thaw. ~**se** vpr thaw

desheredar vt disinherit

deshidratar vt dehydrate. ~**se** vpr become dehydrated

deshielo m thaw

deshilachado a frayed

deshincha|do a ⟨neumático⟩ flat. ~**r** vt deflate. ~**rse** vpr go down

deshollina|dor m (chimney-)sweep. ~**r** vt sweep

deshon|esto a dishonest; (obsceno) indecent. ~**or** m, ~**ra** f disgrace. ~**rar** vt dishonour

deshora f. **a** ~ (a hora desacostumbrada) at an unusual time; (a hora inoportuna) at an inconvenient time; (a hora avanzada) very late

deshuesar vt bone ⟨carne⟩; stone ⟨fruta⟩

desidia f laziness

desierto a deserted. ● m desert

designa|ción f designation. ~**r** vt designate; (fijar) fix

desigual a unequal; ⟨terreno⟩ uneven; (distinto) different. ~**dad** f inequality

desilusi|ón f disappointment; (pérdida de ilusiones) disillusionment. ~**onar** vt disappoint; (quitar las ilusiones) disillusion. ~**onarse** vpr become disillusioned

desinfecta|nte m disinfectant. ~**r** vt disinfect

desinfestar vt decontaminate

desinflar vt deflate. ~**se** vpr go down

desinhibido a uninhibited

desintegra|ción f disintegration. ~**r** vt disintegrate. ~**rse** vpr disintegrate

desinter|és m impartiality; (generosidad) generosity. ~**esado** a impartial; (liberal) generous

desistir vi. ~ **de** give up

desleal a disloyal. ~**tad** f disloyalty

desleír [51] vt thin down, dilute

deslenguado a foul-mouthed

desligar [12] vt untie; (separar) separate; (fig, librar) free. ~**se** vpr break away; (de un compromiso) free o.s.

deslizar [10] vt slide, slip. ~**se** vpr slide, slip; ⟨tiempo⟩ slide by, pass; (fluir) flow

deslucido a tarnished; (gastado) worn out; (fig) undistinguished

deslumbrar vt dazzle

deslustrar vt tarnish

desmadr|ado a unruly. ~**arse** vpr get out of control. ~**e** m excess

desmán m outrage

desmandarse vpr get out of control

desmantelar vt dismantle; (despojar) strip

desmañado a clumsy

desmaquillador m make-up remover

desmay|ado a unconscious. ~**ar** vi lose heart. ~**arse** vpr faint. ~**o** m faint; (estado) unconsciousness; (fig) depression

desmedido a excessive

desmedrarse vpr waste away

desmejorarse vpr deteriorate

desmelenado a dishevelled

desmembrar vt (fig) divide up

desmemoriado *a* forgetful

desmentir [4] *vt* deny. ~se *vpr* contradict o.s.; (*desdecirse*) go back on one's word

desmenuzar [10] *vt* crumble; chop ⟨*carne etc*⟩

desmerecer [11] *vt* be unworthy of. ● *vi* deteriorate

desmesurado *a* excessive; (*enorme*) enormous

desmigajar *vt*, **desmigar** [12] *vt* crumble

desmonta|ble *a* collapsible. ~**r** *vt* (*quitar*) remove; (*desarmar*) take to pieces; (*derribar*) knock down; (*allanar*) level. ● *vi* dismount

desmoralizar [10] *vt* demoralize

desmoronar *vt* wear away; (*fig*) make inroads into. ~se *vpr* crumble

desmovilizar [10] *vt/i* demobilize

desnatar *vt* skim

desnivel *m* unevenness; (*fig*) difference, inequality

desnud|ar *vt* strip; undress, strip ⟨*persona*⟩. ~arse *vpr* get undressed. ~ez *f* nudity. ~o *a* naked; (*fig*) bare. ● *m* nude

desnutri|ción *f* malnutrition. ~do *a* undernourished

desobed|ecer [11] *vt* disobey. ~iencia *f* disobedience. ~iente *a* disobedient

desocupa|do *a* ⟨*asiento etc*⟩ vacant, free; (*sin trabajo*) unemployed; (*ocioso*) idle. ~r *vt* vacate

desodorante *m* deodorant

desoír [50] *vt* take no notice of

desola|ción *f* desolation; (*fig*) distress. ~do *a* desolate; ⟨*persona*⟩ sorry, sad. ~r *vt* ruin; (*desconsolar*) distress

desollar *vt* skin; (*fig, criticar*) criticize; (*fig, hacer pagar demasiado, fam*) fleece

desorbitante *a* excessive

desorden *m* disorder, untidiness; (*confusión*) confusion. ~ado *a* untidy. ~ar *vt* disarrange, make a mess of

desorganizar [10] *vt* disorganize; (*trastornar*) disturb

desorienta|do *a* confused. ~r *vt* disorientate. ~rse *vpr* lose one's bearings

desovar *vi* ⟨*pez*⟩ spawn; ⟨*insecto*⟩ lay eggs

despabila|do *a* wide awake; (*listo*) quick. ~r *vt* (*despertar*) wake up;

(*avivar*) brighten up. ~rse *vpr* wake up; (*avivarse*) brighten up. **¡despabílate!** get a move on!

despaci|o *adv* slowly. ● *int* easy does it! ~to *adv* slowly

despach|ar *vt* finish; (*tratar con*) deal with; (*vender*) sell; (*enviar*) send; (*despedir*) send away; issue ⟨*billete*⟩. ● *vi* hurry up. ~arse *vpr* get rid; (*terminar*) finish. ~o *m* dispatch; (*oficina*) office; (*venta*) sale; (*del teatro*) box office

despampanante *a* stunning

desparejado *a* odd

desparpajo *m* confidence; (*descaro*) impudence

desparramar *vt* scatter; spill ⟨*líquidos*⟩; squander ⟨*fortuna*⟩

despavorido *a* terrified

despectivo *a* disparaging; ⟨*sentido etc*⟩ pejorative

despecho *m* spite. **a ~ de** in spite of. **por ~** out of spite

despedazar [10] *vt* tear to pieces

despedi|da *f* goodbye, farewell. ~da de soltero stag-party. ~r [5] *vt* say goodbye, see off; dismiss ⟨*empleado*⟩; evict ⟨*inquilino*⟩; (*arrojar*) throw; give off ⟨*olor etc*⟩. ~rse *vpr*. ~rse de say goodbye to

despeg|ado *a* cold, indifferent. ~ar [12] *vt* unstick. ● *vi* ⟨*avión*⟩ take off. ~o *m* indifference. ~ue *m* take-off

despeinar *vt* ruffle the hair of

despeja|do *a* clear; ⟨*persona*⟩ wide awake. ~r *vt* clear; (*aclarar*) clarify. ● *vi* clear. ~rse *vpr* (*aclararse*) become clear; ⟨*cielo*⟩ clear; ⟨*tiempo*⟩ clear up; ⟨*persona*⟩ liven up

despellejar *vt* skin

despensa *f* pantry, larder

despeñadero *m* cliff

desperdici|ar *vt* waste. ~o *m* waste. ~os *mpl* rubbish. **no tener ~o** be good all the way through

desperezarse [10] *vpr* stretch

desperfecto *m* flaw

desperta|dor *m* alarm clock. ~r [1] *vt* wake up; (*fig*) awaken. ~rse *vpr* wake up

despiadado *a* merciless

despido *m* dismissal

despierto *a* awake; (*listo*) bright

despilfarr|ar *vt* waste. ~o *m* squandering; (*gasto innecesario*) extravagance

despista|do *a* (*con estar*) confused; (*con ser*) absent-minded. ~r *vt* throw off the scent; (*fig*) mislead. ~**rse** *vpr* go wrong; (*fig*) get confused

despiste *m* swerve; (*error*) mistake; (*confusión*) muddle

desplaza|do *a* out of place. ~**miento** *m* displacement; (*de opinión etc*) swing, shift. ~**r** [10] *vt* displace. ~**rse** *vpr* travel

despl|egar [1 & 12] *vt* open out; spread (*alas*); (*fig*) show. ~**iegue** *m* opening; (*fig*) show

desplomarse *vpr* lean; (*caerse*) collapse

desplumar *vt* pluck; (*fig, fam*) fleece

despobla|do *m* deserted area. ~**r** [2] *vt* depopulate

despoj|ar *vt* deprive (*persona*); strip (*cosa*). ~**o** *m* plundering; (*botín*) booty. ~**os** *mpl* left-overs; (*de res*) offal; (*de ave*) giblets

desposado *a & m* newly-wed

déspota *m & f* despot

despreci|able *a* despicable; (*cantidad*) negligible. ~**ar** *vt* despise; (*rechazar*) scorn. ~**o** *m* contempt

desprend|er *vt* remove; give off (*olor*). ~**erse** *vpr* fall off; (*fig*) part with; (*deducirse*) follow. ~**imiento** *m* loosening; (*generosidad*) generosity

despreocupa|ción *f* carelessness. ~**do** *a* unconcerned; (*descuidado*) careless. ~**rse** *vpr* not worry

desprestigiar *vt* discredit

desprevenido *a* unprepared. **coger a uno** ~ catch s.o. unawares

desproporci|ón *f* disproportion. ~**onado** *a* disproportionate

despropósito *m* irrelevant remark

desprovisto *a*. ~ **de** lacking, without

después *adv* after, afterwards; (*más tarde*) later; (*a continuación*) then. ~ **de** after. ~ **de comer** after eating. ~ **de todo** after all. ~ **que** after. **poco** ~ soon after. **una semana** ~ a week later

desquiciar *vt* (*fig*) disturb

desquit|ar *vt* compensate. ~**arse** *vpr* make up for; (*vengarse*) take revenge. ~**e** *m* compensation; (*venganza*) revenge

destaca|do *a* outstanding. ~**r** [7] *vt* emphasize. ● *vi* stand out. ~**rse** *vpr* stand out

destajo *m* piece-work. **hablar a** ~ talk nineteen to the dozen

destap|ar *vt* uncover; open (*botella*). ~**arse** *vpr* reveal one's true self. ~**e** *m* (*fig*) permissiveness

destartalado *a* (*habitación*) untidy; (*casa*) rambling

destell|ar *vi* sparkle. ~**o** *m* sparkle; (*de estrella*) twinkle; (*fig*) glimmer

destemplado *a* out of tune; (*agrio*) harsh; (*tiempo*) unsettled; (*persona*) out of sorts

desteñir [5 & 22] *vt* fade; (*manchar*) discolour. ● *vi* fade. ~**se** *vpr* fade; (*color*) run

desterra|do *m* exile. ~**r** [1] *vt* banish

destetar *vt* wean

destiempo *m*. **a** ~ at the wrong moment

destierro *m* exile

destil|ación *f* distillation. ~**ar** *vt* distil. ~**ería** *f* distillery

destin|ar *vt* destine; (*nombrar*) appoint. ~**atario** *m* addressee. ~**o** *m* (*uso*) use, function; (*lugar*) destination; (*empleo*) position; (*suerte*) destiny. **con** ~**o a** going to, bound for. **dar** ~**o a** find a use for

destitu|ción *f* dismissal. ~**ir** [17] *vt* dismiss

destornilla|dor *m* screwdriver. ~**r** *vt* unscrew

destreza *f* skill

destripar *vt* rip open

destroz|ar [10] *vt* ruin; (*fig*) shatter. ~**o** *m* destruction. **causar** ~**os**, **hacer** ~**os** ruin

destru|cción *f* destruction. ~**ctivo** *a* destructive. ~**ir** [17] *vt* destroy; demolish (*edificio*)

desunir *vt* separate

desus|ado *a* old-fashioned; (*insólito*) unusual. ~**o** *m* disuse. **caer en** ~**o** become obsolete

desvaído *a* pale; (*borroso*) blurred; (*persona*) dull

desvalido *a* needy, destitute

desvalijar *vt* rob; burgle (*casa*)

desvalorizar [10] *vt* devalue

desván *m* loft

desvanec|er [11] *vt* make disappear; tone down (*colores*); (*borrar*) blur; (*fig*) dispel. ~**erse** *vpr* disappear; (*desmayarse*) faint. ~**imiento** *m* (*med*) fainting fit

desvariar [20] *vi* be delirious; (*fig*) talk nonsense

desvel|ar *vt* keep awake. ~**arse** *vpr* stay awake, have a sleepless night. ~**o** *m* insomnia, sleeplessness

desvencijar vt break; (agotar) exhaust

desventaja f disadvantage

desventura f misfortune. ~do a unfortunate

desverg|onzado a impudent, cheeky. ~üenza f impudence, cheek

desvestirse [5] vpr undress

desv|iación f deviation; (auto) diversion. ~iar [20] vt deflect, turn aside. ~iarse vpr be deflected; (del camino) make a detour; (del tema) stray. ~ío m diversion; (frialdad) indifference

desvivirse vpr long (por for); (afanarse) strive, do one's utmost

detall|ar vt relate in detail. ~e m detail; (fig) gesture. ~ista m & f retailer. al ~e in detail; (al por menor) retail. con todo ~e in great detail. en ~es in detail. ¡qué ~e! how thoughtful!

detect|ar vt detect. ~ive m detective

deten|ción f stopping; (jurid) arrest; (en la cárcel) detention. ~er [40] vt stop; (jurid) arrest; (encarcelar) detain; (retrasar) delay. ~erse vpr stop; (entretenerse) spend a lot of time. ~idamente adv carefully. ~ido a (jurid) under arrest; (minucioso) detailed. ● m prisoner

detergente a & m detergent

deterior|ar vt damage, spoil. ~arse vpr deteriorate. ~o m damage

determina|ción f determination; (decisión) decison. ~nte a decisive. ~r vt determine; (decidir) decide; (fijar) fix. tomar una ~ción make a decision

detestar vt detest

detonar vi explode

detrás adv behind; (en la parte posterior) on the back. ~ de behind. por ~ on the back; (detrás de) behind

detrimento m detriment. en ~ de to the detriment of

detrito m debris

deud|a f debt. ~or m debtor

devalua|ción f devaluation. ~r [21] vt devalue

devanar vt wind

devasta|dor a devastating. ~r vt devastate

devoción f devotion

devol|ución f return; (com) repayment, refund. ~ver [5] (pp devuelto) vt return; (com) repay,

refund; restore (edificio etc). ● vi be sick

devorar vt devour

devoto a devout; (amigo etc) devoted. ● m enthusiast

di vb véase **dar**

día m day. ~ de fiesta (public) holiday. ~ del santo saint's day. ~ festivo (public) holiday. ~ hábil, ~ laborable working day. al ~ up to date. al ~ siguiente (on) the following day. ¡buenos ~s! good morning! dar los buenos ~s say good morning. de ~ by day. el ~ de hoy today. el ~ de mañana tomorrow. en pleno ~ in broad daylight. en su ~ in due course. todo el santo ~ all day long. un ~ de estos one of these days. un ~ sí y otro no every other day. vivir al ~ live from hand to mouth

diab|etes f diabetes. ~ético a diabetic

diab|lo m devil. ~lura f mischief. ~ólico a diabolical

diácono m deacon

diadema f diadem

diáfano a diaphanous

diafragma m diaphragm

diagn|osis f diagnosis. ~osticar [7] vt diagnose. ~óstico a diagnostic

diagonal a & f diagonal

diagrama m diagram

dialecto m dialect

diálisis f dialysis

di|alogar [12] vi talk. ~álogo m dialogue

diamante m diamond

diámetro m diameter

diana f reveille; (blanco) bull's-eye

diapasón m (para afinar) tuning fork

diapositiva f slide, transparency

diari|amente adv every day. ~o a daily. ● m newspaper; (libro) diary. a ~o daily. ~o hablado (en la radio) news bulletin. de ~o everyday, ordinary

diarrea f diarrhoea

diatriba f diatribe

dibuj|ar vt draw. ~o m drawing. ~os animados cartoon (film)

diccionario m dictionary

diciembre m December

dictado m dictation

dictad|or m dictator. ~ura f dictatorship

dictamen m opinion; (*informe*) report

dictar vt dictate; pronounce ⟨*sentencia etc*⟩

dich|a f happiness. ~o a said; (*susodicho*) aforementioned. • m saying. ~oso a happy; (*afortunado*) fortunate. ~o y hecho no sooner said than done. mejor ~o rather. por ~a fortunately

didáctico a didactic

dieci|nueve a & m nineteen. ~ocho a & m eighteen. ~séis a & m sixteen. ~siete a & m seventeen

diente m tooth; (*de tenedor*) prong; (*de ajo*) clove. ~ de león dandelion. hablar entre ~s mumble

diesel /'disel/ a diesel

diestr|a f right hand. ~o a (*derecho*) right; (*hábil*) skillful

dieta f diet

diez a & m ten

diezmar vt decimate

difama|ción f (*con palabras*) slander; (*por escrito*) libel. ~r vt (*hablando*) slander; (*por escrito*) libel

diferen|cia f difference; (*desacuerdo*) disagreement. ~ciar vt differentiate between. • vi differ. ~ciarse vpr differ. ~te a different

difer|ido a (*TV etc*) recorded. ~ir [4] vt postpone, defer. • vi differ

difícil a difficult. ~ultad f difficulty; (*problema*) problem. ~icultar vt make difficult

difteria f diphtheria

difundir vt spread; (*TV etc*) broadcast. ~se vpr spread

difunto a late, deceased. • m deceased

difusión f spreading

dige|rir [4] vt digest. ~stión f digestion. ~stivo a digestive

digital a digital; (*de los dedos*) finger

dignarse vpr deign. dígnese Vd be so kind as

dign|atario m dignitary. ~idad f dignity; (*empleo*) office. ~o a worthy; (*apropiado*) appropriate

digo vb véase decir

digresión f digression

dije vb véase decir

dila|ción f delay. ~tación f dilation, expansion. ~tado a extensive; ⟨*tiempo*⟩ long. ~tar vt expand; (*med*) dilate; (*prolongar*) prolong. ~tarse vpr expand; (*med*) dilate; (*extenderse*) extend. sin ~ción immediately

dilema m dilemma

diligen|cia f diligence; (*gestión*) job; (*historia*) stagecoach. ~te a diligent

dilucidar vt explain; solve ⟨*misterio*⟩

diluir [17] vt dilute

diluvio m flood

dimensión f dimension; (*tamaño*) size

diminut|ivo a & m diminutive. ~o a minute

dimi|sión f resignation. ~tir vt/i resign

Dinamarca f Denmark

dinamarqués a Danish. • m Dane

din|ámica f dynamics. ~ámico a dynamic. ~amismo m dynamism

dinamita f dynamite

dínamo m, **dinamo** m dynamo

dinastía f dynasty

dineral m fortune

dinero m money. ~ efectivo cash. ~ suelto change

dinosaurio m dinosaur

diócesis f diocese

dios m god. ~a f goddess. ¡D~ mío! good heavens! ¡gracias a D~! thank God! ¡válgame D~! bless my soul!

diploma m diploma

diplomacia f diplomacy

diplomado a qualified

diplomático a diplomatic. • m diplomat

diptongo m diphthong

diputa|ción f delegation. ~ción provincial county council. ~do m delegate; (*pol, en España*) member of the Cortes; (*pol, en Inglaterra*) Member of Parliament; (*pol, en Estados Unidos*) congressman

dique m dike

direc|ción f direction; (*señas*) address; (*los que dirigen*) management; (*pol*) leadership. ~ción prohibida no entry. ~ción única one-way. ~ta f (*auto*) top gear. ~tiva f directive, guideline. ~tivo m executive. ~to a direct; (*línea*) straight; ⟨*tren*⟩ through. ~tor m director; (*mus*) conductor; (*de escuela etc*) headmaster; (*de periódico*) editor; (*gerente*) manager. ~tora f (*de escuela etc*) headmistress. en ~to (*TV etc*) live. llevar la ~ción de direct

dirig|ente a ruling. • m & f leader; (*de empresa*) manager. ~ible a & m dirigible. ~ir [14] vt direct; (*mus*) conduct; run ⟨*empresa etc*⟩; address

⟨carta etc⟩. ∼**irse** *vpr* make one's way; (*hablar*) address

discernir [1] *vt* distinguish

disciplina *f* discipline. ∼**r** *vt* discipline. ∼**rio** *a* disciplinary

discípulo *m* disciple; (*alumno*) pupil

disco *m* disc; (*mus*) record; (*deportes*) discus; (*de teléfono*) dial; (*auto*) lights; (*rail*) signal

disconforme *a* not in agreement

discontinuo *a* discontinuous

discord|ante *a* discordant. ∼**e** *a* discordant. ∼**ia** *f* discord

discoteca *f* discothèque, disco (*fam*); (*colección de discos*) record library

discreción *f* discretion

discrepa|ncia *f* discrepancy; (*desacuerdo*) disagreement. ∼**r** *vi* differ

discreto *a* discreet; (*moderado*) moderate; (*color*) subdued

discrimina|ción *f* discrimination. ∼**r** *vt* (*distinguir*) discriminate between; (*tratar injustamente*) discriminate against

disculpa *f* apology; (*excusa*) excuse. ∼**r** *vt* excuse, forgive. ∼**rse** *vpr* apologize. **dar** ∼**s** make excuses. **pedir** ∼**s** apologize

discurrir *vt* think up. ● *vi* think (**en** about); ⟨*tiempo*⟩ pass

discurs|ante *m* speaker. ∼**ar** *vi* speak (**sobre** about). ∼**o** *m* speech

discusión *f* discussion; (*riña*) argument. **eso no admite** ∼ there can be no argument about that

discuti|ble *a* debatable. ∼**r** *vt* discuss; (*argumentar*) argue about; (*contradecir*) contradict. ● *vi* discuss; (*argumentar*) argue

disec|ar [7] *vt* dissect; stuff ⟨*animal muerto*⟩. ∼**ción** *f* dissection

disemina|ción *f* dissemination. ∼**r** *vt* disseminate, spread

disentería *f* dysentery

disenti|miento *m* dissent, disagreement. ∼**r** [4] *vi* disagree (**de** with) (**en** on)

diseñ|ador *m* designer. ∼**ar** *vt* design. ∼**o** *m* design; (*fig*) sketch

disertación *f* dissertation

disfraz *m* disguise; (*vestido*) fancy dress. ∼**ar** [10] *vt* disguise. ∼**arse** *vpr*. ∼**arse de** disguise o.s. as

disfrutar *vt* enjoy. ● *vi* enjoy o.s. ∼ **de** enjoy

disgregar [12] *vt* disintegrate

disgust|ar *vt* displease; (*molestar*) annoy. ∼**arse** *vpr* get annoyed, get

upset; ⟨*dos personas*⟩ fall out. ∼**o** *m* annoyance; (*problema*) trouble; (*repugnancia*) disgust; (*riña*) quarrel; (*dolor*) sorrow, grief

disiden|cia *f* disagreement, dissent. ∼**te** *a* & *m* & *f* dissident

disímil *a* (*LAm*) dissimilar

disimular *vt* conceal. ● *vi* pretend

disipa|ción *f* dissipation; (*de dinero*) squandering. ∼**r** *vt* dissipate; (*derrochar*) squander

diskette *m* floppy disk

dislocarse [7] *vpr* dislocate

disminu|ción *f* decrease. ∼**ir** [17] *vi* diminish

disociar *vt* dissociate

disolver [2, *pp* **disuelto**] *vt* dissolve. ∼**se** *vpr* dissolve

disonante *a* dissonant

dispar *a* different

disparar *vt* fire. ● *vi* shoot (**contra** at)

disparat|ado *a* absurd. ∼**ar** *vi* talk nonsense. ∼**e** *m* silly thing; (*error*) mistake. **decir** ∼**es** talk nonsense. **¡qué** ∼**e!** how ridiculous! **un** ∼**e** (*mucho*, *fam*) a lot, an awful lot (*fam*)

disparidad *f* disparity

disparo *m* (*acción*) firing; (*tiro*) shot

dispensar *vt* distribute; (*disculpar*) excuse. **¡Vd dispense!** forgive me

dispers|ar *vt* scatter, disperse. ∼**arse** *vpr* scatter, disperse. ∼**ión** *f* dispersion. ∼**o** *a* scattered

dispon|er [34] *vt* arrange; (*preparar*) prepare. ● *vi*. ∼**er de** have; (*vender etc*) dispose of. ∼**erse** *vpr* get ready. ∼**ibilidad** *f* availability. ∼**ible** *a* available

disposición *f* arrangement; (*aptitud*) talent; (*disponibilidad*) disposal; (*jurid*) order, decree. ∼ **de ánimo** frame of mind. **a la** ∼ **de** at the disposal of. **a su** ∼ at your service

dispositivo *m* device

dispuesto *a* ready; (*hábil*) clever; (*inclinado*) disposed; (*servicial*) helpful

disputa *f* dispute. ∼**r** *vt* dispute. ● *vi*. ∼**r por** argue about; (*competir para*) compete for. **sin** ∼ undoubtedly

distan|cia *f* distance. ∼**ciar** *vt* space out; (*en deportes*) outdistance. ∼**ciarse** *vpr* ⟨*dos personas*⟩ fall out. ∼**te** *a* distant. **a** ∼**cia** from a distance. **guardar las** ∼**cias** keep one's distance

distar *vi* be away; (*fig*) be far. **dista 5 kilómetros** it's 5 kilometres away

distin|ción f distinction. **~guido** a distinguished; (en cartas) Honoured. **~guir** [13] vt/i distinguish. **~guirse** vpr distinguish o.s.; (diferenciarse) differ; (verse) be visible. **~tivo** a distinctive. ● m badge. **~to** a different; (claro) distinct

distorsión f distortion; (med) sprain

distra|cción f amusement; (descuido) absent-mindedness, inattention. **~er** [41] vt distract; (divertir) amuse; embezzle (fondos). ● vi be entertaining. **~erse** vpr amuse o.s.; (descuidarse) not pay attention. **~ído** a amusing; (desatento) absent-minded

distribu|ción f distribution. **~idor** m distributor, agent. **~idor automático** vending machine. **~ir** [17] vt distribute

distrito m district

disturbio m disturbance

disuadir vt dissuade

diurético a & m diuretic

diurno a daytime

divagar [12] vi (al hablar) digress

diván m settee, sofa

diverg|encia f divergence. **~ente** a divergent. **~ir** [14] vi diverge

diversidad f diversity

diversificar [7] vt diversify

diversión f amusement, entertainment; (pasatiempo) pastime

diverso a different

diverti|do a amusing; (que tiene gracia) funny; (agradable) enjoyable. **~r** [4] vt amuse, entertain. **~rse** vpr enjoy o.s.

dividir vt divide; (repartir) share out

divin|idad f divinity. **~o** a divine

divisa f emblem. **~s** fpl foreign exchange

divisar vt make out

divis|ión f division. **~or** m divisor. **~orio** a dividing

divorci|ado a divorced. ● m divorcee. **~ar** vt divorce. **~arse** vpr get divorced. **~o** m divorce

divulgar [12] vt divulge; (propagar) spread. **~se** vpr become known

do m C; (solfa) doh

dobl|adillo m hem; (de pantalón) turn-up (Brit), cuff (Amer). **~ado** a double; (plegado) folded; (película) dubbed. **~ar** vt double; (plegar) fold; (torcer) bend; turn (esquina); dub (película). ● vi turn; (campana) toll. **~arse** vpr double; (encorvarse) bend; (ceder) give in. **~e** a double. ● m

double; (pliegue) fold. **~egar** [12] vt (fig) force to give in. **~egarse** vpr give in. **el ~e** twice as much

doce a & m twelve. **~na** f dozen. **~no** a twelfth

docente a teaching. ● m & f teacher

dócil a obedient

doct|o a learned. **~or** m doctor. **~orado** m doctorate. **~rina** f doctrine

document|ación f documentation, papers. **~al** a & m documentary. **~ar** vt document. **~arse** vpr gather information. **~o** m document. **D~o Nacional de Identidad** national identity card

dogm|a m dogma. **~ático** a dogmatic

dólar m dollar

dol|er [2] vi hurt, ache; (fig) grieve. **me duele la cabeza** my head hurts. **le duele el estómago** he has a pain in his stomach. **~erse** vpr regret; (quejarse) complain. **~or** m pain; (sordo) ache; (fig) sorrow. **~oroso** a painful. **~or de cabeza** headache. **~or de muelas** toothache

domar vt tame; break in (caballo)

dom|esticar [7] vt domesticate. **~éstico** a domestic. ● m servant

domicilio m home. **a ~** at home. **servicio a ~** home delivery service

domina|ción f domination. **~nte** a dominant; (persona) domineering. **~r** vt dominate; (contener) control; (conocer) have a good knowledge of. ● vi dominate; (destacarse) stand out. **~rse** vpr control o.s.

domin|go m Sunday. **~guero** a Sunday. **~ical** a Sunday

dominio m authority; (territorio) domain; (fig) good knowledge

dominó m (juego) dominoes

don m talent, gift; (en un sobre) Mr. **~ Pedro** Pedro. **tener ~ de lenguas** have a gift for languages. **tener ~ de gentes** have a way with people

donación f donation

donaire m grace, charm

dona|nte m (de sangre) donor. **~r** vt donate

doncella f (criada) maid

donde adv where

dónde adv where? **¿hasta ~?** how far? **¿por ~?** whereabouts?; (¿por qué camino?) which way? **¿a ~ vas?** where are you going? **¿de ~ eres?** where are you from?

dondequiera *adv* anywhere; (*en todas partes*) everywhere. ~ **que** wherever. **por** ~ everywhere

doña *f* (*en un sobre*) Mrs. ~ **María** María

dora|do *a* golden; (*cubierto de oro*) gilt. ~**dura** *f* gilding. ~**r** *vt* gilt; (*culin*) brown

dormi|lón *m* sleepyhead. ● *a* lazy. ~**r** [6] *vt* send to sleep. ● *vi* sleep. ~**rse** *vpr* go to sleep. ~**tar** *vi* doze. ~**torio** *m* bedroom. ~**r la siesta** have an afternoon nap, have a siesta. **echarse a dormir** go to bed

dors|al *a* back. ● *m* (*en deportes*) number. ~**o** *m* back

dos *a & m* two. ~**cientos** *a & m* two hundred. **cada** ~ **por tres** every five minutes. **de** ~ **en** ~ in twos, in pairs. **en un** ~ **por tres** in no time. **los dos, las dos** both (of them)

dosi|ficar [7] *vt* dose; (*fig*) measure out. ~**s** *f* dose

dot|ado *a* gifted. ~**ar** *vt* give a dowry; (*proveer*) endow (**de** with). ~**e** *m* dowry

doy *vb véase* **dar**

dragar [12] *vt* dredge

drago *m* dragon tree

dragón *m* dragon

dram|a *m* drama; (*obra de teatro*) play. ~**ático** *a* dramatic. ~**atizar** [10] *vt* dramatize. ~**aturgo** *m* playwright

drástico *a* drastic

droga *f* drug. ~**dicto** *m* drug addict. ~**do** *a* drugged. ● *m* drug addict. ~**r** [12] *vt* drug. ~**rse** *vpr* take drugs. ~**ta** *m & f* (*fam*) drug addict

droguería *f* hardware shop (*Brit*), hardware store (*Amer*)

dromedario *m* dromedary

ducha *f* shower. ~**rse** *vpr* have a shower

dud|a *f* doubt. ~**ar** *vt/i* doubt. ~**oso** *a* doubtful; (*sospechoso*) dubious. **poner en** ~**a** a question. **sin** ~**a** (**alguna**) without a doubt

duelo *m* duel; (*luto*) mourning

duende *m* imp

dueñ|a *f* owner, proprietress; (*de una pensión*) landlady. ~**o** *m* owner, proprietor; (*de una pensión*) landlord

duermo *vb véase* **dormir**

dul|ce *a* sweet; (*agua*) fresh; (*suave*) soft, gentle. ● *m* sweet. ~**zura** *f* sweetness; (*fig*) gentleness

duna *f* dune

dúo *m* duet, duo

duodécimo *a & m* twelfth

duplica|do *a* in duplicate. ● *m* duplicate. ~**r** [7] *vt* duplicate. ~**rse** *vpr* double

duque *m* duke. ~**sa** *f* duchess

dura|ción *f* duration, length. ~**dero** *a* lasting

durante *prep* during, in; (*medida de tiempo*) for. ~ **todo el año** all year round

durar *vi* last

durazno *m* (*LAm, fruta*) peach

dureza *f* hardness, toughness; (*med*) hard patch

durmiente *a* sleeping

duro *a* hard; (*culin*) tough; (*fig*) harsh. ● *adv* hard. ● *m* five-peseta coin. **ser** ~ **de oído** be hard of hearing

E

e *conj* and

ebanista *m & f* cabinet-maker

ébano *m* ebony

ebri|edad *f* drunkenness. ~**o** *a* drunk

ebullición *f* boiling

eccema *m* eczema

eclesiástico *a* ecclesiastical. ● *m* clergyman

eclipse *m* eclipse

eco *m* echo. **hacer(se)** ~ echo

ecolog|ía *f* ecology. ~**ista** *m & f* ecologist

economato *m* cooperative store

econ|omía *f* economy; (*ciencia*) economics. ~**ómicamente** *adv* economically. ~**ómico** *a* economic(al); (*no caro*) inexpensive. ~**omista** *m & f* economist. ~**omizar** [10] *vt/i* economize

ecuación *f* equation

ecuador *m* equator. **el E**~ Ecuador

ecuánime *a* level-headed; (*imparcial*) impartial

ecuanimidad *f* equanimity

ecuatoriano *a & m* Ecuadorian

ecuestre *a* equestrian

echar *vt* throw; post (*carta*); give off (*olor*); pour (*líquido*); sprout (*hojas etc*); (*despedir*) throw out; dismiss (*empleado*); (*poner*) put on; put out (*raíces*); show (*película*). ~**se** *vpr* throw o.s.; (*tumbarse*) lie down. ~ **a** start. ~ **a perder** spoil. ~ **de menos**

miss. ∼se atrás (*fig*) back down. echárselas de feign

edad *f* age. ∼ avanzada old age. E∼ de Piedra Stone Age. E∼ Media Middle Ages. ¿qué ∼ tiene? how old is he?

edición *f* edition; (*publicación*) publication

edicto *m* edict

edific|ación *f* building. ∼ante *a* edifying. ∼ar [7] *vt* build; (*fig*) edify. ● io *m* building; (*fig*) structure

Edimburgo *m* Edinburgh

edit|ar *vt* publish. ∼or *a* publishing. ● *m* publisher. ∼orial *a* editorial. ● *m* leading article. ● *f* publishing house

edredón *m* eiderdown

educa|ción *f* upbringing; (*modales*) (good) manners; (*enseñanza*) education. ∼do *a* polite. ∼dor *m* teacher. ∼r [7] *vt* bring up; (*enseñar*) educate. ∼tivo *a* educational. bien ∼do polite. falta de ∼ción rudeness, bad manners. mal ∼do rude

edulcorante *m* sweetener

EE.UU. *abrev* (*Estados Unidos*) USA, United States (of America)

efect|ivamente *adv* really; (*por supuesto*) indeed. ∼ivo *a* effective; (*auténtico*) real; (*empleo*) permanent. ● *m* cash. ∼o *m* effect; (*impresión*) impression. ∼os *mpl* belongings; (*com*) goods. ∼uar [21] *vt* carry out, effect; make ⟨*viaje, compras etc*⟩. en ∼o in fact; (*por supuesto*) indeed

efervescente *a* effervescent; ⟨*bebidas*⟩ fizzy

efica|cia *f* effectiveness; (*de persona*) efficiency. ∼z *a* effective; ⟨*persona*⟩ efficient

eficien|cia *f* efficiency. ∼te *a* efficient

efigie *f* effigy

efímero *a* ephemeral

efluvio *m* outflow

efusi|ón *n* effusion. ∼vo *a* effusive; ⟨*gracias*⟩ warm

Egeo *m*. mar ∼ Aegean Sea

égida *f* aegis

egipcio *a* & *m* Egyptian

Egipto *m* Egypt

ego|céntrico *a* egocentric. ● *m* egocentric person. ∼ísmo *m* selfishness. ∼ísta *a* selfish. ● *m* selfish person

egregio *a* eminent

egresar *vi* (*LAm*) leave; (*univ*) graduate

eje *m* axis; (*tec*) axle

ejecu|ción *f* execution; (*mus etc*) performance. ∼tante *m* & *f* executor; (*mus etc*) performer. ∼tar *vt* carry out; (*mus etc*) perform; (*matar*) execute

ejecutivo *m* director, manager

ejempl|ar *a* exemplary. ● *m* (*ejemplo*) example, specimen; (*libro*) copy; (*revista*) issue, number. ∼ificar [7] *vt* exemplify. ∼o *m* example. dar ∼o set an example. por ∼o for example. sin ∼ unprecedented

ejerc|er [9] *vt* exercise; practise ⟨*profesión*⟩; exert ⟨*influencia*⟩. ● *vi* practise. ∼icio *m* exercise; (*de una profesión*) practice. ∼itar *vt* exercise. ∼itarse *vpr* exercise. hacer ∼icios take exercise

ejército *m* army

el *art def m* (*pl* los) the. ● *pron* (*pl* los) the one. ∼ de Antonio Antonio's. ∼ que whoever, the one

él *pron* (*persona*) he; (*persona con prep*) him; (*cosa*) it. **el libro de** ∼ his book

elabora|ción *f* processing; (*fabricación*) manufacture. ∼r *vt* process; manufacture ⟨*producto*⟩; (*producir*) produce

el|asticidad *f* elasticity. ∼ástico *a* & *m* elastic

elec|ción *f* choice; (*de político etc*) election. ∼ciones *fpl* (*pol*) election. ∼tor *m* voter. ∼torado *m* electorate. ∼toral *a* electoral

electrici|dad *f* electricity. ∼sta *m* & *f* electrician

eléctrico *a* electric; (*de la electricidad*) electrical

electri|ficar [7] *vt*, **electrizar** [10] *vt* electrify

electrocutar *vt* electrocute

electrodo *m* electrode

electrodoméstico *a* electrical household. ∼s *mpl* electrical household appliances

electrólisis *f* electrolysis

electrón *m* electron

electróni|ca *f* electronics. ∼o *a* electronic

elefante *m* elephant

elegan|cia *f* elegance. ∼te *a* elegant

elegía *f* elegy

elegi|ble *a* eligible. ∼do *a* chosen. ∼r [5 & 14] *vt* choose; (*por votación*) elect

element|al *a* elementary. **~o** *m* element; *(persona)* person, bloke *(fam)*. **~os** *mpl (nociones)* basic principles

elenco *m (en el teatro)* cast

eleva|ción *f* elevation; *(de precios)* rise, increase; *(acción)* raising. **~dor** *m (LAm)* lift. **~r** *vt* raise; *(promover)* promote

elimina|ción *f* elimination. **~r** *vt* eliminate. **~toria** *f* preliminary heat

el|ipse *f* ellipse. **~íptico** *a* elliptical

élite /e'lit, e'lite/ *f* elite

elixir *m* elixir

elocución *f* elocution

elocuen|cia *f* eloquence. **~te** *a* eloquent

elogi|ar *vt* praise. **~o** *m* praise

elote *m (Mex)* corn on the cob

eludir *vt* avoid, elude

ella *pron (persona)* she; *(persona con prep)* her; *(cosa)* it. **~s** *pron pl* they; *(con prep)* them. **el libro de ~** her book. **el libro de ~s** their book

ello *pron* it

ellos *pron pl* they; *(con prep)* them. **el libro de ~** their book

emaciado *a* emaciated

emana|ción *f* emanation. **~r** *vi* emanate *(de* from); *(originarse)* originate *(de* from, in)

emancipa|ción *f* emancipation. **~do** *a* emancipated. **~r** *vt* emancipate. **~rse** *vpr* become emancipated

embadurnar *vt* smear

embajad|a *f* embassy. **~or** *m* ambassador

embalar *vt* pack

embaldosar *vt* tile

embalsamar *vt* embalm

embalse *m* dam; *(pantano)* reservoir

embaraz|ada *a* pregnant. **● f** pregnant woman. **~ar** [10] *vt* hinder. **~o** *m* hindrance; *(de mujer)* pregnancy. **~oso** *a* awkward, embarrassing

embar|cación *f* boat. **~cadero** *m* jetty, pier. **~car** [7] *vt* embark *(personas)*; ship *(mercancías)*. **~carse** *vpr* embark. **~carse en** *(fig)* embark upon

embargo *m* embargo; *(jurid)* seizure. **sin ~** however

embarque *m* loading

embarullar *vt* muddle

embaucar *vt* deceive

embeber *vt* absorb; *(empapar)* soak. **● vi** shrink. **~se** *vpr* be absorbed

embelesar *vt* delight. **~se** *vpr* be delighted

embellecer [11] *vt* embellish

embesti|da *f* attack. **~r** [5] *vt/i* attack

emblema *m* emblem

embobar *vt* amaze

embobecer [11] *vt* make silly. **~se** *vpr* get silly

embocadura *f (de un río)* mouth

emboquillado *a* tipped

embolsar *vt* pocket

emborrachar *vt* get drunk. **~se** *vpr* get drunk

emborrascarse [7] *vpr* get stormy

emborronar *vt* blot

embosca|da *f* ambush. **~rse** [7] *vpr* lie in wait

embotar *vt* blunt; *(fig)* dull

embotella|miento *m (de vehículos)* traffic jam. **~r** *vt* bottle

embrague *m* clutch

embriag|ar [12] *vt* get drunk; *(fig)* intoxicate; *(fig, enajenar)* enrapture. **~arse** *vpr* get drunk. **~uez** *f* drunkenness; *(fig)* intoxication

embrión *m* embryo

embroll|ar *vt* mix up; involve *(personas)*. **~arse** *vpr* get into a muddle; *(en un asunto)* get involved. **~o** *m* tangle; *(fig)* muddle. **~ón** *m* troublemaker

embromar *vt* make fun of; *(engañar)* fool

embruja|do *a* bewitched; *(casa etc)* haunted. **~r** *vt* bewitch

embrutecer [11] *vt* brutalize

embuchar *vt* wolf *(comida)*

embudo *m* funnel

embuste *m* lie. **~ro** *a* deceitful. **● m** liar

embuti|do *m (culin)* sausage. **~r** *vt* stuff

emergencia *f* emergency; *(acción de emerger)* emergence. **en caso de ~** in case of emergency

emerger [14] *vi* appear, emerge; *(submarino)* surface

emigra|ción *f* emigration. **~nte** *m & f* emigrant. **~r** *vi* emigrate

eminen|cia *f* eminence. **~te** *a* eminent

emisario *m* emissary

emis|ión *f* emission; *(de dinero)* issue; *(TV etc)* broadcast. **~or** *a* issuing; *(TV etc)* broadcasting. **~ora** *f* radio station

emitir vt emit; let out ⟨grito⟩; (TV etc) broadcast; ⟨expresar⟩ express; ⟨poner en circulación⟩ issue

emoci|ón f emotion; ⟨excitación⟩ excitement. **~onado** a moved. **~onante** a exciting; ⟨conmovedor⟩ moving. **~onar** vt excite; ⟨conmover⟩ move. **~onarse** vpr get excited; ⟨conmoverse⟩ be moved. **¡qué ~ón!** how exciting!

emotivo a emotional; ⟨conmovedor⟩ moving

empacar [7] vt (LAm) pack

empacho m indigestion; ⟨vergüenza⟩ embarrassment

empadronar vt register. **~se** vpr register

empalagoso a sickly; ⟨demasiado amable⟩ ingratiating; ⟨demasiado sentimental⟩ mawkish

empalizada f fence

empalm|ar vt connect, join. • vi meet. **~e** m junction; ⟨de trenes⟩ connection

empanad|a f ⟨savoury⟩ pie. **~illa** f ⟨small⟩ pie. **~o** a fried in breadcrumbs

empanizado a (Mex) fried in breadcrumbs

empantanar vt flood. **~se** vpr become flooded; (fig) get bogged down

empañar vt mist; dull ⟨metales etc⟩; (fig) tarnish. **~se** vpr ⟨cristales⟩ steam up

empapar vt soak; ⟨absorber⟩ soak up. **~se** vpr be soaked

empapela|do m wallpaper. **~r** vt paper; ⟨envolver⟩ wrap (in paper)

empaquetar vt package; pack together ⟨personas⟩

emparedado m sandwich

emparejar vt match; ⟨nivelar⟩ make level. **~se** vpr pair off

empast|ar vt fill ⟨muela⟩. **~e** m filling

empat|ar vi draw. **~e** m draw

empedernido a inveterate; ⟨insensible⟩ hard

empedrar [1] vt pave

empeine m instep

empeñ|ado a in debt; ⟨decidido⟩ determined; ⟨acalorado⟩ heated. **~ar** vt pawn; pledge ⟨palabras⟩; ⟨principiar⟩ start. **~arse** vpr ⟨endeudarse⟩ get into debt; ⟨meterse⟩ get involved; ⟨estar decidido a⟩ insist (en on). **~o** m pledge; ⟨resolución⟩ determination. **casa de ~s** pawnshop

empeorar vt make worse. • vi get worse. **~se** vpr get worse

empequeñecer [11] vt dwarf; (fig) belittle

empera|dor m emperor. **~triz** f empress

empezar [1 & 10] vt/i start, begin. **para ~** to begin with

empina|do a upright; ⟨cuesta⟩ steep. **~r** vt raise. **~rse** vpr ⟨persona⟩ stand on tiptoe; ⟨animal⟩ rear

empírico a empirical

emplasto m plaster

emplaza|miento m ⟨jurid⟩ summons; ⟨lugar⟩ site. **~r** [10] vt summon; ⟨situar⟩ site

emple|ado m employee. **~ar** vt use; employ ⟨persona⟩; spend ⟨tiempo⟩. **~arse** vpr be used; ⟨persona⟩ be employed. **~o** m use; ⟨trabajo⟩ employment; ⟨puesto⟩ job

empobrecer [11] vt impoverish. **~se** vpr become poor

empolvar vt powder

empoll|ar vt incubate ⟨huevos⟩; ⟨estudiar, fam⟩ swot up (Brit), grind away at (Amer). • vi ⟨ave⟩ sit; ⟨estudiante⟩ swot (Brit), grind away (Amer). **~ón** m swot

emponzoñar vt poison

emporio m emporium; ⟨LAm, almacén⟩ department store

empotra|do a built-in, fitted. **~r** vt fit

emprendedor a enterprising

emprender vt undertake; set out on ⟨viaje etc⟩. **~la con uno** pick a fight with s.o.

empresa f undertaking; (com) company, firm. **~rio** m impresario; (com) contractor

empréstito m loan

empuj|ar vt push; press ⟨botón⟩. **~e** m push, shove; (fig) drive. **~ón** m push, shove

empuñar vt grasp; take up ⟨pluma, espada⟩

emular vt emulate

emulsión f emulsion

en prep in; ⟨sobre⟩ on; ⟨dentro⟩ inside, in; ⟨con dirección⟩ into; ⟨medio de transporte⟩ by. **~ casa** at home. **~ coche** by car. **~ 10 días** in 10 days. **de pueblo ~ pueblo** from town to town

enagua f petticoat

enajena|ción f alienation; ⟨éxtasis⟩ rapture. **~r** vt alienate; ⟨volver loco⟩

drive mad; *(fig, extasiar)* enrapture. ~ción mental insanity

enamora|do *a* in love. ● *m* lover. ~r *vt* win the love of. ~rse *vpr* fall in love (de with)

enan|ito *m* dwarf. ~o a & *m* dwarf

enardecer [11] *vt* inflame. ~se *vpr* get excited (por about)

encabeza|miento *m* heading; *(de periódico)* headline. ~r [10] *vt* introduce *(escrito)*; *(poner título a)* entitle; head *(una lista)*; lead *(revolución etc)*; *(empadronar)* register

encadenar *vt* chain; *(fig)* tie down

encaj|ar *vt* fit; fit together *(varias piezas)*. ● *vi* fit; *(estar de acuerdo)* tally. ~arse *vpr* squeeze into. ~e *m* lace; *(acción de encajar)* fitting

encajonar *vt* box; *(en sitio estrecho)* squeeze in

encalar *vt* whitewash

encallar *vt* run aground; *(fig)* get bogged down

encaminar *vt* direct. ~se *vpr* make one's way

encandilar *vt (pasmar)* bewilder; *(estimular)* stimulate

encanecer [11] *vi* go grey

encant|ado *a* enchanted; *(hechizado)* bewitched; *(casa etc)* haunted. ~ador *a* charming. ● *m* magician. ~amiento *m* magic. ~ar *vt* bewitch; *(fig)* charm, delight. ~o *m* magic; *(fig)* delight. ¡~ado! pleased to meet you! me ~a la leche I love milk

encapotado *a (cielo)* overcast

encapricharse *vpr*. ~ con take a fancy to

encarar *vt* face. ~se *vpr*. ~se con face

encarcelar *vt* imprison

encarecer [11] *vt* put up the price of; *(alabar)* praise. ● *vi* go up

encarg|ado *a* in charge. ● *m* manager, attendant, person in charge. ~ar [12] *vt* entrust; *(pedir)* order. ~arse *vpr* take charge (de of). ~o *m* job; *(com)* order; *(recado)* errand. hecho de ~o made to measure

encariñarse *vpr*. ~ con take to, become fond of

encarna|ción *f* incarnation. ~do *a* incarnate; *(rojo)* red. ● *m* red

encarnizado *a* bitter

encarpetar *vt* file; *(LAm, dar carpetazo)* shelve

encarrilar *vt* put back on the rails; *(fig)* direct, put on the right road

encasillar *vt* pigeonhole

encastillarse *vpr*. ~ en *(fig)* stick to

encauzar [10] *vt* channel

encend|edor *m* lighter. ~er [1] *vt* light; *(pegar fuego a)* set fire to; switch on, turn on *(aparato eléctrico)*; *(fig)* arouse. ~erse *vpr* light; *(prender fuego)* catch fire; *(excitarse)* get excited; *(ruborizarse)* blush. ~ido *a* lit; *(aparato eléctrico)* on; *(rojo)* bright red. ● *m (auto)* ignition

encera|do *a* waxed. ● *m (pizarra)* blackboard. ~r *vt* wax

encerr|ar [1] *vt* shut in; *(con llave)* lock up; *(fig, contener)* contain. ~ona *f* trap

encía *f* gum

encíclica *f* encyclical

enciclop|edia *f* encyclopaedia. ~édico *a* encyclopaedic

encierro *m* confinement; *(cárcel)* prison

encima *adv* on top; *(arriba)* above. ~ de on, on top of; *(sobre)* over; *(además de)* besides, as well as. por ~ on top; *(a la ligera)* superficially. por ~ de todo above all

encina *f* holm oak

encinta *a* pregnant

enclave *m* enclave

enclenque *a* weak; *(enfermizo)* sickly

encog|er [14] *vt* shrink; *(contraer)* contract. ~erse *vpr* shrink. ~erse de hombros shrug one's shoulders. ~ido *a* shrunk; *(fig, tímido)* timid

encolar *vt* glue; *(pegar)* stick

encolerizar [10] *vt* make angry. ~se *vpr* get angry, lose one's temper

encomendar [1] *vt* entrust

encomi|ar *vt* praise. ~o *m* praise

encono *m* bitterness, ill will

encontra|do *a* contrary, conflicting. ~r [2] *vt* find; *(tropezar con)* meet. ~rse *vpr* meet; *(hallarse)* be. no ~rse feel uncomfortable

encorvar *vt* bend, curve. ~se *vpr* stoop

encrespado *a (pelo)* curly; *(mar)* rough

encrucijada *f* crossroads

encuaderna|ción *f* binding. ~dor *m* bookbinder. ~r *vt* bind

encuadrar *vt* frame

encub|ierto *a* hidden. ~rir [pp encubierto] *vt* hide, conceal; shelter *(delincuente)*

encuentro *m* meeting; *(colisión)* crash; *(en deportes)* match; *(mil)* skirmish

encuesta *f* survey; *(investigación)* inquiry

encumbra|do *a* eminent. **~r** *vt* *(fig, elevar)* exalt. **~rse** *vpr* rise

encurtidos *mpl* pickles

encharcar [7] *vt* flood. **~se** *vpr* be flooded

enchuf|ado *a* switched on. **~ar** *vt* plug in; fit together *(tubos etc)*. **~e** *m* socket; *(clavija)* plug; *(de tubos etc)* joint; *(fig, empleo, fam)* cushy job; *(influencia, fam)* influence. **tener ~e** have friends in the right places

endeble *a* weak

endemoniado *a* possessed; *(malo)* wicked

enderezar [10] *vt* straighten out; *(poner vertical)* put upright (again); *(fig, arreglar)* put right, sort out; *(dirigir)* direct. **~se** *vpr* straighten out

endeudarse *vpr* get into debt

endiablado *a* possessed; *(malo)* wicked

endomingarse [12] *vpr* dress up

endosar *vt* endorse *(cheque etc)*; *(fig, fam)* lumber

endrogarse [12] *vpr* *(Mex)* get into debt

endulzar [10] *vt* sweeten; *(fig)* soften

endurecer [11] *vt* harden. **~se** *vpr* harden; *(fig)* become hardened

enema *m* enema

enemi|go *a* hostile. ● *m* enemy. **~stad** *f* enmity. **~star** *vt* make an enemy of. **~starse** *vpr* fall out (con with)

en|ergía *f* energy. **~érgico** *a* *(persona)* lively; *(decisión)* forceful

energúmeno *m* madman

enero *m* January

enervar *vt* enervate

enésimo *a* nth, umpteenth *(fam)*

enfad|adizo *a* irritable. **~ado** *a* cross, angry. **~ar** *vt* make cross, anger; *(molestar)* annoy. **~arse** *vpr* get cross. **~o** *m* anger; *(molestia)* annoyance

énfasis *m invar* emphasis, stress. **poner ~** stress, emphasize

enfático *a* emphatic

enferm|ar *vi* fall ill. **~edad** *f* illness. **~era** *f* nurse. **~ería** *f* sick bay. **~ero** *m* (male) nurse. **~izo** *a* sickly. **~o** *a* ill. ● *m* patient

enflaquecer [11] *vt* make thin. ● *vi* lose weight

enfo|car [7] *vt* shine on; focus *(lente etc)*; *(fig)* consider. **~que** *m* focus; *(fig)* point of view

enfrascarse [7] *vpr* *(fig)* be absorbed

enfrentar *vt* face, confront; *(poner frente a frente)* bring face to face. **~se** *vpr*. **~se con** confront; *(en deportes)* meet

enfrente *adv* opposite. **~ de** opposite. **de ~** opposite

enfria|miento *m* cooling; *(catarro)* cold. **~r** [20] *vt* cool (down); *(fig)* cool down. **~rse** *vpr* go cold; *(fig)* cool off

enfurecer [11] *vt* infuriate. **~se** *vpr* lose one's temper; *(mar)* get rough

enfurruñarse *vpr* sulk

engalanar *vt* adorn. **~se** *vpr* dress up

enganchar *vt* hook; hang up *(ropa)*. **~se** *vpr* get caught; *(mil)* enlist

engañ|ar *vt* deceive, trick; *(ser infiel)* be unfaithful. **~arse** *vpr* be wrong, be mistaken; *(no admitir la verdad)* deceive o.s. **~o** *m* deceit, trickery; *(error)* mistake. **~oso** *a* deceptive; *(persona)* deceitful

engarzar [10] *vt* string *(cuentas)*; set *(joyas)*; *(fig)* link

engatusar *vt* *(fam)* coax

engendr|ar *vt* breed; *(fig)* produce. **~o** *m* *(monstruo)* monster; *(fig)* brainchild

englobar *vt* include

engomar *vt* glue

engordar *vt* fatten. ● *vi* get fatter, put on weight

engorro *m* nuisance

engranaje *m* *(auto)* gear

engrandecer [11] *vt* *(enaltecer)* exalt, raise

engrasar *vt* grease; *(con aceite)* oil; *(ensuciar)* make greasy

engreído *a* arrogant

engrosar [2] *vt* swell. ● *vi* *(persona)* get fatter; *(río)* swell

engullir [22] *vt* gulp down

enharinar *vt* sprinkle with flour

enhebrar *vt* thread

enhorabuena *f* congratulations. **dar la ~** congratulate

enigm|a *m* enigma. **~ático** *a* enigmatic

enjabonar *vt* soap; *(fig, fam)* butter up

enjalbegar [12] *vt* whitewash

enjambre *m* swarm

enjaular vt put in a cage

enjuag|ar [12] vt rinse (out). ∼**a-torio** m mouthwash. ∼**ue** m rinsing; (para la boca) mouthwash

enjugar [12] vt dry; (limpiar) wipe; cancel (deuda)

enjuiciar vt pass judgement on

enjuto a (persona) skinny

enlace m connection; (matrimonial) wedding

enlatar vt tin, can

enlazar [10] vt tie together; (fig) relate, connect

enlodar vt, **enlodazar** [10] vt cover in mud

enloquecer [11] vt drive mad. ● vi go mad. ∼**se** vpr go mad

enlosar vt (con losas) pave; (con baldosas) tile

enlucir [11] vt plaster

enluta|do a in mourning. ∼**r** vt dress in mourning; (fig) sadden

enmarañar vt tangle (up), entangle; (confundir) confuse. ∼**se** vpr get into a tangle; (confundirse) get confused

enmarcar [7] vt frame

enmascarar vt mask. ∼**se de** masquerade as

enm|endar vt correct. ∼**endarse** vpr mend one's way. ∼**ienda** f correction; (de ley etc) amendment

enmohecerse [11] vpr (con óxido) go rusty; (con hongos) go mouldy

enmudecer [11] vi be dumbstruck; (callar) say nothing

ennegrecer [11] vt blacken

ennoblecer [11] vt ennoble; (fig) add style to

enoj|adizo a irritable. ∼**ado** a angry, cross. ∼**ar** vt make cross, anger; (molestar) annoy. ∼**arse** vpr get cross. ∼**o** m anger; (molestia) annoyance. ∼**oso** a annoying

enorgullecerse [11] vpr be proud

enorm|e a enormous; (malo) wicked. ∼**emente** adv enormously. ∼**idad** f immensity; (atrocidad) enormity. **me gusta una** ∼**idad** I like it enormously

enrabiar vt infuriate

enraizar [10 & 20] vi take root

enrarecido a rarefied

enrasar vt make level

enred|adera f creeper. ∼**adero** a climbing. ∼**ar** vt tangle (up), entangle; (confundir) confuse; (comprometer a uno) involve, implicate; (sembrar la discordia) cause trouble

between. ● vi get up to mischief. ∼**ar con** fiddle with, play with. ∼**arse** vpr get into a tangle; (confundirse) get confused; (persona) get involved. ∼**o** m tangle; (fig) muddle, mess

enrejado m bars

enrevesado a complicated

enriquecer [11] vt make rich; (fig) enrich. ∼**se** vpr get rich

enrojecer [11] vt turn red, redden. ∼**se** vpr (persona) go red, blush

enrolar vt enlist

enrollar vt roll (up); wind (hilo etc)

enroscar [7] vt coil; (atornillar) screw in

ensalad|a f salad. ∼**era** f salad bowl. ∼**illa** f Russian salad. **armar una** ∼**a** make a mess

ensalzar [10] vt praise; (enaltecer) exalt

ensambladura f, **ensamblaje** m (acción) assembling; (efecto) joint

ensamblar vt join

ensanch|ar vt widen; (agrandar) enlarge. ∼**arse** vpr get wider. ∼**e** m widening; (de ciudad) new district

ensangrentar [1] vt stain with blood

ensañarse vpr. ∼ **con** treat cruelly

ensartar vt string (cuentas etc)

ensay|ar vt test; rehearse (obra de teatro etc). ∼**arse** vpr rehearse. ∼**o** m test, trial; (composición literaria) essay

ensenada f inlet, cove

enseña|nza f education; (acción de enseñar) teaching. ∼**nza media** secondary education. ∼**r** vt teach; (mostrar) show

enseñorearse vpr take over

enseres mpl equipment

ensillar vt saddle

ensimismarse vpr be lost in thought

ensoberbecerse [11] vpr become conceited

ensombrecer [11] vt darken

ensordecer [11] vt deafen. ● vi go deaf

ensortijar vt curl (pelo etc)

ensuciar vt dirty. ∼**se** vpr get dirty

ensueño m dream

entablar vt (empezar) start

entablillar vt put in a splint

entalegar [12] vt put into a bag; (fig) hoard

entallar vt fit (un vestido). ● vi fit

entarimado m parquet

ente m entity, being; (persona rara, fam) odd person; (com) firm, company

entend|er [1] vt understand; (*opinar*) believe, think; (*querer decir*) mean. ● vi understand. **~erse** vpr make o.s. understood; (*comprenderse*) be understood. **~er de** know all about. **~erse con** get on with. **~ido** a understood; (*enterado*) well-informed. ● interj agreed!, OK! (*fam*). **~i-miento** m understanding. **a mi ~er** in my opinion. **dar a ~er** hint. **no darse por ~ido** pretend not to understand, turn a deaf ear

entenebrecer [11] vt darken. **~se** vpr get dark

enterado a well-informed; (*que sabe*) aware. **no darse por ~** pretend not to understand, turn a deaf ear

enteramente adv entirely, completely

enterar vt inform. **~se** vpr. **~se de** find out about, hear of. **¡entérate!** listen! **¿te enteras?** do you understand?

entereza f (*carácter*) strength of character

enternecer [11] vt (*fig*) move, touch. **~se** vpr be moved, be touched

entero a entire, whole; (*firme*) firm. **por ~** entirely, completely

enterra|dor m gravedigger. **~r** [1] vt bury

entibiar vt cool. **~se** vpr cool down; (*fig*) cool off

entidad f entity; (*organización*) organization; (*com*) company

entierro m burial; (*ceremonia*) funeral

entona|ción f intonation; (*fig*) arrogance. **~r** vt intone. ● vi (*mus*) be in tune; (*colores*) match. **~rse** vpr (*fortalecerse*) tone o.s. up; (*engreírse*) be arrogant

entonces adv then. **en aquel ~, por aquel ~** at that time, then

entontecer [11] vt make silly. **~se** vpr get silly

entornar vt half close; leave ajar (*puerta*)

entorpecer [11] vt (*frío etc*) numb; (*dificultar*) hinder

entra|da f entrance; (*acceso*) admission, entry; (*billete*) ticket; (*de datos, tec*) input. **~do** a. **~do en años** elderly. **ya ~da la noche** late at night. **~nte** a next, coming. **dar ~da a** (*admitir*) admit. **de ~da** right away.

entraña f (*fig*) heart. **~s** fpl entrails; (*fig*) heart. **~ble** a (*cariño etc*) deep; (*amigo*) close. **~r** vt involve

entrar vt put; (*traer*) bring. ● vi go in, enter; (*venir*) come in, enter; (*empezar*) start, begin. **no ~ ni salir en** have nothing to do with

entre prep (*de dos personas o cosas*) between; (*más de dos*) among(st)

entreab|ierto a half-open. **~rir** [pp entreabierto] vt half open

entreacto m interval

entrecano a (*pelo*) greying; (*persona*) who is going grey

entrecejo m forehead. **arrugar el ~, fruncir el ~** frown

entrecerrar [1] vt (*Amer*) half close

entrecortado a (*voz*) faltering; (*respiración*) laboured

entrecruzar [10] vt intertwine

entrega f handing over; (*de mercancías etc*) delivery; (*de novela etc*) instalment; (*dedicación*) commitment. **~r** [12] vt hand over, deliver, give. **~rse** vpr surrender, give o.s. up; (*dedicarse*) devote o.s (a to)

entrelazar [10] vt intertwine

entremés m hors-d'oeuvre; (*en el teatro*) short comedy

entremet|er vt insert. **~erse** vpr interfere. **~ido** a interfering

entremezclar vt mix

entrena|dor m trainer. **~miento** m training. **~r** vt train. **~rse** vpr train

entrepierna f crotch

entresacar [7] vt pick out

entresuelo m mezzanine

entretanto adv meanwhile

entretejer vt interweave

entreten|er [40] vt entertain, amuse; (*detener*) delay, keep; (*mantener*) keep alive, keep going. **~erse** vpr amuse o.s.; (*tardar*) delay, linger. **~ido** a entertaining. **~imiento** m entertainment; (*mantenimiento*) upkeep

entrever [43] vt make out, glimpse

entrevista f interview; (*reunión*) meeting. **~rse** vpr have an interview

entristecer [11] vt sadden, make sad. **~se** vpr be sad

entromet|erse vpr interfere. **~ido** a interfering

entroncar [7] vi be related

entruchada f, **entruchado** m (*fam*) plot

entumec|erse [11] vpr go numb. **~ido** a numb

enturbiar *vt* cloud

entusi|asmar *vt* fill with enthusiasm; *(gustar mucho)* delight. ~**asmarse** *vpr*. ~**asmarse con** get enthusiastic about; *(ser aficionado a)* be mad about, love. ~**asmo** *m* enthusiasm. ~**asta** *a* enthusiastic. ● *m & f* enthusiast. ~**ástico** *a* enthusiastic

enumera|ción *f* count, reckoning. ~**r** *vt* enumerate

enuncia|ción *f* enunciation. ~**r** *vt* enunciate

envainar *vt* sheathe

envalentonar *vt* encourage. ~**se** *vpr* be brave, pluck up courage

envanecer [11] *vt* make conceited. ~**se** *vpr* be conceited

envas|ado *a* tinned. ● *m* packaging. ~**ar** *vt* package; *(en latas)* tin, can; *(en botellas)* bottle. ~**e** *m* packing; *(lata)* tin, can; *(botella)* bottle

envejec|er [11] *vt* make old. ● *vi* get old, grow old. ~**erse** *vpr* get old, grow old. ~**ido** *a* aged, old

envenenar *vt* poison

envergadura *f (alcance)* scope

envés *m* wrong side

envia|do *a* sent. ● *m* representative; *(de la prensa)* correspondent. ~**r** *vt* send

enviciar *vt* corrupt

envidi|a *f* envy; *(celos)* jealousy. ~**able** *a* enviable. ~**ar** *vt* envy, be envious of. ~**oso** *a* envious. **tener** ~**a a** envy

envilecer [11] *vt* degrade

envío *m* sending, dispatch; *(de mercancías)* consignment; *(de dinero)* remittance. ~ **contra reembolso** cash on delivery. **gastos** *mpl* **de** ~ postage and packing (costs)

enviudar *vi* ⟨*mujer*⟩ become a widow, be widowed; ⟨*hombre*⟩ become a widower, be widowed

env|oltura *f* wrapping. ~**olver** [2, *pp* **envuelto**] *vt* wrap; *(cubrir)* cover; *(fig, acorralar)* corner; *(fig, enredar)* involve; *(mil)* surround. ~**olvimiento** *m* involvement. ~**uelto** *a* wrapped (up)

enyesar *vt* plaster; *(med)* put in plaster

enzima *f* enzyme

épica *f* epic

epicentro *m* epicentre

épico *a* epic

epid|emia *f* epidemic. ~**émico** *a* epidemic

epil|epsia *f* epilepsy. ~**éptico** *a* epileptic

epílogo *m* epilogue

episodio *m* episode

epístola *f* epistle

epitafio *m* epitaph

epíteto *m* epithet

epítome *m* epitome

época *f* age; *(período)* period. **hacer** ~ make history, be epoch-making

equidad *f* equity

equilátero *a* equilateral

equilibr|ar *vt* balance. ~**io** *m* balance; *(de balanza)* equilibrium. ~**ista** *m & f* tightrope walker

equino *a* horse, equine

equinoccio *m* equinox

equipaje *m* luggage *(esp Brit)*, baggage *(esp Amer)*; *(de barco)* crew

equipar *vt* equip; *(de ropa)* fit out

equiparar *vt* make equal; *(comparar)* compare

equipo *m* equipment; *(en deportes)* team

equitación *f* riding

equivale|ncia *f* equivalence. ~**nte** *a* equivalent. ~**r** [42] *vi* be equivalent; *(significar)* mean

equivoca|ción *f* mistake, error. ~**do** *a* wrong. ~**r** [7] *vt* mistake. ~**rse** *vpr* be mistaken, be wrong, make a mistake. ~**rse de** be wrong about. ~**rse de número** dial the wrong number. **si no me equivoco** if I'm not mistaken

equívoco *a* equivocal; *(sospechoso)* suspicious. ● *m* ambiguity; *(juego de palabras)* pun; *(doble sentido)* double meaning

era *f* era. ● *vb* véase **ser**

erario *m* treasury

erección *f* erection; *(fig)* establishment

eremita *m* hermit

eres *vb* véase **ser**

erguir [48] *vt* raise. ~ **la cabeza** hold one's head high. ~**se** *vpr* straighten up

erigir [14] *vt* erect. ~**se** *vpr* set o.s. up (en as)

eriza|do *a* prickly. ~**rse** [10] *vpr* stand on end

erizo *m* hedgehog; *(de mar)* sea urchin. ~ **de mar**, ~ **marino** sea urchin

ermita *f* hermitage. ~**ño** *m* hermit

erosi|ón f erosion. **~onar** vt erode

er|ótico a erotic. **~otismo** m eroticism

errar [1, la i inicial se escribe y] vt miss. ● vi wander; (equivocarse) make a mistake, be wrong

errata f misprint

erróneo a erroneous, wrong

error m error, mistake. **estar en un ~** be wrong, be mistaken

eructar vi belch

erudi|ción f learning, erudition. **~to** a learned

erupción f eruption; (med) rash

es vb véase **ser**

esa a véase **ese**

ésa pron véase **ése**

esbelto a slender, slim

esboz|ar [10] vt sketch, outline. **~o** m sketch, outline

escabeche m pickle. **en ~** pickled

escabroso a (terreno) rough; (asunto) difficult; (atrevido) crude

escabullirse [22] vpr slip away

escafandra f, **escafandro** m diving-suit

escala f scale; (escalera de mano) ladder; (de avión) stopover. **~da** f climbing; (pol) escalation. **~r** vt scale; break into (una casa). ● vi (pol) escalate. **hacer ~ en** stop at. **vuelo sin ~s** non-stop flight

escaldar vt scald

escalera f staircase, stairs; (de mano) ladder. **~ de caracol** spiral staircase. **~ de incendios** fire escape. **~ mecánica** escalator. **~ plegable** step-ladder

escalfa|do a poached. **~r** vt poach

escalinata f flight of steps

escalofrío m shiver

escal|ón m step; (de escalera interior) stair; (de escala) rung. **~onar** vt spread out

escalope m escalope

escam|a f scale; (de jabón) flake; (fig) suspicion. **~oso** a scaly

escamotear vt make disappear; (robar) steal, pinch (fam); disregard (dificultad)

escampar vi stop raining

esc|andalizar [10] vt scandalize, shock. **~andalizarse** vpr be shocked. **~ándalo** m scandal; (alboroto) uproar. **~andaloso** a scandalous; (alborotador) noisy

Escandinavia f Scandinavia

escandinavo a & m Scandinavian

escaño m bench; (pol) seat

escapa|da f escape; (visita) flying visit. **~do a** in a hurry. **~r** vi escape. **~rse** vpr escape; (líquido, gas) leak. **dejar ~r** let out

escaparate m (shop) window. **ir de ~s** go window-shopping

escapatoria f (fig, fam) way out

escape m (de gas, de líquido) leak; (fuga) escape; (auto) exhaust

escarabajo m beetle

escaramuza f skirmish

escarbar vt scratch; pick (dientes, herida etc); (fig, escudriñar) delve (en into)

escarcha f frost. **~do a** (fruta) crystallized

escarlat|a a invar scarlet. **~ina** f scarlet fever

escarm|entar [1] vt punish severely. ● vi learn one's lesson. **~iento** m punishment; (lección) lesson

escarn|ecer [11] vt mock. **~io** m ridicule

escarola f endive

escarpa f slope. **~do a** steep

escas|ear vi be scarce. **~ez** f scarcity, shortage; (pobreza) poverty. **~o** a scarce; (poco) little; (insuficiente) short; (muy justo) barely

escatimar vt be sparing with

escayola f plaster. **~r** vt put in plaster

escena f scene; (escenario) stage. **~rio** m stage; (en el cine) scenario; (fig) scene

escénico a scenic

escenografía f scenery

esc|epticismo m scepticism. **~éptico** a sceptical. ● m sceptic

esclarecer [11] vt (fig) throw light on, clarify

esclavina f cape

esclav|itud f slavery. **~izar** [10] vt enslave. **~o** m slave

esclerosis f sclerosis

esclusa f lock

escoba f broom

escocer [2 & 9] vt hurt. ● vi sting

escocés a Scottish. ● m Scotsman

Escocia f Scotland

escog|er [14] vt choose, select. **~ido** a chosen; (de buena calidad) choice

escolar a school. ● m schoolboy. ● f schoolgirl. **~idad** f schooling

escolta f escort

escombros mpl rubble

escond|er vt hide. **~erse** vpr hide. **~idas, a ~idas** secretly. **~ite** m hiding place; (juego) hide-and-seek. **~rijo** m hiding place

escopeta f shotgun. **~zo** m shot

escoplo m chisel

escoria f slag; (fig) dregs

Escorpión m Scorpio

escorpión m scorpion

escot|ado a low-cut. **~adura** f low neckline. **~ar** vt cut out. ● vi pay one's share. **~e** m low neckline. **ir a ~e, pagar a ~e** share the expenses

escozor m pain

escri|bano m clerk. **~biente** m clerk. **~bir** [pp **escrito**] vt/i write. **~bir a máquina** type. **~birse** vpr write to each other; (deletrearse) be spelt. **~to** a written. ● m writing; (documento) document. **~tor** m writer. **~torio** m desk; (oficina) office. **~tura** f (hand)writing; (documento) document; (jurid) deed. **¿cómo se escribe...?** how do you spell...? **poner por ~to** put into writing

escr|úpulo m scruple; (escrupulosidad) care, scrupulousness. **~upuloso** a scrupulous

escrut|ar vt scrutinize; count (votos). **~inio** m count. **hacer el ~inio** count the votes

escuadr|a f (instrumento) square; (mil) squad; (naut) fleet. **~ón** m squadron

escuálido a skinny; (sucio) squalid

escuchar vt listen to. ● vi listen

escudilla f bowl

escudo m shield. **~ de armas** coat of arms

escudriñar vt examine

escuela f school. **~ normal** teachers' training college

escueto a simple

escuincle m (Mex, perro) stray dog; (Mex, muchacho, fam) child, kid (fam)

escul|pir vt sculpture. **~tor** m sculptor. **~tora** f sculptress. **~tura** f sculpture; (en madera) carving

escupir vt/i spit

escurr|eplatos m invar plate-rack. **~idizo** a slippery. **~ir** vt drain; wring out (ropa). ● vi drip; (ser resbaladizo) be slippery. **~irse** vpr slip

ese a (f **esa**, mpl **esos**, fpl **esas**) that; (en plural) those

ése pron (f **ésa**, mpl **ésos**, fpl **ésas**) that one; (en plural) those; (primero de dos) the former. **ni por ésas** on no account

esencia f essence. **~l** a essential. **lo ~l** the main thing

esf|era f sphere; (de reloj) face. **~érico** a spherical

esfinge f sphinx

esf|orzarse [2 & 10] vpr make an effort. **~uerzo** m effort

esfumarse vpr fade away; (persona) vanish

esgrim|a f fencing. **~ir** vt brandish; (fig) use

esguince m swerve; (med) sprain

eslab|ón m link. **~onar** vt link (together)

eslavo a Slav, Slavonic

eslogan m slogan

esmalt|ar vt enamel; varnish (uñas); (fig) adorn. **~e** m enamel. **~e de uñas, ~e para las uñas** nail varnish (Brit), nail polish (Amer)

esmerado a careful

esmeralda f emerald

esmerarse vpr take care (**en** over)

esmeril m emery

esmero m care

esmoquin m dinner jacket, tuxedo (Amer)

esnob a invar snobbish. ● m & f (pl **esnobs**) snob. **~ismo** m snobbery

esnórkel m snorkel

eso pron that. **¡~ es!** that's it! **~ mismo** exactly. **¡~ no!** certainly not! **¡~ sí!** of course. **a ~ de** about. **en ~** at that moment. **¿no es ~?** isn't that right? **por ~** therefore. **y ~ que** although

esos a pl véase **ese**

ésos pron pl véase **ése**

espabila|do a bright. **~r** vt snuff (vela); (avivar) brighten up; (despertar) wake up. **~rse** vpr wake up; (apresurarse) hurry up

espaci|al a space. **~ar** vt space out. **~o** m space. **~oso** a spacious

espada f sword. **~s** fpl (en naipes) spades

espagueti m spaghetti

espald|a f back. **~illa** f shoulder-blade. **a ~as de uno** behind s.o.'s back. **a las ~as on** on s.o.'s back. **tener las ~as anchas** be broad-shouldered. **volver la ~a a uno, volver las ~as a uno** give s.o. the cold shoulder

espant|ada f stampede. **~adizo** a timid, timorous. **~ajo** m, **~apájaros** m invar scarecrow. **~ar** vt frighten; (ahuyentar) frighten away. **~arse** vpr be frightened; (ahuyentarse) be frightened away. **~o** m terror; (horror) horror. **~oso** a frightening; (muy grande) terrible. **¡qué ~ajo!** what a sight!

España f Spain

español a Spanish. ● m (persona) Spaniard; (lengua) Spanish. **los ~es** the Spanish. **~izado** a Hispanicized

esparadrapo m sticking-plaster, plaster (Brit)

esparci|do a scattered; (fig) widespread. **~r** [9] vt scatter; (difundir) spread. **~rse** vpr be scattered; (divertirse) enjoy o.s.

espárrago m asparagus

esparto m esparto (grass)

espasm|o m spasm. **~ódico** a spasmodic

espátula f spatula; (en pintura) palette knife

especia f spice

especial a special. **~idad** f speciality (Brit), specialty (Amer). **~ista** a & m & f specialist. **~ización** f specialization. **~izar** [10] vt specialize. **~izarse** vpr specialize. **~mente** adv especially. **en ~** especially

especie f kind, sort; (en biología) species; (noticia) piece of news. **en ~** in kind

especifica|ción f specification. **~r** [7] vt specify

específico a specific

espect|áculo m sight; (diversión) entertainment, show. **~ador** m & f spectator. **~acular** a spectacular

espectro m spectre; (en física) spectrum

especula|ción f speculation. **~dor** m speculator. **~r** vi speculate. **~tivo** a speculative

espej|ismo m mirage. **~o** m mirror. **~o retrovisor** (auto) rear-view mirror

espeleólogo m potholer

espeluznante a horrifying

espera f wait. **sala f de ~** waiting room

espera|nza f hope. **~r** vt hope; (aguardar) wait for; (creer) expect. ● vi hope; (aguardar) wait. **~r en uno** trust in s.o. **en ~ de** awaiting. **espero**

que no I hope not. **espero que sí** I hope so

esperma f sperm

esperpento m fright; (disparate) nonsense

espes|ar vt thicken. **~arse** vpr thicken. **~o** a thick; (pasta etc) stiff. **~or** m, **~ura** f thickness; (bot) thicket

espetón m spit

esp|ía f spy. **~iar** [20] vt spy on. ● vi spy

espiga f (de trigo etc) ear

espina f thorn; (de pez) bone; (dorsal) spine; (astilla) splinter; (fig, dificultad) difficulty. **~ dorsal** spine

espinaca f spinach

espinazo m spine

espinilla f shin; (med) blackhead

espino m hawthorn. **~ artificial** barbed wire. **~so** a thorny; (pez) bony; (fig) difficult

espionaje m espionage

espiral a & f spiral

espirar vt/i breathe out

esp|iritismo m spiritualism. **~iritoso** a spirited. **~iritista** m & f spiritualist. **~íritu** m spirit; (mente) mind; (inteligencia) intelligence. **~iritual** a spiritual. **~iritualismo** m spiritualism

espita f tap, faucet (Amer)

espl|éndido a splendid; (persona) generous. **~endor** m splendour

espliego m lavender

espolear vt (fig) spur on

espoleta f fuse

espolvorear vt sprinkle

esponj|a f sponge; (tejido) towelling. **~oso** a spongy. **pasar la ~a** forget about it

espont|aneidad f spontaneity. **~áneo** a spontaneous

esporádico a sporadic

espos|a f wife. **~as** fpl handcuffs. **~ar** vt handcuff. **~o** m husband. **los ~os** the couple

espuela f spur; (fig) incentive. **dar de ~s** spur on

espum|a f foam; (en bebidas) froth; (de jabón) lather. **~ar** vt skim. ● vi foam; (bebidas) froth; (jabón) lather. **~oso** a (vino) sparkling. **echar ~a** foam, froth

esqueleto m skeleton

esquem|a m outline. **~ático** a sketchy

esquí m (pl esquís) ski; (el deporte) skiing. ∼**ador** m skier. ∼**iar** [20] vi ski

esquilar vt shear

esquimal a & m Eskimo

esquina f corner

esquirol m blackleg

esquiv|ar vt avoid. ∼**o** a aloof

esquizofrénico a & m schizophrenic

esta a véase **este**

ésta pron véase **éste**

estab|ilidad f stability. ∼**ilizador** m stabilizer. ∼**ilizar** [10] vt stabilize. ∼**le** a stable

establec|er [11] vt establish. ∼**erse** vpr settle; (com) start a business. ∼**imiento** m establishment

establo m cowshed

estaca f stake; (para apalear) stick. ∼**da** f (cerca) fence

estación f station; (del año) season; (de vacaciones) resort. ∼ **de servicio** service station

estaciona|miento m parking. ∼**r** vt station; (auto) park. ∼**rio** a stationary

estadio m stadium; (fase) stage

estadista m statesman. ● f stateswoman

estadístic|a f statistics. ∼**o** a statistical

estado m state. ∼ **civil** marital status. ∼ **de ánimo** frame of mind. ∼ **de cuenta** bank statement. ∼ **mayor** (mil) staff. **en buen** ∼ in good condition. **en** ∼ (interesante) pregnant

Estados Unidos mpl United States

estadounidense a American, United States. ● m & f American

estafa f swindle. ∼**r** vt swindle

estafeta f (oficina de correos) (sub-) post office

estala|ctita f stalactite. ∼**gmita** f stalagmite

estall|ar vi explode; ⟨olas⟩ break; ⟨guerra, epidemia etc⟩ break out; (fig) burst. ∼**ar en llanto** burst into tears. ∼**ar de risa** burst out laughing. ∼**ido** m explosion; (de guerra, epidemia etc) outbreak; (de risa etc) outburst

estamp|a f print; (aspecto) appearance. ∼**ado** a printed. ● m printing; (tela) cotton print. ∼**ar** vt stamp; (imprimir) print. **dar a la** ∼**a** (imprimir) print; (publicar) publish. **la viva** ∼**a** the image

estampía. de ∼**ía** suddenly

estampido m explosion

estampilla f stamp; (Mex) (postage) stamp

estanca|do a stagnant. ∼**miento** m stagnation. ∼**r** [7] vt stem; (com) turn into a monopoly

estanci|a f stay; (Arg, finca) ranch, farm; (cuarto) room. ∼**ero** m (Arg) farmer

estanco a watertight. ● m tobacconist's (shop)

estandarte m standard, banner

estanque m lake; (depósito de agua) reservoir

estanquero m tobacconist

estante m shelf. ∼**ría** f shelves; (para libros) bookcase

estañ|o m tin. ∼**adura** f tin-plating

estar [27] vi be; (quedarse) stay; (estar en casa) be in. ¿**estamos**? alright? **estamos a 29 de noviembre** it's the 29th of November. ∼ **para** be about to. ∼ **por** remain to be; (con ganas de) be tempted to; (ser partidario de) be in favour of. ∼**se** vpr stay. ¿**cómo está Vd?, ¿cómo estás?** how are you?

estarcir [9] vt stencil

estatal a state

estático a static; (pasmado) dumbfounded

estatua f statue

estatura f height

estatut|ario a statutory. ∼**o** m statute

este m east; (viento) east wind. ● a (f **esta**, mpl **estos**, fpl **estas**) this; (en plural) these. ● int (LAm) well, er

éste pron (f **ésta**, mpl **éstos**, fpl **éstas**) this one; (en plural) these; (segundo de dos) the latter

estela f wake; (arquit) carved stone

estera f mat; (tejido) matting

est|éreo a stereo. ∼**ereofónico** a stereo, stereophonic

esterilla f mat

estereotip|ado a stereotyped. ∼**o** m stereotype

est|éril a sterile; ⟨mujer⟩ infertile; ⟨terreno⟩ barren. ∼**erilidad** f sterility; (de mujer) infertility; (de terreno) barrenness

esterlina a sterling. **libra** f ∼ pound sterling

estético a aesthetic

estevado a bow-legged

estiércol m dung; (abono) manure

estigma *m* stigma. ~**s** *mpl* (*relig*) stigmata

estilarse *vpr* be used

estilista *m* & *f* stylist. ~**izar** [10] *vt* stylize. ~**o** *m* style. **por el** ~**o** of that sort

estilográfica *f* fountain pen

estima *f* esteem. ~**do** *a* esteemed. ~**do señor** (*en cartas*) Dear Sir. ~**r** *vt* esteem; have great respect for (*persona*); (*valorar*) value; (*juzgar*) think

estimulante *a* stimulating. ● *m* stimulant. ~**imular** *vt* stimulate; (*incitar*) incite. ~**ímulo** *m* stimulus

estipular *vt* stipulate

estirado *a* stretched; (*persona*) haughty. ~**ar** *vt* stretch; (*fig*) stretch out. ~**ón** *m* pull, tug; (*crecimiento*) sudden growth

estirpe *m* stock

estival *a* summer

esto *pron neutro* this; (*este asunto*) this business. **en** ~ at this point. **en** ~ **de** in this business of. **por** ~ therefore

estofa *f* class. **de baja** ~ (*gente*) low-class

estofado *a* stewed. ● *m* stew. ~**r** *vt* stew

estoicismo *m* stoicism. ~**o** *a* stoical. ● *m* stoic

estómago *m* stomach. **dolor** *m* **de** ~ stomach-ache

estorbar *vt* hinder, obstruct; (*molestar*) bother, annoy. ● *vi* be in the way. ~**o** *m* hindrance; (*molestia*) nuisance

estornino *m* starling

estornudar *vi* sneeze. ~**o** *m* sneeze

estos *a mpl véase* **este**

éstos *pron mpl véase* **éste**

estoy *vb véase* **estar**

estrabismo *m* squint

estrafalario *a* outlandish

estragar [12] *vt* devastate. ~**o** *m* devastation. **hacer** ~**os** devastate

estragón *m* tarragon

estrambótico *a* outlandish

estrangulación *f* strangulation. ~**dor** *m* strangler; (*auto*) choke. ~**miento** *m* blockage; (*auto*) bottleneck. ~**r** *vt* strangle

estraperlo *m* black market. **comprar algo de** ~ buy sth on the black market

estratagema *f* stratagem

estratega *m* & *f* strategist. ~**ia** *f* strategy

estratégicamente *adv* strategically. ~**o** *a* strategic

estrato *m* stratum

estratosfera *f* stratosphere

estrechar *vt* make narrower; take in (*vestido*); (*apretar*) squeeze; hug (*persona*). ~**ar la mano a uno** shake hands with s.o. ~**arse** *vpr* become narrower; (*apretarse*) squeeze up. ~**ez** *f* narrowness; (*apuro*) tight spot; (*falta de dinero*) want. ~**o** *a* narrow; (*vestido etc*) tight; (*fig, íntimo*) close. ● *m* straits. ~**o de miras. de miras** ~**as** narrow-minded

estregar [1 & 12] *vt* rub

estrella *f* star. ~ **de mar** ~**mar** *m* starfish

estrellar *vt* smash; fry (*huevos*). ~**se** *vpr* smash; (*fracasar*) fail. ~**se contra** crash into

estremecer [11] *vt* shake. ~**erse** *vpr* tremble (**de** with). ~**imiento** *m* shaking

estrenar *vt* use for the first time; wear for the first time (*vestido etc*); show for the first time (*película*). ~**arse** *vpr* make one's début; (*película*) have its première; (*obra de teatro*) open. ~**o** *m* first use; (*de película*) première; (*de obra de teatro*) first night

estreñido *a* constipated. ~**miento** *m* constipation

estrépito *m* din. ~**epitoso** *a* noisy; (*fig*) resounding

estreptomicina *f* streptomycin

estrés *m* stress

estría *f* groove

estribar *vt* rest (**en** on); (*consistir*) lie (**en** in)

estribillo *m* refrain; (*muletilla*) catchphrase

estribo *m* stirrup; (*de vehículo*) step; (*contrafuerte*) buttress. **perder los** ~**s** lose one's temper

estribor *m* starboard

estricto *a* strict

estridente *a* strident, raucous

estrofa *f* strophe

estropajo *m* scourer. ~**so** *a* (*carne etc*) tough; (*persona*) slovenly

estropear *vt* spoil; (*romper*) break. ~**se** *vpr* be damaged; (*fruta etc*) go bad; (*fracasar*) fail

estructura *f* structure. ~**l** *a* structural

estruendo *m* din; (*de mucha gente*) uproar. **∼so** *a* deafening

estrujar *vt* squeeze; (*fig*) drain

estuario *m* estuary

estuco *m* stucco

estuche *m* case

estudi|ante *m & f* student. **∼antil** *a* student. **∼ar** *vt* study. **∼o** *m* study; (*de artista*) studio. **∼oso** *a* studious

estufa *f* heater; (*LAm*) cooker

estupefac|ción *f* astonishment. **∼iente** *a* astonishing. • *m* narcotic. **∼to** *a* astonished

estupendo *a* marvellous; (*hermoso*) beautiful

est|upidez *f* stupidity; (*acto*) stupid thing. **∼úpido** *a* stupid

estupor *m* amazement

esturión *m* sturgeon

estuve *vb véase* **estar**

etapa *f* stage. **hacer ∼ en** break the journey at. **por ∼s** in stages

etc *abrev* (*etcétera*) etc

etcétera *adv* et cetera

éter *m* ether

etéreo *a* ethereal

etern|amente *adv* eternally. **∼idad** *f* eternity. **∼izar** [10] *vt* drag out. **∼izarse** *vpr* be interminable. **∼o** *a* eternal

étic|a *f* ethics. **∼o** *a* ethical

etimología *f* etymology

etiqueta *f* ticket, tag; (*ceremonial*) etiquette. **de ∼** formal

étnico *a* ethnic

eucalipto *m* eucalyptus

eufemismo *m* euphemism

euforia *f* euphoria

Europa *f* Europe

europe|o *a & m* European. **∼izar** [10] *vt* Europeanize

eutanasia *f* euthanasia

evacua|ción *f* evacuation. **∼r** [21 *o regular*] *vt* evacuate

evadir *vt* avoid. **∼se** *vpr* escape

evalua|r [21] *vt* evaluate

evang|élico *a* evangelical. **∼elio** *m* gospel. **∼elista** *m & f* evangelist

evapora|ción *f* evaporation. **∼r** *vi* evaporate. **∼rse** *vpr* evaporate; (*fig*) disappear

evasi|ón *f* evasion; (*fuga*) escape. **∼vo** *a* evasive

evento *m* event. **a todo ∼** at all events

eventual *a* possible. **∼idad** *f* eventuality

eviden|cia *f* evidence. **∼ciar** *vt* show. **∼ciarse** *vpr* be obvious. **∼te** *a* obvious. **∼temente** *adv* obviously. **poner en ∼cia** show; (*fig*) make a fool of

evitar *vt* avoid; (*ahorrar*) spare

evocar [7] *vt* evoke

evolu|ción *f* evolution. **∼onado** *a* fully-developed. **∼onar** *vi* evolve; (*mil*) manoeuvre

ex *pref* ex-, former

exacerbar *vt* exacerbate

exact|amente *adv* exactly. **∼itud** *f* exactness. **∼o** *a* exact; (*preciso*) accurate; (*puntual*) punctual. **¡∼!** con **∼itud** exactly!. exactly

exagera|ción *f* exaggeration. **∼do** *a* exaggerated. **∼r** *vt/i* exaggerate

exalta|do *a* exalted; (*fanático*) fanatical. **∼r** *vt* exalt. **∼rse** *vpr* get excited

exam|en *m* examination; (*escol, univ*) exam(ination). **∼inador** *m* examiner. **∼inar** *vt* examine. **∼inarse** *vpr* take an exam

exánime *a* lifeless

exaspera|ción *f* exasperation. **∼r** *vt* exasperate. **∼rse** *vpr* get exasperated

excava|ción *f* excavation. **∼dora** *f* digger. **∼r** *vt* excavate

excede|ncia *f* leave of absence. **∼nte** *a & m* surplus. **∼r** *vi* exceed. **∼rse** *vpr* go too far. **∼rse a sí mismo** excel o.s.

excelen|cia *f* excellence; (*tratamiento*) Excellency. **∼te** *a* excellent

exc|entricidad *f* eccentricity. **∼éntrico** *a & m* eccentric

excepci|ón *f* exception. **∼onal** *a* exceptional. **a ∼ón de, con ∼ón de** except (for)

except|o *prep* except (for). **∼uar** [21] *vt* except

exces|ivo *a* excessive. **∼o** *m* excess. **∼o de equipaje** excess luggage (*esp Brit*), excess baggage (*esp Amer*)

excita|ble *a* excitable. **∼ción** *f* excitement. **∼nte** *a* exciting. • *m* stimulant. **∼r** *vt* excite; (*incitar*) incite. **∼rse** *vpr* get excited

exclama|ción *f* exclamation. **∼r** *vi* exclaim

exclu|ir [17] *vt* exclude. **∼sión** *f* exclusion. **∼siva** *f* sole right; (*en la prensa*) exclusive (story). **∼sive**

adv exclusive; (*exclusivamente*) exclusively. ~**sivo** *a* exclusive

excomu|lgar [12] *vt* excommunicate. ~**nión** *f* excommunication

excremento *m* excrement

exculpar *vt* exonerate; (*jurid*) acquit

excursi|ón *f* excursion, trip. ~**onista** *m* & *f* day-tripper. **ir de** ~**ón** go on an excursion

excusa *f* excuse; (*disculpa*) apology. ~**r** *vt* excuse. **presentar sus** ~**s** apologize

execra|ble *a* loathsome. ~**r** *vt* loathe

exento *a* exempt; (*libre*) free

exequias *fpl* funeral rites

exhala|ción *f* shooting star. ~**r** *vt* exhale, breath out; give off (*olor etc*). ~**rse** *vpr* hurry. **como una** ~**ción** at top speed

exhaust|ivo *a* exhaustive. ~**o** *a* exhausted

exhibi|ción *f* exhibition. ~**cionista** *m* & *f* exhibitionist. ~**r** *vt* exhibit

exhortar *vt* exhort (**a** to)

exhumar *vt* exhume; (*fig*) dig up

exig|encia *f* demand. ~**ente** *a* demanding. ~**ir** [14] *vt* demand. **tener muchas** ~**encias** be very demanding

exiguo *a* meagre

exil|(i)ado *a* exiled. ● *m* exile. ~**(i)arse** *vpr* go into exile. ~**io** *m* exile

eximio *a* distinguished

eximir *vt* exempt; (*liberar*) free

existencia *f* existence. ~**s** *fpl* stock

existencial *a* existential. ~**ismo** *m* existentialism

exist|ente *a* existing. ~**ir** *vi* exist

éxito *m* success. **no tener** ~ fail. **tener** ~ be successful

exitoso *a* successful

éxodo *m* exodus

exonerar *vt* (*de un empleo*) dismiss; (*de un honor etc*) strip

exorbitante *a* exorbitant

exorci|smo *m* exorcism. ~**zar** [10] *vt* exorcise

exótico *a* exotic

expan|dir *vt* expand; (*fig*) spread. ~**dirse** *vpr* expand. ~**sión** *f* expansion. ~**sivo** *a* expansive

expatria|do *a* & *m* expatriate. ~**r** *vt* banish. ~**rse** *vpr* emigrate; (*exiliarse*) go into exile

expectativa *f*. **estar a la** ~ be on the lookout

expedición *f* dispatch; (*cosa expedida*) shipment; (*mil, científico etc*) expedition

expediente *m* expedient; (*jurid*) proceedings; (*documentos*) record, file

expedi|r [5] *vt* dispatch, send; issue (*documento*). ~**to** *a* clear

expeler *vt* expel

expende|dor *m* dealer. ~**dor automático** vending machine. ~**duría** *f* shop; (*de billetes*) ticket office. ~**r** *vt* sell

expensas *fpl*. **a** ~ **de** at the expense of. **a mis** ~ at my expense

experiencia *f* experience

experiment|al *a* experimental. ~**ar** *vt* test, experiment with; (*sentir*) experience. ~**o** *m* experiment

experto *a* & *m* expert

expiar [20] *vt* atone for

expirar *vi* expire; (*morir*) die

explana|da *f* levelled area; (*paseo*) esplanade. ~**r** *vt* level

explayar *vt* extend. ~**se** *vpr* spread out, extend; (*hablar*) be long-winded; (*confiarse*) confide (**a** in)

expletivo *m* expletive

explica|ción *f* explanation. ~**r** [7] *vt* explain. ~**rse** *vpr* understand; (*hacerse comprender*) explain o.s. **no me lo explico** I can't understand it

explícito *a* explicit

explora|ción *f* exploration. ~**dor** *m* explorer; (*muchacho*) boy scout. ~**r** *vt* explore. ~**torio** *a* exploratory

explosi|ón *f* explosion; (*fig*) outburst. ~**onar** *vt* blow up. ~**vo** *a* & *m* explosive

explota|ción *f* working; (*abuso*) exploitation. ~**r** *vt* work (*mina*); farm (*tierra*); (*abusar*) exploit. ● *vi* explode

expone|nte *m* exponent; (*de cuadros etc*) exhibition; (*en escaparate etc*) display; (*explicación*) exposition, explanation

exposición *f* exposure; (*de cuadros etc*) exhibition; (*en escaparate etc*) display; (*explicación*) exposition, explanation

expresamente *adv* specifically

expres|ar *vt* express. ~**arse** *vpr* express o.s. ~**ión** *f* expression. ~**ivo** *a* expressive; (*cariñoso*) affectionate

expreso *a* express. ● *m* express messenger; (*tren*) express

exprimi|dor *m* squeezer. ~**r** *vt* squeeze; (*explotar*) exploit

expropiar *vt* expropriate

expuesto *a* on display; (*lugar etc*) exposed; (*peligroso*) dangerous. **estar** ~ **a** be liable to

expuls|ar *vt* expel; throw out (*persona*); send off (*jugador*). ~**ión** *f* expulsion

expurgar [12] *vt* expurgate

exquisit|o *a* exquisite. ~**amente** *adv* exquisitely

extasiar [20] *vt* enrapture

éxtasis *m invar* ecstasy

extático *a* ecstatic

extend|er [1] *vt* spread (out); draw up (*documento*). ~**erse** *vpr* spread; (*paisaje etc*) extend, stretch; (*tenderse*) stretch out. ~**ido** *a* spread out; (*generalizado*) widespread; (*brazos*) outstretched

extens|amente *adv* widely; (*detalladamente*) in full. ~**ión** *f* extension; (*amplitud*) expanse; (*mus*) range. ~**o** *a* extensive

extenuar [21] *vt* exhaust

exterior *a* external, exterior; (*del extranjero*) foreign; (*aspecto etc*) outward. ● *m* exterior; (*países extranjeros*) abroad. ~**izar** [10] *vt* show

extermin|ación *f* extermination. ~**ar** *vt* exterminate. ~**io** *m* extermination

externo *a* external; (*signo etc*) outward. ● *m* day pupil

extin|ción *f* extinction. ~**guir** [13] *vt* extinguish. ~**guirse** *vpr* die out; (*fuego*) go out. ~**to** *a* extinguished; (*raza etc*) extinct. ~**tor** *m* fire extinguisher

extirpa|r *vt* uproot; extract (*muela etc*); remove (*tumor*). ~**ción** *f* (*fig*) eradication

extorsi|ón *f* (*fig*) inconvenience. ~**onar** *vt* inconvenience

extra *a invar* extra; (*de buena calidad*) good-quality; (*huevos*) large. **paga** *f* ~ bonus

extrac|ción *f* extraction; (*de lotería*) draw. ~**to** *m* extract

extradición *f* extradition

extraer [41] *vt* extract

extranjero *a* foreign. ● *m* foreigner; (*países*) foreign countries. **del** ~ from abroad. **en el** ~, **por el** ~ abroad

extrañ|ar *vt* surprise; (*encontrar extraño*) find strange; (*LAm, echar de menos*) miss; (*desterrar*) banish. ~**arse** *vpr* be surprised (**de** at); (*2 personas*) grow apart. ~**eza** *f* strangeness; (*asombro*) surprise. ~**o** *a* strange. ● *m* stranger

extraoficial *a* unofficial

extraordinario *a* extraordinary. ● *m* (*correo*) special delivery; (*plato*) extra dish; (*de periódico etc*) special edition. **horas** *fpl* **extraordinarias** overtime

extrarradio *m* suburbs

extrasensible *a* extra-sensory

extraterrestre *a* extraterrestrial. ● *m* alien

extravagan|cia *f* oddness, eccentricity. ~**te** *a* odd, eccentric

extravertido *a* & *m* extrovert

extrav|iado *a* lost; (*lugar*) isolated. ~**iar** [20] *vt* lose. ~**iarse** *vpr* get lost; (*objetos*) be missing. ~**ío** *m* loss

extremar *vt* overdo. ~**se** *vpr* make every effort

extremeño *a* from Extremadura. ● *m* person from Extremadura

extrem|idad *f* extremity. ~**idades** *fpl* extremities. ~**ista** *a* & *m* & *f* extremist. ~**o** *a* extreme. ● *m* end; (*colmo*) extreme. **en** ~ extremely. **en último** ~**o** as a last resort

extrovertido *a* & *m* extrovert

exuberan|cia *f* exuberance. ~**te** *a* exuberant

exulta|ción *f* exultation. ~**r** *vi* exult

eyacular *vt/i* ejaculate

F

fa *m* F; (*solfa*) fah

fabada *f* Asturian stew

fábrica *f* factory. **marca** *f* **de** ~ trade mark

fabrica|ción *f* manufacture. ~**ción en serie** mass production. ~**nte** *m* & *f* manufacturer. ~**r** [7] *vt* manufacture; (*inventar*) fabricate

fábula *f* fable; (*mentira*) story, lie; (*chisme*) gossip

fabuloso *a* fabulous

facci|ón *f* faction. ~**ones** *fpl* (*de la cara*) features

faceta *f* facet

fácil *a* easy; (*probable*) likely; (*persona*) easygoing

facili|dad f ease; (*disposición*) aptitude. ~**dades** fpl facilities. ~**tar** vt facilitate; (*proporcionar*) provide

fácilmente adv easily

facistol m lectern

facón m (*Arg*) gaucho knife

facsímil(e) m facsimile

factible a feasible

factor m factor

factoría f agency; (*esp LAm, fábrica*) factory

factura f bill, invoice; (*hechura*) manufacture. ~**r** vt (*hacer la factura*) invoice; (*cobrar*) charge; (*en ferrocarril*) register (*Brit*), check (*Amer*)

facultad f faculty; (*capacidad*) ability; (*poder*) power. ~**tivo** a optional

facha f (*aspecto, fam*) look

fachada f façade; (*fig, apariencia*) show

faena f job. ~**s domésticas** housework

fagot m bassoon; (*músico*) bassoonist

faisán m pheasant

faja f (*de tierra*) strip; (*corsé*) corset; (*mil etc*) sash

fajo m bundle; (*de billetes*) wad

falang|e f (*política española*) Falange. ~**ista** m & f Falangist

falda f skirt; (*de montaña*) side

fálico a phallic

fals|ear vt falsify, distort. ~**edad** f falseness; (*mentira*) lie, falsehood. ~**ificación** f forgery. ~**ificador** m forger. ~**ificar** [7] vt forge. ~**o** a false; (*equivocado*) wrong; (*falsificado*) fake

falt|a f lack; (*ausencia*) absence; (*escasez*) shortage; (*defecto*) fault, defect; (*culpa*) fault; (*error*) mistake; (*en fútbol etc*) foul; (*en tenis*) fault. ~**ar** vi be lacking; (*estar ausente*) be absent. ~**o** a lacking (**de** in). a ~**a de** for lack of. **echar en** ~**a** miss. **hacer** ~**a** be necessary. **me hace** ~**a** I need. **¡no** ~**aba más!** don't mention it! (*naturalmente*) of course! **sacar** ~**as** find fault

falla f (*incl geol*) fault. ~**r** vi fail; (*romperse*) break, give way; (*motor, tiro etc*) miss. **sin** ~**r** without fail

fallec|er [11] vi die. ~**ido** a late. • m deceased

fallido a vain; (*fracasado*) unsuccessful

fallo m failure; (*defecto*) fault; (*jurid*) sentence

fama f fame; (*reputación*) reputation. **de mala** ~ of ill repute. **tener** ~ **de** have the reputation of

famélico a starving

familia f family. ~ **numerosa** large family. ~**r** a familiar; (*de la familia*) family; (*sin ceremonia*) informal. ~**ridad** f familiarity. ~**rizarse** [10] vpr become familiar (**con** with)

famoso a famous

fanático a fanatical. • m fanatic

fanfarr|ón a boastful. • m braggart. ~**onada** f boasting; (*dicho*) boast. ~**onear** vi show off

fango m mud. ~**so** a muddy

fantas|ear vi daydream; (*imaginar*) fantasize. ~**ía** f fantasy. **de** ~ fancy

fantasma m ghost

fantástico a fantastic

fantoche m puppet

faringe f pharynx

fardo m bundle

farfullar vi jabber, gabble

farmac|éutico a pharmaceutical. • m chemist (*Brit*), pharmacist, druggist (*Amer*). ~**ia** f (*ciencia*) pharmacy; (*tienda*) chemist's (shop) (*Brit*), pharmacy, drugstore (*Amer*)

faro m lighthouse; (*aviac*) beacon; (*auto*) headlight

farol m lantern; (*de la calle*) street lamp. ~**a** f street lamp. ~**ita** f small street lamp

farsa f farce

fas adv. **por** ~ **o por nefas** rightly or wrongly

fascículo m instalment

fascina|ción f fascination. ~**r** vt fascinate

fascis|mo m fascism. ~**ta** a & m & f fascist

fase f phase

fastidi|ar vt annoy; (*estropear*) spoil. ~**arse** vpr (*aguantarse*) put up with it; (*hacerse daño*) hurt o.s. ~**o** m nuisance; (*aburrimiento*) boredom. ~**oso** a annoying. **¡para que te** ~**es!** so there! **¡qué** ~**o!** what a nuisance!

fatal a fateful; (*mortal*) fatal; (*pésimo, fam*) terrible. ~**idad** f fate; (*desgracia*) misfortune. ~**ista** m & f fatalist

fatig|a f fatigue. ~**as** fpl troubles. ~**ar** [12] vt tire. ~**arse** vpr get tired. ~**oso** a tiring

fatuo a fatuous

fauna f fauna

fausto a lucky
favor m favour. **~able** a favourable. **a ~ de, en ~ de** in favour of. **haga el ~ de** would you be so kind as to, please. **por ~** please
favorec|edor a flattering. **~er** [11] vt favour; ⟨vestido, peinado etc⟩ suit. **~ido** a favoured
favorit|ismo m favouritism. **~o** a & m favourite
faz f face
fe f faith. **dar ~ de** certify. **de buena ~** in good faith
fealdad f ugliness
febrero m February
febril a feverish
fecund|ación f fertilization. **~ación artificial** artificial insemination. **~ar** vt fertilize. **~o** a fertile; ⟨fig⟩ prolific
fecha f date. **~r** vt date. **a estas ~s** now; ⟨todavía⟩ still. **hasta la ~** so far. **poner la ~** date
fechoría f misdeed
federa|ción f federation. **~l** a federal
feísimo a hideous
felici|dad f happiness. **~dades** fpl best wishes; ⟨congratulaciones⟩ congratulations. **~tación** f congratulation. **~tar** vt congratulate. **~tarse** vpr be glad
feligr|és m parishioner. **~esía** f parish
felino a & m feline
feliz a happy; ⟨afortunado⟩ lucky. **¡Felices Pascuas!** Happy Christmas! **¡F~ Año Nuevo!** Happy New Year!
felpudo a plush. ● m doormat
femeni|l a feminine. **~no** a feminine; ⟨biol, bot⟩ female. ● m feminine. **feminidad** f femininity. **feminista** a & m & f feminist
fen|omenal a phenomenal. **~ómeno** m phenomenon; ⟨monstruo⟩ freak
feo a ugly; ⟨desagradable⟩ nasty; ⟨malo⟩ bad
féretro m coffin
feria f fair; ⟨verbena⟩ carnival; ⟨descanso⟩ holiday; ⟨Mex, cambio⟩ change. **~do** a. **día ~do** holiday
ferment|ación f fermentation. **~ar** vt/i ferment. **~o** m ferment
fero|cidad f ferocity. **~z** a fierce; ⟨persona⟩ savage
férreo a iron. **vía férrea** railway ⟨Brit⟩, railroad ⟨Amer⟩

ferreter|ía f ironmonger's (shop) ⟨Brit⟩, hardware store ⟨Amer⟩. **~o** m ironmonger ⟨Brit⟩, hardware dealer ⟨Amer⟩
ferro|bús m local train. **~carril** m railway ⟨Brit⟩, railroad ⟨Amer⟩. **~viario** a rail. ● m railwayman ⟨Brit⟩, railroad worker ⟨Amer⟩
fértil a fertile
fertili|dad f fertility. **~zante** m fertilizer. **~zar** [10] vt fertilize
férvido a fervent
ferv|iente a fervent. **~or** m fervour
festej|ar vt celebrate; entertain ⟨persona⟩; court ⟨novia etc⟩; ⟨Mex, golpear⟩ beat. **~o** m entertainment; ⟨celebración⟩ celebration
festiv|al m festival. **~idad** f festivity. **~o** a festive; ⟨humorístico⟩ humorous. **día ~o** feast day, holiday
festonear vt festoon
fétido a stinking
feto m foetus
feudal a feudal
fiado m. **al ~** on credit. **~r** m fastener; ⟨jurid⟩ guarantor
fiambre m cold meat
fianza f ⟨dinero⟩ deposit; ⟨objeto⟩ surety. **bajo ~** on bail. **dar ~** pay a deposit
fiar [20] vt guarantee; ⟨vender⟩ sell on credit; ⟨confiar⟩ confide. ● vi trust. **~se** vpr. **~se de** trust
fiasco m fiasco
fibra f fibre; ⟨fig⟩ energy. **~ de vidrio** fibreglass
fic|ción f fiction. **~ticio** a fictitious; ⟨falso⟩ false
ficha f token; ⟨tarjeta⟩ index card; ⟨en los juegos⟩ counter. **~ar** vt file. **~ero** m card index. **estar ~ado** have a (police) record
fidedigno a reliable
fidelidad f faithfulness. **alta ~** hi-fi ⟨fam⟩, high fidelity
fideos mpl noodles
fiebre f fever. **~ del heno** hay fever. **tener ~** have a temperature
fiel a faithful; ⟨memoria, relato etc⟩ reliable. ● m believer; ⟨de balanza⟩ needle. **los ~es** the faithful
fieltro m felt
fier|a f wild animal; ⟨persona⟩ brute. **~o** a fierce; ⟨cruel⟩ cruel. **estar hecho una ~a** be furious
fierro m ⟨LAm⟩ iron
fiesta f party; ⟨día festivo⟩ holiday. **~s** fpl celebrations. **~ nacional**

figura 101 flato

bank holiday (*Brit*), national holiday

figura *f* figure; (*forma*) shape; (*en obra de teatro*) character; (*en naipes*) court-card. **~r** *vt* feign; (*representar*) represent. ● *vi* figure; (*ser importante*) be important. **~rse** *vpr* imagine. ¡**figúrate!** just imagine! **~tivo** *a* figurative

fij|ación *f* fixing. **~ar** *vt* fix; stick (*sello*); post (*cartel*). **~arse** *vpr* settle; (*fig, poner atención*) notice. ¡**fíjate!** just imagine! **~o** *a* fixed; (*firme*) stable; (*persona*) settled. **de ~o** certainly

fila *f* line; (*de soldados etc*) file; (*en el teatro, cine etc*) row; (*cola*) queue. **ponerse en ~** line up

filamento *m* filament

fil|antropía *f* philanthropy. **~antrópico** *a* philanthropic. **~ántropo** *m* philanthropist

filarmónico *a* philharmonic

filat|elia *f* stamp collecting, philately. **~élico** *a* philatelic. ● *m* stamp collector, philatelist

filete *m* fillet

filfa *f* (*fam*) hoax

filial *a* filial. ● *f* subsidiary

filigrana *f* filigree (work); (*en papel*) watermark

Filipinas *fpl*. **las (islas) ~** the Philippines

filipino *a* Philippine, Filipino

filmar *vt* film

filo *m* edge; (*de hoja*) cutting edge; (*Mex, hambre*) hunger. **al ~ de las doce** at exactly twelve o'clock. **dar ~ a, sacar ~ a** sharpen

filología *f* philology

filón *m* vein; (*fig*) gold-mine

fil|osofía *f* philosophy. **~osófico** *a* philosophical. **~ósofo** *m* philosopher

filtr|ar *vt* filter. **~arse** *vpr* filter; (*dinero*) disappear. **~o** *m* filter; (*bebida*) philtre

fin *m* end; (*objetivo*) aim. **~ de semana** weekend. **a ~ de** in order to. **a ~ de cuentas** all things considered. **a ~ de que** in order that. **a ~es de** at the end of. **al ~** finally. **al ~ y al cabo** after all. **dar ~ a** end. **en ~** in short. **poner ~ a** end. **por ~** finally. **sin ~** endless

final *a* final, last. ● *m* end. ● *f* final. **~idad** *f* aim. **~ista** *m* & *f* finalist. **~izar** [10] *vt/i* end. **~mente** *adv* finally

financi|ar *vt* finance. **~ero** *a* financial. ● *m* financier

finca *f* property; (*tierras*) estate; (*LAm, granja*) farm

finés *a* Finnish. ● *m* Finn; (*lengua*) Finnish

fingi|do *a* false. **~r** [14] *vt* feign; (*simular*) simulate. ● *vi* pretend. **~rse** *vpr* pretend to be

finito *a* finite

finlandés *a* Finnish. ● *m* (*persona*) Finn; (*lengua*) Finnish

Finlandia *f* Finland

fin|o *a* fine; (*delgado*) slender; (*astuto*) shrewd; (*sentido*) keen; (*cortés*) polite; (*jerez*) dry. **~ura** *f* fineness; (*astucia*) shrewdness; (*de sentido*) keenness; (*cortesía*) politeness

fiordo *m* fiord

firma *f* signature; (*empresa*) firm

firmamento *m* firmament

firmar *vt* sign

firme *a* firm; (*estable*) stable, steady; (*persona*) steadfast. ● *m* (*pavimento*) (road) surface. ● *adv* hard. **~za** *f* firmness. **de ~** hard. **en ~** firm, definite

fisc|al *a* fiscal. ● *m* & *f* public prosecutor. **~o** *m* treasury

fisg|ar [12] *vt* pry into (*asunto*); spy on (*persona*). ● *vi* pry. **~ón** *a* prying. ● *m* busybody

físic|a *f* physics. **~o** *a* physical. ● *m* physique; (*persona*) physicist

fisi|ología *f* physiology. **~ológico** *a* physiological. **~ólogo** *m* physiologist

fisioterap|euta *m* & *f* physiotherapist. **~ia** *f* physiotherapy. **~ista** *m* & *f* (*fam*) physiotherapist

fisonom|ía *f* physiognomy, face. **~ista** *m* & *f*. **ser buen ~ista** be good at remembering faces

fisura *f* (*Med*) fracture

fláccido *a* flabby

flaco *a* thin, skinny; (*débil*) weak

flagelo *m* scourge

flagrante *a* flagrant. **en ~** redhanded

flamante *a* splendid; (*nuevo*) brand-new

flamenco *a* flamenco; (*de Flandes*) Flemish. ● *m* (*música etc*) flamenco

flan *m* crème caramel

flaqueza *f* thinness; (*debilidad*) weakness

flash *m* flash

flato *m*, **flatulencia** *f* flatulence

flaut|a f flute. ● m & f (*músico*) flautist, flutist (*Amer*). ~**in** m piccolo. ~**ista** m & f flautist, flutist (*Amer*)

fleco m fringe

flecha f arrow

flem|a f phlegm. ~**ático** a phlegmatic

flequillo m fringe

fletar vt charter

flexib|ilidad f flexibility. ~**le** a flexible. ● m flex, cable

flirte|ar vi flirt. ~**o** m flirting

floj|ear vi ease up. ~**o** a loose; (*poco fuerte*) weak; (*viento*) light; (*perezoso*) lazy

flor f flower; (*fig*) cream. ~**a** f flora. ~**al** a floral. ~**ecer** [11] vi flower, bloom; (*fig*) flourish. ~**eciente** a (*fig*) flourishing. ~**ero** m flower vase. ~**ido** a flowery; (*selecto*) select; (*lenguaje*) florid. ~**ista** m & f florist

flota f fleet

flot|ador m float. ~**ar** vi float. ~**e** m. **a** ~**e** afloat

flotilla f flotilla

fluctua|ción f fluctuation. ~**r** [21] vi fluctuate

flu|idez f fluidity; (*fig*) fluency. ~**ido** a fluid; (*fig*) fluent. ● m fluid. ~**ir** [17] vi flow. ~**jo** m flow. ~**o y reflujo** ebb and flow

fluorescente a fluorescent

fluoruro m fluoride

fluvial a river

fobia f phobia

foca f seal

foc|al a focal. ~**o** m focus; (*lámpara*) floodlight; (*LAm, bombilla*) light bulb

fogón m (*cocina*) cooker

fogoso a spirited

folio m leaf

folkl|ore m folklore. ~**órico** a folk

follaje m foliage

follet|ín m newspaper serial. ~**o** m pamphlet

follón m (*lío*) mess; (*alboroto*) row

fomentar vt foment, stir up

fonda f (*pensión*) boarding-house

fondo m bottom; (*parte más lejana*) bottom, end; (*de escenario, pintura etc*) background; (*profundidad*) depth. ~**s** mpl funds, money. **a** ~ thoroughly. **en el** ~ deep down

fonética f phonetics. ~**o** a phonetic

fono m (*LAm, del teléfono*) earpiece

fontaner|ía plumbing. ~**o** m plumber

footing /'futin/ m jogging

forastero a alien. ● m stranger

forceje|ar vi struggle. ~**o** m struggle

fórceps m invar forceps

forense a forensic

forjar vt forge

forma f form, shape; (*horma*) mould; (*modo*) way; (*de zapatero*) last. ~**s** fpl conventions. ~**ción** f formation; (*educación*) training. **dar** ~ **a** shape; (*expresar*) formulate. **de** ~ **que** so (that). **de todas** ~**s** anyway. **estar en** ~ be in good form. **guardar** ~**s** keep up appearances

formal a formal; (*de fiar*) reliable; (*serio*) serious. ~**idad** f formality; (*fiabilidad*) reliability; (*seriedad*) seriousness

formar vt form; (*hacer*) make; (*enseñar*) train. ~**se** vpr form; (*desarrollarse*) develop

formato m format

formidable a formidable; (*muy grande*) enormous; (*muy bueno, fam*) marvellous

fórmula f formula; (*receta*) recipe

formular vt formulate; make (*queja etc*); (*expresar*) express

fornido a well-built

forraje m fodder. ~**ar** vt/i forage

forr|ar vt (*en el interior*) line; (*en el exterior*) cover. ~**o** m lining; (*cubierta*) cover. ~**o del freno** brake lining

fortale|cer [11] vt strengthen. ~**za** f strength; (*mil*) fortress; (*fuerza moral*) fortitude

fortificar [7] vt fortify

fortuito a fortuitous. **encuentro** m ~ chance meeting

fortuna f fortune; (*suerte*) luck. **por** ~ fortunately

forz|ado a hard. ~**ar** [2 & 10] vt force. ~**osamente** adv necessarily. ~**oso** a inevitable; (*necesario*) necessary

fosa f grave

fosfato m phosphate

fósforo m phosphorus; (*cerilla*) match

fósil a & m fossil

fosilizarse [10] vpr fossilize

foso m ditch

foto f photo, photograph. **sacar** ~**s** take photographs

fotocopia f photocopy. ~**dora** f photocopier. ~**r** vt photocopy

fotogénico a photogenic

fotografía f photography; (foto) photograph. ~ografiar [20] vt photograph. ~ográfico a photographic. ~ógrafo m photographer. sacar ~ografías take photographs

foyer m foyer

frac m (pl fraques o fracs) tails

fracas|ar vi fail. ~o m failure

fracción f fraction; (pol) faction

fractura f fracture. ~r vt fracture, break. ~rse vpr fracture, break

fragan|cia f fragrance. ~te a fragrant

fragata f frigate

fr|ágil a fragile; (débil) weak. ~agilidad f fragility; (debilidad) weakness

fragment|ario a fragmentary. ~o m fragment

fragor m din

fragoso a rough

fragua f forge. ~r [15] vt forge; (fig) concoct. ● vi harden

fraile m friar; (monje) monk

frambuesa f raspberry

francés a French. ● m (persona) Frenchman; (lengua) French

Francia f France

franco a frank; (com) free. ● m (moneda) franc

francotirador m sniper

franela f flannel

franja f border; (fleco) fringe

franque|ar vt clear; stamp (carta); overcome (obstáculo). ~o m stamping; (cantidad) postage

franqueza f frankness; (familiaridad) familiarity

franquis|mo m General Franco's regime; (política) Franco's policy. ~ta a pro-Franco

frasco m small bottle

frase f phrase; (oración) sentence. ~ hecha set phrase

fratern|al a fraternal. ~idad f fraternity

fraud|e m fraud. ~ulento a fraudulent

fray m brother, friar

frecuen|cia f frequency. ~tar vt frequent. ~te a frequent. con ~cia frequently

frega|dero m sink. ~r [1 & 12] vt scrub; wash up (los platos); mop (el suelo); (LAm, fig, molestar, fam) annoy

freír [51, pp frito] vt fry; (fig, molestar, fam) annoy. ~se vpr fry; (persona) be very hot, be boiling (fam)

frenar vt brake; (fig) check

fren|esí m frenzy. ~ético a frenzied

freno m (de caballería) bit; (auto) brake; (fig) check

frente m front. ● f forehead. ~ a opposite; (en contra de) opposed to. ~ por ~ opposite; (en un choque) head-on. al ~ at the head; (hacia delante) forward. arrugar la ~ frown. de ~ forward. hacer ~ a face (cosa); stand up to (persona)

fresa f strawberry

fresc|a f fresh air. ~o a (frío) cool; (nuevo) fresh; (descarado) cheeky. ● m fresh air; (frescor) coolness; (mural) fresco; (persona) impudent person. ~or m coolness. ~ura f freshness; (frío) coolness; (descaro) cheek. al ~o in the open air. hacer ~o be cool. tomar el ~o get some fresh air

fresno m ash (tree)

friable a friable

frialdad f coldness; (fig) indifference

fricci|ón f rubbing; (fig, tec) friction; (masaje) massage. ~onar vt rub

frigidez f coldness; (fig) frigidity

frígido a frigid

frigorífico m refrigerator, fridge (fam)

fríjol m bean. ~es refritos (Mex) purée of black beans

frío a & m cold. coger ~ catch cold. hacer ~ be cold

frisar vi. ~ en be getting on for, be about

frito a fried; (exasperado) exasperated. me tiene ~ I'm sick of him

fr|ivolidad f frivolity. ~ívolo a frivolous

fronda f foliage

fronter|a f frontier; (fig) limit. ~izo a frontier. ~o a opposite

frontón m pelota court

frotar vt rub; strike (cerilla)

fructífero a fruitful

frugal a frugal

fruncir [9] vt gather (tela); wrinkle (piel)

fruslería f trifle

frustra|ción f frustration. ~r vt frustrate. ~rse vpr (fracasar) fail. quedar ~do be disappointed

frut|a f fruit. ~ería f fruit shop. ~ero a fruit. ● m fruiterer; (recipiente) fruit bowl. ~icultura f fruit-growing. **~illa** f (LAm) strawberry. **~o** m fruit

fucsia f fuchsia

fuego m fire. **~s artificiales** fireworks. **a ~ lento** on a low heat. **tener ~** have a light

fuente f fountain; (manantial) spring; (plato) serving dish; (fig) source

fuera adv out; (al exterior) outside; (en otra parte) away; (en el extranjero) abroad. ● vb véase **ir** y **ser**. **~ de** outside; (excepto) except for, besides. **por ~** on the outside

fuerte a strong; (color) bright; (sonido) loud; (dolor) severe; (duro) hard; (grande) large; (lluvia, nevada) heavy. ● m fort; (fig) strong point. ● adv hard; (con hablar etc) loudly; (mucho) a lot

fuerza f strength; (poder) power; (en física) force; (mil) forces. **~ de voluntad** will-power. **a ~ de** by dint of, by means of. **a la ~** by necessity. **por ~** by force; (por necesidad) by necessity. **tener ~s para** have the strength to

fuese vb véase **ir** y **ser**

fug|a f flight, escape; (de gas etc) leak; (mus) fugue. **~arse** [12] vpr flee, escape. **~az** a fleeting. **~itivo** a & m fugitive. **ponerse en ~a** take to flight

fui vb véase **ir** y **ser**

fulano m so-and-so. **~, mengano y zutano** Tom, Dick and Harry

fulgor m brilliance; (fig) splendour

fulminar vt strike by lightning; (fig, mirar) look daggers at

fuma|dor a smoking. ● m smoker. **~r** vt/i smoke. **~rse** vpr smoke; (fig, gastar) squander. **~rada** f puff of smoke. **~r en pipa** smoke a pipe. **prohibido ~r** no smoking

funámbulo m tightrope walker

funci|ón f function; (de un cargo etc) duties; (de teatro) show, performance. **~onal** a functional. **~onar** vi work, function. **~onario** m civil servant. **no ~ona** out of order

funda f cover. **~ de almohada** pillowcase

funda|ción f foundation. **~mental** a fundamental. **~mentar** vt lay the foundations of; (fig) base. **~mento** m foundation. **~r** vt found; (fig) base. **~rse** vpr be based

fundi|ción f melting; (de metales) smelting; (taller) foundry. **~r** vt melt; smelt (metales); cast (objeto); blend (colores); (fusionar) merge. **~rse** vpr melt; (unirse) merge

fúnebre a funeral; (sombrío) gloomy

funeral a funeral. ● m funeral. **~es** mpl funeral

funicular a & m funicular

furg|ón m van. **~oneta** f van

fur|ia f fury; (violencia) violence. **~ibundo** a furious. **~ioso** a furious. **~or** m fury

furtivo a furtive

furúnculo m boil

fuselaje m fuselage

fusible m fuse

fusil m gun. **~ar** vt shoot

fusión f melting; (unión) fusion; (com) merger

fútbol m football

futbolista m footballer

fútil a futile

futur|ista a futuristic. ● m & f futurist. **~o** a & m future

G

gabán m overcoat

garbardina f raincoat; (tela) gabardine

gabinete m (pol) cabinet; (en museo etc) room; (de dentista, médico etc) consulting room

gacela f gazelle

gaceta f gazette

gachas fpl porridge

gacho a drooping

gaélico a Gaelic

gafa f hook. **~s** fpl glasses, spectacles. **~s de sol** sun-glasses

gaf|ar vt hook; (fam) bring bad luck to. **~e** m jinx

gaita f bagpipes

gajo m (de naranja, nuez etc) segment

gala|s fpl finery, best clothes. **estar de ~** be dressed up. **hacer ~ de** show off

galán m (en el teatro) male lead; (enamorado) lover

galante a gallant. **~ar** vt court. **~ría** f gallantry

galápago m turtle

galardón m reward

galaxia f galaxy

galeón m galleon

galera f galley

galería f gallery

Gales m Wales. **país de ~** Wales

gal|és a Welsh. ● m Welshman; (lengua) Welsh. **~esa** f Welshwoman

galgo m greyhound

Galicia f Galicia

galimatías m invar (fam) gibberish

galón m gallon; (cinta) braid; (mil) stripe

galop|ar vi gallop. **~e** m gallop

galvanizar [10] vt galvanize

gallard|ía f elegance. **~o** a elegant

gallego a & m Galician

galleta f biscuit (Brit), cookie (Amer)

gall|ina f hen, chicken; (fig, fam) coward. **~o** m cock

gama f scale; (fig) range

gamba f prawn (Brit), shrimp (Amer)

gamberro m hooligan

gamuza f (piel) chamois leather

gana f wish, desire; (apetito) appetite. **de buena ~** willingly. **de mala ~** reluctantly. **no me da la ~** I don't feel like it. **tener ~s de** (+ infinitivo) feel like (+ gerundio)

ganad|ería f cattle raising; (ganado) livestock. **~o** m livestock. **~o de cerda** pigs. **~o lanar** sheep. **~o vacuno** cattle

ganar vt earn; (en concurso, juego etc) win; (alcanzar) reach; (aventajar) beat. ● vi (vencer) win; (mejorar) improve. **~se la vida** earn a living. **salir ganando** come out better off

ganch|illo m crochet. **~o** m hook. **~oso** a, **~udo** a hooked. **echar el ~o a** hook. **hacer ~illo** crochet. **tener ~o** be very attractive

gandul a & m & f good-for-nothing

ganga f bargain; (buena situación) easy job, cushy job (fam)

gangrena f gangrene

gans|ada f silly thing. **~o** m goose

gañi|do m yelping. **~r** [22] vi yelp

garabat|ear vt/i (garrapatear) scribble. **~o** m (garrapato) scribble

garaj|e m garage. **~ista** m & f garage attendant

garant|e m & f guarantor. **~ía** f guarantee. **~ir** [24] vt (esp LAm), **~izar** [10] vt guarantee

garapiñado a. **almendras** fpl **garapiñadas** sugared almonds

garbanzo m chick-pea

garbo m poise; (de escrito) style. **~so** a elegant

garfio m hook

garganta f throat; (desfiladero) gorge; (de botella) neck

gárgaras fpl. **hacer ~** gargle

gargarismo m gargle

gárgola f gargoyle

garita f hut; (de centinela) sentry box

garito m gambling den

garra f (de animal) claw; (de ave) talon

garrafa f carafe

garrapata f tick

garrapat|ear vi scribble. **~o** m scribble

garrote m club, cudgel; (tormento) garrotte

gárrulo a garrulous

garúa f (LAm) drizzle

garza f heron

gas m gas. **con ~** fizzy. **sin ~** still

gasa f gauze

gaseosa f lemonade

gasfitero m (Arg) plumber

gas|óleo m diesel. **~olina** f petrol (Brit), gasoline (Amer), gas (Amer). **~olinera** f petrol station (Brit), gas station (Amer); (lancha) motor boat. **~ómetro** m gasometer

gast|ado a spent; (vestido etc) worn out. **~ador** m spendthrift. **~ar** vt spend; (consumir) use; (malgastar) waste; wear (vestido etc); crack (broma). ● vi spend. **~arse** vpr wear out. **~o** m expense; (acción de gastar) spending

gástrico a gastric

gastronomía f gastronomy

gat|a f cat. **a ~as** on all fours. **~ear** vi crawl

gatillo m trigger; (de dentista) (dental) forceps

gat|ito m kitten. **~o** m cat. **dar ~o por liebre** take s.o. in

gaucho a & m Gaucho

gaveta f drawer

gavilla f sheaf; (de personas) band, gang

gaviota f seagull

gazpacho m gazpacho, cold soup

géiser m geyser

gelatina f gelatine; (jalea) jelly

gelignita f gelignite

gema f gem

gemelo m twin. **~s** mpl (anteojos) binoculars; (de camisa) cuff-links. **G~s** Gemini

gemido m groan

Géminis mpl Gemini

gemir [5] *vi* groan; ‹*animal*› whine, howl

gen *m*, **gene** *m* gene

geneal|ogía *f* genealogy. ~**ógico** *a* genealogical. **árbol** *m* ~**ógico** family tree

generación *f* generation

general *a* general; (*corriente*) common. ● *m* general. ~**ísimo** *m* generalissimo, supreme commander. ~**ización** *f* generalization. ~**izar** [10] *vt/i* generalize. ~**mente** *adv* generally. **en** ~ in general. **por lo** ~ generally

generar *vt* generate

género *m* type, sort; (*biol*) genus; (*gram*) gender; (*producto*) product. ~**s de punto** knitwear. ~ **humano** mankind

generos|idad *f* generosity. ~**o** *a* generous; ‹*vino*› full-bodied

génesis *f* genesis

genétic|a *f* genetics. ~**o** *a* genetic

genial *a* brilliant; (*agradable*) pleasant

genio *m* temper; (*carácter*) nature; (*talento, persona*) genius

genital *a* genital. ~**es** *mpl* genitals

gente *f* people; (*nación*) nation; (*familia, fam*) family; (*Mex, persona*) person

gentil *a* charming; (*pagano*) pagan. ~**eza** *f* elegance; (*encanto*) charm; (*amabilidad*) kindness

gentío *m* crowd

genuflexión *f* genuflection

genuino *a* genuine

ge|ografía *f* geography. ~**ográfico** *a* geographical. ~**ógrafo** *m* geographer

ge|ología *f* geology. ~**ólogo** *m* geologist

geom|etría *f* geometry. ~**étrico** *a* geometrical

geranio *m* geranium

geren|cia *f* management. ~**te** *m* manager

geriatría *f* geriatrics

germánico *a & m* Germanic

germen *m* germ

germicida *f* germicide

germinar *vi* germinate

gestación *f* gestation

gesticula|ción *f* gesticulation. ~**r** *vi* gesticulate; (*hacer muecas*) grimace

gesti|ón *f* step; (*administración*) management. ~**onar** *vt* take steps to arrange; (*dirigir*) manage

gesto *m* expression; (*ademán*) gesture; (*mueca*) grimace

Gibraltar *m* Gibraltar

gibraltareño *a & m* Gibraltarian

gigante *a* gigantic. ● *m* giant. ~**sco** *a* gigantic

gimn|asia *f* gymnastics. ~**asio** *m* gymnasium, gym (*fam*). ~**asta** *m & f* gymnast. ~**ástica** *f* gymnastics

gimotear *vi* whine

ginebra *f* gin

Ginebra *f* Geneva

ginec|ología *f* gynaecology. ~**ólogo** *m* gynaecologist

gira *f* excursion; (*a varios sitios*) tour

girar *vt* spin; (*por giro postal*) transfer. ● *vi* rotate, go round; ‹*camino etc*› turn

girasol *m* sunflower

gir|atorio *a* revolving. ~**o** *m* turn; (*com*) draft; (*locución*) expression. ~**o postal** postal order

giroscopio *m* gyroscope

gis *m* chalk

gitano *a & m* gypsy

glacia|l *a* icy. ~**r** *m* glacier

gladiador *m* gladiator

glándula *f* gland

glasear *vt* glaze; (*culin*) ice

glicerina *f* glycerine

glicina *f* wisteria

glob|al *a* global; (*fig*) overall. ~**o** *m* globe; (*aeróstato, juguete*) balloon

glóbulo *m* globule; (*med*) corpuscle

gloria *f* glory. ~**rse** *vpr* boast (de about)

glorieta *f* bower; (*auto*) roundabout (*Brit*), (traffic) circle (*Amer*)

glorificar [7] *vt* glorify

glorioso *a* glorious

glosario *m* glossary

glot|ón *a* gluttonous. ● *m* glutton. ~**onería** *f* gluttony

glucosa *f* glucose

gnomo /'nomo/ *m* gnome

gob|ernación *f* government. ~**ernador** *a* governing. ● *m* governor. ~**ernante** *a* governing. ~**ernar** [1] *vt* govern; (*dirigir*) manage, direct. ~**ierno** *m* government; (*dirección*) management, direction. ~**ierno de la casa** housekeeping. **Ministerio** *m* **de la G~ernación** Home Office (*Brit*), Department of the Interior (*Amer*)

goce *m* enjoyment

gol *m* goal

golf *m* golf

golfo *m* gulf; *(niño)* urchin; *(holgazán)* layabout

golondrina *f* swallow

golos|ina *f* titbit; *(dulce)* sweet. ~o *a* fond of sweets

golpe *m* blow; *(puñetazo)* punch; *(choque)* bump; *(de emoción)* shock; *(acceso)* fit; *(en fútbol)* shot; *(en golf, en tenis, de remo)* stroke. ~ar *vt* hit; *(dar varios golpes)* beat; *(con mucho ruido)* bang; *(con el puño)* punch. ● *vi* knock. ~ de estado coup d'etat. ~ de fortuna stroke of luck. ~ de mano raid. ~ de vista glance. ~ militar military coup. de ~ suddenly. de un ~ at one go

gom|a *f* rubber; *(para pegar)* glue; *(anillo)* rubber band; *(elástico)* elastic. ~a de borrar rubber. ~a de pegar glue. ~a espuma foam rubber. ~ita *f* rubber band

gongo *m* gong

gord|a *f (Mex)* thick tortilla. ~iflón *m (fam)*, ~inflón *m (fam)* fatty. ~o *a* *(persona)* fat; *(carne)* fatty; *(grande)* large, big. ● *m* first prize. ~ura *f* fatness; *(grasa)* fat

gorila *f* gorilla

gorje|ar *vi* chirp. ~o *m* chirping

gorra *f* cap

gorrión *m* sparrow

gorro *m* cap; *(de niño)* bonnet

got|a *f* drop; *(med)* gout. ~ear *vi* drip. ~eo *m* dripping. ~era *f* leak. ni ~ nothing

gótico *a* Gothic

gozar [10] *vt* enjoy. ● *vi*. ~ de enjoy. ~se *vpr* enjoy

gozne *m* hinge

gozo *m* pleasure; *(alegría)* joy. ~so *a* delighted

graba|ción *f* recording. ~do *m* engraving, print; *(en libro)* illustration. ~r* vt* engrave; record *(discos etc)*

gracejo *m* wit

graci|a *f* grace; *(favor)* favour; *(humor)* wit. ~as *fpl* thanks. ¡~as! thank you!, thanks! ~oso *a* funny. ● *m* fool, comic character. dar las ~as thank. hacer ~a amuse; *(gustar)* please. ¡muchas ~as! thank you very much! tener ~a be funny

grad|a *f* step; *(línea)* row; *(de anfiteatro)* tier. ~ación *f* gradation. ~o *m* degree; *(escol)* year *(Brit)*, grade *(Amer)*; *(voluntad)* willingness

gradua|ción *f* graduation; *(de alcohol)* proof. ~do *m* graduate. ~l *a*

gradual. ~r [21] *vt* graduate; *(medir)* measure; *(univ)* confer a degree on. ~rse *vpr* graduate

gráfic|a *f* graph. ~o *a* graphic. ● *m* graph

grajo *m* rook

gram|ática *f* grammar. ~atical *a* grammatical

gramo *m* gram, gramme *(Brit)*

gramófono *m* record-player, gramophone *(Brit)*, phonograph *(Amer)*

gran *a véase* grande

grana *f (color)* scarlet

granada *f* pomegranate; *(mil)* grenade

granate *m* garnet

Gran Bretaña *f* Great Britain

grande *a (delante de nombre en singular gran)* big, large; *(alto)* tall; *(fig)* great. ● *m* grandee. ~za *f* greatness

grandioso *a* magnificent

granel *m.* a ~ in bulk; *(suelto)* loose; *(fig)* in abundance

granero *m* barn

granito *m* granite; *(grano)* small grain

graniz|ado *m* iced drink. ~ar [10] *vi* hail. ~o *m* hail

granj|a *f* farm. ~ero *m* farmer

grano *m* grain; *(semilla)* seed; *(de café)* bean; *(med)* spot. ~s *mpl* cereals

granuja *m & f* rogue

gránulo *m* granule

grapa *f* staple

gras|a *f* grease; *(culin)* fat. ~iento *a* greasy

gratifica|ción *f (propina)* tip; *(de sueldo)* bonus. ~r [7] *vt (dar propina)* tip

gratis *adv* free

gratitud *f* gratitude

grato *a* pleasant; *(bienvenido)* welcome

gratuito *a* free; *(fig)* uncalled for

grava *f* gravel

grava|men *m* obligation. ~r *vt* tax; *(cargar)* burden

grave *a* serious; *(pesado)* heavy; *(sonido)* low; *(acento)* grave. ~dad *f* gravity

gravilla *f* gravel

gravita|ción *f* gravitation. ~r *vi* gravitate; *(apoyarse)* rest *(sobre* on); *(fig, pesar)* weigh *(sobre* on)

gravoso *a* onerous; *(costoso)* expensive

graznar vi ⟨cuervo⟩ caw; ⟨pato⟩ quack

Grecia f Greece

gregario a gregarious

greguería f uproar

gremio m union

greña f mop of hair. ~**udo** a unkempt

gresca f uproar; ⟨riña⟩ quarrel

griego a & m Greek

grieta f crack

grifo m tap, faucet (Amer); ⟨animal fantástico⟩ griffin

grilletes mpl shackles

grillo m cricket; ⟨bot⟩ shoot. ~**s** mpl shackles

grima f. **dar** ~ annoy

gringo m (LAm) Yankee ⟨fam⟩, American

gripe f flu ⟨fam⟩, influenza

gris a grey. ● m grey; ⟨policía, fam⟩ policeman

grit|ar vt shout (for); ⟨como protesta⟩ boo. ● vi shout. ~**ería** f, ~**erío** m uproar. ~**o** m shout; ⟨de dolor, sorpresa⟩ cry; ⟨chillido⟩ scream. **dar** ~**s** shout

grosella f redcurrant. ~ **negra** blackcurrant

groser|ía f coarseness; ⟨palabras etc⟩ coarse remark. ~**o** a coarse; ⟨descortés⟩ rude

grosor m thickness

grotesco a grotesque

grúa f crane

grues|a f gross. ~**o** a thick; ⟨persona⟩ fat, stout. ● m thickness; ⟨fig⟩ main body

grulla f crane

grumo m clot; ⟨de leche⟩ curd

gruñi|do m grunt; ⟨fig⟩ grumble. ~**r** [22] vi grunt; ⟨perro⟩ growl; ⟨refunfuñar⟩ grumble

grupa f hindquarters

grupo m group

gruta f grotto

guacamole m (Mex) avocado purée

guadaña f scythe

guagua f trifle; ⟨esp LAm, autobús, fam⟩ bus

guante m glove

guapo a good-looking; ⟨chica⟩ pretty; ⟨elegante⟩ smart

guarapo m (LAm) sugar cane liquor

guarda m & f guard; ⟨de parque etc⟩ keeper. ● f protection. ~**barros** m invar mudguard. ~**bosque** m gamekeeper. ~**costas** m invar coastguard

vessel. ~**dor** a careful. ● m keeper. ~**espaldas** m invar bodyguard. ~**meta** m invar goalkeeper. ~**r** vt keep; ⟨vigilar⟩ guard; ⟨proteger⟩ protect; ⟨reservar⟩ save, keep. ~**rse** vpr be on one's guard. ~**rse de** (+ infinitivo) avoid (+ gerundio). ~**rropa** m wardrobe; ⟨en local público⟩ cloakroom. ~**vallas** m invar (LAm) goalkeeper

guardería f nursery

guardia f guard; ⟨custodia⟩ care. ● f guard. **G**~ **Civil** Civil Guard. ~ **municipal** policeman. ~ **de tráfico** traffic policeman. **estar de** ~ be on duty. **estar en** ~ be on one's guard. **montar la** ~ mount guard

guardián m guardian; ⟨de parque etc⟩ keeper; ⟨de edificio⟩ caretaker

guardilla f attic

guar|ecer [11] ⟨albergar⟩ give shelter to. ~**ecerse** vpr take shelter. ~**ida** f den, lair; ⟨de personas⟩ hideout

guarn|ecer [11] vt provide; ⟨adornar⟩ decorate; ⟨culin⟩ garnish. ~**ición** m decoration; ⟨de caballo⟩ harness; ⟨culin⟩ garnish; ⟨mil⟩ garrison; ⟨de piedra preciosa⟩ setting

guarro m pig

guasa f joke; ⟨ironía⟩ irony

guaso a (Arg) coarse

guasón a humorous. ● m joker

Guatemala f Guatemala

guatemalteco a from Guatemala. ● m person from Guatemala

guateque m party

guayaba f guava; ⟨dulce⟩ guava jelly

guayabera f (Mex) shirt

gubernamental a, **gubernativo** a governmental

güero a (Mex) fair

guerr|a f war; ⟨método⟩ warfare. ~**a civil** civil war. ~**ear** vi wage war. ~**ero** a war; ⟨belicoso⟩ fighting. ● m warrior. ~**illa** f band of guerillas. ~**illero** m guerilla. **dar** ~**a** annoy

guía m & f guide. ● f guidebook; ⟨de teléfonos⟩ directory; ⟨de ferrocarriles⟩ timetable

guiar [20] vt guide; ⟨llevar⟩ lead; ⟨auto⟩ drive. ~**se** vpr be guided (por by)

guij|arro m pebble. ~**o** m gravel

guillotina f guillotine

guind|a f morello cherry. ~**illa** f chilli

guiñapo m rag; ⟨fig, persona⟩ reprobate

guiñ|ar vt/i wink. **~o** m wink. **hacer ~os** wink

guil|ón m hyphen, dash; (de película etc) script. **~onista** m & f scriptwriter

guirnalda f garland

güiro m (LAm) gourd

guisa f manner, way. **a ~ de** as. **de tal ~** in such a way

guisado m stew

guisante m pea. **~ de olor** sweet pea

guis|ar vt/i cook. **~o** m dish

güisqui m whisky

guitarr|a f guitar. **~ista** m & f guitarist

gula f gluttony

gusano m worm; (larva de mosca) maggot

gustar vt taste. ● vi please. **¿te gusta?** do you like it? **me gusta el vino** I like wine

gusto m taste; (placer) pleasure. **~so** a tasty; (agradable) pleasant. **a ~** comfortable. **a mi ~** to my liking. **buen ~** (good) taste. **con mucho ~** with pleasure. **dar ~** please. **mucho ~** pleased to meet you

gutural a guttural

H

ha vb véase **haber**

haba f broad bean; (de café etc) bean

Habana f. **la ~** Havana

haban|era f habanera, Cuban dance. **~ero** a from Havana. ● m person from Havana. **~o** m (puro) Havana

haber v aux [30] have. ● v impersonal (presente s & pl **hay**, imperfecto s & pl **había**, pretérito s & pl **hubo**) be. **hay 5 bancos en la plaza** there are 5 banks in the square. **hay que hacerlo** it must be done, you have to do it. **he aquí** here is, here are. **no hay de qué** don't mention it, not at all. **¿qué hay?** (¿qué pasa?) what's the matter?; (¿qué tal?) how are you?

habichuela f bean

hábil a skilful; (listo) clever; (adecuado) suitable

habilidad f skill; (astucia) cleverness

habilita|ción f qualification. **~r** vt qualify

habita|ble a habitable. **~ción** f room; (casa etc) dwelling; (cuarto de dormir) bedroom; (en biología) habitat. **~ción de matrimonio**, **~ción doble** double room. **~ción individual**, **~ción sencilla** single room. **~do** a inhabited. **~nte** m inhabitant. **~r** vt live in. ● vi live

hábito m habit

habitual a usual, habitual; (cliente) regular. **~mente** adv usually

habituar [21] vt accustom. **~se** vpr. **~se a** get used to

habla f speech; (idioma) language; (dialecto) dialect. **al ~** (al teléfono) speaking. **ponerse al ~ con** get in touch with. **~dor** a talkative. ● m chatterbox. **~duría** f rumour. **~durías** fpl gossip. **~nte** a speaking. ● m & f speaker. **~r** vt speak. ● vi speak, talk (con to). **~rse** vpr speak. **¡ni ~r!** out of the question! **se ~ español** Spanish spoken

hacedor m creator, maker

hacendado m landowner; (LAm) farmer

hacendoso a hard-working

hacer [31] vt do; (fabricar, producir etc) make; (en matemáticas) make, be. ● v impersonal (con expresiones meteorológicas) be; (con determinado periodo de tiempo) ago. **~se** vpr become; (acostumbrarse) get used (a to); (estar hecho) be made. **~ de** act as. **~se a la mar** put to sea. **~se el sordo** pretend to be deaf. **hace buen tiempo** it's fine weather. **hace calor** it's hot. **hace frío** it's cold. **hace poco** recently. **hace 7 años** 7 years ago. **hace sol** it's sunny. **hace viento** it's windy. **¿qué le vamos a ~?** what are we going to do?

hacia prep towards; (cerca de) near; (con tiempo) at about. **~ abajo** down(wards). **~ arriba** up(wards). **~ las dos** at about two o'clock

hacienda f country estate; (en LAm) ranch; (LAm, ganado) livestock; (pública) treasury. **Ministerio de H~** Ministry of Finance; (en Gran Bretaña) Exchequer; (en Estados Unidos) Treasury. **ministro m de H~** Minister of Finance; (en Gran Bretaña) Chancellor of the Exchequer; (en Estados Unidos) Secretary of the Treasury

hacinar vt stack

hacha f axe; (antorcha) torch

hachís m hashish

hada f fairy. **cuento** m **de** ~s fairy tale
hado m fate
hago vb véase **hacer**
Haití m Haiti
halag|ar [12] vt flatter. ~**üeño** a flattering
halcón m falcon
hálito m breath
halo m halo
hall /xol/ m hall
halla|r vt find; (descubrir) discover. ~**rse** vpr be. ~**zgo** m discovery
hamaca f hammock; (asiento) deckchair
hambr|e f hunger; (de muchos) famine. ~**iento** a starving. **tener** ~**e** be hungry
Hamburgo m Hamburg
hamburguesa f hamburger
hamp|a f underworld. ~**ón** m thug
handicap /'xandikap/ m handicap
hangar m hangar
haragán a lazy, idle. ● m layabout
harap|iento a in rags. ~**o** m rag
harina f flour
harpa f harp
hart|ar vt satisfy; (fastidiar) annoy. ~**arse** vpr (comer) eat one's fill; (cansarse) get fed up (de with). ~**azgo** m surfeit. ~**o** a full; (cansado) tired; (fastidiado) fed up (de with). ● adv enough; (muy) very. ~**ura** f surfeit; (abundancia) plenty; (de deseo) satisfaction
hasta prep as far as; (con tiempo) until, till; (Mex) not until. ● adv even. ¡~ **la vista!** goodbye!, see you! (fam). ¡~ **luego!** see you later! ¡~ **mañana!** see you tomorrow! ¡~ **pronto!** see you soon!
hast|iar [20] vt annoy; (cansar) weary, tire; (aburrir) bore. ~**iarse** vpr get fed up (de with). ~**ío** m weariness; (aburrimiento) boredom; (asco) disgust
hat|illo m bundle (of belongings); (ganado) small flock. ~**o** m belongings; (ganado) flock, herd
haya f beech (tree). ● vb véase **haber**
Haya f. **la** ~ the Hague
haz m bundle; (de trigo) sheaf; (de rayos) beam
hazaña f exploit
hazmerreír m laughing-stock
he vb véase **haber**
hebdomadario a weekly
hebilla f buckle

hebra f thread; (fibra) fibre
hebreo a Hebrew; (actualmente) Jewish. ● m Hebrew; (actualmente) Jew; (lengua) Hebrew
hecatombe f (fig) disaster
hechi|cera f witch. ~**cería** f witchcraft. ~**cero** a magic. ● m wizard. ~**zar** [10] vt cast a spell on; (fig) fascinate. ~**zo** m witchcraft; (un acto de brujería) spell; (fig) fascination
hech|o pp de **hacer**. ● a mature; (terminado) finished; (vestidos etc) ready-made; (culin) done. ● m fact; (acto) deed; (cuestión) matter; (suceso) event. ~**ura** f making; (forma) form; (del cuerpo) build; (calidad de fabricación) workmanship. **de** ~**o** in fact
hed|er [1] vi stink. ~**iondez** f stench. ~**iondo** a stinking, smelly. ~**or** m stench
hela|da f freeze; (escarcha) frost. ~**dera** f (LAm) refrigerator, fridge (Brit, fam). ~**dería** f ice-cream shop. ~**do** a frozen; (muy frío) very cold. ● m ice-cream. ~**dora** f freezer. ~**r** [1] vt freeze. ~**rse** vpr freeze
helecho m fern
hélice f spiral; (propulsor) propeller
heli|cóptero m helicopter. ~**puerto** m heliport
hembra f female; (mujer) woman
hemisferio m hemisphere
hemorragia f haemorrhage
hemorroides fpl haemorrhoids, piles
henchir [5] vt fill. ~**se** vpr stuff o.s.
hend|er [1] vt split. ~**idura** f crack, split; (geol) fissure
heno m hay
heráldica f heraldry
herb|áceo a herbaceous. ~**olario** m herbalist. ~**oso** a grassy
hered|ad f country estate. ~**ar** vt/i inherit. ~**era** f heiress. ~**ero** m heir. ~**itario** a hereditary
hereje m heretic. ~**ía** f heresy
herencia f inheritance; (fig) heritage
heri|da f injury. ~**do** a injured, wounded. ● m injured person. ~**r** [4] vt injure, wound; (fig) hurt. ~**rse** vpr hurt o.s. **los** ~**dos** the injured; (cantidad) the number of injured
herman|a f sister. ~**a política** sister-in-law. ~**astra** f stepsister. ~**astro** m stepbrother. ~**dad** f brotherhood. ~**o** m brother. ~**o**

político brother-in-law. ∼os ge- melos twins

hermético a hermetic; (fig) water- tight

hermos|o a beautiful; (espléndido) splendid; (hombre) handsome. ∼ura f beauty

hernia f hernia

héroe m hero

hero|ico a heroic. ∼ína f heroine; (droga) heroin. ∼ísmo m heroism

herr|adura f horseshoe. ∼amienta f tool. ∼ería f smithy. ∼ero m black- smith. ∼umbre f rust

herv|idero m (manantial) spring; (fig) hotbed; (multitud) throng. ∼ir [4] vt/i boil. ∼or m boiling; (fig) ar- dour

heterogéneo a heterogeneous

heterosexual a & m & f hetero- sexual

hex|agonal a hexagonal. ∼ágono m hexagon

hiato m hiatus

hiberna|ción f hibernation. ∼r vi hibernate

hibisco m hibiscus

híbrido a & m hybrid

hice vb véase hacer

hidalgo m nobleman

hidrata|nte a moisturizing. ∼r vt hydrate; (crema etc) moisturize. crema f ∼nte moisturizing cream

hidráulico a hydraulic

hidroavión m seaplane

hidroeléctrico a hydroelectric

hidrófilo a absorbent

hidr|ofobia f rabies. ∼ófobo a rabid

hidrógeno m hydrogen

hidroplano m seaplane

hiedra f ivy

hiel f (fig) bitterness

hielo m ice; (escarcha) frost; (fig) coldness

hiena f hyena; (fig) brute

hierba f grass; (culin, med) herb. ∼buena f mint. mala ∼ weed; (gente) bad people, evil people

hierro m iron

hígado m liver

higi|ene f hygiene. ∼énico a hy- gienic

hig|o m fig. ∼uera f fig tree

hij|a f daughter. ∼a política daugh- ter-in-law. ∼astra f stepdaughter. ∼astro m stepson. ∼o m son. ∼o

político son-in-law. ∼os mpl sons; (chicos y chicas) children

hilar vt spin. ∼ delgado split hairs

hilaridad f laughter, hilarity

hilera f row; (mil) file

hilo m thread; (elec) wire; (de líquido) trickle; (lino) linen

hilv|án m tacking. ∼anar vt tack; (fig, bosquejar) outline

himno m hymn. ∼ nacional anthem

hincapié m. hacer ∼ en stress, insist on

hincar [7] vt drive in. ∼se vpr sink into. ∼se de rodillas kneel down

hincha f (fam) grudge; (aficionado, fam) fan

hincha|do a inflated; (med) swollen; (persona) arrogant. ∼r vt inflate, blow up. ∼rse vpr swell up; (fig, comer mucho, fam) gorge o.s. ∼zón f swelling; (fig) arrogance

hindi m Hindi

hindú a Hindu

hiniesta f (bot) broom

hinojo m fennel

hiper... pref hyper...

hiper|mercado m hypermarket. ∼sensible a hypersensitive. ∼ten- sión f high blood pressure

hípico a horse

hipn|osis f hypnosis. ∼ótico a hyp- notic. ∼otismo m hypnotism. ∼oti- zador m hypnotist. ∼otizar [10] vt hypnotize

hipo m hiccup. tener ∼ have hiccups

hipocondríaco a & m hypochondriac

hip|ocresía f hypocrisy. ∼ócrita a hypocritical. ● m & f hypocrite

hipodérmico a hypodermic

hipódromo m racecourse

hipopótamo m hippopotamus

hipoteca f mortgage. ∼r [7] vt mort- gage

hip|ótesis f invar hypothesis. ∼oté- tico a hypothetical

hiriente a offensive, wounding

hirsuto a shaggy

hirviente a boiling

hispánico a Hispanic

hispano... pref Spanish

Hispanoamérica f Spanish America

hispano|americano a Spanish American. ∼hablante a, ∼par- lante a Spanish-speaking

hist|eria f hysteria. ∼érico a hys- terical. ∼erismo m hysteria

hist|oria f history; (cuento) story. ∼oriador m historian. ∼órico a his- torical. ∼orieta f tale; (con dibujos) strip cartoon. **pasar a la** ~**oria** go down in history

hito *m* milestone

hizo *vb véase* **hacer**

hocico *m* snout; (*fig, de enfado*) grimace

hockey *m* hockey. ~ **sobre hielo** ice hockey

hogar *m* hearth; (*fig*) home. ~**eño** *a* home; (*persona*) home-loving

hogaza *f* large loaf

hoguera *f* bonfire

hoja *f* leaf; (*de papel, metal etc*) sheet; (*de cuchillo, espada etc*) blade. ~ **de afeitar** razor blade. ~**lata** *f* tin. ~**latería** *f* tinware. ~**latero** *m* tin-smith

hojaldre *m* puff pastry, flaky pastry

hojear *vt* leaf through; (*leer superficialmente*) glance through

hola *int* hello!

Holanda *f* Holland

holand|és *a* Dutch. ● *m* Dutchman; (*lengua*) Dutch. ~**esa** *f* Dutchwoman

holg|ado *a* loose; (*fig*) comfortable. ~**ar** [2 & 12] *vt* (*no trabajar*) not work, have a day off; (*sobrar*) be unnecessary. ~**azán** *a* lazy. ● *m* idler. ~**ura** *f* looseness; (*fig*) comfort; (*en mecánica*) play. **huelga decir que** needless to say

holocausto *m* holocaust

hollín *m* soot

hombre *m* man; (*especie humana*) man(kind). ● *int* Good Heavens!; (*de duda*) well. ~ **de estado** statesman. ~ **de negocios** businessman. ~ **rana** frogman. **el ~ de la calle** the man in the street

hombr|era *f* epaulette; (*almohadilla*) shoulder pad. ~**o** *m* shoulder

hombruno *a* masculine

homenaje *m* homage; (*fig*) tribute. **rendir** ~ **a** pay tribute to

home|ópata *m* homoeopath. ~**opatía** *f* homoeopathy. ~**opático** *a* homoeopathic

homicid|a *a* murderous. ● *m & f* murderer. ~**io** *m* murder

homogéneo *a* homogeneous

homosexual *a & m & f* homosexual. ~**idad** *f* homosexuality

hond|o *a* deep. ~**onada** *f* hollow. ~**ura** *f* depth

Honduras *fpl* Honduras

hondureño *a & m* Honduran

honest|idad *f* decency. ~**o** *a* proper

hongo *m* fungus; (*culin*) mushroom; (*venenoso*) toadstool

hon|or *m* honour. ~**orable** *a* honourable. ~**orario** *a* honorary. ~**orarios** *mpl* fees. ~**ra** *f* honour; (*buena fama*) good name. ~**radez** *f* honesty. ~**rado** *a* honest. ~**rar** *vt* honour. ~**rarse** *vpr* be honoured

hora *f* hour; (*momento determinado, momento oportuno*) time. ~ **avanzada** late hour. ~ **punta** rush hour. ~**s** *fpl* **de trabajo** working hours. ~**s** *fpl* **extraordinarias** overtime. **a estas** ~**s** now. **¿a qué** ~? at what time? when? **de** ~ **en** ~ hourly. **de última** ~ last-minute. **en buena** ~ at the right time. **media** ~ half an hour. **¿qué** ~ **es?** what time is it? **¿tiene Vd** ~? can you tell me the time?

horario *a* time; (*cada hora*) hourly. ● *m* timetable. **a** ~ (*LAm*) on time

horca *f* gallows

horcajadas *fpl*. **a** ~ astride

horchata *f* tiger-nut milk

horda *f* horde

horizont|al *a & f* horizontal. ~**e** *m* horizon

horma *f* mould; (*para fabricar calzado*) last; (*para conservar forma del calzado*) shoe-tree

hormiga *f* ant

hormigón *m* concrete

hormigue|ar *vt* tingle; (*bullir*) swarm. **me** ~**a la mano** I've got pins and needles in my hand. ~**o** *m* tingling; (*fig*) anxiety

hormiguero *m* anthill; (*de gente*) swarm

hormona *f* hormone

horn|ada *f* batch. ~**ero** *m* baker. ~**illo** *m* cooker. ~**o** *m* oven; (*para ladrillos, cerámica etc*) kiln; (*tec*) furnace

horóscopo *m* horoscope

horquilla *f* pitchfork; (*para el pelo*) hairpin

horr|endo *a* awful. ~**ible** *a* horrible. ~**ipilante** *a* terrifying. ~**or** *m* horror; (*atrocidad*) atrocity. ~**orizar** [10] *vt* horrify. ~**orizarse** *vpr* be horrified. ~**oroso** *a* horrifying. **¡qué** ~**or!** how awful!

hort|aliza *f* vegetable. ~**elano** *m* market gardener. ~**icultura** *f* horticulture

hosco *a* surly; (*lugar*) gloomy

hospeda|je m lodging. **~r** vt put up. **~rse** vpr lodge

hospital m hospital

hospital|ario m hospitable. **~idad** f hospitality

hostal m boarding-house

hostería f inn

hostia f (relig) host; (golpe, fam) punch

hostigar [12] vt whip; (fig, excitar) urge; (fig, molestar) pester

hostil a hostile. **~idad** f hostility

hotel m hotel. **~ero** a hotel. ● m hotelier

hoy adv today. **~ (en) día** nowadays. **~ mismo** this very day. **~ por ~** for the time being. **de ~ en adelante** from now on

hoy|a f (sepultura) grave. **~o** m hole; (sepultura) grave. **~uelo** m dimple

hoz f sickle; (desfiladero) pass

hube vb véase **haber**

hucha f money box

hueco a hollow; (vacío) empty; (esponjoso) spongy; (resonante) resonant. ● m hollow

huelg|a f strike. **~a de brazos caídos** sit-down strike. **~a de celo** work-to-rule. **~a de hambre** hunger strike. **~uista** m & f striker. **declarar la ~a, declararse en ~a** come out on strike

huelo vb véase **oler**

huella f footprint; (de animal, vehículo etc) track. **~ dactilar, ~ digital** fingerprint

huérfano a orphaned. ● m orphan. **~ de** without

huero a empty

huert|a f market garden (Brit), truck farm (Amer); (terreno de regadío) irrigated plain. **~o** m vegetable garden; (de árboles frutales) orchard

huesa f grave

hueso m bone; (de fruta) stone. **~so** a bony

huésped m guest; (que paga) lodger; (animal) host

huesudo a bony

huev|a f roe. **~era** f eggcup. **~o** m egg. **~o duro** hard-boiled egg. **~o escalfado** poached egg. **~o estrellado, ~o frito** fried egg. **~o pasado por agua** boiled egg. **~os revueltos** scrambled eggs

hui|da f flight, escape. **~dizo** a (tímido) shy; (fugaz) fleeting. **~r** [17] vt/i flee, run away; (evitar) avoid

huipil m (Mex) embroidered smock

huitlacoche m (Mex) edible black fungus

hule m oilcloth, oilskin

human|idad f mankind; (fig) humanity. **~idades** fpl humanities. **~ismo** m humanism. **~ista** m & f humanist. **~itario** a humanitarian. **~o** a human; (benévolo) humane. ● m human (being)

hum|areda f cloud of smoke. **~ear** vi smoke; (echar vapor) steam

humed|ad f dampness (en meteorología) humidity. **~ecer** [11] vt moisten. **~ecerse** vpr become moist

húmedo a damp; (clima) humid; (mojado) wet

humi|ldad f humility. **~lde** a humble. **~llación** f humiliation. **~llar** vt humiliate. **~llarse** vpr humble o.s.

humo m smoke; (vapor) steam; (gas nocivo) fumes. **~s** mpl conceit

humor m mood, temper; (gracia) humour. **~ismo** m humour. **~ista** m & f humorist. **~ístico** a humorous. **estar de mal ~** be in a bad mood

hundi|do a sunken. **~miento** m sinking. **~r** vt sink; destroy (edificio). **~rse** vpr sink; (edificio) collapse

húngaro a & m Hungarian

Hungría f Hungary

huracán m hurricane

huraño a unsociable

hurg|ar [12] vt poke; (fig) stir up. **~ón** m poker

hurón m ferret. ● a unsociable

hurra int hurray!

hurraca f magpie

hurtadillas fpl a **~** stealthily

hurt|ar vt steal. **~o** m theft; (cosa robada) stolen object

husmear vt sniff out; (fig) pry into

huyo vb véase **huir**

I

Iberia f Iberia

ibérico a Iberian

ibero a & m Iberian

íbice m ibex, mountain goat

Ibiza f Ibiza

iceberg /iθ'ber/ m iceberg

icono m icon

ictericia f jaundice

ida f outward journey; (salida) departure. **de ∼ y vuelta** return (Brit), round-trip (Amer)

idea f idea; (opinión) opinion. **cambiar de ∼** change one's mind. **no tener la más remota ∼, no tener la menor ∼** not have the slightest idea, not have a clue (fam)

ideal a ideal; (imaginario) imaginary. ● m ideal. **∼ista** m & f idealist. **∼izar** [10] vt idealize

idear vt think up, conceive; (inventar) invent

ídem pron & adv the same

idéntico a identical

identi|dad f identity. **∼ficación** f identification. **∼ficar** [7] vt identify. **∼ficarse** vpr. **∼ficarse con** identify with

ideo|logía f ideology. **∼ógico** a ideological

idílico a idyllic

idilio m idyll

idioma m language. **∼ático** a idiomatic

idiosincrasia f idiosyncrasy

idiot|a a idiotic. ● m & f idiot. **∼ez** f idiocy

idiotismo m idiom

idolatrar vt worship; (fig) idolize

ídolo m idol

idóneo a suitable (**para** for)

iglesia f church

iglú m igloo

ignición f ignition

ignomini|a f ignominy, disgrace. **∼oso** a ignominious

ignora|ncia f ignorance. **∼nte** a ignorant. ● m ignoramus. **∼r** vt not know, be unaware of

igual a equal; (mismo) the same; (similar) like; (llano) even; (liso) smooth. ● adv easily. ● m equal. **∼ que** (the same) as. **al ∼ que** the same as. **da ∼, es ∼** it doesn't matter

igual|ar vt make equal; (ser igual) equal; (allanar) level. **∼arse** vpr be equal. **∼dad** f equality. **∼mente** adv equally; (también) also, likewise; (respuesta de cortesía) the same to you

ijada f flank

ilegal a illegal

ilegible a illegible

ilegítimo a illegitimate

ileso a unhurt

ilícito a illicit

ilimitado a unlimited

ilógico a illogical

ilumina|ción f illumination; (alumbrado) lighting; (fig) enlightenment. **∼r** vt light (up); (fig) enlighten. **∼rse** vpr light up

ilusi|ón f illusion; (sueño) dream; (alegría) joy. **∼onado** a excited. **∼onar** vt give false hope. **∼onarse** vpr have false hopes. **hacerse ∼ones** build up one's hopes. **me hace ∼ón** I'm thrilled; I'm looking forward to (algo en el futuro)

ilusionis|mo m conjuring. **∼ta** m & f conjurer

iluso a easily deceived. ● m dreamer. **∼rio** a illusory

ilustra|ción f learning; (dibujo) illustration. **∼do** a learned; (con dibujos) illustrated. **∼r** vt explain; (instruir) instruct; (añadir dibujos etc) illustrate. **∼rse** vpr acquire knowledge. **∼tivo** a illustrative

ilustre a illustrious

imagen f image; (TV etc) picture

imagina|ble a imaginable. **∼ción** f imagination. **∼r** vt imagine. **∼rse** vpr imagine. **∼rio** m imaginary. **∼tivo** a imaginative

imán m magnet

imantar vt magnetize

imbécil a stupid. ● m & f imbecile, idiot

imborrable a indelible; (recuerdo etc) unforgettable

imbuir [17] vt imbue (**de** with)

imita|ción f imitation. **∼r** vt imitate

impacien|cia f impatience. **∼tarse** vpr lose one's patience. **∼te** a impatient; (intranquilo) anxious

impacto m impact

impar a odd

imparcial a impartial. **∼idad** f impartiality

impartir vt impart

impasible a impassive

impávido a fearless; (impasible) impassive

impecable a impeccable

impedi|do a disabled. **∼menta** f (esp mil) baggage. **∼mento** m hindrance. **∼r** [5] vt prevent; (obstruir) hinder

impeler vt drive

impenetrable a impenetrable

impenitente a unrepentant

impensa|ble a unthinkable. **∼do** a unexpected

imperar vi reign

imperativo a imperative; ⟨persona⟩ imperious

imperceptible a imperceptible

imperdible m safety pin

imperdonable a unforgivable

imperfec|ción f imperfection. ∼to a imperfect

imperial a imperial. ●f upper deck. ∼ismo m imperialism

imperio m empire; (poder) rule; (fig) pride. ∼so a imperious

impermeable a waterproof. ●m raincoat

impersonal a impersonal

impertérrito a undaunted

impertinen|cia f impertinence. ∼te a impertinent

imperturbable a imperturbable

ímpetu m impetus; (impulso) impulse; (impetuosidad) impetuosity

impetuos|idad f impetuosity; (violencia) violence. ∼o a impetuous; (violento) violent

impío a ungodly; ⟨acción⟩ irreverent

implacable a implacable

implantar vt introduce

implica|ción f implication. ∼r [7] vt implicate; (significar) imply

implícito a implicit

implora|ción f entreaty. ∼r vt implore

imponderable a imponderable; (inapreciable) invaluable

impon|ente a imposing; (fam) terrific. ∼er [34] vt impose; (requerir) demand; deposit ⟨dinero⟩. ∼erse vpr be imposed; (hacerse obedecer) assert o.s.; (hacerse respetar) command respect. ∼ible a taxable

impopular a unpopular. ∼idad f unpopularity

importa|ción f import; (artículo) import. ∼dor a importing. ●m importer

importa|ncia f importance; (tamaño) size. ∼nte a important; (en cantidad) considerable. ∼r vt import; (valer) cost. ●vi be important, matter. ¡le importa...? would you mind...? **no** ∼ it doesn't matter

importe m price; (total) amount

importun|ar vt bother. ∼o a troublesome; (inoportuno) inopportune

imposib|ilidad f impossibility. ∼le a impossible. **hacer lo** ∼**le** do all one can

imposición f imposition; (impuesto) tax

impostor m & f impostor

impotable a undrinkable

impoten|cia f impotence. ∼te a powerless, impotent

impracticable a impracticable; (intransitable) unpassable

impreca|ción f curse. ∼r [7] vt curse

imprecis|ión f vagueness. ∼o a imprecise

impregnar vt impregnate; (empapar) soak; (fig) cover

imprenta f printing; (taller) printing house, printer's

imprescindible a indispensable, essential

impresi|ón f impression; (acción de imprimir) printing; (tirada) edition; (huella) imprint. ∼onable a impressionable. ∼onante a impressive; (espantoso) frightening. ∼onar vt impress; (conmover) move; (foto) expose. ∼onarse vpr be impressed; (conmover) be moved

impresionis|mo m impressionism. ∼ta a & m & f impressionist

impreso a printed. ●m printed paper, printed matter. ∼ra f printer

imprevis|ible a unforseeable. ∼to a unforeseen

imprimir [pp impreso] vt impress; print ⟨libro etc⟩

improbab|ilidad f improbability. ∼le a unlikely, improbable

improcedente a unsuitable

improductivo a unproductive

improperio m insult. ∼s mpl abuse

impropio m improper

improvis|ación f improvisation. ∼adamente adv suddenly. ∼ado a improvised. ∼ar vt improvise. ∼o a. **de** ∼o suddenly

impruden|cia f imprudence. ∼te a imprudent

impúdico a immodest; (desvergonzado) shameless. ∼udor m immodesty; (desvergüenza) shamelessness

impuesto a imposed. ●m tax. ∼ **sobre el valor añadido** VAT, value added tax

impugnar vt contest; (refutar) refute

impulsar vt impel

impuls|ividad f impulsiveness. ∼ivo a impulsive. ∼o m impulse

impun|e *a* unpunished. ~idad *f* impunity

impur|eza *f* impurity. ~o *a* impure

imputa|ción *f* charge. ~r *vt* attribute; (*acusar*) charge

inacabable *a* interminable

inaccesible *a* inaccessible

inaceptable *a* unacceptable

inacostumbrado *a* unaccustomed

inactiv|idad *f* inactivity. ~o *a* inactive

inadaptado *a* maladjusted

inadecuado *a* inadequate; (*inapropiado*) unsuitable

inadmisible *a* inadmissible; (*intolerable*) intolerable

inadvert|ido *a* unnoticed. ~encia *f* inadvertence

inagotable *a* inexhaustible

inaguantable *a* unbearable; (*persona*) insufferable

inaltera|ble unchangeable; (*color*) fast; (*carácter*) calm. ~do *a* unchanged

inanimado *a* inanimate

inaplicable *a* inapplicable

inapreciable *a* imperceptible

inapropiado *a* inappropriate

inarticulado *a* inarticulate

inasequible *a* out of reach

inaudito *a* unheard-of

inaugura|ción *f* inauguration. ~l *a* inaugural. ~r *vt* inaugurate

inca *a* Incan. ● *m & f* Inca. ~ico *a* Incan

incalculable *a* incalculable

incandescen|cia *f* incandescence. ~te *a* incandescent

incansable *a* tireless

incapa|cidad *f* incapacity. ~citar *vt* incapacitate. ~z *a* incapable

incauto *a* unwary; (*fácil de engañar*) gullible

incendi|ar *vt* set fire to. ~arse *vpr* catch fire. ~ario *a* incendiary. ● *m* arsonist. ~o *m* fire

incentivo *m* incentive

incertidumbre *f* uncertainty

incesante *a* incessant

incest|o *m* incest. ~uoso *a* incestuous

inciden|cia *f* incidence; (*incidente*) incident. ~tal *a* incidental. ~te *m* incident

incidir *vi* fall; (*influir*) influence

incienso *m* incense

incierto *a* uncertain

incinera|ción *f* incineration; (*de cadáveres*) cremation. ~dor *m* incinerator. ~r *vt* incinerate; cremate (*cadáver*)

incipiente *a* incipient

incisión *f* incision

incisivo *a* incisive. ● *m* incisor

incitar *vt* incite

incivil *a* rude

inclemen|cia *f* harshness. ~te *a* harsh

inclina|ción *f* slope; (*de la cabeza*) nod; (*fig*) inclination. ~r *vt* incline. ~rse *vpr* lean; (*encorvarse*) stoop; (*en saludo*) bow; (*fig*) be inclined. ~rse a (*parecerse*) resemble

inclu|ido *a* included; (*precio*) inclusive; (*en cartas*) enclosed. ~ir [17] *vt* include; (*en cartas*) enclose. ~sión *f* inclusion. ~sive *adv* inclusive. hasta el lunes ~sive up to and including Monday. ~so *a* included; (*en cartas*) enclosed. ● *adv* including; (*hasta*) even

incógnito *a* unknown. de ~ incognito

incoheren|cia *f* incoherence. ~te *a* incoherent

incoloro *a* colourless

incólume *a* unharmed

incomestible *a*, incomible *a* uneatable, inedible

incomodar *vt* inconvenience; (*molestar*) bother. ~se *vpr* trouble o.s.; (*enfadarse*) get angry

incómodo *a* uncomfortable; (*inoportuno*) inconvenient

incomparable *a* incomparable

incompatib|ilidad *f* incompatibility. ~le *a* incompatible

incompeten|cia *f* incompetence. ~te *a* incompetent

incompleto *a* incomplete

incompren|dido *a* misunderstood. ~sible *a* incomprehensible. ~sión *f* incomprehension

incomunicado *a* isolated; (*preso*) in solitary confinement

inconcebible *a* inconceivable

inconciliable *a* irreconcilable

inconcluso *a* unfinished

incondicional *a* unconditional

inconfundible *a* unmistakable

incongruente *a* incongruous

inconmensurable *a* (*fam*) enormous

inconscien|cia *f* unconsciousness; (*irreflexión*) recklessness. ~te *a* unconscious; (*irreflexivo*) reckless

inconsecuente *a* inconsistent
inconsiderado *a* inconsiderate
inconsistente *a* insubstantial
inconsolable *a* unconsolable
inconstan|cia *f* inconstancy. ~te *a* changeable; ⟨persona⟩ fickle
incontable *a* countless
incontaminado *a* uncontaminated
incontenible *a* irrepressible
incontestable *a* indisputable
incontinen|cia *f* incontinence. ~te *a* incontinent
inconvenien|cia *f* disadvantage. ~te *a* inconvenient; ⟨inapropiado⟩ inappropriate; ⟨incorrecto⟩ improper. ● *m* difficulty; ⟨desventaja⟩ drawback
incorpora|ción *f* incorporation. ~r *vt* incorporate; ⟨culin⟩ mix. ~rse *upr* sit up; join ⟨sociedad, regimiento etc⟩
incorrecto *a* incorrect; ⟨acción⟩ improper; ⟨descortés⟩ discourteous
incorregible *a* incorrigible
incorruptible *a* incorruptible
incrédulo *a* incredulous
increíble *a* incredible
increment|ar *vt* increase. ~o *m* increase
incriminar *vt* incriminate
incrustar *vt* encrust
incuba|ción *f* incubation. ~dora *f* incubator. ~r *vt* incubate; ⟨fig⟩ hatch
incuestionable *a* unquestionable
inculcar [7] *vt* inculcate
inculpar *vt* accuse; ⟨culpar⟩ blame
inculto *a* uncultivated; ⟨persona⟩ uneducated
incumplimiento *m* non-fulfilment; ⟨de un contrato⟩ breach
incurable *a* incurable
incurrir *vi*. ~ en incur; fall into ⟨error⟩; commit ⟨crimen⟩
incursión *f* raid
indaga|ción *f* investigation. ~r [12] *vt* investigate
indebido *a* undue
indecen|cia *f* indecency. ~te *a* indecent
indecible *a* inexpressible
indecis|ión *f* indecision. ~o *a* undecided
indefenso *a* defenceless
indefini|ble *a* indefinable. ~do *a* indefinite
indeleble *a* indelible
indelicad|eza *f* indelicacy. ~o *a* indelicate; ⟨falto de escrúpulo⟩ unscrupulous

indemn|e *a* undamaged; ⟨persona⟩ unhurt. ~idad *f* indemnity. ~izar [10] *vt* indemnify, compensate
independ|encia *f* independence. ~iente *a* independent
independizarse [10] *upr* become independent
indescifrable *a* indecipherable, incomprehensible
indescriptible *a* indescribable
indeseable *a* undesirable
indestructible *a* indestructible
indetermina|ble *a* indeterminable. ~do *a* indeterminate
India *f*. la ~ India. las ~s *fpl* the Indies
indica|ción *f* indication; ⟨sugerencia⟩ suggestion. ~ciones *fpl* directions. ~dor *m* indicator; ⟨tec⟩ gauge. ~r [7] *vt* show, indicate; ⟨apuntar⟩ point at; ⟨hacer saber⟩ point out; ⟨aconsejar⟩ advise. ~tivo *a* indicative. ● *m* indicative; ⟨al teléfono⟩ dialling code
índice *m* indication; ⟨dedo⟩ index finger; ⟨de libro⟩ index; ⟨catálogo⟩ catalogue; ⟨aguja⟩ pointer
indicio *m* indication, sign; ⟨vestigio⟩ trace
indiferen|cia *f* indifference. ~te *a* indifferent. me es ~te it's all the same to me
indígena *a* indigenous. ● *m & f* native
indigen|cia *f* poverty. ~te *a* needy
indigest|ión *f* indigestion. ~o *a* undigested; ⟨difícil de digerir⟩ indigestible
indign|ación *f* indignation. ~ado *a* indignant. ~ar *vt* make indignant. ~arse *upr* be indignant. ~o *a* unworthy; ⟨despreciable⟩ contemptible
indio *a & m* Indian
indirect|a *f* hint. ~o *a* indirect
indisciplina *f* lack of discipline. ~do *a* undisciplined
indiscre|ción *f* indiscretion. ~to *a* indiscreet
indiscutible *a* unquestionable
indisoluble *a* indissoluble
indispensable *a* indispensable
indisp|oner [34] *vt* ⟨enemistar⟩ set against. ~onerse *upr* fall out; ⟨ponerse enfermo⟩ fall ill. ~osición *f* indisposition. ~uesto *a* indisposed
indistinto *a* indistinct
individu|al *a* individual; ⟨cama⟩ single. ~alidad *f* individuality. ~alista *m & f* individualist. ~alizar [10]

vt individualize. ∿o *a* & *m* individual

índole*f* nature; (*clase*) type

indolen|cia *f* indolence. ∿te *a* indolent

indoloro*a* painless

indomable*a* untameable

indómito*a* indomitable

Indonesia*f*Indonesia

inducir[47] *vt* induce; (*deducir*) infer

indudable *a* undoubted. ∿mente *adv* undoubtedly

indulgen|cia *f* indulgence. ∿te *a* indulgent

indult|ar *vt* pardon; exempt (*de un pago etc*). ∿o*m* pardon

industria*f* industry. ∿l *a* industrial. ● *m* industrialist. ∿lización *f* industrialization. ∿lizar [10] *vt* industrialize

industriarse*vpr* do one's best

industrioso*a* industrious

inédito *a* unpublished; (*fig*) unknown

ineducado*a* impolite

inefable*a* inexpressible

ineficaz*a* ineffective

ineficiente*a* inefficient

inelegible*a* ineligible

ineludible *a* inescapable, unavoidable

inept|itud*f*ineptitude. ∿o*a* inept

inequívoco*a* unequivocal

iner|cia*f*inertia

inerme*a* unarmed; (*fig*) defenceless

inerte*a* inert

inesperado*a* unexpected

inestable*a* unstable

inestimable*a* inestimable

inevitable*a* inevitable

inexacto *a* inaccurate; (*incorrecto*) incorrect; (*falso*) untrue

inexistente*a* non-existent

inexorable*a* inexorable

inexper|iencia*f* inexperience. ∿to *a* inexperienced

inexplicable*a* inexplicable

infalible*a* infallible

infam|ar *vt* defame. ∿atorio *a* defamatory. ∿e *a* infamous; (*fig, muy malo, fam*) awful. ∿ia*f*infamy

infancia*f*infancy

infant|a*f* infanta, princess. ∿e*m* infante, prince; (*mil*) infantryman. ∿ería *f* infantry. ∿il *a* (*de niño*) child's; (*como un niño*) infantile

infarto*m* coronary (thrombosis)

infatigable*a* untiring

infatua|ción*f* conceit. ∿rse *vpr* get conceited

infausto*a* unlucky

infec|ción *f* infection. ∿cioso *a* infectious. ∿tar *vt* infect. ∿tarse *vpr* become infected. ∿to *a* infected; (*fam*) disgusting

infecundo*a* infertile

infeli|cidad*f*unhappiness. ∿z*a* unhappy

inferior *a* inferior. ● *m* & *f* inferior. ∿idad*f*lower; (*calidad*) inferiority

inferir[4] *vt* infer; (*causar*) cause

infernal*a* infernal, hellish

infestar*vt* infest; (*fig*) inundate

infi|delidad *f* unfaithfulness. ∿el *a* unfaithful

infierno*m* hell

infiltra|ción *f* infiltration. ∿rse *vpr* infiltrate

ínfimo*a* lowest

infini|dad *f* infinity. ∿tivo *m* infinitive. ∿to *a* infinite. ● *m* infinite; (*en matemáticas*) infinity. una ∿dad de countless

inflación*f*inflation; (*fig*) conceit

inflama|ble*a* (in)flammable. ∿ción *f* inflammation. ∿r *vt* set on fire; (*fig, med*) inflame. ∿rse *vpr* catch fire; (*med*) become inflamed

inflar *vt* inflate; (*fig, exagerar*) exaggerate

inflexi|ble *a* inflexible. ∿ón *f* inflexion

infligir[14] *vt* inflict

influ|encia*f* influence. ∿enza *f* flu (*fam*), influenza. ∿ir [17] *vt/i* influence. ∿jo *m* influence. ∿yente *a* influential

informa|ción *f* information. ∿ciones *fpl* (*noticias*) news; (*de teléfonos*) directory enquiries. ∿dor *m* informant

informal *a* informal; (*incorrecto*) incorrect

inform|ante *m* & *f* informant. ∿ar *vt/i* inform. ∿arse *vpr* find out. ∿ática *f* information technology. ∿ativo*a* informative

informe *a* shapeless. ● *m* report; (*información*) information

infortun|ado *a* unfortunate. ∿io *m* misfortune

infracción*f*infringement

infraestructura*f*infrastructure

infranqueable *a* impassable; (*fig*) insuperable

infrarrojo*a* infrared

infrecuente *a* infrequent
infringir [14] *vt* infringe
infructuoso *a* fruitless
infundado *a* unfounded
infu|ndir *vt* instil. ~**sión** *f* infusion
ingeniar *vt* invent
ingenier|ía *f* engineering. ~**o** *m* engineer
ingenio *m* ingenuity; (*agudeza*) wit; (*LAm, de azúcar*) refinery. ~**so** *a* ingenious
ingenu|idad *f* ingenuousness. ~**o** *a* ingenuous
ingerir [4] *vt* swallow
Inglaterra *f* England
ingle *f* groin
ingl|és *a* English. ● *m* Englishman; (*lengua*) English. ~**esa** *f* Englishwoman
ingrat|itud *f* ingratitude. ~**o** *a* ungrateful;(*desagradable*)thankless
ingrediente *m* ingredient
ingres|ar *vt* deposit. ● *vi*. ~**ar en** come in, enter; join (*sociedad*). ~**o** *m* entry; (*en sociedad, hospital etc*) admission. ~**os** *mpl* income
inh|ábil *a* unskillful; (*no apto*) unfit. ~**abilidad** *f* unskillfulness
inhabitable *a* uninhabitable
inhala|ción *f* inhalation. ~**dor** *m* inhaler. ~**r** *vt* inhale
inherente *a* inherent
inhibi|ción *f* inhibition. ~**r** *vt* inhibit
inhospitalario *a*, **inhóspito** *a* inhospitable
inhumano *a* inhuman
inicia|ción *f* beginning. ~**l** *a & f* initial. ~**r** *vt* initiate; (*comenzar*) begin, start. ~**tiva** *f* initiative
inicio *m* beginning
inicuo *a* iniquitous
inigualado *a* unequalled
ininterrumpido *a* continuous
injer|encia *f* interference. ~**ir** [4] *vt* insert. ~**irse** *vpr* interfere
injert|ar *vt* graft. ~**to** *m* graft
injuri|a *f* insult; (*ofensa*) offence. ~**ar** *vt* insult. ~**oso** *a* offensive
injust|icia *f* injustice. ~**o** *a* unjust
inmaculado *a* immaculate
inmaduro *a* unripe; (*persona*) immature
inmediaciones *fpl* neighbourhood
inmediat|amente *adv* immediately. ~**o** *a* immediate; (*contiguo*) next
inmejorable *a* excellent

inmemorable *a* immemorial
inmens|idad *f* immensity. ~**o** *a* immense
inmerecido *a* undeserved
inmersión *f* immersion
inmigra|ción *f* immigration. ~**nte** *a & m* immigrant. ~**r** *vt* immigrate
inminen|cia *f* imminence. ~**te** *a* imminent
inmiscuirse [17] *vpr* interfere
inmobiliario *a* property
inmoderado *a* immoderate
inmodesto *a* immodest
inmolar *vt* sacrifice
inmoral *a* immoral. ~**idad** *f* immorality
inmortal *a* immortal. ~**izar** [10] *vt* immortalize
inmóvil *a* immobile
inmueble *a*. **bienes** ~**s** property
inmund|icia *f* filth. ~**icias** *fpl* rubbish. ~**o** *a* filthy
inmun|e *a* immune. ~**idad** *f* immunity. ~**ización** *f* immunization. ~**izar** [10] *vt* immunize
inmuta|ble *a* unchangeable. ~**rse** *vpr* turn pale
innato *a* innate
innecesario *a* unnecessary
innegable *a* undeniable
innoble *a* ignoble
innova|ción *f* innovation. ~**r** *vt/i* innovate
innumerable *a* innumerable
inocen|cia *f* innocence. ~**tada** *f* practical joke. ~**te** *a* innocent. ~**tón** *a* naïve
inocuo *a* innocuous
inodoro *a* odourless. ● *m* toilet
inofensivo *a* inoffensive
inolvidable *a* unforgettable
inoperable *a* inoperable
inopinado *a* unexpected
inoportuno *a* untimely; (*incómodo*) inconvenient
inorgánico *a* inorganic
inoxidable *a* stainless
inquebrantable *a* unbreakable
inquiet|ar *vt* worry. ~**arse** *vpr* get worried. ~**o** *a* worried; (*agitado*) restless. ~**ud** *f* anxiety
inquilino *m* tenant
inquirir [4] *vt* enquire into, investigate
insaciable *a* insatiable
insalubre *a* unhealthy
insanable *a* incurable

insatisfecho *a* unsatisfied; *(descontento)* dissatisfied

inscri|bir [*pp* **inscrito**] *vt* inscribe; *(en registro etc)* enrol, register. **~birse** *vpr* register. **~pción** *f* inscription; *(registro)* registration

insect|icida *m* insecticide. **~o** *m* insect

insegur|idad *f* insecurity. **~o** *a* insecure; *(dudoso)* uncertain

insemina|ción *f* insemination. **~r** *vt* inseminate

insensato *a* senseless

insensible *a* insensitive; *(med)* insensible; *(imperceptible)* imperceptible

inseparable *a* inseparable

insertar *vt* insert

insidi|a *f* trap. **~oso** *a* insidious

insigne *a* famous

insignia *f* badge; *(bandera)* flag

insignificante *a* insignificant

insincero *a* insincere

insinua|ción *f* insinuation. **~nte** *a* insinuating. **~r** [21] *vt* insinuate. **~rse** *vpr* ingratiate o.s. **~rse en** creep into

insípido *a* insipid

insist|encia *f* insistence. **~ente** *a* insistent. **~ir** *vi* insist; *(hacer hincapié)* stress

insolación *f* sunstroke

insolen|cia *f* rudeness, insolence. **~te** *a* rude, insolent

insólito *a* unusual

insoluble *a* insoluble

insolven|cia *f* insolvency. **~te** *a & m & f* insolvent

insomn|e *a* sleepless. **~io** *m* insomnia

insondable *a* unfathomable

insoportable *a* unbearable

insospechado *a* unexpected

insostenible *a* untenable

inspec|ción *f* inspection. **~cionar** *vt* inspect. **~tor** *m* inspector

inspira|ción *f* inspiration. **~r** *vt* inspire. **~rse** *vpr* be inspired

instala|ción *f* installation. **~r** *vt* install. **~rse** *vpr* settle

instancia *f* request

instant|ánea *f* snapshot. **~áneo** *a* instantaneous; *(café etc)* instant. **~e** *m* instant. **a cada ~e** constantly. **al ~e** immediately

instar *vt* urge

instaura|ción *f* establishment. **~r** *vt* establish

instiga|ción *f* instigation. **~dor** *m* instigator. **~r** [12] *vt* instigate; *(incitar)* incite

instint|ivo *a* instinctive. **~o** *m* instinct

institu|ción *f* institution. **~cional** *a* institutional. **~ir** [17] *vt* establish. **~to** *m* institute; *(escol)* (secondary) school. **~triz** *f* governess

instru|cción *f* instruction. **~ctivo** *a* instructive. **~ctor** *m* instructor. **~ir** [17] *vt* instruct; *(enseñar)* teach

instrument|ación *f* instrumentation. **~al** *a* instrumental. **~o** *m* instrument; *(herramienta)* tool

insubordina|ción *f* insubordination. **~r** *vt* stir up. **~rse** *vpr* rebel

insuficien|cia *f* insufficiency; *(inadecuación)* inadequacy. **~te** *a* insufficient

insufrible *a* insufferable

insular *a* insular

insulina *f* insulin

insulso *a* tasteless; *(fig)* insipid

insult|ar *vt* insult. **~o** *m* insult

insuperable *a* insuperable; *(excelente)* excellent

insurgente *a* insurgent

insurrec|ción *f* insurrection. **~to** *a* insurgent

intacto *a* intact

intachable *a* irreproachable

intangible *a* intangible

integra|ción *f* integration. **~l** *a* integral; *(completo)* complete; *(pan)* wholemeal *(Brit)*, wholewheat *(Amer)*. **~r** *vt* make up

integridad *f* integrity; *(entereza)* wholeness

íntegro *a* complete; *(fig)* upright

intelect|o *m* intellect. **~ual** *a & m & f* intellectual

inteligen|cia *f* intelligence. **~te** *a* intelligent

inteligible *a* intelligible

intemperancia *f* intemperance

intemperie *f* bad weather. **a la ~** in the open

intempestivo *a* untimely

intenci|ón *f* intention. **~onado** *a* deliberate. **~onal** *a* intentional. **bien ~onado** well-meaning. **mal ~onado** malicious. **segunda ~ón** duplicity

intens|idad *f* intensity. **~ificar** [7] *vt* intensify. **~ivo** *a* intensive. **~o** *a* intense

intent|ar *vt* try. **~o** *m* intent; *(tentativa)* attempt. **de ~o** intentionally
intercalar *vt* insert
intercambio *m* exchange
interceder *vi* intercede
interceptar *vt* intercept
intercesión *f* intercession
interdicto *m* ban
inter|és *m* interest; *(egoísmo)* self-interest. **~esado** *a* interested; *(parcial)* biassed; *(egoísta)* selfish. **~esante** *a* interesting. **~esar** *vt* interest; *(afectar)* concern. ● *vi* be of interest. **~esarse** *vpr* take an interest *(por* in)
interferencia *f* interference. **~ir** [4] *vi* interfere
interino *a* temporary; *(persona)* acting. ● *m* stand-in; *(médico)* locum
interior *a* interior. ● *m* inside. **Ministerio** *m* **del I~** Home Office *(Brit)*, Department of the Interior *(Amer)*
interjección *f* interjection
interlocutor *m* speaker
interludio *m* interlude
intermediario *a & m* intermediary
intermedio *a* intermediate. ● *m* interval
interminable *a* interminable
intermitente *a* intermittent. ● *m* indicator
internacional *a* international
intern|ado *m* *(escol)* boarding-school. **~ar** *vt* intern; *(en manicomio)* commit. **~arse** *vpr* penetrate. **~o** *a* internal; *(escol)* boarding. ● *m* *(escol)* boarder
interpelar *vt* appeal
interponer [34] *vt* interpose. **~se** *vpr* intervene
int|erpretación *f* interpretation. **~erpretar** *vt* interpret. **~érprete** *m* interpreter; *(mus)* performer
interroga|ción *f* question; *(acción)* interrogation; *(signo)* question mark. **~r** [12] *vt* question. **~tivo** *a* interrogative
interru|mpir *vt* interrupt; *(suspender)* stop. **~pción** *f* interruption. **~ptor** *m* switch
intersección *f* intersection
interurbano *a* inter-city; *(conferencia)* long-distance
intervalo *m* interval; *(espacio)* space. **a ~s** at intervals
interven|ir [53] *vt* control; *(med)* operate on. ● *vi* intervene; *(participar)* take part. **~tor** *m* inspector; *(com)* auditor

intestino *m* intestine
intim|ar *vi* become friendly. **~idad** *f* intimacy
intimidar *vt* intimidate
íntimo *a* intimate. ● *m* close friend
intitular *vt* entitle
intolera|ble *a* intolerable. **~nte** *a* intolerant
intoxicar [7] *vt* poison
intranquil|izar [10] *vt* worry. **~o** *a* worried
intransigente *a* intransigent
intransitable *a* impassable
intransitivo *a* intransitive
intratable *a* intractable
intrépido *a* intrepid
intriga *f* intrigue. **~nte** *a* intriguing. **~r** [12] *vt/i* intrigue
intrincado *a* intricate
intrínseco *a* intrinsic
introduc|ción *f* introduction. **~ir** [47] *vt* introduce; *(meter)* insert. **~irse** *vpr* get into; *(entrometerse)* interfere
intromisión *f* interference
introvertido *a & m* introvert
intrus|ión *f* intrusion. **~o** *a* intrusive. ● *m* intruder
intui|ción *f* intuition. **~r** [17] *vt* sense. **~tivo** *a* intuitive
inunda|ción *f* flooding. **~r** *vt* flood
inusitado *a* unusual
in|útil *a* useless; *(vano)* futile. **~utilidad** *f* uselessness
invadir *vt* invade
inv|alidez *f* invalidity; *(med)* disablement. **~álido** *a & m* invalid
invaria|ble *a* invariable. **~do** *a* unchanged
invas|ión *f* invasion. **~or** *a* invading. ● *m* invader
invectiva *f* invective
invencible *a* invincible
inven|ción *f* invention. **~tar** *vt* invent
inventario *m* inventory
invent|iva *f* inventiveness. **~ivo** *a* inventive. **~or** *m* inventor
invernadero *m* greenhouse
invernal *a* winter
inverosímil *a* improbable
inversión *f* inversion; *(com)* investment
inverso *a* inverse; *(contrario)* opposite. **a la inversa** the other way round
invertebrado *a & m* invertebrate

inverti|do a inverted; (*homosexual*) homosexual. ● m homosexual. ~**r** [4] vt reverse; (*volcar*) turn upside down; (*com*) invest; spend ⟨*tiempo*⟩

investidura f investiture

investiga|ción f investigation; (*univ*) research. ~**dor** m investigator. ~**r** [12] vt investigate

investir [5] vt invest

inveterado a inveterate

invicto a unbeaten

invierno m winter

inviolable a inviolate

invisib|ilidad f invisibility. ~**le** a invisible

invita|ción f invitation. ~**do** m guest. ~**r** vt invite. **te invito a una copa** I'll buy you a drink

invoca|ción f invocation. ~**r** [7] vt invoke

involuntario a involuntary

invulnerable a invulnerable

inyec|ción f injection. ~**tar** vt inject

ion m ion

ir [49] vi go; ⟨*ropa*⟩ (*convenir*) suit. ● m going. ~**se** vpr go away. ~ **a hacer** be going to do. ~ **a pie** walk. ~ **de paseo** go for a walk. ~ **en coche** go by car. **no me va ni me viene** it's all the same to me. **no vaya a ser que** in case. **¡qué va!** nonsense! **va mejorando** it's gradually getting better. **¡vamos!**, **¡vámonos!** come on! let's go! **¡vaya!** fancy that! **¡vete a saber!** who knows? **¡ya voy!** I'm coming!

ira f anger. ~**cundo** a irascible

Irak m Iraq

Irán m Iran

iraní & m & f Iranian

iraquí a & m & f Iraqi

iris m (*anat*) iris; (*arco iris*) rainbow

Irlanda f Ireland

irland|és a Irish. ● m Irishman; (*lengua*) Irish. ~**esa** f Irishwoman

ir|onía f irony. ~**ónico** a ironic

irracional a irrational

irradiar vt/i radiate

irrazonable a unreasonable

irreal a unreal. ~**idad** f unreality

irrealizable a unattainable

irreconciliable a irreconcilable

irreconocible a unrecognizable

irrecuperable a irretrievable

irreducible a irreducible

irreflexión f impetuosity

irrefutable a irrefutable

irregular a irregular. ~**idad** f irregularity

irreparable a irreparable

irreprimible a irrepressible

irreprochable a irreproachable

irresistible a irresistible

irresoluto a irresolute

irrespetuoso a disrespectful

irresponsable a irresponsible

irrevocable a irrevocable

irriga|ción f irrigation. ~**r** [12] vt irrigate

irrisorio a derisive; (*insignificante*) ridiculous

irrita|ble a irritable. ~**ción** f irritation. ~**r** vt irritate. ~**rse** vpr get annoyed

irrumpir vi burst (**en** in)

irrupción f irruption

isla f island. **las I** ~**s Británicas** the British Isles

Islam m Islam

islámico a Islamic

islandés a Icelandic. ● m Icelander; (*lengua*) Icelandic

Islandia f Iceland

isleño a island. ● m islander

Israel m Israel

israelí & m Israeli

istmo /'ismo/ m isthmus

Italia f Italy

italiano a & m Italian

itinerario a itinerary

IVA abrev (*impuesto sobre el valor añadido*) VAT, value added tax

izar [10] vt hoist

izquierd|a f left(-hand); (*pol*) left (-wing). ~**ista** m & f leftist. ~**o** a left. **a la** ~**a** on the left; (*con movimiento*) to the left

J

ja int ha!

jabalí m wild boar

jabalina f javelin

jab|ón m soap. ~**onar** vt soap. ~**onoso** a soapy

jaca f pony

jacinto m hyacinth

jacta|ncia f boastfulness; (*acción*) boasting. ~**rse** vpr boast

jadea|nte a panting. ~**r** vi pant

jaez m harness

jaguar m jaguar

jalea f jelly

jaleo m row, uproar. **armar un** ~ kick up a fuss

jalón m (LAm, tirón) pull; (Mex, trago) drink

Jamaica f Jamaica

jamás adv never; (en frases afirmativas) ever

jamelgo m nag

jamón m ham. ~ **de York** boiled ham. ~ **serrano** cured ham

Japón m. **el** ~ Japan

japonés a & m Japanese

jaque m check. ~ **mate** checkmate

jaqueca f migraine. **dar** ~ bother

jarabe m syrup

jardín m garden. ~ **de la infancia** kindergarten, nursery school

jardiner|ía f gardening. ~**o** m gardener

jarocho a (Mex) from Veracruz

jarr|a f jug. ~**o** m jug. **echar un** ~**o de agua fría** a throw cold water on. **en** ~**as** with hands on hips

jaula f cage

jauría f pack of hounds

jazmín m jasmine

jef|a f boss. ~**atura** f leadership; (sede) headquarters. ~**e** m boss; (pol etc) leader. ~**e de camareros** head waiter. ~**e de estación** stationmaster. ~**e de ventas** sales manager

jengibre m ginger

jeque m sheikh

jer|arquía f hierarchy. ~**árquico** a hierarchical

jerez m sherry. **al** ~ with sherry

jerga f coarse cloth; (argot) jargon

jerigonza f jargon; (galimatías) gibberish

jeringa f syringe; (LAm, molestia) nuisance. ~**r** [12] vt (fig, molestar, fam) annoy

jeroglífico m hieroglyph(ic)

jersey m (pl **jerseys**) jersey

Jerusalén m Jerusalem

Jesucristo m Jesus Christ. **antes de** ~ BC, before Christ

jesuita a & m & f Jesuit

Jesús m Jesus. ● int good heavens!; (al estornudar) bless you!

jícara f small cup

jilguero m goldfinch

jinete m rider, horseman

jipijapa f straw hat

jirafa f giraffe

jirón m shred, tatter

jitomate m (Mex) tomato

jocoso a funny, humorous

jorna|da f working day; (viaje) journey; (etapa) stage. ~**l** m day's wage;

(trabajo) day's work. ~**lero** m day labourer

joroba f hump. ~**do** a hunchbacked. ● m hunchback. ~**r** vt annoy

jota f letter J; (danza) jota, popular dance; (fig) iota. **ni** ~ nothing

joven (pl **jóvenes**) a young. ● m young man, youth. ● f young woman, girl

jovial a jovial

joy|a f jewel. ~**as** fpl jewellery. ~**ería** f jeweller's (shop). ~**ero** m jeweller; (estuche) jewellery box

juanete m bunion

jubil|ación f retirement. ~**ado** a retired. ~**ar** vt pension off. ~**arse** vpr retire. ~**eo** m jubilee

júbilo m joy

jubiloso a jubilant

judaísmo m Judaism

judía f Jewish woman; (alubia) bean. ~ **blanca** haricot bean. ~ **escarlata** runner bean. ~ **verde** French bean

judicial a judicial

judío a Jewish. ● m Jewish man

judo m judo

juego m game; (de niños, tec) play; (de azar) gambling; (conjunto) set. ● vb véase **jugar**. **estar en** ~ be at stake. **estar fuera de** ~ be offside. **hacer** ~ match

juerga f spree

jueves m Thursday

juez m judge. ~ **de instrucción** examining magistrate. ~ **de línea** linesman

juga|dor m player; (en juegos de azar) gambler. ~**r** [3] vt play. ● vi play; (a juegos de azar) gamble; (apostar) bet. ~**rse** vpr risk. ~**r al fútbol** play football

juglar m minstrel

jugo m juice; (de carne) gravy; (fig) substance. ~**so** a juicy; (fig) substantial

juguet|e m toy. ~**ear** vi play. ~**ón** a playful

juicio m judgement; (opinión) opinion; (razón) reason. ~**so** a wise. **a mi** ~ in my opinion

juliana f vegetable soup

julio m July

junco m rush, reed

jungla f jungle

junio m June

junt|a f meeting; (consejo) board, committee; (pol) junta; (tec) joint. ~**ar** vt join; (reunir) collect. ~**arse**

vpr join; ⟨*gente*⟩ meet. ∼o *a* joined; (*en plural*) together. ∼o *a* next to. ∼ura *f* joint. por ∼o all together

jura|do *a* sworn. ● *m* jury; (*miembro de jurado*) juror. ∼mento *m* oath. ∼r *vt/i* swear. ∼r en falso commit perjury. jurárselas a uno have it in for s.o. prestar ∼mento take the oath

jurel *m* (type of) mackerel

jurídico *a* legal

juris|dicción *f* jurisdiction. ∼prudencia *f* jurisprudence

justamente *a* exactly; (*con justicia*) fairly

justicia *f* justice

justifica|ción *f* justification. ∼r [7] *vt* justify

justo *a* fair, just; (*exacto*) exact; (*ropa*) tight. ● *adv* just. ∼ a tiempo just in time

juven|il *a* youthful. ∼tud *f* youth; (*gente joven*) young people

juzga|do *m* (*tribunal*) court. ∼r [12] *vt* judge. a ∼r por judging by

K

kilo *m*, kilogramo *m* kilo, kilogram

kil|ometraje *m* distance in kilometres, mileage. ∼ométrico *a* (*fam*) endless. ∼ómetro *m* kilometre. ∼ómetro cuadrado square kilometre

kilovatio *m* kilowatt

kiosco *m* kiosk

L

la *m* A; (*solfa*) lah. ● *art def f* the. ● *pron* (*ella*) her; (*Vd*) you; (*ello*) it. ∼ de the one. ∼ de Vd your one, yours. ∼ que whoever, the one

laberinto *m* labyrinth, maze

labia *f* glibness

labio *m* lip

labor *m* work; (*tarea*) job. ∼able *a* working. ∼ar *vi* work. ∼es *fpl* de aguja needlework. ∼es *fpl* de ganchillo crochet. ∼es *fpl* de punto knitting. ∼es *fpl* domésticas housework

laboratorio *m* laboratory

laborioso *a* laborious

laborista *a* Labour. ● *m & f* member of the Labour Party

labra|do *a* worked; (*madera*) carved; (*metal*) wrought; (*tierra*) ploughed. ∼dor *m* farmer; (*obrero*) labourer. ∼nza *f* farming. ∼r *vt* work; carve (*madera*); cut (*piedra*); till (*la tierra*); (*fig, causar*) cause

labriego *m* peasant

laca *f* lacquer

lacayo *m* lackey

lacerar *vt* lacerate

lacero *m* lassoer; (*cazador*) poacher

lacio *a* straight; (*flojo*) limp

lacón *m* shoulder of pork

lacónico *a* laconic

lacra *f* scar

lacr|ar *vt* seal. ∼e *m* sealing wax

lactante *a* breast-fed

lácteo *a* milky. productos *mpl* ∼s dairy products

ladear *vt/i* tilt. ∼se *vpr* lean

ladera *f* slope

ladino *a* astute

lado *m* side. al ∼ near. al ∼ de at the side of, beside. los de al ∼ the next door neighbours. por otro ∼ on the other hand. por todos ∼s on all sides. por un ∼ on the one hand

ladr|ar *vi* bark. ∼ido *m* bark

ladrillo *m* brick; (*de chocolate*) block

ladrón *a* thieving. ● *m* thief

lagart|ija *f* (small) lizard. ∼o *m* lizard

lago *m* lake

lágrima *f* tear

lagrimoso *a* tearful

laguna *f* small lake; (*fig, omisión*) gap

laico *a* lay

lamé *m* lamé

lamedura *f* lick

lament|able *a* lamentable, pitiful. ∼ar *vt* be sorry about. ∼arse *vpr* lament; (*quejarse*) complain. ∼o *m* moan

lamer *vt* lick; ⟨*olas etc*⟩ lap

lámina *f* sheet; (*foto*) plate; (*dibujo*) picture

lamina|do *a* laminated. ∼r *vt* laminate

lámpara *f* lamp; (*bombilla*) bulb; (*lamparón*) grease stain. ∼ de pie standard lamp

lamparón *m* grease stain

lampiño *a* clean-shaven, beardless

lana *f* wool. ∼r *a*. ganado *m* ∼r sheep. de ∼ wool(len)

lanceta *f* lancet

lancha *f* boat. ∼ motora *f* motor boat. ∼ salvavidas lifeboat

lanero a wool(len)

langost|a f (crustáceo marino) lobster; (insecto) locust. ~ino m prawn

languide|cer [11] vi languish. ~z f languor

lánguido a languid; (decaído) listless

lanilla f nap; (tela fina) flannel

lanudo a woolly

lanza f lance, spear

lanza|llamas m invar flamethrower. ~miento m throw; (acción de lanzar) throwing; (de proyectil, de producto) launch. ~r [10] vt throw; (de un avión) drop; launch (proyectil, producto). ~rse vpr fling o.s.

lapicero m (propelling) pencil

lápida f memorial tablet. ~ sepulcral tombstone

lapidar vt stone

lápiz m pencil; (grafito) lead. ~ de labios lipstick

Laponia f Lapland

lapso m lapse

larg|a f. a la ~a in the long run. dar ~as put off. ~ar [12] vt slacken; (dar, fam) give; (fam) deal ‹bofetada etc›. ~arse vpr (fam) go away, clear off (fam). ~o a long; (demasiado) too long. ● m length. ¡~o! go away! ~ueza f generosity. a lo ~o lengthwise. a lo ~o de along. tener 100 metros de ~o be 100 metres long

laring|e f larynx. ~itis f laryngitis

larva f larva

las art def fpl the. ● pron them. ~ de those, the ones. ~ de Vd your ones, yours. ~ que whoever, the ones

lascivo a lascivious

láser m laser

lástima f pity; (queja) complaint. dar ~ be pitiful. ella me da ~ I feel sorry for her. ¡qué ~! what a pity!

lastim|ado a hurt; (envase) hurt. ~arse vpr hurt o.s. ~ero a doleful. ~oso a pitiful

lastre m ballast

lata f tinplate; (envase) tin (esp Brit); can; (molestia, fam) nuisance. dar la ~ be a nuisance. ¡qué ~! what a nuisance!

latente a latent

lateral a side, lateral

latido m beating; (cada golpe) beat

latifundio m large estate

latigazo m (golpe) lash; (chasquido) crack

látigo m whip

latín m Latin. saber ~ (fam) not be stupid

latino a Latin. L~américa f Latin America. ~americano a & m Latin American

latir vi beat; ‹herida› throb

latitud f latitude

latón m brass

latoso a annoying; (pesado) boring

laucha f (Arg) mouse

laúd m lute

laudable a laudable

laureado a honoured; (premiado) prize-winning

laurel m laurel; (culin) bay

lava f lava

lava|ble a washable. ~bo m wash-basin; (retrete) toilet. ~dero m sink, wash-basin. ~do m washing. ~do de cerebro brainwashing. ~do en seco dry-cleaning. ~dora f washing machine. ~ndería f laundry. ~ndería automática launderette, laundromat (esp Amer). ~parabrisas m invar windscreen washer (Brit), windshield washer (Amer). ~platos m & f invar dishwasher; (Mex, fregadero) sink. ~r vt wash. ~r en seco dry-clean. ~rse vpr have a wash. ~rse las manos (incl fig) wash one's hands. ~tiva f enema. ~vajillas m & f invar dishwasher

lax|ante a & m laxative. ~o a loose

laz|ada f bow. ~o m knot; (lazada) bow; (fig, vínculo) tie; (cuerda con nudo corredizo) lasso; (trampa) trap

le pron (acusativo, él) him; (acusativo, Vd) you; (dativo, él) (to) him; (dativo, ella) (to) her; (dativo, ello) (to) it; (dativo, Vd) (to) you

leal a loyal; (fiel) faithful. ~tad f loyalty; (fidelidad) faithfulness

lebrel m greyhound

lección f lesson; (univ) lecture

lect|or m reader; (univ) language assistant. ~ura f reading

leche f milk; (golpe) bash. ~ condensada condensed milk. ~ desnatada skimmed milk. ~ en polvo powdered milk. ~ra f (vasija) milk jug. ~ría f dairy. ~ro a milk, dairy. ● m milkman. ~ sin desnatar whole milk. tener mala ~ be spiteful

lecho m bed

lechoso a milky

lechuga f lettuce

lechuza f owl

leer [18] vt/i read

legación *f* legation
legado *m* legacy; *(enviado)* legate
legajo *m* bundle, file
legal *a* legal. **~idad** *f* legality. **~izar** [10] *vt* legalize; *(certificar)* authenticate. **~mente** *adv* legally
legar [12] *vt* bequeath
legendario *a* legendary
legible *a* legible
legi|ón *f* legion. **~onario** *m* legionary
legisla|ción *f* legislation. **~dor** *m* legislator. **~r** *vi* legislate. **~tura** *f* legislature
leg|itimidad *f* legitimacy. **~ítimo** *a* legitimate; *(verdadero)* real
lego *a* lay; *(ignorante)* ignorant. ● *m* layman
legua *f* league
legumbre *f* vegetable
lejan|ía *f* distance. **~o** *a* distant
lejía *f* bleach
lejos *adv* far. **~ de** far from. **a lo ~** in the distance. **desde ~** from a distance, from afar
lelo *a* stupid
lema *m* motto
lencería *f* linen; *(de mujer)* lingerie
lengua *f* tongue; *(idioma)* language. **irse de la ~** talk too much. **morderse la ~** hold one's tongue. **tener mala ~** have a vicious tongue
lenguado *m* sole
lenguaje *m* language
lengüeta *f (de zapato)* tongue
lengüetada *f*, **lengüetazo** *m* lick
lente *f* lens. **~s** *mpl* glasses. **~s de contacto** contact lenses
lentej|a *f* lentil. **~uela** *f* sequin
lentilla *f* contact lens
lent|itud *f* slowness. **~o** *a* slow
leña *f* firewood. **~ador** *m* woodcutter. **~o** *m* log
Leo *m* Leo
le|ón *m* lion. **León** Leo. **~ona** *f* lioness
leopardo *m* leopard
leotardo *m* thick tights
lepr|a *f* leprosy. **~oso** *m* leper
lerdo *a* dim; *(torpe)* clumsy
les *pron (acusativo)* them; *(acusativo, Vds)* you; *(dativo)* (to) them; *(dativo, Vds)* (to) you
lesbia(na) *f* lesbian
lesbiano *a*, **lesbio** *a* lesbian
lesi|ón *f* wound. **~onado** *a* injured. **~onar** *vt* injure; *(dañar)* damage
letal *a* lethal

letanía *f* litany
let|árgico *a* lethargic. **~argo** *m* lethargy
letr|a *f* letter; *(escritura)* handwriting; *(de una canción)* words, lyrics. **~a de cambio** bill of exchange. **~a de imprenta** print. **~ado** *a* learned. **~ero** *m* notice; *(cartel)* poster
letrina *f* latrine
leucemia *f* leukaemia
levadizo *a*. **puente** *m* **~** drawbridge
levadura *f* yeast. **~ en polvo** baking powder
levanta|miento *m* lifting; *(sublevación)* uprising. **~r** *vt* raise, lift; *(construir)* build; *(recoger)* pick up; *(separar)* take off. **~rse** *vpr* get up; *(ponerse de pie)* stand up; *(erguirse, sublevarse)* rise up
levante *m* east; *(viento)* east wind. **L~** Levant
levar *vt* weigh *(ancla)*. ● *vi* set sail
leve *a* light; *(enfermedad etc)* slight; *(de poca importancia)* trivial. **~dad** *f* lightness; *(fig)* slightness
léxico *m* vocabulary
lexicografía *f* lexicography
ley *f* law; *(parlamentaria)* act. **plata** *f* **de ~** sterling silver
leyenda *f* legend
liar [20] *vt* tie; *(envolver)* wrap up; roll *(cigarillo)*; *(fig, confundir)* confuse; *(fig, enredar)* involve. **~se** *vpr* get involved
libanés *a* & *m* Lebanese
Líbano *m*. **el ~** Lebanon
libel|ista *m* & *f* satirist. **~o** *m* satire
libélula *f* dragonfly
libera|ción *f* liberation. **~dor** *a* liberating. ● *m* liberator
liberal *a* & *m* & *f* liberal. **~idad** *f* liberality. **~mente** *adv* liberally
liber|ar *vt* free. **~tad** *f* freedom. **~tad de cultos** freedom of worship. **~tad de imprenta** freedom of the press. **~tad provisional** bail. **~tar** *vt* free. **en ~tad** free
libertino *m* libertine
Libia *f* Libya
libido *m* libido
libio *a* & *m* Libyan
libra *f* pound. **~ esterlina** pound sterling
Libra *f* Libra
libra|dor *m (com)* drawer. **~r** *vt* free; *(de un peligro)* rescue. **~rse** *vpr* free o.s. **~rse de** get rid of

libre *a* free; (*aire*) open; (*en natación*) freestyle. ~ de impuestos tax-free. ● *m* (*Mex*) taxi

librea*f* livery

libr|ería*f* bookshop (*Brit*), bookstore (*Amer*); (*mueble*) bookcase. ~ero *m* bookseller. ~eta *f* notebook. ~o *m* book. ~o de a bordo logbook. ~o de bolsillo paperback. ~o de ejercicios exercise book. ~o de reclamaciones complaints book

licencia *f* permission; (*documento*) licence. ~do *m* graduate. ~ para manejar (*LAm*) driving licence. ~r *vt* (*mil*) discharge; (*echar*) dismiss. ~tura*f* degree

licencioso *a* licentious

liceo *m* (*esp LAm*) (secondary) school

licita|dor *m* bidder. ~r *vt* bid for

licito*a* legal; (*permisible*) permissible

licor *m* liquid; (*alcohólico*) liqueur

licua|dora *f* liquidizer. ~r [21] liquefy

lid*f* fight. en buena ~ by fair means

líder *m* leader

liderato *m*, liderazgo *m* leadership

lidia *f* bullfighting; (*lucha*) fight; (*LAm, molestia*) nuisance. ~r *vt/i* fight

liebre*f* hare

lienzo *m* linen; (*del pintor*) canvas; (*muro, pared*) wall

liga *f* garter; (*alianza*) league; (*mezcla*) mixture. ~dura *f* bond; (*mus*) slur; (*med*) ligature. ~mento *m* ligament. ~r [12] *vt* tie; (*fig*) join; (*mus*) slur. ● *vi* mix. ~r con (*fig*) pick up. ~rse *vpr* (*fig*) commit o.s.

liger|eza *f* lightness; (*agilidad*) agility; (*rapidez*) swiftness; (*de carácter*) fickleness. ~o *a* light; (*rápido*) quick; (*ágil*) agile; (*superficial*) superficial; (*de poca importancia*) slight. ● *adv* quickly. a la ~a lightly, superficially

liguero*m* suspender belt

lija *f* dogfish; (*papel de lija*) sandpaper. ~r *vt* sand

lila*f* lilac

Lima*f* Lima

lima *f* file; (*fruta*) lime. ~duras *fpl* filings. ~r *vt* file (down)

limbo*m* limbo

limita|ción *f* limitation. ~do *a* limited. ~r *vt* limit. ~r con border on. ~tivo*a* limiting

límite*m* limit. ~ de velocidad speed limit

limítrofe *a* bordering

limo*m* mud

lim|ón *m* lemon. ~onada*f* lemonade

limosn|a *f* alms. ~ear *vi* beg. pedir ~a beg

limpia *f* cleaning. ~botas *m invar* bootblack. ~parabrisas *m invar* windscreen wiper (*Brit*), windshield wiper (*Amer*). ~pipas *m invar* pipecleaner. ~r *vt* clean; (*enjugar*) wipe

limpi|eza *f* cleanliness; (*acción de limpiar*) cleaning. ~eza en seco dry-cleaning. ~o *a* clean; (*cielo*) clear; (*fig, honrado*) honest. ● *adv* fairly. en ~o (*com*) net. jugar ~o play fair

linaje *m* lineage; (*fig, clase*) kind

lince *m* lynx

linchar *vt* lynch

lind|ante *a* bordering (con on). ~ar *vi* border (con on). ~e *f* boundary. ~ero*m* border

lindo *a* pretty, lovely. de lo ~ (*fam*) a lot

línea *f* line. en ~s generales in broad outline. guardar la ~ watch one's figure

lingote*m* ingot

lingü|ista *m* & *f* linguist. ~ística *f* linguistics. ~ístico*a* linguistic

lino*m* flax; (*tela*) linen

linóleo *m*, linóleum *m* lino, linoleum

linterna*f* lantern; (*de bolsillo*) torch, flashlight (*Amer*)

lío *m* bundle; (*jaleo*) fuss; (*embrollo*) muddle; (*amorío*) affair

liquen*m* lichen

liquida|ción *f* liquidation; (*venta especial*) (clearance) sale. ~r*vt* liquify; (*com*) liquidate; settle (*cuenta*)

líquido*a* liquid; (*com*) net. ● *m* liquid

lira*f* lyre; (*moneda italiana*) lira

líric|a*f* lyric poetry. ~o*a* lyric(al)

lirio *m* iris. ~ de los valles lily of the valley

lirón *m* dormouse; (*fig*) sleepyhead. dormir como un ~ sleep like a log

Lisboa*f* Lisbon

lisia|do *a* disabled. ~r *vt* disable; (*herir*) injure

liso*a* smooth; (*pelo*) straight; (*tierra*) flat; (*sencillo*) plain

lisonj|a *f* flattery. ~eador *a* flattering. ● *m* flatterer. ~ear *vt* flatter. ~ero*a* flattering

lista *f* stripe; (*enumeración*) list; (*de platos*) menu. ~ de correos poste

restante. ∼**do** a striped. **a** ∼**s** striped
listo a clever; (*preparado*) ready
listón m ribbon; (*de madera*) strip
lisura f smoothness
litera f (*en barco*) berth; (*en tren*)
sleeper; (*en habitación*) bunk bed
literal a literal
litera|rio a literary. ∼**tura** f lit-
erature
litig|ar [12] *vi* dispute; (*jurid*) litigate.
∼**io** m dispute; (*jurid*) litigation
litografía f (*arte*) lithography; (*cuadro*) lithograph
litoral a coastal. ● m coast
litro m litre
lituano a & m Lithuanian
liturgia f liturgy
liviano a fickle, inconstant
lívido a livid
lizo m warp thread
lo *art def neutro.* ∼ **importante** what
is important, the important thing.
● *pron* (*él*) him; (*ello*) it. ∼ **que** what-
(ever), that which
loa f praise. ∼**ble** a praiseworthy. ∼**r**
vt praise
lobo m wolf
lóbrego a gloomy
lóbulo m lobe
local a local. ● m premises; (*lugar*)
place. ∼**idad** f locality; (*de un
espectáculo*) seat; (*entrada*) ticket.
∼**izar** [10] *vt* localize; (*encontrar*)
find, locate
loción f lotion
loco a mad; (*fig*) foolish. ● m lunatic.
∼ **de alegría** mad with joy. **estar** ∼
por be crazy about. **volverse** ∼ go
mad
locomo|ción f locomotion. ∼**tora** f
locomotive
locuaz a talkative
locución f expression
locura f madness; (*acto*) crazy thing.
con ∼ madly
locutor m announcer
locutorio m (*de teléfono*) telephone
booth
lod|azal m quagmire. ∼**o** m mud
logaritmo m logarithm, log
lógic|a f logic. ∼**o** a logical
logística f logistics
logr|ar *vt* get; win (*premio*). ∼ **hacer**
manage to do. ∼**o** m achievement;
(*de premio*) winning; (*éxito*) success
loma f small hill
lombriz f worm

lomo m back; (*de libro*) spine;
(*doblez*) fold. ∼ **de cerdo** loin of pork
lona f canvas
loncha f slice; (*de tocino*) rasher
londinense a from London. ● m Lon-
doner
Londres m London
loneta f thin canvas
longánimo a magnanimous
longaniza f sausage
longev|idad f longevity. ∼**o** a long-
lived
longitud f length; (*geog*) longitude
lonja f slice; (*de tocino*) rasher; (*com*)
market
lord m (*pl* **lores**) lord
loro m parrot
los *art def mpl* the. ● *pron* them. ∼ **de
Antonio** Antonio's. ∼ **que** whoever,
the ones
losa f slab; (*baldosa*) flagstone. ∼
sepulcral tombstone
lote m share
lotería f lottery
loto m lotus
loza f crockery
lozano a fresh; (*vegetación*) lush;
(*persona*) lively
lubri(fi)ca|nte a lubricating. ● m
lubricant. ∼**r** [7] *vt* lubricate
lucero m (*estrella*) bright star; (*planeta*) Venus
lucid|ez f lucidity. ∼**o** a splendid
lúcido a lucid
luciérnaga f glow-worm
lucimiento m brilliance
lucir [11] *vt* (*fig*) show off. ● *vi* shine;
(*lámpara*) give off light; (*joya*)
sparkle. ∼**se** *vpr* (*fig*) shine, excel
lucr|ativo a lucrative. ∼**o** m gain
lucha f fight. ∼**dor** m fighter. ∼**r** *vi*
fight
luego *adv* then; (*más tarde*) later.
● *conj* therefore. ∼ **que** as soon as.
desde ∼ of course
lugar m place. ∼ **común** cliché.
∼**eño** a village. **dar** ∼ **a** give rise to.
en ∼ **de** instead of. **en primer** ∼ in
the first place. **hacer** ∼ make room.
tener ∼ take place
lugarteniente m deputy
lúgubre a gloomy
lujo m luxury. ∼**so** a luxurious. **de** ∼
de luxe
lujuria f lust
lumbago m lumbago
lumbre f fire; (*luz*) light. ¿**tienes** ∼?
have you got a light?

luminoso *a* luminous; (*fig*) brilliant
luna *f* moon; (*de escaparate*) window; (*espejo*) mirror. ~ **de miel** honeymoon. ~**r** *a* lunar. ● *m* mole. **claro de** ~ moonlight. **estar en la** ~ be miles away
lunes *m* Monday. **cada** ~ **y cada martes** day in, day out
lupa *f* magnifying glass
lúpulo *m* hop
lustr|abotas *m invar* (*LAm*) bootblack. ~**ar** *vt* shine, polish. ~**e** *m* shine; (*fig, esplendor*) splendour. ~**oso** *a* shining. **dar** ~**e a, sacar** ~**e a** polish
luto *m* mourning. **estar de** ~ be in mourning
luxación *f* dislocation
Luxemburgo *m* Luxembourg
luz *f* light; (*electricidad*) electricity. **luces** *fpl* intelligence. ~ **antiniebla** (*auto*) fog light. **a la** ~ **de** in the light of. **a todas luces** obviously. **dar a** ~ give birth. **hacer la** ~ **sobre** shed light on. **sacar a la** ~ bring to light

enough. ~**rse** *vpr* come near; (*ir*) go (round). ~**r** *a* (*conseguir*) manage to. ~**r a saber** find out. ~**r a ser** become
llen|ar *vt* fill (up); (*rellenar*) fill in. ~**o** *a* full. ● *m* (*en el teatro etc*) full house. **de** ~ completely
lleva|dero *a* tolerable. ~**r** *vt* carry; (*inducir, conducir*) lead; (*acompañar*) take; wear ‹ropa›; (*traer*) bring. ~**rse** *vpr* run off with ‹cosa›. ~**rse bien** get on well together. **¿cuánto tiempo** ~**s aquí?** how long have you been here? **llevo 3 años estudiando inglés** I've been studying English for 3 years
llor|ar *vi* cry; ‹ojos› water. ~**iquear** *vi* whine. ~**iqueo** *m* whining. ~**o** *m* crying. ~**ón** *a* whining. ● *m* crybaby. ~**oso** *a* tearful
llov|er [2] *vi* rain. ~**izna** *f* drizzle. ~**iznar** *vi* drizzle
llueve *vb véase* **llover**
lluvia *f* rain; (*fig*) shower. ~**oso** *a* rainy; ‹clima› wet

LL

llaga *f* wound; (*úlcera*) ulcer
llama *f* flame; (*animal*) llama
llamada *f* call; (*golpe*) knock; (*señal*) sign
llama|do *a* known as. ~**miento** *m* call. ~**r** *vt* call; (*por teléfono*) ring (up). ● *vi* call; (*golpear en la puerta*) knock; (*tocar el timbre*) ring. ~**rse** *vpr* be called. ~**r por teléfono** ring (up), telephone. **¿cómo te** ~**s?** what's your name?
llamarada *f* blaze; (*fig*) blush; (*fig, de pasión etc*) outburst
llamativo *a* loud, gaudy
llamear *vi* blaze
llan|eza *f* simplicity. ~**o** *a* flat, level; (*persona*) natural; (*sencillo*) plain. ● *m* plain
llanta *f* (*auto*) (wheel) rim; (*LAm, neumático*) tyre
llanto *m* weeping
llanura *f* plain
llave *f* key; (*para tuercas*) spanner; (*grifo*) tap (*Brit*), faucet (*Amer*); (*elec*) switch. ~ **inglesa** monkey wrench. ~**ro** *m* key-ring. **cerrar con** ~ lock. **echar la** ~ lock up
llega|da *f* arrival. ~**r** [12] *vi* arrive, come; (*alcanzar*) reach; (*bastar*) be

M

maca *f* defect; (*en fruta*) bruise
macabro *a* macabre
macaco *a* (*LAm*) ugly. ● *m* macaque (monkey)
macadam *m*, **macadán** *m* Tarmac (*P*)
macanudo *a* (*fam*) great
macarrón *m* macaroon. ~**es** *mpl* macaroni
macerar *vt* macerate
maceta *f* mallet; (*tiesto*) flowerpot
macilento *a* wan
macizo *a* solid. ● *m* mass; (*de plantas*) bed
macrobiótico *a* macrobiotic
mácula *f* stain
macuto *m* knapsack
mach /mak/ *m*. (**número de**) ~ Mach (number)
machac|ar [7] *vt* crush. ● *vi* go on (**en** about). ~**ón** *a* boring. ● *m* bore
machamartillo. a ~ *adv* firmly
machaqueo *m* crushing
machet|azo *m* blow with a machete; (*herida*) wound from a machete. ~**e** *m* machete
mach|ista *m* male chauvinist. ~**o** *a* male; (*varonil*) macho
machón *m* buttress
machucar [7] *vt* crush; (*estropear*) damage

madeja f skein

madera m (vino) Madeira. ● f wood; (naturaleza) nature. ~ble a yielding timber. ~je m, ~men m woodwork

madero m log; (de construcción) timber

madona f Madonna

madr|astra f stepmother. ~e f mother. ~eperla f mother-of-pearl. ~eselva f honeysuckle

madrigal m madrigal

madriguera f den; (de liebre) burrow

madrileño a of Madrid. ● m person from Madrid

madrina f godmother; (en una boda) chief bridesmaid

madroño m strawberry-tree

madrug|ada f dawn. ~ador a who gets up early. ● m early riser. ~ar [12] vi get up early. ~ón m. darse un ~ón get up very early

madur|ación f maturing; (de fruta) ripening. ~ar vt/i mature; (fruta) ripen. ~ez f maturity; (de fruta) ripeness. ~o a mature; (fruta) ripe

maestr|a f teacher. ~ía f skill. ~o m master. ~a, ~o (de escuela) schoolteacher

mafia f Mafia

magdalena f madeleine, small sponge cake

magia f magic

mágico a magic; (maravilloso) magical

magín m (fam) imagination

magisterio m teaching (profession); (conjunto de maestros) teachers

magistrado m magistrate; (juez) judge

magistral a teaching; (bien hecho) masterly; (lenguaje) pedantic

magistratura f magistracy

magn|animidad f magnanimity. ~ánimo a magnanimous

magnate m magnate

magnesia f magnesia. ~ efervescente milk of magnesia

magnético a magnetic

magneti|smo m magnetism. ~zar [10] vt magnetize

magnetofón m, **magnetófono** m tape recorder

magnificencia f magnificence

magnífico a magnificent

magnitud f magnitude

magnolia f magnolia

mago m magician. los (tres) reyes ~s the Magi

magr|a f slice of ham. ~o a lean; (tierra) poor; (persona) thin

magulla|dura f bruise. ~r vt bruise

mahometano a & m Muhammadan

maíz m maize, corn (Amer)

majada f sheepfold; (estiércol) manure; (LAm) flock of sheep

majader|ía f silly thing. ~o m idiot; (mano del mortero) pestle. ● a stupid

majador m crusher

majagranzas m idiot

majar vt crush; (molestar) bother

majest|ad f majesty. ~uoso a majestic

majo a nice

mal adv badly; (poco) poorly; (difícilmente) hardly; (equivocadamente) wrongly. ● a see **malo**. ● m evil; (daño) harm; (enfermedad) illness. ~ que bien somehow (or other). de ~ en peor worse and worse. hacer ~ en be wrong to. ¡menos ~! thank goodness!

malabar a. juegos ~es juggling. ~ismo m juggling. ~ista m & f juggler

malaconsejado a ill-advised

malacostumbrado a with bad habits

malagueño a of Málaga. ● m person from Málaga

malamente adv badly; (fam) hardly enough

malandanza f misfortune

malapata m & f nuisance

malaria f malaria

Malasia f Malaysia

malasombra m & f clumsy person

malavenido a incompatible

malaventura f misfortune. ~do a unfortunate

malayo a Malay(an)

malbaratar vt sell off cheap; (malgastar) squander

malcarado a ugly

malcasado a unhappily married; (infiel) unfaithful

malcomer vi eat poorly

malcriad|eza f (LAm) bad manners. ~o a (niño) spoilt

maldad f evil; (acción) wicked thing

maldecir [46 pero imperativo **maldice**, futuro y condicional regulares, pp **maldecido** o **maldito**] vt curse. ● vi speak ill (de of); (quejarse) complain (de about)

maldici|ente a backbiting; (que blasfema) foul-mouthed. ~ón f curse

maldit|a f tongue. **¡~a sea!** damn it! **~o** a damned. ● m (en el teatro) extra

maleab|ilidad f malleability. **~le** a malleable

malea|nte a wicked. ● m vagrant. **~r** vt damage; (pervertir) corrupt. **~rse** vpr be spoilt; (pervertirse) be corrupted

malecón m breakwater; (rail) embankment; (para atracar) jetty

maledicencia f slander

maleficio m curse

maléfico a evil

malestar m indisposition; (fig) uneasiness

malet|a f (suit)case; (auto) boot, trunk (Amer); (LAm, lío de ropa) bundle; (LAm, de bicicleta) saddlebag. **hacer la ~a** pack one's bags. ● m & f (fam) bungler. **~ero** m porter; (auto) boot, trunk (Amer). **~ín** m small case

malevolencia f malevolence

malévolo a malevolent

maleza f weeds; (matorral) undergrowth

malgasta|dor a wasteful. ● m spendthrift. **~r** vt waste

malgeniado a (LAm) bad-tempered

malhablado a foul-mouthed

malhadado a unfortunate

malhechor m criminal

malhumorado a bad-tempered

malici|a f malice. **~arse** vpr suspect. **~as** fpl (fam) suspicions. **~oso** a malicious

malign|idad f malice; (med) malignancy. **~o** a malignant; (persona) malicious

malintencionado a malicious

malmandado a disobedient

malmirado a (con estar) disliked; (con ser) inconsiderate

malo a (delante de nombre masculino en singular **mal**) bad; (enfermo) ill. **~ de difícil. estar de malas** be out of luck; (malhumorado) be in a bad mood. **lo ~ es que** the trouble is that. **ponerse a malas con uno** fall out with s.o. **por las malas** by force

malogr|ar vt waste; (estropear) spoil. **~arse** vpr fall through. **~o** m failure

maloliente a smelly

malparto m miscarriage

malpensado a nasty, malicious

malquerencia f dislike

malquist|ar vt set against. **~arse** vpr fall out. **~o** a disliked

malsano a unhealthy; (enfermizo) sickly

malsonante a ill-sounding; (grosero) offensive

malta f malt; (cerveza) beer

maltés a & m Maltese

maltratar vt ill-treat

maltrecho a battered

malucho a (fam) poorly

malva f mallow. **(color de) ~** a invar mauve

malvado a wicked

malvavisco m marshmallow

malvender vt sell off cheap

malversa|ción f embezzlement. **~dor** a embezzling. ● m embezzler. **~r** vt embezzle

Malvinas fpl. **las islas ~** the Falkland Islands

malla f mesh. **cota de ~** coat of mail

mallo m mallet

Mallor|ca f Majorca. **~quín** a & m Majorcan

mama f teat; (de mujer) breast

mamá f mum(my)

mama|da f sucking. **~r** vt suck; (fig) grow up with; (engullir) gobble

mamario a mammary

mamarrach|adas fpl nonsense. **~o** m clown; (cosa ridícula) (ridiculous) sight

mameluco a Brazilian half-breed; (necio) idiot

mamífero a mammalian. ● m mammal

mamola f. **hacer la ~** chuck (under the chin); (fig) make fun of

mamotreto m notebook; (libro voluminoso) big book

mampara f screen

mamporro m blow

mampostería f masonry

mamut m mammoth

maná f manna

manada f herd; (de lobos) pack. **en ~** in crowds

manager /'manaʒer/ m manager

mana|ntial m spring; (fig) source. **~r** vi flow; (fig) abound. ● vt run with

manaza f big hand; (sucia) dirty hand. **ser un ~s** be clumsy

manceb|a f concubine. **~ía** f brothel. **~o** m youth; (soltero) bachelor

mancera f plough handle

mancilla f stain. **~r** vt stain

manco a (de una mano) one-handed; (de las dos manos) handless; (de un *brazo*) one-armed; (*de los dos brazos*) armless

mancomún *adv*. de ~ jointly

mancomún|adamente *adv* jointly. ~ar *vt* unite; (*jurid*) make jointly liable. ~arse *vpr* unite. ~idad *f* union

mancha *f* stain

Mancha *f*. la ~ la Mancha (region of Spain). el canal de la ~ the English Channel

mancha|do *a* dirty; (*animal*) spotted. ~r *vt* stain. ~rse *vpr* get dirty

manchego *a* of la Mancha. ● *m* person from la Mancha

manchón *m* large stain

manda *f* legacy

manda|dero *m* messenger. ~miento *m* order; (*relig*) commandment. ~r *vt* order; (*enviar*) send; (*gobernar*) rule. ● *vi* be in command. ¿mande? (*esp LAm*) pardon?

mandarín *m* mandarin

mandarin|a *f* (*naranja*) mandarin; (*lengua*) Mandarin. ~o *m* mandarin tree

mandat|ario *m* attorney. ~o *m* order; (*jurid*) power of attorney

mandíbula *f* jaw

mandil *m* apron

mandioca *f* cassava

mando *m* command; (*pol*) term of office. ~ a distancia remote control. los ~s the leaders

mandolina *f* mandolin

mandón *a* bossy

manducar [7] *vt* (*fam*) stuff oneself with

manecilla *f* needle; (*de reloj*) hand

manej|able *a* manageable. ~ar *vt* handle; (*fig*) manage; (*LAm, conducir*) drive. ~arse *vpr* behave. ~o *m* handling; (*intriga*) intrigue

manera *f* way. ~s *fpl* manners. de ~ que so (that). de ninguna ~ not at all. de otra ~ otherwise. de todas ~s anyway

manga *f* sleeve; (*tubo de goma*) hose-(pipe); (*red*) net; (*para colar*) filter

mangante *m* beggar; (*fam*) scrounger

mangle *m* mangrove

mango *m* handle; (*fruta*) mango

mangonear *vt* boss about. ● *vi* (*entrometerse*) interfere

manguera *f* hose(pipe)

manguito *m* muff

manía *f* mania; (*antipatía*) dislike

maniaco *a*, **maníaco** *a* maniac(al). ● *m* maniac

maniatar *vt* tie s.o.'s hands

maniático *a* maniac(al); (*fig*) crazy

manicomio *m* lunatic asylum

manicura *f* manicure; (*mujer*) manicurist

manido *a* stale; (*carne*) high

manifesta|ción *f* manifestation; (*pol*) demonstration. ~nte *m* demonstrator. ~r [1] *vi* manifest; (*pol*) state. ~rse *vpr* show; (*pol*) demonstrate

manifiesto *a* clear; (*error*) obvious; (*verdad*) manifest. ● *m* manifesto

manilargo *a* light-fingered

manilla *f* bracelet; (*de hierro*) handcuffs

manillar *m* handlebar(s)

maniobra *f* manoeuvring; (*rail*) shunting; (*fig*) manoeuvre. ~r *vt* operate; (*rail*) shunt. ● *vi* manoeuvre. ~s *fpl* (*mil*) manoeuvres

manipula|ción *f* manipulation. ~r *vt* manipulate

maniquí *m* dummy. ● *f* model

manirroto *a* extravagant. ● *m* spendthrift

manita *f* little hand

manivela *f* crank

manjar *m* (*special*) dish

mano *f* hand; (*de animales*) front foot; (*de perros, gatos*) front paw. ~ de obra work force. ¡~s arriba! hands up! a ~ by hand; (*próximo*) handy. de segunda ~ second hand. echar una ~ lend a hand. tener buena ~ para be good at

manojo *m* bunch

manose|ar *vt* handle; (*fig*) overwork. ~o *m* handling

manotada *f*, **manotazo** *m* slap

manote|ar *vi* gesticulate. ~o *m* gesticulation

mansalva. a ~ *adv* without risk

mansarda *f* attic

mansedumbre *f* gentleness; (*de animal*) tameness

mansión *f* stately home

manso *a* gentle; (*animal*) tame

manta *f* blanket. ~ eléctrica electric blanket. a ~ (de Dios) a lot

mantec|a *f* fat; (*LAm*) butter. ~ado *m* bun; (*helado*) ice-cream. ~oso *a* greasy

mantel *m* tablecloth; (*del altar*) altar cloth. ~ería *f* table linen

manten|er [40] *vt* support; (*conservar*) keep; (*sostener*) maintain. **~erse** *vpr* remain. **~ de/con** live off. **~imiento** *m* maintenance

mantequ|era *f* butter churn. **~ería** *f* dairy. **~illa** *f* butter

mantilla *f* mantilla

manto *m* cloak

mantón *m* shawl

manual *a & m* manual

manubrio *m* crank

manufactura *f* manufacture; (*fábrica*) factory

manuscrito *a* handwritten. ● *m* manuscript

manutención *f* maintenance

manzana *f* apple. **~r** *m* (*apple*) orchard

manzanilla *f* camomile tea; (*vino*) manzanilla, pale dry sherry

manzano *m* apple tree

maña *f* skill. **~s** *fpl* cunning

mañan|a *f* morning; (*el día siguiente*) tomorrow. ● *m* future. ● *adv* tomorrow. **~ero** *a* who gets up early. ● *m* early riser. **~a por la ~a** tomorrow morning. **pasado ~a** the day after tomorrow. **por la ~a** in the morning

mañoso *a* clever; (*astuto*) crafty

mapa *m* map. **~mundi** *m* map of the world

mapache *m* racoon

mapurite *m* skunk

maqueta *f* scale model

maquiavélico *a* machiavellian

maquilla|je *m* make-up. **~r** *vt* make up. **~rse** *vpr* make up

máquina *f* machine; (*rail*) engine. **~ de escribir** typewriter. **~ fotográfica** camera

maquin|ación *f* machination. **~al** *a* mechanical. **~aria** *f* machinery. **~ista** *m & f* operator; (*rail*) engine driver

mar *m & f* sea. **alta ~** high seas. **la ~ de** (*fam*) lots of

maraña *f* thicket; (*enredo*) tangle; (*embrollo*) muddle

maravedí *m* (*pl* maravedís, maravedises) maravedi, old Spanish coin

maravill|a *f* wonder. **~ar** *vt* astonish. **~arse** *vpr* be astonished (**con** at). **~oso** *a* marvellous, wonderful. **a ~a, a las mil ~as** marvellously. **contar/decir ~as** speak wonderfully of. **hacer ~as** work wonders

marbete *m* label

marca *f* mark; (*de fábrica*) trademark; (*deportes*) record. **~do** *a* marked. **~dor** *m* marker; (*deportes*) scoreboard. **~r** [7] *vt* mark; (*señalar*) show; (*anotar*) note down; score (*un gol*); dial (*número de teléfono*). ● *vi* score. **de ~** brand name; (*fig*) excellent. **de ~ mayor** (*fam*) first-class

marcial *a* martial

marciano *a & m* Martian

marco *m* frame; (*moneda alemana*) mark; (*deportes*) goal-posts

marcha *f* (*incl mus*) march; (*auto*) gear; (*curso*) course. **a toda ~** at full speed. **dar/hacer ~ atrás** put into reverse. **poner en ~** start; (*fig*) set in motion

marchante *m* (*f* marchanta) dealer; (*LAm, parroquiano*) client

marchar *vi* go; (*funcionar*) work, go. **~se** *vpr* go away, leave

marchit|ar *vt* wither. **~arse** *vpr* wither. **~o** *a* withered

marea *f* tide. **~do** *a* sick; (*en el mar*) seasick; (*aturdido*) dizzy; (*borracho*) drunk. **~r** *vt* sail, navigate; (*baquetear*) annoy. **~rse** *vpr* feel sick; (*en un barco*) be seasick; (*estar aturdido*) feel dizzy; (*irse la cabeza*) feel faint; (*emborracharse*) get slightly drunk

marejada *f* swell; (*fig*) wave

maremagno *m* (*de cosas*) sea; (*de gente*) (noisy) crowd

mareo *m* sickness; (*en el mar*) seasickness; (*aturdimiento*) dizziness; (*fig, molestia*) nuisance

marfil *m* ivory. **~eño** *a* ivory. **torre** *f* **de ~** ivory tower

margarina *f* margarine

margarita *f* pearl; (*bot*) daisy

marg|en *m* margin; (*borde*) edge, border; (*de un río*) bank; (*de un camino*) side; (*nota marginal*) marginal note. **~inado** *a* on the edge. ● *m* outcast. **~inal** *a* marginal. **~inar** *vt* (*excluir*) exclude; (*dejar márgenes*) leave margins; (*poner notas*) write notes in the margin. **al ~en** (*fig*) outside

mariachi (*Mex*) *m* (*música popular de Jalisco*) Mariachi; (*conjunto popular*) Mariachi band

mariano *a* Marian

marica *f* (*hombre afeminado*) sissy; (*urraca*) magpie

maricón *m* homosexual, queer (*sl*)

marid|aje m married life; (fig) harmony. ~**o** m husband

mariguana f, **marihuana** f marijuana

marimacho m mannish woman

marimandona f bossy woman

marimba f (type of) drum; (LAm, especie de xilofón) marimba

marimorena f (fam) row

marin|a f coast; (cuadro) seascape; (conjunto de barcos) navy; (arte de navegar) seamanship; ~**era** f seamanship; (conjunto de marineros) crew. ~**ero** a marine; (barco) seaworthy. ● m sailor. ~**o** a marine. ~**a de guerra** navy. ~**a mercante** merchant navy. **a la** ~**era** in tomato and garlic sauce. **azul** ~**o** navy blue

marioneta f puppet. ~**s** fpl puppet show

maripos|a f butterfly. ~**ear** vi be fickle; (galantear) flirt. ~**ón** m flirt. ~**a nocturna** moth

mariquita f ladybird, ladybug (Amer)

marisabidilla f know-all

mariscador m shell-fisher

mariscal m marshal

maris|co m seafood, shellfish. ~**quero** m (persona que pesca mariscos) seafood fisherman; (persona que vende mariscos) seafood seller

marital a marital

marítimo a maritime; (ciudad etc) coastal, seaside

maritornes f uncouth servant

marmit|a f pot. ~**ón** m kitchen boy

mármol m marble

marmol|era f marblework, marbles. ~**ista** m & f marble worker

marmóreo a marble

marmota f marmot

maroma f rope; (LAm, función de volatines) tightrope walking

marqu|és m marquess. ~**esa** f marchioness. ~**esina** f glass canopy

marquetería f marquetry

marrajo a (toro) vicious; (persona) cunning. ● m shark

marran|a f sow. ~**ada** f filthy thing; (cochinada) dirty trick. ~**o** a filthy. ● m hog

marrar vt (errar) miss; (fallar) fail

marrón a & m brown

marroquí a & m & f Moroccan. ● m (tafilete) morocco

marrubio m (bot) horehound

Marruecos m Morocco

marruller|ía f cajolery. ~**o** a cajoling. ● m cajoler

marsopa f porpoise

marsupial a & m marsupial

marta f marten

martajar vt (Mex) grind (maíz)

Marte m Mars

martes m Tuesday

martill|ada f blow with a hammer. ~**ar** vt hammer. ~**azo** m blow with a hammer. ~**ear** vt hammer. ~**eo** m hammering. ~**o** m hammer

martín m **pescador** kingfisher

martinete m (macillo del piano) hammer; (mazo) drop hammer

martingala f (ardid) trick

mártir m & f martyr

martir|io m martyrdom. ~**izar** [10] vt martyr; (fig) torment, torture. ~**ologio** m martyrology

marxis|mo m Marxism. ~**ta** a & m & f Marxist

marzo m March

más adv & a (comparativo) more; (superlativo) most. ~ **caro** dearer. ~ **curioso** more curious. **el** ~ **caro** the dearest; (de dos) the dearer. **el** ~ **curioso** the most curious; (de dos) the more curious. ● conj and, plus. ● m plus (sign). ~ **bien** rather. ~ **de** (cantidad indeterminada) more than. ~ **o menos** more or less. ~ **que** more than. ~ **y** ~ more and more. **a lo** ~ at (the) most. **de** ~ too many. **es** ~ moreover. **no** ~ no more

masa f dough; (cantidad) mass; (física) mass. **en** ~ en masse

masacre f massacre

masaj|e m massage. ~**ista** m masseur. ● f masseuse

masca|da f (LAm) plug of tobacco. ~**dura** f chewing. ~**r** [7] vt chew

máscara f mask; (persona) masked figure/person

mascar|ada f masquerade. ~**illa** f mask. ~**ón** m (large) mask

mascota f mascot

masculin|idad f masculinity. ~**o** a masculine; (sexo) male. ● m masculine

mascullar [3] vt mumble

masilla f putty

masivo a massive, large-scale

mas|ón m (free)mason. ~**onería** f (free)masonry. ~**ónico** a masonic

masoquis|mo m masochism. ~**ta** a masochistic. ● m & f masochist

mastate m (Mex) loincloth

mastelero m topmast

mastica|ción f chewing. ~r [7] vt chew; (fig) chew over

mástil m mast; (palo) pole; (en instrumentos de cuerda) neck

mastín m mastiff

mastitis f mastitis

mastodonte m mastodon

mastoides a & f mastoid

mastuerzo m cress

masturba|ción f masturbation. ~rse vpr masturbate

mata f grove; (arbusto) bush

matad|ero m slaughterhouse. ~or a killing. ● m killer; (torero) matador

matadura f sore

matamoscas m invar fly swatter

mata|nza f killing. ~r vt kill (personas); slaughter (reses). ~rife m butcher. ~rse vpr commit suicide; (en un accidente) be killed. **estar a** ~r **con uno** be deadly enemies with s.o.

matarratas m invar cheap liquor

matasanos m invar quack

matasellos m invar postmark

match m match

mate a matt, dull; (sonido) dull. ● m (ajedrez) (check)mate; (LAm, bebida) maté

matemátic|as fpl mathematics, maths (fam), math (Amer, fam). ~o a mathematical. ● m mathematician

materia f matter; (material) material. ~ **prima** raw material. **en** ~ **de** on the question of

material a & m material. ~idad f material nature. ~ismo m materialism. ~ista a materialistic. ● m & f materialist. ~izar [10] vt materialize. ~izarse vpr materialize. ~mente adv materially; (absolutamente) absolutely

matern|al a maternal; (como de madre) motherly. ~idad f motherhood; (casa de maternidad) maternity home. ~o a motherly; (lengua) mother

matin|al a morning. ~ée m matinée

matiz m shade. ~ación f combination of colours. ~ar [10] vt blend (colores); (introducir variedad) vary; (teñir) tinge (**de** with)

matojo m bush

mat|ón m bully. ~onismo m bullying

matorral m scrub; (conjunto de matas) thicket

matra|ca f rattle. ~quear vt rattle; (dar matraca) pester. **dar** ~ca pester. **ser un(a)** ~ca be a nuisance

matraz m flask

matriarca|do m matriarchy. ~l a matriarchal

matr|ícula f (lista) register, list; (acto de matricularse) registration; (auto) registration number. ~icular vt register. ~icularse vpr enrol, register

matrimoni|al a matrimonial. ~o m marriage; (pareja) married couple

matritense a from Madrid

matriz f matrix; (anat) womb, uterus

matrona f matron; (partera) midwife

Matusalén m Methuselah. **más viejo que** ~ as old as Methuselah

matute m smuggling. ~ro m smuggler

matutino a morning

maula f piece of junk

maull|ar vi miaow. ~ido m miaow

mauritano a & m Mauritanian

mausoleo m mausoleum

maxilar a maxillary. **hueso** ~ jaw(bone)

máxima f maxim

máxime adv especially

máximo a maximum; (más alto) highest. ● m maximum

maya f daisy; (persona) Maya Indian

mayestático a majestic

mayo m May; (palo) maypole

mayólica f majolica

mayonesa f mayonnaise

mayor a (más grande, comparativo) bigger; (más grande, superlativo) biggest; (de edad, comparativo) older; (de edad, superlativo) oldest; (adulto) grown-up; (principal) main, major; (mus) major. ● m & f boss; (adulto) adult. ~al m foreman; (pastor) head shepherd. ~azgo m entailed estate. **al por** ~ wholesale

mayordomo m butler

mayor|ía f majority. ~ista m & f wholesaler. ~mente adv especially

mayúscul|a f capital (letter). ~o a capital; (fig, grande) big

maza f mace

mazacote m hard mass

mazapán m marzipan

mazmorra f dungeon

mazo m mallet; (manojo) bunch

mazorca f. ~ **de maíz** corn on the cob

me pron (acusativo) me; (dativo) (to) me; (reflexivo) (to) myself

meandro *m* meander

mecánic|a *f* mechanics. ~**o** *a* mechanical. ● *m* mechanic

mecani|smo *m* mechanism. ~**zación** *f* mechanization. ~**zar** [10] *vt* mechanize

mecanograf|ía *f* typing. ~**iado** *a* typed, typewritten. ~**iar** [20] *vt* type

mecanógrafo *m* typist

mecate *m* (*LAm*) (*pita*) rope

mecedora *f* rocking chair

mecenazgo *m* patronage

mecer [9] *vt* rock; swing ⟨*columpio*⟩. ~**se** *vpr* rock; (*en un columpio*) swing

mecha *f* (*de vela*) wick; (*de mina*) fuse

mechar *vt* stuff, lard

mechero *m* (cigarette) lighter

mechón *m* (*de pelo*) lock

medall|a *f* medal. ~**ón** *m* medallion; (*relicario*) locket

media *f* stocking; (*promedio*) average

mediación *f* mediation

mediado *a* half full; ⟨*trabajo etc*⟩ halfway through. **a** ~**s de marzo** in the middle of March

mediador *m* mediator

medialuna *f* croissant

median|amente *adv* fairly. ~**era** *f* party wall. ~**ero** *a* ⟨*muro*⟩ party. ~**a** *f* average circumstances. ~**o** *a* average, medium; (*mediocre*) mediocre

medianoche *f* midnight; (*culin*) small sandwich

mediante *prep* through, by means of

mediar *vi* mediate; (*llegar a la mitad*) be halfway (**en** through)

mediatizar [10] *vt* annex

medic|ación *f* medication. ~**amento** *m* medicine. ~**ina** *f* medicine. ~**inal** *a* medicinal. ~**inar** *vt* administer medicine

medición *f* measurement

médico *a* medical. ● *m* doctor. ~ **de cabecera** GP, general practitioner

medid|a *f* measurement; (*unidad*) measure; (*disposición*) measure, step; (*prudencia*) moderation. ~**or** *m* (*LAm*) meter. **a la** ~**a** made to measure. **a** ~**a que** as. **en cierta** ~**a** to a certain point

mediero *m* share-cropper

medieval *a* medieval. ~**ista** *m* & *f* medievalist

medio *a* half (a); (*mediano*) average. ~ **litro** half a litre. ● *m* middle; (*manera*) means; (*en deportes*)

half(-back). **en** ~ in the middle (**de** of). **por** ~ **de** through

mediocr|e *a* (*mediano*) average; (*de escaso mérito*) mediocre. ~**idad** *f* mediocrity

mediodía *m* midday, noon; (*sur*) south

medioevo *m* Middle Ages

Medio Oriente *m* Middle East

medir [5] *vt* measure; weigh up ⟨*palabras etc*⟩. ● *vi* measure, be. ~**se** *vpr* (*moderarse*) be moderate

medita|bundo *a* thoughtful. ~**ción** *f* meditation. ~**r** *vt* think about. ● *vi* meditate

Mediterráneo *m* Mediterranean

mediterráneo *a* Mediterranean

médium *m* & *f* medium

medrar *vi* thrive

medroso *a* (*con estar*) frightened; (*con ser*) fearful

médula *f* marrow

medusa *f* jellyfish

mefítico *a* noxious

mega... *pref* mega...

megáfono *m* megaphone

megal|ítico *a* megalithic. ~**ito** *m* megalith

megal|omanía *f* megalomania. ~**ómano** *m* megalomaniac

mejicano *a* & *m* Mexican

Méjico *m* Mexico

mejido *a* ⟨*huevo*⟩ beaten

mejilla *f* cheek

mejillón *m* mussel

mejor *a* & *adv* (*comparativo*) better; (*superlativo*) best. ~**a** *f* improvement. ~**able** *a* improvable. ~**amiento** *m* improvement. ~ **dicho** rather. **a lo** ~ perhaps. **tanto** ~ so much the better

mejorana *f* marjoram

mejorar *vt* improve, better. ● *vi* get better

mejunje *m* mixture

melanc|olía *f* melancholy. ~**ólico** *a* melancholic

melaza *f* molasses, treacle (*Amer*)

melen|a *f* long hair; (*de león*) mane. ~**udo** *a* long-haired

melifluo *a* mellifluous

melillense *a* of/from Melilla. ● *m* person from Melilla

melindr|e *m* (*mazapán*) sugared marzipan cake; (*masa frita con miel*) honey fritter. ~**oso** *a* affected

melocot|ón *m* peach. ~**onero** *m* peach tree

mel|odía f melody. ~**ódico** a melodic. ~**odioso** a melodious

melodram|a m melodrama. ~**áticamente** adv melodramatically. ~**ático** a melodramatic

melómano m music lover

mel|ón m melon; (*bobo*) fool. ~**onada** f something stupid

meloncillo m (*animal*) mongoose

melos|idad f sweetness. ~**o** a sweet

mella f notch. ~**do** a jagged. ~**r** vt notch

mellizo a & m twin

membran|a f membrane. ~**oso** a membranous

membrete m letterhead

membrill|ero m quince tree. ~**o** m quince

membrudo a burly

memez f something silly

memo a stupid. ● m idiot

memorable a memorable

memorando m, **memorándum** m notebook; (*nota*) memorandum

memoria f memory; (*informe*) report; (*tesis*) thesis. ~**s** fpl (*recuerdos personales*) memoirs. **de** ~ from memory

memorial m memorial. ~**ista** m amanuensis

memor|ión m good memory. ~**ista** a having a good memory. ~**ístico** a memory

mena f ore

menaje m furnishings

menci|ón f mention. ~**onado** a aforementioned. ~**onar** vt mention

menda|cidad f mendacity. ~**z** a lying

mendi|cante a & m mendicant. ~**cidad** f begging. ~**gar** [12] vt beg (for). ● vi beg. ~**go** m beggar

mendrugo m (*pan*) hard crust; (*zoquete*) blockhead

mene|ar vt move, shake. ~**arse** vpr move, shake. ~**o** m movement, shake

menester m need. ~**oso** a needy. **ser** ~ be necessary

menestra f stew

menestral m artesan

mengano m so-and-so

mengua f decrease; (*falta*) lack; (*descrédito*) discredit. ~**do** a miserable; (*falto de carácter*) spineless. ~**nte** a decreasing; (*luna*) waning; (*marea*) ebb. ● f (*del mar*) ebb tide;

(*de un río*) low water. ~**r** [15] vt/i decrease, diminish

meningitis f meningitis

menisco m meniscus

menjurje m mixture

menopausia f menopause

menor a (*más pequeño, comparativo*) smaller; (*más pequeño, superlativo*) smallest; (*más joven, comparativo*) younger; (*más joven*) youngest; (*mus*) minor. ● m & f (*menor de edad*) minor. **al por** ~ retail

Menorca f Minorca

menorquín a & m Minorcan

menos a (*comparativo*) less; (*comparativo, con plural*) fewer; (*superlativo*) least; (*superlativo, con plural*) fewest. ● adv (*comparativo*) less; (*superlativo*) least. ● prep except. ~**cabar** vt lessen; (*fig, estropear*) damage. ~**cabo** m lessening. ~**preciable** a contemptible. ~**preciar** vt despise. ~**precio** m contempt. **a** ~ **que** unless. **al** ~ at least. **ni mucho** ~ far from it. **por lo** ~ at least

mensaje m message. ~**ro** m messenger

menso a (*Mex*) stupid

menstru|ación f menstruation. ~**al** a menstrual. ~**ar** [21] vi menstruate. ~**o** m menstruation

mensual a monthly. ~**idad** f monthly pay

ménsula f bracket

mensurable a measurable

menta f mint

mental a mental. ~**idad** f mentality. ~**mente** adv mentally

mentar [1] vt mention, name

mente f mind

mentecato a stupid. ● m idiot

mentir [4] vi lie. ~**a** f lie. ~**oso** a lying. ● m liar. **de** ~**ijillas** for a joke

mentís m invar denial

mentol m menthol

mentor m mentor

menú m menu

menudear vi happen frequently

menudencia f trifle

menudeo m retail trade

menudillos mpl giblets

menudo a tiny; (*lluvia*) fine; (*insignificante*) insignificant. ~**s** mpl giblets. **a** ~ often

meñique a (*dedo*) little. ● m little finger

meollo m brain; (*médula*) marrow; (*parte blanda*) soft part; (*fig, inteligencia*) brains

meramente *adv* merely

mercachifle *m* hawker; (*fig*) profiteer

mercader *m* (*LAm*) merchant

mercado *m* market. **M~ Común** Common Market. **~ negro** black market

mercan|cía *f* article. **~cías** *fpl* goods, merchandise. **~te** *a & m* merchant. **~til** *a* mercantile, commercial. **~tilismo** *m* mercantilism

mercar [7] *vt* buy

merced *f* favour. **su/vuestra ~** your honour

mercenario *a & m* mercenary

mercer|ía *f* haberdashery, notions (*Amer*). **~o** *m* haberdasher

mercurial *a* mercurial

Mercurio *m* Mercury

mercurio *m* mercury

merec|edor *a* deserving. **~er** [11] *vt* deserve. ● *vi* be deserving. **~ida-mente** *adv* deservedly. **~ido** *a* well deserved. **~imiento** *m* (*mérito*) merit

merend|ar [1] vt have as an afternoon snack. ● *vi* have an afternoon snack. **~ero** *m* snack bar; (*lugar*) picnic area

merengue *m* meringue

meretriz *f* prostitute

mergo *m* cormorant

meridian|a *f* (*diván*) couch. **~o** *a* midday; (*fig*) dazzling. ● *m* meridian

meridional *a* southern. ● *m* southerner

merienda *f* afternoon snack

merino *a* merino

mérito *m* merit; (*valor*) worth

meritorio *a* meritorious. ● *m* unpaid trainee

merlo *m* black wrasse

merluza *f* hake

merma *f* decrease. **~r** *vt/i* decrease, reduce

mermelada *f* jam

mero *a* mere; (*Mex, verdadero*) real. ● *adv* (*Mex, precisamente*) exactly; (*Mex, verdaderamente*) really. ● *m* grouper

merode|ador *a* marauding. ● *m* marauder. **~ar** *vi* maraud. **~o** *m* marauding

merovingio *a & m* Merovingian

mes *m* month; (*mensualidad*) monthly pay

mesa *f* table; (*para escribir o estudiar*) desk. **poner la ~** lay the table

mesana *f* (*palo*) mizen-mast

mesarse *vpr* tear at one's hair

mesenterio *m* mesentery

meseta *f* plateau; (*descansillo*) landing

mesiánico *a* Messianic

Mesías *m* Messiah

mesilla *f* small table. **~ de noche** bedside table

mesón *m* inn

mesoner|a *f* landlady. **~o** *m* landlord

mestiz|aje *m* crossbreeding. **~o** *a* (*persona*) half-caste; (*animal*) crossbred. ● *m* (*persona*) half-caste; (*animal*) cross-breed

mesura *f* moderation. **~do** *a* moderate

meta *f* goal; (*de una carrera*) finish

metabolismo *m* metabolism

metacarpiano *m* metacarpal

metafísic|a *f* metaphysics. **~o** *a* metaphysical

met|áfora *f* metaphor. **~afórico** *a* metaphorical

met|al *m* metal; (*instrumentos de latón*) brass; (*de la voz*) timbre. **~álico** *a* (*objeto*) metal; (*sonido*) metallic. **~alizarse** [10] *vpr* (*fig*) become mercenary

metal|urgia *f* metallurgy. **~úrgico** *a* metallurgical

metam|órfico *a* metamorphic. **~orfosear** *vt* transform. **~orfosis** *f* metamorphosis

metano *m* methane

metatarsiano *m* metatarsal

metátesis *f* invar metathesis

metedura *f*. **~ de pata** blunder

mete|órico *a* meteoric. **~orito** *m* meteorite. **~oro** *m* meteor. **~oro-logía** *f* meteorology. **~orológico** *a* meteorological. **~orólogo** *m* meteorologist

meter *vt* put, place; (*ingresar*) deposit; score (*un gol*); (*enredar*) involve; (*causar*) make. **~se** *vpr* get; (*entrometerse*) meddle. **~se con uno** pick a quarrel with s.o.

meticulos|idad *f* meticulousness. **~o** *a* meticulous

metido *m* reprimand. ● *a*. **~ en años** getting on. **estar muy ~ con uno** be well in with s.o.

metilo *m* methyl

metódico *a* methodical

metodis|mo *m* Methodism. **~ta** *a & m & f* Methodist

método m method

metodología f methodology

metomentodo m busybody

metraje m length. **de largo ~** ⟨*película*⟩ feature

metrall|a f shrapnel. **~eta** f submachine gun

métric|a f metrics. **~o** a metric; ⟨*verso*⟩ metrical

metro m metre; ⟨*tren*⟩ underground, subway (*Amer*). **~ cuadrado** square metre

metrónomo m metronome

metr|ópoli f metropolis. **~opolitano** a metropolitan. ● m metropolitan; ⟨*tren*⟩ underground, subway (*Amer*)

mexicano a & m (*LAm*) Mexican

México m (*LAm*) Mexico. **~ D. F.** Mexico City

mezcal m (*Mex*) (type of) brandy

mezc|la f ⟨*acción*⟩ mixing; ⟨*substancia*⟩ mixture; ⟨*argamasa*⟩ mortar. **~lador** m mixer. **~lar** vt mix; shuffle ⟨*los naipes*⟩. **~larse** vpr mix; ⟨*intervenir*⟩ interfere. **~olanza** f mixture

mezquin|dad f meanness. **~o** a mean; ⟨*escaso*⟩ meagre. ● m mean person

mezquita f mosque

mi a my. ● m (*mus*) E; (*solfa*) mi

mí pron me

miaja f crumb

miasma m miasma

miau m miaow

mica f ⟨*silicato*⟩ mica; (*Mex, embriaguez*) drunkenness

mico m (long-tailed) monkey

micro... pref micro...

microbio m microbe

micro: **~biología** f microbiology. **~cosmo** m microcosm. **~film(e)** m microfilm

micrófono m microphone

micrómetro m micrometer

microonda f microwave. **horno m de ~s** microwave oven

microordenador m microcomputer

microsc|ópico a microscopic. **~opio** m microscope

micro: **~surco** m long-playing record. **~taxi** m minicab

miedo m fear. **~so** a fearful. **dar ~** frighten. **morirse de ~** be scared to death. **tener ~** be frightened

miel f honey

mielga f lucerne, alfalfa (*Amer*)

miembro m limb; (*persona*) member

mientras conj while. ● adv meanwhile. **~ que** whereas. **~ tanto** in the meantime

miércoles m Wednesday. **~ de ceniza** Ash Wednesday

mierda f (*vulgar*) shit

mies f corn, grain (*Amer*)

miga f crumb; (*fig, meollo*) essence. **~jas** fpl crumbs. **~r** [12] vt crumble

migra|ción f migration. **~torio** a migratory

mijo m millet

mil a & m a/one thousand. **~es de** thousands of. **~ novecientos noventa y dos** nineteen ninety-two. **~ pesetas** a thousand pesetas

milagro m miracle. **~so** a miraculous

milano m kite

mildeu m, **mildiu** m mildew

milen|ario a millenial. **~io** m millennium

milenrama f milfoil

milésimo a & m thousandth

mili f (*fam*) military service

milicia f soldiering; (*gente armada*) militia

mili|gramo m milligram. **~litro** m millilitre

milímetro m millimetre

militante a militant

militar a military. ● m soldier. **~ismo** m militarism. **~ista** a militaristic. ● m & f militarist. **~izar** [10] vt militarize

milonga f (*Arg, canción*) popular song; (*Arg, baile*) popular dance

milord m. **vivir como un ~** live like a lord

milpiés m invar woodlouse

milla f mile

millar m thousand. **a ~es** by the thousand

mill|ón m million. **~onada** f fortune. **~onario** m millionaire. **~onésimo** a & m millionth. **un ~n de libros** a million books

mimar vt spoil

mimbre m & f wicker. **~arse** vpr sway. **~ra** f osier. **~ral** m osier-bed

mimetismo m mimicry

mímic|a f mime. **~o** a mimic

mimo m mime; (*a un niño*) spoiling; (*caricia*) caress

mimosa f mimosa

mina f mine. **~r** vt mine; (*fig*) undermine

minarete m minaret

mineral m mineral; (*mena*) ore. ~**ogía** f mineralogy. ~**ogista** m & f mineralogist

miner|ía f mining. ~**o** a mining. ● m miner

mini... *pref* mini...

miniar vt paint in miniature

miniatura f miniature

minifundio m smallholding

minimizar [10] vt minimize

mínim|o a & m minimum. ~**um** m minimum

minino m (*fam*) cat, puss (*fam*)

minio m red lead

minist|erial a ministerial. ~**erio** m ministry. ~**ro** m minister

minor|ación f diminution. ~**a** f minority. ~**idad** f minority. ~**ista** m & f retailer

minucia f trifle. ~**osidad** f thoroughness. ~**oso** a thorough; (*con muchos detalles*) detailed

minué m minuet

minúscul|a f small letter, lower case letter. ~**o** a tiny

minuta f draft; (*menú*) menu

minut|ero m minute hand. ~**o** m minute

mío a & pron mine. **un amigo** ~ a friend of mine

miop|e a short-sighted. ● m & f short-sighted person. ~**ía** f shortsightedness

mira f sight; (*fig, intención*) aim. ~**da** f look. ~**do** a thought of; (*comedido*) considerate; (*cirunspecto*) circumspect. ~**dor** m windowed balcony; (*lugar*) viewpoint. ~**miento** m consideration. ~**r** vt look at; (*observar*) watch; (*considerar*) consider. ~**r fijamente** a stare at. ● vi look; (*edificio etc*) face. ~**rse** vpr (*personas*) look at each other. **a la** ~ **on the lookout. con** ~**s a** with a view to. **echar una** ~**da a** a glance at

mirilla f peephole

miriñaque m crinoline

mirlo m blackbird

mirón a nosey. ● m nosey-parker; (*espectador*) onlooker

mirra f myrrh

mirto m myrtle

misa f mass

misal m missal

mis|antropía f misanthropy. ~**antrópico** a misanthropic. ~**ántropo** m misanthropist

miscelánea f miscellany; (*Mex, tienda*) corner shop

miser|able a very poor; (*lastimoso*) miserable; (*tacaño*) mean. ~**ia** f extreme poverty; (*suciedad*) squalor

misericordi|a f pity; (*piedad*) mercy. ~**oso** a merciful

mísero a very poor; (*lastimoso*) miserable; (*tacaño*) mean

misil m missile

misi|ón f mission. ~**onal** a missionary. ~**onero** m missionary

misiva f missive

mism|amente adv just. ~**ísimo** a very same. ~**o** a same; (*después de pronombre personal*) myself, yourself, himself, herself, itself, ourselves, yourselves, themselves; (*enfático*) very. ● adv right. **ahora** ~ right now. **aquí** ~ right here

mis|oginia f misogyny. ~**ógino** m misogynist

misterio m mystery. ~**so** a mysterious

místic|a f mysticism. ~**o** a mystical

mistifica|ción f falsidication; (*engaño*) trick. ~**r** [7] vt falsify; (*engañar*) deceive

mitad f half; (*centro*) middle

mítico a mythical

mitiga|ción f mitigation. ~**r** [12] vt mitigate; quench (*sed*); relieve (*dolor etc*)

mitin m meeting

mito m myth. ~**logía** f mythology. ~**lógico** a mythological

mitón m mitten

mitote m (*LAm*) Indian dance

mitra f mitre. ~**do** m prelate

mixteca f (*Mex*) southern Mexico

mixt|o a mixed. ● m passenger and goods train; (*cerilla*) match. ~**ura** f mixture

mnemotécnic|a f mnemonics. ~**o** a mnemonic

moaré m moiré

mobiliario m furniture

moblaje m furniture

moca m mocha

moce|dad f youth. ~**ro** m young people. ~**tón** m strapping lad

moción f motion

moco m mucus

mochales a invar. **estar** ~ be round the bend

mochila f rucksack

mocho a blunt. ● m butt end

mochuelo m little owl

moda f fashion. ~l a modal. ~les mpl manners. ~lidad f kind. de ~ in fashion

model|ado m modelling. ~ador m modeller. ~ar vt model; (fig, configurar) form. ~o m model

modera|ción f moderation. ~do a moderate. ~r vt moderate; reduce ⟨velocidad⟩. ~rse vpr control oneself

modern|amente adv recently. ~idad f modernity. ~ismo m modernism. ~ista m & f modernist. ~izar [10] vt modernize. ~o a modern

modest|ia f modesty. ~o a modest

modicidad f reasonableness

módico a moderate

modifica|ción f modification. ~r [7] vt modify

modismo m idiom

modist|a f dressmaker. ~o m & f designer

modo m manner, way; (gram) mood; (mus) mode. ~ de ser character. de ~ que so that. de ningún ~ certainly not. de todos ~s anyhow

modorr|a f drowsiness. ~o a drowsy

modoso a well-behaved

modula|ción f modulation. ~dor m modulator. ~r vt modulate

módulo m module

mofa f mockery. ~rse vpr. ~rse de make fun of

mofeta f skunk

moflet|e m chubby cheek. ~udo a with chubby cheeks

mogol m Mongol. el Gran M~ the Great Mogul

moh|ín m grimace. ~ino a sulky. hacer un ~ín pull a face

moho m mould; (óxido) rust. ~so a mouldy; ⟨metales⟩ rusty

moisés m Moses basket

mojado a damp, wet

mojama f salted tuna

mojar vt wet; (empapar) soak; (humedecer) moisten, dampen. ● vi. ~ en get involved in

mojicón m blow in the face; (bizcocho) sponge cake

mojiganga f masked ball; (en el teatro) farce

mojigat|ería f hypocrisy. ~o m hypocrite

mojón m boundary post; (señal) signpost

molar m molar

mold|e m mould; (aguja) knitting needle. ~ear vt mould, shape; (fig) form. ~ura f moulding

mole f mass, bulk. ● m (Mex, guisado) (Mexican) stew with chili sauce

mol|écula f molecule. ~ecular a molecular

mole|dor a grinding. ● m grinder; (persona) bore. ~r [2] grind; (hacer polvo) pulverize

molest|ar vt annoy; (incomodar) bother. ¿le ~a que fume? do you mind if I smoke? no ~ar do not disturb. ● vi be a nuisance. ~arse vpr bother; (ofenderse) take offence. ~ia f bother, nuisance; (inconveniente) inconvenience; (incomodidad) discomfort. ~o a annoying; (inconveniente) inconvenient; (ofendido) offended

molicie f softness; (excesiva comodidad) easy life

molido a ground; (fig, muy cansado) worn out

molienda f grinding

molin|ero m miller. ~ete m toy windmill. ~illo m mill; (juguete) toy windmill. ~o m (water) mill. ~o de viento windmill

molusco m mollusc

mollar a soft

molleja f gizzard

mollera f (de la cabeza) crown; (fig, sesera) brains

moment|áneamente adv momentarily; (por el momento) right now. ~áneo a momentary. ~o m moment; (mecánica) momentum

momi|a f mummy. ~ficación f mummification. ~ficar [7] vt mummify. ~ficarse vpr become mummified

momio a lean. ● m bargain; (trabajo) cushy job

monaca|l a monastic. ~to m monasticism

monada f beautiful thing; (de un niño) charming way; (acción tonta) silliness

monaguillo m altar boy

mon|arca m & f monarch. ~arquía f monarchy. ~árquico a monarchic(al). ~arquismo m monarchism

mon|asterio m monastery. ~ástico a monastic

monda f pruning; (peladura) peel

mond|adientes m invar toothpick. ~adura f pruning; (peladura) peel.

∼ar *vt* peel ⟨*fruta etc*⟩; dredge ⟨*un río*⟩. ∼o ⟨*sin pelo*⟩ bald; ⟨*sin dinero*⟩ broke; ⟨*sencillo*⟩ plain

mondongo *m* innards

moned|a *f* coin; ⟨*de un país*⟩ currency. **∼ero** *m* minter; ⟨*portamonedas*⟩ purse

monetario *a* monetary

mongol *a* & *m* Mongolian

mongolismo *m* Down's syndrome

monigote *m* weak character; ⟨*muñeca*⟩ rag doll; ⟨*dibujo*⟩ doodle

monises *mpl* money, dough (*fam*)

monitor *m* monitor

monj|a *f* nun. **∼e** *m* monk. **∼il** *a* nun's; ⟨*como de monja*⟩ like a nun

mono *m* monkey; ⟨*sobretodo*⟩ overalls. ● *a* pretty

mono... *pref* mono...

monocromo *a* & *m* monochrome

monóculo *m* monocle

mon|ogamia *f* monogamy. **∼ógamo** *a* monogamous

monografía *f* monograph

monograma *m* monogram

monol|ítico *a* monolithic. **∼ito** *m* monolith

mon|ologar [12] *vi* soliloquize. **∼ólogo** *m* monologue

monoman|ía *f* monomania. **∼iaco** *m* monomaniac

monoplano *m* monoplane

monopoli|o *m* monopoly. **∼zar** [10] *vt* monopolize

monos|ilábico *a* monosyllabic. **∼ílabo** *m* monosyllable

monoteís|mo *m* monotheism. **∼ta** *a* monotheistic. ● *m* & *f* monotheist

mon|otonía *f* monotony. **∼ótono** *a* monotonous

monseñor *m* monsignor

monserga *f* boring talk

monstruo *m* monster. **∼sidad** *f* monstrosity. **∼so** *a* monstrous

monta *f* mounting; ⟨*valor*⟩ value

montacargas *m invar* service lift

monta|do *a* mounted. **∼dor** *m* fitter. **∼je** *m* assembly; ⟨*cine*⟩ montage; ⟨*teatro*⟩ staging; production

montañ|a *f* mountain. **∼ero** *a* mountaineer. **∼és** *a* mountain. ● *m* highlander. **∼ismo** *m* mountaineering. **∼oso** *a* mountainous. **∼a rusa** big dipper

montaplatos *m invar* service lift

montar *vt* ride; ⟨*subirse*⟩ get on; ⟨*ensamblar*⟩ assemble; cock ⟨*arma*⟩; set up ⟨*una casa, un negocio*⟩. ● *vi*

ride; ⟨*subirse a*⟩ mount. **∼ a caballo** ride a horse

montaraz *a* ⟨*animales*⟩ wild; ⟨*personas*⟩ mountain

monte *m* ⟨*montaña*⟩ mountain; ⟨*terreno inculto*⟩ scrub; ⟨*bosque*⟩ forest. **∼ de piedad** pawn-shop. **ingeniero *m* de ∼s** forestry expert

montepío *m* charitable fund for dependents

monter|a *f* cloth cap. **∼o** *m* hunter

montés *a* wild

Montevideo *m* Montevideo

montevideano *a* & *m* Montevidean

montículo *m* hillock

montón *m* heap, pile. **a montones** in abundance, lots of

montuoso *a* hilly

montura *f* mount; ⟨*silla*⟩ saddle

monument|al *a* monumental; ⟨*fig, muy grande*⟩ enormous. **∼o** *m* monument

monzón *m* & *f* monsoon

moñ|a *f* hair ribbon. **∼o** *m* bun

moque|o *m* runny nose. **∼ro** *m* handkerchief

moqueta *f* fitted carpet

moquillo *m* distemper

mora *f* mulberry; ⟨*zarzamora*⟩ blackberry

morada *f* dwelling

morado *a* purple

morador *m* inhabitant

moral *m* mulberry tree. ● *f* morals. ● *a* moral. **∼eja** *f* moral. **∼idad** *f* morality. **∼ista** *m* & *f* moralist. **∼izadora** moralizing. ● *m* moralist. **∼izar** [10] *vt* moralize

morapio *m* (*fam*) cheap red wine

morar *vi* live

moratoria *f* moratorium

morbidez *f* softness

mórbido *a* soft; ⟨*malsano*⟩ morbid

morbo *m* illness. **∼sidad** *f* morbidity. **∼so** *a* unhealthy

morcilla *f* black pudding

morda|cidad *f* bite. **∼za** *f* biting

mordaza *f* gag

mordazmente *adv* bitingly

morde|dura *f* bite. **∼r** [2] *vt* bite; ⟨*fig, quitar porciones a*⟩ eat into; ⟨*denigrar*⟩ gossip about. ● *vi* bite

mordis|car [7] *vt* nibble (at). ● *vi* nibble. **∼co** *m* bite. **∼quear** *vt* nibble (at)

morelense *a* (*Mex*) from Morelos. ● *m* & *f* person from Morelos

morena f (geol) moraine

moreno a dark; (de pelo obscuro) dark-haired; (de raza negra) negro

morera f mulberry tree

morería f Moorish lands; (barrio) Moorish quarter

moretón m bruise

morfema m morpheme

morfin|a f morphine. **~ómano** a morphine. ● m morphine addict

morfol|ogía f morphology. **~ógico** a morphological

moribundo a moribund

morillo m andiron

morir [6] (pp muerto) vi die; (fig, extinguirse) die away; (fig, terminar) end. **~se** vpr die. **~se de hambre** starve to death; (fig) be starving. **se muere por una flauta** she's dying to have a flute

moris|co a Moorish. ● m Moor. **~ma** f Moors

morm|ón m & f Mormon. **~ónico** a Mormon. **~onismo** m Mormonism

moro a Moorish. ● m Moor

moros|idad f dilatoriness. **~o** a dilatory

morrada f butt; (puñetazo) punch

morral m (mochila) rucksack; (del cazador) gamebag; (para caballos) nosebag

morralla f rubbish

morrillo m nape of the neck

morriña f homesickness

morro m snout

morrocotudo a (esp Mex) (fam) terrific (fam)

morsa f walrus

mortaja f shroud

mortal a & m & f mortal. **~idad** f mortality. **~mente** adv mortally

mortandad f death toll

mortecino a failing; (color) faded

mortero m mortar

mortífero a deadly

mortifica|ción f mortification. **~r** [7] vt (med) damage; (atormentar) plague; (humillar) humiliate. **~rse** vpr (Mex) feel embarassed

mortuorio a death

morueco m ram

moruno a Moorish

mosaico a of Moses, Mosaic. ● m mosaic

mosca f fly. **~rda** f blowfly. **~rdón** m botfly; (mosca de cuerpo azul) bluebottle

moscatel a muscatel

moscón m botfly; (mosca de cuerpo azul) bluebottle

moscovita a & m & f Muscovite

Moscú m Moscow

mosque|arse vpr get cross. **~o** m resentment

mosquete m musket. **~ro** m musketeer

mosquit|ero m mosquito net. **~o** m mosquito; (mosca pequeña) fly, gnat

mostacho m moustache

mostachón m macaroon

mostaza f mustard

mosto m must

mostrador m counter

mostrar [2] vt show. **~se** vpr (show oneself to) be. **se mostró muy amable** he was very kind

mostrenco a ownerless; (animal) stray; (torpe) thick; (gordo) fat

mota f spot, speck

mote m nickname; (lema) motto

motea|do a speckled. **~r** vt speckle

motejar vt call

motel m motel

motete m motet

motín m riot; (rebelión) uprising; (de tropas) mutiny

motiv|ación f motivation. **~ar** vt motivate; (explicar) explain. **~o** m reason. **con ~o de** because of

motocicl|eta f motor cycle, motor bike (fam). **~ista** m & f motorcyclist

motón m pulley

motonave f motor boat

motor a motor. ● m motor, engine. **~a** f motor boat. **~ de arranque** starter motor

motoris|mo m motorcycling. **~ta** m & f motorist; (de una moto) motorcyclist

motorizar [10] vt motorize

motriz a & f motive, driving

move|dizo a movable; (poco firme) unstable; (persona) fickle. **~r** [2] vt move; shake (la cabeza); (provocar) cause. **~rse** vpr move; (darse prisa) hurry up. **arenas** fpl **~dizas** quicksand

movi|ble a movable. **~do** a moved; (foto) blurred; (inquieto) fidgety

móvil a movable. ● m motive

movili|dad f mobility. **~zación** f mobilization. **~zar** [10] vt mobilize

movimiento m movement, motion; (agitación) bustle

moza f girl; (sirvienta) servant, maid. **~lbete** m young lad

mozárabe *a* Mozarabic. ● *m & f* Mozarab

moz|o *m* boy, lad. ~**uela** *f* young girl. ~**uelo** *m* young boy/lad

muaré *m* moiré

mucam|a *f* (*Arg*) servant. ~**o** *m* (*Arg*) servant

mucos|idad *f* mucus. ~**o** *a* mucous

muchach|a *f* girl; (*sirvienta*) servant, maid. ~**o** *m* boy, lad; (*criado*) servant

muchedumbre *f* crowd

muchísimo *a* very much. ● *adv* a lot

mucho *a* much (*pl* many), a lot of. ● *pron* a lot; (*personas*) many (people). ● *adv* a lot, very much; (*de tiempo*) long, a long time. **ni ~ menos** by no means. **por ~ que** however much

muda *f* change of clothing; (*de animales*) moult. ~**ble** *a* changeable; (*personas*) fickle. ~**nza** *f* change; (*de casa*) removal. ~**r** *vt/i* change. ~**rse** (*de ropa*) change one's clothes; (*de casa*) move (house)

mudéjar *a & m & f* Mudéjar

mud|ez *f* dumbness. ~**o** *a* dumb; (*callado*) silent

mueble *a* movable. ● *m* piece of furniture

mueca *f* grimace, face. **hacer una ~** pull a face

muela *f* (*diente*) tooth; (*diente molar*) molar; (*piedra de afilar*) grindstone; (*piedra de molino*) millstone

muelle *a* soft. ● *m* spring; (*naut*) wharf; (*malecón*) jetty

muérdago *m* mistletoe

muero *vb véase* **morir**

muert|e *f* death; (*homicidio*) murder. ~**o** *a* dead; (*matado, fam*) killed; (*colores*) pale. ● *m* dead person; (*cadáver*) body, corpse

muesca *f* nick; (*ranura*) slot

muestra *f* sample; (*prueba*) proof; (*modelo*) model; (*seal*) sign. ~**rio** *m* collection of samples

muestro *vb véase* **mostrar**

muevo *vb véase* **mover**

mugi|do *m* moo. ~**r** [14] *vi* moo; (*fig*) roar

mugr|e *m* dirt. ~**iento** *a* dirty, filthy

mugrón *m* sucker

muguete *m* lily of the valley

mujer *f* woman; (*esposa*) wife. ● *int* my dear! ~**iego** *a* ⟨*hombre*⟩ fond of the women. ~**il** *a* womanly. ~**ío** *m* (crowd of) women. ~**zuela** *f* prostitute

mújol *m* mullet

mula *f* mule; (*Mex*) unsaleable goods. ~**da** *f* drove of mules

mulato *a & m* mulatto

mulero *m* muleteer

mulet|a *f* crutch; (*fig*) support; (*toreo*) stick with a red flag

mulo *m* mule

multa *f* fine. ~**r** *vt* fine

**multi... ** *pref* multi...

multicolor *a* multicolour(ed)

multicopista *m* copying machine

multiforme *a* multiform

multilateral *a* multilateral

multilingüe *a* multilingual

multimillonario *m* multimillion-aire

múltiple *a* multiple

multiplic|ación *f* multiplication. ~**ar** [7] *vt* multiply. ~**arse** *vpr* multiply; (*fig*) go out of one's way. ~**idad** *f* multiplicity

múltiplo *a & m* multiple

multitud *f* multitude, crowd. ~**inario** *a* multitudinous

mulli|do *a* soft. ● *m* stuffing. ~**r** [22] *vt* soften

mund|ano *a* wordly; (*de la sociedad elegante*) society. ● *m* socialite. ~**ial** *a* world-wide. **la segunda guerra ~ial** the Second World War. ~**illo** *m* world, circles. ~**o** *m* world. ~**ología** *f* worldly wisdom. **todo el ~o** everybody

munición *f* ammunition; (*provisiones*) supplies

municip|al *a* municipal. ~**alidad** *f* municipality. ~**io** *m* municipality; (*ayuntamiento*) town council

mun|ificencia *f* munificence. ~**ífico** *a* munificent

muñe|ca *f* (*anat*) wrist; (*juguete*) doll; (*maniquí*) dummy. ~**co** *m* boy doll. ~**quera** *f* wristband

muñón *m* stump

mura|l *a* mural, wall. ● *m* mural. ~**lla** *f* (city) wall. ~**r** *vt* wall

murciélago *m* bat

murga *f* street band; (*lata*) bore, nuisance. **dar la ~** bother, be a pain (*fam*)

murmullo *m* (*de personas*) whisper(ing), murmur(ing); (*del agua*) rippling; (*del viento*) sighing, rustle

murmura|ción *f* gossip. ~**dor** *a* gossiping. ● *m* gossip. ~**r** *vi* murmur; (*hablar en voz baja*) whisper; (*quejarse en voz baja*) mutter; (*criticar*) gossip muro *m* wall

murri|a *f* depression. ~o *a* depressed

mus *m* card game

musa *f* muse

musaraña *f* shrew

muscula|r *a* muscular. ~tura *f* muscles

músculo *m* muscle

musculoso *a* muscular

muselina *f* muslin

museo *m* museum. ~ de arte art gallery

musgaño *m* shrew

musgo *m* moss. ~so *a* mossy

música *f* music

musical *a & m* musical

músico *a* musical. ● *m* musician

music|ología *f* musicology. ~ólogo *m* musicologist

musitar *vt/i* mumble

muslímico *a* Muslim

muslo *m* thigh

mustela *a* weasel

musti|arse *vpr* wither, wilt. ~o *a* ‹plantas› withered; ‹cosas› faded; ‹personas› gloomy; (*Mex, hipócrita*) hypocritical

musulmán *a & m* Muslim

muta|bilidad *f* mutability. ~ción *f* change; (*en biología*) mutation

mutila|ción *f* mutilation. ~do *a* crippled. ● *m* cripple. ~r *vt* mutilate; cripple, maim ‹*persona*›

mutis *m* (*en el teatro*) exit. ~mo *m* silence

mutu|alidad *f* mutuality; (*asociación*) friendly society. ~amente *adv* mutually. ~o *a* mutual

muy *adv* very; (*demasiado*) too

N

nab|a *f* swede. ~o *m* turnip

nácar *m* mother-of-pearl

nac|er [11] *vi* be born; ‹*huevo*› hatch; ‹*planta*› sprout. ~ido *a* born. ~iente *a* ‹*sol*› rising. ~imiento *m* birth; (*de río*) source; (*belén*) crib. dar ~imiento a give rise to. lugar *m* de ~imiento place of birth. recien ~ido newborn. volver a ~er have a narrow escape

naci|ón *f* nation. ~onal *a* national. ~onalidad *f* nationality. ~onalismo *m* nationalism. ~onalista *m & f* nationalist. ~onalizar [10] *vt*

nationalize. ~onalizarse *vpr* become naturalized

nada *pron* nothing, not anything. ● *adv* not at all. ¡~ de eso! nothing of the sort! antes de ~ first of all. ¡de ~! (*después de ‘gracias’*) don't mention it! para ~ (not) at all. por ~ del mundo not for anything in the world

nada|dor *m* swimmer. ~r *vi* swim

nadería *f* trifle

nadie *pron* no one, nobody

nado *adv.* a ~ swimming

nafta *f* (*LAm, gasolina*) petrol, (*Brit*), gas (*Amer*)

nailon *m* nylon

naipe *m* (playing) card. juegos *mpl* de ~s card games

nalga *f* buttock. ~s *fpl* bottom

nana *f* lullaby

Nápoles *m* Naples

naranj|a *f* orange. ~ada *f* orangeade. ~al *m* orange grove. ~o *m* orange tree

narcótico *a & m* narcotic

nariz *f* nose; (*orificio de la nariz*) nostril. ¡narices! rubbish!

narra|ción *f* narration. ~dor *m* narrator. ~r *vt* tell. ~tivo *a* narrative

nasal *a* nasal

nata *f* cream

natación *f* swimming

natal *a* birth; ‹*pueblo etc*› home. ~idad *f* birth rate

natillas *fpl* custard

natividad *f* nativity

nativo *a & m* native

nato *a* born

natural *a* natural. ● *m* native. ~eza *f* nature; (*nacionalidad*) nationality; (*ciudadanía*) naturalization. ~eza muerta still life. ~idad *f* naturalness. ~ista *m & f* naturalist. ~izar [10] *vt* naturalize. ~izarse *vpr* become naturalized. ~mente *adv* naturally. ● *int* of course!

naufrag|ar [12] *vi* ‹*barco*› sink; ‹*persona*› be shipwrecked; (*fig*) fail. ~io *m* shipwreck

náufrago *a* shipwrecked. ● *m* shipwrecked person

náusea *f* nausea. dar ~s a uno make s.o. feel sick. sentir ~s feel sick

nauseabundo *a* sickening

náutico *a* nautical

navaja *f* penknife; (*de afeitar*) razor. ~zo *m* slash

naval *a* naval

Navarra f Navarre

nave f ship; (de iglesia) nave. ~ **espacial** spaceship. **quemar las** ~s burn one's boats

navega|ble a navigable; ⟨barco⟩ seaworthy. ~**ción** f navigation. ~**nte** m & f navigator. ~**r** [12] vi sail; ⟨avión⟩ fly

Navid|ad f Christmas. ~**eño** a Christmas. **en** ~**ades** at Christmas. **¡feliz** ~**ad!** Happy Christmas! **por** ~**ad** at Christmas

navío m ship

nazi a & m & f Nazi

neblina f mist

nebuloso a misty; (fig) vague

necedad f foolishness. **decir** ~**es** talk nonsense. **hacer una** ~ do sth stupid

necesari|amente adv necessarily. ~**o** a necessary

necesi|dad f necessity; (pobreza) poverty. ~**dades** fpl hardships. **por** ~**dad** (out) of necessity. ~**tado** a in need (de of); (pobre) needy. ~**tar** vt need. ● vi. ~**tar de** need

necio a silly. ● m idiot

necrología f obituary column

néctar m nectar

nectarina f nectarine

nefasto a unfortunate, ominous

nega|ción f negation; (desmentimiento) denial; (gram) negative. ~**do** a incompetent. ~**r** [1 & 12] vt deny; (rehusar) refuse. ~**rse** vpr. ~**rse** a refuse. ~**tiva** f negative; (acción) denial; (acción de rehusar) refusal. ~**tivo** a & m negative

negligen|cia f negligence. ~**te** a negligent

negoci|able a negotiable. ~**ación** f negotiation. ~**ante** m & f dealer. ~**ar** vt/i negotiate. ~**ar en** trade in. ~**o** m business; (com, trato) deal. ~**os** mpl business. **hombre** m **de** ~**os** businessman

negr|a f Negress; (mus) crotchet. ~**o** a black; ⟨persona⟩ Negro. ● m (color) black; ⟨persona⟩ Negro. ~**ura** f blackness. ~**uzco** a blackish

nene m & f baby, child

nenúfar m water lily

neo... pref neo...

neocelandés a from New Zealand. ● m New Zealander

neolítico a Neolithic

neón m neon

nepotismo m nepotism

nervio m nerve; (tendón) sinew; (bot) vein. ~**sidad** f, ~**sismo** m nervousness; (impaciencia) impatience. ~**so** a nervous; (de temperamento) highly-strung. **crispar los** ~s **a uno** (fam) get on s.o.'s nerves. **ponerse** ~**so** get excited

neto a clear; ⟨verdad⟩ simple; (com) net

neumático a pneumatic. ● m tyre

neumonía f pneumonia

neuralgia f neuralgia

neur|ología f neurology. ~**ólogo** m neurologist

neur|osis f neurosis. ~**ótico** a neurotic

neutr|al a neutral. ~**alidad** f neutrality. ~**alizar** [10] vt neutralize. ~**o** a neutral; (gram) neuter

neutrón m neutron

neva|da f snowfall. ~**r** [1] vi snow. ~**sca** f blizzard

nevera f fridge (Brit, fam), refrigerator

nevisca f light snowfall. ~**r** [7] vi snow lightly

nexo m link

ni conj nor, neither; (ni siquiera) not even. ~... ~ neither... nor. ~ **que** as if. ~ **siquiera** not even

Nicaragua f Nicaragua

nicaragüense a & m & f Nicaraguan

nicotina f nicotine

nicho m niche

nido m nest; (de ladrones) den; (escondrijo) hiding-place

niebla f fog; (neblina) mist. **hay** ~ it's foggy

niet|a f granddaughter. ~**o** m grandson. ~**os** mpl grandchildren

nieve f snow; (LAm, helado) ice-cream

Nigeria f Nigeria. ~**no** a Nigerian

niki m T-shirt

nilón m nylon

nimbo m halo

nimi|edad f triviality. ~**o** a insignificant

ninfa f nymph

ninfea f water lily

ningún véase **ninguno**

ninguno a (delante de nombre masculino en singular **ningún**) no, not any. ● pron none; (persona) no-one, nobody; (de dos) neither. **de ninguna manera, de ningún modo** by no means. **en ninguna parte** nowhere

niñ|a f (little) girl. **~ada** f childish thing. **~era** f nanny. **~ería** f childish thing. **~ez** f childhood. **~o** a childish. ● m (little) boy. **de ~o** as a child. **desde ~o** from childhood

níquel m nickel

níspero m medlar

nitidez f clearness

nítido a clear; (foto) sharp

nitrato m nitrate

nítrico a nitric

nitrógeno m nitrogen

nivel m level; (fig) standard. **~ar** vt level. **~arse** vpr become level. **~ de vida** standard of living

no adv not; (como respuesta) no. ¿~? isn't it? **~ más** only. **¡a que ~!** I bet you don't! **¡cómo ~!** of course! **Felipe ~ tiene hijos** Felipe has no children. **¡que ~!** certainly not!

nob|iliario a noble. **~le** a & m & f noble. **~leza** f nobility

noción f notion. **nociones** fpl rudiments

nocivo a harmful

nocturno a nocturnal; (clase) evening; (tren etc) night. ● m nocturne

noche f night. **~ vieja** New Year's Eve. **~ a ~** at night. **hacer ~** spend the night. **media ~** midnight. **por la ~** at night

Nochebuena f Christmas Eve

nodo m (Esp, película) newsreel

nodriza f nanny

nódulo m nodule

nogal m walnut(-tree)

nómada a nomadic. ● m & f nomad

nombr|adía f fame. **~ado** a famous; (susodicho) aforementioned. **~amiento** m appointment. **~ar** vt appoint; (citar) mention. **~e** m name; (gram) noun; (fama) renown. **~e de pila** Christian name. **en ~e de** in the name of. **no tener ~e** be unspeakable. **poner de ~e** call

nomeolvides m invar forget-me-not

nómina f payroll

nominal|l a nominal. **~tivo** a & m nominative. **~tivo a** (cheque etc) made out to

nona a odd. ● m odd number

nonada f trifle

nono a ninth

nordeste a (región) north-eastern; (viento) north-easterly. ● m north-east

nórdico a northern. ● m northerner

noria f water-wheel; (en una feria) ferris wheel

norma f rule

normal a normal. ● f teachers' training college. **~idad** f normality (Brit), normalcy (Amer). **~izar** [10] vt normalize. **~mente** adv normally, usually

Normandía f Normandy

noroeste a (región) north-western; (viento) north-westerly. ● m north-west

norte m north; (viento) north wind; (fig, meta) aim

Norteamérica f (North) America

norteamericano a & m (North) American

norteño a northern. ● m northerner

Noruega f Norway

noruego a & m Norwegian

nos pron (acusativo) us; (dativo) (to) us; (reflexivo) (to) ourselves; (recíproco) (to) each other

nosotros pron we; (con prep) us

nost|algia f nostalgia; (de casa, de patria) homesickness. **~álgico** a nostalgic

nota f note; (de examen etc) mark. **~ble** a notable. **~ción** f notation. **~r** vt notice; (apuntar) note down. **de mala ~** notorious. **de ~** famous. **digno de ~** notable. **es de ~r** it should be noted. **hacerse ~r** stand out

notario m notary

notici|a f (piece of) news. **~as** fpl news. **~ario** m news. **~ero** a news. **atrasado de ~as** behind the times. **tener ~as de** hear from

notifica|ción f notification. **~r** [7] vt notify

notori|edad f notoriety. **~o** a well-known; (evidente) obvious

novato m novice

novecientos a & m nine hundred

noved|ad f newness; (noticia) news; (cambio) change; (moda) latest fashion. **~oso** a (LAm) novel. **sin ~ad** no news

novel|a f novel. **~ista** m & f novelist

noveno a ninth

novent|a a & m ninety; (nonagésimo) ninetieth. **~ón** a & m ninety-year-old

novia f girlfriend; (prometida) fiancée; (en boda) bride. **~zgo** m engagement

novicio m novice

noviembre m November

novilunio *m* new moon

novill|a *f* heifer. **~o** *m* bullock. **hacer ~os** play truant

novio *m* boyfriend; (*prometido*) fiancé; (*en boda*) bridegroom. **los ~s** the bride and groom

novísimo *a* very new

nub|arrón *m* large dark cloud. **~e** *f* cloud; (*de insectos etc*) swarm. **~lado** *a* cloudy, overcast. ● *m* cloud. **~lar** *vt* cloud. **~larse** *vpr* become cloudy. **~loso** *a* cloudy

nuca *f* back of the neck

nuclear *a* nuclear

núcleo *m* nucleus

nudillo *m* knuckle

nudis|mo *m* nudism. **~ta** *m* & *f* nudist

nudo *m* knot; (*de asunto etc*) crux. **~so** *a* knotty. **tener un ~ en la garganta** have a lump in one's throat

nuera *f* daughter-in-law

nuestro *a* our; (*pospuesto al sustantivo*) of ours. ● *pron* ours. **~ coche** our car. **un coche ~** a car of ours

nueva *f* (piece of) news. **~s** *fpl* news. **~mente** *adv* newly; (*de nuevo*) again

Nueva York *f* New York

Nueva Zelanda *f*, **Nueva Zelandia** *f* (*LAm*) New Zealand

nueve *a* & *m* nine

nuevo *a* new. **de ~** again

nuez *f* nut; (*del nogal*) walnut; (*anat*) Adam's apple. **~ de Adán** Adam's apple. **~ moscada** nutmeg

nul|idad *f* incompetence; (*persona, fam*) nonentity. **~o** *a* useless; (*jurid*) null and void

num|eración *f* numbering. **~eral** *a* & *m* numeral. **~erar** *vt* number. **~érico** *a* numerical

número *m* number; (*arábigo, romano*) numeral; (*de zapatos etc*) size. **sin ~** countless

numeroso *a* numerous

nunca *adv* never, not ever. **~ (ja)más** never again. **casi ~** hardly ever. **más que ~** more than ever

nupcia|l *a* nuptial. **~s** *fpl* wedding. **banquete ~l** wedding breakfast

nutria *f* otter

nutri|ción *f* nutrition. **~do** *a* nourished, fed; (*fig*) large; (*aplausos*) loud; (*fuego*) heavy. **~r** *vt* nourish, feed; (*fig*) feed. **~tivo** *a* nutritious. **valor** *m* **~tivo** nutritional value

nylon *m* nylon

Ñ

ña *f* (*LAm, fam*) Mrs

ñacanina *f* (*Arg*) poisonous snake

ñame *m* yam

ñapindá *m* (*Arg*) mimosa

ñato *adj* (*LAm*) snub-nosed

ño *m* (*LAm, fam*) Mr

ñoñ|ería *f*, **~ez** *f* insipidity. **~o** *a* insipid; (*tímido*) bashful; (*quisquilloso*) prudish

ñu *m* gnu

O

o *conj* or. **~ bien** rather. **~... ~** either... or. **~ sea** in other words

oasis *m invar* oasis

obcecar [7] *vt* blind

obed|ecer [11] *vt/i* obey. **~iencia** *f* obedience. **~iente** *a* obedient

obelisco *m* obelisk

obertura *f* overture

obes|idad *f* obesity. **~o** *a* obese

obispo *m* bishop

obje|ción *f* objection. **~tar** *vt/i* object

objetiv|idad *f* objectivity. **~o** *a* objective. ● *m* objective; (*foto etc*) lens

objeto *m* object

objetor *m* objector. **~ de conciencia** conscientious objector

oblicuo *a* oblique; (*mirada*) sidelong

obliga|ción *f* obligation; (*com*) bond. **~do** *a* obliged; (*forzoso*) obligatory; **~r** [12] *vt* force, oblige. **~rse** *vpr* **~rse a** undertake to. **~torio** *a* obligatory

oboe *m* oboe; (*músico*) oboist

obra *f* work; (*de teatro*) play; (*construcción*) building. **~ maestra** masterpiece. **en ~s** under construction. **por ~ de** thanks to. **~r** *vt* do; (*construir*) build

obrero *a* labour; (*clase*) working. ● *m* workman; (*en fábrica*) worker

obscen|idad *f* obscenity. **~o** *a* obscene

obscu... *véase* oscu...

obsequi|ar *vt* lavish attention on. **~ar con** give, present with. **~o** *m* gift, present; (*agasajo*) attention. **~oso** *a* obliging. **en ~o de** in honour of

observa|ción f observation; (*objeción*) objection. ∼dor m observer. ∼ncia f observance. ∼nte a observant. ∼r vt observe; (*notar*) notice. ∼rse vpr be noted. ∼torio m observatory. hacer una ∼ción make a remark

obses|ión f obsession. ∼ionar vt obsess. ∼ivo a obsessive. ∼o a obsessed

obst|aculizar [10] vt hinder. ∼áculo m obstacle

obstante. no ∼ adv however, nevertheless. ● prep in spite of

obstar vi. ∼ para prevent

obstétrico a obstetric

obstina|ción f obstinacy. ∼do a obstinate. ∼rse vpr be obstinate. ∼rse en (+ *infintivo*) persist in (+ *gerundio*)

obstru|cción f obstruction. ∼ir [17] vt obstruct

obtener [40] vt get, obtain

obtura|dor m (*foto*) shutter. ∼r vt plug; fill ⟨*muela etc*⟩

obtuso a obtuse

obviar vt remove

obvio a obvious

oca f goose

ocasi|ón f occasion; (*oportunidad*) opportunity; (*motivo*) cause. ∼onal a chance. ∼onar vt cause. aprovechar la ∼ón take the opportunity. con ∼ón de on the occasion of. de ∼ón bargain; (*usado*) secondhand. en ∼ones sometimes. perder una ∼ón miss a chance

ocaso m sunset; (*fig*) decline

occident|al a western. ● m & f westerner. ∼e m west

océano m ocean

ocio m idleness; (*tiempo libre*) leisure time. ∼sidad f idleness. ∼so a idle; (*inútil*) pointless

oclusión f occlusion

octano m octane. índice m de ∼ octane number, octane rating

octav|a f octave. ∼o a & m eighth

octogenario a & m octogenarian, eighty-year-old

oct|ogonal a octagonal. ∼ógono m octagon

octubre m October

oculista m & f oculist, optician

ocular a eye

ocult|ar vt hide. ∼arse vpr hide. ∼o a hidden; (*secreto*) secret

ocupa|ción f occupation. ∼do a occupied; ⟨*persona*⟩ busy. ∼nte m occupant. ∼r vt occupy. ∼rse vpr look after

ocurr|encia f occurrence, event; (*idea*) idea; (*que tiene gracia*) witty remark. ∼ir vi happen. ∼irse vpr occur. ¿qué ∼e? what's the matter? se me ∼e que it occurs to me that

ochent|a a & m eighty. ∼ón a & m eighty-year-old

ocho a & m eight. ∼cientos a & m eight hundred

oda f ode

odi|ar vt hate. ∼o m hatred. ∼oso a hateful

odisea f odyssey

oeste m west; (*viento*) west wind

ofen|der vt offend; (*insultar*) insult. ∼derse vpr take offence. ∼sa f offence. ∼siva f offensive. ∼sivo a offensive

oferta f offer; (*en subasta*) bid; (*regalo*) gift. ∼s de empleo situations vacant. en ∼ on (special) offer

oficial a official. ● m skilled worker; (*funcionario*) civil servant; (*mil*) officer. ∼a f skilled (woman) worker

oficin|a f office. ∼a de colocación employment office. ∼a de Estado government office. ∼a de turismo tourist office. ∼ista m & f office worker. horas fpl de ∼a business hours

oficio m job; (*profesión*) profession; (*puesto*) post. ∼so a (*no oficial*) unofficial

ofrec|er [11] vt offer; give ⟨*fiesta, banquete etc*⟩; (*prometer*) promise. ∼erse vpr ⟨*persona*⟩ volunteer; ⟨*cosa*⟩ occur. ∼imiento m offer

ofrenda f offering. ∼r vt offer

ofusca|ción f blindness; (*confusión*) confusion. ∼r [7] vt blind; (*confundir*) confuse. ∼rse vpr be dazzled

ogro m ogre

oi|ble a audible. ∼da f hearing. ∼do m hearing; (*anat*) ear. al ∼do in one's ear. de ∼das by hearsay. de ∼do by ear. duro de ∼do hard of hearing

oigo vb *véase* oír

oír [50] vt hear. ∼ misa go to mass. ¡oiga! listen!; (*al teléfono*) hello!

ojal m buttonhole

ojalá int I hope so! ● conj if only

ojea|da f glance. ∼r vt eye; (*para inspeccionar*) see; (*ahuyentar*) scare away. **dar una** ∼**da a, echar una** ∼**da a** glance at

ojeras *fpl* (*del ojo*) bags

ojeriza *f* ill will. **tener** ∼ a have a grudge against

ojete *m* eyelet

ojo *m* eye; (*de cerradura*) keyhole; (*de un puente*) span. ¡∼! careful!

ola *f* wave

olé *int* bravo!

olea|da *f* wave. ∼**je** *m* swell

óleo *m* oil; (*cuadro*) oil painting

oleoducto *m* oil pipeline

oler [2, *las formas que empezarían por* **ue** *se escriben* **hue**] *vt* smell; (*curiosear*) pry into; (*descubrir*) discover. ● *vi* smell (**a** of)

olfat|ear *vt* smell, sniff; (*fig*) sniff out. ∼**o** *m* (sense of) smell; (*fig*) intuition

olimpiada *f*, **olimpíada** *f* Olympic games, Olympics

olímpico *a* (*juegos*) Olympic

oliv|a *f* olive; (*olivo*) olive tree. ∼**ar** *m* olive grove. ∼**om** olive tree

olmo *m* elm (tree)

olor *m* smell. ∼**oso** *a* sweet-smelling

olvid|adizo *a* forgetful. ∼**ar** *vt* forget; ∼**arse** *vpr* forget; (*estar olvidado*) be forgotten. ∼**om** oblivion; (*acción de olvidar*) forgetfulness. **se me** ∼**ó** I forgot

olla *f* pot, casserole; (*guisado*) stew. ∼ **a/de presión,** ∼ **exprés** pressure cooker. ∼ **podrida** Spanish stew

ombligo *m* navel

ominoso *a* awful, abominable

omi|sión *f* omission; (*olvido*) forgetfulness. ∼**tir** *vt* omit

ómnibus *a* omnibus

omnipotente *a* omnipotent

omóplato *m*, **omoplato** *m* shoulder blade

once *a* & *m* eleven

ond|a *f* wave. ∼**a corta** short wave. ∼**a larga** long wave. ∼**ear** *vi* wave; (*agua*) ripple. ∼**ulación** *f* undulation; (*del pelo*) wave. ∼**ular** *vi* wave. **longitud** *f* **de** ∼**a** wavelength

oneroso *a* onerous

ónice *m* onyx

onomástico *a*. **día** ∼, **fiesta onomástica** name-day

ONU *abrev* (*Organización de las Naciones Unidas*) UN, United Nations

onza *f* ounce

opa *a* (*LAm*) stupid

opaco *a* opaque; (*fig*) dull

ópalo *m* opal

opción *f* option

ópera *f* opera

opera|ción *f* operation; (*com*) transaction. ∼**dor** *m* operator; (*cirujano*) surgeon; (*TV*) cameraman. ∼**r** *vt* operate on; work (*milagro etc*). ● *vi* operate; (*com*) deal. ∼**rse** *vpr* occur; (*med*) have an operation. ∼**torio** *a* operative

opereta *f* operetta

opin|ente *a* opposing. ∼**ión** *f* opinion. **la** ∼**ión pública** public opinion

opio *m* opium

opone|nte *a* opposing. ● *m* & *f* opponent. ∼**r** *vt* oppose; offer (*resistencia*); raise (*objeción*). ∼**rse** *vpr* be opposed; (*dos personas*) oppose each other

oporto *m* port (wine)

oportun|idad *f* opportunity; (*cualidad de oportuno*) timeliness. ∼**ista** *m* & *f* opportunist. ∼**o** *a* opportune; (*apropiado*) suitable

oposi|ción *f* opposition. ∼**ciones** *fpl* competition, public examination. ∼**tor** *m* candidate

opres|ión *f* oppression; (*ahogo*) difficulty in breathing. ∼**ivo** *a* oppressive. ∼**o** *a* oppressed. ∼**or** *m* oppressor

oprimir *vt* squeeze; press (*botón etc*); (*ropa*) be too tight for; (*fig*) oppress

oprobio *m* disgrace

optar *vi* choose. ∼ **por** opt for

óptic|a *f* optics; (*tienda*) optician's (shop). ∼**o** *a* optic(al). ● *m* optician

optimis|mo *m* optimism. ∼**ta** *a* optimistic. ● *m* & *f* optimist

opuesto *a* opposite; (*enemigo*) opposed

opulen|cia *f* opulence. ∼**to** *a* opulent

oración *f* prayer; (*discurso*) speech; (*gram*) sentence

oráculo *m* oracle

orador *m* speaker

oral *a* oral

orar *vi* pray

oratori|a *f* oratory. ∼**o** *a* oratorical. ● *m* (*mus*) oratorio

orbe *m* orb

órbita *f* orbit

orden *m* & *f* order; (*Mex, porción*) portion. ∼**ado** *a* tidy. ∼ **del día** agenda. **órdenes** *fpl* **sagradas** Holy Orders. **a sus órdenes** (*esp Mex*) can

I help you? **en ~** in order. **por ~** in turn

ordenador *m* computer

ordena|nza *f* order. ● *m* (*mil*) orderly. **~r** *vt* put in order; (*mandar*) order; (*relig*) ordain

ordeñar *vt* milk

ordinal *a & m* ordinal

ordinario *a* ordinary; (*grosero*) common

orear *vt* air

orégano *m* oregano

oreja *f* ear

orfanato *m* orphanage

orfebre *m* goldsmith, silversmith

orfeón *m* choral society

orgánico *a* organic

organigrama *m* flow chart

organillo *m* barrel-organ

organismo *m* organism

organista *m & f* organist

organiza|ción *f* organization. **~dor** *m* organizer. **~r** [10] *vt* organize. **~rse** *vpr* get organized

órgano *m* organ

orgasmo *m* orgasm

orgía *f* orgy

orgullo *m* pride. **~so** *a* proud

orientación *f* direction

oriental *a & m & f* oriental

orientar *vt* position. **~se** *vpr* point; (*persona*) find one's bearings

oriente *m* east. **O~ Medio** Middle East

orificio *m* hole

orig|en *m* origin. **~inal** *a* original; (*excéntrico*) odd. **~inalidad** *f* originality. **~inar** *vt* give rise to. **~inario** *a* original; (*nativo*) native. **dar ~en a** give rise to. **ser ~inario de** come from

orilla *f* (*del mar*) shore; (*de río*) bank; (*borde*) edge

orín *m* rust

orina *f* urine. **~l** *m* chamber-pot. **~r** *vi* urinate

oriundo *a*. **~ de** (*persona*) (originating) from; (*animal etc*) native to

orla *f* border

ornamental *a* ornamental

ornitología *f* ornithology

oro *m* gold. **~s** *mpl* Spanish card suit. **~ de ley** 9 carat gold. **hacerse de ~** make a fortune. **prometer el ~ y el moro** promise the moon

oropel *m* tinsel

orquesta *f* orchestra. **~l** *a* orchestral. **~r** *vt* orchestrate

orquídea *f* orchid

ortiga *f* nettle

ortodox|ia *f* orthodoxy. **~o** *a* orthodox

ortografía *f* spelling

ortop|edia *f* orthopaedics. **~édico** *a* orthopaedic

oruga *f* caterpillar

orzuelo *m* sty

os *pron* (*acusativo*) you; (*dativo*) (to) you; (*reflexivo*) (to) yourselves; (*recíproco*) (to) each other

osad|ía *f* boldness. **~o** *a* bold

oscila|ción *f* swinging; (*de precios*) fluctuation; (*tec*) oscillation. **~r** *vi* swing; (*precio*) fluctuate; (*tec*) oscillate; (*fig, vacilar*) hesitate

oscur|ecer [11] *vi* darken; (*fig*) obscure. **~ecerse** *vpr* grow dark; (*nublarse*) cloud over. **~idad** *f* darkness; (*fig*) obscurity. **~o** *a* dark; (*fig*) obscure. **a ~as** in the dark

óseo *a* bony

oso *m* bear. **~ de felpa, ~ de peluche** teddy bear

ostensible *a* obvious

ostent|ación *f* ostentation. **~ar** *vt* show off; (*mostrar*) show. **~oso** *a* ostentatious

osteoartritis *f* osteoarthritis

oste|ópata *m & f* osteopath. **~opatía** *f* osteopathy

ostión *m* (*esp Mex*) oyster

ostra *f* oyster

ostracismo *m* ostracism

Otan *abrev* (*Organización del Tratado del Atlántico Norte*) NATO, North Atlantic Treaty Organization

otear *vt* observe; (*escudriñar*) scan, survey

otitis *f* inflammation of the ear

otoño *m* autumn (*Brit*), fall (*Amer*)

otorga|miento *m* granting; (*documento*) authorization. **~r** [12] *vt* give; (*jurid*) draw up

otorrinolaringólogo *m* ear, nose and throat specialist

otro *a* other; (*uno más*) another. ● *pron* another (one); (*en plural*) others; (*otra persona*) someone else. **el ~** the other. **el uno al ~** one another, each other

ovación *f* ovation

oval *a* oval

óvalo *m* oval

ovario *m* ovary

oveja *f* sheep; (*hembra*) ewe

overol *m* (*LAm*) overalls

ovino a sheep

ovillo m ball. **hacerse un ~** curl up

OVNI abrev (objeto volante no identificado) UFO, unidentified flying object

ovulación f ovulation

oxida|ción f rusting. **~r** vi rust. **~rse** vpr go rusty

óxido m oxide

oxígeno m oxygen

oye vb véase oír

oyente a listening. ● m & f listener

ozono m ozone

P

pabellón m bell tent; (edificio) building; (de instrumento) bell; (bandera) flag

pabilo m wick

paceño a from La Paz. ● m person from La Paz

pacer [11] vi graze

pacien|cia f patience. **~te** a & m & f patient

pacificar [7] vt pacify; reconcile ‹dos personas›. **~se** vpr calm down

pacífico a peaceful. **el (Océano** m**) P~** the Pacific (Ocean)

pacifis|mo m pacifism. **~ta** a & m & f pacifist

pact|ar vi agree, make a pact. **~o** m pact, agreement

pachucho a ‹fruta› overripe; ‹persona› poorly

padec|er [11] vt/i suffer (de from); (soportar) bear. **~imiento** m suffering; (enfermedad) ailment

padrastro m stepfather

padre a (fam) great. ● m father. **~s** mpl parents

padrino m godfather; (en boda) best man

padrón m census

paella f paella

paga f pay, wages. **~ble** a, **~dero** a payable

pagano a & m pagan

pagar [12] vt pay; pay for ‹compras›. ● vi pay. **~é** m IOU

página f page

pago m payment

pagoda f pagoda

país m country; (región) region. **~ natal** native land. **el P~ Vasco** the Basque Country. **los P~es Bajos** the Low Countries

paisa|je m countryside. **~no** a of the same country. ● m compatriot

paja f straw; (fig) nonsense

pajarera f aviary

pájaro m bird. **~ carpintero** woodpecker

paje m page

Pakistán m. **el ~** Pakistan

pala f shovel; (laya) spade; (en deportes) bat; (de tenis) racquet

palabr|a f word; (habla) speech. **~ota** f swear-word. **decir ~otas** swear. **pedir la ~a** ask to speak. **soltar ~otas** swear. **tomar la ~a** (begin to) speak

palacio m palace; (casa grande) mansion

paladar m palate

paladino a clear; (público) public

palanca f lever; (fig) influence. **~ de cambio (de velocidades)** gear lever (Brit), gear shift (Amer)

palangana f wash-basin

palco m (en el teatro) box

Palestina f Palestine

palestino a & m Palestinian

palestra f (fig) arena

paleta f (de pintor) palette; (de albañil) trowel

paleto m yokel

paliativo a & m palliative

palide|cer [11] vi turn pale. **~z** f paleness

pálido a pale

palillo m small stick; (de dientes) toothpick

palique m. **estar de ~** be chatting

paliza f beating

palizada f fence; (recinto) enclosure

palma f (de la mano) palm; (árbol) palm (tree); (de dátiles) date palm. **~s** fpl applause. **dar ~da** f slap. **~das** fpl applause. **dar ~(da)s** clap. **tocar las ~s** clap

palmera f date palm

palmo m span; (fig, pequeña cantidad) small amount. **~ a ~** inch by inch

palmote|ar vi clap, applaud. **~o** m clapping, applause

palo m stick; (del teléfono etc) pole; (mango) handle; (de golf) club; (golpe) blow; (de naipes) suit; (mástil) mast

paloma f pigeon, dove

palomitas fpl popcorn

palpa|ble a palpable. **~r** vt feel

palpita|ción f palpitation. ~**nte** a throbbing. ~**r** vi throb; (latir) beat
palta f (LAm) avocado pear
pal|údico a marshy; (de paludismo) malarial. ~**udismo** m malaria
pamp|a f pampas. ~**ear** vi (LAm) travel across the pampas. ~**ero** a of the pampas
pan m bread; (barra) loaf. ~ **integral** wholemeal bread (Brit), wholewheat bread (Amer). ~ **tostado** toast. ~ **rallado** breadcrumbs. **ganarse el** ~ earn one's living
pana f corduroy
panacea f panacea
panader|ía f bakery; (tienda) baker's (shop). ~**o** m baker
panal m honeycomb
Panamá f Panama
panameño a & m Panamanian
pancarta f placard
panda m panda; (pandilla) gang
pander|eta f (small) tambourine. ~**o** m tambourine
pandilla f gang
panecillo m (bread) roll
panel m panel
panfleto m pamphlet
pánico m panic
panor|ama m panorama. ~**ámico** a panoramic
panqué m (LAm) pancake
pantaletas fpl (LAm) underpants, knickers
pantal|ón m trousers. ~**ones** mpl trousers. ~**ón corto** shorts. ~**ón tejano**, ~**ón vaquero** jeans
pantalla f screen; (de lámpara) (lamp)shade
pantano m marsh; (embalse) reservoir. ~**so** a boggy
pantera f panther
pantomima f pantomime
pantorrilla f calf
pantufla f slipper
panucho m (Mex) stuffed tortilla
panz|a f belly. ~**ada** f (hartazgo, fam) bellyful; (golpe, fam) blow in the belly. ~**udo** a fat, pot-bellied
pañal m nappy (Brit), diaper (Amer)
pañ|ería f draper's (shop). ~**o** m material; (de lana) woollen cloth; (trapo) cloth. ~**o de cocina** dishcloth; (para secar) tea towel. ~**o higiénico** sanitary towel. **en** ~**os menores** in one's underclothes
pañuelo m handkerchief; (de cabeza) scarf

papa m pope. ● f (esp LAm) potato. ~**s francesas** (LAm) chips
papá m dad(dy). ~**s** mpl parents. **P~ Noel** Father Christmas
papada f (de persona) double chin
papado m papacy
papagayo m parrot
papal a papal
papanatas m invar simpleton
paparrucha f (tontería) silly thing
papaya f pawpaw
papel m paper; (en el teatro etc) role. ~ **carbón** carbon paper. ~ **celofán** celophane paper. ~ **de calcar** carbon paper. ~ **de embalar**, ~ **de envolver** wrapping paper. ~ **de plata** silver paper. ~ **de seda** tissue paper. ~**era** f waste-paper basket. ~**ería** f stationer's (shop). ~**eta** f ticket; (para votar) paper. ~ **higiénico** toilet paper. ~ **pintado** wallpaper. ~ **secante** blotting paper. **blanco como el** ~ as white as a sheet. **desempeñar un** ~, **hacer un** ~ play a role
paperas fpl mumps
paquebote m packet (boat)
paquete m packet; (paquebote) packet (boat); (Mex, asunto difícil) difficult job. ~ **postal** parcel
paquistaní a & m Pakistani
par a equal; (número) even. ● m couple; (dos cosas iguales) pair; (igual) equal; (título) peer. **a la** ~ at the same time; (monedas) at par. **al** ~ **que** at the same time. **a** ~**es** two by two. **de** ~ **en** ~ wide open. **sin** ~ without equal
para prep for; (hacia) towards; (antes del infinitivo) (in order) to. ~ **con** to(wards). **¿** ~ **qué?** why? ~ **que** so that
parabienes mpl congratulations
parábola f (narración) parable
parabrisas m invar windscreen (Brit), windshield (Amer)
paraca f (LAm) strong wind (from the Pacific)
paraca|ídas m invar parachute. ~**idista** m & f parachutist; (mil) paratrooper
parachoques m invar bumper (Brit), fender (Amer); (rail) buffer
parad|a f (acción) stopping; (sitio) stop; (de taxis) rank; (mil) parade. ~**ero** m whereabouts; (alojamiento) lodging. ~**o** a stationary; (obrero) unemployed; (lento) slow. **dejar** ~**o**

confuse. **tener mal** ~**ero** come to a sticky end
paradoja *f* paradox
parador *m* state-owned hotel
parafina *f* paraffin
par|afrasear *vt* paraphrase. ~**áfra-sis** *f invar* paraphrase
paraguas *m invar* umbrella
Paraguay *m* Paraguay
paraguayo *a & m* Paraguayan
paraíso *m* paradise; (*en el teatro*) gallery
paralel|a *f* parallel (line). ~**as** *fpl* parallel bars. ~**o** *a & m* parallel
par|álisis *f invar* paralysis. ~**alítico** *a* paralytic. ~**alizar**[10] *vt* paralyse
paramilitar *a* paramilitary
páramo *m* barren plain
parang|ón *m* comparison. ~**onar** *vt* compare
paraninfo *m* hall
paranoi|a *f* paranoia. ~**co** *a* paranoiac
parapeto *m* parapet; (*fig*) barricade
parapléjico *a & m* paraplegic
parar *vt/i* stop. ~**se** *vpr* stop. **sin** ~ continuously
pararrayos *m invar* lightning conductor
parásito *a* parasitic. ● *m* parasite
parasol *m* parasol
parcela *f* plot. ~**r** *vt* divide into plots
parcial *a* partial. ~**idad** *f* prejudice; (*pol*) faction. **a tiempo** ~ part-time
parco *a* sparing, frugal
parche *m* patch
pardo *a* brown
parear *vt* pair off
parec|er *m* opinion; (*aspecto*) appearance. ● *vi* [11] seem; (*asemejarse*) look like; (*aparecer*) appear. ~**erse** *vpr* resemble, look like. ~**ido** *a* similar. ● *m* similarity. **al** ~**er** apparently. **a mi** ~**er** in my opinion. **bien** ~**ido** good-looking. **me** ~**e** I think. **¿qué te parece?** what do you think? **según** ~**e** apparently
pared *f* wall. ~**ón** *m* thick wall; (*de ruinas*) standing wall. ~ **por medio** next door. **llevar al** ~**ón** shoot
parej|a *f* pair; (*hombre y mujer*) couple; (*la otra persona*) partner. ~**o** *a* alike, the same; (*liso*) smooth
parente|la *f* relations. ~**sco** *m* relationship
paréntesis *m invar* parenthesis; (*signo ortográfico*) bracket. **entre** ~ (*fig*) by the way

paria *m & f* outcast
paridad *f* equality
pariente *m & f* relation, relative
parihuela *f*, **parihuelas** *fpl* stretcher
parir *vt* give birth to. ● *vi* have a baby, give birth
París *m* Paris
parisiense *a & m & f*, **parisino** *a & m* Parisian
parking /'parkin/ *m* car park (*Brit*), parking lot (*Amer*)
parlament|ar *vi* discuss. ~**ario** *a* parliamentary. ● *m* member of parliament (*Brit*), congressman (*Amer*). ~**o** *m* parliament
parlanchín *a* talkative. ● *m* chatterbox
parmesano *a* Parmesan
paro *m* stoppage; (*desempleo*) unemployment; (*pájaro*) tit
parodia *f* parody. ~**r** *vt* parody
parpadear *vi* blink; (*luz*) flicker; (*estrella*) twinkle
párpado *m* eyelid
parque *m* park. ~ **de atracciones** funfair. ~ **infantil** children's playground. ~ **zoológico** zoo, zoological gardens
parqué *m* parquet
parquedad *f* frugality; (*moderación*) moderation
parra *f* grapevine
párrafo *m* paragraph
parrilla *f* grill; (*LAm, auto*) radiator grill. ~**da** *f* grill. **a la** ~ grilled
párroco *m* parish priest
parroqui|a *f* parish; (*iglesia*) parish church. ~**no** *m* parishioner; (*cliente*) customer
parsimoni|a *f* thrift. ~**oso** *a* thrifty
parte *m* message; (*informe*) report. ● *f* part; (*porción*) share; (*lado*) side; (*jurid*) party. **dar** ~ report. **de mi** ~ for me. **de** ~ **de** from. **¿de** ~ **de quién?** (*al teléfono*) who's speaking? **en cualquier** ~ anywhere. **en gran** ~ largely. **en** ~ partly. **en todas** ~**s** everywhere. **la mayor** ~ the majority. **ninguna** ~ nowhere. **por otra** ~ on the other hand. **por todas** ~**s** everywhere
partera *f* midwife
partición *f* sharing out
participa|ción *f* participation; (*noticia*) notice; (*de lotería*) lottery ticket. ~**nte** *a* participating. ● *m & f* participant. ~**r** *vt* notify. ● *vi* take part

participio *m* participle

partícula *f* particle

particular *a* particular; ⟨*clase*⟩ private. ● *m* matter. **~idad** *f* peculiarity. **~izar** [10] *vt* distinguish; ⟨*detallar*⟩ give details about. **en ~** in particular. **nada de ~** nothing special

partida *f* departure; ⟨*en registro*⟩ entry; ⟨*documento*⟩ certificate; ⟨*juego*⟩ game; ⟨*de gente*⟩ group. **mala ~** dirty trick

partidario *a* & *m* partisan. **~ de** keen on

parti|do *a* divided. ● *m* ⟨*pol*⟩ party; ⟨*encuentro*⟩ match, game; ⟨*equipo*⟩ team. **~r** *vt* divide; ⟨*romper*⟩ break; ⟨*repartir*⟩ share; crack ⟨*nueces*⟩. ● *vi* leave; ⟨*empezar*⟩ start. **~rse** *vpr* ⟨*romperse*⟩ break; ⟨*dividirse*⟩ split. **a ~r de** (starting) from

partitura *f* ⟨*mus*⟩ score

parto *m* birth; ⟨*fig*⟩ creation. **estar de ~** be in labour

párvulo *m*. **colegio de ~s** nursery school

pasa *f* raisin. **~ de Corinto** currant. **~ de Esmirna** sultana

pasa|ble *a* passable. **~da** *f* passing; ⟨*de puntos*⟩ row. **~dero** *a* passable. **~dizo** *m* passage. **~do** *a* past; ⟨*día, mes etc*⟩ last; ⟨*anticuado*⟩ old-fashioned; ⟨*comida*⟩ bad, off. **~do mañana** the day after tomorrow. **~dor** *m* bolt; ⟨*de pelo*⟩ hair-slide; ⟨*culin*⟩ strainer. **de ~da** in passing. **el lunes ~do** last Monday

pasaje *m* passage; ⟨*naut*⟩ crossing; ⟨*viajeros*⟩ passengers. **~ro** *a* passing. ● *m* passenger

pasamano(s) *m* handrail; ⟨*barandilla de escalera*⟩ banister(s)

pasamontañas *m invar* Balaclava (helmet)

pasaporte *m* passport

pasar *vt* pass; ⟨*poner*⟩ put; ⟨*filtrar*⟩ strain; spend ⟨*tiempo*⟩; ⟨*tragar*⟩ swallow; show ⟨*película*⟩; ⟨*tolerar*⟩ tolerate, overlook; give ⟨*mensaje, enfermedad*⟩. ● *vi* pass; ⟨*suceder*⟩ happen; ⟨*ir*⟩ go; ⟨*venir*⟩ come; ⟨*tiempo*⟩ go by. **~ de** have no interest in. **~se** *vpr* pass; ⟨*terminarse*⟩ be over; ⟨*flores*⟩ wither; ⟨*comida*⟩ go bad; spend ⟨*tiempo*⟩; ⟨*excederse*⟩ go too far. **~lo bien** have a good time. **~ por alto** leave out. **como si no hubiese pasado nada** as if nothing had

happened. **lo que pasa es que** the fact is that. **pase lo que pase** whatever happens. **¡pase Vd!** come in!, go in! **¡que lo pases bien!** have a good time! **¿qué pasa?** what's the matter?, what's happening?

pasarela *f* footbridge; ⟨*naut*⟩ gangway

pasatiempo *m* hobby, pastime

pascua *f* ⟨*fiesta de los hebreos*⟩ Passover; ⟨*de Resurrección*⟩ Easter; ⟨*Navidad*⟩ Christmas. **~s** *fpl* Christmas. **hacer la ~ a uno** mess things up for s.o. **¡y santas ~s!** and that's that!

pase *m* pass

pase|ante *m* & *f* passer-by. **~ar** *vt* take for a walk; ⟨*exhibir*⟩ show off. ● *vi* go for a walk; ⟨*en coche etc*⟩ go for a ride. **~arse** *vpr* go for a walk; ⟨*en coche etc*⟩ go for a ride. **~o** *m* walk; ⟨*en coche etc*⟩ ride; ⟨*calle*⟩ avenue. **~o marítimo** promenade. **dar un ~o** for a walk. **¡vete a ~o!** ⟨*fam*⟩ go away!, get lost! ⟨*fam*⟩

pasillo *m* passage

pasión *f* passion

pasiv|idad *f* passiveness. **~o** *a* passive

pasm|ar *vt* astonish. **~arse** *vpr* be astonished. **~o** *m* astonishment. **~oso** *a* astonishing

paso *a* ⟨*fruta*⟩ dried ● *m* step; ⟨*acción de pasar*⟩ passing; ⟨*huella*⟩ footprint; ⟨*manera de andar*⟩ gait; ⟨*camino*⟩ way through; ⟨*entre montañas*⟩ pass; ⟨*estrecho*⟩ strait(s). **~ a nivel** level crossing ⟨*Brit*⟩, grade crossing ⟨*Amer*⟩. **~ de cebra** Zebra crossing. **~ de peatones** pedestrian crossing. **~ elevado** flyover. **a cada ~** at every turn. **a dos ~s** very near. **al ~ que** at the same time as. **a ~ lento** slowly. **ceda el ~** give way. **de ~** in passing. **de ~ por** on the way through. **prohibido el ~** no entry

pasodoble *m* ⟨*baile*⟩ pasodoble

pasota *m* & *f* drop-out

pasta *f* paste; ⟨*masa*⟩ dough; ⟨*dinero, fam*⟩ money. **~s** *fpl* pasta; ⟨*pasteles*⟩ pastries. **~ de dientes**, **~ dentífrica** toothpaste

pastar *vt/i* graze

pastel *m* cake; ⟨*empanada*⟩ pie; ⟨*lápiz*⟩ pastel. **~ería** *f* cakes; ⟨*tienda*⟩ cake shop, confectioner's

paste(u)rizar [10] *vt* pasteurize

pastiche *m* pastiche

pastilla *f* pastille; ⟨*de jabón*⟩ bar; ⟨*de chocolate*⟩ piece

pastinaca f parsnip

pasto m pasture; (*hierba*) grass; (*Mex, césped*) lawn. ~r m shepherd; (*relig*) minister. ~ral a pastoral

pata f leg; (*pie*) paw, foot. ~s arriba upside down. a cuatro ~s on all fours. meter la ~ put one's foot in it. tener mala ~ have bad luck

pataca f Jerusalem artichoke

pata|da f kick. ~lear vt stamp; (*niño pequeño*) kick

pataplum int crash!

patata f potato. ~s fritas chips (*Brit*), French fries (*Amer*). ~s fritas (a la inglesa) (potato) crisps (*Brit*), potato chips (*Amer*)

patent|ar vt patent. ~e a obvious. ● f licence. ~e de invención patent

patern|al a paternal; (*cariño etc*) fatherly. ~idad f paternity. ~o a paternal; (*cariño etc*) fatherly

patético a moving

patillas fpl sideburns

patín m skate; (*juguete*) scooter

pátina f patina

patina|dero m skating rink. ~dor m skater. ~je m skating. ~r vi skate; (*deslizarse*) slide. ~zo m skid; (*fig, fam*) blunder

patio m patio. ~ de butacas stalls (*Brit*), orchestra (*Amer*)

pato m duck

patol|ogía f pathology. ~ógico a pathological

patoso a clumsy

patraña f hoax

patria f native land

patriarca m patriarch

patrimonio m inheritance; (*fig*) heritage

patri|ota a patriotic. ● m & f patriot. ~ótico a patriotic. ~otismo m patriotism

patrocin|ar vt sponsor. ~io m sponsorship

patr|ón m patron; (*jefe*) boss; (*de pensión etc*) landlord; (*modelo*) pattern. ~onato m patronage; (*fundación*) trust, foundation

patrulla f patrol; (*fig, cuadrilla*) group. ~rvt/i patrol

paulatinamente adv slowly

pausa f pause. ~do a slow

pauta f guideline

paviment|ar vt pave. ~o m pavement

pavo m turkey. ~ real peacock

pavor m terror. ~oso a terrifying

payas|ada f buffoonery. ~o m clown

paz f peace. La P~ La Paz

peaje m toll

peatón m pedestrian

pebet|a f (*LAm*) little girl. ~e m little boy

peca f freckle

peca|do m sin; (*defecto*) fault. ~dor m sinner. ~minoso a sinful. ~r [7] vi sin

pecoso a freckled

pectoral a pectoral; (*para la tos*) cough

peculiar a peculiar, particular. ~idad f peculiarity

pech|era f front. ~ero m bib. ~o m chest; (*de mujer*) breast; (*fig, corazón*) heart. ~uga f breast. dar el ~o breast-feed (*a un niño*); (*afrontar*) confront. tomar a ~o take to heart

pedagogo m teacher

pedal m pedal. ~ear vi pedal

pedante a pedantic

pedazo m piece, bit. a ~s in pieces. hacer ~s break to pieces. hacerse ~s fall to pieces

pedernal m flint

pedestal m pedestal

pedestre a pedestrian

pediatra m & f paediatrician

pedicuro m chiropodist

pedi|do m order. ~r [5] vt ask (for); (*com, en restaurante*) order. ● vi ask. ~r prestado borrow

pegadizo a sticky; (*mus*) catchy

pegajoso a sticky

pega|r [12] vt stick (on); (*coser*) sew on; give (*enfermedad etc*); (*juntar*) join; (*golpear*) hit; (*dar*) give. ● vi stick. ~rse vpr stick; (*pelearse*) hit each other. ~r fuego a set fire to. ~tina f sticker

pein|ado m hairstyle. ~ar vt comb. ~arse vpr comb one's hair. ~e m comb. ~eta f ornamental comb

p.ej. abrev (*por ejemplo*) e.g., for example

pela|do a (*fruta*) peeled; (*cabeza*) bald; (*número*) exactly; (*terreno*) barren. ● m bare patch. ~dura f (*acción*) peeling; (*mondadura*) peelings

pela|je m (*de animal*) fur; (*fig, aspecto*) appearance. ~mbre m (*de animal*) fur; (*de persona*) thick hair

pelar vt cut the hair; (*mondar*) peel; (*quitar el pellejo*) skin

peldaño *m* step; *(de escalera de mano)* rung

pelea *f* fight; *(discusión)* quarrel. ~r *vi* fight. ~rse *vpr* fight

peletería *f* fur shop

peliagudo *a* difficult, tricky

pelícano *m*, **pelicano** *m* pelican

película *f* film *(esp Brit)*, movie *(Amer)*. ~ **de dibujos (animados)** cartoon (film). ~ **en colores** colour film

peligro *m* danger; *(riesgo)* risk. ~so *a* dangerous. **poner en** ~**endanger**

pelirrojo *a* red-haired

pelma *m & f*, **pelmazo** *m* bore, nuisance

pelo *m* hair; *(de barba o bigote)* whisker. ~ón *a* bald; *(rapado)* with very short hair. **no tener** ~**os en la lengua** be outspoken. **tomar el** ~ **o a uno** pull s.o.'s leg

pelota *f* ball; *(juego vasco)* pelota. ~ **vasca** pelota. **en** ~(**s**) **naked**

pelotera *f* squabble

pelotilla *f*. **hacer la** ~ **a** ingratiate o.s. with

peluca *f* wig

peludo *a* hairy

peluquer|ía *f* *(de mujer)* hairdresser's; *(de hombre)* barber's. ~o *m (de mujer)* hairdresser; *(de hombre)* barber

pelusa *f* down; *(celos, fam)* jealousy

pelvis *f* pelvis

pella *f* lump

pelleja *f*, **pellejo** *m* skin

pellizc|ar[7] *vt* pinch. ~o *m* pinch

pena *f* sadness; *(dificultad)* difficulty. ~ **de muerte** death penalty. **a duras** ~**s** with difficulty. **da** ~ **que** it's a pity that. **me da** ~ **que** I'm sorry that. **merecer la** ~ be worthwhile. **¡qué** ~! what a pity! **valer la** ~ be worthwhile

penacho *m* tuft; *(fig)* plume

penal *a* penal; *(criminal)* criminal. ● *m* prison. ~**idad** *f* suffering; *(jurid)* penalty. ~**izar**[10] *vt* penalize

penalty *m* penalty

penar *vt* punish. ● *vi* suffer. ~ **por** long for

pend|er *vi* hang. ~**iente** *a* hanging; *(terreno)* sloping; *(cuenta)* outstanding; *(fig)* *(asunto etc)* pending. ● *m* earring. ● *f* slope

pendón *m* banner

péndulo *a* hanging. ● *m* pendulum

pene *m* penis

penetra|nte *a* penetrating; *(sonido)* piercing; *(herida)* deep. ~r *vt* penetrate; *(fig)* pierce; *(entender)* understand. ● *vi* penetrate; *(entrar)* go into

penicilina *f* penicillin

pen|ínsula *f* peninsula. **península Ibérica** Iberian Peninsula. ~**insular** *a* peninsular

penique *m* penny

peniten|cia *f* penitence; *(castigo)* penance. ~**te** *a & m & f* penitent

penoso *a* painful; *(difícil)* difficult

pensa|do *a* thought. ~**dor** *m* thinker. ~**miento** *m* thought. ~r [1] *vt* think; *(considerar)* consider. ● *vi* think. ~r **en** think about. ~**tivo** *a* thoughtful. **bien** ~**do** all things considered. **cuando menos se piensa** when least expected. **menos** ~**do** least expected. **¡ni** ~**rlo!** certainly not! **pienso que sí** I think so

pensi|ón *f* pension; *(casa de huéspedes)* guest-house. ~**ón completa** full board. ~**onista** *m & f* pensioner; *(huésped)* lodger; *(escol)* boarder

pentágono *m* pentagon

pentagrama *m* stave

Pentecostés *m* Whitsun; *(fiesta judía)* Pentecost

penúltimo *a & m* penultimate, last but one

penumbra *f* half-light

penuria *f* shortage

peña *f* rock; *(de amigos)* group; *(club)* club. ~ón *m* rock. **el peñón de Gibraltar** The Rock (of Gibraltar)

peón *m* labourer; *(en ajedrez)* pawn; *(en damas)* piece; *(juguete)* (spinning) top

peonía *f* peony

peonza *f* (spinning) top

peor *a* *(comparativo)* worse; *(superlativo)* worst. ● *adv* worse. ~ **que** ~ worse and worse. **lo** ~ the worst thing. **tanto** ~ so much the worse

pepin|illo *m* gherkin. ~o *m* cucumber. **(no) me importa un** ~o I couldn't care less

pepita *f* pip

pepitoria *f* fricassee

pequeñ|ez *f* smallness; *(minucia)* trifle. ~**ito** *a* very small, tiny. ~o *a* small, little. **de** ~o as a child. **en** ~o in miniature

pequinés *m* *(perro)* Pekinese

pera *f* *(fruta)* pear. ~**l** *m* pear (tree)

percance *m* setback

percatarse *vpr*. ~ **de** notice

perc|epción f perception. **∼eptible** a perceptible. **∼eptivo** a perceptive. **∼ibir** vt perceive; earn ⟨dinero⟩

percusión f percussion

percutir vt tap

percha f hanger; (de aves) perch. de ∼ off the peg

perde|dor a losing. ● m loser. **∼r** [1] vt lose; (malgastar) waste; miss ⟨tren etc⟩. ● vi lose; ⟨tela⟩ fade. **∼rse** vpr get lost; (desaparecer) disappear; (desperdiciarse) be wasted; (estropearse) be spoilt. **echar(se) a ∼r** spoil

pérdida f loss; (de líquido) leak; (de tiempo) waste

perdido a lost

perdiz f partridge

perd|ón m pardon, forgiveness. ● int sorry! **∼onar** vt excuse, forgive; ⟨jurid⟩ pardon. **¡∼one (Vd)!** sorry! **pedir ∼ón** apologize

perdura|ble a lasting. **∼r** vi last

perece|dero a perishable. **∼r** [11] vi perish

peregrin|ación f pilgrimage. **∼ar** vi go on a pilgrimage; (fig, fam) travel. **∼o** a strange. ● m pilgrim

perejil m parsley

perengano m so-and-so

perenne a everlasting; (bot) perennial

perentorio a peremptory

perez|a f laziness. **∼oso** a lazy

perfec|ción f perfection. **∼cionamiento** m perfection; (mejora) improvement. **∼cionar** vt perfect; (mejorar) improve. **∼cionista** m & f perfectionist. **∼tamente** adv perfectly. ● int of course! **∼to** a perfect; (completo) complete. **a la ∼ción** perfectly, to perfection

perfidia f treachery

pérfido a treacherous

perfil m profile; (contorno) outline; **∼es** mpl (fig, rasgos) features. **∼ado** a (bien terminado) well-finished. **∼ar** vt draw in profile; (fig) put the finishing touches to

perfora|ción f perforation. **∼do** m perforation. **∼dora** f punch. **∼r** vt pierce, perforate; punch ⟨papel, tarjeta etc⟩

perfum|ar vt perfume. **∼arse** vpr put perfume on. **∼e** m perfume, scent. **∼ería** f perfumery

pergamino m parchment

pericia f expertise

pericón m popular Argentinian dance

perif|eria f (de población) outskirts. **∼érico** a peripheral

perilla f (barba) goatee

perímetro m perimeter

periódico a periodic(al). ● m newspaper

periodis|mo m journalism. **∼ta** m & f journalist

período m, **periodo** m period

periquito m budgerigar

periscopio m periscope

perito a & m expert

perju|dicar [7] vt harm; (desfavorecer) not suit. **∼dicial** a harmful. **∼icio** m harm. **en ∼icio de** to the detriment of

perjur|ar vi perjure o.s. **∼io** m perjury

perla f pearl. **de ∼s** adv very well. ● a excellent

permane|cer [11] vi remain. **∼ncia** f permanence; (estancia) stay. **∼nte** a permanent. ● f perm

permeable a permeable

permi|sible a permissible. **∼sivo** a permissive. **∼so** m permission; (documento) licence; (mil etc) leave. **∼so de conducción**, **∼so de conducir** driving licence (Brit), driver's license (Amer). **∼tir** vt allow, permit. **∼tirse** vpr be allowed. **con ∼so** excuse me. **¿me ∼te?** may I?

permutación f exchange; (math) permutation

pernicioso a pernicious; ⟨persona⟩ wicked

pernio m hinge

perno m bolt

pero conj but. ● m fault; (objeción) objection

perogrullada f platitude

perol m pan

peronista m & f follower of Juan Perón

perorar vi make a speech

perpendicular a & f perpendicular

perpetrar vt perpetrate

perpetu|ar [21] vt perpetuate. **∼o** a perpetual

perplej|idad f perplexity. **∼o** a perplexed

perr|a f (animal) bitch; (moneda) coin, penny (Brit), cent (Amer); (rabieta) tantrum. **∼era** f kennel. **∼ería** f (mala jugada) dirty trick; (palabra) harsh word. **∼o** a awful

● m dog. ∼o corredor hound. ∼o de aguas spaniel. ∼o del hortelano dog in the manger. ∼o galgo greyhound. de ∼os awful. estar sin una ∼a be broke

persa a & m & f Persian

perse|cución f pursuit; (tormento) persecution. ∼guir [5 & 13] vt pursue; (atormentar) persecute

perseve|ncia f perseverance. ∼nte a persevering. ∼r vi persevere

persiana f (Venetian) blind

persist|encia f persistence. ∼ente a persistent. ∼ir vi persist

person|a f person. ∼as fpl people. ∼aje m (persona importante) important person; (de obra literaria) character. ∼al a personal; (para una persona) single. ● m staff. ∼alidad f personality. ∼arse vpr appear in person. ∼ificar [7] vt personify. ∼ificación f personification

perspectiva f perspective

perspica|cia f shrewdness; (de vista) keen eye-sight. ∼z a shrewd; (vista) keen

persua|dir vt persuade. ∼sión f persuasion. ∼sivo a persuasive

pertenecer [11] vi belong

pertinaz a persistent

pertinente a relevant

perturba|ción f disturbance. ∼r vt perturb

Perú m. el ∼ Peru

peruano a & m Peruvian

perver|sión f perversion. ∼so a perverse. ● m pervert. ∼tir [4] vt pervert

pervivir vi live on

pesa f weight. ∼dez f weight; (de cabeza etc) heaviness; (lentitud) sluggishness; (cualidad de fastidioso) tediousness; (cosa fastidiosa) bore, nuisance

pesadilla f nightmare

pesad|o a heavy; (lento) slow; (duro) hard; (aburrido) boring, tedious. ∼umbre f (pena) sorrow

pésame m sympathy, condolences

pesar vt/i weigh. ● m sorrow; (remordimiento) regret. a ∼ de (que) in spite of. me pesa que I'm sorry that. pese a (que) in spite of

pesario m pessary

pesca f fishing; (peces) fish; (pescado) catch. ∼da f hake. ∼dería f fish shop. ∼dilla f whiting. ∼do m fish. ∼dor a fishing. ● m fisherman. ∼r

[7] vt catch. ● vi fish. ir de ∼ go fishing

pescuezo m neck

pesebre m manger

pesero m (Mex) minibus taxi

peseta f peseta; (Mex) twenty-five centavos

pesimis|mo m pessimism. ∼ta a pessimistic. ● m & f pessimist

pésimo a very bad, awful

peso m weight; (moneda) peso. ∼ bruto gross weight. ∼ neto net weight. a ∼ by weight. de ∼ influential

pesquero a fishing

pesquisa f inquiry

pestaña f eyelash. ∼ear vi blink. sin ∼ear without batting an eyelid

pest|e f plague; (hedor) stench. ∼icida m pesticide. ∼ilencia f pestilence; (hedor) stench

pestillo m bolt

pestiño m pancake with honey

petaca f tobacco case; (LAm, maleta) suitcase

pétalo m petal

petardo m firework

petición f request; (escrito) petition. a ∼ de at the request of

petirrojo m robin

petrificar [7] vt petrify

petr|óleo m oil. ∼olero a oil. ● m oil tanker. ∼olífero a oil-bearing

petulante a arrogant

peyorativo a pejorative

pez f fish; (substancia negruzca) pitch. ∼ espada swordfish

pezón m nipple; (bot) stalk

pezuña f hoof

piada f chirp

piadoso a compassionate; (devoto) devout

pian|ista m & f pianist. ∼o m piano. ∼o de cola grand piano

piar [20] vi chirp

pib|a f (LAm) little girl. ∼e m (LAm) little boy

picad|illo m mince; (guiso) stew. ∼o a perforated; (carne) minced; (ofendido) offended; (mar) choppy; (diente) bad. ∼ura f bite, sting; (de polilla) moth hole

picante a hot; (palabras etc) cutting

picaporte m door-handle; (aldaba) knocker

picar [7] vt prick, pierce; (ave) peck; (insecto, pez) bite; (avispa) sting; (comer poco) pick at; mince (carne).

● *vi* prick; ⟨*ave*⟩ peck; ⟨*insecto, pez*⟩ bite; ⟨*sol*⟩ scorch; ⟨*sabor fuerte*⟩ be hot. ∼ **alto** aim high

picard|ear *vt* corrupt. ∼**ía** *f* wickedness; ⟨*travesura*⟩ naughty thing

picaresco *a* roguish; ⟨*literatura*⟩ picaresque

pícaro *a* villainous; ⟨*niño*⟩ mischievous. ● *m* rogue

picatoste *m* toast; ⟨*frito*⟩ fried bread

picazón *f* itch

pico *m* beak; ⟨*punta*⟩ corner; ⟨*herramienta*⟩ pickaxe; ⟨*cima*⟩ peak. ∼**tear** *vt* peck; ⟨*comer, fam*⟩ pick at. **y** ∼ ⟨*con tiempo*⟩ a little after; ⟨*con cantidad*⟩ a little more than

picudo *a* pointed

pich|ona *f* ⟨*fig*⟩ darling; ∼**ón** *m* pigeon

pido *vb véase* **pedir**

pie *m* foot; ⟨*bot, de vaso*⟩ stem. ∼ **cuadrado** square foot. **a cuatro** ∼**s** on all fours. **al** ∼ **de la letra** literally. **a** ∼ **on** foot. **a** ∼(**s**) **juntillas** ⟨*fig*⟩ firmly. **buscarle tres** ∼**s al gato** split hairs. **de** ∼ standing (up). **de** ∼**s a cabeza** from head to foot. **en** ∼ standing (up). **ponerse de/en** ∼ stand up

piedad *f* pity; ⟨*relig*⟩ piety

piedra *f* stone; ⟨*de mechero*⟩ flint; ⟨*granizo*⟩ hailstone

piel *f* skin; ⟨*cuero*⟩ leather. **artículos de** ∼ leather goods

pienso *vb véase* **pensar**

pierdo *vb véase* **perder**

pierna *f* leg. **estirar las** ∼**s** stretch one's legs

pieza *f* piece; ⟨*parte*⟩ part; ⟨*obra teatral*⟩ play; ⟨*moneda*⟩ coin; ⟨*habitación*⟩ room. ∼ **de recambio** spare part

pífano *m* fife

pigment|ación *f* pigmentation. ∼**o** *m* pigment

pigmeo *a & m* pygmy

pijama *m* pyjamas

pila *f* ⟨*montón*⟩ pile; ⟨*recipiente*⟩ basin; ⟨*eléctrica*⟩ battery. ∼ **bautismal** font

píldora *f* pill

pilot|ar *vt* pilot. ∼**o** *m* pilot

pilla|je *m* pillage. ∼**r** *vt* pillage; ⟨*alcanzar, agarrar*⟩ catch; ⟨*atropellar*⟩ run over

pillo *a* wicked. ● *m* rogue

pim|entero *m* ⟨*vasija*⟩ pepper-pot. ∼**entón** *m* paprika, cayenne pepper.

∼**ienta** *f* pepper. ∼**iento** *m* pepper. **grano** *m* **de** ∼**ienta** peppercorn

pináculo *m* pinnacle

pinar *m* pine forest

pincel *m* paintbrush. ∼**ada** *f* brushstroke. **la última** ∼**ada** ⟨*fig*⟩ the finishing touch

pinch|ar *vt* pierce, prick; puncture ⟨*neumático*⟩; ⟨*fig, incitar*⟩ push; ⟨*med, fam*⟩ give an injection to. ∼**azo** *m* prick; ⟨*en neumático*⟩ puncture. ∼**itos** *mpl* kebab(s); ⟨*tapas*⟩ savoury snacks. ∼**o** *m* point

ping|ajo *m* rag. ∼**o** *m* rag

ping-pong *m* table tennis, pingpong

pingüino *m* penguin

pino *m* pine (tree)

pint|a *f* spot; ⟨*fig, aspecto*⟩ appearance. ∼**ada** *f* graffiti. ∼**ar** *vt* paint. ∼**arse** *vpr* put on make-up. ∼**or** *m* painter. ∼**or de brocha gorda** painter and decorator. ∼**oresco** *a* picturesque. ∼**ura** *f* painting. **no** ∼**a nada** ⟨*fig*⟩ it doesn't count. **tener** ∼**a de** look like

pinza *f* ⟨clothes-⟩peg ⟨*Brit*⟩, ⟨clothes-⟩pin ⟨*Amer*⟩; ⟨*de cangrejo etc*⟩ claw. ∼**s** *fpl* tweezers

pinzón *m* chaffinch

piñ|a *f* pine cone; ⟨*ananás*⟩ pineapple; ⟨*fig, grupo*⟩ group. ∼**ón** *m* ⟨*semilla*⟩ pine nut

pío *a* pious; ⟨*caballo*⟩ piebald. ● *m* chirp. **no decir** (**ni**) ∼ not say a word

piocha *f* pickaxe

piojo *m* louse

pionero *m* pioneer

pipa *f* pipe; ⟨*semilla*⟩ seed; ⟨*de girasol*⟩ sunflower seed

pipián *m* ⟨*LAm*⟩ stew

pique *m* resentment; ⟨*rivalidad*⟩ rivalry. **irse a** ∼ sink

piqueta *f* pickaxe

piquete *m* picket

piragua *f* canoe

pirámide *f* pyramid

pirata *m & f* pirate

Pirineos *mpl* Pyrenees

piropo *m* ⟨*fam*⟩ compliment

piruet|a *f* pirouette. ∼**ear** *vi* pirouette

pirulí *m* lollipop

pisa|da *f* footstep; ⟨*huella*⟩ footprint. ∼**papeles** *m invar* paperweight. ∼**r** *vt* tread on; ⟨*apretar*⟩ press; ⟨*fig*⟩ walk over. ● *vi* tread. **no** ∼**r el césped** keep off the grass

piscina f swimming pool; (*para peces*) fish-pond

Piscis m Pisces

piso m floor; (*vivienda*) flat (*Brit*), apartment (*Amer*); (*de zapato*) sole

pisotear vt trample (on)

pista f track; (*fig, indicio*) clue. ~ **de aterrizaje** runway. ~ **de baile** dance floor. ~ **de hielo** skating-rink. ~ **de tenis** tennis court

pistacho m pistachio (nut)

pisto m fried vegetables

pistol|a f pistol. ~**era** f holster. ~**ero** m gunman

pistón m piston

pit|ar vt whistle at. ● vi blow a whistle; (*auto*) sound one's horn. ~**ido** m whistle

pitill|era f cigarette case. ~**o** m cigarette

pito m whistle; (*auto*) horn

pitón m python

pitorre|arse vpr. ~**arse de** make fun of. ~**o** m teasing

pitorro m spout

pivote m pivot

pizarr|a f slate; (*encerrado*) blackboard. ~**ón** m (*LAm*) blackboard

pizca f (*fam*) tiny piece; (*de sal*) pinch. **ni** ~ not at all

pizz|a f pizza. ~**ería** f pizzeria

placa f plate; (*conmemorativa*) plaque; (*distintivo*) badge

pláceme m congratulations

place|ntero a pleasant. ~**r** [32] vt please. **me** ~ I like. ● m pleasure

plácido a placid

plaga f plague; (*fig, calamidad*) disaster; (*fig, abundancia*) glut. ~**r** [12] vt fill

plagi|ar vt plagiarize. ~**o** m plagiarism

plan m plan; (*med*) course of treatment. **a todo** ~ on a grand scale. **en** ~ **de** as

plana f (*llanura*) plain; (*página*) page. **en primera** ~ on the front page

plancha f iron; (*lámina*) sheet. ~**do** m ironing. ~**r** vt/i iron. **a la** ~ grilled. **tirarse una** ~ put one's foot in it

planeador m glider

planear vt plan. ● vi glide

planeta m planet. ~**rio** a planetary. ● m planetarium

planicie f plain

planifica|ción f planning. ~**r** [7] vt plan

planilla f (*LAm*) list

plano a flat. ● m plane; (*de ciudad*) plan. **primer** ~ foreground; (*foto*) close-up

planta f (*anat*) sole; (*bot, fábrica*) plant; (*plano*) ground plan; (*piso*) floor. ~ **baja** ground floor (*Brit*), first floor (*Amer*)

planta|ción f plantation. ~**do** a planted. ~**r** vt plant; deal (*golpe*). ~**r en la calle** throw out. ~**rse** vpr stand; (*fig*) stand firm. **bien** ~**do** good-looking

plantear vt (*exponer*) expound; (*causar*) create; raise (*cuestión*)

plantilla f insole; (*modelo*) pattern; (*personal*) personnel

plaqué m plate

plasma m plasma

plástico a & m plastic

plata f silver; (*fig, dinero, fam*) money. ~ **de ley** sterling silver. ~ **alemana** nickel silver

plataforma f platform

plátano m plane (tree); (*fruta*) banana; (*platanero*) banana tree

platea f stalls (*Brit*), orchestra (*Amer*)

plateado a silver-plated; (*color de plata*) silver

pl|ática f chat, talk. ~**aticar** [7] vi chat, talk

platija f plaice

platillo m saucer; (*mus*) cymbal. ~ **volante** flying saucer

platino m platinum. ~**s** mpl (*auto*) points

plato m plate; (*comida*) dish; (*parte de una comida*) course

platónico a platonic

plausible a plausible; (*loable*) praiseworthy

playa f beach; (*fig*) seaside

plaza f square; (*mercado*) market; (*sitio*) place; (*empleo*) job. ~ **de toros** bullring

plazco vb véase **placer**

plazo m period; (*pago*) instalment; (*fecha*) date. **comprar a** ~**s** buy on hire purchase (*Brit*), buy on the installment plan (*Amer*)

plazuela f little square

pleamar f high tide

plebe f common people. ~**yo** a & m plebeian

plebiscito m plebiscite

plectro *m* plectrum

plega|ble *a* pliable; ⟨silla etc⟩ folding. ∼r [1 & 12] *vt* fold. ∼rse *vpr* bend; (fig) give way

pleito *m* (court) case; (fig) dispute

plenilunio *m* full moon

plen|itud *f* fullness; (fig) height. ∼o a full. **en** ∼**o día** in broad daylight. **en** ∼**o verano** at the height of the summer

pleuresía *f* pleuresy

plieg|o *m* sheet. ∼**ue** *m* fold; (en ropa) pleat

plinto *m* plinth

plisar *vt* pleat

plom|ero *m* (esp LAm) plumber. ∼o *m* lead; (elec) fuse. **de** ∼**o** lead

pluma *f* feather; (para escribir) pen. ∼ **estilográfica** fountain pen. ∼**je** *m* plumage

plúmbeo *a* leaden

plum|ero *m* feather duster; (para plumas, lápices etc) pencil-case. ∼**ón** *m* down

plural *a & m* plural. ∼**idad** *f* plurality; (mayoría) majority. **en** ∼ in the plural

pluriempleo *m* having more than one job

plus *m* bonus

pluscuamperfecto *m* pluperfect

plusvalía *f* appreciation

plut|ocracia *f* plutocracy. ∼**ócrata** *m & f* plutocrat. ∼**ocrático** *a* plutocratic

plutonio *m* plutonium

pluvial *a* rain

pobla|ción *f* population; (ciudad) city, town; (pueblo) village. ∼**do** a populated. ● *m* village. ∼**r** [2] *vt* populate; (habitar) inhabit. ∼**rse** *vpr* get crowded

pobre *a* poor. ● *m & f* poor person; (fig) poor thing. ¡∼**cito**! poor (little) thing! ¡∼ **de mí**! poor (old) me! ∼**za** *f* poverty

pocilga *f* pigsty

poción *f* potion

poco *a* not much, little; (en plural) few; (unos) a few. ● *m* (a) little. ● *adv* little, not much; (con adjetivo) not very; (poco tiempo) not long. ∼ **a** ∼ little by little, gradually. **a** ∼ **de** soon after. **dentro de** ∼ soon. **hace** ∼ not long ago. **poca cosa** nothing much. **por** ∼ (fam) nearly

podar *vt* prune

poder [33] *vi* be able. **no pudo venir** he couldn't come. ¿**puedo hacer algo**? can I do anything? ¿**puedo pasar**? may I come in? ● *m* power. ∼**es** *mpl* **públicos** authorities. ∼**oso** *a* powerful. **en el** ∼ in power. **no** ∼ **con** not be able to cope with; (no aguantar) not be able to stand. **no** ∼ **más** be exhausted; (estar harto de algo) not be able to manage any more. **no** ∼ **menos que** not be able to help. **puede que** it is possible that. **puede ser** it is possible. ¿**se puede** ...? may I ...?

podrido *a* rotten

po|ema *m* poem. ∼**esía** *f* poetry; (poema) poem. ∼**eta** *m* poet. ∼**ético** *a* poetic

polaco *a* Polish. ● *m* Pole; (lengua) Polish

polar *a* polar. **estrella** ∼ polestar

polarizar [10] *vt* polarize

polca *f* polka

polea *f* pulley

pol|émica *f* controversy. ∼**émico** *a* polemic(al). ∼**emizar** [10] *vi* argue

polen *m* pollen

policía *f* police (force); (persona) policewoman. ● *m* policeman. ∼**co** *a* police; (novela etc) detective

policlínica *f* clinic, hospital

policromo, polícromo *a* polychrome

polideportivo *m* sports centre

poliéster *m* polyester

poliestireno *m* polystyrene

polietileno *m* polythene

pol|igamia *f* polygamy. ∼**ígamo** *a* polygamous

polígloto *a & f* polyglot

polígono *m* polygon

polilla *f* moth

polio(mielitis) *f* polio(myelitis)

pólipo *m* polyp

politécnic|a *f* polytechnic. ∼**o** *a* polytechnic

polític|a *f* politics. ∼**o** *a* political; (pariente) -in-law. ● *m* politician. **padre** *m* ∼ father-in-law

póliza *f* document; (de seguros) policy

polo *m* pole; (helado) ice lolly (Brit); (juego) polo. ∼ **helado** ice lolly (Brit). ∼ **norte** North Pole

Polonia *f* Poland

poltrona *f* armchair

polución *f* (contaminación) pollution

polv|areda *f* cloud of dust; (fig, escándalo) scandal. ∼**era** *f* compact.

~o *m* powder; (*suciedad*) dust. ~os *mpl* powder. en ~o powdered. estar hecho ~o be exhausted. quitar el ~o dust

pólvora *f* gunpowder; (*fuegos artificiales*) fireworks

polvor|iento *a* dusty. ~ón *m* Spanish Christmas shortcake

poll|ada *f* brood. ~era *f* (*para niños*) baby-walker; (*LAm, falda*) skirt. ~ería *f* poultry shop. ~o *m* chicken; (*gallo joven*) chick

pomada *f* ointment

pomelo *m* grapefruit

pómez *a*. piedra *f* ~ pumice stone

pomp|a *f* bubble; (*esplendor*) pomp. ~as fúnebres funeral. ~oso *a* pompous; (*espléndido*) splendid

pómulo *m* cheek; (*hueso*) cheekbone

poncha|do *a* (*Mex*) punctured, flat. ~r *vt* (*Mex*) puncture

ponche *m* punch

poncho *m* poncho

ponderar *vt* (*alabar*) speak highly of

poner [34] *vt* put; put on (*ropa, obra de teatro, TV etc*); (*suponer*) suppose; lay (*la mesa, un huevo*); (*hacer*) make; (*contribuir*) contribute; give (*nombre*); show (*película, interés*); open (*una tienda*); equip (*una casa*). ● *vi* lay. ~se *vpr* put o.s.; (*volverse*) get; put on (*ropa*); (*sol*) set. ~ con (*al teléfono*) put through to. ~ en claro clarify. ~ por escrito put into writing. ~ una multa fine. ~se a start to. ~se a mal con uno fall out with s.o. pongamos let's suppose

pongo *vb véase* poner

poniente *m* west; (*viento*) west wind

pont|ificado *m* pontificate. ~ifical *a* pontifical. ~ificar [7] *vi* pontificate. ~ífice *m* pontiff

pontón *m* pontoon

popa *f* stern

popelín *m* poplin

popul|acho *m* masses. ~ar *a* popular; (*lenguaje*) colloquial. ~aridad *f* popularity. ~arizar [10] *vt* popularize. ~oso *a* populous

póquer *m* poker

poquito *m* a little bit. ● *adv* a little

por *prep* for; (*para*) (in order) to; (*a través de*) through; (*a causa de*) because of; (*como agente*) by; (*en matemática*) times; (*como función*) as; (*en lugar de*) instead of. ~ la calle along the street. ~ mí as for me, for my part. ~ si in case. ~ todo el país

throughout the country. **50 kilómetros ~ hora** 50 kilometres per hour

porcelana *f* china

porcentaje *m* percentage

porcino *a* pig. ● *m* small pig

porción *f* portion; (*de chocolate*) piece

pordiosero *m* beggar

porf|ía *f* persistence; (*disputa*) dispute. ~iado *a* persistent. ~iar [20] *vi* insist. a ~ía in competition

pormenor *m* detail

pornogr|afía *f* pornography. ~áfico *a* pornographic

poro *m* pore. ~so *a* porous

poroto *m* (*LAm, judía*) bean

porque *conj* because; (*para que*) so that

porqué *m* reason

porquer|ía *f* filth; (*basura*) rubbish; (*grosería*) dirty trick

porra *f* club; (*culin*) fritter

porrón *m* wine jug (with a long spout)

portaaviones *m invar* aircraft-carrier

portada *f* façade; (*de libro*) title page

portador *m* bearer

porta|equipaje(s) *m invar* boot (*Brit*), trunk (*Amer*); (*encima del coche*) roof-rack. ~estandarte *m* standard-bearer

portal *m* hall; (*puerta principal*) main entrance; (*soportal*) porch

porta|lámparas *m invar* socket. ~ligas *m invar* suspender belt. ~monedas *m invar* purse

portarse *vpr* behave

portátil *a* portable

portavoz *m* megaphone; (*fig, persona*) spokesman

portazgo *m* toll

portazo *m* bang. dar un ~ slam the door

porte *m* transport; (*precio*) carriage. ~ador *m* carrier

portento *m* marvel

porteño *a* (*de Buenos Aires*) from Buenos Aires. ● *m* person from Buenos Aires

porter|ía *f* caretaker's lodge, porter's lodge; (*en deportes*) goal. ~o *m* caretaker, porter; (*en deportes*) goalkeeper. ~o automático intercom (*fam*)

portezuela *f* small door; (*auto*) door

pórtico *m* portico

portilla f gate; (en barco) porthole. ∼o m opening

portorriqueño a Puerto Rican

Portugal m Portugal

portuguésa & m Portuguese

porvenir m future

posada f guest house; (mesón) inn

posaderas fpl (fam) bottom

posar vt put. ● vi (pájaro) perch; (modelo) sit. ∼se vpr settle

posdata f postscript

poseedor m owner. ∼er [18] vt have, own; (saber) know well. ∼ído a possessed. ∼sión f possession. ∼sionar vt. ∼sionar de hand over. ∼sionarse vpr. ∼sionarse de take possession of. ∼sivo a possessive

posfechar vt postdate

posguerra f post-war years

posibilidad f possibility. ∼le a possible. de ser ∼le if possible. en lo ∼le as far as possible. hacer todo lo ∼le para do everything possible to. si es ∼le if possible

posición f position

positivo a positive

poso m sediment

posponer [34] vt put after; (diferir) postpone

posta f. a ∼ on purpose

postal a postal. ● f postcard

poste m pole

postergar [12] vt pass over; (diferir) postpone

posteridad f posterity. ∼or a back; (ulterior) later. ∼ormente adv later

postigo m door; (contraventana) shutter

postizo a false, artificial. ● m hairpiece

postrado a prostrate. ∼r vt prostrate. ∼rse vpr prostrate o.s.

postre m dessert, sweet (Brit). de ∼ for dessert

postular vt postulate; collect (dinero)

póstumo a posthumous

postura f position, stance

potable a drinkable; (agua) drinking

potaje m vegetable stew

potasio m potassium

pote m jar

potencia f power. ∼cial a & m potential. ∼te a powerful. en ∼cia potential

potingue m (fam) concoction

potra f filly. ∼o m colt; (en gimnasia) horse. tener ∼a be lucky

pozo m well; (hoyo seco) pit; (de mina) shaft

pozole m (Mex) stew

práctica f practice; (destreza) skill. en la ∼ in practice. poner en ∼ put into practice

practicable a practicable. ∼nte m & f nurse. ∼r [7] vt practise; play (deportes); (ejecutar) carry out

práctico a practical; (diestro) skilled. ● m practitioner

pradera f meadow; (terreno grande) prairie. ∼o m meadow

pragmático a pragmatic

preámbulo m preamble

precario a precarious

precaución f precaution; (cautela) caution. con ∼ cautiously

precaver vt guard against

precedencia f precedence; (prioridad) priority. ∼nte a preceding. ● m precedent. ∼r vt/i precede

precepto m precept. ∼r m tutor

preciado a valuable; (estimado) esteemed. ∼rse vpr boast

precinto m seal

precio m price. ∼ de venta al público retail price. al ∼ de at the cost of. no tener ∼ be priceless. ¿qué ∼ tiene? how much is it?

preciosidad f value; (cosa preciosa) beautiful thing. ∼o a precious; (bonito) beautiful. ¡es una ∼idad! it's beautiful!

precipicio m precipice

precipitación f precipitation. ∼damente adv hastily. ∼do a hasty. ∼r vt hurl; (acelerar) accelerate; (apresurar) hasten. ∼rse vpr throw o.s.; (correr) rush; (actuar sin reflexionar) act rashly

precisamente a exactly. ∼ar vt require; (determinar) determine. ∼ión f precision; (necesidad) need. ∼o a precise; (necesario) necessary

preconcebido a preconceived

precoz a early; (niño) precocious

precursor m forerunner

predecesor m predecessor

predecir [46]; o [46, pero imperativo predice, futuro y condicional regulares] vt foretell

predestinación f predestination. ∼r vt predestine

prédica f sermon

predicamento m influence

predicar [7] vt/i preach

predicción f prediction; (*del tiempo*) forecast
predilec|ción f predilection. ~**to** a favourite
predisponer [34] vt predispose
predomin|ante a predominant. ~**ar** vt dominate. ● vi predominate. ~**io** m predominance
preeminente a pre-eminent
prefabricado a prefabricated
prefacio m preface
prefect|o m prefect. ~**ura** f prefecture
prefer|encia f preference. ~**ente** a preferential. ~**ible** a preferable. ~**ido** a favourite. ~**ir** [4] vt prefer. **de** ~**encia** preferably
prefigurar vt foreshadow
prefij|ar vt fix beforehand; (*gram*) prefix. ~**o** m prefix; (*telefónico*) dialling code
preg|ón m announcement. ~**onar** vt announce
pregunta f question. ~**r** vt/i ask. ~**rse** vpr wonder. **hacer** ~**s** ask questions
prehistórico a prehistoric
preju|icio m prejudice. ~**zgar** [12] vt prejudge
prelado m prelate
preliminar a & m preliminary
preludio m prelude
premarital a, **prematrimonial** a premarital
prematuro a premature
predita|ción f premeditation. ~**r** vt premeditate
premi|ar vt give a prize to; (*recompensar*) reward. ~**o** m prize; (*recompensa*) reward; (*com*) premium. ~**o gordo** first prize
premonición f premonition
premura f urgency; (*falta*) lack
prenatal a antenatal
prenda f pledge; (*de vestir*) article of clothing, garment; (*de cama etc*) linen. ~**s** fpl (*cualidades*) talents; (*juego*) forfeits. ~**r** vt captivate. ~**rse** vpr be captivated (**de** by); (*enamorarse*) fall in love (**de** with)
prender vt capture; (*sujetar*) fasten. ● vi catch; (*arraigar*) take root. ~**se** vpr (*encenderse*) catch fire
prensa f press. ~**r** vt press
preñado a pregnant; (*fig*) full
preocupa|ción f worry. ~**do** a worried. ~**r** vt worry. ~**rse** vpr worry.

~**rse de** look after. **¡no te preocupes!** don't worry!
prepara|ción f preparation. ~**do** a prepared. ● m preparation. ~**r** vt prepare. ~**rse** vpr get ready. ~**tivo** a preparatory. ● m preparation. ~**torio** a preparatory
preponderancia f preponderance
preposición f preposition
prepotente a powerful; (*fig*) presumptuous
prerrogativa f prerogative
presa f (*acción*) capture; (*cosa*) catch; (*embalse*) dam
presagi|ar vt presage. ~**o** m omen; (*premonición*) premonition
présbita a long-sighted
presb|iteriano a & m Presbyterian. ~**iterio** m presbytery. ~**ítero** m priest
prescindir vi. ~ **de** do without; (*deshacerse de*) dispense with
prescri|bir (*pp* prescrito) vt prescribe. ~**pción** f prescription
presencia f presence; (*aspecto*) appearance. ~**r** vt be present at; (*ver*) witness. **en** ~ **de** in the presence of
presenta|ble a presentable. ~**ción** f presentation; (*aspecto*) appearance; (*de una persona a otra*) introduction. ~**dor** m presenter. ~**r** vt present; (*ofrecer*) offer; (*hacer conocer*) introduce; show (*película*). ~**rse** vpr present o.s.; (*hacerse conocer*) introduce o.s.; (*aparecer*) turn up
presente a present; (*este*) this. ● m present. **los** ~**s** those present. **tener** ~ remember
presenti|miento m presentiment; (*de algo malo*) foreboding. ~**r** [4] vt have a presentiment of
preserva|ción f preservation. ~**r** vt preserve. ~**tivo** m condom
presiden|cia f presidency; (*de asamblea*) chairmanship. ~**cial** a presidential. ~**ta** f (woman) president. ~**te** m president; (*de asamblea*) chairman. ~**te del gobierno** leader of the government, prime minister
presidi|ario m convict. ~**o** m prison
presidir vt preside over
presilla f fastener
presi|ón f pressure. ~**onar** vt press; (*fig*) put pressure on. **a** ~**ón** under pressure. **hacer** ~**ón** press
preso a under arrest; (*fig*) stricken. ● m prisoner

presta|do *a (a uno)* lent; *(de uno)* borrowed. **~mista** *m & f* moneylender. **pedir ~do** borrow

préstamo *m* loan; *(acción de pedir prestado)* borrowing

prestar *vt* lend; give *(ayuda etc)*; pay *(atención)*. ● *vi* lend

prestidigita|ción *f* conjuring. **~dor** *m* magician

prestigio *m* prestige. **~so** *a* prestigious

presu|mido *a* presumptuous. **~mir** *vt* presume. ● *vi* be conceited. **~nción** *f* presumption. **~nto** *a* presumed. **~ntuoso** *a* presumptuous

presup|oner [34] *vt* presuppose. **~uesto** *m* budget

presuroso *a* quick

preten|cioso *a* pretentious. **~der** *vt* try to; *(afirmar)* claim; *(solicitar)* apply for; *(cortejar)* court. **~dido** *a* so-called. **~diente** *m* pretender; *(a una mujer)* suitor. **~sión** *f* pretension; *(aspiración)* aspiration

pretérito *m* preterite, past

pretexto *m* pretext. **a ~ de** on the pretext of

prevalec|er [11] *vi* prevail. **~iente** *a* prevalent

prevalerse [42] *vpr* take advantage

preven|ción *f* prevention; *(prejuicio)* prejudice. **~ido** *a* ready; *(precavido)* cautious. **~ir** [53] *vt* prepare; *(proveer)* provide; *(precaver)* prevent; *(advertir)* warn. **~tivo** *a* preventive

prever [43] *vt* foresee; *(prepararse)* plan

previo *a* previous

previs|ible *a* predictable. **~ión** *f* forecast; *(prudencia)* prudence. **~ión de tiempo** weather forecast. **~to** *a* foreseen

prima *f (pariente)* cousin; *(cantidad)* bonus

primario *a* primary

primate *m* primate; *(fig, persona)* important person

primavera *f* spring. **~l** *a* spring

primer *a véase* **primero**

primer|a *f (auto)* first (gear); *(en tren etc)* first class. **~o** *a (delante de nombre masculino en singular* **primer***)* first; *(principal)* main; *(anterior)* former; *(mejor)* best. ● *n* (the) first. ● *adv* first. **~a enseñanza** primary education. **a ~os de** at the beginning of. **de ~a** first-class

primitivo *a* primitive

primo *m* cousin; *(fam)* fool. **hacer el ~** be taken for a ride

primogénito *a & m* first-born, eldest

primor *m* delicacy; *(cosa)* beautiful thing

primordial *a* basic

princesa *f* princess

principado *m* principality

principal *a* principal. ● *m (jefe)* head, boss *(fam)*

príncipe *m* prince

principi|ante *m & f* beginner. **~ar** *vt/i* begin, start. **~o** *m* beginning; *(moral, idea)* principle; *(origen)* origin. **al ~o** at first. **a ~o(s) de** at the beginning of. **dar ~o a** a start. **desde el ~o** from the outset. **en ~o** in principle. **~os** *mpl (nociones)* rudiments

pring|oso *a* greasy. **~ue** *m* dripping; *(mancha)* grease mark

prior *m* prior. **~ato** *m* priory

prioridad *f* priority

prisa *f* hurry, haste. **a ~** quickly. **a toda ~** *(fam)* as quickly as possible. **correr ~** be urgent. **darse ~** hurry (up). **de ~** quickly. **tener ~** be in a hurry

prisi|ón *f* prison; *(encarcelamiento)* imprisonment. **~onero** *m* prisoner

prism|a *m* prism. **~áticos** *mpl* binoculars

priva|ción *f* deprivation. **~do** *a (particular)* private. **~r** *vt* deprive (de of); *(prohibir)* prevent (de from). ● *vi* be popular. **~tivo** *a* exclusive (de to)

privilegi|ado *a* privileged; *(muy bueno)* exceptional. **~o** *m* privilege

pro *prep* for. ● *m* advantage. ● *pref* pro-. **el ~ y el contra** the pros and cons. **en ~ de** on behalf of. **los ~s y los contras** the pros and cons

proa *f* bows

probab|ilidad *f* probability. **~le** *a* probable, likely. **~lemente** *adv* probably

proba|dor *m* fitting-room. **~r** [2] *vt* try; try on *(ropa)*; *(demostrar)* prove. ● *vi* try. **~rse** *vpr* try on

probeta *f* test-tube

problem|a *m* problem. **~ático** *a* problematic

procaz *a* insolent

proced|encia *f* origin. **~ente** *a (razonable)* reasonable. **~ente de** (coming) from. **~er** *m* conduct. ● *vi* proceed. **~er contra** start legal proceedings against. **~er de** come from.

~**imiento** *m* procedure; (*sistema*) process; (*jurid*) proceedings

procesador *m.* ~ **de textos** word processor

procesal *a.* ~ **costas** ~**es** legal costs

procesamiento *m* processing. ~ **de textos** word-processing

procesar *vt* prosecute

procesión *f* procession

proceso *m* process; (*jurid*) trial; (*transcurso*) course

proclama *f* proclamation. ~**ción** *f* proclamation. ~**r** *vt* proclaim

procreación *f* procreation. ~**r** *vt* procreate

procurador *m* attorney, solicitor. ~**r** *vt* try; (*obtener*) get; (*dar*) give

prodigar [12] *vt* lavish. ~**se** *vpr* do one's best

prodigio *m* prodigy; (*milagro*) miracle. ~**ioso** *a* prodigious

pródigo *a* prodigal

producción *f* production. ~**ir** [47] *vt* produce; (*causar*) cause. ~**irse** *vpr* (*aparecer*) appear; (*suceder*) happen. ~**tivo** *a* productive. ~**to** *m* product. ~**tor** *m* producer. ~**to derivado** by-product. ~**tos agrícolas** farm produce. ~**tos de belleza** cosmetics. ~**tos de consumo** consumer goods

proeza *f* exploit

profanación *f* desecration. ~**ar** *vt* desecrate. ~**o** *a* profane

profecía *f* prophecy

proferir [4] *vt* utter; hurl (*insultos etc*)

profesar *vt* profess; practise (*profesión*). ~**ión** *f* profession. ~**ional** *a* professional. ~**or** *m* teacher; (*en universidad etc*) lecturer. ~**orado** *m* teaching profession; (*conjunto de profesores*) staff

profeta *m* prophet. ~**ético** *a* prophetic. ~**etizar** [10] *vt/i* prophesize

prófugo *a* fugitive

profundidad *f* depth. ~**o** *a* deep; (*fig*) profound

profusión *f* profusion. ~**o** *a* profuse. **con** ~**ión** profusely

progenie *f* progeny

programa *m* programme; (*de ordenador*) program; (*de estudios*) curriculum. ~**ción** *f* programming; (*TV etc*) programmes; (*en periódico*) TV guide. ~**r** *vt* programme; program (*ordenador*). ~**dor** *m* computer programmer

progresar *vi* (make) progress. ~**ión** *f* progression. ~**ista** *a* progressive. ~**ivo** *a* progressive. ~**o** *m* progress. **hacer** ~**os** make progress

prohibición *f* prohibition. ~**do** *a* forbidden. ~**r** *vt* forbid. ~**tivo** *a* prohibitive

prójimo *m* fellow man

prole *f* offspring

proletariado *m* proletariat. ~**o** *a* & *m* proletarian

proliferación *f* proliferation. ~**iferar** *vi* proliferate. ~**ífico** *a* prolific

prolijo *a* long-winded, extensive

prólogo *m* prologue

prolongar [12] *vt* prolong; (*alargar*) lengthen. ~**se** *vpr* go on

promedio *m* average

promesa *f* promise. ~**ter** *vt/i* promise. ~**terse** *vpr* (*novios*) get engaged. ~**térselas muy felices** have high hopes. ~**tida** *f* fiancée. ~**tido** *a* promised; (*novios*) engaged. ● *m* fiancé

prominencia *f* prominence. ~**te** *a* prominent

promiscuidad *f* promiscuity. ~**o** *a* promiscuous

promoción *f* promotion

promontorio *m* promontory

promotor *m* promoter. ~**ver** [2] *vt* promote; (*causar*) cause

promulgar [12] *vt* promulgate

pronombre *m* pronoun

pronosticar [7] *vt* predict. ~**óstico** *m* prediction; (*del tiempo*) forecast; (*med*) prognosis

prontitud *f* quickness. ~**o** *a* quick; (*preparado*) ready. ● *adv* quickly; (*dentro de poco*) soon; (*temprano*) early. ● *m* urge. **al** ~**o** at first. **de** ~**o** suddenly. **por lo** ~**o** for the time being; (*al menos*) anyway. **tan** ~**o como** as soon as

pronunciación *f* pronunciation. ~**miento** *m* revolt. ~**r** *vt* pronounce; deliver (*discurso*). ~**rse** *vpr* be pronounced; (*declararse*) declare o.s.; (*sublevarse*) rise up

propagación *f* propagation

propaganda *f* propaganda; (*anuncios*) advertising

propagar [12] *vt/i* propagate. ~**se** *vpr* spread

propano *m* propane

propasarse *vpr* go too far

propensión *f* inclination. ~**o** *a* inclined

propiamente adv exactly

propici|ar vt (provocar) cause, bring about. ~o a favourable

propie|dad f property; (posesión) possession. ~tario m owner

propina f tip

propio a own; (característico) typical; (natural) natural; (apropiado) proper. de ~ on purpose. el médico ~ the doctor himself

proponer [34] vt propose. ~se vpr propose

proporci|ón f proportion. ~onado a proportioned. ~onal a proportional. ~onar vt proportion; (facilitar) provide

proposición f proposition

propósito m intention. a ~ (adrede) on purpose; (de paso) incidentally. a ~ de with regard to. de ~ on purpose

propuesta f proposal

propuls|ar vt propel; (fig) promote. ~ión f propulsion. ~ión a chorro jet propulsion

prórroga f extension

prorrogar [12] vt extend

prorrumpir vi burst out

prosa f prose. ~ico a prosaic

proscri|bir (pp proscrito) vt banish; (prohibido) ban. ~to a banned. ● m exile; (persona) outlaw

prosecución f continuation

proseguir [5 & 13] vt/i continue

prospección f prospecting

prospecto m prospectus

prosper|ar vi prosper. ~idad f prosperity; (éxito) success

próspero a prosperous. ¡P~ Año Nuevo! Happy New Year!

prostit|ución f prostitution. ~uta f prostitute

protagonista m & f protagonist

prote|cción f protection. ~ctor a protective. ● m protector; (patrocinador) patron. ~ger [14] vt protect. ~gida f protégée. ~gido a protected. ● m protegé

proteína f protein

protesta f protest; (declaración) protestation

protestante a & m & f (relig) Protestant

protestar vt/i protest

protocolo m protocol

protuberan|cia f protuberance. ~te a protuberant

provecho m benefit. ¡buen ~! enjoy your meal! de ~ useful. en ~ de to the benefit of. sacar ~ de benefit from

proveer [18] (pp proveído y provisto) vt supply, provide

provenir [53] vi come (de from)

proverbi|al a proverbial. ~o m proverb

providencia f providence. ~l a providential

provincia f province. ~l a, ~no a provincial

provisi|ón f provision; (medida) measure. ~onal a provisional

provisto a provided (de with)

provoca|ción f provocation. ~r [7] vt provoke; (causar) cause. ~tivo a provocative

próximamente adv soon

proximidad f proximity

próximo a next; (cerca) near

proyec|ción f projection. ~tar vt hurl; cast (luz); show (película). ~til m missile. ~to m plan. ~to de ley bill. ~tor m projector. en ~to planned

pruden|cia f prudence. ~nte a prudent, sensible

prueba f proof; (examen) test; (de ropa) fitting. a ~ on trial. a ~ de proof against. a ~ de agua waterproof. en ~ de in proof of. poner a ~ test

pruebo vb véase **probar**

psicoan|álisis f psychoanalysis. ~alista m & f psychoanalyst. ~alizar [10] vt psychoanalyse

psicodélico a psychedelic

psic|ología f psychology. ~ológico a psychological. ~ólogo m psychologist

psicópata m & f psychopath

psicosis f psychosis

psique f psyche

psiqui|atra m & f psychiatrist. ~atría f psychiatry. ~átrico a psychiatric

psíquico a psychic

ptas, pts abrev (pesetas) pesetas

púa f sharp point; (bot) thorn; (de erizo) quill; (de peine) tooth; (mus) plectrum

pubertad f puberty

publica|ción f publication. ~r [7] vt publish; (anunciar) announce

publici|dad f publicity; (com) advertising. ~tario a advertising

público a public. • m public; (de espectáculo etc) audience. **dar al ~** publish

puchero m cooking pot; (guisado) stew. **hacer ~s** (fig, fam) pout

pude vb véase **poder**

púdico a modest

pudiente a rich

pudín m pudding

pudor m modesty. **~oso** a modest

pudrir (pp podrido) vt rot; (fig, molestar) annoy. **~se** vpr rot

puebl|ecito m small village. **~o** m town; (aldea) village; (nación) nation, people

puedo vb véase **poder**

puente m bridge; (fig, fam) long weekend. **~ colgante** suspension bridge. **~ levadizo** drawbridge. **hacer ~** (fam) have a long weekend

puerco a filthy; (grosero) coarse. • m pig. **~ espín** porcupine

pueril a childish

puerro m leek

puerta f door; (en deportes) goal; (de ciudad) gate. **~ principal** main entrance. **a ~ cerrada** behind closed doors

puerto m port; (fig, refugio) refuge; (entre montañas) pass. **~ franco** free port

Puerto Rico m Puerto Rico

puertorriqueño a & m Puerto Rican

pues adv (entonces) then; (bueno) well. • conj since

puest|a f setting; (en juegos) bet. **~a de sol** sunset. **~a en escena** staging. **~a en marcha** starting. **~o** a put; (vestido) dressed. • m place; (empleo) position, job; (en mercado etc) stall. • conj. **~o que** since. **~o de socorro** first aid post

pugna f fight. **~r** vt fight

puja f effort; (en subasta) bid. **~r** vt struggle; (en subasta) bid

pulcro a neat

pulga f flea; (de juego) tiddly-wink. **tener malas ~s** be bad-tempered

pulga|da f inch. **~r** m thumb; (del pie) big toe

puli|do a neat. **~mentar** vt polish. **~mento** m polishing; (substancia) polish. **~r** vt polish; (suavizar) smooth

pulm|ón m lung. **~onar** a pulmonary. **~onía** f pneumonia

pulpa f pulp

pulpería f (LAm) grocer's shop (Brit), grocery store (Amer)

púlpito m pulpit

pulpo m octopus

pulque m (Mex) pulque, alcoholic Mexican drink

pulsa|ción f pulsation. **~dor** a pulsating. • m button. **~r** vt (mus) play

pulsera f bracelet; (de reloj) strap

pulso m pulse; (muñeca) wrist; (firmeza) steady hand; (fuerza) strength; (fig, tacto) tact. **tomar el ~ a uno** take s.o.'s pulse

pulular vi teem with

pulveriza|dor m (de perfume) atomizer. **~r** [10] vt pulverize; atomize (líquido)

pulla f cutting remark

pum int bang!

puma m puma

puna f puna, high plateau

punitivo a punitive

punta f point; (extremo) tip; (clavo) (small) nail. **estar de ~** be in a bad mood. **estar de ~ con uno** be at odds with s.o. **ponerse de ~ con uno** fall out with s.o.. **sacar ~ a** sharpen; (fig) find fault with

puntada f stitch

puntal m prop, support

puntapié m kick

puntear vt mark; (mus) pluck

puntera f toe

puntería f aim; (destreza) marksmanship

puntiagudo a sharp, pointed

puntilla f (encaje) lace. **de ~s** on tiptoe

punto m point; (señal) dot; (de examen) mark; (lugar) spot, place; (de taxis) stand; (momento) moment; (punto final) full stop (Brit), period (Amer); (puntada) stitch; (de tela) mesh. **~ de admiración** exclamation mark. **~ de arranque** starting point. **~ de exclamación** exclamation mark. **~ de interrogación** question mark. **~ de vista** point of view. **~ final** full stop. **~ muerto** (auto) neutral (gear). **~ y aparte** full stop, new paragraph (Brit), period, new paragraph (Amer). **~ y coma** semicolon. **a ~** on time; (listo) ready. **a ~ de** on the point of. **de ~** knitted. **dos ~s** colon. **en ~** exactly. **hacer ~** knit. **hasta cierto ~** to a certain extent

puntuación f punctuation; (*en deportes, acción*) scoring; (*en deportes, número de puntos*) score

puntual a punctual; (*exacto*) accurate. ~**idad** f punctuality; (*exactitud*) accuracy

puntuar [21] vt punctuate. ● vi score

punza|da f prick; (*dolor*) pain; (*fig*) pang. ~**nte** a sharp. ~**r** [10] vt prick

puñado m handful. **a** ~**s** by the handful

puñal m dagger. ~**ada** f stab

puñ|etazo m punch. ~**o** m fist; (*de ropa*) cuff; (*mango*) handle. **de su** ~**o (y letra)** in his own handwriting

pupa f spot; (*en los labios*) cold sore. **hacer** ~ hurt. **hacerse** ~ hurt o.s.

pupila f pupil

pupitre m desk

puquío m (*Arg*) spring

puré m purée; (*sopa*) thick soup. ~ **de patatas** mashed potatoes

pureza f purity

purga f purge. ~**r** [12] vt purge. ~**torio** m purgatory

purifica|ción f purification. ~**r** [7] vt purify

purista m & f purist

puritano a puritanical. ● m puritan

puro a pure; (*cielo*) clear; (*fig*) simple. ● m cigar. **de** ~ **so. de pura casualidad** by sheer chance

púrpura f purple

purpúreo a purple

pus m pus

puse vb véase **poner**

pusilánime a cowardly

pústula f spot

puta f whore

putrefacción f putrefaction

pútrido a rotten, putrid

Q

que pron rel (*personas, sujeto*) who; (*personas, complemento*) whom; (*cosas*) which, that. ● conj that. ¡~ **tengan Vds buen viaje!** have a good journey! ¡~ **venga!** let him come! ~ **venga o no venga** whether he comes or not. **a** ~ I bet. **creo** ~ **tiene razón** I think (that) he is right. **de** ~ from which. **yo** ~ **tú** if I were you

qué a (*con sustantivo*) what; (*con a o adv*) how. ● pron what. ¡~ **bonito!**

how nice. ¿**en** ~ **piensas?** what are you thinking about?

quebra|da f gorge; (*paso*) pass. ~**dizo** a fragile. ~**do** a broken; (*com*) bankrupt. ● m (*math*) fraction. ~**dura** f fracture; (*hondonada*) gorge. ~**ntar** vt break; (*debilitar*) weaken. ~**nto** m (*pérdida*) loss; (*daño*) damage. ~**r** [1] vt break. ● vi break; (*com*) go bankrupt. ~**rse** vpr break

quechua a & m & f Quechuan

queda f curfew

quedar vi stay, remain; (*estar*) be; (*faltar, sobrar*) be left. ~ **bien** come off well. ~**se** vpr stay. ~ **con** arrange to meet. ~ **en** agree to. ~ **en nada** come to nothing. ~ **por** (+ *infinitivo*) remain to be (+ *pp*)

quehacer m job. ~**es domésticos** household chores

quej|a f complaint; (*de dolor*) moan. ~**arse** vpr complain (**de** about); (*gemir*) moan. ~**ido** m moan. ~**oso** a complaining

quema|do a burnt; (*fig, fam*) bitter. ~**dor** m burner. ~**dura** f burn. ~**r** vt burn; (*prender fuego a*) set fire to. ● vi burn. ~**rse** vpr burn o.s.; (*consumirse*) burn up; (*con el sol*) get sunburnt. ~**rropa** adv. **a** ~**rropa** point-blank

quena f Indian flute

quepo vb véase **caber**

queque m (*Mex*) cake

querella f (*riña*) quarrel, dispute; (*jurid*) charge

quer|er [35] vt want; (*amar*) love; (*necesitar*) need. ~**er decir** mean. ~**ido** a dear; (*amado*) loved. ● m darling; (*amante*) lover. **como quiera que** since; (*de cualquier modo*) however. **cuando quiera** que whenever. **donde quiera** wherever. ¿**quieres darme ese libro?** would you pass me that book? **quiere llover** it's trying to rain. ¿**quieres un helado?** would you like an ice-cream? **quisiera ir a la playa** I'd like to go to the beach. **sin** ~**er** without meaning to

queroseno m kerosene

querubín m cherub

ques|adilla f cheesecake; (*Mex, empanadilla*) pie. ~**o** m cheese. ~**o de bola** Edam cheese

quiá int never!, surely not!

quicio m frame. **sacar de** ~ **a uno** infuriate s.o.

quiebra f break; (fig) collapse; (com) bankruptcy

quiebro m dodge

quien pron rel (sujeto) who; (complemento) whom

quién pron interrogativo (sujeto) who; (tras preposición) whom. ¿de ~? whose. ¿de ~ son estos libros? whose are these books?

quienquiera pron whoever

quiero vb véase **querer**

quiet|o a still; (inmóvil) motionless; (carácter etc) calm. ~ud f stillness

quijada f jaw

quilate m carat

quilla f keel

quimera f (fig) illusion

químic|a f chemistry. ~o a chemical. ● m chemist

quincalla f hardware; (de adorno) trinket

quince a & m fifteen. ~ días a fortnight. ~na f fortnight. ~nal a fortnightly

quincuagésimo a fiftieth

quiniela f pools coupon. ~s fpl (football) pools

quinientos a & m five hundred

quinino m quinine

quinqué m oil-lamp; (fig, fam) shrewdness

quinquenio m (period of) five years

quinta f (casa) villa

quintaesencia f quintessence

quintal m a hundred kilograms

quinteto m quintet

quinto a & m fifth

quiosco m kiosk; (en jardín) summerhouse; (en parque etc) bandstand

quirúrgico a surgical

quise vb véase **querer**

quisque pron. cada ~ (fam) (absolutely) everybody

quisquill|a f trifle; (camarón) shrimp. ~oso a irritable; (chinchorrero) fussy

quita|manchas m invar stain remover. ~nieves m invar snow plough. ~r vt remove, take away; take off (ropa); (robar) steal. ~ndo (a excepción de, fam) apart from. ~rse vpr be removed; take off (ropa). ~rse de (no hacerlo más) stop. ~rse de en medio get out of the way. ~sol m invar sunshade

Quito m Quito

quizá(s) adv perhaps

quórum m quorum

R

rábano m radish. ~ picante horse-radish. **me importa un ~** I couldn't care less

rabi|a f rabies; (fig) rage. ~ar vi (de dolor) be in great pain; (estar enfadado) be furious; (fig, tener ganas fam) long. ~ar por algo long for sth. ~ar por hacer algo long to do sth. ~eta f tantrum. **dar ~a** infuriate

rabino m Rabbi

rabioso a rabid; (furioso) furious; (dolor etc) violent

rabo m tail

racial a racial

racimo m bunch

raciocinio m reason; (razonamiento) reasoning

ración f share, ration; (de comida) portion

racional a rational. ~izar [10] vt rationalize

racionar vt (limitar) ration; (repartir) ration out

racis|mo m racism. ~ta a racist

racha f gust of wind; (fig) spate

radar m radar

radiación f radiation

radiactiv|idad f radioactivity. ~o a radioactive

radiador m radiator

radial a radial

radiante a radiant

radical a & m & f radical

radicar [7] vi (estar) be. ~ en (fig) lie in

radio m radius; (de rueda) spoke; (elemento metálico) radium. ● f radio

radioactiv|idad f radioactivity. ~o a radioactive

radio|difusión f broadcasting. ~emisora** f radiostation. ~escucha** m & f listener

radiografía f radiography

radi|ología f radiology. ~ólogo m radiologist

radioterapia f radiotherapy

radioyente m & f listener

raer [36] vt scrape off

ráfaga f (de viento) gust; (de luz) flash; (de ametralladora) burst

rafia f raffia

raído a threadbare

raigambre f roots; (fig) tradition
raíz f root. a ~ de immediately after. **echar raíces** (fig) settle
raja f split; (culin) slice. ~r vt split. ~rse vpr split; (fig) back out
rajatabla. a ~ vigorously
ralea f sort
ralo a sparse
ralla|dor m grater. ~r vt grate
rama f branch. ~je m branches. ~l m branch. **en ~** raw
rambla f gully; (avenida) avenue
ramera f prostitute
ramifica|ción f ramification. ~rse [7] vpr branch out
ramilla f twig
ramillete m bunch
ramo m branch; (de flores) bouquet
rampa f ramp, slope
ramplón a vulgar
rana f frog. **ancas** fpl **de ~** frogs' legs. **no ser ~** not be stupid
rancio a rancid; (vino) old; (fig) ancient
ranch|ero m cook; (LAm, jefe de rancho) farmer. ~o m (LAm) ranch, farm
rango m rank
ranúnculo m buttercup
ranura f groove; (para moneda) slot
rapar vt shave; crop (pelo)
rapaz a rapacious; (ave) of prey. ● m bird of prey
rapidez f speed
rápido a fast, quick. ● adv quickly. ● m (tren) express. ~s mpl rapids
rapiña f robbery. **ave** f **de ~** bird of prey
rapsodia f rhapsody
rapt|ar vt kidnap. ~o m kidnapping; (de ira etc) fit; (éxtasis) ecstasy
raqueta f racquet
raramente adv seldom, rarely
rarefacción f rarefaction
rar|eza f rarity; (cosa rara) oddity. ~o a rare; (extraño) odd. **es ~o que** it is strange that. **¡qué ~o!** how strange!
ras m. **a ~ de** level with
rasar vt level; (rozar) graze
rasca|cielos m invar skyscraper. ~dura f scratch. ~r [7] vt scratch; (raspar) scrape
rasgar [12] vt tear
rasgo m stroke. ~s mpl (facciones) features
rasguear vt strum; (fig, escribir) write

rasguñ|ar vt scratch. ~o m scratch
raso a (llano) flat; (liso) smooth; (cielo) clear; (cucharada etc) level; (vuelo etc) low. ● m satin. **al ~** in the open air. **soldado** m **~** private
raspa f (de pescado) backbone
raspa|dura f scratch; (acción) scratching. ~r vt scratch; (rozar) scrape
rastr|a f rake. **a ~as** dragging. ~ear vt track. ~eo m dragging. ~ero a creeping; (vuelo) low. ~illar vt rake. ~illo m rake. ~o m rake; (huella) track; (señal) sign. **el R~o** the flea market in Madrid. **ni ~o** not a trace
rata f rat
rate|ar vt steal. ~ría f pilfering. ~ro m petty thief
ratifica|ción f ratification. ~r [7] vt ratify
rato m moment, short time. ~s **libres** spare time. **a ~s** at times. **hace un ~** a moment ago. **¡hasta otro ~!** (fam) see you soon! **pasar mal ~** have a rough time
rat|ón m mouse. ~onera f mouse-trap; (madriguera) mouse hole
raud|al m torrent; (fig) floods. ~o a swift
raya f line; (lista) stripe; (de pelo) parting. ~r vt rule. ● vi border (con on). **a ~s** striped. **pasar de la ~** go too far
rayo m ray; (descarga eléctrica) light-ning. ~s X X-rays
raza f race; (de animal) breed. **de ~** (caballo) thoroughbred; (perro) pedigree
raz|ón f reason. **a ~ón de** at the rate of. **perder la ~ón** go out of one's mind. **tener ~ón** be right. ~onable a reasonable. ~onamiento m reas-oning. ~onar vt reason out. ● vi reason
re m D; (solfa) re
reac|ción f reaction. ~cionario a & m reactionary. ~ción **en cadena** chain reaction. ~tor m reactor; (avión) jet
real a real; (de rey etc) royal. ● m real, old Spanish coin
realce m relief; (fig) splendour
realidad f reality; (verdad) truth. **en ~** in fact
realis|mo m realism. ~ta a realistic. ● m & f realist; (monárquico) royalist
realiza|ción f fulfilment. ~r [10] vt carry out; make (viaje); achieve

⟨meta⟩; ⟨vender⟩ sell. ~rse vpr ⟨plan etc⟩ be carried out; ⟨sueño, predicción etc⟩ come true; ⟨persona⟩ fulfil o.s.

realzar [10] vt ⟨fig⟩ enhance

reanima|ción f revival. ~r vt revive. ~rse vpr revive

reanudar vt resume; renew ⟨amistad⟩

reaparecer [11] vi reappear

rearm|ar vt rearm. ~e m rearmament

reavivar vt revive

rebaja f reduction. ~do a ⟨precio⟩ reduced. ~r vt lower. en ~s in the sale

rebanada f slice

rebaño m herd; ⟨de ovejas⟩ flock

rebasar vt exceed; ⟨dejar atrás⟩ leave behind

rebatir vt refute

rebel|arse vpr rebel. ~de a rebellious. ● m rebel. ~día f rebelliousness. ~ión f rebellion

reblandecer [11] vt soften

rebosa|nte a overflowing. ~r vi overflow; ⟨abundar⟩ abound

rebot|ar vt bounce; ⟨rechazar⟩ repel. ● vi bounce; ⟨bala⟩ ricochet. ~e m bounce, rebound. de ~e on the rebound

rebozar [10] vt wrap up; ⟨culin⟩ coat in batter

rebullir [22] vi stir

rebusca|do a affected. ~r [7] vt search thoroughly

rebuznar vi bray

recabar vt claim

recado m errand; ⟨mensaje⟩ message. dejar ~ leave a message

reca|er [29] vi fall back; ⟨med⟩ relapse; ⟨fig⟩ fall. ~ída f relapse

recalcar [7] vt squeeze; ⟨fig⟩ stress

recalcitrante a recalcitrant

recalentar [1] vt ⟨de nuevo⟩ reheat; ⟨demasiado⟩ overheat

recamar vt embroider

recámara f small room; ⟨de arma de fuego⟩ chamber; ⟨LAm, dormitorio⟩ bedroom

recambio m change; ⟨de pluma etc⟩ refill. ~s mpl spare parts. de ~ spare

recapitula|ción f summing up. ~r vt sum up

recarg|ar [12] vt overload; ⟨aumentar⟩ increase; recharge ⟨batería⟩. ~o m increase

recat|ado a modest. ~ar vt hide. ~arse vpr hide o.s. away; ⟨actuar

discretamente⟩ act discreetly. ~o m prudence; ⟨modestia⟩ modesty. sin ~arse, sin ~o openly

recauda|ción f ⟨cantidad⟩ takings. ~dor m tax collector. ~r vt collect

recel|ar vt/i suspect. ~o m distrust; ⟨temor⟩ fear. ~oso a suspicious

recepción f reception. ~onista m & f receptionist

receptáculo m receptacle

recept|ivo a receptive. ~or m receiver

recesión f recession

receta f recipe; ⟨med⟩ prescription

recib|imiento m ⟨acogida⟩ welcome. ~ir vt receive; ⟨acoger⟩ welcome. ● vi entertain. ~irse vpr graduate. ~o m receipt. acusar ~o acknowledge receipt

reci|én adv recently; ⟨casado, nacido etc⟩ newly. ~ente a recent; ⟨culin⟩ fresh

recinto m enclosure

recio a strong; ⟨voz⟩ loud. ● adv hard; ⟨en voz alta⟩ loudly

recipiente m ⟨persona⟩ recipient; ⟨cosa⟩ receptacle

recíproco a reciprocal. a la recíproca vice versa

recital m recital; ⟨de poesías⟩ reading. ~r vt recite

reclama|ción f claim; ⟨queja⟩ complaint. ~r vt claim. ● vi appeal

reclinar vi lean. ~se vpr lean

reclu|ir [17] vt shut away. ~sión f seclusion; ⟨cárcel⟩ prison. ~so m prisoner

recluta m recruit. ● f recruitment. ~miento m recruitment; ⟨conjunto de reclutas⟩ recruits. ~r vt recruit

recobrar vt recover. ~se vpr recover

recodo m bend

recog|er [14] vt collect; pick up ⟨cosa caída⟩; ⟨cosechar⟩ harvest; ⟨dar asilo⟩ shelter. ~erse vpr withdraw; ⟨ir a casa⟩ go home; ⟨acostarse⟩ go to bed. ~ida f collection; ⟨cosecha⟩ harvest. ~ido a withdrawn; ⟨pequeño⟩ small

recolección f harvest

recomenda|ción f recommendation. ~r [1] vt recommend; ⟨encomendar⟩ entrust

recomenzar [1 & 10] vt/i start again

recompensa f reward. ~r vt reward

recomponer [34] vt mend

reconcilia|ción f reconciliation. ~r vt reconcile. ~rse vpr be reconciled

recóndito a hidden

reconoc|er [11] *vt* recognize; (*admitir*) acknowledge; (*examinar*) examine. ~**imiento** *m* recognition; (*admisión*) acknowledgement; (*agradecimiento*) gratitude; (*examen*) examination

reconozco *vb véase* **reconocer**

reconquista *f* reconquest. ~**r** *vt* reconquer; (*fig*) win back

reconsiderar *vt* reconsider

reconstitu|ir [17] *vt* reconstitute. ~**yente** *m* tonic

reconstru|cción *f* reconstruction. ~**ir** [17] *vt* reconstruct

récord /'rekor/ *m* record. **batir un ~** break a record

recordar [2] *vt* remember; (*hacer acordar*) remind; (*LAm, despertar*) wake up. ●*vi* remember. **que yo recuerde** as far as I remember. **si mal no recuerdo** if I remember rightly

recorr|er *vt* tour ⟨*país*⟩; (*pasar por*) travel through; cover ⟨*distancia*⟩; (*registrar*) look over. ~**ido** *m* journey; (*itinerario*) route

recort|ado *a* jagged. ~**ar** *vt* cut (out). ~**e** *m* cutting (out); (*de periódico etc*) cutting

recoser *vt* mend

recostar [2] *vt* lean. ~**se** *vpr* lie back

recoveco *m* bend; (*rincón*) nook

recre|ación *f* recreation. ~**ar** *vt* re-create; (*divertir*) entertain. ~**arse** *vpr* amuse o.s. ~**ativo** *a* recreational. ~**o** *m* recreation; (*escol*) break

recrimina|ción *f* recrimination. ~**r** *vt* reproach

recrudecer [11] *vi* increase, worsen, get worse

recta *f* straight line

rect|angular *a* rectangular; ⟨*triángulo*⟩ right-angled. ~**ángulo** *a* rectangular; ⟨*triángulo*⟩ right-angled. ●*m* rectangle

rectifica|ción *f* rectification. ~**r** [7] *vt* rectify

rect|itud *f* straightness; (*fig*) honesty. ~**o** *a* straight; (*fig, justo*) fair; (*fig, honrado*) honest. ●*m* rectum. **todo ~o** straight on

rector *a* governing. ●*m* rector

recuadro *m* (*en periódico*) box

recubrir [*pp* **recubierto**] *vt* cover

recuerdo *m* memory; (*regalo*) souvenir. ●*vb véase* **recordar**. ~**s** *mpl* (*saludos*) regards

recupera|ción *f* recovery. ~**r** *vt* recover. ~**rse** *vpr* recover. ~**r el tiempo perdido** make up for lost time

recur|rir *vi*. ~**rir a** resort to ⟨*cosa*⟩; turn to ⟨*persona*⟩. ~**so** *m* resort; (*medio*) resource; (*jurid*) appeal. ~**sos** *mpl* resources

recusar *vt* refuse

rechaz|ar [10] *vt* repel; reflect ⟨*luz*⟩; (*no aceptar*) refuse; (*negar*) deny. ~**o** *m*. **de ~o** on the rebound; (*fig*) consequently

rechifla *f* booing; (*burla*) derision

rechinar *vi* squeak; ⟨*madera etc*⟩ creak; ⟨*dientes*⟩ grind

rechistar *vt* murmur. **sin ~** without saying a word

rechoncho *a* stout

red *f* network; (*malla*) net; (*para equipaje*) luggage rack; (*fig, engaño*) trap

redac|ción *f* editing; (*conjunto de redactores*) editorial staff; (*oficina*) editorial office; (*escol, univ*) essay. ~**tar** *vt* write. ~**tor** *m* writer; (*de periódico*) editor

redada *f* casting; (*de policía*) raid

redecilla *f* small net; (*para el pelo*) hairnet

rededor *m*. **al ~**, **en ~** around

reden|ción *f* redemption. ~**tor** *a* redeeming

redil *f* sheepfold

redimir *vt* redeem

rédito *m* interest

redoblar *vt* redouble; (*doblar*) bend back

redoma *f* flask

redomado *a* sly

redond|a *f* (*de imprenta*) roman (type); (*mus*) semibreve (*Brit*), whole note (*Amer*). ~**amente** *adv* (*categóricamente*) flatly. ~**ear** *vt* round off. ~**el** *m* circle; (*de plaza de toros*) arena. ~**o** *a* round; (*completo*) complete. ●*m* circle. **a la ~a** around. **en ~o** round; (*categóricamente*) flatly

reduc|ción *f* reduction. ~**ido** *a* reduced; (*limitado*) limited; (*pequeño*) small; ⟨*precio*⟩ low. ~**ir** [47] *vt* reduce. ~**irse** *vpr* be reduced; (*fig*) amount

reduje *vb véase* **reducir**

redundan|cia *f* redundancy. ~**te** *a* redundant

reduplicar [7] *vt* (*aumentar*) redouble

reduzco *vb véase* **reducir**

reedificar [7] *vt* reconstruct

reembols|ar *vt* reimburse. ~**o** *m* repayment. **contra** ~**o** cash on delivery

reemplaz|ar [10] *vt* replace. ~**o** *m* replacement

reemprender *vt* start again

reenviar [20] *vt*, **reexpedir** [5] *vt* forward

referencia *f* reference; (*información*) report. **con** ~ **a** with reference to. **hacer** ~ **a** refer to

referéndum *m* (*pl* **referéndums**) referendum

referir [4] *vt* tell; (*remitir*) refer. ~**se** *vpr* refer. **por lo que se refiere a** as regards

refiero *vb véase* **referir**

refilón. de ~ obliquely

refin|amiento *m* refinement. ~**ar** *vt* refine. ~**ería** *f* refinery

reflector *m* reflector; (*proyector*) searchlight

reflej|ar *vt* reflect. ~**o** *a* reflected; (*med*) reflex. ● *m* reflection; (*med*) reflex; (*en el pelo*) highlights

reflexi|ón *f* reflection. ~**onar** *vi* reflect. ~**vo** *a* (*persona*) thoughtful; (*gram*) reflexive. **con** ~**ón** on reflection. **sin** ~**ón** without thinking

reflujo *m* ebb

reforma *f* reform. ~**s** *fpl* (*reparaciones*) repairs. ~**r** *vt* reform. ~**rse** *vpr* reform

reforzar [2 & 10] *vt* reinforce

refrac|ción *f* refraction. ~**tar** *vt* refract. ~**tario** *a* heat-resistant

refrán *m* saying

refregar [1 & 12] *vt* rub

refrenar *vt* rein in (*caballo*); (*fig*) restrain

refrendar *vt* endorse

refresc|ar [7] *vt* refresh; (*enfriar*) cool. ● *vi* get cooler. ~**arse** *vpr* refresh o.s.; (*salir*) go out for a walk. ~**o** *m* cold drink. ~**os** *mpl* refreshments

refrigera|ción *f* refrigeration; (*aire acondicionado*) air-conditioning. ~**r** *vt* refrigerate. ~**dor** *m*, ~**dora** *f* refrigerator

refuerzo *m* reinforcement

refugi|ado *m* refugee. ~**arse** *vpr* take refuge. ~**o** *m* refuge, shelter

refulgir [14] *vi* shine

refundir *vt* (*fig*) revise, rehash

refunfuñar *vi* grumble

refutar *vt* refute

regadera *f* watering-can; (*Mex, ducha*) shower

regala|damente *adv* very well. ~**do** *a* as a present, free; (*cómodo*) comfortable. ~**r** *vt* give; (*agasajar*) treat very well. ~**rse** *vpr* indulge o.s.

regaliz *m* liquorice

regalo *m* present, gift; (*placer*) joy; (*comodidad*) comfort

regañ|adientes, **a** ~**adientes** reluctantly. ~**ar** *vt* scold. ● *vi* moan; (*dos personas*) quarrel. ~**o** *m* (*reprensión*) scolding

regar [1 & 12] *vt* water

regata *f* regatta

regate *m* dodge; (*en deportes*) dribbling. ~**ar** *vt* haggle over; (*economizar*) economize on. ● *vi* haggle; (*en deportes*) dribble. ~**o** *m* haggling; (*en deportes*) dribbling

regazo *m* lap

regencia *f* regency

regenerar *vt* regenerate

regente *m & f* regent; (*director*) manager

régimen *m* (*pl* **regímenes**) rule; (*pol*) regime; (*med*) diet. ~ **alimenticio** diet

regimiento *m* regiment

regio *a* royal

regi|ón *f* region. ~**onal** *a* regional

regir [5 & 14] *vt* rule; govern (*país*); run (*colegio, empresa*). ● *vi* apply, be in force

registr|ado *a* registered. ~**ador** *m* recorder; (*persona*) registrar. ~**ar** *vt* register; (*grabar*) record; (*examinar*) search. ~**arse** *vpr* register; (*darse*) be reported. ~**o** *m* (*acción de registrar*) registration; (*libro*) register; (*cosa anotada*) entry; (*inspección*) search. ~**o civil** (*oficina*) register office

regla *f* ruler; (*norma*) rule; (*menstruación*) period, menstruation. ~**mentación** *f* regulation. ~**mentar** *vt* regulate. ~**mentario** *a* obligatory. ~**mento** *m* regulations. **en** ~ in order. **por** ~ **general** as a rule

regocij|ar *vt* delight. ~**arse** *vpr* be delighted. ~**o** *m* delight. ~**os** *mpl* festivities

regode|arse *vpr* be delighted. ~**o** *m* delight

regordete *a* chubby

regres|ar *vi* return. ~**ión** *f* regression. ~**ivo** *a* backward. ~**o** *m* return

reguer|a f irrigation ditch. ∼o m irrigation ditch; (*señal*) trail

regula|dor m control. ∼r a regular; (*mediano*) average; (*no bueno*) so-so. • vt regulate; (*controlar*) control. ∼ridad f regularity. con ∼ridad regularly. por lo ∼r as a rule

rehabilita|ción f rehabilitation; (*en un empleo etc*) reinstatement. ∼r f rehabilitate; (*al empleo etc*) reinstate

rehacer [31] vt redo; (*repetir*) repeat; (*reparar*) repair. ∼se vpr recover

rehén m hostage

rehogar [12] vt sauté

rehuir [17] vt avoid

rehusar vt/i refuse

reimpr|esión f reprinting. ∼imir (*pp reimpreso*) vt reprint

reina f queen. ∼do m reign. ∼nte a ruling; (*fig*) prevailing. ∼r vi reign; (*fig*) prevail

reincidir vi relapse, repeat an offence

reino m kingdom. R∼ Unido United Kingdom

reinstaurar vt restore

reintegr|ar vt reinstate (*persona*); refund (*cantidad*). ∼arse vpr return. ∼o m refund

reír [51] vi laugh. ∼se vpr laugh. ∼se de laugh at. echarse a ∼ burst out laughing

reivindica|ción f claim. ∼r [7] vt claim; (*restaurar*) restore

rej|a f grille, grating. ∼illa f grille, grating; (*red*) luggage rack; (*de mimbre*) wickerwork. entre ∼as behind bars

rejuvenecer [11] vt/i rejuvenate. ∼se vpr be rejuvenated

relaci|ón f relation(ship); (*relato*) tale; (*lista*) list. ∼onado a concerning. ∼onar vt relate (con to). ∼onarse vpr be connected. bien ∼onado well-connected. con ∼ón a, en ∼ón a in relation to. hacer ∼ón a refer to

relaja|ción f relaxation; (*aflojamiento*) slackening. ∼do a loose. ∼r vt relax; (*aflojar*) slacken. ∼rse vpr relax

relamerse vpr lick one's lips

relamido a overdressed

rel|ámpago m (flash of) lightning. ∼ampaguear vi thunder; (*fig*) sparkle

relatar vt tell, relate

relativ|idad f relativity. ∼o a relative. en lo ∼o a in relation to

relato m tale; (*informe*) report

relegar [12] vt relegate. ∼ al olvido forget about

relev|ante a outstanding. ∼ar vt relieve; (*substituir*) replace. ∼o m relief. carrera f de ∼os relay race

relieve m relief; (*fig*) importance. de ∼ important. poner de ∼ emphasize

religi|ón f religion. ∼osa f nun. ∼oso a religious. • m monk

relinch|ar vi neigh. ∼o m neigh

reliquia f relic

reloj m clock; (*de bolsillo o pulsera*) watch. ∼ de caja grandfather clock. ∼ de pulsera wrist-watch. ∼ de sol sundial. ∼ despertador alarm clock. ∼ería f watchmaker's (shop). ∼ero m watchmaker

reluci|ente a shining. ∼r [11] vi shine; (*destellar*) sparkle

relumbrar vi shine

rellano m landing

rellen|ar vt refill; (*culin*) stuff; fill in (*formulario*). ∼o a full up; (*culin*) stuffed. • m filling; (*culin*) stuffing

remach|ar vt rivet; (*fig*) drive home. ∼e m rivet

remangar [12] vt roll up

remanso m pool; (*fig*) haven

remar vi row

remat|ado a (*total*) complete; (*niño*) very naughty. ∼ar vt finish off; (*agotar*) use up; (*com*) sell off cheap. ∼e m end; (*fig*) finishing touch. de ∼e completely

remedar vt imitate

remedi|ar vt remedy; (*ayudar*) help; (*poner fin a*) put a stop to; (*fig, resolver*) solve. ∼o m remedy; (*fig*) solution. como último ∼o as a last resort. no hay más ∼o there's no other way. no tener más ∼o have no choice

remedo m imitation

rem|endar [1] vt repair. ∼iendo m patch; (*fig, mejora*) improvement

remilg|ado a fussy; (*afectado*) affected. ∼o m fussiness; (*afectación*) affectation

reminiscencia f reminiscence

remirar vt look again at

remisión f sending; (*referencia*) reference; (*perdón*) forgiveness

remiso a remiss

remit|e m sender's name and address. ∼ente m sender. ∼ir vt send; (*referir*) refer. • vi diminish

remo m oar

remoj|ar vt soak; (fig, fam) celebrate. **~o** m soaking. **poner a ~o** soak

remolacha f beetroot. **~ azucarera** sugar beet

remolcar [7] vt tow

remolino m swirl; (de aire etc) whirl; (de gente) throng

remolque m towing; (cabo) towrope; (vehículo) trailer. **a ~** on tow. **dar a ~** a tow

remontar vt mend. **~se** vpr soar; (con tiempo) go back to

rémora f (fig) hindrance

remord|er [2] vi (fig) worry. **~imiento** m remorse. **tener ~imientos** feel remorse

remoto a remote

remover [2] vt move; stir (líquido); turn over (tierra); (quitar) remove; (fig, activar) revive

remozar [10] vt rejuvenate (persona); renovate (edificio etc)

remunera|ción f remuneration. **~r** vt remunerate

renac|er [11] vi be reborn; (fig) revive. **~imiento** m rebirth. **R~** Renaissance

renacuajo m tadpole; (fig) tiddler

rencilla f quarrel

rencor m bitterness. **~oso** a (estar) resentful; (ser) spiteful. **guardar ~** a have a grudge against

rendi|ción f surrender. **~do** a submissive; (agotado) exhausted

rendija f crack

rendi|miento m efficiency; (com) yield. **~r** [5] vt yield; (vencer) defeat; (agotar) exhaust; pay (homenaje). • vi pay; (producir) produce. **~rse** vpr surrender

renega|do a & m renegade. **~r** [1 & 12] vt deny. • vi grumble. **~r de** renounce (fe etc); disown (personas)

RENFE abrev (Red Nacional de los Ferrocarriles Españoles) Spanish National Railways

renglón m line; (com) item. **a ~ seguido** straight away

reno m reindeer

renombr|ado a renowned. **~e** m renown

renova|ción f renewal; (de edificio) renovation; (de cuarto) decorating. **~r** vt renew; renovate (edificio); decorate (cuarto)

rent|a f income; (alquiler) rent; (deuda) national debt. **~able** a profitable. **~ar** vt produce, yield; (LAm, alquilar) rent, hire. **~a vitalicia** (life) annuity. **~ista** m & f person of independent means

renuncia f renunciation. **~r** vi. **~r a** renounce, give up

reñi|do a hard-fought. **~r** [5 & 22] vt tell off. • vi quarrel. **estar ~do con** be incompatible with (cosas); be on bad terms with (personas)

reo m & f culprit; (jurid) accused. **~ de Estado** person accused of treason. **~ de muerte** prisoner sentenced to death

reojo adv. **mirar de ~** look out of the corner of one's eye at; (fig) look askance at

reorganizar [10] vt reorganize

repanchigarse [12] vpr, **repantigarse** [12] vpr sprawl out

repar|ación f repair; (acción) repairing; (fig, compensación) reparation. **~ar** vt repair; (fig) make amends for; (notar) notice. • vi. **~ar en** notice; (hacer caso de) pay attention to. **~o** m fault; (objeción) objection. **poner ~os** raise objections

repart|ición f division. **~idor** m delivery man. **~imiento** m distribution. **~ir** vt distribute, share out; deliver (cartas, leche etc); hand out (folleto, premio). **~o** m distribution; (de cartas, leche etc) delivery; (actores) cast

repas|ar vt go over; check (cuenta); revise (texto); (leer a la ligera) glance through; (coser) mend. • vi go back. **~o** m revision; (de ropa) mending. **dar un ~o** look through

repatria|ción f repatriation. **~r** vt repatriate

repecho m steep slope

repel|ente a repulsive. **~er** vt repel

repensar [1] vt reconsider

repent|e adv. **de ~** suddenly. **~ino** a sudden

repercu|sión f repercussion. **~tir** vi reverberate; (fig) have repercussions (**en** on)

repertorio m repertoire; (lista) index

repeti|ción f repetition; (mus) repeat. **~damente** adv repeatedly. **~r** [5] vt repeat; copy; (imitar) copy. • vi. **~r de** have a second helping of. **¡que se repita!** encore!

repi|car [7] vt ring (campanas). **~que** m peal

repisa f shelf. ∼ **de chimenea** mantlepiece

repito vb véase **repetir**

replegarse [1 & 12] vpr withdraw

repleto a full up

réplica a answer; (copia) replica

replicar [7] vi answer

repliegue m crease; (mil) withdrawal

repollo m cabbage

reponer [34] vt replace; revive (obra de teatro); (contestar) reply. ∼**se** vpr recover

report|aje m report. ∼**ero** m reporter

repos|ado a quiet; (sin prisa) unhurried. ∼**ar** vi rest. ∼**arse** vpr settle. ∼**o** m rest

repost|ar vt replenish; refuel (avión); fill up (coche etc). ∼**ería** f cake shop

repren|der vt reprimand. ∼**sible** a reprehensible

represalia f reprisal. **tomar** ∼**s** retaliate

representa|ción f representation; (en el teatro) performance. **en** ∼**ción de** representing. ∼**nte** m representative; (actor) actor. •**f** representative; (actriz) actress. ∼**r** vt represent; perform (obra de teatro); play (papel); (aparentar) look. ∼**rse** vpr imagine. ∼**tivo** a representative

represi|ón f repression. ∼**vo** a repressive

reprimenda f reprimand

reprimir vt supress. ∼**se** vpr stop o.s.

reprobar [2] vt condemn; reproach (persona)

réprobo a & m reprobate

reproch|ar vt reproach. ∼**e** m reproach

reproduc|ción f reproduction. ∼**ir** [47] vt reproduce. ∼**tor** a reproductive

reptil m reptile

rep|ública f republic. ∼**ublicano** a & m republican

repudiar vt repudiate

repuesto m store; (auto) spare (part). **de** ∼ in reserve

repugna|ncia f disgust. ∼**nte** a repugnant. ∼**r** vt disgust

repujar vt emboss

repuls|a f rebuff. ∼**ión** f repulsion. ∼**ivo** a repulsive

reputa|ción f reputation. ∼**do** a reputable. ∼**r** vt consider

requebrar [1] vt flatter

requemar vt scorch; (culin) burn; tan (piel)

requeri|miento m request; (jurid) summons. ∼**r** [4] vt need; (pedir) ask

requesón m cottage cheese

requete... pref extremely

requiebro m compliment

réquiem m (pl réquiems) m requiem

requis|a f inspection; (mil) requisition. ∼**ar** vt requisition. ∼**ito** m requirement

res f animal. ∼ **lanar** sheep. ∼ **vacuna** (vaca) cow; (toro) bull; (buey) ox. **carne de** ∼ (Mex) beef

resabido a well-known; (persona) pedantic

resabio m (unpleasant) after-taste; (vicio) bad habit

resaca f undercurrent; (después de beber alcohol) hangover

resaltar vi stand out. **hacer** ∼ emphasise

resarcir [9] vt repay; (compensar) compensate. ∼**se** vpr make up for

resbal|adizo a slippery. ∼**ar** vi slip; (auto) skid; (líquido) trickle. ∼**arse** vpr slip; (auto) skid; (líquido) trickle. ∼**ón** m slip; (de vehículo) skid

rescat|ar vt ransom; (recuperar) recapture; (fig) recover. ∼**e** m ransom; (recuperación) recapture; (salvamento) rescue

rescindir vt cancel

rescoldo m embers

resecar [7] vt dry up; (med) remove. ∼**se** vpr dry up

resenti|do a resentful. ∼**miento** m resentment. ∼**rse** vpr feel the effects; (debilitarse) be weakened; (ofenderse) take offence (**de at**)

reseña f account; (en periódico) report, review. ∼**r** vt describe; (en periódico) report on, review

resero m (Arg) herdsman

reserva f reservation; (provisión) reserve(s). ∼**ción** f reservation. ∼**do** a reserved. ∼**r** vt reserve; (guardar) keep, save. ∼**rse** vpr save o.s. a ∼ **de** except for. a ∼ **de que** unless. **de** ∼ in reserve

resfria|do m cold; (enfriamiento) chill. ∼**r** vt. ∼**r a** uno give s.o. a cold. ∼**rse** vpr catch a cold; (fig) cool off

resguard|ar vt protect. ∼**arse** vpr protect o.s.; (fig) take care. ∼**o** m protection; (garantía) guarantee; (recibo) receipt

resid|encia f residence; (*univ*) hall of residence, dormitory (*Amer*); (*de ancianos etc*) home. ~**encial** a residential. ~**ente** a & m & f resident. ~**ir** vi reside; (*fig*) lie

residu|al a residual. ~**o** m remainder. ~**os** mpl waste

resigna|ción f resignation. ~**damente** adv with resignation. ~**r** vt resign. ~**rse** vpr resign o.s. (a, con to)

resina f resin

resist|encia f resistence. ~**ente** a resistent. ~**ir** vt resist; (*soportar*) bear. • vi resist. **oponer** ~**encia** a resist

resma f ream

resobado a trite

resol|ución f resolution; (*solución*) solution; (*decisión*) decision. ~**ver** [2] (*pp* resuelto) resolve; solve (*problema etc*). ~**verse** vpr be solved; (*resultar bien*) work out; (*decidirse*) make up one's mind

resollar [2] vi breathe heavily. **sin** ~ without saying a word

resona|ncia f resonance. ~**nte** a resonant; (*fig*) resounding. ~**r** [2] vi resound. **tener** ~**ncia** cause a stir

resopl|ar vi puff; (*por enfado*) snort; (*por cansancio*) pant. ~**ido** m heavy breathing; (*de enfado*) snort; (*de cansancio*) panting

resorte m spring. **tocar (todos los)** ~**s** (*fig*) pull strings

respald|ar vt back; (*escribir*) endorse. ~**arse** vpr lean back. ~**o** m back

respect|ar vi concern. ~**ivo** a respective. ~**o** m respect. **al** ~**o** on the matter. (**con**) ~**o** a as regards. **en/ por lo que** ~ a as regards

respet|able a respectable. • m audience. ~**ar** vt respect. ~**o** m respect. ~**uoso** a respectful. **de** ~**o** best. **faltar al** ~**o** a be disrespectful to. **hacerse** ~**ar** command respect

respingo m start

respir|ación f breathing; (*med*) respiration; (*ventilación*) ventilation. ~**ador** a respiratory. ~**ar** vi breathe; (*fig*) breathe a sigh of relief. **no** ~ (*no hablar*) not say a word. ~**o** m breathing; (*fig*) rest

respland|ecer [11] vi shine. ~**eciente** a shining. ~**or** m brilliance; (*de llamas*) glow

responder vi answer; (*replicar*) answer back; (*fig*) reply, respond. ~ **de** answer for

responsab|ilidad f responsibility. ~**le** a responsible. **hacerse** ~**le de** assume responsibilty for

respuesta f reply, answer

resquebra|dura f crack. ~**jar** vt crack. ~**jarse** vpr crack

resquemor m (*fig*) uneasiness

resquicio m crack; (*fig*) possibility

resta f subtraction

restablecer [11] vt restore. ~**se** vpr recover

restallar vi crack

restante a remaining. **lo** ~ the rest

restar vt take away; (*substraer*) subtract. • vi be left

restaura|ción f restoration. ~**nte** m restaurant. ~**r** vt restore

restitu|ción f restitution. ~**ir** [17] vt return; (*restaurar*) restore

resto m rest, remainder; (*en matemática*) remainder. ~**s** mpl remains; (*de comida*) leftovers

restorán m restaurant

restregar [1 & 12] vt rub

restri|cción f restriction. ~**ngir** [14] vt restrict, limit

resucitar vt resuscitate; (*fig*) revive. • vi return to life

resuelto a resolute

resuello m breath; (*respiración*) breathing

resulta|do m result. ~**r** vi result; (*salir*) turn out; (*ser*) be; (*ocurrir*) happen; (*costar*) come to

resum|en m summary. ~**ir** vt summarize; (*recapitular*) sum up; (*abreviar*) abridge. **en** ~**en** in short

resur|gir [14] vi reappear; (*fig*) revive. ~**gimiento** m resurgence. ~**rección** f resurrection

retaguardia f (*mil*) rearguard

retahíla f string

retal m remnant

retama f, **retamo** m (*LAm*) broom

retar vt challenge

retardar vt slow down; (*demorar*) delay

retazo m remnant; (*fig*) piece, bit

retemblar [1] vi shake

rete... pref extremely

reten|ción f retention. ~**er** [40] vt keep; (*en la memoria*) retain; (*no dar*) withhold

reticencia f insinuation; (*reserva*) reticence, reluctance

retina f retina

retintín m ringing. **con** ~ (*fig*) sarcastically

retir|ada f withdrawal. **~ado** a secluded; (*jubilado*) retired. **~ar** vt move away; (*quitar*) remove; withdraw (*dinero*); (*jubilar*) pension off. **~arse** vpr draw back; (*mil*) withdraw; (*jubilarse*) retire; (*acostarse*) go to bed. **~o** m retirement; (*pensión*) pension; (*lugar apartado*) retreat

reto m challenge

retocar [7] vt retouch

retoño m shoot

retoque m (*acción*) retouching; (*efecto*) finishing touch

retor|cer [2 & 9] vt twist; wring (*ropa*). **~erse** vpr get twisted up; (*de dolor*) writhe. **~imiento** m twisting; (*de ropa*) wringing

retóric|a f rhetoric; (*grandilocuencia*) grandiloquence. **~o** m rhetorical

retorn|ar vt/i return. **~o** m return

retortijón m twist; (*de tripas*) stomach cramp

retoz|ar [10] vi romp, frolic. **~ón** a playful

retractar vt retract. **~se** vpr retract

retra|er [41] vt retract. **~erse** vpr withdraw. **~ído** a retiring

retransmitir vt relay

retras|ado a behind; (*reloj*) slow; (*poco desarrollado*) backward; (*anticuado*) old-fashioned; (*med*) mentally retarded. **~ar** vt delay; put back (*reloj*); (*retardar*) slow down. • vi fall behind; (*reloj*) be slow. **~arse** vpr be behind; (*reloj*) be slow. **~o** m delay; (*poco desarrollo*) backwardness; (*de reloj*) slowness. **~os** mpl arrears. **con 5 minutos de ~o** 5 minutes late. **traer ~o** be late

retrat|ar vt paint a portrait of; (*foto*) photograph; (*fig*) portray. **~ista** m & f portrait painter. **~o** m portrait; (*fig, descripción*) description. **ser el vivo ~o de** be the living image of

retreparse vpr lean back

retreta f retreat

retrete m toilet

retribu|ción f payment. **~ir** [17] vt pay

retroce|der vi move back; (*fig*) back down. **~so** m backward movement; (*de arma de fuego*) recoil; (*med*) relapse

retrógrado a & m (*pol*) reactionary

retropropulsión f jet propulsion

retrospectivo a retrospective

retrovisor m rear-view mirror

retumbar vt echo; (*trueno etc*) boom

reuma m, **reúma** m rheumatism

reum|ático a rheumatic. **~atismo** m rheumatism

reuni|ón f meeting; (*entre amigos*) reunion. **~r** [23] vt join together; (*recoger*) gather (together). **~rse** vpr join together; (*personas*) meet

rev|álida f final exam. **~alidar** vt confirm; (*escol*) take an exam in

revancha f revenge. **tomar la ~** get one's own back

revela|ción f revelation. **~do** m developing. **~dor** a revealing. **~r** vt reveal; (*foto*) develop

revent|ar [1] vi burst; (*tener ganas*) be dying to. **~arse** vpr burst. **~ón** m burst; (*auto*) puncture

reverbera|ción f (*de luz*) reflection; (*de sonido*) reverberation. **~r** vi (*luz*) be reflected; (*sonido*) reverberate

reveren|cia f reverence; (*muestra de respeto*) bow; (*muestra de respeto de mujer*) curtsy. **~ciar** vt revere. **~do** a respected; (*relig*) reverend. **~te** a reverent

revers|ible a reversible. **~o** m reverse

revertir [4] vi revert

revés m wrong side; (*desgracia*) misfortune; (*en deportes*) backhand. **al ~** the other way round; (*con lo de arriba abajo*) upside down; (*con lo de dentro fuera*) inside out

revesti|miento m coating. **~r** [5] vt cover; put on (*ropa*); (*fig*) take on

revis|ar vt check; overhaul (*mecanismo*); service (*coche etc*). **~ión** f check(ing); (*inspección*) inspection; (*de coche etc*) service. **~or** m inspector

revist|a f magazine; (*inspección*) inspection; (*artículo*) review; (*espectáculo*) revue. **~ero** m critic; (*mueble*) magazine rack. **pasar ~a a** inspect

revivir vi come to life again

revocar [7] vt revoke; whitewash (*pared*)

revolcar [2 & 7] vt knock over. **~se** vpr roll

revolotear vi flutter

revoltijo m, **revoltillo** m mess. **~ de huevos** scrambled eggs

revoltoso a rebellious; (*niño*) naughty

revoluci|ón f revolution. **~onar** vt revolutionize. **~onario** a & m revolutionary

revolver [2, pp **revuelto**] vt mix; stir ‹líquido›; (desordenar) mess up; (pol) stir up. **~se** vpr turn round. **~se contra** turn on

revólver m revolver

revoque m (con cal) whitewashing

revuelo m fluttering; (fig) stir

revuelt|a f turn; (de calle etc) bend; (motín) revolt; (conmoción) disturbance. **~o** a mixed up; ‹líquido› cloudy; ‹mar› rough; ‹tiempo› unsettled; ‹huevos› scrambled

rey m king. **~es** mpl king and queen

reyerta f quarrel

rezagarse [12] vpr fall behind

rez|ar [10] vt say. ● vi pray; (decir) say. **~o** m praying; (oración) prayer

rezongar [12] vi grumble

rezumar vt/i ooze

ría f estuary

riachuelo m stream

riada f flood

ribera f bank

ribete m border; (fig) embellishment

ricino. **aceite de ~** castor oil

rico a rich; (culin, fam) delicious. ● m rich person

rid|ículo a ridiculous. **~iculizar** [10] vt ridicule

riego m watering; (irrigación) irrigation

riel m rail

rienda f rein

riesgo m risk. **a ~ de** at the risk of. **correr (el) ~ de** run the risk of

rifa f raffle. **~r** vt raffle. **~rse** vpr (fam) quarrel over

rifle m rifle

rigidez f rigidity; (fig) inflexibility

rígido a rigid; (fig) inflexible

rig|or m strictness; (exactitud) exactness; (de clima) severity. **~uroso** a rigorous. **de ~or** compulsory. **en ~or** strictly speaking

rima f rhyme. **~r** vt/i rhyme

rimbombante a resounding; ‹lenguaje› pompous; (fig, ostentoso) showy

rimel m mascara

rincón m corner

rinoceronte m rhinoceros

riña f quarrel; (pelea) fight

riñ|ón m kidney. **~onada** f loin; (guiso) kidney stew

río m river; (fig) stream. ● vb véase **reír**. **~ abajo** downstream. **~ arriba** upstream

rioja m Rioja wine

riqueza f wealth; (fig) richness. **~s** fpl riches

riquísimo a delicious

risa f laugh. **desternillarse de ~** split one's sides laughing. **la ~** laughter

risco m cliff

ris|ible a laughable. **~otada** f guffaw

ristra f string

risueño a smiling; (fig) happy

rítmico a rhythmic(al)

ritmo m rhythm; (fig) rate

rit|o m rite; (fig) ritual. **~ual** a & m ritual. **de ~ual** customary

rival a & m & f rival. **~idad** f rivalry. **~izar** [10] vi rival

riz|ado a curly. **~ar** [10] vt curl; ripple ‹agua›. **~o** m curl; (en agua) ripple. **~oso** a curly

róbalo m bass

robar vt steal ‹cosa›; rob ‹persona›; (raptar) kidnap

roble m oak (tree)

roblón m rivet

robo m theft; (fig, estafa) robbery

robot (pl **robots**) m robot

robust|ez f strength. **~o** a strong

roca f rock

roce m rubbing; (toque ligero) touch; (señal) mark; (fig, entre personas) contact

rociar [20] vt spray

rocín m nag

rocío m dew

rodaballo m turbot

rodado m (Arg, vehículo) vehicle

rodaja f disc; (culin) slice

roda|je m (de película) shooting; (de coche) running in. **~r** [2] vt shoot ‹película›; run in ‹coche›; (recorrer) travel. ● vi roll; ‹coche› run; (hacer una película) shoot

rode|ar vt surround. **~arse** vpr surround o.s. (**de** with). **~o** m long way round; (de ganado) round-up. **andar con ~os** beat about the bush. **sin ~os** plainly

rodill|a f knee. **~era** f knee-pad. **de ~as** kneeling

rodillo m roller; (culin) rolling-pin

rododendro m rhododendron

rodrigón m stake

roe|dor m rodent. **~r** [37] vt gnaw

rogar [2 & 12] *vt/i* ask; (*relig*) pray. se ruega a los Sres pasajeros... passengers are requested.... se ruega no fumar please do not smoke

roj|ete *m* rouge. ~ez *f* redness. ~izo *a* reddish. ~o *a & m* red. ponerse ~o blush

roll|izo *a* round; (*persona*) plump. ~o *m* roll; (*de cuerda*) coil; (*culin*, *rodillo*) rolling-pin; (*fig*, *pesadez*, *fam*) bore

romance *a* Romance. ● *m* Romance language; (*poema*) romance. hablar en ~ speak plainly

rom|ánico *a* Romanesque; (*lengua*) Romance. ~ano *a & m* Roman. a la ~ana (*culin*) (deep-)fried in batter

rom|anticismo *m* romanticism. ~ántico *a* romantic

romería *f* pilgrimage

romero *m* rosemary

romo *a* blunt; (*nariz*) snub; (*fig*, *torpe*) dull

rompe|cabezas *m invar* puzzle; (*con tacos de madera*) jigsaw (puzzle). ~nueces *m invar* nutcrackers. ~olas *m invar* breakwater

romp|er (*pp* roto) *vt* break; break off (*relaciones etc*). ● *vi* break; (*sol*) break through. ~erse *vpr* break. ~er a burst out. ~imiento *m* (*de relaciones etc*) breaking off

ron *m* rum

ronc|ar [7] *vi* snore. ~o *a* hoarse

roncha *f* lump; (*culin*) slice

ronda *f* round; (*patrulla*) patrol; (*carretera*) ring road. ~lla *f* group of serenaders; (*invención*) story. ~r *vt/i* patrol

rondón *adv*. de ~ unannounced

ronquedad *f*, **ronquera** *f* hoarseness

ronquido *m* snore

ronronear *vi* purr

ronzal *m* halter

roña *f* (*suciedad*) grime. ~oso *a* dirty; (*oxidado*) rusty; (*tacaño*) mean

rop|a *f* clothes, clothing. ~a blanca linen; (*ropa interior*) underwear. ~a de cama bedclothes. ~a hecha ready-made clothes. ~a interior underwear. ~aje *m* robes; (*excesivo*) heavy clothing. ~ero *m* wardrobe

ros|a *a invar* pink. ● *f* rose; (*color*) pink. ~áceo *a* pink. ~ado *a* rosy. ● *m* (*vino*) rosé. ~al *m* rose-bush

rosario *m* rosary; (*fig*) series

rosbif *m* roast beef

rosc|a *f* coil; (*de tornillo*) thread; (*de pan*) roll. ~o *m* roll

rosetón *m* rosette

rosquilla *f* doughnut; (*oruga*) grub

rostro *m* face

rota|ción *f* rotation. ~tivo *a* rotary

roto *a* broken

rótula *f* kneecap

rotulador *m* felt-tip pen

rótulo *m* sign; (*etiqueta*) label

rotundo *a* emphatic

rotura *f* break

roturar *vt* plough

roza *f* groove. ~dura *f* scratch

rozagante *a* showy

rozar [10] *vt* rub against; (*ligeramente*) brush against; (*ensuciar*) dirty; (*fig*) touch on. ~se *vpr* rub; (*con otras personas*) mix

Rte. *abrev* (*Remite(nte)*) sender

rúa *f* (small) street

rubéola *f* German measles

rubí *m* ruby

rubicundo *a* ruddy

rubio *a* (*pelo*) fair; (*persona*) fair-haired; (*tabaco*) Virginian

rubor *m* blush; (*fig*) shame. ~izado *a* blushing; (*fig*) ashamed. ~izar [10] *vt* make blush. ~izarse *vpr* blush

rúbrica *f* red mark; (*de firma*) flourish; (*título*) heading

rudeza *f* roughness

rudiment|al *a* rudimentary. ~os *mpl* rudiments

rudo *a* rough; (*sencillo*) simple

rueda *f* wheel; (*de mueble*) castor; (*de personas*) ring; (*culin*) slice. ~ de prensa press conference

ruedo *m* edge; (*redondel*) arena

ruego *m* request; (*súplica*) entreaty. ● *vb véase* rogar

rufi|án *m* pimp; (*granuja*) villain. ~anesco *a* roguish

rugby *m* Rugby

rugi|do *m* roar. ~r [14] *vi* roar

ruibarbo *m* rhubarb

ruido *m* noise; (*alboroto*) din; (*escándalo*) commotion. ~so *a* noisy; (*fig*) sensational

ruin *a* despicable; (*tacaño*) mean

ruina *f* ruin; (*colapso*) collapse

ruindad *f* meanness

ruinoso *a* ruinous

ruiseñor *m* nightingale

ruleta *f* roulette

rulo *m* (*culin*) rolling-pin; (*del pelo*) curler

Rumania *f* Romania

rumano *a & m* Romanian

rumba *f* rumba

rumbo *m* direction; (*fig*) course; (*fig, generosidad*) lavishness. ~**so** *a* lavish. **con** ~ **a** in the direction of. **hacer** ~ **a** head for

rumia|nte *a & m* ruminant. ~**r** *vt* chew; (*fig*) chew over. ● *vi* ruminate

rumor *m* rumour; (*ruido*) murmur. ~**ear** *vpr* be rumoured. ~**oso** *a* murmuring

runr|ún *m* rumour; (*ruido*) murmur. ~**unearse** *vpr* be rumoured

ruptura *f* break; (*de relaciones etc*) breaking off

rural *a* rural

Rusia *f* Russia

ruso *a & m* Russian

rústico *a* rural; (*de carácter*) coarse. **en rústica** paperback

ruta *f* route; (*camino*) road; (*fig*) course

rutilante *a* shining

rutina *f* routine. ~**rio** *a* routine

S

S.A. *abrev* (*Sociedad Anónima*) Ltd, Limited, plc, Public Limited Company

sábado *m* Saturday

sabana *f* (*esp LAm*) savannah

sábana *f* sheet

sabandija *f* bug

sabañón *m* chilblain

sabático *a* sabbatical

sab|elotodo *m & f invar* know-all (*fam*). ~**er** [38] *vt* know; (*ser capaz de*) be able to, know how to; (*enterarse de*) learn. ● *vi*. ~**er a** taste of. ~**er** *m* knowledge. ~**ido** *a* well-known. ~**iduría** *f* wisdom; (*conocimientos*) knowledge. **a** ~**er si** I wonder if. **¡haberlo** ~**ido!** if only I'd known! **hacer** ~**er** let know. **no sé cuántos** what's-his-name. **para que lo sepas** let me tell you. **¡qué sé yo!** how should I know? **que yo sepa** as far as I know. **¿**~**es nadar?** can you swim? **un no sé qué** a certain sth. **¡yo qué sé!** how should I know?

sabiendas *adv*. **a** ~ knowingly; (*a propósito*) on purpose

sabio *a* learned; (*prudente*) wise

sabor *m* taste, flavour; (*fig*) flavour. ~**ear** *vt* taste; (*fig*) savour

sabot|aje *m* sabotage. ~**eador** *m* saboteur. ~**ear** *vt* sabotage

sabroso *a* tasty; (*fig, substancioso*) meaty

sabueso *m* (*perro*) bloodhound; (*fig, detective*) detective

saca|corchos *m invar* corkscrew. ~**puntas** *m invar* pencil-sharpener

sacar [7] *vt* take out; put out (*parte del cuerpo*); (*quitar*) remove; take (*foto*); win (*premio*); get (*billete, entrada etc*); withdraw (*dinero*); reach (*solución*); draw (*conclusión*); make (*copia*). ~ **adelante** bring up (*niño*); carry on (*negocio*)

sacarina *f* saccharin

sacerdo|cio *m* priesthood. ~**tal** *a* priestly. ~**te** *m* priest

saciar *vt* satisfy

saco *m* bag; (*anat*) sac; (*LAm, chaqueta*) jacket; (*de mentiras*) pack. ~ **de dormir** sleeping-bag

sacramento *m* sacrament

sacrific|ar [7] *vt* sacrifice. ~**arse** *vpr* sacrifice o.s. ~**io** *m* sacrifice

sacr|ilegio *m* sacrilege. ~**ílego** *a* sacrilegious

sacro *a* sacred, holy. ~**santo** *a* sacrosanct

sacudi|da *f* shake; (*movimiento brusco*) jolt, jerk; (*fig*) shock. ~**da eléctrica** electric shock. ~**r** *vt* shake; (*golpear*) beat; (*ahuyentar*) chase away. ~**rse** *vpr* shake off; (*fig*) get rid of

sádico *a* sadistic. ● *m* sadist

sadismo *m* sadism

saeta *f* arrow; (*de reloj*) hand

safari *m* safari

sagaz *a* shrewd

Sagitario *m* Sagittarius

sagrado *a* sacred, holy. ● *m* sanctuary

Sahara *m*, **Sáhara** /'saxara/ *m* Sahara

sainete *m* short comedy

sal *f* salt

sala *f* room; (*en teatro*) house. ~ **de espectáculos** concert hall, auditorium. ~ **de espera** waiting-room. ~ **de estar** living-room. ~ **de fiestas** nightclub

sala|do *a* salty; (*agua del mar*) salt; (*vivo*) lively; (*encantador*) cute; (*fig*) witty. ~**r** *vt* salt

salario *m* wages

salazón *f* (*carne*) salted meat; (*pescado*) salted fish

salchich|a *f* (pork) sausage. **~ón** *m* salami

sald|ar *vt* pay ⟨*cuenta*⟩; ⟨*vender*⟩ sell off; ⟨*fig*⟩ settle. **~o** *m* balance; ⟨*venta*⟩ sale; ⟨*lo que queda*⟩ remnant

salero *m* salt-cellar

salgo *vb véase* **salir**

sali|da *f* departure; ⟨*puerta*⟩ exit, way out; ⟨*de gas, de líquido*⟩ leak; ⟨*de astro*⟩ rising; ⟨*com, posibilidad de venta*⟩ opening; ⟨*chiste*⟩ witty remark; ⟨*fig*⟩ way out. **~da de emergencia** emergency exit. **~ente** *a* projecting; ⟨*fig*⟩ outstanding. **~r** [52] *vi* leave; ⟨*de casa etc*⟩ go out; ⟨*revista etc*⟩ be published; ⟨*resultar*⟩ turn out; ⟨*astro*⟩ rise; ⟨*aparecer*⟩ appear. **~rse** *vpr* leave; ⟨*recipiente, líquido etc*⟩ leak. **~r adelante** get by. **~rse con la suya** get one's own way

saliva *f* saliva

salmo *m* psalm

salm|ón *m* salmon. **~onete** *m* red mullet

salmuera *f* brine

salón *m* lounge, sitting-room. **~ de actos** assembly hall. **~ de fiestas** dancehall

salpica|dero *m* ⟨*auto*⟩ dashboard. **~dura** *f* splash; ⟨*acción*⟩ splashing. **~r** [7] *vt* splash; ⟨*fig*⟩ sprinkle

sals|a *f* sauce; ⟨*para carne asada*⟩ gravy; ⟨*fig*⟩ spice. **~a verde** parsley sauce. **~era** *f* sauce-boat

salt|amontes *m invar* grasshopper. **~ar** *vt* jump (over); ⟨*fig*⟩ miss out. ● *vi* jump; ⟨*romperse*⟩ break; ⟨*líquido*⟩ spurt out; ⟨*desprenderse*⟩ come off; ⟨*pelota*⟩ bounce; ⟨*estallar*⟩ explode. **~eador** *m* highwayman. **~ear** *vt* rob; ⟨*culin*⟩ sauté. ● *vi* skip through

saltimbanqui *m* acrobat

salt|o *m* jump; ⟨*al agua*⟩ dive. **~o de agua** waterfall. **~ón** *a* ⟨*ojos*⟩ bulging. ● *m* grasshopper. **a ~os** by jumping; ⟨*fig*⟩ by leaps and bounds. **de un ~o** with one jump

salud *f* health; ⟨*fig*⟩ welfare. ● *int* cheers! **~able** *a* healthy

salud|ar *vt* greet, say hello to; ⟨*mil*⟩ salute. **~o** *m* greeting; ⟨*mil*⟩ salute. **~os** *mpl* best wishes. **le ~a atentamente** ⟨*en cartas*⟩ yours faithfully

salva *f* salvo; ⟨*de aplausos*⟩ thunders

salvación *f* salvation

salvado *m* bran

Salvador *m*. **El ~** El Salvador

salvaguardia *f* safeguard

salvaje *a* ⟨*planta, animal*⟩ wild; ⟨*primitivo*⟩ savage. ● *m & f* savage

salvamanteles *m invar* table-mat

salva|mento *m* rescue. **~r** *vt* save, rescue; ⟨*atravesar*⟩ cross; ⟨*recorrer*⟩ travel; ⟨*fig*⟩ overcome. **~rse** *vpr* save o.s. **~vidas** *m invar* lifebelt. **chaleco** *m* **~vidas** life-jacket

salvia *f* sage

salvo *a* safe. ● *adv & prep* except (for). **~ que** unless. **~conducto** *m* safe-conduct. **a ~** out of danger. **poner a ~** put in a safe place

samba *f* samba

San *a* Saint, St. **~ Miguel** St Michael

sana|r *vt* cure. ● *vi* recover. **~torio** *m* sanatorium

sanci|ón *f* sanction. **~onar** *vt* sanction

sancocho *m* ⟨*LAm*⟩ stew

sandalia *f* sandal

sándalo *m* sandalwood

sandía *f* water melon

sandwich /'sambitʃ/ *m* (*pl* **sandwichs, sandwiches**) sandwich

sanear *vt* drain

sangr|ante *a* bleeding; ⟨*fig*⟩ flagrant. **~ar** *vt/i* bleed. **~e** *f* blood. **a ~e fría** in cold blood

sangría *f* ⟨*bebida*⟩ sangria

sangriento *a* bloody

sangu|ijuela *f* leech. **~íneo** *a* blood

san|idad *f* health. **~itario** *a* sanitary. **~o** *a* healthy; ⟨*seguro*⟩ sound. **~o y salvo** safe and sound. **cortar por lo ~o** settle things once and for all

santiamén *m*. **en un ~** in an instant

sant|idad *f* sanctity. **~ificar** [7] *vt* sanctify. **~iguar** [15] *vt* make the sign of the cross over. **~iguarse** *vpr* cross o.s. **~o** *a* holy; ⟨*delante de nombre*⟩ Saint, St. ● *m* saint; ⟨*día*⟩ saint's day, name day. **~uario** *m* sanctuary. **~urrón** *a* sanctimonious, hypocritical

saña *f* fury; ⟨*crueldad*⟩ cruelty. **~oso** *a*, **~udo** *a* furious

sapo *m* toad; ⟨*bicho, fam*⟩ small animal, creature

saque *m* ⟨*en tenis*⟩ service; ⟨*en fútbol*⟩ throw-in; ⟨*inicial en fútbol*⟩ kick-off

saque|ar *vt* loot. **~o** *m* looting

sarampión *m* measles

sarape *m* ⟨*Mex*⟩ blanket

sarc|asmo *m* sarcasm. **~ástico** *a* sarcastic

sardana *f* Catalonian dance

sardina *f* sardine

sardo *a* & *m* Sardinian

sardónico *a* sardonic

sargento *m* sergeant

sarmiento *m* vine shoot

sarpullido *m* rash

sarta *f* string

sartén *f* frying-pan (*Brit*), fry-pan (*Amer*)

sastre *m* tailor. **~ría** *f* tailoring; (*tienda*) tailor's (shop)

Satanás *m* Satan

satánico *a* satanic

satélite *m* satellite

satinado *a* shiny

sátira *f* satire

satírico *a* satirical. ● *m* satirist

satisf|acción *f* satisfaction. **~acer** [31] *vt* satisfy; (*pagar*) pay; (*gustar*) please; meet (*gastos, requisitos*). **~acerse** *vpr* satisfy o.s.; (*vengarse*) take revenge. **~actorio** *a* satisfactory. **~echo** *a* satisfied. **~echo de sí mismo** smug

satura|ción *f* saturation. **~r** *vt* saturate

Saturno *m* Saturn

sauce *m* willow. **~ llorón** weeping willow

saúco *m* elder

savia *f* sap

sauna *f* sauna

saxofón *m*, **saxófono** *m* saxophone

saz|ón *f* ripeness; (*culin*) seasoning. **~onado** *a* ripe; (*culin*) seasoned. **~onar** *vt* ripen; (*culin*) season. **en ~ón** in season

se *pron* (*él*) him; (*ella*) her; (*Vd*) you; (*reflexivo, él*) himself; (*reflexivo, ella*) herself; (*reflexivo, ello*) itself; (*reflexivo, uno*) oneself; (*reflexivo, Vd*) yourself; (*reflexivo, ellos, ellas*) themselves; (*reflexivo, Vds*) yourselves; (*recíproco*) (to) each other. **~ dice** people say, they say, it is said (**que** that). **~ habla español** Spanish spoken

sé *vb véase* **saber** *y* **ser**

sea *vb véase* **ser**

sebo *m* tallow; (*culin*) suet

seca|dor *m* drier; (*de pelo*) hair-drier. **~nte** *a* drying. ● *m* blotting-paper. **~r** [7] *vt* dry. **~rse** *vpr* dry; (*río etc*) dry up; (*persona*) dry o.s.

sección *f* section

seco *a* dry; (*frutos, flores*) dried; (*flaco*) thin; (*respuesta*) curt; (*escueto*) plain. **a secas** just. **en ~** (*bruscamente*) suddenly. **lavar en ~** dry-clean

secre|ción *f* secretion. **~tar** *vt* secrete

secretar|ía *f* secretariat. **~io** *m* secretary

secreto *a* & *m* secret

secta *f* sect. **~rio** *a* sectarian

sector *m* sector

secuela *f* consequence

secuencia *f* sequence

secuestr|ar *vt* confiscate; kidnap (*persona*); hijack (*avión*). **~o** *m* seizure; (*de persona*) kidnapping; (*de avión*) hijack(ing)

secular *a* secular

secundar *vt* second, help. **~io** *a* secondary

sed *f* thirst. ● *vb véase* **ser**. **tener ~** be thirsty. **tener ~ de** (*fig*) be hungry for

seda *f* silk

sedante *a* & *m*, **sedativo** *a* & *m* sedative

sede *f* seat; (*relig*) see

sedentario *a* sedentary

sedic|ión *f* sedition. **~oso** *a* seditious

sediento *a* thirsty

sediment|ar *vi* deposit. **~arse** *vpr* settle. **~o** *m* sediment

seduc|ción *f* seduction. **~ir** [47] *vt* seduce; (*atraer*) attract. **~tor** *a* seductive. ● *m* seducer

sega|dor *m* harvester. **~dora** *f* harvester, mower. **~r** [1 & 12] *vt* reap

seglar *a* secular. ● *m* layman

segmento *m* segment

segoviano *m* person from Segovia

segrega|ción *f* segregation. **~r** [12] *vt* segregate

segui|da *f*. **en ~da** immediately. **~do** *a* continuous; (*en plural*) consecutive. ● *adv* straight; (*después*) after. **todo ~do** straight ahead. **~dor** *a* following. ● *m* follower. **~r** [5 & 13] *vt* follow (*continuar*) continue

según *prep* according to. ● *adv* it depends; (*a medida que*) as

segundo *a* second. ● *m* second; (*culin*) second course

segur|amente *adv* certainly; (*muy probablemente*) surely. **~idad** *f* safety; (*certeza*) certainty; (*aplomo*) confidence. ~idad en sí mismo self-confidence. ~idad social social security. ~o a safe; (cierto) certain, sure; (firme) secure; (de fiar) reliable. ●adv for certain. ●m insurance; (dispositivo de seguridad) safety device. ~o de sí mismo self-confident. ~o de terceros third-party insurance

seis a & m six. ~cientos a & m six hundred

seísmo m earthquake

selec|ción f selection. ~cionar vt select, choose. ~tivo a selective. ~to a selected; (fig) choice

selva f forest; (jungla) jungle

sell|ar vt stamp; (cerrar) seal. ~o m stamp; (en documento oficial) seal; (fig, distintivo) hallmark

semáforo m semaphore; (auto) traffic lights; (rail) signal

semana f week. ~l a weekly. ~rio a & m weekly. S~ Santa Holy Week

semántic|a f semantics. ~o a semantic

semblante m face; (fig) look

sembrar [1] vt sow; (fig) scatter

semeja|nte a similar; (tal) such. ●m fellow man; (cosa) equal. ~nza f similarity. ~r vi seem. ~rse vpr look alike. a ~nza de like. tener ~nza con resemble

semen m semen. ~tal a stud. ●m stud animal

semestr|al a half-yearly. ~e m six months

semibreve m semibreve (Brit), whole note (Amer)

semic|ircular a semicircular. ~írculo m semicircle

semicorchea f semiquaver (Brit), sixteenth note (Amer)

semifinal f semifinal

semill|a f seed. ~ero m nursery; (fig) hotbed

seminario m (univ) seminar; (relig) seminary

sem|ita a Semitic. ●m Semite. ~ítico a Semitic

sémola f semolina

senado m senate; (fig) assembly. ~r m senator

sencill|ez f simplicity. ~o a simple; (uno solo) single

senda f, sendero m path

sendos apl each

seno m bosom. ~ materno womb

sensaci|ón f sensation. ~onal a sensational

sensat|ez f good sense. ~o a sensible

sensi|bilidad f sensibility. ~ble a sensitive; (notable) notable; (lamentable) lamentable. ~tivo a (órgano) sense

sensual a sensual. ~idad f sensuality

senta|do a sitting (down). dar algo por ~do take something for granted. ~r [1] vt place; (establecer) establish. ●vi suit; (de medidas) fit; (comida) agree with. ~rse vpr sit (down); (sedimento) settle

sentencia f saying; (jurid) sentence. ~r vt sentence

sentido a deeply felt; (sincero) sincere; (sensible) sensitive. ●m sense; (dirección) direction. ~ común common sense. ~ del humor sense of humour. ~ único one-way. doble ~ double meaning. no tener ~ not make sense. perder el ~ faint. sin ~ unconscious; (cosa) senseless

sentim|ental a sentimental. ~iento m feeling; (sentido) sense; (pesar) regret

sentir [4] vt feel; (oír) hear; (lamentar) be sorry for. ●vi feel; (lamentarse) be sorry. ●m (opinión) opinion. ~se vpr feel. lo siento I'm sorry

seña f sign. ~s fpl (dirección) address; (descripción) description

señal f sign; (rail etc) signal; (telefónico) tone; (com) deposit. ~ado a notable. ~ar vt signal; (poner señales en) mark; (apuntar) point out; (manecilla, aguja) point to; (determinar) fix. ~arse vpr stand out. dar ~es de show signs of. en ~ de as a token of

señero a alone; (sin par) unique

señor m man; (caballero) gentleman; (delante de nombre propio) Mr; (tratamiento directo) sir. ~a f lady, woman; (delante de nombre propio) Mrs; (esposa) wife; (tratamiento directo) madam. ~ial a (casa) stately. ~ita f young lady; (delante de nombre propio) Miss; (tratamiento directo) miss. ~ito m young gentleman. el ~ alcalde the mayor. el ~ Mr. muy ~ mío Dear Sir. ¡no ~! certainly not! ser ~ de be master of, control

señuelo m lure

sepa vb véase saber

separa|ción f separation. **~do** a separate. **~r** vt separate; (*apartar*) move away; (*de empleo*) dismiss. **~rse** vpr separate; (*amigos*) part. **~tista** a & m & f separatist. **por ~do** separately

septentrional a north(ern)

séptico a septic

septiembre m September

séptimo a seventh

sepulcro m sepulchre

sepult|ar vt bury. **~ura** f burial; (*tumba*) grave. **~urero** m gravedigger

sequ|edad f dryness. **~ía** f drought

séquito m entourage; (*fig*) aftermath

ser [39] vi be. ● m being. **~ de** be made of; (*provenir de*) come from; (*pertenecer a*) belong to. **~ humano** human being. **a no ~ que** unless. **¡así sea!** so be it! **es más what is** more. **lo que sea** anything. **no sea que, no vaya a ~ que** in case. **o sea** in other words. **sea lo que fuere** be that as it may. **sea... sea** either... or. **siendo así que** since. **soy yo** it's me

seren|ar vt calm down. **~arse** vpr calm down; (*tiempo*) clear up. **~ata** f serenade. **~idad** f serenity. **~o** a (*cielo*) clear; (*tiempo*) fine; (*fig*) calm. ● m night watchman. **al ~o** in the open

seri|al m serial. **~e** f series. **fuera de ~e** (*fig, extraordinario*) special. **producción** f **en ~** mass production

seri|edad f seriousness. **~o** a serious; (*confiable*) reliable. **en ~o** seriously. **poco ~o** frivolous

sermón m sermon

serp|enteante a winding. **~entear** vi wind. **~iente** f snake. **~iente de cascabel** rattlesnake

serrano a mountain; (*jamón*) cured

serr|ar [1] vt saw. **~ín** m sawdust. **~ucho** m (hand)saw

servi|cial a helpful. **~cio** m service; (*conjunto*) set; (*aseo*) toilet. **~cio a domicilio** delivery service. **~dor** m servant. **~dumbre** f servitude; (*criados*) servants, staff. **~l** a servile. **su (seguro) ~dor** (*en cartas*) yours faithfully

servilleta f serviette, (table) napkin

servir [5] vt serve; (*ayudar*) help; (*en restaurante*) wait on. ● vi serve; (*ser útil*) be of use. **~se** vpr help o.s. **~se de** use. **no ~ de nada** be useless. **para ~le** at your service. **sírvase sentarse** please sit down

sesear vi pronounce the Spanish c as an s

sesent|a a & m sixty. **~ón** a & m sixty-year-old

seseo m pronunciation of the Spanish c as an s

sesg|ado a slanting. **~o** m slant; (*fig, rumbo*) turn

sesión f session; (*en el cine*) showing; (*en el teatro*) performance

ses|o m brain; (*fig*) brains. **~udo** a inteligent; (*sensato*) sensible

seta f mushroom

sete|cientos a & m seven hundred. **~nta** a & m seventy. **~ntón** a & m seventy-year-old

setiembre m September

seto m fence; (*de plantas*) hedge. **~ vivo** hedge

seudo... pref pseudo...

seudónimo m pseudonym

sever|idad f severity. **~o** a severe; (*disciplina, profesor etc*) strict

Sevilla f Seville

sevillan|as fpl popular dance from Seville. **~o** m person from Seville

sexo m sex

sext|eto m sextet. **~o** a sixth

sexual a sexual. **~idad** f sexuality

si m (*mus*) B; (*solfa*) te. ● conj if; (*dubitativo*) whether. **~ no** or else. **por ~ (acaso)** in case

sí pron reflexivo (*él*) himself; (*ella*) herself; (*ello*) itself; (*uno*) oneself; (*Vd*) yourself; (*ellos, ellas*) themselves; (*Vds*) yourselves; (*recíproco*) each other

sí adv yes. ● m consent

Siamés a & m Siamese

Sicilia f Sicily

sida m Aids

siderurgia f iron and steel industry

sidra f cider

siega f harvesting; (*época*) harvest time

siembra f sowing; (*época*) sowing time

siempre adv always. **~ que** if. **como ~** as usual. **de ~** (*acostumbrado*) usual. **lo de ~** the same old story. **para ~** for ever

sien f temple

siento vb véase **sentar** y **sentir**

sierra f saw; (*cordillera*) mountain range

siervo m slave

siesta f siesta

siete a & m seven

sífilis f syphilis

sifón m U-bend; (de soda) syphon

sigilo m secrecy

sigla f initials, abbreviation

siglo m century; (época) time, age; (fig, mucho tiempo, fam) ages; (fig, mundo) world

significa|ción f meaning; (importancia) significance. ~**do** a (conocido) well-known. ● m meaning. ~**r** [7] vt mean; (expresar) express. ~**rse** vpr stand out. ~**tivo** a significant

signo m sign. ~ **de admiración** exclamation mark. ~ **de interrogación** question mark

sigo vb véase **seguir**

siguiente a following, next. **lo** ~ the following

sílaba f syllable

silb|ar vt/i whistle. ~**ato** m, ~**ido** m whistle

silenci|ador m silencer. ~**ar** vt hush up. ~**o** m silence. ~**oso** a silent

sílfide f sylph

silicio m silicon

silo m silo

silueta f silhouette; (dibujo) outline

silvestre a wild

sill|a f chair; (de montar) saddle; (relig) see. ~**a de ruedas** wheelchair. ~**ín** m saddle. ~**ón** m armchair

simb|ólico a symbolic(al). ~**olismo** m symbolism. ~**olizar** [10] vt symbolize

símbolo m symbol

sim|etría f symmetry. ~**étrico** a symmetric(al)

simiente f seed

similar a similar

simp|atía f liking; (cariño) affection; (fig, amigo) friend. ~**ático** a nice, likeable; (amable) kind. ~**atizante** m & f sympathizer. ~**atizar** [10] vi get on (well together). **me es** ~**ático** I like

simpl|e a simple; (mero) mere. ~**eza** f simplicity; (tontería) stupid thing; (insignificancia) trifle. ~**icidad** f simplicity. ~**ificar** [7] vt simplify. ~**ón** m simpleton

simposio m symposium

simula|ción f simulation. ~**r** vt feign

simultáneo a simultaneous

sin prep without. ~ **que** without

sinagoga f synagogue

sincer|idad f sincerity. ~**o** a sincere

síncopa f (mus) syncopation

sincopar vt syncopate

sincronizar [10] vt synchronize

sindica|l a (trade-)union. ~**lista** m & f trade-unionist. ~**to** m trade union

síndrome m syndrome

sinfín m endless number

sinf|onía f symphony. ~**ónico** a symphonic

singular a singular; (excepcional) exceptional. ~**izar** [10] vt single out. ~**izarse** vpr stand out

siniestro a sinister; (desgraciado) unlucky. ● m disaster

sinnúmero m endless number

sino m fate. ● conj but; (salvo) except

sínodo m synod

sinónimo a synonymous. ● m synonym

sinrazón f wrong

sintaxis f syntax

síntesis f invar synthesis

sint|ético a synthetic. ~**etizar** [10] vt synthesize; (resumir) summarize

síntoma f sympton

sintomático a symptomatic

sinton|ía f (en la radio) signature tune. ~**izar** [10] vt (con la radio) tune (in)

sinuoso a winding

sinvergüenza m & f scoundrel

sionis|mo m Zionism. ~**ta** m & f Zionist

siquiera conj even if. ● adv at least. **ni** ~ not even

sirena f siren

Siria f Syria

sirio a & m Syrian

siroco m sirocco

sirvienta f, **sirviente** m servant

sirvo vb véase **servir**

sise|ar vt/i hiss. ~**o** m hissing

sísmico a seismic

sismo m earthquake

sistem|a m system. ~**ático** a systematic. **por** ~**a** as a rule

sitiar vt besiege; (fig) surround

sitio m place; (espacio) space; (mil) siege. **en cualquier** ~ anywhere

situa|ción f position. ~**r** [21] vt situate; (poner) put; (depositar) deposit. ~**rse** vpr be successful, establish o.s.

slip /es'lip/ m (pl slips /es'lip/) underpants, briefs

slogan /es'logan/ m (pl slogans /es'logan/) slogan

smoking /es'mokin/ m (pl smokings /es'mokin/) dinner jacket (Brit), tuxedo (Amer)

sobaco m armpit

sobar vt handle; knead ‹masa›
soberan|ía f sovereignty. ‹o a sovereign; (fig) supreme. ● m sovereign
soberbi|a f pride; (altanería) arrogance. ‹o a proud; (altivo) arrogant
soborn|ar vt bribe. ‹o m bribe
sobra f surplus. ‹s fpl leftovers. ‹do a more than enough. ‹nte a surplus. ‹r vi be left over; (estorbar) be in the way. **de** ‹ more than enough
sobrasada f Majorcan sausage
sobre prep on; (encima de) on top of; (más o menos) about; (por encima de) above; (sin tocar) over; (además de) on top of. ● m envelope. ‹cargar [12] vt overload. ‹coger [14] vt startle. ‹cogerse vpr be startled. ‹cubierta f dust cover. ‹dicho a aforementioned. ‹entender [1] vt understand, infer. ‹entendido a implicit. ‹humano a superhuman. ‹llevar vt bear. ‹mesa f. ● de ‹mesa after-dinner. ‹natural a supernatural. ‹nombre m nickname. ‹pasar vt exceed. ‹poner [34] vt superimpose; (fig, anteponer) put before. ‹ponerse vpr overcome. ‹pujar vt surpass. ‹saliente a (fig) outstanding. ● m excellent mark. ‹salir [52] vi stick out; (fig) stand out. ‹saltar vt startle. ‹salto m fright. ‹sueldo m bonus. ‹todo m overall; (abrigo) overcoat. ‹ todo above all, especially. ‹venir [53] vi happen. ‹viviente a surviving. ● m & f survivor. ‹vivir vi survive. ‹volar vt fly over
sobriedad f restraint
sobrin|a f niece. ‹o m nephew
sobrio a moderate, sober
socarr|ón a sarcastic; (taimado) sly. ‹onería f sarcasm
socavar vt undermine
soci|able a sociable. ‹al a social. ‹aldemocracia f social democracy. ‹aldemócrata m & f social democrat. ‹alismo m socialism. ‹alista a & m & f socialist. ‹alizar [10] vt nationalize. ‹edad f society; (com) company. ‹edad anónima limited company. ‹o m member; (com) partner. ‹ología f sociology. ‹ólogo m sociologist
socorr|er vt help. ‹o m help
soda f (bebida) soda (water)
sodio m sodium
sofá m sofa, settee

sofistica|ción f sophistication. ‹do a sophisticated. ‹r [7] vt adulterate
sofoca|ción f suffocation. ‹nte a (fig) stifling. ‹r [7] vt suffocate; (fig) stifle. ‹rse vpr suffocate; (ruborizarse) blush
soga f rope
soja f soya (bean)
sojuzgar [12] vt subdue
sol m sun; (luz solar) sunlight; (mus) G; (solfa) soh. **al ‹** in the sun. **día** m **de ‹** sunny day. **hace ‹, hay ‹** it is sunny. **tomar el ‹** sunbathe
solamente adv only
solapa f lapel; (de bolsillo etc) flap. ‹do a sly. ‹r vt/i overlap
solar a solar. ● m plot
solariego a ‹casa› ancestral
solaz m relaxation
soldado m soldier. ‹ raso private
solda|dor m welder; (utensilio) soldering iron. ‹r [2] vt weld, solder
solea|do a sunny. ‹r vt put in the sun
soledad f solitude; (aislamiento) loneliness
solemn|e a solemn. ‹idad f solemnity; (ceremonia) ceremony
soler [2] vi be in the habit of. **suele despertarse a las 6** he usually wakes up at 6 o'clock
sol|icitar vt request; apply for ‹empleo›; attract ‹atención›. ‹ícito a solicitous. ‹icitud f (atención) concern; (petición) request; (para un puesto) application
solidaridad f solidarity
solid|ez f solidity; (de color) fastness. ‹ificar [7] vt solidify. ‹ificarse vpr solidify
sólido a solid; ‹color› fast; (robusto) strong. ● m solid
soliloquio m soliloquy
solista m & f soloist
solitario a solitary; (aislado) lonely. ● m recluse; (juego, diamante) solitaire
solo a (sin compañía) alone; (aislado) lonely; (único) only; (mus) solo; (café) black. ● m solo; (juego) solitaire. **a solas** alone
sólo adv only. ‹ **que** only. **aunque** ‹ **sea** even if it is only. **con** ‹ **que** if; (con tal que) as long as. **no** ‹... **sino también** not only... but also... **tan** ‹ only
solomillo m sirloin
solsticio m solstice

soltar [2] *vt* let go of; (*dejar caer*) drop; (*dejar salir, decir*) let out; give (*golpe etc*). ~**se** *vpr* come undone; (*librarse*) break loose

solter|**a** *f* single woman. ~**o** *a* single. ● *m* bachelor. **apellido** *m* **de** ~**a** maiden name

soltura *f* looseness; (*agilidad*) agility; (*en hablar*) ease, fluency

solu|**ble** *a* soluble. ~**ción** *f* solution. ~**cionar** *vt* solve; settle (*huelga, asunto*)

solvent|**ar** *vt* resolve; settle (*deuda*). ~**e** *a & m* solvent

sollo *m* sturgeon

solloz|**ar** [10] *vi* sob. ~**o** *m* sob

sombr|**a** *f* shade; (*imagen oscura*) shadow. ~**eado** *a* shady. **a la** ~**a** in the shade

sombrero *m* hat. ~ **hongo** bowler hat

sombrío *a* sombre

somero *a* shallow

someter *vt* subdue; subject (*persona*); (*presentar*) submit. ~**se** *vpr* give in

somn|**oliento** *a* sleepy. ~**ífero** *m* sleeping-pill

somos *vb véase* **ser**

son *m* sound. ● *vb véase* **ser**

sonámbulo *m* sleepwalker

sonar [2] *vt* blow; ring (*timbre*). ● *vi* sound; (*timbre, teléfono etc*) ring; (*reloj*) strike; (*pronunciarse*) be pronounced; (*mus*) play; (*fig, ser conocido*) be familiar. ~**se** *vpr* blow one's nose. ~ **a** sound like

sonata *f* sonata

sonde|**ar** *vt* sound; (*fig*) sound out. ~**o** *m* sounding; (*fig*) poll

soneto *m* sonnet

sónico *a* sonic

sonido *m* sound

sonoro *a* sonorous; (*ruidoso*) loud

sonr|**eír** [51] *vi* smile. ~**eírse** *vpr* smile. ~**iente** *a* smiling. ~**isa** *f* smile

sonroj|**ar** *vt* make blush. ~**arse** *vpr* blush. ~**o** *m* blush

sonrosado *a* rosy, pink

sonsacar [7] *vt* wheedle out

soñ|**ado** *a* dream. ~**ador** *m* dreamer. ~**ar** [2] *vi* dream (**con** of). **¡ni** ~**arlo!** not likely! (**que**) **ni** ~**ado** marvellous

sopa *f* soup

sopesar *vt* (*fig*) weigh up

sopl|**ar** *vt* blow; blow out (*vela*); blow off (*polvo*); (*inflar*) blow up. ● *vi* blow. ~**ete** *m* blowlamp. ~**o** *m* puff; (*fig, momento*) moment

soporífero *a* soporific. ● *m* sleeping-pill

soport|**al** *m* porch. ~**ales** *mpl* arcade. ~**ar** *vt* support; (*fig*) bear. ~**e** *m* support

soprano *f* soprano

sor *f* sister

sorb|**er** *vt* suck; sip (*bebida*); (*absorber*) absorb. ~**ete** *m* sorbet, water-ice. ~**o** *m* swallow; (*pequeña cantidad*) sip

sord|**amente** *adv* silently, dully. ~**era** *f* deafness

sórdido *a* squalid; (*tacaño*) mean

sordo *a* deaf; (*silencioso*) quiet. ● *m* deaf person. ~**mudo** *a* deaf and dumb. **a la sorda, a sordas** on the quiet. **hacerse el** ~ turn a deaf ear

sorna *f* sarcasm. **con** ~ sarcastically

soroche *m* (*LAm*) mountain sickness

sorpren|**dente** *a* surprising. ~**nder** *vt* surprise; (*coger desprevenido*) catch. ~**sa** *f* surprise

sorte|**ar** *vt* draw lots for; (*rifar*) raffle; (*fig*) avoid. ● *vi* draw lots; (*con moneda*) toss up. ~**o** *m* draw; (*rifa*) raffle; (*fig*) avoidance

sortija *f* ring; (*de pelo*) ringlet

sortilegio *m* witchcraft; (*fig*) spell

sos|**egado** *a* calm. ~**egar** [1 & 12] *vt* calm. ● *vi* rest. ~**iego** *m* calmness. **con** ~**iego** calmly

soslayo. al ~, **de** ~ sideways

soso *a* tasteless; (*fig*) dull

sospech|**a** *f* suspicion. ~**ar** *vt/i* suspect. ~**oso** *a* suspicious. ● *m* suspect

sost|**én** *m* support; (*prenda femenina*) bra (*fam*), brassière. ~**ener** [40] *vt* support; (*sujetar*) hold; (*mantener*) maintain; (*alimentar*) sustain. ~**enerse** *vpr* support o.s.; (*continuar*) remain. ~**enido** *a* sustained; (*mus*) sharp. ● *m* (*mus*) sharp

sota *f* (*de naipes*) jack

sótano *m* basement

sotavento *m* lee

soto *m* grove; (*matorral*) thicket

soviético *a* (*historia*) Soviet

soy *vb véase* **ser**

Sr *abrev* (*Señor*) Mr. ~ **a** *abrev* (*Señora*) Mrs. ~**ta** *abrev* (*Señorita*) Miss

su *a* (*de él*) his; (*de ella*) her; (*de ello*) its; (*de uno*) one's; (*de Vd*) your; (*de ellos, de ellas*) their; (*de Vds*) your

suav|e *a* smooth; (*fig*) gentle; (*color, sonido*) soft. ~**idad** *f* smoothness, softness. ~**izar** [10] *vt* smooth, soften

subalimentado *a* underfed

subalterno *a* secondary; (*persona*) auxiliary

subarrendar [1] *vt* sublet

subasta *f* auction; (*oferta*) tender. ~**r** *vt* auction

sub|campeón *m* runner-up. ~**consciencia** *f* subconscious. ~**consciente** *a* & *m* subconscious. ~**continente** *m* subcontinent. ~**desarrollado** *a* under-developed. ~**director** *m* assistant manager

súbdito *m* subject

sub|dividir *vt* subdivide. ~**estimar** *vt* underestimate. ~**gerente** *m* & *f* assistant manager

subi|da *f* ascent; (*aumento*) rise; (*pendiente*) slope. ~**do** *a* (*precio*) high; (*color*) bright; (*olor*) strong. ~**r** *vt* go up; (*poner*) put; (*llevar*) take up; (*aumentar*) increase. ● *vi* go up. ~**r** *a* get into (*coche*); get on (*autobús, avión, barco, tren*); (*aumentar*) increase. ~**rse** *vpr* climb up. ~**rse** *a* get on (*tren etc*)

súbito *a* sudden. ● *adv* suddenly. **de ~** suddenly

subjetivo *a* subjective

subjuntivo *a* & *m* subjunctive

subleva|ción *f* uprising. ~**r** *vt* incite to rebellion. ~**rse** *vpr* rebel

sublim|ar *vt* sublimate. ~**e** *a* sublime

submarino *a* underwater. ● *m* submarine

subordinado *a* & *m* subordinate

subrayar *vt* underline

subrepticio *a* surreptitious

subsanar *vt* remedy; overcome (*dificultad*)

subscri|bir *vt* (*pp* subscrito) sign. ~**birse** *vpr* subscribe. ~**pción** *f* subscription

subsidi|ario *a* subsidiary. ~**o** *m* subsidy. ~**o de paro** unemployment benefit

subsiguiente *a* subsequent

subsist|encia *f* subsistence. ~**ir** *vi* subsist; (*perdurar*) survive

substanci|a *f* substance. ~**al** *a* important. ~**oso** *a* substantial

substantivo *m* noun

substitu|ción *f* substitution. ~**ir** [17] *vt/i* substitute. ~**to** *a* & *m* substitute

substraer [41] *vt* take away

subterfugio *m* subterfuge

subterráneo *a* underground. ● *m* (*bodega*) cellar; (*conducto*) underground passage

subtítulo *m* subtitle

suburb|ano *a* suburban. ● *m* suburban train. ~**io** *m* suburb; (*en barrio pobre*) slum

subvenci|ón *f* grant. ~**onar** *vt* subsidize

subver|sión *f* subversion. ~**sivo** *a* subversive. ~**tir** [4] *vt* subvert

subyugar [12] *vt* subjugate; (*fig*) subdue

succión *f* suction

suce|der *vi* happen; (*seguir*) follow; (*substituir*) succeed. ~**dido** *m* event. **lo ~dido** what happened. ~**sión** *f* succession. ~**sivo** *a* successive; (*consecutivo*) consecutive. ~**so** *m* event; (*incidente*) incident. ~**sor** *m* successor. **en lo ~sivo** in future. **lo que ~de es que** the trouble is that. **¿qué ~de?** what's the matter?

suciedad *f* dirt; (*estado*) dirtiness

sucinto *a* concise; (*prenda*) scanty

sucio *a* dirty; (*vil*) mean; (*conciencia*) guilty. **en ~** in rough

sucre *m* (*unidad monetaria del Ecuador*) sucre

suculento *a* succulent

sucumbir *vi* succumb

sucursal *f* branch (office)

Sudáfrica *m* & *f* South Africa

sudafricano *a* & *m* South African

Sudamérica *f* South America

sudamericano *a* & *m* South American

sudar *vt* work hard for. ● *vi* sweat

sud|este *m* south-east; (*viento*) south-east wind. ~**oeste** *m* south-west; (*viento*) south-west wind

sudor *m* sweat

Suecia *f* Sweden

sueco *a* Swedish. ● *m* (*persona*) Swede; (*lengua*) Swedish. **hacerse el ~** pretend not to hear

suegr|a *f* mother-in-law. ~**o** *m* father-in-law. **mis ~os** my in-laws

suela *f* sole

sueldo *m* salary

suelo *m* ground; (*dentro de edificio*) floor; (*tierra*) land. ● *vb véase* **soler**

suelto *a* loose; (*libre*) free; (*sin pareja*) odd; (*lenguaje*) fluent. ● *m* (*en periódico*) item; (*dinero*) change

sueño *m* sleep; (*ilusión*) dream. **tener ~** be sleepy

suero m serum; (de leche) whey
suerte f luck; (destino) fate; (azar) chance. **de otra ~** otherwise. **de ~ que** so. **echar ~s** draw lots. **por ~** fortunately. **tener ~** be lucky
suéter m jersey
suficien|cia f sufficiency; (presunción) smugness; (aptitud) suitability. **~te** a sufficient; (presumido) smug. **~temente** adv enough
sufijo m suffix
sufragio m (voto) vote
sufri|do a (persona) long-suffering; (tela) hard-wearing. **~miento** m suffering. **~r** vt suffer; (experimentar) undergo; (soportar) bear. • vi suffer
suge|rencia f suggestion. **~rir** [4] vt suggest. **~stión** f suggestion. **~stionable** a impressionable. **~stionar** vt influence. **~stivo** a (estimulante) stimulating; (atractivo) attractive
suicid|a a suicidal. • m & f suicide; (fig) maniac. **~arse** vpr commit suicide. **~io** m suicide
Suiza f Switzerland
suizo a Swiss. • m Swiss; (bollo) bun
suje|ción f subjection. **~tador** m fastener; (de pelo, papeles etc) clip; (prenda femenina) bra, (fam), brassière. **~tapapeles** m invar paper-clip. **~tar** vt fasten; (agarrar) hold; (fig) restrain. **~tarse** vpr subject o.s.; (ajustarse) conform. **~to** a fastened; (susceptible) subject. • m individual
sulfamida f sulpha (drug)
sulfúrico a sulphuric
sult|án m sultan. **~ana** f sultana
suma f sum; (total) total. **en ~** in short. **~mente** adv extremely. **~r** vt add (up); (fig) gather. • vi add up. **~rse** vpr. **~rse a** join in
sumario a brief. • m summary; (jurid) indictment
sumergi|ble m submarine. • a submersible. **~r** [14] vt submerge
sumidero m drain
suministr|ar vt supply. **~o** m supply; (acción) supplying
sumir vt sink; (fig) plunge
sumis|ión f submission. **~o** a submissive
sumo a greatest; (supremo) supreme. **a lo ~** at the most
suntuoso a sumptuous
supe vb véase **saber**

superar vt surpass; (vencer) overcome; (dejar atrás) get past. **~se** vpr excel o.s.
superchería f swindle
superestructura f superstructure
superfici|al a superficial. **~e** f surface; (extensión) area. **de ~e** surface
superfluo a superfluous
superhombre m superman
superintendente m superintendent
superior a superior; (más alto) higher; (mejor) better; (piso) upper. • m superior. **~idad** f superiority
superlativo a & m superlative
supermercado m supermarket
supersónico a supersonic
supersti|ción f superstition. **~oso** a superstitious
supervis|ión f supervision. **~or** m supervisor
superviviente a surviving. • m & f survivor
suplantar vt supplant
suplement|ario a supplementary. **~o** m supplement
suplente a & m & f substitute
súplica f entreaty; (petición) request
suplicar [7] vt beg
suplicio m torture
suplir vt make up for; (reemplazar) replace
supo|ner [34] vt suppose; (significar) mean; (costar) cost. **~sición** f supposition
supositorio m suppository
suprem|acía f supremacy. **~o** a supreme; (momento etc) critical
supr|esión f suppression. **~imir** vt suppress; (omitir) omit
supuesto a supposed. • m assumption. **~ que** if. **¡por ~!** of course!
sur m south; (viento) south wind
surc|ar [7] vt plough. **~o** m furrow; (de rueda) rut; (en la piel) wrinkle
surgir [14] vi spring up; (elevarse) loom up; (aparecer) appear; (dificultad, oportunidad) arise, crop up
surrealis|mo m surrealism. **~ta** a & m & f surrealist
surti|do a well-stocked; (variado) assorted. • m assortment, selection. **~dor** m (de gasolina) petrol pump (Brit), gas pump (Amer). **~r** vt supply; have (efecto). **~rse** vpr provide o.s. (de with)
susceptib|ilidad f susceptibility; (sensibilidad) sensitivity. **~le** a susceptible; (sensible) sensitive

suscitar vt provoke; arouse ⟨curiosidad, interés, sospechas⟩

suscr... véase **subscr...**

susodicho a aforementioned

suspen|der vt hang (up); (interrumpir) suspend; (univ etc) fail. **~derse** vpr stop. **~sión** f suspension. **~so** a hanging; (pasmado) amazed; (univ etc) failed. ● m fail. **en ~so** pending

suspicaz a suspicious

suspir|ar vi sigh. **~o** m sigh

sust... véase **subst...**

sustent|ación f support. **~ar** vt support; (alimentar) sustain; (mantener) maintain. **~o** m support; (alimento) sustenance

susto m fright. **caerse del ~** be frightened to death

susurr|ar vi ⟨persona⟩ whisper; ⟨agua⟩ murmur; ⟨hojas⟩ rustle. **~o** m (de persona) whisper; (de agua) murmur; (de hojas) rustle

sutil a fine; (fig) subtle. **~eza** f fineness; (fig) subtlety

suyo a & pron (de él) his; (de ella) hers; (de ello) its; (de uno) one's; (de Vd) yours; (de ellos, de ellas) theirs; (de Vds) yours. **un amigo ~** a friend of his, a friend of theirs, etc

T

taba f (anat) ankle-bone; (juego) jacks

tabac|alera f (state) tobacconist. **~alero** a tobacco. **~o** m tobacco; (cigarillos) cigarettes; (rapé) snuff

tabalear vi drum (with one's fingers)

Tabasco m Tabasco (**P**)

tabern|a f bar. **~ero** m barman; (dueño) landlord

tabernáculo m tabernacle

tabique m (thin) wall

tabl|a f plank; (de piedra etc) slab; (estante) shelf; (de vestido) pleat; (lista) list; (índice) index; (en matemática etc) table. **~ado** m platform; (en el teatro) stage. **~ao** m place where flamenco shows are held. **~as reales** backgammon. **~ero** m board. **~ero de mandos** dashboard. **hacer ~a rasa de** disregard

tableta f tablet; (de chocolate) bar

tabl|illa f small board. **~ón** m plank. **~ón de anuncios** notice board (esp Brit), bulletin board (Amer)

tabú m taboo

tabular vt tabulate

taburete m stool

tacaño a mean

tacita f small cup

tácito a tacit

taciturno a taciturn; (triste) miserable

taco m plug; (LAm, tacón) heel; (de billar) cue; (de billetes) book; (fig, lío, fam) mess; (Mex, culin) filled tortilla

tacógrafo m tachograph

tacón m heel

táctic|a f tactics. **~o** a tactical

táctil a tactile

tacto m touch; (fig) tact

tacuara f (Arg) bamboo

tacurú m (small) ant

tacha f fault; (clavo) tack. **poner ~s a** find fault with. **sin ~** flawless

tachar vt (borrar) rub out; (con raya) cross out. **~ de** accuse of

tafia f (LAm) rum

tafilete m morocco

tahúr m card-sharp

Tailandia f Thailand

tailandés a & m Thai

taimado a sly

taj|ada f slice. **~ante** a sharp. **~o** m slash; (fig, trabajo, fam) job; (culin) chopping block. **sacar ~ada** profit

Tajo m Tagus

tal a such; (ante sustantivo en singular) such a. ● pron (persona) someone; (cosa) such a thing. ● adv so; (de tal manera) in such a way. **~ como** the way. **~ cual** (tal como) the way; (regular) fair. **~ para cual** (fam) two of a kind. **con ~ que** as long as. **¿qué ~?** how are you? **un ~** a certain

taladr|ar vt drill. **~o** m drill; (agujero) drill hole

talante m mood. **de buen ~** willingly

talar vt fell; (fig) destroy

talco m talcum powder

talcualillo a (fam) so so

talega f, **talego** m sack

talento m talent

TALGO m high-speed train

talismán m talisman

tal|ón m heel; (recibo) counterfoil; (cheque) cheque. **~onario** m receipt book; (de cheques) cheque book

talla f carving; (grabado) engraving; (de piedra preciosa) cutting; (estatura) height; (medida) size; (palo) measuring stick; (*Arg, charla*) gossip. ∿do *a* carved. ● *m* carving. ∿dor *m* engraver

tallarín *m* noodle

talle *m* waist; (*figura*) figure; (*medida*) size

taller *m* workshop; (*de pintor etc*) studio

tallo *m* stem, stalk

tamal *m* (*LAm*) tamale

tamaño *a* (*tan grande*) so big a; (*tan pequeño*) so small a. ● *m* size. de ∿ natural life-size

tambalearse *vpr* (*persona*) stagger; (*cosa*) wobble

también *adv* also, too

tambor *m* drum. ∿ del freno brake drum. ∿ilear *vi* drum

Támesis *m* Thames

tamiz *m* sieve. ∿ar[10] *vt* sieve

tampoco *adv* nor, neither, not either

tampón *m* tampon; (*para entintar*) ink-pad

tan *adv* so. tan... ∿ as... as

tanda *f* group; (*capa*) layer; (*de obreros*) shift

tangente *a* & *f* tangent

Tánger *m* Tangier

tangible *a* tangible

tango *m* tango

tanque *m* tank; (*camión, barco*) tanker

tante|ar *vt* estimate; (*ensayar*) test; (*fig*) weigh up. ● *vi* score. ∿o *m* estimate; (*prueba*) test; (*en deportes*) score

tanto *a* (*en singular*) so much; (*en plural*) so many; (*comparación en singular*) as much; (*comparación en plural*) as many. ● *pron* so much; (*en plural*) so many. ● *adv* so much; (*tiempo*) so long. ● *m* certain amount; (*punto*) point; (*gol*) goal. ∿ como as well as; (*cantidad*) as much as. ∿ más... cuanto que all the more... because. ∿ si... como si whether... or. a ∿s de sometime in. en ∿, entre ∿ meanwhile. en ∿ que while. entre ∿ meanwhile. estar al ∿ de be up to date with. hasta ∿ que until. no es para ∿ it's not as bad as all that. otro ∿ the same; (*el doble*) as much again. por (lo) ∿ so. un ∿ *adv* somewhat

tañer[22] *vt* play

tapa *f* lid; (*de botella*) top; (*de libro*) cover. ∿s *fpl* savoury snacks

tapacubos *m invar* hub-cap

tapa|dera *f* cover, lid; (*fig*) cover. ∿r *vt* cover; (*abrigar*) wrap up; (*obturar*) plug; put the top on (*botella*)

taparrabo(s) *m invar* loincloth; (*bañador*) swimming-trunks

tapete *m* (*de mesa*) table cover; (*alfombra*) rug

tapia *f* wall. ∿r *vt* enclose

tapicería *f* tapestry; (*de muebles*) upholstery

tapioca *f* tapioca

tapiz *m* tapestry. ∿ar [10] *vt* hang with tapestries; upholster (*muebles*)

tap|ón *m* stopper; (*corcho*) cork; (*med*) tampon; (*tec*) plug. ∿onazo *m* pop

taqu|igrafía *f* shorthand. ∿ígrafo *m* shorthand writer

taquill|a *f* ticket office; (*archivador*) filing cabinet; (*fig, dinero*) takings. ∿ero *m* clerk, ticket seller. ● *a* box-office

tara *f* (*peso*) tare; (*defecto*) defect

taracea *f* marquetry

tarántula *f* tarantula

tararear *vt/i* hum

tarda|nza *f* delay. ∿r *vi* take; (*mucho tiempo*) take a long time. a más ∿r at the latest. sin ∿r without delay

tard|e *adv* late. ● *f* (*antes del atardecer*) afternoon; (*después del atardecer*) evening. ∿e o temprano sooner or later. ∿ío a late. de ∿e en ∿e from time to time. por la ∿e in the afternoon

tardo *a* (*torpe*) slow

tarea *f* task, job

tarifa *f* rate, tariff

tarima *f* platform

tarjeta *f* card. ∿ de crédito credit card. ∿ postal postcard

tarro *m* jar

tarta *f* cake; (*torta*) tart. ∿ helada ice-cream gateau

tartamud|ear *vi* stammer. ∿o *a* stammering. ● *m* stammerer. es ∿o he stammers

tártaro *m* tartar

tarugo *m* chunk

tasa *f* valuation; (*precio*) fixed price; (*índice*) rate. ∿r *vt* fix a price for; (*limitar*) ration; (*evaluar*) value

tasca *f* bar

tatarabuel|a *f* great-great-grandmother. ∿o *m* great-great-grandfather

tatua|je *m* (*acción*) tattooing; (*dibujo*) tattoo. ∿r[21] *vt* tattoo

taurino a bullfighting

Tauro m Taurus

tauromaquia f bullfighting

tax|i m taxi. ~**ímetro** m taxi meter. ~**ista** m & f taxi-driver

tayuyá m (Arg) water melon

taz|a f cup. ~**ón** m bowl

te pron (acusativo) you; (dativo) (to) you; (reflexivo) (to) yourself

té m tea. **dar el** ~ bore

tea f torch

teatr|al a theatre; (exagerado) theatrical. ~**alizar** [10] vt dramatize. ~**o** m theatre; (literatura) drama. **obra** f ~**al** play

tebeo m comic

teca f teak

tecla f key. ~**do** m keyboard. **tocar la** ~, **tocar una** ~ pull strings

técnica f technique

tecn|icismo m technicality

técnico a technical. ● m technician

tecnol|ogía f technology. ~**ógico** a technological

tecolote m (Mex) owl

tecomate m (Mex) earthenware cup

tech|ado m roof. ~**ar** vt roof. ~**o** m (interior) ceiling; (exterior) roof. ~**umbre** f roofing. **bajo** ~**ado** indoors

teja f tile. ~**do** m roof. **a toca** ~ cash

teje|dor m weaver. ~**r** vt weave; (hacer punto) knit

tejemaneje m (fam) fuss; (intriga) scheming

tejido m material; (anat, fig) tissue. ~**s** mpl textiles

tejón m badger

tela f material; (de araña) web; (en líquido) skin

telar m loom. ~**es** mpl textile mill

telaraña f spider's web, cobweb

tele f (fam) television

tele|comunicación f telecommunication. ~**diario** m television news. ~**dirigido** a remote-controlled. ~**férico** m cable-car; (tren) cable-railway

tel|efonear vt/i telephone. ~**efónico** a telephone. ~**efonista** m & f telephonist. ~**éfono** m telephone. **al** ~**éfono** on the phone

tel|egrafía f telegraphy. ~**egrafiar** [20] vt telegraph. ~**egráfico** a telegraphic. ~**égrafo** m telegraph

telegrama m telegram

telenovela f television soap opera

teleobjetivo m telephoto lens

telep|atía f telepathy. ~**ático** a telepathic

telesc|ópico a telescopic. ~**opio** m telescope

telesilla m ski-lift, chair-lift

telespectador m viewer

telesquí m ski-lift

televi|dente m & f viewer. ~**sar** vt televise. ~**sión** f television. ~**sor** m television (set)

télex m telex

telón m curtain. ~ **de acero** (historia) Iron Curtain

tema m subject; (mus) theme

tembl|ar [1] vi shake; (de miedo) tremble; (de frío) shiver; (fig) shudder. ~**or** m shaking; (de miedo) trembling; (de frío) shivering. ~**or de tierra** earthquake. ~**oroso** a trembling

temer vt be afraid (of). ● vi be afraid. ~**se** vpr be afraid

temerario a reckless

tem|eroso a frightened. ~**ible** a fearsome. ~**or** m fear

témpano m floe

temperamento m temperament

temperatura f temperature

temperie f weather

tempest|ad f storm. ~**uoso** a stormy. **levantar** ~**ades** (fig) cause a storm

templ|ado a moderate; (tibio) warm; ‹clima, tiempo› mild; (valiente) courageous; (listo) bright. ~**anza** f moderation; (de clima o tiempo) mildness. ~**ar** vt temper; (calentar) warm; (mus) tune. ~**e** m tempering; (temperatura) temperature; (humor) mood

templ|ete m niche; (pabellón) pavilion. ~**o** m temple

tempora|da f time; (época) season. ~**l** a temporary. ● m (tempestad) storm; (período de lluvia) rainy spell

tempran|ero a ‹frutos› early. ~**o** a & adv early. **ser** ~**ero** be an early riser

tena|cidad f tenacity

tenacillas fpl tongs

tenaz a tenacious

tenaza f, **tenazas** fpl pliers; (para arrancar clavos) pincers; (para el fuego, culin) tongs

tende|ncia f tendency. ~**nte** a. ~**nte a** aimed at. ~**r** [1] vt spread (out); hang out ‹ropa a secar›; (colocar) lay. ● vi have a tendency (a to). ~**rse** vpr stretch out

tender|ete m stall. ~**o** m shop-keeper

tendido a spread out; ⟨ropa⟩ hung out; ⟨persona⟩ stretched out. ● m (en plaza de toros) front rows. ~**s** mpl ⟨ropa lavada⟩ washing

tendón m tendon

tenebroso a gloomy; (turbio) shady

tenedor m fork; (poseedor) holder

tener [40] vt have (got); (agarrar) hold; be ⟨años, calor, celos, cuidado, frío, ganas, hambre, miedo, razón, sed etc⟩. **¡ten cuidado!** be careful! **tengo calor** I'm hot. **tiene 3 años** he's 3 (years old). ~**se** vpr stand up; (considerarse) consider o.s., think o.s. ~ **al corriente**, ~ **al día** keep up to date. ~ **2 cm de largo** be 2 cms long. ~ **a uno por** consider s.o. ~ **que** have (got) to. **tenemos que comprar pan** we've got to buy some bread. **¡ahí tienes!** there you are! **no ~ nada que ver con** have nothing to do with. **¿qué tienes?** what's the matter (with you)? **¡tenga!** here you are!

tengo vb véase **tener**

teniente m lieutenant. ~ **de alcalde** deputy mayor

tenis m tennis. ~**ta** m & f tennis player

tenor m sense; (mus) tenor. **a este** ~ in this fashion

tens|ión f tension; (presión) pressure; (arterial) blood pressure; (elec) voltage; (de persona) tenseness. ~**o** a tense

tentación f temptation

tentáculo m tentacle

tenta|dor a tempting. ~**r** [1] vt feel; (seducir) tempt

tentativa f attempt

tenue a thin; (luz, voz) faint

teñi|do m dye. ~**r** [5 & 22] vt dye; (fig) tinge (**de** with). ~**rse** vpr dye one's hair

te|ología f theology. ~**ológico** a theological. ~**ólogo** m theologian

teorema m theorem

te|oría f theory. ~**órico** a theoretical

tepache m (Mex) (alcoholic) drink

tequila f tequila

TER m high-speed train

terap|éutico a therapeutic. ~**ia** f therapy

tercer a véase **tercero**. ~**a** f (auto) third (gear). ~**o** a (delante de nombre masculino en singular **tercer**) third. ● m third party

terceto m trio

terciar vi mediate. ~ **en** join in. ~**se** vpr occur

tercio m third

terciopelo m velvet

terco a obstinate

tergiversar vt distort

terma|l a thermal. ~**s** fpl thermal baths

termes m invar termite

térmico a thermal

termina|ción f ending; (conclusión) conclusion. ~**l** a & m terminal. ~**nte** a categorical. ~**r** vt finish, end. ~**rse** vpr come to an end. ~**r por** end up

término m end; (palabra) term; (plazo) period. ~ **medio** average. ~ **municipal** municipal district. **dar** ~ **a** finish off. **en último** ~ as a last resort. **estar en buenos** ~**s con** be on good terms with. **llevar a** ~ carry out. **poner** ~ **a** put an end to. **primer** ~ foreground

terminología f terminology

termita f termite

termo m Thermos flask (P), flask

termómetro m thermometer

termo|nuclear a thermonuclear. ~**sifón** m boiler. ~**stato** m thermostat

terner|a f (carne) veal. ~**o** m calf

ternura f tenderness

terquedad f stubbornness

terracota f terracotta

terrado m flat roof

terraplén m embankment

terrateniente m & f landowner

terraza f terrace; (terrado) flat roof

terremoto m earthquake

terre|no a earthly. ● m land; (solar) plot; (fig) field. ~**stre** a earthly; (mil) ground

terr|ible a terrible. ~**iblemente** adv awfully. ~**ífico** a terrifying

territori|al a territorial. ~**o** m territory

terrón m (de tierra) clod; (culin) lump

terror m terror. ~**ífico** a terrifying. ~**ismo** m terrorism. ~**ista** m & f terrorist

terr|oso a earthy; (color) brown. ~**uño** m land; (patria) native land

terso a polished; (piel) smooth

tertulia f social gathering, get-together (fam). ~**r** vi (LAm) get together. **estar de** ~ chat. **hacer** ~ get together

tesi|na f dissertation. ~**s** f invar thesis; (opinión) theory

tesón m perseverance

tesor|ería f treasury. ~**ero** m treasurer. ~**o** m treasure; (tesorería) treasury; (libro) thesaurus

testa f (fam) head. ~**ferro** m figurehead

testa|mento m will. **T~mento** (relig) Testament. ~**r** vi make a will

testarudo a stubborn

testículo m testicle

testi|ficar [7] vt/i testify. ~**go** m witness. ~**go de vista**, ~**go ocular**, ~**go presencial** eyewitness. ~**monio** m testimony

teta f nipple; (de biberón) teat

tétanos m tetanus

tetera f (para el té) teapot; (Mex, biberón) feeding-bottle

tetilla f nipple; (de biberón) teat

tétrico a gloomy

textil a & m textile

text|o m text. ~**ual** a textual

textura f texture

teyú m (Arg) iguana

tez f complexion

ti pron you

tía f aunt; (fam) woman

tiara f tiara

tibio a lukewarm. **ponerle** ~ **a uno** insult s.o.

tiburón m shark

tic m tic

tiempo m time; (atmosférico) weather; (mus) tempo; (gram) tense; (en deportes) half. **a su** ~ in due course. **a** ~ in time. **¿cuánto** ~? how long? **hace buen** ~ the weather is fine. **hace** ~ some time ago. **mucho** ~ a long time. **perder el** ~ waste time. **¿qué** ~ **hace?** what is the weather like?

tienda f shop; (de campaña) tent. ~ **de comestibles**, ~ **de ultramarinos** grocer's (shop) (Brit), grocery store (Amer)

tiene vb véase **tener**

tienta. a ~**s** gropingly. **andar a** ~**s** grope one's way

tiento m touch; (de ciego) blind person's stick; (fig) tact

tierno a tender; (joven) young

tierra f land; (planeta, elec) earth; (suelo) ground; (geol) soil, earth. **caer**

por ~ (fig) crumble. **por** ~ overland, by land

tieso a stiff; (firme) firm; (engreído) conceited; (orgulloso) proud

tiesto m flowerpot

tifoideo a typhoid

tifón m typhoon

tifus m typhus; (fiebre tifoidea) typhoid (fever); (en el teatro) people with complimentary tickets

tigre m tiger

tijera f. **tijeras** fpl scissors; (de jardín) shears

tijeret|a f (insecto) earwig; (bot) tendril. ~**ear** vt snip

tila f lime(-tree); (infusión) lime tea

tild|ar vt. ~**ar de** (fig) call. ~**e** m tilde

tilín m tinkle. **hacer** ~ appeal

tilingo a (Arg, Mex) silly

tilma f (Mex) poncho

tilo m lime(-tree)

timar vt swindle

timbal m drum; (culin) timbale, meat pie

timbiriche m (Mex) (alcoholic) drink

timbr|ar vt stamp. ~**e** m (sello) stamp; (elec) bell; (sonido) timbre. **tocar el** ~**e** ring the bell

timidez f shyness

tímido a shy

timo m swindle

timón m rudder; (fig) helm

tímpano m kettledrum; (anat) eardrum. ~**s** mpl (mus) timpani

tina f tub. ~**ja** f large earthenware jar

tinglado m (fig) intrigue

tinieblas fpl darkness; (fig) confusion

tino f (habilidad) skill; (moderación) moderation; (tacto) tact

tint|a f ink. ~**e** m dyeing; (color) dye; (fig) tinge. ~**ero** m ink-well. **de buena** ~**a** on good authority

tint|ín m tinkle; (de vasos) chink, clink. ~**inear** vi tinkle; (vasos) chink, clink

tinto a (vino) red

tintorería f dyeing; (tienda) dry cleaner's

tintura f dyeing; (color) dye; (noción superficial) smattering

tío m uncle; (fam) man. ~**s** mpl uncle and aunt

tiovivo m merry-go-round

típico a typical

tipo m type; (persona, fam) person; (figura de mujer) figure; (figura de hombre) build; (com) rate tip|ografía f typography. ∼ográfico a typographic(al). ∼ógrafo m printer

típula f crane-fly, daddy-long-legs

tique m, tiquet m ticket

tiquete m (LAm) ticket

tira f strip. la ∼ de lots of

tirabuzón m corkscrew; (de pelo) ringlet

tirad|a f distance; (serie) series; (de libros etc) edition. ∼o a (barato) very cheap; (fácil, fam) very easy. ∼or m (asa) handle; (juguete) catapult (Brit), slingshot (Amer). de una ∼a at one go

tiran|ía f tyranny. ∼izar [10] vt tyrannize. ∼o a tyrannical. ● m tyrant

tirante a tight; (fig) tense; (relaciones) strained. ● m shoulder strap. ∼s mpl braces (esp Brit), suspenders (Amer)

tirar vt throw; (desechar) throw away; (derribar) knock over; give (golpe, coz etc); (imprimir) print. ● vi (disparar) shoot. ∼se vpr throw o.s.; (tumbarse) lie down. ∼a tend to (be); (parecerse a) resemble. ∼ de pull; (atraer) attract. a todo ∼ at the most. ir tirando get by

tirita f sticking-plaster, plaster (Brit)

tirit|ar vi shiver. ∼ón m shiver

tiro m throw; (disparo) shot; (alcance) range. ∼ a gol shot at goal. a ∼ within range. errar el ∼ miss. pegarse un ∼ shoot o.s.

tiroides m thyroid (gland)

tirón m tug. de un ∼ in one go

tirote|ar vt shoot at. ∼o m shooting

tisana f herb tea

tisis f tuberculosis

tisú m (pl tisus) tissue

títere m puppet. ∼ de guante glove puppet. ∼s mpl puppet show

titilar vi quiver; (estrella) twinkle

titiritero m puppeteer; (acróbata) acrobat; (malabarista) juggler

titube|ante a shaky; (fig) hesitant. ∼ar vi stagger; (cosa) be unstable; (fig) hesitate. ∼o m hesitation

titula|do a (libro) entitled; (persona) qualified. ∼r m headline; (persona) holder. ● vt call. ∼rse vpr be called

título m title; (persona) titled person; (académico) qualification; (univ) degree; (de periódico etc) headline; (derecho) right. a ∼ de as, by way of

tiza f chalk

tiz|nar vt dirty. ∼ne m soot. ∼ón m half-burnt stick; (fig) stain

toall|a f towel. ∼ero m towel-rail

tobillo m ankle

tobogán m slide; (para la nieve) toboggan

tocadiscos m invar record-player

toca|do a (con sombrero) wearing. ● m hat. ∼dor m dressing-table. ∼dor de señoras ladies' room. ∼nte a touching. ∼r [7] vt touch; (mus) play; ring (timbre); (mencionar) touch on; (barco) stop at. ● vi knock; (corresponder a uno) be one's turn. ∼rse vpr touch each other; (cubrir la cabeza) cover one's head. en lo que ∼ a, en lo ∼nte a as for. estar ∼do (de la cabeza) be mad. te ∼ a ti it's your turn

tocateja. a ∼ cash

tocayo m namesake

tocino m bacon

tocólogo m obstetrician

todavía adv still. ∼ no not yet

todo a all; (entero) the whole; (cada) every. ● adv completely, all. ● m whole. ● pron everything, all; (en plural) everyone. ∼ el día all day. ∼ el mundo everyone. ∼ el que anyone who. ∼ incluido all in. ∼ lo contrario quite the opposite. ∼ lo que anything which. ∼s los días every day. ∼s los dos both (of them). ∼s los tres all three. ante ∼ above all. a ∼ esto meanwhile. con ∼ still, however. del ∼ completely. en ∼ el mundo anywhere. estar en ∼ be on the ball. es ∼ uno it's all the same. nosotros ∼s all of us. sobre ∼ above all

toldo m sunshade

tolera|ncia f tolerance. ∼nte a tolerant. ∼r vt tolerate

tolondro m (chichón) lump

toma f taking; (med) dose; (de agua) outlet; (elec) socket; (elec, clavija) plug. ● int well!, fancy that! ∼ de corriente power point. ∼dura f. ∼dura de pelo hoax. ∼r vt take; catch (autobús, tren etc); (beber) drink, have; (comer) eat, have. ● vi take; (dirigirse) go. ∼rse vpr take; (beber) drink, have; (comer) eat, have. ∼r a bien take well. ∼r a mal take badly. ∼r en serio take seriously. ∼rla con uno pick on s.o. ∼r nota take note. ∼r por take for. ∼r y daca give and take. ¿qué va a ~r? what would you like?

tomate m tomato

tomavistas m invar cine-camera

tómbola f tombola

tomillo m thyme

tomo m volume

ton. sin ~ ni son without rhyme or reason

tonada f, tonadilla f tune

tonel m barrel. ~ada f ton. ~aje m tonnage

tónic|a f tonic water; (mus) tonic. ~o a tonic; (sílaba) stressed. ● m tonic

tonificar [7] vt invigorate

tono m tone; (mus, modo) key; (color) shade

tont|ería f silliness; (cosa) silly thing; (dicho) silly remark. ~o a silly. ● m fool, idiot; (payaso) clown. dejarse de ~erías stop wasting time. hacer el ~o act the fool. hacerse el ~o feign ignorance

topacio m topaz

topar vt (animal) butt; (persona) bump into; (fig) run into. ● vi. ~ con run into

tope a maximum. ● m end; (de tren) buffer. hasta los ~s crammed full. ir a ~ go flat out

tópico a topical. ● m cliché

topo m mole

topogr|afía f topography. ~áfico a topographical

toque m touch; (sonido) sound; (de campana) peal; (de reloj) stroke; (fig) crux. ~ de queda curfew. ~tear vt keep fingering, fiddle with. dar el último ~ put the finishing touches

toquilla f shawl

tórax m thorax

torbellino m whirlwind; (de polvo) cloud of dust; (fig) whirl

torcer [2 & 9] vt twist; (doblar) bend; wring out (ropa). ● vi turn. ~se vpr twist; (fig, desviarse) go astray; (fig, frustrarse) go wrong

tordo a dapple grey. ● m thrush

tore|ar vt fight; (evitar) dodge; (entretener) put off. ● vi fight (bulls). ~o m bullfighting. ~ro m bullfighter

torment|a f storm. ~o m torture. ~oso a stormy

tornado m tornado

tornar vt return

tornasolado a irridescent

torneo m tournament

tornillo m screw

torniquete m (entrada) turnstile

torno m lathe; (de alfarero) wheel. en ~ a around

toro m bull. ~s mpl bullfighting. ir a los ~s go to a bullfight

toronja f grapefruit

torpe a clumsy; (estúpido) stupid

torped|ero m torpedo-boat. ~o m torpedo

torpeza f clumsiness; (de inteligencia) slowness

torpor m torpor

torrado m toasted chick-pea

torre f tower; (en ajedrez) castle, rook

torrefac|ción f roasting. ~to a roasted

torren|cial a torrential. ~te m torrent; (circulatorio) bloodstream; (fig) flood

tórrido a torrid

torrija f French toast

torsión f twisting

torso m torso

torta f tart; (bollo, fam) cake; (golpe) slap, punch; (Mex, bocadillo) sandwich. ~zo m slap, punch. no entender ni ~ not understand a word of it. pegarse un ~zo have a bad accident

tortícolis f stiff neck

tortilla f omelette; (Mex, de maíz) tortilla, maize cake. ~ francesa plain omelette

tórtola f turtle-dove

tortuga f tortoise; (de mar) turtle

tortuoso a winding; (fig) devious

tortura f torture. ~r vt torture

torvo a grim

tos f cough. ~ ferina whooping cough

tosco a crude; (persona) coarse

toser vi cough

tósigo m poison

tosquedad f crudeness; (de persona) coarseness

tost|ada f toast. ~ado a (pan) toasted; (café) roasted; (persona) tanned; (marrón) brown. ~ar vt toast (pan); roast (café); tan (piel). ~ón m (pan) crouton; (lata) bore

total a total. ● adv after all. ● m total; (totalidad) whole. ~idad f whole. ~itario a totalitarian. ~izar [10] vt total. ~ que so, to cut a long story short

tóxico a toxic

toxicómano m drug addict

toxina f toxin

tozudo a stubborn

traba f bond; (fig, obstáculo) obstacle. **poner ~s a** hinder

trabaj|ador a hard-working. ● m worker. **~ar** vt work (**de** as); knead (masa); (estudiar) work at; (actor) act. ● vi work. **~o** m work. **~os** mpl hardships. **~os forzados** hard labour. **~oso** a hard. **costar ~o** be difficult. **¿en qué ~as?** what work do you do?

trabalenguas m invar tongue-twister

traba|r vt (sujetar) fasten; (unir) join; (empezar) start; (culin) thicken. **~rse** vpr get tangled up. **trabársele la lengua** get tongue-tied. **~zón** f joining; (fig) connection

trabucar [7] vt mix up

trácala f (Mex) trick

tracción f traction

tractor m tractor

tradici|ón f tradition. **~onal** a traditional. **~onalista** m & f traditionalist

traduc|ción f translation. **~ir** [47] vt translate (al into). **~tor** m translator

traer [41] vt bring; (llevar) carry; (atraer) attract. **traérselas** be difficult

trafica|nte m & f dealer. **~r** [7] vi deal

tráfico m traffic; (com) trade

traga|deras fpl (fam) throat. **tener buenas ~deras** (ser crédulo) swallow anything; (ser tolerante) be easygoing. **~luz** m skylight. **~perras** f invar slot-machine. **~r** [12] vt swallow; (comer mucho) devour; (absorber) absorb; (fig) swallow up. **no (poder) ~r** not be able to stand. **~rse** vpr swallow; (fig) swallow up

tragedia f tragedy

trágico a tragic. ● m tragedian

trag|o m swallow, gulp; (pequeña porción) sip; (fig, disgusto) blow. **~ón** a greedy. ● m glutton. **echar(se) un ~o** have a drink

trai|ción f treachery; (pol) treason. **~cionar** vt betray. **~cionero** a treacherous. **~dor** a treacherous. ● m traitor

traigo vb véase **traer**

traje m dress; (de hombre) suit. ● vb véase **traer**. **~ de baño** swimming-costume. **~ de ceremonia**, **~ de etiqueta**, **~ de noche** evening dress

traj|ín m (transporte) haulage; (jaleo, fam) bustle. **~inar** vt transport. ● vi bustle about

trama f weft; (fig) link; (fig, argumento) plot. **~r** vt weave; (fig) plot

tramitar vt negotiate

trámite m step. **~s** mpl procedure. **en ~** in hand

tramo m (parte) section; (de escalera) flight

tramp|a f trap; (puerta) trapdoor; (fig) trick. **~illa** f trapdoor. **hacer ~a** cheat

trampolín m trampoline; (fig, de piscina) springboard

tramposo a cheating. ● m cheat

tranca f stick; (de puerta) bar

trance m moment; (hipnótico etc) trance. **a todo ~** at all costs

tranco m stride

tranquil|idad f (peace and) quiet; (de espíritu) peace of mind. **~izar** [10] vt reassure. **~o** a quiet; (conciencia) clear; (mar) calm; (despreocupado) thoughtless. **estáte ~o** don't worry

trans... pref (véase también **tras...**) trans...

transacción f transaction; (acuerdo) compromise

transatlántico a transatlantic. ● m (ocean) liner

transbord|ador m ferry. **~ar** vt transfer. **~arse** vpr change. **~o** m transfer. **hacer ~o** change (**en at**)

transcri|bir (pp **transcrito**) vt transcribe. **~pción** f transcription

transcur|rir vi pass. **~so** m course

transeúnte a temporary. ● m & f passer-by

transfer|encia f transfer. **~ir** [4] vt transfer

transfigurar vt transfigure

transforma|ción f transformation. **~dor** m transformer. **~r** vt transform

transfusión f transfusion. **hacer una ~** give a blood transfusion

transgre|dir vt transgress. **~sión** f transgression

transición f transition

transido a overcome

transigir [14] vi give in, compromise

transistor m transistor; (radio) radio

transita|ble a passable. **~r** vi go

transitivo a transitive

tránsito m transit; (tráfico) traffic

transitorio a transitory

translúcido *a* translucent

transmi|sión *f* transmission; (*radio, TV*) broadcast. **~sor** *m* transmitter. **~sora** *f* broadcasting station. **~tir** *vt* transmit; (*radio, TV*) broadcast; (*fig*) pass on

transparen|cia *f* transparency. **~tar** *vt* show. **~te** *a* transparent

transpira|ción *f* perspiration. **~r** *vi* transpire; (*sudar*) sweat

transponer [34] *vt* move. ● *vi* disappear round (*esquina etc*); disappear behind (*montaña etc*). **~se** *vpr* disappear

transport|ar *vt* transport. **~e** *m* transport. **empresa** *f* **de ~es** removals company

transversal *a* transverse; (*calle*) side

tranvía *m* tram

trapacería *f* swindle

trapear *vt* (*LAm*) mop

trapecio *m* trapeze; (*math*) trapezium

trapiche *m* (*para azúcar*) mill; (*para aceitunas*) press

trapicheo *m* fiddle

trapisonda *f* (*jaleo, fam*) row; (*enredo, fam*) plot

trapo *m* rag; (*para limpiar*) cloth. **~s** *mpl* (*fam*) clothes. **a todo ~** out of control

tráquea *f* windpipe, trachea

traquete|ar *vt* bang, rattle. **~o** *m* banging, rattle

tras *prep* after; (*detrás*) behind; (*encima de*) as well as

tras... *pref* (*véase también* **trans...**) trans...

trascende|ncia *f* importance. **~ntal** *a* transcendental; (*importante*) important. **~r** [1] *vi* (*oler*) smell a (*of*); (*saberse*) become known; (*extenderse*) spread

trasegar [1 & 12] *vt* move around

trasero *a* back, rear. ● *m* (*anat*) bottom

trasgo *m* goblin

traslad|ar *vt* move; (*aplazar*) postpone; (*traducir*) translate; (*copiar*) copy. **~o** *m* transfer; (*copia*) copy; (*mudanza*) removal. **dar ~o** send a copy

trasl|úcido *a* translucent. **~ucirse** [11] *vpr* be translucent; (*dejarse ver*) show through; (*fig, revelarse*) be revealed. **~uz** *m*. **al ~uz** against the light

trasmano *m*. **a ~** out of reach; (*fig*) out of the way

trasnochar *vt* (*acostarse tarde*) go to bed late; (*no acostarse*) stay up all night; (*no dormir*) be unable to sleep; (*pernoctar*) spend the night

traspas|ar *vt* pierce; (*transferir*) transfer; (*pasar el límite*) go beyond. **~o** *m* transfer. **se ~a** for sale

traspié *m* trip; (*fig*) slip. **dar un ~** stumble; (*fig*) slip up

trasplant|ar *vt* transplant. **~e** *m* transplanting; (*med*) transplant

trastada *f* stupid thing; (*jugada*) dirty trick, practical joke

traste *m* fret. **dar al ~ con** ruin. **ir al ~** fall through

trastero *m* storeroom

trastienda *f* back room; (*fig*) shrewdness

trasto *m* piece of furniture; (*cosa inútil*) piece of junk; (*persona*) useless person, dead loss (*fam*)

trastorn|ado *a* mad. **~ar** *vt* upset; (*volver loco*) drive mad; (*fig, gustar mucho, fam*) delight. **~arse** *vpr* be upset; (*volverse loco*) go mad. **~o** *m* (*incl med*) upset; (*pol*) disturbance; (*fig*) confusion

trastrocar [2 & 7] *vt* change round

trat|able *a* friendly. **~ado** *m* treatise; (*acuerdo*) treaty. **~amiento** *m* treatment; (*título*) title. **~ante** *m & f* dealer. **~ar** *vt* (*incl med*) treat; deal with (*asunto etc*); (*com*) deal; (*manejar*) handle; (*de tú, de Vd*) address (**de** as); (*llamar*) call. ● *vi* deal (with). **~ar con** have to do with; know (*persona*); (*com*) deal in. **~ar de** be about; (*intentar*) try. **~o** *m* treatment; (*acuerdo*) agreement; (*título*) title; (*relación*) relationship. **¡~o hecho!** agreed! **~os** *mpl* dealings. **¿de qué se ~a?** what's it about?

traum|a *m* trauma. **~ático** *a* traumatic

través *m* (*inclinación*) slant. **a ~ de** through; (*de un lado a otro*) across. **de ~** across; (*de lado*) sideways. **mirar de ~** look askance at

travesaño *m* crosspiece

travesía *f* crossing; (*calle*) side-street

trav|esura *f* prank. **~ieso** *a* (*niño*) mischievous, naughty

trayecto *m* road; (*tramo*) stretch; (*ruta*) route; (*viaje*) journey. **~ria** *f* trajectory; (*fig*) course

traz|a *f* plan; (*aspecto*) look, appearance; (*habilidad*) skill. ~ado *a*. bien ~ado good-looking. mal ~ado unattractive. ● *m* plan. ~ar [10] *vt* draw; (*bosquejar*) sketch. ~o *m* line

trébol *m* clover. ~es *mpl* (*en naipes*) clubs

trece *a & m* thirteen

trecho *m* stretch; (*distancia*) distance; (*tiempo*) while. a ~s in places. de ~ en ~ at intervals

tregua *f* truce; (*fig*) respite

treinta *a & m* thirty

tremendo *a* terrible; (*extraordinario*) terrific

trementina *f* turpentine

tren *m* train; (*equipaje*) luggage. ~ de aterrizaje landing gear. ~ de vida lifestyle

tren|cilla *f* braid. ~za *f* braid; (*de pelo*) plait. ~zar [10] *vt* plait

trepa|dor *a* climbing. ~r *vt/i* climb

tres *a & m* three. ~cientos *a & m* three hundred. ~illo *m* three-piece suite; (*mus*) triplet

treta *f* trick

tri|angular *a* triangular. ~ángulo *m* triangle

trib|al *a* tribal. ~u *f* tribe

tribulación *f* tribulation

tribuna *f* platform; (*de espectadores*) stand

tribunal *m* court; (*de examen etc*) board; (*fig*) tribunal

tribut|ar *vt* pay. ~o *m* tribute; (*impuesto*) tax

triciclo *m* tricycle

tricolor *a* three-coloured

tricornio *a* three-cornered. ● *m* three-cornered hat

tricotar *vt/i* knit

tridimensional *a* three-dimensional

tridente *m* trident

trigésimo *a* thirtieth

trig|al *m* wheat field. ~o *m* wheat

trigonometría *f* trigonometry

trigueño *a* olive-skinned; (*pelo*) dark blonde

trilogía *f* trilogy

trilla|do *a* (*fig, manoseado*) trite; (*fig, conocido*) well-known. ~r *vt* thresh

trimestr|al *a* quarterly. ~e *m* quarter; (*escol, univ*) term

trin|ar *vi* warble. estar que trina be furious

trinchar *vt* carve

trinchera *f* ditch; (*mil*) trench; (*rail*) cutting; (*abrigo*) trench coat

trineo *m* sledge

trinidad *f* trinity

Trinidad *f* Trinidad

trino *m* warble

trío *m* trio

tripa *f* intestine; (*culin*) tripe; (*fig, vientre*) tummy, belly. ~s *fpl* (*de máquina etc*) parts, workings. me duele la ~ I've got tummy-ache. revolver las ~s turn one's stomach

tripicallos *mpl* tripe

tripl|e *a* triple. ● *m*. el ~e (de) three times as much (as). ~icado *a*. por ~icado in triplicate. ~icar [7] *vt* treble

trípode *m* tripod

tríptico *m* triptych

tripula|ción *f* crew. ~nte *m & f* member of the crew. ~r *vt* man

triquitraque *m* (*ruido*) clatter

tris *m* crack; (*de papel etc*) ripping noise. estar en un ~ be on the point of

triste *a* sad; (*paisaje, tiempo etc*) gloomy; (*fig, insignificante*) miserable. ~za *f* sadness

tritón *m* newt

triturar *vt* crush

triunf|al *a* triumphal. ~ante *a* triumphant. ~ar *vi* triumph (de, sobre over). ~o *m* triumph

triunvirato *m* triumvirate

trivial *a* trivial

triza *f* piece. hacer algo ~s smash sth to pieces

trocar [2 & 7] *vt* (ex)change

trocear *vt* cut up, chop

trocito *m* small piece

trocha *f* narrow path; (*atajo*) short cut

trofeo *m* trophy

tromba *f* waterspout. ~ de agua heavy downpour

trombón *m* trombone; (*músico*) trombonist

trombosis *f* invar thrombosis

trompa *f* horn; (*de orquesta*) French horn; (*de elefante*) trunk; (*hocico*) snout; (*juguete*) spinning top; (*anat*) tube. ● *m* horn player. coger una ~ (*fam*) get drunk

trompada *f*, trompazo *m* bump

trompet|a *f* trumpet; (*músico*) trumpeter, trumpet player; (*clarín*) bugle. ~illa *f* ear-trumpet

trompicar [7] *vi* trip

trompo m (*juguete*) (spinning) top

trona|da f thunder storm. ~r vt (*Mex*) shoot. • vi thunder

tronco m trunk. dormir como un ~ sleep like a log

tronchar vt bring down; (*fig*) cut short. ~se de risa laugh a lot

trono m throne

trop|a f troops. ~el m mob. ser de ~a be in the army

tropero m (*Arg, vaquero*) cowboy

tropez|ar [1 & 10] vi trip; (*fig*) slip up. ~ar con run into. ~ón m stumble; (*fig*) slip

tropical a tropical

trópico a tropical. • m tropic

tropiezo m slip; (*desgracia*) mishap

trot|ar vi trot. ~e m trot; (*fig*) toing and froing. al ~e trotting; (*de prisa*) in a rush. de mucho ~e hard-wearing

trozo m piece, bit. a ~s in bits

truco m knack; (*ardid*) trick. coger el ~ get the knack

trucha f trout

trueno m thunder; (*estampido*) bang

trueque m exchange. aun a ~ de even at the expense of

trufa f truffle. ~r vt stuff with truffles

truhán m rogue; (*gracioso*) jester

truncar [7] vt truncate; (*fig*) cut short

tu a your

tú pron you

tuba f tuba

tubérculo m tuber

tuberculosis f tuberculosis

tub|ería f pipes; (*oleoducto etc*) pipeline. ~o m tube. ~o de ensayo test tube. ~o de escape (*auto*) exhaust (pipe). ~ular a tubular

tuerca f nut

tuerto a one-eyed, blind in one eye. • m one-eyed person

tuétano m marrow; (*fig*) heart. hasta los ~s completely

tufo m fumes; (*olor*) bad smell

tugurio m hovel, slum

tul m tulle

tulipán m tulip

tulli|do a paralysed. ~r [22] vt cripple

tumba f grave, tomb

tumb|ar vt knock down, knock over; (*fig, en examen, fam*) fail; (*pasmar, fam*) overwhelm. ~arse vpr lie down. ~o m jolt. dar un ~o tumble. ~ona f settee; (*sillón*) armchair; (*de lona*) deckchair

tumefacción f swelling

tumido a swollen

tumor m tumour

tumulto m turmoil; (*pol*) riot

tuna f prickly pear; (*de estudiantes*) student band

tunante m & f rogue

túnel m tunnel

Túnez m (*ciudad*) Tunis; (*país*) Tunisia

túnica f tunic

Tunicia f Tunisia

tupé m toupee; (*fig*) nerve

tupido a thick

turba f peat; (*muchedumbre*) mob

turba|ción f disturbance, upset; (*confusión*) confusion. ~do a upset

turbante m turban

turbar vt upset; (*molestar*) disturb. ~se vpr be upset

turbina f turbine

turbi|o a cloudy; ⟨vista⟩ blurred; ⟨asunto etc⟩ unclear. ~ón m squall

turbulen|cia f turbulence; (*disturbio*) disturbance. ~te a turbulent; ⟨persona⟩ restless

turco a Turkish. • m Turk; (*lengua*) Turkish

tur|ismo m tourism; (*coche*) car. ~ista m & f tourist. ~ístico a touristic. oficina f de ~ismo tourist office

turn|arse vpr take turns (para to). ~o m turn; (*de trabajo*) shift. por ~o in turn

turquesa f turquoise

Turquía f Turkey

turrón m nougat

turulato a (*fam*) stunned

tutear vt address as tú. ~se vpr be on familiar terms

tutela f (*jurid*) guardianship; (*fig*) protection

tuteo m use of the familiar tú

tutor m guardian; (*escol*) form master

tuve vb *véase* tener

tuyo a & pron yours. un amigo ~ a friend of yours

U

u conj or

ubicuidad f ubiquity

ubre f udder

ucraniano a & m Ukranian

Ud abrev (*Usted*) you

uf int phew!; (*de repugnancia*) ugh!

ufan|arse *vpr* be proud (**con**, **de** of); (*jactarse*) boast (**con**, **de** about). **~o** *a* proud

ujier *m* usher

úlcera *f* ulcer

ulterior *a* later; (*lugar*) further. **~mente** *adv* later, subsequently

últimamente *adv* (*recientemente*) recently; (*al final*) finally; (*en último caso*) as a last resort

ultim|ar *vt* complete. **~átum** *m* ultimatum

último *a* last; (*más reciente*) latest; (*más lejano*) furthest; (*más alto*) top; (*más bajo*) bottom; (*fig, extremo*) extreme. **estar en las últimas** be on one's last legs; (*sin dinero*) be down to one's last penny. **por ~** finally. **ser lo ~** (*muy bueno*) be marvellous; (*muy malo*) be awful. **vestido a la última** dressed in the latest fashion

ultra *a* ultra, extreme

ultraj|ante *a* outrageous. **~e** *m* outrage

ultramar *m* overseas countries. **de ~**, **en ~** overseas

ultramarino *a* overseas. **~s** *mpl* groceries. **tienda de ~s** grocer's (shop) (*Brit*), grocery store (*Amer*)

ultranza. a ~ (*con decisión*) decisively; (*extremo*) extreme

ultra|sónico *a* ultrasonic. **~violeta** *a invar* ultraviolet

ulular *vi* howl; (*búho*) hoot

umbilical *a* umbilical

umbral *m* threshold

umbrío *a*, **umbroso** *a* shady

un *art indef* *m* (*pl* **unos**) a. **• a** one. **~os** *a pl* some

una *art indef* *a*. **la ~** one o'clock

un|ánime *a* unanimous. **~animidad** *f* unanimity

undécimo *a* eleventh

ung|ir [14] *vt* anoint. **~üento** *m* ointment

únic|amente *adv* only. **~o** *a* only; (*fig, incomparable*) unique

unicornio *m* unicorn

unid|ad *f* unit; (*cualidad*) unity. **~o** *a* united

unifica|ción *f* unification. **~r** [7] *vt* unite, unify

uniform|ar *vt* standardize; (*poner uniforme a*) put into uniform. **~e** *a & m* uniform. **~idad** *f* uniformity

uni|génito *a* only. **~lateral** *a* unilateral

uni|ón *f* union; (*cualidad*) unity; (*tec*) joint. **~r** *vt* join; mix (*líquidos*). **~rse** *vpr* join together

unísono *m* unison. **al ~** in unison

unitario *a* unitary

universal *a* universal

universi|dad *f* university. **U~dad a Distancia** Open University. **~tario** *a* university

universo *m* universe

uno *a* one; (*en plural*) some. **• pron** one; (*alguien*) someone, somebody. **• m** one. **~ a otro** each other. **~ y otro** both. **(los) ~s... (los) otros** some... others

untar *vt* grease; (*med*) rub; (*fig, sobornar*, *fam*) bribe

uña *f* nail; (*de animal*) claw; (*casco*) hoof

upa *int* up!

uranio *m* uranium

Urano *m* Uranus

urban|idad *f* politeness. **~ismo** *m* town planning. **~ístico** *a* urban. **~ización** *f* development. **~izar** [10] *vt* civilize; develop (*terreno*). **~o** *a* urban

urbe *f* big city

urdimbre *f* warp

urdir *vt* (*fig*) plot

urg|encia *f* urgency; (*emergencia*) emergency; (*necesidad*) urgent need. **~ente** *a* urgent. **~ir** [14] *vi* be urgent. **carta/~ente** express letter

urinario *m* urinal

urna *f* urn; (*pol*) ballot box

urraca *f* magpie

URSS *abrev* (*historia*) (*Unión de Repúblicas Socialistas Soviéticas*) USSR, Union of Soviet Socialist Republics

Uruguay *m*. **el ~** Uruguay

uruguayo *a & m* Uruguayan

us|ado *a* used; (*ropa etc*) worn. **~anza** *f* usage, custom. **~ar** *vt* use; (*llevar*) wear. **~o** *m* use; (*costumbre*) usage, custom. **al ~o** (*de moda*) in fashion; (*a la manera de*) in the style of. **de ~o externo** for external use

usted *pron* you

usual *a* usual

usuario *a* user

usur|a *f* usury. **~ero** *m* usurer

usurpar *vt* usurp

usuta *f* (*Arg*) sandal

utensilio *m* tool; (*de cocina*) utensil. **~s** *mpl* equipment

útero *m* womb

útil a useful. **~es** mpl implements
utili|dad f usefulness. **~tario** a utilitarian; ⟨coche⟩ utility. **~zación** f use, utilization. **~zar** [10] vt use, utilize
uva f grape. **~ pasa** raisin. **mala ~** bad mood

V

vaca f cow; ⟨carne⟩ beef
vacaciones fpl holiday(s). **estar de ~** be on holiday. **ir de ~** go on holiday
vaca|nte a vacant. ●f vacancy. **~r** [7] vi fall vacant
vaci|ar [20] vt empty; ⟨ahuecar⟩ hollow out; ⟨en molde⟩ cast; ⟨afilar⟩ sharpen. **~edad** f emptiness; ⟨tontería⟩ silly thing, frivolity
vacila|ción f hesitation. **~nte** a unsteady; ⟨fig⟩ hesitant. **~r** vi sway; ⟨dudar⟩ hesitate; ⟨fam⟩ tease
vacío a empty; ⟨vanidoso⟩ vain. ●m empty space; ⟨estado⟩ emptiness; ⟨en física⟩ vacuum; ⟨fig⟩ void
vacuidad f emptiness; ⟨tontería⟩ silly thing, frivolity
vacuna f vaccine. **~ción** f vaccination. **~r** vt vaccinate
vacuno a bovine
vacuo a empty
vade m folder
vad|ear vt ford. **~o** m ford
vaga|bundear vi wander. **~bundo** a vagrant; ⟨perro⟩ stray. ●m tramp. **~r** [12] vi wander (about)
vagina f vagina
vago a vague; ⟨holgazán⟩ idle; ⟨foto⟩ blurred. ●m idler
vag|ón m carriage; ⟨de mercancías⟩ truck, wagon. **~ón restaurante** dining-car. **~oneta** f truck
vahído m dizzy spell
vaho m breath; ⟨vapor⟩ steam. **~s** mpl inhalation
vaina f sheath; ⟨bot⟩ pod
vainilla f vanilla
vaivén m swaying; ⟨de tráfico⟩ coming and going; ⟨fig, de suerte⟩ change. **vaivenes** mpl ⟨fig⟩ ups and downs
vajilla f dishes, crockery. **lavar la ~** wash up
vale m voucher; ⟨pagaré⟩ IOU. **~dero** a valid
valenciano a from Valencia

valent|ía f courage; ⟨acción⟩ brave deed. **~ón** m braggart
valer [42] vt be worth; ⟨costar⟩ cost; ⟨fig, significar⟩ mean. ●vi be worth; ⟨costar⟩ cost; ⟨servir⟩ be of use; ⟨ser valedero⟩ be valid; ⟨estar permitido⟩ be allowed. ●m worth. **~ la pena** be worthwhile, be worth it. **¿cuánto vale?** how much is it? **no ~ para nada** be useless. **¡vale!** all right!, OK! ⟨fam⟩ **¿vale?** all right?, OK? ⟨fam⟩
valeroso a courageous
valgo vb véase **valer**
valía f worth
validez f validity. **dar ~ a** validate
válido a valid
valiente a brave; ⟨valentón⟩ boastful; ⟨en sentido irónico⟩ fine. ●m brave person; ⟨valentón⟩ braggart
valija f case; ⟨de correos⟩ mailbag. **~ diplomática** diplomatic bag
val|ioso a valuable. **~or** m value, worth; ⟨descaro, fam⟩ nerve. **~ores** mpl securities. **~oración** f valuation. **~orar** vt value. **conceder ~or a** attach importance to. **objetos** mpl **de ~or** valuables. **sin ~or** worthless
vals m invar waltz
válvula f valve
valla f fence; ⟨fig⟩ barrier
valle m valley
vampiro m vampire
vanagloriarse [20 o regular] vpr boast
vanamente adv uselessly, in vain
vandalismo m vandalism
vándalo m vandal
vanguardia f vanguard. **de ~** ⟨en arte, música etc⟩ avant-garde
vanid|ad f vanity. **~oso** a vain
vano a vain; ⟨inútil⟩ useless. **en ~** in vain
vapor m steam; ⟨gas⟩ vapour; ⟨naut⟩ steamer. **~izador** m spray. **~izar** [10] vaporize. **al ~** ⟨culin⟩ steamed
vaquer|ía f dairy. **~o** m cow-herd, cowboy. **~os** mpl jeans
vara f stick; ⟨de autoridad⟩ staff; ⟨medida⟩ yard
varar vi run aground
varia|ble a & f variable. **~ción** f variation. **~nte** f version. **~ntes** fpl hors d'oeuvres. **~r** [20] vt change; ⟨dar variedad a⟩ vary. ●vi vary; ⟨cambiar⟩ change
varice f varicose vein

varicela f chickenpox

varicoso a having varicose veins

variedad f variety

varilla f stick; (de metal) rod

vario a varied; (en plural) several

varita f wand

variz f varicose vein

var|ón a male. ● m man; (niño) boy. ∼**onil** a manly

vasc|o a & m Basque. ∼**ongado** a Basque. ∼**uence** a & m Basque. las V∼**ongadas** the Basque provinces

vasectomía f vasectomy

vaselina f Vaseline (P), petroleum jelly

vasija f pot, container

vaso m glass; (anat) vessel

vástago m shoot; (descendiente) descendant; (varilla) rod

vasto a vast

Vaticano m Vatican

vatic|inar vt prophesy. ∼**io** m prophesy

vatio m watt

vaya vb véase **ir**

Vd abrev (Usted) you

vecin|dad f neighbourhood, vicinity; (vecinos) neighbours. ∼**dario** m inhabitants, neighbourhood. ∼**o** a neighbouring; (de al lado) next-door. ● m neighbour

veda|do m preserve. ∼**do de caza** game preserve. ∼**r** vt prohibit

vega f fertile plain

vegeta|ción f vegetation. ∼**l** a vegetable. ● m plant, vegetable. ∼**r** vi grow; (persona) vegetate. ∼**riano** a & m vegetarian

vehemente a vehement

vehículo m vehicle

veinte a & m twenty. ∼**na** f score

veinti|cinco a & m twenty-five. ∼**cuatro** a & m twenty-four. ∼**dós** a & m twenty-two. ∼**nueve** a & m twenty-nine; ∼**ocho** a & m twenty-eight. ∼**séis** a & m twenty-six. ∼**siete** a & m twenty-seven. ∼**trés** a & m twenty-three. ∼**ún** a twenty-one. ∼**uno** a & m (delante de nombre masculino **veintún**) twenty-one

vejar vt humiliate; (molestar) vex

vejez f old age

vejiga f bladder; (med) blister

vela f (naut) sail; (de cera) candle; (falta de sueño) sleeplessness; (vigilia) vigil. **pasar la noche en** ∼ have a sleepless night

velada f evening party

vela|do a veiled; (foto) blurred. ∼**r** vt watch over; (encubrir) veil; (foto) blur. ● vi stay awake, not sleep. ∼**r por** look after. ∼**rse** vpr (foto) blur

velero m sailing-ship

veleta f weather vane

velo m veil

veloc|idad f speed; (auto etc) gear. ∼**ímetro** m speedometer. ∼**ista** m & f sprinter. **a toda** ∼**idad** at full speed

velódromo m cycle-track

veloz a fast, quick

vell|o m down. ∼**ón** m fleece. ∼**udo** a hairy

vena f vein; (en madera) grain. **estar de/en** ∼ be in the mood

venado m deer; (culin) venison

vencedor a winning. ● m winner

vencejo m (pájaro) swift

venc|er [9] vt beat; (superar) overcome. ● vi win; (plazo) expire. ∼**erse** vpr collapse; (persona) control o.s. ∼**ido** a beaten; (com, atrasado) in arrears. **darse por** ∼**ido** give up. **los** ∼**idos** mpl (en deportes etc) the losers

venda f bandage. ∼**je** m dressing. ∼**r** vt bandage

vendaval m gale

vende|dor a selling. ● m seller, salesman. ∼**dor ambulante** pedlar. ∼**r** vt sell. ∼**rse** vpr sell. ∼**rse caro** play hard to get. **se** ∼ **for sale**

vendimia f grape harvest; (de vino) vintage, year

Venecia f Venice

veneciano a Venetian

veneno m poison; (fig, malevolencia) spite. ∼**so** a poisonous

venera f scallop shell

venera|ble a venerable. ∼**ción** f reverence. ∼**r** vt revere

venéreo a venereal

venero m (yacimiento) seam; (de agua) spring; (fig) source

venezolano a & m Venezuelan

Venezuela f Venezuela

venga|nza f revenge. ∼**r** [12] vt avenge. ∼**rse** vpr take revenge (de, por for) (de, en on). ∼**tivo** a vindictive

vengo vb véase **venir**

venia f (permiso) permission

venial a venial

veni|da f arrival; (vuelta) return. ∼**dero** a coming. ∼**r** [53] vi come; (estar, ser) be. ∼**r a para** come to. ∼**r**

bien suit. **la semana que viene** next
week. **¡venga!** come on!
venta f sale; (*posada*) inn. **en ~** for
sale
ventaj|a f advantage. **~oso** a ad-
vantageous
ventan|a f window; (*de la nariz*) nos-
tril. **~illa** f window
ventarrón m (*fam*) strong wind
ventear vt (*olfatear*) sniff
ventero m innkeeper
ventila|ción f ventilation. **~dor** m
fan. **~r** vt air
vent|isca f blizzard. **~olera** f gust of
wind. **~osa** f sucker. **~osidad** f
wind, flatulence. **~oso** a windy
ventrílocuo m ventriloquist
ventrudo a pot-bellied
ventur|a f happiness; (*suerte*) luck.
~oso a happy, lucky. **a la ~a** at random. **echar la buena ~a a uno** tell
s.o.'s fortune. **por ~a** by chance;
(*afortunadamente*) fortunately
Venus f Venus
ver [43] vt see; watch ‹*televisión*›. ● vi
see. **~se** vpr see o.s.; (*encontrarse*)
find o.s.; ‹*dos personas*› meet. **a mi
(modo de) ~** in my view. **a ~** let's
see. **de buen ~** good-looking. **dejarse ~** show. **¡hábráse visto!** did
you ever! **no poder ~** not be able to
stand. **no tener nada que ~ con**
have nothing to do with. **¡para que
veas!** so there! **vamos a ~** let's see.
ya lo veo that's obvious. **ya ~ás**
you'll see. **ya ~emos** we'll see
ver|a f edge; (*de río*) bank
veracruzano a from Veracruz
veran|eante m & f tourist, holiday-
maker. **~ear** vi spend one's holiday.
~eo m (summer) holiday. **~iego** a
summer. **~o** m summer. **casa** f **de
~eo** summer-holiday home. **ir de
~eo** go on holiday. **lugar** m **de ~eo**
holiday resort
veras fpl. **de ~** really
veraz a truthful
verbal a verbal
verbena f (*bot*) verbena; (*fiesta*) fair;
(*baile*) dance
verbo m verb. **~so** a verbose
verdad f truth. **¿~?** isn't it?, aren't
they?, won't it? etc. **~eramente** adv
really. **~ero** a true; (*fig*) real. **a decir
~** to tell the truth. **de ~** really. **la
pura ~** the plain truth. **si bien es ~
que** although

verd|e a green; ‹*fruta etc*› unripe;
‹*chiste etc*› dirty, blue. ● m green;
(*hierba*) grass. **~or** m greenness
verdugo m executioner; (*fig*) tyrant
verdu|lería f greengrocer's (shop).
~lero m greengrocer. **~ra** f (green)
vegetable(s)
vereda f path; (*LAm, acera*) pavement (*Brit*), sidewalk (*Amer*)
veredicto m verdict
vergel m large garden; (*huerto*)
orchard
verg|onzoso a shameful; (*tímido*)
shy. **~üenza** f shame; (*timidez*) shyness. **¡es una ~üenza!** it's a disgrace! **me da ~üenza** I'm ashamed;
(*tímido*) I'm shy about. **tener ~üenza**
be ashamed; (*tímido*) be shy
verídico a true
verifica|ción f verification. **~r** [7] vt
check. **~rse** vpr take place; (*resultar
verdad*) come true
verja f grating; (*cerca*) railings;
(*puerta*) iron gate
vermú m, **vermut** m vermouth
vernáculo a vernacular
verosímil a likely; ‹*relato etc*› cred-
ible
verraco m boar
verruga f wart
versado a versed
versar vi turn. **~ sobre** be about
versátil a versatile; (*fig*) fickle
versión f version; (*traducción*) translation
verso m verse; (*línea*) line
vértebra f vertebra
verte|dero m rubbish tip; (*de-
saguadero*) drain. **~dor** m drain. **~r**
[1] vt pour; (*derramar*) spill. ● vi flow
vertical a & f vertical
vértice f vertex
vertiente f slope
vertiginoso a dizzy
vértigo m dizziness; (*med*) vertigo.
de ~ (*fam*) amazing
vesania f rage; (*med*) insanity
vesícula f blister. **~ biliar** gall-
bladder
vespertino a evening
vestíbulo m hall; (*de hotel, teatro etc*)
foyer
vestido m (*de mujer*) dress; (*ropa*)
clothes
vestigio m trace. **~s** mpl remains
vest|imenta f clothing. **~ir** [5] vt
(*ponerse*) put on; (*llevar*) wear;
dress ‹*niño etc*›. ● vi dress; (*llevar*)

wear. **~irse** *vpr* get dressed; (*llevar*) wear. **~uario** *m* wardrobe; (*cuarto*) dressing-room

Vesuvio *m* Vesuvius

vetar *vt* veto

veterano *a* veteran

veterinari|a *f* veterinary science. **~o** *a* veterinary. ● *m* vet (*fam*), veterinary surgeon (*Brit*), veterinarian (*Amer*)

veto *m* veto. **poner el ~ a** veto

vetusto *a* ancient

vez *f* time; (*turno*) turn. **a la ~** at the same time; (*de una vez*) in one go. **alguna que otra ~** from time to time. **alguna ~** sometimes; (*en preguntas*) ever. **algunas veces** sometimes. **a su ~** in (his) turn. **a veces** sometimes. **cada ~ más** more and more. **de una ~** in one go. **de una ~ para siempre** once and for all. **de ~ en cuando** from time to time. **dos veces** twice. **2 veces** 4 2 times 4. **en ~ de** instead of. **érase una ~, había una ~** once upon a time. **muchas veces** often. **otra ~** again. **pocas veces, rara ~** rarely. **repetidas veces** again and again. **tal ~** perhaps. **una ~ (que)** once

vía *f* road; (*rail*) line; (*anat*) tract; (*fig*) way. ● *prep* via. **~ aérea** by air. **~ de comunicación** *f* means of communication. **~ férrea** railway (*Brit*), railroad (*Amer*). **~ rápida** fast lane. **estar en ~s de** be in the process of

viab|ilidad *f* viability. **~le** *a* viable

viaducto *m* viaduct

viaj|ante *m* & *f* commercial traveller. **~ar** *vi* travel. **~e** *m* journey; (*corto*) trip. **~e de novios** honeymoon. **~ero** *m* traveller; (*pasajero*) passenger. **¡buen ~e!** have a good journey!

víbora *f* viper

vibra|ción *f* vibration. **~nte** *a* vibrant. **~r** *vt/i* vibrate

vicario *m* vicar

vice... *pref* vice-...

viceversa *adv* vice versa

vici|ado *a* corrupt; (*aire*) stale. **~ar** *vt* corrupt; (*estropear*) spoil. **~o** *m* vice; (*mala costumbre*) bad habit. **~oso** *a* dissolute; (*círculo*) vicious

vicisitud *f* vicissitude

víctima *f* victim; (*de un accidente*) casualty

victori|a *f* victory. **~oso** *a* victorious

vid *f* vine

vida *f* life; (*duración*) lifetime. **¡~ mía!** my darling! **de por ~** for life. **en mi ~** never (in my life). **en ~ de** during the lifetime of. **estar en ~** be alive

vídeo *m* video recorder

video|cinta *f* videotape. **~juego** *m* video game

vidriar *vt* glaze

vidri|era *f* stained glass window; (*puerta*) glass door; (*LAm, escaparate*) shop window. **~ería** *f* glass works. **~ero** *m* glazier. **~o** *m* glass. **~oso** *a* glassy

vieira *f* scallop

viejo *a* old. ● *m* old person

Viena *f* Vienna

viene *vb véase* venir

viento *m* wind. **hacer ~** be windy

vientre *f* belly; (*matriz*) womb; (*intestino*) bowels. **llevar un niño en el ~** be pregnant

viernes *m* Friday. **V~ Santo** Good Friday

viga *f* beam; (*de metal*) girder

vigen|cia *f* validity; (*ley*) in force. **entrar en ~cia** come into force

vigésimo *a* twentieth

vigía *f* (*torre*) watch-tower; (*persona*) lookout

vigil|ancia *f* vigilance. **~ante** *a* vigilant. ● *m* watchman, supervisor. **~ar** *vt* keep an eye on. ● *vi* be vigilant; (*vigía etc*) keep watch. **~ia** *f* vigil; (*relig*) fasting

vigor *m* vigour; (*vigencia*) force. **~oso** *a* vigorous. **entrar en ~** come into force

vil *a* vile. **~eza** *f* vileness; (*acción*) vile deed

vilipendiar *vt* abuse

vilo. en ~ in the air

villa *f* town; (*casa*) villa. **la V~** Madrid

villancico *m* (Christmas) carol

villano *a* rustic; (*grosero*) coarse

vinagre *m* vinegar. **~ra** *f* vinegar bottle. **~ras** *fpl* cruet. **~ta** *f* vinaigrette (sauce)

vincular *vt* bind

vínculo *m* bond

vindicar [7] *vt* avenge; (*justificar*) vindicate

vine *vb véase* venir

vinicult|or *m* wine-grower. **~ura** *f* wine growing

vino *m* wine. ~ **de Jerez** sherry. ~ **de la casa** house wine. ~ **de mesa** table wine

viña *f*, **viñedo** *m* vineyard

viola *f* viola; (*músico*) viola player

violación *f* violation; (*de una mujer*) rape

violado *a & m* violet

violar *vt* violate; break ⟨*ley*⟩; rape ⟨*mujer*⟩

violen|cia *f* violence; (*fuerza*) force; (*embarazo*) embarrassment. ~**tar** *vt* force; break into ⟨*casa etc*⟩. ~**tarse** *vpr* force o.s. ~**to** *a* violent; (*fig*) awkward. **hacer** ~**cia** a force

violeta *a invar & f* violet

violl|ín *m* violin; (*músico*) violinist. ~**inista** *m & f* violinist. ~**ón** *m* double bass; (*músico*) double-bass player. ~**onc(h)elista** *m & f* cellist. ~**onc(h)elo** *m* cello

vira|je *m* turn. ~**r** *vt* turn. ● *vi* turn; (*fig*) change direction

virgen *a & f* virgin. ~**inal** *a* virginal. ~**inidad** *f* virginity

Virgo *m* Virgo

viril *a* virile. ~**idad** *f* virility

virtual *a* virtual

virtud *f* virtue; (*capacidad*) ability. **en** ~ **de** by virtue of

virtuoso *a* virtuous. ● *m* virtuoso

viruela *f* smallpox. **picado de** ~**s** pock-marked

virulé. a la ~ (*fam*) crooked; (*estropeado*) damaged

virulento *a* virulent

virus *m invar* virus

visa|do *m* visa. ~**r** *vt* endorse

vísceras *fpl* entrails

viscos|a *f* viscose. ~**o** *a* viscous

visera *f* visor; (*de gorra*) peak

visib|ilidad *f* visibility. ~**le** *a* visible

visig|odo *a* Visigothic. ● *m* Visigoth. ~**ótico** *a* Visigothic

visillo *m* (*cortina*) net curtain

visi|ón *f* vision; (*vista*) sight. ~**onaria** *a & m* visionary

visita *f* visit; (*persona*) visitor. ~ **de cumplido** courtesy call. ~**nte** *m & f* visitor. ~**r** *vt* visit. **tener** ~ have visitors

vislumbr|ar *vt* glimpse. ~**e** *f* glimpse; (*resplandor, fig*) glimmer

viso *m* sheen; (*aspecto*) appearance

visón *m* mink

visor *m* viewfinder

víspera *f* day before, eve

vista *f* sight, vision; (*aspecto, mirada*) look; (*panorama*) view. **apartar la** ~ look away; (*fig*) turn a blind eye. **a primera** ~, **a simple** ~ at first sight. **clavar la** ~ **en** stare at. **con** ~**s a** with a view to. **en** ~ **de** in view of, considering. **estar a la** ~ be obvious. **hacer la** ~ **gorda** turn a blind eye. **perder de** ~ lose sight of. **tener a la** ~ have in front of one. **volver la** ~ **atrás** look back

vistazo *m* glance. **dar/echar un** ~ a glance at

visto *a* seen; (*corriente*) common; (*considerado*) considered. ● *vb véase* **vestir.** ~ **bueno** passed. ~ **que** since. **bien** ~ acceptable. **está** ~ **que** it's obvious that. **lo nunca** ~ an unheard-of thing. **mal** ~ unacceptable. **por lo** ~ apparently

vistoso *a* colourful, bright

visual *a* visual. ● *f* glance. **echar una** ~ a have a look at

vital *a* vital. ~**icio** *a* life. ● *m* (life) annuity. ~**idad** *f* vitality

vitamina *f* vitamin

viticult|or *m* wine-grower. ~**ura** *f* wine growing

vitorear *vt* cheer

vítreo *a* vitreous

vitrina *f* showcase

vituper|ar *vt* censure. ~**io** *m* censure. ~**ios** *mpl* abuse

viud|a *f* widow. ~**ez** *f* widowhood. ~**o** *a* widowed. ● *m* widower

viva *m* cheer

vivacidad *f* liveliness

vivamente *adv* vividly; (*sinceramente*) sincerely

vivaz *a* (*bot*) perennial; (*vivo*) lively

víveres *mpl* supplies

vivero *m* nursery; (*fig*) hotbed

viveza *f* vividness; (*de inteligencia*) sharpness; (*de carácter*) liveliness

vívido *a* true

vívido *a* vivid

vivienda *f* housing; (*casa*) house; (*piso*) flat

viviente *a* living

vivificar [7] *vt* (*animar*) enliven

vivir *vt* live through. ● *vi* live. ● *m* life. ~ **de** live on. **de mal** ~ dissolute. **¡viva!** hurray! **¡viva el rey!** long live the king!

vivisección *f* vivisection

vivo *a* alive; (*viviente*) living; ⟨*color*⟩ bright; (*listo*) clever; (*fig*) lively. **a lo** ~, **al** ~ vividly

Vizcaya *f* Biscay

vizconde *m* viscount. ∼**sa** *f* viscountess

vocab|lo *m* word. ∼**ulario** *m* vocabulary

vocación *f* vocation

vocal *a* vocal. ● *f* vowel. ● *m & f* member. ∼**ista** *m & f* vocalist

voce|ar *vt* call ‹mercancías›; (*fig*) proclaim. ● *vi* shout. ∼**río** *m* shouting

vociferar *vi* shout

vodka *m & f* vodka

vola|da *f* flight. ∼**dor** *a* flying. ● *m* rocket. ∼**ndas, en** ∼**ndas** in the air; (*fig, rápidamente*) very quickly. ∼**nte** *a* flying. ● *m* (*auto*) steering-wheel; (*nota*) note; (*rehilete*) shuttlecock; (*tec*) flywheel. ∼**r** [2] *vt* blow up. ● *vi* fly; (*desaparecer, fam*) disappear

volátil *a* volatile

volcán *m* volcano. ∼**ico** *a* volcanic

vol|car [2 & 7] *vt* knock over; (*adrede*) empty out. ● *vi* overturn. ∼**carse** *vpr* fall over; (*vehículo*) overturn; (*fig*) do one's utmost. ∼**carse en** throw o.s. into

vol(e)ibol *m* volleyball

volquete *m* tipper, dump truck

voltaje *m* voltage

volte|ar *vt* turn over; (*en el aire*) toss; ring ‹campanas›. ∼**reta** *f* somersault

voltio *m* volt

voluble *a* (*fig*) fickle

volum|en *m* volume; (*importancia*) importance. ∼**inoso** *a* voluminous

voluntad *f* will; (*fuerza de voluntad*) will-power; (*deseo*) wish; (*intención*) intention. **buena** ∼ goodwill. **mala** ∼ ill will

voluntario *a* voluntary. ● *m* volunteer. ∼**so** *a* willing; (*obstinado*) wilful

voluptuoso *a* voluptuous

volver [2, *pp* **vuelto**] *vt* turn; (*de arriba a abajo*) turn over; (*devolver*) restore. ● *vi* return; (*fig*) revert. ∼**se** *vpr* turn round; (*regresar*) return; (*hacerse*) become. ∼ **a hacer algo** do sth again. ∼ **en sí** come round

vomit|ar *vt* bring up. ● *vi* be sick, vomit. ∼**ivo** *m* emetic. ● *a* disgusting

vómito *m* vomit; (*acción*) vomiting

vorágine *f* maelstrom

voraz *a* voracious

vos *pron* (*LAm*) you

vosotros *pron* you; (*reflexivo*) yourselves. **el libro de** ∼ your book

vot|ación *f* voting; (*voto*) vote. ∼**ante** *m & f* voter. ∼**ar** *vt* vote for.

● *vi* vote. ∼**o** *m* vote; (*relig*) vow; (*maldición*) curse. **hacer** ∼**os por** hope for

voy *vb véase* **ir**

voz *f* voice; (*grito*) shout; (*rumor*) rumour; (*palabra*) word. ∼ **pública** public opinion. **aclarar la** ∼ clear one's throat. **a media** ∼ softly. **a una** ∼ unanimously. **dar voces** shout. **en** ∼ **alta** loudly

vuelco *m* upset. **el corazón me dio un** ∼ my heart missed a beat

vuelo *m* flight; (*acción*) flying; (*de ropa*) flare. **al** ∼ in flight; (*fig*) in passing

vuelta *f* turn; (*curva*) bend; (*paseo*) walk; (*revolución*) revolution; (*regreso*) return; (*dinero*) change. **a la** ∼ on one's return; (*de página*) over the page. **a la** ∼ **de la esquina** round the corner. **dar la** ∼ **al mundo** go round the world. **dar una** ∼ go for a walk. **estar de** ∼ be back. **¡hasta la** ∼! see you soon!

vuelvo *vb véase* **volver**

vuestro *a* your. ● *pron* yours. **un amigo** ∼ a friend of yours

vulg|ar *a* vulgar; ‹persona› common. ∼**aridad** *f* ordinariness; (*trivialidad*) triviality; (*grosería*) vulgarity. ∼**arizar** [10] *vt* popularize. ∼**o** *m* common people

vulnerab|ilidad *f* vulnerability. ∼**le** *a* vulnerable

W

wáter *m* toilet

whisky /'wiski/ *m* whisky

X

xenofobia *f* xenophobia

xilófono *m* xylophone

Y

y *conj* and

ya *adv* already; (*ahora*) now; (*luego*) later; (*en seguida*) immediately; (*pronto*) soon. ● *int* of course! ∼ **no** no longer. ∼ **que** since. **¡**∼**, **∼**!** oh yes!, all right!

yacaré *m* (*LAm*) alligator

yac|er [44] *vi* lie. ∼**imiento** *m* deposit; (*de petróleo*) oilfield

yanqui *m & f* American, Yank(ee)

yate *m* yacht

yegua *f* mare

yeísmo *m* pronunciation of the Spanish *ll* like the Spanish *y*

yelmo *m* helmet

yema *f* (*bot*) bud; (*de huevo*) yolk; (*golosina*) sweet. ~ del dedo fingertip

yergo *vb véase* **erguir**

yermo *a* uninhabited; (*no cultivable*) barren. ● *m* wasteland

yerno *m* son-in-law

yerro *m* mistake. ● *vb véase* **errar**

yerto *a* stiff

yeso *m* gypsum; (*arquit*) plaster. ~ mate plaster of Paris

yo *pron* I. ● *m* ego. ~ mismo I myself. soy ~ it's me

yodo *m* iodine

yoga *m* yoga

yogur *m* yog(h)urt

York. de ~ (*jamón*) cooked

yuca *f* yucca

Yucatán *m* Yucatán

yugo *m* yoke

Yugoslavia *f* Yugoslavia

yugoslavo *a & m* Yugoslav

yunque *m* anvil

yunta *f* yoke

yuxtaponer [34] *vt* juxtapose

yuyo *m* (*Arg*) weed

Z

zafarse *vpr* escape; get out of (*obligación etc*)

zafarrancho *m* (*confusión*) mess; (*riña*) quarrel

zafio *a* coarse

zafiro *m* sapphire

zaga *f* rear. no ir en ~ not be inferior

zaguán *m* hall

zaherir [4] *vt* hurt one's feelings

zahorí *m* clairvoyant; (*de agua*) water diviner

zaino *a* (*caballo*) chestnut; (*vaca*) black

zalamer|ía *f* flattery. ~o *a* flattering. ● *m* flatterer

zamarra *f* (*piel*) sheepskin; (*prenda*) sheepskin jacket

zamarrear *vt* shake

zamba *f* (*esp LAm*) South American dance; (*samba*) samba

zambulli|da *f* dive. ~r [22] *vt* plunge. ~rse *vpr* dive

zamparse *vpr* fall; (*comer*) gobble up

zanahoria *f* carrot

zancad|a *f* stride. ~illa *f* trip. echar la ~illa a uno, poner la ~illa a uno trip s.o. up

zanc|o *m* stilt. ~udo *a* long-legged. ● *m* (*LAm*) mosquito

zanganear *vi* idle

zángano *m* drone; (*persona*) idler

zangolotear *vt* fiddle with. ● *vi* rattle; (*persona*) fidget

zanja *f* ditch. ~r *vt* (*fig*) settle

zapapico *m* pickaxe

zapat|ear *vt/i* tap with one's feet. ~ería *f* shoe shop; (*arte*) shoe-making. ~ero *m* shoemaker; (*el que remienda zapatos*) cobbler. ~illa *f* slipper. ~illas deportivas trainers. ~o *m* shoe

zaragata *f* turmoil

Zaragoza *f* Saragossa

zarand|a *f* sieve. ~ear *vt* sieve; (*sacudir*) shake

zarcillo *m* earring

zarpa *f* claw, paw

zarpar *vi* weigh anchor

zarza *f* bramble. ~mora *f* blackberry

zarzuela *f* musical, operetta

zascandil *m* scatterbrain

zenit *m* zenith

zigzag *m* zigzag. ~uear *vi* zigzag

zinc *m* zinc

zipizape *m* (*fam*) row

zócalo *m* skirting-board; (*pedestal*) plinth

zodiaco *m*, **zodíaco** *m* zodiac

zona *f* zone; (*área*) area

zoo *m* zoo. ~logía *f* zoology. ~lógico *a* zoological

zoólogo *m* zoologist

zopenco *a* stupid. ● *m* idiot

zoquete *m* (*de madera*) block; (*persona*) blockhead

zorr|a *f* fox; (*hembra*) vixen. ~o *m* fox

zozobra *f* (*fig*) anxiety. ~r *vi* be ship-wrecked; (*fig*) be ruined

zueco *m* clog

zulú *a & m* Zulu

zumb|ar *vt* (*fam*) give (*golpe etc*). ● *vi* buzz. ~ido *m* buzzing

zumo *m* juice

zurci|do *m* darning. ~r [9] *vt* darn

zurdo *a* left-handed; (*mano*) left

zurrar *vt* (*fig, dar golpes, fam*) beat up

zurriago *m* whip

zutano *m* so-and-so

TEST YOURSELF WITH WORD GAMES

This section contains a number of word games which will help you to use your dictionary more effectively and to build up your knowledge of Spanish vocabulary and usage in a fun and entertaining way. You will find answers to all puzzles and games at the end of the section.

1 X files

A freak power cut in the office has caused all the computers to go down. When they are re-booted, all the words on the screen have become mysteriously jumbled. Use the **English to Spanish** side of the dictionary to help you decipher these Spanish names of everyday office and computer equipment.

ZIPLÁ

ÓCNAJ

AERODONRD

PRACATE

ODCSI

MOAG

GLOBAFÍRO

TAPALLAN

2 Odd meaning Out

Watch out: one word can have different meanings. In the following exercise, only two of the suggested translations are correct. Use the dictionary to spot the odd one out, then find the correct Spanish translation for it.

vela	sail
	veil
	candle

bote	boot
	jar
	boat

talón	cheque
	heel
	talon

suave	smooth
	suave
	soft

muelle	wharf
	mussel
	jetty

bufete	buffet
	writing desk
	lawyer's office

3 Mystery Word

The following crossword is composed entirely of musical instruments. Put the Spanish translation of the pictures of instruments in the right boxes to form the name of a Spanish composer in the vertical column.

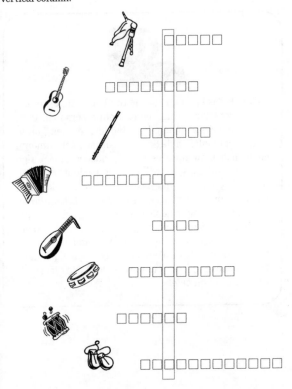

4 Doña Paquita's shooting stars

Doña Paquita is very good at predicting the future, but she is not very good at using the subjunctive. Help her to replace the verbs between brackets with the correct part of the present subjunctive.

Aries: Estás en el apogeo de tu vida, tanto en tu carrera profesional como en el ámbito personal. Pero tienes que evitar que todo (echarse) a perder. Con la influencia maléfica de Saturnio situado actualmente en tu astro, siempre es posible que (suceder) algo negativo. Además, los aries son impacientes por naturaleza y quieren que las cosas (hacerse) lo antes posible. Por lo tanto te aconsejo que no (precipitarse) a la hora de tomar decisiones importantes. Aunque tu situación económica te (parecer) segura, no (contar) con el apoyo de los demás. Sin embargo, con el aspecto favorable de Venus es muy posible que dentro de poco (conocer) a tu pareja ideal. ¡No (dejar) de reconocerlo! ¡Suerte!

5 Write it right

A mother and daughter are getting a little bit annoyed with each other. In the fraught atmosphere, many of the Spanish accents and other punctuation have been left out of the dialogue. You have a box full of characters to be substituted or added in the right place in the text. They must all be used up.

— ¡Raquel! ¿Donde estás?

— Aquí, mama. ¿Que pasa? Por que me gritas así?

— Porque tu no me haces caso. Mira, ¿cuando vas a ordenar tu habitación?

—Cuando tenga tiempo. Quizá manana. No me des la lata ahora!

—Eso me dices todos los días, pero jamas lo haces. No me ayudas nada en la casa y encima me contestas mal. Eres una sinver-guenza y pienso decirselo a tu padre cuando vuelva.

—Perdon, mama. Lo siento. Me pasé, lo se.

6 Crowded suitcase

You are at the airport on your way to visit your Welsh cousins in
Patagonia when you are told that your suitcase is overweight.
Luckily, you had packed a number of things you did not need
because you had forgotten that it was wintertime in the southern
hemisphere. Decide which 5 items to jettison from your luggage.

gafas de sol   calcetines de lana   alpargatas   camisón

esterilla   cepillo de dientes   camiseta

crema bronceadora   camisa de manga corta   cinturón

bañador   abrigo   unas revistas

pantalón corto   bufanda

7 Crossword

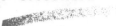

Across
1. we inhabit
7. dative of 'them'
9. scarcely
10. the letter 'n' as spoken (or written)
11. evade – present subjunctive
    (1st or 3rd person singular)
13. reindeer, in reverse
14. swim! – polite imperative (singular)
15. nor
16. clear
18. religious sister
20. go! – familiar imperative (plural)
21. I heard
22. woman's name
23. do! – familiar imperative (singular)
24. sarcasm

Down
2. mountaineers
3. to be unaware of
4. absence
5. wave (figurative
   sense)
6. paths
8. present subjunctive
   of 'ser' (1st or 3rd
   person singular)
12. you (singular) will
    be worth
13. half of the number
    eleven
17. they were hearing
19. ounce

8 Liar, liar

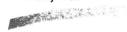

Miguel is telling his parents what he did on his day off while his younger brother Félix was meant to be at school, but he makes a blunder. Once the truth is out, as punishment they both have to write out the story with the correct plural endings and pronouns. Use the verb tables at the back of the dictionary to help you make the necessary alterations to the text.

Iba andando a la playa cuando de repente me encontré con Paco. Me acompañó hasta la tienda de la esquina donde dijo:

– Mira, ¿quieres que te preste mi bicicleta para que llegues más rápido?

Estaba muy cansado y no quería seguir caminando así que acepté con mucho gusto y me fui contentísimo por el camino. Me costó un poco controlar la bici porque era tan grande y casi me caigo un par de veces. La gente me miraba como si estuviera loco y varias personas me gritaban "¡Bravo!"

Cuando estaba ya en la playa se me salieron los pies de los pedales y perdí el control. Bajaba a toda velocidad hacia el agua, de repente frené y–¡plaf! –me caí al agua.

Más tarde, me dio vergüenza devolverle la bicicleta a Paco y naturalmente se echó a reír:

—Pero, ¿qué pasó?–me dijo–¿te diste un buen baño?

Le contesté:

—Fue culpa de él—y dije dándome la vuelta hacia atrás —¡Nunca más voy a montar en un tándem contigo, Félix!

9 Hidden words—false friends

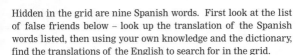

Hidden in the grid are nine Spanish words. First look at the list of false friends below – look up the translation of the Spanish words listed, then using your own knowledge and the dictionary, find the translations of the English to search for in the grid.

O	S	É	T	R	O	C	S	E	D
H	I	G	A	E	C	Í	J	A	O
A	D	O	R	A	R	H	D	E	L
F	O	B	I	N	S	A	H	O	M
N	F	T	É	P	N	L	E	P	A
Ú	R	E	L	A	V	E	Ú	O	S
T	E	R	P	T	O	T	I	T	É
A	C	M	D	Z	A	A	S	I	T
M	E	A	C	R	X	P	O	N	U
S	R	O	J	O	N	Í	A	E	L

English	Spanish	
pie	pie	....
dote	dote	....
red	red	....
tuna	atún	....
lid	lid	....
fin	fin	....
rude	rudo	....
mole	mole	....
tea	tea	....

10 Word Families

It's good to build up word families to increase your vocabulary, but it's important to know the part of speech of each word and how it can fit into a sentence. Pick the right word from each family to go in the space. Everything you need to know for this exercise is in the dictionary.

le falta . . . . .

> preparado
> preparación
> preparó

tuvieron que . . . .

> esconder
> escondrijo
> esconderse

una mujer . . . en años

> entrada
> entró
> entrante

no se hace así en la . . .

> actualmente
> actualidad
> actualización

y por . . . agregarle el agua

> ultimar
> últimamente
> último

la industria . . . de esa región

> floreciente
> florista
> florida

su timidez me . . . .

> desconcierto
> desconcertante
> deconcierta

11 My life's a mess

Pilar Jiménez has a busy schedule but she is a creature of habit and likes to stick to her daily routine. The order of her normal workday has been muddled up in the sentences below. Link up the matching halves of each sentence in the two columns and then try to put the complete sentences in sequence. Be careful, some can link up with more than one of the other column, so you'll have to do them all before you can be sure which go together best.

sólo lee el periódico	para comer
llega a casa	lee la correspondencia
nunca toma café durante	antes de las nueve y media
normalmente saca al perro	muy cansada
le gusta	durante el viaje de vuelta
primero	antes de acostarse
suele salir a mediodía	una reunión
prefiere ducharse antes	por la mañana
siempre entra al trabajo	dar una vuelta antes de volver a la oficina
insiste en tener las reuniones	de cenar

12 Recipe of the Week

The printers have left out some important words in this recipe.
Can you supply the missing words from the jumble below?

COCINA: Receta de la semana

Limpiar y lavar los . . . . y cortarlos en rodajas finas.
Calentar el . . . . . . en una sartén de hierro y freír la . . . . .
picada, los puerros y dos dientes de . . . . . Agregar el vaso de . . . .
. . . . y dejar cocer a . . . . lento durante 10 minutos. Sazonar con
. . . . , ... y . . . . . . picado.
En otra sartén aparte, saltear los trocitos de . . . . . en el resto
del aceite de oliva hasta que empiecen a dorarse. Regar con dos
cucharadas de . . . . . y dejar cocer unos minutos más. Incorporar
las . . . . y la . . . . . .
Distribuir los puerros uniformemente en platos calientes y
colocar el pollo salteado encima. Salar al gusto. Servir
acompañado de una guarnición de . . . . . . al vapor.

puerros   aceite de oliva   **fuego**

cebolla   ajo   vino blanco   **sal**

pimienta   **pollo**   **perejil**   jerez

aceitunas   **nata**   patatas

13 Link-up

The Spanish nouns on the left-hand side are all made up of two separate words but they have been split apart. Try to link up the two halves of each compound, then do the same for the English compounds in the right-hand columns. Now you can match up the Spanish compounds with their English translations.

espanta	minas	mine	sport
sujeta	corchos	pencil	cleaner
porta	pipas	birth	screw
agua	césped	paper	sweeper
saca	aviones	flame	day
draga	años	spoil	crow
lanza	puntas	lawn	sharpener
limpia	fiestas	aircraft	thrower
corta	papeles	pipe	clip
cumple	llamas	scare	carrier
saca	pájaros	cork	mower

Answers

1. lápiz   disco
   cajón   goma
   ordenador   bolígrafo
   carpeta   pantalla

2. veil – velo   suave – zalamero
   boot – bota   mussel – mejillón
   talon – garra   buffet – bufé

3. gaita   laúd
   guitarra   pandereta
   flauta   tambor
   acordeón   castañuelas
   The composer's name is Granados (1867-1916)

4. se eche   parezca
   suceda   cuentes
   se hagan   conozcas
   te precipites   dejes

5. — ¡Raquel! ¿Dónde estás?
   — Aquí, mamá. ¿Qué pasa? ¿Por qué me gritas así?
   — Porque tú no me haces caso. Mira, ¿cuándo vas a ordenar tu
      habitación?
   — Cuando tenga tiempo. Quizá mañana. ¡No me des la lata ahora!
   — Eso me dices todos los días, pero jamás lo haces. No me
      ayudas nada en la casa y encima me contestas mal. Eres una
      sinvergüenza y pienso decírselo a tu padre cuando vuelva.
   — Perdón, mamá. Lo siento. Me pasé, lo sé.

6. alpargatas
   esterilla
   crema bronceadora
   camisa de manga corta
   pantalón corto

7. Crossword answers
Across   1 habitamos   7 les   9 apenas   10 ene   11 evada
            13 oner (=reno)   14 nade   15 ni   16 claro   18 sor   20 id
            21 oí   22 Marisa   23 haz   24 sarcasmo

Down   2 alpinistas 3 ignorar 4 ausencia 5 oleada 6 senderos
8 sea 12 valdrás 13 on (from 'once') 17 oían 19 onza

8. There are two boys going to the beach, the narrator and Félix. The bike
   is a tandem.

   Íbamos   nos encontramos   Nos acompañó   nos dijo

   —Mirad, ¿queréis que os preste. . . ?

   Estábamos muy cansados y no queríamos   aceptamos

   y nos fuimos contentísimos   Nos costó

   casi nos caemos   nos miraba

   como si estuviéramos locos   nos gritaban

   estábamos   se nos salieron   perdimos el control

   Bajábamos   frenamos   Nos dio vergüenza

   ¿os disteis un buen baño?

   Note that the second person plural verb endings given here are all the
   `vosotros' form used in Spain. In Latin America this would be replaced
   by the 'ustedes' form, as follows:

   —Miren, ¿quieren que les preste ...?

   ¿se dieron un buen baño?

9.

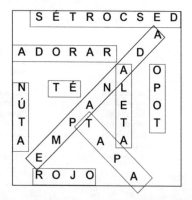

foot	empanada
dowry	adorar
	(= dote on)
net	rojo
torch	té
fight	tapa
end	aleta
rough	descortés
prickly pear	atún
mass, bulk	topo

10. preparación
esconderse
entrada
actualidad
último
floreciente
desconcierta

11. siempre entra al trabajo antes de las nueve y media
primero lee la correspondencia
insiste en tener las reuniones por la mañana
nunca toma café durante una reunión
suele salir a mediodía para comer
le gusta dar una vuelta antes de volver a la oficina
sólo lee el periódico durante el viaje de vuelta
llega a casa muy cansada
prefiere ducharse antes de cenar
normalmente saca al perro antes de acostarse

12.

Limpiar y lavar los PUERROS y cortarlos en rodajas finas.
Calentar el ACEITE DE OLIVA en una sartén de hierro y freír la
CEBOLLA picada, los puerros y dos dientes de AJO. Agregar el vaso de
VINO BLANCO y dejar cocer a FUEGO lento durante 10 minutos. Sazonar
con SAL, PIMIENTA y PEREJIL picado.
En otra sartén aparte, saltear los trocitos de POLLO en el resto del aceite
de oliva hasta que empiecen a dorarse. Regar con dos cucharadas de JEREZ
y dejar cocer unos minutos más. Incorporar las ACEITUNAS y la NATA.
Distribuir los puerros uniformemente en platos calientes y colocar el
pollo salteado encima. Salar al gusto. Servir acompañado de una guarnición de PATATAS al vapor.

13.

espantapájaros	=	scarecrow
sujetapapeles	=	paper clip
portaaviones	=	aircraft carrier
aguafiestas	=	spoilsport
sacacorchos	=	corkscrew
dragaminas	=	minesweeper
lanzallamas	=	flame thrower
cumpleaños	=	birthday
limpiapipas	=	pipe cleaner
cortacésped	=	lawn-mower
sacapuntas	=	pencil sharpener

ENGLISH–SPANISH
INGLÉS–ESPAÑOL

A

a /ə, eɪ/ *indef art* (*before vowel* **an**) un *m*; una *f*

aback /ə'bæk/ *adv.* **be taken ~** quedar desconcertado

abacus /'æbəkəs/ *n* ábaco *m*

abandon /ə'bændən/ *vt* abandonar.
● *n* abandono *m*, desenfado *m*. **~ed** *a* abandonado; ⟨*behaviour*⟩ perdido.
~ment *n* abandono *m*

abase /ə'beɪs/ *vt* degradar. **~ment** *n* degradación *f*

abashed /ə'bæʃt/ *a* confuso

abate /ə'beɪt/ *vt* disminuir. ● *vi* disminuir; ⟨*storm etc*⟩ calmarse.
~ment *n* disminución *f*

abattoir /'æbətwɑ:(r)/ *n* matadero *m*

abbess /'æbɪs/ *n* abadesa *f*

abbey /'æbɪ/ *n* abadía *f*

abbot /'æbət/ *n* abad *m*

abbreviat|e /ə'bri:vɪeɪt/ *vt* abreviar.
~ion /-'eɪʃn/ *n* abreviatura *f*; (*act*) abreviación *f*

ABC /'eɪbi:'si:/ *n* abecé *m*, abecedario *m*

abdicat|e /'æbdɪkeɪt/ *vt/i* abdicar.
~ion /-'eɪʃn/ *n* abdicación *f*

abdom|en /'æbdəmən/ *n* abdomen *m*. **~inal** /-'dɒmɪnl/ *a* abdominal

abduct /æb'dʌkt/ *vt* secuestrar.
~ion /-ʃn/ *n* secuestro *m*. **~or** *n* secuestrador *m*

aberration /æbə'reɪʃn/ *n* aberración *f*

abet /ə'bet/ *vt* (*pt* **abetted**) (*jurid*) ser cómplice de

abeyance /ə'beɪəns/ *n*. **in ~** en suspenso

abhor /əb'hɔ:(r)/ *vt* (*pt* **abhorred**) aborrecer. **~rence** /-'hɒrəns/ *n* aborrecimiento *m*; (*thing*) abominación *f*.
~rent /-'hɒrənt/ *a* aborrecible

abide /ə'baɪd/ *vt* (*pt* **abided**) soportar. ● *vi* (*old use*, *pt* **abode**) morar.
~ by atenerse a; cumplir ⟨*promise*⟩

abiding /ə'baɪdɪŋ/ *a* duradero, permanente

ability /ə'bɪlətɪ/ *n* capacidad *f*; (*cleverness*) habilidad *f*

abject /'æbdʒekt/ *a* (*wretched*) miserable; (*vile*) abyecto

ablaze /ə'bleɪz/ *a* en llamas

able /'eɪbl/ *a* (**-er, -est**) capaz. **be ~** poder; (*know how to*) saber

ablutions /ə'blu:ʃnz/ *npl* ablución *f*

ably /'eɪblɪ/ *adv* hábilmente

abnormal /æb'nɔ:ml/ *a* anormal.
~ity /-'mælətɪ/ *n* anormalidad *f*

aboard /ə'bɔ:d/ *adv* a bordo. ● *prep* a bordo de

abode /ə'bəʊd/ *see* **abide**. ● *n* (*old use*) domicilio *m*

abolish /ə'bɒlɪʃ/ *vt* suprimir, abolir

abolition /æbə'lɪʃn/ *n* supresión *f*, abolición *f*

abominable /ə'bɒmɪnəbl/ *a* abominable

abominat|e /ə'bɒmɪneɪt/ *vt* abominar. **~ion** /-'neɪʃn/ *n* abominación *f*

aborigin|al /æbə'rɪdʒənl/ *a & n* aborigen (*m & f*), indígena (*m & f*).
~es /-i:z/ *npl* aborígenes *mpl*

abort /ə'bɔ:t/ *vt* hacer abortar. ● *vi* abortar. **~ion** /-ʃn/ *n* aborto *m* provocado; (*fig*) aborto *m*. **~ionist** *n* abortista *m & f*. **~ive** *a* abortivo; (*fig*) fracasado

abound /ə'baʊnd/ *vi* abundar (**in** de, en)

about /ə'baʊt/ *adv* (*approximately*) alrededor de; (*here and there*) por todas partes; (*in existence*) por aquí.
~ here por aquí. **be ~ to** estar a punto de. **be up and ~** estar levantado. ● *prep* sobre; (*around*) alrededor de; (*somewhere in*) en. **talk ~** hablar de. **~-face** *n* (*fig*) cambio *m* rotundo. **~-turn** *n* (*fig*) cambio *m* rotundo

above /ə'bʌv/ *adv* arriba. ● *prep* encima de; (*more than*) más de. **~ all** sobre todo. **~-board** *a* honrado.

● *adv* abiertamente. ~-mentioned *a* susodicho

abrasi|on /ə'breɪʒn/ *n* abrasión *f.* ~ve /ə'breɪsɪv/ *a & n* abrasivo (*m*); (*fig*) agresivo, brusco

abreast /ə'brest/ *adv* de frente. keep ~ of mantenerse al corriente de

abridge /ə'brɪdʒ/ *vt* abreviar. ~ment *n* abreviación *f*; (*abstract*) resumen *m*

abroad /ə'brɔːd/ *adv* (*be*) en el extranjero; (*go*) al extranjero; (*far and wide*) por todas partes

abrupt /ə'brʌpt/ *a* brusco. ~ly *adv* (*suddenly*) repentinamente; (*curtly*) bruscamente. ~ness *n* brusquedad *f*

abscess /'æbsɪs/ *n* absceso *m*

abscond /əb'skɒnd/ *vi* fugarse

absen|ce /'æbsəns/ *n* ausencia *f*; (*lack*) falta *f*. ~t /'æbsənt/ *a* ausente. /æb'sent/ *vr.* ~ o.s. ausentarse. ~tly *adv* distraídamente. ~t-minded *a* distraído. ~t-mindedness *n* distracción *f*, despiste *m*

absentee /æbsən'tiː/ *n* ausente *m & f*. ~ism *n* absentismo *m*

absinthe /'æbsɪnθ/ *n* ajenjo *m*

absolute /'æbsəluːt/ *a* absoluto. ~ly *adv* absolutamente

absolution /æbsə'luːʃn/ *n* absolución *f*

absolve /əb'zɒlv/ *vt* (*from sin*) absolver; (*from obligation*) liberar

absor|b /əb'zɔːb/ *vt* absorber. ~bent *a* absorbente. ~ption *n* absorción *f*

abstain /əb'steɪn/ *vi* abstenerse (from de)

abstemious /əb'stiːmɪəs/ *a* abstemio

abstention /əb'stenʃn/ *n* abstención *f*

abstinen|ce /'æbstɪnəns/ *n* abstinencia *f*. ~t *a* abstinente

abstract /'æbstrækt/ *a* abstracto. ● *n* (*quality*) abstracto *m*; (*summary*) resumen *m*. /əb'strækt/ *vt* extraer; (*summarize*) resumir. ~ion /-ʃn/ *n* abstracción *f*

abstruse /əb'struːs/ *a* abstruso

absurd /əb'sɜːd/ *a* absurdo. ~ity *n* absurdo *m*, disparate *m*

abundan|ce /ə'bʌndəns/ *n* abundancia *f*. ~t *a* abundante

abuse /ə'bjuːz/ *vt* (*misuse*) abusar de; (*ill-treat*) maltratar; (*insult*) insultar. /ə'bjuːs/ *n* abuso *m*; (*insults*) insultos *mpl*

abusive /ə'bjuːsɪv/ *a* injurioso

abut /ə'bʌt/ *vi* (*pt* abutted) confinar (on con)

abysmal /ə'bɪzml/ *a* abismal; (*bad, fam*) pésimo; (*fig*) profundo

abyss /ə'bɪs/ *n* abismo *m*

acacia /ə'keɪʃə/ *n* acacia *f*

academic /ækə'demɪk/ *a* académico; (*pej*) teórico. ● *n* universitario *m*, catedrático *m*. ~ian /-də'mɪʃn/ *n* académico *m*

academy /ə'kædəmɪ/ *n* academia *f*. ~ of music conservatorio *m*

accede /ək'siːd/ *vi*. ~ to acceder a (*request*); tomar posesión de (*office*). ~ to the throne subir al trono

accelerat|e /ək'seləreɪt/ *vt* acelerar. ~ion /-'reɪʃn/ *n* aceleración *f*. ~or *n* acelerador *m*

accent /'æksənt/ *n* acento *m*. /æk'sent/ *vt* acentuar

accentuate /æk'sentʃʊeɪt/ *vt* acentuar

accept /ək'sept/ *vt* aceptar. ~able *a* aceptable. ~ance *n* aceptación *f*; (*approval*) aprobación *f*

access /'ækses/ *n* accceso *m*. ~ibility /-ɪ'bɪlətɪ/ *n* accesibilidad *f*. ~ible /ək'sesəbl/ *a* accesible; (*person*) tratable

accession /æk'seʃn/ *n* (*to power, throne etc*) ascenso *m*; (*thing added*) adquisición *f*

accessory /ək'sesərɪ/ *a* accesorio. ● *n* accesorio *m*, complemento *m*; (*jurid*) cómplice *m & f*

accident /'æksɪdənt/ *n* accidente *m*; (*chance*) casualidad *f*. by ~ por accidente, por descuido, sin querer; (*by chance*) por casualidad. ~al /-'dentl/ *a* accidental, fortuito. ~ally /-'dentlɪ/ *adv* por accidente, por descuido, sin querer; (*by chance*) por casualidad

acclaim /ə'kleɪm/ *vt* aclamar. ● *n* aclamación *f*

acclimatiz|ation /əklaɪmətar'zeɪʃn/ *n* aclimatación *f*. ~e /ə'klaɪmətaɪz/ *vt* aclimatar. ● *vi* aclimatarse

accolade /'ækəleɪd/ *n* (*of knight*) acolada *f*; (*praise*) encomio *m*

accommodat|e /ə'kɒmədeɪt/ *vt* (*give hospitality to*) alojar; (*adapt*) acomodar; (*supply*) proveer; (*oblige*) complacer. ~ing *a* complaciente. ~ion /-'deɪʃn/ *n* alojamiento *m*; (*rooms*) habitaciones *fpl*

accompan|iment /ə'kʌmpənɪmənt/ *n* acompañamiento *m*. ~ist *n*

acompañante *m & f.* ~y /ə'kʌmpəni/
vt acompañar

accomplice /ə'kʌmplɪs/ *n* cómplice
m & f

accomplish /ə'kʌmplɪʃ/ *vt* (*complete*) acabar; (*achieve*) realizar;
(*carry out*) llevar a cabo. ~ed *a* consumado. ~ment *n* realización *f*;
(*ability*) talento *m*; (*thing achieved*)
triunfo *m*, logro *m*

accord /ə'kɔːd/ *vi* concordar. •*vt*
conceder. •*n* acuerdo *m*; (*harmony*)
armonía *f*. of one's own ~ espontáneamente. ~ance *n*. in ~ance
with de acuerdo con

according /ə'kɔːdɪŋ/ *adv*. ~ to
según. ~ly *adv* en conformidad;
(*therefore*) por consiguiente

accordion /ə'kɔːdiən/ *n* acordeón *m*

accost /ə'kɒst/ *vt* abordar

account /ə'kaunt/ *n* cuenta *f*; (*description*) relato *m*; (*importance*) importancia *f*. on ~ of a causa de. on
no ~ de ninguna manera. on this ~
por eso. take into ~ tener en cuenta.
•*vt* considerar. ~ for dar cuenta de,
explicar

accountab|ility /əkauntə'bɪləti/ *n*
responsabilidad *f*. ~le a responsable
(for de)

accountan|cy /ə'kauntənsi/ *n* contabilidad *f*. ~t *n* contable *m & f*

accoutrements /ə'kuːtrəmənts/ *npl*
equipo *m*

accredited /ə'kredɪtɪd/ *a* acreditado; (*authorized*) autorizado

accrue /ə'kruː/ *vi* acumularse

accumulat|e /ə'kjuːmjuleɪt/ *vt* acumular. ~*vi* acumularse. ~ion
/-'leɪʃn/ *n* acumulación *f*. ~or *n* (*elec*)
acumulador *m*

accura|cy /'ækjərəsi/ *n* exactitud *f*,
precisión *f*. ~te *a* exacto, preciso

accus|ation /ækjuː'zeɪʃn/ *n* acusación *f*. ~e *vt* acusar

accustom /ə'kʌstəm/ *vt* acostumbrar. ~ed *a* acostumbrado. get
~ed (to) acostumbrarse (a)

ace /eɪs/ *n* as *m*

acetate /'æsɪteɪt/ *n* acetato *m*

ache /eɪk/ *n* dolor *m*. •*vi* doler. my
leg ~s me duele la pierna

achieve /ə'tʃiːv/ *vt* realizar; lograr
(*success*). ~ment *n* realización *f*;
(*feat*) éxito *m*; (*thing achieved*) proeza
f, logro *m*

acid /'æsɪd/ *a & n* ácido (*m*). ~ity
/ə'sɪdəti/ *n* acidez *f*

acknowledge /ək'nɒlɪdʒ/ *vt* reconocer. ~ receipt of acusar recibo de.
~ment *n* reconocimiento *m*; (*com*)
acuse *m* de recibo

acme /'ækmɪ/ *n* cima *f*

acne /'ækni/ *n* acné *m*

acorn /'eɪkɔːn/ *n* bellota *f*

acoustic /ə'kuːstɪk/ *a* acústico. ~s
npl acústica *f*

acquaint /ə'kweɪnt/ *vt*. ~ s.o. with
poner a uno al corriente de. be ~ed
with conocer (*person*); saber (*fact*).
~ance *n* conocimiento *m*; (*person*)
conocido *m*

acquiesce /ækwɪ'es/ *vi* consentir (in
en). ~nce *n* aquiescencia *f*, consentimiento *m*

acqui|re /ə'kwaɪə(r)/ *vt* adquirir;
aprender (*language*). ~re a taste
for tomar gusto a. ~sition
/ækwɪ'zɪʃn/ *n* adquisición *f*. ~sitive
/-'kwɪzətɪv/ *a* codicioso

acquit /ə'kwɪt/ *vt* (*pt* acquitted) absolver; ~ o.s. well defenderse bien,
tener éxito. ~tal *n* absolución *f*

acre /'eɪkə(r)/ *n* acre *m*. ~age *n*
superficie *f* (en acres)

acrid /'ækrɪd/ *a* acre

acrimon|ious /ækrɪ'məunɪəs/ *a*
cáustico, mordaz. ~y /'ækrɪməni/ *n*
acrimonia *f*, acritud *f*

acrobat /'ækrəbæt/ *n* acróbata *m & f*. ~ic /-'bætɪk/ *a* acrobático. ~ics
/-'bætɪks/ *npl* acrobacia *f*

acronym /'ækrənɪm/ *n* acrónimo *m*,
siglas *fpl*

across /ə'krɒs/ *adv & prep* (*side to
side*) de un lado al otro; (*on other side*)
del otro lado de; (*crosswise*) a través.
go or walk ~ atravesar

act /ækt/ *n* acto *m*; (*action*) acción *f*;
(*in variety show*) número *m*; (*decree*)
decreto *m*. •*vt* hacer (*part, role*). •*vi*
actuar; (*pretend*) fingir; (*function*)
funcionar. ~ as actuar de. ~ for representar. ~ing *a* interino. •*n* (*of
play*) representación *f*; (*by actor*)
interpretación *f*; (*profession*) profesión *f* de actor

action /'ækʃn/ *n* acción *f*; (*jurid*) demanda *f*; (*plot*) argumento *m*. out of
~ (*on sign*) no funciona. put out of
~ inutilizar. take ~ tomar medidas

activate /'æktɪveɪt/ *vt* activar

activ|e /'æktɪv/ *a* activo; (*energetic*)
enérgico; (*volcano*) en actividad.
~ity /-'tɪvəti/ *n* actividad *f*

act|or /'æktə(r)/ n actor m. **~ress**n
actriz f

actual /'æktʃʊəl/ a verdadero. **~ity**
/-'ælətɪ/ n realidad f. **~ly** adv en
realidad, efectivamente; (even) incluso

actuary /'æktʃʊərɪ/ n actuario m

actuate /'æktʃʊeɪt/ vt accionar, impulsar

acumen /'ækjʊmen/ n perspicacia f

acupunctur|e /'ækjʊpʌŋktʃə(r)/ n
acupuntura f. **~ist** n acupunturista
m & f

acute /ə'kjuːt/ a agudo. **~ly** adv agu-
damente. **~ness** n agudeza f

ad /æd/ n (fam) anuncio m

AD /eɪ'diː/ abbr (Anno Domini) d.J.C.

adamant /'ædəmənt/ a inflexible

Adam's apple /'ædəmz'æpl/ n nuez
f (de Adán)

adapt /ə'dæpt/ vt adaptar. **●**vi
adaptarse

adaptab|ility /ədæptə'bɪlətɪ/ n
adaptabilidad f. **~le** /ə'dæptəbl/ a
adaptable

adaptation /ædæp'teɪʃn/ n adaptación f; (of book etc) versión f

adaptor /ə'dæptə(r)/ n (elec) adapta-
dor m

add /æd/ vt añadir. **●**vi sumar. **~ up**
sumar; (fig) tener sentido. **~ up to**
equivaler a

adder /'ædə(r)/ n víbora f

addict /'ædɪkt/ n adicto m; (fig) entusiasta m & f. **~ed** /ə'dɪktɪd/ a.
~ed to adicto a; (fig) fanático de.
~ion /-ʃn/ n (med) dependencia f;
(fig) afición f. **~ive** a que crea dependencia

adding machine /'ædɪŋməʃiːn/ n
máquina f de sumar, sumadora f

addition /ə'dɪʃn/ n suma f. in **~**
además. **~al**/-ʃənl/ a suplementario

additive /'ædɪtɪv/ a & n aditivo (m)

address /ə'dres/ n señas fpl, dirección f; (speech) discurso m. **●** vt poner
la dirección; (speak to) dirigirse a.
~ee /ædre'siː/ n destinatario m

adenoids /'ædɪnɔɪdz/ npl vegeta-
ciones fpl adenoideas

adept /'ædept/ a & n experto (m)

adequa|cy /'ædɪkwəsɪ/ n suficiencia
f. **~te** a suficiente, adecuado. **~tely**
adv suficientemente, adecuadamente

adhere /əd'hɪə(r)/ vi adherirse (to
a); observar (rule). **~nce** /-rəns/ n
adhesión f; (to rules) observancia f

adhesion /əd'hiːʒn/ n adherencia f

adhesive /əd'hiːsɪv/ a & n adhesivo
(m)

ad infinitum /ædɪnfɪ'naɪtəm/ adv
hasta el infinito

adjacent /ə'dʒeɪsnt/ a contiguo

adjective /'ædʒɪktɪv/ n adjetivo m

adjoin /ə'dʒɔɪn/ vt lindar con. **~ing**
a contiguo

adjourn /ə'dʒɜːn/ vt aplazar; suspender (meeting etc). **●**vi sus-
penderse. **~ to**trasladarse a

adjudicate /ə'dʒuːdɪkeɪt/ vt juzgar.
●vi actuar como juez

adjust /ə'dʒʌst/ vt ajustar
(machine); (arrange) arreglar. **●**vi.
~ (to) adaptarse (a). **~able** a ajus-
table. **~ment** n adaptación f; (tec)
ajuste m

ad lib /æd'lɪb/ a improvisado. **●**vi
(pt **-libbed**) (fam) improvisar

administer /əd'mɪnɪstə(r)/ vt administrar, dar, proporcionar

administrat|ion /ədmɪnɪ'streɪʃn/ n
administración f. **~or** n administrador m

admirable /'ædmərəbl/ a admirable

admiral /'ædmərəl/ n almirante m

admiration /ædmə'reɪʃn/ n admiración f

admire /əd'maɪə(r)/ vt admirar. **~r**
/-'maɪərə(r)/ n admirador m; (suitor)
enamorado m

admissible /əd'mɪsəbl/ a admisible

admission /əd'mɪʃn/ n admisión f;
(entry) entrada f

admit /əd'mɪt/ vt (pt **admitted**)
dejar entrar; (acknowledge) admitir,
reconocer. **~ to** confesar. **be ~ted**
(to hospital etc) ingresar. **~tance** n
entrada f. **~tedly**adv es verdad que

admoni|sh /əd'mɒnɪʃ/ vt reprender;
(advise) aconsejar. **~tion** /-'nɪʃn/ n
reprensión f

ado /ə'duː/ n alboroto m; (trouble)
dificultad f. **without more ~** en
seguida, sin más

adolescen|ce /ædə'lesns/ n adoles-
cencia f. **~ta** & n adolescente (m & f)

adopt /ə'dɒpt/ vt adoptar. **~ed** a
(child) adoptivo. **~ion** /-ʃn/ n
adopción f. **~ive** a adoptivo

ador|able /ə'dɔːrəbl/ a adorable.
~ation /ædə'reɪʃn/ n adoración f.
~e /ə'dɔː(r)/ vt adorar

adorn /ə'dɔːn/ vt adornar. **~ment** n
adorno m

adrenalin /ə'drenəlɪn/ n adrenalina
f

adrift /əˈdrɪft/ *a & adv* a la deriva

adroit /əˈdrɔɪt/ *a* diestro

adulation /ædjʊˈleɪʃn/ *n* adulación *f*

adult /ˈædʌlt/ *a & n* adulto (*m*)

adulterat|ion /ədʌltəˈreɪʃn/ *n* adulteración *f*. **~e** /əˈdʌltəreɪt/ *vt* adulterar

adulter|er /əˈdʌltərə(r)/ *n* adúltero *m*. **~ess** *n* adúltera *f*. **~ous** *a* adúltero. **~y** *n* adulterio *m*

advance /ədˈvɑːns/ *vt* adelantar. • *vi* adelantarse. • *n* adelanto *m*. **in ~** con anticipación, por adelantado. **~d** *a* avanzado; (*studies*) superior. **~ment** *n* adelanto *m*; (*in job*) promoción *f*

advantage /ədˈvɑːntɪdʒ/ *n* ventaja *f*. **take ~ of** aprovecharse de; abusar de (*person*). **~ous** /ædvənˈteɪdʒəs/ *a* ventajoso

advent /ˈædvənt/ *n* venida *f*. **A~** *n* adviento *m*

adventur|e /ədˈventʃə(r)/ *n* aventura *f*. **~er** *n* aventurero *m*. **~ous** *a* (*persona*) aventurero; (*cosa*) arriesgado; (*fig, bold*) llamativo

adverb /ˈædvɜːb/ *n* adverbio *m*

adversary /ˈædvəsərɪ/ *n* adversario *m*

advers|e /ˈædvɜːs/ *a* adverso, contrario, desfavorable. **~ity** /ədˈvɜːsətɪ/ *n* infortunio *m*

advert /ˈædvɜːt/ *n* (*fam*) anuncio *m*. **~ise** /ˈædvətaɪz/ *vt* anunciar. • *vi* hacer publicidad; (*seek, sell*) poner un anuncio. **~isement** /ədˈvɜːtɪsmənt/ *n* anuncio *m*. **~iser** /-ə(r)/ *n* anunciante *m & f*

advice /ədˈvaɪs/ *n* consejo *m*; (*report*) informe *m*

advis|able /ədˈvaɪzəbl/ *a* aconsejable. **~e** *vt* aconsejar; (*inform*) avisar. **~e against** aconsejar en contra de. **~er** *n* consejero *m*; (*consultant*) asesor *m*. **~ory** *a* consultivo

advocate /ˈædvəkət/ *n* defensor *m*; (*jurid*) abogado *m*. /ˈædvəkeɪt/ *vt* recomendar

aegis /ˈiːdʒɪs/ *n* égida *f*. **under the ~ of** bajo la tutela de, patrocinado por

aeon /ˈiːən/ *n* eternidad *f*

aerial /ˈeərɪəl/ *a* aéreo. • *n* antena *f*

aerobatics /eərəˈbætɪks/ *npl* acrobacia *f* aérea

aerobics /eəˈrɒbɪks/ *npl* aeróbica *f*

aerodrome /ˈeərədrəʊm/ *n* aeródromo *m*

aerodynamic /eərəʊdaɪˈnæmɪk/ *a* aerodinámico

aeroplane /ˈeərəpleɪn/ *n* avión *m*

aerosol /ˈeərəsɒl/ *n* aerosol *m*

aesthetic /iːsˈθetɪk/ *a* estético

afar /əˈfɑː(r)/ *adv* lejos

affable /ˈæfəbl/ *a* afable

affair /əˈfeə(r)/ *n* asunto *m*. **(love) ~** aventura *f*, amorío *m*. **~s** *npl* (*business*) negocios *mpl*

affect /əˈfekt/ *vt* afectar; (*pretend*) fingir

affect|ation /æfekˈteɪʃn/ *n* afectación *f*. **~ed** *a* afectado, amanerado

affection /əˈfekʃn/ *n* cariño *m*; (*disease*) afección *f*. **~ate** /-ʃənət/ *a* cariñoso

affiliat|e /əˈfɪlɪeɪt/ *vt* afiliar. **~ion** /-ˈeɪʃn/ *n* afiliación *f*

affinity /əˈfɪnətɪ/ *n* afinidad *f*

affirm /əˈfɜːm/ *vt* afirmar. **~ation** /æfəˈmeɪʃn/ *n* afirmación *f*

affirmative /əˈfɜːmətɪv/ *a* afirmativo. • *n* respuesta *f* afirmativa

affix /əˈfɪks/ *vt* sujetar; añadir (*signature*); pegar (*stamp*)

afflict /əˈflɪkt/ *vt* afligir. **~ion** /-ʃn/ *n* aflicción *f*, pena *f*

affluen|ce /ˈæfluəns/ *n* riqueza *f*. **~t** *a* rico. • *n* (*geog*) afluente *m*

afford /əˈfɔːd/ *vt* permitirse; (*provide*) dar

affray /əˈfreɪ/ *n* reyerta *f*

affront /əˈfrʌnt/ *n* afrenta *f*, ofensa *f*. • *vt* afrentar, ofender

afield /əˈfiːld/ *adv*. **far ~** muy lejos

aflame /əˈfleɪm/ *adv & a* en llamas

afloat /əˈfləʊt/ *adv* a flote

afoot /əˈfʊt/ *adv*. **sth is ~** se está tramando algo

aforesaid /əˈfɔːsed/ *a* susodicho

afraid /əˈfreɪd/ *a*. **be ~** tener miedo (**of** *a*); (*be sorry*) sentir, lamentar

afresh /əˈfreʃ/ *adv* de nuevo

Africa /ˈæfrɪkə/ *n* África *f*. **~n** *a & n* africano (*m*)

after /ˈɑːftə(r)/ *adv* después; (*behind*) detrás. • *prep* después de; (*behind*) detrás de. **be ~** (*seek*) buscar, andar en busca de. • *conj* después de que. • *a* posterior

afterbirth /ˈɑːftəbɜːθ/ *n* placenta *f*

after-effect /ˈɑːftərɪfekt/ *n* consecuencia *f*, efecto *m* secundario

aftermath /ˈɑːftəmæθ/ *n* secuelas *fpl*

afternoon /ɑːftəˈnuːn/ *n* tarde *f*

aftershave /'ɑ:ftəʃeɪv/ n loción f para después del afeitado

afterthought /'ɑ:ftəθɔ:t/ n ocurrencia f tardía

afterwards /'ɑ:ftəwədz/ adv después

again /ə'gen/ adv otra vez; (besides) además. ~ and ~ una y otra vez

against /ə'genst/ prep contra, en contra de

age /eɪdʒ/ n edad f. of ~ mayor de edad. under ~ menor de edad. ● vt/i (pres p ageing) envejecer. ~d /'eɪdʒd/ a de ... años. ~d 10 de 10 años, que tiene 10 años. ~d /'eɪdʒɪd/ a viejo, anciano. ~less a siempre joven; (eternal) eterno, inmemorial. ~s (fam) siglos mpl

agency /'eɪdʒənsɪ/ n agencia f, organismo m, oficina f; (means) mediación f

agenda /ə'dʒendə/ npl orden m del día

agent /'eɪdʒənt/ n agente m & f; (representative) representante m & f

agglomeration /əglɒmə'reɪʃn/ n aglomeración f

aggravat|e /'ægrəveɪt/ vt agravar; (irritate, fam) irritar. ~ion /-'veɪʃn/ n agravación f, (irritation, fam) irritación f

aggregate /'ægrɪgət/ a total. ● n conjunto m. /'ægrɪgeɪt/ vt agregar. ● vi ascender a

aggress|ion /ə'greʃn/ n agresión f. ~ive a agresivo. ~iveness n agresividad f. ~or n agresor a

aggrieved /ə'gri:vd/ a apenado, ofendido

aghast /ə'gɑ:st/ a horrorizado

agil|e /'ædʒaɪl/ a ágil. ~ity /ə'dʒɪlətɪ/ n agilidad f

agitat|e /'ædʒɪteɪt/ vt agitar. ~ion /-'teɪʃn/ n agitación f, excitación f. ~or n agitador m

agnostic /æg'nɒstɪk/ a & n agnóstico (m). ~ism /-sɪzəm/ n agnosticismo m

ago /ə'gəʊ/ adv hace. a long time ~ hace mucho tiempo. 3 days ~ hace 3 días

agog /ə'gɒg/ a ansioso

agon|ize /'ægənaɪz/ vi atormentarse. ~izing a atroz, angustioso, doloroso. ~y n dolor m (agudo); (mental) angustia f

agree /ə'gri:/ vt acordar. ● vi estar de acuerdo; (of figures) concordar; (get on) entenderse. ~ with (of food etc) sentar bien a. ~able /ə'gri:əbl/ a agradable. be ~able (willing) estar de acuerdo. ~d a (time, place) convenido. ~ment /ə'gri:mənt/ n acuerdo m. in ~ment de acuerdo

agricultur|al /ægrɪ'kʌltʃərəl/ a agrícola. ~e /'ægrɪkʌltʃə(r)/ n agricultura f

aground /ə'graʊnd/ adv. run ~ (of ship) varar, encallar

ahead /ə'hed/ adv delante; (of time) antes de. be ~ ir delante

aid /eɪd/ vt ayudar. ● n ayuda f. in ~ of a beneficio de

aide /eɪd/ n (Amer) ayudante m & f

AIDS /eɪdz/ n (med) SIDA m

ail /eɪl/ vt afligir. ~ing a enfermo. ~ment n enfermedad f

aim /eɪm/ vt apuntar; (fig) dirigir. ● vi apuntar; (fig) pretender. ● n puntería f; (fig) propósito m. ~less a, ~lessly adv sin objeto, sin rumbo

air /eə(r)/ n aire m. be on the ~ estar en el aire. put on ~s darse aires. ● vt airear. ● a (base etc) aéreo. ~borne a en el aire; (mil) aerotransportado. ~conditioned a climatizado, con aire acondicionado. ~craft /'eəkrɑ:ft/ n (pl invar) avión m. ~field /'eəfi:ld/ n aeródromo m. A~ Force fuerzas fpl aéreas. ~gun /'eəgʌn/ n escopeta f de aire comprimido. ~lift /'eəlɪft/ n puente m aéreo. ~line /'eəlaɪn/ n línea f aérea. ~lock /'eəlɒk/ n (in pipe) burbuja f de aire; (chamber) esclusa f de aire. ~ mail n correo m aéreo. ~man /'eəmən/ (pl -men) n aviador m. ~port /'eəpɔ:t/ n aeropuerto m. ~tight /'eətaɪt/ a hermético. ~worthy /'eəwɜ:ðɪ/ a en condiciones de vuelo. ~y /'eərɪ/ a (-ier, -iest) aireado; (manner) ligero

aisle /aɪl/ n nave f lateral; (gangway) pasillo m

ajar /ə'dʒɑ:(r)/ adv & a entreabierto

akin /ə'kɪn/ a semejante (a to)

alabaster /'æləbɑ:stə(r)/ n alabastro m

alacrity /ə'lækrətɪ/ n prontitud f

alarm /ə'lɑ:m/ n alarma f; (clock) despertador m. ● vt asustar. ~ist n alarmista m & f

alas /ə'læs/ int ¡ay!, ¡ay de mí!

albatross /'ælbətrɒs/ n albatros m

albino /æl'bi:nəʊ/ a & n albino (m)

album /'ælbəm/ n álbum m

alchemist /'ælkəmɪst/ n alquimista m & f. ∼n alquimia f

alcohol /'ælkəhɒl/ n alcohol m. ∼ic /-'hɒlɪk/ a & n alcohólico (m). ∼ism n alcoholismo m

alcove /'ælkəʊv/ n nicho m

ale /eɪl/ n cerveza f

alert /ə'lɜ:t/ a vivo; (watchful) vigilante. ● n alerta f. on the ∼ alerta. ● vt avisar. ∼ness n vigilancia f

algebra /'ældʒɪbrə/ n álgebra f

Algeria /æl'dʒɪərɪə/ n Argelia f. ∼n a & n argelino (m)

alias /'eɪlɪəs/ n (pl -ases) alias m invar. ● adv alias

alibi /'ælɪbaɪ/ n (pl -is) coartada f

alien /'eɪlɪən/ n extranjero m. ● a ajeno

alienat|e /'eɪlɪəneɪt/ vt enajenar. ∼ion /-'neɪʃn/ n enajenación f

alight¹ /ə'laɪt/ vi bajar; ⟨bird⟩ posarse

alight² /ə'laɪt/ a ardiendo; ⟨light⟩ encendido

align /ə'laɪn/ vt alinear. ∼ment n alineación f

alike /ə'laɪk/ a parecido, semejante. look or be ∼ parecerse. ● adv de la misma manera

alimony /'ælɪmənɪ/ n pensión f alimenticia

alive /ə'laɪv/ a vivo. ∼ to sensible a. ∼ with lleno de

alkali /'ælkəlaɪ/ n (pl -is) álcali m. ∼ne a alcalino

all /ɔ:l/ a & pron todo. ∼ but one todos excepto uno. ∼ of it todo. ● adv completamente. ∼ but casi. ∼ in (fam) rendido. ∼ of a sudden de pronto. ∼ over (finished) acabado; (everywhere) por todas partes. ∼ right! ¡vale! be ∼ for estar a favor de. not at ∼ de ninguna manera; (after thanks!) ¡no hay de qué!

allay /ə'leɪ/ vt aliviar ⟨pain⟩; aquietar ⟨fears etc⟩

all-clear /ɔ:l'klɪə(r)/ n fin m de (la) alarma

allegation /ælɪ'geɪʃn/ n alegato m

allege /ə'ledʒ/ vt alegar. ∼dly /-ɪdlɪ/ adv según se dice, supuestamente

allegiance /ə'li:dʒəns/ n lealtad f

allegor|ical /ælɪ'gɒrɪkl/ a alegórico. ∼y /'ælɪgərɪ/ n alegoría f

allerg|ic /ə'lɜ:dʒɪk/ a alérgico. ∼y /'ælədʒɪ/ n alergia f

alleviat|e /ə'li:vɪeɪt/ vt aliviar. ∼ion /-'eɪʃn/ n alivio m

alley /'ælɪ/ (pl -eys) n callejuela f; (for bowling) bolera f

alliance /ə'laɪəns/ n alianza f

allied /'ælaɪd/ a aliado

alligator /'ælɪgeɪtə(r)/ n caimán m

allocat|e /'æləkeɪt/ vt asignar; (share out) repartir. ∼ion /-'keɪʃn/ n asignación f; (share) ración f; (distribution) reparto m

allot /ə'lɒt/ vt (pt allotted) asignar. ∼ment n asignación f; (share) ración f; (land) parcela f

all-out /ɔ:l'aʊt/ a máximo

allow /ə'laʊ/ vt permitir; (grant) conceder; (reckon on) prever; (agree) admitir. ∼ for tener en cuenta. ∼ance /ə'laʊəns/ n concesión f; (pension) pensión f; (com) rebaja f. make ∼ances for ser indulgente con; (take into account) tener en cuenta

alloy /'ælɔɪ/ n aleación f. /ə'lɔɪ/ vt alear

all-round /ɔ:l'raʊnd/ a completo

allude /ə'lu:d/ vi aludir

allure /ə'lʊə(r)/ vt atraer. ● n atractivo m

allusion /ə'lu:ʒn/ n alusión f

ally /'ælaɪ/ n aliado m. /ə'laɪ/ vt aliarse

almanac /'ɔ:lmənæk/ n almanaque m

almighty /ɔ:l'maɪtɪ/ a todopoderoso; (big, fam) enorme. ● n. the A∼ el Todopoderoso m

almond /'ɑ:mənd/ n almendra f; (tree) almendro (m)

almost /'ɔ:lməʊst/ adv casi

alms /ɑ:mz/ n limosna f

alone /ə'ləʊn/ a solo. ● adv sólo, solamente

along /ə'lɒŋ/ prep por, a lo largo de. ● adv. ∼ with junto con. all ∼ todo el tiempo. come ∼ venga

alongside /ə'lɒŋ'saɪd/ adv (naut) al costado. ● prep al lado de

aloof /ə'lu:f/ adv apartado. ● a reservado. ∼ness n reserva f

aloud /ə'laʊd/ adv en voz alta

alphabet /'ælfəbet/ n alfabeto m. ∼ical /-'betɪkl/ a alfabético

alpine /'ælpaɪn/ a alpino

Alps /ælps/ npl. the ∼ los Alpes mpl

already /ɔ:l'redɪ/ adv ya

Alsatian /æl'seɪʃn/ n (geog) alsaciano m; (dog) pastor m alemán

also /'ɔːlsəʊ/ adv también; (moreover) además

altar /'ɔːltə(r)/ n altar m

alter /'ɔːltə(r)/ vt cambiar. ● vi cambiarse. ~ation /-'reɪʃn/ n modificación f; (to garment) arreglo m

alternate /ɔːl'tɜːnət/ a alterno. /'ɔːltəneɪt/ vt/i alternar. ~ly adv alternativamente

alternative /ɔːl'tɜːnətɪv/ a alternativo. ● n alternativa f. ~ly adv en cambio, por otra parte

although /ɔːl'ðəʊ/ conj aunque

altitude /'æltɪtjuːd/ n altitud f

altogether /ɔːltə'geðə(r)/ adv completamente; (on the whole) en total

altruis|m /'æltruːɪzəm/ n altruismo m. ~t /'æltruːɪst/ n altruista m & f. ~tic /-'ɪstɪk/ a altruista

aluminium /æljʊ'mɪnɪəm/ n aluminio m

always /'ɔːlweɪz/ adv siempre

am /æm/ see **be**

a.m. /'eɪem/ abbr (ante meridiem) de la mañana

amalgamate /ə'mælgəmeɪt/ vt amalgamar. ● vi amalgamarse

amass /ə'mæs/ vt amontonar

amateur /'æmətə(r)/ n aficionado m. ● a no profesional; (in sports) amateur. ~ish a (pej) torpe, chapucero

amaz|e /ə'meɪz/ vt asombrar. ~ed a asombrado, estupefacto. **be** ~ed at quedarse asombrado de, asombrarse de. ~ement n asombro m. ~ingly adv extraordinariamente

ambassador /æm'bæsədə(r)/ n embajador m

amber /'æmbə(r)/ n ámbar m; (auto) luz f amarilla

ambidextrous /æmbɪ'dekstrəs/ a ambidextro

ambience /'æmbɪəns/ n ambiente m

ambigu|ity /æmbɪ'gjuːətɪ/ n ambigüedad f. ~ous /æm'bɪgjʊəs/ a ambiguo

ambit /'æmbɪt/ n ámbito m

ambiti|on /æm'bɪʃn/ n ambición f. ~ous a ambicioso

ambivalen|ce /æm'bɪvələns/ n ambivalencia f. ~t a ambivalente

amble /'æmbl/ vi andar despacio, andar sin prisa

ambulance /'æmbjʊləns/ n ambulancia f

ambush /'æmbʊʃ/ n emboscada f. ● vt tender una emboscada a

amen /ɑː'men/ int amén

amenable /ə'miːnəbl/ a. ~ to (responsive) sensible a, flexible a

amend /ə'mend/ vt enmendar. ~ment n enmienda f. ~s npl. **make** ~s reparar

amenities /ə'miːnətɪz/ npl atractivos mpl, comodidades fpl, instalaciones fpl

America /ə'merɪkə/ n América; (North America) Estados mpl Unidos. ~n a & n americano (m); (North American) estadounidense (m & f). ~nism n americanismo m. ~nize vt americanizar

amethyst /'æmɪθɪst/ n amatista f

amiable /'eɪmɪəbl/ a simpático

amicabl|e /'æmɪkəbl/ a amistoso. ~y adv amistosamente

amid(st) /ə'mɪd(st)/ prep entre, en medio de

amiss /ə'mɪs/ a malo. ● adv mal. **sth** ~ algo que no va bien. **take sth** ~ llevar algo a mal

ammonia /ə'məʊnɪə/ n amoníaco m, amoniaco m

ammunition /æmjʊ'nɪʃn/ n municiones fpl

amnesia /æm'niːzɪə/ n amnesia f

amnesty /'æmnəstɪ/ n amnistía f

amok /ə'mɒk/ adv. **run** ~ volverse loco

among(st) /ə'mʌŋ(st)/ prep entre

amoral /eɪ'mɒrəl/ a amoral

amorous /'æmərəs/ a amoroso

amorphous /ə'mɔːfəs/ a amorfo

amount /ə'maʊnt/ n cantidad f; (total) total m, suma f. ● vi. ~ **to** sumar; (fig) equivaler a, significar

amp(ere) /'æmp(eə(r))/ n amperio m

amphibi|an /æm'fɪbɪən/ n anfibio m. ~ous a anfibio

amphitheatre /'æmfɪθɪətə(r)/ n anfiteatro m

ampl|e /'æmpl/ a (-er, -est) amplio; (enough) suficiente; (plentiful) abundante. ~y adv ampliamente, bastante

amplif|ier /'æmplɪfaɪə(r)/ n amplificador m. ~y vt amplificar

amputat|e /'æmpjʊteɪt/ vt amputar. ~ion /-'teɪʃn/ n amputación f

amus|e /ə'mjuːz/ vt divertir. ~ement n diversión f. ~ing a divertido

an /ən, æn/ see **a**

anachronism /ə'nækrənɪzəm/ n anacronismo m

anaemi|a /ə'niːmɪə/ n anemia f. ~c a anémico

anaesthe|sia /ænɪs'θiːzɪə/ n anestesia f. **~tic** /ænɪs'θetɪk/ n anestésico m. **~tist** /ə'niːsθɪtɪst/ n anestesista m & f

anagram /'ænəɡræm/ n anagrama m

analogy /ə'næləʤɪ/ n analogía f

analys|e /'ænəlaɪz/ vt analizar. **~is** /ə'næləsɪs/ n (pl -yses /-siːz/) n análisis m. **~t** /'ænəlɪst/ n analista m & f

analytic(al) /ænə'lɪtɪk(əl)/ a analítico

anarch|ist /'ænəkɪst/ n anarquista m & f. **~y** n anarquía f

anathema /ə'næθəmə/ n anatema m

anatom|ical /ænə'tɒmɪkl/ a anatómico. **~y** /ə'nætəmɪ/ n anatomía f

ancestor /'ænsestə(r)/ n antepasado m. **~ral** /-'sestrəl/ a ancestral. **~ry** /'ænsestrɪ/ n ascendencia f

anchor /'æŋkə(r)/ n ancla f. • vt anclar; (fig) sujetar. • vi anclar

anchovy /'æntʃəvɪ/ n (fresh) boquerón m; (tinned) anchoa f

ancient /'emʃənt/ a antiguo, viejo

ancillary /æn'sɪlərɪ/ a auxiliar

and /ənd, ænd/ conj y; (before i- and hi-) e. **go ~ see him** vete a verle. **more ~ more** siempre más, cada vez más. **try ~ come** ven si puedes, trata de venir

Andalusia /ændə'luːzjə/ f Andalucía f

anecdote /'ænɪkdəʊt/ n anécdota f

anew /ə'njuː/ adv de nuevo

angel /'eɪnʤl/ n ángel m. **~ic** /æn'ʤelɪk/ a angélico

anger /'æŋɡə(r)/ n ira f. • vt enojar

angle¹ /'æŋɡl/ n ángulo m; (fig) punto m de vista

angle² /'æŋɡl/ vi pescar con caña. **~ for** (fig) buscar. **~r** /-ə(r)/ n pescador m

Anglican /'æŋɡlɪkən/ a & n anglicano (m)

Anglo-... /'æŋɡləʊ/ pref anglo...

Anglo-Saxon /'æŋɡləʊ'sæksn/ a & n anglosajón (m)

angr|ily /'æŋɡrɪlɪ/ adv con enojo. **~y** /'æŋɡrɪ/ a (-ier, -iest) enojado. **get ~y** enfadarse

anguish /'æŋɡwɪʃ/ n angustia f

angular /'æŋɡjʊlə(r)/ a angular; ⟨face⟩ anguloso

animal /'ænɪməl/ a & n animal (m)

animat|e /'ænɪmət/ a vivo. /'ænɪmeɪt/ vt animar. **~ion** /-'meɪʃn/ n animación f

animosity /ænɪ'mɒsətɪ/ n animosidad f

aniseed /'ænɪsiːd/ n anís m

ankle /'æŋkl/ n tobillo m. **~ sock** escarpín m, calcetín m

annals /'ænlz/ npl anales mpl

annex /ə'neks/ vt anexionar. **~ation** /ænek'seɪʃn/ n anexión f

annexe /'æneks/ n anexo m, dependencia f

annihilat|e /ə'naɪəleɪt/ vt aniquilar. **~ion** /-'leɪʃn/ n aniquilación f

anniversary /ænɪ'vɜːsərɪ/ n aniversario m

annotat|e /'ænəteɪt/ vt anotar. **~ion** /-'teɪʃn/ n anotación f

announce /ə'naʊns/ vt anunciar, comunicar. **~ment** n anuncio m, aviso m, declaración f. **~r** /-ə(r)/ n (radio, TV) locutor m

annoy /ə'nɔɪ/ vt molestar. **~ance** n disgusto m. **~ed** a enfadado. **~ing** a molesto

annual /'ænjʊəl/ a anual. • n anuario m. **~ly** adv cada año

annuity /ə'njuːətɪ/ n anualidad f. **life ~** renta f vitalicia

annul /ə'nʌl/ vt (pt annulled) anular. **~ment** n anulación f

anoint /ə'nɔɪnt/ vt ungir

anomal|ous /ə'nɒmələs/ a anómalo. **~y** n anomalía f

anon /ə'nɒn/ adv (old use) dentro de poco

anonymous /ə'nɒnɪməs/ a anónimo

anorak /'ænəræk/ n anorac m

another /ə'nʌðə(r)/ a & pron otro (m). **~ 10 minutes** 10 minutos más. **in ~ way** de otra manera. **one ~** unos a otros

answer /'ɑːnsə(r)/ n respuesta f; (solution) solución f. • vt contestar a; escuchar, oír ⟨prayer⟩. **~ the door** abrir la puerta. • vi contestar. **~ back** replicar. **~ for** ser responsable de. **~able** a responsable. **~ing-machine** n contestador m automático

ant /ænt/ n hormiga f

antagoni|sm /æn'tæɡənɪzəm/ n antagonismo m. **~stic** /-'nɪstɪk/ a antagónico, opuesto. **~ze** /æn'tæɡənaɪz/ vt provocar la enemistad de

Antarctic /æn'tɑːktɪk/ a antártico. • n Antártico m

ante-... /'ænti/ *pref* ante...

antecedent /ænti'si:dnt/ *n* antecedente *m*

antelope /'æntɪləʊp/ *n* antílope *m*

antenatal /'æntɪneɪtl/ *a* prenatal

antenna /æn'tenə/ *n* antena *f*

anthem /'ænθəm/ *n* himno *m*

anthill /'ænthɪl/ *n* hormiguero *m*

anthology /æn'θɒlədʒɪ/ *n* antología *f*

anthropolog|ist /ænθrə'pɒlədʒɪst/ *n* antropólogo *m*. ~y *n* antropología *f*

anti-... /'ænti/ *pref* anti... ~**aircraft** *a* antiaéreo

antibiotic /æntɪbaɪ'ɒtɪk/ *a & n* antibiótico (*m*)

antibody /'æntɪbɒdɪ/ *n* anticuerpo *m*

antic /'æntɪk/ *n* payasada *f*, travesura *f*

anticipat|e /æn'tɪsɪpeɪt/ *vt* anticiparse a; (*foresee*) prever; (*forestall*) prevenir. ~**ion** /-'peɪʃn/ *n* anticipación *f*; (*expectation*) esperanza *f*

anticlimax /æntɪ'klaɪmæks/ *n* decepción *f*

anticlockwise /æntɪ'klɒkwaɪz/ *adv & a* en sentido contrario al de las agujas del reloj, hacia la izquierda

anticyclone /æntɪ'saɪkləʊn/ *n* anticiclón *m*

antidote /'æntɪdəʊt/ *m* antídoto *m*

antifreeze /'æntɪfri:z/ *n* anticongelante *m*

antipathy /æn'tɪpəθɪ/ *n* antipatía *f*

antiquarian /æntɪ'kweərɪən/ *a & n* anticuario (*m*)

antiquated /'æntɪkweɪtɪd/ *a* anticuado

antique /æn'ti:k/ *a* antiguo. ● *n* antigüedad *f*. ~ **dealer** anticuario *m*. ~ **shop** tienda *f* de antigüedades

antiquity /æn'tɪkwətɪ/ *n* antigüedad *f*

anti-Semitic /æntɪsɪ'mɪtɪk/ *a* antisemítico

antiseptic /æntɪ'septɪk/ *a & n* antiséptico (*m*)

antisocial /æntɪ'səʊʃl/ *a* antisocial

antithesis /æn'tɪθəsɪs/ *n* (*pl* -eses /-si:z/) antítesis *f*

antler /'æntlər/ *n* cornamenta *f*

anus /'eɪnəs/ *n* ano *m*

anvil /'ænvɪl/ *n* yunque *m*

anxiety /æŋ'zaɪətɪ/ *n* ansiedad *f*; (*worry*) inquietud *f*; (*eagerness*) anhelo *m*

anxious /'æŋkʃəs/ *a* inquieto; (*eager*) deseoso. ~**ly** *adv* con inquietud; (*eagerly*) con impaciencia

any /'enɪ/ *a* algún *m*; (*negative*) ningún *m*; (*whatever*) cualquier; (*every*) todo. **at** ~ **moment** en cualquier momento. **have you** ~ **wine?** ¿tienes vino? ● *pron* alguno; (*negative*) ninguno. **have we** ~? ¿tenemos algunos? **not** ~ ninguno. ● *adv* (*a little*) un poco, algo. **is it** ~ **better?** ¿está algo mejor? **it isn't** ~ **good** no sirve para nada

anybody /'enɪbɒdɪ/ *pron* alguien; (*after negative*) nadie. ~ **can do it** cualquiera sabe hacerlo, cualquiera puede hacerlo

anyhow /'enɪhaʊ/ *adv* de todas formas; (*in spite of all*) a pesar de todo; (*badly*) de cualquier modo

anyone /'enɪwʌn/ *pron* alguien; (*after negative*) nadie

anything /'enɪθɪŋ/ *pron* algo; (*whatever*) cualquier cosa; (*after negative*) nada. ~ **but** todo menos

anyway /'enɪweɪ/ *adv* de todas formas

anywhere /'enɪweə(r)/ *adv* en cualquier parte; (*after negative*) en ningún sitio; (*everywhere*) en todas partes. ~ **else** en cualquier otro lugar. ~ **you go** dondequiera que vayas

apace /ə'peɪs/ *adv* rápidamente

apart /ə'pɑ:t/ *adv* aparte; (*separated*) apartado, separado. ~ **from** aparte de. **come** ~ romperse. **take** ~ desmontar

apartheid /ə'pɑ:theɪt/ *n* segregación *f* racial, apartheid *m*

apartment /ə'pɑ:tmənt/ *n* (*Amer*) apartamento *m*

apath|etic /æpə'θetɪk/ *a* apático, indiferente. ~**y** /'æpəθɪ/ *n* apatía *f*

ape /eɪp/ *n* mono *m*. ● *vt* imitar

aperient /ə'pɪərɪənt/ *a & n* laxante (*m*)

aperitif /ə'perətɪf/ *n* aperitivo *m*

aperture /'æpətʃʊə(r)/ *n* abertura *f*

apex /'eɪpeks/ *n* ápice *m*

aphorism /'æfərɪzəm/ *n* aforismo *m*

aphrodisiac /æfrə'dɪzɪæk/ *a & n* afrodisíaco (*m*), afrodisiaco (*m*)

apiece /ə'pi:s/ *adv* cada uno

aplomb /ə'plɒm/ *n* aplomo *f*

apolog|etic /əplə'dʒetɪk/ *a* lleno de disculpas. **be** ~**etic** disculparse. ~**ize** /ə'pɒlədʒaɪz/ *vi* disculparse (for de). ~y /ə'pɒlədʒɪ/ n disculpa f; (poor specimen) birria f

apople|ctic /ˌæpə'plektɪk/ a apoplético. ~xy /'æpəpleksɪ/ n apoplejía f

apostle /ə'pɒsl/ n apóstol m

apostrophe /ə'pɒstrəfɪ/ n (punctuation mark) apóstrofo m

appal /ə'pɔːl/ vt (pt appalled) horrorizar. ~ling a espantoso

apparatus /ˌæpə'reɪtəs/ n aparato m

apparel /ə'pærəl/ n ropa f, indumentaria f

apparent /ə'pærənt/ a aparente; (clear) evidente. ~ly adv por lo visto

apparition /ˌæpə'rɪʃn/ n aparición f

appeal /ə'piːl/ vi apelar; (attract) atraer. ● n llamamiento m; (attraction) atractivo m; (jurid) apelación f. ~ing a atrayente

appear /ə'pɪə(r)/ vi aparecer; (arrive) llegar; (seem) parecer; (on stage) actuar. ~ance n aparición f; (aspect) aspecto m

appease /ə'piːz/ vt aplacar; (pacify) apaciguar

append /ə'pend/ vt adjuntar. ~age /ə'pendɪdʒ/ n añadidura f

appendicitis /əpendɪ'saɪtɪs/ n apendicitis f

appendix /ə'pendɪks/ n (pl -ices /-siːz/) (of book) apéndice m. (pl -ixes) (anat) apéndice m

appertain /ˌæpə'teɪn/ vi relacionarse (to con)

appetite /'æpɪtaɪt/ n apetito m

appetiz|er /'æpɪtaɪzə(r)/ n aperitivo m. ~ing a apetitoso

applau|d /ə'plɔːd/ vt/i aplaudir. ~se n aplausos mpl

apple /'æpl/ n manzana f. ~tree n manzano m

appliance /ə'plaɪəns/ n aparato m. **electrical** ~ electrodoméstico m

applicable /'æplɪkəbl/ a aplicable; (relevant) pertinente

applicant /'æplɪkənt/ n candidato m, solicitante m & f

application /ˌæplɪ'keɪʃn/ n aplicación f; (request) solicitud f. ~ form formulario m (de solicitud)

appli|ed /ə'plaɪd/ a aplicado. ~y /ə'plaɪ/ vt aplicar. ● vi aplicarse; (ask) dirigirse. ~y for solicitar ⟨job etc⟩

appoint /ə'pɔɪnt/ vt nombrar; (fix) señalar. ~ment n cita f; (job) empleo m

apportion /ə'pɔːʃn/ vt repartir

apposite /'æpəzɪt/ a apropiado

apprais|al /ə'preɪzl/ n evaluación f. ~e vt evaluar

appreciable /ə'priːʃəbl/ a sensible; (considerable) considerable

appreciat|e /ə'priːʃɪeɪt/ vt apreciar; (understand) comprender; (be grateful for) agradecer. ● vi (increase value) aumentar en valor. ~ion /-'eɪʃn/ n aprecio m; (gratitude) agradecimiento m. ~ive /ə'priːʃɪətɪv/ a (grateful) agradecido

apprehen|d /ˌæprɪ'hend/ vt detener; (understand) comprender. ~sion /-ʃn/ n detención f; (fear) recelo m

apprehensive /ˌæprɪ'hensɪv/ a aprensivo

apprentice /ə'prentɪs/ n aprendiz m. ● vt poner de aprendiz. ~ship n aprendizaje m

approach /ə'prəʊtʃ/ vt acercarse a. ● vi acercarse. ● n acercamiento m; (to problem) enfoque m; (access) acceso m. **make** ~es to dirigirse a. ~able a accesible

approbation /ˌæprə'beɪʃn/ n aprobación f

appropriate /ə'prəʊprɪət/ a apropiado. /ə'prəʊprɪeɪt/ vt apropiarse de. ~ly adv apropiadamente

approval /ə'pruːvl/ n aprobación f. **on** ~ a prueba

approv|e /ə'pruːv/ vt/i aprobar. ~ingly adv con aprobación

approximat|e /ə'prɒksɪmət/ a aproximado. /ə'prɒksɪmeɪt/ vt aproximarse a. ~ely adv aproximadamente. ~ion /-'meɪʃn/ n aproximación f

apricot /'eɪprɪkɒt/ n albaricoque m, chabacano m (Mex). ~tree n albaricoquero m, chabacano m (Mex)

April /'eɪprəl/ n abril m. ~ **fool!** ¡inocentón!

apron /'eɪprən/ n delantal m

apropos /'æprəpəʊ/ adv a propósito

apse /æps/ n ábside m

apt /æpt/ a apropiado; (pupil) listo. **be** ~ **to** tener tendencia a

aptitude /'æptɪtjuːd/ n aptitud f

aptly /'æptlɪ/ adv acertadamente

aqualung /'ækwəlʌŋ/ n pulmón m acuático

aquarium /ə'kweərɪəm/ n (pl -ums) acuario m

Aquarius /ə'kweərɪəs/ n Acuario m

aquatic /ə'kwætɪk/ a acuático

aqueduct /'ækwɪdʌkt/ n acueducto m

aquiline /'ækwɪlaɪn/ a aquilino

Arab /'ærəb/ a & n árabe m. ~**ian** /ə'reɪbɪən/ a árabe. ~**ic** /'ærəbɪk/ a & n árabe (m). ~**ic numerals** números mpl arábigos

arable /'ærəbl/ a cultivable

arbiter /'ɑːbɪtə(r)/ n árbitro m

arbitrary /'ɑːbɪtrərɪ/ a arbitrario

arbitrat|e /'ɑːbɪtreɪt/ vi arbitrar. ~**ion** /-'treɪʃn/ n arbitraje m. ~**or** n árbitro m

arc /ɑːk/ n arco m

arcade /ɑː'keɪd/ n arcada f; (around square) soportales mpl; (shops) galería f. **amusement** ~ galería f de atracciones

arcane /ɑː'keɪn/ a misterioso

arch[1] /ɑːtʃ/ n arco m. ● vt arquear. ● vi arquearse

arch[2] /ɑːtʃ/ a malicioso

archaeolog|ical /ɑːkɪə'lɒdʒɪkl/ a arqueológico. ~**ist** /ɑːkɪ'ɒlədʒɪst/ n arqueólogo m. ~**y** /ɑːkɪ'ɒlədʒɪ/ n arqueología f

archaic /ɑː'keɪɪk/ a arcaico

archbishop /ɑːtʃ'bɪʃəp/ n arzobispo m

arch-enemy /ɑːtʃ'enəmɪ/ n enemigo m jurado

archer /'ɑːtʃə(r)/ n arquero m. ~**y** n tiro m al arco

archetype /'ɑːkɪtaɪp/ n arquetipo m

archipelago /ɑːkɪ'pelagəʊ/ n (pl -os) archipiélago m

architect /'ɑːkɪtekt/ n arquitecto m. ~**ure** /'ɑːkɪtektʃə(r)/ n arquitectura f. ~**ural** /-'tektʃərəl/ a arquitectónico

archiv|es /'ɑːkaɪvz/ npl archivo m. ~**ist** /-ɪvɪst/ n archivero m

archway /'ɑːtʃweɪ/ n arco m

Arctic /'ɑːktɪk/ a ártico. ● n Ártico m

arctic /'ɑːktɪk/ a glacial

ardent /'ɑːdənt/ a ardiente, fervoroso, apasionado. ~**ly** adv ardientemente

ardour /'ɑːdə(r)/ n ardor m, fervor m, pasión f

arduous /'ɑːdjʊəs/ a arduo

are /ɑː(r)/ see **be**

area /'eərɪə/ n (surface) superficie f; (region) zona f; (fig) campo m

arena /ə'riːnə/ n arena f; (in circus) pista f; (in bullring) ruedo m

aren't /ɑːnt/ = **are not**

Argentin|a /ɑːdʒən'tiːnə/ n Argentina f. ~**ian** /-'tɪnɪən/ a & n argentino (m)

arguable /'ɑːgjʊəbl/ a discutible

argue /'ɑːgjuː/ vi discutir; (reason) razonar

argument /'ɑːgjʊmənt/ n disputa f; (reasoning) argumento m. ~**ative** /-'mentətɪv/ a discutidor

arid /'ærɪd/ a árido

Aries /'eəriːz/ n Aries m

arise /ə'raɪz/ vi (pt arose, pp arisen) levantarse; (fig) surgir. ~ **from** resultar de

aristocra|cy /ærɪ'stɒkrəsɪ/ n aristocracia f. ~**t** /'ærɪstəkræt/ n aristócrata m & f. ~**tic** /-'krætɪk/ a aristocrático

arithmetic /ə'rɪθmətɪk/ n aritmética f

ark /ɑːk/ n (relig) arca f

arm[1] /ɑːm/ n brazo m. ~ **in** ~ cogidos del brazo

arm[2] /ɑːm/ n. ~**s** npl armas fpl. ● vt armar

armada /ɑː'mɑːdə/ n armada f

armament /'ɑːməmənt/ n armamento m

armchair /ɑː'mtʃeə(r)/ n sillón m

armed robbery /ɑːmd'rɒbərɪ/ n robo m a mano armada

armful /'ɑːmfʊl/ n brazada f

armistice /'ɑːmɪstɪs/ n armisticio m

armlet /'ɑːmlɪt/ n brazalete m

armour /'ɑːmə(r)/ n armadura f. ~**ed** a blindado

armoury /'ɑːmərɪ/ n arsenal m

armpit /'ɑːmpɪt/ n sobaco m, axila f

army /'ɑːmɪ/ n ejército m

aroma /ə'rəʊmə/ n aroma m. ~**tic** /ærə'mætɪk/ a aromático

arose /ə'rəʊz/ see **arise**

around /ə'raʊnd/ adv alrededor; (near) cerca. **all** ~ por todas partes. ● prep alrededor de; (with time) a eso de

arouse /ə'raʊz/ vt despertar

arpeggio /ɑː'pedʒɪəʊ/ n arpegio m

arrange /ə'reɪndʒ/ vt arreglar; (fix) fijar. ~**ment** n arreglo m; (agreement) acuerdo m; (pl, plans) preparativos mpl

array /ə'reɪ/ vt (dress) ataviar; (mil) formar. ● n atavío m; (mil) orden m; (fig) colección f, conjunto m

arrears /ə'rɪəz/ npl atrasos mpl. **in** ~ atrasado en pagos

arrest /ə'rest/ vt detener; llamar ⟨attention⟩. ● n detención f. **under** ~ detenido

arriv|al /ə'raɪvl/ n llegada f. **new** ~**al** recién llegado m. ~**e** /ə'raɪv/ vi llegar

arrogan|ce /'ærəgəns/ n arrogancia f. ~**t** a arrogante. ~**tly** adv con arrogancia

arrow /'ærəʊ/ n flecha f

arsenal /'ɑːsənl/ n arsenal m

arsenic /'ɑːsnɪk/ n arsénico m

arson /'ɑːsn/ n incendio m provocado. ~**ist** n incendiario m

art[1] /ɑːt/ n arte m. **A**~**s** npl (Univ) Filosofía y Letras fpl. **fine** ~**s** bellas artes fpl

art[2] /ɑːt/ ⟨old use, with thou⟩ = are

artefact /'ɑːtɪfækt/ n artefacto m

arterial /ɑː'tɪərɪəl/ a arterial. ~ **road** n carretera f nacional

artery /'ɑːtərɪ/ n arteria f

artesian /ɑː'tiːzjən/ a. ~ **well** pozo m artesiano

artful /'ɑːtfʊl/ a astuto. ~**ness** n astucia f

art gallery /'ltgælərɪ/ n museo m de pinturas, pinacoteca f, galería f de arte

arthriti|c /ɑː'θrɪtɪk/ a artrítico. ~**s** /ɑː'θraɪtɪs/ n artritis f

artichoke /'ɑːtɪtʃəʊk/ n alcachofa f. **Jerusalem** ~ pataca f

article /'ɑːtɪkl/ n artículo m. ~ **of clothing** prenda f de vestir. **leading** ~ artículo de fondo

articulat|e /ɑː'tɪkjʊlət/ a articulado; ⟨person⟩ elocuente. /ɑː'tɪkjʊlent/ vt/i articular. ~**ed lorry** n camión m con remolque. ~**ion** /-'leɪʃn/ n articulación f

artifice /'ɑːtɪfɪs/ n artificio m

artificial /ɑːtɪ'fɪʃl/ a artificial; ⟨hair etc⟩ postizo

artillery /ɑː'tɪlərɪ/ n artillería f

artisan /ɑː'tɪ'zæn/ n artesano m

artist /'ɑːtɪst/ n artista m & f

artiste /ɑː'tiːst/ n (in theatre) artista m & f

artist|ic /ɑː'tɪstɪk/ a artístico. ~**ry** n arte m, habilidad f

artless /'ɑːtlɪs/ a ingenuo

arty /'ɑːtɪ/ a (fam) que se las da de artista

as /æz, əz/ adv & conj como; ⟨since⟩ ya que; ⟨while⟩ mientras. ~ **big** ~ tan grande como. ~ **far** ~ ⟨distance⟩ hasta; ⟨qualitative⟩ en cuanto a. ~

far ~ **I know** que yo sepa. ~ **if** como si. ~ **long** ~ mientras. ~ **much** ~ tanto como. ~ **soon** ~ tan pronto como. ~ **well** también

asbestos /æz'bestɒs/ n amianto m, asbesto m

ascen|d /ə'send/ vt/i subir. ~**t** /ə'sent/ n subida f

ascertain /æsə'teɪn/ vt averiguar

ascetic /ə'setɪk/ a ascético. ● n asceta m & f

ascribe /ə'skraɪb/ vt atribuir

ash[1] /æʃ/ n ceniza f

ash[2] /æʃ/ n. ~**(-tree)** fresno m

ashamed /ə'ʃeɪmd/ a avergonzado. **be** ~ avergonzarse

ashen /'æʃn/ a ceniciento

ashore /ə'ʃɔː(r)/ adv a tierra. **go** ~ desembarcar

ash: ~**tray** /'æʃtreɪ/ n cenicero m. **A**~ **Wednesday** n Miércoles m de Ceniza

Asia /'eɪʃə/ n Asia f. ~**n** a & n asiático (m). ~**tic** /-ɪ'ætɪk/ a asiático

aside /ə'saɪd/ adv a un lado. ● n (in theatre) aparte m

asinine /'æsɪnaɪn/ a estúpido

ask /ɑːsk/ vt pedir; preguntar ⟨question⟩; ⟨invite⟩ invitar. ~ **about** enterarse de. ~ **after** pedir noticias de. ~ **for help** pedir ayuda. ~ **for trouble** buscarse problemas. ~ **s.o. in** invitar a uno a pasar

askance /ə'skæns/ adv. **look** ~ **at** mirar de soslayo

askew /ə'skjuː/ adv & a ladeado

asleep /ə'sliːp/ adv & a dormido. **fall** ~ dormirse, quedar dormido

asparagus /ə'spærəgəs/ n espárrago m

aspect /'æspekt/ n aspecto m; ⟨of house etc⟩ orientación f

aspersions /ə'spɜːʃnz/ npl. **cast** ~ **on** difamar

asphalt /'æsfælt/ n asfalto m. ● vt asfaltar

asphyxia /æs'fɪksɪə/ n asfixia f. ~**te** /əs'fɪksɪeɪt/ vt asfixiar. ~**tion** /-'eɪʃn/ n asfixia f

aspic /'æspɪk/ n gelatina f

aspir|ation /æspə'reɪʃn/ n aspiración f. ~**e** /ə'spaɪə(r)/ vi aspirar

aspirin /'æsprɪn/ n aspirina f

ass /æs/ n asno m; (fig, fam) imbécil m

assail /ə'seɪl/ vt asaltar. ~**ant** n asaltador m

assassin /ə'sæsɪn/ n asesino m. **~ate** /ə'sæsɪneɪt/ vt asesinar. **~ation** /-'eɪʃn/ n asesinato m

assault /ə'sɔːlt/ n (mil) ataque m; (jurid) atentado m. ● vt asaltar

assemblage /ə'semblɪdʒ/ n (of things) colección f; (of people) reunión f; (mec) montaje m

assemble /ə'sembl/ vt reunir; (mec) montar. ● vi reunirse

assembly /ə'semblɪ/ n reunión f; (pol etc) asamblea f. **~ line** n línea f de montaje

assent /ə'sent/ n asentimiento m. ● vi asentir

assert /ə'sɜːt/ vt afirmar; hacer valer ⟨one's rights⟩. **~ion** /-ʃn/ n afirmación f. **~ive** a positivo, firme

assess /ə'ses/ vt valorar; (determine) determinar; fijar ⟨tax etc⟩. **~ment** n valoración f

asset /'æset/ n (advantage) ventaja f; (pl, com) bienes mpl

assiduous /ə'sɪdjʊəs/ a asiduo

assign /ə'saɪn/ vt asignar; (appoint) nombrar

assignation /æsɪg'neɪʃn/ n asignación f; (meeting) cita f

assignment /ə'saɪnmənt/ n asignación f, misión f; (task) tarea f

assimilat|e /ə'sɪmɪleɪt/ vt asimilar. ● vi asimilarse. **~ion** /-'eɪʃn/ n asimilación f

assist /ə'sɪst/ vt/i ayudar. **~ance** n ayuda f. **~ant** /ə'sɪstənt/ n ayudante m & f; (shop) dependienta f, dependiente m. ● a auxiliar, adjunto

associat|e /ə'səʊʃɪeɪt/ vt asociar. ● vi asociarse. /ə'səʊʃɪət/ a asociado. ● n colega m & f; (com) socio m. **~ion** /-'eɪʃn/ n asociación f. **A~ion football** n fútbol m

assort|ed /ə'sɔːtɪd/ a surtido. **~ment** n surtido m

assume /ə'sjuːm/ vt suponer; tomar ⟨power, attitude⟩; asumir ⟨role, burden⟩

assumption /ə'sʌmpʃn/ n suposición f. **the A~** la Asunción f

assur|ance /ə'ʃʊərəns/ n seguridad f; (insurance) seguro m. **~e** /ə'ʃʊə(r)/ vt asegurar. **~ed** a seguro. **~edly** /-rɪdlɪ/ adv seguramente

asterisk /'æstərɪsk/ n asterisco m

astern /ə'stɜːn/ adv a popa

asthma /'æsmə/ n asma f. **~tic** /-'mætɪk/ a & n asmático (m)

astonish /ə'stɒnɪʃ/ vt asombrar. **~ing** a asombroso. **~ment** n asombro m

astound /ə'staʊnd/ vt asombrar

astray /ə'streɪ/ adv & a. **go ~** extraviarse. **lead ~** llevar por mal camino

astride /ə'straɪd/ adv a horcajadas. ● prep a horcajadas sobre

astringent /ə'strɪndʒənt/ a astringente; (fig) austero. ● n astringente m

astrolog|er /ə'strɒlədʒə(r)/ n astrólogo m. **~y** n astrología f

astronaut /'æstrənɔːt/ n astronauta m & f

astronom|er /ə'strɒnəmə(r)/ n astrónomo m. **~ical** /æstrə'nɒmɪkl/ a astronómico. **~y** /ə'strɒnəmɪ/ n astronomía f

astute /ə'stjuːt/ a astuto. **~ness** n astucia f

asunder /ə'sʌndə(r)/ adv en pedazos; (in two) en dos

asylum /ə'saɪləm/ n asilo m. **lunatic ~** manicomio m

at /ət, æt/ prep a. **~ home** en casa. **~ night** por la noche. **~ Robert's** en casa de Roberto. **~ once** en seguida; (simultaneously) a la vez. **~ sea** en el mar. **~ the station** en la estación. **~ times** a veces. **not ~ all** nada; (after thanks) ¡de nada!

ate /et/ see **eat**

atheis|m /'eɪθɪzəm/ n ateísmo m. **~t** /'eɪθɪɪst/ n ateo m

athlet|e /'æθliːt/ n atleta m & f. **~ic** /-'letɪk/ a atlético. **~ics** /-'letɪks/ npl atletismo m

Atlantic /ət'læntɪk/ a & n atlántico (m). ● n. **~ (Ocean)** (Océano m) Atlántico m

atlas /'ætləs/ n atlas m

atmospher|e /'ætməsfɪə(r)/ n atmósfera f; (fig) ambiente m. **~ic** /-'ferɪk/ a atmosférico. **~ics** /-'ferɪks/ npl parásitos mpl

atom /'ætəm/ n átomo m. **~ic** /ə'tɒmɪk/ a atómico

atomize /'ætəmaɪz/ vt atomizar. **~r** /'ætəmaɪzə(r)/ n atomizador m

atone /ə'təʊn/ vi. **~ for** expiar. **~ment** n expiación f

atroci|ous /ə'trəʊʃəs/ a atroz. **~ty** /ə'trɒsətɪ/ n atrocidad f

atrophy /'ætrəfɪ/ n atrofia f

attach /ə'tætʃ/ vt sujetar; adjuntar ⟨document etc⟩. **be ~ed to** (be fond of) tener cariño a

attaché /əˈtæʃeɪ/ n agregado m. ~ **case** maletín m

attachment /əˈtætʃmənt/ n (affection) cariño m; (tool) accesorio m

attack /əˈtæk/ n ataque m. ● vt/i atacar. ~**er** n agresor m

attain /əˈteɪn/ vt conseguir. ~**able** a alcanzable. ~**ment** n logro m. ~**ments** npl conocimientos mpl, talento m

attempt /əˈtempt/ vt intentar. ● n tentativa f; (attack) atentado m

attend /əˈtend/ vt asistir a; (escort) acompañar. ● vi prestar atención. ~ **to** (look after) ocuparse de. ~**ance** n asistencia f; (people present) concurrencia f. ~**ant** /əˈtendənt/ a concomitante. ● n encargado m; (servant) sirviente m

attention /əˈtenʃn/ n atención f. ~! (mil) ¡firmes! **pay** ~ prestar atención

attentive /əˈtentɪv/ a atento. ~**ness** n atención f

attenuate /əˈtenjʊeɪt/ vt atenuar

attest /əˈtest/ vt atestiguar. ● vi dar testimonio. ~**ation** /æteˈsteɪʃn/ n testimonio m

attic /ˈætɪk/ n desván m

attire /əˈtaɪə(r)/ n atavío m. ● vt vestir

attitude /ˈætɪtjuːd/ n postura f

attorney /əˈtɜːnɪ/ n (pl -eys) apoderado m; (Amer) abogado m

attract /əˈtrækt/ vt atraer. ~**ion** /-ʃn/ n atracción f; (charm) atractivo m

attractive /əˈtræktɪv/ a atractivo; (interesting) atrayente. ~**ness** n atractivo m

attribute /əˈtrɪbjuːt/ vt atribuir. /ˈætrɪbjuːt/ n atributo m

attrition /əˈtrɪʃn/ n desgaste m

aubergine /ˈəʊbəʒiːn/ n berenjena f

auburn /ˈɔːbən/ a castaño

auction /ˈɔːkʃn/ n subasta f. ● vt subastar. ~**eer** /-əˈnɪə(r)/ n subastador m

audacious /ɔːˈdeɪʃəs/ a audaz. ~**ty** /-æsəti/ n audacia f

audible /ˈɔːdəbl/ a audible

audience /ˈɔːdɪəns/ n (interview) audiencia f; (teatro, radio) público m

audio-visual /ˈɔːdɪəʊˈvɪʒʊəl/ a audiovisual

audit /ˈɔːdɪt/ n revisión f de cuentas. ● vt revisar

audition /ɔːˈdɪʃn/ n audición f. ● vt dar audición a

auditor /ˈɔːdɪtə(r)/ n interventor m de cuentas

auditorium /ɔːdɪˈtɔːrɪəm/ n sala f, auditorio m

augment /ɔːgˈment/ vt aumentar

augur /ˈɔːgə(r)/ vt augurar. **it** ~**s well** es de buen agüero

august /ɔːˈgʌst/ a augusto

August /ˈɔːgəst/ n agosto m

aunt /ɑːnt/ n tía f

au pair /əʊˈpeə(r)/ n chica f au pair

aura /ˈɔːrə/ n atmósfera f, halo m

auspices /ˈɔːspɪsɪz/ npl auspicios mpl

auspicious /ɔːˈspɪʃəs/ a propicio

auster|e /ɔːˈstɪə(r)/ a austero. ~**ity** /-erətɪ/ n austeridad f

Australia /ɒˈstreɪlɪə/ n Australia f. ~**n** a & n australiano (m)

Austria /ˈɒstrɪə/ n Austria f. ~**n** a & n austríaco (m)

authentic /ɔːˈθentɪk/ a auténtico. ~**ate** /ɔːˈθentɪkeɪt/ vt autenticar. ~**ity** /-ənˈtɪsətɪ/ n autenticidad f

author /ˈɔːθə(r)/ n autor m. ~**ess** n autora f

authoritarian /ɔːθɒrɪˈteərɪən/ a autoritario

authoritative /ɔːˈθɒrɪtətɪv/ a autorizado; (manner) autoritario

authority /ɔːˈθɒrətɪ/ n autoridad f; (permission) autorización f

authoriz|ation /ɔːθəraɪˈzeɪʃn/ n autorización f. ~**e** /ˈɔːθəraɪz/ vt autorizar

authorship /ˈɔːθəʃɪp/ n profesión f de autor; (origin) paternidad f literaria

autistic /ɔːˈtɪstɪk/ a autista

autobiography /ɔːtəʊbaɪˈɒgrəfɪ/ n autobiografía f

autocra|cy /ɔːˈtɒkrəsɪ/ n autocracia f. ~**t** /ˈɔːtəkræt/ n autócrata m & f. ~**tic** /-ˈkrætɪk/ a autocrático

autograph /ˈɔːtəgrɑːf/ n autógrafo m. ● vt firmar

automat|e /ˈɔːtəmeɪt/ vt automatizar. ~**ic** /ɔːtəˈmætɪk/ a automático. ~**ion** /-ˈmeɪʃn/ n automatización f. ~**on** /ɔːˈtɒmətən/ n autómata m

automobile /ˈɔːtəməbiːl/ n (Amer) coche m, automóvil m

autonom|ous /ɔːˈtɒnəməs/ a autónomo. ~**y** n autonomía f

autopsy /ˈɔːtɒpsɪ/ n autopsia f

autumn /ˈɔːtəm/ n otoño m. ~**al** /-ˈtʌmnəl/ a de otoño, otoñal

auxiliary /ɔːgˈzɪlɪərɪ/ a auxiliar. • n asistente m; (verb) verbo m auxiliar; (pl, troops) tropas fpl auxiliares

avail /əˈveɪl/ vt/i servir. ∼ o.s. of aprovecharse de. • n ventaja f. to no ∼ inútil

availab|ility /əveɪləˈbɪlətɪ/ n disponibilidad f. ∼le /əˈveɪləbl/ a disponible

avalanche /ˈævəlɑːnʃ/ n avalancha f

avaric|e /ˈævərɪs/ n avaricia f. ∼ious /-ˈrɪʃəs/ a avaro

avenge /əˈvendʒ/ vt vengar

avenue /ˈævənjuː/ n avenida f; (fig) vía f

average /ˈævərɪdʒ/ n promedio m. on ∼ por término medio. • a medio. • vt calcular el promedio de. • vi alcanzar un promedio de

avers|e /əˈvɜːs/ a enemigo (to de). be ∼e to sentir repugnancia por, no gustarle. ∼ion /-ʃn/ n repugnancia f

avert /əˈvɜːt/ vt (turn away) apartar; (ward off) desviar

aviary /ˈeɪvɪərɪ/ n pajarera f

aviation /eɪvɪˈeɪʃn/ n aviación f

aviator /ˈeɪvɪeɪtə(r)/ n (old use) aviador m

avid /ˈævɪd/ a ávido. ∼ity /-ˈvɪdətɪ/ n avidez f

avocado /ævəˈkɑːdəʊ/ n (pl -os) aguacate m

avoid /əˈvɔɪd/ vt evitar. ∼able a evitable. ∼ance n el evitar m

avuncular /əˈvʌŋkjʊlə(r)/ a de tío

await /əˈweɪt/ vt esperar

awake /əˈweɪk/ vt/i (pt awoke, pp awoken) despertar. • a despierto. wide ∼ completamente despierto; (fig) despabilado. ∼n /əˈweɪkən/ vt/i despertar. ∼ning n el despertar m

award /əˈwɔːd/ vt otorgar; (jurid) adjudicar. • n premio m; (jurid) adjudicación f; (scholarship) beca f

aware /əˈweə(r)/ a consciente. are you ∼ that? ¿te das cuenta de que? ∼ness n conciencia f

awash /əˈwɒʃ/ a inundado

away /əˈweɪ/ adv (absent) fuera; (far) lejos; (persistently) sin parar. • a & n. ∼ (match) partido m fuera de casa

awe /ɔː/ n temor m. ∼some a imponente. ∼struck a atemorizado

awful /ˈɔːfʊl/ a terrible, malísimo. ∼ly adv terriblemente

awhile /əˈwaɪl/ adv un rato

awkward /ˈɔːkwəd/ a difícil; (inconvenient) inoportuno; (clumsy) desmañado; (embarrassed) incómodo. ∼ly adv con dificultad; (clumsily) de manera torpe. ∼ness n dificultad f; (discomfort) molestia f; (clumsiness) torpeza f

awning /ˈɔːnɪŋ/ n toldo m

awoke, awoken /əˈwəʊk, əˈwəʊkən/ see awake

awry /əˈraɪ/ adv & a ladeado. go ∼ salir mal

axe /æks/ n hacha f. • vt (pres p axing) cortar con hacha; (fig) recortar

axiom /ˈæksɪəm/ n axioma m

axis /ˈæksɪs/ n (pl axes /-iːz/) eje m

axle /ˈæksl/ n eje m

ay(e) /aɪ/ adv & n sí (m)

B

BA abbr see bachelor

babble /ˈbæbl/ vi balbucir; (chatter) parlotear; (of stream) murmullar. • n balbuceo m; (chatter) parloteo m; (of stream) murmullo m

baboon /bəˈbuːn/ n mandril m

baby /ˈbeɪbɪ/ n niño m, bebé m; (Amer, sl) chica f. ∼ish /ˈbeɪbɪʃ/ a infantil. ∼sit vi cuidar a los niños, hacer de canguro. ∼sitter n persona f que cuida a los niños, canguro m

bachelor /ˈbætʃələ(r)/ n soltero m. B∼ of Arts (BA) licenciado m en filosofía y letras. B∼ of Science (BSc) licenciado m en ciencias

back /bæk/ n espalda f; (of car) parte f trasera; (of chair) respaldo m; (of cloth) revés m; (of house) parte f de atrás; (of animal, book) lomo m; (of hand, document) dorso m; (football) defensa m & f. ∼ of beyond en el quinto pino. • a trasero; (taxes) atrasado. • adv atrás; (returned) de vuelta. • vt apoyar; (betting) apostar a; dar marcha atrás a (car). • vi retroceder; (car) dar marcha atrás. ∼ down vi volverse atrás. ∼ out vi retirarse. ∼ up vi (auto) retroceder. ∼ache /ˈbækeɪk/ n dolor m de espalda. ∼bencher n (pol) diputado m sin poder ministerial. ∼biting /ˈbækbaɪtɪŋ/ n maledicencia f. ∼bone /ˈbækbəʊn/ n columna f vertebral; (fig) pilar m. ∼chat /ˈbæktʃæt/ n impertinencias fpl.

~**date** /bæk'deɪt/ vt antedatar. ~**er** /'bæk.ə(r)/ n partidario m; (com) financiador m. ~**fire** /bæk'faɪə(r)/ vi (auto) petardear; (fig) fallar, salir el tiro por la culata. ~**gammon** /bæk'gæmən/ n backgamon m. ~**ground** /'bækgraʊnd/ n fondo m; (environment) antecedentes mpl. ~**hand** /'bækhænd/ n (sport) revés m. ~**handed** a dado con el dorso de la mano; (fig) equívoco, ambiguo. ~**hander** n (sport) revés m; (fig) ataque m indirecto; (bribe, sl) soborno m. ~**ing** /'bækɪŋ/ n apoyo m. ~**lash** /bæk'læʃ/ n reacción f. ~**log** /'bæklɒg/ n atrasos mpl. ~**side** /bæk'saɪd/ n (fam) trasero m. ~**stage** /bæk'steɪdʒ/ a de bastidores. ●adv entre bastidores. ~**stroke** /'bækstrəʊk/ n (tennis etc) revés m; (swimming) braza f de espaldas. ~**up** n apoyo m. ~**ward** /'bækwəd/ a ⟨step etc⟩ hacia atrás; (retarded) atrasado. ~**wards** /'bækwədz/ adv hacia atrás; (fall) de espaldas; (back to front) al revés. **go ~wards and forwards** ir de acá para allá. ~**water** /'bækwɔ:tə(r)/ n agua f estancada; (fig) lugar m apartado

bacon /'beɪkən/ n tocino m

bacteria /bæk'tɪərɪə/ npl bacterias fpl. ~**l** a bacteriano

bad /bæd/ a (worse, worst) malo; (serious) grave; (harmful) nocivo; ⟨language⟩ indecente. **feel ~** sentirse mal

bade /beɪd/ see **bid**

badge /bædʒ/ n distintivo m, chapa f

badger /'bædʒə(r)/ n tejón m. ●vt acosar

bad: ~**ly** adv mal. **want ~ly** desear muchísimo. ~**ly off** mal de dinero. ~**-mannered** a mal educado

badminton /'bædmɪntən/ n bádminton m

bad-tempered /bæd'tempəd/ a (always) de mal genio; (temporarily) de mal humor

baffle /'bæfl/ vt desconcertar

bag /bæg/ n bolsa f; (handbag) bolso m. ●vt (pt bagged) ensacar; (take) coger (not LAm), agarrar (LAm). ~**s** npl (luggage) equipaje m. ~**s of** (fam) montones de

baggage /'bægɪdʒ/ n equipaje m

baggy /'bægɪ/ a ⟨clothes⟩ holgado

bagpipes /'bægpaɪps/ npl gaita f

Bahamas /bə'hɑ:məz/ npl. **the ~** las Bahamas fpl

bail[1] /beɪl/ n caución f, fianza f. ●vt poner en libertad bajo fianza. ~ **s.o. out** obtener la libertad de uno bajo fianza

bail[2] /beɪl/ n (cricket) travesaño m

bail[3] /beɪl/ vt (naut) achicar

bailiff /'beɪlɪf/ n alguacil m; (estate) administrador m

bait /beɪt/ n cebo m. ●vt cebar; (torment) atormentar

bak|e /beɪk/ vt cocer al horno. ●vi cocerse. ~**er** n panadero m. ~**ery** /'beɪkərɪ/ n panadería f. ~**ing** n cocción f; (batch) hornada f. ~**ing-powder** n levadura f en polvo

balance /'bæləns/ n equilibrio m; (com) balance m; (sum) saldo m; (scales) balanza f; (remainder) resto m. ●vt equilibrar; (com) saldar; nivelar ⟨budget⟩. ●vi equilibrarse; (com) saldarse. ~**d** a equilibrado

balcony /'bælkənɪ/ n balcón m

bald /bɔ:ld/ a (-er, -est) calvo; ⟨tyre⟩ desgastado

balderdash /'bɔ:ldədæʃ/ n tonterías fpl

bald: ~**ly** adv escuetamente. ~**ness** n calvicie f

bale /beɪl/ n bala f, fardo m. ●vi. ~ **out** lanzarse en paracaídas

Balearic /bælɪ'ærɪk/ a. ~ **Islands** Islas fpl Baleares

baleful /'beɪlfʊl/ a funesto

balk /bɔ:k/ vt frustrar. ●vi. ~ (**at**) resistirse (a)

ball[1] /bɔ:l/ n bola f; (tennis etc) pelota f; (football etc) balón m; (of yarn) ovillo m

ball[2] /bɔ:l/ (dance) baile m

ballad /'bæləd/ n balada f

ballast /'bæləst/ n lastre m

ball: ~**-bearing** n cojinete m de bolas. ~**cock** n llave f de bola

ballerina /bælə'ri:nə/ f bailarina f

ballet /'bæleɪ/ n ballet m

ballistic /bə'lɪstɪk/ a balístico. ~**s** n balística f

balloon /bə'lu:n/ n globo m

balloonist /bə'lu:nɪst/ n aeronauta m & f

ballot /'bælət/ n votación f. ~ (**-paper**) n papeleta f. ~**-box** n urna f

ball-point /'bɔ:lpɔɪnt/ n. ~ (**pen**) bolígrafo m

ballroom /'bɔ:lru:m/ n salón m de baile

ballyhoo /bælɪ'hu:/ n (publicity) publicidad f sensacionalista; (uproar) jaleo m

balm /ba:m/ n bálsamo m. ~y a (mild) suave; (sl) chiflado

baloney /bə'ləʊnɪ/ n (sl) tonterías fpl

balsam /'bɔ:lsəm/ n bálsamo m

balustrade /bælə'streɪd/ n barandilla f

bamboo /bæm'bu:/ n bambú m

bamboozle /bæm'bu:zl/ vt engatusar

ban /bæn/ vt (pt banned) prohibir. ~ **from** excluir de. ● n prohibición f

banal /bə'na:l/ a banal. ~ity /-ælətɪ/ n banalidad f

banana /bə'na:nə/ n plátano m, banana f (LAm). ~-**tree** plátano m, banano m

band¹ /bænd/ n banda f

band² /bænd/ n (mus) orquesta f; (military, brass) banda f. ● vi. ~ **together** juntarse

bandage /'bændɪdʒ/ n venda f. ● vt vendar

b & b abbr (bed and breakfast) cama f y desayuno

bandit /'bændɪt/ n bandido m

bandstand /'bændstænd/ n quiosco m de música

bandwagon /'bændwægən/ n. **jump on the** ~ (fig) subirse al carro

bandy¹ /'bændɪ/ a (-ier, -iest) patizambo

bandy² /'bændɪ/ vt. ~ **about** repetir. **be bandied about** estar en boca de todos

bandy-legged /'bændɪlegd/ a patizambo

bane /beɪn/ n (fig) perdición f. ~**ful** a funesto

bang /bæŋ/ n (noise) ruido m; (blow) golpe m; (of gun) estampido m; (of door) golpe m. ● vt/i golpear. ● adv exactamente. ● int ¡pum!

banger /'bæŋə(r)/ n petardo m; (culin, sl) salchicha f

bangle /'bæŋgl/ n brazalete m

banish /'bænɪʃ/ vt desterrar

banisters /'bænɪstəz/ npl barandilla f

banjo /'bændʒəʊ/ n (pl -os) banjo m

bank¹ /bæŋk/ n (of river) orilla f. ● vt cubrir (fire). ● vi (aviat) ladearse

bank² /bæŋk/ n banco m. ● vt depositar. ~ **on** vt contar con. ~ **with**

tener una cuenta con. ~**er** n banquero m. ~ **holiday** n día m festivo, fiesta f. ~**ing** n (com) banca f. ~-**note** /'bæŋknəʊt/ n billete m de banco

bankrupt /'bæŋkrʌpt/ a & n quebrado (m). ● vt hacer quebrar. ~**cy** n bancarrota f, quiebra f

banner /'bænə(r)/ n bandera f; (in demonstration) pancarta f

banns /bænz/ npl amonestaciones fpl

banquet /'bæŋkwɪt/ n banquete m

bantamweight /'bæntəmweɪt/ n peso m gallo

banter /'bæntə(r)/ n chanza f. ● vi chancearse

bap /bæp/ n panecillo m blando

baptism /'bæptɪzəm/ n bautismo m; (act) bautizo m

Baptist /'bæptɪst/ n bautista m & f

baptize /bæp'taɪz/ vt bautizar

bar /ba:(r)/ n barra f; (on window) reja f; (of chocolate) tableta f; (of soap) pastilla f; (pub) bar m; (mus) compás m; (jurid) abogacía f; (fig) obstáculo m. ● vt (pt barred) atrancar (door); (exclude) excluir; (prohibit) prohibir. ● prep excepto

barbar|ian /ba:'beərɪən/ a & n bárbaro (m). ~**ic** /ba:'bærɪk/ a bárbaro. ~**ity** /-ətɪ/ n barbaridad f. ~**ous** /'ba:bərəs/ a bárbaro

barbecue /'ba:bɪkju:/ n barbacoa f. ● vt asar a la parrilla

barbed /ba:bd/ a. ~ **wire** alambre m de espinas

barber /'ba:bə(r)/ n peluquero m, barbero m

barbiturate /ba:'bɪtjʊrət/ n barbitúrico m

bare /beə(r)/ a (-er, est) desnudo; (room) con pocos muebles; (mere) simple; (empty) vacío. ● vt desnudar; (uncover) descubrir. ~ **one's teeth** mostrar los dientes. ~**back** /'beəbæk/ adv a pelo. ~-**faced** /'beəfeɪst/ a descarado. ~**foot** a descalzo. ~**headed** /'beəhedɪd/ a descubierto. ~**ly** adv apenas. ~**ness** n desnudez f

bargain /'ba:gɪn/ n (agreement) pacto m; (good buy) ganga f. ● vi negociar; (haggle) regatear. ~ **for** esperar, contar con

barge /ba:dʒ/ n barcaza f. ● vi. ~ **in** irrumpir

baritone /'bærɪtəʊn/ n barítono m

barium /'beərɪəm/ n bario m

bark¹ /bɑːk/ n (of dog) ladrido m. ● vi ladrar

bark² /bɑːk/ n (of tree) corteza f

barley /ˈbɑːlɪ/ n cebada f. **~-water** n hordiate m

barmaid /ˈbɑːmeɪd/ n camarera f. **~man** /ˈbɑːmən/ n (pl **-men**) camarero m

barmy /ˈbɑːmɪ/ a (sl) chiflado

barn /bɑːn/ n granero m

barometer /bəˈrɒmɪtə(r)/ n barómetro m

baron /ˈbærən/ n barón m. **~ess** n baronesa f

baroque /bəˈrɒk/ a & n barroco (m)

barracks /ˈbærəks/ npl cuartel m

barrage /ˈbærɑːʒ/ n (mil) barrera f; (dam) presa f; (of questions) bombardeo m

barrel /ˈbærəl/ n tonel m; (of gun) cañón m. **~-organ** n organillo m

barren /ˈbærən/ a estéril. **~ness** n esterilidad f, aridez f

barricade /bærɪˈkeɪd/ n barricada f. ● vt cerrar con barricadas

barrier /ˈbærɪə(r)/ n barrera f

barring /ˈbɑːrɪŋ/ prep salvo

barrister /ˈbærɪstə(r)/ n abogado m

barrow /ˈbærəʊ/ n carro m; (wheelbarrow) carretilla f

barter /ˈbɑːtə(r)/ n trueque m. ● vt trocar

base /beɪs/ n base f. ● vt basar. ● a vil

baseball /ˈbeɪsbɔːl/ n béisbol m

baseless /ˈbeɪslɪs/ a infundado

basement /ˈbeɪsmənt/ n sótano m

bash /bæʃ/ vt golpear. ● n golpe m. **have a ~** (sl) probar

bashful /ˈbæʃfl/ a tímido

basic /ˈbeɪsɪk/ a básico, fundamental. **~ally** adv fundamentalmente

basil /ˈbæzl/ n albahaca f

basilica /bəˈzɪlɪkə/ n basílica f

basin /ˈbeɪsn/ n (for washing) palangana f; (for food) cuenco m; (geog) cuenca f

basis /ˈbeɪsɪs/ n (pl **bases** /-siːz/) base f

bask /bɑːsk/ vi asolearse; (fig) gozar (**in** de)

basket /ˈbɑːskɪt/ n cesta f; (big) cesto m. **~ball** /ˈbɑːskɪtbɔːl/ n baloncesto m

Basque /bɑːsk/ a & n vasco (m). **~ Country** n País m Vasco. **~ Provinces** npl Vascongadas fpl

bass¹ /beɪs/ a bajo. ● n (mus) bajo m

bass² /bæs/ n (marine fish) róbalo m; (freshwater fish) perca f

bassoon /bəˈsuːn/ n fagot m

bastard /ˈbɑːstəd/ a & n bastardo (m). **you ~!** (fam) ¡cabrón!

baste /beɪst/ vt (sew) hilvanar; (culin) lard(e)ar

bastion /ˈbæstɪən/ n baluarte m

bat¹ /bæt/ n bate m; (for table tennis) raqueta f. **off one's own ~** por sí solo. ● vt (pt **batted**) golpear. ● vi batear

bat² /bæt/ n (mammal) murciélago m

bat³ /bæt/ vt. **without ~ting an eyelid** sin pestañear

batch /bætʃ/ n (of people) grupo m; (of papers) lío m; (of goods) remesa f; (of bread) hornada f

bated /ˈbeɪtɪd/ a. **with ~ breath** con aliento entrecortado

bath /bɑːθ/ n (pl **-s** /bɑːðz/) baño m; (tub) bañera f; (pl, swimming pool) piscina f. ● vt bañar. ● vi bañarse

bathe /beɪð/ vt bañar. ● vi bañarse. ● n baño m. **~r** /-ə(r)/ n bañista m & f

bathing /ˈbeɪðɪŋ/ n baños mpl. **~ costume** n traje m de baño

bathroom /ˈbɑːθrʊm/ n cuarto m de baño

batman /ˈbætmən/ n (pl **-men**) (mil) ordenanza f

baton /ˈbætən/ n (mil) bastón m; (mus) batuta f

batsman /ˈbætsmən/ n (pl **-men**) bateador m

battalion /bəˈtælɪən/ n batallón m

batter¹ /ˈbætə(r)/ vt apalear

batter² /ˈbætə(r)/ n batido m para rebozar, albardilla f

batter: **~ed** a (car etc) estropeado; (wife etc) golpeado. **~ing** n (fam) bombardeo m

battery /ˈbætərɪ/ n (mil, auto) batería f; (of torch, radio) pila f

battle /ˈbætl/ n batalla f; (fig) lucha f. ● vi luchar. **~axe** /ˈbætlæks/ n (woman, fam) arpía f. **~field** /ˈbætlfiːld/ n campo m de batalla. **~ments** /ˈbætlmənts/ npl almenas fpl. **~ship** /ˈbætlʃɪp/ n acorazado m

batty /ˈbætɪ/ a (sl) chiflado

baulk /bɔːlk/ vt frustrar. ● vi. **~ (at)** resistirse (a)

bawd|iness /ˈbɔːdɪnəs/ n obscenidad f. **~y** /ˈbɔːdɪ/ a (**-ier**, **-iest**) obsceno, verde

bawl /bɔːl/ vt/i gritar

bay¹ /beɪ/ n (geog) bahía f

bay² /beɪ/ n (bot) laurel m

bay³ /beɪ/ n (of dog) ladrido m. **keep at** ~ mantener a raya. ● vi ladrar

bayonet /'beɪənet/ n bayoneta f

bay window /beɪ'wɪndəu/ n ventana f saladiza

bazaar /bə'zɑ:(r)/ n bazar m

BC /bi:'si:/ abbr (before Christ) a. de C., antes de Cristo

be /bi:/ vi (pres am, are, is; pt was, were; pp been) (position or temporary) estar; (permanent) ser. ~ **cold/hot, etc** tener frío/calor, etc. ~ **reading/singing, etc** (aux) leer/cantar, etc. ~ **that as it may** sea como fuere. **he is 30** (age) tiene 30 años. **he is to come** (must) tiene que venir. **how are you?** ¿cómo estás? **how much is it?** ¿cuánto vale?, ¿cuánto es? **have been to** have been to estado en. **it is cold/hot, etc** (weather) hace frío/calor, etc

beach /bi:tʃ/ n playa f

beachcomber /'bi:tʃkəumə(r)/ n raquero m

beacon /'bi:kən/ n faro m

bead /bi:d/ n cuenta f; (of glass) abalorio m

beak /bi:k/ n pico m

beaker /'bi:kə(r)/ n jarra f, vaso m

beam /bi:m/ n viga f; (of light) rayo m; (naut) bao m. ● vt emitir. ● vi irradiar; (smile) sonreír. ~**ends** npl. **be on one's ~ends** no tener más dinero. ~**ing** a radiante

bean /bi:n/ n judía f; (broad bean) haba f; (of coffee) grano m

beano /'bi:nəu/ n (pl -os) (fam) juerga f

bear¹ /beə(r)/ vt (pt bore, pp borne) llevar; parir (niño); (endure) soportar. ~ **right** torcer a la derecha. ~ **in mind** tener en cuenta. ~ **with** tener paciencia con

bear² /beə(r)/ n oso m

bearable /'beərəbl/ a soportable

beard /bɪəd/ n barba f. ~**ed** a barbudo

bearer /'beərə(r)/ n portador m; (of passport) poseedor m

bearing /'beərɪŋ/ n comportamiento m; (relevance) relación f; (mec) cojinete m. **get one's** ~**s** orientarse

beast /bi:st/ n bestia f; (person) bruto m. ~**ly** /'bi:stlɪ/ a (-ier, -iest) bestial; (fam) horrible

beat /bi:t/ vt (pt **beat**, pp **beaten**) golpear; (culin) batir; (defeat) derrotar; (better) sobrepasar; (baffle) dejar perplejo. ~ **a retreat** (mil) batirse en retirada. ~ **it** (sl) largarse. ● vi (heart) latir. ● n latido m; (mus) ritmo m; (of policeman) ronda f. ~ **up** dar una paliza a; (culin) batir. ~**er** n batidor m. ~**ing** n paliza f

beautician /bju:'tɪʃn/ n esteticista m & f

beautiful /'bju:tɪfl/ a hermoso. ~**ly** adv maravillosamente

beautify /'bju:tɪfaɪ/ vt embellecer

beauty /'bju:tɪ/ n belleza f. ~ **parlour** n salón m de belleza. ~ **spot** (on face) lunar m; (site) lugar m pintoresco

beaver /'bi:və(r)/ n castor m

became /bɪ'keɪm/ see **become**

because /bɪ'kɒz/ conj porque. ● adv. ~ **of** a causa de

beck /bek/ n. **be at the** ~ **and call of** estar a disposición de

beckon /'bekən/ vt/i. ~ **(to)** hacer señas (a)

become /bɪ'kʌm/ vt (pt became, pp become) (clothes) sentar bien. ● vi hacerse, llegar a ser, volverse, convertirse en. **what has** ~ **of her?** ¿qué es de ella?

becoming /bɪ'kʌmɪŋ/ a (clothes) favorecedor

bed /bed/ n cama f; (layer) estrato m; (of sea, river) fondo m; (of flowers) macizo m. ● vi (pt bedded). ~ **down** acostarse. ~ **and breakfast (b & b)** cama y desayuno. ~**bug**/'bedbʌg/ n chinche f. ~**clothes** /'bedkləuðz/ npl, ~**ding** n ropa f de cama

bedevil /bɪ'devl/ vt (pt bedevilled) (torment) atormentar

bedlam /'bedləm/ n confusión f, manicomio m

bed: ~**pan** /'bedpæn/ n orinal m de cama. ~**post** /'bedpəust/ n columna f de la cama

bedraggled /bɪ'drægld/ a sucio

bed: ~**ridden** /'bedrɪdn/ a encamado. ~**room** /'bedrum/ n dormitorio m, habitación f. ~**side** /'bedsaɪd/ n cabecera f. ~**sitting-room** /bed'sɪtɪŋru:m/ n salón m con cama, estudio m. ~**spread** /'bedspred/ n colcha f. ~**time** /'bedtaɪm/ n hora f de acostarse

bee /bi:/ n abeja f. **make a** ~**line for** ir en línea recta hacia

beech /biːtʃ/ n haya f

beef /biːf/ n carne f de vaca, carne f de res (LAm). ● vi (sl) quejarse.

~burger /'biːfbɜːgə(r)/ n hamburguesa f

beefeater /'biːfiːtə(r)/ n alabardero m de la torre de Londres

beefsteak /biːfsteɪk/ n filete m, bistec m, bife m (Arg)

beefy /'biːfɪ/ a (-ier, -iest) musculoso

beehive /biːhaɪv/ n colmena f

been /biːn/ see **be**

beer /bɪə(r)/ n cerveza f

beet /biːt/ n remolacha f

beetle /'biːtl/ n escarabajo m

beetroot /'biːtruːt/ n invar remolacha f

befall /bɪ'fɔːl/ vt (pt befell, pp befallen) acontecer a. ● vi acontecer

befit /bɪ'fɪt/ vt (pt befitted) convenir a

before /bɪ'fɔː(r)/ prep (time) antes de; (place) delante de. ~ leaving antes de marcharse. ● adv (place) delante; (time) antes. a week ~ una semana antes. the week ~ la semana anterior. ● conj (time) antes de que. ~ he leaves antes de que se vaya. ~hand /bɪ'fɔːhænd/ adv de antemano

befriend /bɪ'frend/ vt ofrecer amistad a

beg /beg/ vt/i (pt begged) mendigar; (entreat) suplicar; (ask) pedir. ~ s.o.'s pardon pedir perdón a uno. I ~ your pardon! ¡perdone Vd! I ~ your pardon? ¿cómo? it's going ~ging no lo quiere nadie

began /bɪ'gæn/ see **begin**

beget /bɪ'get/ vt (pt begot, pp begotten, pres p begetting) engendrar

beggar /'begə(r)/ n mendigo m; (sl) individuo m, tío m (fam)

begin /bɪ'gɪn/ vt/i (pt began, pp begun, pres p beginning) comenzar, empezar. ~ner n principiante m & f. ~ning n principio m

begot,begotten /bɪ'gɒt, bɪ'gɒtn/ see **beget**

begrudge /bɪ'grʌdʒ/ vt envidiar; (give) dar de mala gana

beguile /bɪ'gaɪl/ vt engañar, seducir; (entertain) entretener

begun /bɪ'gʌn/ see **begin**

behalf /bɪ'hɑːf/ n. on ~ of de parte de, en nombre de

behav|e /bɪ'heɪv/ vi comportarse, portarse. ~ (o.s.) portarse bien.

~iour /bɪ'heɪvjə(r)/ n comportamiento m

behead /bɪ'hed/ vt decapitar

beheld /bɪ'held/ see **behold**

behind /bɪ'haɪnd/ prep detrás de. ● adv detrás; (late) atrasado. ● n (fam) trasero m

behold /bɪ'həʊld/ vt (pt beheld) (old use) mirar, contemplar

beholden /bɪ'həʊldən/ a agradecido

being /'biːɪŋ/ n ser m. come into ~ nacer

belated /bɪ'leɪtɪd/ a tardío

belch /beltʃ/ vi eructar. ● vt. ~ out arrojar (smoke)

belfry /'belfrɪ/ n campanario m

Belgi|an /'beldʒən/ a & n belga (m & f). ~um /'beldʒəm/ n Bélgica f

belie /bɪ'laɪ/ vt desmentir

belie|f /bɪ'liːf/ n (trust) fe f; (opinion) creencia f. ~ve /bɪ'liːv/ vt/i creer. make ~ve fingir. ~ver /-ə(r)/ n creyente m & f; (supporter) partidario m

belittle /bɪ'lɪtl/ vt empequeñecer; (fig) despreciar

bell /bel/ n campana f; (on door) timbre m

belligerent /bɪ'lɪdʒərənt/ a & n beligerante (m & f)

bellow /'beləʊ/ vt gritar. ● vi bramar

bellows /'beləʊz/ npl fuelle m

belly /'belɪ/ n vientre m. ~ful /'belɪfʊl/ n panzada f. have a ~ful of (sl) estar harto de

belong /bɪ'lɒŋ/ vi pertenecer; (club) ser socio (to de)

belongings /bɪ'lɒŋɪŋz/ npl pertenencias fpl. personal ~ efectos mpl personales

beloved /bɪ'lʌvɪd/ a & n querido (m)

below /bɪ'ləʊ/ prep debajo de; (fig) inferior a. ● adv abajo

belt /belt/ n cinturón m; (area) zona f. ● vt (fig) rodear; (sl) pegar

bemused /bɪ'mjuːzd/ a perplejo

bench /bentʃ/ n banco m. the B~ (jurid) la magistratura f

bend /bend/ vt (pt & pp bent) doblar; torcer (arm, leg). ● vi doblarse; (road) torcerse. ● n curva f. ~ down/over inclinarse

beneath /bɪ'niːθ/ prep debajo de; (fig) inferior a. ● adv abajo

benediction /benɪ'dɪkʃn/ n bendición f

benefactor /'benɪfæktə(r)/ n bienhechor m, benefactor m

beneficial /benɪ'fɪʃl/ *a* provechoso
beneficiary /benɪ'fɪʃərɪ/ *a & n* beneficiario (*m*)
benefit /'benɪfɪt/ *n* provecho *m*, ventaja *f*; (*allowance*) subsidio *m*; (*financial gain*) beneficio *m*. ●*vt* (*pt* **benefited**, *pres p* **benefiting**) aprovechar. ●*vi* aprovecharse
benevolen|ce /bɪ'nevələns/ *n* benevolencia *f*. ~**ta** benévolo
benign /bɪ'naɪn/ *a* benigno
bent /bent/ *see* **bend**. ●*n* inclinación *f*. ●*a* encorvado; (*sl*) corrompido
bequeath /bɪ'kwiːð/ *vt* legar
bequest /bɪ'kwest/ *n* legado *m*
bereave|d /bɪ'riːvd/ *n*. the ~**d** la familia *f* del difunto. ~**ment** *n* pérdida *f*; (*mourning*) luto *m*
bereft /bɪ'reft/ *a*. ~ **of** privado de
beret /'bereɪ/ *n* boina *f*
Bermuda /bə'mjuːdə/ *n* Islas *fpl* Bermudas
berry /'berɪ/ *n* baya *f*
berserk /bə'sɜːk/ *a*. **go** ~ volverse loco, perder los estribos
berth /bɜːθ/ *n* litera *f*; (*anchorage*) amarradero *m*. **give a wide** ~ **to** evitar. ●*vi* atracar
beseech /bɪ'siːtʃ/ *vt* (*pt* **besought**) suplicar
beset /bɪ'set/ *vt* (*pt* **beset**, *pres p* **besetting**) acosar
beside /bɪ'saɪd/ *prep* al lado de. **be ~ o.s.** estar fuera de sí
besides /bɪ'saɪdz/ *prep* además de; (*except*) excepto. ●*adv* además
besiege /bɪ'siːdʒ/ *vt* asediar; (*fig*) acosar
besought /bɪ'sɔːt/ *see* **beseech**
bespoke /bɪ'spəʊk/ *a* (*tailor*) que confecciona a la medida
best /best/ *a* (el) mejor. **the ~ thing is to...** lo mejor es... ●*adv* (lo) mejor. **like** ~ preferir. ●*n* lo mejor. **at** ~ a lo más. **do one's** ~ hacer todo lo posible. **make the** ~ **of** contentarse con. ~ **man** *n* padrino *m* (de boda)
bestow /bɪ'stəʊ/ *vt* conceder
bestseller /best'selə(r)/ *n* éxito *m* de librería, bestseller *m*
bet /bet/ *n* apuesta *f*. ●*vt/i* (*pt* **bet** or **betted**) apostar
betray /bɪ'treɪ/ *vt* traicionar. ~**al** *n* traición *f*
betroth|al /bɪ'trəʊðəl/ *n* esponsales *mpl*. ~**ed** prometido

better /'betə(r)/ *a & adv* mejor. ~ **off** en mejores condiciones; (*richer*) más rico. **get** ~ mejorar. **all the** ~ tanto mejor. **I'd** ~ más vale que. **the** ~ **part of** la mayor parte de. **the sooner the** ~ cuanto antes mejor. ●*vt* mejorar; (*beat*) sobrepasar. ●*n* superior *m*. **get the** ~ **of** vencer a. **one's** ~**s** sus superiores *mpl*
between /bɪ'twiːn/ *prep* entre. ●*adv* en medio
beverage /'bevərɪdʒ/ *n* bebida *f*
bevy /'bevɪ/ *n* grupo *m*
beware /bɪ'weə(r)/ *vi* tener cuidado. ●*int* ¡cuidado!
bewilder /bɪ'wɪldə(r)/ *vt* desconcertar. ~**ment** *n* aturdimiento *m*
bewitch /bɪ'wɪtʃ/ *vt* hechizar
beyond /bɪ'jɒnd/ *prep* más allá de; (*fig*) fuera de. ~ **doubt** sin lugar a duda. ~ **reason** irrazonable. ●*adv* más allá
bias /'baɪəs/ *n* predisposición *f*; (*prejudice*) prejuicio *m*; (*sewing*) sesgo *m*. ●*vt* (*pt* **biased**) influir en. ~**ed** *a* parcial
bib /bɪb/ *n* babero *m*
Bible /'baɪbl/ *n* Biblia *f*
biblical /'bɪblɪkl/ *a* bíblico
bibliography /bɪblɪ'ɒgrəfɪ/ *n* bibliografía *f*
biceps /'baɪseps/ *n* bíceps *m*
bicker /'bɪkə(r)/ *vi* altercar
bicycle /'baɪsɪkl/ *n* bicicleta *f*. ●*vi* ir en bicicleta
bid /bɪd/ *n* (*offer*) oferta *f*; (*attempt*) tentativa *f*. ●*vi* hacer una oferta. ●*vt* (*pt* **bid**, *pres p* **bidding**) ofrecer; (*pt* **bid**, *pp* **bidden**, *pres p* **bidding**) mandar; dar (*welcome*, *good-day etc*). ~**der** *n* postor *m*. ~**ding** *n* (*at auction*) ofertas *fpl*; (*order*) mandato *m*
bide /baɪd/ *vt*. ~ **one's time** esperar el momento oportuno
biennial /baɪ'enɪəl/ *a* bienal. ●*n* (*event*) bienal *f*; (*bot*) planta *f* bienal
bifocals /baɪ'fəʊklz/ *npl* gafas *fpl* bifocales, anteojos *mpl* bifocales (*LAm*)
big /bɪg/ *a* (**bigger**, **biggest**) grande; (*generous*, *sl*) generoso. ●*adv*. **talk** ~ fanfarronear
bigam|ist /'bɪgəmɪst/ *n* bígamo *m*. ~**ous** *a* bígamo. ~**y** *n* bigamia *f*
big-headed /bɪg'hedɪd/ *a* engreído
bigot /'bɪgət/ *n* fanático *m*. ~**ed** *a* fanático. ~**ry** *n* fanatismo *m*
bigwig /'bɪgwɪg/ *n* (*fam*) pez *m* gordo

bike /baɪk/ n (fam) bicicleta f, bici f (fam)

bikini /bɪˈkiːnɪ/ n (pl **-is**) biquini m, bikini m

bilberry /ˈbɪlbərɪ/ n arándano m

bile /baɪl/ n bilis f

bilingual /barˈlɪŋgwəl/ a bilingüe

bilious /ˈbɪlɪəs/ a (med) bilioso

bill¹ /bɪl/ n cuenta f; (invoice) factura f; (notice) cartel m; (Amer, banknote) billete m; (pol) proyecto m de ley. ● vt pasar la factura; (in theatre) anunciar

bill² /bɪl/ n (of bird) pico m

billet /ˈbɪlɪt/ n (mil) alojamiento m. ● vt alojar

billiards /ˈbɪlɪədz/ n billar m

billion /ˈbɪlɪən/ n billón m; (Amer) mil millones mpl

billy-goat /ˈbɪlɪgəʊt/ n macho m cabrio

bin /bɪn/ n recipiente m; (for rubbish) cubo m; (for waste paper) papelera f

bind /baɪnd/ vt (pt **bound**) atar; encuadernar ‹book›; (jurid) obligar. ● n (sl) lata f. ~**ing** /ˈbaɪndɪŋ/ n (of books) encuadernación f; (braid) ribete m

binge /bɪndʒ/ n (sl) (of food) comilona f; (of drink) borrachera f. **go on a** ~ ir de juerga

bingo /ˈbɪŋgəʊ/ n bingo m

binoculars /bɪˈnɒkjʊləz/ npl prismáticos mpl

biochemistry /baɪəʊˈkemɪstrɪ/ n bioquímica f

biograph|er /barˈɒgrəfə(r)/ n biógrafo m. ~**y** n biografía f

biolog|ical /baɪəˈlɒdʒɪkl/ a biológico. ~**ist** n biólogo m. ~**y** /barˈɒlədʒɪ/ n biología f

biped /ˈbaɪped/ n bípedo m

birch /bɜːtʃ/ n (tree) abedul m; (whip) férula f

bird /bɜːd/ n ave f; (small) pájaro m; (fam) tipo m; (girl, sl) chica f

Biro /ˈbaɪərəʊ/ n (pl **-os**) (P) bolígrafo m, biromen m (Arg)

birth /bɜːθ/ n nacimiento m. ~**certificate** n partida f de nacimiento. ~**control** n control m de la natalidad. ~**day** /ˈbɜːθdeɪ/ n cumpleaños m invar. ~**mark** /ˈbɜːθmɑːk/ n marca f de nacimiento. ~**rate** n natalidad f. ~**right** /ˈbɜːθraɪt/ n derechos mpl de nacimiento

biscuit /ˈbɪskɪt/ n galleta f

bisect /barˈsekt/ vt bisecar

bishop /ˈbɪʃəp/ n obispo m

bit¹ /bɪt/ n trozo m; (quantity) poco m

bit² /bɪt/ see **bite**

bit³ /bɪt/ n (of horse) bocado m; (mec) broca f

bitch /bɪtʃ/ n perra f; (woman, fam) mujer f maligna, bruja f (fam). ● vi (fam) quejarse (**about** de). ~**y** a malintencionado

bit|e /baɪt/ vt/i (pt **bit**, pp **bitten**) morder. ~**e one's nails** morderse las uñas. ● n mordisco m; (mouthful) bocado m; (of insect etc) picadura f. ~**ing** /ˈbaɪtɪŋ/ a mordaz

bitter /ˈbɪtə(r)/ a amargo; (of weather) glacial. **to the** ~ **end** hasta el final. ● n cerveza f amarga. ~**ly** adv amargamente. **it's** ~**ly cold** hace un frío glacial. ~**ness** n amargor m; (resentment) amargura f

bizarre /bɪˈzɑː(r)/ a extraño

blab /blæb/ vi (pt **blabbed**) chismear

black /blæk/ a (**-er**, **-est**) negro. ~ **and blue** amoratado. ● n negro m. ● vt ennegrecer; limpiar ‹shoes›. ~ **out** desmayarse; (make dark) apagar las luces de

blackball /ˈblækbɔːl/ vt votar en contra de

blackberry /ˈblækbərɪ/ n zarzamora f

blackbird /ˈblækbɜːd/ n mirlo m

blackboard /ˈblækbɔːd/ n pizarra f

blackcurrant /blækˈkʌrənt/ n casis f

blacken /ˈblækən/ vt ennegrecer. ● vi ennegrecerse

blackguard /ˈblægɑːd/ n canalla m

blackleg /ˈblækleg/ n esquirol m

blacklist /ˈblæklɪst/ vt poner en la lista negra

blackmail /ˈblækmeɪl/ n chantaje m. ● vt chantajear. ~**er** n chantajista m & f

black-out /ˈblækaʊt/ n apagón m; (med) desmayo m; (of news) censura f

blacksmith /ˈblæksmɪθ/ n herrero m

bladder /ˈblædə(r)/ n vejiga f

blade /bleɪd/ n hoja f; (razor-blade) cuchilla f. ~ **of grass** brizna f de hierba

blame /bleɪm/ vt echar la culpa a. **be to** ~ tener la culpa. ● n culpa f. ~**less** a inocente

bland /blænd/ a (**-er**, **-est**) suave

blandishments /'blændɪʃmənts/ *npl* halagos *mpl*

blank /blæŋk/ *a* en blanco; ‹cartridge› sin bala; (*fig*) vacío. ~ **verse** *n* verso *m* suelto. ● *n* blanco *m*

blanket /'blæŋkɪt/ *n* manta *f*; (*fig*) capa *f*. ● *vt* (*pt* **blanketed**) (*fig*) cubrir (**in, with** de)

blare /bleə(r)/ *vi* sonar muy fuerte. ● *n* estrépito *m*

blarney /'blɑːnɪ/ *n* coba *f*. ● *vt* dar coba

blasé /'blɑːzeɪ/ *a* hastiado

blasphem|e /blæs'fiːm/ *vt/i* blasfemar. ~**er** *n* blasfemador *m*. ~**ous** /'blæsfəməs/ *a* blasfemo. ~**y** /'blæsfəmɪ/ *n* blasfemia *f*

blast /blɑːst/ *n* explosión *f*; (*gust*) ráfaga *f*; (*sound*) toque *m*. ● *vt* volar. ~**ed** *a* maldito. ~**-furnace** *n* alto horno *m*. ~**-off** *n* (*of missile*) despegue *m*

blatant /'bleɪtnt/ *a* patente; (*shameless*) descarado

blaze /bleɪz/ *n* llamarada *f*; (*of light*) resplandor *m*; (*fig*) arranque *m*. ● *vi* arder en llamas; (*fig*) brillar. ~ **a trail** abrir un camino

blazer /'bleɪzə(r)/ *n* chaqueta *f*

bleach /bliːtʃ/ *n* lejía *f*; (*for hair*) decolorante *m*. ● *vt* blanquear; decolorar ‹hair›. ● *vi* blanquearse

bleak /bliːk/ *a* (-er, -est) desolado; (*fig*) sombrío

bleary /'blɪərɪ/ *a* ‹eyes› nublado; (*indistinct*) indistinto

bleat /bliːt/ *n* balido *m*. ● *vi* balar

bleed /bliːd/ *vt/i* (*pt* **bled**) sangrar

bleep /bliːp/ *n* pitido *m*. ~**er** *n* busca *m*, buscapersonas *m*

blemish /'blemɪʃ/ *n* tacha *f*

blend /blend/ *n* mezcla *f*. ● *vt* mezclar. ● *vi* combinarse

bless /bles/ *vt* bendecir. ~ **you!** (*on sneezing*) ¡Jesús! ~**ed** *a* bendito. **be** ~**ed with** estar dotado de. ~**ing** *n* bendición *f*; (*advantage*) ventaja *f*

blew /bluː/ *see* **blow**

blight /blaɪt/ *n* añublo *m*, tizón *m*; (*fig*) plaga *f*. ● *vt* añublar, atizonar; (*fig*) destrozar

blighter /'blaɪtə(r)/ *n* (*sl*) tío *m* (*fam*), sinvergüenza *m*

blind /blaɪnd/ *a* ciego. ~ **alley** *n* callejón *m* sin salida. ● *n* persiana *f*; (*fig*) pretexto *m*. ● *vt* cegar. ~**fold** /'blaɪndfəʊld/ *a* & *adv* con los ojos vendados. ● *n* venda *f*. ● *vt* vendar

los ojos. ~**ly** *adv* a ciegas. ~**ness** *n* ceguera *f*

blink /blɪŋk/ *vi* parpadear; (*of light*) centellear

blinkers /'blɪŋkəz/ *npl* anteojeras *fpl*; (*auto*) intermitente *m*

bliss /blɪs/ *n* felicidad *f*. ~**ful** *a* feliz. ~**fully** *adv* felizmente; (*completely*) completamente

blister /'blɪstə(r)/ *n* ampolla *f*. ● *vi* formarse ampollas

blithe /blaɪð/ *a* alegre

blitz /blɪts/ *n* bombardeo *m* aéreo. ● *vt* bombardear

blizzard /'blɪzəd/ *n* ventisca *f*

bloated /'bləʊtɪd/ *a* hinchado (**with** de)

bloater /'bləʊtə(r)/ *n* arenque *m* ahumado

blob /blɒb/ *n* gota *f*; (*stain*) mancha *f*

bloc /blɒk/ *n* (*pol*) bloque *m*

block /blɒk/ *n* bloque *m*; (*of wood*) zoquete *m*; (*of buildings*) manzana *f*, cuadra *f* (*LAm*); (*in pipe*) obstrucción *f*. **in** ~ **letters** en letra de imprenta. **traffic** ~ embotellamiento *m*. ● *vt* obstruir. ~**ade** /blɒ'keɪd/ *n* bloqueo *m*. ● *vt* bloquear. ~**age** *n* obstrucción *f*

blockhead /'blɒkhed/ *n* (*fam*) zopenco *m*

bloke /bləʊk/ *n* (*fam*) tío *m* (*fam*), tipo *m*

blond /blɒnd/ *a* & *n* rubio (*m*). ~**e** *a* & *n* rubia (*f*)

blood /blʌd/ *n* sangre *f*. ~ **count** *n* recuento *m* sanguíneo. ~**-curdling** *a* horripilante

bloodhound /'blʌdhaʊnd/ *n* sabueso *m*

blood: ~ **pressure** *n* tensión *f* arterial. **high** ~ **pressure** hipertensión *f*. ~**shed** /'blʌdʃed/ *n* efusión *f* de sangre, derramamiento *m* de sangre, matanza *f*. ~**shot** /'blʌdʃɒt/ *a* sanguinolento; ‹eye› inyectado de sangre. ~**stream** /'blʌdstriːm/ *n* sangre *f*

bloodthirsty /'blʌdθɜːstɪ/ *a* sanguinario

bloody /'blʌdɪ/ *a* (-ier, -iest) sangriento; (*stained*) ensangrentado; (*sl*) maldito. ~**y-minded** *a* (*fam*) terco

bloom /bluːm/ *n* flor *f*. ● *vi* florecer

bloomer /'bluːmə(r)/ *n* (*sl*) metedura *f* de pata

blooming a floreciente; (fam) maldito

blossom /'blɒsəm/ n flor f. • vi florecer. ~ **out** (into) (fig) llegar a ser

blot /blɒt/ n borrón m. • vt (pt blotted) manchar; (dry) secar. ~ **out** oscurecer

blotch /blɒtʃ/ n mancha f. ~**y** a lleno de manchas

blotter /'blɒtə(r)/ n, **blotting-paper** /'blɒtɪŋpeɪpə(r)/ n papel m secante

blouse /blaʊz/ n blusa f

blow¹ /bləʊ/ vt (pt blew, pp blown) soplar; fundir ⟨fuse⟩; tocar ⟨trumpet⟩. • vi soplar; ⟨fuse⟩ fundirse; ⟨sound⟩ sonar. • n (puff) soplo m. ~ **down** vt derribar. ~ **out** apagar ⟨candle⟩. ~ **over** pasar. ~ **up** vt inflar; ⟨explode⟩ volar; ⟨photo⟩ ampliar. • vi ⟨explode⟩ estallar; ⟨burst⟩ reventar

blow² /bləʊ/ n (incl fig) golpe m

blow-dry /'bləʊdraɪ/ vt secar con secador

blowlamp /'bləʊlæmp/ n soplete m

blow: ~**out** n (of tyre) reventón m. ~**up** n (photo) ampliación f

blowzy /'blaʊzɪ/ a desaliñado

blubber /'blʌbə(r)/ n grasa f de ballena. • vt aporrear

bludgeon /'blʌdʒən/ n cachiporra f. • vt aporrear

blue /blu:/ a (-er, -est) azul; ⟨joke⟩ verde. • n azul m. **out of the** ~ totalmente inesperado. ~**s** npl. **have the** ~**s** tener tristeza

bluebell /'blu:bel/ n campanilla f

bluebottle /'blu:bɒtl/ n moscarda f

blueprint /'blu:prɪnt/ n ferroprusiato m; (fig, plan) anteproyecto m

bluff /blʌf/ a ⟨person⟩ brusco. • n (poker) farol m. • vt engañar. • vi (poker) tirarse un farol

blunder /'blʌndə(r)/ vi cometer un error. • n metedura f de pata

blunt /blʌnt/ a desafilado; ⟨person⟩ directo, abrupto. • vt desafilar. ~**ly** adv francamente. ~**ness** n embotadura f; (fig) franqueza f, brusquedad f

blur /blɜ:(r)/ n impresión f indistinta. • vt (pt blurred) hacer borroso

blurb /blɜ:b/ n resumen m publicitario

blurt /blɜ:t/ vt. ~ **out** dejar escapar

blush /blʌʃ/ vi ruborizarse. • n sonrojo m

bluster /'blʌstə(r)/ vi ⟨weather⟩ bramar; ⟨person⟩ fanfarronear. ~**y** a tempestuoso

boar /bɔ:(r)/ n verraco m

board /bɔ:d/ n tabla f, tablero m; (for notices) tablón m; (food) pensión f; (admin) junta f. ~ **and lodging** casa y comida. **above** ~ correcto. **full** ~ pensión f completa. **go by the** ~ ser abandonado. • vt alojar; ⟨naut⟩ embarcar en. • vi alojarse (**with** en casa de); (at school) ser interno. ~**er** n huésped m; (schol) interno m. ~**inghouse** n casa f de huéspedes, pensión f. ~**ing-school** n internado m

boast /bəʊst/ vt enorgullecerse de. • vi jactarse. • n jactancia f. ~**er** n jactancioso m. ~**ful** a jactancioso

boat /bəʊt/ n barco m; (large) navío m; (small) barca f

boater /'bəʊtə(r)/ n (hat) canotié m

boatswain /'bəʊsn/ n contramaestre m

bob¹ /bɒb/ vi (pt bobbed) menearse, subir y bajar. ~ **up** presentarse súbitamente

bob² /bɒb/ n invar (sl) chelín m

bobbin /'bɒbɪn/ n carrete m; (in sewing machine) canilla f

bobby /'bɒbɪ/ n (fam) policía m, poli m (fam)

bobsleigh /'bɒbsleɪ/ n bob(sleigh) m

bode /bəʊd/ vi presagiar. ~ **well/ill** ser de buen/mal agüero

bodice /'bɒdɪs/ n corpiño m

bodily /'bɒdɪlɪ/ a físico, corporal. • adv físicamente; (in person) en persona

body /'bɒdɪ/ n cuerpo m. ~**guard** /'bɒdɪgɑ:d/ n guardaespaldas m invar. ~**work** n carrocería f

boffin /'bɒfɪn/ n (sl) científico m

bog /bɒg/ n ciénaga f. • vt (pt bogged). **get** ~**ged down** empantanarse

bogey /'bəʊgɪ/ n duende m; (nuisance) pesadilla f

boggle /'bɒgl/ vi sobresaltarse. **the mind** ~**s** ¡no es posible!

bogus /'bəʊgəs/ a falso

bogy /'bəʊgɪ/ n duende m; (nuisance) pesadilla f

boil¹ /bɔɪl/ vt/i hervir. **be** ~**ing hot** estar ardiendo; ⟨weather⟩ hacer mucho calor. ~ **away** evaporarse. ~ **down to** reducirse a. ~ **over** rebosar

boil² /bɔɪl/ n furúnculo m

boiled /'bɔɪld/ a hervido; ⟨egg⟩ pasado por agua

boiler /'bɔɪlə(r)/ n caldera f. ~ **suit** n mono m

boisterous /'bɔɪstərəs/ a ruidoso, bullicioso

bold /bəʊld/ a (-er, -est) audaz. ~**ness** n audacia f

Bolivia /bə'lɪvɪə/ n Bolivia f. ~**n** a & n boliviano (m)

bollard /'bɒləd/ n (naut) noray m; (Brit, auto) poste m

bolster /'bəʊlstə(r)/ n cabezal m. ● vt. ~ **up** sostener

bolt /bəʊlt/ n cerrojo m; (for nut) perno m; (lightning) rayo m; (leap) fuga f. ● vt echar el cerrojo a ⟨door⟩; engullir ⟨food⟩. ● vi fugarse. ● adv. ~ **upright** rígido

bomb /bɒm/ n bomba f. ● vt bombardear. ~**ard** /bɒm'bɑːd/ vt bombardear

bombastic /bɒm'bæstɪk/ a ampuloso

bomb: ~**er** /'bɒmə(r)/ n bombardero m. ~**ing** n bombardeo m. ~**shell** n bomba f

bonanza /bə'nænzə/ n bonanza f

bond /bɒnd/ n (agreement) obligación f; (link) lazo m; (com) bono m

bondage /'bɒndɪdʒ/ n esclavitud f

bone /bəʊn/ n hueso m; (of fish) espina f. ● vt deshuesar. ~-**dry** a completamente seco. ~ **idle** a holgazán

bonfire /'bɒnfaɪə(r)/ n hoguera f

bonnet /'bɒnɪt/ n gorra f; (auto) capó m, tapa f del motor (Mex)

bonny /'bɒnɪ/ a (-ier, -iest) bonito

bonus /'bəʊnəs/ n prima f; (fig) plus m

bony /'bəʊnɪ/ a (-ier, -iest) huesudo; ⟨fish⟩ lleno de espinas

boo /buː/ int ¡bu! ● vt/i abuchear

boob /buːb/ n (mistake, sl) metedura f de pata. ● vi (sl) meter la pata

booby /'buːbɪ/ n bobo m. ~ **trap** trampa f; (mil) trampa f explosiva

book /bʊk/ n libro m; (of cheques etc) talonario m; (notebook) libreta f; (exercise book) cuaderno m; (pl, com) cuentas fpl. ● vt (enter) registrar; (reserve) reservar. ● vi reservar. ~**able** a que se puede reservar. ~**case** /'bʊkkeɪs/ n estantería f, librería f. ~-**ing-office** (in theatre) taquilla f; (rail) despacho m de billetes. ~**let** /'bʊklɪt/ n folleto m

bookkeeping /'bʊkkiːpɪŋ/ n contabilidad f

bookmaker /'bʊkmeɪkə(r)/ n corredor m de apuestas

book: ~**mark** /'bʊkmɑː(r)k/ n señal f. ~**seller** /'bʊkselə(r)/ n librero m. ~**shop** /'bʊkʃɒp/ n librería f. ~**stall** /'bʊkstɔːl/ n quiosco m de libros. ~**worm** /'bʊkwɜːm/ n (fig) ratón m de biblioteca

boom /buːm/ vi retumbar; (fig) prosperar. ● n estampido m; (com) auge m

boon /buːn/ n beneficio m

boor /bʊə(r)/ n patán m. ~**ish** a grosero

boost /buːst/ vt estimular; reforzar ⟨morale⟩; aumentar ⟨price⟩; (publicize) hacer publicidad por. ● n empuje m. ~**er** n (med) revacunación f

boot /buːt/ n bota f; (auto) maletero m, baúl m (LAm). **get the** ~ (sl) ser despedido

booth /buːð/ n cabina f; (at fair) puesto m

booty /'buːtɪ/ n botín m

booze /buːz/ vi (fam) beber mucho. ● n (fam) alcohol m; (spree) borrachera f

border /'bɔːdə(r)/ n borde m; (frontier) frontera f; (in garden) arriate m. ● vi. ~ **on** lindar con

borderline /'bɔːdəlaɪn/ n línea f divisoria. ~ **case** n caso m dudoso

bore[1] /bɔː(r)/ vt (tec) taladrar. ● vi taladrar

bore[2] /bɔː(r)/ vt (annoy) aburrir. ● n (person) pelmazo m; (thing) lata f

bore[3] /bɔː(r)/ see **bear**[1]

boredom /'bɔːdəm/ n aburrimiento m

boring /'bɔːrɪŋ/ a aburrido, pesado

born /bɔːn/ a nato. **be** ~ nacer

borne /bɔːn/ see **bear**[1]

borough /'bʌrə/ n municipio m

borrow /'bɒrəʊ/ vt pedir prestado

Borstal /'bɔːstl/ n reformatorio m

bosh /bɒʃ/ int & n (sl) tonterías (fpl)

bosom /'bʊzəm/ n seno m. ~ **friend** n amigo m íntimo

boss /bɒs/ n (fam) jefe m. ● vt. ~ (**about**) (fam) dar órdenes a. ~**y** /'bɒsɪ/ a mandón

botan|ical /bə'tænɪkl/ a botánico. ~**ist** /'bɒtənɪst/ n botánico m. ~**y** /'bɒtənɪ/ n botánica f

botch /bɒtʃ/ vt chapucear. ● n chapuza f

both /bəʊθ/ a & pron ambos (mpl), los dos (mpl). ● adv al mismo tiempo, a la vez

bother /'bɒðə(r)/ vt molestar; (worry) preocupar. ~ it! int ¡caramba! ● vi molestarse. ~ about preocuparse de. ~ doing tenerse la molestia de hacer. ● n molestia f

bottle /'bɒtl/ n botella; (for baby) biberón m. ● vt embotellar. ~ up (fig) reprimir. ~neck /'bɒtlnek/ n (traffic jam) embotellamiento m. ~opener n destapador m, abrebotellas m invar; (corkscrew) sacacorchos m invar

bottom /'bɒtəm/ n fondo m; (of hill) pie m; (buttocks) trasero m. ● a último, inferior. ~less a sin fondo

bough /baʊ/ n rama f

bought /bɔ:t/ see **buy**

boulder /'bəʊldə(r)/ n canto m

boulevard /'bu:ləva:d/ n bulevar m

bounc|e /baʊns/ vt hacer rebotar. ● vi rebotar; (person) saltar; (cheque, sl) ser rechazado. ● n rebote m. ~ing /'baʊnsɪŋ/ a robusto

bound[1] /baʊnd/ vi saltar. ● n salto m

bound[2] /baʊnd/ n. out of ~s zona f prohibida

bound[3] /baʊnd/ a. be ~ for dirigirse a

bound[4] /baʊnd/ see **bind**. ~ to obligado a; (certain) seguro de

boundary /'baʊndərɪ/ n límite m

boundless /'baʊndləs/ a ilimitado

bountiful /'baʊntɪfl/ a abundante

bouquet /bʊ'keɪ/ n ramo m; (perfume) aroma m; (of wine) buqué m, nariz f

bout /baʊt/ n período m; (med) ataque m; (sport) encuentro m

bow[1] /bəʊ/ n (weapon, mus) arco m; (knot) lazo m

bow[2] /baʊ/ n reverencia f. ● vi inclinarse. ● vt inclinar

bow[3] /baʊ/ n (naut) proa f

bowels /'baʊəlz/ npl intestinos mpl; (fig) entrañas fpl

bowl[1] /bəʊl/ n cuenco m; (for washing) palangana f; (of pipe) cazoleta f

bowl[2] /bəʊl/ n (ball) bola f. ● vt (cricket) arrojar. ● vi (cricket) arrojar la pelota. ~ over derribar

bow-legged /bəʊ'legɪd/ a estevado

bowler[1] /'bəʊlə(r)/ n (cricket) lanzador m

bowler[2] /'bəʊlə(r)/ n. ~ (hat) hongo m, bombín m

bowling /'bəʊlɪŋ/ n bolos mpl

bow-tie /bəʊ'taɪ/ n corbata f de lazo, pajarita f

box[1] /bɒks/ n caja f; (for jewels etc) estuche m; (in theatre) palco m

box[2] /bɒks/ vt boxear contra. ~ s.o.'s ears dar una manotada a uno. ● vi boxear. ~er n boxeador m. ~ing n boxeo m

box: B~ing Day n el 26 de diciembre. ~-office n taquilla f. ~-room n trastero m

boy /bɔɪ/ n chico m, muchacho m; (young) niño m

boycott /'bɔɪkɒt/ vt boicotear. ● n boicoteo m

boy: ~-friend n novio m. ~-hood n niñez f. ~ish a de muchacho; (childish) infantil

bra /brɑ:/ n sostén m, sujetador m

brace /breɪs/ n abrazadera f; (dental) aparato m. ● vt asegurar. ~ o.s. prepararse. ~s npl tirantes mpl

bracelet /'breɪslɪt/ n pulsera f

bracing /'breɪsɪŋ/ a vigorizante

bracken /'brækən/ n helecho m

bracket /'brækɪt/ n soporte m; (group) categoría f; (typ) paréntesis m invar. **square** ~s corchetes mpl. ● vt poner entre paréntesis; (join together) agrupar

brag /bræg/ vi (pt bragged) jactarse (about de)

braid /breɪd/ n galón m; (of hair) trenza f

brain /breɪn/ n cerebro m. ● vt romper la cabeza

brain-child /'breɪntʃaɪld/ n invento m

brain: ~ drain (fam) fuga f de cerebros. ~-less a estúpido. ~s npl (fig) inteligencia f

brainstorm /'breɪnstɔ:m/ n ataque m de locura; (Amer, brainwave) idea f genial

brainwash /'breɪnwɒʃ/ vt lavar el cerebro

brainwave /'breɪnweɪv/ n idea f genial

brainy /'breɪnɪ/ a (-ier, -iest) inteligente

braise /breɪz/ vt cocer a fuego lento

brake /breɪk/ n freno m. **disc** ~ freno de disco. **hand** ~ freno de mano. ● vt/i frenar. ~ **fluid** n líquido m de freno. ~ **lining** n forro m del freno. ~ **shoe** n zapata f del freno

bramble /'bræmbl/ n zarza f

bran /bræn/ n salvado m

branch /brɑ:ntʃ/ n rama f; (of road) bifurcación f; (com) sucursal m; (fig) ramo m. ● vi. ~ off bifurcarse. ~ out ramificarse

brand /brænd/ n marca f; (iron) hierro m. ● vt marcar; (reputation) tildar de

brandish /'brændɪʃ/ vt blandir

brand-new /brænd'nju:/ a flamante

brandy /'brændɪ/ n coñac m

brash /bræʃ/ a descarado

brass /brɑːs/ n latón m. **get down to ~ tacks** (fig) ir al grano. **top ~** (sl) peces mpl gordos. ~**y** a (-ier, -iest) descarado

brassière /'bræsjeə(r)/ n sostén m, sujetador m

brat /bræt/ n (pej) mocoso m

bravado /brə'vɑːdəʊ/ n bravata f

brave /breɪv/ a (-er, -est) valiente. ● n (Red Indian) guerrero m indio. ● vt afrontar. ~**ry** /-ərɪ/ n valentía f, valor m

brawl /brɔːl/ n alboroto m. ● vi pelearse

brawn /brɔːn/ n músculo m; (strength) fuerza f muscular. ~**y** a musculoso

bray /breɪ/ n rebuzno m. ● vi rebuznar

brazen /'breɪzn/ a descarado

brazier /'breɪzɪə(r)/ n brasero m

Brazil /brə'zɪl/ n el Brasil m. ~**ian** a & n brasileño (m)

breach /briːtʃ/ n violación f; (of contract) incumplimiento m; (gap) brecha f. ● vt abrir una brecha en

bread /bred/ n pan m. **loaf of ~** pan. ~**crumbs** /'bredkrʌmz/ npl migajas fpl; (culin) pan rallado. ~**line** n. **on the ~line** en la miseria

breadth /bredθ/ n anchura f

bread-winner /'bredwɪnə(r)/ n sostén m de la familia, cabeza f de familia

break /breɪk/ vt (pt **broke**, pp **broken**) romper; quebrantar (law); batir (record); comunicar (news); interrumpir (journey). ● vi romperse; (news) divulgarse. ● n ruptura f; (interval) intervalo m; (chance, fam) oportunidad f; (in weather) cambio m. ~ **away** escapar. ~ **down** vt derribar; analizar (figures). ● vi estropearse; (auto) averiarse; (med) sufrir un colapso; (cry) deshacerse en lágrimas. ~ **into** forzar (house etc); (start doing) ponerse a. ~ **off** interrumpirse. ~ **out** (war, disease) estallar; (run away) escaparse. ~ **up**

romperse; (schools) terminar. ~**able** a frágil. ~**age** n rotura f

breakdown /'breɪkdaʊn/ n (tec) falla f; (med) colapso m, crisis f nerviosa; (of figures) análisis f

breaker /'breɪkə(r)/ n (wave) cachón m

breakfast /'brekfəst/ n desayuno m

breakthrough /'breɪkθruː/ n adelanto m

breakwater /'breɪkwɔːtə(r)/ n rompeolas m invar

breast /brest/ n pecho m; (of chicken etc) pechuga f. ~**stroke** n braza f de pecho

breath /breθ/ n aliento m, respiración f. **out of ~** sin aliento. **under one's ~** a media voz. ~**alyser** /'breθəlaɪzə(r)/ n alcoholímetro m

breath|e /briːð/ vt/i respirar. ~**er** /'briːðə(r)/ n descanso m, pausa f. ~**ing** n respiración f

breathtaking /'breθteɪkɪŋ/ a impresionante

bred /bred/ see **breed**

breeches /'brɪtʃɪz/ npl calzones mpl

breed /briːd/ vt/i (pt **bred**) reproducirse; (fig) engendrar. ● n raza f. ~**er** n criador m. ~**ing** n cría f; (manners) educación f

breez|e /briːz/ n brisa f. ~**y** a de mucho viento; (person) despreocupado. **it is** ~**y** hace viento

Breton /'bretən/ a & n bretón (m)

brew /bruː/ vt hacer. ● vi fermentar; (tea) reposar; (fig) prepararse. ● n infusión f. ~**er** n cervecero m. ~**ery** n fábrica f de cerveza, cervecería f

bribe /braɪb/ n soborno m. ● vt sobornar. ~**ry** /-ərɪ/ n soborno m

brick /brɪk/ n ladrillo m. ● vt. ~ **up** tapar con ladrillos. ~**layer** /'brɪkleɪə(r)/ n albañil m

bridal /'braɪdl/ a nupcial

bride /braɪd/ m novia f. ~**groom** /'braɪdgrʊm/ n novio m. ~**smaid** /'braɪdzmeɪd/ n dama f de honor

bridge[1] /brɪdʒ/ n puente m; (of nose) caballete m. ● vt tender un puente sobre. ~ **a gap** llenar un vacío

bridge[2] /brɪdʒ/ n (cards) bridge m

bridle /'braɪdl/ n brida f. ● vt embridar. ~**path** n camino m de herradura

brief /briːf/ a (-er, -est) breve. ● n (jurid) escrito m. ● vt dar instrucciones a. ~**case** n /'briːfkeɪs/ n maletín m. ~**ly** adv brevemente. ~**s** npl (*man's*) calzoncillos *mpl*; (*woman's*) bragas *fpl*

brigad|e /brɪ'geɪd/ *n* brigada *f*. ~**ier** /-ə'dɪə(r)/ *n* general *m* de brigada

bright /braɪt/ *a* (**-er, -est**) brillante, claro; (*clever*) listo; (*cheerful*) alegre. ~**en** /'braɪtn/ *vt* aclarar; hacer más alegre (*house etc*). ●*vi* (*weather*) aclararse; (*face*) animarse. ~**ly** *adv* brillantemente. ~**ness** *n* claridad *f*

brillian|ce /'brɪljəns/ *n* brillantez *f*, brillo *m*. ~**t** *a* brillante

brim /brɪm/ *n* borde *m*; (*of hat*) ala *f*. ●*vi* (*pt* **brimmed**). ~ **over** desbordarse

brine /braɪn/ *n* salmuera *f*

bring /brɪŋ/ *vt* (*pt* **brought**) traer (*thing*); conducir (*person, vehicle*). ~ **about** causar. ~ **back** devolver. ~ **down** derribar; rebajar (*price*). ~ **off** lograr. ~ **on** causar. ~ **out** sacar; lanzar (*product*); publicar (*book*). ~ **round/to** hacer volver en sí (*unconscious person*). ~ **up** (*med*) vomitar; educar (*children*); plantear (*question*)

brink /brɪŋk/ *n* borde *m*

brisk /brɪsk/ *a* (**-er, -est**) enérgico, vivo. ~**ness** *n* energía *f*

bristl|e /'brɪsl/ *n* cerda *f*. ●*vi* erizarse. ~**ing with** erizado de

Brit|ain /'brɪtən/ *n* Gran Bretaña *f*. ~**ish** /'brɪtɪʃ/ *a* británico. **the** ~**ish** los británicos. ~**on** /'brɪtən/ *n* británico *m*

Brittany /'brɪtənɪ/ *n* Bretaña *f*

brittle /'brɪtl/ *a* frágil, quebradizo

broach /brəʊtʃ/ *vt* abordar (*subject*); espitar (*cask*)

broad /brɔːd/ *a* (**-er, -est**) ancho. **in** ~ **daylight** en pleno día. ~ **bean** *n* haba *f*

broadcast /'brɔːdkɑːst/ *n* emisión *f*. ●*vt* (*pt* **broadcast**) emitir. ●*vi* hablar por la radio. ~**ing** *a* de radiodifusión. ●*n* radio-difusión *f*

broad|en /'brɔːdn/ *vt* ensanchar. ●*vi* ensancharse. ~**ly** *adv* en general. ~**-minded** *a* de miras amplias, tolerante, liberal

brocade /brə'keɪd/ *n* brocado *m*

broccoli /'brɒkəlɪ/ *n invar* brécol *m*

brochure /'brəʊʃə(r)/ *n* folleto *m*

brogue /brəʊg/ *n* abarca *f*; (*accent*) acento *m* regional

broke /brəʊk/ *see* **break**. ●*a* (*sl*) sin blanca

broken /'brəʊkən/ *see* **break**. ●*a*. ~ **English** inglés *m* chapurreado. ~**hearted** *a* con el corazón destrozado

broker /'brəʊkə(r)/ *n* corredor *m*

brolly /'brɒlɪ/ *n* (*fam*) paraguas *m invar*

bronchitis /brɒŋ'kaɪtɪs/ *n* bronquitis *f*

bronze /brɒnz/ *n* bronce *m*. ●*vt* broncear. ●*vi* broncearse

brooch /brəʊtʃ/ *n* broche *m*

brood /bruːd/ *n* cría *f*; (*joc*) prole *m*. ●*vi* empollar; (*fig*) meditar. ~**y** *a* contemplativo

brook¹ /brʊk/ *n* arroyo *m*

brook² /brʊk/ *vt* soportar

broom /bruːm/ *n* hiniesta *f*; (*brush*) escoba *f*. ~**stick** /'bruːmstɪk/ *n* palo *m* de escoba

broth /brɒθ/ *n* caldo *m*

brothel /'brɒθl/ *n* burdel *m*

brother /'brʌðə(r)/ *n* hermano *m*. ~**hood** *n* fraternidad *f*, (*relig*) hermandad *f*. ~**-in-law** *n* cuñado *m*. ~**ly** *a* fraternal

brought /brɔːt/ *see* **bring**

brow /braʊ/ *n* frente *f*; (*of hill*) cima *f*

browbeat /'braʊbiːt/ *vt* (*pt* **-beat**, *pp* **-beaten**) intimidar

brown /braʊn/ *a* (**-er, -est**) marrón; (*skin*) moreno; (*hair*) castaño. ●*n* marrón *m*. ●*vt* poner moreno; (*culin*) dorar. ●*vi* ponerse moreno; (*culin*) dorarse. **be** ~**ed off** (*sl*) estar hasta la coronilla

Brownie /'braʊnɪ/ *n* niña *f* exploradora

browse /braʊz/ *vi* (*in a shop*) curiosear; (*animal*) pacer

bruise /bruːz/ *n* magulladura *f*. ●*vt* magullar; machucar (*fruit*). ●*vi* magullarse; (*fruit*) machucarse

brunch /brʌntʃ/ *n* (*fam*) desayuno *m* tardío

brunette /bruː'net/ *n* morena *f*

brunt /brʌnt/ *n*. **the** ~ **of** lo más fuerte de

brush /brʌʃ/ *n* cepillo *m*; (*large*) escoba; (*for decorating*) brocha *f*; (*artist's*) pincel *m*; (*skirmish*) escaramuza *f*. ●*vt* cepillar. ~ **against** rozar. ~ **aside** rechazar. ~ **off** (*rebuff*) desairar. ~ **up (on)** refrescar

brusque /bruːsk/ *a* brusco. ~**ly** *adv* bruscamente

Brussels /'brʌslz/ *n* Bruselas *f*. ~ **sprout** col *m* de Bruselas

brutal /'bru:tl/ *a* brutal. ∼**ity** /-'tæləti/ *n* brutalidad *f*

brute /bru:t/ *n* bestia *f*. ∼ **force** fuerza *f* bruta

BSc *abbr see* **bachelor**

bubble /'bʌbl/ *n* burbuja *f*. ● *vi* burbujear. ∼ **over** desbordarse

bubbly /'bʌblɪ/ *a* burbujeante. ● *n* (*fam*) champaña *m*, champán *m* (*fam*)

buck[1] /bʌk/ *a* macho. ● *n* (*deer*) ciervo *m*. ● *vi* (*of horse*) corcovear. ∼ **up** (*hurry, sl*) darse prisa; (*cheer up, sl*) animarse

buck[2] /bʌk/ (*Amer, sl*) dólar *m*

buck[3] /bʌk/ *n*. **pass the** ∼ **to s.o.** echarle a uno el muerto

bucket /'bʌkɪt/ *n* cubo *m*

buckle /'bʌkl/ *n* hebilla *f*. ● *vt* abrochar. ● *vi* torcerse. ∼ **down to** dedicarse con empeño a

bud /bʌd/ *n* brote *m*. ● *vi* (*pt* **budded**) brotar.

Buddhis|m /'bʊdɪzəm/ *n* budismo *m*. ∼**t** /'bʊdɪst/ *a & n* budista (*m & f*)

budding /'bʌdɪŋ/ *a* (*fig*) en ciernes

buddy /'bʌdɪ/ *n* (*fam*) compañero *m*, amigote *m* (*fam*)

budge /bʌdʒ/ *vt* mover. ● *vi* moverse

budgerigar /'bʌdʒərɪgɑ:(r)/ *n* periquito *m*

budget /'bʌdʒɪt/ *n* presupuesto *m*. ● *vi* (*pt* **budgeted**) presupuestar

buff /bʌf/ *n* (*colour*) color *m* de ante; (*fam*) aficionado *m*. ● *vt* pulir

buffalo /'bʌfələʊ/ *n* (*pl* **-oes** *or* **-o**) búfalo *m*

buffer /'bʌfə(r)/ *n* parachoques *m invar*. ∼ **state** estado *m* tapón

buffet[1] /'bʊfeɪ/ *n* (*meal, counter*) bufé *m*. /'bʌfɪt/ *n* golpe *m*; (*slap*) bofetada *f*. ● *vt* (*pt* **buffeted**) golpear

buffoon /bə'fu:n/ *n* payaso *m*, bufón *m*

bug /bʌg/ *n* bicho *m*; (*germ, sl*) microbio *m*; (*device, sl*) micrófono *m* oculto. ● *vt* (*pt* **bugged**) ocultar un micrófono en; intervenir ⟨*telephone*⟩; (*Amer, sl*) molestar

bugbear /'bʌgbeə(r)/ *n* pesadilla *f*

buggy /'bʌgɪ/ *n*. **baby** ∼ (*esp Amer*) cochecito *m* de niño

bugle /'bju:gl/ *n* corneta *f*

build /bɪld/ *vt/i* (*pt* **built**) construir. ∼ **up** *vt* urbanizar; (*increase*) aumentar. ● *n* (*of person*) figura *f*, tipo *m*. ∼**er** *n* constructor *m*. ∼**up** *n* aumento *m*; (*of gas etc*) acumulación *f*; (*fig*) propaganda *f*

built /bɪlt/ *see* **build**. ∼**-in** *a* empotrado. ∼**-up area** *n* zona *f* urbanizada

bulb /bʌlb/ *n* bulbo *m*; (*elec*) bombilla *f*. ∼**ous** *a* bulboso

Bulgaria /bʌl'geərɪə/ *n* Bulgaria *f*. ∼**n** *a & n* búlgaro (*m*)

bulge /bʌldʒ/ *n* protuberancia *f*. ● *vi* pandearse; (*jut out*) sobresalir. ∼**ing** *a* abultado; ⟨*eyes*⟩ saltón

bulk /bʌlk/ *n* bulto *m*, volumen *m*. **in** ∼ a granel; (*loose*) suelto. **the** ∼ **of** la mayor parte de. ∼**y** *a* voluminoso

bull /bʊl/ *n* toro *m*

bulldog /'bʊldɒg/ *n* buldog *m*

bulldozer /'bʊldəʊzə(r)/ *n* oruga *f* aplanadora, bulldozer *m*

bullet /'bʊlɪt/ *n* bala *f*

bulletin /'bʊlətɪn/ *n* anuncio *m*; (*journal*) boletín *m*

bullet-proof /'bʊlɪtpru:f/ *a* a prueba de balas

bullfight /'bʊlfaɪt/ *n* corrida *f* (de toros). ∼**er** *n* torero *m*

bullion /'bʊljən/ *n* (*gold*) oro *m* en barras; (*silver*) plata *f* en barras

bull: ∼**ring** /'bʊlrɪŋ/ *n* plaza *f* de toros. ∼**'s-eye** *n* centro *m* del blanco, diana *f*

bully /'bʊlɪ/ *n* matón *m*. ● *vt* intimidar. ∼**ing** *n* intimidación *f*

bum[1] /bʌm/ *n* (*bottom, sl*) trasero *m*

bum[2] /bʌm/ *n* (*Amer, sl*) holgazán *m*

bumble-bee /'bʌmblbi:/ *n* abejorro *m*

bump /bʌmp/ *vt* chocar contra. ● *vi* dar sacudidas. ● *n* choque *m*; (*swelling*) chichón *m*. ∼ **into** chocar contra; (*meet*) encontrar

bumper /'bʌmpə(r)/ *n* parachoques *m invar*. ● *a* abundante. ∼ **edition** edición *f* especial

bumpkin /'bʌmpkɪn/ *n* patán *m*, paleto *m* (*fam*)

bumptious /'bʌmpʃəs/ *a* presuntuoso

bun /bʌn/ *n* bollo *m*; (*hair*) moño *m*

bunch /bʌntʃ/ *n* manojo *m*; (*of people*) grupo *m*; (*of bananas, grapes*) racimo *m*; (*of flowers*) ramo *m*

bundle /'bʌndl/ *n* bulto *m*; (*of papers*) legajo *m*; (*of nerves*) manojo *m*. ● *vt*. ∼ **up** atar

bung /bʌŋ/ *n* tapón *m*. ● *vt* tapar; (*sl*) tirar

bungalow /'bʌŋgələʊ/ *n* casa *f* de un solo piso, chalé *m*, bungalow *m*

bungle /'bʌŋgl/ *vt* chapucear

bunion /'bʌnjən/ n juanete m

bunk /bʌŋk/ n litera f

bunker /'bʌŋkə(r)/ n carbonera f; (golf) obstáculo m; (mil) refugio m, búnker m

bunkum /'bʌŋkəm/ n tonterías fpl

bunny /'bʌnɪ/ n conejito m

buoy /bɔɪ/ n boya f. ● vt.~ **up** hacer flotar; (fig) animar

buoyan|cy /'bɔɪənsɪ/ n flotabilidad f; (fig) optimismo m. ~**t** /'bɔɪənt/ a boyante; (fig) alegre

burden /'bɜːdn/ n carga f. ● vt cargar (**with** de). ~**some** a pesado

bureau /'bjʊərəʊ/ n (pl -eaux /-əʊz/) escritorio m; (office) oficina f

bureaucra|cy /bjʊə'rɒkrəsɪ/ n burocracia f. ~**t** /'bjʊərəkræt/ n burócrata m & f. ~**tic** /-'krætɪk/ a burocrático

burgeon /'bɜːdʒən/ vi brotar; (fig) crecer

burgl|ar /'bɜːglə(r)/ n ladrón m. ~**ary** n robo m con allanamiento de morada. ~**e** /'bɜːgl/ vt robar con allanamiento

Burgundy /'bɜːgəndɪ/ n Borgoña f; (wine) vino m de Borgoña

burial /'berɪəl/ n entierro m

burlesque /bɜː'lesk/ n burlesco m

burly /'bɜːlɪ/ a (-ier, -iest) corpulento

Burm|a /'bɜːmə/ Birmania f. ~**ese** /-'miːz/ a & n birmano (m)

burn /bɜːn/ vt (pt **burned** or **burnt**) quemar. ● vi quemarse. ~ **down** destruir con fuego. ● n quemadura f. ~**er** n quemador m. ~**ing** a ardiente; (food) que quema; (question) candente

burnish /'bɜːnɪʃ/ vt lustrar, pulir

burnt /bɜːnt/ see **burn**

burp /bɜːp/ n (fam) eructo m. ● vi (fam) eructar

burr /bɜː(r)/ n (bot) erizo m

burrow /'bʌrəʊ/ n madriguera f. ● vt excavar

bursar /'bɜːsə(r)/ n tesorero m. ~**y** /'bɜːsərɪ/ n beca f

burst /bɜːst/ vt (pt **burst**) reventar. ● vi reventarse; (tyre) pincharse. ● n reventón m; (mil) ráfaga f; (fig) explosión f. ~ **of laughter** carcajada f

bury /'berɪ/ vt enterrar; (hide) ocultar

bus /bʌs/ n (pl **buses**) autobús m, camión m (Mex). ● vi (pt **bussed**) ir en autobús

bush /bʊʃ/ n arbusto m; (land) monte m. ~**y** a espeso

busily /'bɪzɪlɪ/ adv afanosamente

business /'bɪznɪs/ n negocio m; (com) negocios mpl; (profession) ocupación f; (fig) asunto m. **mind one's own** ~ ocuparse de sus propios asuntos. ~**like** a práctico, serio. ~**man** n hombre m de negocios

busker /'bʌskə(r)/ n músico m ambulante

bus-stop /'bʌsstɒp/ n parada f de autobús

bust[1] /bʌst/ n busto m; (chest) pecho m

bust[2] /bʌst/ vt (pt **busted** or **bust**) (sl) romper. ● vi romperse. ● a roto. **go** ~ (sl) quebrar

bustle /'bʌsl/ vi apresurarse. ● n bullicio m

bust-up /'bʌstʌp/ n (sl) riña f

busy /'bɪzɪ/ a (-ier, -iest) ocupado; (street) concurrido. ● vt.~ **o.s. with** ocuparse de

busybody /'bɪzɪbɒdɪ/ n entrometido m

but /bʌt/ conj pero; (after negative) sino. ● prep menos. ~ **for** si no fuera por. **last** ~ **one** penúltimo. ● adv solamente

butane /'bjuːteɪn/ n butano m

butcher /'bʊtʃə(r)/ n carnicero m. ● vt matar; (fig) hacer una carnicería con. ~**y** n carnicería f, matanza f

butler /'bʌtlə(r)/ n mayordomo m

butt /bʌt/ n (of gun) culata f; (of cigarette) colilla f; (target) blanco m. ● vi topar. ~ **in** interrumpir

butter /'bʌtə(r)/ n mantequilla f. ● vt untar con mantequilla. ~ **up** vt (fam) lisonjear, dar jabón a. ~**bean** n judía f

buttercup /'bʌtəkʌp/ n ranúnculo m

butter-fingers /'bʌtəfɪŋgəz/ n manazas m invar, torpe m

butterfly /'bʌtəflaɪ/ n mariposa f

buttock /'bʌtək/ n nalga f

button /'bʌtn/ n botón m. ● vt abotonar. ● vi abotonarse. ~**hole** /'bʌtnhəʊl/ n ojal m. ● vt (fig) detener

buttress /'bʌtrɪs/ n contrafuerte m. ● vt apoyar

buxom /'bʌksəm/ a (woman) rollizo

buy /baɪ/ vt (pt **bought**) comprar. ● n compra f. ~**er** n comprador m

buzz /bʌz/ n zumbido m; (phone call, fam) llamada f. ● vi zumbar. ~ **off** (sl) largarse. ~**er** n timbre m

by /baɪ/ *prep* por; *(near)* cerca de; *(before)* antes de; *(according to)* según. ~ **and large** en conjunto, en general. ~ **car** en coche. ~ **oneself** por sí solo

bye-bye /'baɪbaɪ/ *int (fam)* ¡adiós!

by-election /'baɪlekʃn/ *n* elección *f* parcial

bygone /'baɪgɒn/ *a* pasado

by-law /'baɪlɔ:/ *n* reglamento *m* (local)

bypass /'baɪpɑ:s/ *n* carretera *f* de circunvalación. ● *vt* evitar

by-product /'baɪprɒdʌkt/ *n* subproducto *m*

bystander /'baɪstændə(r)/ *n* espectador *m*

byword /'baɪwɜ:d/ *n* sinónimo *m*. **be a ~ for** ser conocido por

C

cab /kæb/ *n* taxi *m*; *(of lorry, train)* cabina *f*

cabaret /'kæbəreɪ/ *n* espectáculo *m*

cabbage /'kæbɪdʒ/ *n* col *m*, repollo *m*

cabin /'kæbɪn/ *n* cabaña *f*; *(in ship)* camarote *m*; *(in plane)* cabina *f*

cabinet /'kæbɪnɪt/ *n* *(cupboard)* armario *m*; *(for display)* vitrina *f*. **C~** *(pol)* gabinete *m*. ~**-maker** *n* ebanista *m & f*

cable /'keɪbl/ *n* cable *m*. ● *vt* cablegrafiar. ~ **railway** *n* funicular *m*

cache /kæʃ/ *n* *(place)* escondrijo *m*; *(things)* reservas *fpl* escondidas. ● *vt* ocultar

cackle /'kækl/ *n* *(of hen)* cacareo *m*; *(laugh)* risotada *f*. ● *vi* cacarear; *(laugh)* reírse a carcajadas

cacophon|ous /kə'kɒfənəs/ *a* cacofónico. ~**y** *n* cacofonía *f*

cactus /'kæktəs/ *n* *(pl* **-ti** /-taɪ/) cacto *m*

cad /kæd/ *n* sinvergüenza *m*. ~**dish** *a* desvergonzado

caddie /'kædɪ/ *n* *(golf)* portador *m* de palos

caddy /'kædɪ/ *n* cajita *f*

cadence /'keɪdəns/ *n* cadencia *f*

cadet /kə'det/ *n* cadete *m*

cadge /kædʒ/ *vt/i* gorronear. ~**r** /-ə(r)/ *n* gorrón *m*

Caesarean /sɪ'zeərɪən/ *a* cesáreo. ~ **section** *n* cesárea *f*

café /'kæfeɪ/ *n* cafetería *f*

cafeteria /kæfɪ'tɪərɪə/ *n* autoservicio *m*

caffeine /'kæfi:n/ *n* cafeína *f*

cage /keɪdʒ/ *n* jaula *f*. ● *vt* enjaular

cagey /'keɪdʒɪ/ *a (fam)* evasivo

Cairo /'kaɪərəʊ/ *n* el Cairo *m*

cajole /kə'dʒəʊl/ *vt* engatusar. ~**ry** *n* engatusamiento *m*

cake /keɪk/ *n* pastel *m*, tarta *f*; *(sponge)* bizcocho *m*. ~ **of soap** pastilla *f* de jabón. ~**d** *a* incrustado

calamit|ous /kə'læmɪtəs/ *a* desastroso. ~**y** /kə'læmətɪ/ *n* calamidad *f*

calcium /'kælsɪəm/ *n* calcio *m*

calculat|e /'kælkjuleɪt/ *vt/i* calcular; *(Amer)* suponer. ~**ing** *a* calculador. ~**ion** /-'leɪʃn/ *n* cálculo *m*. ~**or** *n* calculadora *f*

calculus /'kælkjʊləs/ *n* *(pl* **-li**) cálculo *m*

calendar /'kælɪndə(r)/ *n* calendario *m*

calf[1] /kɑ:f/ *n* *(pl* **calves**) ternero *m*

calf[2] /kɑ:f/ *n* *(pl* **calves**) *(of leg)* pantorrilla *f*

calibre /'kælɪbə(r)/ *n* calibre *m*

calico /'kælɪkəʊ/ *n* calicó *m*

call /kɔ:l/ *vt/i* llamar. ● *n* llamada *f*; *(shout)* grito *m*; *(visit)* visita *f*. **be on** ~ estar de guardia. **long distance** ~ conferencia *f*. ~ **back** *vt* hacer volver; *(on phone)* volver a llamar. ● *vi* volver; *(on phone)* volver a llamar. ~ **for** pedir; *(fetch)* ir a buscar. ~ **off** cancelar. ~ **on** visitar. ~ **out** dar voces. ~ **together** convocar. ~ **up** *(mil)* llamar al servicio militar; *(phone)* llamar. ~**-box** *n* cabina *f* telefónica. ~**er** *n* visita *f*; *(phone)* el que llama *m*. ~**ing** *n* vocación *f*

callous /'kæləs/ *a* insensible, cruel. ~**ness** *n* crueldad *f*

callow /'kæləʊ/ *a* (**-er, -est**) inexperto

calm /kɑ:m/ *a* (**-er, -est**) tranquilo; *(weather)* calmoso. ● *n* tranquilidad *f*, calma *f*. ● *vt* calmar. ● *vi* calmarse. ~**ness** *n* tranquilidad *f*, calma *f*

calorie /'kælərɪ/ *n* caloría *f*

camber /'kæmbə(r)/ *n* curvatura *f*

came /keɪm/ *see* **come**

camel /'kæml/ *n* camello *m*

camellia /kə'mi:lɪə/ *n* camelia *f*

cameo /'kæmɪəʊ/ *n* *(pl* **-os**) camafeo *m*

camera /'kæmərə/ *n* máquina *f* (fotográfica); *(TV)* cámara *f*. ~**man** *n* *(pl* **-men**) operador *m*, cámara *m*

camouflage /'kæməflɑːʒ/ *n* camuflaje *m*. ● *vt* encubrir; (*mil*) camuflar

camp[1] /kæmp/ *n* campamento *m*. ● *vi* acamparse

camp[2] /kæmp/ *a* (*affected*) amanerado

campaign /kæm'peɪn/ *n* campaña *f*. ● *vi* hacer campaña

camp: ∼**-bed** *n* catre *m* de tijera. ∼**er** *n* campista *m & f*; (*vehicle*) caravana *f*. ∼**ing** *n* camping *m*. **go** ∼**ing** hacer camping. ∼**site** /'kæmpsaɪt/ *n* camping *m*

campus /'kæmpəs/ *n* (*pl* **-puses**) ciudad *f* universitaria

can[1] /kæn/ *v aux* (*pt* **could**) (*be able to*) poder; (*know how to*) saber. ∼**not** (*neg*), ∼**'t** (*neg, fam*). **I** ∼**not**/ ∼**'t go** no puedo ir

can[2] /kæn/ *n* lata *f*. ● *vt* (*pt* **canned**) enlatar. ∼**ned music** música *f* grabada

Canad|a /'kænədə/ *n* el Canadá *m*. ∼**ian** /kə'neɪdɪən/ *a & n* canadiense (*m & f*)

canal /kə'næl/ *n* canal *m*

canary /kə'neərɪ/ *n* canario *m*

cancel /'kænsl/ *vt/i* (*pt* **cancelled**) anular; cancelar ⟨*contract etc*⟩; suspender ⟨*appointment etc*⟩; (*delete*) tachar. ∼**lation** /-'leɪʃn/ *n* cancelación *f*

cancer /'kænsə(r)/ *n* cáncer *m*. **C**∼ *n* (*astr*) Cáncer *m*. ∼**ous** *a* canceroso

candid /'kændɪd/ *a* franco

candida|cy /'kændɪdəsɪ/ *n* candidatura *f*. ∼**te** /'kændɪdeɪt/ *n* candidato *m*

candle /'kændl/ *n* vela *f*. ∼**stick** /'kændlstɪk/ *n* candelero *m*

candour /'kændə(r)/ *n* franqueza *f*

candy /'kændɪ/ *n* (*Amer*) caramelo *m*. ∼**floss** *n* algodón *m* de azúcar

cane /keɪn/ *n* caña *f*; (*for baskets*) mimbre *m*; (*stick*) bastón *m*. ● *vt* (*strike*) castigar con palmeta

canine /'keɪnaɪn/ *a* canino

canister /'kænɪstə(r)/ *n* bote *m*

cannabis /'kænəbɪs/ *n* cáñamo *m* índico, hachís *m*, mariguana *f*

cannibal /'kænɪbl/ *n* caníbal *m*. ∼**ism** *n* canibalismo *m*

cannon /'kænən/ *n invar* cañón *m*. ∼ **shot** cañonazo *m*

cannot /'kænət/ *see* **can**[1]

canny /'kænɪ/ *a* astuto

canoe /kə'nuː/ *n* canoa *f*, piragua *f*. ● *vi* ir en canoa. ∼**ist** *n* piragüista *m & f*

canon /'kænən/ *n* canon *m*; (*person*) canónigo *m*. ∼**ize** /'kænənaɪz/ *vt* canonizar

can-opener /'kænəʊpnə(r)/ *n* abrelatas *m invar*

canopy /'kænəpɪ/ *n* dosel *m*; (*of parachute*) casquete *m*

cant /kænt/ *n* jerga *f*

can't /kɑːnt/ *see* **can**[1]

cantankerous /kæn'tæŋkərəs/ *a* malhumorado

canteen /kæn'tiːn/ *n* cantina *f*; (*of cutlery*) juego *m*; (*flask*) cantimplora *f*

canter /'kæntə(r)/ *n* medio galope *m*. ● *vi* ir a medio galope

canvas /'kænvəs/ *n* lona *f*; (*artist's*) lienzo *m*

canvass /'kænvəs/ *vi* hacer campaña, solicitar votos. ∼**ing** *n* solicitación *f* (de votos)

canyon /'kænjən/ *n* cañón *m*

cap /kæp/ *n* gorra *f*; (*lid*) tapa *f*; (*of cartridge*) cápsula *f*; (*academic*) birrete *m*; (*of pen*) capuchón *m*; (*mec*) casquete *m*. ● *vt* (*pt* **capped**) tapar, poner cápsula a; (*outdo*) superar

capab|ility /keɪpə'bɪlətɪ/ *n* capacidad *f*. ∼**le** /'keɪpəbl/ *a* capaz. ∼**ly** *adv* competentemente

capacity /kə'pæsətɪ/ *n* capacidad *f*; (*function*) calidad *f*

cape[1] /keɪp/ *n* (*cloak*) capa *f*

cape[2] /keɪp/ *n* (*geog*) cabo *m*

caper[1] /'keɪpə(r)/ *vi* brincar. ● *n* salto *m*; (*fig*) travesura *f*

caper[2] /'keɪpə(r)/ *n* (*culin*) alcaparra *f*

capital /'kæpɪtl/ *a* capital. ∼ **letter** *n* mayúscula *f*. ● *n* (*town*) capital *f*; (*money*) capital *m*

capitalis|m /'kæpɪtəlɪzəm/ *n* capitalismo *m*. ∼**t** *a & n* capitalista (*m & f*)

capitalize /'kæpɪtəlaɪz/ *vt* capitalizar; (*typ*) escribir con mayúsculas. ∼ **on** aprovechar

capitulat|e /kə'pɪtʃʊleɪt/ *vi* capitular. ∼**ion** /-'leɪʃn/ *n* capitulación *f*

capon /'keɪpən/ *n* capón *m*

capricious /kə'prɪʃəs/ *a* caprichoso

Capricorn /'kæprɪkɔːn/ *n* Capricornio *m*

capsicum /'kæpsɪkəm/ *n* pimiento *m*

capsize /kæp'saɪz/ vt hacer zozobrar. ● vi zozobrar

capsule /'kæpsjuːl/ n cápsula f

captain /'kæptɪn/ n capitán m. ● vt capitanear

caption /'kæpʃn/ n (heading) título m; (of cartoon etc) leyenda f

captivate /'kæptɪvett/ vt encantar

captiv|e /'kæptɪv/ a & n cautivo (m). ~ity /-'tɪvətɪ/ n cautiverio m, cautividad f

capture /'kæptʃə(r)/ vt prender; llamar (attention); (mil) tomar. ● n apresamiento m; (mil) toma f

car /kɑː(r)/ n coche m, carro m (LAm)

carafe /kə'ræf/ n jarro m, garrafa f

caramel /'kærəməl/ n azúcar m quemado; (sweet) caramelo m

carat /'kærət/ n quilate m

caravan /'kærəvæn/ n caravana f

carbohydrate /kɑːbəʊ'haɪdreɪt/ n hidrato m de carbono

carbon /'kɑːbən/ n carbono m; (paper) carbón m. ~ **copy** copia f al carbón

carburettor /kɑːbjʊ'retə(r)/ n carburador m

carcass /'kɑːkəs/ n cadáver m, esqueleto m

card /kɑːd/ n tarjeta f; (for games) carta f; (membership) carnet m; (records) ficha f

cardboard /'kɑːdbɔːd/ n cartón m

cardiac /'kɑːdɪæk/ a cardíaco

cardigan /'kɑːdɪgən/ n chaqueta f de punto, rebeca f

cardinal /'kɑːdɪnl/ a cardinal. ● n cardenal m

card-index /'kɑːdɪndeks/ n fichero m

care /keə(r)/ n cuidado m; (worry) preocupación f; (protection) cargo m. ~ **of** a cuidado de, en casa de. **take** ~ **of** cuidar de (person); ocuparse de (matter). ● vi interesarse. **I don't** ~ me es igual. ~ **about** interesarse por. ~ **for** cuidar de; (like) querer

career /kə'rɪə(r)/ n carrera f. ● vi correr a toda velocidad

carefree /'keəfriː/ a despreocupado

careful /'keəfʊl/ a cuidadoso; (cautious) prudente. ~**ly** adv con cuidado

careless /'keəlɪs/ a negligente; (not worried) indiferente. ~**ly** adv descuidadamente. ~**ness** n descuido m

caress /kə'res/ n caricia f. ● vt acariciar

caretaker /'keəteɪkə(r)/ n vigilante m; (of flats etc) portero m

car-ferry /'kɑːferɪ/ n transbordador m de coches

cargo /'kɑːgəʊ/ n (pl -oes) carga f

Caribbean /kærɪ'biːən/ a caribe. ~ **Sea** n mar m Caribe

caricature /'kærɪkətʃʊə(r)/ n caricatura f. ● vt caricaturizar

carnage /'kɑːnɪdʒ/ n carnicería f, matanza f

carnal /'kɑːnl/ a carnal

carnation /kɑː'neɪʃn/ n clavel m

carnival /'kɑːnɪvl/ n carnaval m

carol /'kærəl/ n villancico m

carouse /kə'raʊz/ vi correrse una juerga

carousel /kærə'sel/ n tiovivo m

carp¹ /kɑːp/ n invar carpa f

carp² /kɑːp/ vi. ~ **at** quejarse de

car park /'kɑːpɑːk/ n aparcamiento m

carpent|er /'kɑːpɪntə(r)/ n carpintero m. ~**ry** n carpintería f

carpet /'kɑːpɪt/ n alfombra f. **be on the** ~ (fam) recibir un rapapolvo; (under consideration) estar sobre el tapete. ● vt alfombrar. ~**-sweeper** n escoba f mecánica

carriage /'kærɪdʒ/ n coche m; (mec) carro m; (transport) transporte m; (cost, bearing) porte m

carriageway /'kærɪdʒweɪ/ n calzada f, carretera f

carrier /'kærɪə(r)/ n transportista m & f; (company) empresa f de transportes; (med) portador m. ~**-bag** bolsa f

carrot /'kærət/ n zanahoria f

carry /'kærɪ/ vt llevar; transportar (goods); (involve) llevar consigo, implicar. ● vi (sounds) llegar, oírse. ~ **off** llevarse. ~ **on** continuar; (complain, fam) quejarse. ~ **out** realizar; cumplir (promise, threat). ~**-cot** n capazo m

cart /kɑːt/ n carro m. ● vt acarrear; (carry, fam) llevar

cartilage /'kɑːtɪlɪdʒ/ n cartílago m

carton /'kɑːtən/ n caja f (de cartón)

cartoon /kɑː'tuːn/ n caricatura f, chiste m; (strip) historieta f; (film) dibujos mpl animados. ~**ist** n caricaturista m & f

cartridge /'kɑːtrɪdʒ/ n cartucho m

carve /kɑːv/ vt tallar; trinchar (meat)

cascade /kæsˈkeɪd/ n cascada f. ● vi caer en cascadas

case /keɪs/ n caso m; (jurid) proceso m; (crate) cajón m; (box) caja f; (suitcase) maleta f. **in any** ～ en todo caso. **in** ～ **he comes** por si viene. **in** ～ **of** en caso de. **lower** ～ caja f baja, minúscula f. **upper** ～ caja f alta, mayúscula f

cash /kæʃ/ n dinero m efectivo. **pay (in)** ～ pagar al contado. ● vt cobrar. ～ **in (on)** aprovecharse de. ～ **desk** n caja f

cashew /kæʃuː/ n anacardo m

cashier /kæˈʃɪə(r)/ n cajero m

cashmere /kæʃˈmɪə(r)/ n casimir m, cachemir m

casino /kəˈsiːnəʊ/ n (pl -os) casino m

cask /kɑːsk/ n barril m

casket /ˈkɑːskɪt/ n cajita f

casserole /ˈkæsərəʊl/ n cacerola f; (stew) cazuela f

cassette /kəˈset/ n casete m

cast /kɑːst/ vt (pt cast) arrojar; fundir (metal); dar (vote); (in theatre) repartir. ● n lanzamiento m; (in play) reparto m; (mould) molde m

castanets /kæstəˈnets/ npl castañuelas fpl

castaway /ˈkɑːstəweɪ/ n náufrago m

caste /kɑːst/ n casta f

cast: ～ **iron** n hierro m fundido. ～ **-iron** a de hierro fundido; (fig) sólido

castle /ˈkɑːsl/ n castillo m; (chess) torre f

cast-offs /ˈkɑːstɒfs/ npl desechos mpl

castor /ˈkɑːstə(r)/ n ruedecilla f

castor oil /kɑːstərˈɔɪl/ n aceite m de ricino

castor sugar /kɑːstəˈʃʊgə(r)/ n azúcar m extrafino

castrat|e /kæˈstreɪt/ vt castrar. ～**ion** /-ʃn/ n castración f

casual /ˈkæʒʊəl/ a casual; (meeting) fortuito; (work) ocasional; (attitude) despreocupado; (clothes) informal, de sport. ～**ly** adv de paso

casualt|y /ˈkæʒʊəltɪ/ n accidente m; (injured) víctima f, herido m; (dead) víctima f, muerto m. ～**ies** npl (mil) bajas fpl

cat /kæt/ n gato m

cataclysm /ˈkætəklɪzəm/ n cataclismo m

catacomb /ˈkætəkuːm/ n catacumba f

catalogue /ˈkætəlɒg/ n catálogo m. ● vt catalogar

catalyst /ˈkætəlɪst/ n catalizador m

catamaran /kætəməˈræn/ n catamarán m

catapult /ˈkætəpʌlt/ n catapulta f; (child's) tirador m, tirachinos m invar

cataract /ˈkætərækt/ n catarata f

catarrh /kəˈtɑː(r)/ n catarro m

catastroph|e /kəˈtæstrəfɪ/ n catástrofe m. ～**ic** /kætəˈstrɒfɪk/ a catastrófico

catch /kætʃ/ vt (pt caught) coger (not LAm), agarrar; (grab) asir; tomar (train, bus); (unawares) sorprender; (understand) comprender; contraer (disease). ～ **a cold** resfriarse. ～ **sight of** avistar. ● vi (get stuck) engancharse; (fire) prenderse. ● n cogida f; (of fish) pesca f; (on door) pestillo m; (on window) cerradura f. ～ **on** (fam) hacerse popular. ～ **up** poner al día. ～ **up with** alcanzar; ponerse al corriente de (news etc)

catching /ˈkætʃɪŋ/ a contagioso

catchment /ˈkætʃmənt/ n. ～ **area** n zona f de captación

catch-phrase /ˈkætʃfreɪz/ n eslogan m

catchword /ˈkætʃwɜːd/ n eslogan m, consigna f

catchy /ˈkætʃɪ/ a pegadizo

catechism /ˈkætɪkɪzəm/ n catecismo m

categorical /kætɪˈgɒrɪkl/ a categórico

category /ˈkætɪgərɪ/ n categoría f

cater /ˈkeɪtə(r)/ vi proveer comida a. ～ **for** proveer a (needs). ～**er** n proveedor m

caterpillar /ˈkætəpɪlə(r)/ n oruga f

cathedral /kəˈθiːdrəl/ n catedral f

catholic /ˈkæθəlɪk/ a universal. **C**～ a & n católico (m). **C**～**ism** /kəˈθɒlɪsɪzəm/ n catolicismo m

catnap /ˈkætnæp/ n sueñecito m

cat's eyes /ˈkætsaɪz/ npl catafotos mpl

cattle /ˈkætl/ npl ganado m (vacuno)

cat|ty /ˈkætɪ/ a malicioso. ～**walk** /ˈkætwɔːk/ n pasarela f

caucus /ˈkɔːkəs/ n comité m electoral

caught /kɔːt/ see **catch**

cauldron /ˈkɔːldrən/ n caldera f

cauliflower /ˈkɒlɪflaʊə(r)/ n coliflor f

cause /kɔ:z/ n causa f, motivo m. ● vt causar

causeway /ˈkɔ:zweɪ/ n calzada f elevada, carretera f elevada

caustic /ˈkɔ:stɪk/ a & n cáustico (m)

cauterize /ˈkɔ:təraɪz/ vt cauterizar

caution /ˈkɔ:ʃn/ n cautela f; (warning) advertencia f. ● vt advertir; (jurid) amonestar

cautious /ˈkɔ:ʃəs/ a cauteloso, prudente. ∼ly adv con precaución, cautelosamente

cavalcade /kævəlˈkeɪd/ n cabalgata f

cavalier /kævəˈlɪə(r)/ a arrogante

cavalry /ˈkævəlrɪ/ n caballería f

cave /keɪv/ n cueva f. ● vi. ∼ in hundirse. ∼-man n (pl -men) troglodita m

cavern /ˈkævən/ n caverna f, cueva f

caviare /ˈkævɪɑ:(r)/ n caviar m

caving /ˈkeɪvɪŋ/ n espeleología f

cavity /ˈkævətɪ/ n cavidad f; (in tooth) caries f

cavort /kəˈvɔ:t/ vi brincar

cease /si:s/ vt/i cesar. ● n. without ∼ sin cesar. ∼-fire n tregua f, alto m el fuego. ∼less a incesante

cedar /ˈsi:də(r)/ n cedro m

cede /si:d/ vt ceder

cedilla /sɪˈdɪlə/ n cedilla f

ceiling /ˈsi:lɪŋ/ n techo m

celebrat|e /ˈselɪbreɪt/ vt celebrar. ● vi divertirse. ∼ed a célebre. ∼ion /-ˈbreɪʃn/ n celebración f; (party) fiesta f

celebrity /sɪˈlebrətɪ/ n celebridad f

celery /ˈselərɪ/ n apio m

celestial /sɪˈlestjəl/ a celestial

celiba|cy /ˈselɪbəsɪ/ n celibato m. ∼te /ˈselɪbət/ a & n célibe (m & f)

cell /sel/ n celda f; (biol) célula f; (elec) pila f

cellar /ˈselə(r)/ n sótano m; (for wine) bodega f

cell|ist /ˈtʃelɪst/ n violonc(h)elo m & f, violonc(h)elista m & f. ∼o /ˈtʃeləʊ/ n (pl -os) violonc(h)elo m

Cellophane /ˈseləfeɪn/ n (P) celofán m (P)

cellular /ˈseljʊlə(r)/ a celular

celluloid /ˈseljʊlɔɪd/ n celuloide m

cellulose /ˈseljʊləʊs/ n celulosa f

Celt /kelt/ n celta m & f. ∼ic a céltico m

cement /sɪˈment/ n cemento m. ● vt cementar; (fig) consolidar

cemetery /ˈsemətrɪ/ n cementerio m

cenotaph /ˈsenətɑ:f/ n cenotafio m

censor /ˈsensə(r)/ n censor m. ● vt censurar. ∼ship n censura f

censure /ˈsenʃə(r)/ n censura f. ● vt censurar

census /ˈsensəs/ n censo m

cent /sent/ n centavo m

centenary /senˈti:nərɪ/ n centenario m

centigrade /ˈsentɪɡreɪd/ a centígrado

centilitre /ˈsentɪli:tə(r)/ n centilitro m

centimetre /ˈsentɪmi:tə(r)/ n centímetro m

centipede /ˈsentɪpi:d/ n ciempiés m invar

central /ˈsentrəl/ a central; (of town) céntrico. ∼ heating n calefacción f central. ∼ize vt centralizar. ∼ly adv (situated) en el centro

centre /ˈsentə(r)/ n centro m. ● vt (pt centred) vi concentrarse

centrifugal /senˈtrɪfjʊɡəl/ a centrífugo

century /ˈsentʃərɪ/ n siglo m

ceramic /sɪˈræmɪk/ a cerámico. ∼s npl cerámica f

cereal /ˈsɪərɪəl/ n cereal m

cerebral /ˈserɪbrəl/ a cerebral

ceremon|ial /serɪˈməʊnɪəl/ a & n ceremonial (m). ∼ious /-ˈməʊnɪəs/ a ceremonioso. ∼y /ˈserɪmənɪ/ n ceremonia f

certain /ˈsɜ:tn/ a cierto. for ∼ seguro. make ∼ of asegurarse de. ∼ly adv desde luego. ∼ty n certeza f

certificate /səˈtɪfɪkət/ n certificado m; (of birth, death etc) partida f

certify /ˈsɜ:tɪfaɪ/ vt certificar

cessation /seˈseɪʃən/ n cesación f

cesspit /ˈsespɪt/ n, **cesspool** /ˈsespu:l/ n pozo m negro; (fam) sentina f

chafe /tʃeɪf/ vt rozar. ● vi rozarse; (fig) irritarse

chaff /tʃæf/ vt zumbarse de

chaffinch /ˈtʃæfɪntʃ/ n pinzón m

chagrin /ˈʃæɡrɪn/ n disgusto m

chain /tʃeɪn/ n cadena f. ● vt encadenar. ∼ reaction n reacción f en cadena. ∼-smoker n fumador m que siempre tiene un cigarillo encendido. ∼ store n sucursal m

chair /tʃeə(r)/ n silla f; (univ) cátedra f. ● vt presidir. ∼-lift n telesilla m

chairman /ˈtʃeəmən/ n (pl -men) presidente m

chalet /ˈʃæleɪ/ n chalé m

chalice /ˈtʃælɪs/ n cáliz m

chalk /tʃɔːk/ n creta f; (stick) tiza f. ~y a cretáceo

challeng|e /'tʃælɪndʒ/ n desafío m; (fig) reto m. ● vt desafiar; (question) poner en duda. ~ing a estimulante

chamber /'tʃeɪmbə(r)/ n (old use) cámara f. ~maid /'tʃeɪmbəmeɪd/ n camarera f. ~pot n orinal m. ~s npl despacho m, bufete m

chameleon /kə'miːljən/ n camaleón m

chamois /'ʃæmɪ/ n gamuza f

champagne /ʃæm'peɪn/ n champaña m, champán m (fam)

champion /'tʃæmpɪən/ n campeón m. ● vt defender. ~ship n campeonato m

chance /tʃɑːns/ n casualidad f; (likelihood) probabilidad f; (opportunity) oportunidad f; (risk) riesgo m. by ~ por casualidad. ● a fortuito. ● vt arriesgar. ● vi suceder. ~ upon tropezar con

chancellor /'tʃɑːnsələ(r)/ n canciller m; (univ) rector m. C~ of the Exchequer Ministro m de Hacienda

chancy /'tʃɑːnsɪ/ a arriesgado; (uncertain) incierto

chandelier /ʃændə'lɪə(r)/ n araña f (de luces)

change /tʃeɪndʒ/ vt cambiar; (substitute) reemplazar. ~ one's mind cambiar de idea. ● vi cambiarse. ● n cambio m; (small coins) suelto m. ~ of life menopausia f. ~able a cambiable; (weather) variable. ~over n cambio m

channel /'tʃænl/ n canal m; (fig) medio m. the C~ Islands npl las islas fpl Anglonormandas. the (English) C~ el canal de la Mancha. ● vt (pt channelled) acanalar; (fig) encauzar

chant /tʃɑːnt/ n canto m. ● vt/i cantar; (fig) salmodiar

chao|s /'keɪɒs/ n caos m, desorden m. ~tic /-'ɒtɪk/ a caótico, desordenado

chap¹ /tʃæp/ n (crack) grieta f. ● vt (pt chapped) agrietar. ● vi agrietarse

chap² /tʃæp/ n (fam) hombre m, tío m (fam)

chapel /'tʃæpl/ n capilla f

chaperon /'ʃæpərəʊn/ n acompañanta f. ● vt acompañar

chaplain /'tʃæplɪn/ n capellán m

chapter /'tʃæptə(r)/ n capítulo m

char¹ /tʃɑː(r)/ vt (pt charred) carbonizar

char² /tʃɑː(r)/ n asistenta f

character /'kærəktə(r)/ n carácter m; (in play) personaje m. in ~ característico

characteristic /kærəktə'rɪstɪk/ a característico. ~ally adv típicamente

characterize /'kærəktəraɪz/ vt caracterizar

charade /ʃə'rɑːd/ n charada f, farsa f

charcoal /'tʃɑːkəʊl/ n carbón m vegetal; (for drawing) carboncillo m

charge /tʃɑːdʒ/ n precio m; (elec, mil) carga f; (jurid) acusación f; (task, custody) encargo m; (responsibility) responsabilidad f. in ~ of responsable de, encargado de. take ~ of encargarse de. ● vt pedir; (elec, mil) cargar; (jurid) acusar; (entrust) encargar. ● vi cargar; (money) cobrar. ~able a a cargo (de)

chariot /'tʃærɪət/ n carro m

charisma /kə'rɪzmə/ n carisma m. ~tic /-'mætɪk/ a carismático

charitable /'tʃærɪtəbl/ a caritativo

charity /'tʃærɪtɪ/ n caridad f; (society) institución f benéfica

charlatan /'ʃɑːlətən/ n charlatán n

charm /tʃɑːm/ n encanto m; (spell) hechizo m; (on bracelet) dije m, amuleto m. ● vt encantar. ~ing a encantador

chart /tʃɑːt/ n (naut) carta f de marear; (table) tabla f. ● vt poner en una carta de marear

charter /'tʃɑːtə(r)/ n carta f. ● vt conceder carta a, estatuir; alquilar (bus, train); fletar (plane, ship). ~ed accountant n contador m titulado. ~ flight n vuelo m charter

charwoman /'tʃɑːwʊmən/ n (pl -women) asistenta f

chary /'tʃeərɪ/ a cauteloso

chase /tʃeɪs/ vt perseguir. ● vi correr. ● n persecución f. ~ away, ~ off ahuyentar

chasm /'kæzəm/ n abismo m

chassis /'ʃæsɪ/ n chasis m

chaste /tʃeɪst/ a casto

chastise /tʃæs'taɪz/ vt castigar

chastity /'tʃæstɪtɪ/ n castidad f

chat /tʃæt/ n charla f. have a ~ charlar. ● vi (pt chatted) charlar

chattels /'tʃætlz/ n bienes mpl muebles

chatter /'tʃætə(r)/ n charla f. ● vi charlar. his teeth are ~ing le

castañetean los dientes. ~**box**
/'tʃætəbɒks/ n parlanchín m

chatty a hablador; ⟨style⟩ familiar

chauffeur /'ʃəʊfə(r)/ n chófer m

chauvinis|m /'ʃəʊvɪnɪzəm/ n
patriotería f; (male) machismo m. ~**t**
/'ʃəʊvɪnɪst/ n patriotero m; (male)
machista m & f

cheap /tʃiːp/ a (-er, -est) barato;
(poor quality) de baja calidad; ⟨rate⟩
económico. ~**en** /'tʃiːpən/ vt
abaratar. ~**(ly)** adv barato, a bajo
precio. ~**ness** n baratura f

cheat /tʃiːt/ vt defraudar; (deceive)
engañar. ● vi (at cards) hacer
trampas. ● n trampa f; (person)
tramposo m

check¹ /tʃek/ vt comprobar; (examine) inspeccionar; (curb) detener;
(chess) dar jaque a. ● vi comprobar.
● n comprobación f; (of tickets) control m; (curb) freno m; (chess) jaque
m; (bill, Amer) cuenta f. ~ **in** registrarse; (at airport) facturar el
equipaje. ~ **out** pagar la cuenta y
marcharse. ~ **up** comprobar. ~ **up
on** investigar

check² /tʃek/ n (pattern) cuadro m.
~**ed** a a cuadros

checkmate /'tʃekmeɪt/ n jaque m
mate. ● vt dar mate a

check-up /'tʃekʌp/ n examen m

cheek /tʃiːk/ n mejilla f; (fig) descaro
m. ~**bone** n pómulo m. ~**y** a
descarado

cheep /tʃiːp/ vi piar

cheer /tʃɪə(r)/ n alegría f; (applause)
viva m. ● vt alegrar; (applaud)
aplaudir. ● vi alegrarse; (applaud)
aplaudir. ~ **up!** ¡ánimate! ~**ful** a
alegre. ~**fulness** n alegría f

cheerio /tʃɪərɪ'əʊ/ int (fam) ¡adiós!,
¡hasta luego!

cheer : ~**less** /'tʃɪəlɪs/ a triste. ~**s!**
¡salud!

cheese /tʃiːz/ n queso m

cheetah /'tʃiːtə/ n guepardo m

chef /ʃef/ n cocinero m

chemical /'kemɪkl/ a químico. ● n
producto m químico

chemist /'kemɪst/ n farmacéutico m;
(scientist) químico m. ~**ry** n química
f. ~**'s (shop)** n farmacia f

cheque /tʃek/ n cheque m, talón m.
~**book** n talonario m

chequered /'tʃekəd/ a a cuadros;
(fig) con altibajos

cherish /'tʃerɪʃ/ vt cuidar; (love)
querer; abrigar ⟨hope⟩

cherry /'tʃerɪ/ n cereza f. ~**tree** n
cerezo m

cherub /'tʃerəb/ n (pl -im) (angel)
querubín m

chess /tʃes/ n ajedrez m. ~**board** n
tablero m de ajedrez

chest /tʃest/ n pecho m; (box) cofre
m, cajón m. ~ **of drawers** n cómoda
f

chestnut /'tʃesnʌt/ n castaña f. ~
tree n castaño m

chew /tʃuː/ vt masticar; (fig) rumiar.
~**ing-gum** n chicle m

chic /ʃiːk/ a elegante. ● n elegancia f

chick /tʃɪk/ n polluelo m. ~**en**
/'tʃɪkɪn/ n pollo m. ● a (sl) cobarde.
● vi. ~**en out** (sl) retirarse. ~**en-
pox** n varicela f

chicory /'tʃɪkərɪ/ n (in coffee) achicoria f; (in salad) escarola f

chide /tʃaɪd/ vt (pt chided) reprender

chief /tʃiːf/ n jefe m. ● a principal.
~**ly** adv principalmente

chilblain /'tʃɪlbleɪn/ n sabañón m

child /tʃaɪld/ n (pl children
/'tʃɪldrən/) niño m; (offspring) hijo
m. ~**birth** /'tʃaɪldbɜːθ/ n parto m.
~**hood** n niñez f. ~**ish** a infantil.
~**less** a sin hijos. ~**like** a inocente,
infantil

Chile /'tʃɪlɪ/ n Chile m. ~**an** a & n
chileno (m)

chill /tʃɪl/ n frío m; (illness) resfriado
m. ● a frío. ● vt enfriar; refrigerar
⟨food⟩

chilli /'tʃɪlɪ/ n (pl -ies) chile m

chilly /'tʃɪlɪ/ a frío

chime /tʃaɪm/ n carillón m. ● vt tocar ⟨bells⟩; dar ⟨hours⟩. ● vi repicar

chimney /'tʃɪmnɪ/ n (pl -eys) chimenea f. ~**pot** n cañón m de chimenea.
~**sweep** n deshollinador m

chimpanzee /tʃɪmpæn'ziː/ n chimpancé m

chin /tʃɪn/ n barbilla f

china /'tʃaɪnə/ n porcelana f

Chin|a /'tʃaɪnə/ n China f. ~**ese**
/-'niːz/ a & n chino (m)

chink¹ /tʃɪŋk/ n (crack) grieta f

chink² /tʃɪŋk/ n (sound) tintín m. ● vt
hacer tintinear. ● vi tintinear

chip /tʃɪp/ n pedacito m; (splinter) astilla f; (culin) patata f frita; (gambling) ficha f. **have a ~ on one's
shoulder** guardar rencor. ● vt (pt

chipped) desportillar. ●vi desportillarse. ~ in (fam) interrumpir; (with money) contribuir

chiropodist /kɪˈrɒpədɪst/ n callista m & f

chirp /tʃɜːp/ n pío m. ●vi piar

chirpy /ˈtʃɜːpɪ/ a alegre

chisel /ˈtʃɪzl/ n formón m. ●vt (pt chiselled) cincelar

chit /tʃɪt/ n vale m, nota f

chit-chat /ˈtʃɪttʃæt/ n cháchara f

chivalr|ous a /ˈʃɪvəlrəs/ a caballeroso. ~y /ˈʃɪvəlrɪ/ n caballerosidad f

chive /tʃaɪv/ n cebollino m

chlorine /ˈklɔːriːn/ n cloro m

chock /tʃɒk/ n calzo m. ~-a-block a, ~-full a atestado

chocolate /ˈtʃɒklɪt/ n chocolate m; (individual sweet) bombón m

choice /tʃɔɪs/ n elección f; (preference) preferencia f. ●a escogido

choir /kwaɪə(r)/ n coro m. ~boy /ˈkwaɪəbɔɪ/ n niño m de coro

choke /tʃəʊk/ vt sofocar. ●vi sofocarse. ●n (auto) estrangulador m, estárter m

cholera /ˈkɒlərə/ n cólera m

cholesterol /kəˈlestərɒl/ n colesterol m

choose /tʃuːz/ vt/i (pt chose, pp chosen) elegir. ~y /ˈtʃuːzɪ/ a (fam) exigente

chop /tʃɒp/ vt (pt chopped) cortar. ●n (culin) chuleta f. ~ down talar. ~ off cortar. ~per n hacha f; (butcher's) cuchilla f; (sl) helicóptero m

choppy /ˈtʃɒpɪ/ a picado

chopstick /ˈtʃɒpstɪk/ n palillo m (chino)

choral /ˈkɔːrəl/ a coral

chord /kɔːd/ n cuerda f; (mus) acorde m

chore /tʃɔː(r)/ n tarea f, faena f. household ~s npl faenas fpl domésticas

choreographer /kɒrɪˈɒɡrəfə(r)/ n coreógrafo m

chorister /ˈkɒrɪstə(r)/ n (singer) corista m & f

chortle /ˈtʃɔːtl/ n risita f alegre. ●vi reírse alegremente

chorus /ˈkɔːrəs/ n coro m; (of song) estribillo m

chose, chosen /tʃəʊz, ˈtʃəʊzn/ see choose

Christ /kraɪst/ n Cristo m

christen /ˈkrɪsn/ vt bautizar. ~ing n bautizo m

Christian /ˈkrɪstjən/ a & n cristiano (m). ~ name n nombre m de pila

Christmas /ˈkrɪsməs/ n Navidad f; (period) Navidades fpl. ●a de Navidad, navideño. ~-box n aguinaldo m. ~ day n día m de Navidad. ~ Eve n Nochebuena f. Father ~ n Papá m Noel. Happy ~! ¡Felices Pascuas!

chrom|e /krəʊm/ n cromo m. ~ium /ˈkrəʊmɪəm/ n cromo m. ~ium plating n cromado m

chromosome /ˈkrəʊməsəʊm/ n cromosoma m

chronic /ˈkrɒnɪk/ a crónico; (bad, fam) terrible

chronicle /ˈkrɒnɪkl/ n crónica f. ●vt historiar

chronolog|ical /krɒnəˈlɒdʒɪkl/ a cronológico. ~y /krəˈnɒlədʒɪ/ n cronología f

chrysanthemum /krɪˈsænθəməm/ n crisantemo m

chubby /ˈtʃʌbɪ/ a (-ier, -iest) regordete; (face) mofletudo

chuck /tʃʌk/ vt (fam) arrojar. ~ out tirar

chuckle /ˈtʃʌkl/ n risa f ahogada. ●vi reírse entre dientes

chuffed /tʃʌft/ a (sl) contento

chug /tʃʌɡ/ vi (pt chugged) (of motor) traquetear

chum /tʃʌm/ n amigo m, compinche m. ~my a. be ~my (2 people) ser muy amigos. be ~my with ser muy amigo de

chump /tʃʌmp/ n (sl) tonto m. ~ chop n chuleta f

chunk /tʃʌŋk/ n trozo m grueso. ~y /ˈtʃʌŋkɪ/ a macizo

church /tʃɜːtʃ/ n iglesia f. ~yard /ˈtʃɜːtʃjɑːd/ n cementerio m

churlish /ˈtʃɜːlɪʃ/ a grosero

churn /ˈtʃɜːn/ n (for milk) lechera f, cántara f; (for butter) mantequera f. ●vt agitar. ~ out producir en profusión

chute /ʃuːt/ n tobogán m

chutney /ˈtʃʌtnɪ/ n (pl -eys) condimento m agridulce

cider /ˈsaɪdə(r)/ n sidra f

cigar /sɪˈɡɑː(r)/ n puro m

cigarette /sɪɡəˈret/ n cigarillo m. ~holder n boquilla f

cine-camera /ˈsɪnɪkæmərə/ n cámara f, tomavistas m invar

cinema /ˈsɪnəmə/ n cine m

cinnamon /'sɪnəmən/ n canela f

cipher /'saɪfə(r)/ n (math, fig) cero m; (secret system) cifra f

circle /'sɜːkl/ n círculo m; (in theatre) anfiteatro m. ● vt girar alrededor de. ● vi dar vueltas

circuit /'sɜːkɪt/ n circuito m; (chain) cadena f

circuitous /sɜː'kjuːɪtəs/ a indirecto

circular /'sɜːkjələ(r)/ a & n circular (f)

circularize /'sɜːkjələraɪz/ vt enviar circulares a

circulat|e /'sɜːkjəleɪt/ vt hacer circular. ~ion /-'leɪʃn/ n circulación f; (of journals) tirada f

circumcis|e /'sɜːkəmsaɪz/ vt circuncidar. ~ion /-'sɪʒn/ n circuncisión f

circumference /sə'kʌmfərəns/ n circunferencia f

circumflex /'sɜːkəmfleks/ a & n circunflejo (m)

circumspect /'sɜːkəmspekt/ a circunspecto

circumstance /'sɜːkəmstəns/ n circunstancia f. ~s (means) npl situación f económica

circus /'sɜːkəs/ n circo m

cistern /'sɪstən/ n depósito m; (of WC) cisterna f

citadel /'sɪtədl/ n ciudadela f

citation /saɪ'teɪʃn/ n citación f

cite /saɪt/ vt citar

citizen /'sɪtɪzn/ n ciudadano m; (inhabitant) habitante m & f. ~ship n ciudadanía f

citrus /'sɪtrəs/ n. ~ fruits cítricos mpl

city /'sɪtɪ/ n ciudad f; the C~ el centro m financiero de Londres

civic /'sɪvɪk/ a cívico. ~s npl cívica f

civil /'sɪvl/ a civil, cortés

civilian /sɪ'vɪlɪən/ a & n civil (m & f). ~ clothes npl traje m de paisano

civility /sɪ'vɪlɪtɪ/ n cortesía f

civiliz|ation /sɪvɪlaɪ'zeɪʃn/ n civilización f. ~e /'sɪvəlaɪz/ vt civilizar.

civil: ~ servant n funcionario m. ~ service n administración f pública

civvies /'sɪvɪz/ npl. in ~ (sl) en traje m de paisano

clad /klæd/ see **clothe**

claim /kleɪm/ vt reclamar; (assert) pretender. ● n reclamación f; (right) derecho m; (jurid) demanda f. ~ant n demandante m & f; (to throne) pretendiente m

clairvoyant /kleə'vɔɪənt/ n clarividente m & f

clam /klæm/ n almeja f

clamber /'klæmbə(r)/ vi trepar a gatas

clammy /'klæmɪ/ a (-ier, -iest) húmedo

clamour /'klæmə(r)/ n clamor m. ● vi. ~ for pedir a voces

clamp /klæmp/ n abrazadera f; (auto) cepo m. ● vt sujetar con abrazadera. ~ down on reprimir

clan /klæn/ n clan m

clandestine /klæn'destɪn/ a clandestino

clang /klæŋ/ n sonido m metálico

clanger /'klæŋə(r)/ n (sl) metedura f de pata

clap /klæp/ vt (pt clapped) aplaudir; batir (hands). ● n palmada f; (of thunder) trueno m

claptrap /'klæptræp/ n charlatanería f, tonterías fpl

claret /'klærət/ n clarete m

clarif|ication /klærɪfɪ'keɪʃn/ n aclaración f. ~y /'klærɪfaɪ/ vt aclarar. ● vi aclararse

clarinet /klærɪ'net/ n clarinete m

clarity /'klærətɪ/ n claridad f

clash /klæʃ/ n choque m; (noise) estruendo m; (contrast) contraste m; (fig) conflicto m. ● vt golpear. ● vi encontrarse; (dates) coincidir; (opinions) estar en desacuerdo; (colours) desentonar

clasp /klɑːsp/ n cierre m. ● vt agarrar; apretar (hand); (fasten) abrochar

class /klɑːs/ n clase f. **evening** ~ n clase nocturna. ● vt clasificar

classic /'klæsɪk/ a & n clásico (m). ~al a clásico. ~s npl estudios mpl clásicos

classification /klæsɪfɪ'keɪʃn/ n clasificación f. ~y /'klæsɪfaɪ/ vt clasificar

classroom /'klɑːsruːm/ n aula f

classy /'klɑːsɪ/ a (sl) elegante

clatter /'klætə(r)/ n estrépito m. ● vi hacer ruido

clause /klɔːz/ n cláusula f; (gram) oración f

claustrophobia /klɔːstrə'fəʊbɪə/ n claustrofobia f

claw /klɔː/ n garra f; (of cat) uña f; (of crab) pinza f; (device) garfio m. ● vt arañar

clay /kleɪ/ n arcilla f

clean /kliːn/ *a* (-er, -est) limpio; ⟨*stroke*⟩ neto. ● *adv* completamente. ● *vt* limpiar. ● *vi* hacer la limpieza. **~ up** hacer la limpieza. **~-cut** *a* bien definido. **~er** *n* mujer *f* de la limpieza. **~liness** /ˈklenlɪnɪs/ *n* limpieza *f*

cleanse /klenz/ *vt* limpiar; (*fig*) purificar. **~ing cream** *n* crema *f* desmaquilladora

clear /klɪə(r)/ *a* (-er, -est) claro; (*transparent*) transparente; (*without obstacles*) libre; (*profit*) neto; ⟨*sky*⟩ despejado. **keep ~ of** evitar. ● *adv* claramente. ● *vt* despejar; liquidar ⟨*goods*⟩; (*jurid*) absolver; (*jump over*) saltar por encima de; quitar ⟨*table*⟩. ● *vi* ⟨*weather*⟩ despejarse; ⟨*fog*⟩ disolverse. **~ off** *vi* (*sl*), **~ out** *vi* (*sl*) largarse. **~ up** *vt* (*tidy*) poner en orden; aclarar ⟨*mystery*⟩; ● *vi* ⟨*weather*⟩ despejarse

clearance /ˈklɪərəns/ *n* espacio *m* libre; (*removal of obstructions*) despeje *m*; (*authorization*) permiso *m*; (*by customs*) despacho *m*; (*by security*) acreditación *f*. **~ sale** *n* liquidación *f*

clearing /ˈklɪərɪŋ/ *n* claro *m*

clearly /ˈklɪəlɪ/ *adv* evidentemente

clearway /ˈklɪəweɪ/ *n* carretera *f* en la que no se permite parar

cleavage /ˈkliːvɪdʒ/ *n* escote *m*; (*fig*) división *f*

cleave /kliːv/ *vt* (*pt* cleaved, clove or cleft; *pp* cloven or cleft) hender. ● *vi* henderse

clef /klef/ *n* (*mus*) clave *f*

cleft /kleft/ *see* cleave

clemen|cy /ˈklemənsɪ/ *n* clemencia *f*. **~ta** clemente

clench /klentʃ/ *vt* apretar

clergy /ˈklɜːdʒɪ/ *n* clero *m*. **~man** *n* (*pl* -men) clérigo *m*

cleric /ˈklerɪk/ *n* clérigo *m*. **~al** *a* clerical; (*of clerks*) de oficina

clerk /klɑːk/ *n* empleado *m*; (*jurid*) escribano *m*

clever /ˈklevə(r)/ *a* (-er, -est) listo; (*skilful*) hábil. **~ly** *adv* inteligentemente; (*with skill*) hábilmente. **~ness** *n* inteligencia *f*

cliché /ˈkliːʃeɪ/ *n* tópico *m*, frase *f* hecha

click /klɪk/ *n* golpecito *m*. ● *vi* chascar; (*sl*) llevarse bien

client /ˈklaɪənt/ *n* cliente *m* & *f*

clientele /kliːənˈtel/ *n* clientela *f*

cliff /klɪf/ *n* acantilado *m*

climat|e /ˈklaɪmɪt/ *n* clima *m*. **~ic** /-ˈmætɪk/ *a* climático

climax /ˈklaɪmæks/ *n* punto *m* culminante

climb /klaɪm/ *vt* subir ⟨*stairs*⟩; trepar ⟨*tree*⟩; escalar ⟨*mountain*⟩. ● *vi* subir. ● *n* subida *f*. **~ down** bajar; (*fig*) volverse atrás, rajarse. **~er** *n* (*sport*) alpinista *m* & *f*; (*plant*) trepadora *f*

clinch /klɪntʃ/ *vt* cerrar ⟨*deal*⟩

cling /klɪŋ/ *vi* (*pt* clung) agarrarse; (*stick*) pegarse

clinic /ˈklɪnɪk/ *n* clínica *f*. **~al** /ˈklɪnɪkl/ *a* clínico

clink /klɪŋk/ *n* sonido *m* metálico. ● *vt* hacer tintinear. ● *vi* tintinear

clinker /ˈklɪŋkə(r)/ *n* escoria *f*

clip¹ /klɪp/ *n* (*for paper*) sujetapapeles *m invar*; (*for hair*) horquilla *f*. ● *vt* (*pt* clipped) (*join*) sujetar

clip² /klɪp/ *n* (*with scissors*) tijeretada *f*; (*blow, fam*) golpe *m*. ● *vt* (*pt* clipped) (*cut*) cortar; (*fam*) golpear. **~pers** /ˈklɪpəz/ *npl* (*for hair*) maquinilla *f* para cortar el pelo; (*for nails*) cortauñas *m invar*. **~ping** *n* recorte *m*

clique /kliːk/ *n* pandilla *f*

cloak /kləʊk/ *n* capa *f*. **~room** /ˈkləʊkruːm/ *n* guardarropa *m*; (*toilet*) servicios *mpl*

clobber /ˈklɒbə(r)/ *n* (*sl*) trastos *mpl*. ● *vt* (*sl*) dar una paliza a

clock /klɒk/ *n* reloj *m*. **grandfather ~** reloj de caja. ● *vi*. **~ in** fichar, registrar la llegada. **~wise** /ˈklɒkwaɪz/ *a* & *adv* en el sentido de las agujas del reloj, a la derecha. **~work** /ˈklɒkwɜːk/ *n* mecanismo *m* de relojería. **like ~work** con precisión

clod /klɒd/ *n* terrón *m*

clog /klɒg/ *n* zueco *m*. ● *vt* (*pt* clogged) atascar. ● *vi* atascarse

cloister /ˈklɔɪstə(r)/ *n* claustro *m*

close¹ /kləʊs/ *a* (-er, -est) cercano; (*together*) apretado; (*friend*) íntimo; (*weather*) bochornoso; (*link etc*) estrecho; (*game, battle*) reñido. **have a ~ shave** (*fig*) escaparse de milagro. ● *adv* cerca. ● *n* recinto *m*

close² /kləʊz/ *vt* cerrar. ● *vi* cerrarse; (*end*) terminar. ● *n* fin *m*. **~d shop** *n* empresa *f* que emplea solamente a miembros del sindicato

close: ~**ly** adv de cerca; (with attention) atentamente; (exactly) exactamente. ~**ness** n proximidad f; (togetherness) intimidad f

closet /'klɒzɪt/ n (Amer) armario m

close-up /'kləʊsʌp/ n (cinema etc) primer plano m

closure /'kləʊʒə(r)/ n cierre m

clot /klɒt/ n (culin) grumo m; (med) coágulo m; (sl) tonto m. ●vi (pt **clotted**) cuajarse

cloth /klɒθ/ n tela f; (duster) trapo m; (table-cloth) mantel m

cloth|e /kləʊð/ vt (pt **clothed** or **clad**) vestir. ~**es** /kləʊðz/ npl, ~**ing** n ropa f

cloud /klaʊd/ n nube f. ●vi nublarse. ~**burst** /'klaʊdbɜːst/ n chaparrón m. ~**y** a (-**ier**, -**iest**) nublado; (liquid) turbio

clout /klaʊt/ n bofetada f. ●vt abofetear

clove[1] /kləʊv/ n clavo m

clove[2] /kləʊv/ n. ~ **of garlic** n diente m de ajo

clove[3] /kləʊv/ see **cleave**

clover /'kləʊvə(r)/ n trébol m

clown /klaʊn/ n payaso m. ●vi hacer el payaso

cloy /klɔɪ/ vt empalagar

club /klʌb/ n club m; (weapon) porra f; (at cards) trébol m. ●vt (pt **clubbed**) aporrear. ●vi. ~ **together** reunirse, pagar a escote

cluck /klʌk/ vi cloquear

clue /kluː/ n pista f; (in crosswords) indicación f. **not to have a** ~ no tener la menor idea

clump /klʌmp/ n grupo m. ●vt agrupar. ●vi pisar fuertemente

clums|iness /'klʌmzɪnɪs/ n torpeza f. ~**y** /'klʌmzɪ/ a (-**ier**, -**iest**) torpe

clung /klʌŋ/ see **cling**

cluster /'klʌstə(r)/ n grupo m. ●vi agruparse

clutch /klʌtʃ/ vt agarrar. ●n (auto) embrague m

clutter /'klʌtə(r)/ n desorden m. ●vt llenar desordenadamente

coach /kəʊtʃ/ n autocar m; (of train) vagón m; (horse-drawn) coche m; (sport) entrenador m. ●vt dar clases particulares; (sport) entrenar

coagulate /kəʊ'ægjʊleɪt/ vt coagular. ●vi coagularse

coal /kəʊl/ n carbón m. ~**field** /'kəʊlfiːld/ n yacimiento m de carbón

coalition /kəʊə'lɪʃn/ n coalición f

coarse /kɔːs/ a (-**er**, -**est**) grosero; (material) basto. ~**ness** n grosería f; (texture) basteza f

coast /kəʊst/ n costa f. ●vi (with cycle) deslizarse cuesta abajo; (with car) ir en punto muerto. ~**al** a costero. ~**er** /'kəʊstə(r)/ n (ship) barco m de cabotaje; (for glass) posavasos m invar. ~**guard** /'kəʊstgɑːd/ n guardacostas m invar. ~**line** /'kəʊstlaɪn/ n litoral m

coat /kəʊt/ n abrigo m; (jacket) chaqueta f; (of animal) pelo m; (of paint) mano f. ●vt cubrir, revestir. ~**ing** n capa f. ~ **of arms** n escudo m de armas

coax /kəʊks/ vt engatusar

cob /kɒb/ n (of corn) mazorca f

cobble[1] /'kɒbl/ n guijarro m, adoquín m. ●vt empedrar con guijarros, adoquinar

cobble[2] /'kɒbl/ vt (mend) remendar. ~**r** /'kɒblə(r)/ n (old use) remendón m

cobweb /'kɒbweb/ n telaraña f

cocaine /kə'keɪn/ n cocaína f

cock /kɒk/ n gallo m; (mec) grifo m; (of gun) martillo m. ●vt amartillar (gun); aguzar (ears). ~**-and-bull story** n patraña f. ~**erel** /'kɒkərəl/ n gallo m. ~**-eyed** a (sl) torcido

cockle /'kɒkl/ n berberecho m

cockney /'kɒknɪ/ a & n (pl -**eys**) londinense (m & f) (del este de Londres)

cockpit /'kɒkpɪt/ n (in aircraft) cabina f del piloto

cockroach /'kɒkrəʊtʃ/ n cucaracha f

cocksure /kɒk'ʃʊə(r)/ a presuntuoso

cocktail /'kɒkteɪl/ n cóctel m. **fruit** ~ macedonia f de frutas

cock-up /'kɒkʌp/ n (sl) lío m

cocky /'kɒkɪ/ a (-**ier**, -**iest**) engreído

cocoa /'kəʊkəʊ/ n cacao m; (drink) chocolate m

coconut /'kəʊkənʌt/ n coco m

cocoon /kə'kuːn/ n capullo m

cod /kɒd/ n (pl **cod**) bacalao m, abadejo m

coddle /'kɒdl/ vt mimar; (culin) cocer a fuego lento

code /kəʊd/ n código m; (secret) cifra f

codify /'kəʊdɪfaɪ/ vt codificar

cod-liver oil /'kɒdlɪvə(r)ɒɪl/ n aceite m de hígado de bacalao

coeducational /kəʊedʒʊ'keɪʃənl/ a mixto

coerc|e /kəʊˈɜːs/ vt obligar. **∼ion** /-ʃn/ n coacción f

coexist /kəʊɪɡˈzɪst/ vi coexistir. **∼ence** n coexistencia f

coffee /ˈkɒfɪ/ n café m. **∼mill** n molinillo m de café. **∼pot** n cafetera f

coffer /ˈkɒfə(r)/ n cofre m

coffin /ˈkɒfɪn/ n ataúd m

cog /kɒɡ/ n diente m; (fig) pieza f

cogent /ˈkəʊdʒənt/ a convincente

cohabit /kəʊˈhæbɪt/ vi cohabitar

coherent /kəʊˈhɪərənt/ a coherente

coil /kɔɪl/ vt enrollar. ● n rollo m; (one ring) vuelta f

coin /kɔɪn/ n moneda f. ● vt acuñar. **∼age** n sistema m monetario

coincide /kəʊɪnˈsaɪd/ vi coincidir

coinciden|ce /kəʊˈɪnsɪdəns/ n casualidad f. **∼tal** /-ˈdentl/ a casual; (coinciding) coincidente

coke /kəʊk/ n (coal) coque m

colander /ˈkʌləndə(r)/ n colador m

cold /kəʊld/ a (-er, -est) frío. **be ∼** tener frío. **it is ∼** hace frío. ● n frío m; (med) resfriado m. **have a ∼** estar constipado. **∼-blooded** a insensible. **∼cream** n crema f. **∼feet** (fig) mieditis f. **∼ness** n frialdad f. **∼shoulder** vt tratar con frialdad. **∼sore** n herpes m labial. **∼storage** n conservación f en frigorífico

coleslaw /ˈkəʊlslɔː/ n ensalada f de col

colic /ˈkɒlɪk/ n cólico m

collaborat|e /kəˈlæbəreɪt/ vi colaborar. **∼ion** /-ˈreɪʃn/ n colaboración f. **∼or** n colaborador m

collage /ˈkɒlɑːʒ/ n collage m

collaps|e /kəˈlæps/ vi derrumbarse; (med) sufrir un colapso. ● n derrumbamiento m; (med) colapso m. **∼ible** /kəˈlæpsəbl/ a plegable

collar /ˈkɒlə(r)/ n cuello m; (for animals) collar m. ● vt (fam) hurtar. **∼bone** n clavícula f

colleague /ˈkɒliːɡ/ n colega m & f

collect /kəˈlekt/ vt reunir; (hobby) coleccionar; (pick up) recoger; recaudar ⟨rent⟩. ● vi ⟨people⟩ reunirse; ⟨things⟩ acumularse. **∼ed** /kəˈlektɪd/ a reunido; ⟨person⟩ tranquilo. **∼ion** /-ʃn/ n colección f; (in church) colecta f; (of post) recogida f. **∼ive** /kəˈlektɪv/ a colectivo. **∼or** n coleccionista m & f; (of taxes) recaudador m

college /ˈkɒlɪdʒ/ n colegio m; (of art, music etc) escuela f; (univ) colegio m mayor

collide /kəˈlaɪd/ vi chocar

colliery /ˈkɒlɪərɪ/ n mina f de carbón

collision /kəˈlɪʒn/ n choque m

colloquial /kəˈləʊkwɪəl/ a familiar. **∼ism** n expresión f familiar

collusion /kəˈluːʒn/ n connivencia f

colon /ˈkəʊlən/ n (gram) dos puntos mpl; (med) colon m

colonel /ˈkɜːnl/ n coronel m

colon|ial /kəˈləʊnɪəl/ a colonial. **∼ize** /ˈkɒlənaɪz/ vt colonizar. **∼y** /ˈkɒlənɪ/ n colonia f

colossal /kəˈlɒsl/ a colosal

colour /ˈkʌlə(r)/ n color m. **off ∼** (fig) indispuesto. ● a de color(es), en color(es). ● vt colorar; (dye) teñir. ● vi (blush) sonrojarse. **∼ bar** n barrera f racial. **∼-blind** a daltoniano. **∼ed** /ˈkʌləd/ a de color. **∼ful** a lleno de color; (fig) pintoresco. **∼less** a incoloro. **∼s** npl (flag) bandera f

colt /kəʊlt/ n potro m

column /ˈkɒləm/ n columna f. **∼ist** /ˈkɒləmnɪst/ n columnista m & f

coma /ˈkəʊmə/ n coma m

comb /kəʊm/ n peine m. ● vt peinar; (search) registrar

combat /ˈkɒmbæt/ n combate m. ● vt (pt combated) combatir. **∼ant** /-ətənt/ n combatiente m & f

combination /kɒmbɪˈneɪʃn/ n combinación f

combine /kəmˈbaɪn/ vt combinar. ● vi combinarse. /ˈkɒmbaɪn/ n asociación f. **∼harvester** n cosechadora f

combustion /kəmˈbʌstʃən/ n combustión f

come /kʌm/ vi (pt came, pp come) venir; (occur) pasar. **∼ about** ocurrir. **∼ across** encontrarse con ⟨person⟩; encontrar ⟨object⟩. **∼ apart** deshacerse. **∼ away** marcharse. **∼ back** volver. **∼ by** obtener; (pass) pasar. **∼ down** bajar. **∼ in** entrar. **∼ in for** recibir. **∼ into** heredar ⟨money⟩. **∼ off** desprenderse; (succeed) tener éxito. **∼ off it!** (fam) ¡no me vengas con eso! **∼ out** salir; (result) resultar. **∼ round** (after fainting) volver en sí; (be converted) cambiar de idea. **∼ to** llegar a ⟨decision etc⟩. **∼ up** subir; (fig) salir. **∼ up with** proponer ⟨idea⟩

comeback /ˈkʌmbæk/ n retorno m; (retort) réplica f

comedian /kəˈmiːdɪən/ n cómico m

comedown /'kʌmdaʊn/ n revés m

comedy /'kɒmədɪ/ n comedia f

comely /'kʌmlɪ/ a (-ier, -iest) (old use) bonito

comet /'kɒmɪt/ n cometa m

comeuppance /kʌm'ʌpəns/ n (Amer) merecido m

comf|ort /'kʌmfət/ n bienestar m; (consolation) consuelo m. ● vt consolar. ～ortable a cómodo; (wealthy) holgado. ～y /'kʌmfɪ/ a (fam) cómodo

comic /'kɒmɪk/ a cómico. ● n cómico m; (periodical) tebeo m. ～al a cómico. ～ strip n historieta f

coming /'kʌmɪŋ/ n llegada f. ● a próximo; (week, month etc) que viene. ～ and going n ir y venir

comma /'kɒmə/ n coma f

command /kə'mɑːnd/ n orden f; (mastery) dominio m. ● vt mandar; (deserve) merecer

commandeer /kɒmən'dɪə(r)/ vt requisar

commander /kə'mɑːndə(r)/ n comandante m

commanding /kə'mɑːndɪŋ/ a imponente

commandment /kə'mɑːndmənt/ n mandamiento m

commando /kə'mɑːndəʊ/ n (pl -os) comando m

commemorat|e /kə'meməreɪt/ vt conmemorar. ～ion /-'reɪʃn/ n conmemoración f. ～ive /-ətɪv/ a conmemorativo

commence /kə'mens/ vt/i empezar. ～ment n principio m

commend /kə'mend/ vt alabar; (entrust) encomendar. ～able a loable. ～ation /kɒmen'deɪʃn/ n elogio m

commensurate /kə'menʃərət/ a proporcionado

comment /'kɒment/ n observación f. ● vi hacer observaciones

commentary /'kɒmentrɪ/ n comentario m; (radio, TV) reportaje m

commentat|e /'kɒmənteɪt/ vi narrar. ～or n (radio, TV) locutor m

commerce /'kɒmɜːs/ n comercio m. ～ial /kə'mɜːʃl/ a comercial. ● n anuncio m. ～ialize vt comercializar

commiserat|e /kə'mɪzəreɪt/ vt compadecer. ● vi compadecerse (with de). ～ion /-'reɪʃn/ n conmiseración f

commission /kə'mɪʃn/ n comisión f. out of ～ fuera de servicio. ● vt encargar; (mil) nombrar

commissionaire /kəmɪʃə'neə(r)/ n portero m

commissioner /kə'mɪʃənə(r)/ n comisario m; (of police) jefe m

commit /kə'mɪt/ vt (pt committed) cometer; (entrust) confiar. ～ o.s. comprometerse. ～ to memory aprender de memoria. ～ment n compromiso m

committee /kə'mɪtɪ/ n comité m

commodity /kə'mɒdətɪ/ n producto m, artículo m

common /'kɒmən/ a (-er, -est) común; (usual) corriente; (vulgar) ordinario. ● n ejido m

commoner /'kɒmənə(r)/ n plebeyo m

common: ～ law n derecho m consuetudinario. ～ly adv comúnmente. C～ Market n Mercado m Común

commonplace /'kɒmənpleɪs/ a banal. ● n banalidad f

common: ～-room n sala f común, salón m común. ～ sense n sentido m común

Commonwealth /'kɒmənwelθ/ n. the ～ la Mancomunidad f Británica

commotion /kə'məʊʃn/ n confusión f

communal /'kɒmjʊnl/ a comunal

commune¹ /'kɒmjuːn/ n comuna f

commune² /kə'mjuːn/ vi comunicarse

communicat|e /kə'mjuːnɪkeɪt/ vt comunicar. ● vi comunicarse. ～ion /-'keɪʃn/ n comunicación f. ～ive /-ətɪv/ a comunicativo

communion /kə'mjuːnɪən/ n comunión f

communiqué /kə'mjuːnɪkeɪ/ n comunicado m

communis|m /'kɒmjʊnɪsəm/ n comunismo m. ～t /'kɒmjʊnɪst/ n comunista m & f

community /kə'mjuːnətɪ/ n comunidad f. ～ centre n centro m social

commute /kə'mjuːt/ vi viajar diariamente. ● vt (jurid) conmutar. ～r /-ə(r)/ n viajero m diario

compact /kəm'pækt/ a compacto. /'kɒmpækt/ n (for powder) polvera f. ～ disc /'kɒm-/ n disco m compacto

companion /kəm'pænɪən/ n compañero m. ～ship n compañerismo m

company /'kʌmpənɪ/ n compañía f; (guests, fam) visita f; (com) sociedad f

compar|able /'kɒmpərəbl/ a comparable. ～ative /kəm'pærətɪv/ a comparativo; (*fig*) relativo. ● *n* (*gram*) comparativo *m*. ~e /kəm'peə(r)/ *vt* comparar. ● *vi* poderse comparar. ~ison /kəm'pærɪsn/ *n* comparación *f*

compartment /kəm'pɑːtmənt/ *n* compartimiento *m*; (*on train*) departamento *m*

compass /'kʌmpəs/ *n* brújula *f*. ~es *npl* compás *m*

compassion /kəm'pæʃn/ *n* compasión *f*. ~ate *a* compasivo

compatib|ility /kəmpætə'bɪlətɪ/ *n* compatibilidad *f*. ~le /kəm'pætəbl/ *a* compatible

compatriot /kəm'pætrɪət/ *n* compatriota *m* & *f*

compel /kəm'pel/ *vt* (*pt* compelled) obligar. ~ling *a* irresistible

compendium /kəm'pendɪəm/ *n* compendio *m*

compensat|e /'kɒmpənseɪt/ *vt* compensar; (*for loss*) indemnizar. ● *vi* compensar. ~ion /-'seɪʃn/ *n* compensación *f*; (*financial*) indemnización *f*

compère /'kɒmpeə(r)/ *n* presentador *m*. ● *vt* presentar

compete /kəm'piːt/ *vi* competir

competen|ce /'kɒmpətəns/ *n* competencia *f*, aptitud *f*. ~t /'kɒmpɪtənt/ *a* competente, capaz

competit|ion /kɒmpə'tɪʃn/ *n* (*contest*) concurso *m*; (*com*) competencia *f*. ~ive /kəm'petətɪv/ *a* competidor; (*price*) competitivo. ~or /kəm'petɪtə(r)/ *n* competidor *m*; (*in contest*) concursante *m* & *f*

compile /kəm'paɪl/ *vt* compilar. ~r /-ə(r)/ *n* recopilador *m*, compilador *m*

complacen|cy /kəm'pleɪsənsɪ/ *n* satisfacción *f* de sí mismo. ~t /kəm'pleɪsnt/ *a* satisfecho de sí mismo

complain /kəm'pleɪn/ *vi*. ~ (about) quejarse (de). ~ of (*med*) sufrir de. ~t /kəm'pleɪnt/ *n* queja *f*; (*med*) enfermedad *f*

complement /'kɒmplɪmənt/ *n* complemento *m*. ● *vt* complementar. ~ary /-'mentrɪ/ *a* complementario

complete /kəm'pliːt/ *a* completo; (*finished*) acabado; (*downright*) total. ● *vt* acabar; llenar (*a form*). ~ly *adv* completamente. ~ion /-ʃn/ *n* conclusión *f*

complex /'kɒmpleks/ *a* complejo. ● *n* complejo *m*

complexion /kəm'plekʃn/ *n* tez *f*; (*fig*) aspecto *m*

complexity /kəm'pleksətɪ/ *n* complejidad *f*

complian|ce /kəm'plaɪəns/ *n* sumisión *f*. in ~ce with de acuerdo con. ~t *a* sumiso

complicat|e /'kɒmplɪkeɪt/ *vt* complicar. ~ed *a* complicado. ~ion /-'keɪʃn/ *n* complicación *f*

complicity /kəm'plɪsətɪ/ *n* complicidad *f*

compliment /'kɒmplɪmənt/ *n* cumplido *m*; (*amorous*) piropo *m*. ● *vt* felicitar. ~ary /-'mentrɪ/ *a* halagador; (*given free*) de favor. ~s *npl* saludos *mpl*

comply /kəm'plaɪ/ *vi*. ~ with conformarse con

component /kəm'pəʊnənt/ *a* & *n* componente (*m*)

compose /kəm'pəʊz/ *vt* componer. ~ o.s. tranquilizarse. ~d *a* sereno

compos|er /kəm'pəʊzə(r)/ *n* compositor *m*. ~ition /kɒmpə'zɪʃn/ *n* composición *f*

compost /'kɒmpɒst/ *n* abono *m*

composure /kəm'pəʊʒə(r)/ *n* serenidad *f*

compound[1] /'kɒmpaʊnd/ *n* compuesto *m*. ● *a* compuesto; (*fracture*) complicado. /kəm'paʊnd/ *vt* componer; agravar (*problem etc*). ● *vi* (*settle*) arreglarse

compound[2] /'kɒmpaʊnd/ *n* (*enclosure*) recinto *m*

comprehen|d /kɒmprɪ'hend/ *vt* comprender. ~sion /kɒmprɪ'henʃn/ *n* comprensión *f*

comprehensive /kɒmprɪ'hensɪv/ *a* extenso; (*insurance*) a todo riesgo. ~ school *n* instituto *m*

compress /'kɒmpres/ *n* (*med*) compresa *f*. /kəm'pres/ *vt* comprimir; (*fig*) condensar. ~ion /-ʃn/ *n* compresión *f*

comprise /kəm'praɪz/ *vt* comprender

compromise /'kɒmprəmaɪz/ *n* acuerdo *m*, acomodo *m*, arreglo *m*. ● *vt* comprometer. ● *vi* llegar a un acuerdo

compuls|ion /kəm'pʌlʃn/ *n* obligación *f*, impulso *m*. ~ive /kəm'pʌlsɪv/ *a* compulsivo. ~ory /kəm'pʌlsərɪ/ *a* obligatorio

compunction /kəmˈpʌŋkʃn/ n remordimiento m

computer /kəmˈpjuːtə(r)/ n ordenador m. ~ize vt instalar ordenadores en. be ~ized tener ordenador

comrade /ˈkɒmreɪd/ n camarada m & f. ~ship n camaradería f

con¹ /kɒn/ vt (pt **conned**) (fam) estafar. ● n (fam) estafa f

con² /kɒn/ see **pro and con**

concave /ˈkɒŋkeɪv/ a cóncavo

conceal /kənˈsiːl/ vt ocultar. ~ment n encubrimiento m

concede /kənˈsiːd/ vt conceder

conceit /kənˈsiːt/ n vanidad f. ~ed a engreído

conceiv|able /kənˈsiːvəbl/ a concebible. ~ably adv. **may** ~ably es concebible que. ~e /kənˈsiːv/ vt/i concebir

concentrat|e /ˈkɒnsəntreɪt/ vt concentrar. ● vi concentrarse. ~ion /-ˈtreɪʃn/ n concentración f. ~ion **camp** n campo m de concentración

concept /ˈkɒnsept/ n concepto m

conception /kənˈsepʃn/ n concepción f

conceptual /kənˈseptʃʊəl/ a conceptual

concern /kənˈsɜːn/ n asunto m; (worry) preocupación f; (com) empresa f. ● vt tener que ver con; (deal with) tratar de. **as far as I'm** ~ed en cuanto a mí. **be** ~ed **about** preocuparse por. ~ing prep acerca de

concert /ˈkɒnsət/ n concierto m. **in** ~ de común acuerdo. ~ed /kənˈsɜːtɪd/ a concertado

concertina /kɒnsəˈtiːnə/ n concertina f

concerto /kənˈtʃɜːtəʊ/ n (pl -os) concierto m

concession /kənˈseʃn/ n concesión f

conciliat|e /kənˈsɪlɪeɪt/ vt conciliar. ~ion /-ˈeɪʃn/ n conciliación f

concise /kənˈsaɪs/ a conciso. ~ly adv concisamente. ~ness n concisión f

conclu|de /kənˈkluːd/ vt concluir. ● vi concluirse. ~ding a final. ~sion n conclusión f

conclusive /kənˈkluːsɪv/ a decisivo. ~ly adv concluyentemente

concoct /kənˈkɒkt/ vt confeccionar; (fig) inventar. ~ion /-ʃn/ n mezcla f; (drink) brebaje m

concourse /ˈkɒŋkɔːs/ n (rail) vestíbulo m

concrete /ˈkɒŋkriːt/ n hormigón m. ● a concreto. ● vt cubrir con hormigón

concur /kənˈkɜː(r)/ vi (pt **concurred**) estar de acuerdo

concussion /kənˈkʌʃn/ n conmoción f cerebral

condemn /kənˈdem/ vt condenar. ~ation /kɒndemˈneɪʃn/ n condenación f, condena f; (censure) censura f

condens|ation /kɒndenˈseɪʃn/ n condensación f. ~e /kənˈdens/ vt condensar. ● vi condensarse

condescend /kɒndɪˈsend/ vi dignarse (**to** a). ~ing a superior

condiment /ˈkɒndɪmənt/ n condimento m

condition /kənˈdɪʃn/ n condición f. **on** ~ **that** a condición de que. ● vt condicionar. ~al a condicional. ~er n acondicionador m; (for hair) suavizante m

condolences /kənˈdəʊlənsɪz/ npl pésame m

condom /ˈkɒndɒm/ n condón m

condone /kənˈdəʊn/ vt condonar

conducive /kənˈdjuːsɪv/ a. be ~ to ser favorable a

conduct /kənˈdʌkt/ vt conducir; dirigir (orchestra). /ˈkɒndʌkt/ n conducta f. ~or /kənˈdʌktə(r)/ n director m; (of bus) cobrador m. ~ress n cobradora f

cone /kəʊn/ n cono m; (for ice-cream) cucurucho m

confectioner /kənˈfekʃənə(r)/ n pastelero m. ~y n dulces mpl, golosinas fpl

confederation /kənfedəˈreɪʃn/ n confederación f

confer /kənˈfɜː(r)/ vt (pt **conferred**) conferir. ● vi consultar

conference /ˈkɒnfərəns/ n congreso m

confess /kənˈfes/ vt confesar. ● vi confesarse. ~ion /-ʃn/ n confesión f. ~ional n confes(i)onario m. ~or n confesor m

confetti /kənˈfeti/ n confeti m, confetis mpl

confide /kənˈfaɪd/ vt/i confiar

confiden|ce /ˈkɒnfɪdəns/ n confianza f; (secret) confidencia f. ~ce **trick** n estafa f, timo m. ~t /ˈkɒnfɪdənt/ a seguro

confidential /kɒnfɪ'denʃl/ a confidencial

confine /kən'faɪn/ vt confinar; (limit) limitar. ~ment n (imprisonment) prisión f; (med) parto m

confines /'kɒnfaɪnz/ npl confines mpl

confirm /kən'fɜ:m/ vt confirmar. ~ation n confirmación f. ~ed a inveterado

confiscat|e /'kɒnfɪskeɪt/ vt confiscar. ~ion /-'keɪʃn/ n confiscación f

conflagration /kɒnflə'greɪʃn/ n conflagración f

conflict /'kɒnflɪkt/ n conflicto m. /kən'flɪkt/ vi chocar. ~ing /kən-/ a contradictorio

conform /kən'fɔ:m/ vt conformar. ●vi conformarse. ~ist n conformista m & f

confound /kən'faʊnd/ vt confundir. ~ed a (fam) maldito

confront /kən'frʌnt/ vt hacer frente a; (face) enfrentarse con. ~ation /kɒnfrʌn'teɪʃn/ n confrontación f

confus|e /kən'fju:z/ vt confundir. ~ing a desconcertante. ~ion /-ʒn/ n confusión f

congeal /kən'dʒi:l/ vt coagular. ●vi coagularse

congenial /kən'dʒi:nɪəl/ a simpático

congenital /kən'dʒenɪtl/ a congénito

congest|ed /kən'dʒestɪd/ a congestionado. ~ion /-tʃən/ n congestión f

congratulat|e /kən'grætjʊleɪt/ vt felicitar. ~ions /-'leɪʃnz/ npl felicitaciones fpl

congregat|e /'kɒŋgrɪgeɪt/ vi congregarse. ~ion /-'geɪʃn/ n asamblea f; (relig) fieles mpl, feligreses mpl

congress /'kɒŋgres/ n congreso m. C~ (Amer) el Congreso

conic(al) /'kɒnɪk(l)/ a cónico

conifer /'kɒnɪfə(r)/ n conífera f

conjecture /kən'dʒektʃə(r)/ n conjetura f. ●vt conjeturar. ●vi hacer conjeturas

conjugal /'kɒndʒʊgl/ a conyugal

conjugat|e /'kɒndʒʊgeɪt/ vt conjugar. ~ion /-'geɪʃn/ n conjugación f

conjunction /kən'dʒʌŋkʃn/ n conjunción f

conjur|e /'kʌndʒə(r)/ vi hacer juegos de manos. ●vt. ~e up evocar. ~or n prestidigitador m

conk /kɒŋk/ vi. ~ out (sl) fallar; (person) desmayarse

conker /'kɒŋkə(r)/ n (fam) castaña f de Indias

conman /'kɒnmæn/ n (fam) estafador m, timador m

connect /kə'nekt/ vt juntar; (elec) conectar. ●vi unirse; (elec) conectarse. ~ with (train) enlazar con. ~ed a unido; (related) relacionado. be ~ed with tener que ver con, estar emparentado con

connection /kə'nekʃn/ n unión f; (rail) enlace m; (elec, mec) conexión f; (fig) relación f. in ~ with a propósito de, con respecto a. ~s npl relaciones fpl

conniv|ance /kə'naɪvəns/ n connivencia f. ~e /kə'naɪv/ vi. ~e at hacer la vista gorda a

connoisseur /kɒnə'sɜ:(r)/ n experto m

connot|ation /kɒnə'teɪʃn/ n connotación f. ~e /kə'nəʊt/ vt connotar; (imply) implicar

conquer /'kɒŋkə(r)/ vt conquistar; (fig) vencer. ~or n conquistador m

conquest /'kɒŋkwest/ n conquista f

conscience /'kɒnʃəns/ n conciencia f

conscientious /kɒnʃɪ'enʃəs/ a concienzudo

conscious /'kɒnʃəs/ a consciente; (deliberate) intencional. ~ly adv a sabiendas. ~ness n conciencia f; (med) conocimiento m

conscript /'kɒnskrɪpt/ n recluta m. /kən'skrɪpt/ vt reclutar. ~ion /kən'skrɪpʃn/ n reclutamiento m

consecrat|e /'kɒnsɪkreɪt/ vt consagrar. ~ion /-'kreɪʃn/ n consagración f

consecutive /kən'sekjʊtɪv/ a sucesivo

consensus /kən'sensəs/ n consenso m

consent /kən'sent/ vi consentir. ●n consentimiento m

consequen|ce /'kɒnsɪkwəns/ n consecuencia f. ~t /'kɒnsɪkwənt/ a consiguiente. ~tly adv por consiguiente

conservation /kɒnsə'veɪʃn/ n conservación f, preservación f. ~ist /kɒnsə'veɪʃənɪst/ n conservacionista m & f

conservative /kən'sɜ:vətɪv/ a conservador; (modest) prudente, moderado. C~ a & n conservador (m)

conservatory /kən'sɜ:vətrɪ/ *n* (*greenhouse*) invernadero *m*

conserve /kən'sɜ:v/ *vt* conservar

consider /kən'sɪdə(r)/ *vt* considerar; (*take into account*) tomar en cuenta. **∼able** /kən'sɪdərəbl/ *a* considerable. **∼ably** *adv* considerablemente

considerat|e /kən'sɪdərət/ *a* considerado. **∼ion** /-'reɪʃn/ *n* consideración *f*

considering /kən'sɪdərɪŋ/ *prep* en vista de

consign /kən'saɪn/ *vt* consignar; (*send*) enviar. **∼ment** *n* envío *m*

consist /kən'sɪst/ *vi.* **∼ of** consistir en

consistency /kən'sɪstənsɪ/ *n* consistencia *f*; (*fig*) coherencia *f*

consistent /kən'sɪstənt/ *a* coherente; (*unchanging*) constante. **∼ with** compatible con. **∼ly** *adv* constantemente

consolation /kɒnsə'leɪʃn/ *n* consuelo *m*

console /kən'səʊl/ *vt* consolar

consolidat|e /kən'sɒlɪdeɪt/ *vt* consolidar. ● *vi* consolidarse. **∼ion** /-'deɪʃn/ *n* consolidación *f*

consonant /'kɒnsənənt/ *n* consonante *f*

consort /'kɒnsɔ:t/ *n* consorte *m & f*. /kən'sɔ:t/ *vi.* **∼ with** asociarse con

consortium /kən'sɔ:tɪəm/ *n* (*pl* **-tia**) consorcio *m*

conspicuous /kən'spɪkjʊəs/ *a* (*easily seen*) visible; (*showy*) llamativo; (*noteworthy*) notable

conspir|acy /kən'spɪrəsɪ/ *n* complot *m*, conspiración *f*. **∼e** /kən'spaɪə(r)/ *vi* conspirar

constab|le /'kʌnstəbl/ *n* policía *m*, guardia *m*. **∼ulary** /kən'stæbjʊlərɪ/ *n* policía *f*

constant /'kɒnstənt/ *a* constante. **∼ly** *adv* constantemente

constellation /kɒnstə'leɪʃn/ *n* constelación *f*

consternation /kɒnstə'neɪʃn/ *n* consternación *f*

constipat|ed /'kɒnstɪpeɪtɪd/ *a* estreñido. **∼ion** /-'peɪʃn/ *n* estreñimiento *m*

constituen|cy /kən'stɪtjʊənsɪ/ *n* distrito *m* electoral. **∼t** /kən'stɪtjʊənt/ *n* componente *m*; (*pol*) elector *m*

constitut|e /'kɒnstɪtju:t/ *vt* constituir. **∼ion** /-'tju:ʃn/ *n* constitución *f*. **∼ional** /-'tju:ʃənl/ *a* constitucional. ● *n* paseo *m*

constrain /kən'streɪn/ *vt* forzar, obligar, constreñir. **∼t** /kən'streɪnt/ *n* fuerza *f*

constrict /kən'strɪkt/ *vt* apretar. **∼ion** /-ʃn/ *n* constricción *f*

construct /kən'strʌkt/ *vt* construir. **∼ion** /-ʃn/ *n* construcción *f*. **∼ive** /kən'strʌktɪv/ *a* constructivo

construe /kən'stru:/ *vt* interpretar; (*gram*) construir

consul /'kɒnsl/ *n* cónsul *m*. **∼ar** /-jʊlə(r)/ *a* consular. **∼ate** /-ət/ *n* consulado *m*

consult /kən'sʌlt/ *vt/i* consultar. **∼ant** /kən'sʌltənt/ *n* asesor *m*; (*med*) especialista *m & f*; (*tec*) consejero *m* técnico. **∼ation** /kɒnsəl'teɪʃn/ *n* consulta *f*

consume /kən'sju:m/ *vt* consumir; (*eat*) comer; (*drink*) beber. **∼r** /-ə(r)/ *n* consumidor *m*. ● *a* de consumo. **∼rism** /kən'sju:mərɪzəm/ *n* protección *f* del consumidor, consumismo *m*

consummat|e /'kɒnsəmeɪt/ *vt* consumar. **∼ion** /-'meɪʃn/ *n* consumación *f*

consumption /kən'sʌmpʃn/ *n* consumo *m*; (*med*) tisis *f*

contact /'kɒntækt/ *n* contacto *m*. ● *vt* ponerse en contacto con

contagious /kən'teɪdʒəs/ *a* contagioso

contain /kən'teɪn/ *vt* contener. **∼ o.s.** contenerse. **∼er** *n* recipiente *m*; (*com*) contenedor *m*

contaminat|e /kən'tæmɪneɪt/ *vt* contaminar. **∼ion** /-'neɪʃn/ *n* contaminación *f*

contemplat|e /'kɒntəmpleɪt/ *vt* contemplar; (*consider*) considerar. **∼ion** /-'pleɪʃn/ *n* contemplación *f*

contemporary /kən'tempərərɪ/ *a & n* contemporáneo (*m*)

contempt /kən'tempt/ *n* desprecio *m*. **∼ible** *a* despreciable. **∼uous** /-tjʊəs/ *a* desdeñoso

contend /kən'tend/ *vt* sostener. ● *vi* contender. **∼er** *n* contendiente *m & f*

content[1] /kən'tent/ *a* satisfecho. ● *vt* contentar

content[2] /'kɒntent/ *n* contenido *m*

contented /kən'tentɪd/ *a* satisfecho

contention /kən'tenʃn/ *n* contienda *f*; (*opinion*) opinión *f*, argumento *m*

contentment /kən'tentmənt/ *n* contento *m*

contest /'kɒntest/ n (*competition*) concurso m; (*fight*) contienda f. /kən'test/ vt disputar. **∼ant** n contendiente m & f, concursante m & f

context /'kɒntekst/ n contexto m

continent /'kɒntɪnənt/ n continente m. the C∼ Europa f. **∼al** /-'nentl/ a continental

contingency /kən'tɪndʒənsɪ/ n contingencia f

contingent /kən'tɪndʒənt/ a & n contingente (m)

continu|al /kən'tɪnjʊəl/ a continuo. **∼ance** /kən'tɪnjʊəns/ n continuación f. **∼ation** /-ʊ'eɪʃn/ n continuación f. **∼e** /kən'tɪnju:/ vt/i continuar; (*resume*) seguir. **∼ed** a continuo. **∼ity** /kɒntɪ'nju:ətɪ/ n continuidad f. **∼ity girl** (*cinema, TV*) secretaria f de rodaje. **∼ous** /kən'tɪnjʊəs/ a continuo. **∼ously** adv continuamente

contort /kən'tɔ:t/ vt retorcer. **∼ion** /-ʃn/ n contorsión f. **∼ionist** /-ʃənɪst/ n contorsionista m & f

contour /'kɒntʊə(r)/ n contorno m. **∼ line** n curva f de nivel

contraband /'kɒntrəbænd/ n contrabando m

contracepti|on /kɒntrə'sepʃn/ n contracepción f. **∼ve** /kɒntrə'septɪv/ a & n anticonceptivo (m)

contract /'kɒntrækt/ n contrato m. /kən'trækt/ vt contraer. ● vi contraerse. **∼ion** /kən'trækʃn/ n contracción f. **∼or** /kən'træktə(r)/ n contratista m & f

contradict /kɒntrə'dɪkt/ vt contradecir. **∼ion** /-ʃn/ n contradicción f. **∼ory** a contradictorio

contraption /kən'træpʃn/ n (*fam*) artilugio m

contrary /'kɒntrərɪ/ a & n contrario (m). on the ∼ al contrario. ● adv. ∼ to contrariamente a. /kən'treərɪ/ a terco

contrast /'kɒntrɑ:st/ n contraste m. /kən'trɑ:st/ vt poner en contraste. ● vi contrastar. **∼ing** a contrastante

contraven|e /kɒntrə'vi:n/ vt contravenir. **∼tion** /-'venʃn/ n contravención f

contribut|e /kən'trɪbju:t/ vt/i contribuir. **∼e to** escribir para ⟨*newspaper*⟩. **∼ion** /kɒntrɪ'bju:ʃn/ n contribución f; (*from salary*) cotización f. **∼or** n contribuyente m & f; (*to newspaper*) colaborador m

contrite /'kɒntraɪt/ a arrepentido, pesaroso

contriv|ance /kən'traɪvəns/ n invención f. **∼e** /kən'traɪv/ vt idear. **∼e to** conseguir

control /kən'trəʊl/ vt (*pt controlled*) controlar. ● n control m. **∼s** npl (*mec*) mandos mpl

controvers|ial /kɒntrə'vɜ:ʃl/ a polémico, discutible. **∼y** /'kɒntrəvɜ:sɪ/ n controversia f

conundrum /kə'nʌndrəm/ n adivinanza f; (*problem*) enigma m

conurbation /kɒnɜ:'beɪʃn/ n conurbación f

convalesce /kɒnvə'les/ vi convalecer. **∼nce** n convalecencia f. **∼nt** a & n convaleciente (m & f). **∼nt home** n casa f de convalecencia

convector /kən'vektə(r)/ n estufa f de convección

convene /kən'vi:n/ vt convocar. ● vi reunirse

convenien|ce /kən'vi:nɪəns/ n conveniencia f, comodidad f. all modern **∼ces** todas las comodidades. at your **∼ce** según le convenga. **∼ces** npl servicios mpl. **∼t** /kən'vi:nɪənt/ a cómodo; ⟨*place*⟩ bien situado; ⟨*time*⟩ oportuno. be **∼t** convenir. **∼tly** adv convenientemente

convent /'kɒnvənt/ n convento m

convention /kən'venʃn/ n convención f; (*meeting*) congreso m. **∼al** a convencional

converge /kən'vɜ:dʒ/ vi convergir

conversant /kən'vɜ:sənt/ a. ∼ with versado en

conversation /kɒnvə'seɪʃn/ n conversación f. **∼al** a de la conversación. **∼alist** n hábil conversador m

converse[1] /kən'vɜ:s/ vi conversar

converse[2] /'kɒnvɜ:s/ a converso. ● n lo contrario. **∼ly** adv a la inversa

conver|sion /kən'vɜ:ʃn/ n conversión f. **∼t** /kən'vɜ:t/ vt convertir. /'kɒnvɜ:t/ n converso m. **∼tible** /kən'vɜ:tɪbl/ a convertible. ● n (*auto*) descapotable m

convex /'kɒnveks/ a convexo

convey /kən'veɪ/ vt llevar; transportar ⟨*goods*⟩; comunicar ⟨*idea, feeling*⟩. **∼ance** n transporte m. **∼or belt** n cinta f transportadora

convict /kən'vɪkt/ *vt* condenar. /'kɒnvɪkt/ *n* presidiario *m*. ∼**ion** /kən'vɪkʃn/ *n* condena *f*; (*belief*) creencia *f*

convinc|e /kən'vɪns/ *vt* convencer. ∼**ing** *a* convincente

convivial /kən'vɪvɪəl/ *a* alegre

convoke /kən'vəʊk/ *vt* convocar

convoluted /'kɒnvəluːtɪd/ *a* enrollado; (*argument*) complicado

convoy /'kɒnvɔɪ/ *n* convoy *m*

convuls|e /kən'vʌls/ *vt* convulsionar. **be** ∼**ed with laughter** desternillarse de risa. ∼**ion** /-ʃn/ *n* convulsión *f*

coo /kuː/ *vi* arrullar

cook /kʊk/ *vt* cocinar; (*alter, fam*) falsificar. ∼ **up** (*fam*) inventar. ● *n* cocinero *m*

cooker /'kʊkə(r)/ *n* cocina *f*

cookery /'kʊkərɪ/ *n* cocina *f*

cookie /'kʊkɪ/ *n* (*Amer*) galleta *f*

cool /kuːl/ *a* (**-er, -est**) fresco; (*calm*) tranquilo; (*unfriendly*) frío. ● *n* fresco *m*; (*sl*) calma *f*. ● *vt* enfriar. ● *vi* enfriarse. ∼ **down** (*person*) calmarse. ∼**ly** *adv* tranquilamente. ∼**ness** *n* frescura *f*

coop /kuːp/ *n* gallinero *m*. ● *vt*. ∼ **up** encerrar

co-operat|e /kəʊ'ɒpəreɪt/ *vi* cooperar. ∼**ion** /-'reɪʃn/ *n* cooperación *f*

cooperative /kəʊ'ɒpərətɪv/ *a* cooperativo. ● *n* cooperativa *f*

co-opt /kəʊ'ɒpt/ *vt* cooptar

co-ordinat|e /kəʊ'ɔːdɪneɪt/ *vt* coordinar. ∼**ion** /-'neɪʃn/ *n* coordinación *f*

cop /kɒp/ *vt* (*pt* **copped**) (*sl*) prender. ● *n* (*sl*) policía *m*

cope /kəʊp/ *vi* (*fam*) arreglárselas. ∼ **with** enfrentarse con

copious /'kəʊpɪəs/ *a* abundante

copper /'kɒpə(r)/ *n* cobre *m*; (*coin*) perra *f*. ● *a* de cobre

copper /'kɒpə(r)/ *n* (*sl*) policía *m*

coppice /'kɒpɪs/ *n*, **copse** /kɒps/ *n* bosquecillo *m*

Coptic /'kɒptɪk/ *a* copto

copulat|e /'kɒpjʊleɪt/ *vi* copular. ∼**ion** /-'leɪʃn/ *n* cópula *f*

copy /'kɒpɪ/ *n* copia *f*; (*typ*) material *m*. ● *vt* copiar

copyright /'kɒpɪraɪt/ *n* derechos *mpl* de autor

copy-writer /'kɒpɪraɪtə(r)/ *n* redactor *m* de textos publicitarios

coral /'kɒrəl/ *n* coral *m*

cord /kɔːd/ *n* cuerda *f*; (*fabric*) pana *f*. ∼**s** *npl* pantalones *mpl* de pana

cordial /'kɔːdɪəl/ *a & n* cordial (*m*)

cordon /'kɔːdn/ *n* cordón *m*. ● *vt*. ∼ **off** acordonar

corduroy /'kɔːdərɔɪ/ *n* pana *f*

core /kɔː(r)/ *n* (*of apple*) corazón *m*; (*fig*) meollo *m*

cork /kɔːk/ *n* corcho *m*. ● *vt* taponar. ∼**screw** /'kɔːkskruː/ *n* sacacorchos *m invar*

corn /kɔːn/ *n* (*wheat*) trigo *m*; (*Amer*) maíz *m*; (*seed*) grano *m*

corn /kɔːn/ *n* (*hard skin*) callo *m*

corned /kɔːnd/ *a*. ∼ **beef** *n* carne *f* de vaca en lata

corner /'kɔːnə(r)/ *n* ángulo *m*; (*inside*) rincón *m*; (*outside*) esquina *f*; (*football*) saque *m* de esquina. ● *vt* arrinconar; (*com*) acaparar. ∼**stone** *n* piedra *f* angular

cornet /'kɔːnɪt/ *n* (*mus*) corneta *f*; (*for ice-cream*) cucurucho *m*

cornflakes /'kɔːnfleɪks/ *npl* copos *mpl* de maíz

cornflour /'kɔːnflaʊə(r)/ *n* harina *f* de maíz

cornice /'kɔːnɪs/ *n* cornisa *f*

cornucopia /kɔːnjʊ'kəʊpɪə/ *n* cuerno *m* de la abundancia

Corn|ish /'kɔːnɪʃ/ *a* de Cornualles. ∼**wall** /'kɔːnwəl/ *n* Cornualles *m*

corny /'kɔːnɪ/ *a* (*trite, fam*) gastado; (*mawkish*) sentimental, sensiblero

corollary /kə'rɒlərɪ/ *n* corolario *m*

coronary /'kɒrənərɪ/ *n* trombosis *f* coronaria

coronation /kɒrə'neɪʃn/ *n* coronación *f*

coroner /'kɒrənə(r)/ *n* juez *m* de primera instancia

corporal /'kɔːpərəl/ *n* cabo *m*

corporal /'kɔːpərəl/ *a* corporal

corporate /'kɔːpərət/ *a* corporativo

corporation /kɔːpə'reɪʃn/ *n* corporación *f*; (*of town*) ayuntamiento *m*

corps /kɔː(r)/ *n* (*pl* **corps** /kɔːz/) cuerpo *m*

corpse /kɔːps/ *n* cadáver *m*

corpulent /'kɔːpjʊlənt/ *a* gordo, corpulento

corpuscle /'kɔːpʌsl/ *n* glóbulo *m*

corral /kə'rɑːl/ *n* (*Amer*) corral *m*

correct /kə'rekt/ *a* correcto; (*time*) exacto. ● *vt* corregir. ∼**ion** /-ʃn/ *n* corrección *f*

correlat|e /'kɒrəleɪt/ *vt* poner en correlación. **~ion** /-'leɪʃn/ *n* correlación *f*

correspond /kɒrɪ'spɒnd/ *vi* corresponder; (*write*) escribirse. **~ence** *n* correspondencia *f*. **~ent** *n* corresponsal *m & f*

corridor /'kɒrɪdɔ:(r)/ *n* pasillo *m*

corroborate /kə'rɒbəreɪt/ *vt* corroborar

corro|de /kə'rəʊd/ *vt* corroer. ● *vi* corroerse. **~sion** *n* corrosión *f*

corrugated /'kɒrəgeɪtɪd/ *a* ondulado. **~ iron** *n* hierro *m* ondulado

corrupt /kə'rʌpt/ *a* corrompido. ● *vt* corromper. **~ion** /-ʃn/ *n* corrupción *f*

corset /'kɔ:sɪt/ *n* corsé *m*

Corsica /'kɔ:sɪkə/ *n* Córcega *f*. **~n** *a & n* corso (*m*)

cortège /'kɔ:teɪʒ/ *n* cortejo *m*

cos /kɒs/ *n* lechuga *f* romana

cosh /kɒʃ/ *n* cachiporra *f*. ● *vt* aporrear

cosiness /'kəʊzɪnɪs/ *n* comodidad *f*

cosmetic /kɒz'metɪk/ *a & n* cosmético (*m*)

cosmic /'kɒzmɪk/ *a* cósmico

cosmonaut /'kɒzmənɔ:t/ *n* cosmonauta *m & f*

cosmopolitan /kɒzmə'pɒlɪtən/ *a & n* cosmopolita (*m & f*)

cosmos /'kɒzmɒs/ *n* cosmos *m*

Cossack /'kɒsæk/ *a & n* cosaco (*m*)

cosset /'kɒsɪt/ *vt* (*pt* **cosseted**) mimar

cost /kɒst/ *vi* (*pt* **cost**) costar, valer. ● *vt* (*pt* **costed**) calcular el coste de. ● *n* precio *m*. **at all ~s** cueste lo que cueste. **to one's ~** a sus expensas. **~s** *npl* (*jurid*) costas *fpl*

Costa Rica /kɒstə'ri:kə/ *n* Costa *f* Rica. **~n** *a & n* costarricense (*m & f*), costarriqueño (*m*)

costly /'kɒstlɪ/ *a* (**-ier, -iest**) caro, costoso

costume /'kɒstju:m/ *n* traje *m*

cosy /'kəʊzɪ/ *a* (**-ier, -iest**) cómodo; (*place*) acogedor. ● *n* cubierta *f* (de tetera)

cot /kɒt/ *n* cuna *f*

cottage /'kɒtɪdʒ/ *n* casita *f* de campo. **~ cheese** *n* requesón *m*. **~ industry** *n* industria *f* casera. **~ pie** *n* carne *f* picada con puré de patatas

cotton /'kɒtn/ *n* algodón *m*. ● *vi*. **~ on** (*sl*) comprender. **~ wool** *n* algodón hidrófilo

couch /kaʊtʃ/ *n* sofá *m*. ● *vt* expresar

couchette /ku:'ʃet/ *n* litera *f*

cough /kɒf/ *vi* toser. ● *n* tos *f*. **~ up** (*sl*) pagar. **~ mixture** *n* jarabe *m* para la tos

could /kʊd, kəd/ *pt of* **can**

couldn't /'kʊdnt/ = **could not**

council /'kaʊnsl/ *n* consejo *m*; (*of town*) ayuntamiento *m*. **~ house** *n* vivienda *f* protegida. **~lor** /'kaʊnsələ(r)/ *n* concejal *m*

counsel /'kaʊnsl/ *n* consejo *m*; (*pl invar*) (*jurid*) abogado *m*. **~lor** *n* consejero *m*

count¹ /kaʊnt/ *n* recuento *m*. ● *vt/i* contar

count² /kaʊnt/ *n* (*nobleman*) conde *m*

countdown /'kaʊntdaʊn/ *n* cuenta *f* atrás

countenance /'kaʊntɪnəns/ *n* semblante *m*. ● *vt* aprobar

counter /'kaʊntə(r)/ *n* (*in shop etc*) mostrador *m*; (*token*) ficha *f*. ● *adv*. **~ to** en contra de. ● *a* opuesto. ● *vt* oponerse a; parar ⟨*blow*⟩. ● *vi* contraatacar

counter... /'kaʊntə(r)/ *pref* contra...

counteract /kaʊntər'ækt/ *vt* contrarrestar

counter-attack /'kaʊntərətæk/ *n* contraataque *m*. ● *vt/i* contraatacar

counterbalance /'kaʊntəbæləns/ *n* contrapeso *m*. ● *vt/i* contrapesar

counterfeit /'kaʊntəfɪt/ *a* falsificado. ● *n* falsificación *f*. ● *vt* falsificar

counterfoil /'kaʊntəfɔɪl/ *n* talón *m*

counterpart /'kaʊntəpɑ:t/ *n* equivalente *m*; (*person*) homólogo *m*

counter-productive /'kaʊntəprə'dʌktɪv/ *a* contraproducente

countersign /'kaʊntəsaɪn/ *vt* refrendar

countess /'kaʊntɪs/ *n* condesa *f*

countless /'kaʊntlɪs/ *a* innumerable

countrified /'kʌntrɪfaɪd/ *a* rústico

country /'kʌntrɪ/ *n* (*native land*) país *m*; (*countryside*) campo *m*. **~ folk** *n* gente *f* del campo. **go to the ~** ir al campo; (*pol*) convocar elecciones generales

countryman /'kʌntrɪmən/ *n* (*pl* **-men**) campesino *m*; (*of one's own country*) compatriota *m*

countryside /'kʌntrɪsaɪd/ *n* campo *m*

county /'kaʊntɪ/ *n* condado *m*, provincia *f*

coup /ku:/ n golpe m

coupé /'ku:peɪ/ n cupé m

couple /'kʌpl/ n (of things) par m; (of people) pareja f; (married) matrimonio m. a ~ of un par de. ● vt unir; (tec) acoplar. ● vi copularse

coupon /'ku:pɒn/ n cupón m

courage /'kʌrɪdʒ/ n valor m. ~ous /kə'reɪdʒəs/ a valiente. ~ously adv valientemente

courgette /kʊə'ʒet/ n calabacín m

courier /'kʊrɪə(r)/ n mensajero m; (for tourists) guía m & f

course /kɔ:s/ n curso m; (behaviour) conducta f; (aviat, naut) rumbo m; (culin) plato m; (for golf) campo m. in due ~ a su debido tiempo. in the ~ of en el transcurso de, durante. of ~ desde luego, por supuesto

court /kɔ:t/ n corte f; (tennis) pista f; (jurid) tribunal m. ● vt cortejar; buscar (danger)

courteous /'kɜ:tɪəs/ a cortés

courtesan /kɔ:tɪ'zæn/ n (old use) cortesana f

courtesy /'kɜ:təsɪ/ n cortesía f

court: ~ier /'kɔ:tɪə(r)/ n (old use) cortesano m. ~ martial n (pl courts martial) consejo m de guerra. ~-martial vt (pt ~-martialled) juzgar en consejo de guerra. ~ship /'kɔ:tʃɪp/ n cortejo m

courtyard /'kɔ:tjɑ:d/ n patio m

cousin /'kʌzn/ n primo m. first ~ primo carnal. second ~ primo segundo

cove /kəʊv/ n cala f

covenant /'kʌvənənt/ n acuerdo m

Coventry /'kɒvntrɪ/ n. send to ~ hacer el vacío

cover /'kʌvə(r)/ vt cubrir; (journalism) hacer un reportaje sobre. ~ up cubrir; (fig) ocultar. ● n cubierta f; (shelter) abrigo m; (lid) tapa f; (for furniture) funda f; (pretext) pretexto m; (of magazine) portada f. ~age /'kʌvərɪdʒ/ n reportaje m. ~ charge n precio m del cubierto. ~ing n cubierta f. ~ing letter n carta f explicatoria, carta f adjunta

covet /'kʌvɪt/ vt codiciar

cow /kaʊ/ n vaca f

coward /'kaʊəd/ n cobarde m. ~ly a cobarde. ~ice /'kaʊədɪs/ n cobardía f

cowboy /'kaʊbɔɪ/ n vaquero m

cower /'kaʊə(r)/ vi encogerse, acobardarse

cowl /kaʊl/ n capucha f; (of chimney) sombrerete m

cowshed /'kaʊʃed/ n establo m

coxswain /'kɒksn/ n timonel m

coy /kɔɪ/ a (-er, -est) (falsamente) tímido, remilgado

crab¹ /kræb/ n cangrejo m

crab² /kræb/ vi (pt crabbed) quejarse

crab-apple /'kræbæpl/ n manzana f silvestre

crack /kræk/ n grieta f; (noise) crujido m; (of whip) chasquido m; (joke, sl) chiste m. ● a (fam) de primera. ● vt agrietar; chasquear (whip, fingers); cascar (nut); gastar (joke); resolver (problem). ● vi agrietarse. get ~ing (fam) darse prisa. ~ down on (fam) tomar medidas enérgicas contra. ~ up vi fallar; (person) volverse loco. ~ed /krækt/ a (sl) chiflado

cracker /'krækə(r)/ n petardo m; (culin) galleta f (soso); (culin, Amer) galleta f

crackers /'krækəz/ a (sl) chiflado

crackl|e /'krækl/ vi crepitar. ● n crepitación f, crujido m. ~ing /'kræklɪŋ/ n crepitación f, crujido m; (of pork) chicharrón m

crackpot /'krækpɒt/ n (sl) chiflado m

cradle /'kreɪdl/ n cuna f. ● vt acunar

craft /krɑ:ft/ n destreza f; (technique) arte f; (cunning) astucia f. ● n invar (boat) barco m

craftsman /'krɑ:ftsmən/ n (pl -men) artesano m. ~ship n artesanía f

crafty /'krɑ:ftɪ/ a (-ier, -iest) astuto

crag /kræg/ n despeñadero m. ~gy a peñascoso

cram /kræm/ vt (pt crammed) rellenar. ~ with llenar de. ● vi (for exams) empollar. ~-full a atestado

cramp /kræmp/ n calambre m

cramped /kræmpt/ a apretado

cranberry /'krænbərɪ/ n arándano m

crane /kreɪn/ n grúa f; (bird) grulla f. ● vt estirar (neck)

crank¹ /kræŋk/ n manivela f

crank² /kræŋk/ n (person) excéntrico m. ~y a excéntrico

cranny /'krænɪ/ n grieta f

crash /kræʃ/ n accidente m; (noise) estruendo m; (collision) choque m; (com) quiebra f. ● vt estrellar. ● vi quebrar con estrépito; (*have accident*) tener un accidente; ⟨*car etc*⟩ chocar; (*fail*) fracasar. ~ **course** *n* curso *m* intensivo. ~**-helmet** *n* casco *m* protector. ~**-land** *vi* hacer un aterrizaje de emergencia, hacer un aterrizaje forzoso

crass /kræs/ *a* craso, burdo

crate /kreɪt/ *n* cajón *m*. ● *vt* embalar

crater /'kreɪtə(r)/ *n* cráter *m*

cravat /krə'væt/ *n* corbata *f*, fular *m*

crav|e /kreɪv/ *vi*. ~**e for** anhelar. ~**ing** *n* ansia *f*

crawl /krɔːl/ *vi* andar a gatas; (*move slowly*) avanzar lentamente; (*drag o.s.*) arrastrarse. ● *n* (*swimming*) crol *m*. **at a** ~ a paso lento. ~ **to** humillarse ante. ~ **with** hervir de

crayon /'kreɪən/ *n* lápiz *m* de color

craze /kreɪz/ *n* manía *f*

craz|iness /'kreɪzɪnɪs/ *n* locura *f*. ~**y** /'kreɪzɪ/ *a* (**-ier**, **-iest**) loco. **be** ~**y about** andar loco por. ~**y paving** *n* enlosado *m* irregular

creak /kriːk/ *n* crujido *m*; (*of hinge*) chirrido *m*. ● *vi* crujir; ⟨*hinge*⟩ chirriar

cream /kriːm/ *n* crema *f*; (*fresh*) nata *f*. ● *a* (*colour*) color de crema. ● *vt* (*remove*) desnatar; (*beat*) batir. ~ **cheese** *n* queso *m* de nata. ~**y** *a* cremoso

crease /kriːs/ *n* pliegue *m*; (*crumple*) arruga *f*. ● *vt* plegar; (*wrinkle*) arrugar. ● *vi* arrugarse

creat|e /kriː'eɪt/ *vt* crear. ~**ion** /-ʃn/ *n* creación *f*. ~**ive** *a* creativo. ~**or** *n* creador *m*

creature /'kriːtʃə(r)/ *n* criatura *f*, bicho *m*, animal *m*

crèche /kreʃ/ *n* guardería *f* infantil

credence /'kriːdns/ *n* creencia *f*, fe *f*

credentials /krɪ'denʃlz/ *npl* credenciales *mpl*

credib|ility /kredə'bɪlətɪ/ *n* credibilidad *f*. ~**le** /'kredəbl/ *a* creíble

credit /'kredɪt/ *n* crédito *m*; (*honour*) honor *m*. **take the** ~ **for** atribuirse el mérito de. ● *vt* (*pt* **credited**) acreditar; (*believe*) creer. ~ **s.o. with** atribuir a uno. ~**able** *a* loable. ~ **card** *n* tarjeta *f* de crédito. ~**or** *n* acreedor *m*

credulous /'kredjʊləs/ *a* crédulo

creed /kriːd/ *n* credo *m*

creek /kriːk/ *n* ensenada *f*. **up the** ~ (*sl*) en apuros

creep /kriːp/ *vi* (*pt* **crept**) arrastrarse; ⟨*plant*⟩ trepar. ● *n* (*sl*) persona *f* desagradable. ~**er** *n* enredadera *f*. ~**s** /kriːps/ *npl*. **give s.o. the** ~**s** dar repugnancia a uno

cremat|e /krɪ'meɪt/ *vt* incinerar. ~**ion** /-ʃn/ *n* cremación *f*. ~**orium** /kremə'tɔːrɪəm/ *n* (*pl* **-ia**) crematorio *m*

Creole /'kriːəʊl/ *a* & *n* criollo (*m*)

crêpe /kreɪp/ *n* crespón *m*

crept /krept/ *see* **creep**

crescendo /krɪ'ʃendəʊ/ *n* (*pl* **-os**) crescendo *m*

crescent /'kresnt/ *n* media luna *f*; (*street*) calle *f* en forma de media luna

cress /kres/ *n* berro *m*

crest /krest/ *n* cresta *f*; (*coat of arms*) blasón *m*

Crete /kriːt/ *n* Creta *f*

cretin /'kretɪn/ *n* cretino *m*

crevasse /krɪ'væs/ *n* grieta *f*

crevice /'krevɪs/ *n* grieta *f*

crew[1] /kruː/ *n* tripulación *f*; (*gang*) pandilla *f*

crew[2] /kruː/ *see* **crow**[2]

crew: ~ **cut** *n* corte *m* al rape. ~ **neck** *n* cuello *m* redondo

crib /krɪb/ *n* cuna *f*; (*relig*) belén *m*; (*plagiarism*) plagio *m*. ● *vt/i* (*pt* **cribbed**) plagiar

crick /krɪk/ *n* calambre *m*; (*in neck*) tortícolis *f*

cricket[1] /'krɪkɪt/ *n* críquet *m*

cricket[2] /'krɪkɪt/ *n* (*insect*) grillo *m*

cricketer /'krɪkɪtə(r)/ *n* jugador *m* de críquet

crim|e /kraɪm/ *n* crimen *m*; (*acts*) criminalidad *f*. ~**inal** /'krɪmɪnl/ *a* & *n* criminal (*m*)

crimp /krɪmp/ *vt* rizar

crimson /'krɪmzn/ *a* & *n* carmesí (*m*)

cringe /krɪndʒ/ *vi* encogerse; (*fig*) humillarse

crinkle /'krɪŋkl/ *vt* arrugar. ● *vi* arrugarse. ● *n* arruga *f*

crinoline /'krɪnəlɪn/ *n* miriñaque *m*

cripple /'krɪpl/ *n* lisiado *m*, mutilado *m*. ● *vt* lisiar; (*fig*) paralizar

crisis /'kraɪsɪs/ *n* (*pl* **crises** /'kraɪsiːz/) crisis *f*

crisp /krɪsp/ *a* (**-er**, **-est**) (*culin*) crujiente; ⟨*air*⟩ vigorizador. ~**s** *npl* patatas *fpl* fritas a la inglesa

criss-cross /'krɪskrɒs/ *a* entrecruzado. ● *vt* entrecruzar. ● *vi* entrecruzarse

criterion /kraɪˈtɪərɪən/ n (pl **-ia**) criterio m

critic /ˈkrɪtɪk/ n crítico m

critical /ˈkrɪtɪkl/ a crítico. ~**ly** adv críticamente; (ill) gravemente

critici|sm /ˈkrɪtɪsɪzəm/ n crítica f. ~**ze** /ˈkrɪtɪsaɪz/ vt/i criticar

croak /krəʊk/ n (of person) gruñido m; (of frog) canto m. ● vi gruñir; (frog) croar

crochet /ˈkrəʊʃeɪ/ n croché m, ganchillo m. ● vt hacer ganchillo

crock[1] /krɒk/ n (person, fam) vejancón m; (old car) cacharro m

crock[2] /krɒk/ n vasija f de loza

crockery /ˈkrɒkərɪ/ n loza f

crocodile /ˈkrɒkədaɪl/ n cocodrilo m. ~ **tears** npl lágrimas fpl de cocodrilo

crocus /ˈkrəʊkəs/ n (pl **-es**) azafrán m

crony /ˈkrəʊnɪ/ n amigote m

crook /krʊk/ n (fam) maleante m & f, estafador m, criminal m; (stick) cayado m; (of arm) pliegue m

crooked /ˈkrʊkɪd/ a torcido; (winding) tortuoso; (dishonest) poco honrado

croon /kru:n/ vt/i canturrear

crop /krɒp/ n cosecha f; (fig) montón m. ● vt (pt **cropped**) vi cortar. ~ **up** surgir

cropper /ˈkrɒpər/ n. **come a** ~ (fall, fam) caer; (fail, fam) fracasar

croquet /ˈkrəʊkeɪ/ n croquet m

croquette /krəˈket/ n croqueta f

cross /krɒs/ n cruz f; (of animals) cruce m. ● vt/i cruzar; (oppose) contrariar. ~ **off** tachar. ~ **o.s.** santiguarse. ~ **out** tachar. ~ **s.o.'s mind** ocurrírsele a uno. ● a enfadado. **talk at** ~ **purposes** hablar sin entenderse

crossbar /ˈkrɒsbɑː(r)/ n travesaño m

cross-examine /krɒsɪɡˈzæmɪn/ vt interrogar

cross-eyed /ˈkrɒsaɪd/ a bizco

crossfire /ˈkrɒsfaɪə(r)/ n fuego m cruzado

crossing /ˈkrɒsɪŋ/ n (by boat) travesía f; (on road) paso m para peatones

crossly /ˈkrɒslɪ/ adv con enfado

cross-reference /krɒsˈrefrəns/ n referencia f

crossroads /ˈkrɒsrəʊdz/ n cruce m (de carreteras)

cross-section /krɒsˈsekʃn/ n sección f transversal; (fig) muestra f representativa

crosswise /ˈkrɒswaɪz/ adv al través

crossword /ˈkrɒswɜːd/ n crucigrama m

crotch /krɒtʃ/ n entrepiernas fpl

crotchety /ˈkrɒtʃɪtɪ/ a de mal genio

crouch /kraʊtʃ/ vi agacharse

crow[1] /krəʊ/ n cuervo m. **as the** ~ **flies** en línea recta

crow[2] /krəʊ/ vi (pt **crew**) cacarear

crowbar /ˈkrəʊbɑː(r)/ n palanca f

crowd /kraʊd/ n muchedumbre f. ● vt amontonar; (fill) llenar. ● vi amontonarse; (gather) reunirse. ~**ed** a atestado

crown /kraʊn/ n corona f; (of hill) cumbre f; (of head) coronilla f. ● vt coronar; poner una corona a (tooth). C~ **Court** n tribunal m regional. C~ **prince** n príncipe m heredero

crucial /ˈkruːʃl/ a crucial

crucifix /ˈkruːsɪfɪks/ n crucifijo m. ~**ion** /-ˈfɪkʃn/ n crucifixión f

crucify /ˈkruːsɪfaɪ/ vt crucificar

crude /kruːd/ a (**-er, -est**) (raw) crudo; (rough) tosco; (vulgar) ordinario

cruel /krʊəl/ a (**crueller, cruellest**) cruel. ~**ty** n crueldad f

cruet /ˈkruːɪt/ n vinagreras fpl

cruise /kruːz/ n crucero m. ● vi hacer un crucero; (of car) circular lentamente. ~**r** n crucero m

crumb /krʌm/ n migaja f

crumble /ˈkrʌmbl/ vt desmenuzar. ● vi desmenuzarse; (collapse) derrumbarse

crummy /ˈkrʌmɪ/ a (**-ier, -iest**) (sl) miserable

crumpet /ˈkrʌmpɪt/ n bollo m blando

crumple /ˈkrʌmpl/ vt arrugar; estrujar (paper). ● vi arrugarse

crunch /krʌntʃ/ vt hacer crujir; (bite) ronzar, morder, masticar. ● n crujido m; (fig) momento m decisivo

crusade /kruːˈseɪd/ n cruzada f. ~**r** /-ə(r)/ n cruzado m

crush /krʌʃ/ vt aplastar; arrugar (clothes); estrujar (paper). ● n (crowd) aglomeración f. **have a** ~ **on** (sl) estar perdido por. **orange** ~ n naranjada f

crust /krʌst/ n corteza f. ~**y** a (bread) de corteza dura; (person) malhumorado

crutch /krʌtʃ/ n muleta f; (anat) entrepiernas fpl

crux /krʌks/ n (pl **cruxes**) punto m más importante, quid m, busilis m

cry /kraɪ/ n grito m. **be a far ~ from** (fig) distar mucho de. ● vi llorar; (call out) gritar. **~ off** rajarse. **~ baby** n llorón m

crypt /krɪpt/ n cripta f

cryptic /ˈkrɪptɪk/ a enigmático

crystal /ˈkrɪstl/ n cristal m. **~lize** vt cristalizar. ● vi cristalizarse

cub /kʌb/ n cachorro m. **C~** (Scout) n niño m explorador

Cuba /ˈkjuːbə/ n Cuba f. **~n** a & n cubano (m)

cubby-hole /ˈkʌbɪhəʊl/ n casilla f; (room) chiribitil m, cuchitril m

cub|e /kjuːb/ n cubo m. **~ic** a cúbico

cubicle /ˈkjuːbɪkl/ n cubículo m; (changing room) caseta f

cubis|m /ˈkjuːbɪzm/ n cubismo m. **~t** a & n cubista (m & f)

cuckold /ˈkʌkəʊld/ n cornudo m

cuckoo /ˈkʊkuː/ n cuco m, cuclillo m

cucumber /ˈkjuːkʌmbə(r)/ n pepino m

cuddl|e /ˈkʌdl/ vt abrazar. ● vi abrazarse. ● n abrazo m. **~y** a mimoso

cudgel /ˈkʌdʒl/ n porra f. ● vt (pt **cudgelled**) aporrear

cue¹ /kjuː/ n indicación f; (in theatre) pie m

cue² /kjuː/ n (in billiards) taco m

cuff /kʌf/ n puño m; (blow) bofetada f. **speak off the ~** hablar de improviso. ● vt abofetear. **~-link** n gemelo m

cul-de-sac /ˈkʌldəsæk/ n callejón m sin salida

culinary /ˈkʌlɪnərɪ/ a culinario

cull /kʌl/ vt coger (flowers); entresacar (animals)

culminat|e /ˈkʌlmɪneɪt/ vi culminar. **~ion** /-ˈneɪʃn/ n culminación f

culottes /kʊˈlɒts/ npl falda f pantalón

culprit /ˈkʌlprɪt/ n culpable m

cult /kʌlt/ n culto m

cultivat|e /ˈkʌltɪveɪt/ vt cultivar. **~ion** /-ˈveɪʃn/ n cultivo m; (fig) cultura f

cultur|al /ˈkʌltʃərəl/ a cultural. **~e** /ˈkʌltʃə(r)/ n cultura f; (bot etc) cultivo m. **~ed** a cultivado; (person) culto

cumbersome /ˈkʌmbəsəm/ a incómodo; (heavy) pesado

cumulative /ˈkjuːmjʊlətɪv/ a cumulativo

cunning /ˈkʌnɪŋ/ a astuto. ● n astucia f

cup /kʌp/ n taza f; (prize) copa f

cupboard /ˈkʌbəd/ n armario m

Cup Final /kʌpˈfaɪnl/ n final f del campeonato

cupful /ˈkʌpfʊl/ n taza f

cupidity /kjuːˈpɪdɪtɪ/ n codicia f

curable /ˈkjʊərəbl/ a curable

curate /ˈkjʊərət/ n coadjutor m

curator /kjʊəˈreɪtə(r)/ n (of museum) conservador m

curb /kɜːb/ n freno m. ● vt refrenar

curdle /ˈkɜːdl/ vt cuajar. ● vi cuajarse; (milk) cortarse

curds /kɜːdz/ npl cuajada f, requesón m

cure /kjʊə(r)/ vt curar. ● n cura f

curfew /ˈkɜːfjuː/ n queda f; (signal) toque m de queda

curio /ˈkjʊərɪəʊ/ n (pl **-os**) curiosidad f

curio|us /ˈkjʊərɪəs/ a curioso. **~sity** /-ˈɒsɪtɪ/ n curiosidad f

curl /kɜːl/ vt rizar (hair). **~ o.s. up** acurrucarse. ● vi (hair) rizarse; (paper) arrollarse. ● n rizo m. **~er** /ˈkɜːlə(r)/ n bigudí m, rulo m. **~y** /ˈkɜːlɪ/ a (-ier, -iest) rizado

currant /ˈkʌrənt/ n pasa f de Corinto

currency /ˈkʌrənsɪ/ n moneda f; (acceptance) uso m (corriente)

current /ˈkʌrənt/ a & n corriente (f). **~ events** asuntos mpl de actualidad. **~ly** adv actualmente

curriculum /kəˈrɪkjʊləm/ n (pl **-la**) programa m de estudios. **~ vitae** n curriculum m vitae

curry¹ /ˈkʌrɪ/ n curry m

curry² /ˈkʌrɪ/ vt. **~ favour with** congraciarse con

curse /kɜːs/ n maldición f; (oath) palabrota f. ● vt maldecir. ● vi decir palabrotas

cursory /ˈkɜːsərɪ/ a superficial

curt /kɜːt/ a brusco

curtail /kɜːˈteɪl/ vt abreviar; reducir (expenses)

curtain /ˈkɜːtn/ n cortina f; (in theatre) telón m

curtsy /ˈkɜːtsɪ/ n reverencia f. ● vi hacer una reverencia

curve /kɜːv/ n curva f. ● vt encurvar. ● vi encurvarse; (road) torcerse

cushion /'kʊʃn/ n cojín m. ● vt amortiguar ‹a blow›; (fig) proteger

cushy /'kʊʃɪ/ a (-ier, -iest) (fam) fácil

custard /'kʌstəd/ n natillas fpl

custodian /kʌ'stəʊdɪən/ n custodio m

custody /'kʌstədɪ/ n custodia f. be in ~ (jurid) estar detenido

custom /'kʌstəm/ n costumbre f; (com) clientela f

customary /'kʌstəmərɪ/ a acostumbrado

customer /'kʌstəmə(r)/ n cliente m

customs /'kʌstəmz/ npl aduana f. ~ officer n aduanero m

cut /kʌt/ vt/i (pt cut, pres p cutting) cortar; reducir ‹prices›. ● n corte m; (reduction) reducción f. ~ across atravesar. ~ back, ~ down reducir. ~ in interrumpir. ~ off cortar; (phone) desconectar; (fig) aislar. ~ out recortar; (omit) suprimir. ~ through atravesar. ~ up cortar en pedazos. be ~ up about (fig) afligirse por

cute /kju:t/ a (-er, -est) (fam) listo; (Amer) mono

cuticle /'kju:tɪkl/ n cutícula f

cutlery /'kʌtlərɪ/ n cubiertos mpl

cutlet /'kʌtlɪt/ n chuleta f

cut-price /'kʌtpraɪs/ a a precio reducido

cut-throat /'kʌtθrəʊt/ a despiadado

cutting /'kʌtɪŋ/ a cortante; ‹remark› mordaz. ● n (from newspaper) recorte m; (of plant) esqueje m

cyanide /'saɪənaɪd/ n cianuro m

cybernetics /saɪbə'netɪks/ n cibernética f

cyclamen /'sɪkləmən/ n ciclamen m

cycle /'saɪkl/ n ciclo m; (bicycle) bicicleta f. ● vi ir en bicicleta

cyclic(al) /'saɪklɪk(l)/ a cíclico

cycling /'saɪklɪŋ/ n ciclismo m. ~st n ciclista m & f

cyclone /'saɪkləʊn/ n ciclón m

cylinder /'sɪlɪndə(r)/ n cilindro m. ~er head (auto) n culata f. ~rical /'lɪndrɪkl/ a cilíndrico

cymbal /'sɪmbl/ n címbalo m

cynic /'sɪnɪk/ n cínico m. ~al a cínico. ~ism /-sɪzəm/ n cinismo m

cypress /'saɪprəs/ n ciprés m

Cypr|iot /'sɪprɪət/ a & n chipriota (m & f). ~us /'saɪprəs/ n Chipre f

cyst /sɪst/ n quiste m

czar /zɑ:(r)/ n zar m

Czech /tʃek/ a & n checo (m). the ~ Republic n la república f Checa

Czechoslovak /tʃekəʊ'sləʊvæk/ a & n (history) checoslovaco (m). ~ia /-ə'vækɪə/ n (history) Checoslovaquia f

D

dab /dæb/ vt (pt dabbed) tocar ligeramente. ● n toque m suave. a ~ of un poquito de

dabble /'dæbl/ vi. ~ in meterse (superficialmente) en. ~r /ə(r)/ n aficionado m

dad /dæd/ n (fam) papá m. ~dy n (children's use) papá m. ~dy-long-legs n típula f

daffodil /'dæfədɪl/ n narciso m

daft /dɑ:ft/ a (-er, -est) tonto

dagger /'dægə(r)/ n puñal m

dahlia /'deɪlɪə/ n dalia f

daily /'deɪlɪ/ a diario. ● adv diariamente, cada día. ● n diario m; (cleaner, fam) asistenta f

dainty /'deɪntɪ/ a (-ier, -iest) delicado

dairy /'deərɪ/ n vaquería f; (shop) lechería f. ● a lechero

dais /'deɪs/ n estrado m

daisy /'deɪzɪ/ n margarita f

dale /deɪl/ n valle m

dally /'dælɪ/ vi tardar; (waste time) perder el tiempo

dam /dæm/ n presa f. ● vt (pt dammed) embalsar

damag|e /'dæmɪdʒ/ n daño m; (pl, jurid) daños mpl y perjuicios mpl. ● vt (fig) dañar, estropear. ~ing a perjudicial

damask /'dæməsk/ n damasco m

dame /deɪm/ n (old use) dama f; (Amer, sl) chica f

damn /dæm/ vt condenar; (curse) maldecir. ● int ¡córcholis! ● a maldito. ● n. I don't care a ~ (no) me importa un comino. ~ation /-'neɪʃn/ n condenación f, perdición f

damp /dæmp/ n humedad f. ● a (-er, -est) húmedo. ● vt mojar; (fig) ahogar. ~er /'dæmpə(r)/ n apagador m, sordina f; (fig) aguafiestas m invar. ~ness n humedad f

damsel /'dæmzl/ n (old use) doncella f

dance /dɑ:ns/ vt/i bailar. ● n baile m. ~-hall n salón m de baile. ~r

/-ə(r)/ n bailador m; (professional) bailarín m

dandelion /'dændılaıən/ n diente m de león

dandruff /'dændrʌf/ n caspa f

dandy /'dændı/ n petimetre m

Dane /deın/ n danés m

danger /'deındʒə(r)/ n peligro m; (risk) riesgo m. ~ous a peligroso

dangle /'dæŋgl/ vt balancear. ● vi suspender, colgar

Danish /'deınıʃ/ a danés. ● m (lang) danés m

dank /dæŋk/ a (-er, -est) húmedo, malsano

dare /deə(r)/ vt desafiar. ● vi atreverse a. I ~ say probablemente. ● n desafío m

daredevil /'deədevl/ n atrevido m

daring /'deərıŋ/ a atrevido

dark /dɑːk/ a (-er, -est) oscuro; (gloomy) sombrío; (skin, hair) moreno. ● n oscuridad f; (nightfall) atardecer. in the ~ a oscuras. ~en /'dɑːkən/ vt oscurecer. ● vi oscurecerse. ~ horse n persona f de talentos desconocidos. ~ness n oscuridad f. ~room n cámara f oscura

darling /'dɑːlıŋ/ a querido. ● n querido m

darn /dɑːn/ vt zurcir

dart /dɑːt/ n dardo m. ● vi lanzarse; (run) precipitarse. ~board /'dɑːtbɔːd/ n blanco m. ~s npl los dardos mpl

dash /dæʃ/ vi precipitarse. ~ off marcharse apresuradamente. ~ out salir corriendo. ● vt lanzar; (break) romper; defraudar (hopes). ● n carrera f; (small amount) poquito m; (stroke) raya f. cut a ~ causar sensación

dashboard /'dæʃbɔːd/ n tablero m de mandos

dashing /'dæʃıŋ/ a vivo; (showy) vistoso

data /'deıtə/ npl datos mpl. ~ processing n proceso m de datos

date¹ /deıt/ n fecha f; (fam) cita f. to ~ hasta la fecha. ● vt fechar; (go out with, fam) salir con. ● vi datar; (be old-fashioned) quedar anticuado

date² /deıt/ n (fruit) dátil m

dated /'deıtıd/ a pasado de moda

daub /dɔːb/ vt embadurnar

daughter /'dɔːtə(r)/ n hija f. ~-in-law n nuera f

daunt /dɔːnt/ vt intimidar

dauntless /'dɔːntlıs/ a intrépido

dawdle /'dɔːdl/ vi andar despacio; (waste time) perder el tiempo. ~r /-ə(r)/ n rezagado m

dawn /dɔːn/ n amanecer m. ● vi amanecer; (fig) nacer. it ~ed on me that caí en la cuenta de que, comprendí que

day /deı/ n día m; (whole day) jornada f; (period) época f. ~-break n amanecer m. ~-dream n ensueño m. ● vi soñar despierto. ~-light /'deılaıt/ n luz f del día. ~-time /'deıtaım/ n día m

daze /deız/ vt aturdir. ● n aturdimiento m. in a ~ aturdido

dazzle /'dæzl/ vt deslumbrar

deacon /'diːkən/ n diácono m

dead /ded/ a muerto; (numb) entumecido. ~ centre justo en medio. ● adv completamente. ~ beat rendido. ~ on time justo a tiempo. ~ slow muy lento. stop ~ parar en seco. ~ n muertos mpl. in the ~ of night en plena noche. the ~ los muertos mpl. ~en /'dedn/ vt amortiguar (sound, blow); calmar (pain). ~ end n callejón m sin salida. ~ heat n empate m

deadline /'dedlaın/ n fecha f tope, fin m de plazo

deadlock /'dedlɒk/ n punto m muerto

deadly /'dedlı/ a (-ier, -iest) mortal; (harmful) nocivo; (dreary) aburrido

deadpan /'dedpæn/ a impasible

deaf /def/ a (-er, -est) sordo. ~en /'defn/ vt ensordecer. ~ening a ensordecedor. ~mute n sordomudo m. ~ness n sordera f

deal /diːl/ n (transaction) negocio m; (agreement) pacto m; (of cards) reparto m; (treatment) trato m; (amount) cantidad f. a great ~ muchísimo. ● vt (pt dealt) distribuir; (give ⟨a blow, cards⟩). ● vi. ~ in comerciar en. ~ with tratar con ⟨person⟩; tratar de ⟨subject etc⟩; ocuparse de ⟨problem etc⟩. ~er n comerciante m. ~ings /'diːlıŋz/ npl trato m

dean /diːn/ n deán m; (univ) decano m

dear /dıə(r)/ a (-er, -est) querido; (expensive) caro. ● n querido m; (child) pequeño m. ● adv caro. ● int ¡Dios mío! ~ me! ¡Dios mío! ~ly adv tiernamente; *(pay)* caro; *(very much)* muchísimo

dearth /dɜ:θ/ *n* escasez *f*

death /deθ/ *n* muerte *f*. ~ **duty** *n* derechos *mpl* reales. ~**ly** *a* mortal; ‹silence› profundo. ● *adv* como la muerte. ~**'s head** *n* calavera *f*. ~**trap** *n* lugar *m* peligroso.

débâcle /deɪˈbɑːkl/ *n* fracaso *m*, desastre *m*

debar /dɪˈbɑː(r)/ *vt* (*pt* **debarred**) excluir

debase /dɪˈbeɪs/ *vt* degradar

debat|able /dɪˈbeɪtəbl/ *a* discutible. ~**e** /dɪˈbeɪt/ *n* debate *m*. ● *vt* debatir, discutir. ● *vi* discutir; *(consider)* considerar

debauch /dɪˈbɔːtʃ/ *vt* corromper. ~**ery** *n* libertinaje *m*

debilit|ate /dɪˈbɪlɪteɪt/ *vt* debilitar. ~**y** /dɪˈbɪlətɪ/ *n* debilidad *f*

debit /ˈdebɪt/ *n* debe *m*. ● *vt*. ~ **s.o.'s account** cargar en cuenta a uno

debonair /debəˈneə(r)/ *a* alegre

debris /ˈdebriː/ *n* escombros *mpl*

debt /det/ *n* deuda *f*. **be in** ~ tener deudas. ~**or** *n* deudor *m*

debutante /ˈdebjuːtɑːnt/ *n* (old use) debutante *f*

decade /ˈdekeɪd/ *n* década *f*

decaden|ce /ˈdekədəns/ *n* decadencia *f*. ~**t** /ˈdekədənt/ *a* decadente

decant /dɪˈkænt/ *vt* decantar. ~**er** /ə(r)/ *n* garrafa *f*

decapitate /dɪˈkæpɪteɪt/ *vt* decapitar

decay /dɪˈkeɪ/ *vi* decaer; ‹tooth› cariarse. ● *n* decadencia *f*; *(of tooth)* caries *f*

deceased /dɪˈsiːst/ *a* difunto

deceit /dɪˈsiːt/ *n* engaño *m*. ~**ful** *a* falso. ~**fully** *adv* falsamente

deceive /dɪˈsiːv/ *vt* engañar

December /dɪˈsembə(r)/ *n* diciembre *m*

decen|cy /ˈdiːsənsɪ/ *n* decencia *f*. ~**t** /ˈdiːsnt/ *a* decente; *(good, fam)* bueno; *(kind, fam)* amable. ~**tly** *adv* decentemente

decentralize /diːˈsentrəlaɪz/ *vt* descentralizar

decepti|on /dɪˈsepʃn/ *n* engaño *m*. ~**ve** /dɪˈseptɪv/ *a* engañoso

decibel /ˈdesɪbel/ *n* decibel(io) *m*

decide /dɪˈsaɪd/ *vt/i* decidir. ~**d** /-ɪd/ *a* resuelto; *(unquestionable)*

indudable. ~**dly** /-ɪdlɪ/ *adv* decididamente; *(unquestionably)* indudablemente

decimal /ˈdesɪml/ *a & n* decimal *(f)*. ~ **point** *n* coma *f (decimal)*

decimate /ˈdesɪmeɪt/ *vt* diezmar

decipher /dɪˈsaɪfə(r)/ *vt* descifrar

decision /dɪˈsɪʒn/ *n* decisión *f*

decisive /dɪˈsaɪsɪv/ *a* decisivo; *(manner)* decidido. ~**ly** *adv* de manera decisiva

deck /dek/ *n* cubierta *f*; *(of cards, Amer)* baraja *f*. **top** ~ *(of bus)* imperial *m*. ● *vt* adornar. ~**-chair** *n* tumbona *f*

declaim /dɪˈkleɪm/ *vt* declamar

declar|ation /dekləˈreɪʃn/ *n* declaración *f*. ~**e** /dɪˈkleə(r)/ *vt* declarar

decline /dɪˈklaɪn/ *vt* rehusar; *(gram)* declinar. ● *vi* disminuir; *(deteriorate)* deteriorarse; *(fall)* bajar. ● *n* decadencia *f*; *(decrease)* disminución *f*; *(fall)* baja *f*

decode /diːˈkəʊd/ *vt* descifrar

decompos|e /diːkəmˈpəʊz/ *vt* descomponer. ● *vi* descomponerse. ~**i-tion** /-ɒmpəˈzɪʃn/ *n* descomposición *f*

décor /ˈdeɪkɔː(r)/ *n* decoración *f*

decorat|e /ˈdekəreɪt/ *vt* decorar; empapelar y pintar ‹room›. ~**ion** /-ˈreɪʃn/ *n* *(act)* decoración *f*; *(ornament)* adorno *m*. ~**ive** /-ətɪv/ *a* decorativo. ~**or** /ˈdekəreɪtə(r)/ *n* pintor *m* decorador. **interior** ~**or** decorador *m* de interiores

decorum /dɪˈkɔːrəm/ *n* decoro *m*

decoy /ˈdiːkɔɪ/ *n* señuelo *m*. /dɪˈkɔɪ/ *vt* atraer con señuelo

decrease /dɪˈkriːs/ *vt* disminuir. ● *vi* disminuirse. /ˈdiːkriːs/ *n* disminución *f*

decree /dɪˈkriː/ *n* decreto *m*; *(jurid)* sentencia *f*. ● *vt* (*pt* **decreed**) decretar

decrepit /dɪˈkrepɪt/ *a* decrépito

decry /dɪˈkraɪ/ *vt* denigrar

dedicat|e /ˈdedɪkeɪt/ *vt* dedicar. ~**ion** /-ˈkeɪʃn/ *n* dedicación *f*; *(in book)* dedicatoria *f*

deduce /dɪˈdjuːs/ *vt* deducir

deduct /dɪˈdʌkt/ *vt* deducir. ~**ion** /-ʃn/ *n* deducción *f*

deed /diːd/ *n* hecho *m*; *(jurid)* escritura *f*

deem /diːm/ *vt* juzgar, considerar

deep /di:p/ *a* (**-er**, **est**) *adv* profundo. **get into ~ waters** meterse en honduras. **go off the ~ end** enfadarse. ● *adv* profundamente. **be ~ in thought** estar absorto en sus pensamientos. **~en** /'di:pən/ *vt* profundizar. ● *vi* hacerse más profundo. **~freeze** *n* congelador *m*. **~ly** *adv* profundamente

deer /dɪə(r)/ *n invar* ciervo *m*

deface /dɪ'feɪs/ *vt* desfigurar

defamation /defə'meɪʃn/ *n* difamación *f*

default /dɪ'fɔ:lt/ *vi* faltar. ● *n*. **by ~** en rebeldía. **in ~ of** en ausencia de

defeat /dɪ'fi:t/ *vt* vencer; (*frustrate*) frustrar. ● *n* derrota *f*; (*of plan etc*) fracaso *m*. **~ism** /dɪ'fi:tɪzm/ *n* derrotismo *m*. **~ist** /dɪ'fi:tɪst/ *n* derrotista *m & f*

defect /'di:fekt/ *n* defecto *m*. /dɪ'fekt/ *vi* desertar. **~ to** pasar a. **~ion** /dɪ'fekʃn/ *n* deserción *f*. **~ive** /dɪ'fektɪv/ *a* defectuoso

defence /dɪ'fens/ *n* defensa *f*. **~less** *a* indefenso

defend /dɪ'fend/ *vt* defender. **~ant** *n* (*jurid*) acusado *m*

defensive /dɪ'fensɪv/ *a* defensivo. ● *n* defensiva *f*

defer /dɪ'fɜ:(r)/ *vt* (*pt* **deferred**) aplazar

deferen|ce /'defərəns/ *n* deferencia *f*. **~tial** /-'renʃl/ *a* deferente

defian|ce /dɪ'faɪəns/ *n* desafío *m*. **in ~ce** a despecho de. **~t** *a* desafiante. **~tly** *adv* con tono retador

deficien|cy /dɪ'fɪʃənsɪ/ *n* falta *f*. **~t** /dɪ'fɪʃnt/ *a* deficiente. **be ~t in** carecer de

deficit /'defɪsɪt/ *n* déficit *m*

defile /dɪ'faɪl/ *vt* ensuciar; (*fig*) deshonrar

define /dɪ'faɪn/ *vt* definir

definite /'defɪnɪt/ *a* determinado; (*clear*) claro; (*firm*) categórico. **~ly** *adv* claramente; (*certainly*) seguramente

definition /defɪ'nɪʃn/ *n* definición *f*

definitive /dɪ'fɪnətɪv/ *a* definitivo

deflat|e /dɪ'fleɪt/ *vt* desinflar. ● *vi* desinflarse. **~ion** /-ʃn/ *n* (*com*) deflación *f*

deflect /dɪ'flekt/ *vt* desviar. ● *vi* desviarse

deform /dɪ'fɔ:m/ *vt* deformar. **~ed** *a* deforme. **~ity** *n* deformidad *f*

defraud /dɪ'frɔ:d/ *vt* defraudar

defray /dɪ'freɪ/ *vt* pagar

defrost /di:'frɒst/ *vt* descongelar

deft /deft/ *a* (**-er**, **-est**) hábil. **~ness** *n* destreza *f*

defunct /dɪ'fʌŋkt/ *a* difunto

defuse /di:'fju:z/ *vt* desactivar ⟨*bomb*⟩; (*fig*) calmar

defy /dɪ'faɪ/ *vt* desafiar; (*resist*) resistir

degenerate /dɪ'dʒenəreɪt/ *vi* degenerar. /dɪ'dʒenərət/ *a & n* degenerado (*m*)

degrad|ation /degrə'deɪʃn/ *n* degradación *f*. **~e** /dɪ'greɪd/ *vt* degradar

degree /dɪ'gri:/ *n* grado *m*; (*univ*) licenciatura *f*; (*rank*) rango *m*. **to a certain ~** hasta cierto punto. **to a ~** (*fam*) sumamente

dehydrate /di:'haɪdreɪt/ *vt* deshidratar

de-ice /di:'aɪs/ *vt* descongelar

deign /deɪn/ *vi*. **~ to** dignarse

deity /'di:ɪtɪ/ *n* deidad *f*

deject|ed /dɪ'dʒektɪd/ *a* desanimado. **~ion** /-ʃn/ *n* abatimiento *m*

delay /dɪ'leɪ/ *vt* retardar; (*postpone*) aplazar. ● *vi* demorarse. ● *n* demora *f*

delectable /dɪ'lektəbl/ *a* deleitable

delegat|e /'delɪgeɪt/ *vt* delegar. /'delɪgət/ *n* delegado *m*. **~ion** /-'geɪʃn/ *n* delegación *f*

delet|e /dɪ'li:t/ *vt* tachar. **~ion** /-ʃn/ *n* tachadura *f*

deliberat|e /dɪ'lɪbəreɪt/ *vt/i* deliberar. /dɪ'lɪbərət/ *a* intencionado; (*steps etc*) pausado. **~ely** *adv* a propósito. **~ion** /-'reɪʃn/ *n* deliberación *f*

delica|cy /'delɪkəsɪ/ *n* delicadeza *f*; (*food*) manjar *m*; (*sweet food*) golosina *f*. **~te** /'delɪkət/ *a* delicado

delicatessen /delɪkə'tesn/ *n* charcutería *f* fina

delicious /dɪ'lɪʃəs/ *a* delicioso

delight /dɪ'laɪt/ *n* placer *m*. ● *vt* encantar. ● *vi* deleitarse. **~ed** *a* encantado. **~ful** *a* delicioso

delineat|e /dɪ'lɪnɪeɪt/ *vt* delinear. **~ion** /-'eɪʃn/ *n* delineación *f*

delinquen|cy /dɪ'lɪŋkwənsɪ/ *n* delincuencia *f*. **~t** /dɪ'lɪŋkwənt/ *a & n* delincuente (*m & f*)

deliri|ous /dɪ'lɪrɪəs/ *a* delirante. **~um** *n* delirio *m*

deliver /dɪ'lɪvə(r)/ *vt* entregar; (*utter*) pronunciar; (*aim*) lanzar; (*set free*) librar; (*med*) asistir al parto de.

~ance n liberación f. ~y n entrega f; (of post) reparto m; (med) parto m

delta /'deltə/ n (geog) delta m

delude /dɪ'luːd/ vt engañar. ~ o.s. engañarse

deluge /'deljuːdʒ/ n diluvio m

delusion /dɪ'luːʒn/ n ilusión f

de luxe /dɪ'lʌks/ a de lujo

delve /delv/ vi cavar. ~ into (investigate) investigar

demagogue /'deməgɒg/ n demagogo m

demand /dɪ'mɑːnd/ vt exigir. ● n petición f; (claim) reclamación f; (com) demanda f. in ~ muy popular, muy solicitado. on ~ a solicitud. ~ing a exigente. ~s npl exigencias fpl

demarcation /diːmɑː'keɪʃn/ n demarcación f

demean /dɪ'miːn/ vt. ~ o.s. degradarse. ~our /dɪ'miːnə(r)/ n conducta f

demented /dɪ'mentɪd/ a demente

demerara /demə'reərə/ n. ~ (sugar) n azúcar m moreno

demise /dɪ'maɪz/ n fallecimiento m

demo /'deməʊ/ n (pl -os) (fam) manifestación f

demobilize /diː'məʊbəlaɪz/ vt desmovilizar

democra|cy /dɪ'mɒkrəsɪ/ n democracia f. ~t /'deməkræt/ n demócrata m & f. ~tic /-'krætɪk/ a democrático

demoli|sh /dɪ'mɒlɪʃ/ vt derribar. ~tion /demə'lɪʃn/ n demolición f

demon /'diːmən/ n demonio m

demonstrat|e /'demənstreɪt/ vt demostrar. ● vi manifestarse, hacer una manifestación. ~ion /-'streɪʃn/ n demostración f; (pol etc) manifestación f

demonstrative /dɪ'mɒnstrətɪv/ a demostrativo

demonstrator /'demənstreɪtə(r)/ n demostrador m; (pol etc) manifestante m & f

demoralize /dɪ'mɒrəlaɪz/ vt desmoralizar

demote /dɪ'məʊt/ vt degradar

demure /dɪ'mjʊə(r)/ a recatado

den /den/ n (of animal) guarida f, madriguera f

denial /dɪ'naɪəl/ n denegación f; (statement) desmentimiento m

denigrate /'denɪgreɪt/ vt denigrar

denim /'denɪm/ n dril m (de algodón azul grueso). ~s npl pantalón m vaquero

Denmark /'denmɑːk/ n Dinamarca f

denomination /dɪnɒmɪ'neɪʃn/ n denominación f; (relig) secta f

denote /dɪ'nəʊt/ vt denotar

denounce /dɪ'naʊns/ vt denunciar

dens|e /dens/ a (-er, -est) espeso; (person) torpe. ~ely adv densamente. ~ity n densidad f

dent /dent/ n abolladura f. ● vt abollar

dental /'dentl/ a dental. ~ surgeon n dentista m & f

dentist /'dentɪst/ n dentista m & f. ~ry n odontología f

denture /'dentʃə(r)/ n dentadura f postiza

denude /dɪ'njuːd/ vt desnudar; (fig) despojar

denunciation /dɪnʌnsɪ'eɪʃn/ n denuncia f

deny /dɪ'naɪ/ vt negar; desmentir (rumour); (disown) renegar

deodorant /diː'əʊdərənt/ a & n desodorante (m)

depart /dɪ'pɑːt/ vi marcharse; (train etc) salir. ~ from apartarse de

department /dɪ'pɑːtmənt/ n departamento m; (com) sección f. ~ store n grandes almacenes mpl

departure /dɪ'pɑːtʃə(r)/ n partida f; (of train etc) salida f. ~ from (fig) desviación f

depend /dɪ'pend/ vi depender. ~ on depender de; (rely) contar con. ~able a seguro. ~ant n /dɪ'pendənt/ n familiar m & f dependiente. ~ence n dependencia f. ~ent a dependiente. be ~ent on depender de

depict /dɪ'pɪkt/ vt pintar; (in words) describir

deplete /dɪ'pliːt/ vt agotar

deplor|able /dɪ'plɔːrəbl/ a lamentable. ~e /dɪ'plɔː(r)/ vt lamentar

deploy /dɪ'plɔɪ/ vt desplegar. ● vi desplegarse

depopulate /diː'pɒpjʊleɪt/ vt despoblar

deport /dɪ'pɔːt/ vt deportar. ~ation /diːpɔː'teɪʃn/ n deportación f

depose /dɪ'pəʊz/ vt deponer

deposit /dɪ'pɒzɪt/ vt (pt deposited) depositar. ● n depósito m. ~or n depositante m & f

depot /'depəʊ/ n depósito m; (Amer) estación f

deprav|e /dɪˈpreɪv/ vt depravar. ~ity /-ˈprævətɪ/ n depravación f

deprecate /ˈdeprɪkeɪt/ vt desaprobar

depreciat|e /dɪˈpriːʃɪeɪt/ vt depreciar. ● vi depreciarse. ~ion /-ˈeɪʃn/ n depreciación f

depress /dɪˈpres/ vt deprimir; (press down) apretar. ~ion /-ʃn/ n depresión f

depriv|ation /deprɪˈveɪʃn/ n privación f. ~e /dɪˈpraɪv/ vt. ~ of privar de

depth /depθ/ n profundidad f. be out of one's ~ perder pie; (fig) meterse en honduras. in the ~s of en lo más hondo de

deputation /depjʊˈteɪʃn/ n diputación f

deputize /ˈdepjʊtaɪz/ vi. ~ for sustituir a

deputy /ˈdepjʊtɪ/ n sustituto m. ~ chairman n vicepresidente m

derail /dɪˈreɪl/ vt hacer descarrilar. ~ment n descarrilamiento m

deranged /dɪˈreɪndʒd/ a (mind) trastornado

derelict /ˈderəlɪkt/ a abandonado

deri|de /dɪˈraɪd/ vt mofarse de. ~sion /-ˈrɪʒn/ n mofa f. ~sive a burlón. ~sory /dɪˈraɪsərɪ/ a mofador; (offer etc) irrisorio

deriv|ation /derɪˈveɪʃn/ n derivación f. ~ative /dɪˈrɪvətɪv/ a & n derivado (m). ~e /dɪˈraɪv/ vt/i derivar

derogatory /dɪˈrɒɡətrɪ/ a despectivo

derv /dɜːv/ n gasóleo m

descen|d /dɪˈsend/ vt/i descender, bajar. ~dant n descendiente m & f. ~t /dɪˈsent/ n descenso m; (lineage) descendencia f

descri|be /dɪsˈkraɪb/ vt describir. ~ption /-ˈkrɪpʃn/ n descripción f. ~ptive /-ˈkrɪptɪv/ a descriptivo

desecrat|e /ˈdesɪkreɪt/ vt profanar. ~ion /-ˈkreɪʃn/ n profanación f

desert[1] /dɪˈzɜːt/ vt abandonar. ● vi (mil) desertar

desert[2] /ˈdezət/ a & n desierto (m)

deserter /dɪˈzɜːtə(r)/ n desertor m

deserts /dɪˈzɜːts/ npl lo merecido. get one's ~ llevarse su merecido

deserv|e /dɪˈzɜːv/ vt merecer. ~edly adv merecidamente. ~ing a (person) digno de; (action) meritorio

design /dɪˈzaɪn/ n diseño m; (plan) proyecto m; (pattern) modelo m; (aim) propósito m. have ~s on poner la mira en. ● vt diseñar; (plan) proyectar

designat|e /ˈdezɪɡneɪt/ vt designar; (appoint) nombrar. ~ion /-ˈneɪʃn/ n denominación f; (appointment) nombramiento m

designer /dɪˈzaɪnə(r)/ n diseñador m; (of clothing) modisto m; (in theatre) escenógrafo m

desirab|ility /dɪzaɪərəˈbɪlətɪ/ n conveniencia f. ~le /dɪˈzaɪrəbl/ a deseable

desire /dɪˈzaɪə(r)/ n deseo m. ● vt desear

desist /dɪˈzɪst/ vi desistir

desk /desk/ n escritorio m; (at school) pupitre m; (in hotel) recepción f; (com) caja f

desolat|e /ˈdesələt/ a desolado; (uninhabited) deshabitado. ~ion /-ˈleɪʃn/ n desolación f

despair /dɪˈspeə(r)/ n desesperación f. ● vi. ~ of desesperarse de

desperat|e /ˈdespərət/ a desesperado; (dangerous) peligroso. ~ely adv desesperadamente. ~ion /-ˈreɪʃn/ n desesperación f

despicable /dɪˈspɪkəbl/ a despreciable

despise /dɪˈspaɪz/ vt despreciar

despite /dɪˈspaɪt/ prep a pesar de

desponden|cy /dɪˈspɒndənsɪ/ n abatimiento m. ~t /dɪˈspɒndənt/ a desanimado

despot /ˈdespɒt/ n déspota m

dessert /dɪˈzɜːt/ n postre m. ~spoon n cuchara f de postre

destination /destɪˈneɪʃn/ n destino m

destine /ˈdestɪn/ vt destinar

destiny /ˈdestɪnɪ/ n destino m

destitute /ˈdestɪtjuːt/ a indigente. ~ of desprovisto de

destroy /dɪˈstrɔɪ/ vt destruir

destroyer /dɪˈstrɔɪə(r)/ n (naut) destructor m

destructi|on /dɪˈstrʌkʃn/ n destrucción f. ~ve a destructivo

desultory /ˈdesəltrɪ/ a irregular

detach /dɪˈtætʃ/ vt separar. ~able a separable. ~ed a separado. ~ed house n chalet m. ~ment /dɪˈtætʃmənt/ n separación f; (mil) destacamento m; (fig) indiferencia f

detail /'di:teɪl/ n detalle m. ● vt detallar; (mil) destacar. ~ed a detallado

detain /dɪ'teɪn/ vt detener; (delay) retener. ~ee /di:ter'ni:/ n detenido m

detect /dɪ'tekt/ vt percibir; (discover) descubrir. ~ion /-ʃn/ n descubrimiento m, detección f. ~or n detector m

detective /dɪ'tektɪv/ n detective m. ~ story n novela f policíaca

detention /dɪ'tenʃn/ n detención f

deter /dɪ'tɜ:(r)/ vt (pt deterred) disuadir; (prevent) impedir

detergent /dɪ'tɜ:dʒənt/ a & n detergente (m)

deteriorat|e /dɪ'tɪərɪəreɪt/ vi deteriorarse. ~ion /-'reɪʃn/ n deterioro m

determination /dɪtɜ:mɪ'neɪʃn/ n determinación f

determine /dɪ'tɜ:mɪn/ vt determinar; (decide) decidir. ~d a determinado; (resolute) resuelto

deterrent /dɪ'terənt/ n fuerza f de disuasión

detest /dɪ'test/ vt aborrecer. ~able a odioso

detonat|e /'detəneɪt/ vt hacer detonar. ● vi detonar. ~ion /-'neɪʃn/ n detonación f. ~or n detonador m

detour /'di:tʊə(r)/ n desviación f

detract /dɪ'trækt/ vi. ~ from (lessen) disminuir

detriment /'detrɪmənt/ n perjuicio m. ~al /-'mentl/ a perjudicial

devalu|ation /di:vælju'eɪʃn/ n desvalorización f. ~e /di:'vælju:/ vt desvalorizar

devastat|e /'devəsteɪt/ vt devastar. ~ing a devastador; (fig) arrollador

develop /dɪ'veləp/ vt desarrollar; contraer (illness); urbanizar (land). ● vi desarrollarse; (show) aparecerse. ~er n (foto) revelador m. ~ing country n país m en vías de desarrollo. ~ment n desarrollo m. (new) ~ment novedad f

deviant /'di:vɪənt/ a desviado

deviat|e /'di:vɪeɪt/ vi desviarse. ~ion /-'eɪʃn/ n desviación f

device /dɪ'vaɪs/ n dispositivo m; (scheme) estratagema f

devil /'devl/ n diablo m. ~ish a diabólico

devious /'di:vɪəs/ a tortuoso

devise /dɪ'vaɪz/ vt idear

devoid /dɪ'vɔɪd/ a. ~ of desprovisto de

devolution /di:və'lu:ʃn/ n descentralización f; (of power) delegación f

devot|e /dɪ'vəʊt/ vt dedicar. ~ed a leal. ~edly adv con devoción f. ~ee /devə'ti:/ n partidario m. ~ion /-ʃn/ n dedicación f. ~ions npl (relig) oraciones fpl

devour /dɪ'vaʊə(r)/ vt devorar

devout /dɪ'vaʊt/ a devoto

dew /dju:/ n rocío m

dext|erity /dek'sterəti/ n destreza f. ~(e)rous /'dekstrəs/ a diestro

diabet|es /daɪə'bi:ti:z/ n diabetes f. ~ic /-'betɪk/ a & n diabético (m)

diabolical /daɪə'bɒlɪkl/ a diabólico

diadem /'daɪədem/ n diadema f

diagnos|e /'daɪəgnəʊz/ vt diagnosticar. ~is /,daɪəg'nəʊsɪs/ n (pl -oses /-si:z/) diagnóstico m

diagonal /daɪ'ægənl/ a & n diagonal (f)

diagram /'daɪəgræm/ n diagrama m

dial /'daɪəl/ n cuadrante m; (on phone) disco m. ● vt (pt dialled) marcar

dialect /'daɪəlekt/ n dialecto m

dial: ~ling code n prefijo m. ~ling tone n señal f para marcar

dialogue /'daɪəlɒg/ n diálogo m

diameter /daɪ'æmɪtə(r)/ n diámetro m

diamond /'daɪəmənd/ n diamante m; (shape) rombo m. ~s npl (cards) diamantes mpl

diaper /'daɪəpə(r)/ n (Amer) pañal m

diaphanous /daɪ'æfənəs/ a diáfano

diaphragm /'daɪəfræm/ n diafragma m

diarrhoea /daɪə'rɪə/ n diarrea f

diary /'daɪərɪ/ n diario m; (book) agenda f

diatribe /'daɪətraɪb/ n diatriba f

dice /daɪs/ n invar dado m. ● vt (culin) cortar en cubitos

dicey /'daɪsɪ/ a (sl) arriesgado

dictat|e /dɪk'teɪt/ vt/i dictar. ~es /'dɪkteɪts/ npl dictados mpl. ~ion /dɪk'teɪʃn/ n dictado m

dictator /dɪk'teɪtə(r)/ n dictador m. ~ship n dictadura f

diction /'dɪkʃn/ n dicción f

dictionary /'dɪkʃənərɪ/ n diccionario m

did /dɪd/ see **do**

didactic /daɪ'dæktɪk/ a didáctico

diddle /'dɪdl/ vt (sl) estafar

didn't /'dɪdnt/ = **did not**

die[1] /daɪ/ vi (pres p **dying**) morir. **be dying** to morirse por. ~ **down** disminuir. ~ **out** extinguirse

die[2] /daɪ/ n (tec) cuño m

die-hard /'daɪhɑːd/ n intransigente m & f

diesel /'diːzl/ n (fuel) gasóleo m. ~ **engine** n motor m diesel

diet /'daɪət/ n alimentación f; (restricted) régimen m. ● vi estar a régimen. ~**etic** /daɪə'tetɪk/ a dietético. ~**itian** n dietético m

differ /'dɪfə(r)/ vi ser distinto; (disagree) no estar de acuerdo. ~**ence** /'dɪfrəns/ n diferencia f; (disagreement) desacuerdo m. ~**ent** /'dɪfrənt/ a distinto, diferente

differentia|l /dɪfə'renʃl/ a & n diferencial (f). ~**te** /dɪfə'renʃɪeɪt/ vt diferenciar. ● vi diferenciarse

differently /'dɪfrəntlɪ/ adv de otra manera

difficult /'dɪfɪkəlt/ a difícil. ~**y** n dificultad f

diffiden|ce /'dɪfɪdəns/ n falta de confianza. ~**t** /'dɪfɪdənt/ a que falta confianza

diffus|e /dɪ'fjuːs/ a difuso. /dɪ'fjuːz/ vt difundir. ● vi difundirse. ~**ion** /-ʒn/ n difusión f

dig /dɪg/ n (poke) empujón m; (poke with elbow) codazo m; (remark) indirecta f; (archaeol) excavación f. ● vt (pt **dug**, pres p **digging**) cavar; (thrust) empujar. ● vi cavar. ~ **out** extraer. ~ **up** desenterrar. ~**s** npl (fam) alojamiento m

digest /'daɪdʒest/ n resumen m. ● vt digerir. ~**ible** a digerible. ~**ion** /-∫n/ n digestión f. ~**ive** a digestivo

digger /'dɪgə(r)/ n (mec) excavadora f

digit /'dɪdʒɪt/ n cifra f; (finger) dedo m. ~**al** /'dɪdʒɪtl/ a digital

dignif|ied /'dɪgnɪfaɪd/ a solemne. ~**y** /'dɪgnɪfaɪ/ vt dignificar

dignitary /'dɪgnɪtərɪ/ n dignatario m

dignity /'dɪgnɪtɪ/ n dignidad f

digress /daɪ'gres/ vi divagar. ~ **from** apartarse de. ~**ion** /-∫n/ n digresión f

dike /daɪk/ n dique m

dilapidated /dɪ'læpɪdeɪtɪd/ a ruinoso

dilat|e /daɪ'leɪt/ vt dilatar. ● vi dilatarse. ~**ion** /-∫n/ n dilatación f

dilatory /'dɪlətərɪ/ a dilatorio, lento

dilemma /daɪ'lemə/ n dilema m

diligen|ce /'dɪlɪdʒəns/ n diligencia f. ~**t** /'dɪlɪdʒənt/ a diligente

dilly-dally /'dɪlɪdælɪ/ vi (fam) perder el tiempo

dilute /daɪ'ljuːt/ vt diluir

dim /dɪm/ a (**dimmer**, **dimmest**) (weak) débil; (dark) oscuro; (stupid, fam) torpe. ● vt (pt **dimmed**) amortiguar. ● vi apagarse. ~ **the headlights** bajar los faros

dime /daɪm/ n (Amer) moneda f de diez centavos

dimension /daɪ'menʃn/ n dimensión f

diminish /dɪ'mɪnɪʃ/ vt/i disminuir

diminutive /dɪ'mɪnjʊtɪv/ a diminuto. ● n diminutivo m

dimness /'dɪmnɪs/ n debilidad f; (of room etc) oscuridad f

dimple /'dɪmpl/ n hoyuelo m

din /dɪn/ n jaleo m

dine /daɪn/ vi cenar. ~**r** /-ə(r)/ n comensal m & f; (rail) coche m restaurante

dinghy /'dɪŋgɪ/ n (inflatable) bote m neumático

din|giness /'dɪndʒɪnɪs/ n suciedad f. ~**y** /'dɪndʒɪ/ a (-**ier**, -**iest**) miserable, sucio

dining-room /'daɪnɪŋruːm/ n comedor m

dinner /'dɪnə(r)/ n cena f. ~-**jacket** n esmoquin m. ~ **party** n cena f

dinosaur /'daɪnəsɔː(r)/ n dinosaurio m

dint /dɪnt/ n. **by** ~ **of** a fuerza de

diocese /'daɪəsɪs/ n diócesis f

dip /dɪp/ vt (pt **dipped**) sumergir. ● vi bajar. ~ **into** hojear ⟨book⟩. ● n (slope) inclinación f; (in sea) baño m

diphtheria /dɪf'θɪərɪə/ n difteria f

diphthong /'dɪfθɒŋ/ n diptongo m

diploma /dɪ'pləʊmə/ n diploma m

diplomacy /dɪ'pləʊməsɪ/ n diplomacia f

diplomat /'dɪpləmæt/ n diplomático m. ~**ic** /-'mætɪk/ a diplomático

dipstick /'dɪpstɪk/ n (auto) varilla f del nivel de aceite

dire /daɪə(r)/ a (-**er**, -**est**) terrible; ⟨need, poverty⟩ extremo

direct /dɪ'rekt/ a directo. ● adv directamente. ● vt dirigir; (show the way) indicar

direction /dɪ'rekʃn/ n dirección f. ~**s** npl instrucciones fpl

directly /dɪ'rektlɪ/ adv directamente; (at once) en seguida. ● conj (fam) en cuanto

director /dɪˈrektə(r)/ n director m

directory /dɪˈrektərɪ/ n guía f

dirge /dɜːdʒ/ n canto m fúnebre

dirt /dɜːt/ n suciedad f. ~-**track** n (sport) pista f de ceniza. ~**y** /'dɜːtɪ/ a (-**ier**, -**iest**) sucio. ~**y trick** n mala jugada f. ~**y word** n palabrota f. ● vt ensuciar

disability /dɪsəˈbɪlətɪ/ n invalidez f

disable /dɪsˈeɪbl/ vt incapacitar. ~**d** a minusválido

disabuse /dɪsəˈbjuːz/ vt desengañar

disadvantage /dɪsədˈvɑːntɪdʒ/ n desventaja f. ~**d** a desventajado

disagree /dɪsəˈgriː/ vi no estar de acuerdo; ⟨food, climate⟩ sentar mal a. ~**able** /dɪsəˈgriːəbl/ a desagradable. ~**ment** n desacuerdo m; ⟨quarrel⟩ riña f

disappear /dɪsəˈpɪə(r)/ vi desaparecer. ~**ance** n desaparición f

disappoint /dɪsəˈpɔɪnt/ vt desilusionar, decepcionar. ~**ment** n desilusión f, decepción f

disapprov|al /dɪsəˈpruːvl/ n desaprobación f. ~**e** /dɪsəˈpruːv/ vi. ~ **of** desaprobar

disarm /dɪsˈɑːm/ vt/i desarmar. ~**a-ment** n desarme m

disarray /dɪsəˈreɪ/ n desorden m

disast|er /dɪˈzɑːstə(r)/ n desastre m. ~**rous** a catastrófico

disband /dɪsˈbænd/ vt disolver. ● vi disolverse

disbelief /dɪsbɪˈliːf/ n incredulidad f

disc /dɪsk/ n disco m

discard /dɪsˈkɑːd/ vt descartar; abandonar ⟨beliefs etc⟩

discern /dɪˈsɜːn/ vt percibir. ~**ible** a perceptible. ~**ing** a perspicaz

discharge /dɪsˈtʃɑːdʒ/ vt descargar; cumplir ⟨duty⟩; ⟨dismiss⟩ despedir; poner en libertad ⟨prisoner⟩; ⟨mil⟩ licenciar. /'dɪstʃɑːdʒ/ n descarga f; ⟨med⟩ secreción f; ⟨mil⟩ licenciamiento m; ⟨dismissal⟩ despedida f

disciple /dɪˈsaɪpl/ n discípulo m

disciplin|arian /dɪsəplɪˈneərɪən/ n ordenancista m & f. ~**ary** a disciplinario. ~**e** /'dɪsɪplɪn/ n disciplina f. ● vt disciplinar; ⟨punish⟩ castigar

disc jockey /'dɪskdʒɒkɪ/ n ⟨on radio⟩ pinchadiscos m & f invar

disclaim /dɪsˈkleɪm/ vt desconocer. ~**er** n renuncia f

disclos|e /dɪsˈkləʊz/ vt revelar. ~**ure** /-ʒə(r)/ n revelación f

disco /'dɪskəʊ/ n (pl -**os**) ⟨fam⟩ discoteca f

discolo|ur /dɪsˈkʌlə(r)/ vt decolorar. ● vi decolorarse. ~**ration** /-'reɪʃn/ n decoloración f

discomfort /dɪsˈkʌmfət/ n malestar m; ⟨lack of comfort⟩ incomodidad f

disconcert /dɪskənˈsɜːt/ vt desconcertar

disconnect /dɪskəˈnekt/ vt separar; ⟨elec⟩ desconectar

disconsolate /dɪsˈkɒnsələt/ a desconsolado

discontent /dɪskənˈtent/ n descontento m. ~**ed** a descontento

discontinue /dɪskənˈtɪnjuː/ vt interrumpir

discord /'dɪskɔːd/ n discordia f; ⟨mus⟩ disonancia f. ~**ant** /-'skɔːd-ənt/ a discorde; ⟨mus⟩ disonante

discothèque /'dɪskətek/ n discoteca f

discount /'dɪskaʊnt/ n descuento m. /dɪsˈkaʊnt/ vt hacer caso omiso de; ⟨com⟩ descontar

discourage /dɪsˈkʌrɪdʒ/ vt desanimar; ⟨dissuade⟩ disuadir

discourse /'dɪskɔːs/ n discurso m

discourteous /dɪsˈkɜːtɪəs/ a descortés

discover /dɪsˈkʌvə(r)/ vt descubrir. ~**y** n descubrimiento m

discredit /dɪsˈkredɪt/ vt (pt discredited) desacreditar. ● n descrédito m

discreet /dɪsˈkriːt/ a discreto. ~**ly** adv discretamente

discrepancy /dɪˈskrepənsɪ/ n discrepancia f

discretion /dɪˈskreʃn/ n discreción f

discriminat|e /dɪsˈkrɪmɪneɪt/ vt/i discriminar. ~**e between** distinguir entre. ~**ing** a perspicaz. ~**ion** /-'neɪʃn/ n discernimiento m; ⟨bias⟩ discriminación f

discus /'dɪskəs/ n disco m

discuss /dɪsˈkʌs/ vt discutir. ~**ion** /-ʃn/ n discusión f

disdain /dɪsˈdeɪn/ n desdén m. ● vt desdeñar. ~**ful** a desdeñoso

disease /dɪˈziːz/ n enfermedad f. ~**d** a enfermo

disembark /dɪsɪmˈbɑːk/ vt/i desembarcar

disembodied /dɪsɪmˈbɒdɪd/ a incorpóreo

disenchant /dɪsɪn'tʃɑːnt/ *vt* desencantar. ∼**ment** *n* desencanto *m*

disengage /dɪsɪn'geɪdʒ/ *vt* soltar. ∼ **the clutch** desembragar. ∼**ment** *n* soltura *f*

disentangle /dɪsɪn'tæŋgl/ *vt* desenredar

disfavour /dɪs'feɪvə(r)/ *n* desaprobación *f*. **fall into** ∼ ⟨*person*⟩ caer en desgracia; ⟨*custom, word*⟩ caer en desuso

disfigure /dɪs'fɪgə(r)/ *vt* desfigurar

disgorge /dɪs'gɔːdʒ/ *vt* arrojar; ⟨*river*⟩ descargar; ⟨*fig*⟩ restituir

disgrace /dɪs'greɪs/ *n* deshonra *f*; ⟨*disfavour*⟩ desgracia *f*. ● *vt* deshonrar. ∼**ful** *a* vergonzoso

disgruntled /dɪs'grʌntld/ *a* descontento

disguise /dɪs'gaɪz/ *vt* disfrazar. ● *n* disfraz *m*. **in** ∼ disfrazado

disgust /dɪs'gʌst/ *n* repugnancia *f*, asco *m*. ● *vt* repugnar, dar asco. ∼**ing** *a* repugnante, asqueroso

dish /dɪʃ/ *n* plato *m*. ● *vt*. ∼ **up** servir. ∼**cloth** /'dɪʃklɒθ/ *n* bayeta *f*

dishearten /dɪs'hɑːtn/ *vt* desanimar

dishevelled /dɪ'ʃevld/ *a* desaliñado; ⟨*hair*⟩ despeinado

dishonest /dɪs'ɒnɪst/ *a* ⟨*person*⟩ poco honrado; ⟨*means*⟩ fraudulento. ∼**y** *n* falta *f* de honradez

dishonour /dɪs'ɒnə(r)/ *n* deshonra *f*. ● *vt* deshonrar. ∼**able** *a* deshonroso. ∼**ably** *adv* deshonrosamente

dishwasher /'dɪʃwɒʃə(r)/ *n* lavaplatos *m* & *f*

disillusion /dɪsɪ'luːʒn/ *vt* desilusionar. ∼**ment** *n* desilusión *f*

disincentive /dɪsɪn'sentɪv/ *n* freno *m*

disinclined /dɪsɪn'klaɪnd/ *a* poco dispuesto

disinfect /dɪsɪn'fekt/ *vt* desinfectar. ∼**ant** *n* desinfectante *m*

disinherit /dɪsɪn'herɪt/ *vt* desheredar

disintegrate /dɪs'ɪntɪgreɪt/ *vt* desintegrar. ● *vi* desintegrarse

disinterested /dɪs'ɪntrəstɪd/ *a* desinteresado

disjointed /dɪs'dʒɔɪntɪd/ *a* inconexo

disk /dɪsk/ *n* disco *m*

dislike /dɪs'laɪk/ *n* aversión *f*. ● *vt* tener aversión a

dislocat|e /'dɪsləkeɪt/ *vt* dislocar(se) ⟨*limb*⟩. ∼**ion** /-'keɪʃn/ *n* dislocación *f*

dislodge /dɪs'lɒdʒ/ *vt* sacar; ⟨*oust*⟩ desalojar

disloyal /dɪs'lɔɪəl/ *a* desleal. ∼**ty** *n* deslealtad *f*

dismal /'dɪzməl/ *a* triste; ⟨*bad*⟩ fatal

dismantle /dɪs'mæntl/ *vt* desarmar

dismay /dɪs'meɪ/ *n* consternación *f*. ● *vt* consternar

dismiss /dɪs'mɪs/ *vt* despedir; ⟨*reject*⟩ rechazar. ∼**al** *n* despedida *f*; ⟨*of idea*⟩ abandono *m*

dismount /dɪs'maʊnt/ *vi* apearse

disobedien|ce /dɪsə'biːdɪəns/ *n* desobediencia *f*. ∼**t** /dɪsə'biːdɪənt/ *a* desobediente

disobey /dɪsə'beɪ/ *vt/i* desobedecer

disorder /dɪs'ɔːdə(r)/ *n* desorden *m*; ⟨*ailment*⟩ trastorno *m*. ∼**ly** *a* desordenado

disorganize /dɪs'ɔːgənaɪz/ *vt* desorganizar

disorientate /dɪs'ɔːrɪənteɪt/ *vt* desorientar

disown /dɪs'əʊn/ *vt* repudiar

disparaging /dɪs'pærɪdʒɪŋ/ *a* despreciativo. ∼**ly** *adv* con desprecio

disparity /dɪs'pærətɪ/ *n* disparidad *f*

dispassionate /dɪs'pæʃənət/ *a* desapasionado

dispatch /dɪs'pætʃ/ *vt* enviar. ● *n* envío *m*; ⟨*report*⟩ despacho *m*. ∼**rider** *n* correo *m*

dispel /dɪs'pel/ *vt* (*pt* **dispelled**) disipar

dispensable /dɪs'pensəbl/ *a* prescindible

dispensary /dɪs'pensərɪ/ *n* farmacia *f*

dispensation /dɪspen'seɪʃn/ *n* distribución *f*; ⟨*relig*⟩ dispensa *f*

dispense /dɪs'pens/ *vt* distribuir; ⟨*med*⟩ preparar; ⟨*relig*⟩ dispensar; administrar ⟨*justice*⟩. ∼ **with** prescindir de. ∼**r** /-ə(r)/ *n* ⟨*mec*⟩ distribuidor *m* automático; ⟨*med*⟩ farmacéutico *m*

dispers|al /dɪs'pɜːsl/ *n* dispersión *f*. ∼**e** /dɪ'spɜːs/ *vt* dispersar. ● *vi* dispersarse

dispirited /dɪs'pɪrɪtɪd/ *a* desanimado

displace /dɪs'pleɪs/ *vt* desplazar

display /dɪs'pleɪ/ *vt* mostrar; exhibir ⟨*goods*⟩; manifestar ⟨*feelings*⟩. ● *n* exposición *f*, ⟨*of feelings*⟩ manifestación *f*; ⟨*pej*⟩ ostentación *f*

displeas|e /dɪs'pliːz/ *vt* desagradar. **be** ∼**ed with** estar disgustado con. ∼**ure** /-'pleʒə(r)/ *n* desagrado *m*

dispos|able /dɪsˈpəʊzəbl/ a desechable. ~**al** n (of waste) eliminación f. **at s.o.'s** ~**al** a la disposición de uno. ~**e** /dɪsˈpəʊz/ vt disponer. **be well** ~**ed towards** estar bien dispuesto hacia. ● vi. ~**e of** deshacerse de

disposition /dɪspəˈzɪʃn/ n disposición f

disproportionate /dɪsprəˈpɔːʃənət/ a desproporcionado

disprove /dɪsˈpruːv/ vt refutar

dispute /dɪsˈpjuːt/ vt disputar. ● n disputa f. **in** ~ disputado

disqualif|ication /dɪskwɒlɪfɪˈkeɪʃn/ n descalificación f. ~**y** /dɪsˈkwɒlɪfaɪ/ vt incapacitar. (sport) descalificar

disquiet /dɪsˈkwaɪət/ n inquietud f

disregard /dɪsrɪˈɡɑːd/ vt no hacer caso de. ● n indiferencia f (**for** a)

disrepair /dɪsrɪˈpeə(r)/ n mal estado m

disreputable /dɪsˈrepjʊtəbl/ a de mala fama

disrepute /dɪsrɪˈpjuːt/ n descrédito m

disrespect /dɪsrɪsˈpekt/ n falta f de respeto

disrobe /dɪsˈrəʊb/ vt desvestir. ● vi desvestirse

disrupt /dɪsˈrʌpt/ vt interrumpir; trastornar (plans). ~**ion** /-ʃn/ n interrupción f; (disorder) desorganización f. ~**ive** a desbaratador

dissatisfaction /dɪsætɪsˈfækʃn/ n descontento m

dissatisfied /dɪˈsætɪsfaɪd/ a descontento

dissect /dɪˈsekt/ vt disecar. ~**ion** /-ʃn/ n disección f

disseminat|e /dɪˈsemɪneɪt/ vt diseminar. ~**ion** /-ˈneɪʃn/ n diseminación f

dissent /dɪˈsent/ vi disentir. ● n disentimiento m

dissertation /dɪsəˈteɪʃn/ n disertación f; (univ) tesis f

disservice /dɪsˈsɜːvɪs/ n mal servicio m

dissident /ˈdɪsɪdənt/ a & n disidente (m & f)

dissimilar /dɪˈsɪmɪlə(r)/ a distinto

dissipate /ˈdɪsɪpeɪt/ vt disipar; (fig) desvanecer. ~**d** a disoluto

dissociate /dɪˈsəʊʃɪeɪt/ vt disociar

dissolut|e /ˈdɪsəluːt/ a disoluto. ~**ion** /dɪsəˈluːʃn/ n disolución f

dissolve /dɪˈzɒlv/ vt disolver. ● vi disolverse

dissuade /dɪˈsweɪd/ vt disuadir

distan|ce /ˈdɪstəns/ n distancia f. **from a** ~**ce** desde lejos. **in the** ~**ce** a lo lejos. ~**t** /ˈdɪstənt/ a lejano; (aloof) frío

distaste /dɪsˈteɪst/ n aversión f. ~**ful** a desagradable

distemper[1] /dɪˈstempə(r)/ n (paint) temple m. ● vt pintar al temple

distemper[2] /dɪˈstempə(r)/ n (of dogs) moquillo m

distend /dɪsˈtend/ vt dilatar. ● vi dilatarse

distil /dɪsˈtɪl/ vt (pt distilled) destilar. ~**lation** /-ˈleɪʃn/ n destilación f. ~**lery** /dɪsˈtɪlərɪ/ n destilería f

distinct /dɪsˈtɪŋkt/ a distinto; (clear) claro; (marked) marcado. ~**ion** /-ʃn/ n distinción f; (in exam) sobresaliente m. ~**ive** a distintivo. ~**ly** adv claramente

distinguish /dɪsˈtɪŋgwɪʃ/ vt/i distinguir. ~**ed** a distinguido

distort /dɪsˈtɔːt/ vt torcer. ~**ion** /-ʃn/ n deformación f

distract /dɪsˈtrækt/ vt distraer. ~**ed** a aturdido. ~**ing** a molesto. ~**ion** /-ʃn/ n distracción f; (confusion) aturdimiento m

distraught /dɪsˈtrɔːt/ a aturdido

distress /dɪsˈtres/ n angustia f; (poverty) miseria f; (danger) peligro m. ● vt afligir. ~**ing** a penoso

distribut|e /dɪsˈtrɪbjuːt/ vt distribuir. ~**ion** /-ˈbjuːʃn/ n distribución f. ~**or** n distribuidor m; (auto) distribuidor m de encendido

district /ˈdɪstrɪkt/ n distrito m; (of town) barrio m

distrust /dɪsˈtrʌst/ n desconfianza f. ● vt desconfiar de

disturb /dɪsˈtɜːb/ vt molestar; (perturb) inquietar; (move) desordenar; (interrupt) interrumpir. ~**ance** n disturbio m; (tumult) alboroto m. ~**ed** a trastornado. ~**ing** a inquietante

disused /dɪsˈjuːzd/ a fuera de uso

ditch /dɪtʃ/ n zanja f; (for irrigation) acequia f. ● vt (sl) abandonar

dither /ˈdɪðə(r)/ vi vacilar

ditto /ˈdɪtəʊ/ adv ídem

divan /dɪˈvæn/ n diván m

dive /daɪv/ *vi* tirarse de cabeza; (*rush*) meterse (precipitadamente); (*underwater*) bucear. ● *n* salto *m*; (*of plane*) picado *m*; (*place, fam*) taberna *f*. ~**r** *n* saltador *m*; (*underwater*) buzo *m*

diverge /daɪˈvɜːdʒ/ *vi* divergir. ~**nt** /daɪˈvɜːdʒənt/ *a* divergente

divers|e /daɪˈvɜːs/ *a* diverso. ~**ify** /daɪˈvɜːsɪfaɪ/ *vt* diversificar. ~**ity** /daɪˈvɜːsəti/ *n* diversidad *f*

diver|sion /daɪˈvɜːʃn/ *n* desvío *m*; (*distraction*) diversión *f*. ~**t** /daɪˈvɜːt/ *vt* desviar; (*entertain*) divertir

divest /daɪˈvest/ *vt*. ~ **of** despojar de

divide /dɪˈvaɪd/ *vt* dividir. ● *vi* dividirse

dividend /ˈdɪvɪdend/ *n* dividendo *m*

divine /dɪˈvaɪn/ *a* divino

diving-board /ˈdaɪvɪŋbɔːd/ *n* trampolín *m*

diving-suit /ˈdaɪvɪŋsuːt/ *n* escafandra *f*

divinity /dɪˈvɪnɪti/ *n* divinidad *f*

division /dɪˈvɪʒn/ *n* división *f*

divorce /dɪˈvɔːs/ *n* divorcio *m*. ● *vt* divorciarse de; (*judge*) divorciar. ● *vi* divorciarse. ~**e** /dɪvɔːˈsiː/ *n* divorciado *m*

divulge /daɪˈvʌldʒ/ *vt* divulgar

DIY *abbr see* **do-it-yourself**

dizz|iness /ˈdɪzɪnɪs/ *n* vértigo *m*. ~**y** /ˈdɪzɪ/ *a* (**-ier, -iest**) mareado; (*speed*) vertiginoso. **be** or **feel** ~**y** marearse

do /duː/ *vt* (*3 sing pres* **does**, *pt* **did**, *pp* **done**) hacer; (*swindle, sl*) engañar. ● *vi* hacer; (*fare*) ir; (*be suitable*) convenir; (*be enough*) bastar. ● *n* (*pl* **dos** *or* **do's**) (*fam*) fiesta *f*. ● *v aux*. ~ **you speak Spanish? Yes I** ~ ¿habla Vd español? Sí. **doesn't he?, don't you?** ¿verdad? ~ **come in!** (*emphatic*) ¡pase Vd! ~ **away with** abolir. ~ **in** (*exhaust, fam*) agotar; (*kill, sl*) matar. ~ **out** (*clean*) limpiar. ~ **up** abotonar (*coat etc*); renovar (*house*). ~ **with** tener que ver con; (*need*) necesitar. ~ **without** prescindir de. ~**ne for** (*fam*) arruinado. ~**ne in** (*fam*) agotado. **well** ~**ne** (*culin*) bien hecho. **well** ~**ne!** ¡muy bien!

docile /ˈdəʊsaɪl/ *a* dócil

dock[1] /dɒk/ *n* dique *m*. ● *vt* poner en dique. ● *vi* atracar al muelle

dock[2] /dɒk/ *n* (*jurid*) banquillo *m* de los acusados

dock: ~**er** *n* estibador *m*. ~**yard** /ˈdɒkjɑːd/ *n* astillero *m*

doctor /ˈdɒktə(r)/ *n* médico *m*, doctor *m*; (*univ*) doctor *m*. ● *vt* castrar (*cat*); (*fig*) adulterar

doctorate /ˈdɒktərət/ *n* doctorado *m*

doctrine /ˈdɒktrɪn/ *n* doctrina *f*

document /ˈdɒkjʊmənt/ *n* documento *m*. ~**ary** /-ˈmentrɪ/ *a & n* documental (*m*)

doddering /ˈdɒdərɪŋ/ *a* chocho

dodge /dɒdʒ/ *vt* esquivar. ● *vi* esquivarse. ● *n* regate *m*; (*fam*) truco *m*

dodgems /ˈdɒdʒəmz/ *npl* autos *mpl* de choque

dodgy /ˈdɒdʒɪ/ *a* (**-ier, -iest**) (*awkward*) difícil

does /dʌz/ *see* **do**

doesn't /ˈdʌznt/ = **does not**

dog /dɒg/ *n* perro *m*. ● *vt* (*pt* **dogged**) perseguir. ~**-collar** *n* (*relig, fam*) alzacuello *m*. ~**-eared** *a* (*book*) sobado

dogged /ˈdɒgɪd/ *a* obstinado

doghouse /ˈdɒghaʊs/ *n* (*Amer*) perrera *f*. **in the** ~ (*sl*) en desgracia

dogma /ˈdɒgmə/ *n* dogma *m*. ~**tic** /-ˈmætɪk/ *a* dogmático

dogsbody /ˈdɒgzbɒdɪ/ *n* (*fam*) burro *m* de carga

doh /dəʊ/ *n* (*mus, first note of any musical scale*) do *m*

doily /ˈdɔɪlɪ/ *n* tapete *m*

doings /ˈduːɪŋz/ *npl* (*fam*) actividades *fpl*

do-it-yourself /duːɪtjɔːˈself/ (*abbr* **DIY**) *n* bricolaje *m*. ~ **enthusiast** *n* manitas *m*

doldrums /ˈdɒldrəmz/ *npl*. **be in the** ~ estar abatido

dole /dəʊl/ *vt*. ~ **out** distribuir. ● *n* (*fam*) subsidio *m* de paro. **on the** ~ (*fam*) parado

doleful /ˈdəʊlfl/ *a* triste

doll /dɒl/ *n* muñeca *f*. ● *vt*. ~ **up** (*fam*) emperejilar

dollar /ˈdɒlə(r)/ *n* dólar *m*

dollop /ˈdɒləp/ *n* (*fam*) masa *f*

dolphin /ˈdɒlfɪn/ *n* delfín *m*

domain /dəʊˈmeɪn/ *n* dominio *m*; (*fig*) campo *m*

dome /dəʊm/ *n* cúpula *f*. ~**d** *a* abovedado

domestic /dəˈmestɪk/ *a* doméstico; (*trade, flights, etc*) nacional

domesticated (*animal*) domesticado

domesticity /dɒme'stɪsəti/ *n* domesticidad *f*

domestic: ~ **science** *n* economía *f* doméstica. ~ **servant** *n* doméstico *m*

dominant /'dɒmɪnənt/ *a* dominante

dominat|e /'dɒmɪneɪt/ *vt/i* dominar. ~**ion** /-'neɪʃn/ *n* dominación *f*

domineer /dɒmɪ'nɪə(r)/ *vt* tiranizar

Dominican Republic /dəmɪnɪkən rɪ'pʌblɪk/ *n* República *f* Dominicana

dominion /də'mɪnjən/ *n* dominio *m*

domino /'dɒmɪnəʊ/ *n* (*pl* ~**es**) ficha *f* de dominó. ~**es** *npl* (*game*) dominó *m*

don[1] /dɒn/ *n* profesor *m*

don[2] /dɒn/ *vt* (*pt* **donned**) ponerse

donat|e /dəʊ'neɪt/ *vt* donar. ~**ion** /-ʃn/ *n* donativo *m*

done /dʌn/ *see* **do**

donkey /'dɒŋkɪ/ *n* burro *m*. ~**work** *n* trabajo *m* penoso

donor /'dəʊnə(r)/ *n* donante *m & f*

don't /dəʊnt/ = **do not**

doodle /'du:dl/ *vi* garrapatear

doom /du:m/ *n* destino *m*; (*death*) muerte *f*. ● *vt*. **be** ~**ed to** ser condenado a

doomsday /'du:mzdeɪ/ *n* día *m* del juicio final

door /dɔ:(r)/ *n* puerta *f*. ~**man** /'dɔ:mən/ *n* (*pl* **-men**) portero *m*. ~**mat** /'dɔ:mæt/ *n* felpudo *m*. ~**step** /'dɔ:step/ *n* peldaño *m*. ~**way** /'dɔ:weɪ/ *n* entrada *f*

dope /dəʊp/ *n* (*fam*) droga *f*; (*idiot, sl*) imbécil *m*. ● *vt* (*fam*) drogar. ~**y** *a* (*sl*) torpe

dormant /'dɔ:mənt/ *a* inactivo

dormer /'dɔ:mə(r)/ *n*. ~ (**window**) buhardilla *f*

dormitory /'dɔ:mɪtrɪ/ *n* dormitorio *m*

dormouse /'dɔ:maʊs/ *n* (*pl* **-mice**) lirón *m*

dos|age /'dəʊsɪdʒ/ *n* dosis *f*. ~**e** /dəʊs/ *n* dosis *f*

doss /dɒs/ *vi* (*sl*) dormir. ~**-house** *n* refugio *m*

dot /dɒt/ *n* punto *m*. **on the** ~ en punto. ● *vt* (*pt* **dotted**) salpicar. **be** ~**ted with** estar salpicado de

dote /dəʊt/ *vi*. ~ **on** adorar

dotted line /dɒtɪd'laɪn/ *n* línea *f* de puntos

dotty /'dɒtɪ/ *a* (**-ier, -iest**) (*fam*) chiflado

double /'dʌbl/ *a* doble. ● *adv* doble, dos veces. ● *n* doble *m*; (*person*) doble

m & f. **at the** ~ corriendo. ● *vt* doblar; redoblar *(efforts etc)*. ● *vi* doblarse. ~**-bass** *n* contrabajo *m*. ~ **bed** *n* cama *f* de matrimonio. ~**breasted** *a* cruzado. ~ **chin** *n* papada *f*. ~**cross** *vt* traicionar. ~**dealing** *n* doblez *m & f*. ~**decker** *n* autobús *m* de dos pisos. ~ **Dutch** *n* galimatías *m*. ~**jointed** *a* con articulaciones dobles. ~**s** *npl* (*tennis*) doble *m*

doubt /daʊt/ *n* duda *f*. ● *vt* dudar; (*distrust*) dudar de, desconfiar de. ~**ful** *a* dudoso. ~**less** *adv* sin duda

doubly /'dʌblɪ/ *adv* doblemente

dough /dəʊ/ *n* masa *f*; (*money, sl*) dinero *m*, pasta *f* (*sl*)

doughnut /'dəʊnʌt/ *n* buñuelo *m*

douse /daʊs/ *vt* mojar; apagar *(fire)*

dove /dʌv/ *n* paloma *f*

dowager /'daʊədʒə(r)/ *n* viuda *f* (con bienes o título del marido)

dowdy /'daʊdɪ/ *a* (**-ier, -iest**) poco atractivo

down[1] /daʊn/ *adv* abajo. ~ **with** abajo. **come** ~ bajar. **go** ~ bajar; *(sun)* ponerse. ● *prep* abajo. ● *a* (*sad*) triste. ● *vt* derribar; (*drink, fam*) beber

down[2] /daʊn/ *n* (*feathers*) plumón *m*

down-and-out /'daʊnənd'aʊt/ *n* vagabundo *m*

downcast /'daʊnkɑ:st/ *a* abatido

downfall /'daʊnfɔ:l/ *n* caída *f*; (*fig*) perdición *f*

downgrade /daʊn'greɪd/ *vt* degradar

down-hearted /daʊn'hɑ:tɪd/ *a* abatido

downhill /daʊn'hɪl/ *adv* cuesta abajo

down payment /'daʊnpeɪmənt/ *n* depósito *m*

downpour /'daʊnpɔ:(r)/ *n* aguacero *m*

downright /'daʊnraɪt/ *a* completo; (*honest*) franco. ● *adv* completamente

downs /daʊnz/ *npl* colinas *fpl*

downstairs /daʊn'steəz/ *adv* abajo. /'daʊnsteəz/ *a* de abajo

downstream /'daʊnstri:m/ *adv* río abajo

down-to-earth /daʊntʊ'ɜ:θ/ *a* práctico

downtrodden /'daʊntrɒdn/ *a* oprimido

down: ~ **under** en las antípodas; (*in Australia*) en Australia. ~**ward** /'daʊnwəd/ *a & adv*, ~**wards** *adv* hacia abajo

dowry /'daʊərɪ/ *n* dote *f*

doze /daʊz/ *vi* dormitar. ~ **off** dormirse, dar una cabezada. ● *n* sueño *m* ligero

dozen /'dʌzn/ *n* docena *f*. ~**s of** (*fam*) miles de, muchos

Dr *abbr* (*Doctor*) Dr, Doctor *m*. ~ **Broadley** (el) Doctor Broadley

drab /dræb/ *a* monótono

draft /drɑːft/ *n* borrador *m*; (*outline*) bosquejo *m*; (*com*) letra *f* de cambio; (*Amer, mil*) reclutamiento *m*; (*Amer, of air*) corriente *f* de aire. ● *vt* bosquejar; (*mil*) destacar; (*Amer, conscript*) reclutar

drag /dræg/ *vt* (*pt* **dragged**) arrastrar; rastrear (*river*). ● *vi* arrastrarse por el suelo. ● *n* (*fam*) lata *f*. in ~ (*man, sl*) vestido de mujer

dragon /'drægən/ *n* dragón *m*

dragon-fly /'drægənflaɪ/ *n* libélula *f*

drain /dreɪn/ *vt* desaguar; apurar (*tank, glass*); (*fig*) agotar. ● *vi* escurrirse. ● *n* desaguadero *m*. **be a ~ on** agotar. ~**ing-board** *n* escurridero *m*

drama /'drɑːmə/ *n* drama *m*; (*art*) arte *m* teatral. ~**tic** /drə'mætɪk/ *a* dramático. ~**tist** /'dræmətɪst/ *n* dramaturgo *m*. ~**tize** /'dræmətaɪz/ *vt* adaptar al teatro; (*fig*) dramatizar

drank /dræŋk/ *see* **drink**

drape /dreɪp/ *vt* cubrir; (*hang*) colgar. ~**s** *npl* (*Amer*) cortinas *fpl*

drastic /'dræstɪk/ *a* drástico

draught /drɑːft/ *n* corriente *f* de aire. ~ **beer** *n* cerveza *f* de barril. ~**s** *n pl* (*game*) juego *m* de damas

draughtsman /'drɑːftsmən/ *n* (*pl* **-men**) diseñador *m*

draughty /'drɑːftɪ/ *a* lleno de corrientes de aire

draw /drɔː/ *vt* (*pt* **drew**, *pp* **drawn**) tirar; (*attract*) atraer; dibujar (*picture*); trazar (*line*); retirar (*money*). ~ **the line at** trazar el límite. ● *vi* (*sport*) empatar; dibujar (*pictures*); (*in lottery*) sortear. ● *n* (*sport*) empate *m*; (*in lottery*) sorteo *m*. ~ **in** (*days*) acortarse. ~ **out** sacar (*money*). ~ **up** pararse; redactar (*document*); acercar (*chair*)

drawback /'drɔːbæk/ *n* desventaja *f*

drawbridge /'drɔːbrɪdʒ/ *n* puente *m* levadizo

drawer /drɔː(r)/ *n* cajón *m*. ~**s** /drɔːz/ *npl* calzoncillos *mpl*; (*women's*) bragas *fpl*

drawing /'drɔːɪŋ/ *n* dibujo *m*. ~**-pin** *n* chinche *m*, chincheta *f*

drawing-room /'drɔːɪŋruːm/ *n* salón *m*

drawl /drɔːl/ *n* habla *f* lenta

drawn /drɔːn/ *see* **draw**. ● *a* (*face*) ojeroso

dread /dred/ *n* terror *m*. ● *vt* temer. ~**ful** /'dredfl/ *a* terrible. ~**fully** *adv* terriblemente

dream /driːm/ *n* sueño *m*. ● *vt/i* (*pt* **dreamed** *or* **dreamt**) soñar. ● *a* ideal. ~ **up** idear. ~**er** *n* soñador *m*. ~**y** *a* soñador

drear|iness /'drɪərɪnɪs/ *n* tristeza *f*; (*monotony*) monotonía *f*. ~**y** /'drɪərɪ/ *a* (**-ier, -iest**) triste; (*boring*) monótono

dredge¹ /dredʒ/ *n* draga *f*. ● *vt* dragar

dredge² /dredʒ/ *n* (*culin*) espolvorear

dredger¹ /'dredʒə(r)/ *n* draga *f*

dredger² /'dredʒə(r)/ *n* (*for sugar*) espolvoreador *m*

dregs /dregz/ *npl* heces *fpl*; (*fig*) hez *f*

drench /drentʃ/ *vt* empapar

dress /dres/ *n* vestido *m*; (*clothing*) ropa *f*. ● *vt* vestir; (*decorate*) adornar; (*med*) vendar; (*culin*) aderezar, aliñar. ● *vi* vestirse. ~ **circle** *n* primer palco *m*

dresser¹ /'dresə(r)/ *n* (*furniture*) aparador *m*

dresser² /'dresə(r)/ *n* (*in theatre*) camarero *m*

dressing /'dresɪŋ/ *n* (*sauce*) aliño *m*; (*bandage*) vendaje *m*. ~**-case** *n* neceser *m*. ~**-down** *n* rapapolvo *m*, reprensión *f*. ~**-gown** *n* bata *f*. ~**-room** *n* tocador *m*; (*in theatre*) camarín *m*. ~**-table** *n* tocador *m*

dressmak|er /'dresmeɪkə(r)/ *n* modista *m & f*. ~**ing** *n* costura *f*

dress rehearsal /'dresrɪhɜːsl/ *n* ensayo *m* general

dressy /'dresɪ/ *a* (**-ier, -iest**) elegante

drew /druː/ *see* **draw**

dribble /'drɪbl/ *vi* gotear; (*baby*) babear; (*in football*) regatear

dribs and drabs /drɪbzn'dræbz/ *npl*. **in ~** poco a poco, en cantidades pequeñas

drie|d /draɪd/ a ⟨food⟩ seco; ⟨fruit⟩ paso. **~r** /'draɪə(r)/ n secador m

drift /drɪft/ vi ir a la deriva; ⟨snow⟩ amontonarse. ● n ⟨movement⟩ dirección f; ⟨of snow⟩ montón m; ⟨meaning⟩ significado m. **~er** n persona f sin rumbo. **~wood** /'drɪftwʊd/ n madera f flotante

drill /drɪl/ n ⟨tool⟩ taladro m; ⟨training⟩ ejercicio m; ⟨fig⟩ lo normal. ● vt taladrar, perforar; ⟨train⟩ entrenar. ● vi entrenarse

drily /'draɪlɪ/ adv secamente

drink /drɪŋk/ vt/i ⟨pt **drank**, pp **drunk**⟩ beber. ● n bebida f. **~able** a bebible; ⟨water⟩ potable. **~er** n bebedor m. **~ing-water** n agua f potable

drip /drɪp/ vi ⟨pt **dripped**⟩ gotear. ● n gota f; ⟨med⟩ goteo m intravenoso; ⟨person, sl⟩ mentecato m. **~-dry** a que no necesita plancharse

dripping /'drɪpɪŋ/ n ⟨culin⟩ pringue m

drive /draɪv/ vt ⟨pt **drove**, pp **driven**⟩ empujar; conducir, manejar ⟨LAm⟩ ⟨car etc⟩. **~ in** clavar ⟨nail⟩. **~ s.o. mad** volver loco a uno. ● vi conducir. **~ in** ⟨in car⟩ entrar en coche. ● n paseo m; ⟨road⟩ calle f; ⟨private road⟩ camino m de entrada; ⟨fig⟩ energía f; ⟨pol⟩ campaña f. **~ at** querer decir. **~r** /'draɪvə(r)/ n conductor m, chófer m ⟨LAm⟩

drivel /'drɪvl/ n tonterías fpl

driving /'draɪvɪŋ/ n conducción f. **~-licence** n carné m de conducir. **~school** n autoescuela f

drizzl|e /'drɪzl/ n llovizna f. ● vi lloviznar. **~y** a lloviznoso

dromedary /'drɒmədərɪ/ n dromedario m

drone /drəʊn/ n ⟨noise⟩ zumbido m; ⟨bee⟩ zángano m. ● vi zumbar; ⟨fig⟩ hablar en voz monótona; ⟨idle, fam⟩ holgazanear

drool /druːl/ vi babear

droop /druːp/ vt inclinar. ● vi inclinarse; ⟨flowers⟩ marchitarse

drop /drɒp/ n gota f; ⟨fall⟩ caída f; ⟨of cliff⟩ precipicio m. ● vt ⟨pt **dropped**⟩ dejar caer; ⟨lower⟩ bajar. ● vi caer. **~ in on** pasar por casa de. **~ off** ⟨sleep⟩ dormirse. **~ out** retirarse; ⟨student⟩ abandonar los estudios. **~-out** n marginado m

droppings /'drɒpɪŋz/ npl excremento m

dross /drɒs/ n escoria f

drought /draʊt/ n sequía f

drove[1] /drəʊv/ see **drive**

drove[2] /drəʊv/ n manada f

drown /draʊn/ vt ahogar. ● vi ahogarse

drowsy /'draʊzɪ/ a soñoliento

drudge /drʌdʒ/ n esclavo m del trabajo. **~ry** /-ərɪ/ n trabajo m pesado

drug /drʌg/ n droga f; ⟨med⟩ medicamento m. ● vt ⟨pt **drugged**⟩ drogar. **~ addict** n toxicómano m

drugstore /'drʌgstɔː(r)/ n ⟨Amer⟩ farmacia f ⟨que vende otros artículos también⟩

drum /drʌm/ n tambor m; ⟨for oil⟩ bidón m. ● vi ⟨pt **drummed**⟩ tocar el tambor. ● vt. **~ into s.o.** inculcar en la mente de uno. **~mer** n tambor m; ⟨in group⟩ batería f. **~s** npl batería f. **~stick** /'drʌmstɪk/ n baqueta f; ⟨culin⟩ pierna f ⟨de pollo⟩

drunk /drʌŋk/ see **drink**. ● a borracho. **get ~** emborracharse. **~ard** n borracho m. **~en** a borracho. **~enness** n embriaguez f

dry /draɪ/ a ⟨**drier**, **driest**⟩ seco. ● vt secar. ● vi secarse. **~ up** ⟨fam⟩ secar los platos. **~-clean** vt limpiar en seco. **~-cleaner** n tintorero m. **~-cleaner's** ⟨shop⟩ tintorería f. **~ness** n sequedad f

dual /'djuːəl/ a doble. **~-carriageway** n autovía f, carretera f de doble calzada. **~-purpose** a de doble uso

dub /dʌb/ vt ⟨pt **dubbed**⟩ doblar ⟨film⟩; ⟨nickname⟩ apodar

dubious /'djuːbɪəs/ a dudoso; ⟨person⟩ sospechoso

duchess /'dʌtʃɪs/ n duquesa f

duck[1] /dʌk/ n pato m

duck[2] /dʌk/ vt sumergir; bajar ⟨head etc⟩. ● vi agacharse

duckling /'dʌklɪŋ/ n patito m

duct /dʌkt/ n conducto m

dud /dʌd/ a inútil; ⟨cheque⟩ sin fondos; ⟨coin⟩ falso

due /djuː/ a ⟨debido; ⟨expected⟩ esperado. **~ to** debido a. ● adv. **~ north** n derecho hacia el norte. **~s** npl derechos mpl

duel /'djuːəl/ n duelo m

duet /djuː'et/ n dúo m

duffle /'dʌfl/ a. **~ bag** n bolsa f de lona. **~-coat** n trenca f

dug /dʌg/ see **dig**

duke /djuːk/ n duque m

dull /dʌl/ a (-er, -est) ⟨weather⟩ gris; ⟨colour⟩ apagado; ⟨person, play, etc⟩ pesado; ⟨sound⟩ sordo; ⟨stupid⟩ torpe. ●vt aliviar ⟨pain⟩; entorpecer ⟨mind⟩

duly /'dju:lɪ/ adv debidamente

dumb /dʌm/ a (-er, -est) mudo; (fam) estúpido

dumbfound /dʌm'faʊnd/ vt pasmar

dummy /'dʌmɪ/ n muñeco m; (of tailor) maniquí m; (of baby) chupete m. ● a falso. ~ run n prueba f

dump /dʌmp/ vt descargar; (fam) deshacerse de. ● n vertedero m; (mil) depósito m; (fam) lugar m desagradable. **be down in the ~s** estar deprimido

dumpling /'dʌmplɪŋ/ n bola f de masa hervida

dumpy /'dʌmpɪ/ a (-ier, -iest) regordete

dunce /dʌns/ n burro m

dung /dʌŋ/ n excremento m; (manure) estiércol m

dungarees /dʌŋgə'ri:z/ npl mono m, peto m

dungeon /'dʌndʒən/ n calabozo m

dunk /dʌŋk/ vt remojar

duo /'dju:əʊ/ n dúo m

dupe /dju:p/ vt engañar. ● n inocentón m

duplicat|e /'dju:plɪkət/ a & n duplicado (m). /'dju:plɪkeɪt/ vt duplicar; (on machine) reproducir. ~or n multicopista f

duplicity /dju:'plɪsətɪ/ n doblez f

durable /'djʊərəbl/ a resistente; (enduring) duradero

duration /djʊ'reɪʃn/ n duración f

duress /djʊ'res/ n coacción f

during /'djʊərɪŋ/ prep durante

dusk /dʌsk/ n crepúsculo m

dusky /'dʌskɪ/ a (-ier, -iest) oscuro

dust /dʌst/ n polvo m. ● vt quitar el polvo a; (sprinkle) espolvorear

dustbin /'dʌstbɪn/ n cubo m de la basura

dust-cover /'dʌstkʌvə(r)/ n sobrecubierta f

duster /'dʌstə(r)/ n trapo m

dust-jacket /'dʌstdʒækɪt/ n sobrecubierta f

dustman /'dʌstmən/ n (pl -men) basurero m

dustpan /'dʌstpæn/ n recogedor m

dusty /'dʌstɪ/ a (-ier, -iest) polvoriento

Dutch /dʌtʃ/ a & n holandés (m). **go ~** pagar a escote. ~**man** m holandés m. ~**woman** n holandesa f

dutiful /'dju:tɪfl/ a obediente

duty /'dju:tɪ/ n deber m; (tax) derechos mpl de aduana. **on ~** de servicio. ~**-free** a libre de impuestos

duvet /'dju:veɪ/ n edredón m

dwarf /dwɔ:f/ n (pl -s) enano m. ● vt empequeñecer

dwell /dwel/ vi (pt dwelt) morar. ~ **on** dilatarse. ~**er** n habitante m & f. ~**ing** n morada f

dwindle /'dwɪndl/ vi disminuir

dye /daɪ/ vt (pres p dyeing) teñir. ● n tinte m

dying /'daɪɪŋ/ see **die**

dynamic /daɪ'næmɪk/ a dinámico. ~**s** npl dinámica f

dynamite /'daɪnəmaɪt/ n dinamita f. ● vt dinamitar

dynamo /'daɪnəməʊ/ n dinamo f, dínamo f

dynasty /'dɪnəstɪ/ n dinastía f

dysentery /'dɪsəntrɪ/ n disentería f

dyslexia /dɪs'leksɪə/ n dislexia f

E

each /i:tʃ/ a cada. ● pron cada uno. ~ **one** cada uno. ~ **other** uno a otro, el uno al otro. **they love ~ other** se aman

eager /'i:gə(r)/ a impaciente; (enthusiastic) ávido. ~**ly** adv con impaciencia. ~**ness** n impaciencia f, ansia f

eagle /'i:gl/ n águila f

ear¹ /ɪə(r)/ n oído m; (outer) oreja f

ear² /ɪə(r)/ n (of corn) espiga f

ear: ~**ache** /'ɪəreɪk/ n dolor m de oído. ~**drum** n tímpano m

earl /ɜ:l/ n conde m

early /'ɜ:lɪ/ a (-ier, -iest) temprano; (before expected time) prematuro. **in the ~ spring** a principios de la primavera. ● adv temprano; (ahead of time) con anticipación

earmark /'ɪəmɑ:k/ vt. ~ **for** destinar a

earn /ɜ:n/ vt ganar; (deserve) merecer

earnest /'ɜ:nɪst/ a serio. **in ~** en serio

earnings /'ɜ:nɪŋz/ npl ingresos mpl; (com) ganacias fpl

ear: ~**phones** /'ɪəfəʊnz/ npl auricular m. ~**-ring** n pendiente m

earshot /'ɪəʃɒt/ *n*. **within** ~ al alcance del oído

earth /ɜ:θ/ *n* tierra *f*. ● *vt* (*elec*) conectar a tierra. ~**ly** *a* terrenal

earthenware /'ɜ:θnweə(r)/ *n* loza *f* de barro

earthquake /'ɜ:θkweɪk/ *n* terremoto *m*

earthy /'ɜ:θɪ/ *a* terroso; (*coarse*) grosero

earwig /'ɪəwɪɡ/ *n* tijereta *f*

ease /i:z/ *n* facilidad *f*; (*comfort*) tranquilidad *f*. **at** ~ a gusto; (*mil*) en posición de descanso. **ill at** ~ molesto. **with** ~ fácilmente. ● *vt* calmar; aliviar (*pain*); tranquilizar ⟨*mind*⟩; (*loosen*) aflojar. ● *vi* calmarse; (*lessen*) disminuir

easel /'i:zl/ *n* caballete *m*

east /i:st/ *n* este *m*, oriente *m*. ● *a* del este, oriental. ● *adv* hacia el este.

Easter /'i:stə(r)/ *n* Semana *f* Santa; (*relig*) Pascua *f* de Resurrección. ~ **egg** *n* huevo *m* de Pascua

east: ~**erly** *a* este; ⟨*wind*⟩ del este. ~**ern** *a* del este, oriental. ~**ward** *adv*, ~**wards** *adv* hacia el este

easy /'i:zɪ/ *a* (**-ier, -iest**) fácil; (*relaxed*) tranquilo. **go** ~ **on** (*fam*) tener cuidado con. **take it** ~ no preocuparse. ● *int* ¡despacio! ~ **chair** *n* sillón *m*. ~**-going** *a* acomodadizo

eat /i:t/ *vt*/*i* (*pt* **ate**, *pp* **eaten**) comer. ~ **into** corroer. ~**able** *a* comestible. ~**er** *n* comedor *m*

eau-de-Cologne /ˌəʊdəkə'ləʊn/ *n* agua *f* de colonia

eaves /i:vz/ *npl* alero *m*

eavesdrop /'i:vzdrɒp/ *vi* (*pt* **-dropped**) escuchar a escondidas

ebb /eb/ *n* reflujo *m*. ● *vi* bajar; (*fig*) decaer

ebony /'ebənɪ/ *n* ébano *m*

ebullient /ɪ'bʌlɪənt/ *a* exuberante

EC /i:'si:/ *abbr* (*European Community*) CE (Comunidad *f* Europea)

eccentric /ɪk'sentrɪk/ *a* & *n* excéntrico (*m*). ~**ity** /eksen'trɪsətɪ/ *n* excentricidad *f*

ecclesiastical /ɪkli:zɪ'æstɪkl/ *a* eclesiástico

echelon /'eʃəlɒn/ *n* escalón *m*

echo /'ekəʊ/ *n* (*pl* **-oes**) eco *m*. ● *vt* (*pt* **echoed**, *pres p* **echoing**) repetir; (*imitate*) imitar. ● *vi* hacer eco

eclectic /ɪk'lektɪk/ *a* & *n* ecléctico (*m*)

eclipse /ɪ'klɪps/ *n* eclipse *m*. ● *vt* eclipsar

ecology /ɪ'kɒlədʒɪ/ *n* ecología *f*

econom|**ic** /i:kə'nɒmɪk/ *a* económico. ~**ical** *a* económico. ~**ics** *n* economía *f*. ~**ist** /ɪ'kɒnəmɪst/ *n* economista *m* & *f*. ~**ize** /ɪ'kɒnəmaɪz/ *vi* economizar. ~**y** /ɪ'kɒnəmɪ/ *n* economía *f*

ecsta|**sy** /'ekstəsɪ/ *n* éxtasis *f*. ~**tic** /ɪk'stætɪk/ *a* extático. ~**tically** *adv* con éxtasis

Ecuador /'ekwədɔ:(r)/ *n* el Ecuador *m*

ecumenical /i:kju:'menɪkl/ *a* ecuménico

eddy /'edɪ/ *n* remolino *m*

edge /edʒ/ *n* borde *m*, margen *m*; (*of knife*) filo *m*; (*of town*) afueras *fpl*. **have the** ~ **on** (*fam*) llevar la ventaja a. **on** ~ nervioso. ● *vt* ribetear; (*move*) mover poco a poco. ● *vi* avanzar cautelosamente. ~**ways** *adv* de lado

edging /'edʒɪŋ/ *n* borde *m*; (*sewing*) ribete *m*

edgy /'edʒɪ/ *a* nervioso

edible /'edɪbl/ *a* comestible

edict /'i:dɪkt/ *n* edicto *m*

edifice /'edɪfɪs/ *n* edificio *m*

edify /'edɪfaɪ/ *vt* edificar

edit /'edɪt/ *vt* dirigir ⟨*newspaper*⟩; preparar una edición de ⟨*text*⟩; (*write*) redactar; montar ⟨*film*⟩. ~**ed by** *a* cargo de. ~**ion** /ɪ'dɪʃn/ *n* edición *f*. ~**or** /'edɪtə(r)/ *n* (*of newspaper*) director *m*; (*of text*) redactor *m*. ~**orial** /edɪ'tɔ:rɪəl/ *a* editorial. ● *n* artículo *m* de fondo. ~**or in chief** *n* jefe *m* de redacción

educat|**e** /'edʒʊkeɪt/ *vt* instruir, educar. ~**ed** *a* culto. ~**ion** /-'keɪʃn/ *n* enseñanza *f*; (*culture*) cultura *f*; (*upbringing*) educación *f*. ~**ional** /-'keɪʃənl/ *a* instructivo

EEC /i:i:'si:/ *abbr* (*European Economic Community*) CEE (Comunidad *f* Económica Europea)

eel /i:l/ *n* anguila *f*

eerie /'ɪərɪ/ *a* (**-ier, -iest**) misterioso

efface /ɪ'feɪs/ *vt* borrar

effect /ɪ'fekt/ *n* efecto *m*. **in** ~ efectivamente. **take** ~ entrar en vigor. ● *vt* efectuar

effective /ɪ'fektɪv/ *a* eficaz; (*striking*) impresionante; (*mil*) efectivo. ~**ly** *adv* eficazmente. ~**ness** *n* eficacia *f*

effeminate /ɪˈfemɪnət/ a afeminado

effervescent /efəˈvesnt/ a efervescente

effete /ɪˈfiːt/ a agotado

efficien|cy /ɪˈfɪʃənsɪ/ n eficiencia f; (mec) rendimiento m. ∼t /ɪˈfɪʃnt/ a eficiente. ∼tly adv eficientemente

effigy /ˈefɪdʒɪ/ n efigie f

effort /ˈefət/ n esfuerzo m. ∼less a fácil

effrontery /ɪˈfrʌntərɪ/ n descaro m

effusive /ɪˈfjuːsɪv/ a efusivo

e.g. /ˈiːˈdʒiː/ abbr (exempli gratia) p.ej., por ejemplo

egalitarian /ɪɡælɪˈteərɪən/ a & n igualitario (m)

egg[1] /eɡ/ n huevo m

egg[3] /eɡ/ vt. ∼ on (fam) incitar

egg-cup /ˈeɡkʌp/ n huevera f

egg-plant /ˈeɡplɑːnt/ n berenjena f

eggshell /ˈeɡʃel/ n cáscara f de huevo

ego /ˈiːɡəʊ/ n (pl -os) yo m. ∼ism n egoísmo m. ∼ist n egoísta m & f. ∼centric /iːɡəʊˈsentrɪk/ a egocéntrico. ∼tism n egotismo m. ∼tist n egotista m & f

Egypt /ˈiːdʒɪpt/ n Egipto m. ∼ian /ɪˈdʒɪpʃən/ a & n egipcio (m)

eh /eɪ/ int (fam) ¡eh!

eiderdown /ˈaɪdədaʊn/ n edredón m

eight /eɪt/ a & n ocho (m)

eighteen /eɪˈtiːn/ a & n dieciocho (m). ∼th a & n decimoctavo (m)

eighth /eɪtθ/ a & n octavo (m)

eight|ieth /ˈeɪtɪəθ/ a & n ochenta (m), octogésimo (m). ∼y /ˈeɪtɪ/ a & n ochenta (m)

either /ˈaɪðə(r)/ a cualquiera de los dos; (negative) ninguno de los dos; (each) cada. ● pron uno u otro; (with negative) ni uno ni otro. ● adv (negative) tampoco. ● conj o. ∼ he or o él o; (with negative) ni él ni

ejaculate /ɪˈdʒækjʊleɪt/ vt/i (exclaim) exclamar

eject /ɪˈdʒekt/ vt expulsar, echar

eke /iːk/ vt. ∼ out hacer bastar; (increase) complementar

elaborate /ɪˈlæbərət/ a complicado. /ɪˈlæbəreɪt/ vt elaborar. ● vi explicarse

elapse /ɪˈlæps/ vi (of time) transcurrir

elastic /ɪˈlæstɪk/ a & n elástico (m). ∼ band n goma f (elástica)

elasticity /ɪlæˈstɪsətɪ/ n elasticidad f

elat|ed /ɪˈleɪtɪd/ a regocijado. ∼ion /-ʃn/ n regocijo m

elbow /ˈelbəʊ/ n codo m

elder[1] /ˈeldə(r)/ a & n mayor (m)

elder[2] /ˈeldə(r)/ n (tree) saúco m

elderly /ˈeldəlɪ/ a mayor, anciano

eldest /ˈeldɪst/ a & n el mayor (m)

elect /ɪˈlekt/ vt elegir. ∼ to do decidir hacer. ● a electo. ∼ion /-ʃn/ n elección f

elector /ɪˈlektə(r)/ n elector m. ∼al a electoral. ∼ate n electorado m

electric /ɪˈlektrɪk/ a eléctrico. ∼al a eléctrico. ∼ blanket n manta f eléctrica. ∼ian /ɪlekˈtrɪʃn/ n electricista m & f. ∼ity /ɪlekˈtrɪsətɪ/ n electricidad f

electrify /ɪˈlektrɪfaɪ/ vt electrificar; (fig) electrizar

electrocute /ɪˈlektrəkjuːt/ vt electrocutar

electrolysis /ɪlekˈtrɒlɪsɪs/ n electrólisis f

electron /ɪˈlektrɒn/ n electrón m

electronic /ɪlekˈtrɒnɪk/ a electrónico. ∼s n electrónica f

elegan|ce /ˈelɪɡəns/ n elegancia f. ∼t /ˈelɪɡənt/ a elegante. ∼tly adv elegantemente

element /ˈelɪmənt/ n elemento m. ∼ary /-ˈmentrɪ/ a elemental

elephant /ˈelɪfənt/ n elefante m

elevat|e /ˈelɪveɪt/ vt elevar. ∼ion /-ˈveɪʃn/ n elevación f. ∼or /ˈelɪveɪtə(r)/ n (Amer) ascensor m

eleven /ɪˈlevn/ a & n once (m). ∼th a & n undécimo (m)

elf /elf/ n (pl elves) duende m

elicit /ɪˈlɪsɪt/ vt sacar

eligible /ˈelɪdʒəbl/ a elegible. be ∼ for tener derecho a

eliminat|e /ɪˈlɪmɪneɪt/ vt eliminar. ∼ion /-ˈneɪʃn/ n eliminación f

élite /eɪˈliːt/ n elite f, élite m

elixir /ɪˈlɪksɪə(r)/ n elixir m

ellip|se /ɪˈlɪps/ n elipse f. ∼tical a elíptico

elm /elm/ n olmo m

elocution /eləˈkjuːʃn/ n elocución f

elongate /ˈiːlɒŋɡeɪt/ vt alargar

elope /ɪˈləʊp/ vi fugarse con el amante. ∼ment n fuga f

eloquen|ce /ˈeləkwəns/ n elocuencia f. ∼t /ˈeləkwənt/ a elocuente. ∼tly adv con elocuencia

El Salvador /elˈsælvədɔː(r)/ n El Salvador m

else /els/ *adv* más. **everybody** ∼ todos los demás. **nobody** ∼ ningún otro, nadie más. **nothing** ∼ nada más. **or** ∼ o bien. **somewhere** ∼en otra parte

elsewhere /els'weə(r)/ *adv* en otra parte

elucidate /ɪ'lu:sɪdeɪt/ *vt* aclarar

elude /ɪ'lu:d/ *vt* eludir

elusive /ɪ'lu:sɪv/ *a* esquivo

emaciated /ɪ'meɪʃɪeɪtɪd/ *a* esquelético

emanate /'eməneɪt/ *vi* emanar

emancipat|e /ɪ'mænsɪpeɪt/ *vt* emancipar. ∼**ion** /-'peɪʃn/ *n* emancipación *f*

embalm /ɪm'bɑ:m/ *vt* embalsamar

embankment /ɪm'bæŋkmənt/ *n* terraplén *m*; (*of river*) dique *m*

embargo /ɪm'bɑ:gəʊ/ *n* (*pl* **-oes**) prohibición *f*

embark /ɪm'bɑ:k/ *vt* embarcar. ●*vi* embarcarse. ∼ **on** (*fig*) emprender. ∼**ation** /emba:'keɪʃn/ *n* (*of people*) embarco *m*; (*of goods*) embarque *m*

embarrass /ɪm'bærəs/ *vt* desconcertar; (*shame*) dar vergüenza. ∼**ment** *n* desconcierto *m*; (*shame*) vergüenza *f*

embassy /'embəsɪ/ *n* embajada *f*

embed /ɪm'bed/ *vt* (*pt* **embedded**) embutir; (*fig*) fijar

embellish /ɪm'belɪʃ/ *vt* embellecer. ∼**ment** *n* embellecimiento *m*

embers /'embəz/ *npl* ascua *f*

embezzle /ɪm'bezl/ *vt* desfalcar. ∼**ment** *n* desfalco *m*

embitter /ɪm'bɪtə(r)/ *vt* amargar

emblem /'embləm/ *n* emblema *m*

embod|iment /ɪm'bɒdɪmənt/ *n* encarnación *f*. ∼**y** /ɪm'bɒdɪ/ *vt* encarnar; (*include*) incluir

emboss /ɪm'bɒs/ *vt* grabar en relieve, repujar. ∼**ed** *a* en relieve, repujado

embrace /ɪm'breɪs/ *vt* abrazar; (*fig*) abarcar. ●*vi* abrazarse. ●*n* abrazo *m*

embroider /ɪm'brɔɪdə(r)/ *vt* bordar. ∼**y** *n* bordado *m*

embroil /ɪm'brɔɪl/ *vt* enredar

embryo /'embrɪəʊ/ *n* (*pl* **-os**) embrión *m*. ∼**nic** /-'ɒnɪk/ *a* embrionario

emend /ɪ'mend/ *vt* enmendar

emerald /'emərəld/ *n* esmeralda *f*

emerge /ɪ'mɜ:dʒ/ *vi* salir. ∼**nce** /-əns/ *n* aparición *f*

emergency /ɪ'mɜ:dʒənsɪ/ *n* emergencia *f*. **in an** ∼en caso de emergencia. ∼ **exit** *n* salida *f* de emergencia

emery /'emərɪ/ *n* esmeril *m*. ∼**board** *n* lima *f* de uñas

emigrant /'emɪgrənt/ *n* emigrante *m & f*

emigrat|e /'emɪgreɪt/ *vi* emigrar. ∼**ion** /-'greɪʃn/ *n* emigración *f*

eminen|ce /'emɪnəns/ *n* eminencia *f*. ∼**t** /'emɪnənt/ *a* eminente. ∼**tly** *adv* eminentemente

emissary /'emɪsərɪ/ *n* emisario *m*

emission /ɪ'mɪʃn/ *n* emisión *f*

emit /ɪ'mɪt/ *vt* (*pt* **emitted**) emitir

emollient /ɪ'mɒlɪənt/ *a & n* emoliente (*m*)

emotion /ɪ'məʊʃn/ *n* emoción *f*. ∼**onal** *a* emocional; (*person*) emotivo; (*moving*) conmovedor. ∼**ve** /ɪ'məʊtɪv/ *a* emotivo

empathy /'empəθɪ/ *n* empatía *f*

emperor /'empərə(r)/ *n* emperador *m*

emphasi|s /'emfəsɪs/ *n* (*pl* ∼**ses** /-si:z/) énfasis *m*. ∼**ze** /'emfəsaɪz/ *vt* subrayar; (*single out*) destacar

emphatic /ɪm'fætɪk/ *a* categórico; (*resolute*) decidido

empire /'empaɪə(r)/ *n* imperio *m*

empirical /ɪm'pɪrɪkl/ *a* empírico

employ /ɪm'plɔɪ/ *vt* emplear. ∼**ee** /emplɔɪ'i:/ *n* empleado *m*. ∼**er** *n* patrón *m*. ∼**ment** *n* empleo *m*. ∼**ment agency** *n* agencia *f* de colocaciones

empower /ɪm'paʊə(r)/ *vt* autorizar (**to do** a hacer)

empress /'empris/ *n* emperatriz *f*

empt|ies /'emptɪz/ *npl* envases *mpl*. ∼**iness** *n* vacío *m*. ∼**y** /'emptɪ/ *a* vacío; (*promise*) vano. **on an** ∼**y stomach** con el estómago vacío. ●*vt* vaciar. ●*vi* vaciarse

emulate /'emjʊleɪt/ *vt* emular

emulsion /ɪ'mʌlʃn/ *n* emulsión *f*

enable /ɪ'neɪbl/ *vt*. ∼ **s.o. to** permitir a uno

enact /ɪ'nækt/ *vt* (*jurid*) decretar; (*in theatre*) representar

enamel /ɪ'næml/ *n* esmalte *m*. ●*vt* (*pt* **enamelled**) esmaltar

enamoured /ɪ'næməd/ *a*. **be** ∼ **of** estar enamorado de

encampment /ɪn'kæmpmənt/ *n* campamento *m*

encase /ɪn'keɪs/ *vt* encerrar

enchant /ɪnˈtʃɑːnt/ vt encantar. ~ing a encantador. ~ment n encanto m

encircle /ɪnˈsɜːkl/ vt rodear

enclave /ˈenkleɪv/ n enclave m

enclos|e /ɪnˈkləʊz/ vt cercar ⟨land⟩; (with letter) adjuntar; (in receptacle) encerrar. ~ed a ⟨space⟩ encerrado; (com) adjunto. ~ure /ɪnˈkləʊʒə(r)/ n cercamiento m; (area) recinto m; (com) documento m adjunto

encompass /ɪnˈkʌmpəs/ vt cercar; (include) abarcar

encore /ˈɒŋkɔː/ int ¡bis! • n bis m, repetición f

encounter /ɪnˈkaʊntə(r)/ vt encontrar. • n encuentro m

encourage /ɪnˈkʌrɪdʒ/ vt animar; (stimulate) estimular. ~ment n estímulo m

encroach /ɪnˈkrəʊtʃ/ vi. ~ on invadir ⟨land⟩; quitar ⟨time⟩. ~ment n usurpación f

encumb|er /ɪnˈkʌmbə(r)/ vt (hamper) estorbar; (burden) cargar. be ~ered with estar cargado de. ~rance n estorbo m; (burden) carga f

encyclical /ɪnˈsɪklɪkl/ n encíclica f

encyclopaedi|a /ɪnˌsaɪkləˈpiːdɪə/ n enciclopedia f. ~c a enciclopédico

end /end/ n fin m; (furthest point) extremo m. **in the ~** por fin. **make ~s meet** poder llegar a fin de mes. **no ~** (fam) muy. **no ~ of** muchísimos. **on ~** de pie; (consecutive) seguido. • vt/i terminar, acabar

endanger /ɪnˈdeɪndʒə(r)/ vt arriesgar

endear|ing /ɪnˈdɪərɪŋ/ a simpático. ~ment n palabra f cariñosa

endeavour /ɪnˈdevə(r)/ n tentativa f. • vi. ~ **to** esforzarse por

ending /ˈendɪŋ/ n fin m

endive /ˈendɪv/ n escarola f, endibia f

endless /ˈendlɪs/ a interminable; ⟨patience⟩ infinito

endorse /ɪnˈdɔːs/ vt endosar; (fig) aprobar. ~ment n endoso m; (fig) aprobación f; (auto) nota f de inhabilitación

endow /ɪnˈdaʊ/ vt dotar

endur|able /ɪnˈdjʊərəbl/ a aguantable. ~ance n resistencia f. ~e /ɪnˈdjʊə(r)/ vt aguantar. • vi durar. ~ing a perdurable

enemy /ˈenəmɪ/ n & a enemigo (m)

energ|etic /enəˈdʒetɪk/ a enérgico. ~y /ˈenədʒɪ/ n energía f

enervat|e /ˈenəːveɪt/ vt debilitar. ~ing a debilitante

enfold /ɪnˈfəʊld/ vt envolver; (in arms) abrazar

enforce /ɪnˈfɔːs/ vt aplicar; (impose) imponer; hacer cumplir ⟨law⟩. ~d a forzado

engage /ɪnˈgeɪdʒ/ vt emplear ⟨staff⟩; (reserve) reservar; ocupar ⟨attention⟩; (mec) hacer engranar. • vi (mec) engranar. ~d a prometido; (busy) ocupado. **get ~d** prometerse. ~ment n compromiso m; (undertaking) obligación f

engaging /ɪnˈgeɪdʒɪŋ/ a atractivo

engender /ɪnˈdʒendə(r)/ vt engendrar

engine /ˈendʒɪn/ n motor m; (of train) locomotora f. ~-driver n maquinista m

engineer /endʒɪˈnɪə(r)/ n ingeniero m; (mechanic) mecánico m. • vt (contrive, fam) lograr. ~ing n ingeniería f

England /ˈɪŋglənd/ n Inglaterra f

English /ˈɪŋglɪʃ/ a inglés. • n (lang) inglés m; (people) ingleses mpl. ~man n inglés m. ~woman n inglesa f. **the ~ Channel** n el canal m de la Mancha

engrav|e /ɪnˈgreɪv/ vt grabar. ~ing n grabado m

engrossed /ɪnˈgrəʊst/ a absorto

engulf /ɪnˈgʌlf/ vt tragar(se)

enhance /ɪnˈhɑːns/ vt aumentar

enigma /ɪˈnɪgmə/ n enigma m. ~tic /enɪgˈmætɪk/ a enigmático

enjoy /ɪnˈdʒɔɪ/ vt gozar de. ~ **o.s.** divertirse. **I ~ reading** me gusta la lectura. ~able a agradable. ~ment n placer m

enlarge /ɪnˈlɑːdʒ/ vt agrandar; (foto) ampliar. • vi agrandarse. ~ **upon** extenderse sobre. ~ment n (foto) ampliación f

enlighten /ɪnˈlaɪtn/ vt aclarar; (inform) informar. ~ment n aclaración f. **the E~ment** n el siglo m de las luces

enlist /ɪnˈlɪst/ vt alistar; (fig) conseguir. • vi alistarse

enliven /ɪnˈlaɪvn/ vt animar

enmity /ˈenmətɪ/ n enemistad f

ennoble /ɪˈnəʊbl/ vt ennoblecer

enorm|ity /ɪˈnɔːmətɪ/ n enormidad f. ~ous /ɪˈnɔːməs/ a enorme

enough /ɪˈnʌf/ a & adv bastante. ● n bastante m, suficiente m. ● int ¡basta!

enquir|e /ɪnˈkwaɪə(r)/ vt/i preguntar. ~e about informarse de. ~y n pregunta f; (investigation) investigación f

enrage /ɪnˈreɪdʒ/ vt enfurecer

enrapture /ɪnˈræptʃə(r)/ vt extasiar

enrich /ɪnˈrɪtʃ/ vt enriquecer

enrol /ɪnˈrəʊl/ vt (pt **enrolled**) inscribir; matricular ⟨student⟩. ● vi inscribirse; ⟨student⟩ matricularse. ~ment n inscripción f; (of student) matrícula f

ensconce /ɪnˈskɒns/ vt. ~ o.s. arrellanarse

ensemble /ɒnˈsɒmbl/ n conjunto m

enshrine /ɪnˈʃraɪn/ vt encerrar

ensign /ˈensaɪn/ n enseña f

enslave /ɪnˈsleɪv/ vt esclavizar

ensue /ɪnˈsjuː/ vi resultar, seguirse

ensure /ɪnˈʃʊə(r)/ vt asegurar

entail /ɪnˈteɪl/ vt suponer; acarrear ⟨trouble etc⟩

entangle /ɪnˈtæŋgl/ vt enredar. ~ment n enredo m; (mil) alambrada f

enter /ˈentə(r)/ vt entrar en; ⟨write⟩ escribir; matricular ⟨school etc⟩; hacerse socio de ⟨club⟩. ● vi entrar

enterprise /ˈentəpraɪz/ n empresa f; (fig) iniciativa f

enterprising /ˈentəpraɪzɪŋ/ a emprendedor

entertain /entəˈteɪn/ vt divertir; recibir ⟨guests⟩; abrigar ⟨ideas, hopes⟩; (consider) considerar. ~ment n diversión f; (performance) espectáculo m; (reception) recepción f

enthral /ɪnˈθrɔːl/ vt (pt **enthralled**) cautivar

enthuse /ɪnˈθjuːz/ vi. ~ over entusiasmarse por

enthusias|m /ɪnˈθjuːzɪæzəm/ n entusiasmo m. ~tic /-ˈæstɪk/ a entusiasta; ⟨thing⟩ entusiástico. ~tically /-ˈæstɪklɪ/ adv con entusiasmo. ~t /ɪnˈθjuːzɪæst/ n entusiasta m & f

entice /ɪnˈtaɪs/ vt atraer. ~ment n atracción f

entire /ɪnˈtaɪə(r)/ a entero. ~ly adv completamente. ~ty /ɪnˈtaɪərətɪ/ n. in its ~ty en su totalidad

entitle /ɪnˈtaɪtl/ vt titular; ⟨give a right⟩ dar derecho a. be ~d to tener derecho a. ~ment n derecho m

entity /ˈentɪtɪ/ n entidad f

entomb /ɪnˈtuːm/ vt sepultar

entrails /ˈentreɪlz/ npl entrañas fpl

entrance[1] /ˈentrəns/ n entrada f; (right to enter) admisión f

entrance[2] /ɪnˈtrɑːns/ vt encantar

entrant /ˈentrənt/ n participante m & f; (in exam) candidato m

entreat /ɪnˈtriːt/ vt suplicar. ~y n súplica f

entrench /ɪnˈtrentʃ/ vt atrincherar

entrust /ɪnˈtrʌst/ vt confiar

entry /ˈentrɪ/ n entrada f; (of street) bocacalle f; (note) apunte m

entwine /ɪnˈtwaɪn/ vt entrelazar

enumerate /ɪˈnjuːməreɪt/ vt enumerar

enunciate /ɪˈnʌnsɪeɪt/ vt pronunciar; (state) enunciar

envelop /ɪnˈveləp/ vt (pt **enveloped**) envolver

envelope /ˈenvələʊp/ n sobre m

enviable /ˈenvɪəbl/ a envidiable

envious /ˈenvɪəs/ a envidioso. ~ly adv con envidia

environment /ɪnˈvaɪərənmənt/ n medio m ambiente. ~al /-ˈmentl/ a ambiental

envisage /ɪnˈvɪzɪdʒ/ vt prever; (imagine) imaginar

envoy /ˈenvɔɪ/ n enviado m

envy /ˈenvɪ/ n envidia f. ● vt envidiar

enzyme /ˈenzaɪm/ n enzima f

epaulette /ˈepəʊlet/ n charretera f

ephemeral /ɪˈfemərəl/ a efímero

epic /ˈepɪk/ n épica f. ● a épico

epicentre /ˈepɪsentə(r)/ n epicentro m

epicure /ˈepɪkjʊə(r)/ n sibarita m & f; (gourmet) gastrónomo m

epidemic /epɪˈdemɪk/ n epidemia f. ● a epidémico

epilep|sy /ˈepɪlepsɪ/ n epilepsia f. ~tic /-ˈleptɪk/ a & n epiléptico (m)

epilogue /ˈepɪlɒg/ n epílogo m

episode /ˈepɪsəʊd/ n episodio m

epistle /ɪˈpɪsl/ n epístola f

epitaph /ˈepɪtɑːf/ n epitafio m

epithet /ˈepɪθet/ n epíteto m

epitom|e /ɪˈpɪtəmɪ/ n epítome m, personificación f. ~ize vt epitomar, personificar, ser la personificación de

epoch /ˈiːpɒk/ n época f. ~-making a que hace época

equal /ˈiːkwəl/ a & n igual (m & f). ~ to ⟨a task⟩ a la altura de. ● vt (pt **equalled**) ser igual a; (math) ser. ~ity /ɪˈkwɒlətɪ/ n igualdad f. ~ize

/'i:kwəlaɪz/ vt/i igualar. ∼izer /-ə(r)/ n (sport) tanto m de empate. ∼ly adv igualmente

equanimity /ekwə'nɪmətɪ/ n ecuanimidad f

equate /ɪ'kweɪt/ vt igualar

equation /ɪ'kweɪʒn/ n ecuación f

equator /ɪ'kweɪtə(r)/ n ecuador m. ∼ial /ekwə'tɔ:rɪəl/ a ecuatorial

equestrian /ɪ'kwestrɪən/ a ecuestre

equilateral /i:kwɪ'lætərl/ a equilátero

equilibrium /i:kwɪ'lɪbrɪəm/ n equilibrio m

equinox /'i:kwɪnɒks/ n equinoccio m

equip /ɪ'kwɪp/ vt (pt equipped) equipar. ∼ment n equipo m

equitable /'ekwɪtəbl/ a equitativo

equity /'ekwətɪ/ n equidad f; (pl, com) acciones fpl ordinarias

equivalen|ce /ɪ'kwɪvələns/ n equivalencia f. ∼t /ɪ'kwɪvəkl/ a & n equivalente (m)

equivocal /ɪ'kwɪvəkl/ a equívoco

era /'ɪərə/ n era f

eradicate /ɪ'rædɪkeɪt/ vt extirpar

erase /ɪ'reɪz/ vt borrar. ∼r /-ə(r)/ n borrador m

erect /ɪ'rekt/ a erguido. ● vt levantar. ∼ion /-ʃn/ n erección f, montaje m

ermine /'ɜ:mɪn/ n armiño m

ero|de /ɪ'rəʊd/ vt desgastar. ∼sion /-ʒn/ n desgaste m

erotic /ɪ'rɒtɪk/ a erótico. ∼ism /-sɪzəm/ n erotismo m

err /ɜ:(r)/ vi errar; (sin) pecar

errand /'erənd/ n recado m

erratic /ɪ'rætɪk/ a irregular; ⟨person⟩ voluble

erroneous /ɪ'rəʊnɪəs/ a erróneo

error /'erə(r)/ n error m

erudit|e /'eru:daɪt/ a erudito. ∼ion /-'dɪʃn/ n erudición f

erupt /ɪ'rʌpt/ vi estar en erupción; (fig) estallar. ∼ion /-ʃn/ n erupción f

escalat|e /'eskəleɪt/ vt intensificar. ● vi intensificarse. ∼ion /-'leɪʃn/ n intensificación f

escalator /'eskəleɪtə(r)/ n escalera f mecánica

escapade /eskə'peɪd/ n aventura f

escap|e /ɪ'skeɪp/ vi escaparse. ● vt evitar. ● n fuga f, (avoidance) evasión f. **have a narrow ∼e** escapar por un pelo. ∼ism /ɪ'skeɪpɪzəm/ n escapismo m

escarpment /ɪs'kɑ:pmənt/ n escarpa f

escort /'eskɔ:t/ n acompañante m; (mil) escolta f. /ɪ'skɔ:t/ vt acompañar; (mil) escoltar

Eskimo /'eskɪməʊ/ n (pl -os, -o) esquimal (m & f)

especial /ɪ'speʃl/ a especial. ∼ly adv especialmente

espionage /'espɪənɑ:ʒ/ n espionaje m

esplanade /esplə'neɪd/ n paseo m marítimo

Esq. /ɪ'skweɪə(r)/ abbr (Esquire) (in address). **E. Ashton, ∼** Sr. D. E. Ashton

essay /'eseɪ/ n ensayo m; (at school) composición f

essence /'esns/ n esencia f. **in ∼** esencialmente

essential /ɪ'senʃl/ a esencial. ● n lo esencial. ∼ly adv esencialmente

establish /ɪ'stæblɪʃ/ vt establecer; (prove) probar. ∼ment n establecimiento m. **the E∼ment** los que mandan, el sistema m

estate /ɪ'steɪt/ n finca f; (possessions) bienes mpl. ∼ **agent** n agente m inmobiliario. ∼ **car** n furgoneta f

esteem /ɪ'sti:m/ vt estimar. ● n estimación f, estima f

estimat|e /'estɪmət/ n cálculo m; (com) presupuesto m. /'estɪmeɪt/ vt calcular. ∼ion /-'meɪʃn/ n estima f, estimación f; (opinion) opinión f

estranged /ɪs'treɪndʒd/ a alejado

estuary /'estʃʊərɪ/ n estuario m

etc. /et'setrə/ abbr (et cetera) etc., etcétera

etching /'etʃɪŋ/ n aguafuerte m

eternal /ɪ'tɜ:nl/ a eterno

eternity /ɪ'tɜ:nətɪ/ n eternidad f

ether /'i:θə(r)/ n éter m

ethereal /ɪ'θɪərɪəl/ a etéreo

ethic /'eθɪk/ n ética f. ∼s npl ética f. ∼al a ético

ethnic /'eθnɪk/ a étnico

ethos /'i:θɒs/ n carácter m distintivo

etiquette /'etɪket/ n etiqueta f

etymology /etɪ'mɒlədʒɪ/ n etimología f

eucalyptus /ju:kə'lɪptəs/ n (pl -tuses) eucalipto m

eulogy /'ju:lədʒɪ/ n encomio m

euphemism /'ju:fəmɪzəm/ n eufemismo m

euphoria /ju:'fɔ:rɪə/ n euforia f

Europe /'juərəp/ n Europa f. ~an /-'pɪən/ a & n europeo (m)

euthanasia /ju:θə'neɪzɪə/ n eutanasia f

evacuat|e /ɪ'vækjʊeɪt/ vt evacuar; desocupar ⟨building⟩. ~ion /-'eɪʃn/ n evacuación f

evade /ɪ'veɪd/ vt evadir

evaluate /ɪ'væljʊeɪt/ vt evaluar

evangeli|cal /i:væn'dʒelɪkl/ a evangélico. ~st /ɪ'vændʒəlɪst/ n evangelista m & f

evaporat|e /ɪ'væpəreɪt/ vi evaporarse. ~ion /-'reɪʃn/ n evaporación f

evasion /ɪ'veɪʒn/ n evasión f

evasive /ɪ'veɪsɪv/ a evasivo

eve /i:v/ n víspera f

even /'i:vn/ a regular; ⟨flat⟩ llano; ⟨surface⟩ liso; ⟨amount⟩ igual; ⟨number⟩ par. **get** ~ **with** desquitarse con. ● vt nivelar. ~ **up** igualar. ● adv aun, hasta, incluso. ~ **if** aunque. ~ **so** aun así. **not** ~ ni siquiera

evening /'i:vnɪŋ/ n tarde f; ⟨after dark⟩ noche f. ~ **class** n clase f nocturna. ~ **dress** n ⟨man's⟩ traje m de etiqueta; ⟨woman's⟩ traje m de noche

evensong /'i:vnsɒŋ/ n vísperas fpl

event /ɪ'vent/ n acontecimiento m; ⟨sport⟩ prueba f. **in the** ~ **of** en caso de. ~**ful** a lleno de acontecimientos

eventual /ɪ'ventʃʊəl/ a final, definitivo. ~**ity** /-'ælətɪ/ n eventualidad f. ~**ly** adv finalmente

ever /'evə(r)/ adv jamás, nunca; ⟨at all times⟩ siempre. ~ **after** desde entonces. ~ **since** desde entonces. ● conj después de que. ~ **so** ⟨fam⟩ muy. **for** ~ para siempre. **hardly** ~ casi nunca

evergreen /'evəgri:n/ a de hoja perenne. ● n árbol m de hoja perenne

everlasting /evə'lɑːstɪŋ/ a eterno

every /'evrɪ/ a cada, todo. ~ **child** todos los niños. ~ **one** cada uno. ~ **other day** cada dos días

everybody /'evrɪbɒdɪ/ pron todo el mundo

everyday /'evrɪdeɪ/ a todos los días

everyone /'evrɪwʌn/ pron todo el mundo. ~ **else** todos los demás

everything /'evrɪθɪŋ/ pron todo

everywhere /'evrɪweə(r)/ adv en todas partes

evict /ɪ'vɪkt/ vt desahuciar. ~**ion** /-ʃn/ n desahucio m

eviden|ce /'evɪdəns/ n evidencia f; ⟨proof⟩ pruebas fpl; ⟨jurid⟩ testimonio m. ~**ce of** señales de. **in** ~**ce** visible. ~**t** /'evɪdənt/ a evidente. ~**tly** adv evidentemente

evil /'i:vl/ a malo. ● n mal m, maldad f

evocative /ɪ'vɒkətɪv/ a evocador

evoke /ɪ'vəʊk/ vt evocar

evolution /i:və'lu:ʃn/ n evolución f

evolve /ɪ'vɒlv/ vt desarrollar. ● vi desarrollarse, evolucionar

ewe /ju:/ n oveja f

ex... /eks/ pref ex...

exacerbate /ɪg'zæsəbeɪt/ vt exacerbar

exact /ɪg'zækt/ a exacto. ● vt exigir ⟨from a⟩. ~**ing** a exigente. ~**itude** n exactitud f. ~**ly** adv exactamente

exaggerat|e /ɪg'zædʒəreɪt/ vt exagerar. ~**ion** /-'reɪʃn/ n exageración f

exalt /ɪg'zɔːlt/ vt exaltar

exam /ɪg'zæm/ n ⟨fam⟩ examen m. ~**ination** /ɪgzæmɪ'neɪʃn/ n examen m. ~**ine** /ɪg'zæmɪn/ vt examinar; interrogar ⟨witness⟩. ~**iner** /-ə(r)/ n examinador m

example /ɪg'zɑːmpl/ n ejemplo m. **make an** ~ **of** infligir castigo ejemplar a

exasperat|e /ɪg'zæspəreɪt/ vt exasperar. ~**ion** /-'reɪʃn/ n exasperación f

excavat|e /'ekskəveɪt/ vt excavar. ~**ion** /-'veɪʃn/ n excavación f

exceed /ɪk'si:d/ vt exceder. ~**ingly** adv extremadamente

excel /ɪk'sel/ vi ⟨pt **excelled**⟩ sobresalir. ● vt superar

excellen|ce /'eksələns/ n excelencia f. ~**t** /'eksələnt/ a excelente. ~**tly** adv excelentemente

except /ɪk'sept/ prep excepto, con excepción de. ~ **for** con excepción de. ● vt exceptuar. ~**ing** prep con excepción de

exception /ɪk'sepʃən/ n excepción f. **take** ~ **to** ofenderse por. ~**al** /ɪk'sepʃənl/ a excepcional. ~**ally** adv excepcionalmente

excerpt /'eksɜːpt/ n extracto m

excess /ɪk'ses/ n exceso m. /'ekses/ a excedente. ~ **fare** n suplemento m. ~ **luggage** n exceso m de equipaje

excessive /ɪk'sesɪv/ a excesivo. ~**ly** adv excesivamente

exchange /ɪkˈstʃeɪndʒ/ vt cambiar. ● n cambio m. **(telephone)** ~ central f telefónica

exchequer /ɪksˈtʃekə(r)/ n (pol) erario m, hacienda f

excise[1] /ˈeksaɪz/ n impuestos mpl indirectos

excise[2] /ekˈsaɪz/ vt quitar

excit|able /ɪkˈsaɪtəbl/ a excitable. ~e /ɪkˈsaɪt/ vt emocionar; (stimulate) excitar. ~ed a entusiasmado. ~ement n emoción f; (enthusiasm) entusiasmo m. ~ing a emocionante

excla|im /ɪkˈskleɪm/ vi exclamar. ~mation /eksklə'meɪʃn/ n exclamación f. ~mation mark n signo m de admiración f, punto m de exclamación

exclu|de /ɪkˈskluːd/ vt excluir. ~sion /-ʒən/ n exclusión f

exclusive /ɪkˈskluːsɪv/ a exclusivo; ⟨club⟩ selecto. ~ of excluyendo. ~ly adv exclusivamente

excommunicate /ekskəˈmjuːnɪkeɪt/ vt excomulgar

excrement /ˈekskrɪmənt/ n excremento m

excruciating /ɪkˈskruːʃɪeɪtɪŋ/ a atroz, insoportable

excursion /ɪkˈskɜːʃn/ n excursión f

excus|able a /ɪkˈskjuːzəbl/ a perdonable. ~e /ɪkˈskjuːz/ vt perdonar. ~e from dispensar de. ~e me! ¡perdón! /ɪkˈskjuːs/ n excusa f

ex-directory /eksdɪˈrektərɪ/ a que no está en la guía telefónica

execrable /ˈeksɪkrəbl/ a execrable

execut|e /ˈeksɪkjuːt/ vt ejecutar. ~ion /eksɪˈkjuːʃn/ n ejecución f. ~ioner n verdugo m

executive /ɪgˈzekjʊtɪv/ a & n ejecutivo (m)

executor /ɪgˈzekjʊtə(r)/ n (jurid) testamentario m

exemplary /ɪgˈzemplərɪ/ a ejemplar

exemplify /ɪgˈzemplɪfaɪ/ vt ilustrar

exempt /ɪgˈzempt/ a exento. ● vt dispensar. ~ion /-ʃn/ n exención f

exercise /ˈeksəsaɪz/ n ejercicio m. ● vt ejercer. ● vi hacer ejercicios. ~ book n cuaderno m

exert /ɪgˈzɜːt/ vt ejercer. ~ o.s. esforzarse. ~ion /-ʃn/ n esfuerzo m

exhal|ation /ekshəˈleɪʃn/ n exhalación f. ~e /eksˈheɪl/ vt/i exhalar

exhaust /ɪgˈzɔːst/ vt agotar. ● n (auto) tubo m de escape. ~ed a agotado. ~ion /-stʃən/ n agotamiento m. ~ive /ɪgˈzɔːstɪv/ a exhaustivo

exhibit /ɪgˈzɪbɪt/ vt exponer; (jurid) exhibir; (fig) mostrar. ● n objeto m expuesto; (jurid) documento m

exhibition /eksɪˈbɪʃn/ n exposición f; (act of showing) demostración f; (univ) beca f. ~ist n exhibicionista m & f

exhibitor /ɪgˈzɪbɪtə(r)/ n expositor m

exhilarat|e /ɪgˈzɪləreɪt/ vt alegrar. ~ion /-ˈreɪʃn/ n regocijo m

exhort /ɪgˈzɔːt/ vt exhortar

exile /ˈeksaɪl/ n exilio m; (person) exiliado m. ● vt desterrar

exist /ɪgˈzɪst/ vi existir. ~ence n existencia f. in ~ence existente

existentialism /egzɪsˈtenʃəlɪzəm/ n existencialismo m

exit /ˈeksɪt/ n salida f

exodus /ˈeksədəs/ n éxodo m

exonerate /ɪgˈzɒnəreɪt/ vt disculpar

exorbitant /ɪgˈzɔːbɪtənt/ a exorbitante

exorcis|e /ˈeksɔːsaɪz/ vt exorcizar. ~m /-sɪzəm/ n exorcismo m

exotic /ɪgˈzɒtɪk/ a exótico

expand /ɪkˈspænd/ vt extender; dilatar ⟨metal⟩; (develop) desarrollar. ● vi extenderse; (develop) desarrollarse; ⟨metal⟩ dilatarse

expanse /ɪkˈspæns/ n extensión f

expansion /ɪkˈspænʃn/ n extensión f; (of metal) dilatación f

expansive /ɪkˈspænsɪv/ a expansivo

expatriate /eksˈpætrɪət/ a & n expatriado (m)

expect /ɪkˈspekt/ vt esperar; (suppose) suponer; (demand) contar con. I ~ so supongo que sí

expectan|cy /ɪkˈspektənsɪ/ n esperanza f. life ~cy esperanza f de vida. ~t /ɪkˈspektənt/ a expectante. ~t mother n futura madre f

expectation /ekspekˈteɪʃn/ n esperanza f

expedien|cy /ɪkˈspiːdɪənsɪ/ n conveniencia f. ~t /ɪkˈspiːdɪənt/ a conveniente

expedite /ˈekspɪdaɪt/ vt acelerar

expedition /ekspɪˈdɪʃn/ n expedición f. ~ary a expedicionario

expel /ɪkˈspel/ vt (pt expelled) expulsar

expend /ɪkˈspend/ vt gastar. ~able a prescindible

expenditure /ɪk'spendɪtʃə(r)/ n gastos mpl

expens|e /ɪk'spens/ n gasto m; (fig) costa f. **at s.o.'s ~e** a costa de uno. **~ive** /ɪk'spensɪv/ a caro. **~ively** adv costosamente

experience /ɪk'spɪərɪəns/ n experiencia. ● vt experimentar. **~d** a experto

experiment /ɪk'sperɪmənt/ n experimento m. ● vi experimentar. **~al** /-'mentl/ a experimental

expert /'ekspɜːt/ a & n experto (m). **~ise** /ekspɜː'tiːz/ n pericia f. **~ly** adv hábilmente

expir|e /ɪk'spaɪə(r)/ vi expirar. **~y** n expiración f

expla|in /ɪk'spleɪn/ vt explicar. **~nation** /eksplə'neɪʃn/ n explicación f. **~natory** /ɪks'plænətərɪ/ a explicativo

expletive /ɪk'spliːtɪv/ n palabrota f

explicit /ɪk'splɪsɪt/ a explícito

explode /ɪk'spləʊd/ vt hacer explotar; (tec) explosionar. ● vi estallar

exploit /'eksplɔɪt/ n hazaña f. /ɪk'splɔɪt/ vt explotar. **~ation** /eksplɔɪ'teɪʃn/ n explotación f

explor|ation /eksplə'reɪʃn/ n exploración f. **~atory** /ɪk'splɒrətrɪ/ a exploratorio. **~e** /ɪk'splɔː(r)/ vt explorar. **~er** n explorador m

explosi|on /ɪk'spləʊʒn/ n explosión f. **~ve** a & n explosivo (m)

exponent /ɪk'spəʊnənt/ n exponente m

export /ɪk'spɔːt/ vt exportar. /'ekspɔːt/ n exportación f. **~er** /ɪks'pɔːtə(r)/ exportador m

expos|e /ɪk'spəʊz/ vt exponer; (reveal) descubrir. **~ure** /-ʒə(r)/ n exposición f. **die of ~ure** morir de frío

expound /ɪk'spaʊnd/ vt exponer

express¹ /ɪk'spres/ vt expresar

express² /ɪk'spres/ a expreso; (letter) urgente. ● adv (by express post) por correo urgente. ● n (train) rápido m, expreso m

expression /ɪk'spreʃn/ n expresión f

expressive /ɪk'spresɪv/ a expresivo

expressly /ɪk'spreslɪ/ adv expresamente

expulsion /ɪk'spʌlʃn/ n expulsión f

expurgate /'ekspəgeɪt/ vt expurgar

exquisite /'ekskwɪzɪt/ a exquisito. **~ly** adv primorosamente

ex-serviceman /eks'sɜːvɪsmən/ n (pl -men) excombatiente m

extant /ek'stænt/ a existente

extempore /ek'stempərɪ/ a improvisado. ● adv de improviso

exten|d /ɪk'stend/ vt extender; (prolong) prolongar; ensanchar (house). ● vi extenderse. **~sion** n extensión f; (of road, time) prolongación f; (building) anejo m; (com) prórroga f

extensive /ɪk'stensɪv/ a extenso. **~ly** adv extensamente

extent /ɪk'stent/ n extensión f; (fig) alcance m. **to a certain ~** hasta cierto punto

extenuate /ɪk'stenjʊeɪt/ vt atenuar

exterior /ɪk'stɪərɪə(r)/ a & n exterior (m)

exterminat|e /ɪk'stɜːmɪneɪt/ vt exterminar. **~ion** /-'neɪʃn/ n exterminio m

external /ɪk'stɜːnl/ a externo. **~ly** adv externamente

extinct /ɪk'stɪŋkt/ a extinto. **~ion** /-ʃn/ n extinción f

extinguish /ɪk'stɪŋgwɪʃ/ vt extinguir. **~er** n extintor m

extol /ɪk'stəʊl/ vt (pt extolled) alabar

extort /ɪk'stɔːt/ vt sacar por la fuerza. **~ion** /-ʃn/ n exacción f. **~ionate** /ɪk'stɔːʃənət/ a exorbitante

extra /'ekstrə/ a suplementario. ● adv extraordinariamente. ● n suplemento m; (cinema) extra m & f

extract /'ekstrækt/ n extracto m. /ɪk'strækt/ vt extraer; (fig) arrancar. **~ion** /-ʃn/ n extracción f; (lineage) origen m

extradit|e /'ekstrədaɪt/ vt extraditar. **~ion** /-'dɪʃn/ n extradición f

extramarital /ekstrə'mærɪtl/ a fuera del matrimonio

extramural /ekstrə'mjʊərəl/ a fuera del recinto universitario; (for external students) para estudiantes externos

extraordinary /ɪk'strɔːdnrɪ/ a extraordinario

extra-sensory /ekstrə'sensərɪ/ a extrasensorial

extravagan|ce /ɪk'strævəgəns/ n prodigalidad f, extravagancia f. **~t** /ɪk'strævəgənt/ a pródigo, extravagante

extrem|e /ɪk'striːm/ a & n extremo (m). **~ely** adv extremadamente. **~ist** n extremista m & f. **~ity** /ɪk'stremətɪ/ n extremidad f

extricate /'ekstrɪkeɪt/ vt desenredar, librar

extrovert /'ekstrəvɜ:t/ n extrovertido m

exuberan|ce /ɪg'zju:bərəns/ n exuberancia f. **~t** /ɪg'zju:bərənt/ a exuberante

exude /ɪg'zju:d/ vt rezumar

exult /ɪg'zʌlt/ vi exultar

eye /aɪ/ n ojo m. **keep an ~ on** no perder de vista. **see ~ to ~** estar de acuerdo con. ● vt (pt **eyed**, pres p **eyeing**) mirar. **~ball** /'aɪbɔ:l/ n globo m del ojo. **~brow** /'aɪbraʊ/ n ceja f. **~ful** /'aɪfʊl/ n (fam) espectáculo m sorprendente. **~lash** /'aɪlæʃ/ n pestaña f. **~let** /'aɪlɪt/ n ojete m. **~lid** /'aɪlɪd/ n párpado m. **~opener** n (fam) revelación f. **~shadow** n sombra f de ojos, sombreador m. **~sight** /'aɪsaɪt/ n vista f. **~sore** /'aɪsɔ:(r)/ n (fig, fam) monstruosidad f, horror m. **~witness** /'aɪwɪtnɪs/ n testigo m ocular

F

fable /'feɪbl/ n fábula f

fabric /'fæbrɪk/ n tejido m, tela f

fabrication /fæbrɪ'keɪʃn/ n invención f

fabulous /'fæbjʊləs/ a fabuloso

facade /fə'sɑ:d/ n fachada f

face /feɪs/ n cara f, rostro m; (of watch) esfera f; (aspect) aspecto m. **~down(wards)** boca abajo. **~up-(wards)** boca arriba. **in the ~ of** frente a. **lose ~** quedar mal. **pull ~s** hacer muecas. ● vt mirar hacia; (house) dar a; (confront) enfrentarse con. ● vi volverse. **~ up to** enfrentarse con. **~ flannel** n paño m (para lavarse la cara). **~less** a anónimo. **~lift** n cirugía f estética en la cara

facet /'fæsɪt/ n faceta f

facetious /fə'si:ʃəs/ a chistoso, gracioso

facial /'feɪʃl/ a facial. ● n masaje m facial

facile /'fæsaɪl/ a fácil

facilitate /fə'sɪlɪteɪt/ vt facilitar

facility /fə'sɪlɪtɪ/ n facilidad f

facing /'feɪsɪŋ/ n revestimiento m. **~s** npl (on clothes) vueltas fpl

facsimile /fæk'sɪmɪlɪ/ n facsímile m

fact /fækt/ n hecho m. **as a matter of ~, in ~** en realidad, a decir verdad

faction /'fækʃn/ n facción f

factor /'fæktə(r)/ n factor m

factory /'fæktərɪ/ n fábrica f

factual /'fæktʃʊəl/ a basado en hechos, factual

faculty /'fækəltɪ/ n facultad f

fad /fæd/ n manía f, capricho m

fade /feɪd/ vi (colour) descolorarse; (flowers) marchitarse; (light) apagarse; (memory, sound) desvanecerse

faeces /'fi:si:z/ npl excrementos mpl

fag¹ /fæg/ n (chore, colour) faena f; (cigarette, sl) cigarillo m, pitillo m

fag² /fæg/ n (homosexual, Amer, sl) marica m

fagged /fægd/ a. **~ (out)** rendido

fah /fɑ:/ n (mus, fourth note of any musical scale) fa m

fail /feɪl/ vi fallar; (run short) acabarse. **he ~ed to arrive** no llegó. ● vt no aprobar (exam); suspender (candidate); (disappoint) fallar. **~ s.o.** (words etc) faltarle a uno. ● n. **without ~** sin falta

failing /'feɪlɪŋ/ n defecto m. ● prep a falta de

failure /'feɪljə(r)/ n fracaso m; (person) fracasado m; (med) ataque m; (mec) fallo m. **~ to do** dejar m de hacer

faint /feɪnt/ a (-er, -est) (weak) débil; (indistinct) indistinto. **feel ~** estar mareado. **the ~est idea** la más remota idea. ● vi desmayarse. ● n desmayo m. **~hearted** a pusilánime, cobarde. **~ly** adv (weakly) débilmente; (indistinctly) indistintamente. **~ness** n debilidad f

fair¹ /feə(r)/ a (-er, -est) (just) justo; (weather) bueno; (amount) razonable; (hair) rubio; (skin) blanco. **~ play** n juego m limpio. ● adv limpio

fair² /feə(r)/ n feria f

fair: ~ly adv (justly) justamente; (rather) bastante. **~ness** n justicia f

fairy /'feərɪ/ n hada f. **~land** n país m de las hadas. **~ story**, **~tale** cuento m de hadas

fait accompli /feɪtə'kɒmpli:/ n hecho m consumado

faith /feɪθ/ n (trust) confianza f; (relig) fe f. **~ful** a fiel. **~fully** adv fielmente. **~fulness** n fidelidad f. **~healing** n curación f por la fe

fake /feɪk/ n falsificación f; (person) impostor m. ● a falso. ● vt falsificar; (pretend) fingir

fakir /ˈfeɪkɪə(r)/ n faquir m

falcon /ˈfɔːlkən/ n halcón m

Falkland /ˈfɔːlklənd/ n. **the ~ Islands** npl las islas fpl Malvinas

fall /fɔːl/ vi (pt **fell**, pp **fallen**) caer. ● n caída f; (autumn, Amer) otoño m; (in price) baja f. ~ **back on** recurrir a. ~ **down** (fall) caer; (be unsuccessful) fracasar. ~ **for** (fam) enamorarse de ⟨person⟩; (fam) dejarse engañar por ⟨trick⟩. ~ **in** (mil) formar filas. ~ **off** (diminish) disminuir. ~ **out** (quarrel) reñir (with con); (drop out) caer. ~ **over** caer(se). ~ **over sth** tropezar con algo. ~ **short** ser insuficiente. ~ **through** fracasar

fallacy /ˈfæləsɪ/ n error m

fallible /ˈfælɪbl/ a falible

fallout /ˈfɔːlaʊt/ n lluvia f radiactiva

fallow /ˈfæləʊ/ a en barbecho

false /fɔːls/ a falso. ~**hood** n mentira f. ~**ly** adv falsamente. ~**ness** n falsedad f

falsetto /fɔːlˈsetəʊ/ n (pl -os) falsete m

falsify /ˈfɔːlsɪfaɪ/ vt falsificar

falter /ˈfɔːltə(r)/ vi vacilar

fame /feɪm/ n fama f. ~**d** a famoso

familiar /fəˈmɪlɪə(r)/ a familiar. **be ~ with** conocer. ~**ity** /-ˈærətɪ/ n familiaridad f. ~**ize** vt familiarizar

family /ˈfæməlɪ/ n familia f. ● a de (la) familia, familiar

famine /ˈfæmɪn/ n hambre f, hambruna f (LAm)

famished /ˈfæmɪʃt/ a hambriento

famous /ˈfeɪməs/ a famoso. ~**ly** adv (fam) a las mil maravillas

fan[1] /fæn/ n abanico m; (mec) ventilador m. ● vt (pt **fanned**) abanicar; soplar ⟨fire⟩. ● vi. ~ **out** desparramarse en forma de abanico

fan[2] /fæn/ n (of person) admirador m; (enthusiast) aficionado m, entusiasta m & f

fanatic /fəˈnætɪk/ n fanático m. ~**al** a fanático. ~**ism** /-sɪzəm/ n fanatismo m

fan belt /ˈfænbelt/ n correa f de ventilador

fancier /ˈfænsɪə(r)/ n aficionado m

fanciful /ˈfænsɪfl/ a (imaginative) imaginativo; (unreal) imaginario

fancy /ˈfænsɪ/ n fantasía f; (liking) gusto m. **take a ~ to** tomar cariño a ⟨person⟩; aficionarse a ⟨thing⟩. ● a de lujo; (extravagant) excesivo. ● vt (imagine) imaginar; (believe) creer; (want, fam) apetecer a. ~ **dress** n disfraz m

fanfare /ˈfænfeə(r)/ n fanfarria f

fang /fæŋ/ n (of animal) colmillo m; (of snake) diente m

fanlight /ˈfænlaɪt/ n montante m

fantasize /ˈfæntəsaɪz/ vi fantasear

fantastic /fænˈtæstɪk/ a fantástico

fantasy /ˈfæntəsɪ/ n fantasía f

far /fɑː(r)/ adv lejos; (much) mucho. **as ~ as** hasta. **as ~ as I know** que yo sepa. **by ~** con mucho. ● a (further, furthest or farther, farthest) lejano

far-away /ˈfɑːrəweɪ/ a lejano

farce /fɑːs/ n farsa f. ~**ical** a ridículo

fare /feə(r)/ n (for transport) tarifa f; (food) comida f. ● vi irle. **how did you ~?** ¿qué tal te fue?

Far East /fɑː(r)ˈiːst/ n Extremo/Lejano Oriente m

farewell /feəˈwel/ int & n adiós (m)

far-fetched /fɑːˈfetʃt/ a improbable

farm /fɑːm/ n granja f. ● vt cultivar. ~ **out** arrendar. ● vi ser agricultor. ~**er** n agricultor m. ~**house** n granja f. ~**ing** n agricultura f. ~**yard** n corral m

far: ~**off** a lejano. ~**reaching** a trascendental. ~**seeing** a clarividente. ~**sighted** a hipermétrope; (fig) clarividente

farther, farthest /ˈfɑːðə(r), ˈfɑːðəst/ see **far**

fascinat|e /ˈfæsɪneɪt/ vt fascinar. ~**ion** /-ˈneɪʃn/ n fascinación f

fascis|m /ˈfæʃɪzəm/ n fascismo m. ~**t** /ˈfæʃɪst/ a & n fascista (m & f)

fashion /ˈfæʃn/ n (manner) manera f; (vogue) moda f. ~**able** a de moda

fast[1] /fɑːst/ a (-er, -est) rápido; (clock) adelantado; (secure) fijo; (colours) sólido. ● adv rápidamente; (securely) firmemente. ~ **asleep** profundamente dormido

fast[2] /fɑːst/ vi ayunar. ● n ayuno m

fasten /ˈfɑːsn/ vt/i sujetar; cerrar ⟨windows, doors⟩; abrochar ⟨belt etc⟩. ~**er** n, ~**ing** n (on box, window) cierre m; (on door) cerrojo m

fastidious /fæˈstɪdɪəs/ a exigente, minucioso

fat /fæt/ n grasa f. ● a (fatter, fattest) gordo; ⟨meat⟩ que tiene mucha grasa; ⟨thick⟩ grueso. a ~ lot of (sl) muy poco

fatal /'feɪtl/ a mortal; ⟨fateful⟩ fatídico

fatalis|m /'feɪtəlɪzəm/ n fatalismo m. ~t n fatalista m & f

fatality /fə'tælətɪ/ n calamidad f; ⟨death⟩ muerte f

fatally /'feɪtlɪ/ adv mortalmente; ⟨by fate⟩ fatalmente

fate /feɪt/ n destino m; ⟨one's lot⟩ suerte f. ~d a predestinado. ~ful a fatídico

fat-head /'fæthed/ n imbécil m

father /'fɑ:ðə(r)/ n padre m. ~hood m paternidad f. ~-in-law m (pl fathers-in-law) m suegro m. ~ly a paternal

fathom /'fæðəm/ n braza f. ● vt. ~ (out) comprender

fatigue /fə'ti:g/ n fatiga f. ● vt fatigar

fat|ness n gordura f. ~ten vt/i engordar. ~tening a que engorda. ~ty a graso. ● n (fam) gordinflón m

fatuous /'fætjʊəs/ a fatuo

faucet /'fɔ:sɪt/ n (Amer) grifo m

fault /fɔ:lt/ n defecto m; ⟨blame⟩ culpa f; ⟨tennis⟩ falta f; ⟨geol⟩ falla f. at ~ culpable. ● vt criticar. ~less a impecable. ~y a defectuoso

fauna /'fɔ:nə/ n fauna f

faux pas /fəʊ'pɑ:/ (pl faux pas /fəʊ'pɑ:/) n metedura f de pata, paso m en falso

favour /'feɪvə(r)/ n favor m. ● vt favorecer; ⟨support⟩ estar a favor de; ⟨prefer⟩ preferir. ~able a favorable. ~ably adv favorablemente

favourit|e /'feɪvərɪt/ a & n preferido (m). ~ism n favoritismo m

fawn¹ /fɔ:n/ n cervato m. ● a color de cervato, beige, beis

fawn² /fɔ:n/ vi. ~ on adular

fax /fæks/ n telefacsímil m, fax m

fear /fɪə(r)/ n miedo m. ● vt temer. ~ful a ⟨frightening⟩ espantoso; ⟨frightened⟩ temeroso. ~less a intrépido. ~lessness n intrepidez f. ~some a espantoso

feasib|ility /fi:zə'bɪlətɪ/ n viabilidad f. ~le /'fi:zəbl/ a factible; ⟨likely⟩ posible

feast /fi:st/ n ⟨relig⟩ fiesta f; ⟨meal⟩ banquete m, comilona f. ● vt banquetear, festejar. ~ on regalarse con

feat /fi:t/ n hazaña f

feather /'feðə(r)/ n pluma f. ● vt. ~ one's nest hacer su agosto. ~-brained a tonto. ~weight n peso m pluma

feature /'fi:tʃə(r)/ n ⟨on face⟩ facción f; ⟨characteristic⟩ característica f; ⟨in newspaper⟩ artículo m; ~ ⟨film⟩ película f principal, largometraje m. ● vt presentar; ⟨give prominence to⟩ destacar. ● vi figurar

February /'februərɪ/ n febrero m

feckless /'feklɪs/ a inepto; ⟨irresponsible⟩ irreflexivo

fed /fed/ see feed. ● a. ~ up (sl) harto ⟨with de⟩

federal /'fedərəl/ a federal

federation /fedə'reɪʃn/ n federación f

fee /fi:/ n ⟨professional⟩ honorarios mpl; ⟨enrolment⟩ derechos mpl; ⟨club⟩ cuota f

feeble /'fi:bl/ a (-er, -est) débil. ~-minded a imbécil

feed /fi:d/ vt (pt fed) dar de comer a; ⟨supply⟩ alimentar. ● vi comer. ● n ⟨for animals⟩ pienso m; ⟨for babies⟩ comida f. ~back n reacciones fpl, comentarios mpl

feel /fi:l/ vt (pt felt) sentir; ⟨touch⟩ tocar; ⟨think⟩ parecerle. do you ~ it's a good idea? te parece buena idea? I ~ it is necessary me parece necesario. ~ as if tener la impresión de que. ~ hot/hungry tener calor/hambre. ~ like ⟨want, fam⟩ tener ganas de. ~ up to sentirse capaz de

feeler /'fi:lə(r)/ n ⟨of insects⟩ antena f. put out a ~ (fig) hacer un sondeo

feeling /'fi:lɪŋ/ n sentimiento m; ⟨physical⟩ sensación f

feet /fi:t/ see foot

feign /feɪn/ vt fingir

feint /feɪnt/ n finta f

felicitous /fə'lɪsɪtəs/ a feliz, oportuno

feline /'fi:laɪn/ a felino

fell¹ /fel/ see fall

fell² /fel/ vt derribar

fellow /'feləʊ/ n ⟨fam⟩ tipo m; ⟨comrade⟩ compañero m; ⟨society⟩ socio m. ~-countryman n compatriota m & f. ~ passenger/traveller n compañero m de viaje. ~ship n compañerismo m; ⟨group⟩ asociación f

felony /'felənɪ/ n crimen m

felt¹ /felt/ n fieltro m

felt² /felt/ see feel

female /'fi:meɪl/ a hembra; ⟨voice, sex etc⟩ femenino. ● n mujer f; ⟨animal⟩ hembra f

femini|ne /'femənɪn/ a & n femenino (m). ~**nity** /-'nɪnətɪ/ n feminidad f. ~**st** n feminista m & f

fenc|e /fens/ n cerca f; ⟨person, sl⟩ perista m & f ⟨fam⟩. ● vt. ~**e** (**in**) encerrar, cercar. ● vi ⟨sport⟩ practicar la esgrima. ~**er** n esgrimidor m. ~**ing** n ⟨sport⟩ esgrima f

fend /fend/ vi. ~ **for o.s.** valerse por sí mismo. ● vt. ~ **off** defenderse de

fender /'fendə(r)/ n guardafuego m; ⟨mudguard, Amer⟩ guardabarros m invar; ⟨naut⟩ defensa f

fennel /'fenl/ n hinojo m

ferment /'fɜːment/ n fermento m; ⟨fig⟩ agitación f. /fə'ment/ vt/i fermentar. ~**ation** /-'teɪʃn/ n fermentación f

fern /fɜːn/ n helecho m

feroci|ous /fə'rəʊʃəs/ a feroz. ~**ty** /fə'rɒsətɪ/ n ferocidad f

ferret /'ferɪt/ n hurón m. ● vi ⟨pt **ferreted**⟩ huronear. ● vt. ~ **out** descubrir

ferry /'ferɪ/ n ferry m. ● vt transportar

fertil|e /'fɜːtaɪl/ a fértil; ⟨biol⟩ fecundo. ~**ity** /-'tɪlətɪ/ n fertilidad f; ⟨biol⟩ fecundidad f

fertilize /'fɜːtəlaɪz/ vt abonar; ⟨biol⟩ fecundar. ~**r** n abono m

fervent /'fɜːvənt/ a ferviente

fervour /'fɜːvə(r)/ n fervor m

fester /'festə(r)/ vi enconarse

festival /'festɪvl/ n fiesta f; ⟨of arts⟩ festival m

festive /'festɪv/ a festivo. ~ **season** n temporada f de fiestas

festivity /fe'stɪvətɪ/ n festividad f

festoon /fe'stuːn/ vi. ~ **with** adornar de

fetch /fetʃ/ vt ⟨go for⟩ ir a buscar; ⟨bring⟩ traer; ⟨be sold for⟩ venderse por

fetching /'fetʃɪŋ/ a atractivo

fête /feɪt/ n fiesta f. ● vt festejar

fetid /'fetɪd/ a fétido

fetish /'fetɪʃ/ n fetiche m; ⟨psych⟩ obsesión f

fetter /'fetə(r)/ vt encadenar. ~**s** npl grilletes mpl

fettle /'fetl/ n condición f

feud /fjuːd/ n enemistad f ⟨inveterada⟩

feudal /fjuːdl/ a feudal. ~**ism** n feudalismo m

fever /'fiːvə(r)/ n fiebre f. ~**ish** a febril

few /fjuː/ a pocos. ● n pocos mpl. **a** ~ unos (pocos). **a good** ~, **quite a** ~ ⟨fam⟩ muchos. ~**er** a & n menos. ~**est** a & n el menor número de

fiancé /fr'ɒnseɪ/ n novio m. ~**e** /fr'ɒnseɪ/ n novia f

fiasco /fr'æskəʊ/ n ⟨pl -**os**⟩ fiasco m

fib /fɪb/ n mentirijilla f. ~**ber** n mentiroso m

fibre /'faɪbə(r)/ n fibra f. ~**glass** n fibra f de vidrio

fickle /'fɪkl/ a inconstante

fiction /'fɪkʃn/ n ficción f. (**works of**) ~ novelas fpl. ~**al** a novelesco

fictitious /fɪk'tɪʃəs/ a ficticio

fiddle /'fɪdl/ n ⟨fam⟩ violín m; ⟨swindle, sl⟩ trampa f. ● vt ⟨sl⟩ falsificar. ~ **with** juguetear con, toquetear, manosear. ~**r** n ⟨fam⟩ violinista m & f; ⟨cheat, sl⟩ tramposo m

fidelity /fr'delətɪ/ n fidelidad f

fidget /'fɪdʒɪt/ vi ⟨pt **fidgeted**⟩ moverse, ponerse nervioso. ~ **with** juguetear con. ● n azogado m. ~**y** a azogado

field /fiːld/ n campo m. ~ **day** n gran ocasión f. ~ **glasses** npl gemelos mpl. **F~ Marshal** n mariscal m de campo, capitán m general. ~**work** n investigaciones fpl en el terreno

fiend /fiːnd/ n demonio m. ~**ish** a diabólico

fierce /fɪəs/ a ⟨-er, -est⟩ feroz; ⟨attack⟩ violento. ~**ness** n ferocidad f, violencia f

fiery /'faɪərɪ/ a ⟨-ier, -iest⟩ ardiente

fifteen /fɪf'tiːn/ a & n quince (m). ~**th** a & n quince (m), decimoquinto (m). ● n ⟨fraction⟩ quinzavo m

fifth /fɪfθ/ a & n quinto (m). ~ **column** n quinta columna f

fift|ieth /'fɪftɪəθ/ a & n cincuenta (m). ~**y** a & n cincuenta (m). ~**y-**~**y** mitad y mitad, a medias. **a** ~**y-**~**y chance** una posibilidad f de cada dos

fig /fɪg/ n higo m

fight /faɪt/ vt/i ⟨pt **fought**⟩ luchar; ⟨quarrel⟩ disputar. ~ **shy of** evitar. ● n lucha f; ⟨quarrel⟩ disputa f; ⟨mil⟩ combate m. ~ **back** defenderse. ~ **off** rechazar ⟨attack⟩; luchar contra ⟨illness⟩. ~**er** n luchador m; ⟨mil⟩ combatiente m & f; ⟨aircraft⟩ avión m de caza. ~**ing** n luchas fpl

figment /'fɪgmənt/ n invención f

figurative /'fɪgjʊrətɪv/ a figurado

figure /'fɪgə(r)/ n (number) cifra f; (diagram) figura f; (shape) forma f; (of woman) tipo m. ● vt imaginar. ● vi figurar. **that ~s** (Amer, fam) es lógico. **~ out** explicarse. **~head** n testaferro m, mascarón m de proa. **~ of speech** n tropo m, figura f. **~s** npl (arithmetic) aritmética f

filament /'fɪləmənt/ n filamento m

filch /fɪltʃ/ vt hurtar

file[1] /faɪl/ n carpeta f; (set of papers) expediente m. ● vt archivar (papers)

file[2] /faɪl/ n (row) fila f. ● vi. **~ in** entrar en fila. **~ past** desfilar ante

file[3] /faɪl/ n (tool) lima f. ● vt limar

filings /'faɪlɪŋz/ npl limaduras fpl

fill /fɪl/ vt llenar. ● vi llenarse. **~ in** rellenar (form). **~ out** (get fatter) engordar. **~ up** (auto) llenar, repostar. ● n. **eat one's ~** hartarse de comer. **have had one's ~ of** estar harto de

fillet /'fɪlɪt/ n filete m. ● vt (pt filleted) cortar en filetes

filling /'fɪlɪŋ/ n (in tooth) empaste m. **~ station** n estación f de servicio

film /fɪlm/ n película f. ● vt filmar. **~ star** n estrella f de cine. **~-strip** n tira f de película

filter /'fɪltə(r)/ n filtro m. ● vt filtrar. ● vi filtrarse. **~-tipped** a con filtro

filth /fɪlθ/ n inmundicia f. **~iness** n inmundicia f. **~y** a inmundo

fin /fɪn/ n aleta f

final /'faɪnl/ a último; (conclusive) decisivo. ● n (sport) final f. **~s** npl (schol) exámenes mpl de fin de curso

finale /fɪ'nɑːlɪ/ n final m

final: **~ist** n finalista m & f. **~ize** vt concluir. **~ly** adv (lastly) finalmente, por fin; (once and for all) definitivamente

financ|e /'faɪnæns/ n finanzas fpl. ● vt financiar. **~ial** /faɪ'nænʃl/ a financiero. **~ially** adv económicamente. **~ier** /faɪ'nænsɪə(r)/ n financiero m

finch /fɪntʃ/ n pinzón m

find /faɪnd/ vt (pt found) encontrar. **~ out** enterarse de. **~er** n el m que encuentra, descubridor m. **~ings** npl resultados mpl

fine[1] /faɪn/ a (-er, -est) fino; (excellent) excelente. ● adv muy bien; (small) en trozos pequeños

fine[2] /faɪn/ n multa f. ● vt multar

fine: **~ arts** npl bellas artes fpl. **~ly** adv (admirably) espléndidamente; (cut) en trozos pequeños. **~ry** /'faɪnərɪ/ n galas fpl

finesse /fɪ'nes/ n tino m

finger /'fɪŋgə(r)/ n dedo m. ● vt tocar. **~-nail** n uña f. **~print** n huella f dactilar. **~-stall** n dedil m. **~-tip** n punta f del dedo

finicking /'fɪnɪkɪŋ/ a, **finicky** /'fɪnɪkɪ/ a melindroso

finish /'fɪnɪʃ/ vt/i terminar. **~ doing** terminar de hacer. **~ up doing** terminar por hacer. ● n fin m; (of race) llegada f, meta f; (appearance) acabado m

finite /'faɪnaɪt/ a finito

Fin|land /'fɪnlənd/ n Finlandia f. **~n** n finlandés m. **~nish** a & n finlandés (m)

fiord /fjɔːd/ n fiordo m

fir /fɜː(r)/ n abeto m

fire /faɪə(r)/ n fuego m; (conflagration) incendio m. ● vt disparar (bullet etc); (dismiss) despedir; (fig) excitar, enardecer, inflamar. ● vi tirar. **~-arm** n arma f de fuego. **~-brigade** n cuerpo m de bomberos. **~-cracker** n (Amer) petardo m. **~-department** n (Amer) cuerpo m de bomberos. **~-engine** n coche m de bomberos. **~-escape** n escalera f de incendios. **~-light** n lumbre f. **~-man** n bombero m. **~-place** n chimenea f. **~-side** n hogar m. **~ station** n parque m de bomberos. **~-wood** n leña f. **~-work** n fuego m artificial

firing-squad /'faɪərɪŋskwɒd/ n pelotón m de ejecución

firm[1] /fɜːm/ n empresa f

firm[2] /fɜːm/ a (-er, -est) firme. **~ly** adv firmemente. **~ness** n firmeza f

first /fɜːst/ a primero. **at ~ hand** directamente. **at ~ sight** a primera vista. ● n primero m. ● adv primero; (first time) por primera vez. **~ of all** ante todo. **~ aid** n primeros auxilios mpl. **~-born** a primogénito. **~-class** a de primera clase. **~ floor** n primer piso m; (Amer) planta f baja. **F~ Lady** n (Amer) Primera Dama f. **~ly** adv en primer lugar. **~ name** n nombre m de pila. **~-rate** a excelente

fiscal /'fɪskl/ a fiscal

fish /fɪʃ/ n (usually invar) (alive in water) pez m; (food) pescado m. ● vi pescar. **~ for** pescar. **~ out** (take out, fam) sacar. **go ~ing** ir de pesca.

~**erman** /'fɪʃəmən/ n pescador m.
~**ing** n pesca f. ~**ing-rod** n caña f de
pesca. ~**monger** n pescadero m. ~**shop** n pescadería f. ~**y** a ⟨smell⟩ a
pescado; ⟨questionable, fam⟩ sospechoso

fission /'fɪʃn/ n fisión f

fist /fɪst/ n puño m

fit¹ /fɪt/ a (fitter, fittest) conveniente; ⟨healthy⟩ sano; ⟨good
enough⟩ adecuado; ⟨able⟩ capaz. ~n
⟨of clothes⟩ corte m. ●vt (pt fitted)
⟨adapt⟩ adaptar; ⟨be the right size for⟩
sentar bien a; ⟨install⟩ colocar. ●vi
encajar; ⟨in certain space⟩ caber;
⟨clothes⟩ sentar. ~ out equipar. ~
up equipar

fit² /fɪt/ n ataque m

fitful /'fɪtfl/ a irregular

fitment /'fɪtmənt/ n mueble m

fitness /'fɪtnɪs/ n ⟨buena⟩ salud f; ⟨of
remark⟩ conveniencia f

fitting /'fɪtɪŋ/ a apropiado. ●n ⟨of
clothes⟩ prueba f. ~s /'fɪtɪŋz/ npl ⟨in
house⟩ accesorios mpl

five /faɪv/ a & n cinco (m). ~r
/'faɪvə(r)/ n (fam) billete m de cinco
libras

fix /fɪks/ vt ⟨make firm, attach,
decide⟩ fijar; ⟨mend, deal with⟩ arreglar. ●n. in a ~ en un aprieto. ~ation
/-eɪʃn/ n fijación f. ~ed a ⟨skirt⟩
fijo

fixture /'fɪkstʃə(r)/ n ⟨sport⟩ partido
m. ~s ⟨in house⟩ accesorios mpl

fizz /fɪz/ vi burbujear. ●n efervescencia f. ~le /'fɪzl/ vi burbujear.
~le out fracasar. ~y a efervescente;
⟨water⟩ con gas

flab /flæb/ n (fam) flaccidez f

flabbergast /'flæbəɡɑːst/ vt pasmar

flabby /'flæbɪ/ a flojo

flag /flæɡ/ n bandera f. ●vt (pt
flagged). ~ down hacer señales de
parada a. ●vi (pt flagged) ⟨weaken⟩
flaquear; ⟨interest⟩ decaer; ⟨conversation⟩ languidecer

flagon /'flæɡən/ n botella f grande,
jarro m

flag-pole /'flæɡpəʊl/ n asta f de
bandera

flagrant /'fleɪɡrənt/ a ⟨glaring⟩
flagrante; ⟨scandalous⟩ escandaloso

flagstone /'flæɡstəʊn/ n losa f

flair /fleə(r)/ n don m ⟨for de⟩

flak|e /fleɪk/ n copo m; ⟨of paint,
metal⟩ escama f. ●vi desconcharse.

~**e out** (fam) caer rendido. ~**y** a
escamoso

flamboyant /flæm'bɔɪənt/ a ⟨clothes⟩ vistoso; ⟨manner⟩ extravagante

flame /fleɪm/ n llama f. ●vi llamear

flamingo /flə'mɪŋɡəʊ/ n (pl -o(e)s)
flamenco m

flammable /'flæməbl/ a inflamable

flan /flæn/ n tartaleta f, tarteleta f

flank /flæŋk/ n ⟨of animal⟩ ijada f,
flanco m; ⟨of person⟩ costado m; ⟨of
mountain⟩ falda f; ⟨mil⟩ flanco m

flannel /'flænl/ n franela f (de lana);
⟨for face⟩ paño m (para lavarse la
cara). ~**ette** n franela f (de algodón),
muletón m

flap /flæp/ vi (pt flapped) ondear;
⟨wings⟩ aletear; ⟨become agitated,
fam⟩ ponerse nervioso. ●vt sacudir;
batir ⟨wings⟩. ●n ⟨of pocket⟩ cartera
f; ⟨of table⟩ ala f. **get into a** ~ ponerse
nervioso

flare /fleə(r)/ ●n llamarada f; ⟨mil⟩
bengala f; ⟨in skirt⟩ vuelo m. ●vi. ~
up llamear; ⟨fighting⟩ estallar; ⟨person⟩ encolerizarse. ~**d** a ⟨skirt⟩
acampanado

flash /flæʃ/ ●vi brillar; ⟨on and off⟩
destellar. ●vt despedir; ⟨aim torch⟩
dirigir; ⟨flaunt⟩ hacer ostentación
de. ~ **past** pasar como un rayo. ●n
relámpago m; ⟨of news, camera⟩ flash
m. ~**back** n escena f retrospectiva.
~**light** n ⟨torch⟩ linterna f

flashy /'flæʃɪ/ a ostentoso

flask /flɑːsk/ n frasco m; ⟨vacuum
flask⟩ termo m

flat¹ /flæt/ a (flatter, flattest) llano;
⟨tyre⟩ desinflado; ⟨refusal⟩ categórico; ⟨fare, rate⟩ fijo; ⟨mus⟩
desafinado. ●adv. ~ **out** ⟨at top
speed⟩ a toda velocidad

flat² /flæt/ n ⟨rooms⟩ piso m, apartamento m; ⟨tyre⟩ (fam) pinchazo m;
⟨mus⟩ bemol m

flat: ~**ly** adv categóricamente.
~**ness** n llanura f. ~**ten** /'flætn/ vt
allanar, aplanar. ●vi allanarse,
aplanarse

flatter /'flætə(r)/ vt adular. ~**er** n
adulador m. ~**ing** a ⟨person⟩ lisonjero; ⟨clothes⟩ favorecedor. ~**y** n
adulación f

flatulence /'flætjʊləns/ n flatulencia f

flaunt /flɔːnt/ vt hacer ostentación
de

flautist /'flɔːtɪst/ n flautista m & f

flavour /'fleɪvə(r)/ n sabor m. ● vt condimentar. ~ing n condimento m

flaw /flɔː/ n defecto m. ~less a perfecto

flax /flæks/ n lino m. ~en a de lino; ⟨hair⟩ rubio

flea /fliː/ n pulga f

fleck /flek/ n mancha f, pinta f

fled /fled/ see **flee**

fledged /fledʒd/ a. **fully** ~ ⟨doctor etc⟩ hecho y derecho; ⟨member⟩ de pleno derecho

fledg(e)ling /'fledʒlɪŋ/ n pájaro m volantón

flee /fliː/ vi (pt **fled**) huir. ● vt huir de

fleece /fliːs/ n vellón m. ● vt ⟨rob⟩ desplumar

fleet /fliːt/ n ⟨naut, aviat⟩ flota f; ⟨of cars⟩ parque m

fleeting /'fliːtɪŋ/ a fugaz

Flemish /'flemɪʃ/ a & n flamenco (m)

flesh /fleʃ/ n carne f. **in the** ~ en persona. **one's own** ~ **and blood** los de su sangre. ~y a ⟨fruit⟩ carnoso

flew /fluː/ see **fly**

flex /fleks/ vt doblar; flexionar ⟨muscle⟩. ● n ⟨elec⟩ cable m, flexible m

flexib|ility /fleksə'bɪlətɪ/ n flexibilidad f. ~le /'fleksəbl/ a flexible

flexitime /'fleksɪtaɪm/ n horario m flexible

flick /flɪk/ n golpecito m. ● vt dar un golpecito a. ~ **through** hojear

flicker /'flɪkə(r)/ vi temblar; ⟨light⟩ parpadear. ● n temblor m; ⟨of hope⟩ resquicio m; ⟨of light⟩ parpadeo m

flick: ~**-knife** n navaja f de muelle. ~**s** npl cine m

flier /'flaɪə(r)/ n aviador m; ⟨circular, Amer⟩ prospecto m, folleto m

flies /flaɪz/ npl ⟨on trousers, fam⟩ bragueta f

flight /flaɪt/ n vuelo m; ⟨fleeing⟩ huida f, fuga f. ~ **of stairs** tramo m de escalera f. **put to** ~ poner en fuga. **take (to)** ~ darse a la fuga. ~**-deck** n cubierta f de vuelo

flighty /'flaɪtɪ/ a (**-ier, -iest**) frívolo

flimsy /'flɪmzɪ/ a (**-ier, -iest**) flojo, débil, poco substancioso

flinch /flɪntʃ/ vi ⟨draw back⟩ retroceder (**from** ante). **without** ~**ing** ⟨without wincing⟩ sin pestañear

fling /flɪŋ/ vt (pt **flung**) arrojar. ● n. **have a** ~ echar una cana al aire

flint /flɪnt/ n pedernal m; ⟨for lighter⟩ piedra f

flip /flɪp/ vt (pt **flipped**) dar un golpecito a. ~ **through** hojear. ● n golpecito m. ~ **side** n otra cara f

flippant /'flɪpənt/ a poco serio; ⟨disrespectful⟩ irrespetuoso

flipper /'flɪpə(r)/ n aleta f

flirt /flɜːt/ vi coquetear. ● n ⟨woman⟩ coqueta f; ⟨man⟩ mariposón m, coqueto m. ~**ation** /-'teɪʃn/ n coqueteo m

flit /flɪt/ vi (pt **flitted**) revolotear

float /fləʊt/ vi flotar. ● vt hacer flotar. ● n flotador m; ⟨on fishing line⟩ corcho m; ⟨cart⟩ carroza f

flock /flɒk/ n ⟨of birds⟩ bandada f; ⟨of sheep⟩ rebaño m; ⟨of people⟩ muchedumbre f, multitud f. ● vi congregarse

flog /flɒg/ vt (pt **flogged**) ⟨beat⟩ azotar; ⟨sell, sl⟩ vender

flood /flʌd/ n inundación f; ⟨fig⟩ torrente m. ● vt inundar. ● vi ⟨building etc⟩ inundarse; ⟨river⟩ desbordar

floodlight /'flʌdlaɪt/ n foco m. ● vt (pt **floodlit**) iluminar (con focos)

floor /flɔː(r)/ n suelo m; ⟨storey⟩ piso m; ⟨for dancing⟩ pista f. ● vt ⟨knock down⟩ derribar; ⟨baffle⟩ confundir

flop /flɒp/ vi (pt **flopped**) dejarse caer pesadamente; ⟨fail, sl⟩ fracasar. ● n ⟨sl⟩ fracaso m. ~**py** a flojo

flora /'flɔːrə/ n flora f

floral /'flɔːrəl/ a floral

florid /'flɒrɪd/ a florido

florist /'flɒrɪst/ n florista m & f

flounce /flaʊns/ n volante m

flounder[1] /'flaʊndə(r)/ vi avanzar con dificultad, no saber qué hacer

flounder[2] /'flaʊndə(r)/ n ⟨fish⟩ platija f

flour /flaʊə(r)/ n harina f

flourish /'flʌrɪʃ/ vi prosperar. ● vt blandir. ● n ademán m elegante; ⟨in handwriting⟩ rasgo m. ~**ing** a próspero

floury /'flaʊərɪ/ a harinoso

flout /flaʊt/ vt burlarse de

flow /fləʊ/ vi correr; ⟨hang loosely⟩ caer. ~ **into** ⟨river⟩ desembocar en. ● n flujo m; ⟨jet⟩ chorro m; ⟨stream⟩ corriente f; ⟨of words, tears⟩ torrente m. ~**chart** n organigrama m

flower /'flaʊə(r)/ n flor f. ~**bed** n macizo m de flores. ~**ed** a floreado, de flores. ~**y** a florido

flown /fləʊn/ *see* **fly**[1]

flu /fluː/ *n* (*fam*) gripe *f*

fluctuat|e /'flʌktjʊeɪt/ *vi* fluctuar. ~**ion** /-eɪʃn/ *n* fluctuación *f*

flue /fluː/ *n* humero *m*

fluen|cy /'fluːənsɪ/ *n* facilidad *f*. ~**t** *a* (*style*) fluido; (*speaker*) elocuente. **be** ~**t** (**in a language**) hablar (un idioma) con soltura. ~**tly** *adv* con fluidez; (*lang*) con soltura

fluff /flʌf/ *n* pelusa *f*. ~**y** *a* (**-ier, -iest**) velloso

fluid /'fluːɪd/ *a & n* fluido (*m*)

fluke /fluːk/ *n* (*stroke of luck*) chiripa *f*

flung /flʌŋ/ *see* **fling**

flunk /flʌŋk/ *vt* (*Amer, fam*) ser suspendido en (*exam*); suspender (*person*). ● *vi* (*fam*) ser suspendido

fluorescent /flʊə'resnt/ *a* fluorescente

fluoride /flʊəraɪd/ *n* fluoruro *m*

flurry /'flʌrɪ/ *n* (*squall*) ráfaga *f*; (*fig*) agitación *f*

flush[1] /flʌʃ/ *vi* ruborizarse. ● *vt* limpiar con agua. ~ **the toilet** tirar de la cadena. ● *n* (*blush*) rubor *m*; (*fig*) emoción *f*

flush[2] /flʌʃ/ *a*. ~ (**with**) a nivel (con)

flush[3] /flʌʃ/ *vt/i*. ~ **out** (*drive out*) echar fuera

fluster /'flʌstə(r)/ *vt* poner nervioso

flute /fluːt/ *n* flauta *f*

flutter /'flʌtə(r)/ *vi* ondear; (*bird*) revolotear. ● *n* (*of wings*) revoloteo *m*; (*fig*) agitación *f*

flux /flʌks/ *n* flujo *m*. **be in a state of** ~ estar siempre cambiando

fly[1] /flaɪ/ *vi* (*pt* **flew**, *pp* **flown**) volar; (*passenger*) ir en avión; (*flag*) flotar; (*rush*) correr. ● *vt* pilotar (*aircraft*); transportar en avión (*passengers, goods*); izar (*flag*). ● *n* (*of trousers*) bragueta *f*

fly[2] /flaɪ/ *n* mosca *f*

flyer /'flaɪə(r)/ *n* aviador *m*; (*circular, Amer*) prospecto *m*, folleto *m*

flying /'flaɪɪŋ/ *a* volante; (*hasty*) relámpago *invar*. ● *n* (*activity*) aviación *f*. ~ **visit** *n* visita *f* relámpago

fly: ~**leaf** *n* guarda *f*. ~**over** *n* paso *m* elevado. ~**weight** *n* peso *m* mosca

foal /fəʊl/ *n* potro *m*

foam /fəʊm/ *n* espuma *f*. ~(**rubber**) *n* goma *f* espuma. ● *vi* espumar

fob /fɒb/ *vt* (*pt* **fobbed**). ~ **off on s.o.** (*palm off*) encajar a uno

focal /'fəʊkl/ *a* focal

focus /'fəʊkəs/ *n* (*pl* **-cuses** *or* **-ci** /-saɪ/) foco *m*; (*fig*) centro *m*. **in** ~ enfocado. **out of** ~ desenfocado. ● *vt/i* (*pt* **focused**) enfocar(se); (*fig*) concentrar

fodder /'fɒdə(r)/ *n* forraje *m*

foe /fəʊ/ *n* enemigo *m*

foetus /'fiːtəs/ *n* (*pl* **-tuses**) feto *m*

fog /fɒg/ *n* niebla *f*. ● *vt* (*pt* **fogged**) envolver en niebla; (*photo*) velar. ● *vi*. ~ (**up**) empañarse; (*photo*) velarse

fog(e)y /'fəʊgɪ/ *n*. **be an old** ~ estar chapado a la antigua

foggy /'fɒgɪ/ *a* (**-ier, -iest**) nebuloso. **it is** ~ hay niebla

foghorn /'fɒghɔːn/ *n* sirena *f* de niebla

foible /'fɔɪbl/ *n* punto *m* débil

foil[1] /fɔɪl/ *vt* (*thwart*) frustrar

foil[2] /fɔɪl/ *n* papel *m* de plata; (*fig*) contraste *m*

foist /fɔɪst/ *vt* encajar (**on** a)

fold[1] /fəʊld/ *vt* doblar; cruzar (*arms*). ● *vi* doblarse; (*fail*) fracasar. ● *n* pliegue *m*

fold[2] /fəʊld/ *n* (*for sheep*) redil *m*

folder /'fəʊldə(r)/ *n* (*file*) carpeta *f*; (*leaflet*) folleto *m*

folding /'fəʊldɪŋ/ *a* plegable

foliage /'fəʊlɪɪdʒ/ *n* follaje *m*

folk /fəʊk/ *n* gente *f*. ● *a* popular. ~**lore** *n* folklore *m*. ~**s** *npl* (*one's relatives*) familia *f*

follow /'fɒləʊ/ *vt/i* seguir. ~ **up** seguir; (*investigate further*) investigar. ~**er** *n* seguidor *m*. ~**ing** *n* partidarios *mpl*. ● *a* siguiente. ● *prep* después de

folly /'fɒlɪ/ *n* locura *f*

foment /fə'ment/ *vt* fomentar

fond /fɒnd/ *a* (**-er, -est**) (*loving*) cariñoso; (*hope*) vivo. **be** ~ **of s.o.** tener(le) cariño a uno. **be** ~ **of sth** ser aficionado a algo

fondle /'fɒndl/ *vt* acariciar

fondness /'fɒndnɪs/ *n* cariño *m*; (*for things*) afición *f*

font /fɒnt/ *n* pila *f* bautismal

food /fuːd/ *n* alimento *m*, comida *f*. ~ **processor** *n* robot *m* de cocina, batidora *f*

fool /fuːl/ *n* tonto *m*. ● *vt* engañar. ● *vi* hacer el tonto

foolhardy /'fuːlhɑːdɪ/ *a* temerario

foolish /'fuːlɪʃ/ *a* tonto. ~**ly** *adv* tontamente. ~**ness** *n* tontería *f*

foolproof /'fu:lpru:f/ *a* infalible, a toda prueba, a prueba de tontos

foot /fʊt/ *n* (*pl* **feet**) pie *m*; (*measure*) pie *m* (= 30,48 cm); (*of animal, furniture*) pata *f*. **get under s.o.'s feet** estorbar a uno. **on** ∼ a pie. **on/to one's feet** de pie. **put one's** ∼ **in it** meter la pata. ● *vt* pagar ⟨*bill*⟩. ∼ **it** ir andando

footage /'fʊtɪdʒ/ *n* (*of film*) secuencia *f*

football /'fʊtbɔ:l/ *n* (*ball*) balón *m*; (*game*) fútbol *m*. ∼**er** *n* futbolista *m* & *f*

footbridge /'fʊtbrɪdʒ/ *n* puente *m* para peatones

foothills /'fʊthɪlz/ *npl* estribaciones *fpl*

foothold /'fʊthəʊld/ *n* punto *m* de apoyo *m*

footing /'fʊtɪŋ/ *n* pie *m*

footlights /'fʊtlaɪts/ *npl* candilejas *fpl*

footloose /'fʊtlu:s/ *a* libre

footman /'fʊtmən/ *n* lacayo *m*

footnote /'fʊtnəʊt/ *n* nota *f* (al pie de la página)

foot: ∼**path** *n* (*in country*) senda *f*; (*in town*) acera *f*, vereda *f* (Arg), banqueta *f* (Mex). ∼**print** *n* huella *f*. ∼**sore** *a*. **be** ∼**sore** tener los pies doloridos. ∼**step** *n* paso *m*. ∼**stool** *n* escabel *m*. ∼**wear** *n* calzado *m*

for /fɔ:(r)/, *unstressed* /fə(r)/ *prep* (*expressing purpose*) para; (*on behalf of*) por; (*in spite of*) a pesar de; (*during*) durante; (*in favour of*) a favor de. **he has been in Madrid** ∼ **two months** hace dos meses que está en Madrid. ● *conj* ya que

forage /'fɒrɪdʒ/ *vi* forrajear. ● *n* forraje *m*

foray /'fɒreɪ/ *n* incursión *f*

forbade /fə'bæd/ *see* **forbid**

forbear /fɔ:'beər/ *vt/i* (*pt* **forbore**, *pp* **forborne**) contenerse. ∼**ance** *n* paciencia *f*

forbid /fə'bɪd/ *vt* (*pt* **forbade**, *pp* **forbidden**) prohibir (**s.o. to do** a uno hacer). ∼ **s.o. sth** prohibir algo a uno

forbidding /fə'bɪdɪŋ/ *a* imponente

force /fɔ:s/ *n* fuerza *f*. **come into** ∼ entrar en vigor. **the** ∼**s** las fuerzas *fpl* armadas. ● *vt* forzar. ∼ **on** imponer a. ∼**d** *a* forzado. ∼**feed** *vt* alimentar a la fuerza. ∼**ful** /'fɔ:sfʊl/ *a* enérgico

forceps /'fɔ:seps/ *n invar* tenazas *fpl*; (*for obstetric use*) fórceps *m invar*; (*for dental use*) gatillo *m*

forcible /'fɔ:səbl/ *a* a la fuerza. ∼**y** *adv* a la fuerza

ford /fɔ:d/ *n* vado *m*, botadero *m* (Mex). ● *vt* vadear

fore /fɔ:(r)/ *a* anterior. ● *n*. **come to the** ∼ hacerse evidente

forearm /'fɔ:rɑ:m/ *n* antebrazo *m*

foreboding /fɔ:'bəʊdɪŋ/ *n* presentimiento *m*

forecast /'fɔ:kɑ:st/ *vt* (*pt* **forecast**) pronosticar. ● *n* pronóstico *m*

forecourt /'fɔ:kɔ:t/ *n* patio *m*

forefathers /'fɔ:fɑ:ðəz/ *npl* antepasados *mpl*

forefinger /'fɔ:fɪŋgə(r)/ *n* (dedo *m*) índice *m*

forefront /'fɔ:frʌnt/ *n* vanguardia *f*. **in the** ∼ a/en vanguardia, en primer plano

foregone /'fɔ:gɒn/ *a*. ∼ **conclusion** resultado *m* previsto

foreground /'fɔ:graʊnd/ *n* primer plano *m*

forehead /'fɒrɪd/ *n* frente *f*

foreign /'fɒrən/ *a* extranjero; ⟨*trade*⟩ exterior; ⟨*travel*⟩ al extranjero, en el extranjero. ∼**er** *n* extranjero *m*. **F**∼ **Secretary** *n* ministro *m* de Asuntos Exteriores

foreman /'fɔ:mən/ *n* capataz *m*, caporal *m*

foremost /'fɔ:məʊst/ *a* primero. ● *adv*. **first and** ∼ ante todo

forensic /fə'rensɪk/ *a* forense

forerunner /'fɔ:rʌnə(r)/ *n* precursor *m*

foresee /fɔ:'si:/ *vt* (*pt* **-saw**, *pp* **-seen**) prever. ∼**able** *a* previsible

foreshadow /fɔ:'ʃædəʊ/ *vt* presagiar

foresight /'fɔ:saɪt/ *n* previsión *f*

forest /'fɒrɪst/ *n* bosque *m*

forestall /fɔ:'stɔ:l/ *vt* anticiparse a

forestry /'fɒrɪstrɪ/ *n* silvicultura *f*

foretaste /'fɔ:teɪst/ *n* anticipación *f*

foretell /fɔ:'tel/ *vt* (*pt* **foretold**) predecir

forever /fə'revə(r)/ *adv* para siempre

forewarn /fɔ:'wɔ:n/ *vt* prevenir

foreword /'fɔ:wɜ:d/ *n* prefacio *m*

forfeit /'fɔ:fɪt/ *n* (*penalty*) pena *f*; (*in game*) prenda *f*; (*fine*) multa *f*. ● *vt* perder

forgave /fə'geɪv/ *see* **forgive**

forge¹ /fɔːdʒ/ n fragua f. ● vt fraguar; ⟨copy⟩ falsificar

forge² /fɔːdʒ/ vi avanzar. **~ahead** adelantarse rápidamente

forge|r /ˈfɔːdʒə(r)/ n falsificador m. **~ry** n falsificación f

forget /fəˈget/ vt (pt **forgot**, pp **forgotten**) olvidar. **~ o.s.** propasarse, extralimitarse. ● vi olvidar(se). **I forgot** se me olvidó. **~ful** a olvidadizo. **~ful of** olvidando. **~menot** n nomeolvides f invar

forgive /fəˈgɪv/ vt (pt **forgave**, pp **forgiven**) perdonar. **~ness** n perdón m

forgo /fɔːˈgəʊ/ vt (pt **forwent**, pp **forgone**) renunciar a

fork /fɔːk/ n tenedor m; (for digging) horca f; (in road) bifurcación f. ● vi ⟨road⟩ bifurcarse. **~ out** (sl) aflojar la bolsa (fam), pagar. **~ed** a ahorquillado; ⟨road⟩ bifurcado. **~lift truck** n carretilla f elevadora

forlorn /fəˈlɔːn/ a (hopeless) desesperado; (abandoned) abandonado. **~ hope** n empresa f desesperada

form /fɔːm/ n forma f; (document) impreso m, formulario m; (schol) clase f. ● vt formar. ● vi formarse

formal /ˈfɔːml/ a formal; ⟨person⟩ formalista; ⟨dress⟩ de etiqueta. **~ity** /-ˈmælətɪ/ n formalidad f. **~ly** adv oficialmente

format /ˈfɔːmæt/ n formato m

formation /fɔːˈmeɪʃn/ n formación f

formative /ˈfɔːmətɪv/ a formativo

former /ˈfɔːmə(r)/ a anterior; (first of two) primero. **~ly** adv antes

formidable /ˈfɔːmɪdəbl/ a formidable

formless /ˈfɔːmlɪs/ a informe

formula /ˈfɔːmjʊlə/ n (pl **-ae** /-iː/ or **-as**) fórmula f

formulate /ˈfɔːmjʊleɪt/ vt formular

fornicat|e /ˈfɔːnɪkeɪt/ vi fornicar. **~ion** /-ˈkeɪʃn/ n fornicación f

forsake /fəˈseɪk/ vt (pt **forsook**, pp **forsaken**) abandonar

fort /fɔːt/ n (mil) fuerte m

forte /ˈfɔːteɪ/ n (talent) fuerte m

forth /fɔːθ/ adv en adelante. **and so ~** y así sucesivamente. **go back and ~** ir y venir

forthcoming /fɔːθˈkʌmɪŋ/ a próximo, venidero; (sociable, fam) comunicativo

forthright /ˈfɔːθraɪt/ a directo

forthwith /fɔːθˈwɪθ/ adv inmediatamente

fortieth /ˈfɔːtɪɪθ/ a cuarenta, cuadragésimo. ● n cuadragésima parte f

fortif|ication /fɔːtɪfɪˈkeɪʃn/ n fortificación f. **~y** /ˈfɔːtɪfaɪ/ vt fortificar

fortitude /ˈfɔːtɪtjuːd/ n valor m

fortnight /ˈfɔːtnaɪt/ n quince días mpl, quincena f. **~ly** a bimensual. ● adv cada quince días

fortress /ˈfɔːtrɪs/ n fortaleza f

fortuitous /fɔːˈtjuːɪtəs/ a fortuito

fortunate /ˈfɔːtʃənət/ a afortunado. **be ~** tener suerte. **~ly** adv afortunadamente

fortune /ˈfɔːtʃuːn/ n fortuna f. **have the good ~ to** tener la suerte de. **~teller** n adivino m

forty /ˈfɔːtɪ/ a & n cuarenta (m). **~ winks** un sueñecito m

forum /ˈfɔːrəm/ n foro m

forward /ˈfɔːwəd/ a delantero; (advanced) precoz; (pert) impertinente. ● n (sport) delantero m. ● adv adelante. **come ~** presentarse. **go ~** avanzar. ● vt hacer seguir ⟨letter⟩; enviar ⟨goods⟩; (fig) favorecer. **~ness** n precocidad f

forwards /ˈfɔːwədz/ adv adelante

fossil /ˈfɒsl/ a & n fósil (m)

foster /ˈfɒstə(r)/ vt (promote) fomentar; criar ⟨child⟩. **~child** n hijo m adoptivo. **~mother** n madre f adoptiva

fought /fɔːt/ see **fight**

foul /faʊl/ a (**-er, -est**) ⟨smell, weather⟩ asqueroso; (dirty) sucio; ⟨language⟩ obsceno; ⟨air⟩ viciado. **~ play** n (sport) jugada f sucia; (crime) delito m. ● n (sport) falta f. ● vt ensuciar; manchar ⟨reputation⟩. **~-mouthed** a obsceno

found¹ /faʊnd/ see **find**

found² /faʊnd/ vt fundar

found³ /faʊnd/ vt (tec) fundir

foundation /faʊnˈdeɪʃn/ n fundación f; (basis) fundamento. **~s** npl (archit) cimientos mpl

founder¹ /ˈfaʊndə(r)/ n fundador m

founder² /ˈfaʊndə(r)/ vi ⟨ship⟩ hundirse

foundry /ˈfaʊndrɪ/ n fundición f

fountain /ˈfaʊntɪn/ n fuente f. **~pen** n estilográfica f

four /fɔː(r)/ a & n cuatro (m). **~fold** a cuádruple. ● adv cuatro veces. **~poster** n cama f con cuatro columnas

foursome /'fɔːsəm/ n grupo m de cuatro personas

fourteen /'fɔːtiːn/ a & n catorce (m). ~**th** a & n catorce (m), decimocuarto (m). ● n (fraction) catorceavo m

fourth /fɔːθ/ a & n cuarto (m)

fowl /faʊl/ n nave f

fox /fɒks/ n zorro m, zorra f. ● vt (baffle) dejar perplejo; (deceive) engañar

foyer /'fɔɪeɪ/ n (hall) vestíbulo m

fraction /'frækʃn/ n fracción f

fractious /'frækʃəs/ a díscolo

fracture /'fræktʃə(r)/ n fractura f. ● vt fracturar. ● vi fracturarse

fragile /'frædʒaɪl/ a frágil

fragment /'frægmənt/ n fragmento m. ~**ary** a fragmentario

fragran|ce /'freɪgrəns/ n fragancia f. ~**t** a fragante

frail /freɪl/ a (-er, -est) frágil

frame /freɪm/ n (of picture, door, window) marco m; (of spectacles) montura f; (fig, structure) estructura f; (temporary state) estado m. ~ **of mind** estado m de ánimo. ● vt enmarcar; (fig) formular; (jurid, sl) incriminar falsamente. ~**up** n (sl) complot m

framework /'freɪmwɜːk/ n estructura f; (context) marco m

France /frɑːns/ n Francia f

franchise /'fræntʃaɪz/ n (pol) derecho m a votar; (com) concesión f

Franco... /'frænkəʊ/ pref franco...

frank /fræŋk/ a sincero. ● vt franquear. ~**ly** adv sinceramente. ~**ness** n sinceridad f

frantic /'fræntɪk/ a frenético. ~ **with** loco de

fraternal /frə'tɜːnl/ a fraternal

fraternity /frə'tɜːnɪtɪ/ n fraternidad f; (club) asociación f

fraternize /'frætənaɪz/ vi fraternizar

fraud /frɔːd/ n (deception) fraude m; (person) impostor m. ~**ulent** a fraudulento

fraught /frɔːt/ a (tense) tenso. ~ **with** cargado de

fray[1] /freɪ/ vt desgastar. ● vi deshilacharse

fray[2] /freɪ/ n riña f

freak /friːk/ n (caprice) capricho m; (monster) monstruo m; (person) chalado m. ● a anormal. ~**ish** a anormal

freckle /'frekl/ n peca f. ~**d** a pecoso

free /friː/ a (freer /'friːə(r)/, freest /'friːɪst/) libre; (gratis) gratis; (lavish) generoso. ~ **kick** n golpe m franco. ~ **of charge** gratis. ~ **speech** n libertad f de expresión. **give a** ~ **hand** dar carta blanca. ● vt (pt freed) (set at liberty) poner en libertad; (relieve from) liberar (from of de); (untangle) desenredar; (loosen) soltar

freedom /'friːdəm/ n libertad f

freehold /'friːhəʊld/ n propiedad f absoluta

freelance /'friːlɑːns/ a independiente

freely /'friːlɪ/ adv libremente

Freemason /'friːmeɪsn/ n masón m. ~**ry** n masonería f

free-range /'friːreɪndʒ/ a (eggs) de granja

freesia /'friːzjə/ n fresia f

freeway /'friːweɪ/ n (Amer) autopista f

freez|e /'friːz/ vt (pt froze, pp frozen) helar; congelar (food, wages). ● vi helarse, congelarse; (become motionless) quedarse inmóvil. ● n helada f; (of wages, prices) congelación f. ~**er** n congelador m. ~**ing** a glacial. ● n congelación f. **below** ~**ing** bajo cero

freight /freɪt/ n (goods) mercancías fpl; (hire of ship etc) flete m. ~**er** n (ship) buque m de carga

French /frentʃ/ a francés. ● n (lang) francés m. ~**man** n francés m. ~-**speaking** a francófono. ~ **window** n puertaventana f. ~**woman** f francesa f

frenz|ied /'frenzɪd/ a frenético. ~**y** n frenesí m

frequency /'friːkwənsɪ/ n frecuencia f

frequent /frɪ'kwent/ vt frecuentar. /'friːkwənt/ a frecuente. ~**ly** adv frecuentemente

fresco /'freskəʊ/ n (pl -o(e)s) fresco m

fresh /freʃ/ a (-er, -est) fresco; (different, additional) nuevo; (cheeky) fresco, descarado; (water) dulce. ~**en** vi refrescar. ~**en up** (person) refrescarse. ~**ly** adv recientemente. ~**man** n estudiante m de primer año. ~**ness** n frescura f

fret /fret/ vi (pt fretted) inquietarse. ~**ful** a (discontented) quejoso; (irritable) irritable

Freudian /'frɔɪdjən/ *a* freudiano
friar /'fraɪə(r)/ *n* fraile *m*
friction /'frɪkʃn/ *n* fricción *f*
Friday /'fraɪdeɪ/ *n* viernes *m*. **Good** ~ Viernes Santo
fridge /frɪdʒ/ *n* (*fam*) nevera *f*, refrigerador *m*, refrigeradora *f*
fried /fraɪd/ *see* **fry**¹. ● *a* frito
friend /frend/ *n* amigo *m*. **~liness** /'frendlɪnɪs/ *n* simpatía *f*. **~ly** *a* (**-ier, -iest**) simpático. **F~ly Society** *n* mutualidad *f*. **~ship** /'frendʃɪp/ *n* amistad *f*
frieze /fri:z/ *n* friso *m*
frigate /'frɪgət/ *n* fragata *f*
fright /fraɪt/ *n* susto *m*; (*person*) espantajo *m*; (*thing*) horror *m*
frighten /'fraɪtn/ *vt* asustar. ~**ed** *a* asustado. **be** ~**ed** tener miedo (**of** de)
frightful /'fraɪtfl/ *a* espantoso, horrible. ~**ly** *adv* terriblemente
frigid /'frɪdʒɪd/ *a* frío; (*psych*) frígido. ~**ity** /-'dʒɪdətɪ/ *n* frigidez *f*
frill /frɪl/ *n* volante *m*. ~**s** *npl* (*fig*) adornos *mpl*. **with no** ~**s** sencillo
fringe /frɪndʒ/ *n* (*sewing*) fleco *m*; (*ornamental border*) franja *f*; (*of hair*) flequillo *m*; (*of area*) periferia *f*; (*of society*) margen *m*. ~ **benefits** *npl* beneficios *mpl* suplementarios. ~ **theatre** *n* teatro *m* de vanguardia
frisk /frɪsk/ *vt* (*search*) cachear
frisky /'frɪskɪ/ *a* (**-ier, -iest**) retozón; (*horse*) fogoso
fritter¹ /'frɪtə(r)/ *vt*. ~ **away** desperdiciar
fritter² /'frɪtə(r)/ *n* buñuelo *m*
frivol|ity /frɪ'vɒlətɪ/ *n* frivolidad *f*. ~**ous** /'frɪvələs/ *a* frívolo
frizzy /'frɪzɪ/ *a* crespo
fro /frəʊ/ *see* **to and fro**
frock /frɒk/ *n* vestido *m*; (*of monk*) hábito *m*
frog /frɒg/ *n* rana *f*. **have a** ~ **in one's throat** tener carraspera
frogman /'frɒgmən/ *n* hombre *m* rana
frolic /'frɒlɪk/ *vi* (*pt* **frolicked**) retozar. ● *n* broma *f*
from /frɒm/, *unstressed* /frəm/ *prep* de; (*with time, prices, etc*) a partir de; (*habit, conviction*) por; (*according to*) según. **take** ~ (*away from*) quitar a
front /frʌnt/ *n* parte *f* delantera; (*of building*) fachada *f*; (*of clothes*) delantera *f*; (*mil, pol*) frente *f*; (*of book*) principio *m*; (*fig, appearance*) apariencia *f*; (*sea front*) paseo *m* marítimo. **in** ~ **of** delante de. **put a bold** ~ **on** hacer de tripas corazón, mostrar firmeza. ● *a* delantero; (*first*) primero. ~**age** *n* fachada *f*. ~**al** *a* frontal; (*attack*) de frente. ~ **door** *n* puerta *f* principal. ~ **page** *n* (*of newspaper*) primera plana *f*
frontier /'frʌntɪə(r)/ *n* frontera *f*
frost /frɒst/ *n* (*freezing*) helada *f*; (*frozen dew*) escarcha *f*. ~**-bite** *n* congelación *f*. ~**-bitten** *a* congelado. ~**ed** *a* (*glass*) esmerilado
frosting /'frɒstɪŋ/ *n* (*icing, Amer*) azúcar *m* glaseado
frosty *a* (*weather*) de helada; (*window*) escarchado; (*fig*) glacial
froth /frɒθ/ *n* espuma *f*. ● *vi* espumar. ~**y** *a* espumoso
frown /fraʊn/ *vi* fruncir el entrecejo. ~ **on** desaprobar. ● *n* ceño *m*
froze /frəʊz/, **frozen** /'frəʊzn/ *see* **freeze**
frugal /'fru:gl/ *a* frugal. ~**ly** *adv* frugalmente
fruit /fru:t/ *n* (*bot, on tree, fig*) fruto *m*; (*as food*) fruta *f*. ~**erer** *n* frutero *m*. ~**ful** /'fru:tfl/ *a* fértil; (*fig*) fructífero. ~**less** *a* infructuoso. ~ **machine** *n* (máquina *f*) tragaperras *m*. ~ **salad** *n* macedonia *f* de frutas. ~**y** /'fru:tɪ/ *a* (*taste*) que sabe a fruta
fruition /fru:'ɪʃn/ *n*. **come to** ~ realizarse
frump /frʌmp/ *n* espantajo *m*
frustrat|e /frʌ'streɪt/ *vt* frustrar. ~**ion** /-ʃn/ *n* frustración *f*; (*disappointment*) decepción *f*
fry¹ /fraɪ/ *vt* (*pt* **fried**) freír. ● *vi* freírse
fry² /fraɪ/ *n* (*pl* **fry**). **small** ~ gente *f* de poca monta
frying-pan /'fraɪɪŋpæn/ *n* sartén *f*
fuchsia /'fju:ʃə/ *n* fucsia *f*
fuddy-duddy /'fʌdɪdʌdɪ/ *n*. **be a** ~ (*sl*) estar chapado a la antigua
fudge /fʌdʒ/ *n* dulce *m* de azúcar
fuel /'fju:əl/ *n* combustible *m*; (*for car engine*) carburante *m*; (*fig*) pábulo *m*. ● *vt* (*pt* **fuelled**) alimentar de combustible
fugitive /'fju:dʒɪtɪv/ *a & n* fugitivo (*m*)
fugue /fju:g/ *n* (*mus*) fuga *f*
fulfil /fʊl'fɪl/ *vt* (*pt* **fulfilled**) cumplir (con) (*promise, obligation*); satisfacer (*condition*); realizar (*hopes, plans*); llevar a cabo (*task*). ~**ment**

n (*of promise, obligation*) cumplimiento *m*; (*of conditions*) satisfacción *f*; (*of hopes, plans*) realización *f*; (*of task*) ejecución *f*
full /fʊl/ *a* (**-er, -est**) lleno; (*bus, hotel*) completo; (*skirt*) amplio; (*account*) detallado. **at ∼ speed** a máxima velocidad. **be ∼ (up)** (*with food*) no poder más. **in ∼ swing** en plena marcha. ● *n*. **in ∼** sin quitar nada. **to the ∼** completamente. **write in ∼** escribir con todas las letras. **∼ back** *n* (*sport*) defensa *m & f*. **∼-blooded** *a* vigoroso. **∼ moon** *n* plenilunio *m*. **∼-scale** *a* (*drawing*) de tamaño natural; (*fig*) amplio. **∼ stop** *n* punto *m*; (*at end of paragraph, fig*) punto *m* final. **∼ time** *a* de jornada completa. **∼y** *adv* completamente
fulsome /'fʊlsəm/ *a* excesivo
fumble /'fʌmbl/ *vi* buscar (torpemente)
fume /fjuːm/ *vi* humear; (*fig, be furious*) estar furioso. **∼s** *npl* humo *m*
fumigate /'fjuːmɪgeɪt/ *vt* fumigar
fun /fʌn/ *n* (*amusement*) diversión *f*; (*merriment*) alegría *f*. **for ∼** en broma. **have ∼** divertirse. **make ∼ of** burlarse de
function /'fʌŋkʃn/ *n* (*purpose, duty*) función *f*; (*reception*) recepción *f*. ● *vi* funcionar. **∼al** *a* funcional
fund /fʌnd/ *n* fondo *m*. ● *vt* proveer fondos para
fundamental /fʌndə'mentl/ *a* fundamental
funeral /'fjuːnərəl/ *n* funeral *m*, funerales *mpl*. ● *a* fúnebre
fun-fair /'fʌnfeə(r)/ *n* parque *m* de atracciones
fungus /'fʌŋgəs/ *n* (*pl* **-gi** /-gaɪ/) hongo *m*
funicular /fjuː'nɪkjʊlə(r)/ *n* funicular *m*
funk /fʌŋk/ *m* (*fear, sl*) miedo *m*; (*state of depression, Amer, sl*) depresión *f*. **be in a (blue) ∼** tener (mucho) miedo; (*Amer*) estar (muy) deprimido. ● *vi* rajarse
funnel /'fʌnl/ *n* (*for pouring*) embudo *m*; (*of ship*) chimenea *f*
funn|ily /'fʌnɪlɪ/ *adv* graciosamente; (*oddly*) curiosamente. **∼y** *a* (**-ier, -iest**) divertido, gracioso; (*odd*) curioso, raro. **∼y-bone** *n* cóndilo *m* del húmero. **∼y business** *n* engaño *m*

fur /fɜː(r)/ *n* pelo *m*; (*pelt*) piel *f*; (*in kettle*) sarro *m*
furbish /'fɜːbɪʃ/ *vt* pulir; (*renovate*) renovar
furious /'fjʊərɪəs/ *a* furioso. **∼ly** *adv* furiosamente
furnace /'fɜːnɪs/ *n* horno *m*
furnish /'fɜːnɪʃ/ *vt* (*with furniture*) amueblar; (*supply*) proveer. **∼ings** *npl* muebles *mpl*, mobiliario *m*
furniture /'fɜːnɪtʃə(r)/ *n* muebles *mpl*, mobiliario *m*
furrier /'fʌrɪə(r)/ *n* peletero *m*
furrow /'fʌrəʊ/ *n* surco *m*
furry /'fɜːrɪ/ *a* peludo
furthe|r /'fɜːðə(r)/ *a* más lejano; (*additional*) nuevo. ● *adv* más lejos; (*more*) además. ● *vt* fomentar. **∼rmore** *adv* además. **∼rmost** *a* más lejano. **∼st** *a* más lejano. ● *adv* más lejos
furtive /'fɜːtɪv/ *a* furtivo
fury /'fjʊərɪ/ *n* furia *f*
fuse[1] /fjuːz/ *vt* (*melt*) fundir; (*fig, unite*) fusionar. **∼ the lights** fundir los plomos. ● *vi* fundirse; (*fig*) fusionarse. ● *n* fusible *m*, plomo *m*
fuse[2] /fjuːz/ *n* (*of bomb*) mecha *f*
fuse-box /'fjuːzbɒks/ *n* caja *f* de fusibles
fuselage /'fjuːzəlɑːʒ/ *n* fuselaje *m*
fusion /'fjuːʒn/ *n* fusión *f*
fuss /fʌs/ *n* (*commotion*) jaleo *m*. **kick up a ∼** armar un lío, armar una bronca, protestar. **make a ∼ of** tratar con mucha atención. **∼y** *a* (**-ier, -iest**) (*finicky*) remilgado; (*demanding*) exigente; (*ornate*) recargado
fusty /'fʌstɪ/ *a* (**-ier, -iest**) que huele a cerrado
futile /'fjuːtaɪl/ *a* inútil, vano
future /'fjuːtʃə(r)/ *a* futuro. ● *n* futuro *m*, porvenir *m*; (*gram*) futuro *m*. **in ∼** en lo sucesivo, de ahora en adelante
futuristic /fjuːtʃə'rɪstɪk/ *a* futurista
fuzz /fʌz/ *n* (*fluff*) pelusa *f*; (*police, sl*) policía *f*, poli *f* (*fam*)
fuzzy /'fʌzɪ/ *a* (*hair*) crespo; (*photograph*) borroso

G

gab /gæb/ *n* charla *f*. **have the gift of the ∼** tener un pico de oro
gabardine /gæbə'diːn/ *n* gabardina *f*

gabble /'gæbl/ vt decir atropelladamente. ● vi hablar atropelladamente. ● n torrente m de
palabras

gable /'geɪbl/ n aguilón m

gad /gæd/ vi (pt gadded). ~ about
callejear

gadget /'gædʒɪt/ n chisme m

Gaelic /'geɪlɪk/ a & n gaélico (m)

gaffe /gæf/ n plancha f, metedura f
de pata

gag /gæg/ n mordaza f; (joke) chiste
m. ● vt (pt gagged) amordazar

gaga /'ga:ga:/ a (sl) chocho

gaiety /'geɪətɪ/ n alegría f

gaily /'geɪlɪ/ adv alegremente

gain /geɪn/ vt ganar; (acquire)
adquirir; (obtain) conseguir. ● vi
(clock) adelantar. ● n ganancia f; (increase) aumento m. ~ful a lucrativo

gainsay /geɪn'seɪ/ vt (pt gainsaid)
(formal) negar

gait /geɪt/ n modo m de andar

gala /'ga:lə/ n fiesta f; (sport)
competición f

galaxy /'gæləksɪ/ n galaxia f

gale /geɪl/ n vendaval m; (storm)
tempestad f

gall /gɔ:l/ n bilis f; (fig) hiel f; (impudence) descaro m

gallant /'gælənt/ a (brave) valiente;
(chivalrous) galante. ~ry n valor m

gall-bladder /'gɔ:lblædə(r)/ n vesícula f biliar

galleon /'gælɪən/ n galeón m

gallery /'gælərɪ/ n galería f

galley /'gælɪ/ n (ship) galera f;
(ship's kitchen) cocina f. ~ (proof) n
(typ) galerada f

Gallic /'gælɪk/ a gálico. ~ism n gali-
cismo m

gallivant /'gælɪvænt/ vi (fam) callejear

gallon /'gælən/ n galón m (imperial = 4,546l; Amer = 3,785l)

gallop /'gæləp/ n galope m. ● vi (pt
galloped) galopar

gallows /'gæləʊz/ n horca f

galore /gə'lɔ:(r)/ adv en abundancia

galosh /gə'lɒʃ/ n chanclo m

galvanize /'gælvənaɪz/ vt galvanizar

gambit /'gæmbɪt/ n (in chess) gam-
bito m; (fig) táctica f

gamble /'gæmbl/ vt/i jugar. ~e on
contar con. ● n (venture) empresa f
arriesgada; (bet) jugada f; (risk)

riesgo m. ~er n jugador m. ~ing n
juego m

game¹ /geɪm/ n juego m; (match)
partido m; (animals, birds) caza f. ● a
valiente. ~ for listo para

game² /geɪm/ a (lame) cojo

gamekeeper /'geɪmki:pə(r)/ n
guardabosque m

gammon /'gæmən/ n jamón m ahumado

gamut /'gæmət/ n gama f

gamy /'geɪmɪ/ a manido

gander /'gændə(r)/ n ganso m

gang /gæŋ/ n pandilla f; (of workmen) equipo m. ● vi. ~ up unirse (on
contra)

gangling /'gæŋglɪŋ/ a larguirucho

gangrene /'gæŋgri:n/ n gangrena f

gangster /'gæŋstə(r)/ n bandido m,
gangster m

gangway /'gæŋweɪ/ n pasillo m; (of
ship) pasarela f

gaol /dʒeɪl/ n cárcel f. ~bird n criminal m empedernido. ~er n carcelero
m

gap /gæp/ n vacío m; (breach) brecha
f; (in time) intervalo m; (deficiency)
laguna f; (difference) diferencia f

gape /geɪp/ vi quedarse boquiabierto; (be wide open) estar muy
abierto. ~ing a abierto; (person)
boquiabierto

garage /'gæra:ʒ/ n garaje m; (petrol
station) gasolinera f; (for repairs)
taller m. ● vt dejar en (el) garaje

garb /ga:b/ n vestido m

garbage /'ga:bɪdʒ/ n basura f

garble /'ga:bl/ vt mutilar

garden /'ga:dn/ n (of flowers) jardín
m; (of vegetables/fruit) huerto m. ● vi
trabajar en el jardín/huerto. ~er
n jardinero/hortelano m. ~ing n
jardinería/horticultura f

gargantuan /ga:'gæntjʊən/ a gigantesco

gargle /'ga:gl/ vi hacer gárgaras. n
gargarismo m

gargoyle /'ga:gɔɪl/ n gárgola f

garish /'geərɪʃ/ a chillón

garland /'ga:lənd/ n guirnalda f

garlic /'ga:lɪk/ n ajo m

garment /'ga:mənt/ n prenda f (de
vestir)

garnet /'ga:nɪt/ n granate m

garnish /'ga:nɪʃ/ vt aderezar. ● n
aderezo m

garret /'gærət/ n guardilla f,
buhardilla f

garrison /'gærɪsn/ n guarnición f

garrulous /'gærələs/ a hablador

garter /'ga:tə(r)/ n liga f

gas /gæs/ n (pl **gases**) gas m; (med) anestésico m; (petrol, Amer, fam) gasolina f. ● vt (pt **gassed**) asfixiar con gas. ● vi (fam) charlar. ~ **fire** n estufa f de gas

gash /gæʃ/ n cuchillada f. ● vt acuchillar

gasket /'gæskɪt/ n junta f

gas: ~ **mask** n careta f antigás a invar. ~ **meter** n contador m de gas

gasoline /'gæsəli:n/ n (petrol, Amer) gasolina f

gasometer /gæ'sɒmɪtə(r)/ n gasómetro m

gasp /ga:sp/ vi jadear; (with surprise) quedarse boquiabierto. ● n jadeo m

gas: ~ **ring** n hornillo m de gas. ~ **station** n (Amer) gasolinera f

gastric /'gæstrɪk/ a gástrico

gastronomy /gæ'strɒnəmɪ/ n gastronomía f

gate /geɪt/ n puerta f; (of metal) verja f; (barrier) barrera f

gateau /'gætəʊ/ n (pl **gateaux**) tarta f

gate: ~**crasher** n intruso m (que ha entrado sin ser invitado o sin pagar). ~**way** n puerta f

gather /'gæðə(r)/ vt reunir ⟨people, things⟩; (accumulate) acumular; (pick up) recoger; recoger ⟨flowers⟩; (fig, infer) deducir; (sewing) fruncir. ~ **speed** acelerar. ● vi ⟨people⟩ reunirse; ⟨things⟩ acumularse. ~**ing** n reunión f

gauche /gəʊʃ/ a torpe

gaudy /'gɔ:dɪ/ a (-**ier**, -**iest**) chillón

gauge /geɪdʒ/ n (measurement) medida f; (rail) entrevía f; (instrument) indicador m. ● vt medir; (fig) estimar

gaunt /gɔ:nt/ a macilento; (grim) lúgubre

gauntlet /'gɔ:ntlɪt/ n. **run the ~ of** estar sometido a

gauze /gɔ:z/ n gasa f

gave /geɪv/ see **give**

gawk /gɔ:k/ vi. ~ **at** mirar como un tonto

gawky /'gɔ:kɪ/ a (-**ier**, -**iest**) torpe

gawp /gɔ:p/ vi. ~ **at** mirar como un tonto

gay /geɪ/ a (-**er**, -**est**) (joyful) alegre; (homosexual, fam) homosexual, gay (fam)

gaze /geɪz/ vi. ~ **(at)** mirar (fijamente). ● n mirada f (fija)

gazelle /gə'zel/ n gacela f

gazette /gə'zet/ n boletín m oficial, gaceta f

gazump /gə'zʌmp/ vt aceptar un precio más elevado de otro comprador

GB abbr see **Great Britain**

gear /gɪə(r)/ n equipo m; (tec) engranaje m; (auto) marcha f. **in ~** engranado. **out of ~** desengranado. ● vt adaptar. ~**box** n (auto) caja f de cambios

geese /gi:s/ see **goose**

geezer /'gi:zə(r)/ n (sl) tipo m

gelatine /'dʒeləti:n/ n gelatina f

gelignite /'dʒelɪgnaɪt/ n gelignita f

gem /dʒem/ n piedra f preciosa

Gemini /'dʒemɪnaɪ/ n (astr) Gemelos mpl, Géminis mpl

gen /dʒen/ n (sl) información f

gender /'dʒendə(r)/ n género m

gene /dʒi:n/ n gene m

genealogy /dʒi:nɪ'ælədʒɪ/ n genealogía f

general /'dʒenərəl/ a general. ● n general m. **in ~** generalmente. ~ **election** n elecciones fpl generales

generaliz|ation /dʒenərəlaɪ'zeɪʃn/ n generalización f. ~**e** vt/i generalizar

generally /'dʒenərəlɪ/ adv generalmente

general practitioner /'dʒenərəl præk'tɪʃənə(r)/ n médico m de cabecera

generate /'dʒenəreɪt/ vt producir; (elec) generar

generation /dʒenə'reɪʃn/ n generación f

generator /'dʒenəreɪtə(r)/ n (elec) generador m

genero|sity /dʒenə'rɒsətɪ/ n generosidad f. ~**us** /'dʒenərəs/ a generoso; (plentiful) abundante

genetic /dʒɪ'netɪk/ a genético. ~**s** n genética f

Geneva /dʒɪ'ni:və/ n Ginebra f

genial /'dʒi:nɪəl/ a simpático, afable; ⟨climate⟩ suave, templado

genital /'dʒenɪtl/ a genital. ~**s** npl genitales mpl

genitive /'dʒenɪtɪv/ a & n genitivo (m)

genius /'dʒi:nɪəs/ n (pl -**uses**) genio m

genocide /'dʒenəsaɪd/ n genocidio m

genre /ʒɑːŋr/ n género m

gent /dʒent/ n (sl) señor m. **~s** n aseo m de caballeros

genteel /dʒenˈtiːl/ a distinguido; (excessively refined) cursi

gentle /ˈdʒentl/ a (-er, -est) (mild, kind) amable, dulce; (slight) ligero; (hint) discreto

gentlefolk /ˈdʒentlfəʊk/ npl gente f de buena familia

gentleman /ˈdʒentlmən/ n señor m; (well-bred) caballero m

gentleness /ˈdʒentlnɪs/ n amabilidad f

gentlewoman /ˈdʒentlwʊmən/ n señora f (de buena familia)

gently /ˈdʒentlɪ/ adv amablemente; (slowly) despacio

gentry /ˈdʒentrɪ/ npl pequeña aristocracia f

genuflect /ˈdʒenjuːflekt/ vi doblar la rodilla

genuine /ˈdʒenjʊɪn/ a verdadero; (person) sincero

geograph|er /dʒɪˈɒɡrəfə(r)/ n geógrafo m. **~ical** /dʒɪəˈɡræfɪkl/ a geográfico. **~y** /dʒɪˈɒɡrəfɪ/ n geografía f

geolog|ical /dʒɪəˈlɒdʒɪkl/ a geológico. **~ist** n geólogo m. **~y** /dʒɪˈɒlədʒɪ/ n geología f

geometr|ic(al) /dʒɪəˈmetrɪk(l)/ a geométrico. **~y** /dʒɪˈɒmɪtrɪ/ n geometría f

geranium /dʒəˈreɪnɪəm/ n geranio m

geriatrics /dʒerɪˈætrɪks/ n geriatría f

germ /dʒɜːm/ n (rudiment, seed) germen m; (med) microbio m

German /ˈdʒɜːmən/ a & n alemán (m). **~ic** /dʒəˈmænɪk/ a germánico. **~ measles** n rubéola f. **~ shepherd (dog)** n (perro m) pastor m alemán. **~y** n Alemania f

germicide /ˈdʒɜːmɪsaɪd/ n germicida m

germinate /ˈdʒɜːmɪneɪt/ vi germinar. ● vt hacer germinar

gerrymander /ˈdʒerɪmændə(r)/ n falsificación f electoral

gestation /dʒeˈsteɪʃn/ n gestación f

gesticulate /dʒeˈstɪkjʊleɪt/ vi hacer ademanes, gesticular

gesture /ˈdʒestʃə(r)/ n ademán m; (fig) gesto m

get /get/ vt (pt & pp **got**, pp Amer **gotten**, pres p **getting**) obtener,

tener; (catch) coger (not LAm), agarrar (esp LAm); (buy) comprar; (find) encontrar; (fetch) buscar, traer; (understand, sl) comprender, caer (fam). **~s.o. to do sth** conseguir que uno haga algo. ● vi (go) ir; (become) hacerse; (start to) empezar a; (manage) conseguir. **~ married** casarse. **~ ready** prepararse. **~ about** (person) salir mucho; (after illness) levantarse. **~ along** (manage) ir tirando; (progress) hacer progresos. **~ along with** llevarse bien con. **~ at** (reach) llegar a; (imply) querer decir. **~ away** salir; (escape) escaparse. **~ back** vi volver. ● vt (recover) recobrar. **~ by** (manage) ir tirando; (pass) pasar. **~ down** bajar; (depress) deprimir. **~ in** entrar; subir (vehicle); (arrive) llegar. **~ off** bajar de (train, car etc); (leave) irse; (jurid) salir absuelto. **~ on** (progress) hacer progresos; (succeed) tener éxito. **~ on with** (be on good terms with) llevarse bien con; (continue) seguir. **~ out** (person) salir; (take out) sacar. **~ out of** (fig) librarse de. **~ over** reponerse de (illness). **~ round** soslayar (difficulty etc); engatusar (person). **~ through** (pass) pasar; (finish) terminar; (on phone) comunicar con. **~ up** levantarse; (climb) subir; (organize) preparar. **~away** n huida f. **~-up** n traje m

geyser /ˈɡiːzə(r)/ n calentador m de agua; (geog) géiser m

Ghana /ˈɡɑːnə/ n Ghana f

ghastly /ˈɡɑːstlɪ/ a (-ier, -iest) horrible; (pale) pálido

gherkin /ˈɡɜːkɪn/ n pepinillo m

ghetto /ˈɡetəʊ/ n (pl -os) (Jewish quarter) judería f; (ethnic settlement) barrio m pobre habitado por un grupo étnico

ghost /ɡəʊst/ n fantasma m. **~ly** a espectral

ghoulish /ˈɡuːlɪʃ/ a macabro

giant /ˈdʒaɪənt/ n gigante m. ● a gigantesco

gibberish /ˈdʒɪbərɪʃ/ n jerigonza f

gibe /dʒaɪb/ n mofa f

giblets /ˈdʒɪblɪts/ npl menudillos mpl

Gibraltar /dʒɪˈbrɔːltə(r)/ n Gibraltar m

gidd|iness /ˈɡɪdɪnɪs/ n vértigo m. **~y** a (-ier, -iest) mareado; (speed) vertiginoso. **be/feel ~y** estar/sentirse mareado

ift /gɪft/ n regalo m; (ability) don m.
~ed a dotado de talento. **~-wrap** vt
envolver para regalo

ig /gɪg/ n (fam) concierto m

igantic /dʒaɪˈgæntɪk/ a gigantesco

iggle /ˈgɪgl/ vi reírse tontamente.
● n risita f. the **~s** la risa f tonta

ild /gɪld/ vt dorar

ills /gɪlz/ npl agallas fpl

ilt /gɪlt/ a dorado. **~-edged** a (com)
de máxima garantía

immick /ˈgɪmɪk/ n truco m

in /dʒɪn/ n ginebra f

inger /ˈdʒɪndʒə(r)/ n jengibre m.
● a rojizo. ● vt. **~ up** animar. **~ ale**
n, **~ beer** n cerveza f de jengibre.
~bread n pan m de jengibre

ingerly /ˈdʒɪndʒəlɪ/ adv cautelosamente

ingham /ˈgɪŋəm/ n guinga f

ipsy /ˈdʒɪpsɪ/ n gitano m

iraffe /dʒɪˈrɑːf/ n jirafa f

irder /ˈgɜːdə(r)/ n viga f

irdle /ˈgɜːdl/ n (belt) cinturón m;
(corset) corsé m

irl /gɜːl/ n chica f, muchacha f;
(child) niña f. **~friend** n amiga f; (of
boy) novia f. **~hood** n (up to adolescence) niñez f; (adolescence) juventud f. **~ish** a de niña; (boy)
afeminado

iro /ˈdʒaɪrəʊ/ n (pl -os) giro m (ban-
cario)

irth /gɜːθ/ n circunferencia f

ist /dʒɪst/ n lo esencial invar

ive /gɪv/ vt (pt gave, pp given) dar;
(deliver) entregar; regalar (present);
prestar (aid, attention); (grant) conceder; (yield) ceder; (devote) dedicar.
~ o.s. to darse a. ● vi dar; (yield)
ceder; (stretch) estirarse. ● n elasticidad f. **~ away** regalar; descubrir
(secret). **~ back** devolver. **~ in**
(yield) rendirse. **~ off** emitir. **~ o.s.
up** entregarse (a). **~ out** distribuir;
(announce) anunciar; (become used
up) agotarse. **~ over** (devote) dedicar; (stop, fam) dejar (de). **~ up**
(renounce) renunciar a; (yield) ceder

iven /ˈgɪvn/ see **give**. ● a dado. **~
name** n nombre m de pila

lacier /ˈglæsɪə(r)/ n glaciar m.

lad /glæd/ a contento. **~den** vt alegrar

lade /gleɪd/ n claro m

ladiator /ˈglædɪeɪtə(r)/ n gladiador
m

gladiolus /glædɪˈəʊləs/ n (pl -li
/-laɪ/) estoque m, gladiolo m, gla-
díolo m

gladly /ˈglædlɪ/ adv alegremente;
(willingly) con mucho gusto

glamorize /ˈglæməraɪz/ vt embellecer. **~rous** a atractivo. **~ur** n encanto m

glance /glɑːns/ n ojeada f. ● vi. **~ at**
dar un vistazo a

gland /glænd/ n glándula f

glare /gleə(r)/ vi deslumbrar; (stare
angrily) mirar airadamente. ● n
deslumbramiento m; (stare, fig)
mirada f airada. **~ing** a deslumbra-
dor; (obvious) manifiesto

glass /glɑːs/ n (material) vidrio m;
(without stem or for wine) vaso m;
(with stem) copa f; (for beer) caña f;
(mirror) espejo m. **~es** npl (spectacles) gafas fpl, anteojos (LAm) mpl.
~y a vítreo

glaze /gleɪz/ vt poner cristales a
(windows, doors); vidriar (pottery).
● n barniz m; (for pottery) esmalte m.
~d a (object) vidriado; (eye) vidrioso

gleam /gliːm/ n destello m. ● vi
destellar

glean /gliːn/ vt espigar

glee /gliː/ n regocijo m. **~ club** n
orfeón m. **~ful** a regocijado

glen /glen/ n cañada f

glib /glɪb/ a de mucha labia; (reply)
fácil. **~ly** adv con poca sinceridad

glide /glaɪd/ vi deslizarse; (plane)
planear. **~er** n planeador m. **~ing**
n planeo m

glimmer /ˈglɪmə(r)/ n destello m.
● vi destellar

glimpse /glɪmps/ n vislumbre f.
catch a ~ of vislumbrar. ● vt vislumbrar

glint /glɪnt/ n destello m. ● vi destellar

glisten /ˈglɪsn/ vi brillar

glitter /ˈglɪtə(r)/ vi brillar. ● n brillo
m

gloat /gləʊt/ vi. **~ on/over** rego-
dearse

global /ˈgləʊbl/ a (world-wide)
mundial; (all-embracing) global

globe /gləʊb/ n globo m

globule /ˈglɒbjuːl/ n glóbulo m

gloom /gluːm/ n oscuridad f; (sadness, fig) tristeza f. **~y** a (-ier, -iest)
triste; (pessimistic) pesimista

glorify /ˈglɔːrɪfaɪ/ vt glorificar

glorious /'glɔːrɪəs/ *a* espléndido; ⟨*deed, hero etc*⟩ glorioso

glory /'glɔːrɪ/ *n* gloria *f*; ⟨*beauty*⟩ esplendor *m*. ● *vi*. ~ **in** enorgullecerse de. ~**hole** *n* ⟨*untidy room*⟩ leonera *f*

gloss /glɒs/ *n* lustre *m*. ● *a* brillante. ● *vi*. ~ **over** ⟨*make light of*⟩ minimizar; ⟨*cover up*⟩ encubrir

glossary /'glɒsərɪ/ *n* glosario *m*

glossy /'glɒsɪ/ *a* brillante

glove /glʌv/ *n* guante *m*. ~ **compartment** *n* ⟨*auto*⟩ guantera *f*, gaveta *f*. ~**d** *a* enguantado

glow /gləʊ/ *vi* brillar; ⟨*with health*⟩ rebosar de; ⟨*with passion*⟩ enardecerse. ● *n* incandescencia *f*; ⟨*of cheeks*⟩ rubor *m*

glower /'glaʊə(r)/ *vi*. ~ **(at)** mirar airadamente

glowing /'gləʊɪŋ/ *a* incandescente; ⟨*account*⟩ entusiasta; ⟨*complexion*⟩ rojo; ⟨*with health*⟩ rebosante de

glucose /'gluːkəʊs/ *n* glucosa *f*

glue /gluː/ *n* cola *f*. ● *vt* (*pres p* **gluing**) pegar

glum /glʌm/ *a* (**glummer, glummest**) triste

glut /glʌt/ *n* superabundancia *f*

glutton /'glʌtn/ *n* glotón *m*. ~**ous** *a* glotón. ~**y** *n* glotonería *f*

glycerine /'glɪsəriːn/ *n* glicerina *f*

gnarled /nɑːld/ *a* nudoso

gnash /næʃ/ *vt*. ~ **one's teeth** rechinar los dientes

gnat /næt/ *n* mosquito *m*

gnaw /nɔː/ *vt/i* roer

gnome /nəʊm/ *n* gnomo *m*

go /gəʊ/ *vi* (*pt* **went**, *pp* **gone**) ir; ⟨*leave*⟩ irse; ⟨*work*⟩ funcionar; ⟨*become*⟩ hacerse; ⟨*be sold*⟩ venderse; ⟨*vanish*⟩ desaparecer. ~ **ahead!** ¡adelante! ~ **bad** pasarse. ~ **riding** montar a caballo. ~ **shopping** ir de compras. **be** ~**ing to do** ir a hacer. ● *n* (*pl* **goes**) ⟨*energy*⟩ energía *f*. **be on the** ~ trabajar sin cesar. **have a** ~ intentar. **it's your** ~ te toca a ti. **make a** ~ **of** tener éxito en. ~ **across** cruzar. ~ **away** irse. ~ **back** volver. ~ **back on** faltar a ⟨*promise etc*⟩. ~ **by** pasar. ~ **down** bajar; ⟨*sun*⟩ ponerse. ~ **for** buscar, traer; ⟨*like*⟩ gustar; ⟨*attack, sl*⟩ atacar. ~ **in** entrar. ~ **in for** presentarse para ⟨*exam*⟩. ~ **off** ⟨*leave*⟩ irse; ⟨*go bad*⟩ pasarse; ⟨*explode*⟩ estallar. ~ **on** seguir; ⟨*happen*⟩ pasar. ~ **out** salir; ⟨*light, fire*⟩ apagarse. ~ **over** ⟨*check*⟩

examinar. ~ **round** ⟨*be enough*⟩ ser bastante. ~ **through** ⟨*suffer*⟩ sufrir; ⟨*check*⟩ examinar. ~ **under** hundirse. ~ **up** subir. ~ **without** pasarse sin

goad /gəʊd/ *vt* aguijonear

go-ahead /'gəʊəhed/ *n* luz *f* verde. ● *a* dinámico

goal /gəʊl/ *n* fin *m*, objeto *m*; ⟨*sport*⟩ gol *m*. ~**ie** *n* ⟨*fam*⟩ portero *m*. ~**keeper** *n* portero *m*. ~**post** *n* poste *m* (de la portería)

goat /gəʊt/ *n* cabra *f*

goatee /gəʊˈtiː/ *n* perilla *f*, barbas *fpl* de chivo

gobble /'gɒbl/ *vt* engullir

go-between /'gəʊbɪtwiːn/ *n* intermediario *m*

goblet /'gɒblɪt/ *n* copa *f*

goblin /'gɒblɪn/ *n* duende *m*

God /gɒd/ *n* Dios *m*. ~**-forsaken** *a* olvidado de Dios

god /gɒd/ *n* dios *m*. ~**child** *n* ahijado *m*. ~**daughter** *n* ahijada *f*. ~**dess** /'gɒdɪs/ *n* diosa *f*. ~**father** *n* padrino *m*. ~**ly** *a* devoto. ~**mother** *n* madrina *f*. ~**send** *n* beneficio *m* inesperado. ~**son** *n* ahijado *m*

go-getter /gəʊˈgetə(r)/ *n* persona *f* ambiciosa

goggle /'gɒgl/ *vi*. ~ **(at)** mirar con los ojos desmesuradamente abiertos

goggles /'gɒglz/ *npl* gafas *fpl* protectoras

going /'gəʊɪŋ/ *n* camino *m*; ⟨*racing*⟩ ⟨*estado m del*⟩ terreno *m*. **it is slow/hard** ~ es lento/difícil. ● *a* ⟨*price*⟩ actual; ⟨*concern*⟩ en funcionamiento. ~**s-on** *npl* actividades *fpl* anormales, tejemaneje *m*

gold /gəʊld/ *n* oro *m*. ● *a* de oro. ~**en** /'gəʊldən/ *a* de oro; ⟨*in colour*⟩ dorado; ⟨*opportunity*⟩ único. ~**en wedding** *n* bodas *fpl* de oro. ~**fish** *n invar* pez *m* de colores, carpa *f* dorada. ~**mine** *n* mina *f* de oro; ⟨*fig*⟩ fuente *f* de gran riqueza. ~**-plated** *a* chapado en oro. ~**smith** *n* orfebre *m*

golf /gɒlf/ *n* golf *m*. ~**-course** *n* campo *m* de golf. ~**er** *n* jugador *m* de golf

golly /'gɒlɪ/ *int* ¡caramba!

golosh /gəˈlɒʃ/ *n* chanclo *m*

gondol|**a** /'gɒndələ/ *n* góndola *f*. ~**ier** /gɒndəˈlɪə(r)/ *n* gondolero *m*

gone /gɒn/ *see* **go**. ● *a* pasado. ~ **six o'clock** después de las seis

gong /gɒŋ/ *n* gong(o) *m*

good /gʊd/ a (**better**, **best**) bueno, (before masculine singular noun) buen. ~ **afternoon!** (before dark) ¡buenas tardes!; (after dark) ¡buenas noches! G~ **Friday** n Viernes m Santo. ~ **morning!** ¡buenos días! ~ **name** n (buena) reputación f. ~ **night!** ¡buenas noches! a ~ **deal** bastante. as ~ as (almost) casi. be ~ **with** entender. do ~ hacer bien. **feel** ~ sentirse bien. **have a** ~ **time** divertirse. **it is** ~ **for you** le sentará bien. **o** n bien m. **for** ~ para siempre. **it is no** ~ **shouting/etc** es inútil gritar/etc.

goodbye /gʊd'baɪ/ int ¡adiós! **o** n adiós m. **say** ~ **to** despedirse de

good: ~-**for-nothing** a & n inútil (m). ~-**looking** a guapo

goodness /'gʊdnɪs/ n bondad f. ~!, ~ **gracious!**, ~ **me!**, **my** ~! ¡Dios mío!

goods /gʊdz/ npl (merchandise) mercancías fpl

goodwill /gʊd'wɪl/ n buena voluntad f

goody /'gʊdɪ/ n (culin, fam) golosina f; (in film) bueno m. ~-**goody** n mojigato m

gooey /'gu:ɪ/ a (**gooier**, **gooiest**) (sl) pegajoso; (fig) sentimental

goof /gu:f/ vi (Amer, blunder) cometer una pifia. ~**y** a (sl) necio

goose /gu:s/ n (pl **geese**) oca f

gooseberry /'gʊzbərɪ/ n uva f espina, grosella f

goose-flesh /'gu:sfleʃ/ n, **goose-pimples** /'gu:spɪmplz/ n carne f de gallina

gore /gɔ:(r)/ n sangre f. **o** vt cornear

gorge /gɔ:dʒ/ n (geog) garganta f. **o** vt. ~ **o.s.** hartarse (**on** de)

gorgeous /'gɔ:dʒəs/ a magnífico

gorilla /gə'rɪlə/ n gorila m

gormless /'gɔ:mlɪs/ a (sl) idiota

gorse /gɔ:s/ n aulaga f

gory /'gɔ:rɪ/ a (-**ier**, -**iest**) (covered in blood) ensangrentado; (horrific, fig) horrible

gosh /gɒʃ/ int ¡caramba!

go-slow /gəʊ'sləʊ/ n huelga f de celo

gospel /'gɒspl/ n evangelio m

gossip /'gɒsɪp/ n (idle chatter) charla f; (tittle-tattle) comadreo m; (person) chismoso m. **o** vi (pt **gossiped**) (chatter) charlar; (repeat scandal) comadrear. ~**y** a chismoso

got /gɒt/ see **get**. **have** ~ tener. **have** ~ **to do** tener que hacer

Gothic /'gɒθɪk/ a (archit) gótico; (people) godo

gouge /gaʊdʒ/ vt. ~ **out** arrancar

gourmet /'gʊəmeɪ/ n gastrónomo m

gout /gaʊt/ n (med) gota f

govern /'gʌvn/ vt/i gobernar

governess /'gʌvənɪs/ n institutriz f

government /'gʌvənmənt/ n gobierno m. ~**al** /gʌvən'mentl/ a gubernamental

governor /'gʌvənə(r)/ n gobernador m

gown /gaʊn/ n vestido m; (of judge, teacher) toga f

GP abbr see **general practitioner**

grab /græb/ vt (pt **grabbed**) agarrar

grace /greɪs/ n gracia f. ~**ful** a elegante

gracious /'greɪʃəs/ a (kind) amable; (elegant) elegante

gradation /grə'deɪʃn/ n gradación f

grade /greɪd/ n clase f, categoría f; (of goods) clase f, calidad f; (on scale) grado m; (school mark) nota f; (class, Amer) curso m. ~ **school** n (Amer) escuela f primaria. **o** vt clasificar; (schol) calificar

gradient /'greɪdɪənt/ n (slope) pendiente f

gradual /'grædʒʊəl/ a gradual. ~**ly** adv gradualmente

graduat|e /'grædʒʊət/ n (univ) licenciado. **o** vi /'grædʒʊeɪt/ licenciarse. **o** vt graduar. ~**ion** /-'eɪʃn/ n entrega f de títulos

graffiti /grə'fi:tɪ/ npl pintada f

graft[1] /grɑ:ft/ n (med, bot) injerto m. **o** vt injertar

graft[2] /grɑ:ft/ n (bribery, fam) corrupción f

grain /greɪn/ n grano m

gram /græm/ n gramo m

gramma|r /'græmə(r)/ n gramática f. ~**tical** /grə'mætɪkl/ a gramatical

gramophone /'græməfəʊn/ n tocadiscos m invar

grand /grænd/ a (-**er**, -**est**) magnífico; (excellent, fam) estupendo. ~-**child** n nieto m. ~-**daughter** n nieta f

grandeur /'grændʒə(r)/ n grandiosidad f

grandfather /'grændfɑ:ðə(r)/ n abuelo m

grandiose /'grændɪəʊs/ a grandioso

grand: ~**mother** n abuela f. ~-**parents** npl abuelos mpl. ~ **piano** n piano m de cola. ~**son** n nieto m

grandstand /'grænstænd/ n tribuna f

granite /'grænɪt/ n granito m

granny /'grænɪ/ n (fam) abuela f, nana f (fam)

grant /grɑ:nt/ vt conceder; (give) donar; (admit) admitir (**that** que). **take for** ∼**ed** dar por sentado. ● n concesión f; (univ) beca f

granulated /'grænjʊleɪtɪd/ a. ∼ **sugar** n azúcar m granulado

granule /'grænu:l/ n gránulo m

grape /greɪp/ n uva f

grapefruit /'greɪpfru:t/ n invar toronja f, pomelo m

graph /grɑ:f/ n gráfica f

graphic /'græfɪk/ a gráfico

grapple /'græpl/ vi. ∼ **with** intentar vencer

grasp /grɑ:sp/ vt agarrar. ● n (hold) agarro m; (strength of hand) apretón m; (reach) alcance m; (fig) comprensión f

grasping /'grɑ:spɪŋ/ a avaro

grass /grɑ:s/ n hierba f. ∼**hopper** n saltamontes m invar. ∼**land** n pradera f. ∼ **roots** npl base f popular. ● a popular. ∼**y** a cubierto de hierba

grate /greɪt/ n (fireplace) parrilla f. ● vt rallar. ∼ **one's teeth** hacer rechinar los dientes. ● vi rechinar

grateful /'greɪtfl/ a agradecido. ∼**ly** adv con gratitud

grater /'greɪtə(r)/ n rallador m

gratif|ied /'grætɪfaɪd/ a contento. ∼**y** vt satisfacer; (please) agradar a. ∼**ying** a agradable

grating /'greɪtɪŋ/ n reja f

gratis /'grɑ:tɪs/ a & adv gratis (a invar)

gratitude /'grætɪtju:d/ n gratitud f

gratuitous /grə'tju:ɪtəs/ a gratuito

gratuity /grə'tju:ətɪ/ n (tip) propina f; (gift of money) gratificación f

grave[1] /greɪv/ n sepultura f

grave[2] /greɪv/ a (-er, -est) (serious) serio. /grɑ:v/ a. ∼ **accent** n acento m grave

grave-digger /'greɪvdɪgə(r)/ n sepulturero m

gravel /'grævl/ n grava f

gravely /'greɪvlɪ/ a (seriously) seriamente

grave: ∼**stone** n lápida f. ∼**yard** n cementerio m

gravitat|e /'grævɪteɪt/ vi gravitar. ∼**ion** /-'teɪʃn/ n gravitación f

gravity /'grævɪtɪ/ n gravedad f

gravy /'greɪvɪ/ n salsa f

graze[1] /greɪz/ vt/i (eat) pacer

graze[2] /greɪz/ vt (touch) rozar; (scrape) raspar. ● n rozadura f

greas|e /gri:s/ n grasa f. ● vt engrasar. ∼**e-paint** n maquillaje m ∼**e-proof paper** n papel m a prueba de grasa, apergaminado m. ∼**y** a grasiento

great /greɪt/ a (-er, -est) grande, (before singular noun) gran; (very good, fam) estupendo. **G**∼ **Britain** n Gran Bretaña f. ∼**-grandfather** n bisabuelo m. ∼**-grandmother** n bisabuela f. ∼**ly** /'greɪtlɪ/ adv (very) muy; (much) mucho. ∼**ness** n grandeza f

Greece /gri:s/ n Grecia f

greed /gri:d/ n avaricia f; (for food) glotonería f. ∼**y** a avaro; (for food) glotón

Greek /gri:k/ a & n griego (m)

green /gri:n/ a (-er, -est) verde; (fig) crédulo. ● n verde m; (grass) céspe[d] m. ∼ **belt** n zona f verde. ∼**ery** n verdor m. ∼ **fingers** npl habilidad f con las plantas

greengage /'gri:ngeɪdʒ/ n (plum) claudia f

greengrocer /'gri:ngrəʊsə(r)/ n verdulero m

greenhouse /'gri:nhaʊs/ n invernadero m

green: ∼ **light** n luz f verde. ∼**s** npl verduras fpl

Greenwich Mean Time /grenɪtʃ 'mi:ntaɪm/ n hora f media de Greenwich

greet /gri:t/ vt saludar; (receive) recibir. ∼**ing** n saludo m. ∼**ings** npl (in letter) recuerdos mpl

gregarious /grɪ'geərɪəs/ a gregario

grenade /grɪ'neɪd/ n granada f

grew /gru:/ see **grow**

grey /greɪ/ a & n (-er, -est) gris (m). ● vi (hair) encanecer

greyhound /'greɪhaʊnd/ n galgo m

grid /grɪd/ n reja f; (network, elec) re[d] f; (culin) parrilla f; (on map) cuadrícula f

grief /gri:f/ n dolor m. **come to** ∼ (person) sufrir un accidente; (fail) fracasar

grievance /'gri:vns/ n queja f

grieve /gri:v/ vt afligir. ● vi afligirse. ∼ **for** llorar

grievous /'gri:vəs/ a doloroso; (serious) grave

rill /grɪl/ n (cooking device) parrilla *f*; (food) parrillada *f*, asado *m*, asada *f*. ● vt asar a la parrilla; (interrogate) interrogar

rille /grɪl/ n rejilla *f*

rim /grɪm/ a (**grimmer, grimmest**) severo

rimace /'grɪməs/ n mueca *f*. ● vi hacer muecas

rim|e /graɪm/ n mugre *f*. **~y** a mugriento

rin /grɪn/ vt (pt **grinned**) sonreír. ● n sonrisa *f* (abierta)

rind /graɪnd/ vt (pt **ground**) moler (coffee, corn etc); (pulverize) pulverizar; (sharpen) afilar. **~ one's teeth** hacer rechinar los dientes. ● n faena *f*

rip /grɪp/ vt (pt **gripped**) agarrar; (interest) captar la atención de. ● n (hold) agarro *m*; (strength of hand) apretón *m*. **come to ~s** encararse (**with** a/con)

ripe /graɪp/ n. **~s** npl (med) cólico *n*

risly /'grɪzlɪ/ a (-ier, -iest) horrible

ristle /'grɪsl/ n cartílago *m*

rit /grɪt/ n arena *f*; (fig) valor *m*, aguante *m*. ● vt (pt **gritted**) echar arena en (road). **~ one's teeth** (fig) acorazarse

rizzle /'grɪzl/ vi lloriquear

roan /grəʊn/ vi gemir. ● n gemido *m*

rocer /'grəʊsə(r)/ n tendero *m*. **~ies** npl comestibles mpl. **~y** n tienda *f* de comestibles

rog /grɒg/ n grog *m*

roggy /'grɒgɪ/ a (weak) débil; (unsteady) inseguro; (ill) malucho

roin /grɔɪn/ n ingle *f*

room /gruːm/ n mozo *m* de caballos; (bridegroom) novio *m*. ● vt almohazar (horses); (fig) preparar. **well-~ed** a bien arreglado

roove /gruːv/ n ranura *f*; (in record) surco *m*

rope /grəʊp/ vi (find one's way) moverse a tientas. **~ for** buscar a tientas

ross /grəʊs/ a (-er, -est) (coarse) grosero; (com) bruto; (fat) grueso; (flagrant) grave. ● n invar gruesa *f*. **~ly** adv groseramente; (very) enormemente

rotesque /grəʊ'tesk/ a grotesco

rotto /'grɒtəʊ/ n (pl -oes) gruta *f*

grotty /'grɒtɪ/ a (sl) desagradable; (dirty) sucio

grouch /graʊtʃ/ vi (grumble, fam) rezongar

ground[1] /graʊnd/ n suelo *m*; (area) terreno *m*; (reason) razón *f*; (elec, Amer) toma *f* de tierra. ● vt varar (ship); prohibir despegar (aircraft). **~s** npl jardines mpl; (sediment) poso *m*

ground[2] /graʊnd/ see **grind**

ground: **~ floor** n planta *f* baja. **~ rent** n alquiler *m* del terreno

grounding /'graʊndɪŋ/ n base *f*, conocimientos mpl (**in** de)

groundless /'graʊndlɪs/ a infundado

ground: **~sheet** n tela *f* impermeable. **~swell** n mar *m* de fondo. **~work** n trabajo *m* preparatorio

group /gruːp/ n grupo *m*. ● vt agrupar. ● vi agruparse

grouse[1] /graʊs/ n invar (bird) urogallo *m*. **red ~** lagópodo *m* escocés

grouse[2] /graʊs/ vi (grumble, fam) rezongar

grove /grəʊv/ n arboleda *f*. **lemon ~** n limonar *m*. **olive ~** n olivar *m*. **orange ~** n naranjal *m*. **pine ~** n pinar *m*

grovel /'grɒvl/ vi (pt **grovelled**) arrastrarse, humillarse. **~ling** a servil

grow /grəʊ/ vi (pt **grew**, pp **grown**) crecer; (cultivated plant) cultivarse; (become) volverse, ponerse. ● vt cultivar. **~ up** hacerse mayor. **~er** n cultivador *m*

growl /graʊl/ vi gruñir. ● n gruñido *m*

grown /grəʊn/ see **grow**. ● a adulto. **~-up** a & n adulto (*m*)

growth /grəʊθ/ n crecimiento *m*; (increase) aumento *m*; (development) desarrollo *m*; (med) tumor *m*

grub /grʌb/ n (larva) larva *f*; (food, sl) comida *f*

grubby /'grʌbɪ/ a (-ier, -iest) mugriento

grudg|e /grʌdʒ/ vt dar de mala gana; (envy) envidiar. **~e doing** molestarle hacer. **he ~ed paying** le molestó pagar. ● n rencor *m*. **bear/have a ~e against s.o.** guardar rencor a alguien. **~ingly** adv de mala gana

gruelling /'gruːəlɪŋ/ a agotador

gruesome /'gru:səm/ a horrible

gruff /grʌf/ a (**-er, -est**) ⟨manners⟩ brusco; ⟨voice⟩ ronco

grumble /'grʌmbl/ vi rezongar

grumpy /'grʌmpɪ/ a (**-ier, -iest**) malhumorado

grunt /grʌnt/ vi gruñir. ● n gruñido m

guarant|ee /gærən'ti:/ n garantía f. ● vt garantizar. **~or** n garante m & f

guard /gɑːd/ vt proteger; ⟨watch⟩ vigilar. ● vi. **~ against** guardar de. ● n ⟨vigilance, mil group⟩ guardia f; ⟨person⟩ guardia m; ⟨on train⟩ jefe m de tren

guarded /'gɑːdɪd/ a cauteloso

guardian /'gɑːdɪən/ n guardián m; ⟨of orphan⟩ tutor m

guer(r)illa /gə'rɪlə/ n guerrillero m. **~ warfare** n guerra f de guerrillas

guess /ges/ vt/i adivinar; ⟨suppose, Amer⟩ creer. ● n conjetura f. **~work** n conjetura(s) f(pl)

guest /gest/ n invitado m; ⟨in hotel⟩ huésped m. **~house** n casa f de huéspedes

guffaw /gʌ'fɔ:/ n carcajada f. ● vi reírse a carcajadas

guidance /'gaɪdəns/ n ⟨advice⟩ consejos mpl; ⟨information⟩ información f

guide /gaɪd/ n ⟨person⟩ guía m & f; ⟨book⟩ guía f. **Girl G~** exploradora f, guía f ⟨fam⟩. ● vt guiar. **~book** n guía f. **~d missile** n proyectil m teledirigido. **~lines** npl pauta f

guild /gɪld/ n gremio m

guile /gaɪl/ n astucia f

guillotine /'gɪləti:n/ n guillotina f

guilt /gɪlt/ n culpabilidad f. **~y** a culpable

guinea-pig /'gɪnɪpɪg/ n ⟨including fig⟩ cobaya f

guise /gaɪz/ n ⟨external appearance⟩ apariencia f; ⟨style⟩ manera f

guitar /gɪ'tɑ:(r)/ n guitarra f. **~ist** n guitarrista m & f

gulf /gʌlf/ n ⟨part of sea⟩ golfo m; ⟨hollow⟩ abismo m

gull /gʌl/ n gaviota f

gullet /'gʌlɪt/ n esófago m

gullible /'gʌləbl/ a crédulo

gully /'gʌlɪ/ n ⟨ravine⟩ barranco m

gulp /gʌlp/ vt. **~ down** tragarse de prisa. ● vi tragar; ⟨from fear etc⟩ sentir dificultad para tragar. ● n trago m

gum¹ /gʌm/ n goma f; ⟨for chewing⟩ chicle m. ● vt ⟨pt **gummed**⟩ engomar

gum² /gʌm/ n ⟨anat⟩ encía f. **~boil** /'gʌmbɔɪl/ n flemón m

gumboot /'gʌmbu:t/ n bota f de agua

gumption /'gʌmpʃn/ n ⟨fam⟩ iniciativa f; ⟨common sense⟩ sentido m común

gun /gʌn/ n ⟨pistol⟩ pistola f; ⟨rifle⟩ fusil m; ⟨large⟩ cañón m. ● vt ⟨pt **gunned**⟩. **~ down** abatir a tiros. **~fire** n tiros mpl

gunge /gʌndʒ/ n ⟨sl⟩ materia f sucia (y pegajosa)

gun: ~man /'gʌnmən/ n pistolero m. **~ner** /'gʌnə(r)/ n artillero m. **~powder** n pólvora f. **~shot** n disparo m

gurgle /'gɜːgl/ n ⟨of liquid⟩ gorgoteo m; ⟨of baby⟩ gorjeo m. ● vi ⟨liquid⟩ gorgotear; ⟨baby⟩ gorjear

guru /'goru:/ n ⟨pl **-us**⟩ mentor m

gush /gʌʃ/ vi. **~ (out)** salir a borbotones. ● n ⟨of liquid⟩ chorro m; ⟨fig⟩ torrente m. **~ing** a efusivo

gusset /'gʌsɪt/ n escudete m

gust /gʌst/ n ráfaga f; ⟨of smoke⟩ bocanada f

gusto /'gʌstəʊ/ n entusiasmo m

gusty /'gʌstɪ/ a borrascoso

gut /gʌt/ n tripa f, intestino m. ● vt ⟨pt **gutted**⟩ destripar; ⟨fire⟩ destruir. **~s** npl tripas fpl; ⟨courage, fam⟩ valor m

gutter /'gʌtə(r)/ n ⟨on roof⟩ canalón m; ⟨in street⟩ cuneta f; ⟨slum, fig⟩ arroyo m. **~snipe** n golfillo m

guttural /'gʌtərəl/ a gutural

guy /gaɪ/ n ⟨man, fam⟩ hombre m, tío m ⟨fam⟩

guzzle /'gʌzl/ vt/i soplarse, tragarse

gym /dʒɪm/ n ⟨gymnasium, fam⟩ gimnasio m; ⟨gymnastics, fam⟩ gimnasia f

gymkhana /dʒɪmkɑ:nə/ n gincana f, gymkhana f

gymnasium /dʒɪm'neɪzɪəm/ n gimnasio m

gymnast /'dʒɪmnæst/ n gimnasta m & f. **~ics** npl gimnasia f

gym-slip /'dʒɪmslɪp/ n túnica f ⟨de gimnasia⟩

gynaecolog|ist /gaɪnɪ'kɒlədʒɪst/ n ginecólogo m. **~y** n ginecología f

gypsy /'dʒɪpsɪ/ n gitano m

gyrate /dʒaɪə'reɪt/ vi girar

gyroscope /'dʒaɪərəskəʊp/ n giroscopio m

H

haberdashery /hæbə'dæʃərɪ/ n mercería f

habit /'hæbɪt/ n costumbre f; (costume, relig) hábito m. **be in the ~ of** (+ gerund) tener la costumbre de (+ infinitive), soler (+ infinitive). **get into the ~ of** (+ gerund) acostumbrarse a (+ infinitive)

habitable /'hæbɪtəbl/ a habitable

habitat /'hæbɪtæt/ n hábitat m

habitation /hæbɪ'teɪʃn/ n habitación f

habitual /hə'bɪtjʊəl/ a habitual; (smoker, liar) inveterado. **~ly** adv de costumbre

hack /hæk/ n (old horse) jamelgo m; (writer) escritorzuelo m. ● vt cortar. **~ to pieces** cortar en pedazos

hackney /'hæknɪ/ a. **~ carriage** n coche m de alquiler, taxi m

hackneyed /'hæknɪd/ a manido

had /hæd/ see **have**

haddock /'hædək/ n invar eglefino m. **smoked ~** n eglefino m ahumado

haemorrhage /'hemərɪdʒ/ n hemorragia f

haemorrhoids /'hemərɔɪdz/ npl hemorroides fpl, almorranas fpl

hag /hæg/ n bruja f

haggard /'hægəd/ a ojeroso

haggle /'hægl/ vi regatear

Hague /heɪg/ n. **The ~** La Haya f

hail[1] /heɪl/ n granizo m. ● vi granizar

hail[2] /heɪl/ vt (greet) saludar; llamar ‹taxi›. ● vi. **~ from** venir de

hailstone /'heɪlstəʊn/ n grano m de granizo

hair /heə(r)/ n pelo m. **~brush** n cepillo m para el pelo. **~cut** n corte m de pelo. **have a ~cut** cortarse el pelo. **~do** n (fam) peinado m. **~dresser** n peluquero m. **~dresser's (shop)** n peluquería f. **~dryer** n secador m. **~pin** n horquilla f. **~pin bend** n curva f cerrada. **~raising** a espeluznante. **~style** n peinado m

hairy /'heərɪ/ a (-ier, -iest) peludo; (terrifying, sl) espeluznante

hake /heɪk/ n invar merluza f

halcyon /'hælsɪən/ a sereno. **~ days** npl época f feliz

hale /heɪl/ a robusto

half /hɑːf/ n (pl halves) mitad f. ● a medio. **~ a dozen** media docena f. **~ an hour** media hora f. ● adv medio, a medias. **~-back** n (sport) medio m. **~-caste** a & n mestizo (m). **~-hearted** a poco entusiasta. **~-term** n vacaciones fpl de media trimestre. **~-time** n (sport) descanso m. **~-way** a medio. ● adv a medio camino. **~-wit** n imbécil m & f. **at ~-mast** a media asta

halibut /'hælɪbət/ n invar hipogloso m, halibut m

hall /hɔːl/ n (room) sala f; (mansion) casa f solariega; (entrance) vestíbulo m. **~ of residence** n colegio m mayor

hallelujah /hælɪ'luːjə/ int & n aleluya (f)

hallmark /'hɔːlmɑːk/ n (on gold etc) contraste m; (fig) sello m (distintivo)

hallo /hə'ləʊ/ int = **hello**

hallow /'hæləʊ/ vt santificar. **H~e'en** n víspera f de Todos los Santos

hallucination /həluːsɪ'neɪʃn/ n alucinación f

halo /'heɪləʊ/ n (pl -oes) aureola f

halt /hɔːlt/ n alto m. ● vt parar. ● vi pararse

halve /hɑːv/ vt dividir por mitad

ham /hæm/ n jamón m; (theatre, sl) racionista m & f

hamburger /'hæmbɜːgə(r)/ n hamburguesa f

hamlet /'hæmlɪt/ n aldea f, caserío m

hammer /'hæmə(r)/ n martillo m. ● vt martill(e)ar; (defeat, fam) machacar

hammock /'hæmək/ n hamaca f

hamper[1] /'hæmpə(r)/ n cesta f

hamper[2] /'hæmpə(r)/ vt estorbar, poner trabas

hamster /'hæmstə(r)/ n hámster m

hand /hænd/ n (including cards) mano f; (of clock) manecilla f; (writing) escritura f, letra f; (worker) obrero m. **at ~** a mano. **by ~** a mano. **lend a ~** echar una mano. **on ~** a mano. **on one's ~s** (fig) en (las) manos de uno. **on the one ~... on the other ~** por un lado... por otro. **out of ~** fuera de control. **to ~** a mano. ● vt dar. **~ down** pasar. **~ in** entregar. **~ over** entregar. **~ out** distribuir. **~bag** n bolso m, cartera f (LAm). **~book** n (manual) manual m; (guidebook) guía f. **~cuffs** npl

esposas *fpl.* **~ful** /'hændfol/ *n* puñado *m*; (*person, fam*) persona *f* difícil. **~-luggage** *n* equipaje *m* de mano. **~-out** *n* folleto *m*; (*money*) limosna *f*

handicap /'hændɪkæp/ *n* desventaja *f*; (*sport*) handicap *m*. ● *vt* (*pt* **handicapped**) imponer impedimentos a

handicraft /'hændɪkrɑːft/ *n* artesanía *f*

handiwork /'hændɪwɜːk/ *n* obra *f*, trabajo *m* manual

handkerchief /'hæŋkətʃɪf/ *n* (*pl* **-fs**) pañuelo *m*

handle /'hændl/ *n* (*of door etc*) tirador *m*; (*of implement*) mango *m*; (*of cup, bag, basket etc*) asa *f*. ● *vt* manejar; (*touch*) tocar; (*control*) controlar

handlebar /'hændlbɑː(r)/ *n* (*on bicycle*) manillar *m*

handshake /'hændʃeɪk/ *n* apretón *m* de manos

handsome /'hænsəm/ *a* (*good-looking*) guapo; (*generous*) generoso; (*large*) considerable

handwriting /'hændraɪtɪŋ/ *n* escritura *f*, letra *f*

handy /'hændɪ/ *a* (**-ier, -iest**) (*useful*) cómodo; (*person*) diestro; (*near*) a mano. **~man** *n* hombre *m* habilidoso

hang /hæŋ/ *vt* (*pt* **hung**) colgar; (*pt* **hanged**) (*capital punishment*) ahorcar. ● *vi* colgar; (*hair*) caer. ● *n*. **get the ~ of sth** coger el truco de algo. **~ about** holgazanear. **~ on** (*hold out*) resistir; (*wait, sl*) esperar. **~ out** *vi* tender; (*live, sl*) vivir. **~ up** (*telephone*) colgar

hangar /'hæŋə(r)/ *n* hangar *m*

hanger /'hæŋə(r)/ *n* (*for clothes*) percha *f*. **~-on** *n* parásito *m*, pegote *m*

hang-gliding /'hæŋglaɪdɪŋ/ *n* vuelo *m* libre

hangman /'hæŋmən/ *n* verdugo *m*

hangover /'hæŋəʊvə(r)/ *n* (*after drinking*) resaca *f*

hang-up /'hæŋʌp/ *n* (*sl*) complejo *m*

hanker /'hæŋkə(r)/ *vi*. **~ after** anhelar. **~ing** *n* anhelo *m*

hanky-panky /'hæŋkɪpæŋkɪ/ *n* (*trickery, sl*) trucos *mpl*

haphazard /hæp'hæzəd/ *a* fortuito. **~ly** *adv* al azar

hapless /'hæplɪs/ *a* desafortunado

happen /'hæpən/ *vi* pasar, suceder, ocurrir. **if he ~s to come** si acaso viene. **~ing** *n* acontecimiento *m*

happ|ily /'hæpɪlɪ/ *adv* felizmente; (*fortunately*) afortunadamente. **~iness** *n* felicidad *f*. **~y** *a* (**-ier, -iest**) feliz. **~y-go-lucky** *a* despreocupado. **~y medium** *n* término *m* medio

harangue /həˈræŋ/ *n* arenga *f*. ● *vt* arengar

harass /'hærəs/ *vt* acosar. **~ment** *n* tormento *m*

harbour /'hɑːbə(r)/ *n* puerto *m*. ● *vt* encubrir (*criminal*); abrigar (*feelings*)

hard /hɑːd/ *a* (**-er, -est**) duro; (*difficult*) difícil. **~ of hearing** duro de oído. ● *adv* mucho; (*pull*) fuerte. **~ by** (muy) cerca. **~ done by** tratado injustamente. **~ up** (*fam*) sin un cuarto. **~board** *n* chapa *f* de madera, tabla *f*. **~-boiled egg** *n* huevo *n* duro. **~en** /'hɑːdn/ *vt* endurecer. ● *vi* endurecerse. **~-headed** *a* realista

hardly /'hɑːdlɪ/ *adv* apenas. **~ ever** casi nunca

hardness /'hɑːdnɪs/ *n* dureza *f*

hardship /'hɑːdʃɪp/ *n* apuro *m*

hard: ~ shoulder *n* arcén *m*. **~ware** *n* ferretería *f*; (*computer*) hardware *m*. **~-working** *a* trabajador

hardy /'hɑːdɪ/ *a* (**-ier, -iest**) (*bold*) audaz; (*robust*) robusto; (*bot*) resistente

hare /heə(r)/ *n* liebre *f*. **~-brained** *a* aturdido

harem /'hɑːriːm/ *n* harén *m*

haricot /'hærɪkəʊ/ *n*. **~ bean** alubia *f*, judía *f*

hark /hɑːk/ *vi* escuchar. **~ back to** volver a

harlot /'hɑːlət/ *n* prostituta *f*

harm /hɑːm/ *n* daño *m*. **there is no ~ in** (+ *gerund*) no hay ningún mal en (+ *infinitive*). ● *vt* hacer daño a (*person*); dañar (*thing*); perjudicar (*interests*). **~ful** *a* perjudicial. **~less** *a* inofensivo

harmonica /hɑːˈmɒnɪkə/ *n* armónica *f*

harmon|ious /hɑːˈməʊnɪəs/ *a* armonioso. **~ize** *vt/i* armonizar. **~y** *n* armonía *f*

harness /'hɑːnɪs/ *n* (*for horses*) guarniciones *fpl*; (*for children*) andadores *mpl*. ● *vt* poner guarniciones a (*horse*); (*fig*) aprovechar

harp /hɑːp/ *n* arpa *f*. ● *vi*. **~ on (about)** machacar. **~ist** /'hɑːpɪst/ *n* arpista *m & f*

harpoon /hɑːˈpuːn/ n arpón m
harpsichord /ˈhɑːpsɪkɔːd/ n clavicémbalo m, clave m
harrowing /ˈhærəʊɪŋ/ a desgarrador
harsh /hɑːʃ/ a (-er, -est) duro, severo; (taste, sound) áspero. ~ly adv severamente. ~ness n severidad f
harvest /ˈhɑːvɪst/ n cosecha f. • vt cosechar. ~er n (person) segador; (machine) cosechadora f
has /hæz/ see have
hash /hæʃ/ n picadillo m. make a ~ of sth hacer algo con los pies, estropear algo
hashish /ˈhæʃiːʃ/ n hachís m
hassle /ˈhæsl/ n (quarrel) pelea f; (difficulty) problema m, dificultad f; (bother, fam) pena f, follón m, lío m. • vt (harass) acosar, dar la lata
haste /heɪst/ n prisa f. in ~ de prisa. make ~ darse prisa
hasten /ˈheɪsn/ vt apresurar. • vi apresurarse, darse prisa
hastily /ˈheɪstɪlɪ/ adv de prisa. ~y a (-ier, -iest) precipitado; (rash) irreflexivo
hat /hæt/ n sombrero m. a ~ trick n tres victorias fpl consecutivas
hatch¹ /hætʃ/ n (for food) ventanilla f; (naut) escotilla f
hatch² /hætʃ/ vt empollar (eggs); tramar (plot). • vi salir del cascarón
hatchback /ˈhætʃbæk/ n (coche m) cincopuertas m invar, coche m con puerta trasera
hatchet /ˈhætʃɪt/ n hacha f
hate /heɪt/ n odio m. • vt odiar. ~ful a odioso
hatred /ˈheɪtrɪd/ n odio m
haughty /ˈhɔːtɪ/ a (-ier, -iest) altivo
haul /hɔːl/ vt arrastrar; transportar (goods). • n (catch) redada f; (stolen goods) botín m; (journey) recorrido m. ~age n transporte m. ~ier n transportista m & f
haunch /hɔːntʃ/ n anca f
haunt /hɔːnt/ vt frecuentar. • n sitio m preferido. ~ed house n casa f frecuentada por fantasmas
Havana /həˈvænə/ n La Habana f
have /hæv/ vt (3 sing pres tense has, pt had) tener; (eat, drink) tomar. ~ it out with resolver el asunto. ~ sth done hacer algo. ~ to do tener que hacer. • v aux haber. ~ just done

acabar de hacer. • n. the ~s and ~-nots los ricos mpl y los pobres mpl
haven /ˈheɪvn/ n puerto m; (refuge) refugio m
haversack /ˈhævəsæk/ n mochila f
havoc /ˈhævək/ n estragos mpl
haw /hɔː/ see hum
hawk¹ /hɔːk/ n halcón m
hawk² /hɔːk/ vt vender por las calles. ~er n vendedor m ambulante
hawthorn /ˈhɔːθɔːn/ n espino m (blanco)
hay /heɪ/ n heno m. ~ fever n fiebre f del heno. ~stack n almiar m
haywire /ˈheɪwaɪə(r)/ a. go ~ (plans) desorganizarse; (machine) estropearse
hazard /ˈhæzəd/ n riesgo m. • vt arriesgar; aventurar (guess). ~ous a arriesgado
haze /heɪz/ n neblina f
hazel /ˈheɪzl/ n avellano m. ~nut n avellana f
hazy /ˈheɪzɪ/ a (-ier, -iest) nebuloso
he /hiː/ pron él. • n (animal) macho m; (man) varón m
head /hed/ n cabeza f; (leader) jefe m; (of beer) espuma f. ~s or tails cara o cruz. • a principal. ~ waiter n jefe m de comedor. • vt encabezar. ~ for dirigirse a. ~ache n dolor m de cabeza. ~dress n tocado m. ~er n (football) cabezazo m. ~ first adv de cabeza. ~gear n tocado m
heading /ˈhedɪŋ/ n título m, encabezamiento m
headlamp /ˈhedlæmp/ n faro m
headland /ˈhedlənd/ n promontorio m
headlight /ˈhedlaɪt/ n faro m
headline /ˈhedlaɪn/ n titular m
headlong /ˈhedlɒŋ/ adv de cabeza; (precipitately) precipitadamente
head: ~master n director m. ~mistress n directora f. ~on a & adv de frente. ~phone n auricular m, audífono m (LAm)
headquarters /hedˈkwɔːtəz/ n (of organization) sede f; (of business) oficina f central; (mil) cuartel m general
headstrong /ˈhedstrɒŋ/ a testarudo
headway /ˈhedweɪ/ n progreso m. make ~ hacer progresos
heady /ˈhedɪ/ a (-ier, -iest) (impetuous) impetuoso; (intoxicating) embriagador

heal /hi:l/ vt curar. ● vi ⟨wound⟩ cicatrizarse; ⟨fig⟩ curarse

health /helθ/ n salud f. ~y a sano

heap /hi:p/ n montón m. ● vt amontonar. ~s of ⟨fam⟩ montones de, muchísimos

hear /hɪə(r)/ vt/i ⟨pt **heard** /hɜ:d/⟩ oír. ~, ~! ¡bravo! **not** ~ **of** ⟨refuse to allow⟩ no querer oír. ~ **about** oír hablar de. ~ **from** recibir noticias de. ~ **of** oír hablar de

hearing /hɪərɪŋ/ n oído m; ⟨of witness⟩ audición f. ~**aid** n audífono m

hearsay /hɪəseɪ/ n rumores mpl. **from** ~ según los rumores

hearse /hɜ:s/ n coche m fúnebre

heart /hɑ:t/ n corazón m. **at** ~ en el fondo. **by** ~ de memoria. **lose** ~ descorazonarse. ~**ache** n pena f. ~ **attack** n ataque m al corazón. ~**break** n pena f. ~**breaking** a desgarrador. ~**broken** a. **be** ~**broken** partírsele el corazón

heartburn /hɑ:tbɜ:n/ n acedía f

hearten /hɑ:tn/ vt animar

heartfelt /hɑ:tfelt/ a sincero

hearth /hɑ:θ/ n hogar m

heartily /hɑ:tɪlɪ/ adv de buena gana; ⟨sincerely⟩ sinceramente

heart ~**less** a cruel. ~**searching** n examen m de conciencia. ~**to-**~ a abierto

hearty /hɑ:tɪ/ a ⟨sincere⟩ sincero; ⟨meal⟩ abundante

heat /hi:t/ n calor m; ⟨contest⟩ eliminatoria f. ● vt calentar. ● vi calentarse. ~**ed** a ⟨fig⟩ acalorado. ~**er** /hɪ:tə(r)/ n calentador m

heath /hi:θ/ n brezal m, descampado m, terreno m baldío

heathen /hi:ðn/ n & a pagano (m)

heather /heðə(r)/ n brezo m

heat ~**ing** n calefacción f. ~**stroke** n insolación f. ~**wave** n ola f de calor

heave /hi:v/ vt ⟨lift⟩ levantar; exhalar ⟨sigh⟩; ⟨throw, fam⟩ lanzar. ● vi ⟨retch⟩ sentir náuseas

heaven /hevn/ n cielo m. ~**ly** a celestial; ⟨astronomy⟩ celeste; ⟨excellent, fam⟩ divino

heav|ily /hevɪlɪ/ adv pesadamente; ⟨smoke, drink⟩ mucho. ~**y** a (**-ier, -iest**) pesado; ⟨sea⟩ grueso; ⟨traffic⟩ denso; ⟨work⟩ duro. ~**yweight** n peso m pesado

Hebrew /hi:bru:/ a & n hebreo (m)

heckle /hekl/ vt interrumpir ⟨speaker⟩

hectic /hektɪk/ a febril

hedge /hedʒ/ n seto m vivo. ● vt rodear con seto vivo. ● vi escaparse por la tangente

hedgehog /hedʒhɒg/ n erizo m

heed /hi:d/ vt hacer caso de. ● n atención f. **pay** ~ **to** hacer caso de. ~**less** a desatento

heel /hi:l/ n talón m; ⟨of shoe⟩ tacón m. **down at** ~, **down at the** ~**s** ⟨Amer⟩ desharrapado

hefty /heftɪ/ a (**-ier, -iest**) ⟨sturdy⟩ fuerte; ⟨heavy⟩ pesado

heifer /hefə(r)/ n novilla f

height /haɪt/ n altura f; ⟨of person⟩ estatura f; ⟨of fame, glory⟩ cumbre f; ⟨of joy, folly, pain⟩ colmo m

heighten /haɪtn/ vt ⟨raise⟩ elevar; ⟨fig⟩ aumentar

heinous /heɪnəs/ a atroz

heir /eə(r)/ n heredero m. ~**ess** n heredera f. ~**loom** /eəlu:m/ n reliquia f heredada

held /held/ see **hold**

helicopter /helɪkɒptə(r)/ n helicóptero m

heliport /helɪpɔ:t/ n helipuerto m

hell /hel/ n infierno m. ~**-bent** a resuelto. ~**ish** a infernal

hello /hə'ləʊ/ int ¡hola!; ⟨telephone, caller⟩ ¡oiga!, ¡bueno! ⟨Mex⟩, ¡hola! ⟨Arg⟩; ⟨telephone, person answering⟩ ¡diga!, ¡bueno! ⟨Mex⟩, ¡hola! ⟨Arg⟩; ⟨surprise⟩ ¡vaya! **say** ~ **to** saludar

helm /helm/ n ⟨of ship⟩ timón m

helmet /helmɪt/ n casco m

help /help/ vt/i ayudar. **he cannot** ~ **laughing** no puede menos de reír. ~ **o.s.** to servirse. **it cannot be** ~**ed** no hay más remedio. ● n ayuda f; ⟨charwoman⟩ asistenta f. ~**er** n ayudante m. ~**ful** a útil; ⟨person⟩ amable

helping /helpɪŋ/ n porción f

helpless /helplɪs/ a ⟨unable to manage⟩ incapaz; ⟨powerless⟩ impotente

helter-skelter /heltə'skeltə(r)/ n tobogán m. ● adv atropelladamente

hem /hem/ n dobladillo m. ● vt ⟨pt **hemmed**⟩ hacer un dobladillo. ~ **in** encerrar

hemisphere /hemɪsfɪə(r)/ n hemisferio m

hemp /hemp/ n ⟨plant⟩ cáñamo m; ⟨hashish⟩ hachís m

hen /hen/ n gallina f

hence /hens/ adv de aquí. ~**forth** adv de ahora en adelante

henchman /hentʃmən/ n secuaz m

henna /'henə/ n alheña f

hen-party /'henpɑ:tɪ/ n (fam) reunión f de mujeres

henpecked /'henpekt/ a dominado por su mujer

her /hɜ:(r)/ pron (accusative) la; (dative) le; (after prep) ella. **I know ~** la conozco. ● a su, sus pl

herald /'herəld/ vt anunciar

heraldry /'herəldrɪ/ n heráldica f

herb /hɜ:b/ n hierba f. **~s** npl hierbas fpl finas

herbaceous /hɜ:'beɪʃəs/ a herbáceo

herbalist /'hɜ:bəlɪst/ n herbolario m

herculean /hɜ:kjʊ'li:ən/ a hercúleo

herd /hɜ:d/ n rebaño m. ● vt. **~ together** reunir

here /hɪə(r)/ adv aquí. **~!** (take this) ¡tenga! **~abouts** adv por aquí. **~after** adv en el futuro. **~by** adv por este medio; (in letter) por la presente

hereditary /hɪ'redɪtərɪ/ a hereditario. **~y** /hɪ'redətɪ/ n herencia f

here|sy /'herəsɪ/ n herejía f. **~tic** n hereje m & f

herewith /hɪə'wɪð/ adv adjunto

heritage /'herɪtɪdʒ/ n herencia f; (fig) patrimonio m

hermetic /hɜ:'metɪk/ a hermético

hermit /'hɜ:mɪt/ n ermitaño m

hernia /'hɜ:nɪə/ n hernia f

hero /'hɪərəʊ/ n (pl -oes) héroe m. **~ic** a heroico

heroin /'herəʊɪn/ n heroína f

hero: **~ine** /'herəʊɪn/ n heroína f. **~ism** /'herəʊɪzm/ n heroísmo m

heron /'herən/ n garza f real

herring /'herɪŋ/ n arenque m

hers /hɜ:z/ poss pron suyo m, suya f, suyos mpl, suyas fpl, de ella

herself /hɜ:'self/ pron ella misma; (reflexive) se; (after prep) sí

hesitant /'hezɪtənt/ a vacilante

hesitate /'hezɪteɪt/ vi vacilar. **~ion** /·'teɪʃn/ n vacilación f

hessian /'hesɪən/ n arpillera f

het /het/ a. **~ up** (sl) nervioso

heterogeneous /hetərəʊ'dʒi:nɪəs/ a heterogéneo

heterosexual /hetərəʊ'seksjʊəl/ a heterosexual

hew /hju:/ vt (pp hewn) cortar; (cut into shape) tallar

hexagon /'heksəgən/ n hexágono m. **~al** /·'ægənl/ a hexagonal

hey /heɪ/ int ¡eh!

heyday /'heɪdeɪ/ n apogeo m

hi /haɪ/ int (fam) ¡hola!

hiatus /haɪ'eɪtəs/ n (pl -tuses) hiato m

hibernat|e /'haɪbəneɪt/ vi hibernar. **~ion** n hibernación f

hibiscus /hɪ'bɪskəs/ n hibisco m

hiccup /'hɪkʌp/ n hipo m. **have (the) ~s** tener hipo. ● vi tener hipo

hide[1] /haɪd/ vt (pt hid, pp hidden) esconder. ● vi esconderse

hide[2] /haɪd/ n piel f, cuero m

hideous /'hɪdɪəs/ a (dreadful) horrible; (ugly) feo

hide-out /'haɪdaʊt/ n escondrijo m

hiding[1] /'haɪdɪŋ/ n (thrashing) paliza f

hiding[2] /'haɪdɪŋ/ n. **go into ~** esconderse

hierarchy /'haɪərɑ:kɪ/ n jerarquía f

hieroglyph /'haɪərəglɪf/ n jeroglífico m

hi-fi /'haɪfaɪ/ a de alta fidelidad. ● n (equipo m de) alta fidelidad (f)

higgledy-piggledy /hɪgldɪ'pɪgldɪ/ adv en desorden

high /haɪ/ a (-er, -est) alto; (price) elevado; (number, speed) grande; (wind) fuerte; (intoxicated, fam) ebrio; (voice) agudo; (meat) manido. **in the ~ season** en plena temporada. ● n alto nivel m. **a (new) ~** un récord m. ● adv alto

highbrow /'haɪbrəʊ/ a & n intelectual (m & f)

higher education /haɪər edʒʊ 'keɪʃn/ n enseñanza f superior

high-falutin /haɪfə'lu:tɪn/ a pomposo

high-handed /haɪ'hændɪd/ a despótico

high jump /'haɪdʒʌmp/ n salto m de altura

highlight /'haɪlaɪt/ n punto m culminante. ● vt destacar

highly /'haɪlɪ/ adv muy; (paid) muy bien. **~ strung** a nervioso

highness /'haɪnɪs/ n (title) alteza f

high: **~-rise building** n rascacielos m. **~ school** n instituto m. **~-speed** a de gran velocidad. **~ spot** n (fam) punto m culminante. **~ street** n calle f mayor. **~-strung** a (Amer) nervioso. **~ tea** n merienda f substanciosa

highway /'haɪweɪ/ n carretera f. **~man** n salteador m de caminos

hijack /'haɪdʒæk/ vt secuestrar. ● n secuestro m. **~er** n secuestrador

hike /haɪk/ n caminata f. ● vi darse la caminata. ~r n excursionista m & f

hilarious /hɪˈleərɪəs/ a (funny) muy divertido

hill /hɪl/ n colina f; (slope) cuesta f. ~billy n rústico m. ~side n ladera f. ~y a montuoso

hilt /hɪlt/ n (of sword) puño m. **to the** ~ totalmente

him /hɪm/ pron le, lo; (after prep) él. **I know** ~ le/lo conozco

himself /hɪmˈself/ pron él mismo; (reflexive) se

hind /haɪnd/ a trasero

hinder /ˈhɪndə(r)/ vt estorbar; (prevent) impedir

hindrance /ˈhɪndrəns/ n obstáculo m

hindsight /ˈhaɪnsaɪt/ n. **with** ~ retrospectivamente

Hindu /hɪnˈduː/ n & a hindú (m & f). ~ism n hinduismo m

hinge /hɪndʒ/ n bisagra f. ● vi. ~ **on** (depend on) depender de

hint /hɪnt/ n indirecta f; (advice) consejo m. ● vt dar a entender. ● vi soltar una indirecta. ~ **at** hacer alusión a

hinterland /ˈhɪntəlænd/ n interior m

hip /hɪp/ n cadera f

hippie /ˈhɪpɪ/ n hippie m & f

hippopotamus /hɪpəˈpɒtəməs/ n (pl -muses or -mi) hipopótamo m

hire /haɪə(r)/ vt alquilar ⟨thing⟩; contratar ⟨person⟩. ● n alquiler m. ~purchase n compra f a plazos

hirsute /ˈhɜːsjuːt/ a hirsuto

his /hɪz/ a su, sus pl. ● poss pron el suyo m, la suya f, los suyos mpl, las suyas fpl

Hispan|ic /hɪˈspænɪk/ a hispánico. ~ist n /ˈhɪspənɪst/ n hispanista m & f. ~o... pref hispano...

hiss /hɪs/ n silbido. ● vt/i silbar

histor|ian /hɪˈstɔːrɪən/ n historiador m. ~ic(al) /hɪˈstɒrɪkl/ a histórico. ~y /ˈhɪstərɪ/ n historia f. **make** ~y pasar a la historia

histrionic /hɪstrɪˈɒnɪk/ a histriónico

hit /hɪt/ vt (pt hit, pres p hitting) golpear; (collide with) chocar con; (find) dar con; (affect) afectar. ~ **it off with** hacer buenas migas con. ● n (blow) golpe m; (fig) éxito m. ~ **on** vi encontrar, dar con

hitch /hɪtʃ/ vt (fasten) atar. ● n (snag) problema m. ~ **a lift**, ~-**hike** vi hacer autostop, hacer dedo (Arg), pedir aventón (Mex). ~-**hiker** n autostopista m & f

hither /ˈhɪðə(r)/ adv acá. ~ **and thither** acá y allá

hitherto /ˈhɪðətuː/ adv hasta ahora

hit-or-miss /ˈhɪtɔːˈmɪs/ a (fam) a la buena de Dios, a ojo

hive /haɪv/ n colmena f. ● vt. ~**off** separar; (industry) desnacionalizar

hoard /hɔːd/ vt acumular. ● n provisión f; (of money) tesoro m

hoarding /ˈhɔːdɪŋ/ n cartelera f, valla f publicitaria

hoar-frost /ˈhɔːfrɒst/ n escarcha f

hoarse /hɔːs/ a (-er, -est) ronco. ~ness n (of voice) ronquera f; (of sound) ronquedad f

hoax /həʊks/ n engaño m. ● vt engañar

hob /hɒb/ n repisa f; (of cooker) fogón m

hobble /ˈhɒbl/ vi cojear

hobby /ˈhɒbɪ/ n pasatiempo m

hobby-horse /ˈhɒbɪhɔːs/ n (toy) caballito m (de niño); (fixation) caballo m de batalla

hobnail /ˈhɒbneɪl/ n clavo m

hob-nob /ˈhɒbnɒb/ vi (pt hob-nobbed). ~ **with** codearse con

hock¹ /hɒk/ n vino m del Rin

hock² /hɒk/ vt (pawn, sl) empeñar

hockey /ˈhɒkɪ/ n hockey m

hodgepodge /ˈhɒdʒpɒdʒ/ n mezcolanza f

hoe /həʊ/ n azada f. ● vt (pres p hoe-ing) azadonar

hog /hɒg/ n cerdo m. ● vt (pt hogged) (fam) acaparar

hoist /hɔɪst/ vt levantar; izar ⟨flag⟩. ● n montacargas m invar

hold¹ /həʊld/ vt (pt held) tener; (grasp) coger (not LAm), agarrar; (contain) contener; mantener ⟨interest⟩; (believe) creer; contener ⟨breath⟩. ~ **one's tongue** callarse. ● vi mantenerse. ● n asidero m; (influence) influencia f. **get** ~ **of** agarrar; (fig, acquire) adquirir. ~ **back** (contain) contener; (conceal) ocultar. ~ **on** (stand firm) resistir; (wait) esperar. ~ **on to** (keep) guardar; (cling to) agarrarse a. ~ **out** vt (offer) ofrecer. ● vi (resist) resistir. ~ **over** aplazar. ~ **up** (support) sostener;

(delay) retrasar; *(rob)* atracar. ~ **with** aprobar

hold² /'həʊld/ n *(of ship)* bodega f

holdall /'həʊldɔːl/ n bolsa f (de viaje)

holder /'həʊldə(r)/ n tenedor m; *(of post)* titular m; *(for object)* soporte m

holding /'həʊldɪŋ/ n *(land)* propiedad f

hold-up /'həʊldʌp/ n atraco m

hole /həʊl/ n agujero m; *(in ground)* hoyo m; *(in road)* bache m. ● vt agujerear

holiday /'hɒlɪdeɪ/ n vacaciones fpl; *(public)* fiesta f. ● vi pasar las vacaciones. ~**maker** n veraneante m

holiness /'həʊlɪnɪs/ n santidad f

Holland /'hɒlənd/ n Holanda f

hollow /'hɒləʊ/ a & n hueco (m). ● vt ahuecar

holly /'hɒlɪ/ n acebo m. ~**hock** n malva f real

holocaust /'hɒləkɔːst/ n holocausto m

holster /'həʊlstə(r)/ n pistolera f

holy /'həʊlɪ/ a (-ier, -iest) santo, grado. H~ **Ghost** n, H~ **Spirit** n Espíritu m Santo. ~ **water** n agua f bendita

homage /'hɒmɪdʒ/ n homenaje m

home /həʊm/ n casa f; *(institution)* asilo m; *(for soldiers)* hogar m; *(native land)* patria f. **feel at** ~ **with** sentirse como en su casa. ● a casera, de casa; *(of family)* de familia; *(pol)* interior; *(match)* de casa. ● adv. **(at)** ~ en casa. H~ **Counties** npl región f alrededor de Londres. ~**land** n patria f. ~**less** a sin hogar. ~**ly** /'həʊmlɪ/ a (-ier, -iest) casero; *(ugly)* feo. H~ **Office** n Ministerio m del Interior. H~ **Secretary** n Ministro m del Interior. ~**sick** a. **be** ~**sick** tener morriña. ~**town** n ciudad f natal. ~ **truths** npl las verdades fpl del barquero, las cuatro verdades fpl. ~**ward** /'həʊmwəd/ a *(journey)* de vuelta. ● adv hacia casa. ~**work** n deberes mpl

homicide /'hɒmɪsaɪd/ n homicidio m

homoeopath|ic /həʊmɪəʊ'pæθɪk/ a homeopático. ~**y** /-'ɒpəθɪ/ n homeopatía f

homogeneous /həʊməʊ'dʒiːnɪəs/ a homogéneo

homosexual /həʊməʊ'seksjʊəl/ a & n homosexual (m)

hone /həʊn/ vt afilar

honest /'ɒnɪst/ a honrado; *(frank)* sincero. ~**ly** adv honradamente. ~**y** n honradez f

honey /'hʌnɪ/ n miel f; *(person, fam)* cielo m, cariño m. ~**comb** n /'hʌnɪkəʊm/ n panal m

honeymoon /'hʌnɪmuːn/ n luna f de miel

honeysuckle /'hʌnɪsʌkl/ n madreselva f

honk /hɒŋk/ vi tocar la bocina

honorary /'ɒnərərɪ/ a honorario

honour /'ɒnə(r)/ n honor m. ● vt honrar. ~**able** a honorable

hood /hʊd/ n capucha f; *(car roof)* capota f; *(car bonnet)* capó m

hoodlum /'huːdləm/ n gamberro m, matón m

hoodwink /'hʊdwɪŋk/ vt engañar

hoof /huːf/ n (pl hoofs or hooves) casco m

hook /hʊk/ n gancho m; *(on garment)* corchete m; *(for fishing)* anzuelo m. **by** ~ **or by crook** por fas o por nefas, por las buenas o por las malas. **get s.o. off the** ~ sacar a uno de un apuro. **off the** ~ *(telephone)* descolgado. ● vt enganchar. ● vi engancharse

hooked /hʊkt/ a ganchudo. ~ **on** *(sl)* adicto a

hooker /'hʊkə(r)/ n *(rugby)* talonador m; *(Amer, sl)* prostituta f

hookey /'hʊkɪ/ n. **play** ~ *(Amer, sl)* hacer novillos

hooligan /'huːlɪgən/ n gamberro m

hoop /huːp/ n aro m

hooray /hʊ'reɪ/ int & n ¡viva! (m)

hoot /huːt/ n *(of horn)* bocinazo m; *(of owl)* ululato m. ● vi tocar la bocina; *(owl)* ulular

hooter /'huːtə(r)/ n *(of car)* bocina f; *(of factory)* sirena f

Hoover /'huːvə(r)/ n (P) aspiradora f. ● vt pasar la aspiradora

hop¹ /hɒp/ vi (pt hopped) saltar a la pata coja. ~ **in** *(fam)* subir. ~ **it** *(sl)* largarse. ~ **out** *(fam)* bajar. ● n salto m; *(flight)* etapa f

hop² /hɒp/ n. ~**(s)** lúpulo m

hope /həʊp/ n esperanza f. ● vt/i esperar. ~ **for** esperar. ~**ful** a esperanzador. ~**fully** adv con optimismo; *(it is hoped)* se espera. ~**less** a desesperado. ~**lessly** adv sin esperanza

hopscotch /'hɒpskɒtʃ/ n tejo m

horde /hɔːd/ n horda f

horizon /hə'raɪzn/ n horizonte m

horizontal /hɒrɪ'zɒntl/ a horizontal. ~**ly** adv horizontalmente

hormone /'hɔːməʊn/ n hormona f

horn /hɔːn/ n cuerno m; (of car) bocina f; (mus) trompa f. ● vt. ~ **in** (sl) entrometerse. ~**ed** a con cuernos

hornet /'hɔːnɪt/ n avispón m

horny /'hɔːnɪ/ a (hands) calloso

horoscope /'hɒrəskəʊp/ n horóscopo m

horri|ble /'hɒrəbl/ a horrible. ~**d** /'hɒrɪd/ a horrible

horrif|ic /hə'rɪfɪk/ a horroroso. ~**y** /'hɒrɪfaɪ/ vt horrorizar

horror /'hɒrə(r)/ n horror m. ~ **film** n película f de miedo

hors-d'oevre /ɔː'dɜːvr/ n entremés m

horse /hɔːs/ n caballo m. ~**back** n. **on ~back** a caballo

horse chestnut /hɔːs'tʃesnʌt/ n castaña f de Indias

horse: ~**man** n jinete m. ~**play** n payasadas fpl. ~**power** n (unit) caballo m (de fuerza). ~**racing** n carreras fpl de caballos

horseradish /'hɔːsrædɪʃ/ n rábano m picante

horse: ~ **sense** n (fam) sentido m común. ~**shoe** /'hɔːsʃuː/ n herradura f

horsy /'hɔːsɪ/ a (face etc) caballuno

horticultur|al /hɔːtɪ'kʌltʃərəl/ a hortícola. ~**e** /'hɔːtɪkʌltʃə(r)/ n horticultura f

hose /həʊz/ n (tube) manga f. ● vt (water) regar con una manga; (clean) limpiar con una manga. ~**pipe** n manga f

hosiery /'həʊzɪərɪ/ n calcetería f

hospice /'hɒspɪs/ n hospicio m

hospitabl|e /hɒ'spɪtəbl/ a hospitalario. ~**y** adv con hospitalidad

hospital /'hɒspɪtl/ n hospital m

hospitality /hɒspɪ'tælətɪ/ n hospitalidad f

host[1] /həʊst/ n. **a ~ of** un montón de

host[2] /həʊst/ n (master of house) huésped m, anfitrión m

host[3] /həʊst/ n (relig) hostia f

hostage /'hɒstɪdʒ/ n rehén m

hostel /'hɒstl/ n (for students) residencia f. **youth ~** albergue m juvenil

hostess /'həʊstɪs/ n huéspeda f, anfitriona f

hostil|e /'hɒstaɪl/ a hostil. ~**ity** n hostilidad f

hot /hɒt/ a (hotter, hottest) caliente; (culin) picante; (news) de última hora. **be/feel ~** tener calor. **in ~ water** (fam) en un apuro. **it is ~** hace calor. ● vt/i. ~ **up** (fam) calentarse

hotbed /'hɒtbed/ n (fig) semillero m

hotchpotch /'hɒtʃpɒtʃ/ n mezcolanza f

hot dog /hɒt'dɒg/ n perrito m caliente

hotel /həʊ'tel/ n hotel m. ~**ier** n hotelero m

hot: ~**head** n impetuoso m. ~-**headed** a impetuoso. ~**house** n invernadero m. ~**line** n teléfono m rojo. ~**plate** n calentador m. ~-**water bottle** n bolsa f de agua caliente

hound /haʊnd/ n perro m de caza. ● vt perseguir

hour /aʊə(r)/ n hora f. ~**ly** a & adv cada hora. ~**ly pay** n sueldo m por hora. **paid ~ly** pagado por hora

house /haʊs/ n (pl -s /'haʊzɪz/) casa f; (theatre building) sala f; (theatre audience) público m; (pol) cámara f. /haʊz/ vt alojar; (keep) guardar. ~**boat** n casa f flotante. ~**breaking** n robo m de casa. ~**hold** /'haʊshəʊld/ n casa f, familia f. ~**holder** n dueño m de una casa; (head of household) cabeza f de familia. ~**keeper** n ama f de llaves. ~**keeping** n gobierno m de la casa. ~**maid** n criada f, mucama f (LAm). **H~ of Commons** n Cámara f de los Comunes. ~-**proud** a meticuloso. ~-**warming** n inauguración f de una casa. ~**wife** /'haʊswaɪf/ n ama f de casa. ~**work** n quehaceres mpl domésticos

housing /'haʊzɪŋ/ n alojamiento m. ~ **estate** n urbanización f

hovel /'hɒvl/ n casucha f

hover /'hɒvə(r)/ vi (bird, threat etc) cernerse; (loiter) rondar. ~**craft** n aerodeslizador m

how /haʊ/ adv cómo. ~ **about a walk?** ¿qué le parece si damos un paseo? ~ **are you?** ¿cómo está Vd? ~ **do you do?** (in introduction) mucho gusto. ~ **long?** ¿cuánto tiempo? ~ **many?** ¿cuántos? ~ **much?** ¿cuánto? ~ **often?** ¿cuántas veces? **and ~!** ¡y cómo!

however /haʊ'evə(r)/ adv (with verb) de cualquier manera que (+

subjunctive); (*with adjective or adverb*) por... que (+ *subjunctive*); (*nevertheless*) no obstante, sin embargo. ∼ **much it rains** por mucho que llueva

howl /haʊl/ n aullido. ● *vi* aullar

howler /ˈhaʊlə(r)/ n (fam) plancha f

HP abbr see **hire-purchase**

hp abbr see **horsepower**

hub /hʌb/ n (of wheel) cubo m; (fig) centro m

hubbub /ˈhʌbʌb/ n barahúnda f

hub-cap /ˈhʌbkæp/ n tapacubos m invar

huddle /ˈhʌdl/ vi apiñarse

hue[1] /hju:/ n (colour) color m

hue[2] /hju:/ n. ∼ **and cry** clamor m

huff /hʌf/ n. **in a** ∼ enojado

hug /hʌg/ vt (pt **hugged**) abrazar; (keep close to) no apartarse de. ● n abrazo m

huge /hju:dʒ/ a enorme. ∼**ly** adv enormemente

hulk /hʌlk/ n (of ship) barco m viejo; (person) armatoste m

hull /hʌl/ n (of ship) casco m

hullabaloo /hʌləbəˈlu:/ n tumulto m

hullo /həˈləʊ/ int = **hello**

hum /hʌm/ vt/i (pt **hummed**) (person) canturrear; (insect, engine) zumbar. ● n zumbido m. ∼ **(or hem) and haw (or ha)** vacilar

human /ˈhju:mən/ a & n humano (m). ∼ **being** n ser m humano

humane /hju:ˈmeɪn/ a humano

humanism /ˈhju:mənɪzəm/ n humanismo m

humanitarian /hju:mænɪˈteərɪən/ a humanitario

humanity /hju:ˈmænətɪ/ n humanidad f

humbl|e /ˈhʌmbl/ a (-er, -est) humilde. ● vt humillar. ∼**y** adv humildemente

humbug /ˈhʌmbʌg/ n (false talk) charlatanería f; (person) charlatán m; (sweet) caramelo m de menta

humdrum /ˈhʌmdrʌm/ a monótono

humid /ˈhju:mɪd/ a húmedo. ∼**ifier** n humedecedor m. ∼**ity** /hju:ˈmɪdətɪ/ n humedad f

humiliat|e /hju:ˈmɪlɪeɪt/ vt humillar. ∼**ion** /-ˈeɪʃn/ n humillación f

humility /hju:ˈmɪlətɪ/ n humildad f

humorist /ˈhju:mərɪst/ n humorista m & f

humo|rous /ˈhju:mərəs/ a divertido. ∼**rously** adv con gracia. ∼**ur** n

humorismo m; (mood) humor m. **sense of** ∼**ur** n sentido m del humor

hump /hʌmp/ n montecillo m; (of the spine) joroba f. **the** ∼ (sl) malhumor m. ● vt encorvarse; (hoist up) llevar al hombro

hunch /hʌntʃ/ vt encorvar. ∼**ed up** encorvado. ● n presentimiento m; (lump) joroba f. ∼**back** /ˈhʌntʃbæk/ n jorobado m

hundred /ˈhʌndrəd/ a ciento, (before noun) cien. ● n ciento m. ∼**fold** a céntuplo. ● adv cien veces. ∼**s of** centenares de. ∼**th** a centésimo. ● n centésimo m, centésima parte f

hundredweight /ˈhʌndrədweɪt/ n 50,8kg; (Amer) 45,36kg

hung /hʌŋ/ see **hang**

Hungar|ian /hʌŋˈgeərɪən/ a & n húngaro (m). ∼**y** /ˈhʌŋgərɪ/ n Hungría f

hunger /ˈhʌŋgə(r)/ n hambre f. ● vi. ∼ **for** tener hambre de. ∼**-strike** n huelga f de hambre

hungr|ily /ˈhʌŋgrəlɪ/ adv ávidamente. ∼**y** a (-ier, -iest) hambriento. **be** ∼**y** tener hambre

hunk /hʌŋk/ n (buen) pedazo m

hunt /hʌnt/ vt/i cazar. ∼ **for** buscar. ● n caza f. ∼**er** n cazador m. ∼**ing** n caza f

hurdle /ˈhɜ:dl/ n (sport) valla f; (fig) obstáculo m

hurdy-gurdy /ˈhɜ:dɪgɜ:dɪ/ n organillo m

hurl /hɜ:l/ vt lanzar

hurly-burly /ˈhɜ:lɪbɜ:lɪ/ n tumulto m

hurrah /huˈrɑ:/, **hurray** /huˈreɪ/ int & n ¡viva! (m)

hurricane /ˈhʌrɪkən/ n huracán m

hurried /ˈhʌrɪd/ a apresurado. ∼**ly** adv apresuradamente

hurry /ˈhʌrɪ/ vi apresurarse, darse prisa. ● vt apresurar, dar prisa a. ● n prisa f. **be in a** ∼ tener prisa

hurt /hɜ:t/ vt/i (pt **hurt**) herir. ● n (injury) herida f; (harm) daño m. ∼**ful** a hiriente; (harmful) dañoso

hurtle /ˈhɜ:tl/ vt lanzar. ● vi. ∼ **along** mover rápidamente

husband /ˈhʌzbənd/ n marido m

hush /hʌʃ/ vt acallar. ● n silencio m. ∼ **up** ocultar (affair). ∼∼ a (fam) muy secreto

husk /hʌsk/ n cáscara f

husky /ˈhʌskɪ/ a (-ier, -iest) (hoarse) ronco; (burly) fornido

hussy /ˈhʌsɪ/ n desvergonzada f

hustle /'hʌsl/ vt (jostle) empujar. ● vi (hurry) darse prisa. ● n empuje m. ~ **and bustle** n bullicio m

hut /hʌt/ n cabaña f

hutch /hʌtʃ/ n conejera f

hyacinth /'haɪəsɪnθ/ n jacinto m

hybrid /'haɪbrɪd/ a & n híbrido (m)

hydrangea /haɪ'dreɪndʒə/ n hortensia f

hydrant /'haɪdrənt/ n. **(fire)** ~ n boca f de riego

hydraulic /haɪ'drɔːlɪk/ a hidráulico

hydroelectric /haɪdrəʊr'lektrɪk/ a hidroeléctrico

hydrofoil /'haɪdrəfɔɪl/ n aerodeslizador m

hydrogen /'haɪdrədʒən/ n hidrógeno m. ~ **bomb** n bomba f de hidrógeno. ~ **peroxide** n peróxido m de hidrógeno

hyena /haɪ'iːnə/ n hiena f

hygien|e /'haɪdʒiːn/ n higiene f. ~**ic** a higiénico

hymn /hɪm/ n himno m

hyper... /'haɪpə(r)/ pref hiper...

hypermarket /'haɪpəmɑːkɪt/ n hipermercado m

hyphen /'haɪfn/ n guión m. ~**ate** vt escribir con guión

hypno|sis /hɪp'nəʊsɪs/ n hipnosis f. ~**tic** /-'nɒtɪk/ a hipnótico. ~**tism** /hɪpnə'tɪzəm/ n hipnotismo m. ~**tist** n hipnotista m & f. ~**tize** vt hipnotizar

hypochondriac /haɪpə'kɒndrɪæk/ n hipocondríaco m

hypocrisy /hɪ'pɒkrəsɪ/ n hipocresía f

hypocrit|e /'hɪpəkrɪt/ n hipócrita m & f. ~**ical** a hipócrita

hypodermic /haɪpə'dɜːmɪk/ a hipodérmico. ● n jeringa f hipodérmica

hypothe|sis /haɪ'pɒθəsɪs/ n (pl -theses /-siːz/) hipótesis f. ~**tical** /-ə'θetɪkl/ a hipotético

hysteri|a /hɪ'stɪərɪə/ n histerismo m. ~**cal** /-'terɪkl/ a histérico. ~**cs** /hɪ'sterɪks/ npl histerismo m. **have** ~**cs** ponerse histérico; (laugh) morir de risa

I

I /aɪ/ pron yo

ice /aɪs/ n hielo m. ● vt helar; glasear (cake). ● vi. ~ **(up)** helarse. ~**berg** n iceberg m, témpano m. ~**cream** n

helado m. ~**cube** n cubito m de hielo. ~ **hockey** n hockey m sobre hielo

Iceland /'aɪslənd/ n Islandia f. ~**er** n islandés m. ~**ic** /-'lændɪk/ a islandés

ice lolly /aɪs'lɒlɪ/ polo m, paleta f (LAm)

icicle /'aɪsɪkl/ n carámbano m

icing /'aɪsɪŋ/ n (sugar) azúcar m glaseado

icon /'aɪkɒn/ n icono m

icy /'aɪsɪ/ a (-ier, -iest) glacial

idea /aɪ'dɪə/ n idea f

ideal /aɪ'dɪəl/ a ideal. ● n ideal m. ~**ism** n idealismo m. ~**ist** n idealista m & f. ~**istic** /-'lɪstɪk/ a idealista. ~**ize** vt idealizar. ~**ly** adv idealmente

identical /aɪ'dentɪkl/ a idéntico

identif|ication /aɪdentɪfɪ'keɪʃn/ n identificación f. ~**y** /aɪ'dentɪfaɪ/ vt identificar. ● vi. ~**y with** identificarse con

identikit /aɪ'dentɪkɪt/ n retrato-robot m

identity /aɪ'dentɪtɪ/ n identidad f

ideolog|ical /aɪdɪə'lɒdʒɪkl/ a ideológico. ~**y** /aɪdɪ'ɒlədʒɪ/ n ideología f

idiocy /'ɪdɪəsɪ/ n idiotez f

idiom /'ɪdɪəm/ n locución f. ~**atic** /-'mætɪk/ a idiomático

idiosyncrasy /ɪdɪəʊ'sɪŋkrəsɪ/ n idiosincrasia f

idiot /'ɪdɪət/ n idiota m & f. ~**ic** /-'ɒtɪk/ a idiota

idle /'aɪdl/ a (-er, -est) ocioso; (lazy) holgazán; (out of work) desocupado; (machine) parado. ● vi (engine) marchar en vacío. ● vt. ~ **away** perder. ~**ness** n ociosidad f. ~**r** /-ə(r)/ n ocioso m

idol /'aɪdl/ n ídolo m. ~**ize** vt idolatrar

idyllic /ɪ'dɪlɪk/ a idílico

i.e. /aɪ'i:/ abbr (id est) es decir

if /ɪf/ conj si

igloo /'ɪgluː/ n iglú m

ignite /ɪg'naɪt/ vt encender. ● vi encenderse

ignition /ɪg'nɪʃn/ n ignición f; (auto) encendido m. ~ **(switch)** n contacto m

ignoramus /ɪgnə'reɪməs/ n (pl -muses) ignorante

ignoran|ce /'ɪgnərəns/ n ignorancia f. ~**t** a ignorante. ~**tly** adv por ignorancia

ignore /ɪg'nɔː(r)/ vt no hacer caso de

ilk /ɪlk/ n ralea f

ill /ɪl/ a enfermo; (bad) malo. ~ **will** n mala voluntad f. ● adv mal. ~ **at ease** inquieto. ● n mal m. ~**advised** a imprudente. ~**bred** a mal educado

illegal /ɪˈliːgl/ a ilegal

illegible /ɪˈledʒəbl/ a ilegible

illegitima|cy /ɪlɪˈdʒɪtɪməsɪ/ n ilegitimidad f. ~**te** a ilegítimo

ill: ~**fated** a malogrado. ~**gotten** a mal adquirido

illitera|cy /ɪˈlɪtərəsɪ/ n analfabetismo m. ~**te** a & n analfabeto (m)

ill: ~**natured** a poco afable. ~**ness** n enfermedad f

illogical /ɪˈlɒdʒɪkl/ a ilógico

ill: ~**starred** a malogrado. ~**treat** vt maltratar

illuminat|e /ɪˈluːmɪneɪt/ vt iluminar. ~**ion** /-ˈneɪʃn/ n iluminación f

illus|ion /ɪˈluːʒn/ n ilusión f. ~**sory** a ilusorio

illustrat|e /ˈɪləstreɪt/ vt ilustrar. ~**ion** n (example) ejemplo m; (picture in book) grabado m, lámina f. ~**ive** a ilustrativo

illustrious /ɪˈlʌstrɪəs/ a ilustre

image /ˈɪmɪdʒ/ n imagen f. ~**ry** n imágenes fpl

imagin|able /ɪˈmædʒɪnəbl/ a imaginable. ~**ary** a imaginario. ~**ation** /-ˈneɪʃn/ n imaginación f. ~**ative** a imaginativo. ~**e** vt imaginar(se)

imbalance /ɪmˈbæləns/ n desequilibrio m

imbecil|e /ˈɪmbəsiːl/ a & n imbécil (m & f). ~**ity** /-ˈsɪlətɪ/ n imbecilidad f

imbibe /ɪmˈbaɪb/ vt embeber; (drink) beber

imbue /ɪmˈbjuː/ vt empapar (**with** de)

imitat|e /ˈɪmɪteɪt/ vt imitar. ~**ion** /-ˈteɪʃn/ n imitación f. ~**or** n imitador m

immaculate /ɪˈmækjʊlət/ a inmaculado

immaterial /ɪməˈtɪərɪəl/ a inmaterial; (unimportant) insignificante

immature /ɪməˈtjʊə(r)/ a inmaduro

immediate /ɪˈmiːdɪət/ a inmediato. ~**ly** adv inmediatamente. ~**ly you hear me** en cuanto me oigas. ● conj en cuanto (+ subj)

immens|e /ɪˈmens/ a inmenso. ~**ely** adv inmensamente; (very much, fam) muchísimo. ~**ity** n inmensidad f

immers|e /ɪˈmɜːs/ vt sumergir. ~**ion** /ɪˈmɜːʃn/ n inmersión f. ~**ion heater** n calentador m de inmersión

immigra|nt /ˈɪmɪgrənt/ a & n inmigrante (m & f). ~**te** vi inmigrar. ~**tion** /-ˈgreɪʃn/ n inmigración f

imminen|ce /ˈɪmɪnəns/ n inminencia f. ~**t** a inminente

immobil|e /ɪˈməʊbaɪl/ a inmóvil. ~**ize** /-bɪlaɪz/ vt inmovilizar

immoderate /ɪˈmɒdərət/ a inmoderado

immodest /ɪˈmɒdɪst/ a inmodesto

immoral /ɪˈmɒrəl/ a inmoral. ~**ity** /ɪməˈrælətɪ/ n inmoralidad f

immortal /ɪˈmɔːtl/ a inmortal. ~**ity** /-ˈtælətɪ/ n inmortalidad f. ~**ize** vt inmortalizar

immun|e /ɪˈmjuːn/ a inmune (**from**, **to** a, contra). ~**ity** n inmunidad f. ~**ization** /ɪmjʊnaɪˈzeɪʃn/ n inmunización f. ~**ize** vt inmunizar

imp /ɪmp/ n diablillo m

impact /ˈɪmpækt/ n impacto m

impair /ɪmˈpeə(r)/ vt perjudicar

impale /ɪmˈpeɪl/ vt empalar

impart /ɪmˈpɑːt/ vt comunicar

impartial /ɪmˈpɑːʃl/ a imparcial. ~**ity** /-ɪˈælətɪ/ n imparcialidad f

impassable /ɪmˈpɑːsəbl/ a ‹barrier etc› infranqueable; ‹road› impracticable

impasse /æmˈpɑːs/ n callejón m sin salida

impassioned /ɪmˈpæʃnd/ a apasionado

impassive /ɪmˈpæsɪv/ a impasible

impatien|ce /ɪmˈpeɪʃəns/ n impaciencia f. ~**t** a impaciente. ~**tly** adv con impaciencia

impeach /ɪmˈpiːtʃ/ vt acusar

impeccable /ɪmˈpekəbl/ a impecable

impede /ɪmˈpiːd/ vt estorbar

impediment /ɪmˈpedɪmənt/ n obstáculo m. (**speech**) ~ n defecto m del habla

impel /ɪmˈpel/ vt (pt **impelled**) impeler

impending /ɪmˈpendɪŋ/ a inminente

impenetrable /ɪmˈpenɪtrəbl/ a impenetrable

imperative /ɪmˈperətɪv/ a imprescindible. ● n (gram) imperativo m

imperceptible /ˌɪmpəˈseptəbl/ a imperceptible.

imperfect /ɪmˈpɜːfɪkt/ a imperfecto. ~**ion** /əˈfekʃn/ n imperfección f

imperial /ɪmˈpɪərɪəl/ a imperial. ~**ism** n imperialismo m

imperil /ɪmˈperəl/ vt (pt imperilled) poner en peligro

imperious /ɪmˈpɪərɪəs/ a imperioso

impersonal /ɪmˈpɜːsənl/ a impersonal

impersonat|e /ɪmˈpɜːsəneɪt/ vt hacerse pasar por; (mimic) imitar. ~**ion** /-ˈneɪʃn/ n imitación f. ~**or** n imitador m

impertinen|ce /ɪmˈpɜːtɪnəns/ n impertinencia f. ~**t** a impertinente. ~**tly** adv impertinentemente

impervious /ɪmˈpɜːvɪəs/ a. ~ **to** impermeable a; (fig) insensible a

impetuous /ɪmˈpetjʊəs/ a impetuoso

impetus /ˈɪmpɪtəs/ n ímpetu m

impinge /ɪmˈpɪndʒ/ vi. ~ **on** afectar a

impish /ˈɪmpɪʃ/ a travieso

implacable /ɪmˈplækəbl/ a implacable

implant /ɪmˈplɑːnt/ vt implantar

implement /ˈɪmplɪmənt/ n herramienta f. /ˈɪmplɪment/ vt realizar

implicat|e /ˈɪmplɪkeɪt/ vt implicar. ~**ion** /-ˈkeɪʃn/ n implicación f

implicit /ɪmˈplɪsɪt/ a (implied) implícito; (unquestioning) absoluto

implied /ɪmˈplaɪd/ a implícito

implore /ɪmˈplɔː(r)/ vt implorar

imply /ɪmˈplaɪ/ vt implicar; (mean) querer decir; (insinuate) dar a entender

impolite /ˌɪmpəˈlaɪt/ a mal educado

imponderable /ɪmˈpɒndərəbl/ a & n imponderable (m)

import /ɪmˈpɔːt/ vt importar. /ˈɪmpɔːt/ n (article) importación f; (meaning) significación f

importan|ce /ɪmˈpɔːtəns/ n importancia f. ~**t** a importante

importation /ˌɪmpɔːˈteɪʃn/ n importación f

importer /ɪmˈpɔːtə(r)/ n importador m

impose /ɪmˈpəʊz/ vt imponer. ● vi. ~ **on** abusar de la amabilidad de

imposing /ɪmˈpəʊzɪŋ/ a imponente

imposition /ˌɪmpəˈzɪʃn/ n imposición f; (fig) molestia f

impossibility /ɪmˌpɒsəˈbɪlətɪ/ n imposibilidad f. ~**le** a imposible

impostor /ɪmˈpɒstə(r)/ n impostor m

impoten|ce /ˈɪmpətəns/ n impotencia f. ~**t** a impotente

impound /ɪmˈpaʊnd/ vt confiscar

impoverish /ɪmˈpɒvərɪʃ/ vt empobrecer

impracticable /ɪmˈpræktɪkəbl/ a impracticable

impractical /ɪmˈpræktɪkl/ a poco práctico

imprecise /ˌɪmprɪˈsaɪs/ a impreciso

impregnable /ɪmˈpregnəbl/ a inexpugnable

impregnate /ˈɪmpregneɪt/ vt impregnar (with de)

impresario /ˌɪmprɪˈsɑːrɪəʊ/ n (pl -os) empresario m

impress /ɪmˈpres/ vt impresionar; (imprint) imprimir. ~ **on s.o.** hacer entender a uno

impression /ɪmˈpreʃn/ n impresión f. ~**able** a impresionable

impressive /ɪmˈpresɪv/ a impresionante

imprint /ˈɪmprɪnt/ n impresión f. /ɪmˈprɪnt/ vt imprimir

imprison /ɪmˈprɪzn/ vt encarcelar. ~**ment** n encarcelamiento m

improbab|ility /ɪmˌprɒbəˈbɪlətɪ/ n improbabilidad f. ~**le** a improbable

impromptu /ɪmˈprɒmptjuː/ a improvisado. ● adv de improviso

improper /ɪmˈprɒpə(r)/ a impropio; (incorrect) incorrecto

impropriety /ˌɪmprəˈpraɪətɪ/ n inconveniencia f

improve /ɪmˈpruːv/ vt mejorar. ● vi mejorar(se). ~**ment** n mejora f

improvis|ation /ˌɪmprəvaɪˈzeɪʃn/ n improvisación f. ~**e** vt/i improvisar

imprudent /ɪmˈpruːdənt/ a imprudente

impuden|ce /ˈɪmpjʊdəns/ n insolencia f. ~**t** a insolente

impulse /ˈɪmpʌls/ n impulso m. **on** ~ sin reflexionar

impulsive /ɪmˈpʌlsɪv/ a irreflexivo. ~**ly** adv sin reflexionar

impunity /ɪmˈpjuːnətɪ/ n impunidad f. **with** ~ impunemente

impur|e /ɪmˈpjʊə(r)/ a impuro. ~**ity** n impureza f

impute /ɪmˈpjuːt/ vt imputar

in /ɪn/ prep en, dentro de. ~ **a firm manner** de una manera terminante.

~ **an hour('s time)** dentro de una hora. ~ **doing** al hacer. ~ **so far as** en cuanto que. ~ **the evening** por la tarde. ~ **the main** por la mayor parte. ~ **the rain** bajo la lluvia. ~ **the sun** al sol. **one** ~ **ten** uno de cada diez. **the best** ~ el mejor de. ● *adv (inside)* dentro; *(at home)* en casa; *(in fashion)* de moda. **the** ~**s and outs of** los detalles *mpl* de

inability /ɪnə'bɪlɪtɪ/ *n* incapacidad *f*

inaccessible /ɪnæk'sesəbl/ *a* inaccesible

inaccura|cy /ɪn'ækjʊrəsɪ/ *n* inexactitud *f*. ~**te** *a* inexacto

inaction /ɪn'ækʃn/ *n* inacción *f*

inactiv|e /ɪn'æktɪv/ *a* inactivo. ~**ity** /-'tɪvətɪ/ *n* inactividad *f*

inadequa|cy /ɪn'ædɪkwəsɪ/ *n* insuficiencia *f*. ~**te** *a* insuficiente

inadmissible /ɪnəd'mɪsəbl/ *a* inadmisible

inadvertently /ɪnəd'vɜ:təntlɪ/ *adv* por descuido

inadvisable /ɪnəd'vaɪzəbl/ *a* no aconsejable

inane /ɪ'neɪn/ *a* estúpido

inanimate /ɪn'ænɪmət/ *a* inanimado

inappropriate /ɪnə'prəʊprɪət/ *a* inoportuno

inarticulate /ɪnɑː'tɪkjʊlət/ *a* incapaz de expresarse claramente

inasmuch as /ɪnəz'mʌtʃəz/ *adv* ya que

inattentive /ɪnə'tentɪv/ *a* desatento

inaudible /ɪn'ɔːdəbl/ *a* inaudible

inaugural /ɪ'nɔ:gjʊrəl/ *a* inaugural

inaugurat|e /ɪ'nɔ:gjʊreɪt/ *vt* inaugurar. ~**ion** /-'reɪʃn/ *n* inauguración *f*

inauspicious /ɪnɔː'spɪʃəs/ *a* poco propicio

inborn /'ɪnbɔːn/ *a* innato

inbred /ɪn'bred/ *a (inborn)* innato

incalculable /ɪn'kælkjʊləbl/ *a* incalculable

incapab|ility /ɪnkeɪpə'bɪlɪtɪ/ *n* incapacidad *f*. ~**le** *a* incapaz

incapacit|ate /ɪnkə'pæsɪteɪt/ *vt* incapacitar. ~**y** *n* incapacidad *f*

incarcerat|e /ɪn'kɑːsəreɪt/ *vt* encarcelar. ~**ion** /-'reɪʃn/ *n* encarcelamiento *m*

incarnat|e /ɪn'kɑːnət/ *a* encarnado. ~**ion** /-'neɪʃn/ *n* encarnación *f*

incautious /ɪn'kɔːʃəs/ *a* incauto. ~**ly** *adv* incautamente

incendiary /ɪn'sendɪərɪ/ *a* incendiario. ● *n (person)* incendiario *m*; *(bomb)* bomba *f* incendiaria

incense[1] /'ɪnsens/ *n* incienso *m*

incense[2] /ɪn'sens/ *vt* enfurecer

incentive /ɪn'sentɪv/ *n* incentivo *m*; *(payment)* prima *f* de incentivo

inception /ɪn'sepʃn/ *n* principio *m*

incertitude /ɪn'sɜ:tɪtju:d/ *n* incertidumbre *f*

incessant /ɪn'sesnt/ *a* incesante. ~**ly** *adv* sin cesar

incest /'ɪnsest/ *n* incesto *m*. ~**uous** /-'sestjʊəs/ *a* incestuoso

inch /ɪntʃ/ *n* pulgada *f* (= 2,54*cm*). ● *vi* avanzar palmo a palmo

incidence /'ɪnsɪdəns/ *n* frecuencia *f*

incident /'ɪnsɪdənt/ *n* incidente *m*

incidental /ɪnsɪ'dentl/ *a* fortuito. ~**ly** *adv* incidentemente; *(by the way)* a propósito

incinerat|e /ɪn'sɪnəreɪt/ *vt* incinerar. ~**or** *n* incinerador *m*

incipient /ɪn'sɪpɪənt/ *a* incipiente

incision /ɪn'sɪʒn/ *n* incisión *f*

incisive /ɪn'saɪsɪv/ *a* incisivo

incite /ɪn'saɪt/ *vt* incitar. ~**ment** *n* incitación *f*

inclement /ɪn'klemənt/ *a* inclemente

inclination /ɪnklɪ'neɪʃn/ *n* inclinación *f*

incline[1] /ɪn'klaɪn/ *vt* inclinar. ● *vi* inclinarse. **be** ~**d to** tener tendencia a

incline[2] /'ɪnklaɪn/ *n* cuesta *f*

inclu|de /ɪn'klu:d/ *vt* incluir. ~**ding** *prep* incluso. ~**sion** /-ʒn/ *n* inclusión *f*

inclusive /ɪn'klu:sɪv/ *a* inclusivo. **be** ~ **of** incluir. ● *adv* inclusive

incognito /ɪnkɒg'ni:təʊ/ *adv* de incógnito

incoherent /ɪnkəʊ'hɪərənt/ *a* incoherente

income /'ɪnkʌm/ *n* ingresos *mpl*. ~ **tax** *n* impuesto *m* sobre la renta

incoming /'ɪnkʌmɪŋ/ *a ‹tide›* ascendente; *‹tenant etc›* nuevo

incomparable /ɪn'kɒmpərəbl/ *a* incomparable

incompatible /ɪnkəm'pætəbl/ *a* incompatible

incompeten|ce /ɪn'kɒmpɪtəns/ *n* incompetencia *f*. ~**t** *a* incompetente

incomplete /ɪnkəm'pli:t/ *a* incompleto

incomprehensible /ɪnkɒmprɪ'hensəbl/ *a* incomprensible

inconceivable /ɪnkən'siːvəbl/ *a* inconcebible

inconclusive /ɪnkən'kluːsɪv/ *a* poco concluyente

incongruous /ɪn'kɒŋgrʊəs/ *a* incongruente

inconsequential /ɪnkɒnsɪ'kwenʃl/ *a* sin importancia

inconsiderate /ɪnkən'sɪdərət/ *a* desconsiderado

inconsisten|cy /ɪnkən'sɪstənsɪ/ *n* inconsecuencia *f*. ~t *a* inconsecuente. be ~t with no concordar con

inconspicuous /ɪnkən'spɪkjʊəs/ *a* que no llama la atención. ~ly *adv* sin llamar la atención

incontinen|ce /ɪn'kɒntɪnəns/ *a* incontinencia *f*. ~t *a* incontinente

inconvenien|ce /ɪnkən'viːnɪəns/ *a* incomodidad *f*; *(drawback)* inconveniente *m*. ~t *a* incómodo; *(time)* inoportuno

incorporat|e /ɪn'kɔːpəreɪt/ *vt* incorporar; *(include)* incluir. ~ion /-'reɪʃn/ *n* incorporación *f*

incorrect /ɪnkə'rekt/ *a* incorrecto

incorrigible /ɪn'kɒrɪdʒəbl/ *a* incorregible

incorruptible /ɪnkə'rʌptəbl/ *a* incorruptible

increase /'ɪnkriːs/ *n* aumento *m* (in, of de). /ɪn'kriːs/ *vt/i* aumentar

increasing /ɪn'kriːsɪŋ/ *a* creciente. ~ly *adv* cada vez más

incredible /ɪn'kredəbl/ *a* increíble

incredulous /ɪn'kredjʊləs/ *a* incrédulo

increment /'ɪnkrɪmənt/ *n* aumento *m*

incriminat|e /ɪn'krɪmɪneɪt/ *vt* acriminar. ~ing *a* acriminador

incubat|e /'ɪnkjʊbeɪt/ *vt* incubar. ~ion /-'beɪʃn/ *n* incubación *f*. ~or *n* incubadora *f*

inculcate /'ɪnkʌlkeɪt/ *vt* inculcar

incumbent /ɪn'kʌmbənt/ *n* titular. ● *a*. be ~ on incumbir a

incur /ɪn'kɜː(r)/ *vt* (*pt* incurred) incurrir en; contraer *(debts)*

incurable /ɪn'kjʊərəbl/ *a* incurable

incursion /ɪn'kɜːʃn/ *n* incursión *f*

indebted /ɪn'detɪd/ *a*. ~ to s.o. estar en deuda con uno

indecen|cy /ɪn'diːsnsɪ/ *n* indecencia *f*. ~t *a* indecente

indecisi|on /ɪndɪ'sɪʒn/ *n* indecisión *f*. ~ve /ɪndɪ'saɪsɪv/ *a* indeciso

indeed /ɪn'diːd/ *adv* en efecto; *(really?)* ¿de veras?

indefatigable /ɪndɪ'fætɪgəbl/ *a* incansable

indefinable /ɪndɪ'faɪnəbl/ *a* indefinible

indefinite /ɪn'defɪnət/ *a* indefinido. ~ly *adv* indefinidamente

indelible /ɪn'delɪbl/ *a* indeleble

indemni|fy /ɪn'demnɪfaɪ/ *vt* indemnizar. ~ty /-ətɪ/ *n* indemnización *f*

indent /ɪn'dent/ *vt* endentar *(text)*. ~ation /-'teɪʃn/ *n* mella *f*

independen|ce /ɪndɪ'pendəns/ *n* independencia *f*. ~t *a* independiente. ~tly *adv* independientemente. ~tly of independientemente de

indescribable /ɪndɪ'skraɪbəbl/ *a* indescriptible

indestructible /ɪndɪ'strʌktəbl/ *a* indestructible

indeterminate /ɪndɪ'tɜːmɪnət/ *a* indeterminado

index /'ɪndeks/ *n* (*pl* indexes) índice *m*. ● *vt* poner índice a; *(enter in the/an index)* poner en el/un índice. ~ finger *n* (dedo *m*) índice *m*. ~linked *a* indexado

India /'ɪndɪə/ *n* la India *f*. ~n *a* & *n* indio (*m*). ~n summer *n* veranillo *m* de San Martín

indicat|e /'ɪndɪkeɪt/ *vt* indicar. ~ion /-'keɪʃn/ *n* indicación *f*. ~ive /ɪn'dɪkətɪv/ *a* & *n* indicativo (*m*). ~or /'ɪndɪkeɪtə(r)/ *n* indicador *m*

indict /ɪn'daɪt/ *vt* acusar. ~ment *n* acusación *f*

indifferen|ce /ɪn'dɪfrəns/ *n* indiferencia *f*. ~t *a* indiferente; *(not good)* mediocre

indigenous /ɪn'dɪdʒɪnəs/ *a* indígena

indigesti|ble /ɪndɪ'dʒestəbl/ *a* indigesto. ~on /-tʃən/ *n* indigestión *f*

indignant /ɪn'dɪgnənt/ *a* indignado. ~tion /-'neɪʃn/ *n* indignación *f*

indignity /ɪn'dɪgnətɪ/ *n* indignidad *f*

indigo /'ɪndɪgəʊ/ *n* añil (*m*)

indirect /ɪndɪ'rekt/ *a* indirecto. ~ly *adv* indirectamente

indiscre|et /ɪndɪ'skriːt/ *a* indiscreto. ~tion /-'kreʃn/ *n* indiscreción *f*

indiscriminate /ɪndɪ'skrɪmɪnət/ *a* indistinto. ~ly *adv* indistintamente

indispensable /ɪndɪ'spensəbl/ *a* imprescindible

indispos|ed /ˌɪndɪsˈpəʊzd/ *a* indispuesto. **~ition** /-əˈzɪʃn/ *n* indisposición *f*

indisputable /ˌɪndɪsˈpjuːtəbl/ *a* indiscutible

indissoluble /ˌɪndɪˈsɒljʊbl/ *a* indisoluble

indistinct /ˌɪndɪˈstɪŋkt/ *a* indistinto

indistinguishable /ˌɪndɪˈstɪŋwɪʃəbl/ *a* indistinguible

individual /ˌɪndɪˈvɪdjʊəl/ *a* individual. ● *n* individuo *m*. **~ist** *n* individualista *m & f*. **~ity** *n* individualidad *f*. **~ly** *adv* individualmente

indivisible /ˌɪndɪˈvɪzəbl/ *a* indivisible

Indo-China /ˌɪndəʊˈtʃaɪnə/ *n* Indochina *f*

indoctrinat|e /ɪnˈdɒktrɪneɪt/ *vt* adoctrinar. **~ion** /-ˈneɪʃn/ *n* adoctrinamiento *m*

indolen|ce /ˈɪndələns/ *n* indolencia *f*. **~t** *a* indolente

indomitable /ɪnˈdɒmɪtəbl/ *a* indomable

Indonesia /ˌɪndəʊˈniːzɪə/ *n* Indonesia *f*. **~n** *a & n* indonesio (*m*)

indoor /ˈɪndɔː(r)/ *a* interior; ⟨clothes etc⟩ de casa; ⟨covered⟩ cubierto. **~s** *adv* dentro; ⟨at home⟩ en casa

induce /ɪnˈdjuːs/ *vt* inducir; ⟨cause⟩ provocar. **~ment** *n* incentivo *m*

induct /ɪnˈdʌkt/ *vt* instalar; ⟨mil, Amer⟩ incorporar

indulge /ɪnˈdʌldʒ/ *vt* satisfacer ⟨desires⟩; complacer ⟨person⟩. ● *vi*. **~ in** entregarse a. **~nce** /ɪnˈdʌldʒəns/ *n* ⟨of desires⟩ satisfacción *f*; ⟨relig⟩ indulgencia *f*. **~nt** *a* indulgente

industrial /ɪnˈdʌstrɪəl/ *a* industrial; ⟨unrest⟩ laboral. **~ist** *n* industrial *m & f*. **~ized** *a* industrializado

industrious /ɪnˈdʌstrɪəs/ *a* trabajador

industry /ˈɪndəstrɪ/ *n* industria *f*; ⟨zeal⟩ aplicación *f*

inebriated /ɪˈniːbrɪeɪtɪd/ *a* borracho

inedible /ɪnˈedɪbl/ *a* incomible

ineffable /ɪnˈefəbl/ *a* inefable

ineffective /ˌɪnɪˈfektɪv/ *a* ineficaz; ⟨person⟩ incapaz

ineffectual /ˌɪnɪˈfektjʊəl/ *a* ineficaz

inefficien|cy /ˌɪnɪˈfɪʃnsɪ/ *n* ineficacia *f*; ⟨of person⟩ incompetencia *f*. **~t** *a* ineficaz; ⟨person⟩ incompetente

ineligible /ɪnˈelɪdʒəbl/ *a* inelegible. **be ~ for** no tener derecho a

inept /ɪˈnept/ *a* inepto

inequality /ˌɪnɪˈkwɒlətɪ/ *n* desigualdad *f*

inert /ɪˈnɜːt/ *a* inerte

inertia /ɪˈnɜːʃə/ *n* inercia *f*

inescapable /ˌɪnɪˈskeɪpəbl/ *a* ineludible

inestimable /ɪnˈestɪməbl/ *a* inestimable

inevitabl|e /ɪnˈevɪtəbl/ *a* inevitable. **~ly** *adv* inevitablemente

inexact /ˌɪnɪɡˈzækt/ *a* inexacto

inexcusable /ˌɪnɪkˈskjuːsəbl/ *a* imperdonable

inexhaustible /ˌɪnɪɡˈzɔːstəbl/ *a* inagotable

inexorable /ɪnˈeksərəbl/ *a* inexorable

inexpensive /ˌɪnɪkˈspensɪv/ *a* económico, barato

inexperience /ˌɪnɪkˈspɪərɪəns/ *n* falta *f* de experiencia. **~d** *a* inexperto

inexplicable /ˌɪnɪkˈsplɪkəbl/ *a* inexplicable

inextricable /ˌɪnɪkˈstrɪkəbl/ *a* inextricable

infallib|ility /ɪnˌfælɪbɪlɪtɪ/ *n* infalibilidad *f*. **~le** *a* infalible

infam|ous /ˈɪnfəməs/ *a* infame. **~y** *n* infamia *f*

infan|cy /ˈɪnfənsɪ/ *n* infancia *f*. **~t** *n* niño *m*. **~tile** /ˈɪnfəntaɪl/ *a* infantil

infantry /ˈɪnfəntrɪ/ *n* infantería *f*

infatuat|ed /ɪnˈfætjʊeɪtɪd/ *a*. **be ~ed with** encapricharse por. **~ion** /-ˈeɪʃn/ *n* encaprichamiento *m*

infect /ɪnˈfekt/ *vt* infectar; ⟨fig⟩ contagiar. **~ s.o. with** contagiar a uno. **~ion** /-ˈfekʃn/ *n* infección *f*; ⟨fig⟩ contagio *m*. **~ious** /ɪnˈfekʃəs/ *a* contagioso

infer /ɪnˈfɜː(r)/ *vt* ⟨pt **inferred**⟩ deducir. **~ence** /ˈɪnfərəns/ *n* deducción *f*

inferior /ɪnˈfɪərɪə(r)/ *a* inferior. ● *n* inferior *m & f*. **~ity** /-ˈɒrətɪ/ *n* inferioridad *f*

infernal /ɪnˈfɜːnl/ *a* infernal. **~ly** *adv* ⟨fam⟩ atrozmente

inferno /ɪnˈfɜːnəʊ/ *n* ⟨pl **-os**⟩ infierno *m*

infertil|e /ɪnˈfɜːtaɪl/ *a* estéril. **~ity** /-ˈtɪlətɪ/ *n* esterilidad *f*

infest /ɪnˈfest/ *vt* infestar. **~ation** /-ˈsteɪʃn/ *n* infestación *f*

infidelity /ɪnfɪ'deləti/ n infidelidad f

infighting /'ɪnfaɪtɪŋ/ n lucha f cuerpo a cuerpo; (fig) riñas fpl (internas)

infiltrat|e /ɪnfɪl'treɪt/ vt infiltrar. • vi infiltrarse. ~ion /-'treɪʃn/ n infiltración f

infinite /'ɪnfɪnət/ a infinito. ~ly adv infinitamente

infinitesimal /ɪnfɪnɪ'tesɪml/ a infinitesimal

infinitive /ɪn'fɪnətɪv/ n infinitivo n

infinity /ɪn'fɪnəti/ n (infinite distance) infinito m; (infinite quantity) infinidad f

infirm /ɪn'fɜ:m/ a enfermizo

infirmary /ɪn'fɜ:məri/ n hospital m; (sick bay) enfermería f

infirmity /ɪn'fɜ:məti/ n enfermedad f; (weakness) debilidad f

inflam|e /ɪn'fleɪm/ vt inflamar. ~mable /ɪn'flæməbl/ a inflamable. ~mation /-ə'meɪʃn/ n inflamación f. ~matory /ɪn'flæmətəri/ a inflamatorio

inflate /ɪn'fleɪt/ vt inflar

inflation /ɪn'fleɪʃn/ n inflación f. ~ary a inflacionario

inflection /ɪn'flekʃn/ n inflexión f

inflexible /ɪn'fleksəbl/ a inflexible

inflict /ɪn'flɪkt/ vt infligir (on a)

inflow /'ɪnfləʊ/ n afluencia f

influence /'ɪnflʊəns/ n influencia f. under the ~ (drunk, fam) borracho. • vt influir, influenciar (esp LAm)

influential /ɪnflʊ'enʃl/ a influyente

influenza /ɪnflʊ'enzə/ n gripe f

influx /'ɪnflʌks/ n afluencia f

inform /ɪn'fɔ:m/ vt informar. keep ~ed tener al corriente

informal /ɪn'fɔ:ml/ a (simple) sencillo, sin ceremonia; (unofficial) oficioso. ~ity /-'mæləti/ n falta f de ceremonia. ~ly adv sin ceremonia

inform|ant /ɪn'fɔ:mənt/ n informador m. ~ation /ɪnfə'meɪʃn/ n información f. ~ative /ɪn'fɔ:mətɪv/ a informativo. ~er /ɪn'fɔ:mə(r)/ n denunciante m

infra-red /ɪnfrə'red/ a infrarrojo

infrequent /ɪn'fri:kwənt/ a poco frecuente. ~ly adv raramente

infringe /ɪn'frɪndʒ/ vt infringir. ~ on usurpar. ~ment n infracción f

infuriate /ɪn'fjʊərɪeɪt/ vt enfurecer

infus|e /ɪn'fju:z/ vt infundir. ~ion /-ʒn/ n infusión f

ingen|ious /ɪn'dʒi:niəs/ a ingenioso. ~uity /ɪndʒɪ'nju:əti/ n ingeniosidad f

ingenuous /ɪn'dʒenjʊəs/ a ingenuo

ingest /ɪn'dʒest/ vt ingerir

ingot /'ɪŋgət/ n lingote m

ingrained /ɪn'greɪnd/ a arraigado

ingratiate /ɪn'greɪʃɪeɪt/ vt. ~ o.s. with congraciarse con

ingratitude /ɪn'grætɪtju:d/ n ingratitud f

ingredient /ɪn'gri:dɪənt/ n ingrediente m

ingrowing /'ɪngrəʊɪŋ/ a. ~ nail n uñero m, uña f encarnada

inhabit /ɪn'hæbɪt/ vt habitar. ~able a habitable. ~ant n habitante m

inhale /ɪn'heɪl/ vt aspirar. • vi (tobacco) aspirar el humo

inherent /ɪn'hɪərənt/ a inherente. ~ly adv intrínsecamente

inherit /ɪn'herɪt/ vt heredar. ~ance n herencia f

inhibit /ɪn'hɪbɪt/ vt inhibir. be ~ed tener inhibiciones. ~ion /-'bɪʃn/ n inhibición f

inhospitable /ɪnhə'spɪtəbl/ a (place) inhóspito; (person) inhospitalario

inhuman /ɪn'hju:mən/ a inhumano. ~e /ɪnhju:'meɪn/ a inhumano. ~ity /ɪnhju:'mænəti/ n inhumanidad f

inimical /ɪ'nɪmɪkl/ a hostil

inimitable /ɪ'nɪmɪtəbl/ a inimitable

iniquit|ous /ɪ'nɪkwɪtəs/ a inicuo. ~y /-əti/ n iniquidad f

initial /ɪ'nɪʃl/ n inicial f. • vt (pt initialled) firmar con iniciales. ~led the document firmó el documento con sus iniciales. • a inicial. ~ly adv al principio

initiat|e /ɪ'nɪʃɪeɪt/ vt iniciar; promover (scheme etc). ~ion /-'eɪʃn/ n iniciación f

initiative /ɪ'nɪʃətɪv/ n iniciativa f

inject /ɪn'dʒekt/ vt inyectar; (fig) injertar (new element). ~ion /-ʃn/ n inyección f

injunction /ɪn'dʒʌŋkʃn/ n (court order) entredicho m

injur|e /'ɪndʒə(r)/ vt (wound) herir; (fig, damage) perjudicar. ~y /'ɪndʒəri/ n herida f; (damage) perjuicio m

injustice /ɪn'dʒʌstɪs/ n injusticia f

ink /ɪŋk/ n tinta f

inkling /'ɪŋklɪŋ/ n atisbo m

ink: ~-well *n* tintero *m.* ~y *a* manchado de tinta

inland /'ɪnlənd/ *a* interior. ● *adv* tierra adentro. I~ Revenue *n* Hacienda *f*

in-laws /'ɪnlɔːz/ *npl* parientes *mpl* políticos

inlay /ɪn'leɪ/ *vt* (*pt* inlaid) taracear, incrustar. /'ɪnleɪ/ *n* taracea *f*, incrustación *f*

inlet /'ɪnlet/ *n* ensenada *f*; (*tec*) entrada *f*

inmate /'ɪnmeɪt/ *n* (*of asylum*) internado *m*; (*of prison*) preso *m*

inn /ɪn/ *n* posada *f*

innards /'ɪnədz/ *npl* tripas *fpl*

innate /ɪ'neɪt/ *a* innato

inner /'ɪnə(r)/ *a* interior; (*fig*) íntimo. ~most *a* más íntimo. ~ tube *n* cámara *f* de aire, llanta *f* (LAm)

innings /'ɪnɪŋz/ *n invar* turno *m*

innkeeper /'ɪnkiːpə(r)/ *n* posadero *m*

innocen|ce /'ɪnəsns/ *n* inocencia *f*. ~t *a* & *n* inocente (*m* & *f*)

innocuous /ɪ'nɒkjʊəs/ *a* inocuo

innovat|e /'ɪnəveɪt/ *vi* innovar. ~ion /-'veɪʃn/ *n* innovación *f*. ~or *n* innovador *m*

innuendo /ɪnjuː'endəʊ/ *n* (*pl* -oes) insinuación *f*

innumerable /ɪ'njuːmərəbl/ *a* innumerable

inoculat|e /ɪ'nɒkjʊleɪt/ *vt* inocular. ~ion /-'leɪʃn/ *n* inoculación *f*

inoffensive /ɪnə'fensɪv/ *a* inofensivo

inoperative /ɪn'ɒpərətɪv/ *a* inoperante

inopportune /ɪn'ɒpətjuːn/ *a* inoportuno

inordinate /ɪ'nɔːdɪnət/ *a* excesivo. ~ly *adv* excesivamente

in-patient /'ɪnpeɪʃnt/ *n* paciente *m* interno

input /'ɪnpʊt/ *n* (*data*) datos *mpl*; (*comput process*) entrada *f*, input *m*; (*elec*) energía *f*

inquest /'ɪnkwest/ *n* investigación *f* judicial

inquir|e /ɪn'kwaɪə(r)/ *vi* preguntar. ~y *n* (*question*) pregunta *f*; (*investigation*) investigación *f*

inquisition /ɪnkwɪ'zɪʃn/ *n* inquisición *f*

inquisitive /ɪn'kwɪzətɪv/ *a* inquisitivo

inroad /'ɪnrəʊd/ *n* incursión *f*

inrush /'ɪnrʌʃ/ *n* irrupción *f*

insan|e /ɪn'seɪn/ *a* loco. ~ity /-'sænətɪ/ *n* locura *f*

insanitary /ɪn'sænɪtərɪ/ *a* insalubre

insatiable /ɪn'seɪʃəbl/ *a* insaciable

inscri|be /ɪn'skraɪb/ *vt* inscribir; dedicar ⟨*book*⟩. ~ption /-ɪpʃn/ *n* inscripción *f*; (*in book*) dedicatoria *f*

inscrutable /ɪn'skruːtəbl/ *a* inescrutable

insect /'ɪnsekt/ *n* insecto *m*. ~icide /ɪn'sektɪsaɪd/ *n* insecticida *f*

insecur|e /ɪnsɪ'kjʊə(r)/ *a* inseguro. ~ity *n* inseguridad *f*

insemination /ɪnsemɪ'neɪʃn/ *n* inseminación *f*

insensible /ɪn'sensəbl/ *a* insensible; (*unconscious*) sin conocimiento

insensitive /ɪn'sensətɪv/ *a* insensible

inseparable /ɪn'sepərəbl/ *a* inseparable

insert /'ɪnsɜːt/ *n* materia *f* insertada. /ɪn'sɜːt/ *vt* insertar. ~ion /-ʃn/ *n* inserción *f*

inshore /ɪn'ʃɔː(r)/ *a* costero

inside /ɪn'saɪd/ *n* interior *m.* ~ out al revés; (*thoroughly*) a fondo. ● *a* interior. ● *adv* dentro. ● *prep* dentro de. ~s *npl* tripas *fpl*

insidious /ɪn'sɪdɪəs/ *a* insidioso

insight /'ɪnsaɪt/ *n* (*perception*) penetración *f*, revelación *f*

insignia /ɪn'sɪgnɪə/ *npl* insignias *fpl*

insignificant /ɪnsɪg'nɪfɪkənt/ *a* insignificante

insincer|e /ɪnsɪn'sɪə(r)/ *a* poco sincero. ~ity /-'serətɪ/ *n* falta *f* de sinceridad *f*

insinuat|e /ɪn'sɪnjʊeɪt/ *vt* insinuar. ~ion /-'eɪʃn/ *n* insinuación *f*

insipid /ɪn'sɪpɪd/ *a* insípido

insist /ɪn'sɪst/ *vt/i* insistir. ~ on insistir en; (*demand*) exigir

insisten|ce /ɪn'sɪstəns/ *n* insistencia *f*. ~t *a* insistente. ~tly *adv* con insistencia

insolen|ce /'ɪnsələns/ *n* insolencia *f*. ~t *a* insolente

insoluble /ɪn'sɒljʊbl/ *a* insoluble

insolvent /ɪn'sɒlvənt/ *a* insolvente

insomnia /ɪn'sɒmnɪə/ *n* insomnio *m.* ~c /-ɪæk/ *n* insomne *m & f*

inspect /ɪn'spekt/ *vt* inspeccionar; revisar ⟨*ticket*⟩. ~ion /-ʃn/ *n* inspección *f*. ~or *n* inspector *m*; (*on train, bus*) revisor *m*

inspir|ation /ɪnspə'reɪʃn/ *n* inspiración *f*. ~e /ɪn'spaɪə(r)/ *vt* inspirar

instability /ɪnstə'bɪlətɪ/ n inestabilidad f

install /ɪn'stɔːl/ vt instalar. ~**ation** /-ə'leɪʃn/ n instalación f

instalment /ɪn'stɔːlmənt/ n (payment) plazo m; (of serial) entrega f

instance /'ɪnstəns/ n ejemplo m; (case) caso m. **for** ~ por ejemplo. **in the first** ~ en primer lugar

instant /'ɪnstənt/ a inmediato; (food) instantáneo. ● n instante m. ~**aneous** /ɪnstən'teɪnɪəs/ a instantáneo. ~**ly** /'ɪnstəntlɪ/ adv inmediatamente

instead /ɪn'sted/ adv en cambio. ~ **of doing** en vez de hacer. ~ **of s.o.** en lugar de uno

instep /'ɪnstep/ n empeine m

instigat|e /'ɪnstɪɡeɪt/ vt instigar. ~**ion** /-'ɡeɪʃn/ n instigación f. ~**or** n instigador m

instil /ɪn'stɪl/ vt (pt **instilled**) infundir

instinct /'ɪnstɪŋkt/ n instinto m. ~**ive** /ɪn'stɪŋktɪv/ a instintivo

institut|e /'ɪnstɪtjuːt/ n instituto m. ● vt establecer; iniciar (enquiry etc). ~**ion** /-'tjuːʃn/ n institución f

instruct /ɪn'strʌkt/ vt instruir; (order) mandar. ~ **s.o. in sth** enseñar algo a uno. ~**ion** /-ʃn/ n instrucción f. ~**ions** /-ʃnz/ npl (for use) modo m de empleo. ~**ive** a instructivo

instrument /'ɪnstrəmənt/ n instrumento m. ~**al** /ɪnstrə'mentl/ a instrumental. **be ~al in** contribuir a. ~**alist** n instrumentalista m & f

insubordinat|e /ɪnsə'bɔːdɪnət/ a insubordinado. ~**ion** /-'neɪʃn/ n insubordinación f

insufferable /ɪn'sʌfərəbl/ a insufrible, insoportable

insufficient /ɪnsə'fɪʃnt/ a insuficiente. ~**ly** adv insuficientemente

insular /'ɪnsjʊlə(r)/ a insular; (narrow-minded) de miras estrechas

insulat|e /'ɪnsjʊleɪt/ vt aislar. ~**ing tape** n cinta f aisladora/aislante. ~**ion** /-'leɪʃn/ n aislamiento m

insulin /'ɪnsjʊlɪn/ n insulina f

insult /ɪn'sʌlt/ vt insultar. /'ɪnsʌlt/ n insulto m

insuperable /ɪn'sjuːpərəbl/ a insuperable

insur|ance /ɪn'ʃʊərəns/ n seguro m. ~**e** vt asegurar. ~**e that** asegurarse de que

insurgent /ɪn'sɜːdʒənt/ a & n insurrecto (m)

insurmountable /ɪnsə'maʊntəbl/ a insuperable

insurrection /ɪnsə'rekʃn/ n insurrección f

intact /ɪn'tækt/ a intacto

intake /'ɪnteɪk/ n (quantity) número m; (mec) admisión f; (of food) consumo m

intangible /ɪn'tændʒəbl/ a intangible

integral /'ɪntɪɡrəl/ a íntegro. **be an** ~ **part of** ser parte integrante de

integrat|e /'ɪntɪɡreɪt/ vt integrar. ● vi integrarse. ~**ion** /-'ɡreɪʃn/ n integración f

integrity /ɪn'teɡrətɪ/ n integridad f

intellect /'ɪntəlekt/ n intelecto m. ~**ual** a & n intelectual (m)

intelligen|ce /ɪn'telɪdʒəns/ n inteligencia f; (information) información f. ~**t** a inteligente. ~**tly** adv inteligentemente. ~**tsia** /ɪntelɪ'dʒentsɪə/ n intelectualidad f

intelligible /ɪn'telɪdʒəbl/ a inteligible

intemperance /ɪn'tempərəns/ n inmoderación f

intend /ɪn'tend/ vt destinar. ~ **to do** tener la intención de hacer. ~**ed** a intencionado. ● n (future spouse) novio m

intense /ɪn'tens/ a intenso; (person) apasionado. ~**ly** adv intensamente; (very) sumamente

intensi|fication /ɪntensɪfɪ'keɪʃn/ n intensificación f. ~**fy** /-faɪ/ vt intensificar

intensity /ɪn'tensətɪ/ n intensidad f

intensive /ɪn'tensɪv/ a intensivo. ~ **care** n asistencia f intensiva, cuidados mpl intensivos

intent /ɪn'tent/ n propósito m. ● a atento. ~ **on** absorto en. ~ **on doing** resuelto a hacer

intention /ɪn'tenʃn/ n intención f. ~**al** a intencional

intently /ɪn'tentlɪ/ adv atentamente

inter /ɪn'tɜː(r)/ vt (pt **interred**) enterrar

inter... /'ɪntə(r)/ pref inter..., entre...

interact /ɪntər'ækt/ vi obrar recíprocamente. ~**ion** /-ʃn/ n interacción f

intercede /ɪntə'siːd/ vi interceder

intercept /ɪntə'sept/ vt interceptar. ~**ion** /-ʃn/ n interceptación f; (in geometry) intersección f

interchange /'ɪntətʃeɪndʒ/ n (road junction) cruce m. **~able** /-'tʃeɪndʒəbl/ a intercambiable

intercom /'ɪntəkɒm/ n intercomunicador m

interconnected /ɪntəkə'nektɪd/ a relacionado

intercourse /'ɪntəkɔːs/ n trato m; (sexual) trato m sexual

interest /'ɪntrest/ n interés m; (advantage) ventaja f. ● vt interesar. **~ed** a interesado. **be ~ed in** interesarse por. **~ing** a interesante

interfere /ɪntə'fɪə(r)/ vi entrometerse. **~ in** entrometerse en. **~ with** entrometerse en, interferir en; interferir (radio). **~nce** n interferencia f

interim a provisional. ● n. **in the ~** entre tanto

interior /ɪn'tɪərɪə(r)/ a & n interior (m)

interjection /ɪntə'dʒekʃn/ n interjección f

interlock /ɪntə'lɒk/ vt/i (tec) engranar

interloper /'ɪntələʊpə(r)/ n intruso m

interlude /'ɪntəluːd/ n intervalo m; (theatre, music) interludio m

intermarr|iage /ɪntə'mærɪdʒ/ n matrimonio m entre personas de distintas razas. **~y** vi casarse (con personas de distintas razas)

intermediary /ɪntə'miːdɪərɪ/ a & n intermediario (m)

intermediate /ɪntə'miːdɪət/ a intermedio

interminable /ɪn'tɜːmɪnəbl/ a interminable

intermission /ɪntə'mɪʃn/ n pausa f; (theatre) descanso m

intermittent /ɪntə'mɪtnt/ a intermitente. **~ly** adv con discontinuidad

intern /ɪn'tɜːn/ vt internar. /'ɪntɜːn/ n (doctor, Amer) interno m

internal /ɪn'tɜːnl/ a interior. **~ly** adv interiormente

international /ɪntə'næʃənl/ a & n internacional (m)

internee /ˌɪntɜː'niː/ n internado m

internment /ɪn'tɜːnmənt/ n internamiento m

interplay /'ɪntəpleɪ/ n interacción f

interpolate /ɪn'tɜːpəleɪt/ vt interpolar

interpret /ɪn'tɜːprɪt/ vt/i interpretar. **~ation** /-'teɪʃn/ n interpretación f. **~er** n intérprete m & f

interrelated /ɪntərɪ'leɪtɪd/ a interrelacionado

interrogat|e /ɪn'terəgeɪt/ vt interrogar. **~ion** /-'geɪʃn/ n interrogación f; (session of questions) interrogatorio m

interrogative /ɪntə'rɒgətɪv/ a & n interrogativo (m)

interrupt /ɪntə'rʌpt/ vt interrumpir. **~ion** /-ʃn/ n interrupción f

intersect /ɪntə'sekt/ vt cruzar. ● vi (roads) cruzarse; (geometry) intersecarse. **~ion** /-ʃn/ n (roads) cruce m; (geometry) intersección f

interspersed /ɪntə'spɜːst/ a disperso. **~ with** salpicado de

intertwine /ɪntə'twaɪn/ vt entrelazar. ● vi entrelazarse

interval /'ɪntəvl/ n intervalo m; (theatre) descanso m. **at ~s** a intervalos

interven|e /ɪntə'viːn/ vi intervenir. **~tion** /-'venʃn/ n intervención f

interview /'ɪntəvjuː/ n entrevista f. ● vt entrevistarse con. **~er** n entrevistador m

intestin|al /ɪnte'staɪnl/ a intestinal. **~e** /ɪn'testɪn/ n intestino m

intimacy /'ɪntɪməsɪ/ n intimidad f

intimate[1] /'ɪntɪmət/ a íntimo

intimate[2] /'ɪntɪmeɪt/ vt (state) anunciar; (imply) dar a entender

intimately /'ɪntɪmətlɪ/ adv íntimamente

intimidat|e /ɪn'tɪmɪdeɪt/ vt intimidar. **~ion** /-'deɪʃn/ n intimidación f

into /'ɪntuː/, unstressed /'ɪntə/ prep en; (translate) a

intolerable /ɪn'tɒlərəbl/ a intolerable

intoleran|ce /ɪn'tɒlərəns/ n intolerancia f. **~t** a intolerante

intonation /ɪntə'neɪʃn/ n entonación f

intoxicat|e /ɪn'tɒksɪkeɪt/ vt embriagar; (med) intoxicar. **~ed** a ebrio. **~ion** /-'keɪʃn/ n embriaguez f; (med) intoxicación f

intra... /'ɪntrə/ pref intra...

intractable /ɪn'træktəbl/ a (person) intratable; (thing) muy difícil

intransigent /ɪn'trænsɪdʒənt/ a intransigente

intransitive /ɪnˈtrænsɪtɪv/ *a* intransitivo

intravenous /ɪntrəˈviːnəs/ *a* intravenoso

intrepid /ɪnˈtrepɪd/ *a* intrépido

intrica|cy /ˈɪntrɪkəsɪ/ *n* complejidad *f*. ∼**te** *a* complejo

intrigu|e /ɪnˈtriːg/ *vt/i* intrigar. ● *n* intriga *f*. ∼**ing** *a* intrigante

intrinsic /ɪnˈtrɪnsɪk/ *a* intrínseco. ∼**ally** *adv* intrínsecamente

introduc|e /ɪntrəˈdjuːs/ *vt* introducir; presentar ⟨person⟩. ∼**tion** /ɪntrəˈdʌkʃn/ *n* introducción *f*; (to person) presentación *f*. ∼**tory** /-tərɪ/ *a* preliminar

introspective /ɪntrəˈspektɪv/ *a* introspectivo

introvert /ˈɪntrəvɜːt/ *n* introvertido *m*

intru|de /ɪnˈtruːd/ *vi* entrometerse; (disturb) molestar. ∼**der** *n* intruso *m*. ∼**sion** *n* intrusión *f*

intuiti|on /ɪntjuːˈɪʃn/ *n* intuición *f*. ∼**ve** /ɪnˈtjuːɪtɪv/ *a* intuitivo

inundat|e /ˈɪnʌndeɪt/ *vt* inundar. ∼**ion** /-ˈdeɪʃn/ *n* inundación *f*

invade /ɪnˈveɪd/ *vt* invadir. ∼**r** /-ə(r)/ *n* invasor *m*

invalid[1] /ˈɪnvəlɪd/ *n* enfermo *m*, inválido *m*

invalid[2] /ɪnˈvælɪd/ *a* nulo. ∼**ate** *vt* invalidar

invaluable /ɪnˈvæljʊəbl/ *a* inestimable

invariabl|e /ɪnˈveərɪəbl/ *a* invariable. ∼**y** *adv* invariablemente

invasion /ɪnˈveɪʒn/ *n* invasión *f*

invective /ɪnˈvektɪv/ *n* invectiva *f*

inveigh /ɪnˈveɪ/ *vi* dirigir invectivas (against contra)

inveigle /ɪnˈveɪgl/ *vt* engatusar, persuadir

invent /ɪnˈvent/ *vt* inventar. ∼**ion** /-ˈvenʃn/ *n* invención *f*. ∼**ive** *a* inventivo. ∼**or** *n* inventor *m*

inventory /ˈɪnvəntərɪ/ *n* inventario *m*

invers|e /ɪnˈvɜːs/ *a & n* inverso (*m*). ∼**ely** *adv* inversamente. ∼**ion** /ɪnˈvɜːʃn/ *n* inversión *f*

invert /ɪnˈvɜːt/ *vt* invertir. ∼**ed commas** *npl* comillas *fpl*

invest /ɪnˈvest/ *vt* invertir. ● *vi.* ∼ **in** hacer una inversión *f*

investigat|e /ɪnˈvestɪgeɪt/ *vt* investigar. ∼**ion** /-ˈgeɪʃn/ *n* investigación

f. **under** ∼**ion** sometido a examen. ∼**or** *n* investigador *m*

inveterate /ɪnˈvetərət/ *a* inveterado

invidious /ɪnˈvɪdɪəs/ *a* (hateful) odioso; (unfair) injusto

invigilat|e /ɪnˈvɪdʒɪleɪt/ *vi* vigilar. ∼**or** *n* celador *m*

invigorate /ɪnˈvɪgəreɪt/ *vt* vigorizar; (stimulate) estimular

invincible /ɪnˈvɪnsɪbl/ *a* invencible

invisible /ɪnˈvɪzəbl/ *a* invisible

invit|ation /ɪnvɪˈteɪʃn/ *n* invitación *f*. ∼**e** /ɪnˈvaɪt/ *vt* invitar; (ask for) pedir. ∼**ing** *a* atrayente

invoice /ˈɪnvɔɪs/ *n* factura *f*. ● *vt* facturar

invoke /ɪnˈvəʊk/ *vt* invocar

involuntary /ɪnˈvɒləntərɪ/ *a* involuntario

involve /ɪnˈvɒlv/ *vt* enredar. ∼**d** *a* (complex) complicado. ∼**d in** embrollado en. ∼**ment** *n* enredo *m*

invulnerable /ɪnˈvʌlnərəbl/ *a* invulnerable

inward /ˈɪnwəd/ *a* interior. ● *adv* interiormente. ∼**s** *adv* hacia/para dentro

iodine /ˈaɪədiːn/ *n* yodo *m*

iota /aɪˈəʊtə/ *n* (amount) pizca *f*

IOU /aɪəʊˈjuː/ *abbr* (I owe you) pagaré *m*

IQ /aɪˈkjuː/ *abbr* (intelligence quotient) cociente *m* intelectual

Iran /ɪˈrɑːn/ *n* Irán *m*. ∼**ian** /ˈreɪnɪən/ *a & n* iraní (*m*)

Iraq /ɪˈrɑːk/ *n* Irak *m*. ∼**i** *a & n* iraquí (*m*)

irascible /ɪˈræsəbl/ *a* irascible

irate /aɪˈreɪt/ *a* colérico

ire /aɪə(r)/ *n* ira *f*

Ireland /ˈaɪələnd/ *n* Irlanda *f*

iris /ˈaɪərɪs/ *n* (anat) iris *m*; (bot) lirio *m*

Irish /ˈaɪərɪʃ/ *a* irlandés. ● *n* (lang) irlandés *m*. ∼**man** *n* irlandés *m*. ∼**woman** *n* irlandesa *f*

irk /ɜːk/ *vt* fastidiar. ∼**some** *a* fastidioso

iron /ˈaɪən/ *n* hierro *m*; (appliance) plancha *f*. ● *a* de hierro. ● *vt* planchar. ∼ **out** allanar. I∼ **Curtain** *n* telón *m* de acero

ironic(al) /aɪˈrɒnɪk(l)/ *a* irónico

ironing-board /ˈaɪənɪŋbɔːd/ *n* tabla *f* de planchar

ironmonger /ˈaɪənmʌŋgə(r)/ *n* ferretero *m*. ∼**y** *n* ferretería *f*

ironwork /ˈaɪənwɜːk/ *n* herraje *m*

irony /'aɪərənɪ/ n ironía f
irrational /ɪ'ræʃənl/ a irracional
irreconcilable /ɪrekən'saɪləbl/ a irreconciliable
irrefutable /ɪrɪ'fju:təbl/ a irrefutable
irregular /ɪ'regjʊlə(r)/ a irregular. ~ity /-'lærətɪ/ n irregularidad f
irrelevan|ce /ɪ'reləvəns/ n inoportunidad f, impertinencia f. ~t a no pertinente
irreparable /ɪ'repərəbl/ a irreparable
irreplaceable /ɪrɪ'pleɪsəbl/ a irreemplazable
irrepressible /ɪrɪ'presəbl/ a irreprimible
irresistible /ɪrɪ'zɪstəbl/ a irresistible
irresolute /ɪ'rezəlu:t/ a irresoluto, indeciso
irrespective /ɪrɪ'spektɪv/ a. ~ of sin tomar en cuenta
irresponsible /ɪrɪ'spɒnsəbl/ a irresponsable
irretrievable /ɪrɪ'tri:vəbl/ a irrecuperable
irreverent /ɪ'revərənt/ a irreverente
irreversible /ɪrɪ'vɜ:səbl/ a irreversible; ⟨decision⟩ irrevocable
irrevocable /ɪ'revəkəbl/ a irrevocable
irrigat|e /'ɪrɪgeɪt/ vt regar; (med) irrigar. ~ion /-'geɪʃn/ n riego m; (med) irrigación f
irritable /'ɪrɪtəbl/ a irritable
irritat|e /'ɪrɪteɪt/ vt irritar. ~ion /-'teɪʃn/ n irritación f
is /ɪz/ see **be**
Islam /'ɪzlɑːm/ n Islam m. ~ic /ɪz'læmɪk/ a islámico
island /'aɪlənd/ n isla f. **traffic** ~ n refugio m (en la calle). ~er n isleño m
isle /aɪl/ n isla f
isolat|e /'aɪsəleɪt/ vt aislar. ~ion /-'leɪʃn/ n aislamiento m
isotope /'aɪsətəʊp/ n isótopo m
Israel /'ɪzreɪl/ n Israel m. ~i /ɪz'reɪlɪ/ a & n israelí (m)
issue /'ɪʃuː/ n asunto m; (outcome) resultado m; (of magazine etc) número m; (of stamps) emisión f; (offspring) descendencia f. **at** ~ en cuestión. **take** ~ **with** oponerse a. ●vt distribuir; emitir ⟨stamps etc⟩; publicar ⟨book⟩. ●vi. ~ **from** salir de

isthmus /'ɪsməs/ n istmo m
it /ɪt/ pron (subject) el, ella, ello; (direct object) lo, la; (indirect object) le; (after preposition) él, ella, ello. ~ **is hot** hace calor. ~ **is me** soy yo. **far from** ~ ni mucho menos. **that's** ~ eso es. **who is** ~? ¿quién es?
italic /ɪ'tælɪk/ a bastardillo m. ~s npl (letra f) bastardilla f
ital|ian /ɪ'tæljən/ a & n italiano (m). I~y /'ɪtəlɪ/ n Italia f
itch /ɪtʃ/ n picazón f. ●vi picar. **I'm** ~**ing to** rabio por. **my arm** ~**es** me pica el brazo. ~**y** a que pica
item /'aɪtəm/ n artículo m; (on agenda) asunto m. **news** ~ n noticia f. ~**ize** vt detallar
itinerant /aɪ'tɪnərənt/ a ambulante
itinerary /aɪ'tɪnərərɪ/ n itinerario m
its /ɪts/ a su, sus (pl). ●pron (el) suyo m, (la) suya f, (los) suyos mpl, (las) suyas fpl
it's /ɪts/ = **it is, it has**
itself /ɪt'self/ pron él mismo, ella misma, ello mismo; (reflexive) se; (after prep) sí mismo, sí misma
ivory /'aɪvərɪ/ n marfil m. ~ **tower** n torre f de marfil
ivy /'aɪvɪ/ n hiedra f

J

jab /dʒæb/ vt (pt jabbed) pinchar; (thrust) hurgonear. ●n pinchazo m
jabber /'dʒæbə(r)/ vi barbullar. ●n farfulla f
jack /dʒæk/ n (mec) gato m; (cards) sota f. ●vt. ~ **up** alzar con gato
jackal /'dʒækl/ n chacal m
jackass /'dʒækæs/ n burro m
jackdaw /'dʒækdɔː/ n grajilla f
jacket /'dʒækɪt/ n chaqueta f, saco m (LAm); (of book) sobrecubierta f, camisa f
jack-knife /'dʒæknaɪf/ n navaja f
jackpot /'dʒækpɒt/ n premio m gordo. **hit the** ~ sacar el premio gordo
jade /dʒeɪd/ n (stone) jade m
jaded /'dʒeɪdɪd/ a cansado
jagged /'dʒægɪd/ a dentado
jaguar /'dʒægjʊə(r)/ n jaguar m
jail /dʒeɪl/ n cárcel m. ~**bird** n criminal m empedernido. ~**er** n carcelero m
jalopy /dʒə'lɒpɪ/ n cacharro m

jam¹ /dʒæm/ vt (pt **jammed**) interferir con ⟨radio⟩; ⟨traffic⟩ embotellar; ⟨people⟩ agolparse en. ● vi obstruirse; ⟨mechanism etc⟩ atascarse. ● n (of people) agolpamiento m; (of traffic) embotellamiento m; (situation, fam) apuro m

jam² /dʒæm/ n mermelada f

Jamaica /dʒə'meɪkə/ n Jamaica f

jamboree /dʒæmbə'riː/ n reunión f

jam-packed /'dʒæm'pækt/ a atestado

jangle /'dʒæŋgl/ n sonido m metálico (y áspero). ● vt/i sonar discordemente

janitor /'dʒænɪtə(r)/ n portero m

January /'dʒænjʊərɪ/ n enero m

Japan /dʒə'pæn/ n el Japón m. ~**ese** /dʒæpə'niːz/ a & n japonés m

jar¹ /dʒɑː(r)/ n tarro m, frasco m

jar² /dʒɑː(r)/ vi (pt **jarred**) ⟨sound⟩ sonar mal; ⟨colours⟩ chillar. ● vt sacudir

jar³ /dʒɑː(r)/ n. **on the** ~ (ajar) entreabierto

jargon /'dʒɑːgən/ n jerga f

jarring /'dʒɑːrɪŋ/ a discorde

jasmine /'dʒæsmɪn/ n jazmín m

jaundice /'dʒɔːndɪs/ n ictericia f. ~**d** a (envious) envidioso; (bitter) amargado

jaunt /dʒɔːnt/ n excursión f

jaunty /'dʒɔːntɪ/ a (-ier, -iest) garboso

javelin /'dʒævəlɪn/ n jabalina f

jaw /dʒɔː/ n mandíbula f. ● vi (talk lengthily, sl) hablar por los codos

jay /dʒeɪ/ n arrendajo m. ~**-walk** vi cruzar la calle descuidadamente

jazz /dʒæz/ n jazz m. ● vt. ~ **up** animar. ~**y** a chillón

jealous /dʒeləs/ a celoso. ~**y** n celos mpl

jeans /dʒiːnz/ npl (pantalones mpl) vaqueros mpl

jeep /dʒiːp/ n jeep m

jeer /dʒɪə(r)/ vt/i. ~ **at** mofarse de, befar; (boo) abuchear. ● n mofa f; (boo) abucheo m

jell /dʒel/ vi cuajar. ~**ied** a en gelatina

jelly /dʒelɪ/ n jalea f. ~**fish** n medusa f

jeopard|ize /'dʒepədaɪz/ vt arriesgar. ~**y** n peligro m

jerk /dʒɜːk/ n sacudida f; (fool, sl) idiota m & f. ● vt sacudir. ~**ily** adv a sacudidas. ~**y** a espasmódico

jersey /'dʒɜːzɪ/ n (pl **-eys**) jersey m

jest /dʒest/ n broma f. ● vi bromear. ~**er** n bufón m

Jesus /'dʒiːzəs/ n Jesús m

jet¹ /dʒet/ n (stream) chorro m; (plane) yet m, avión m de propulsión por reacción

jet² /dʒet/ n (mineral) azabache m. ~**black** a de azabache, como el azabache

jet: ~ **lag** n cansancio m retardado después de un vuelo largo. **have** ~ **lag** estar desfasado. ~**-propelled** a (de propulsión) a reacción

jettison /'dʒetɪsn/ vt echar al mar; (fig, discard) deshacerse de

jetty /'dʒetɪ/ n muelle m

Jew /dʒuː/ n judío m

jewel /'dʒuːəl/ n joya f. ~**led** a enjoyado. ~**ler** n joyero m. ~**lery** n joyas fpl

Jew: ~**ess** n judía f. ~**ish** a judío. ~**ry** /'dʒʊərɪ/ n los judíos mpl

jib¹ /dʒɪb/ n (sail) foque m

jib² /dʒɪb/ vi (pt **jibbed**) rehusar. ~ **at** oponerse a

jiffy /'dʒɪfɪ/ n momentito m. **do sth in a** ~ hacer algo en un santiamén

jig /dʒɪg/ n (dance) giga f

jiggle /'dʒɪgl/ vt zangolotear

jigsaw /'dʒɪgsɔː/ n rompecabezas m invar

jilt /dʒɪlt/ vt plantar, dejar plantado

jingle /'dʒɪŋgl/ vt hacer sonar. ● vi tintinear. ● n tintineo m; (advert) anuncio m cantado

jinx /dʒɪŋks/ n (person) gafe m; (spell) maleficio m

jitter|s /'dʒɪtəz/ npl. **have the** ~**s** estar nervioso. ~**y** /-ərɪ/ a nervioso. **be** ~**y** estar nervioso

job /dʒɒb/ n trabajo m; (post) empleo m, puesto m. **have a** ~ **doing** costar trabajo hacer. **it is a good** ~ **that** menos mal que. ~**centre** n bolsa f de trabajo. ~**less** a sin trabajo.

jockey /'dʒɒkɪ/ n jockey m. ● vi (manoeuvre) maniobrar (**for** para)

jocular /'dʒɒkjʊlə(r)/ a jocoso

jog /dʒɒg/ vt (pt **jogged**) empujar; refrescar ⟨memory⟩. ● vi hacer footing. ~**ging** n jogging m

join /dʒɔɪn/ vt unir, juntar; hacerse socio de ⟨club⟩; hacerse miembro de ⟨political group⟩; alistarse en ⟨army⟩; reunirse con ⟨another person⟩. ● vi ⟨roads etc⟩ empalmar; ⟨rivers⟩ confluir. ~ **in** participar (en). ~ **up** (mil) alistarse. ● n junta

joiner /'dʒɔɪnə(r)/ n carpintero m

joint /dʒɔɪnt/ a común. ~ **author** n coautor m. ● n (join) juntura f; (anat) articulación f; (culin) asado m; (place, sl) garito m; (marijuana, sl) cigarillo m de marijuana. **out of** ~ descoyuntado. ~**ly** adv conjuntamente

joist /dʒɔɪst/ n viga f

jok|e /dʒəʊk/ n broma f; (funny story) chiste m. ● vi bromear. ~**er** n bromista m & f; (cards) comodín m. ~**ingly** adv en broma

joll|ification /dʒɒlɪfɪ'keɪʃn/ n jolgorio m. ~**ity** n jolgorio m. ~**y** a (-ier, -iest) alegre. ● adv (fam) muy

jolt /dʒɒlt/ vt sacudir. ● vt (vehicle) traquetear. ● n sacudida f

Jordan /'dʒɔːdən/ n Jordania f. ~**ian** a & n /-'demɪən/ jordano (m)

jostle /'dʒɒsl/ vt/i empujar(se)

jot /dʒɒt/ n pizca f. ● vt (pt jotted) apuntar. ~**ter** n bloc m

journal /'dʒɜːnl/ n (diary) diario m; (newspaper) periódico m; (magazine) revista f. ~**ese** /dʒɜːnə'liːz/ n jerga f periodística. ~**ism** n periodismo m. ~**ist** n periodista m & f

journey /'dʒɜːnɪ/ n viaje m. ● vi viajar

jovial /'dʒəʊvɪəl/ a jovial

jowl /dʒaʊl/ n (jaw) quijada f; (cheek) mejilla f. **cheek by** ~ muy cerca

joy /dʒɔɪ/ n alegría f. ~**ful** a alegre. ~**ride** n paseo m en coche sin permiso del dueño. ~**ous** a alegre

jubila|nt /'dʒuːbɪlənt/ a jubiloso. ~**tion** /-'leɪʃn/ n júbilo m

jubilee /'dʒuːbɪliː/ n aniversario m especial

Judaism /'dʒuːdeɪɪzəm/ n judaísmo m

judder /'dʒʌdə(r)/ vi vibrar. ● n vibración f

judge /dʒʌdʒ/ n juez m. ● vt juzgar. ~**ment** n juicio m

judicia|l /dʒuː'dɪʃl/ a judicial. ~**ry** n magistratura f

judicious /dʒuː'dɪʃəs/ a juicioso

judo /'dʒuːdəʊ/ n judo m

jug /dʒʌɡ/ n jarra f

juggernaut /'dʒʌɡənɔːt/ n (lorry) camión m grande

juggle /'dʒʌɡl/ vt/i hacer juegos malabares (con). ~**r** n malabarista m & f

juic|e /dʒuːs/ n jugo m, zumo m. ~**y** a jugoso, zumoso; (story etc) (fam) picante

juke-box /'dʒuːkbɒks/ n tocadiscos m invar tragaperras

July /dʒuː'laɪ/ n julio m

jumble /'dʒʌmbl/ vt mezclar. ● n (muddle) revoltijo m. ~ **sale** f de objetos usados, mercadillo m

jumbo /'dʒʌmbəʊ/ a. ~ **jet** n jumbo m

jump /dʒʌmp/ vt/i saltar. ~ **the gun** obrar prematuramente. ~ **the queue** colarse. ● vi saltar; (start) asustarse; (prices) alzarse. ~ **at** apresurarse a aprovechar. ● n salto m; (start) susto m; (increase) aumento m

jumper /'dʒʌmpə(r)/ n jersey m; (dress, Amer) mandil m, falda f con peto

jumpy /'dʒʌmpɪ/ a nervioso

junction /'dʒʌŋkʃn/ n juntura f; (of roads) cruce m, entronque m (LAm); (rail) empalme m, entronque m (LAm)

juncture /'dʒʌŋktʃə(r)/ n momento m; (state of affairs) coyuntura f

June /dʒuːn/ n junio m

jungle /'dʒʌŋgl/ n selva f

junior /'dʒuːnɪə(r)/ a (in age) más joven (**to** que); (in rank) subalterno. ● n menor m. ~ **school** n escuela f

junk /dʒʌŋk/ n trastos mpl viejos. ● vt (fam) tirar

junkie /'dʒʌŋkɪ/ n (sl) drogadicto m

junk shop /'dʒʌŋkʃɒp/ n tienda f de trastos viejos

junta /'dʒʌntə/ n junta f

jurisdiction /dʒʊərɪs'dɪkʃn/ n jurisdicción f

jurisprudence /dʒʊərɪs'pruːdəns/ n jurisprudencia f

juror /'dʒʊərə(r)/ n jurado m

jury /'dʒʊərɪ/ n jurado m

just /dʒʌst/ a (fair) justo. ● adv exactamente; (slightly) apenas; (only) sólo, solamente. ~ **as tall** tan alto (**as** como). ~ **listen!** ¡escucha! **he has** ~ **left** acaba de marcharse

justice /'dʒʌstɪs/ n justicia f. **J~ of the Peace** juez m de paz

justif|iable /dʒʌstɪ'faɪəbl/ a justificable. ~**iably** adv con razón. ~**ication** /dʒʌstɪfɪ'keɪʃn/ n justificación f. ~**y** /'dʒʌstɪfaɪ/ vt justificar

justly /'dʒʌstlɪ/ adv con justicia

jut /dʒʌt/ vi (pt **jutted**). ~ **out** sobresalir

juvenile /'dʒuːvənaɪl/ a juvenil; (childish) infantil. ● n joven m & f. ~ **court** n tribunal m de menores

juxtapose /dʒʌkstə'pəʊz/ vt yuxtaponer

K

kaleidoscope /kə'laɪdəskəʊp/ n calidoscopio m

kangaroo /kæŋgə'ruː/ n canguro m

kapok /'keɪpɒk/ n miraguano m

karate /kə'rɑːtɪ/ n karate m

kebab /kɪ'bæb/ n broqueta f

keel /kiːl/ n (of ship) quilla f. ● vi. ~ **over** volcarse

keen /kiːn/ a (-er, -est) (interest, feeling) vivo; (wind, mind, analysis) penetrante; (edge) afilado; (appetite) bueno; (eyesight) agudo; (eager) entusiasta. **be** ~ **on** gustarle a uno. **he's** ~ **on Shostakovich** le gusta Shostakovich. ~**ly** adv vivamente; (enthusiastically) con entusiasmo. ~**ness** n intensidad f; (enthusiasm) entusiasmo m.

keep /kiːp/ vt (pt **kept**) guardar; cumplir (promise); tener (shop, animals); mantener (family); observar (rule); (celebrate) celebrar; (delay) detener; (prevent) impedir. ● vi (food) conservarse; (remain) quedarse. ● n subsistencia f; (of castle) torreón m. **for** ~**s** (fam) para siempre. ~ **back** vt retener. ● vi no acercarse. ~ **in** no dejar salir. ~ **in with** mantenerse en buenas relaciones con. ~ **out** no dejar entrar. ~ **up** mantener. ~ **up** (**with**) estar al día (en). ~**er** n guarda m

keeping /'kiːpɪŋ/ n cuidado m. **in** ~ **with** de acuerdo con

keepsake /'kiːpseɪk/ n recuerdo m

keg /keg/ n barrilete m

kennel /'kenl/ n perrera f

Kenya /'kenjə/ n Kenia f

kept /kept/ see **keep**

kerb /kɜːb/ n bordillo m

kerfuffle /kə'fʌfl/ n (fuss, fam) lío m

kernel /'kɜːnl/ n almendra f; (fig) meollo m

kerosene /'kerəsiːn/ n queroseno m

ketchup /'ketʃʌp/ n salsa f de tomate

kettle /'ketl/ n hervidor m

key /kiː/ n llave f; (of typewriter, piano etc) tecla f. ● a clave. ● vt. ~ **up** excitar. ~**board** n teclado m. ~**hole** n ojo m de la cerradura. ~**note** n (mus) tónica f; (speech) idea f fundamental. ~**ring** n llavero m. ~**stone** n piedra f clave

khaki /'kɑːkɪ/ a caqui

kibbutz /kɪ'bʊts/ n (pl -**im** /-iːm/ or -**es**) kibbutz m

kick /kɪk/ vt dar una patada a; (animals) tirar una coz a. ● vi dar patadas; (firearm) dar culatazo. ● n patada f; (of animal) coz f; (of firearm) culatazo m; (thrill, fam) placer m. ~ **out** (fam) echar a patadas. ~ **up** armar (fuss etc). ~**back** n culatazo m; (payment) soborno m. ~**off** n (sport) saque m inicial

kid /kɪd/ n (young goat) cabrito m; (leather) cabritilla f; (child, sl) chaval m. ● vt (pt **kidded**) tomar el pelo a. ● vi bromear

kidnap /'kɪdnæp/ vt (pt **kidnapped**) secuestrar. ~**ping** n secuestro m

kidney /'kɪdnɪ/ n riñón m. ● a renal

kill /kɪl/ vt matar; (fig) acabar con. ● n matanza f; (in hunt) pieza(s) f(pl). ~**er** n matador m; (murderer) asesino m. ~**ing** n matanza f; (murder) asesinato m. ● a (funny, fam) para morirse de risa; (tiring, fam) agotador. ~**joy** n aguafiestas m & f invar

kiln /kɪln/ n horno m

kilo /'kiːləʊ/ n (pl -**os**) kilo m

kilogram(me) /'kɪləgræm/ n kilogramo m

kilohertz /'kɪləhɜːts/ n kilohercio m

kilometre /'kɪləmiːtə(r)/ n kilómetro m

kilowatt /'kɪləwɒt/ n kilovatio m

kilt /kɪlt/ n falda f escocesa

kin /kɪn/ n parientes mpl. **next of** ~ pariente m más próximo, parientes mpl más próximos

kind[1] /kaɪnd/ n clase f. ~ **of** (somewhat, fam) un poco. **in** ~ en especie. **be two of a** ~ ser tal para cual

kind[2] /kaɪnd/ a amable

kindergarten /'kɪndəgɑːtn/ n escuela f de párvulos

kind-hearted /kaɪnd'hɑːtɪd/ a bondadoso

kindle /'kɪndl/ vt/i encender(se)

kind: ~**liness** n bondad f. ~**ly** a (-ier, -iest) bondadoso. ● adv bondadosamente; (please) haga el favor de. ~**ness** n bondad f

kindred /'kɪndrɪd/ a emparentado. ~ **spirits** npl almas fpl afines

kinetic /kɪ'netɪk/ a cinético

king /kɪŋ/ n rey m

kingdom /'kɪŋdəm/ n reino m

kingpin /'kɪŋpɪn/ n (person) persona f clave; (thing) piedra f angular

king-size(d) /'kɪŋsaɪz(d)/ a extraordinariamente grande

kink /kɪŋk/ n (in rope) retorcimiento m; (fig) manía f. ~**y** a (fam) pervertido

kiosk /'kiːɒsk/ n quiosco m. **telephone** ~ cabina f telefónica

kip /kɪp/ n (sl) sueño m. • vi (pt kipped) dormir

kipper /'kɪpə(r)/ n arenque m ahumado

kiss /kɪs/ n beso m. • vt/i besar(se)

kit /kɪt/ n avíos mpl; (tools) herramientas fpl. • vt (pt kitted). ~ **out** equipar de. ~**bag** n mochila f

kitchen /'kɪtʃɪn/ n cocina f. ~**ette** /kɪtʃɪ'net/ n cocina f pequeña. ~ **garden** n huerto m

kite /kaɪt/ n (toy) cometa f

kith /kɪθ/ n. ~ **and kin** amigos mpl y parientes mpl

kitten /'kɪtn/ n gatito m

kitty /'kɪtɪ/ n (fund) fondo m común

kleptomaniac /kleptəʊ'meɪnɪæk/ n cleptómano m

knack /næk/ n truco m

knapsack /'næpsæk/ n mochila f

knave /neɪv/ n (cards) sota f

knead /niːd/ vt amasar

knee /niː/ n rodilla f. ~**cap** n rótula f

kneel /niːl/ vi (pt knelt). ~ **(down)** arrodillarse

knees-up /'niːzʌp/ n (fam) baile m

knell /nel/ n toque m de difuntos

knelt /nelt/ see **kneel**

knew /njuː/ see **know**

knickerbockers /'nɪkəbɒkəz/ npl pantalón m bombacho

knickers /'nɪkəz/ npl bragas fpl

knick-knack /'nɪknæk/ n chuchería f

knife /naɪf/ n (pl knives) cuchillo m. • vt acuchillar

knight /naɪt/ n caballero m; (chess) caballo m. • vt conceder el título de Sir a. ~**hood** n título m de Sir

knit /nɪt/ vt (pt knitted or knit) tejer. • vi hacer punto. ~ **one's brow** fruncir el ceño. ~**ting** n labor f de punto. ~**wear** n artículos mpl de punto

knob /nɒb/ n botón m; (of door, drawer etc) tirador m. ~**bly** a nudoso

knock /nɒk/ vt golpear; (criticize) criticar. • vi golpear; (at door) llamar. • n golpe m. ~ **about** vt maltratar. • vi rodar. ~ **down** derribar; atropellar (person); rebajar (prices). ~ **off** vt hacer caer; (complete quickly, fam) despachar; (steal, sl) birlar. • vi (finish work, fam) terminar, salir del trabajo. ~ **out** (by blow) dejar sin conocimiento; (eliminate) eliminar; (tire) agotar. ~ **over** tirar; atropellar (person). ~ **up** preparar de prisa (meal etc). ~**down** a (price) de saldo. ~**er** n aldaba f. ~**kneed** a patizambo. ~**out** n (boxing) knock-out m

knot /nɒt/ n nudo m. • vt (pt knotted) anudar. ~**ty** /'nɒtɪ/ a nudoso

know /nəʊ/ vt (pt knew) saber; (be acquainted with) conocer. • vi saber. • n. **be in the** ~ estar al tanto. ~ **about** entender de (cars etc). ~ **of** saber de. ~**all** n, ~**it-all** (Amer) n sabelotodo m & f. ~**how** n habilidad f. ~**ingly** adv deliberadamente

knowledge /'nɒlɪdʒ/ n conocimiento m; (learning) conocimientos mpl. ~**able** a informado

known /nəʊn/ see **know**. • a conocido

knuckle /'nʌkl/ n nudillo m. • vi. ~ **under** someterse

Koran /kə'rɑːn/ n Corán m, Alcorán m

Korea /kə'rɪə/ n Corea f

kosher /'kəʊʃə(r)/ a preparado según la ley judía

kowtow /kaʊ'taʊ/ vi humillarse (**to** ante)

kudos /'kjuːdɒs/ n prestigio m

L

lab /læb/ n (fam) laboratorio m

label /'leɪbl/ n etiqueta f. • vt (pt labelled) poner etiqueta a; (fig, describe as) describir como

laboratory /lə'bɒrətərɪ/ n laboratorio m

laborious /lə'bɔːrɪəs/ a penoso

labour /'leɪbə(r)/ n trabajo m; (workers) mano f de obra. **in** ~ de parto. • vi trabajar. • vt insistir en

Labour /'leɪbə(r)/ n el partido m laborista. • a laborista

laboured /'leɪbəd/ *a* penoso

labourer /'leɪbərə(r)/ *n* obrero *m*; (*on farm*) labriego *m*

labyrinth /'læbərɪnθ/ *n* laberinto *m*

lace /leɪs/ *n* encaje *m*; (*of shoe*) cordón *m*, agujeta *f* (*Mex*). ● *vt* (*fasten*) atar. ∼ **with** echar a (*a drink*)

lacerate /'læsəreɪt/ *vt* lacerar

lack /læk/ *n* falta *f*. **for** ∼ **of** por falta de. ● *vt* faltarle a uno. **he** ∼**s money** carece de dinero. **be** ∼**ing** faltar

lackadaisical /lækə'deɪzɪkl/ *a* indolente, apático

lackey /'lækɪ/ *n* lacayo *m*

laconic /lə'kɒnɪk/ *a* lacónico

lacquer /'lækə(r)/ *n* laca *f*

lad /læd/ *n* muchacho *m*

ladder /'lædə(r)/ *n* escalera *f* (de mano); (*in stocking*) carrera *f*. ● *vt* hacer una carrera en. ● *vi* hacerse una carrera

laden /'leɪdn/ *a* cargado (**with** de)

ladle /'leɪdl/ *n* cucharón *m*

lady /'leɪdɪ/ *n* señora *f*. **young** ∼ señorita *f*. ∼**bird**, ∼**bug** *n* (*Amer*) mariquita *f*. ∼ **friend** *n* amiga *f*. ∼-**in-waiting** *n* dama *f* de honor. ∼**like** *a* distinguido. ∼**ship** *n* Señora *f*

lag[1] /læg/ *vi* (*pt* **lagged**). ∼ (**behind**) retrasarse. ● *n* (*interval*) intervalo *m*

lag[2] /læg/ *vt* (*pt* **lagged**) revestir (*pipes*)

lager /'lɑːgə(r)/ *n* cerveza *f* dorada

laggard /'lægəd/ *n* holgazán *m*

lagging /'lægɪŋ/ *n* revestimiento *m* calorífugo

lagoon /lə'guːn/ *n* laguna *f*

lah /lɑː/ *n* (*mus, sixth note of any musical scale*) la *m*

laid /leɪd/ *see* **lay**[1]

lain /leɪn/ *see* **lie**[1]

lair /leə(r)/ *n* guarida *f*

laity /'leɪətɪ/ *n* laicado *m*

lake /leɪk/ *n* lago *m*

lamb /læm/ *n* cordero *m*. ∼**swool** *n* lana *f* de cordero

lame /leɪm/ *a* (-**er**, -**est**) cojo; (*excuse*) poco convincente. ∼**ly** *adv* (*argue*) con poca convicción *f*

lament /lə'ment/ *n* lamento *m*. ● *vt/i* lamentarse (de). ∼**able** /'læməntəbl/ *a* lamentable

laminated /'læmɪneɪtɪd/ *a* laminado

lamp /læmp/ *n* lámpara *f*. ∼**post** *n* farol *m*. ∼**shade** *n* pantalla *f*

lance /lɑːns/ *n* lanza *f*. ● *vt* (*med*) abrir con lanceta. ∼-**corporal** *n* cabo *m* interino

lancet /'lɑːnsɪt/ *n* lanceta *f*

land /lænd/ *n* tierra *f*; (*country*) país *m*; (*plot*) terreno *m*. ● *a* terrestre; (*breeze*) de tierra; (*policy, reform*) agrario. ● *vt* desembarcar; (*obtain*) conseguir; dar (*blow*); (*put*) meter. ● *vi* (*from ship*) desembarcar; (*aircraft*) aterrizar; (*fall*) caer. ∼ **up** ir a parar

landed /'lændɪd/ *a* hacendado

landing /'lændɪŋ/ *n* desembarque *m*; (*aviat*) aterrizaje *m*; (*top of stairs*) descanso *m*. ∼-**stage** *n* desembarcadero *m*

landlady /'lændleɪdɪ/ *n* propietaria *f*; (*of inn*) patrona *f*

land-locked /'lændlɒkt/ *a* rodeado de tierra

landlord /'lændlɔːd/ *n* propietario *m*; (*of inn*) patrón *m*

land: ∼**mark** *n* punto *m* destacado. ∼**scape** /'lændskeɪp/ *n* paisaje *m*. ● *vt* ajardinar. ∼**slide** *n* desprendimiento *m* de tierras; (*pol*) victoria *f* arrolladora

lane /leɪn/ *n* (*path, road*) camino *m*; (*strip of road*) carril *m*; (*aviat*) ruta *f*

language /'læŋgwɪdʒ/ *n* idioma *m*; (*speech, style*) lenguaje *m*

langu|**id** /'læŋgwɪd/ *a* lánguido. ∼**ish** /'læŋgwɪʃ/ *vi* languidecer. ∼**or** /'læŋgə(r)/ *n* languidez *f*

lank /læŋk/ *a* larguirucho; (*hair*) lacio. ∼**y** /læŋkɪ/ *a* (-**ier**, -**iest**) larguirucho

lantern /'læntən/ *n* linterna *f*

lap[1] /læp/ *n* regazo *m*

lap[2] /læp/ *n* (*sport*) vuelta *f*. ● *vt/i* (*pt* **lapped**). ∼ **over** traslapar(se)

lap[3] /læp/ *vt* (*pt* **lapped**). ∼ **up** beber a lengüetazos; (*fig*) aceptar con entusiasmo. ● *vi* (*waves*) chapotear

lapel /lə'pel/ *n* solapa *f*

lapse /læps/ *vi* (*decline*) degradarse; (*expire*) caducar; (*time*) transcurrir. ∼ **into** recaer en. ● *n* error *m*; (*of time*) intervalo *m*

larceny /'lɑːsənɪ/ *n* robo *m*

lard /lɑːd/ *n* manteca *f* de cerdo

larder /'lɑːdə(r)/ *n* despensa *f*

large /lɑːdʒ/ *a* (-**er**, -**est**) grande, (*before singular noun*) gran. ● *n*. **at** ∼ en libertad. ∼**ly** *adv* en gran parte. ∼**ness** *n* (gran) tamaño *m*

largesse /lɑː'ʒes/ *n* generosidad *f*

lark[1] /lɑːk/ *n* alondra *f*

lark[2] /lɑːk/ *n* broma *f*; (*bit of fun*) travesura *f*. ● *vi* andar de juerga

larva /'lɑ:və/ n (pl **-vae** /-vi:/) larva f

laryn|gitis /lærin'dʒaitis/ n laringitis f. **~x** /'lærɪŋks/ n laringe f

lascivious /lə'sɪvɪəs/ a lascivo

laser /'leɪzə(r)/ n láser m

lash /læʃ/ vt azotar. **~ out** (spend) gastar. **~ out against** atacar. ● n latigazo m; (eyelash) pestaña f

lashings /'læʃɪŋz/ npl. **~ of** (cream etc, sl) montones de

lass /læs/ n muchacha f

lassitude /'læsɪtju:d/ n lasitud f

lasso /læ'su:/ n (pl **-os**) lazo m

last[1] /lɑ:st/ a último; (week etc) pasado. **~ Monday** n el lunes pasado. **have the ~ word** decir la última palabra. **the ~ straw** n el colmo m. ● adv por último; (most recently) la última vez. **he came ~** llegó el último. ● n último m; (remainder) lo que queda. **~ but one** penúltimo. **at (long) ~** en fin.

last[2] /lɑ:st/ vi durar. **~ out** sobrevivir

last[3] /lɑ:st/ n horma f

lasting /'lɑ:stɪŋ/ a duradero

last: **~ly** adv por último. **~ night** n anoche m

latch /lætʃ/ n picaporte m

late /leɪt/ a (**-er, -est**) (not on time) tarde; (recent) reciente; (former) antiguo, ex; (fruit) tardío; (hour) avanzado; (deceased) difunto. **in ~ July** a fines de julio. **the ~ Dr Phillips** el difunto Dr. Phillips. ● adv tarde. **of ~** últimamente. **~ly** adv últimamente. **~ness** n (delay) retraso m; (of hour) lo avanzado

latent /'leɪtnt/ a latente

lateral /'lætərəl/ a lateral

latest /'leɪtɪst/ a último. **at the ~** a más tardar

lathe /leɪð/ n torno m

lather /'lɑ:ðə(r)/ n espuma f. ● vt enjabonar. ● vi hacer espuma

Latin /'lætɪn/ n (lang) latín m. ● a latino

latitude /'lætɪtju:d/ n latitud m

latrine /lə'tri:n/ n letrina f

latter /'lætə(r)/ a último; (of two) segundo. ● n. **the ~** éste m, ésta f, éstos mpl, éstas fpl. **~-day** a moderno. **~ly** adv últimamente

lattice /'lætɪs/ n enrejado m

laudable /'lɔ:dəbl/ a laudable

laugh /lɑ:f/ vi reír(se) (at de). ● n risa f. **~able** a ridículo. **~ing-stock** n hazmerreír m invar. **~ter**

/'lɑ:ftə(r)/ n (act) risa f; (sound of laughs) risas fpl

launch[1] /lɔ:ntʃ/ vt lanzar. ● n lanzamiento m. **~ (out) into** lanzarse a

launch[2] /lɔ:ntʃ/ n (boat) lancha f

launching pad /'lɔ:ntʃɪŋpæd/ n plataforma f de lanzamiento

laund|er /'lɔ:ndə(r)/ vt lavar (y planchar). **~erette** n lavandería f automática. **~ress** n lavandera f. **~ry** /'lɔ:ndrɪ/ n (place) lavandería f; (dirty clothes) ropa f sucia; (clean clothes) colada f

laurel /'lɒrəl/ n laurel m

lava /'lɑ:və/ n lava f

lavatory /'lævətərɪ/ n retrete m. **public ~** servicios mpl

lavender /'lævəndə(r)/ n lavanda f

lavish /'lævɪʃ/ a (person) pródigo; (plentiful) abundante; (lush) suntuoso. ● vt prodigar. **~ly** adv profusamente

law /lɔ:/ n ley f; (profession, subject of study) derecho m. **~-abiding** a observante de la ley. **~ and order** n orden m público. **~ court** n tribunal m. **~ful** a (permitted by law) lícito; (recognized by law) legítimo. **~fully** adv legalmente. **~less** a sin leyes

lawn /lɔ:n/ n césped m. **~-mower** n cortacésped m. **~ tennis** n tenis m (sobre hierba)

lawsuit /'lɔ:su:t/ n pleito m

lawyer /'lɔɪə(r)/ n abogado m

lax /læks/ a descuidado; (morals etc) laxo

laxative /'læksətɪv/ n laxante m

laxity /'læksətɪ/ n descuido m

lay[1] /leɪ/ vt (pt **laid**) poner (incl table, eggs); tender (trap); formar (plan). **~ hands on** echar mano a. **~ hold of** agarrar. **~ waste** asolar. **~ aside** dejar a un lado. **~ down** dejar a un lado; imponer (condition). **~ into** (sl) dar una paliza a. **~ off** vt despedir (worker); ● vi (fam) terminar. **~ on** (provide) proveer. **~ out** (design) disponer; (display) exponer; desembolsar (money). **~ up** (store) guardar; obligar a guardar cama (person)

lay[2] /leɪ/ a (non-clerical) laico; (opinion etc) profano

lay[3] /leɪ/ see **lie**

layabout /'leɪəbaʊt/ n holgazán m

lay-by /'leɪbaɪ/ n apartadero m

layer /'leɪə(r)/ n capa f

layette /leɪ'et/ n canastilla f

layman /'leɪmən/ n lego m

lay-off /'leɪɒf/ n paro m forzoso

layout /'leɪaʊt/ n disposición f

laze /leɪz/ vi holgazanear; (relax) descansar

laz|iness /'leɪzɪnɪs/ n pereza f. ~y a perezoso. ~y-bones n holgazán m

lb. abbr (pound) libra f

lead¹ /li:d/ vt (pt led) conducir; dirigir (team); llevar (life); (induce) inducir a. ● vi (go first) ir delante; (road) ir, conducir; (in cards) salir. ● n mando m; (clue) pista f; (leash) correa f; (in theatre) primer papel m; (wire) cable m; (example) ejemplo m. **in the** ~ en cabeza. ~ **away** llevar. ~ **up to** preparar el terreno para

lead² /led/ n plomo m; (of pencil) mina f. ~**en** /'ledn/ a de plomo

leader /'li:də(r)/ n jefe m; (leading article) editorial m. ~**ship** n dirección f

leading /'li:dɪŋ/ a principal; (in front) delantero. ~ **article** n editorial m

leaf /li:f/ n (pl leaves) hoja f. ● vi. ~ **through** hojear

leaflet /'li:flɪt/ n folleto m

leafy /'li:fɪ/ a frondoso

league /li:g/ n liga f. **be in** ~ **with** conchabarse con

leak /li:k/ n (hole) agujero m; (of gas, liquid) escape m; (of information) filtración f; (in roof) gotera f; (in boat) vía f de agua. ● vi (receptacle, gas, liquid) salirse; (information) filtrarse; (drip) gotear; (boat) hacer agua. ● vt dejar escapar; filtrar (information). ~**age** n = **leak**. ~**y** a (receptacle) agujereado; (roof) que tiene goteras; (boat) que hace agua

lean¹ /li:n/ vt (pt leaned or leant /lent/) apoyar. ● vi inclinarse. ~ **against** apoyarse en. ~ **on** apoyarse en. ~**out** asomarse (of a). ~ **over** inclinar

lean² /li:n/ a (-er, -est) magro. ● n carne f magra

leaning /'li:nɪŋ/ a inclinado. ● n inclinación f

leanness /'li:nnɪs/ n (of meat) magrez f; (of person) flaqueza f

lean-to /'li:ntu:/ n colgadizo m

leap /li:p/ vi (pt leaped or leapt /lept/) saltar. ● n salto m. ~**-frog** n salto m, saltacabrilla f. ● vi (pt -frogged) jugar a saltacabrilla. ~ **year** n año m bisiesto

learn /lɜ:n/ vt/i (pt learned or learnt) aprender (**to do** a hacer). ~**ed** /'lɜ:nɪd/ a culto. ~**er** /'lɜ:nə(r)/ n principiante m; (apprentice) aprendiz m; (student) estudiante m & f. ~**ing** n saber m

lease /li:s/ n arriendo m. ● vt arrendar

leash /li:ʃ/ n correa f

least /li:st/ a. **the** ~ (smallest amount of) mínimo; (slightest) menor; (smallest) más pequeño. ● n lo menos m. **at** ~ por lo menos. **not in the** ~ en absoluto. ● adv menos

leather /'leðə(r)/ n piel f, cuero m

leave /li:v/ vt (pt left) dejar; (depart from) marcharse de. ~ **alone** dejar de tocar (thing); dejar en paz (person). **be left (over)** quedar. ● vi marcharse; (train) salir. ● n permiso m. **on** ~ (mil) de permiso. **take one's** ~ **of** despedirse de. ~ **out** omitir

leavings /'li:vɪŋz/ npl restos mpl

Leban|on /'lebənən/ n el Líbano m. ~**ese** /-'ni:z/ a & n libanés (m)

lecher /'letʃə(r)/ n libertino m. ~**ous** a lascivo. ~**y** n lascivia f

lectern /'lektɜ:n/ n atril m; (in church) facistol m

lecture /'lektʃə(r)/ n conferencia f; (univ) clase f; (rebuke) sermón m. ● vt/i dar una conferencia (a); (univ) dar clases (a); (rebuke) sermonear. ~**r** n conferenciante m; (univ) profesor m

led /led/ see **lead**¹

ledge /ledʒ/ n repisa f; (of window) antepecho m

ledger /'ledʒə(r)/ n libro m mayor

lee /li:/ n sotavento m; (fig) abrigo m

leech /li:tʃ/ n sanguijuela f

leek /li:k/ n puerro m

leer /'lɪə(r)/ vi. ~ **(at)** mirar impúdicamente. ● n mirada f impúdica

leeway /'li:weɪ/ n deriva f; (fig, freedom of action) libertad f de acción. **make up** ~ recuperar los atrasos

left¹ /left/ a izquierdo. ● adv a la izquierda. ● n izquierda f

left² /left/ see **leave**

left: ~**-hand** a izquierdo. ~**-handed** a zurdo. ~**ist** n izquierdista m & f. ~ **luggage** n consigna f. ~**-overs** npl restos mpl

left-wing /left'wɪŋ/ a izquierdista

leg /leg/ n pierna f; (of animal, furniture) pata f; (of pork) pernil m; (of

lamb) pierna *f*; (*of journey*) etapa *f*.
on its last ~s en las últimas
legacy /'legəsɪ/ *n* herencia *f*
legal /'li:gl/ *a* (*permitted by law*)
lícito; (*recognized by law*) legítimo;
(*affairs etc*) jurídico. **~ aid** *n* abogacía *f* de pobres. **~ity** /-'gælətɪ/ *n*
legalidad *f*. **~ize** *vt* legalizar. **~ly**
adv legalmente
legation /lɪ'geɪʃn/ *n* legación *f*
legend /'ledʒənd/ *n* leyenda *f*. **~ary**
a legendario
leggings /'legɪŋz/ *npl* polainas *fpl*
legib|ility /ledʒəbɪlətɪ/ *n* legibilidad
f. **~le** *a* legible. **~ly** *a* legiblemente
legion /'li:dʒən/ *n* legión *f*
legislat|e /'ledʒɪsleɪt/ *vi* legislar.
~ion /-'leɪʃn/ *n* legislación *f*. **~ive**
a legislativo. **~ure** /-eɪtʃə(r)/ *n*
cuerpo *m* legislativo
legitima|cy /lɪ'dʒɪtɪməsɪ/ *f* legiti-
midad *f*. **~te** *a* legítimo
leisure /'leʒə(r)/ *n* ocio *m*. **at one's
~** cuando tenga tiempo. **~ly** *adv* sin
prisa
lemon /'lemən/ *n* limón *m*. **~ade**
/lemə'neɪd/ *n* (*fizzy*) gaseosa *f* (de
limón); (*still*) limonada *f*
lend /lend/ *vt* (*pt* lent) prestar. **~ itself to** prestarse a. **~er** *n* prestador
m; (*moneylender*) prestamista *m & f*.
~ing *n* préstamo *m*. **~ing library** *n*
biblioteca *f* de préstamo
length /leŋθ/ *n* largo *m*; (*in time*)
duración *f*; (*of cloth*) largo *m*; (*of
road*) tramo *m*. **at ~** (*at last*) por fin.
at (great) ~ detalladamente. **~en**
/'leŋθən/ *vt* alargar. ● *vi* alargarse.
~ways *adv* a lo largo. **~y** *a* largo
lenien|cy /'li:nɪənsɪ/ *n* indulgencia
f. **~t** *a* indulgente. **~tly** *adv* con
indulgencia
lens /lens/ *n* lente *f*. **contact ~es** *npl*
lentillas *fpl*
lent /lent/ *see* lend
Lent /lent/ *n* cuaresma *f*
lentil /'lentl/ *n* (*bean*) lenteja *f*
Leo /'li:əʊ/ *n* (*astr*) Leo *m*
leopard /'lepəd/ *n* leopardo *m*
leotard /'li:ətɑ:d/ *n* leotardo *m*
lep|er /'lepə(r)/ *n* leproso *m*. **~rosy**
/'leprəsɪ/ *n* lepra *f*
lesbian /'lezbɪən/ *n* lesbiana *f*. ● *a*
lesbiano
lesion /'li:ʒn/ *n* lesión *f*
less /les/ *a* (*in quantity*) menos; (*in
size*) menor. ● *adv & prep* menos. **~
than** menos que; (*with numbers*)

menos de. ● *n* menor *m*. **~ and ~**
cada vez menos. **none the ~** sin embargo. **~en** /'lesn/ *vt/i* disminuir.
~er /'lesə(r)/ *a* menor
lesson /'lesn/ *n* clase *f*
lest /lest/ *conj* por miedo de que
let /let/ *vt* (*pt* let, *pres p* letting) dejar; (*lease*) alquilar. **~ me do it**
déjame hacerlo. ● *v aux*. **~'s go!**
¡vamos!, ¡vámonos! **~'s see** (vamos)
a ver. **~'s talk/drink** hable-
mos/bebamos. ● *n* alquiler *m*. **~
down** bajar; (*deflate*) desinflar; (*fig*)
defraudar. **~ go** soltar. **~ in** dejar
entrar. **~ off** disparar (*gun*); (*cause
to explode*) hacer explotar; hacer estallar (*firework*); (*excuse*) perdonar.
~ off steam (*fig*) desfogarse. **~ on**
(*sl*) revelar. **~ o.s. in for** meterse en.
~ out dejar salir. **~ through** dejar
pasar. **~ up** disminuir. **~-down** *n*
desilusión *f*
lethal /'li:θl/ *a* (*dose, wound*) mortal;
(*weapon*) mortífero
letharg|ic /lɪ'tɑ:dʒɪk/ *a* letárgico.
~y /'leθədʒɪ/ *n* letargo *m*
letter /'letə(r)/ *n* (*of alphabet*) letra *f*;
(*written message*) carta *f*. **~-bomb** *n*
carta *f* explosiva. **~-box** *n* buzón *m*.
~-head *n* membrete *m*. **~ing** *n* letras *fpl*
lettuce /'letɪs/ *n* lechuga *f*
let-up /'letʌp/ *n* (*fam*) descanso *m*
leukaemia /lu:'ki:mɪə/ *n* leucemia *f*
level /'levl/ *a* (*flat*) llano; (*on surface*)
horizontal; (*in height*) a nivel; (*in
score*) igual; (*spoonful*) raso. ● *n*
nivel *m*. **be on the ~** (*fam*) ser honrado. ● *vt* (*pt* levelled) nivelar; (*aim*)
apuntar. **~ crossing** *n* paso *m* a
nivel. **~-headed** *a* juicioso
lever /'li:və(r)/ *n* palanca *f*. ● *vt* apalancar. **~age** /'li:vərɪdʒ/ *n* apalan-
camiento *m*
levity /'levətɪ/ *n* ligereza *f*
levy /'levɪ/ *vt* exigir (*tax*). ● *n* impuesto *m*
lewd /lu:d/ *a* (-er, -est) lascivo
lexicography /leksɪ'kɒgrəfɪ/ *n* lexicografía *f*
lexicon /'leksɪkən/ *n* léxico *m*
liable /'laɪəbl/ *a*. **be ~ to do** tener
tendencia a hacer. **~ for** responsable
de. **~ to** susceptible de; expuesto a
(*fine*)
liability /laɪə'bɪlətɪ/ *n* responsabilidad *f*; (*disadvantage, fam*) inconveniente *m*. **liabilities** *npl* (*debts*)
deudas *fpl*

liais|e /lɪˈeɪz/ *vi* hacer un enlace, enlazar. **~on** /lɪˈeɪzɒn/ *n* enlace *m*; (*love affair*) lío *m*

liar /ˈlaɪə(r)/ *n* mentiroso *m*

libel /ˈlaɪbl/ *n* libelo *m*. ● *vt* (*pt* **libelled**) difamar (por escrito)

Liberal /ˈlɪbərəl/ *a & n* liberal (*m & f*)

liberal /ˈlɪbərəl/ *a* liberal; (*generous*) generoso; (*tolerant*) tolerante. **~ly** *adv* liberalmente; (*generously*) generosamente; (*tolerantly*) tolerantemente

liberat|e /ˈlɪbəreɪt/ *vt* liberar. **~ion** /-ˈreɪʃn/ *n* liberación *f*

libertine /ˈlɪbətiːn/ *n* libertino *m*

liberty /ˈlɪbəti/ *n* libertad *f*. **be at ~ to** estar autorizado para. **take liberties** tomarse libertades. **take the ~ of** tomarse la libertad de

libido /lɪˈbiːdəʊ/ *n* (*pl* **-os**) libido *m*

Libra /ˈliːbrə/ *n* (*astr*) Libra *f*

librar|ian /laɪˈbreərɪən/ *n* bibliotecario *m*. **~y** /ˈlaɪbrərɪ/ *n* biblioteca *f*

libretto /lɪˈbretəʊ/ *n* (*pl* **-os**) libreto *m*

Libya /ˈlɪbɪə/ *n* Libia *f*. **~n** *a & n* libio (*m*)

lice /laɪs/ *see* **louse**

licence /ˈlaɪsns/ *n* licencia *f*, permiso *m*; (*fig, liberty*) libertad *f*. **~ plate** (placa *f* de) matrícula *f*. **driving ~** carné *m* de conducir

license /ˈlaɪsns/ *vt* autorizar

licentious /laɪˈsenʃəs/ *a* licencioso

lichen /ˈlaɪkən/ *n* liquen *m*

lick /lɪk/ *vt* lamer; (*defeat, sl*) dar una paliza a. **~ one's chops** relamerse. ● *n* lametón *m*

licorice /ˈlɪkərɪs/ *n* (*Amer*) regaliz *m*

lid /lɪd/ *n* tapa *f*; (*of pan*) cobertera *f*

lido /ˈliːdəʊ/ *n* (*pl* **-os**) piscina *f*

lie[1] /laɪ/ *vi* (*pt* **lay**, *pp* **lain**, *pres p* **lying**) echarse; (*state*) estar echado; (*remain*) quedarse; (*be*) estar, encontrarse; (*in grave*) yacer. **be lying** estar echado. **~ down** acostarse. **~ low** quedarse escondido

lie[2] /laɪ/ *n* mentira *f*. ● *vi* (*pt* **lied**, *pres p* **lying**) mentir. **give the ~ to** desmentir

lie-in /laɪˈɪn/ *n*. **have a ~-in** quedarse en la cama

lieu /ljuː/ *n*. **in ~ of** en lugar de

lieutenant /lefˈtenənt/ *n* (*mil*) teniente *m*

life /laɪf/ *n* (*pl* **lives**) vida *f*. **~belt** *n* cinturón *m* salvavidas. **~boat** *n* lancha *f* de salvamento; (*on ship*) bote *m*

salvavidas. **~buoy** *n* boya *f* salvavidas. **~ cycle** *n* ciclo *m* vital. **~guard** *n* bañero *m*. **~jacket** *n* chaleco *m* salvavidas. **~less** *a* sin vida. **~like** *a* natural. **~line** *n* cuerda *f* salvavidas; (*fig*) cordón *m* umbilical. **~long** *a* de toda la vida. **~-size(d)** *a* de tamaño natural. **~time** *n* vida *f*

lift /lɪft/ *vt* levantar; (*steal, fam*) robar. ● *vi* (*fog*) disiparse. ● *n* ascensor *m*, elevador *m* (*LAm*). **give a ~ to s.o.** llevar a uno en su coche, dar aventón a uno (*LAm*). **~-off** *n* (*aviat*) despegue *m*

ligament /ˈlɪgəmənt/ *n* ligamento *m*

light[1] /laɪt/ *n* luz *f*; (*lamp*) lámpara *f*, luz *f*; (*flame*) fuego *m*; (*headlight*) faro *m*. **bring to ~** sacar a luz. **come to ~** salir a luz. **have you got a ~?** ¿tienes fuego? **the ~s** *npl* (*auto, traffic signals*) el semáforo *m*. ● *a* claro. ● *vt* (*pt* **lit** or **lighted**) encender; (*illuminate*) alumbrar. **~ up** *vt/i* iluminar(se)

light[2] /laɪt/ *a* (**-er**, **-est**) (*not heavy*) ligero

lighten[1] /ˈlaɪtn/ *vt* (*make less heavy*) aligerar

lighten[2] /ˈlaɪtn/ *vt* (*give light to*) iluminar; (*make brighter*) aclarar

lighter /ˈlaɪtə(r)/ *n* (*for cigarettes*) mechero *m*

light-fingered /laɪtˈfɪŋgəd/ *a* largo de uñas

light-headed /laɪtˈhedɪd/ *a* (*dizzy*) mareado; (*frivolous*) casquivano

light-hearted /laɪtˈhɑːtɪd/ *a* alegre

lighthouse /ˈlaɪthaʊs/ *n* faro *m*

lighting /ˈlaɪtɪŋ/ *n* (*system*) alumbrado *m*; (*act*) iluminación *f*

light: **~ly** *adv* ligeramente. **~ness** *n* ligereza *f*

lightning /ˈlaɪtnɪŋ/ *n* relámpago *m*. ● *a* relámpago

lightweight /ˈlaɪtweɪt/ *a* ligero. ● *n* (*boxing*) peso *m* ligero

light-year /ˈlaɪtjɪə(r)/ *n* año *m* luz

like[1] /laɪk/ *a* parecido. ● *prep* como. ● *conj* (*fam*) como. ● *n* igual. **the ~s of you** la gente como tú

like[2] /laɪk/ *vt* gustarle (a uno). **I ~ chocolate** me gusta el chocolate. **I should ~** quisiera. **they ~ swimming** (a ellos) les gusta nadar. **would you ~?** ¿quieres? **~able** *a* simpático. **~s** *npl* gustos *mpl*

likelihood /ˈlaɪklɪhʊd/ *n* probabilidad *f*

likely a (**-ier, -iest**) probable. **he is ~ to come** es probable que venga. ● adv probablemente. **not ~!** ¡ni hablar!

like-minded /laɪkˈmaɪndɪd/ a. **be ~** tener las mismas opiniones

liken /ˈlaɪkən/ vt comparar

likeness /ˈlaɪknɪs/ n parecido m. **be a good ~** parecerse mucho

likewise /ˈlaɪkwaɪz/ adv (also) también; (the same way) lo mismo

liking /ˈlaɪkɪŋ/ n (for thing) afición f; (for person) simpatía f

lilac /ˈlaɪlək/ n lila f. ● a color de lila

lilt /lɪlt/ n ritmo m

lily /ˈlɪlɪ/ n lirio m. **~ of the valley** lirio m de los valles

limb /lɪm/ n miembro m. **out on a ~** aislado

limber /ˈlɪmbə(r)/ vi. **~ up** hacer ejercicios preliminares

limbo /ˈlɪmbəʊ/ n limbo m. **be in ~** (forgotten) estar olvidado

lime[1] /laɪm/ n (white substance) cal f

lime[2] /laɪm/ n (fruit) lima f

lime[3] /laɪm/ n. **~(-tree)** (linden tree) tilo m

limelight /ˈlaɪmlaɪt/ n. **be in the ~** estar muy a la vista

limerick /ˈlɪmərɪk/ n quintilla f humorística

limestone /ˈlaɪmstəʊn/ n caliza f

limit /ˈlɪmɪt/ n límite m. ● vt limitar. **~ation** /-ˈteɪʃn/ n limitación f. **~ed** a limitado. **~ed company** n sociedad f anónima

limousine /ˈlɪməziːn/ n limusina f

limp[1] /lɪmp/ vi cojear. ● n cojera f. **have a ~** cojear

limp[2] /lɪmp/ a (-**er, -est**) flojo

limpid /ˈlɪmpɪd/ a límpido

linctus /ˈlɪŋktəs/ n jarabe m (para la tos)

line[1] /laɪn/ n línea f; (track) vía f; (wrinkle) arruga f; (row) fila f; (of poem) verso m; (rope) cuerda f; (of goods) surtido m; (queue, Amer) cola f. **in ~ with** de acuerdo con. ● vt (on paper etc) rayar; bordear ⟨streets etc⟩. **~ up** alinearse; (in queue) hacer cola

line[2] /laɪn/ vt forrar; (fill) llenar

lineage /ˈlɪnɪɪdʒ/ n linaje m

linear /ˈlɪnɪə(r)/ a lineal

linen /ˈlɪnɪn/ n (sheets etc) ropa f blanca; (material) lino m

liner /ˈlaɪnə(r)/ n transatlántico m

linesman /ˈlaɪnzmən/ n (football) juez m de línea

linger /ˈlɪŋɡə(r)/ vi tardar en marcharse; ⟨smells etc⟩ persistir. **~ over** dilatarse en

lingerie /ˈlænʒərɪ/ n ropa f interior, lencería f

lingo /ˈlɪŋɡəʊ/ n (pl -**os**) idioma m; (specialized vocabulary) jerga f

linguist /ˈlɪŋɡwɪst/ n (specialist in languages) políglota m & f; (specialist in linguistics) lingüista m & f. **~ic** /lɪŋˈɡwɪstɪk/ a lingüístico. **~ics** n lingüística f

lining /ˈlaɪnɪŋ/ n forro m; (auto, brakes) guarnición f

link /lɪŋk/ n (of chain) eslabón m; (fig) lazo m. ● vt eslabonar; (fig) enlazar. **~ up with** reunirse con. **~age** n enlace m

links /lɪŋks/ n invar campo m de golf

lino /ˈlaɪnəʊ/ n (pl -**os**) linóleo m. **~leum** /lɪˈnəʊlɪəm/ n linóleo m

lint /lɪnt/ n (med) hilas fpl; (fluff) pelusa f

lion /ˈlaɪən/ n león m. **the ~'s share** la parte f del león. **~ess** n leona f

lionize /ˈlaɪənaɪz/ vt tratar como a una celebridad

lip /lɪp/ n labio m; (edge) borde m. **pay ~ service to** aprobar de boquilla. **stiff upper ~** n imperturbabilidad f. **~-read** vt/i leer en los labios. **~salve** n crema f para los labios. **~stick** n lápiz m de labios.

liquefy /ˈlɪkwɪfaɪ/ vt/i licuar(se)

liqueur /lɪˈkjʊə(r)/ n licor m

liquid /ˈlɪkwɪd/ a & n líquido (m)

liquidat|e /ˈlɪkwɪdeɪt/ vt liquidar. **~ion** /-ˈdeɪʃn/ n liquidación f

liquidize /ˈlɪkwɪdaɪz/ vt licuar. **~r** n licuadora f

liquor /ˈlɪkə(r)/ n bebida f alcohólica

liquorice /ˈlɪkərɪs/ n regaliz m

lira /ˈlɪərə/ n (pl lire /ˈlɪəreɪ/ or liras) lira f

lisle /laɪl/ n hilo m de Escocia

lisp /lɪsp/ n ceceo m. **speak with a ~** cecear. ● vi cecear

lissom /ˈlɪsəm/ a flexible, ágil

list[1] /lɪst/ n lista f. ● vt hacer una lista de; (enter in a list) inscribir

list[2] /lɪst/ vi (ship) escorar

listen /ˈlɪsn/ vi escuchar. **~ in (to)** escuchar. **~ to** escuchar. **~er** n oyente m & f

listless /ˈlɪstlɪs/ a apático

lit /lɪt/ see light[1]

litany /ˈlɪtənɪ/ n letanía f

literacy /'lıtərəsı/ n capacidad f de leer y escribir

literal /'lıtərəl/ a literal; (fig) prosaico. ~**ly** adv al pie de la letra, literalmente

literary /'lıtərərı/ a literario

literate /'lıtərət/ a que sabe leer y escribir

literature /'lıtərətʃə(r)/ n literatura f; (fig) impresos mpl

lithe /laıð/ a ágil

lithograph /'lıθəgrɑːf/ n litografía f

litigation /lıtı'geıʃn/ n litigio m

litre /'liːtə(r)/ n litro m

litter /'lıtə(r)/ n basura f; (of animals) camada f. ● vt ensuciar; (scatter) esparcir. ~**ed with** lleno de. ~**bin** papelera f

little /'lıtl/ a pequeño; (not much) poco de. n poco m. a ~ un poco. a ~ **water** un poco de agua. ● adv poco. ~ **by** ~ poco a poco. ~ **finger** n meñique m

liturgy /'lıtədʒı/ n liturgia f

live[1] /lıv/ vt/i vivir. ~ **down** lograr borrar. ~ **it up** echar una cana al aire. ~ **on** (feed o.s. on) vivir de; (continue) perdurar. ~ **up to** vivir de acuerdo con; cumplir (a promise)

live[2] /laıv/ a vivo; (wire) con corriente; (broadcast) en directo. **be a ~ wire** ser una persona enérgica

livelihood /'laıvlıhʊd/ n sustento m

livel|iness /'laıvlınıs/ n vivacidad f. ~**y** a (-**ier**, -**iest**) vivo

liven /'laıvn/ vt/i. ~ **up** animar(se); (cheer up) alegrar(se)

liver /'lıvə(r)/ n hígado m

livery /'lıvərı/ n librea f

livestock /'laıvstɒk/ n ganado m

livid /'lıvıd/ a lívido; (angry, fam) furioso

living /'lıvıŋ/ a vivo. ● n vida f. ~**room** n cuarto m de estar, cuarto m de estancia (LAm)

lizard /'lızəd/ n lagartija f; (big) lagarto m

llama /'lɑːmə/ n llama f

load /ləʊd/ n (incl elec) carga f; (quantity) cantidad f; (weight, strain) peso m. ● vt cargar. ~**ed** a (incl dice) cargado; (wealthy, sl) muy rico. ~**s of** (fam) montones de

loaf[1] /ləʊf/ n (pl **loaves**) pan m; (stick of bread) barra f

loaf[2] /ləʊf/ vi. ~ (**about**) holgazanear. ~**er** n holgazán m

loam /ləʊm/ n marga f

loan /ləʊn/ n préstamo m. **on** ~ prestado. ● vt prestar

loath /ləʊθ/ a poco dispuesto (**to** a)

loath|e /ləʊð/ vt odiar. ~**ing** n odio m (**of** a). ~**some** a odioso

lobby /'lɒbı/ n vestíbulo m; (pol) grupo m de presión. ● vt hacer presión sobre

lobe /ləʊb/ n lóbulo m

lobster /'lɒbstə(r)/ n langosta f

local /'ləʊkl/ a local. ● n (pub, fam) bar m. **the** ~**s** los vecinos mpl

local government /ləʊkl'gʌvənmənt/ n gobierno m municipal

locality /ləʊ'kælətı/ n localidad f

localized /'ləʊkəlaızd/ a localizado

locally /'ləʊkəlı/ adv localmente; (nearby) en la localidad

locate /ləʊ'keıt/ vt (situate) situar; (find) encontrar

location /ləʊ'keıʃn/ n colocación f; (place) situación f. **on** ~ fuera del estudio. **to film on** ~ **in Andalusia** rodar en Andalucía

lock[1] /lɒk/ n (of door etc) cerradura f; (on canal) esclusa f. ● vt/i cerrar(se) con llave. ~ **in** encerrar. ~ **out** cerrar la puerta a. ~ **up** encerrar

lock[2] /lɒk/ n (of hair) mechón m. ~**s** npl pelo m

locker /'lɒkə(r)/ n armario m

locket /'lɒkıt/ n medallón m

lock-out /'lɒkaʊt/ n lock-out m

locksmith /'lɒksmıθ/ n cerrajero m

locomotion /ləʊkə'məʊʃn/ n locomoción f

locomotive /ləʊkə'məʊtıv/ n locomotora f

locum /'ləʊkəm/ n interino m

locust /'ləʊkəst/ n langosta f

lodge /lɒdʒ/ n (in park) casa f del guarda; (of porter) portería f. ● vt alojar; presentar (complaint); depositar (money). ● vi alojarse. ~**r** /-ə(r)/ n huésped m

lodgings /'lɒdʒıŋz/ n alojamiento m; (room) habitación f

loft /lɒft/ n desván m

lofty /'lɒftı/ a (-**ier**, -**iest**) elevado; (haughty) altanero

log /lɒg/ n (of wood) leño m; (naut) cuaderno m de bitácora. **sleep like a** ~ dormir como un lirón. ● vt (pt **logged**) apuntar; (travel) recorrer

logarithm /'lɒgərıðəm/ n logaritmo m

log-book /'lɒgbʊk/ n cuaderno m de bitácora; (aviat) diario m de vuelo
loggerheads /'lɒgəhedz/ npl. be at ~ with estar a matar con
logic /'lɒdʒɪk/ a lógica f. ~al a lógico. ~ally adv lógicamente
logistics /lə'dʒɪstɪks/ n logística f
logo /'ləʊgəʊ/ n (pl -os) logotipo m
loin /lɔɪn/ n (culin) solomillo m. ~s npl ijadas fpl
loiter /'lɔɪtə(r)/ vi holgazanear
loll /lɒl/ vi repantigarse
lolli|pop /'lɒlɪpɒp/ n (boiled sweet) piruli m. ~y n (iced) polo m; (money, sl) dinero m
London /'lʌndən/ n Londres m. • a londinense. ~er n londinense m & f
lone /ləʊn/ a solitario. ~ly /'ləʊnlɪ/ a (-ier, -iest) solitario. feel ~ly sentirse muy solo. ~r /'ləʊnə(r)/ n solitario m. ~some a solitario
long /lɒŋ/ a (-er, -est) largo. a ~ time mucho tiempo. how ~ is it? ¿cuánto tiene de largo? in the ~ run a la larga. • adv largo/mucho tiempo. as ~ as (while) mientras; (provided that) con tal que (+ subjunctive). before ~ dentro de poco. so ~! ¡hasta luego! so ~ as (provided that) con tal que (+ subjunctive)
long /lɒŋ/ vi. ~ for anhelar
long-distance /lɒŋ'dɪstəns/ a de larga distancia. ~ (tele)phone call n conferencia f
longer /'lɒŋgə(r)/ adv. no ~er ya no
longevity /lɒn'dʒevətɪ/ n longevidad f
long: ~ face n cara f triste. ~hand n escritura f a mano. ~ johns npl (fam) calzoncillos mpl largos. ~ jump n salto m de longitud
longing /'lɒŋɪŋ/ n anhelo m, ansia f
longitude /'lɒŋgɪtjuːd/ n longitud f
long: ~-playing record n elepé m. ~-range a de gran alcance. ~-sighted a présbita. ~-standing a de mucho tiempo. ~-suffering a sufrido. ~-term a a largo plazo. ~ wave n onda f larga. ~-winded a (speaker etc) prolijo
loo /luː/ n (fam) servicios mpl
look /lʊk/ vt mirar; (seem) parecer; representar (age). • vi mirar; (seem) parecer; (search) buscar. • n mirada f; (appearance) aspecto m. ~ after ocuparse de; cuidar (person). ~ at mirar. ~ down on despreciar. ~ for

buscar. ~ forward to esperar con ansia. ~ in on pasar por casa de. ~ into investigar. ~ like (resemble) parecerse a. ~ on to (room, window) dar a. ~ out tener cuidado. ~ out for buscar; (watch) tener cuidado con. ~ round volver la cabeza. ~ through hojear. ~ up buscar (word); (visit) ir a ver. ~ up to respetar. ~er-on n espectador m. ~ing-glass n espejo m. ~-out n (mil) atalaya f; (person) vigía m. ~s npl belleza f. good ~s mpl belleza f
loom /luːm/ n telar m
loom /luːm/ vi aparecerse
loony /'luːnɪ/ a & n (sl) chiflado (m) (fam), loco (m). ~ bin n (sl) manicomio m
loop /luːp/ n lazo m. • vt hacer presilla con
loophole /'luːphəʊl/ n (in rule) escapatoria f
loose /luːs/ a (-er, -est) (untied) suelto; (not tight) flojo; (inexact) vago; (immoral) inmoral; (not packed) suelto. be at a ~ end, be at ~ ends (Amer) no tener nada que hacer. ~ly adv sueltamente; (roughly) aproximadamente. ~n /'luːsn/ vt (slacken) aflojar; (untie) desatar
loot /luːt/ n botín m. • vt saquear. ~er n saqueador m. ~ing n saqueo m
lop /lɒp/ vt (pt lopped). ~ off cortar
lop-sided /lɒp'saɪdɪd/ a ladeado
loquacious /ləʊ'kweɪʃəs/ a locuaz
lord /lɔːd/ n señor m; (British title) lord m. (good) L~! ¡Dios mío! the L~ el Señor m. the (House of) L~s la Cámara f de los Lores. ~ly señorial; (haughty) altivo. ~ship n señoría f
lore /lɔː(r)/ n tradiciones fpl
lorgnette /lɔː'njet/ n impertinentes mpl
lorry /'lɒrɪ/ n camión m
lose /luːz/ vt/i (pt lost) perder. ~r n perdedor m
loss /lɒs/ n pérdida f. be at a ~ estar perplejo. be at a ~ for words no encontrar palabras. be at a ~ to no saber cómo
lost /lɒst/ see lose. • a perdido. ~ property n, ~ and found (Amer) oficina f de objetos perdidos. get ~ perderse

lot /lɒt/ n (fate) suerte f; (at auction) lote m; (land) solar m. **a ~ (of)** muchos. **quite a ~ of** (fam) bastante. **~s (of)** (fam) muchos. **the ~** todos mpl

lotion /'ləʊʃn/ n loción f

lottery /'lɒtərɪ/ n lotería f

lotto /'lɒtəʊ/ n lotería f

lotus /'ləʊtəs/ n (pl ~-uses) loto m

loud /laʊd/ a (-er, -est) fuerte; (noisy) ruidoso; (gaudy) chillón. **out ~** en voz alta. **~hailer** n megáfono m. **~ly** adv (speak etc) en voz alta; (noisily) ruidosamente. **~speaker** n altavoz m

lounge /laʊndʒ/ vi repantigarse. ● n salón m. **~ suit** n traje m de calle

louse /laʊs/ n (pl lice) piojo m

lousy /'laʊzɪ/ a (-ier, -iest) piojoso; (bad, sl) malísimo

lout /laʊt/ n patán m

lovable /'lʌvəbl/ a adorable

love /lʌv/ n amor m; (tennis) cero m. **be in ~ with** estar enamorado de. **fall in ~ with** enamorarse de. ● vt querer (person); gustarle mucho a uno, encantarle a uno (things). **I ~ milk** me encanta la leche. **~ affair** n amores mpl

lovely /'lʌvlɪ/ a (-ier, -iest) hermoso; (delightful, fam) precioso. **have a ~ time** divertirse

lover /'lʌvə(r)/ n amante m & f

lovesick /'lʌvsɪk/ a atortolado

loving /'lʌvɪŋ/ a cariñoso

low[1] /ləʊ/ a & adv (-er, -est) bajo. ● n (low pressure) área f de baja presión

low[2] /ləʊ/ vi mugir

lowbrow /'ləʊbraʊ/ a poco culto

low-cut /'ləʊkʌt/ a escotado

low-down /'ləʊdaʊn/ a bajo. ● n (sl) informes mpl

lower /'ləʊə(r)/ a & adv see **low**[2]. ● vt bajar. **~ o.s.** envilecerse

low-key /'ləʊ'ki:/ a moderado

lowlands /'ləʊləndz/ npl tierra f baja

lowly /'ləʊlɪ/ a (-ier, -iest) humilde

loyal /'lɔɪəl/ a leal. **~ly** adv lealmente. **~ty** n lealtad f

lozenge /'lɒzɪndʒ/ n (shape) rombo m; (tablet) pastilla f

LP /el'pi:/ abbr (long-playing record) elepé m

Ltd /'lɪmɪtɪd/ abbr (Limited) S.A., Sociedad Anónima

lubrica|nt /'lu:brɪkənt/ n lubricante m. **~te** /-'keɪt/ vt lubricar. **~tion** /-'keɪʃn/ n lubricación f

lucid /'lu:sɪd/ a lúcido. **~ity** /-'sɪdətɪ/ n lucidez f

luck /lʌk/ n suerte f. **bad ~** n mala suerte f. **~ily** /'lʌkɪlɪ/ adv afortunadamente. **~y** a (-ier, -iest) afortunado

lucrative /'lu:krətɪv/ a lucrativo

lucre /'lu:kə(r)/ n (pej) dinero m. **filthy ~** vil metal m

ludicrous /'lu:dɪkrəs/ a ridículo

lug /lʌg/ vt (pt lugged) arrastrar

luggage /'lʌgɪdʒ/ n equipaje m. **~-rack** n rejilla f. **~-van** n furgón m

lugubrious /lu:'gu:brɪəs/ a lúgubre

lukewarm /'lu:kwɔ:m/ a tibio

lull /lʌl/ vt (soothe, send to sleep) adormecer; (calm) calmar. ● n periodo m de calma

lullaby /'lʌləbaɪ/ n canción f de cuna

lumbago /lʌm'beɪgəʊ/ n lumbago m

lumber /'lʌmbə(r)/ n trastos mpl viejos; (wood) maderos mpl. ● vt. **s.o. with** hacer que uno cargue con. **~jack** n leñador m

luminous /'lu:mɪnəs/ a luminoso

lump[1] /lʌmp/ n protuberancia f; (in liquid) grumo m; (of sugar) terrón m; (in throat) nudo m. ● vt. **~ together** agrupar

lump[2] /lʌmp/ vt. **~ it** (fam) aguantarlo

lump: **~ sum** n suma f global. **~y** a (sauce) grumoso; (bumpy) cubierto de protuberancias

lunacy /'lu:nəsɪ/ n locura f

lunar /'lu:nə(r)/ a lunar

lunatic /'lu:nətɪk/ n loco m

lunch /lʌntʃ/ n comida f, almuerzo m. ● vi comer

luncheon /'lʌntʃən/ n comida f, almuerzo m. **~ meat** n carne f en lata. **~ voucher** n vale m de comida

lung /lʌŋ/ n pulmón m

lunge /lʌndʒ/ n arremetida f

lurch[1] /lɜ:tʃ/ vi tambalearse

lurch[2] /lɜ:tʃ/ n. **leave in the ~** dejar en la estacada

lure /ljʊə(r)/ vt atraer. ● n (attraction) atractivo m

lurid /'ljʊərɪd/ a chillón; (shocking) espeluznante

lurk /lɜ:k/ vi esconderse; (in ambush) estar al acecho; (prowl) rondar

luscious /'lʌʃəs/ a delicioso

lush /lʌʃ/ a exuberante. ● n (Amer, sl) borracho m

lust /lʌst/ n lujuria f; (fig) ansia f. ● vi. **~ after** codiciar. **~ful** a lujurioso

lustre /'lʌstə(r)/ n lustre m
lusty /'lʌstɪ/ a (-ier, -iest) fuerte
lute /luːt/ n laúd m
Luxemburg /'lʌksəmbɜːg/ n Luxemburgo m
luxuriant /lʌg'zjʊərɪənt/ a exuberante
luxurious /lʌg'zjʊərɪəs/ a lujoso. ~**y** /'lʌkʃərɪ/ n lujo m. ● a de lujo
lye /laɪ/ n lejía f
lying /'laɪɪŋ/ see lie¹, lie². ● n mentiras fpl
lynch /lɪntʃ/ vt linchar
lynx /lɪŋks/ n lince m
lyre /'laɪə(r)/ n lira f
lyric /'lɪrɪk/ a lírico. ~**al** a lírico. ~**ism** /-sɪzəm/ n lirismo m. ~**s** npl letra f

M

MA abbr (Master of Arts) Master m, grado m universitario entre el de licenciado y doctor
mac /mæk/ n (fam) impermeable m
macabre /mə'kɑːbrə/ a macabro
macaroni /mækə'rəʊnɪ/ n macarrones mpl
macaroon /mækə'ruːn/ n mostachón m
mace¹ /meɪs/ n (staff) maza f
mace² /meɪs/ n (spice) macis f
Mach /mɑːk/ n. ~ (**number**) n (número m de) Mach (m)
machiavellian /mækɪə'velɪən/ a maquiavélico
machinations /mækɪ'neɪʃnz/ npl maquinaciones fpl
machine /mə'ʃiːn/ n máquina f. ● vt (sew) coser a máquina; (tec) trabajar a máquina. ~**gun** n ametralladora f. ~**ry** /mə'ʃiːnərɪ/ n maquinaria f; (working parts, fig) mecanismo m. ~ **tool** n máquina f herramienta
machinist /mə'ʃiːnɪst/ n maquinista m
machismo /mæ'tʃɪzməʊ/ n machismo m. ~**o** a macho
mackerel /'mækrəl/ n invar (fish) caballa f
mackintosh /'mækɪntɒʃ/ n impermeable m
macrobiotic /mækrəʊbaɪ'ɒtɪk/ a macrobiótico
mad /mæd/ a (**madder, maddest**) loco; (foolish) insensato; (dog) rabioso; (angry, fam) furioso. **be** ~

about estar loco por. **like** ~ como un loco; (a lot) muchísimo
Madagascar /mædə'gæskə(r)/ n Madagascar m
madam /'mædəm/ n señora f; (unmarried) señorita f
madcap /'mædkæp/ a atolondrado. ● n locuelo m
madden /'mædn/ vt (make mad) enloquecer; (make angry) enfurecer
made /meɪd/ see make. ~ **to measure** hecho a la medida
Madeira /mə'dɪərə/ n (wine) vino m de Madera
mad: ~**house** n manicomio m. ~**ly** adv (interested, in love etc) locamente; (frantically) como un loco. ~**man** n loco m. ~**ness** n locura f
madonna /mə'dɒnə/ n Virgen f María
madrigal /'mædrɪgl/ n madrigal m
maelstrom /'meɪlstrəm/ n remolino m
maestro /'maɪstrəʊ/ n (pl maestri /-striː/ or os) maestro m
Mafia /'mæfɪə/ n mafia f
magazine /mægə'ziːn/ n revista f; (of gun) recámara f
magenta /mə'dʒentə/ a rojo purpúreo
maggot /'mægət/ n gusano m. ~**y** a agusanado
Magi /'meɪdʒaɪ/ npl. the ~ los Reyes mpl Magos
magic /'mædʒɪk/ n magia f. ● a mágico. ~**al** a mágico. ~**ian** /mə'dʒɪʃn/ n mago m
magisterial /mædʒɪ'stɪərɪəl/ a magistral; (imperious) autoritario
magistrate /'mædʒɪstreɪt/ n magistrado m, juez m
magnanim|ity /mægnə'nɪmətɪ/ n magnanimidad f. ~**ous** /-'nænməs/ a magnánimo
magnate /'mægneɪt/ n magnate m
magnesia /mæg'niːʒə/ n magnesia f
magnet /'mægnɪt/ n imán m. ~**ic** /-'netɪk/ a magnético. ~**ism** n magnetismo m. ~**ize** vt magnetizar
magnificen|ce /mæg'nɪfɪsns/ a magnificencia f. ~**t** a magnífico
magnif|ication /mægnɪfɪ'keɪʃn/ n aumento m. ~**ier** /-'faɪə(r)/ n lupa f, lente f de aumento. ~**y** /-'faɪ/ vt aumentar. ~**ying-glass** n lupa f, lente f de aumento
magnitude /'mægnɪtjuːd/ n magnitud f

magnolia /mæg'nəʊlɪə/ n magnolia f

magnum /'mægnəm/ n botella f de litro y medio

magpie /'mægpaɪ/ n urraca f

mahogany /mə'hɒgənɪ/ n caoba f

maid /meɪd/ n (servant) criada f; (girl, old use) doncella f. **old** ~ solterona f

maiden /'meɪdn/ n doncella f. ●a (aunt) soltera; (voyage) inaugural. ~**hood** n doncellez f, virginidad f, soltería f. ~**ly** adv virginal. ~ **name** n apellido m de soltera

mail¹ /meɪl/ n (armour) correo m; (letters) cartas fpl. ●a postal, de correos. ●vt (post) echar al correo; (send) enviar por correo

mail² /meɪl/ n (armour) (cota f de) malla f

mail: ~**ing list** n lista f de direcciones. ~**man** n (Amer) cartero m. ~ **order** n venta f por correo

maim /meɪm/ vt mutilar

main /meɪn/ n. (water/gas) ~ cañería f principal. **in the** ~ en su mayor parte. **the** ~**s** npl (elec) la red f eléctrica. ●a principal. **a** ~ **road** n una carretera f. ~**land** n continente m. ~**ly** adv principalmente. ~ **spring** n muelle m real; (fig, motive) móvil m principal. ~**stay** n sostén m. ~**stream** n corriente f principal. ~ **street** n calle f principal

maintain /meɪn'teɪn/ vt mantener

maintenance /'meɪntənəns/ n mantenimiento m; (allowance) pensión f alimenticia

maisonette /meɪzə'net/ n (small house) casita f; (part of house) dúplex m

maize /meɪz/ n maíz m

majestic /mə'dʒestɪk/ a majestuoso

majesty /'mædʒəstɪ/ n majestad f

major /'meɪdʒə(r)/ a mayor. **a** ~ **road** una calle f prioritaria. ●n comandante m. ●vi. ~ **in** (univ, Amer) especializarse en

Majorca /mə'jɔːkə/ n Mallorca f

majority /mə'dʒɒrətɪ/ n mayoría f. **the** ~ **of people** la mayoría f de la gente. ●a mayoritario

make /meɪk/ vt/i (pt made) hacer; (manufacture) fabricar; ganar (money); tomar (decision); llegar a (destination). ~ **s.o. do sth** obligar a uno a hacer algo. **be made of** estar hecho de. **I cannot** ~ **anything of it**

no me lo explico. **I** ~ **it two o'clock** yo tengo las dos. ●n fabricación f; (brand) marca f. ~ **as if to** estar a punto de. ~ **believe** fingir. ~ **do** (manage) arreglarse. ~ **do with** (content o.s.) contentarse con. ~ **for** dirigirse a. ~ **good** vi tener éxito. ●vt compensar; (repair) reparar. ~ **it** llegar; (succeed) tener éxito. ~ **it up** (become reconciled) hacer las paces. ~ **much of** dar mucha importancia a. ~ **off** escaparse (**with** con). ~ **out** vt distinguir; (understand) entender; (draw up) extender; (assert) dar a entender. ●vi arreglárselas. ~ **over** ceder (**to** a). ~ **up** formar; (prepare) preparar; inventar (story); (compensate) compensar. ●vi hacer las paces. ~ **up** (one's face) maquillarse. ~ **up for** compensar; recuperar (time). ~ **up to** congraciarse con. ~**believe** a fingido, simulado. ●n ficción f

maker /'meɪkə(r)/ n fabricante m & f. **the M**~ el Hacedor m, el Creador m

makeshift /'meɪkʃɪft/ n expediente m. ●a (temporary) provisional; (improvised) improvisado

make-up /'meɪkʌp/ n maquillaje m

makeweight /'meɪkweɪt/ n complemento m

making /'meɪkɪŋ/ n. **be the** ~ **of** ser la causa del éxito de. **he has the** ~**s of** tiene madera de. **in the** ~ en vías de formación

maladjust|ed /mælə'dʒʌstɪd/ a inadaptado. ~**ment** n inadaptación f

maladministration /mæləd mɪnɪ-'streɪʃn/ n mala administración f

malady /'mælədɪ/ n enfermedad f

malaise /mæ'leɪz/ n malestar m

malaria /mə'leərɪə/ n paludismo m

Malay /mə'leɪ/ a & n malayo (m). ~**sia** n Malasia f

male /meɪl/ a masculino; (bot, tec) macho. ●n macho m; (man) varón m

malefactor /'mælɪfæktə(r)/ n malhechor m

malevolen|ce /mə'levəlns/ n malevolencia f. ~**t** a malévolo

malform|ation /mælfɔː'meɪʃn/ n malformación f. ~**ed** a deforme

malfunction /mæl'fʌŋkʃn/ n funcionamiento m defectuoso. ●vi funcionar mal

malic|e /'mælɪs/ n rencor m. **bear s.o.** ~**e** guardar rencor a uno. ~**ious**

/mə'lɪfəs/ a malévolo. ~**iously** adv con malevolencia

malign /mə'laɪn/ a maligno. ● vt calumniar

malignan|cy /mə'lɪgnənsɪ/ n malignidad f. ~**t** a maligno

malinger /mə'lɪŋgə(r)/ vi fingirse enfermo. ~**er** n enfermo m fingido

malleable /'mælɪəbl/ a maleable

mallet /'mælɪt/ n mazo m

malnutrition /mælnju:'trɪʃn/ n desnutrición f

malpractice /mæl'præktɪs/ n falta f profesional

malt /mɔ:lt/ n malta f

Malt|a /'mɔ:ltə/ n Malta f. ~**ese** /-'ti:z/ a & n maltés (m)

maltreat /mæl'tri:t/ vt maltratar. ~**ment** n maltrato m

malt whisky /mɔ:lt'wɪskɪ/ n güisqui m de malta

mammal /'mæml/ n mamífero m

mammoth /'mæməθ/ n mamut m. ● a gigantesco

man /mæn/ n (pl men) hombre m; (in sports team) jugador m; (chess) pieza f. ~ **in the street** hombre m de la calle. ~ **to** ~ de hombre a hombre. ● vt (pt **manned**) guarnecer (de hombres); tripular (ship); servir (guns)

manacle /'mænəkl/ n manilla f. ● vt poner esposas a

manage /'mænɪdʒ/ vt dirigir; llevar (shop, affairs); (handle) manejar. ● vi arreglárselas. ~ **to do** lograr hacer. ~**able** a manejable. ~**ment** n dirección f

manager /'mænɪdʒə(r)/ n director m; (of actor) empresario m. ~**ess** /-'res/ n directora f. ~**ial** /-'dʒɪərɪəl/ a directivo. ~**ial staff** n personal m dirigente

managing director /mænɪdʒɪŋ daɪ'rektə(r)/ n director m gerente

mandarin /'mændərɪn/ n mandarín m; (orange) mandarina f

mandate /'mændeɪt/ n mandato m

mandatory /'mændətərɪ/ a obligatorio

mane /meɪn/ n (of horse) crin f; (of lion) melena f

manful /'mænfl/ a valiente

manganese /'mæŋgəni:z/ n manganeso m

manger /'meɪndʒə(r)/ n pesebre m

mangle[^1] /'mæŋgl/ n (for wringing) exprimidor m; (for smoothing) máquina f de planchar

mangle[^2] /'mæŋgl/ vt destrozar

mango /'mæŋgəʊ/ n (pl -oes) mango m

mangy /'meɪndʒɪ/ a sarnoso

man: ~**handle** vt maltratar. ~**hole** n registro m. ~**hole cover** n tapa f de registro. ~**hood** n edad f viril; (quality) virilidad f. ~**hour** n horahombre f. ~**hunt** n persecución f

mania /'meɪnɪə/ n manía f. ~**c** /-ɪæk/ n maníaco m

manicur|e /'mænɪkjʊə(r)/ n manicura f. ● vt hacer la manicura a (person). ~**ist** n manicuro m

manifest /'mænɪfest/ a manifiesto. ● vt mostrar. ~**ation** /-'steɪʃn/ n manifestación f

manifesto /mænɪ'festəʊ/ n (pl -os) manifiesto m

manifold /'mænɪfəʊld/ a múltiple

manipulat|e /mə'nɪpjʊleɪt/ vt manipular. ~**ion** /-'leɪʃn/ n manipulación f

mankind /mæn'kaɪnd/ n la humanidad f

man: ~**ly** adv viril. ~**-made** a artificial

mannequin /'mænɪkɪn/ n maniquí m

manner /'mænə(r)/ n manera f; (behaviour) comportamiento m; (kind) clase f. ~**ed** a amanerado. **bad-**~**ed** a mal educado. ~**s** npl (social behaviour) educación f. **have no** ~**s** no tener educación

mannerism /'mænərɪzəm/ n peculiaridad f

mannish /'mænɪʃ/ a (woman) hombruna

manoeuvre /mə'nu:və(r)/ n maniobra f. ● vt/i maniobrar

man-of-war /mænəv'wɔ:(r)/ n buque m de guerra

manor /'mænə(r)/ n casa f solariega

manpower /'mænpaʊə(r)/ n mano f de obra

manservant /'mænsɜ:vənt/ n criado m

mansion /'mænʃn/ n mansión f

man: ~**-size(d)** a grande. ~**slaughter** n homicidio m impremeditado

mantelpiece /'mæntlpi:s/ n repisa f de chimenea

mantilla /mæn'tɪlə/ n mantilla f

mantle /'mæntl/ n manto m

manual /'mænjʊəl/ a manual. ● n (handbook) manual m

manufacture /mænjʊ'fæktʃə(r)/ vt fabricar. ● n fabricación f. ~**r** /-ə(r)/ n fabricante m

manure /mə'njʊə(r)/ n estiércol m

manuscript /'mænjʊskrɪpt/ n manuscrito m

many /'menɪ/ a & n muchos (mpl). ~ **people** mucha gente f. ~ a **time** muchas veces. **a great/good** ~ muchísimos

map /mæp/ n mapa m; (of streets etc) plano m. ● vt (pt **mapped**) levantar un mapa de. ~ **out** organizar

maple /'meɪpl/ n arce m

mar /mɑ:/ vt (pt **marred**) estropear; aguar (enjoyment)

marathon /'mærəθən/ n maratón m

maraud|er /mə'rɔ:də(r)/ n merodeador m. ~**ing** a merodeador

marble /'mɑ:bl/ n mármol m; (for game) canica f

March /mɑ:tʃ/ n marzo m

march /mɑ:tʃ/ vi (mil) marchar. ~ **off** irse. ● vt. ~ **off** (lead away) llevarse. ● n marcha f

marchioness /mɑ:ʃə'nes/ n marquesa f

march-past /'mɑ:tʃpɑ:st/ n desfile m

mare /meə(r)/ n yegua f

margarine /mɑ:dʒə'ri:n/ n margarina f

margin /'mɑ:dʒɪn/ n margen f. ~**al** a marginal. ~**al seat** n (pol) escaño m inseguro. ~**ally** adv muy poco

marguerite /mɑ:gə'ri:t/ n margarita f

marigold /'mærɪgəʊld/ n caléndula f

marijuana /mærɪ'hwɑ:nə/ n marihuana f

marina /mə'ri:nə/ n puerto m deportivo

marina|de /mærɪ'neɪd/ n escabeche m. ~**te** /'mærɪmeɪt/ vt escabechar

marine /mə'ri:n/ a marino. ● n (sailor) soldado m de infantería de marina; (shipping) marina f

marionette /mærɪə'net/ n marioneta f

marital /'mærɪtl/ a marital, matrimonial. ~ **status** n estado m civil

maritime /'mærɪtaɪm/ a marítimo

marjoram /'mɑ:dʒərəm/ n mejorana f

mark[1] /mɑ:k/ n marca f; (trace) huella f; (schol) nota f; (target) blanco m. ● vt marcar; poner nota a (exam). ~ **time** marcar el paso. ~ **out** trazar; escoger (person)

mark[2] /mɑ:k/ n (currency) marco m

marked /mɑ:kt/ a marcado. ~**ly** /-kɪdlɪ/ adv marcadamente

marker /'mɑ:kə(r)/ n marcador m; (for book) registro m

market /'mɑ:kɪt/ n mercado m. **on the** ~ en venta. ● vt (sell) vender; (launch) comercializar. ~ **garden** n huerto m. ~**ing** n marketing m

marking /'mɑ:kɪŋ/ n (marks) marcas fpl

marksman /'mɑ:ksmən/ n tirador m. ~**ship** n puntería f

marmalade /'mɑ:məleɪd/ n mermelada f de naranja

marmot /'mɑ:mət/ n marmota f

maroon /mə'ru:n/ n granate m. ● a de color granate

marooned /mə'ru:nd/ a abandonado; (snow-bound etc) aislado

marquee /mɑ:ki:/ n tienda de campaña f grande; (awning, Amer) marquesina f

marquetry /'mɑ:kɪtrɪ/ n marquetería f

marquis /'mɑ:kwɪs/ n marqués m

marriage /'mærɪdʒ/ n matrimonio m; (wedding) boda f. ~**able** a casadero

married /'mærɪd/ a casado; (life) conjugal

marrow /'mærəʊ/ n (of bone) tuétano m; (vegetable) calabacín m

marry /'mærɪ/ vt casarse con; (give or unite in marriage) casar. ● vi casarse. **get married** casarse

marsh /mɑ:ʃ/ n pantano m

marshal /'mɑ:ʃl/ n (mil) mariscal m; (master of ceremonies) maestro m de ceremonias; (at sports events) oficial m. ● vt (pt **marshalled**) ordenar; formar (troops)

marsh mallow /mɑ:ʃ'mæləʊ/ n (plant) malvavisco m

marshmallow /mɑ:ʃ'mæləʊ/ n (sweet) caramelo m blando

marshy /'mɑ:ʃɪ/ a pantanoso

martial /'mɑ:ʃl/ a marcial. ~ **law** n ley f marcial

Martian /'mɑ:ʃn/ a & n marciano (m)

martinet /mɑ:tɪ'net/ n ordenancista m & f

martyr /'mɑ:tə(r)/ n mártir m & f. ● vt martirizar. ~**dom** n martirio m

marvel /'mɑ:vl/ n maravilla f. ● vi (pt **marvelled**) maravillarse (**at** con, de). ~**lous** /'mɑ:vələs/ a maravilloso

Marxis|m /'mɑ:ksɪzəm/ n marxismo m. ~**ta** & n marxista (m & f)

marzipan /'mɑ:zɪpæn/ n mazapán m

mascara /mæ'skɑ:rə/ n rimel m

mascot /'mæskɒt/ n mascota f

masculin|e /'mæskjʊlɪm/ a & n masculino (m). ~**ity** /-'lɪnətɪ/ n masculinidad f

mash /mæʃ/ n mezcla f; (potatoes, fam) puré m de patatas. ● vt (crush) machacar; (mix) mezclar. ~**ed potatoes** puré m de patatas

mask /mɑ:sk/ n máscara f. ● vt enmascarar

masochis|m /'mæsəkɪzəm/ n masoquismo m. ~**t** n masoquista m & f

mason /'meɪsn/ n (builder) albañil m

Mason /'meɪsn/ n. ~ masón m. ~**ic** /mə'sɒnɪk/ a masónico

masonry /'meɪsnrɪ/ n albañilería f

masquerade /mɑ:skə'reɪd/ n mascarada f. ● vi. ~ **as** hacerse pasar por

mass¹ /mæs/ n masa f; (large quantity) montón m. **the** ~**es** npl las masas fpl. ● vt/i agrupar(se)

mass² /mæs/ n (relig) misa f. **high** ~ misa f mayor

massacre /'mæsəkə(r)/ n masacre f, matanza f. ● vt masacrar

massage /'mæsɑ:ʒ/ n masaje m. ● vt dar masaje a

masseu|r /mæ'sɜ:(r)/ n masajista m. ~**se** /mæ'sɜ:z/ n masajista f

massive /'mæsɪv/ a masivo; (heavy) macizo; (huge) enorme

mass: ~ **media** n medios mpl de comunicación. ~**-produce** vt fabricar en serie

mast /mɑ:st/ n mástil m; (for radio, TV) torre f

master /'mɑ:stə(r)/ n maestro m; (in secondary school) profesor m; (of ship) capitán m. ● vt dominar. ~**-key** n llave f maestra. ~**ly** a magistral. ~**mind** n cerebro m. ● vt dirigir. **M~ of Arts** master m, grado m universitario entre el de licenciado y el de doctor

masterpiece /'mɑ:stəpi:s/ n obra f maestra

master-stroke /'mɑ:stəstrəʊk/ n golpe m maestro

mastery /'mɑ:stərɪ/ n dominio m; (skill) maestría f

masturbat|e /'mæstəbeɪt/ vi masturbarse. ~**ion** /-'beɪʃn/ n masturbación f

mat /mæt/ n estera f; (at door) felpudo m

match¹ /mætʃ/ n (sport) partido m; (equal) igual m; (marriage) matrimonio m; (s.o. to marry) partido m. ● vt emparejar; (equal) igualar; (clothes, colours) hacer juego con. ● vi hacer juego

match² /mætʃ/ n (of wood) fósforo m; (of wax) cerilla f. ~**-box** /'mætʃbɒks/ n (for wooden matches) caja f de fósforos; (for wax matches) caja f de cerillas

matching /'mætʃɪŋ/ a que hace juego

mate¹ /meɪt/ n compañero m; (of animals) macho m, hembra f; (assistant) ayudante m. ● vt/i acoplar(se)

mate² /meɪt/ n (chess) mate m

material /mə'tɪərɪəl/ n material m; (cloth) tela f. ● a material; (fig) importante. ~**istic** /-'lɪstɪk/ a materialista. ~**s** npl materiales mpl. **raw** ~**s** npl materias fpl primas

materialize /mə'tɪərɪəlaɪz/ vi materializarse

maternal /mə'tɜ:nl/ a maternal; (relation) materno

maternity /mə'tɜ:nɪtɪ/ n maternidad f. ● a de maternidad. ~ **clothes** npl vestido m pre-mamá. ~ **hospital** n maternidad f

matey /'meɪtɪ/ a (fam) simpático

mathematic|ian /mæθəmə'tɪʃn/ n matemático m. ~**al** /-'mætɪkl/ a matemático. ~**s** /-'mætɪks/ n & npl matemáticas fpl

maths /mæθs/, **math** (Amer) n & npl matemáticas fpl

matinée /'mætɪneɪ/ n función f de tarde

matriculat|e /mə'trɪkjʊleɪt/ vt/i matricular(se). ~**ion** /-'leɪʃn/ n matriculación f

matrimon|ial /mætrɪ'məʊnɪəl/ a matrimonial. ~**y** /'mætrɪmənɪ/ n matrimonio m

matrix /'meɪtrɪks/ n (pl matrices /-si:z/) matriz f

matron /'meɪtrən/ n (married, elderly) matrona f; (in school) ama f de llaves; (former use, in hospital) enfermera f jefe. ~**ly** a matronil

matt /mæt/ a mate

matted /'mætɪd/ a enmarañado

matter /'mætə(r)/ n (substance) materia f; (affair) asunto m; (pus) pus

m. **as a ~ of fact** en realidad. **no ~**
no importa. **what is the ~?** ¿qué
pasa? ● *vi* importar. **it does not ~**
no importa. **~-of-fact** *a* realista

matting /'mætɪŋ/ *n* estera *f*

mattress /'mætrɪs/ *n* colchón *m*

matur|e /mə'tjʊə(r)/ *a* maduro.
● *vt/i* madurar. **~ity** *n* madurez *f*

maul /mɔːl/ *vt* maltratar

Mauritius /mə'rɪʃəs/ *n* Mauricio *m*

mausoleum /mɔːsə'lɪəm/ *n* mausoleo *m*

mauve /məʊv/ *a & n* color (*m*) de
malva

mawkish /'mɔːkɪʃ/ *a* empalagoso

maxim /'mæksɪm/ *n* máxima *f*

maxim|ize /'mæksɪmaɪz/ *vt* llevar al
máximo. **~um** *a & n* (*pl* **-ima**)
máximo (*m*)

may /meɪ/ *v aux* (*pt* **might**) poder. **~
I smoke?** ¿se permite fumar? ~ **he
be happy** ¡que sea feliz! **he ~/might
come** puede que venga. **I ~/might as
well stay** más vale quedarme. **it ~/
might be true** puede ser verdad

May /meɪ/ *n* mayo *m*. ~ **Day** *n* el primero *m* de mayo

maybe /'meɪbɪ/ *adv* quizá(s)

mayhem /'meɪhem/ *n* (*havoc*) alboroto *m*

mayonnaise /meɪə'neɪz/ *n* mayonesa *f*

mayor /meə(r)/ *n* alcalde *m*, alcaldesa *f*. **~ess** *n* alcaldesa *f*

maze /meɪz/ *n* laberinto *m*

me¹ /miː/ *pron* me; (*after prep*) mí. **he
knows ~** me conoce. **it's ~** soy yo

me² /miː/ *n* (*mus, third note of any
musical scale*) mi *m*

meadow /'medəʊ/ *n* prado *m*

meagre /'miːgə(r)/ *a* escaso

meal¹ /miːl/ *n* comida *f*

meal² /miːl/ *n* (*grain*) harina *f*

mealy-mouthed /miːlɪ'maʊðd/ *a*
hipócrita

mean¹ /miːn/ *vt* (*pt* **meant**) (*intend*)
tener la intención de, querer; (*signify*) querer decir, significar. ~ **to
do** tener la intención de hacer. ~ **
well** tener buenas intenciones. **be
meant for** estar destinado a

mean² /miːn/ *a* (**-er, -est**) (*miserly*)
tacaño; (*unkind*) malo; (*poor*) pobre

mean³ /miːn/ *a* medio. ● *n* medio *m*;
(*average*) promedio *m*

meander /mɪ'ændə(r)/ *vi* (*river*) serpentear; (*person*) vagar

meaning /'miːnɪŋ/ *n* sentido *m*.
~ful *a* significativo. **~less** *a* sin
sentido

meanness /'miːnnɪs/ *n* (*miserliness*)
tacañería *f*; (*unkindness*) maldad *f*

means /miːnz/ *n* medio *m*. **by all ~**
por supuesto. **by no ~** de ninguna
manera. ● *npl* (*wealth*) recursos *mpl*.
~ **test** *n* investigación *f* financial

meant /ment/ *see* **mean**¹

meantime /'miːntaɪm/ *adv* entretanto. **in the ~** entretanto

meanwhile /'miːnwaɪl/ *adv* entretanto

measles /'miːzlz/ *n* sarampión *m*

measly /'miːzlɪ/ *a* (*sl*) miserable

measurable /'meʒərəbl/ *a* mensurable

measure /'meʒə(r)/ *n* medida *f*;
(*ruler*) regla *f*. ● *vt/i* medir. ~ **up to**
estar a la altura de. **~d** *a* (*rhyth-
mical*) acompasado; (*carefully considered*) prudente. **~ment** *n* medida
f

meat /miːt/ *n* carne *f*. **~y** *a* carnoso;
(*fig*) sustancioso

mechanic /mɪ'kænɪk/ *n* mecánico
m. **~al** /mɪ'kænɪkl/ *a* mecánico. **~s**
n mecánica *f*

mechani|sm /'mekənɪzəm/ *n*
mecanismo *m*. **~ze** *vt* mecanizar

medal /'medl/ *n* medalla *f*

medallion /mɪ'dælɪən/ *n* medallón
m

medallist /'medəlɪst/ *n* ganador *m*
de una medalla. **be a gold ~** ganar
una medalla de oro

meddle /'medl/ *vi* entrometerse (**in**
en); (*tinker*) tocar. ~ **with** (*tinker*)
tocar. **~some** *a* entrometido

media /'miːdɪə/ *see* **medium**. ● *npl*.
the ~ *npl* los medios *mpl* de
comunicación

mediat|e /'miːdɪeɪt/ *vi* mediar. **~ion**
/-'eɪʃn/ *n* mediación *f*. **~or** *n* mediador *m*

medical /'medɪkl/ *a* médico; (*student*) de medicina. ● *n* (*fam*)
reconocimiento *m* médico

medicat|ed /'medɪkeɪtɪd/ *a* medi-
cinal. **~ion** /-'keɪʃn/ *n* medicación *f*

medicin|e /'medsɪn/ *n* medicina *f*.
~al /mɪ'dɪsɪnl/ *a* medicinal

medieval /medɪ'iːvl/ *a* medieval

mediocr|e /miːdɪ'əʊkə(r)/ *a* medio-
cre. **~ity** /-'ɒkrətɪ/ *n* mediocridad *f*

meditat|e /'medɪteɪt/ *vt/i* meditar.
~ion /-'teɪʃn/ *n* meditación *f*

Mediterranean /medɪtə'reɪnɪən/ a mediterráneo. ● n. the ~ el Mediterráneo m

medium /'miːdɪəm/ n (pl media) medio m; (pl mediums) (person) médium m. ● a mediano

medley /'medlɪ/ n popurrí m

meek /miːk/ a (-er, -est) manso

meet /miːt/ vt (pt met) encontrar; (bump into s.o.) encontrarse con; (see again) ver; (fetch) ir a buscar; (get to know, be introduced to) conocer. ~ the bill pagar la cuenta. ● vi encontrarse; (get to know) conocerse; (in session) reunirse. ~ with tropezar con (obstacles)

meeting /'miːtɪŋ/ n reunión f; (accidental between two people) encuentro m; (arranged between two people) cita f

megalomania /megələʊ'meɪnɪə/ n megalomanía f

megaphone /'megəfəʊn/ n megáfono m

melancholic /melən'kʊlɪk/ a. ~y /'melənkɒlɪ/ n melancolía f. ● a melancólico

mêlée /'meleɪ/ n pelea f confusa

mellow /'meləʊ/ a (-er, -est) ⟨fruit, person⟩ maduro; ⟨sound, colour⟩ dulce. ● vt/i madurar(se)

melodic /mɪ'lɒdɪk/ a melódico. ~ous /mɪ'ləʊdɪəs/ a melodioso

melodrama /'melədrɑːmə/ n melodrama m. ~tic /-ə'mætɪk/ a melodramático

melody /'melədɪ/ n melodía f

melon /'melən/ n melón m

melt /melt/ vt (make liquid) derretir; fundir ⟨metals⟩. ● vi (become liquid) derretirse; ⟨metals⟩ fundirse. ~ing-pot n crisol m

member /'membə(r)/ n miembro m. M~ of Parliament n diputado m. ~ship n calidad f de miembro; (members) miembros mpl

membrane /'membreɪn/ n membrana f

memento /mɪ'mentəʊ/ n (pl -oes) recuerdo m

memo /'meməʊ/ n (pl -os) (fam) nota f

memoir /'memwɑː(r)/ n memoria f

memorable /'memərəbl/ a memorable

memorandum /memə'rændəm/ n (pl -ums) nota f

memorial /mɪ'mɔːrɪəl/ n monumento m. ● a conmemorativo

memorize /'meməraɪz/ vt aprender de memoria

memory /'memərɪ/ n (faculty) memoria f; (thing remembered) recuerdo m. from ~ de memoria. in ~ of en memoria de

men /men/ see **man**

menace /'menəs/ n amenaza f; (nuisance) pesado m. ● vt amenazar. ~ingly adv de manera amenazadora

menagerie /mɪ'nædʒərɪ/ n casa f de fieras

mend /mend/ vt reparar; (darn) zurcir. ~ one's ways enmendarse. ● n remiendo m. be on the ~ ir mejorando

menfolk /'menfəʊk/ n hombres mpl

menial /'miːnɪəl/ a servil

meningitis /menɪn'dʒaɪtɪs/ n meningitis f

menopause /'menəpɔːz/ n menopausia f

menstruate /'menstrʊeɪt/ vi menstruar. ~ion /-'eɪʃn/ n menstruación f

mental /'mentl/ a mental; ⟨hospital⟩ psiquiátrico

mentality /men'tælətɪ/ n mentalidad f

menthol /'menθɒl/ n mentol m. ~ated a mentolado

mention /'menʃn/ vt mencionar. don't ~ it! ¡no hay de qué! ● n mención f

mentor /'mentɔː(r)/ n mentor m

menu /'menjuː/ n (set meal) menú m; (a la carte) lista f (de platos)

mercantile /'mɜːkəntaɪl/ a mercantil

mercenary /'mɜːsɪnərɪ/ a & n mercenario (m)

merchandise /'mɜːtʃəndaɪz/ n mercancías fpl

merchant /'mɜːtʃənt/ n comerciante m. ● a ⟨ship, navy⟩ mercante. ~ bank n banco m mercantil

merciful /'mɜːsɪfl/ a misericordioso. ~fully adv (fortunately, fam) gracias a Dios. ~less /'mɜːsɪlɪs/ a despiadado

mercurial /mɜː'kjʊərɪəl/ a mercurial; (fig, active) vivo. ~y /'mɜː-kjʊrɪ/ n mercurio m

mercy /'mɜːsɪ/ n compasión f. at the ~ of a merced de

mere /mɪə(r)/ a simple. ~**ly** adv simplemente

merest /'mɪərɪst/ a mínimo

merge /mɜːdʒ/ vt unir; fusionar ⟨companies⟩. ● vi unirse; ⟨companies⟩ fusionarse. ~**r** /-ə(r)/ n fusión f

meridian /mə'rɪdɪən/ n meridiano m

meringue /mə'ræŋ/ n merengue m

merit /'merɪt/ n mérito m. ● vt (pt merited) merecer. ~**orious** /-'tɔː-rɪəs/ a meritorio

mermaid /'mɜːmeɪd/ n sirena f

merr|ily /'merəlɪ/ adv alegremente. ~**iment** /'merɪmənt/ n alegría f. ~**y** /'merɪ/ a (-ier, -iest) alegre. **make** ~ divertirse. ~**y-go-round** n tiovivo m. ~**y-making** n holgorio m

mesh /meʃ/ n malla f; ⟨network⟩ red f

mesmerize /'mezməraɪz/ vt hipnotizar

mess /mes/ n desorden m; ⟨dirt⟩ suciedad f; ⟨mil⟩ rancho m. **make a** ~ **of** chapucear, estropear. ● vt. ~ **up** desordenar; ⟨dirty⟩ ensuciar. ● vi. ~ **about** entretenerse. ~ **with** ⟨tinker with⟩ manosear

message /'mesɪdʒ/ n recado m

messenger /'mesɪndʒə(r)/ n mensajero m

Messiah /mɪ'saɪə/ n Mesías m

Messrs /'mesəz/ npl. ~ **Smith** los señores mpl or Sres. Smith

messy /'mesɪ/ a (-ier, -iest) en desorden; ⟨dirty⟩ sucio

met /met/ see **meet**

metabolism /mɪ'tæbəlɪzəm/ n metabolismo m

metal /'metl/ n metal. ● a de metal. ~**lic** /mɪ'tælɪk/ a metálico

metallurgy /mɪ'tælədʒɪ/ n metalurgia f

metamorphosis /metə'mɔːfəsɪs/ n (pl -phoses /-siːz/) metamorfosis f

metaphor /'metəfə(r)/ n metáfora f. ~**ical** /-'fɒrɪkl/ a metafórico

mete /miːt/ vt. ~ **out** repartir; dar ⟨punishment⟩

meteor /'miːtɪə(r)/ n meteoro m

meteorite /'miːtɪəraɪt/ n meteorito m

meteorolog|ical /miːtɪərə'lɒdʒɪkl/ a meteorológico. ~**y** /-'rɒlədʒɪ/ n meteorología f

meter[1] /'miːtə(r)/ n contador m

meter[2] /'miːtə(r)/ n (Amer) = **metre**

method /'meθəd/ n método m

methodical /mɪ'θɒdɪkl/ a metódico

Methodist /'meθədɪst/ a & n metodista (m & f)

methylated /'meθɪleɪtɪd/ a. ~ **spirit** n alcohol m desnaturalizado

meticulous /mɪ'tɪkjʊləs/ a meticuloso

metre /'miːtə(r)/ n metro m

metric /'metrɪk/ a métrico. ~**ation** /-'keɪʃn/ n cambio m al sistema métrico

metropolis /mɪ'trɒpəlɪs/ n metrópoli f

metropolitan /metrə'pɒlɪtən/ a metropolitano

mettle /'metl/ n valor m

mew /mjuː/ n maullido m. ● vi maullar

mews /mjuːz/ npl casas fpl pequeñas (que antes eran caballerizas)

Mexic|an /'meksɪkən/ a & n mejicano (m); (in Mexico) mexicano (m). ~**o** /-kəʊ/ n Méjico m; (in Mexico) México m

mezzanine /'metsəniːn/ n entresuelo m

mi /miː/ n (mus, third note of any musical scale) mi m

miaow /miː'aʊ/ n & vi = **mew**

mice /maɪs/ see **mouse**

mickey /'mɪkɪ/ n. **take the** ~ **out of** (sl) tomar el pelo a

micro... /'maɪkrəʊ/ pref micro...

microbe /'maɪkrəʊb/ n microbio m

microchip /'maɪkrəʊtʃɪp/ n pastilla f

microfilm /'maɪkrəʊfɪlm/ n microfilme m

microphone /'maɪkrəfəʊn/ n micrófono m

microprocessor /maɪkrəʊ'prəʊse-sə(r)/ n microprocesador m

microscop|e /'maɪkrəskəʊp/ n microscopio m. ~**ic** /-'skɒpɪk/ a microscópico

microwave /'maɪkrəʊweɪv/ n microonda f. ~ **oven** n horno m de microondas

mid /mɪd/ a. **in** ~ **air** en pleno aire. **in** ~ **March** a mediados de marzo. **in** ~ **ocean** en medio del océano

midday /mɪd'deɪ/ n mediodía m

middle /'mɪdl/ a de en medio; ⟨quality⟩ mediano. ● n medio m. **in the** ~ **of** en medio de. ~**aged** a de mediana edad. **M**~ **Ages** npl Edad f Media. ~ **class** n clase f media. ~ **class** a de la clase media. **M**~ **East** n

Oriente *m* Medio. **~man** *n* intermediario *m*

middling /'mɪdlɪŋ/ *a* regular

midge /mɪdʒ/ *n* mosquito *m*

midget /'mɪdʒɪt/ *n* enano *m*. ● *a* minúsculo

Midlands /'mɪdləndz/ *npl* región *f* central de Inglaterra

midnight /'mɪdnaɪt/ *n* medianoche *f*

midriff /'mɪdrɪf/ *n* diafragma *m*; *(fam)* vientre *m*

midst /mɪdst/ *n*. **in our ~** entre nosotros. **in the ~ of** en medio de

midsummer /mɪd'sʌmə(r)/ *n* pleno verano *m*; *(solstice)* solsticio *m* de verano

midway /mɪd'weɪ/ *adv* a medio camino

midwife /'mɪdwaɪf/ *n* comadrona *f*

midwinter /mɪd'wɪntə(r)/ *n* pleno invierno *m*

might /maɪt/ *see* **may**

might² /maɪt/ *n* *(strength)* fuerza *f*; *(power)* poder *m*. **~y** *a* *(strong)* fuerte; *(powerful)* poderoso; *(very great, fam)* enorme. ● *adv* *(fam)* muy

migraine /'miːgreɪn/ *n* jaqueca *f*

migrant /'maɪgrənt/ *a* migratorio. ● *n* *(person)* emigrante *m* & *f*

migrat|e /mar'greɪt/ *vi* emigrar. **~ion** /-ʃn/ *n* migración *f*

mike /maɪk/ *n* *(fam)* micrófono *m*

mild /maɪld/ *a* (-er, -est) *(person)* apacible; *(climate)* templado; *(slight)* ligero; *(taste)* suave; *(illness)* benigno

mildew /'mɪldjuː/ *n* moho *m*

mild: **~ly** *adv (slightly)* ligeramente. **~ness** *n* *(of person)* apacibilidad *f*; *(of climate, illness)* benignidad *f*; *(of taste)* suavidad *f*

mile /maɪl/ *n* milla *f*. **~s better** *(fam)* mucho mejor. **~s too big** *(fam)* demasiado grande. **~age** *n* *(loosely)* kilometraje *m*. **~stone** *n* mojón *m*; *(event, stage, fig)* hito *m*

milieu /mɪ'ljɜː/ *n* ambiente *m*

militant /'mɪlɪtənt/ *a* & *n* militante *(m & f)*

military /'mɪlɪtərɪ/ *a* militar

militate /'mɪlɪteɪt/ *vi* militar *(against* contra)

militia /mɪ'lɪʃə/ *n* milicia *f*

milk /mɪlk/ *n* leche *f*. ● *a* *(product)* lácteo; *(chocolate)* con leche. ● *vt* ordeñar *(cow)*; *(exploit)* chupar. **~man** *n* repartidor *m* de leche. **~**

shake *n* batido *m* de leche. **~y** *a* lechoso. **M~y Way** *n* Vía *f* Láctea

mill /mɪl/ *n* molino *m*; *(for coffee, pepper)* molinillo *m*; *(factory)* fábrica *f*. ● *vt* moler. ● *vi*. **~ about/around** apiñarse, circular

millennium /mɪ'lenɪəm/ *n* *(pl* **-ia** *or* **-iums)** milenio *m*

miller /'mɪlə(r)/ *n* molinero *m*

millet /'mɪlɪt/ *n* mijo *m*

milli... /'mɪlɪ/ *pref* mili...

milligram(me) /'mɪlɪgræm/ *n* miligramo *m*

millimetre /'mɪlɪmiːtə(r)/ *n* milímetro *m*

milliner /'mɪlɪnə(r)/ *n* sombrerero *m*

million /'mɪljən/ *n* millón *m*. **a ~ pounds** un millón *m* de libras. **~aire** *n* millonario *m*

millstone /'mɪlstəʊn/ *n* muela *f* (de molino); *(fig, burden)* losa *f*

mime /maɪm/ *n* pantomima *f*. ● *vt* hacer en pantomima. ● *vi* actuar de mimo

mimic /'mɪmɪk/ *vt* *(pt* **mimicked)** imitar. ● *n* imitador *m*. **~ry** *n* imitación *f*

mimosa /mɪ'məʊzə/ *n* mimosa *f*

minaret /mɪnə'ret/ *n* alminar *m*

mince /mɪns/ *vt* desmenuzar; picar *(meat)*. **not to ~ matters/words** no tener pelos en la lengua. ● *n* carne *f* picada. **~meat** *n* conserva *f* de fruta picada. **make ~meat of s.o.** hacer trizas a uno. **~ pie** *n* pastel *m* con frutas picadas. **~r** *n* máquina *f* de picar carne

mind /maɪnd/ *n* mente *f*; *(sanity)* juicio *m*; *(opinion)* parecer *m*; *(intention)* intención *f*. **be on one's ~** preocuparle a uno. ● *vt* *(look after)* cuidar; *(heed)* hacer caso de. **I don't ~** me da igual. **I don't ~ the noise** no me molesta el ruido. **never ~** no te preocupes, no se preocupe. **~er** *n* cuidador *m*. **~ful** *a* atento *(of* a). **~less** *a* estúpido

mine¹ /maɪn/ *poss pron* (el) mío *m*, (la) mía *f*, (los) míos *mpl*, (las) mías *fpl*. **it is ~** es mío

mine² /maɪn/ *n* mina *f*. ● *vt* extraer. **~field** *n* campo *m* de minas. **~r** *n* minero *m*

mineral /'mɪnərəl/ *a* & *n* mineral *(m)*. **~ (water)** *n* *(fizzy soft drink)* gaseosa *f*. **~ water** *n* *(natural)* agua *f* mineral

minesweeper /'maɪnswiːpə(r)/ n (ship) dragaminas m invar

mingle /'mɪŋgl/ vt/i mezclar(se)

mingy /'mɪndʒɪ/ a tacaño

mini... /'mɪnɪ/ pref mini...

miniature /'mɪnɪtʃə(r)/ a & n miniatura (f)

mini: ~**bus** n microbús m. ~**cab** n taxi m

minim /'mɪnɪm/ n (mus) blanca f

minim|al /'mɪnɪml/ a mínimo. ~**ize** vt minimizar. ~**um** a & n (pl -ima) mínimo (m)

mining /'maɪnɪŋ/ n explotación f. ● a minero

miniskirt /'mɪnɪskɜːt/ n minifalda f

minist|er /'mɪnɪstə(r)/ n ministro m; (relig) pastor m. ~**erial** /-'stɪərɪəl/ a ministerial. ~**ry** n ministerio m

mink /mɪŋk/ n visón m

minor /'maɪnə(r)/ a (incl mus) menor; (of little importance) sin importancia. ● n menor m & f de edad

minority /maɪ'nɒrətɪ/ n minoría f. ● a minoritario

minster /'mɪnstə(r)/ n catedral f

minstrel /'mɪnstrəl/ n juglar m

mint[1] /mɪnt/ n (plant) menta f; (sweet) caramelo m de menta

mint[2] /mɪnt/ n. **the M**~ n casa f de la moneda. **a** ~ un dineral m. ● vt acuñar. **in** ~ **condition** como nuevo

minuet /mɪnjʊ'et/ n minué m

minus /'maɪnəs/ prep menos; (without, fam) sin. ● n (sign) menos m. ~ **sign** n menos m

minuscule /'mɪnəskjuːl/ a minúsculo

minute[1] /'mɪnɪt/ n minuto m. ~**s** npl (of meeting) actas fpl

minute[2] /maɪ'njuːt/ a minúsculo; (detailed) minucioso

minx /mɪŋks/ n chica f descarada

mirac|le /'mɪrəkl/ n milagro m. ~**ulous** /mɪ'rækjʊləs/ a milagroso

mirage /'mɪrɑːʒ/ n espejismo m

mire /'maɪə(r)/ n fango m

mirror /'mɪrə(r)/ n espejo m. ● vt reflejar

mirth /mɜːθ/ n (merriment) alegría f; (laughter) risas fpl

misadventure /mɪsəd'ventʃə(r)/ n desgracia f

misanthropist /mɪ'zænθrəpɪst/ n misántropo m

misapprehension /mɪsæprɪ'henʃn/ n malentendido m

misbehav|e /mɪsbɪ'heɪv/ vi portarse mal. ~**iour** n mala conducta f

miscalculat|e /mɪs'kælkjʊleɪt/ vt/i calcular mal. ~**ion** /-'leɪʃn/ n desacierto m

miscarr|iage /mɪs'kærɪdʒ/ n aborto m. ~**iage of justice** n error m judicial. ~**y** vi abortar

miscellaneous /mɪsə'leɪnɪəs/ a vario

mischief /'mɪstʃɪf/ n (foolish conduct) travesura f; (harm) daño m. **get into** ~ cometer travesuras. **make** ~ armar un lío

mischievous /'mɪstʃɪvəs/ a travieso; (malicious) perjudicial

misconception /mɪskən'sepʃn/ n equivocación f

misconduct /mɪs'kɒndʌkt/ n mala conducta f

misconstrue /mɪskən'struː/ vt interpretar mal

misdeed /mɪs'diːd/ n fechoría f

misdemeanour /mɪsdɪ'miːnə(r)/ n fechoría f

misdirect /mɪsdɪ'rekt/ vt dirigir mal (person)

miser /'maɪzə(r)/ n avaro m

miserable /'mɪzərəbl/ a (sad) triste; (wretched) miserable; (weather) malo

miserly /'maɪzəlɪ/ a avariento

misery /'mɪzərɪ/ n (unhappiness) tristeza f; (pain) sufrimiento m; (poverty) pobreza f; (person, fam) aguafiestas m & f

misfire /mɪs'faɪə(r)/ vi fallar

misfit /'mɪsfɪt/ n (person) inadaptado m; (thing) cosa f mal ajustada

misfortune /mɪs'fɔːtʃuːn/ n desgracia f

misgiving /mɪs'gɪvɪŋ/ n (doubt) duda f; (apprehension) presentimiento m

misguided /mɪs'gaɪdɪd/ a equivocado. **be** ~ equivocarse

mishap /'mɪshæp/ n desgracia f

misinform /mɪsɪn'fɔːm/ vt informar mal

misinterpret /mɪsɪn'tɜːprɪt/ vt interpretar mal

misjudge /mɪs'dʒʌdʒ/ vt juzgar mal

mislay /mɪs'leɪ/ vt (pt **mislaid**) extraviar

mislead /mɪs'liːd/ vt (pt **misled**) engañar. ~**ing** a engañoso

mismanage /mɪsˈmænɪdʒ/ vt administrar mal. ~**ment** n mala administración f

misnomer /mɪsˈnəʊmə(r)/ n nombre m equivocado

misplace /mɪsˈpleɪs/ vt colocar mal; (lose) extraviar

misprint /ˈmɪsprɪnt/ n errata f

misquote /mɪsˈkwəʊt/ vt citar mal

misrepresent /mɪsreprɪˈzent/ vt describir engañosamente

miss[1] /mɪs/ vt (fail to hit) errar; (notice absence of) echar de menos; perder ⟨train⟩. ~ **the point** no comprender. ● n fallo m. ~ **out** omitir

miss[2] /mɪs/ n (pl misses) señorita f

misshapen /mɪsˈʃeɪpən/ a deforme

missile /ˈmɪsaɪl/ n proyectil m

missing /ˈmɪsɪŋ/ a ⟨person⟩ (absent) ausente; ⟨person⟩ (after disaster) desaparecido; (lost) perdido. **be** ~ faltar

mission /ˈmɪʃn/ n misión f. ~**ary** /ˈmɪʃənərɪ/ n misionero m

missive /ˈmɪsɪv/ n misiva f

misspell /mɪsˈspel/ vt (pt misspelt or misspelled) escribir mal

mist /mɪst/ n neblina f, (at sea) bruma f. ● vt/i empañar(se)

mistake /mɪsˈteɪk/ n error m. ● vt (pt mistook, pp mistaken) equivocarse de; (misunderstand) entender mal. ~ **for** tomar por. ~**n** /-ən/ a equivocado. **be** ~**n** equivocarse. ~**nly** adv equivocadamente

mistletoe /ˈmɪsltəʊ/ n muérdago m

mistreat /mɪsˈtriːt/ vt maltratar

mistress /ˈmɪstrɪs/ n (of house) señora f; (primary school teacher) maestra f; (secondary school teacher) profesora f; (lover) amante f

mistrust /mɪsˈtrʌst/ vt desconfiar de. ● n desconfianza f

misty /ˈmɪstɪ/ a (-ier, -iest) nebuloso; ⟨day⟩ de niebla; ⟨glass⟩ empañado. **it is** ~ hay neblina

misunderstand /mɪsʌndəˈstænd/ vt (pt -stood) entender mal. ~**ing** n malentendido m

misuse /mɪsˈjuːz/ vt emplear mal; abusar de ⟨power etc⟩. /mɪsˈjuːs/ n mal uso m; (unfair use) abuso m

mite /maɪt/ n (insect) ácaro m, garrapata f; (child) niño m pequeño

mitigate /ˈmɪtɪgeɪt/ vt mitigar

mitre /ˈmaɪtə(r)/ n (head-dress) mitra f

mitten /ˈmɪtn/ n manopla f; (leaving fingers exposed) mitón m

mix /mɪks/ vt/i mezclar(se). ~ **up** mezclar; (confuse) confundir. ~ **with** frecuentar ⟨people⟩. ● n mezcla f

mixed /mɪkst/ a ⟨school etc⟩ mixto; (assorted) variado. **be** ~ **up** estar confuso

mixer /ˈmɪksə(r)/ n (culin) batidora f. **be a good** ~ tener don de gentes

mixture /ˈmɪkstʃə(r)/ n mezcla f

mix-up /ˈmɪksʌp/ n lío m

moan /məʊn/ n gemido m. ● vi gemir; (complain) quejarse (**about** de). ~**er** n refunfuñador m

moat /məʊt/ n foso m

mob /mɒb/ n (crowd) muchedumbre f; (gang) pandilla f; (masses) populacho m. ● vt (pt mobbed) acosar

mobil|e /ˈməʊbaɪl/ a móvil. ~**e home** n caravana f. ● n móvil m. ~**ity** /məˈbɪlətɪ/ n movilidad f

mobiliz|ation /məʊbɪlaɪˈzeɪʃn/ n movilización f. ~**e** /ˈməʊbɪlaɪz/ vt/i movilizar

moccasin /ˈmɒkəsɪn/ n mocasín m

mocha /ˈmɒkə/ n moca m

mock /mɒk/ vt burlarse de. ● vi burlarse. ● a fingido

mockery /ˈmɒkərɪ/ n burla f. **a** ~ **of** una parodia f de

mock-up /ˈmɒkʌp/ n maqueta f

mode /məʊd/ n (way, method) modo m; (fashion) moda f

model /ˈmɒdl/ n modelo m; (mock-up) maqueta f; (for fashion) maniquí m. ● a (exemplary) ejemplar; ⟨car etc⟩ en miniatura. ● vt (pt modelled) modelar; presentar ⟨clothes⟩. ● vi ser maniquí; (pose) posar. ~**ling** n profesión f de maniquí

moderate /ˈmɒdərət/ a & n moderado (m). /ˈmɒdəreɪt/ vt/i moderar(se). ~**ly** /ˈmɒdərətlɪ/ adv (in moderation) moderadamente; (fairly) medianamente

moderation /mɒdəˈreɪʃn/ n moderación f. **in** ~ con moderación

modern /ˈmɒdn/ a moderno. ~**ize** vt modernizar

modest /ˈmɒdɪst/ a modesto. ~**y** n modestia f

modicum /ˈmɒdɪkəm/ n. **a** ~ **of** un poquito m de

modif|ication /mɒdɪfɪˈkeɪʃn/ n modificación f. ~**y** /-faɪ/ vt/i modificar(se)

modulat|e /'mɒdjʊleɪt/ vt/i modular. ~**ion** /-'leɪʃn/ n modulación f

module /'mɒdju:l/ n módulo m

mogul /'məʊgəl/ n (fam) magnate m

mohair /'məʊheə(r)/ n mohair m

moist /mɔɪst/ a (-er, -est) húmedo. ~**en** /'mɔɪsn/ vt humedecer

moistur|e /'mɔɪstʃə(r)/ n humedad f. ~**ize** /'mɔɪstʃəraɪz/ vt humedecer. ~**izer** n crema f hidratante

molar /'məʊlə(r)/ n muela f

molasses /mə'læsɪz/ n melaza f

mold /məʊld/ (Amer) = **mould**

mole[1] /məʊl/ n (animal) topo m

mole[2] /məʊl/ n (on skin) lunar m

mole[3] /məʊl/ n (breakwater) malecón m

molecule /'mɒlɪkju:l/ n molécula f

molehill /'məʊlhɪl/ n topera f

molest /mə'lest/ vt importunar

mollify /'mɒlɪfaɪ/ vt apaciguar

mollusc /'mɒləsk/ n molusco m

mollycoddle /'mɒlɪkɒdl/ vt mimar

molten /'məʊltən/ a fundido

mom /mɒm/ n (Amer) mamá f

moment /'məʊmənt/ n momento m. ~**arily** /'məʊməntərɪlɪ/ adv momentáneamente. ~**ary** a momentáneo

momentous /mə'mentəs/ a importante

momentum /mə'mentəm/ n momento m; (speed) velocidad f; (fig) ímpetu m

Monaco /'mɒnəkəʊ/ n Mónaco m

monarch /'mɒnək/ n monarca m. ~**ist** n monárquico m. ~**y** n monarquía f

monast|ery /'mɒnəstərɪ/ n monasterio m. ~**ic** /mə'næstɪk/ a monástico

Monday /'mʌndeɪ/ n lunes m

monetar|ist /'mʌnɪtərɪst/ n monetarista m & f. ~**y** a monetario

money /'mʌnɪ/ n dinero m. ~**box** n hucha f. ~**ed** a adinerado. ~**lender** n prestamista m & f. ~**order** n giro m postal. ~**s** npl cantidades fpl de dinero. ~**spinner** n mina f de dinero

mongol /'mɒŋgl/ n & a (med) mongólico (m)

mongrel /'mʌŋgrəl/ n perro m mestizo

monitor /'mɒnɪtə(r)/ n (pupil) monitor m & f; (tec) monitor m. ● vt controlar; escuchar ‹a broadcast›

monk /mʌŋk/ n monje m

monkey /'mʌŋkɪ/ n mono m. ~**nut** n cacahuete m, maní m (LAm). ~**wrench** n llave f inglesa

mono /'mɒnəʊ/ a monofónico

monocle /'mɒnəkl/ n monóculo m

monogram /'mɒnəgræm/ n monograma m

monologue /'mɒnəlɒg/ n monólogo m

monopol|ize /mə'nɒpəlaɪz/ vt monopolizar. ~**y** n monopolio m

monosyllab|ic /mɒnəsɪ'læbɪk/ a monosilábico. ~**le** /-'sɪləbl/ n monosílabo m

monotone /'mɒnətəʊn/ n monotonía f. **speak in a** ~ hablar con una voz monótona

monoton|ous /mə'nɒtənəs/ a monótono. ~**y** n monotonía f

monsoon /mɒn'su:n/ n monzón m

monster /'mɒnstə(r)/ n monstruo m

monstrosity /mɒn'strɒsətɪ/ n monstruosidad f

monstrous /'mɒnstrəs/ a monstruoso

montage /mɒn'tɑ:ʒ/ n montaje m

month /mʌnθ/ n mes m. ~**ly** /'mʌnθlɪ/ a mensual. ● adv mensualmente. ● n (periodical) revista f mensual

monument /'mɒnjʊmənt/ n monumento m. ~**al** /-'mentl/ a monumental

moo /mu:/ n mugido m. ● vi mugir

mooch /mu:tʃ/ vi (sl) haraganear. ● vt (Amer, sl) birlar

mood /mu:d/ n humor m. **be in the** ~ for tener ganas de. **in a good/bad** ~ de buen/mal humor. ~**y** a (-ier, -iest) de humor cambiadizo; (bad-tempered) malhumorado

moon /mu:n/ n luna f. ~**light** n luz f de la luna. ~**lighting** n (fam) pluriempleo m. ~**lit** a iluminado por la luna; ‹night› de luna

moor[1] /mʊə(r)/ n (open land) páramo m

moor[2] /mʊə(r)/ vt amarrar. ~**ings** npl (ropes) amarras fpl; (place) amarradero m

Moor /mʊə(r)/ n moro m

moose /mu:s/ n invar alce m

moot /mu:t/ a discutible. ● vt proponer ‹question›

mop /mɒp/ n fregona f. ~ **of hair** pelambrera f. ● vt (pt mopped) fregar. ~ **(up)** limpiar

mope /məʊp/ vi estar abatido

moped /'məʊped/ n ciclomotor m

moral /'mɒrəl/ a moral. ● n moraleja f. ~s npl moralidad f

morale /mə'rɑːl/ n moral f

moral|ist /'mɒrəlɪst/ n moralista m & f. ~ity /mə'rælətɪ/ n moralidad f. ~ize vi moralizar. ~ly adv moralmente

morass /mə'ræs/ n (marsh) pantano m; (fig, entanglement) embrollo m

morbid /'mɔːbɪd/ a morboso

more /mɔː(r)/ a & n & adv más. ~ and ~ cada vez más. ~ or less más o menos. **once** ~ una vez más. **some** ~ más

moreover /mɔː'rəʊvə(r)/ adv además

morgue /mɔːg/ n depósito m de cadáveres

moribund /'mɒrɪbʌnd/ a moribundo

morning /'mɔːnɪŋ/ n mañana f; (early hours) madrugada f. **at 11 o'clock in the** ~ a las once de la mañana. **in the** ~ por la mañana

Morocc|an /mə'rɒkən/ a & n marroquí (m & f). ~o /-kəʊ/ n Marruecos mpl

moron /'mɔːrɒn/ n imbécil m & f

morose /mə'rəʊs/ a malhumorado

morphine /'mɔːfiːn/ n morfina f

Morse /mɔːs/ n Morse m. ~ (code) n alfabeto m Morse

morsel /'mɔːsl/ n pedazo m; (mouthful) bocado m

mortal /'mɔːtl/ a & n mortal (m). ~ity /-'tælətɪ/ n mortalidad f

mortar /'mɔːtə(r)/ n (all senses) mortero m

mortgage /'mɔːgɪdʒ/ n hipoteca f. ● vt hipotecar

mortify /'mɔːtɪfaɪ/ vt mortificar

mortuary /'mɔːtjʊərɪ/ n depósito m de cadáveres

mosaic /məʊ'zeɪk/ n mosaico m

Moscow /'mɒskəʊ/ n Moscú m

Moses /'məʊzɪz/ a. ~ **basket** n moisés m

mosque /mɒsk/ n mezquita f

mosquito /mɒs'kiːtəʊ/ n (pl -oes) mosquito m

moss /mɒs/ n musgo m. ~y a musgoso

most /məʊst/ a más. **for the** ~ **part** en su mayor parte. ● n la mayoría f. ~ **of** la mayor parte de. **at** ~ a lo más. **make the** ~ **of** aprovechar al máximo. ● adv más; (very) muy. ~ly adv principalmente

MOT abbr (Ministry of Transport). ~ **(test)** ITV, inspección f técnica de vehículos

motel /məʊ'tel/ n motel m

moth /mɒθ/ n mariposa f (nocturna); (in clothes) polilla f. ~ball n bola f de naftalina. ~eaten a apolillado

mother /'mʌðə(r)/ n madre f. ● vt cuidar como a un hijo. ~hood n maternidad f. ~in-law n (pl ~s-in-law) suegra f. ~land n patria f. ~ly adv maternalmente. ~of-pearl n nácar m. **M~'s Day** n el día m de la Madre. ~to-be n futura madre f. ~ **tongue** n lengua f materna

motif /məʊ'tiːf/ n motivo m

motion /'məʊʃn/ n movimiento m; (proposal) moción f. ● vt/i. ~ (to) s.o. **to** hacer señas a uno para que. ~less a inmóvil

motivat|e /'məʊtɪveɪt/ vt motivar. ~ion /-'veɪʃn/ n motivación f

motive /'məʊtɪv/ n motivo m

motley /'mɒtlɪ/ a abigarrado

motor /'məʊtə(r)/ n motor m; (car) coche m. ● a motor; (fem) motora, motriz. ● vi ir en coche. ~ **bike** n (fam) motocicleta f, moto f (fam). ~ **boat** n lancha f motora. ~**cade** /'məʊtəkeɪd/ n (Amer) desfile m de automóviles. ~ **car** n coche m, automóvil m. ~**cycle** n motocicleta f. ~**cyclist** n motociclista m & f. ~**ing** n automovilismo m. ~**ist** n automovilista m & f. ~**ize** vt motorizar. ~**way** n autopista f

mottled /'mɒtld/ a abigarrado

motto /'mɒtəʊ/ n (pl -oes) lema m

mould¹ /məʊld/ n molde m. ● vt moldear

mould² /məʊld/ n (fungus, rot) moho m

moulding /'məʊldɪŋ/ n (on wall etc) moldura f

mouldy /'məʊldɪ/ a mohoso

moult /məʊlt/ vi mudar

mound /maʊnd/ n montículo m; (pile, fig) montón m

mount¹ /maʊnt/ vt/i subir. ● n montura f. ~ **up** aumentar

mount² /maʊnt/ n (hill) monte m

mountain /'maʊntɪn/ n montaña f. ~**eer** /maʊntɪ'nɪə(r)/ n alpinista m & f. ~**eering** n alpinismo m. ~**ous** /'maʊntɪnəs/ a montañoso

mourn /mɔːn/ *vt* llorar. ● *vi* lamentarse. ~ **for** llorar la muerte de. ~**er** *n* persona *f* que acompaña el cortejo fúnebre. ~**ful** *a* triste. ~**ing** *n* luto *m*

mouse /maʊs/ *n* (*pl* **mice**) ratón *m*. ~**trap** *n* ratonera *f*

mousse /muːs/ *n* (*dish*) crema *f* batida

moustache /mə'stɑːʃ/ *n* bigote *m*

mousy /'maʊsɪ/ *a* (*hair*) pardusco; (*fig*) tímido

mouth /maʊð/ *vt* formar con los labios. /maʊθ/ *n* boca *f*. ~**ful** *n* bocado *m*. ~**organ** *n* armónica *f*. ~**piece** *n* (*mus*) boquilla *f*; (*fig, person*) portavoz *f*, vocero *m* (*LAm*). ~**wash** *n* enjuague *m*

movable /'muːvəbl/ *a* móvil, movible

move /muːv/ *vt* mover; mudarse de (*house*); (*with emotion*) conmover; (*propose*) proponer. ● *vi* moverse; (*be in motion*) estar en movimiento; (*progress*) hacer progresos; (*take action*) tomar medidas; (*depart*) irse. ~ (**out**) irse. ● *n* movimiento *m*; (*in game*) jugada *f*; (*player's turn*) turno *m*; (*removal*) mudanza *f*. **on the** ~ **en** movimiento. ~ **along** (hacer) circular. ~ **away** alejarse. ~ **back** (hacer) retroceder. ~ **forward** (hacer) avanzar. ~ **in** instalarse. ~ **on** (hacer) circular. ~ **over** apartarse. ~**ment** /'muːvmənt/ *n* movimiento *m*

movie /'muːvɪ/ *n* (*Amer*) película *f*. **the** ~**s** *npl* el cine *m*

moving /'muːvɪŋ/ *a* en movimiento; (*touching*) conmovedor

mow /məʊ/ *vt* (*pt* **mowed** *or* **mown**) segar. ~ **down** derribar. ~**er** *n* (*for lawn*) cortacésped *m invar*

MP *abbr see* **Member of Parliament**

Mr /'mɪstə(r)/ *abbr* (*pl* **Messrs**) (*Mister*) señor *m*. ~ **Coldbeck** (el) Sr. Coldbeck

Mrs /'mɪsɪz/ *abbr* (*pl* **Mrs**) (*Missis*) señora *f*. ~ **Andrews** (la) Sra. Andrews. **the** ~ **Andrews** (las) Sras. Andrews

Ms /mɪz/ *abbr* (*title of married or unmarried woman*) señora *f*, señorita. **Ms Lawton** (la) Sra. Lawton

much /mʌtʃ/ *a & n* mucho (*m*). ● *adv* mucho; (*before pp*) muy. ~ **as** por mucho que. ~ **the same** más o

menos lo mismo. **so** ~ tanto. **too** ~ demasiado

muck /mʌk/ *n* estiércol *m*; (*dirt, fam*) suciedad *f*. ● *vi*. ~ **about** (*sl*) perder el tiempo. ~ **about with** (*sl*) juguetear con. ● *vt*. ~ **up** (*sl*) echar a perder. ~ **in** (*sl*) participar. ~**y** *a* sucio

mucus /'mjuːkəs/ *n* moco *m*

mud /mʌd/ *n* lodo *m*, barro *m*

muddle /'mʌdl/ *vt* embrollar. ● *vi*. ~ **through** salir del paso. ● *n* desorden *m*; (*mix-up*) lío *m*

muddy /'mʌdɪ/ *a* lodoso; (*hands etc*) cubierto de lodo

mudguard /'mʌdgɑːd/ *n* guardabarros *m invar*

muff /mʌf/ *n* manguito *m*

muffin /'mʌfɪn/ *n* mollete *m*

muffle /'mʌfl/ *vt* tapar; amortiguar (*a sound*). ~**r** *n* (*scarf*) bufanda *f*

mug /mʌg/ *n* tazón *m*; (*for beer*) jarra *f*; (*face, sl*) cara *f*, jeta *f* (*sl*); (*fool, sl*) primo *m*. ● *vt* (*pt* **mugged**) asaltar. ~**ger** *n* asaltador *m*. ~**ging** *n* asalto *m*

muggy /'mʌgɪ/ *a* bochornoso

Muhammadan /mə'hæmɪdən/ *a & n* mahometano (*m*)

mule[1] /mjuːl/ *n* mula *f*, mulo *m*

mule[2] /mjuːl/ *n* (*slipper*) babucha *f*

mull[1] /mʌl/ *vt*. ~ **over** reflexionar sobre

mull[2] /mʌl/ *vt* calentar con especias (*wine*)

multi... /'mʌltɪ/ *pref* multi...

multicoloured /mʌltɪ'kʌləd/ *a* multicolor

multifarious /mʌltɪ'feərɪəs/ *a* múltiple

multinational /mʌltɪ'næʃənl/ *a & n* multinacional (*f*)

multiple /'mʌltɪpl/ *a & n* múltiple (*m*). ~**ication** /mʌltɪplɪ'keɪʃn/ *n* multiplicación *f*. ~**y** /'mʌltɪplaɪ/ *vt/i* multiplicar(se)

multitude /'mʌltɪtjuːd/ *n* multitud *f*

mum[1] /mʌm/ *n* (*fam*) mamá *f* (*fam*)

mum[2] /mʌm/ *a*. **keep** ~ (*fam*) guardar silencio

mumble /'mʌmbl/ *vt* decir entre dientes. ● *vi* hablar entre dientes

mummify /'mʌmɪfaɪ/ *vt/i* momificar(se)

mummy[1] /'mʌmɪ/ *n* (*mother, fam*) mamá *f* (*fam*)

mummy[2] /'mʌmɪ/ *n* momia *f*

mumps /mʌmps/ *n* paperas *fpl*

munch /mʌntʃ/ *vt/i* mascar

mundane /mʌnˈdeɪn/ *a* mundano

municipal /mjuːˈnɪsɪpl/ *a* municipal. **~ity** /-ˈpælətɪ/ *n* municipio *m*

munificent /mjuːˈnɪfɪsənt/ *a* munífico

munitions /mjuːˈnɪʃnz/ *npl* municiones *fpl*

mural /ˈmjʊərəl/ *a & n* mural (*f*)

murder /ˈmɜːdə(r)/ *n* asesinato *m*. ● *vt* asesinar. **~er** *n* asesino *m*. **~ess** *n* asesina *f*. **~ous** *a* homicida

murky /ˈmɜːkɪ/ *a* (**-ier, -iest**) oscuro

murmur /ˈmɜːmə(r)/ *n* murmullo *m*. ● *vt/i* murmurar

muscle /ˈmʌsl/ *n* músculo *m*. ● *vi*. **~ in** (*Amer*, *sl*) meterse por fuerza en

muscular /ˈmʌskjʊlə(r)/ *a* muscular; (*having well-developed muscles*) musculoso

muse /mjuːz/ *vi* meditar

museum /mjuːˈzɪəm/ *n* museo *m*

mush /mʌʃ/ *n* pulpa *f*

mushroom /ˈmʌʃrʊm/ *n* champiñón *m*; (*bot*) seta *f*. ● *vi* (*appear in large numbers*) crecer como hongos

mushy /ˈmʌʃɪ/ *a* pulposo

music /ˈmjuːzɪk/ *n* música *f*. **~al** *a* musical; (*instrument*) de música; (*talented*) que tiene don de música. ● *n* comedia *f* musical. **~ hall** *n* teatro *m* de variedades. **~ian** /mjuːˈzɪʃn/ *n* músico *m*

musk /mʌsk/ *n* almizcle *m*

Muslim /ˈmʊzlɪm/ *a & n* musulmán (*m*)

muslin /ˈmʌzlɪn/ *n* muselina *f*

musquash /ˈmʌskwɒʃ/ *n* ratón *m* almizclero

mussel /ˈmʌsl/ *n* mejillón *m*

must /mʌst/ *v aux* deber, tener que. **he ~ be old** debe ser viejo. **I ~ have done it** debo haberlo hecho. **you ~ go** debes marcharte. ● *n*. **be a ~** ser imprescindible

mustard /ˈmʌstəd/ *n* mostaza *f*

muster /ˈmʌstə(r)/ *vt/i* reunir(se)

musty /ˈmʌstɪ/ *a* (**-ier, -iest**) que huele a cerrado

mutation /mjuːˈteɪʃn/ *n* mutación *f*

mute /mjuːt/ *a & n* mudo (*m*). **~d** *a* (*sound*) sordo; (*criticism*) callado

mutilat|e /ˈmjuːtɪleɪt/ *vt* mutilar. **~ion** /-ˈleɪʃn/ *n* mutilación *f*

mutin|ous /ˈmjuːtɪnəs/ *a* (*sailor etc*) amotinado; (*fig*) rebelde. **~y** *n* motín *m*. ● *vi* amotinarse

mutter /ˈmʌtə(r)/ *vt/i* murmurar

mutton /ˈmʌtn/ *n* cordero *m*

mutual /ˈmjuːtʃʊəl/ *a* mutuo; (*common*, *fam*) común. **~ly** *adv* mutuamente

muzzle /ˈmʌzl/ *n* (*snout*) hocico *m*; (*device*) bozal *m*; (*of gun*) boca *f*. ● *vt* poner el bozal a

my /maɪ/ *a* mi, mis *pl*

myopic /maɪˈɒpɪk/ *a* miope

myriad /ˈmɪrɪəd/ *n* miríada *f*

myself /maɪˈself/ *pron* yo mismo *m*, yo misma *f*; (*reflexive*) me; (*after prep*) mí (mismo) *m*, mí (misma) *f*

myster|ious /mɪˈstɪərɪəs/ *a* misterioso. **~y** /ˈmɪstərɪ/ *n* misterio *m*

mystic /ˈmɪstɪk/ *a & n* místico (*m*). **~al** *a* místico. **~ism** /-sɪzəm/ *n* misticismo *m*

mystif|ication /mɪstɪfɪˈkeɪʃn/ *n* confusión *f*. **~y** /-faɪ/ *vt* dejar perplejo

mystique /mɪˈstiːk/ *n* mística *f*

myth /mɪθ/ *n* mito *m*. **~ical** *a* mítico. **~ology** /mɪˈθɒlədʒɪ/ *n* mitología *f*

N

N *abbr* (*north*) norte *m*

nab /næb/ *vt* (*pt* **nabbed**) (*arrest*, *sl*) coger (*not LAm*), agarrar (*esp LAm*)

nag /næg/ *vt* (*pt* **nagged**) fastidiar; (*scold*) regañar. ● *vi* criticar

nagging /ˈnægɪŋ/ *a* persistente, regañón

nail /neɪl/ *n* clavo *m*; (*of finger, toe*) uña *f*. **pay on the ~** pagar a tocateja. ● *vt* clavar. **~ polish** *n* esmalte *m* para las uñas

naïve /naɪˈiːv/ *a* ingenuo

naked /ˈneɪkɪd/ *a* desnudo. **to the ~ eye** a simple vista. **~ly** *adv* desnudamente. **~ness** *n* desnudez *f*

namby-pamby /næmbɪˈpæmbɪ/ *a & n* ñoño (*m*)

name /neɪm/ *n* nombre *m*; (*fig*) fama *f*. ● *vt* nombrar; (*fix*) fijar. **be ~d after** llevar el nombre de. **~less** *a* anónimo. **~ly** /ˈneɪmlɪ/ *adv* a saber. **~sake** /ˈneɪmseɪk/ *n* (*person*) tocayo *m*

nanny /ˈnænɪ/ *n* niñera *f*. **~-goat** *n* cabra *f*

nap¹ /næp/ *n* (*sleep*) sueñecito *m*; (*after lunch*) siesta *f*. ● *vi* (*pt* **napped**) echarse un sueño. **catch s.o. ~ping** coger a uno desprevenido

nap² /næp/ *n* (*fibres*) lanilla *f*

nape /neɪp/ *n* nuca *f*

napkin /'næpkɪn/ n (at meals) servilleta f; (for baby) pañal m

nappy /'næpɪ/ n pañal m

narcotic /nɑː'kɒtɪk/ a & n narcótico
(m)

narrat|e /nə'reɪt/ vt contar. ~ion
/-ʃn/ n narración f. ~ive /'nærətɪv/
n relato m. ~or /nə'reɪtə(r)/ n na-
rrador m

narrow /'nærəʊ/ a (-er, -est) estrecho. **have a** ~ **escape** escaparse
por los pelos. ● vt estrechar; (limit)
limitar. ● vi estrecharse. ~ly adv
estrechamente; (just) por poco. ~
minded a de miras estrechas.
~ness n estrechez f

nasal /'neɪzl/ a nasal

nast|ily /'nɑːstɪlɪ/ adv desa-
gradablemente; (maliciously) con
malevolencia. ~iness n (malice) malevolencia f. ~y a /'nɑːstɪ/ (-ier,
-iest) desagradable; (malicious)
malévolo; (weather) malo; (taste,
smell) asqueroso; (wound) grave;
(person) antipático

natal /'neɪtl/ a natal

nation /'neɪʃn/ n nación f

national /'næʃənl/ a nacional. ● n
súbdito m. ~ **anthem** n himno m
nacional. ~ism n nacionalismo m.
~ity /næʃə'nælətɪ/ n nacionalidad f.
~ize vt nacionalizar. ~ly adv a nivel
nacional

nationwide /'neɪʃnwaɪd/ a nacional

native /'neɪtɪv/ n natural m & f. **be a**
~ **of** ser natural de. ● a nativo; (country, town) natal; (inborn) innato. ~
speaker of Spanish hispano-
hablante m & f. ~ **language** n lengua f materna

Nativity /nə'tɪvətɪ/ n. **the** ~ la
Natividad f

NATO /'neɪtəʊ/ abbr (North Atlantic
Treaty Organization) OTAN f,
Organización f del Tratado del
Atlántico Norte

natter /'nætə(r)/ vi (fam) charlar.
● n (fam) charla f

natural /'nætʃərəl/ a natural. ~
history n historia f natural. ~ist n
naturalista m & f

naturaliz|ation /nætʃərəlaɪ'zeɪʃn/
n naturalización f. ~e vt naturalizar

naturally /'nætʃərəlɪ/ adv (of
course) naturalmente; (by nature)
por naturaleza

nature /'neɪtʃə(r)/ n naturaleza f;
(kind) género m; (of person) carácter
m

naught /nɔːt/ n (old use) nada f;
(maths) cero m

naught|ily /'nɔːtɪlɪ/ adv mal. ~y a
(-ier, -iest) malo; (child) travieso;
(joke) verde

nause|a /'nɔːzɪə/ n náusea f. ~ate vt
dar náuseas a. ~ous a nauseabundo

nautical /'nɔːtɪkl/ a náutico. ~ **mile**
n milla f marina

naval /'neɪvl/ a naval; (officer) de
marina

Navarre /nə'vɑː(r)/ n Navarra f. ~se
a navarro

nave /neɪv/ n (of church) nave f

navel /'neɪvl/ n ombligo m

navigable /'nævɪgəbl/ a navegable

navigat|e /'nævɪgeɪt/ vt navegar por
(sea etc); gobernar (ship). ● vi
navegar. ~ion n navegación f. ~or n
navegante m

navvy /'nævɪ/ n peón m caminero

navy /'neɪvɪ/ n marina f. ~ (**blue**)
azul m marino

NE abbr (north-east) noreste m

near /'nɪə(r)/ adv cerca. ~ **at hand**
muy cerca. ~ **by** adv cerca. **draw** ~
acercarse. ● prep. ~ (**to**) cerca de.
● a cercano. ● vt acercarse a. ~by a
cercano. **N**~ **East** n Oriente m
Próximo. ~ly /'nɪəlɪ/ adv casi. **not**
~ly **as pretty as** no es ni con mucho
tan guapa como. ~ness /'nɪənɪs/ n
proximidad f

neat /niːt/ a (-er, -est) pulcro; (room
etc) bien arreglado; (clever) diestro;
(ingenious) hábil; (whisky, brandy
etc) solo. ~ly adv pulcramente.
~ness n pulcritud f

nebulous /'nebjʊləs/ a nebuloso

necessar|ies /'nesəsərɪz/ npl lo in-
dispensable. ~ily /nesə'serɪlɪ/ adv
necesariamente. ~y a necesario, imprescindible

necessit|ate /nə'sesɪteɪt/ vt nece-
sitar. ~y /nɪ'sesətɪ/ n necesidad f;
(thing) cosa f indispensable

neck /nek/ n (of person, bottle, dress)
cuello m; (of animal) pescuezo m. ~
and ~ parejos. ~lace /'nekləs/ n
collar m. ~line n escote m. ~tie n
corbata f

nectar /'nektə(r)/ n néctar m

nectarine /nektə'riːn/ n nectarina f

née /neɪ/ a de soltera

need /niːd/ n necesidad f. ● vt necesitar; (demand) exigir. **you ~ not speak** no tienes que hablar

needle /ˈniːdl/ n aguja f. ● vt (annoy, fam) pinchar

needless /ˈniːdlɪs/ a innecesario. **~ly** adv innecesariamente

needlework /ˈniːdlwɜːk/ n costura f; (embroidery) bordado m

needy /ˈniːdɪ/ a (-ier, -iest) necesitado

negation /nɪˈɡeɪʃn/ n negación f

negative /ˈneɡətɪv/ a negativo. ● n (of photograph) negativo m; (word, gram) negativa f. **~ly** adv negativamente

neglect /nɪˈɡlekt/ vt descuidar; no cumplir con (duty). **~ to do** dejar de hacer. ● n descuido m, negligencia f. **(state of) ~** abandono m. **~ful** a descuidado

négligé /ˈneɡlɪʒeɪ/ n bata f, salto m de cama

negligen|ce /ˈneɡlɪdʒəns/ n negligencia f, descuido m. **~t** a descuidado

negligible /ˈneɡlɪdʒəbl/ a insignificante

negotiable /nɪˈɡəʊʃəbl/ a negociable

negotiat|e /nɪˈɡəʊʃɪeɪt/ vt/i negociar. **~ion** /-ˈeɪʃn/ n negociación f. **~or** n negociador m

Negr|ess /ˈniːɡrɪs/ n negra f. **~o** n (pl -oes) negro m. ● a negro

neigh /neɪ/ n relincho m. ● vi relinchar

neighbour /ˈneɪbə(r)/ n vecino m. **~hood** n vecindad f, barrio m. **in the ~hood of** alrededor de. **~ing** a vecino. **~ly** /ˈneɪbəlɪ/ a amable

neither /ˈnaɪðə(r)/ a & pron ninguno m de los dos, ni el uno ni el otro m. ● adv ni. **~ big nor small** ni grande ni pequeño. **~ shall I come** no voy yo tampoco. ● conj tampoco

neon /ˈniːɒn/ n neón m. ● a (lamp etc) de neón

nephew /ˈnevju/ n sobrino m

nepotism /ˈnepətɪzəm/ m nepotismo m

nerve /nɜːv/ n nervio m; (courage) valor m; (calm) sangre f fría; (impudence, fam) descaro m. **~-racking** a exasperante. **~s** npl (before exams etc) nervios mpl

nervous /ˈnɜːvəs/ a nervioso. **be/ feel ~** (afraid) tener miedo (of a).

~ly adv (tensely) nerviosamente; (timidly) tímidamente. **~ness** n nerviosidad f; (fear) miedo m

nervy /ˈnɜːvɪ/ a see **nervous**; (Amer, fam) descarado

nest /nest/ n nido m. ● vi anidar. **~ egg** n (money) ahorros mpl

nestle /ˈnesl/ vi acomodarse. **~ up to** arrimarse a

net /net/ n red f. ● vt (pt netted) coger (not LAm), agarrar (esp LAm). ● a (weight etc) neto

netball /ˈnetbɔːl/ n baloncesto m

Netherlands /ˈneðələndz/ npl. **the ~s** los Países mpl Bajos

netting /ˈnetɪŋ/ n (nets) redes fpl; (wire) malla f; (fabric) tul m

nettle /ˈnetl/ n ortiga f

network /ˈnetwɜːk/ n red f

neuralgia /njʊəˈrældʒɪə/ n neuralgia f

neuro|sis /njʊəˈrəʊsɪs/ n (pl -oses /-siːz/) neurosis f. **~tic** a & n neurótico (m)

neuter /ˈnjuːtə(r)/ a & n neutro (m). ● vt castrar (animals)

neutral /ˈnjuːtral/ a neutral; (colour) neutro; (elec) neutro. **~ (gear)** (auto) punto m muerto. **~ity** /-ˈtrælətɪ/ n neutralidad f

neutron /ˈnjuːtrɒn/ n neutrón m. **~ bomb** n bomba f de neutrones

never /ˈnevə(r)/ adv nunca, jamás; (not, fam) no. **~ again** nunca más. **~ mind** (don't worry) no te preocupes, no se preocupe; (it doesn't matter) no importa. **he ~ smiles** no sonríe nunca. **I ~ saw him** (fam) no le vi. **~-ending** a interminable

nevertheless /nevəðəˈles/ adv sin embargo, no obstante

new /njuː/ a (-er, -est) (new to owner) nuevo (placed before noun); (brand new) nuevo (placed after noun). **~-born** a recién nacido. **~comer** n recién llegado m. **~fangled** a (pej) moderno. **~-laid egg** n huevo m fresco. **~ly** adv nuevamente; (recently) recién. **~ly-weds** npl recién casados mpl. **~ moon** n luna f nueva. **~ness** n novedad f

news /njuːz/ n noticias fpl; (broadcasting, press) informaciones fpl; (on TV) telediario m; (on radio) diario m hablado. **~agent** n vendedor m de periódicos. **~caster** n locutor m. **~letter** n boletín m. **~paper** n periódico m. **~reader** n locutor m.

~**reel** n noticiario m, nodo m (in Spain)

newt /njuːt/ n tritón m

new year /njuːˈjɪə(r)/ n año m nuevo. **N~'s Day** n día m de Año Nuevo. **N~'s Eve** n noche f vieja

New Zealand /njuːˈziːlənd/ n Nueva Zelanda f. **~er** n neozelandés m

next /nekst/ a próximo; ⟨week, month etc⟩ que viene, próximo; (adjoining) vecino; (following) siguiente. ● adv la próxima vez; (afterwards) después. ~ n siguiente m. ~ **to** junto a. ~ **to nothing** casi nada. ~ **door** al lado (**to** de). ~**door** de al lado. ~**best** mejor alternativa f. ~ **of kin** n pariente m más próximo, parientes mpl más próximos

nib /nɪb/ n (of pen) plumilla f

nibble /ˈnɪbl/ vt/i mordisquear. ● n mordisco m

nice /naɪs/ a (-er, -est) agradable; (likeable) simpático; (kind) amable; (pretty) bonito; (weather) bueno; (subtle) sutil. ~**ly** adv agradablemente; (kindly) amablemente; (well) bien

nicety /ˈnaɪsəti/ n (precision) precisión f; (detail) detalle m. **to a** ~ exactamente

niche /nɪtʃ, niːʃ/ n (recess) nicho m; (fig) buena posición f

nick /nɪk/ n corte m pequeño; (prison, sl) cárcel f. **in the** ~ **of time** justo a tiempo. ● vt (steal, arrest, sl) birlar

nickel /ˈnɪkl/ n níquel m; (Amer) moneda f de cinco centavos

nickname /ˈnɪkneɪm/ n apodo m; (short form) diminutivo m. ● vt apodar

nicotine /ˈnɪkətiːn/ n nicotina f

niece /niːs/ n sobrina f

nifty /ˈnɪfti/ a (sl) (smart) elegante

Nigeria /naɪˈdʒɪərɪə/ n Nigeria f. ~**n** a & n nigeriano (m)

niggardly /ˈnɪɡədli/ a ⟨person⟩ tacaño; ⟨thing⟩ miserable

niggling /ˈnɪɡlɪŋ/ a molesto

night /naɪt/ n noche f; (evening) tarde f. ● a nocturno, de noche. ~**cap** n (hat) gorro m de dormir; (drink) bebida f (tomada antes de acostarse). ~**club** n sala f de fiestas, boîte f. ~**dress** n camisón m. ~**fall** n anochecer m. ~**gown** n camisón m

nightingale /ˈnaɪtɪŋɡeɪl/ n ruiseñor m

night: ~**life** n vida f nocturna. ~**ly** adv todas las noches. ~**mare** n pesadilla f. ~**school** n escuela f nocturna. ~**time** n noche f. ~**watchman** n sereno m

nil /nɪl/ n nada f; (sport) cero m

nimble /ˈnɪmbl/ a (-er, -est) ágil

nine /naɪn/ a & n nueve (m)

nineteen /naɪnˈtiːn/ a & n diecinueve (m). ~**th** a & n diecinueve (m), decimonoveno (m)

ninet|ieth /ˈnaɪntɪəθ/ a noventa, nonagésimo. ~**y** a & n noventa (m)

ninth /ˈnaɪnθ/ a & n noveno (m)

nip[1] /nɪp/ vt (pt **nipped**) (pinch) pellizcar; (bite) morder. ● vi (rush, sl) correr. ● n (pinch) pellizco m; (cold) frío m

nip[2] /nɪp/ n (of drink) trago m

nipper /ˈnɪpə(r)/ n (sl) chaval m

nipple /ˈnɪpl/ n pezón m; (of baby's bottle) tetilla f

nippy /ˈnɪpi/ a (-ier, -iest) (nimble, fam) ágil; (quick, sl) rápido; (chilly, fam) fresquito

nitrogen /ˈnaɪtrədʒən/ n nitrógeno m

nitwit /ˈnɪtwɪt/ n (fam) imbécil m & f

no /nəʊ/ a ninguno. ~ **entry** prohibido el paso. ~ **man's land** n tierra f de nadie. ~ **smoking** se prohíbe fumar. ~ **way!** (Amer, fam) ¡ni hablar! ● adv no. ● n (pl **noes**) no m

nobility /nəʊˈbɪlətɪ/ n nobleza f

noble /ˈnəʊbl/ a (-er, -est) noble. ~**man** n noble m

nobody /ˈnəʊbədɪ/ pron nadie m. ● n nadie m. ~ **is there** no hay nadie. **he knows** ~ no conoce a nadie

nocturnal /nɒkˈtɜːnl/ a nocturno

nod /nɒd/ vt (pt **nodded**). ~ **one's head** asentir con la cabeza. ● vi (in agreement) asentir con la cabeza; (in greeting) saludar; (be drowsy) dar cabezadas. ● n inclinación f de cabeza

nodule /ˈnɒdjuːl/ n nódulo m

nois|e /nɔɪz/ n ruido m. ~**eless** a silencioso. ~**ily** /ˈnɔɪzɪlɪ/ adv ruidosamente. ~**y** a (-ier, -iest) ruidoso

nomad /ˈnəʊmæd/ n nómada m & f. ~**ic** /-ˈmædɪk/ a nómada

nominal /ˈnɒmɪnl/ a nominal

nominat|e /ˈnɒmɪneɪt/ vt nombrar; (put forward) proponer. ~**ion** /-ˈneɪʃn/ n nombramiento m

non-... /nɒn/ *pref* no ...

nonagenarian /nəʊnədʒɪˈneərɪən/ *a & n* nonagenario (*m*), noventón (*m*)

nonchalant /ˈnɒnʃələnt/ *a* imperturbable

non-commissioned /nɒnkəˈmɪʃnd/ *a*. ~ **officer** *n* suboficial *m*

non-comittal /nɒnkəˈmɪtl/ *a* evasivo

nondescript /ˈnɒndɪskrɪpt/ *a* inclasificable, anodino

none /nʌn/ *pron* (*person*) nadie, ninguno; (*thing*) ninguno, nada. ~ **of** nada de. ~ **of us** ninguno de nosotros. **I have** ~ no tengo nada. ● *adv* no, de ninguna manera. **he is** ~ **the happier** no está más contento

nonentity /nɒˈnentətɪ/ *n* nulidad *f*

non-existent /nɒnɪgˈzɪstənt/ *a* inexistente

nonplussed /nɒnˈplʌst/ *a* perplejo

nonsense /ˈnɒnsns/ *n* tonterías *fpl*, disparates *mpl*. ~**ical** /-ˈsensɪkl/ *a* absurdo

non-smoker /nɒnˈsməʊkə(r)/ *n* persona *f* que no fuma; (*rail*) departamento *m* de no fumadores

non-starter /nɒnˈstɑːtə(r)/ *n* (*fam*) proyecto *m* imposible

non-stop /nɒnˈstɒp/ *a* ⟨*train*⟩ directo; ⟨*flight*⟩ sin escalas. ● *adv* sin parar; (*by train*) directamente; (*by air*) sin escalas

noodles /ˈnuːdlz/ *npl* fideos *mpl*

nook /nʊk/ *n* rincón *m*

noon /nuːn/ *n* mediodía *m*

no-one /ˈnəʊwʌn/ *pron* nadie. *see* **nobody**

noose /nuːs/ *n* nudo *m* corredizo

nor /nɔː(r)/ *conj* ni, tampoco. **neither blue** ~ **red** ni azul ni rojo. **he doesn't play the piano,** ~ **do I** no sabe tocar el piano, ni yo tampoco

Nordic /ˈnɔːdɪk/ *a* nórdico

norm /nɔːm/ *n* norma *f*; (*normal*) lo normal

normal /ˈnɔːml/ *a* normal. ~**cy** *n* (*Amer*) normalidad *f*. ~**ity** /-ˈmælətɪ/ *n* normalidad *f*. ~**ly** *adv* normalmente

Norman /ˈnɔːmən/ *a & n* normando (*m*)

Normandy /ˈnɔːməndɪ/ *n* Normandía *f*

north /nɔːθ/ *n* norte *m*. ● *a* del norte, norteño. ● *adv* hacia el norte. **N~ America** *n* América *f* del Norte, Norteamérica *f*. **N~ American** *a & n*

norteamericano (*m*). ~**east** *n* nordeste *m*. ~**erly** /ˈnɔːðəlɪ/ *a* del norte. ~**ern** /ˈnɔːðən/ *a* del norte. ~**erner** *n* norteño *m*. **N~ Sea** *n* mar *m* del Norte. ~**ward** *a* hacia el norte. ~**wards** *adv* hacia el norte. ~**west** *n* noroeste *m*

Norway /ˈnɔːweɪ/ *n* Noruega *f*. ~**egian** *a & n* noruego (*m*)

nose /nəʊz/ *n* nariz *f*. ● *vi*. ~ **about** curiosear. ~**bleed** *n* hemorragia *f* nasal. ~**dive** *n* picado *m*

nostalgia /nɒˈstældʒə/ *n* nostalgia *f*. ~**ic** *a* nostálgico

nostril /ˈnɒstrɪl/ *n* nariz *f*; (*of horse*) ollar *m*

nosy /ˈnəʊzɪ/ *a* (**-ier, -iest**) (*fam*) entrometido

not /nɒt/ *adv* no. ~ **at all** no... nada; (*after thank you*) de nada. ~ **yet** aún no. **I do** ~ **know** no sé. **I suppose** ~ supongo que no

notable /ˈnəʊtəbl/ *a* notable. ● *n* (*person*) notabilidad *f*. ~**y** /ˈnəʊtəblɪ/ *adv* notablemente

notary /ˈnəʊtərɪ/ *n* notario *m*

notation /nəʊˈteɪʃn/ *n* notación *f*

notch /nɒtʃ/ *n* muesca *f*. ● *vt*. ~ **up** apuntar ⟨*score etc*⟩

note /nəʊt/ *n* nota *f*; (*banknote*) billete *m*. **take** ~**s** tomar apuntes. ● *vt* notar. ~**book** *n* libreta *f*. ~**d** *a* célebre. ~**paper** *n* papel *m* de escribir. ~**worthy** *a* notable

nothing /ˈnʌθɪŋ/ *pron* nada. **he eats** ~ no come nada. **for** ~ (*free*) gratis; (*in vain*) inútilmente. ● *n* nada *f*; (*person*) nulidad *f*; (*thing of no importance*) fruslería *f*; (*zero*) cero *m*. ● *adv* de ninguna manera. ~ **big** nada grande. ~ **else** nada más. ~ **much** poca cosa

notice /ˈnəʊtɪs/ *n* (*attention*) atención *f*; (*advert*) anuncio *m*; (*sign*) letrero *m*; (*poster*) cartel *m*; (*termination of employment*) despido *m*; (*warning*) aviso *m*. **in** (*advance*) ~ previo aviso *m*. ~ (*of dismissal*) despido *m*. **take** ~ **of** prestar atención a, hacer caso de ⟨*person*⟩; hacer caso de ⟨*thing*⟩. ● *vt* notar. ~**able** *a* evidente. ~**ably** *adv* visiblemente. ~**board** *n* tablón *m* de anuncios

notification /nəʊtɪfɪˈkeɪʃn/ *n* aviso *m*, notificación *f*. ~**y** *vt* avisar

notion /ˈnəʊʃn/ *n* (*concept*) concepto *m*; (*idea*) idea *f*. ~**s** *npl* (*sewing goods etc, Amer*) artículos *mpl* de mercería

notori|ety /ˌnəʊtəˈraɪətɪ/ n notoriedad f; (pej) mala fama f. ∼**ous** /nəʊˈtɔːrɪəs/ a notorio. ∼**ously** adv notoriamente

notwithstanding /ˌnɒtwɪθˈstændɪŋ/ prep a pesar de. ● adv sin embargo

nougat /ˈnuːɡɑː/ n turrón m

nought /nɔːt/ n cero m

noun /naʊn/ n sustantivo m, nombre m

nourish /ˈnʌrɪʃ/ vt alimentar; (incl fig) nutrir. ∼**ment** n alimento m

novel /ˈnɒvl/ n novela f. ● a nuevo. ∼**ist** n novelista m & f. ∼**ty** n novedad f

November /nəʊˈvembə(r)/ n noviembre m

novice /ˈnɒvɪs/ n principiante m & f

now /naʊ/ adv ahora. ∼ **and again**, ∼ **and then** de vez en cuando. **just** ∼ ahora mismo; (a moment ago) hace poco. ● conj ahora que

nowadays /ˈnaʊədeɪz/ adv hoy (en) día

nowhere /ˈnəʊweə(r)/ adv en/por ninguna parte; (after motion towards) a ninguna parte

noxious /ˈnɒkʃəs/ a nocivo

nozzle /ˈnɒzl/ n boquilla f; (tec) tobera f

nuance /ˈnjuːɑːns/ n matiz m

nuclear /ˈnjuːklɪə(r)/ a nuclear

nucleus /ˈnjuːklɪəs/ n (pl -lei /-lɪaɪ/) núcleo m

nude /njuːd/ a & n desnudo (m). **in the** ∼ desnudo

nudge /nʌdʒ/ vt dar un codazo a. ● n codazo m

nudi|sm /ˈnjuːdɪzəm/ n desnudismo m. ∼**st** n nudista m & f. ∼**ty** /ˈnjuːdətɪ/ n desnudez f

nuisance /ˈnjuːsns/ n (thing, event) fastidio m; (person) pesado m. **be a** ∼ dar la lata

null /nʌl/ a nulo. ∼**ify** vt anular

numb /nʌm/ a entumecido. ● vt entumecer

number /ˈnʌmbə(r)/ n número m. ● vt numerar; (count, include) contar. ∼**plate** n matrícula f

numeracy /ˈnjuːmərəsɪ/ n conocimientos mpl de matemáticas

numeral /ˈnjuːmərəl/ n número m

numerate /ˈnjuːmərət/ a que tiene buenos conocimientos de matemáticas

numerical /njuːˈmerɪkl/ a numérico

numerous /ˈnjuːmərəs/ a numeroso

nun /nʌn/ n monja f

nurse /nɜːs/ n enfermera f, enfermero m; (nanny) niñera f. **wet** ∼ n nodriza f. ● vt cuidar; abrigar (hope etc). ∼**maid** n niñera f

nursery /ˈnɜːsərɪ/ n cuarto m de los niños; (for plants) vivero m. (**day**) ∼ n guardería f infantil. ∼ **rhyme** n canción f infantil. ∼ **school** n escuela f de párvulos

nursing home /ˈnɜːsɪŋhəʊm/ n (for old people) asilo m de ancianos

nurture /ˈnɜːtʃə(r)/ vt alimentar

nut /nʌt/ n (walnut, Brazil nut etc) nuez f; (hazelnut) avellana f; (peanut) cacahuete m; (tec) tuerca f; (crazy person, sl) chiflado m. ∼**crackers** npl cascanueces m invar

nutmeg /ˈnʌtmeg/ n nuez f moscada

nutrient /ˈnjuːtrɪənt/ n alimento m

nutrit|ion /njuːˈtrɪʃn/ n nutrición f. ∼**ious** a nutritivo

nuts /nʌts/ a (crazy, sl) chiflado

nutshell /ˈnʌtʃel/ n cáscara f de nuez. **in a** ∼ en pocas palabras

nuzzle /ˈnʌzl/ vt acariciar con el hocico

NW abbr (north-west) noroeste m

nylon /ˈnaɪlɒn/ n nailon m. ∼**s** npl medias fpl de nailon

nymph /nɪmf/ n ninfa f

O

oaf /əʊf/ n (pl **oafs**) zoquete m

oak /əʊk/ n roble m

OAP /ˈəʊeɪpiː/ abbr (old-age pensioner) n pensionista m & f

oar /ɔː(r)/ n remo m. ∼**sman** /ˈɔːzmən/ n (pl -**men**) remero m

oasis /əʊˈeɪsɪs/ n (pl **oases** /-siːz/) oasis m invar

oath /əʊθ/ n juramento m; (swearword) palabrota f

oat|meal /ˈəʊtmiːl/ n harina f de avena. ∼**s** /əʊts/ npl avena f

obedien|ce /əʊˈbiːdɪəns/ n obediencia f. ∼**t** /əʊˈbiːdɪənt/ a obediente. ∼**tly** adv obedientemente

obelisk /ˈɒbəlɪsk/ n obelisco m

obes|e /əʊˈbiːs/ a obeso. ∼**ity** n obesidad f

obey /əʊˈbeɪ/ vt obedecer; cumplir (instructions etc)

obituary /əˈbɪtjʊərɪ/ n necrología f

object /ˈɒbdʒɪkt/ n objeto m. /əbˈdʒekt/ vi oponerse

objection /əbˈdʒekʃn/ n objeción f. ~**able** /əbˈdʒekʃnəbl/ a censurable; (*unpleasant*) desagradable

objective /əbˈdʒektɪv/ a & n objetivo (m). ~**ively** adv objetivamente

objector /əbˈdʒektə(r)/ n objetante m & f

oblig|ation /ɒblɪˈgeɪʃn/ n obligación f. **be under an** ~**ation to** tener obligación de. ~**atory** /əˈblɪgətrɪ/ a obligatorio. ~**e** /əˈblaɪdʒ/ vt obligar; (*do a small service*) hacer un favor a. ~**ed** a agradecido. **much** ~**ed!** ¡muchas gracias! ~**ing** a atento

oblique /əˈbliːk/ a oblicuo

obliterat|e /əˈblɪtəreɪt/ vt borrar. ~**ion** /-ˈreɪʃn/ n borradura f

oblivio|n /əˈblɪvɪən/ n olvido m. ~**us** /əˈblɪvɪəs/ a (*unaware*) inconsciente (**to, of** de)

oblong /ˈɒblɒŋ/ a & n oblongo (m)

obnoxious /əbˈnɒkʃəs/ a odioso

oboe /ˈəʊbəʊ/ n oboe m

obscen|e /əbˈsiːn/ a obsceno. ~**ity** /-ˈenɪtɪ/ n obscenidad f

obscur|e /əbˈskjʊə(r)/ a oscuro. ● vt oscurecer; (*conceal*) esconder; (*confuse*) confundir. ~**ity** n oscuridad f

obsequious /əbˈsiːkwɪəs/ a obsequioso

observan|ce /əbˈzɜːvəns/ n observancia f. ~**t** /əbˈzɜːvənt/ a observador

observation /ɒbzəˈveɪʃn/ n observación f

observatory /əbˈzɜːvətrɪ/ n observatorio m

observe /əbˈzɜːv/ vt observar. ~**r** n observador m

obsess /əbˈses/ vt obsesionar. ~**ion** /-ʃn/ n obsesión f. ~**ive** a obsesivo

obsolete /ˈɒbsəliːt/ a desusado

obstacle /ˈɒbstəkl/ n obstáculo m

obstetrics /əbˈstetrɪks/ n obstetricia f

obstina|cy /ˈɒbstɪnəsɪ/ n obstinación f. ~**te** /ˈɒbstɪnət/ a obstinado. ~**tely** adv obstinadamente

obstreperous /ɒbˈstrepərəs/ a turbulento, ruidoso, protestón

obstruct /əbˈstrʌkt/ vt obstruir. ~**ion** /-ʃn/ n obstrucción f

obtain /əbˈteɪn/ vt obtener. ● vi prevalecer. ~**able** a asequible

obtrusive /əbˈtruːsɪv/ a importuno

obtuse /əbˈtjuːs/ a obtuso

obviate /ˈɒbvɪeɪt/ vt evitar

obvious /ˈɒbvɪəs/ a obvio. ~**ly** obviamente

occasion /əˈkeɪʒn/ n ocasión f, oportunidad f. **on** ~ de vez en cuando. ● vt ocasionar. ~**al** /əˈkeɪʒənl/ a poco frecuente. ~**ally** adv de vez en cuando

occult /ɒˈkʌlt/ a oculto

occup|ant /ˈɒkjʊpənt/ n ocupante m & f. ~**ation** /ɒkjʊˈpeɪʃn/ n ocupación f; (*job*) trabajo m, profesión f. ~**ational** a profesional. ~**ier** n ocupante m & f. ~**y** /ˈɒkjʊpaɪ/ vt ocupar

occur /əˈkɜː(r)/ vi (pt **occurred**) ocurrir, suceder; (*exist*) encontrarse. **it** ~**red to me that** se me ocurrió que. ~**rence** /əˈkʌrəns/ n suceso m, acontecimiento m

ocean /ˈəʊʃn/ n océano m

o'clock /əˈklɒk/ adv. **it is 7** ~ son las siete

octagon /ˈɒktəgən/ n octágono m

octane /ˈɒkteɪn/ n octano m

octave /ˈɒktɪv/ n octava f

October /ɒkˈtəʊbə(r)/ n octubre m

octopus /ˈɒktəpəs/ n (pl **-puses**) pulpo m

oculist /ˈɒkjʊlɪst/ n oculista m & f

odd /ɒd/ a (**-er, -est**) extraño, raro; ⟨*number*⟩ impar; (*one of pair*) sin pareja; (*occasional*) poco frecuente; (*left over*) sobrante. **fifty-**~ unos cincuenta, cincuenta y pico. **the** ~ **one out** la excepción f. ~**ity** n (*thing*) curiosidad f; (*person*) excéntrico m. ~**ly** adv extrañamente. ~**ly enough** por extraño que parezca. ~**ment** /ˈɒdmənt/ n retazo m. ~**s** /ɒdz/ npl probabilidades fpl; (*in betting*) apuesta f. ~**s and ends** retazos mpl. **at** ~**s** de punta, de malas

ode /əʊd/ n oda f

odious /ˈəʊdɪəs/ a odioso

odour /ˈəʊdə(r)/ n olor m. ~**less** a inodoro

of /əv, ɒv/ prep de. **a friend** ~ **mine** un amigo mío. **how kind** ~ **you** es Vd muy amable

off /ɒf/ adv lejos; ⟨*light etc*⟩ apagado; ⟨*tap*⟩ cerrado; ⟨*food*⟩ pasado. ● prep de, desde; (*away from*) fuera de; (*distant from*) lejos de. **be better** ~ estar mejor. **be** ~ marcharse. **day** ~ n día m de asueto, día m libre

offal /ˈɒfl/ n menudos mpl, asaduras fpl

off: ~**beat** *a* insólito. ~ **chance** *n* posibilidad *f* remota. ~ **colour** *a* indispuesto

offen|ce /əˈfens/ *n* ofensa *f*; (*illegal act*) delito *m*. **take** ~**ce** ofenderse. ~**d** /əˈfend/ *vt* ofender. ~**der** *n* delincuente *m & f.* ~**sive** /əˈfensɪv/ *a* ofensivo; (*disgusting*) repugnante. ● *n* ofensiva *f*

offer /ˈɒfə(r)/ *vt* ofrecer. ● *n* oferta *f*. **on** ~ en oferta

offhand /ɒfˈhænd/ *a* (*casual*) desenvuelto; (*brusque*) descortés. ● *adv* de improviso

office /ˈɒfɪs/ *n* oficina *f*; (*post*) cargo *m*

officer /ˈɒfɪsə(r)/ *n* oficial *m*; (*policeman*) policía *f*, guardia *m*; (*of organization*) director *m*

official /əˈfɪʃl/ *a & n* oficial (*m*). ~**ly** *adv* oficialmente

officiate /əˈfɪʃɪeɪt/ *vi* oficiar. ~ **as** desempeñar las funciones de

officious /əˈfɪʃəs/ *a* oficioso

offing /ˈɒfɪŋ/ *n*. **in the** ~ en perspectiva

off: ~**licence** *n* tienda *f* de bebidas alcohólicas. ~**load** *vt* descargar. ~**putting** *a* (*disconcerting, fam*) desconcertante; (*repellent*) repugnante. ~**set** /ˈɒfset/ *vt* (*pt* -**set**, *pres p* -**setting**) contrapesar. ~**shoot** /ˈɒfʃuːt/ *n* retoño *m*; (*fig*) ramificación *f*. ~**side** /ɒfˈsaɪd/ *a* (*sport*) fuera de juego. ~**spring** /ˈɒfsprɪŋ/ *n invar* progenie *f*. ~**stage** *a* entre bastidores. ~**white** *a* blancuzco, color hueso

often /ˈɒfn/ *adv* muchas veces, con frecuencia, a menudo. **how** ~? ¿cuántas veces?

ogle /ˈəʊgl/ *vt* comerse con los ojos

ogre /ˈəʊgə(r)/ *n* ogro *m*

oh /əʊ/ *int* ¡oh!, ¡ay!

oil /ɔɪl/ *n* aceite *m*; (*petroleum*) petróleo *m*. ● *vt* lubricar. ~**field** /ˈɔɪlfiːld/ *n* yacimiento *m* petrolífero. ~**paint-ing** *n* pintura *f* al óleo. ~**rig** /ˈɔɪlrɪg/ *n* plataforma *f* de perforación. ~**skins** /ˈɔɪlskɪnz/ *npl* chubasquero *m*. ~**y** *a* aceitoso; (*food*) grasiento

ointment /ˈɔɪntmənt/ *n* ungüento *m*

OK /əʊˈkeɪ/ *int* ¡vale!, ¡de acuerdo! ● *a* bien; (*satisfactory*) satisfactorio. ● *adv* muy bien

old /əʊld/ *a* (-**er**, -**est**) viejo; (*not modern*) anticuado; (*former*) anti-guo. **how** ~ **is she?** ¿cuántos años

tiene? **she is ten years** ~ tiene diez años. **of** ~ de antaño. ~ **age** *n* vejez *f*. ~**fashioned** *a* anticuado. ~ **maid** *n* soltera *f*. ~**world** *a* antiguo

oleander /əʊlɪˈrændə(r)/ *n* adelfa *f*

olive /ˈɒlɪv/ *n* (*fruit*) aceituna *f*; (*tree*) olivo *m*. ● *a* de oliva; (*colour*) aceitunado

Olympic /əˈlɪmpɪk/ *a* olímpico. ~**s** *npl*, ~ **Games** *npl* Juegos *mpl* Olímpicos

omelette /ˈɒmlɪt/ *n* tortilla *f*, tortilla *f* de huevos (*Mex*)

om|en /ˈəʊmən/ *n* agüero *m*. ~**inous** /ˈɒmɪnəs/ *a* siniestro

omi|ssion /əˈmɪʃn/ *n* omisión *f*. ~**t** /əˈmɪt/ *vt* (*pt* omitted) omitir

omnipotent /ɒmˈnɪpətənt/ *a* omni-potente

on /ɒn/ *prep* en, sobre. ~ **foot** a pie. ~ **Monday** el lunes. ~ **Mondays** los lunes. ~ **seeing** al ver. ~ **the way** de camino. ● *adv* (*light etc*) encendido; (*put on*) puesto, poco natural; (*machine*) en marcha; (*tap*) abierto. ~ **and off** de vez en cuando. ~ **and** ~ sin cesar. **and so** ~ y así sucesivamente. **be** ~ **at** (*fam*) criticar. **go** ~ continuar. **later** ~ más tarde

once /wʌns/ *adv* una vez; (*formerly*) antes. ● *conj* una vez que. **at** ~ en seguida. ~**over** *n* (*fam*) ojeada *f*

oncoming /ˈɒnkʌmɪŋ/ *a* que se acerca; (*traffic*) que viene en sentido contrario, de frente

one /wʌn/ *a & n* uno (*m*). ● *pron* uno. ~ **another** el uno al otro. ~ **by** ~ uno a uno. ~ **never knows** nunca se sabe. **the blue** ~ el azul. **this** ~ éste. ~**off** *a* (*fam*) único

onerous /ˈɒnərəs/ *a* oneroso

one: ~**self** /wʌnˈself/ *pron* (*subject*) uno mismo; (*object*) se; (*after prep*) sí (mismo). **by** ~**self** solo. ~**sided** *a* unilateral. ~**way** *a* (*street*) de dirección única; (*ticket*) de ida

onion /ˈʌnɪən/ *n* cebolla *f*

onlooker /ˈɒnlʊkə(r)/ *n* espectador *m*

only /ˈəʊnlɪ/ *a* único. ~ **son** *n* hijo *m* único. ● *adv* sólo, solamente. ~ **just** apenas. ~ **too** de veras. ● *conj* pero, sólo que

onset /ˈɒnset/ *n* principio *m*; (*attack*) ataque *m*

onslaught /ˈɒnslɔːt/ *n* ataque *m* violento

onus /'əʊnəs/ n responsabilidad f

onward(s) /'ɒnwəd(z)/ a & adv hacia adelante

onyx /'ɒnɪks/ n ónice f

ooze /uːz/ vt/i rezumar

opal /'əʊpl/ n ópalo m

opaque /əʊ'peɪk/ a opaco

open /'əʊpən/ a abierto; (free to all) público; (undisguised) manifiesto; (question) discutible; (view) despejado. ~ sea n alta mar f. ~ secret n secreto m a voces. O~ University n Universidad f a Distancia. **half-~** a medio abierto. **in the ~** al aire libre. • vt/i abrir. ~-**ended** a abierto. ~**er** /'əʊpənə(r)/ n (for tins) abrelatas m invar; (for bottles with caps) abrebotellas m invar; (corkscrew) sacacorchos m invar. **eye-~er** n (fam) revelación f. ~**ing** /'əʊpənɪŋ/ n abertura f; (beginning) principio m; (job) vacante m. ~**ly** /'əʊpənlɪ/ adv abiertamente. ~**minded** a imparcial

opera /'ɒprə/ n ópera f. ~**glasses** npl gemelos mpl de teatro

operate /'ɒpəreɪt/ vt hacer funcionar. • vi funcionar; (medicine etc) operar. ~ **on** (med) operar a

operatic /ɒpə'rætɪk/ a operístico

operation /ɒpə'reɪʃn/ n operación f; (mec) funcionamiento m. **in ~** en vigor. ~**al** /ɒpə'reɪʃnl/ a operacional

operative /'ɒpərətɪv/ a operativo; (law etc) en vigor

operator /'ɒpəreɪtə(r)/ n operario m; (telephonist) telefonista m & f

operetta /ɒpə'retə/ n opereta f

opinion /ə'pɪnɪən/ n opinión f. **in my ~** a mi parecer. ~**ated** a dogmático

opium /'əʊpɪəm/ n opio m

opponent /ə'pəʊnənt/ n adversario m

opportune /'ɒpətjuːn/ a oportuno. ~**ist** /ɒpə'tjuːnɪst/ n oportunista m & f. ~**ity** /ɒpə'tjuːnətɪ/ n oportunidad f

oppose /ə'pəʊz/ vt oponerse a. ~**ed to** en contra de. **be ~ed to** oponerse a. ~**ing** a opuesto

opposite /'ɒpəzɪt/ a opuesto; (facing) de enfrente. • n contrario m. • adv enfrente. • prep enfrente de. ~ **number** n homólogo m

opposition /ɒpə'zɪʃn/ n oposición f; (resistence) resistencia f

oppress /ə'pres/ vt oprimir. ~**ion** /-ʃn/ n opresión f. ~**ive** a (cruel) opresivo; (heat) sofocante. ~**or** n opresor m

opt /ɒpt/ vi. ~ **for** elegir. ~ **out** negarse a participar

optic|al /'ɒptɪkl/ a óptico. ~**ian** /ɒp'tɪʃn/ n óptico m

optimis|m /'ɒptɪmɪzəm/ n optimismo m. ~**t** /'ɒptɪmɪst/ n optimista m & f. ~**tic** /-'mɪstɪk/ a optimista

optimum /'ɒptɪməm/ n lo óptimo, lo mejor

option /'ɒpʃn/ n opción f. ~**al** /'ɒpʃənl/ a facultativo

opulen|ce /'ɒpjʊləns/ n opulencia f. ~**t** /'ɒpjʊlənt/ a opulento

or /ɔː(r)/ conj o; (before Spanish o- and ho-) u; (after negative) ni. ~ **else** si no, o bien

oracle /'ɒrəkl/ n oráculo m

oral /'ɔːrəl/ a oral. • n (fam) examen m oral

orange /'ɒrɪndʒ/ n naranja f; (tree) naranjo m; (colour) color m naranja. • a de color naranja. ~**ade** n naranjada f

orator /'ɒrətə(r)/ n orador m

oratorio /ɒrə'tɔːrɪəʊ/ n (pl -os) oratorio m

oratory /'ɒrətrɪ/ n oratoria f

orb /ɔːb/ n orbe m

orbit /'ɔːbɪt/ n órbita f. • vt orbitar

orchard /'ɔːtʃəd/ n huerto m

orchestra /'ɔːkɪstrə/ n orquesta f. ~**l** /-'kestrəl/ a orquestal. ~**te** /'ɔːkɪstreɪt/ vt orquestar

orchid /'ɔːkɪd/ n orquídea f

ordain /ɔː'deɪn/ vt ordenar

ordeal /ɔː'diːl/ n prueba f dura

order /'ɔːdə(r)/ n orden m; (com) pedido m. **in ~ that** para que. **in ~ to** para. • vt (command) mandar; (com) pedir

orderly /'ɔːdəlɪ/ a ordenado. • n asistente m & f

ordinary /'ɔːdɪnrɪ/ a corriente; (average) medio; (mediocre) ordinario

ordination /ɔːdɪ'neɪʃn/ n ordenación f

ore /ɔː(r)/ n mineral m

organ /'ɔːgən/ n órgano m

organic /ɔː'gænɪk/ a orgánico

organism /'ɔːgənɪzəm/ n organismo m

organist /'ɔːgənɪst/ n organista m & f

organiz|ation /ɔːɡənaɪˈzeɪʃn/ *n* organización *f*. **~e** /ˈɔːɡənaɪz/ *vt* organizar. **~er** organizador *m*

orgasm /ˈɔːɡæzəm/ *n* orgasmo *m*

orgy /ˈɔːdʒɪ/ *n* orgía *f*

Orient /ˈɔːrɪənt/ *n* Oriente *m*. **~al** /-ˈentl/ *a & n* oriental (*m & f*)

orientat|e /ˈɔːrɪənteɪt/ *vt* orientar. **~ion** /-ˈteɪʃn/ *n* orientación *f*

orifice /ˈɒrɪfɪs/ *n* orificio *m*

origin /ˈɒrɪdʒɪn/ *n* origen *m*. **~al** /əˈrɪdʒənl/ *a* original. **~ality** /-ˈnælətɪ/ *n* originalidad *f*. **~ally** *adv* originalmente. **~ate** /əˈrɪdʒɪneɪt/ *vi*. **~ate from** provenir de. **~ator** *n* autor *m*

ormolu /ˈɔːməlʊ/ *n* similor *m*

ornament /ˈɔːnəmənt/ *n* adorno *m*. **~al** /-ˈmentl/ *a* de adorno. **~ation** /-enˈteɪʃn/ *n* ornamentación *f*

ornate /ɔːˈneɪt/ *a* adornado; ⟨*style*⟩ florido

ornithology /ɔːnɪˈθɒlədʒɪ/ *n* ornitología *f*

orphan /ˈɔːfn/ *n* huérfano *m*. ● *vt* dejar huérfano. **~age** *n* orfanato *m*

orthodox /ˈɔːθədɒks/ *a* ortodoxo. **~y** *n* ortodoxia *f*

orthopaedic /ɔːθəˈpiːdɪk/ *a* ortopédico. **~s** *n* ortopedia *f*

oscillate /ˈɒsɪleɪt/ *vi* oscilar

ossify /ˈɒsɪfaɪ/ *vt* osificar. ● *vi* osificarse

ostensibl|e /ɒsˈtensɪbl/ *a* aparente. **~y** *adv* aparentemente

ostentat|ion /ɒstenˈteɪʃn/ *n* ostentación *f*. **~ious** *a* ostentoso

osteopath /ˈɒstɪəpæθ/ *n* osteópata *m & f*. **~y** /-ˈɒpəθɪ/ *n* osteopatía *f*

ostracize /ˈɒstrəsaɪz/ *vt* excluir

ostrich /ˈɒstrɪtʃ/ *n* avestruz *m*

other /ˈʌðə(r)/ *a & n & pron* otro (*m*). **~ than** de otra manera que. **the ~ one** el otro. **~wise** /ˈʌðəwaɪz/ *adv* de otra manera; (*or*) si no

otter /ˈɒtə(r)/ *n* nutria *f*

ouch /aʊtʃ/ *int* ¡ay!

ought /ɔːt/ *v aux* deber. **I ~ to see it** debería verlo. **he ~ to have done it** debería haberlo hecho

ounce /aʊns/ *n* onza *f* (= 28.35 *gr.*)

our /ˈaʊə(r)/ *a* nuestro. **~s** /ˈaʊəz/ *poss pron* el nuestro, la nuestra, los nuestros, las nuestras. **~selves** /aʊəˈselvz/ *pron* (*subject*) nosotros mismos, nosotras mismas; (*reflexive*) nos; (*after prep*) nosotros (mismos), nosotras (mismas)

oust /aʊst/ *vt* expulsar, desalojar

out /aʊt/ *adv* apagado; ⟨*light*⟩ apagado; (*in blossom*) en flor; (*in error*) equivocado. **~and-~** *a* cien por cien. **~ of date** anticuado; (*not valid*) caducado. **~ of doors** fuera. **~ of order** estropeado; (*sign*) no funciona. **~ of pity** por compasión. **~ of place** fuera de lugar; (*fig*) inoportuno. **~ of print** agotado. **~ of sorts** indispuesto. **~ of stock** agotado. **~ of tune** desafinado. **~ of work** parado, desempleado. **be ~** equivocarse. **be ~ of** quedarse sin. **be ~ to** estar resuelto a. **five ~ of six** cinco de cada seis. **made ~ of** hecho de

outbid /aʊtˈbɪd/ *vt* (*pt* -**bid**, *pres p* -**bidding**) ofrecer más que

outboard /ˈaʊtbɔːd/ *a* fuera borda

outbreak /ˈaʊtbreɪk/ *n* (*of anger*) arranque *m*; (*of war*) comienzo *m*; (*of disease*) epidemia *f*

outbuilding /ˈaʊtbɪldɪŋ/ *n* dependencia *f*

outburst /ˈaʊtbɜːst/ *n* explosión *f*

outcast /ˈaʊtkɑːst/ *n* paria *m & f*

outcome /ˈaʊtkʌm/ *n* resultado *m*

outcry /ˈaʊtkraɪ/ *n* protesta *f*

outdated /aʊtˈdeɪtɪd/ *a* anticuado

outdo /aʊtˈduː/ *vt* (*pt* -**did**, *pp* -**done**) superar

outdoor /ˈaʊtdɔː(r)/ *a* al aire libre. **~s** /-ˈdɔːz/ *adv* al aire libre

outer /ˈaʊtə(r)/ *a* exterior

outfit /ˈaʊtfɪt/ *n* equipo *m*; (*clothes*) traje *m*. **~ter** *n* camisero *m*

outgoing /ˈaʊtɡəʊɪŋ/ *a* ⟨*minister etc*⟩ saliente; (*sociable*) abierto. **~s** *npl* gastos *mpl*

outgrow /aʊtˈɡrəʊ/ *vt* (*pt* -**grew**, *pp* -**grown**) crecer más que ⟨*person*⟩; hacerse demasiado grande para ⟨*clothes*⟩. **he's ~n his trousers** le quedan pequeños los pantalones

outhouse /ˈaʊthaʊs/ *n* dependencia *f*

outing /ˈaʊtɪŋ/ *n* excursión *f*

outlandish /aʊtˈlændɪʃ/ *a* extravagante

outlaw /ˈaʊtlɔː/ *n* proscrito *m*. ● *vt* proscribir

outlay /ˈaʊtleɪ/ *n* gastos *mpl*

outlet /ˈaʊtlet/ *n* salida *f*

outline /ˈaʊtlaɪn/ *n* contorno *m*; (*summary*) resumen *m*. ● *vt* trazar; (*describe*) dar un resumen de

outlive /aʊtˈlɪv/ *vt* sobrevivir a

outlook /ˈaʊtlʊk/ *n* perspectiva *f*

outlying /'aʊtlaɪɪŋ/ *a* remoto

outmoded /aʊt'məʊdɪd/ *a* anticuado

outnumber /aʊt'nʌmbə(r)/ *vt* sobrepasar en número

outpatient /aʊt'peɪʃnt/ *n* paciente *m* externo

outpost /'aʊtpəʊst/ *n* avanzada *f*

output /'aʊtpʊt/ *n* producción *f*

outrage /'aʊtreɪdʒ/ *n* ultraje m. ● *vt* ultrajar. ~**ous** /aʊt'reɪdʒəs/ *a* escandaloso, atroz

outright /'aʊtraɪt/ *adv* completamente; (*at once*) inmediatamente; (*frankly*) francamente. ● *a* completo; (*refusal*) rotundo

outset /'aʊtset/ *n* principio *m*

outside /'aʊtsaɪd/ *a & n* exterior (*m*). /aʊt'saɪd/ *adv* fuera. ● *prep* fuera de. ~**r** /aʊt'saɪdə(r)/ *n* forastero *m*; (*in race*) caballo *m* no favorito

outsize /'aʊtsaɪz/ *a* de tamaño extraordinario

outskirts /'aʊtskɜːts/ *npl* afueras *fpl*

outspoken /aʊt'spəʊkn/ *a* franco. be ~ no tener pelos en la lengua

outstanding /aʊt'stændɪŋ/ *a* excepcional; (*not settled*) pendiente; (*conspicuous*) sobresaliente

outstretched /aʊt'stretʃt/ *a* extendido

outstrip /aʊt'strɪp/ *vt* (*pt* -stripped) superar

outward /'aʊtwəd/ *a* externo; (*journey*) de ida. ~**ly** *adv* por fuera, exteriormente. ~**s** /aʊtwədz/ *adv* hacia fuera

outweigh /aʊt'weɪ/ *vt* pesar más que; (*fig*) valer más que

outwit /aʊt'wɪt/ *vt* (*pt* -witted) ser más listo que

oval /'əʊvl/ *a* oval(ado). ● *n* óvalo *m*

ovary /'əʊvərɪ/ *n* ovario *m*

ovation /əʊ'veɪʃn/ *n* ovación *f*

oven /'ʌvn/ *n* horno *m*

over... /'əʊvə(r)/ *prep* por encima de; (*across*) al otro lado de; (*during*) durante; (*more than*) más de. ~ and above por encima de. ● *adv* por encima; (*ended*) terminado; (*more*) más; (*in excess*) de sobra. ~ again otra vez. ~ and ~ una y otra vez. ~ here por aquí. ~ there por allí. all ~ por todas partes

over... /'əʊvə(r)/ *pref* sobre..., super...

overall /'əʊvər'ɔːl/ *a* global; (*length, cost*) total. ● *adv* en conjunto. /'əʊvərɔːl/ *n*, ~**s** *npl* mono *m*

overawe /əʊvər'ɔː/ *vt* intimidar

overbalance /əʊvə'bæləns/ *vt* hacer perder el equilibrio. ● *vi* perder el equilibrio

overbearing /əʊvə'beərɪŋ/ *a* dominante

overboard /'əʊvəbɔːd/ *adv* al agua

overbook /əʊvə'bʊk/ *vt* aceptar demasiadas reservaciones para

overcast /əʊvə'kɑːst/ *a* nublado

overcharge /əʊvə'tʃɑːdʒ/ *vt* (*fill too much*) sobrecargar; (*charge too much*) cobrar demasiado

overcoat /'əʊvəkəʊt/ *n* abrigo *m*

overcome /əʊvə'kʌm/ *vt* (*pt* -came, *pp* -come) superar, vencer. be ~ by estar abrumado de

overcrowded /əʊvə'kraʊdɪd/ *a* atestado (de gente)

overdo /əʊvə'duː/ *vt* (*pt* -did, *pp* -done) exagerar; (*culin*) cocer demasiado

overdose /'əʊvədəʊs/ *n* sobredosis *f*

overdraft /'əʊvədrɑːft/ *n* giro *m* en descubierto

overdraw /əʊvə'drɔː/ *vt* (*pt* -drew, *pp* -drawn) girar en descubierto. be ~n tener un saldo deudor

overdue /əʊvə'djuː/ *a* retrasado; (*belated*) tardío; (*bill*) vencido y no pagado

overestimate /əʊvər'estɪmeɪt/ *vt* sobrestimar

overflow /əʊvə'fləʊ/ *vi* desbordarse. /'əʊvəfləʊ/ *n* (*excess*) exceso *m*; (*outlet*) rebosadero *m*

overgrown /əʊvə'grəʊn/ *a* demasiado grande; (*garden*) cubierto de hierbas

overhang /əʊvə'hæŋ/ *vt* (*pt* -hung) sobresalir por encima de; (*fig*) amenazar. ● *vi* sobresalir. /'əʊvəhæŋ/ *n* saliente *f*

overhaul /əʊvə'hɔːl/ *vt* revisar. /'əʊvəhɔːl/ *n* revisión *f*

overhead /əʊvə'hed/ *adv* por encima. /'əʊvəhed/ *a* de arriba. ~**s** *npl* gastos *mpl* generales

overhear /əʊvə'hɪə(r)/ *vt* (*pt* -heard) oír por casualidad

overjoyed /əʊvə'dʒɔɪd/ *a* muy contento. he was ~ rebosaba de alegría

overland /'əʊvəlænd/ *a* terrestre. ● *adv* por tierra

overlap /əʊvə'læp/ *vt* (*pt* -lapped) traslapar. ● *vi* traslaparse

overleaf /əʊvə'liːf/ *adv* a la vuelta. see ~ véase al dorso

overload /əʊvə'ləʊd/ vt sobrecargar

overlook /əʊvə'lok/ vt dominar; ⟨building⟩ dar a; ⟨forget⟩ olvidar; ⟨oversee⟩ inspeccionar; ⟨forgive⟩ perdonar

overnight /əʊvə'naɪt/ adv por la noche, durante la noche; ⟨fig, instantly⟩ de la noche a la mañana. **stay** ~ pasar la noche. ● a de noche

overpass /'əʊvəpɑːs/ n paso m a desnivel, paso m elevado

overpay /əʊvə'peɪ/ vt (pt **-paid**) pagar demasiado

overpower /əʊvə'paʊə(r)/ vt subyugar; dominar ⟨opponent⟩; ⟨fig⟩ abrumar. ~**ing** a abrumador

overpriced /əʊvə'praɪst/ a demasiado caro

overrate /əʊvə'reɪt/ vt supervalorar

overreach /əʊvə'riːtʃ/ vr. ~ **o.s.** extralimitarse

overreact /əʊvərɪ'ækt/ vi reaccionar excesivamente

overrid|e /əʊvə'raɪd/ vt (pt **-rode**, pp **-ridden**) pasar por encima de. ~**ing** a dominante

overripe /'əʊvəraɪp/ a pasado, demasiado maduro

overrule /əʊvə'ruːl/ vt anular; denegar ⟨claim⟩

overrun /əʊvə'rʌn/ vt (pt **-ran**, pp **-run**, pres p **-running**) invadir; exceder ⟨limit⟩

overseas /əʊvə'siːz/ a de ultramar. ● adv al extranjero, en ultramar

oversee /əʊvə'siː/ vt (pt **-saw**, pp **-seen**) vigilar. ~**r** /'əʊvəsɪə(r)/ n supervisor m

overshadow /əʊvə'ʃædəʊ/ vt ⟨darken⟩ sombrear; ⟨fig⟩ eclipsar

overshoot /əʊvə'ʃuːt/ vt (pt **-shot**) excederse. ~ **the mark** pasarse de la raya

oversight /'əʊvəsaɪt/ n descuido m

oversleep /əʊvə'sliːp/ vi (pt **-slept**) despertarse tarde. **I overslept** se me pegaron las sábanas

overstep /əʊvə'step/ vt (pt **-stepped**) pasar de. ~ **the mark** pasarse de la raya

overt /'əʊvɜːt/ a manifiesto

overtak|e /əʊvə'teɪk/ vt/i (pt **-took**, pp **-taken**) sobrepasar; ⟨auto⟩ adelantar. ~**ing** n adelantamiento m

overtax /əʊvə'tæks/ vt exigir demasiado

overthrow /əʊvə'θrəʊ/ vt (pt **-threw**, pp **-thrown**) derrocar. /'əʊvəθrəʊ/ n derrocamiento m

overtime /'əʊvətaɪm/ n horas fpl extra

overtone /'əʊvətəʊn/ n ⟨fig⟩ matiz m

overture /'əʊvətjʊə(r)/ n obertura f. ~**s** npl ⟨fig⟩ propuestas fpl

overturn /əʊvə'tɜːn/ vt/i volcar

overweight /əʊvə'weɪt/ a demasiado pesado. **be** ~ pesar demasiado, ser gordo

overwhelm /əʊvə'welm/ vt aplastar; ⟨with emotion⟩ abrumar. ~**ing** a aplastante; ⟨fig⟩ abrumador

overwork /əʊvə'wɜːk/ vt hacer trabajar demasiado. ● vi trabajar demasiado. ● n trabajo m excesivo

overwrought /əʊvə'rɔːt/ a agotado, muy nervioso

ovulation /ɒvjʊ'leɪʃn/ n ovulación f

ow|e /əʊ/ vt deber. ~**ing** a debido. ~**ing to** a causa de

owl /aʊl/ n lechuza f, búho m

own /əʊn/ a propio. **get one's** ~ **back** ⟨fam⟩ vengarse. **hold one's** ~ mantenerse firme, saber defenderse. **on one's** ~ por su cuenta. ● vt poseer, tener. ● vi. ~ **up (to)** ⟨fam⟩ confesar. ~**er** n propietario m, dueño m. ~**ership** n posesión f; ⟨right⟩ propiedad f

ox /ɒks/ n (pl **oxen**) buey m

oxide /'ɒksaɪd/ n óxido m

oxygen /'ɒksɪdʒən/ n oxígeno m

oyster /'ɔɪstə(r)/ n ostra f

P

p /piː/ abbr ⟨pence, penny⟩ penique(s) (m(pl))

pace /peɪs/ n paso m. ● vi. ~ **up and down** pasearse de aquí para allá. ~**maker** n ⟨runner⟩ el que marca el paso; ⟨med⟩ marcapasos m invar. **keep** ~ **with** andar al mismo paso que

Pacific /pə'sɪfɪk/ a pacífico. ● n. ~ **(Ocean)** ⟨Océano m⟩ Pacífico m

pacif|ist /'pæsɪfɪst/ n pacifista m & f. ~**y** /'pæsɪfaɪ/ vt apaciguar

pack /pæk/ n fardo m; ⟨of cards⟩ baraja f; ⟨of hounds⟩ jauría f; ⟨of wolves⟩ manada f; ⟨large amount⟩ montón m. ● vt empaquetar; hacer ⟨suitcase⟩; ⟨press down⟩ apretar. ● vi hacer la maleta. ~**age** /'pækɪdʒ/ n paquete m. ● vt empaquetar. ~**age deal** n acuerdo m global. ~**age tour** n viaje *m* organizado. ~ed lunch *n* almuerzo *m* frío. ~ed out (*fam*) de bote en bote. ~et /'pækɪt/ *n* paquete *m*. send ~ing echar a paseo

pact /pækt/ *n* pacto *m*, acuerdo *m*

pad /pæd/ *n* almohadilla *f*; (*for writing*) bloc *m*; (*for ink*) tampón *m*; (*flat, fam*) piso *m*. ● *vt* (*pt* padded) rellenar. ~ding *n* relleno *m*. ● *vi* andar a pasos quedos. launching ~ plataforma *f* de lanzamiento

paddle¹ /'pædl/ *n* canalete *m*

paddle² /'pædl/ *vi* mojarse los pies

paddle-steamer /'pædlstiːmə(r)/ *n* vapor *m* de ruedas

paddock /'pædək/ *n* recinto *m*; (*field*) prado *m*

paddy /'pædɪ/ *n* arroz *m* con cáscara. ~-field *n* arrozal *m*

padlock /'pædlɒk/ *n* candado *m*. ● *vt* cerrar con candado

paediatrician /piːdɪə'trɪʃn/ *n* pediatra *m* & *f*

pagan /'peɪgən/ *a* & *n* pagano (*m*)

page¹ /peɪdʒ/ *n* página *f*. ● *vt* paginar

page² /peɪdʒ/ (*in hotel*) botones *m invar*. ● *vt* llamar

pageant /'pædʒənt/ *n* espectáculo *m* (histórico). ~ry *n* boato *m*

pagoda /pə'gəʊdə/ *n* pagoda *f*

paid /peɪd/ *see* pay. ● *a*. put ~ to (*fam*) acabar con

pail /peɪl/ *n* cubo *m*

pain /peɪn/ *n* dolor *m*. ~ in the neck (*fam*) ⟨*persona*⟩ pesado *m*; ⟨*thing*⟩ lata *f*. be in ~ tener dolores. ~s *npl* (*effort*) esfuerzos *mpl*. be at ~s esmerarse. ● *vt* doler. ~ful /'peɪnfl/ *a* doloroso; (*laborious*) penoso. ~-killer *n* calmante *m*. ~less *a* indoloro. ~staking /'peɪnzteɪkɪŋ/ *a* esmerado

paint /peɪnt/ *n* pintura *f*. ● *vt/i* pintar. ~er *n* pintor *m*. ~ing *n* pintura *f*

pair /peə(r)/ *n* par *m*; (*of people*) pareja *f*. ~ of trousers pantalón *m*, pantalones *mpl*. ● *vi* emparejarse. ~ off emparejarse

pajamas /pə'dʒɑːməz/ *npl* pijama *m*

Pakistan /pɑːkɪ'stɑːn/ *n* el Pakistán *m*. ~i *a* & *n* paquistaní (*m* & *f*)

pal /pæl/ *n* (*fam*) amigo *m*

palace /'pælɪs/ *n* palacio *m*

palatable /'pælətəbl/ *a* sabroso; (*fig*) aceptable. ~e /'pælət/ *n* paladar *m*

palatial /pə'leɪʃl/ *a* suntuoso

palaver /pə'lɑːvə(r)/ *n* (*fam*) lío *m*

pale¹ /peɪl/ *a* (-er, -est) pálido; ⟨*colour*⟩ claro. ● *vi* palidecer

pale² /peɪl/ *n* estaca *f*

paleness /'peɪlnɪs/ *n* palidez *f*

Palestine /'pælɪstaɪn/ *n* Palestina *f*. ~ian /-'stɪnɪən/ *a* & *n* palestino (*m*)

palette /'pælɪt/ *n* paleta *f*. ~-knife *n* espátula *f*

pall¹ /pɔːl/ *n* paño *m* mortuorio; (*fig*) capa *f*

pall² /pɔːl/ *vi*. ~ (on) perder su sabor (para)

pallid /'pælɪd/ *a* pálido

palm /pɑːm/ *n* palma *f*. ● *vt*. ~ off encajar (on a). ~ist /'pɑːmɪst/ *n* quiromántico *m*. P~ Sunday *n* Domingo *m* de Ramos

palpable /'pælpəbl/ *a* palpable

palpitate /'pælpɪteɪt/ *vi* palpitar. ~ion /-'teɪʃn/ *n* palpitación *f*

paltry /'pɔːltrɪ/ *a* (-ier, -iest) insignificante

pamper /'pæmpə(r)/ *vt* mimar

pamphlet /'pæmflɪt/ *n* folleto *m*

pan /pæn/ *n* cacerola *f*; (*for frying*) sartén *f*; (*of scales*) platillo *m*; (*of lavatory*) taza *f*

panacea /pænə'sɪə/ *n* panacea *f*

panache /pə'næʃ/ *n* brío *m*

pancake /'pænkeɪk/ *n* hojuela *f*, crêpe *f*

panda /'pændə/ *n* panda *m*. ~ car *n* coche *m* de la policía

pandemonium /pændɪ'məʊnɪəm/ *n* pandemonio *m*

pander /'pændə(r)/ *vi*. ~ to complacer

pane /peɪn/ *n* (*of glass*) vidrio *m*

panel /'pænl/ *n* panel *m*; (*group of people*) jurado *m*. ~ling *n* paneles *mpl*

pang /pæŋ/ *n* punzada *f*

panic /'pænɪk/ *n* pánico *m*. ● *vi* (*pt* panicked) ser preso de pánico. ~-stricken *a* preso de pánico

panorama /pænə'rɑːmə/ *n* panorama *m*. ~ic /-'ræmɪk/ *a* panorámico

pansy /'pænzɪ/ *n* pensamiento *m*; (*effeminate man, fam*) maricón *m*

pant /pænt/ *vi* jadear

pantechnicon /pæn'teknɪkən/ *n* camión *m* de mudanzas

panther /'pænθə(r)/ *n* pantera *f*

panties /'pæntɪz/ *npl* bragas *fpl*

pantomime /'pæntəmaɪm/ *n* pantomima *f*

pantry /'pæntri/ n despensa f

pants /pænts/ npl (man's underwear, fam) calzoncillos mpl; (woman's underwear, fam) bragas fpl; (trousers, fam) pantalones mpl

papa|cy /'peɪpəsɪ/ n papado m. ∼l a papal

paper /'peɪpə(r)/ n papel m; (newspaper) periódico m; (exam) examen m; (document) documento m. **on** ∼ en teoría. ● vt empapelar, tapizar (LAm). ∼**back** /'peɪpəbæk/ a en rústica. ● n libro m en rústica. ∼**clip** n sujetapapeles m invar, clip m. ∼**weight** /'peɪpəweɪt/ n pisapapeles m invar. ∼**work** n papeleo m, trabajo m de oficina

papier mâché /'pæpɪeɪ'mæʃeɪ/ n cartón m piedra

par /pɑ:(r)/ n par f; (golf) par m. **feel below** ∼ no estar en forma. **on a** ∼ **with** a la par con

parable /'pærəbl/ n parábola f

parachut|e /'pærəʃu:t/ n paracaídas m invar. ● vi lanzarse en paracaídas. ∼**ist** n paracaidista m & f

parade /pə'reɪd/ n desfile m; (street) paseo m; (display) alarde m. ● vi desfilar. ● vt hacer alarde de

paradise /'pærədaɪs/ n paraíso m

paradox /'pærədɒks/ n paradoja f. ∼**ical** /-'dɒksɪkl/ a paradójico

paraffin /'pærəfɪn/ n queroseno m

paragon /'pærəgən/ n dechado m

paragraph /'pærəgrɑ:f/ n párrafo m

parallel /'pærəlel/ a paralelo. ● n paralelo m; (line) paralela f. ● vt ser paralelo a

paraly|se /'pærəlaɪz/ vt paralizar. ∼**sis** /pə'ræləsɪs/ n (pl -ses /-si:z/) parálisis f. ∼**tic** /pærə'lɪtɪk/ a & n paralítico (m)

parameter /pə'ræmɪtə(r)/ n parámetro m

paramount /'pærəmaʊnt/ a supremo

paranoia /pærə'nɔɪə/ n paranoia f

parapet /'pærəpɪt/ n parapeto m

paraphernalia /pærəfə'neɪlɪə/ n trastos mpl

paraphrase /'pærəfreɪz/ n paráfrasis f. ● vt parafrasear

paraplegic /pærə'pli:dʒɪk/ n parapléjico m

parasite /'pærəsaɪt/ n parásito m

parasol /'pærəsɒl/ n sombrilla f

paratrooper /'pærətru:pə(r)/ n paracaidista m

parcel /'pɑ:sl/ n paquete m

parch /pɑ:tʃ/ vt resecar. **be** ∼**ed** tener mucha sed

parchment /'pɑ:tʃmənt/ n pergamino m

pardon /'pɑ:dn/ n perdón m; (jurid) indulto m. **I beg your** ∼! ¡perdone Vd! **I beg your** ∼? ¿cómo?, ¿mande? (Mex). ● vt perdonar

pare /peə(r)/ vt cortar ⟨nails⟩; (peel) pelar, mondar

parent /'peərənt/ n (father) padre m; (mother) madre f; (source) origen m. ∼**s** npl padres mpl. ∼**al** /pə'rentl/ a de los padres

parenthesis /pə'renθəsɪs/ n (pl -theses /-si:z/) paréntesis m invar

parenthood /'peərənthʊd/ n paternidad f, maternidad f

Paris /'pærɪs/ n París m

parish /'pærɪʃ/ n parroquia f; (municipal) municipio m. ∼**ioner** /pə'rɪʃənə(r)/ n feligrés m

Parisian /pə'rɪzɪən/ a & n parisino (m)

parity /'pærətɪ/ n igualdad f

park /pɑ:k/ n parque m. ● vt/i aparcar. ∼ **oneself** vr (fam) instalarse

parka /'pɑ:kə/ n anorak m

parking-meter /'pɑ:kɪŋmi:tə(r)/ n parquímetro m

parliament /'pɑ:ləmənt/ n parlamento m. ∼**ary** /-'mentrɪ/ a parlamentario

parlour /'pɑ:lə(r)/ n salón m

parochial /pə'rəʊkɪəl/ a parroquial; (fig) pueblerino

parody /'pærədɪ/ n parodia f. ● vt parodiar

parole /pə'rəʊl/ n libertad f bajo palabra, libertad f provisional. **on** ∼ libre bajo palabra. ● vt liberar bajo palabra

paroxysm /'pærəksɪzəm/ n paroxismo m

parquet /'pɑ:keɪ/ n. ∼ **floor** parqué m

parrot /'pærət/ n papagayo m

parry /'pærɪ/ vt parar; (avoid) esquivar. ● n parada f

parsimonious /pɑ:sɪ'məʊnɪəs/ a parsimonioso

parsley /'pɑ:slɪ/ n perejil m

parsnip /'pɑ:snɪp/ n pastinaca f

parson /'pɑ:sn/ n cura m, párroco m

part /pɑ:t/ n parte f; (of machine) pieza f; (of serial) entrega f; (in play) papel m; (side in dispute) partido m.

on the ~ of por parte de. ● *adv* en parte. ~ **with** *vt* separarse de. ● *vi* separarse

partake /paːˈteɪk/ *vt* (*pt* **-took**, *pp* **-taken**) participar. ~ **of** compartir

partial /ˈpaːʃl/ *a* parcial. **be ~ to** ser aficionado a. ~**ity** /-ɪˈælətɪ/ *n* parcialidad *f*. ~**ly** *adv* parcialmente

participa|nt /paːˈtɪsɪpənt/ *n* participante *m & f*. ~**te** /paːˈtɪsɪpeɪt/ *vi* participar. ~**tion** /-ˈpeɪʃn/ *n* participación *f*

participle /ˈpaːtɪsɪpl/ *n* participio *m*

particle /ˈpaːtɪkl/ *n* partícula *f*

particular /pəˈtɪkjʊlə(r)/ *a* particular; (*precise*) meticuloso; (*fastidious*) quisquilloso. ● *n*. **in ~** especialmente. ~**ly** *adv* especialmente. ~*s npl* detalles *mpl*

parting /ˈpaːtɪŋ/ *n* separación *f*; (*in hair*) raya *f*. ● *a* de despedida

partisan /paːtɪˈzæn/ *n* partidario *m*

partition /paːˈtɪʃn/ *n* partición *f*; (*wall*) tabique *m*. ● *vt* dividir

partly /ˈpaːtlɪ/ *adv* en parte

partner /ˈpaːtnə(r)/ *n* socio *m*; (*sport*) pareja *f*. ~**ship** *n* asociación *f*; (*com*) sociedad *f*

partridge /ˈpaːtrɪdʒ/ *n* perdiz *f*

part-time /paːtˈtaɪm/ *a & adv* a tiempo parcial

party /ˈpaːtɪ/ *n* reunión *f*, fiesta *f*; (*group*) grupo *m*; (*pol*) partido *m*; (*jurid*) parte *f*. ~ **line** *n* (*telephone*) línea *f* colectiva

pass /paːs/ *vt* pasar; (*in front of*) pasar por delante de; (*overtake*) adelantar; (*approve*) aprobar ⟨*exam, bill, law*⟩; hacer ⟨*remark*⟩; pronunciar ⟨*judgement*⟩. ~ **down** transmitir. ~ **over** pasar por alto de. ~ **round** distribuir. ~ **through** pasar por; (*cross*) atravesar. ~ **up** (*fam*) dejar pasar. ● *vi* pasar; (*in exam*) aprobar. ~ **away** morir. ~ **out** (*fam*) desmayarse. ● *n* (*permit*) permiso *m*; (*in mountains*) puerto *m*, desfiladero *m*; (*sport*) pase *m*; (*in exam*) aprobado *m*. **make a ~ at** (*fam*) hacer proposiciones amorosas a. ~**able** /ˈpaːsəbl/ *a* pasable; ⟨*road*⟩ transitable

passage /ˈpæsɪdʒ/ *n* paso *m*; (*voyage*) travesía *f*; (*corridor*) pasillo *m*; (*in book*) pasaje *m*

passenger /ˈpæsɪndʒə(r)/ *n* pasajero *m*

passer-by /paːsəˈbaɪ/ *n* (*pl* **passers-by**) transeúnte *m & f*

passion /ˈpæʃn/ *n* pasión *f*. ~**ate** *a* apasionado. ~**ately** *adv* apasionadamente

passive /ˈpæsɪv/ *a* pasivo. ~**ness** *n* pasividad *f*

passmark /ˈpaːsmaːk/ *n* aprobado *m*

Passover /ˈpaːsəʊvə(r)/ *n* Pascua *f* de los hebreos

passport /ˈpaːspɔːt/ *n* pasaporte *m*

password /ˈpaːswɜːd/ *n* contraseña *f*

past /paːst/ *a & n* pasado (*m*). **in times ~** en tiempos pasados. **the ~ week** *n* la semana *f* pasada. ● *prep* por delante de; (*beyond*) más allá de. ● *adv* por delante. **drive ~** pasar en coche. **go ~** pasar

paste /peɪst/ *n* pasta *f*; (*adhesive*) engrudo *m*. ● *vt* (*fasten*) pegar; (*cover*) engrudar. ~**board** /ˈpeɪstbɔːd/ *n* cartón *m*. ~ **jewellery** *n* joyas *fpl* de imitación

pastel /ˈpæstl/ *a & n* pastel (*m*)

pasteurize /ˈpæstʃəraɪz/ *vt* pasteurizar

pastiche /pæˈstiːʃ/ *n* pastiche *m*

pastille /ˈpæstl/ *n* pastilla *f*

pastime /ˈpaːstaɪm/ *n* pasatiempo *m*

pastoral /ˈpaːstərəl/ *a* pastoral

pastr|ies *npl* pasteles *mpl*, pastas *fpl*. ~**y** /ˈpeɪstrɪ/ *n* pasta *f*

pasture /ˈpaːstʃə(r)/ *n* pasto *m*

pasty[1] /ˈpæstɪ/ *n* empanada *f*

pasty[2] /ˈpeɪstɪ/ *a* pastoso; (*pale*) pálido

pat[1] /pæt/ *vt* (*pt* **patted**) dar palmaditas en; acariciar ⟨*dog etc*⟩. ● *n* palmadita *f*; (*of butter*) porción *f*

pat[2] /pæt/ *adv* en el momento oportuno

patch /pætʃ/ *n* pedazo *m*; (*period*) período *m*; (*repair*) remiendo *m*; (*piece of ground*) terreno *m*. **not a ~ on** (*fam*) muy inferior a. ● *vt* remendar. ~ **up** arreglar. ~**work** *n* labor *m* de retazos; (*fig*) mosaico *m*. ~**y** *a* desigual

pâté /ˈpæteɪ/ *n* pasta *f*, paté *m*

patent /ˈpeɪtnt/ *a* patente. ● *n* patente *f*. ● *vt* patentar. ~ **leather** *n* charol *m*. ~**ly** *adv* evidentemente

patern|al /pəˈtɜːnl/ *a* paterno. ~**ity** /pəˈtɜːnətɪ/ *n* paternidad *f*

path /paːθ/ *n* (*pl* **-s** /paːðz/) sendero *m*; (*sport*) pista *f*; (*of rocket*) trayectoria *f*; (*fig*) camino *m*

pathetic /pə'θetɪk/ a patético, lastimoso

pathology /pə'θɒlədʒɪ/ n patología f

pathos /'peɪθɒs/ n patetismo m

patien|ce /'peɪʃns/ n paciencia f. ~t /'peɪʃnt/ a & n paciente (m & f). ~tly adv con paciencia

patio /'pætɪəʊ/ n (pl -os) patio m

patriarch /'peɪtrɪɑːk/ n patriarca m

patrician /pə'trɪʃn/ a & n patricio (m)

patriot /'pætrɪət/ n patriota m & f. ~ic /-'ɒtɪk/ a patriótico. ~ism n patriotismo m

patrol /pə'trəʊl/ n patrulla f. ● vt/i patrullar

patron /'peɪtrən/ n (of the arts etc) mecenas m & f; (customer) cliente m & f; (of charity) patrocinador m. ~age /'pætrənɪdʒ/ n patrocinio m; (of shop etc) clientela f. ~ize vt ser cliente de; (fig) tratar con condescendencia

patter¹ /'pætə(r)/ n (of steps) golpeteo m; (of rain) tamborileo m. ● vi correr con pasos ligeros; ⟨rain⟩ tamborilear

patter² /'pætə(r)/ (speech) jerga f; (chatter) parloteo m

pattern /'pætn/ n diseño m; (model) modelo m; (sample) muestra f; (manner) modo m; (in dressmaking) patrón m

paunch /pɔːntʃ/ n panza f

pauper /'pɔːpə(r)/ n indigente m & f, pobre m & f

pause /pɔːz/ n pausa f. ● vi hacer una pausa

pave /peɪv/ vt pavimentar. ~ the way for preparar el terreno para

pavement /'peɪvmənt/ n pavimento m; (at side of road) acera f

pavilion /pə'vɪlɪən/ n pabellón m

paving-stone /'peɪvɪŋstəʊn/ n losa f

paw /pɔː/ n pata f; (of cat) garra f. ● vi tocar con la pata; ⟨person⟩ manosear

pawn¹ /pɔːn/ n (chess) peón m; (fig) instrumento m

pawn² /pɔːn/ vt empeñar. ● n. in ~ en prenda. ~broker /'pɔːnbrəʊkə(r)/ n prestamista m & f. ~shop n monte m de piedad

pawpaw /'pɔːpɔː/ n papaya f

pay /peɪ/ vt (pt paid) pagar; prestar ⟨attention⟩; hacer ⟨compliment, visit⟩. ~ back devolver. ~ cash pagar al contado. ~ in ingresar. ~ off pagar. ~ out pagar. ● vi pagar; (be profitable) rendir. ● n paga f. in the ~

of al servicio de. ~able /'peɪəbl/ a pagadero. ~ment /'peɪmənt/ n pago m. ~-off n (sl) liquidación f; (fig) ajuste m de cuentas. ~roll /'peɪrəʊl/ n nómina f. ~ up pagar

pea /piː/ n guisante m

peace /piːs/ n paz f. ~ of mind tranquilidad f. ~able a pacífico. ~ful /'piːsfl/ a tranquilo. ~maker /'piːsmeɪkə(r)/ n pacificador m

peach /piːtʃ/ n melocotón m, durazno m (LAm); (tree) melocotonero m, duraznero m (LAm)

peacock /'piːkɒk/ n pavo m real

peak /piːk/ n cumbre f; (maximum) máximo m. ~ hours npl horas fpl punta. ~ed cap n gorra f de visera

peaky /'piːkɪ/ a pálido

peal /piːl/ n repique m. ~s of laughter risotadas fpl

peanut /'piːnʌt/ n cacahuete m, maní m (Mex). ~s (sl) una bagatela f

pear /peə(r)/ n pera f; (tree) peral m

pearl /pɜːl/ n perla f. ~y a nacarado

peasant /'peznt/ n campesino m

peat /piːt/ n turba f

pebble /'pebl/ n guijarro m

peck /pek/ vt picotear; (kiss, fam) dar un besito a. ● n picotazo m; (kiss) besito m. ~ish /'pekɪʃ/ a. be ~ish (fam) tener hambre, tener gazuza (fam)

peculiar /pɪ'kjuːlɪə(r)/ a raro; (special) especial. ~ity /-'ærətɪ/ n rareza f; (feature) particularidad f

pedal /'pedl/ n pedal m. ● vi pedalear

pedantic /pɪ'dæntɪk/ a pedante

peddle /'pedl/ vt vender por las calles

pedestal /'pedɪstl/ n pedestal m

pedestrian /pɪ'destrɪən/ n peatón m. ● a de peatones; (dull) prosaico. ~ crossing n paso m de peatones

pedigree /'pedɪɡriː/ n linaje m; (of animal) pedigrí m. ● a ⟨animal⟩ de raza

pedlar /'pedlə(r)/ n buhonero m, vendedor m ambulante

peek /piːk/ vi mirar a hurtadillas

peel /piːl/ n cáscara f. ● vt pelar ⟨fruit, vegetables⟩. ● vi pelarse. ~ings npl peladuras fpl, monda f

peep¹ /piːp/ vi mirar a hurtadillas. ● n mirada f furtiva

peep² /piːp/ ⟨bird⟩ piar. ● n pío m

peep-hole /'piːphəʊl/ n mirilla f

peer¹ /pɪə(r)/ vi mirar. ~ at escudriñar

peer² /pɪə(r)/ n par m, compañero m. ∼**age** n pares mpl

peev|ed /pi:vd/ a (sl) irritado. ∼**ish** /'pi:vɪʃ/ a picajoso

peg /peg/ n clavija f; (for washing) pinza f; (hook) gancho m; (for tent) estaca f. **off the** ∼ de percha. ● vt (pt **pegged**) fijar (precios). ∼ **away at** afanarse por

pejorative /prɪ'dʒɒrətɪv/ a peyorativo, despectivo

pelican /'pelɪkən/ n pelícano m. ∼ **crossing** n paso m de peatones (con semáforo)

pellet /'pelɪt/ n pelotilla f; (for gun) perdigón m

pelt¹ /pelt/ n pellejo m

pelt² /pelt/ vt tirar. ● vi llover a cántaros

pelvis /'pelvɪs/ n pelvis f

pen¹ /pen/ n (enclosure) recinto m

pen² /pen/ (for writing) pluma f, estilográfica f; (ball-point) bolígrafo m

penal /'pi:nl/ a penal. ∼**ize** vt castigar. ∼**ty** /'penltɪ/ n castigo m; (fine) multa f. ∼**ty kick** n (football) penalty m

penance /'penəns/ n penitencia f

pence /pens/ see **penny**

pencil /'pensl/ n lápiz m. ● vt (pt pencilled) escribir con lápiz. ∼**sharpener** n sacapuntas m invar

pendant /'pendənt/ n dije m, medallón m

pending /'pendɪŋ/ a pendiente. ● prep hasta

pendulum /'pendjʊləm/ n péndulo m

penetrat|e /'penɪtreɪt/ vt/i penetrar. ∼**ing** a penetrante. ∼**ion** /-'treɪʃn/ n penetración f

penguin /'peŋgwɪn/ n pingüino m

penicillin /penɪ'sɪlɪn/ n penicilina f

peninsula /pə'nɪnsjʊlə/ n península f

penis /'pi:nɪs/ n pene m

peniten|ce /'penɪtəns/ n penitencia f. ∼**t** /'penɪtənt/ a & n penitente (m & f). ∼**tiary** /penɪ'tenʃərɪ/ n (Amer) cárcel m

pen: ∼**knife** /'pennaɪf/ n (pl penknives) navaja f; (small) cortaplumas m invar. ∼**name** n seudónimo m

pennant /'penənt/ n banderín m

penn|iless /'penɪlɪs/ a sin un céntimo. ∼**y** /'penɪ/ n (pl pennies or pence) penique m

pension /'penʃn/ n pensión f; (for retirement) jubilación f. ● vt pensionar. ∼**able** a con derecho a pensión; (age) de la jubilación. ∼**er** n jubilado m. ∼ **off** jubilar

pensive /'pensɪv/ a pensativo

pent-up /pent'ʌp/ a reprimido; (confined) encerrado

pentagon /'pentəgən/ n pentágono m

Pentecost /'pentɪkɒst/ n Pentecostés m

penthouse /'penthaʊs/ n ático m

penultimate /pen'ʌltɪmət/ a penúltimo

penury /'penjʊərɪ/ n penuria f

peony /'pi:ənɪ/ n peonía f

people /'pi:pl/ npl gente f; (citizens) pueblo m. ∼ **say** se dice. **English** ∼ los ingleses mpl. **my** ∼ (fam) mi familia f. ● vt poblar

pep /pep/ n vigor m. ● vt. ∼ **up** animar

pepper /'pepə(r)/ n pimienta f; (vegetable) pimiento m. ● vt sazonar con pimienta. ∼**y** a picante. ∼**corn** /'pepəkɔːn/ n grano m de pimienta. ∼**corn rent** n alquiler m nominal

peppermint /'pepəmɪnt/ n menta f; (sweet) pastilla f de menta

pep talk /'peptɔːk/ n palabras fpl animadoras

per /pɜ:(r)/ prep por. ∼ **annum** al año. ∼ **cent** por ciento. ∼ **head** por cabeza, por persona. **ten miles** ∼ **hour** diez millas por hora

perceive /pə'si:v/ vt percibir; (notice) darse cuenta de

percentage /pə'sentɪdʒ/ n porcentaje m

percepti|ble /pə'septəbl/ a perceptible. ∼**on** /pə'sepʃn/ n percepción f. ∼**ve** a perspicaz

perch¹ /pɜ:tʃ/ n (of bird) percha f. ● vi posarse

perch² /pɜ:tʃ/ (fish) perca f

percolat|e /'pɜ:kəleɪt/ vt filtrar. ● vi filtrarse. ∼**or** n cafetera f

percussion /pə'kʌʃn/ n percusión f

peremptory /pə'remptərɪ/ a perentorio

perennial /pə'renɪəl/ a & n perenne (m)

perfect /'pɜ:fɪkt/ a perfecto. /pə'fekt/ vt perfeccionar. ∼**ion** /pə'fekʃn/ n perfección f. **to** ∼**ion** a la perfección. ∼**ionist** n perfeccionista m & f. ∼**ly** /'pɜ:fɪktlɪ/ adv perfectamente

perforat|e /'pɜːfəreɪt/ vt perforar. ~ion /-'reɪʃn/ n perforación f

perform /pə'fɔːm/ vt hacer, realizar; representar ⟨play⟩; desempeñar ⟨role⟩; (mus) interpretar. ~ an operation (med) operar. ~ance n ejecución f; (of play) representación f; (of car) rendimiento m; (fuss, fam) jaleo m. ~er n artista m & f

perfume /'pɜːfjuːm/ n perfume m

perfunctory /pə'fʌŋktəri/ a superficial

perhaps /pə'hæps/ adv quizá(s), tal vez

peril /'perəl/ n peligro m. ~ous a arriesgado, peligroso

perimeter /pə'rɪmɪtə(r)/ n perímetro m

period /'pɪərɪəd/ n período m; (lesson) clase f; (gram) punto m. ● a de (la) época. ~ic /-'ɒdɪk/ a periódico. ~ical /pɪərɪ'ɒdɪkl/ n revista f. ~ically /-'ɒdɪklɪ/ adv periódico

peripher|al /pə'rɪfərəl/ a periférico. ~y /pə'rɪfərɪ/ n periferia f

periscope /'perɪskəʊp/ n periscopio m

perish /'perɪʃ/ vi perecer; (rot) estropearse. ~able a perecedero. ~ing a (fam) glacial

perjur|e /'pɜːdʒə(r)/ vr. ~e o.s. perjurarse. ~y n perjurio m

perk[1] /pɜːk/ n gaje m

perk[2] /pɜːk/ vt/i. ~ up vt reanimar. ● vi reanimarse. ~y a alegre

perm /pɜːm/ n permanente f. ● vt hacer una permanente a

permanen|ce /'pɜːmənəns/ n permanencia f. ~t /'pɜːmənənt/ a permanente. ~tly adv permanentemente

permea|ble /'pɜːmɪəbl/ a permeable. ~te /'pɜːmɪeɪt/ vt penetrar; (soak) empapar

permissible /pə'mɪsəbl/ a permisible

permission /pə'mɪʃn/ n permiso m

permissive /pə'mɪsɪv/ a indulgente. ~ness n tolerancia f. ~ society n sociedad f permisiva

permit /pə'mɪt/ vt (pt permitted) permitir. /'pɜːmɪt/ n permiso m

permutation /pɜːmjuː'teɪʃn/ n permutación f

pernicious /pə'nɪʃəs/ a pernicioso

peroxide /pə'rɒksaɪd/ n peróxido m

perpendicular /pɜːpən'dɪkjʊlə(r)/ a & n perpendicular (f)

perpetrat|e /'pɜːpɪtreɪt/ vt cometer. ~or n autor m

perpetua|l /pə'petʃʊəl/ a perpetuo. ~te /pə'petʃʊeɪt/ vt perpetuar. ~tion /-'eɪʃn/ n perpetuación f

perplex /pə'pleks/ vt dejar perplejo. ~ed a perplejo. ~ing a desconcertante. ~ity n perplejidad f

persecut|e /'pɜːsɪkjuːt/ vt perseguir. ~ion /-'kjuːʃn/ n persecución f

persever|ance /pɜːsɪ'vɪərəns/ n perseverancia f. ~e /pɜːsɪ'vɪə(r)/ vi perseverar, persistir

Persian /'pɜːʃn/ a persa. the ~ Gulf n el golfo m Pérsico. ● n persa (m & f); (lang) persa m

persist /pə'sɪst/ vi persistir. ~ence n persistencia f. ~ent a persistente; (continual) continuo. ~ently adv persistentemente

person /'pɜːsn/ n persona f

personal /'pɜːsənl/ a personal

personality /pɜːsə'nælətɪ/ n personalidad f; (on TV) personaje m

personally /'pɜːsənəlɪ/ adv personalmente; (in person) en persona

personify /pə'sɒnɪfaɪ/ vt personificar

personnel /pɜːsə'nel/ n personal m

perspective /pə'spektɪv/ n perspectiva f

perspicacious /pɜːspɪ'keɪʃəs/ a perspicaz

perspir|ation /pɜːspə'reɪʃn/ n sudor m. ~e /pəs'paɪə(r)/ vi sudar

persua|de /pə'sweɪd/ vt persuadir. ~sion n persuasión f. ~sive /pə'sweɪsɪv/ a persuasivo. ~sively adv de manera persuasiva

pert /pɜːt/ a (saucy) impertinente; (lively) animado

pertain /pə'teɪn/ vi. ~ to relacionarse con

pertinent /'pɜːtɪnənt/ a pertinente. ~ly adv pertinentemente

pertly /'pɜːtlɪ/ adv impertinentemente

perturb /pə'tɜːb/ vt perturbar

Peru /pə'ruː/ n el Perú m

perus|al /pə'ruːzl/ n lectura f cuidadosa. ~e /pə'ruːz/ vt leer cuidadosamente

Peruvian /pə'ruːvɪən/ a & n peruano (m)

perva|de /pə'veɪd/ vt difundirse por. ~sive a penetrante

perver|se /pə'vɜːs/ a (stubborn) terco; (wicked) perverso. ~sity n terquedad f; (wickedness) perversidad f.

~sion n perversión f. **~t** /pə'vз:t/ vt pervertir. /'pз:vз:t/ n pervertido m

pessimis|m /'pesɪmɪzəm/ n pesimismo m. **~t** /'pesɪmɪst/ n pesimista m &f. **~tic** /-'mɪstɪk/ a pesimista

pest /pest/ n insecto m nocivo, plaga f; (person) pelma m; (thing) lata f

pester /'pestə(r)/ vt importunar

pesticide /'pestɪsaɪd/ n pesticida f

pet /pet/ n animal m doméstico; (favourite) favorito m. ● a preferido. ● vt (pt petted) acariciar

petal /'petl/ n pétalo m

peter /'pi:tə(r)/ vi. **~ out** (supplies) agotarse; (disappear) desaparecer

petite /pə'ti:t/ a (of woman) chiquita

petition /pɪ'tɪʃn/ n petición f. ● vt dirigir una petición a

pet name /'petneɪm/ n apodo m cariñoso

petrify /'petrɪfaɪ/ vt petrificar. ● vi petrificarse

petrol /'petrəl/ n gasolina f. **~eum** /pɪ'trəʊlɪəm/ n petróleo m. **~ gauge** n indicador m de nivel de gasolina. **~ pump** n (in car) bomba f de gasolina; (at garage) surtidor m de gasolina. **~ station** n gasolinera f. **~ tank** n depósito m de gasolina

petticoat /'petɪkəʊt/ n enaguas fpl

pett|iness /'petɪnɪs/ n mezquindad f. **~y** /'petɪ/ a (-ier, -iest) insignificante; (mean) mezquino. **~y cash** n dinero m para gastos menores. **~y officer** n suboficial m de marina

petulan|ce /'petjʊləns/ n irritabilidad f. **~t** /'petjʊlənt/ a irritable

pew /pju:/ n banco m (de iglesia)

pewter /'pju:tə(r)/ n peltre m

phallic /'fælɪk/ a fálico

phantom /'fæntəm/ n fantasma m

pharmaceutical /fɑ:mə'sju:tɪkl/ a farmacéutico

pharmac|ist /'fɑ:məsɪst/ n farmacéutico m. **~y** /'fɑ:məsɪ/ n farmacia f

pharyngitis /færɪn'dʒaɪtɪs/ n faringitis f

phase /feɪz/ n etapa f. ● vt. **~ in** introducir progresivamente. **~ out** retirar progresivamente

PhD abbr (Doctor of Philosophy) n Doctor m en Filosofía

pheasant /'feznt/ n faisán m

phenomenal /fɪ'nɒmɪnl/ a fenomenal

phenomenon /fɪ'nɒmɪnən/ n (pl -ena) fenómeno m

phew /fju:/ int ¡uy!

phial /'faɪəl/ n frasco m

philanderer /fɪ'lændərə(r)/ n mariposón m

philanthrop|ic /fɪlən'θrɒpɪk/ a filantrópico. **~ist** /fɪ'lænθrəpɪst/ n filántropo m

philatel|ist /fɪ'lætəlɪst/ n filatelista m &f. **~y** /fɪ'lætəlɪ/ n filatelia f

philharmonic /fɪlhɑ:'mɒnɪk/ a filarmónico

Philippines /'fɪlɪpi:nz/ npl Filipinas fpl

philistine /'fɪlɪstaɪn/ a & n filisteo (m)

philosoph|er /fɪ'lɒsəfə(r)/ n filósofo m. **~ical** /-ə'sɒfɪkl/ a filosófico. **~y** /fɪ'lɒsəfɪ/ n filosofía f

phlegm /flem/ n flema f. **~atic** /fleg'mætɪk/ a flemático

phobia /'fəʊbɪə/ n fobia f

phone /fəʊn/ n (fam) teléfono m. ● vt/i llamar por teléfono. **~ back** (caller) volver a llamar; (person called) llamar. **~ box** n cabina f telefónica

phonetic /fə'netɪk/ a fonético. **~s** n fonética f

phoney /'fəʊnɪ/ a (-ier, -iest) (sl) falso. ● n (sl) farsante m &f

phosphate /'fɒsfeɪt/ n fosfato m

phosphorus /'fɒsfərəs/ n fósforo m

photo /'fəʊtəʊ/ n (pl -os) (fam) fotografía f, foto f (fam)

photocopy /'fəʊtəʊkɒpɪ/ n fotocopia f. ● vt fotocopiar

photogenic /fəʊtəʊ'dʒenɪk/ a fotogénico

photograph /'fəʊtəgrɑ:f/ n fotografía f. ● vt hacer una fotografía de, sacar fotos de. **~er** /fə'tɒgrəfə(r)/ n fotógrafo m. **~ic** /-'græfɪk/ a fotográfico. **~y** /fə'tɒgrəfɪ/ n fotografía f

phrase /freɪz/ n frase f, locución f, expresión f. ● vt expresar. **~-book** n libro m de frases

physical /'fɪzɪkl/ a físico

physician /fɪ'zɪʃn/ n médico m

physic|ist /'fɪzɪsɪst/ n físico m. **~s** /'fɪzɪks/ n física f

physiology /fɪzɪ'ɒlədʒɪ/ n fisiología f

physiotherap|ist /fɪzɪəʊ'θerəpɪst/ n fisioterapeuta m & f. **~y** /fɪzɪəʊ-'θerəpɪ/ n fisioterapia f

physique /fɪ'ziːk/ *n* constitución *f*; (*appearance*) físico *m*

pian|ist /'pɪənɪst/ *n* pianista *m* & *f*. **~o** /prˈænəʊ/ *n* (*pl* **-os**) piano *m*

piccolo /'pɪkələʊ/ *n* flautín *m*, píccolo *m*

pick[1] /pɪk/ (*tool*) pico *m*

pick[2] /pɪk/ *vt* escoger; recoger (*flowers etc*); forzar ⟨*a lock*⟩; (*dig*) picar. **~ a quarrel** buscar camorra. **~ holes in** criticar. ● *n* (*choice*) selección *f*; (*the best*) lo mejor. **~ on** *vt* (*nag*) meterse con. **~ out** *vt* escoger; (*identify*) identificar; destacar ⟨*colour*⟩. **~ up** *vt* recoger; (*lift*) levantar; (*learn*) aprender; adquirir ⟨*habit, etc*⟩; obtener ⟨*information*⟩; contagiarse de ⟨*illness*⟩. ● *vi* mejorar; (*med*) reponerse

pickaxe /'pɪkæks/ *n* pico *m*

picket /'pɪkɪt/ *n* (*striker*) huelguista *m* & *f*; (*group of strikers*) piquete *m*; (*stake*) estaca *f*. **~ line** *n* piquete *m*. ● *vt* vigilar por piquetes. ● *vi* estar de guardia

pickle /'pɪkl/ *n* (*in vinegar*) encurtido *m*; (*in brine*) salmuera *f*. **in a ~** (*fam*) en un apuro. ● *vt* encurtir. **~s** *npl* encurtido *m*

pick: **~pocket** /'pɪkpɒkɪt/ *n* ratero *m*. **~-up** *n* (*sl*) ligue *m*; (*truck*) camioneta *f*; (*stylus-holder*) fonocaptor *m*, brazo *m*

picnic/'pɪknɪk/ *n* comida *f* campestre. ● *vi* (*pt* **picnicked**) merendar en el campo

pictorial /pɪk'tɔːrɪəl/ *a* ilustrado

picture /'pɪktʃə(r)/ *n* (*painting*) cuadro *m*; (*photo*) fotografía *f*; (*drawing*) dibujo *m*; (*beautiful thing*) preciosidad *f*; (*film*) película *f*; (*fig*) descripción *f*. **the ~s** *npl* el cine *m*. ● *vt* imaginarse; (*describe*) describir

picturesque /pɪktʃə'resk/ *a* pintoresco

piddling /'pɪdlɪŋ/ *a* (*fam*) insignificante

pidgin /'pɪdʒɪn/ *a.* **~ English** *n* inglés *m* corrompido

pie /paɪ/ *n* empanada *f*; (*sweet*) pastel *m*, tarta *f*

piebald /'paɪbɔːld/ *a* pío

piece /piːs/ *n* pedazo *m*; (*coin*) moneda *f*; (*in game*) pieza *f*. **a ~ of advice** un consejo *m*. **a ~ of news** una noticia *f*. **take to ~s** desmontar. ● *vt*. **~ together** juntar. **~meal** /'piːsmiːl/ *a* gradual; (*unsystematic*)

poco sistemático. —*adv* poco a poco.

~-work *n* trabajo *m* a destajo

pier /pɪə(r)/ *n* muelle *m*

pierc|e /pɪəs/ *vt* perforar. **~ing** *a* penetrante

piety /'paɪətɪ/ *n* piedad *f*

piffl|e /'pɪfl/ *n* (*sl*) tonterías *fpl*. **~ing** *a* (*sl*) insignificante

pig /pɪg/ *n* cerdo *m*

pigeon /'pɪdʒɪn/ *n* paloma *f*; (*culin*) pichón *m*. **~-hole** *n* casilla *f*

pig: **~gy** /'pɪgɪ/ *a* (*greedy, fam*) glotón. **~gy-back** *adv* a cuestas. **~gy bank** *n* hucha *f*. **~-headed** *a* terco

pigment /'pɪgmənt/ *n* pigmento *m*. **~ation** /-'teɪʃn/ *n* pigmentación *f*

pig: **~skin** /'pɪgskɪn/ *n* piel *m* de cerdo. **~sty** /'pɪgstaɪ/ *n* pocilga *f*

pigtail /'pɪgteɪl/ *n* (*plait*) trenza *f*

pike /paɪk/ *n invar* (*fish*) lucio *m*

pilchard /'pɪltʃəd/ *n* sardina *f*

pile[1] /paɪl/ *n* (*heap*) montón *m*. ● *vt* amontonar. **~ it on** exagerar. ● *vi* amontonarse. **~ up** *vt* amontonar. ● *vi* amontonarse. **~s** /paɪlz/ *npl* (*med*) almorranas *fpl*

pile[2] /paɪl/ *n* (*of fabric*) pelo *m*

pile-up /'paɪlʌp/ *n* accidente *m* múltiple

pilfer /'pɪlfə(r)/ *vt/i* hurtar. **~age** *n*, **~ing** *n* hurto *m*

pilgrim /'pɪlgrɪm/ *n* peregrino. **~age** *n* peregrinación *f*

pill /pɪl/ *n* píldora *f*

pillage /'pɪlɪdʒ/ *n* saqueo *m*. ● *vt* saquear

pillar /'pɪlə(r)/ *n* columna *f*. **~-box** *n* buzón *m*

pillion /'pɪlɪən/ *n* asiento *m* trasero. **ride ~** ir en el asiento trasero

pillory /'pɪlərɪ/ *n* picota *f*

pillow /'pɪləʊ/ *n* almohada *f*. **~case** /'pɪləʊkeɪs/ *n* funda *f* de almohada

pilot /'paɪlət/ *n* piloto *m*. ● *vt* pilotar. **~-light** *n* fuego *m* piloto

pimp /pɪmp/ *n* alcahuete *m*

pimple /'pɪmpl/ *n* grano *m*

pin /pɪn/ *n* alfiler *m*; (*mec*) perno *m*. **~s and needles** hormigueo *m*. ● *vt* (*pt* **pinned**) prender con alfileres; (*hold down*) enclavijar; (*fix*) sujetar. **~ s.o. down** obligar a uno a que se decida. **~ up** fijar

pinafore /'pɪnəfɔː(r)/ *n* delantal *m*. **~ dress** *n* mandil *m*

pincers /'pɪnsəz/ *npl* tenazas *fpl*

pinch /pɪntʃ/ vt pellizcar; (*steal, sl*) hurtar. ● vi (*shoe*) apretar. ● n pellizco m; (*small amount*) pizca f. **at a ~** en caso de necesidad

pincushion /'pɪnkʊʃn/ n acerico m

pine[1] /paɪn/ n pino m

pine[2] /paɪn/ vi. **~ away** consumirse. **~ for** suspirar por

pineapple /'paɪnæpl/ n piña f, ananás m

ping /pɪŋ/ n sonido m agudo. **~- pong** /'pɪŋpɒŋ/ n pimpón m, ping-pong m

pinion /'pɪnjən/ vt maniatar

pink /pɪŋk/ a & n color (m) de rosa

pinnacle /'pɪnəkl/ n pináculo m

pin: **~point** vt determinar con precisión f. **~stripe** /'pɪnstraɪp/ n raya f fina

pint /paɪnt/ n pinta f (= 0.57 litre)

pin-up /'pɪnʌp/ n (*fam*) fotografía f de mujer

pioneer /paɪə'nɪə(r)/ n pionero m. ● vt ser el primero, promotor de, promover

pious /'paɪəs/ a piadoso

pip[1] /pɪp/ n (*seed*) pepita f

pip[2] /pɪp/ n (*time signal*) señal f

pip[3] /pɪp/ n (*on uniform*) estrella f

pipe /paɪp/ n tubo m; (*mus*) caramillo m; (*for smoking*) pipa f. ● vt conducir por tuberías. **~down** (*fam*) bajar la voz, callarse. **~-cleaner** n limpiapipas m invar. **~dream** n ilusión f. **~line** /'paɪplaɪn/ n tubería f; (*for oil*) oleoducto m. **in the ~line** en preparación f. **~r** n flautista m & f

piping /'paɪpɪŋ/ n tubería f. **~ hot** muy caliente, hirviendo

piquant /'pi:kənt/ a picante

pique /pi:k/ n resentimiento m

pira|cy /'paɪərəsɪ/ n piratería f. **~te** /'paɪərət/ n pirata m

pirouette /pɪrʊ'et/ n pirueta f. ● vi piruetear

Pisces /'paɪsi:z/ n (*astr*) Piscis m

pistol /'pɪstl/ n pistola f

piston /'pɪstən/ n pistón m

pit /pɪt/ n foso m; (*mine*) mina f; (*of stomach*) boca f. ● vt (*pt* pitted) marcar con hoyos; (*fig*) oponer. **~ o.s. against** medirse con

pitch[1] /pɪtʃ/ n brea f

pitch[2] /pɪtʃ/ (*degree*) grado m; (*mus*) tono m; (*sport*) campo m. ● vt lanzar; armar (*tent*). **~ into** (*fam*) atacar. ● vi caerse; (*ship*) cabecear. **~ in** (*fam*) contribuir. **~ed battle** n batalla f campal

pitch-black /pɪtʃ'blæk/ a oscuro como boca de lobo

pitcher /'pɪtʃə(r)/ n jarro m

pitchfork /'pɪtʃfɔ:k/ n horca f

piteous /'pɪtɪəs/ a lastimoso

pitfall /'pɪtfɔ:l/ n trampa f

pith /pɪθ/ n (*of orange, lemon*) médula f; (*fig*) meollo m

pithy /'pɪθɪ/ a (**-ier, -iest**) conciso

piti|ful /'pɪtɪfl/ a lastimoso. **~less** a despiadado

pittance /'pɪtns/ n sueldo m irrisorio

pity /'pɪtɪ/ n piedad f; (*regret*) lástima f. ● vt compadecerse de

pivot /'pɪvət/ n pivote m. ● vt montonar sobre un pivote. ● vi girar sobre un pivote; (*fig*) depender (**on** de)

pixie /'pɪksɪ/ n duende m

placard /'plækɑ:d/ n pancarta f; (*poster*) cartel m

placate /plə'keɪt/ vt apaciguar

place /pleɪs/ n lugar m; (*seat*) asiento m; (*post*) puesto m; (*house, fam*) casa f. **take ~** tener lugar. ● vt poner, colocar; (*remember*) recordar; (*identify*) identificar. **be ~d** (*in race*) colocarse. **~-mat** n salvamanteles m invar. **~ment** /'pleɪsmənt/ n colocación f

placid /'plæsɪd/ a plácido

plagiari|sm /'pleɪdʒərɪzm/ n plagio m. **~ze** /'pleɪdʒəraɪz/ vt plagiar

plague /pleɪg/ n peste f; (*fig*) plaga f. ● vt atormentar

plaice /pleɪs/ n invar platija f

plaid /plæd/ n tartán m

plain /pleɪn/ a (**-er, -est**) claro; (*simple*) sencillo; (*candid*) franco; (*ugly*) feo. **in ~ clothes** en traje de paisano. ● adv claramente. ● n llanura f. **~ly** adv claramente; (*frankly*) francamente; (*simply*) sencillamente. **~ness** n claridad f; (*simplicity*) sencillez f

plaintiff /'pleɪntɪf/ n demandante m & f

plait /plæt/ vt trenzar. ● n trenza f

plan /plæn/ n proyecto m; (*map*) plano m. ● vt (*pt* planned) planear, proyectar; (*intend*) proponerse

plane[1] /pleɪn/ n (*tree*) plátano m

plane[2] /pleɪn/ n (*level*) nivel m; (*aviat*) avión m. ● a plano

plane³ /pleɪn/ (*tool*) cepillo *m*. ● *vt* cepillar

planet /'plænɪt/ *n* planeta *m*. ~**ary** *a* planetario

plank /plæŋk/ *n* tabla *f*

planning /'plænɪŋ/ *n* planificación *f*. **family** ~ *n* planificación familiar. **town** ~ *n* urbanismo *m*

plant /plɑ:nt/ *n* planta *f*; (*mec*) maquinaria *f*; (*factory*) fábrica *f*. ● *vt* plantar; (*place in position*) colocar. ~**ation** /plænˈteɪʃn/ *n* plantación *f*

plaque /plæk/ *n* placa *f*

plasma /'plæzmə/ *n* plasma *m*

plaster /'plɑːstə(r)/ *n* yeso *m*; (*adhesive*) esparadrapo *m*; (*for setting bones*) escayola *f*. ~ **of Paris** *n* yeso *m* mate. ● *vt* enyesar; (*med*) escayolar ⟨*broken bone*⟩; (*cover*) cubrir (**with** de). ~**ed** *a* (*fam*) borracho

plastic /'plæstɪk/ *a & n* plástico (*m*)

Plasticine /'plæstɪsiːn/ *n* (*P*) pasta *f* de modelar, plastilina *f* (*P*)

plastic surgery /plæstɪk'sɜːdʒərɪ/ *n* cirugía *f* estética

plate /pleɪt/ *n* plato *m*; (*of metal*) chapa *f*; (*silverware*) vajilla *f* de plata; (*in book*) lámina *f*. ● *vt* (*cover with metal*) chapear

plateau /'plætəʊ/ *n* (*pl* plateaux) *n* meseta *f*

plateful /'pleɪtfʊl/ *n* (*pl* -fuls) plato *m*

platform /'plætfɔːm/ *n* plataforma *f*; (*rail*) andén *m*

platinum /'plætɪnəm/ *n* platino *m*

platitude /'plætɪtjuːd/ *n* tópico *m*, perogrullada *f*, lugar *m* común

platonic /plə'tɒnɪk/ *a* platónico

platoon /plə'tuːn/ *n* pelotón *m*

platter /'plætə(r)/ *n* fuente *f*, plato *m* grande

plausible /'plɔːzəbl/ *a* plausible; ⟨*person*⟩ convincente

play /pleɪ/ *vt* jugar; (*act role*) desempeñar el papel de; tocar ⟨*instrument*⟩. ~ **safe** no arriesgarse. ~ **up to** halagar. ● *vi* jugar. ~**ed out** agotado. ● *n* juego *m*; (*drama*) obra *f* de teatro. ~ **on words** *n* juego *m* de palabras. ~ **down** *vt* minimizar. ~ **on** *vt* aprovecharse de. ~ **up** *vi* (*fam*) causar problemas. ~**act** *vi* hacer la comedia. ~**boy** /'pleɪbɔɪ/ *n* calavera *m*. ~**er** *n* jugador *m*; (*mus*) músico *m*. ~**ful** /'pleɪfl/ *a* juguetón. ~**fully** *adv* jugando; (*jokingly*) en broma. ~**ground** /'pleɪgraʊnd/ *n* parque *m* de juegos infantiles; (*in school*) campo

m de recreo. ~**group** *n* jardín *m* de la infancia. ~**ing** /'pleɪɪŋ/ *n* juego *m*. ~**ing-card** *n* naipe *m*. ~**ing-field** *n* campo *m* de deportes. ~**mate** /'pleɪmeɪt/ *n* compañero *m* (de juego). ~**pen** *n* corralito *m*. ~**thing** *n* juguete *m*. ~**wright** /'pleɪraɪt/ *n* dramaturgo *m*

plc /piːel'siː/ *abbr* (*public limited company*) S.A., sociedad *f* anónima

plea /pliː/ *n* súplica *f*; (*excuse*) excusa *f*; (*jurid*) defensa *f*

plead /pliːd/ *vt* (*jurid*) alegar; (*as excuse*) pretextar. ● *vi* suplicar; (*jurid*) abogar. ~ **with** suplicar

pleasant /'plezɪt/ *a* agradable

please /pliːz/ *int* por favor. ● *vt* agradar, dar gusto a. ● *vi* agradar; (*wish*) querer. ~ **o.s.** hacer lo que quiera. **do as you** ~ haz lo que quieras. ~**ed** *a* contento. ~**ed with** satisfecho de. ~**ing** *a* agradable

pleasur|e /'pleʒə(r)/ *n* placer *m*. ~**able** *a* agradable

pleat /pliːt/ *n* pliegue *m*. ● *vt* hacer pliegues en

plebiscite /'plebɪsɪt/ *n* plebiscito *m*

plectrum /'plektrəm/ *n* plectro *m*

pledge /pledʒ/ *n* prenda *f*; (*promise*) promesa *f*. ● *vt* empeñar; (*promise*) prometer

plent|iful /'plentɪfl/ *a* abundante. ~**y** /'plentɪ/ *n* abundancia *f*. ~**y** (of) muchos (de)

pleurisy /'plʊərəsɪ/ *n* pleuresía *f*

pliable /'plaɪəbl/ *a* flexible

pliers /'plaɪəz/ *npl* alicates *mpl*

plight /plaɪt/ *n* situación *f* (difícil)

plimsolls /'plɪmsəlz/ *npl* zapatillas *fpl* de lona

plinth /plɪnθ/ *n* plinto *m*

plod /plɒd/ *vi* (*pt* plodded) caminar con paso pesado; (*work hard*) trabajar laboriosamente. ~**der** *n* empollón *m*

plonk /plɒŋk/ *n* (*sl*) vino *m* peleón

plop /plɒp/ *n* paf *m*. ● *vi* (*pt* plopped) caerse con un paf

plot /plɒt/ *n* complot *m*; (*of novel etc*) argumento *m*; (*piece of land*) parcela *f*. ● *vt* (*pt* plotted) tramar; (*mark out*) trazar. ● *vi* conspirar

plough /plaʊ/ *n* arado *m*. ● *vt*/*i* arar. ~ **through** avanzar laboriosamente por

ploy /plɔɪ/ *n* (*fam*) estratagema *f*, truco *m*

pluck /plʌk/ *vt* arrancar; depilarse ⟨*eyebrows*⟩; desplumar ⟨*bird*⟩; recoger ⟨*flowers*⟩. ~ **up courage** hacer de tripas corazón. ● *n* valor *m*. ~y *a* (-**ier**, -**iest**) valiente

plug /plʌg/ *n* tapón *m*; (*elec*) enchufe *m*; (*auto*) bujía *f*. ● *vt* (*pt* **plugged**) tapar; (*advertise*, *fam*) dar publicidad a. ~ **in** (*elec*) enchufar

plum /plʌm/ *n* ciruela *f*; ⟨*tree*⟩ ciruelo *m*

plumage /'pluːmɪdʒ/ *n* plumaje *m*

plumb /plʌm/ *a* vertical. ● *n* plomada *f*. ● *adv* verticalmente; (*exactly*) exactamente. ● *vt* sondar

plumb|er /'plʌmə(r)/ *n* fontanero *m*. ~**ing** *n* instalación *f* sanitaria, instalación *f* de cañerías

plume /pluːm/ *n* pluma *f*

plum job /plʌm'dʒɒb/ *n* (*fam*) puesto *m* estupendo

plummet /'plʌmɪt/ *n* plomada *f*. ● *vi* caer a plomo, caer en picado

plump /plʌmp/ *a* (-**er**, -**est**) rechoncho. ● *vt*. ~ **for** elegir. ~**ness** *n* gordura *f*

plum pudding /plʌm'pʊdɪŋ/ *n* budín *m* de pasas

plunder /'plʌndə(r)/ *n* (*act*) saqueo *m*; (*goods*) botín *m*. ● *vt* saquear

plunge /plʌndʒ/ *vt* hundir; (*in water*) sumergir. ● *vi* zambullirse; (*fall*) caer. ● *n* salto *m*. ~**er** *n* (*for sink*) desatascador *m*; (*mec*) émbolo *m*. ~**ing** *a* ⟨*neckline*⟩ bajo, escotado

plural /'plʊərəl/ *a* & *n* plural (*m*)

plus /plʌs/ *prep* más. ● *a* positivo. ● *n* signo *m* más; (*fig*) ventaja *f*. **five** ~ más de cinco

plush /plʌʃ/ *n* felpa *f*. ● *a* de felpa, afelpado; (*fig*) lujoso. ~**y** *a* lujoso

plutocrat /'pluːtəkræt/ *n* plutócrata *m* & *f*

plutonium /pluː'təʊnjəm/ *n* plutonio *m*

ply /plaɪ/ *vt* manejar ⟨*tool*⟩; ejercer ⟨*trade*⟩. ~ **s.o. with drink** dar continuamente de beber a uno. ~**wood** *n* contrachapado *m*

p.m. /piː'em/ *abbr* (*post meridiem*) de la tarde

pneumatic /njuː'mætɪk/ *a* neumático

pneumonia /njuː'məʊnjə/ *n* pulmonía *f*

PO /piː'əʊ/ *abbr* (*Post Office*) oficina *f* de correos

poach /pəʊtʃ/ *vt* escalfar ⟨*egg*⟩; cocer ⟨*fish etc*⟩; (*steal*) cazar en vedado. ~**er** *n* cazador *m* furtivo

pocket /'pɒkɪt/ *n* bolsillo *m*; (*of air*, *resistance*) bolsa *f*. **be in** ~ salir ganando. **be out of** ~ salir perdiendo. ● *vt* poner en el bolsillo. ~-**book** *n* (*notebook*) libro *m* de bolsillo; (*purse*, *Amer*) cartera *f*; (*handbag*, *Amer*) bolso *m*. ~-**money** *n* dinero *m* para los gastos personales

pock-marked /'pɒkmɑːkt/ *a* ⟨*face*⟩ picado de viruelas

pod /pɒd/ *n* vaina *f*

podgy /'pɒdʒɪ/ *a* (-**ier**, -**iest**) rechoncho

poem /'pəʊɪm/ *n* poesía *f*

poet /'pəʊɪt/ *n* poeta *m*. ~**ess** *n* poetisa *f*. ~**ic** /-'etɪk/ *a*, ~**ical** /-'etɪkl/ *a* poético. **P**~ **Laureate** *n* poeta laureado. ~**ry** /'pəʊɪtrɪ/ *n* poesía *f*

poignant /'pɔɪnjənt/ *a* conmovedor

point /pɔɪnt/ *n* punto *m*; (*sharp end*) punta *f*; (*significance*) lo importante; (*elec*) toma *f* de corriente. **good** ~**s** cualidades *fpl*. **to the** ~ pertinente. **up to a** ~ hasta cierto punto. **what is the** ~? ¿para qué?, ¿a qué fin? ● *vt* (*aim*) apuntar; (*show*) indicar. ~ **out** señalar. ● *vi* señalar. ~-**blank** *a* & *adv* a boca de jarro, a quemarropa. ~**ed** /'pɔɪntɪd/ *a* puntiagudo; (*fig*) mordaz. ~**er** /'pɔɪntə(r)/ *n* indicador *m*; (*dog*) perro *m* de muestra; (*clue*, *fam*) indicación *f*. ~**less** /'pɔɪntlɪs/ *a* inútil

poise /pɔɪz/ *n* equilibrio *m*; (*elegance*) elegancia *f*; (*fig*) aplomo *m*. ~**d** *a* en equilibrio. ~**d for** listo para

poison /'pɔɪzn/ *n* veneno *m*. ● *vt* envenenar. ~**ous** *a* venenoso; ⟨*chemical etc*⟩ tóxico

poke /pəʊk/ *vt* empujar; atizar ⟨*fire*⟩. ~ **fun at** burlarse de. ~ **out** asomar ⟨*head*⟩. ● *vi* hurgar; (*pry*) meterse. ~ **about** fisgonear. ● *n* empuje *m*

poker[1] /'pəʊkə(r)/ *n* atizador *m*

poker[2] /'pəʊkə(r)/ (*cards*) póquer *m*. ~-**face** *n* cara *f* inmutable

poky /'pəʊkɪ/ *a* (-**ier**, -**iest**) estrecho

Poland /'pəʊlənd/ *n* Polonia *f*

polar /'pəʊlə(r)/ *a* polar. ~ **bear** *n* oso *m* blanco

polarize /'pəʊləraɪz/ *vt* polarizar

Pole /pəʊl/ *n* polaco *m*

pole[1] /pəʊl/ *n* palo *m*; (*for flag*) asta *f*

pole² /pəʊl/ (*geog*) polo *m*. **~-star** *n* estrella *f* polar

polemic /pə'lemɪk/ *a* polémico. ● *n* polémica *f*

police /pə'liːs/ *n* policía *f*. ● *vt* vigilar. **~man** /pə'liːsmən/ *n* (*pl* -men) policía *m*, guardia *m*. **~ record** *n* antecedentes *mpl* penales. **~ state** *n* estado *m* policíaco. **~ station** *n* comisaría *f*. **~woman** /-wʊmən/ *n* (*pl* -women) mujer *m* policía

policy¹ /'pɒlɪsɪ/ *n* política *f*

policy² /'pɒlɪsɪ/ (*insurance*) póliza *f* (de seguros)

polio(myelitis) /'pəʊlɪəʊ(maɪə'laɪtɪs)/ *n* polio(mielitis) *f*

polish /'pɒlɪʃ/ *n* (*for shoes*) betún *m*; (*for floor*) cera *f*; (*for nails*) esmalte *m* de uñas; (*shine*) brillo *m*; (*fig*) finura *f*. **nail ~** esmalte *m* de uñas. ● *vt* pulir; limpiar ‹*shoes*›; encerar ‹*floor*›. **~ off** despachar. **~ed** *a* pulido; ‹*manner*› refinado. **~er** *n* pulidor *m*; (*machine*) pulidora *f*

Polish /'pəʊlɪʃ/ *a* & *n* polaco (*m*)

polite /pə'laɪt/ *a* cortés. **~ly** *adv* cortésmente. **~ness** *n* cortesía *f*

politic|al /pə'lɪtɪkl/ *a* político. **~ian** /pɒlɪ'tɪʃn/ *n* político *m*. **~s** /'pɒlətɪks/ *n* política *f*

polka /'pɒlkə/ *n* polca *f*. **~ dots** *npl* diseño *m* de puntos

poll /pəʊl/ *n* elección *f*; (*survey*) encuesta *f*. ● *vt* obtener ‹*votes*›

pollen /'pɒlən/ *n* polen *m*

polling-booth /'pəʊlɪŋbuːð/ *n* cabina *f* de votar

pollut|e /pə'luːt/ *vt* contaminar. **~ion** /-ʃn/ *n* contaminación *f*

polo /'pəʊləʊ/ *n* polo *m*. **~-neck** *n* cuello *m* vuelto

poltergeist /'pɒltəɡaɪst/ *n* duende *m*

polyester /pɒlɪ'estə(r)/ *n* poliéster *m*

polygam|ist /pə'lɪɡəmɪst/ *n* polígamo *m*. **~ous** *a* polígamo. **~y** /pə'lɪɡəmɪ/ *n* poligamia *f*

polyglot /'pɒlɪɡlɒt/ *a* & *n* políglota (*m* & *f*)

polygon /'pɒlɪɡən/ *n* polígono *m*

polyp /'pɒlɪp/ *n* pólipo *m*

polystyrene /pɒlɪ'staɪriːn/ *n* poliestireno *m*

polytechnic /pɒlɪ'teknɪk/ *n* escuela *f* politécnica

polythene /'pɒlɪθiːn/ *n* polietileno *m*. **~ bag** *n* bolsa *f* de plástico

pomegranate /'pɒmɪɡrænɪt/ *n* (*fruit*) granada *f*

pommel /'pʌml/ *n* pomo *m*

pomp /pɒmp/ *n* pompa *f*

pompon /'pɒmpɒn/ *n* pompón *m*

pompo|sity /pɒm'pɒsətɪ/ *n* pomposidad *f*. **~us** /'pɒmpəs/ *a* pomposo

poncho /'pɒntʃəʊ/ *n* (*pl* -os) poncho *m*

pond /pɒnd/ *n* charca *f*; (*artificial*) estanque *m*

ponder /'pɒndə(r)/ *vt* considerar. ● *vi* reflexionar. **~ous** /'pɒndərəs/ *a* pesado

pong /pɒŋ/ *n* (*sl*) hedor *m*. ● *vi* (*sl*) apestar

pontif|f /'pɒntɪf/ *n* pontífice *m*. **~ical** /-'tɪfɪkl/ *a* pontifical; (*fig*) dogmático. **~icate** /pɒn'tɪfɪkeɪt/ *vi* pontificar

pontoon /pɒn'tuːn/ *n* pontón *m*. **~ bridge** *n* puente *m* de pontones

pony /'pəʊnɪ/ *n* poni *m*. **~-tail** *n* cola *f* de caballo. **~-trekking** *n* excursionismo *m* en poni

poodle /'puːdl/ *n* perro *m* de lanas, caniche *m*

pool¹ /puːl/ *n* charca *f*; (*artificial*) estanque *m*. **(swimming-)~** *n* piscina *f*

pool² /puːl/ *n* (*common fund*) fondos *mpl* comunes; (*snooker*) billar *m* americano. ● *vt* aunar. **~s** *npl* quinielas *fpl*

poor /pʊə(r)/ *a* (**-er, -est**) pobre; (*not good*) malo. **be in ~ health** estar mal de salud. **~ly** *a* (*fam*) indispuesto. ● *adv* pobremente; (*badly*) mal

pop¹ /pɒp/ *n* ruido *m* seco; (*of bottle*) taponazo *m*. ● *vt* (*pt* **popped**) hacer reventar; (*put*) poner. **~ in** *vi* entrar; (*visit*) pasar por. **~ out** *vi* saltar; ‹*person*› salir un rato. **~ up** *vi* surgir, aparecer

pop² /pɒp/ *a* (*popular*) pop *invar*. ● *n* (*fam*) música *f* pop. **~ art** *n* arte *m* pop

popcorn /'pɒpkɔːn/ *n* palomitas *fpl*

pope /pəʊp/ *n* papa *m*

popgun /'pɒpɡʌn/ *n* pistola *f* de aire comprimido

poplar /'pɒplə(r)/ *n* chopo *m*

poplin /'pɒplɪn/ *n* popelina *f*

poppy /'pɒpɪ/ *n* amapola *f*

popular /'pɒpjʊlə(r)/ *a* popular. **~ity** /-'lærətɪ/ *n* popularidad *f*. **~ize** *vt* popularizar

populat|e /'pɒpjʊleɪt/ vt poblar. **~ion**/-'leɪʃn/ n población f; (number of inhabitants) habitantes mpl

porcelain /'pɔ:səlɪn/ n porcelana f

porch /pɔ:tʃ/ n porche m

porcupine /'pɔ:kjʊpaɪn/ n puerco m espín

pore[1] /pɔ:(r)/ n poro m

pore[2] /pɔ:(r)/ vi. **~ over** estudiar detenidamente

pork /pɔ:k/ n cerdo m

porn /pɔ:n/ n (fam) pornografía f. **~ographic** /-ə'græfɪk/ a pornográfico. **~ography** /pɔ:'nɒgrəfɪ/ n pornografía f

porous /'pɔ:rəs/ a poroso

porpoise /'pɔ:pəs/ n marsopa f

porridge /'pɒrɪdʒ/ n gachas fpl de avena

port[1] /pɔ:t/ n puerto m; (porthole) portilla f. **~ of call** puerto de escala

port[2] /pɔ:t/ (naut, left) babor m. ●a de babor

port[3] /pɔ:t/ (wine) oporto m

portable /'pɔ:təbl/ a portátil

portal /'pɔ:tl/ n portal m

portent /'pɔ:tent/ n presagio m

porter /'pɔ:tə(r)/ n portero m; (for luggage) mozo m. **~age** n porte m

portfolio /pɔ:t'fəʊljəʊ/ n (pl -os) cartera f

porthole /'pɔ:thəʊl/ n portilla f

portico /'pɔ:tɪkəʊ/ n (pl -oes) pórtico m

portion /'pɔ:ʃn/ n porción f. ●vt repartir

portly /'pɔ:tlɪ/ a (-ier, -iest) corpulento

portrait /'pɔ:trɪt/ n retrato m

portray /pɔ:'treɪ/ vt retratar; (represent) representar. **~al** n retrato m

Portug|al /'pɔ:tjʊgl/ n Portugal m. **~uese** /-'gi:z/ a & n portugués (m)

pose /pəʊz/ n postura f. ●vt colocar; hacer (question); plantear (problem). ●vi posar. **~ as** hacerse pasar por. **~r** /'pəʊzə(r)/ n pregunta f difícil

posh /pɒʃ/ a (sl) elegante

position /pə'zɪʃn/ n posición f; (job) puesto m; (status) rango m. ●vt colocar

positive /'pɒzətɪv/ a positivo; (real) verdadero; (certain) seguro. ●n (foto) positiva f. **~ly** adv positivamente

possess /pə'zes/ vt poseer. **~ion** /pə'zeʃn/ n posesión f. **take ~ion of**

tomar posesión de. **~ions** npl posesiones fpl; (jurid) bienes mpl. **~ive** /pə'zesɪv/ a posesivo. **~or** n poseedor m

possib|ility /pɒsə'bɪlətɪ/ n posibilidad f. **~le** /'pɒsəbl/ a posible. **~ly** adv posiblemente

post[1] /pəʊst/ n (pole) poste m. ●vt fijar (notice)

post[2] /pəʊst/ (place) puesto m

post[3] /pəʊst/ (mail) correo m. ●vt echar (letter). **keep s.o. ~ed** tener a uno al corriente

post... /pəʊst/ pref post...

post|age /'pəʊstɪdʒ/ n franqueo m. **~al** /'pəʊstl/ a postal. **~al order** n giro m postal. **~box** n buzón m. **~card** /'pəʊstka:d/ n (tarjeta f) postal f. **~code** n código m postal

post-date /pəʊst'deɪt/ vt poner fecha posterior a

poster /'pəʊstə(r)/ n cartel m

poste restante /pəʊst'resta:nt/ n lista f de correos

posteri|or /pɒ'stɪərɪə(r)/ a posterior. ●n trasero m. **~ty** /pɒs'terɪtɪ/ n posteridad f

posthumous /'pɒstjʊməs/ a póstumo. **~ly** adv después de la muerte

post|man /'pəʊstmən/ n (pl -men) cartero m. **~mark** /'pəʊstma:k/ n matasellos m invar. **~master** /'pəʊstma:stə(r)/ n administrador m de correos. **~mistress** /'pəʊstmɪstrɪs/ n administradora f de correos

post-mortem /'pəʊstmɔ:təm/ n autopsia f

Post Office /'pəʊstɒfɪs/ n oficina f de correos, correos mpl

postpone /pəʊst'pəʊn/ vt aplazar. **~ment** n aplazamiento m

postscript /'pəʊstskrɪpt/ n posdata f

postulant /'pɒstjʊlənt/ n postulante m & f

postulate /'pɒstjʊleɪt/ vt postular

posture /'pɒstʃə(r)/ n postura f. ●vi adoptar una postura

posy /'pəʊzɪ/ n ramillete m

pot /pɒt/ n (for cooking) olla f; (for flowers) tiesto m; (marijuana, sl) mariguana f. **go to ~** (sl) echarse a perder. ●vt (pt potted) poner en tiesto

potassium /pə'tæsjəm/ n potasio m

potato /pə'teɪtəʊ/ n (pl -oes) patata f, papa f (LAm)

pot: ∼-**belly** n barriga f. ∼-**boiler** n obra f literaria escrita sólo para ganar dinero

poten|cy /'pəʊtənsɪ/ n potencia f. ∼t /'pəʊtnt/ a potente; ⟨drink⟩ fuerte

potentate /'pəʊtənteɪt/ n potentado m

potential /pəʊ'tenʃl/ a & n potencial (m). ∼**ity** /-ʃɪ'ælətɪ/ n potencialidad f. ∼**ly** adv potencialmente

pot-hole /'pɒthəʊl/ n caverna f; (in road) bache m. ∼r n espeleólogo m

potion /'pəʊʃn/ n poción f

pot: ∼ **luck** n lo que haya. ∼-**shot** n tiro m al azar. ∼**ted** /'pɒtɪd/ see **pot**. ● a ⟨food⟩ en conserva

potter¹ /'pɒtə(r)/ n alfarero m

potter² /'pɒtə(r)/ vi hacer pequeños trabajos agradables, no hacer nada de particular

pottery /'pɒtərɪ/ n cerámica f

potty /'pɒtɪ/ a (-ier, -iest) (sl) chiflado. ● n orinal m

pouch /paʊtʃ/ n bolsa f pequeña

pouffe /puːf/ n ⟨stool⟩ taburete m

poulterer /'pəʊltərə(r)/ n pollero m

poultice /'pəʊltɪs/ n cataplasma f

poultry /'pəʊltrɪ/ n aves fpl de corral

pounce /paʊns/ vi saltar, atacar de repente. ● n salto m, ataque m repentino

pound¹ /paʊnd/ n ⟨weight⟩ libra f (= 454g); ⟨money⟩ libra f (esterlina)

pound² /paʊnd/ n ⟨for cars⟩ depósito m

pound³ /paʊnd/ vt ⟨crush⟩ machacar; ⟨bombard⟩ bombardear. ● vi golpear; ⟨heart⟩ palpitar; ⟨walk⟩ ir con pasos pesados

pour /pɔː(r)/ vt verter. ∼ **out** servir ⟨drink⟩. ● vi fluir; ⟨rain⟩ llover a cántaros. ∼ **in** ⟨people⟩ entrar en tropel. ∼**ing rain** n lluvia f torrencial. ∼ **out** ⟨people⟩ salir en tropel

pout /paʊt/ vi hacer pucheros. ● n puchero m, mala cara f

poverty /'pɒvətɪ/ n pobreza f

powder /'paʊdə(r)/ n polvo m; ⟨cosmetic⟩ polvos mpl. ● vt polvorear; ⟨pulverize⟩ pulverizar. ∼ **one's face** ponerse polvos en la cara. ∼**ed** a en polvo. ∼**y** a polvoriento

power /'paʊə(r)/ n poder m; ⟨elec⟩ corriente f; ⟨energy⟩ energía f; ⟨nation⟩ potencia f. ∼ **cut** n apagón m. ∼**ed** a con motor. ∼**ed by** impulsado por. ∼**ful** a poderoso. ∼**less** a

impotente. ∼-**station** n central f eléctrica

practicable /'præktɪkəbl/ a practicable

practical /'præktɪkl/ a práctico. ∼ **joke** n broma f pesada. ∼**ly** adv prácticamente

practi|ce /'præktɪs/ n práctica f; ⟨custom⟩ costumbre f; ⟨exercise⟩ ejercicio m; ⟨sport⟩ entrenamiento m; ⟨clients⟩ clientela f. **be in** ∼**ce** ⟨doctor, lawyer⟩ ejercer. **be out of** ∼**ce** no estar en forma. **in** ∼**ce** ⟨in fact⟩ en la práctica; ⟨on form⟩ en forma. ∼**se** /'præktɪs/ vt hacer ejercicios en; ⟨put into practice⟩ poner en práctica; ⟨sport⟩ entrenarse en; ejercer ⟨profession⟩. ● vi ejercitarse; ⟨professional⟩ ejercer. ∼**sed** a experto

practitioner /præk'tɪʃənə(r)/ n profesional m & f. **general** ∼ médico m de cabecera. **medical** ∼ médico m

pragmatic /præg'mætɪk/ a pragmático

prairie /'preərɪ/ n pradera f

praise /preɪz/ vt alabar. ● n alabanza f. ∼**worthy** a loable

pram /præm/ n cochecito m de niño

prance /prɑːns/ vi ⟨horse⟩ hacer cabriolas; ⟨person⟩ pavonearse

prank /præŋk/ n travesura f

prattle /'prætl/ vi parlotear. ● n parloteo m

prawn /prɔːn/ n gamba f

pray /preɪ/ vi rezar. ∼**er** /preə(r)/ n oración f. ∼ **for** rogar

pre.. /priː/ pref pre...

preach /priːtʃ/ vt/i predicar. ∼**er** n predicador m

preamble /priː'æmbl/ n preámbulo m

pre-arrange /priːə'reɪndʒ/ vt arreglar de antemano. ∼**ment** n arreglo m previo

precarious /prɪ'keərɪəs/ a precario. ∼**ly** adv precariamente

precaution /prɪ'kɔːʃn/ n precaución f. ∼**ary** a de precaución; ⟨preventive⟩ preventivo

precede /prɪ'siːd/ vt preceder

preceden|ce /'presɪdəns/ n precedencia f. ∼**t** /'presɪdənt/ n precedente m

preceding /prɪ'siːdɪŋ/ a precedente

precept /'priːsept/ n precepto m

precinct /'priːsɪŋkt/ n recinto m. **pedestrian** ∼ zona f peatonal. ∼**s** npl contornos mpl

precious /'preʃəs/ a precioso. ● adv (fam) muy

precipice /'presɪpɪs/ n precipicio m

precipitat|e /prɪ'sɪpɪteɪt/ vt precipitar. /prɪ'sɪpɪtət/ n precipitado m. ● a precipitado. ~ion /-'teɪʃn/ n precipitación f

precipitous /prɪ'sɪpɪtəs/ a escarpado

précis /'preɪsiː/ n (pl précis /-siːz/) resumen m

precis|e /prɪ'saɪs/ a preciso; (careful) meticuloso. ~ely adv precisamente. ~ion /-'sɪʒn/ n precisión f

preclude /prɪ'kluːd/ vt (prevent) impedir; (exclude) excluir

precocious /prɪ'kəʊʃəs/ a precoz. ~ly adv precozmente

preconc|eived /priːkən'siːvd/ a preconcebido. ~eption /-'sepʃn/ n preconcepción f

precursor /priː'kɜːsə(r)/ n precursor m

predator /'predətə(r)/ n animal m de rapiña. ~y a de rapiña

predecessor /'priːdɪsesə(r)/ n predecesor m, antecesor m

predestin|ation /priːdestɪ'neɪʃn/ n predestinación f. ~e /priː'destɪn/ vt predestinar

predicament /prɪ'dɪkəmənt/ n apuro m

predicat|e /'predɪkət/ n predicado m. ~ive /prɪ'dɪkətɪv/ a predicativo

predict /prɪ'dɪkt/ vt predecir. ~ion /-ʃn/ n predicción f

predilection /priːdɪ'lekʃn/ n predilección f

predispose /priːdɪ'spəʊz/ vt predisponer

predomina|nt /prɪ'dɒmɪnənt/ a predominante. ~te /prɪ'dɒmɪneɪt/ vi predominar

pre-eminent /priː'emɪnənt/ a preeminente

pre-empt /priː'empt/ vt adquirir por adelantado, adelantarse a

preen /priːn/ vt limpiar, arreglar. ~ o.s. atildarse

prefab /'priːfæb/ n (fam) casa f prefabricada. ~ricated /-'fæbrɪkeɪtɪd/ a prefabricado

preface /'prefəs/ n prólogo m

prefect /'priːfekt/ n monitor m; (official) prefecto m

prefer /prɪ'fɜː(r)/ vt (pt preferred) preferir. ~able /'prefrəbl/ a preferible. ~ence /'prefrəns/ n preferencia f. ~ential /-ə'renʃl/ a preferente

prefix /'priːfɪks/ n (pl -ixes) prefijo m

pregnan|cy /'pregnənsɪ/ n embarazo m. ~t /'pregnənt/ a embarazada

prehistoric /priːhɪ'stɒrɪk/ a prehistórico

prejudge /priː'dʒʌdʒ/ vt prejuzgar

prejudice /'predʒʊdɪs/ n prejuicio m; (harm) perjuicio m. ● vt predisponer; (harm) perjudicar. ~d a parcial

prelate /'prelət/ n prelado m

preliminar|ies /prɪ'lɪmɪnərɪz/ npl preliminares mpl. ~y /prɪ'lɪmɪnərɪ/ a preliminar

prelude /'preljuːd/ n preludio m

pre-marital /priː'mærɪtl/ a prematrimonial

premature /'premətjʊə(r)/ a prematuro

premeditated /priː'medɪteɪtɪd/ a premeditado

premier /'premɪə(r)/ a primero. ● n (pol) primer ministro

première /'premɪə(r)/ n estreno m

premises /'premɪsɪz/ npl local m. on the ~ en el local

premiss /'premɪs/ n premisa f

premium /'priːmɪəm/ n premio m. at a ~ muy solicitado

premonition /priːmə'nɪʃn/ n presentimiento m

preoccup|ation /priːɒkjʊ'peɪʃn/ n preocupación f. ~ied /-'ɒkjʊpaɪd/ a preocupado

prep /prep/ n deberes mpl

preparation /prepə'reɪʃn/ n preparación f. ~s npl preparativos mpl

preparatory /prɪ'pærətrɪ/ a preparatorio. ~ school n escuela f primaria privada

prepare /prɪ'peə(r)/ vt preparar. ● vi prepararse. ~d to dispuesto a

prepay /priː'peɪ/ vt (pt -paid) pagar por adelantado

preponderance /prɪ'pɒndərəns/ n preponderancia f

preposition /prepə'zɪʃn/ n preposición f

prepossessing /priːpə'zesɪŋ/ a atractivo

preposterous /prɪ'pɒstərəs/ a absurdo

prep school /'prepskuːl/ n escuela f primaria privada

prerequisite /priː'rekwɪzɪt/ n requisito m previo

prerogative /prɪˈrɒgətɪv/ n pre-rrogativa f

Presbyterian /prezbɪˈtɪərɪən/ a & n presbiteriano (m)

prescri|be /prɪˈskraɪb/ vt prescribir; (med) recetar. ~ption /-ˈɪpʃn/ n prescripción f; (med) receta f

presence /ˈprezns/ n presencia f; (attendance) asistencia f. ~ of mind presencia f de ánimo

present¹ /ˈpreznt/ a & n presente (m & f). at ~ actualmente. for the ~ por ahora

present² /ˈpreznt/ n (gift) regalo m

present³ /prɪˈzent/ vt presentar; (give) obsequiar. ~ s.o. with obsequiar a uno con. ~able a presentable. ~ation /prezn'teɪʃn/ n presentación f; (ceremony) ceremonia f de entrega

presently /ˈprezntlɪ/ adv dentro de poco

preserv|ation /prezə'veɪʃn/ n conservación f. ~ative /prɪˈzɜːvətɪv/ n preservativo m. ~e /prɪˈzɜːv/ vt conservar; (maintain) mantener; (culin) poner en conserva. ● n coto m; (jam) confitura f

preside /prɪˈzaɪd/ vi presidir. ~ over presidir

presiden|cy /ˈprezɪdənsɪ/ n presidencia f. ~t /ˈprezɪdənt/ n presidente m. ~tial /-ˈdenʃl/ a presidencial

press /pres/ vt apretar; exprimir (fruit etc); (insist on) insistir en; (iron) planchar. be ~ed for tener poco. ● vi apretar; (time) apremiar; (fig) urgir. ~ on seguir adelante. ● n presión f; (mec, newspapers) prensa f; (printing) imprenta f. ~ conference n rueda f de prensa. ~ cutting n recorte m de periódico. ~ing /ˈpresɪŋ/ a urgente. ~stud n automático m. ~up n plancha f

pressure /ˈpreʃə(r)/ n presión f. ● vt hacer presión sobre. ~-cooker n olla f a presión. ~ group n grupo m de presión

pressurize /ˈpreʃəraɪz/ vt hacer presión sobre

prestig|e /preˈstiːʒ/ n prestigio m. ~ious /preˈstɪdʒəs/ a prestigioso

presum|ably /prɪˈzjuːməblɪ/ adv presumiblemente, probablemente. ~e /prɪˈzjuːm/ vt presumir. ~e (up)on vi abusar de. ~ption /-ˈzʌmpʃn/ n presunción f. ~ptuous /prɪˈzʌmptʃʊəs/ a presuntuoso

presuppose /priːsəˈpəʊz/ vt presuponer

preten|ce /prɪˈtens/ n fingimiento m; (claim) pretensión f; (pretext) pretexto m. ~d /prɪˈtend/ vt/i fingir. ~d to (lay claim) pretender

pretentious /prɪˈtenʃəs/ a pretencioso

pretext /ˈpriːtekst/ n pretexto m

pretty /ˈprɪtɪ/ a (-ier, -iest) adv bonito, lindo (esp LAm); (person) guapo

prevail /prɪˈveɪl/ vi predominar; (win) prevalecer. ~ on persuadir

prevalen|ce /ˈprevələns/ n costumbre f. ~t /ˈprevələnt/ a extendido

prevaricate /prɪˈværɪkeɪt/ vi despistar

prevent /prɪˈvent/ vt impedir. ~able a evitable. ~ion /-ʃn/ n prevención f. ~ive a preventivo

preview /ˈpriːvjuː/ n preestreno m, avance m

previous /ˈpriːvɪəs/ a anterior. ~ to antes de. ~ly adv anteriormente, antes

pre-war /priːˈwɔː(r)/ a de antes de la guerra

prey /preɪ/ n presa f; (fig) víctima f. bird of ~ n ave f de rapiña. ● vi. ~ on alimentarse de; (worry) atormentar

price /praɪs/ n precio m. ● vt fijar el precio de. ~less a inapreciable; (amusing, fam) muy divertido. ~y a (fam) caro

prick /prɪk/ vt/i pinchar. ~ up one's ears aguzar las orejas. ● n pinchazo m

prick|le /ˈprɪkl/ n (bot) espina f; (of animal) púa f; (sensation) picor m. ~y a espinoso; (animal) lleno de púas; (person) quisquilloso

pride /praɪd/ n orgullo m. ~ of place n puesto m de honor. ● vr. ~ o.s. on enorgullecerse de

priest /priːst/ n sacerdote m. ~hood n sacerdocio m. ~ly a sacerdotal

prig /prɪg/ n mojigato m. ~gish a mojigato

prim /prɪm/ a (primmer, primmest) estirado; (prudish) gazmoño

primarily /ˈpraɪmərɪlɪ/ adv en primer lugar

primary /ˈpraɪmərɪ/ a primario; (chief) principal. ~ school n escuela f primaria

prime¹ /praɪm/ vt cebar ⟨gun⟩; ⟨prepare⟩ preparar; aprestar ⟨surface⟩

prime² /praɪm/ a principal; ⟨first rate⟩ excelente. ~ **minister** n primer ministro m. • n. **be in one's** ~ estar en la flor de la vida

primer¹ /'praɪmə(r)/ n ⟨of paint⟩ primera mano f

primer² /'praɪmə(r)/ ⟨book⟩ silabario m

primeval /praɪ'miːvl/ a primitivo

primitive /'prɪmɪtɪv/ a primitivo

primrose /'prɪmrəʊz/ n primavera f

prince /prɪns/ n príncipe m. ~**ly** a principesco. ~**ss** /prɪn'ses/ n princesa f

principal /'prɪnsəpl/ a principal. • n ⟨of school etc⟩ director m

principality /prɪnsɪ'pælətɪ/ n principado m

principally /'prɪnsɪpəlɪ/ adv principalmente

principle /'prɪnsəpl/ n principio m. **in** ~ en principio. **on** ~ por principio

print /prɪnt/ vt imprimir; ⟨write in capitals⟩ escribir con letras de molde. • n ⟨of finger, foot⟩ huella f; ⟨letters⟩ caracteres mpl; ⟨of design⟩ estampado m; ⟨picture⟩ grabado m; ⟨photo⟩ copia f. **in** ~ ⟨book⟩ disponible. **out of** ~ agotado. ~**ed matter** n impresos mpl. ~**er** /'prɪntə(r)/ n impresor m; ⟨machine⟩ impresora f. ~**ing** n tipografía f. ~**out** n listado m

prior /'praɪə(r)/ n prior m. • a anterior. ~ **to** antes de

priority /praɪ'ɒrətɪ/ n prioridad f

priory /'praɪərɪ/ n priorato m

prise /praɪz/ vt apalancar. ~ **open** abrir por fuerza

prism /'prɪzəm/ n prisma m

prison /'prɪzn/ n cárcel m. ~**er** n prisionero m; ⟨in prison⟩ preso m; ⟨under arrest⟩ detenido m. ~ **officer** n carcelero m

pristine /'prɪstiːn/ a prístino

privacy /'prɪvəsɪ/ n intimidad f; ⟨private life⟩ vida f privada. **in** ~ en la intimidad

private /'praɪvət/ a privado; ⟨confidential⟩ personal; ⟨lessons, house⟩ particular; ⟨ceremony⟩ en la intimidad. • n soldado m raso. **in** ~ en privado; ⟨secretly⟩ en secreto. ~ **eye** n ⟨fam⟩ detective m privado. ~**ly** adv

en privado; ⟨inwardly⟩ interiormente

privation /praɪ'veɪʃn/ n privación f

privet /'prɪvɪt/ n alheña f

privilege /'prɪvəlɪdʒ/ n privilegio m. ~**d** a privilegiado

privy /'prɪvɪ/ a. ~ **to** al corriente de

prize /praɪz/ n premio m. • a ⟨idiot etc⟩ de remate. • vt estimar. ~**-fighter** n boxeador m profesional. ~**-giving** n reparto m de premios. ~**-winner** n premiado m

pro /prəʊ/ n. ~**s and cons** el pro m y el contra m

probab|ility /prɒbə'bɪlətɪ/ n probabilidad f. ~**le** /'prɒbəbl/ a probable. ~**ly** adv probablemente

probation /prə'beɪʃn/ n prueba f; ⟨jurid⟩ libertad f condicional. ~**ary** a de prueba

probe /prəʊb/ n sonda f; ⟨fig⟩ encuesta f. • vt sondar. • vi. ~ **into** investigar

problem /'prɒbləm/ n problema m. • a difícil. ~**atic** /-'mætɪk/ a problemático

procedure /prə'siːdʒə(r)/ n procedimiento m

proceed /prə'siːd/ vi proceder. ~**ing** n procedimiento m. ~**ings** /prə'siːdɪŋz/ npl ⟨report⟩ actas fpl; ⟨jurid⟩ proceso m

proceeds /'prəʊsiːdz/ npl ganancias fpl

process /'prəʊses/ n proceso m. **in** ~ **of** en vías de. **in the** ~ **of time** con el tiempo. • vt tratar; revelar ⟨photo⟩. ~**ion** /prə'seʃn/ n desfile m

procla|im /prə'kleɪm/ vt proclamar. ~**mation** /prɒklə'meɪʃn/ n proclamación f

procrastinate /prəʊ'kræstɪneɪt/ vi aplazar, demorar, diferir

procreation /prəʊkrɪ'eɪʃn/ n procreación f

procure /prə'kjʊə(r)/ vt obtener

prod /prɒd/ vt ⟨pt prodded⟩ empujar; ⟨with elbow⟩ dar un codazo a. • vi dar con el dedo. • n empuje m; ⟨with elbow⟩ codazo m

prodigal /'prɒdɪgl/ a pródigo

prodigious /prə'dɪdʒəs/ a prodigioso

prodigy /'prɒdɪdʒɪ/ n prodigio m

produce /prə'djuːs/ vt ⟨show⟩ presentar; ⟨bring out⟩ sacar; poner en escena ⟨play⟩; ⟨cause⟩ causar; ⟨manufacture⟩ producir. /'prɒdjuːs/ n

productos *mpl*. ~er /prəˈdjuːsə(r)/ *n*
productor *m*; (*in theatre*) director *m*
product /ˈprɒdʌkt/ *n* producto *m*.
~ion /prəˈdʌkʃn/ *n* producción *f*; (*of
play*) representación *f*
productive /prəˈdʌktɪv/ *a* pro-
ductivo. ~ity /prɒdʌkˈtɪvətɪ/ *n* pro-
ductividad *f*
profan|e /prəˈfeɪn/ *a* profano; (*blas-
phemous*) blasfemo. ~ity /-ˈfænətɪ/ *n*
profanidad *f*
profess /prəˈfes/ *vt* profesar; (*pretend*) pretender
profession /prəˈfeʃn/ *n* profesión *f*.
~al *a & n* profesional (*m & f*)
professor /prəˈfesə(r)/ *n* catedrático
m; (*Amer*) profesor *m*
proffer /ˈprɒfə(r)/ *vt* ofrecer
proficien|cy /prəˈfɪʃənsɪ/ *n* com-
petencia *f*. ~t /prəˈfɪʃnt/ *a* com-
petente
profile /ˈprəʊfaɪl/ *n* perfil *m*
profit /ˈprɒfɪt/ *n* (*com*) ganancia *f*;
(*fig*) provecho *m*. ● *vi*. ~ **from** sacar
provecho de. ~able *a* provechoso
profound /prəˈfaʊnd/ *a* profundo.
~ly *adv* profundamente
profus|e /prəˈfjuːs/ *a* profuso. ~ely
adv profusamente. ~ion /-ʒn/ *n*
profusión *f*
progeny /ˈprɒdʒənɪ/ *n* progenie *f*
prognosis /prɒgˈnəʊsɪs/ *n* (*pl* -oses)
pronóstico *m*
program(me) /ˈprəʊgræm/ *n* programa *m*. ● *vt* (*pt* **programmed**) pro-
gramar. ~mer *n* programador *m*
progress /ˈprəʊgres/ *n* progreso *m*,
progresos *mpl*; (*development*) desarrollo *m*. **in** ~ en curso. /prəˈgres/ *vi*
hacer progresos; (*develop*) desarrollarse. ~ion /prəˈgreʃn/ *n* pro-
gresión *f*
progressive /prəˈgresɪv/ *a* pro-
gresivo; (*reforming*) progresista.
~ly *adv* progresivamente
prohibit /prəˈhɪbɪt/ *vt* prohibir.
~ive/-bətɪv/ *a* prohibitivo
project /prəˈdʒekt/ *vt* proyectar. ● *vi*
(*stick out*) sobresalir. /ˈprɒdʒekt/ *n*
proyecto *m*
projectile /prəˈdʒektaɪl/ *n* proyectil
m
projector /prəˈdʒektə(r)/ *n* proyector *m*
proletari|an /prəʊlɪˈteərɪən/ *a & n*
proletario (*m*). ~at /prəʊlɪˈteərɪət/ *n*
proletariado *m*

prolifer|ate /prəˈlɪfəreɪt/ *vi* pro-
liferar. ~eration /-ˈreɪʃn/ *n* proliferación *f*. ~ic /prəˈlɪfɪk/ *a* proli-
fico
prologue /ˈprəʊlɒg/ *n* prólogo *m*
prolong /prəˈlɒŋ/ *vt* prolongar
promenade /prɒməˈnɑːd/ *n* paseo
m; (*along beach*) paseo *m* marítimo.
● *vt* pasear. ● *vi* pasearse. ~ **concert**
n concierto *m* (que forma parte de un
festival de música clásica en Londres, en que no todo el público tiene
asientos)
prominen|ce /ˈprɒmɪnəns/ *n* pro-
minencia *f*; (*fig*) importancia *f*. ~t
/ˈprɒmɪnənt/ *a* prominente; (*important*) importante; (*conspicuous*)
conspicuo
promiscu|ity /prɒmɪˈskjuːətɪ/ *n*
libertinaje *m*. ~ous /prəˈmɪskjʊəs/
a libertino
promis|e /ˈprɒmɪs/ *n* promesa *f*.
● *vt/i* prometer. ~ing *a* prometedor;
⟨*person*⟩ que promete
promontory /ˈprɒməntrɪ/ *n* promontorio *m*
promot|e /prəˈməʊt/ *vt* promover.
~ion /-ˈməʊʃn/ *n* promoción *f*
prompt /prɒmpt/ *a* pronto; (*punctual*) puntual. ● *adv* en punto. ● *vt*
incitar; apuntar ⟨*actor*⟩. ~er *n* apun-
tador *m*. ~ly *adv* puntualmente.
~ness *n* prontitud *f*
promulgate /ˈprɒməlgeɪt/ *vt* promulgar
prone /prəʊn/ *a* echado boca abajo.
~ **to** propenso a
prong /prɒŋ/ *n* (*of fork*) diente *m*
pronoun /ˈprəʊnaʊn/ *n* pronombre
m
pronounc|e /prəˈnaʊns/ *vt* pro-
nunciar; (*declare*) declarar. ~ement
n declaración *f*. ~ed /prəˈnaʊnst/ *a*
pronunciado; (*noticeable*) marcado
pronunciation /prənʌnsɪˈeɪʃn/ *n*
pronunciación *f*
proof /pruːf/ *n* prueba *f*; (*of alcohol*)
graduación *f* normal. ● *a*. ~ **against**
a prueba de. ~-**reading** *n* corrección
f de pruebas
prop[1] /prɒp/ *n* puntal *m*; (*fig*) apoyo
m. ● *vt* (*pt* **propped**) apoyar. ~
against (*lean*) apoyar en
prop[2] /prɒp/ (*in theatre*, *fam*) accesorio *m*
propaganda /prɒpəˈgændə/ *n* propaganda *f*

propagat|e /'prɒpəgeɪt/ vt propagar. ● vi propagarse. **∼ion** /-'geɪʃn/ n propagación f

propel /prə'pel/ vt (pt **propelled**) propulsar. **∼ler** /prə'pelə(r)/ n hélice f

propensity /prə'pensəti/ n propensión f

proper /'prɒpə(r)/ a correcto; (suitable) apropiado; (gram) propio; (real, fam) verdadero. **∼ly** adv correctamente

property /'prɒpəti/ n propiedad f; (things owned) bienes mpl. ● a inmobiliario

prophe|cy /'prɒfəsɪ/ n profecía f. **∼sy** /'prɒfɪsaɪ/ vt/i profetizar. **∼t** /'prɒfɪt/ n profeta m. **∼tic** /prə-'fetɪk/ a profético

propitious /prə'pɪʃəs/ a propicio

proportion /prə'pɔːʃn/ n proporción f. **∼al** a, **∼ate** a proporcional

propos|al /prə'pəʊzl/ n propuesta f. **∼al of marriage** oferta f de matrimonio. **∼e** /prə'pəʊz/ vt proponer. ● vi hacer una oferta de matrimonio

proposition /prɒpə'zɪʃn/ n proposición f; (project, fam) asunto m

propound /prə'paʊnd/ vt proponer

proprietor /prə'praɪətə(r)/ n propietario m

propriety /prə'praɪətɪ/ n decoro m

propulsion /prə'pʌlʃn/ n propulsión f

prosaic /prə'zeɪk/ a prosaico

proscribe /prə'skraɪb/ vt proscribir

prose /prəʊz/ n prosa f

prosecut|e /'prɒsɪkjuːt/ vt procesar; (carry on) proseguir. **∼ion** /-'kjuːʃn/ n proceso m. **∼or** n acusador m. **Public P∼or** fiscal m

prospect /'prɒspekt/ n vista f; (expectation) perspectiva f. /prə'spekt/ vi prospectar

prospective /prə'spektɪv/ a probable; (future) futuro

prospector /prə'spektə(r)/ n prospector m, explorador m

prospectus /prə'spektəs/ n prospecto m

prosper /'prɒspə(r)/ vi prosperar. **∼ity** /-'sperətɪ/ n prosperidad f. **∼ous** /'prɒspərəs/ a próspero

prostitut|e /'prɒstɪtjuːt/ n prostituta f. **∼ion** /-'tjuːʃn/ n prostitución f

prostrate /'prɒstreɪt/ a echado boca abajo; (fig) postrado

protagonist /prə'tægənɪst/ n protagonista m & f

protect /prə'tekt/ vt proteger. **∼ion** /-ʃn/ n protección f. **∼ive** /prə'tektɪv/ a protector. **∼or** n protector m

protégé /'prɒtɪʒeɪ/ n protegido m. **∼e** n protegida f

protein /'prəʊtiːn/ n proteína f

protest /'prəʊtest/ n protesta f. **under ∼** bajo protesta. /prə'test/ vt/i protestar. **∼er** n (demonstrator) manifestante m & f

Protestant /'prɒtɪstənt/ a & n protestante (m & f)

protocol /'prəʊtəkɒl/ n protocolo m

prototype /'prəʊtətaɪp/ n prototipo m

protract /prə'trækt/ vt prolongar

protractor /prə'træktə(r)/ n transportador m

protrude /prə'truːd/ vi sobresalir

protuberance /prə'tjuːbərəns/ n protuberancia f

proud /praʊd/ a orgulloso. **∼ly** adv orgullosamente

prove /pruːv/ vt probar. ● vi resultar. **∼n** a probado

provenance /'prɒvənəns/ n procedencia f

proverb /'prɒvɜːb/ n proverbio m. **∼ial** /prə'vɜːbɪəl/ a proverbial

provide /prə'vaɪd/ vt proveer. ● vi. **∼ against** precaverse de. **∼ for** (allow for) prever; mantener (person). **∼d** /prə'vaɪdɪd/ conj. **∼ (that)** con tal que

providen|ce /'prɒvɪdəns/ n providencia f. **∼t** a providente. **∼tial** /prɒvɪ'denʃl/ a providencial

providing /prə'vaɪdɪŋ/ conj. **∼ that** con tal que

provin|ce /'prɒvɪns/ n provincia f; (fig) competencia f. **∼ial** /prə'vɪnʃl/ a provincial

provision /prə'vɪʒn/ n provisión f; (supply) suministro m; (stipulation) condición f. **∼s** npl comestibles mpl

provisional /prə'vɪʒənl/ a provisional. **∼ly** adv provisionalmente

proviso /prə'vaɪzəʊ/ n (pl **-os**) condición f

provo|cation /prɒvə'keɪʃn/ n provocación f. **∼cative** /-'vɒkətɪv/ a provocador. **∼ke** /prə'vəʊk/ vt provocar

prow /praʊ/ n proa f

prowess /'prauɪs/ n habilidad f; (valour) valor m

prowl /praʊl/ vi merodear. ● n ronda f. **be on the ~** merodear. **~er** n merodeador m

proximity /prɒk'sɪmətɪ/ n proximidad f

proxy /'prɒksɪ/ n poder m. **by ~** por poder

prude /pru:d/ n mojigato m

pruden|ce /'pru:dəns/ n prudencia f. **~t** /'pru:dənt/ a prudente. **~tly** adv prudentemente

prudish /'pru:dɪʃ/ a mojigato

prune[1] /pru:n/ n ciruela f pasa

prune[2] /pru:n/ vt podar

pry /praɪ/ vi entrometerse

psalm /sɑ:m/ n salmo m

pseudo- /'sju:dəʊ/ pref seudo...

pseudonym /'sju:dənɪm/ n seudónimo m

psychiatr|ic /saɪkɪ'ætrɪk/ a psiquiátrico. **~ist** /saɪ'kaɪətrɪst/ n psiquiatra m & f. **~y** /saɪ'kaɪətrɪ/ n psiquiatría f

psychic /'saɪkɪk/ a psíquico

psycho-analys|e /saɪkəʊ'ænəlaɪz/ vt psicoanalizar. **~is** /saɪkəʊə'næləsɪs/ n psicoanálisis m. **~t** /-ɪst/ n psicoanalista m & f

psycholog|ical /saɪkə'lɒdʒɪkl/ a psicológico. **~ist** /saɪ'kɒlədʒɪst/ n psicólogo m. **~y** /saɪ'kɒlədʒɪ/ n psicología f

psychopath /'saɪkəpæθ/ n psicópata m & f

pub /pʌb/ n bar m

puberty /'pju:bətɪ/ n pubertad f

pubic /'pju:bɪk/ a pubiano, púbico

public /'pʌblɪk/ a público

publican /'pʌblɪkən/ n tabernero m

publication /pʌblɪ'keɪʃn/ n publicación f

public house /pʌblɪk'haʊs/ n bar m

publicity /pʌb'lɪsətɪ/ n publicidad f

publicize /'pʌblɪsaɪz/ vt publicar, anunciar

publicly /'pʌblɪklɪ/ adv públicamente

public school /pʌblɪk'sku:l/ n colegio m privado; (Amer) instituto m

public-spirited /pʌblɪk'spɪrɪtɪd/ a cívico

publish /'pʌblɪʃ/ vt publicar. **~er** n editor m. **~ing** n publicación f

puck /pʌk/ n (ice hockey) disco m

pucker /'pʌkə(r)/ vt arrugar. ● vi arrugarse

pudding /'pʊdɪŋ/ n postre m; (steamed) budín m

puddle /'pʌdl/ n charco m

pudgy /'pʌdʒɪ/ a (-ier, -iest) rechoncho

puerile /'pjʊəraɪl/ a pueril

puff /pʌf/ n soplo m; (for powder) borla f. ● vt/i soplar. **~ at** chupar ⟨pipe⟩. **~ out** apagar ⟨candle⟩; (swell up) hinchar. **~ed** a (out of breath) sin aliento. **~ pastry** n hojaldre m. **~y** /'pʌfɪ/ a hinchado

pugnacious /pʌg'neɪʃəs/ a belicoso

pug-nosed /'pʌgnəʊzd/ a chato

pull /pʊl/ vt tirar de; sacar ⟨tooth⟩; torcer ⟨muscle⟩. **~ a face** hacer una mueca. **~ a fast one** hacer una mala jugada. **~ down** derribar ⟨building⟩. **~ off** quitarse; (fig) lograr. **~ one's weight** poner de su parte. **~ out** sacar. **~ s.o.'s leg** tomarle el pelo a uno. **~ up** (uproot) desarraigar; (reprimand) reprender. ● vi tirar ⟨at de⟩. **~ away** (auto) alejarse. **~ back** retirarse. **~ in** (enter) entrar; (auto) pararse. **~ o.s. together** tranquilizarse. **~ out** (auto) salirse. **~ through** recobrar la salud. **~ up** (auto) parar. ● n tirón m; (fig) atracción f; (influence) influencia f. **give a ~** tirar

pulley /'pʊlɪ/ n polea f

pullover /'pʊləʊvə(r)/ n jersey m

pulp /pʌlp/ n pulpa f; (for paper) pasta f

pulpit /'pʊlpɪt/ n púlpito m

pulsate /pʌlseɪt/ vi pulsar

pulse /pʌls/ n (med) pulso m

pulverize /'pʌlvəraɪz/ vt pulverizar

pumice /'pʌmɪs/ n piedra f pómez

pummel /'pʌml/ vt (pt pummelled) aporrear

pump[1] /pʌmp/ n bomba f; ● vt sacar con una bomba; (fig) sonsacar. **~ up** inflar

pump[2] /pʌmp/ (plimsoll) zapatilla f de lona; (dancing shoe) escarpín m

pumpkin /'pʌmpkɪn/ n calabaza f

pun /pʌn/ n juego m de palabras

punch[1] /pʌntʃ/ vt dar un puñetazo a; (perforate) perforar; hacer ⟨hole⟩. ● n puñetazo m; (vigour, sl) empuje m; (device) punzón m

punch[2] /pʌntʃ/ (drink) ponche m

punch: **~-drunk** a aturdido a golpes. **~ line** n gracia f. **~-up** n riña f

punctilious /pʌŋk'tɪlɪəs/ a meticuloso

punctual /'pʌŋktʃʊəl/ a puntual. ~ity /-'ælətɪ/ n puntualidad f. ~ly adv puntualmente

punctuat|e /'pʌŋkʃʊeɪt/ vt puntuar. ~ion /-'eɪʃn/ n puntuación f

puncture /'pʌŋktʃə(r)/ n (in tyre) pinchazo m. ● vt pinchar. ● vi pincharse

pundit /'pʌndɪt/ n experto m

pungen|cy /'pʌndʒənsɪ/ n acritud f; (fig) mordacidad f. ~t /'pʌndʒənt/ a acre; (remark) mordaz

punish /'pʌnɪʃ/ vt castigar. ~able a castigable. ~ment n castigo m

punitive /'pju:nɪtɪv/ a punitivo

punk /pʌŋk/ a (music, person) punk

punnet /'pʌnɪt/ n canastilla f

punt¹ /pʌnt/ n (boat) batea f

punt² /pʌnt/ vi apostar. ~er n apostante m & f

puny /'pju:nɪ/ a (-ier, -iest) diminuto; (weak) débil; (petty) insignificante

pup /pʌp/ n cachorro m

pupil¹ /'pju:pl/ n alumno m

pupil² /'pju:pl/ (of eye) pupila f

puppet /'pʌpɪt/ n títere m

puppy /'pʌpɪ/ n cachorro m

purchase /'pɜ:tʃəs/ vt comprar. ● n compra f. ~r n comprador m

pur|e /'pjʊə(r)/ a (-er, -est) puro. ~ely adv puramente. ~ity n pureza f

purée /'pjʊəreɪ/ n puré m

purgatory /'pɜ:gətrɪ/ n purgatorio m

purge /pɜ:dʒ/ vt purgar. ● n purga f

purif|ication /pjʊərɪfɪ'keɪʃn/ n purificación f. ~y /'pjʊərɪfaɪ/ vt purificar

purist /'pjʊərɪst/ n purista m & f

puritan /'pjʊərɪtən/ n puritano m. ~ical /-'tænɪkl/ a puritano

purl /pɜ:l/ n (knitting) punto m del revés

purple /'pɜ:pl/ a purpúreo, morado. ● n púrpura f

purport /pə'pɔ:t/ vt. ~ to be pretender ser

purpose /'pɜ:pəs/ n propósito m; (determination) resolución f. on ~ a propósito. to no ~ en vano. ~-built a construido especialmente. ~ful a (resolute) resuelto. ~ly adv a propósito

purr /pɜ:(r)/ vi ronronear

purse /pɜ:s/ n monedero m; (Amer) bolso m, cartera f (LAm). ● vt fruncir

pursu|e /pə'sju:/ vt perseguir, seguir. ~er n perseguidor m. ~it /pə'sju:t/ n persecución f; (fig) ocupación f

purveyor /pə'veɪə(r)/ n proveedor m

pus /pʌs/ n pus m

push /pʊʃ/ vt empujar; apretar (button). ● vi empujar. ● n empuje m; (effort) esfuerzo m; (drive) dinamismo m. at a ~ en caso de necesidad. get the ~ (sl) ser despedido. ~ aside vt apartar. ~ back vt hacer retroceder. ~ off vi (sl) marcharse. ~ on vi seguir adelante. ~ up vt levantar. ~-button telephone n teléfono m de teclas. ~-chair n sillita f con ruedas. ~ing /'pʊʃɪŋ/ a ambicioso. ~-over n (fam) cosa f muy fácil, pan comido. ~y a (pej) ambicioso

puss /pʊs/ n minino m

put /pʊt/ vt (pt put, pres p putting) poner; (express) expresar; (say) decir; (estimate) estimar; hacer (question). ~ across comunicar; (deceive) engañar. ~ aside poner aparte. ~ away guardar. ~ back devolver; retrasar (clock). ~ by guardar; ahorrar (money). ~ down depositar; (suppress) suprimir; (write) apuntar; (kill) sacrificar. ~ forward avanzar. ~ in introducir; (submit) presentar. ~ in for pedir. ~ off aplazar; (disconcert) desconcertar. ~ on (wear) ponerse; cobrar (speed); encender (light). ~ one's foot down mantenerse firme. ~ out (extinguish) apagar; (inconvenience) incomodar; extender (hand); (disconcert) desconcertar. ~ to sea hacerse a la mar. ~ through (phone) poner. ~ up levantar; subir (price); alojar (guest). ~ up with soportar. stay ~ (fam) no moverse

putrefy /'pju:trɪfaɪ/ vi pudrirse

putt /pʌt/ n (golf) golpe m suave

putty /'pʌtɪ/ n masilla f

put-up /'pʊtʌp/ a. ~ job n confabulación f

puzzl|e /'pʌzl/ n enigma m; (game) rompecabezas m invar. ● vt dejar perplejo. ● vi calentarse los sesos. ~ing a incomprensible; (odd) curioso

pygmy /'pɪgmɪ/ n pigmeo m

pyjamas /pə'dʒɑ:məz/ npl pijama m

pylon /'paɪlən/ n pilón m

pyramid /'pɪrəmɪd/ n pirámide f

python/'paɪθn/ *n* pitón *m*

Q

quack[1]/kwæk/ *n* (*of duck*) graznido *m*

quack[2]/kwæk/ (*person*) charlatán *m*. ~ **doctor***n* curandero *m*

quadrangle/'kwɒdræŋgl/ *n* cuadrilátero *m*; (*court*) patio *m*

quadruped/'kwɒdrʊped/ *n* cuadrúpedo *m*

quadruple/'kwɒdrʊpl/ *a & n* cuádruplo (*m*). ●*vt* cuadruplicar. ~**t** /-plət/ *n* cuatrillizo *m*

quagmire/'kwægmaɪə(r)/ *n* ciénaga *f*; (*fig*) atolladero *m*

quail/kweɪl/ *n* codorniz *f*

quaint/kweɪnt/ *a* (-**er**, -**est**) pintoresco; (*odd*) curioso

quake/kweɪk/ *vi* temblar. ●*n* (*fam*) terremoto *m*

Quaker/'kweɪkə(r)/ *n* cuáquero (*m*)

qualification /kwɒlɪfɪ'keɪʃn/ *n* título *m*; (*requirement*) requisito *m*; (*ability*) capacidad *f*; (*fig*) reserva *f*

qualif|ied/'kwɒlɪfaɪd/ *a* cualificado; (*limited*) limitado; (*with degree, diploma*) titulado. ~**y** /'kwɒlɪfaɪ/ *vt* calificar; (*limit*) limitar. ●*vi* sacar el título; (*sport*) clasificarse; (*fig*) llenar los requisitos

qualitative/'kwɒlɪtətɪv/ *a* cualitativo

quality/'kwɒlɪtɪ/ *n* calidad *f*; (*attribute*) cualidad *f*

qualm/kwɑːm/ *n* escrúpulo *m*

quandary/'kwɒndrɪ/ *n*. in a ~en un dilema

quantitative/'kwɒntɪtətɪv/ *a* cuantitativo

quantity/'kwɒntɪtɪ/ *n* cantidad *f*

quarantine/'kwɒrəntiːn/ *n* cuarentena *f*

quarrel/'kwɒrəl/ *n* riña *f*. ●*vi* (*pt* **quarrelled**) reñir. ~**some** *a* pendenciero

quarry[1]/'kwɒrɪ/ *n* (*excavation*) cantera *f*

quarry[2]/'kwɒrɪ/ *n* (*animal*) presa *f*

quart/kwɔːt/ *n* (poco más de un) litro *m*

quarter/'kwɔːtə(r)/ *n* cuarto *m*; (*of year*) trimestre *m*; (*district*) barrio *m*. from all ~s de todas partes. ●*vt* dividir en cuartos; (*mil*) acuartelar. ~**s** *npl* alojamiento *m*

quartermaster/'kwɔːtəmɑːstə(r)/ *n* intendente *m*

quarter: ~-**final** *n* cuarto *m* de final. ~**ly** *a* trimestral. ●*adv* cada tres meses

quartet/kwɔː'tet/ *n* cuarteto *m*

quartz/kwɔːts/ *n* cuarzo *m*. ●*a* (*watch etc*) de cuarzo

quash/kwɒʃ/ *vt* anular

quasi../'kweɪsaɪ/ *pref* cuasi...

quaver/'kweɪvə(r)/ *vi* temblar. ●*n* (*mus*) corchea *f*

quay/kiː/ *n* muelle *m*

queasy/'kwiːzɪ/ *a* (*stomach*) delicado

queen/kwiːn/ *n* reina *f*. ~ **mother***n* reina *f* madre

queer/kwɪə(r)/ *a* (-**er**, -**est**) extraño; (*dubious*) sospechoso; (*ill*) indispuesto. ●*n* (*sl*) homosexual *m*

quell/kwel/ *vt* reprimir

quench/kwentʃ/ *vt* apagar; sofocar (*desire*)

querulous /'kwerʊləs/ *a* quejumbroso

query/'kwɪərɪ/ *n* pregunta *f*. ●*vt* preguntar; (*doubt*) poner en duda

quest/kwest/ *n* busca *f*

question/'kwestʃən/ *n* pregunta *f*; (*for discussion*) cuestión *f*. in ~en cuestión. out of the ~ imposible. without ~sin duda. ●*vt* preguntar; (*police etc*) interrogar; (*doubt*) poner en duda. ~**able**/'kwestʃənəbl/ *a* discutible. ~ **mark** *n* signo *m* de interrogación. ~**naire** /kwestʃə 'neə(r)/ *n* cuestionario *m*

queue /kjuː/ *n* cola *f*. ●*vi* (*pres p* **queuing**) hacer cola

quibble/'kwɪbl/ *vi* discutir; (*split hairs*) sutilizar

quick/kwɪk/ *a* (-**er**, -**est**) rápido. be ~! ¡date prisa! ●*adv* rápidamente. ●*n*. to the ~ en lo vivo. ~**en** /'kwɪkən/ *vt* acelerar. ●*vi* acelerarse. ~**ly** *adv* rápidamente. ~**sand** /'kwɪksænd/ *n* arena *f* movediza. ~-**tempered** *a* irascible

quid/kwɪd/ *n invar* (*sl*) libra *f* (*esterlina*)

quiet/'kwaɪət/ *a* (-**er**, -**est**) tranquilo; (*silent*) callado; (*discreet*) discreto. ●*n* tranquilidad *f*. on the ~a escondidas. ~**en** /'kwaɪətn/ *vt* calmar. ●*vi* calmarse. ~**ly** *adv* tranquilamente; (*silently*) silenciosamente; (*discreetly*) discretamente. ~**ness***n* tranquilidad *f*

quill /kwɪl/ n pluma f

quilt /kwɪlt/ n edredón m. ●vt acolchar

quince /kwɪns/ n membrillo m

quinine /kwɪˈniːn/ n quinina f

quintessence /kwɪnˈtesns/ n quintaesencia f

quintet /kwɪnˈtet/ n quinteto m

quintuplet /ˈkwɪntjuːplət/ n quintillizo m

quip /kwɪp/ n ocurrencia f

quirk /kwɜːk/ n peculiaridad f

quit /kwɪt/ vt (pt quitted) dejar. ●vi abandonar; (leave) marcharse; (resign) dimitir. ~ doing (cease, Amer) dejar de hacer

quite /kwaɪt/ adv bastante; (completely) totalmente; (really) verdaderamente. ~ (so)! ¡claro! ~ a few bastante

quits /kwɪts/ a a la par. call it ~ darlo por terminado

quiver /ˈkwɪvə(r)/ vi temblar.

quixotic /kwɪkˈsɒtɪk/ a quijotesco

quiz /kwɪz/ n (pl quizzes) serie f de preguntas; (game) concurso m. ●vt (pt quizzed) interrogar. ~zical /ˈkwɪzɪkl/ a burlón

quorum /ˈkwɔːrəm/ n quórum m

quota /ˈkwəʊtə/ n cuota f

quotation /kwəʊˈteɪʃn/ n cita f; (price) presupuesto m. ~ation marks npl comillas fpl. ~e /kwəʊt/ vt citar; (com) cotizar. ●n (fam) cita f; (price) presupuesto m. in ~es entre comillas

quotient /ˈkwəʊʃnt/ n cociente m

R

rabbi /ˈræbaɪ/ n rabino m

rabbit /ˈræbɪt/ n conejo m

rabble /ˈræbl/ n gentío m. the ~ (pej) el populacho m

rabid /ˈræbɪd/ a feroz; (dog) rabioso. ~es /ˈreɪbiːz/ n rabia f

race¹ /reɪs/ n carrera f. ●vt hacer correr (horse); acelerar (engine). ●vi (run) correr, ir corriendo; (rush) ir de prisa

race² /reɪs/ (group) raza f

race: ~course /ˈreɪskɔːs/ n hipódromo m. ~horse /ˈreɪshɔːs/ n caballo m de carreras. ~riots /ˈreɪsraɪəts/ npl disturbios mpl raciales. ~track /ˈreɪstræk/ n hipódromo m

racial /ˈreɪʃl/ a racial. ~ism /-ɪzəm/ n racismo m

racing /ˈreɪsɪŋ/ n carreras fpl. ~ car n coche m de carreras

racis|m /ˈreɪsɪzəm/ n racismo m. ~t /ˈreɪsɪst/ a & n racista (m & f)

rack¹ /ræk/ n (shelf) estante m; (for luggage) rejilla f; (for plates) escurreplatos m invar. ●vt. ~ one's brains devanarse los sesos

rack² /ræk/ n. go to ~ and ruin quedarse en la ruina

racket¹ /ˈrækɪt/ n (for sports) raqueta

racket² /ˈrækɪt/ n (din) alboroto m; (swindle) estafa f. ~eer /-əˈtɪə(r)/ n estafador m

raconteur /rækɒnˈtɜː/ n anecdotista m & f

racy /ˈreɪsɪ/ a (-ier, -iest) vivo

radar /ˈreɪdɑː(r)/ n radar m

radian|ce /ˈreɪdɪəns/ n resplandor m. ~t /ˈreɪdɪənt/ a radiante. ~tly adv con resplandor

radiat|e /ˈreɪdɪeɪt/ vt irradiar. ●vi divergir. ~ion /-ˈeɪʃn/ n radiación f. ~or /ˈreɪdɪeɪtə(r)/ n radiador m

radical /ˈrædɪkl/ a & n radical (m)

radio /ˈreɪdɪəʊ/ n (pl -os) radio f. ●vt transmitir por radio

radioactiv|e /reɪdɪəʊˈæktɪv/ a radiactivo. ~ity /-ˈtɪvətɪ/ n radiactividad f

radiograph|er /reɪdɪˈɒɡrəfə(r)/ n radiógrafo m. ~y n radiografía f

radish /ˈrædɪʃ/ n rábano m

radius /ˈreɪdɪəs/ n (pl -dii /-dɪaɪ/) radio m

raffish /ˈræfɪʃ/ a disoluto

raffle /ˈræfl/ n rifa f

raft /rɑːft/ n balsa f

rafter /ˈrɑːftə(r)/ n cabrio m

rag¹ /ræɡ/ n andrajo m; (for wiping) trapo m; (newspaper) periodicucho m. in ~s (person) andrajoso; (clothes) hecho jirones

rag² /ræɡ/ n (univ) festival m estudiantil; (prank, fam) broma f pesada. ●vt (pt ragged) (sl) tomar el pelo a

ragamuffin /ˈræɡəmʌfɪn/ n granuja m, golfo m

rage /reɪdʒ/ n rabia f; (fashion) moda f. ●vi estar furioso; (storm) bramar

ragged /ˈræɡɪd/ a (person) andrajoso; (clothes) hecho jirones; (edge) mellado

raid /reɪd/ n (mil) incursión f; (by police, etc) redada f; (by thieves) asalto m. ●vt (mil) atacar; (police)

hacer una redada en; ⟨*thieves*⟩ asaltar. **~er** *n* invasor *m*; (*thief*) ladrón
m

rail¹ /reɪl/ *n* barandilla *f*; (*for train*)
riel *m*; (*rod*) barra *f*. **by ~** por
ferrocarril

rail² /reɪl/ *vi*. **~ against, ~ at**
insultar

railing /'reɪlɪŋ/ *n* barandilla *f*; (*fence*)
verja *f*

rail|road /'reɪlrəud/ *n* (*Amer*),
~way /'reɪlweɪ/ *n* ferrocarril *m*.
~wayman *n* (*pl* **-men**) ferroviario
m. **~way station** *n* estación *f* de
ferrocarril

rain /reɪn/ *n* lluvia *f*. ● *vi* llover.
~bow /'reɪnbəu/ *n* arco *m* iris.
~coat /'reɪnkəut/ *n* impermeable *m*.
~fall /'reɪnfɔːl/ *n* precipitación *f*. **~**
water *n* agua *f* de lluvia. **~y** /'reɪnɪ/
a (**-ier, -iest**) lluvioso

raise /reɪz/ *vt* levantar; (*breed*) criar;
obtener ⟨*money etc*⟩; hacer ⟨*question*⟩;
plantear (*problem*); subir (*price*). **~**
one's glass to brindar por. **~ one's**
hat descubrirse. ● *n* (*Amer*) aumento *m*

raisin /'reɪzn/ *n* (*uva f*) pasa *f*

rake¹ /reɪk/ *n* rastrillo *m*. ● *vt*
rastrillar; (*search*) buscar en. **~ up**
remover

rake² /reɪk/ *n* (*man*) calavera *m*

rake-off /'reɪkɒf/ *n* (*fam*) comisión *f*

rally /'rælɪ/ *vt* reunir; (*revive*) reanimar. ● *vi* reunirse; (*in sickness*) re-
cuperarse. ● *n* reunión *f*; (*recovery*)
recuperación *f*; (*auto*) rallye *m*

ram /ræm/ *n* carnero *m*. ● *vt* (*pt*
rammed) (*thrust*) meter por la
fuerza; (*crash into*) chocar con

rambl|e /'ræmbl/ *n* excursión *f* a pie.
● *vi* ir de paseo; (*in speech*) divagar.
~e on divagar. **~er** *n* excursionista
m & *f*. **~ing** *a* ⟨*speech*⟩ divagador

ramification /ræmɪfɪ'keɪʃn/ *n*
ramificación *f*

ramp /ræmp/ *n* rampa *f*

rampage /ræm'peɪdʒ/ *vi* alborotarse. /'ræmpeɪdʒ/ *n*. **go on the ~**
alborotarse

rampant /'ræmpənt/ *a*. **be ~** ⟨*disease etc*⟩ estar extendido

rampart /'ræmpɑːt/ *n* muralla *f*

ramshackle /'ræmʃækl/ *a* desvencijado

ran /ræn/ *see* **run**

ranch /rɑːntʃ/ *n* hacienda *f*

rancid /'rænsɪd/ *a* rancio

rancour /'ræŋkə(r)/ *n* rencor *m*

random /'rændəm/ *a* hecho al azar;
(*chance*) fortuito. ● *n*. **at ~** al azar

randy /'rændɪ/ *a* (**-ier, -iest**)
lujurioso, cachondo (*fam*)

rang /ræŋ/ *see* **ring**²

range /reɪndʒ/ *n* alcance *m*; (*distance*) distancia *f*; (*series*) serie *f*; (*of
mountains*) cordillera *f*; (*extent*)
extensión *f*; (*com*) surtido *m*; (*open
area*) dehesa *f*; (*stove*) cocina *f* económica. ● *vi* extenderse; (*vary*) variar

ranger /'reɪndʒə(r)/ *n* guardabosque
m

rank¹ /ræŋk/ *n* posición *f*, categoría
f; (*row*) fila *f*; (*for taxis*) parada *f*. **the
~ and file** la masa *f*. ● *vt* clasificar.
● *vi* clasificarse. **~s** *npl* soldados
mpl rasos

rank² /ræŋk/ *a* (**-er, -est**) exuberante;
(*smell*) fétido; (*fig*) completo

rankle /ræŋkl/ *vi* (*fig*) causar rencor

ransack /'rænsæk/ *vt* registrar; (*pillage*) saquear

ransom /'rænsəm/ *n* rescate *m*. **hold
s.o. to ~** exigir rescate por uno; (*fig*)
hacer chantaje a uno. ● *vt* rescatar;
(*redeem*) redimir

rant /rænt/ *vi* vociferar

rap /ræp/ *n* golpe *m* seco. ● *vt/i* (*pt
rapped*) golpear

rapacious /rə'peɪʃs/ *a* rapaz

rape /reɪp/ *vt* violar. ● *n* violación *f*

rapid /'ræpɪd/ *a* rápido. **~ity**
/rə'pɪdətɪ/ *n* rapidez *f*. **~s** /'ræpɪdz/
npl rápido *m*

rapist /'reɪpɪst/ *n* violador *m*

rapport /ræ'pɔː(r)/ *n* armonía *f*,
relación *f*

rapt /ræpt/ *a* ⟨*attention*⟩ profundo. **~
in** absorto en

raptur|e /'ræptʃə(r)/ *n* éxtasis *m*.
~ous *a* extático

rare¹ /reə(r)/ *a* (**-er, -est**) raro

rare² /reə(r)/ *a* (*culin*) poco hecho

rarefied /'reərɪfaɪd/ *a* enrarecido

rarely /'reəlɪ/ *adv* raramente

rarity /'reərətɪ/ *n* rareza *f*

raring /'reərɪŋ/ *a* (*fam*). **~ to**
impaciente por

rascal /rɑːskl/ *n* tunante *m* & *f*

rash¹ /ræʃ/ *a* (**-er, -est**) imprudente,
precipitado

rash² /ræʃ/ *n* erupción *f*

rasher /'ræʃə(r)/ *n* loncha *f*

rash|ly /'ræʃlɪ/ *adv* impruden-
temente, a la ligera. **~ness** *n* imprudencia *f*

rasp /rɑːsp/ n (file) escofina f

raspberry /'rɑːzbrɪ/ n frambuesa f

rasping /'rɑːspɪŋ/ a áspero

rat /ræt/ n rata f. ● vi (pt **ratted**). ~ **on** (desert) desertar; (inform on) denunciar, chivarse

rate /reɪt/ n (ratio) proporción f; (speed) velocidad f; (price) precio m; (of interest) tipo m. **at any** ~ de todas formas. **at the** ~ **of** (on the basis of) a razón de. **at this** ~ así. ● vt valorar; (consider) considerar; (deserve, Amer) merecer. ● vi ser considerado. ~**able value** n valor m imponible. ~**payer** /'reɪtpeɪə(r)/ n contribuyente m & f. ~**s** npl (taxes) impuestos mpl municipales

rather /'rɑːðə(r)/ adv mejor dicho; (fairly) bastante; (a little) un poco. ● int claro. **I would** ~ **not** prefiero no

ratif|ication /rætɪfɪ'keɪʃn/ n ratificación f. ~**y** /'rætɪfaɪ/ vt ratificar

rating /'reɪtɪŋ/ n clasificación f; (sailor) marinero m; (number, TV) índice m

ratio /'reɪʃɪəʊ/ n (pl -os) proporción f

ration /'ræʃn/ n ración f. ● vt racionar

rational /'ræʃənəl/ a racional. ~**ize** /'ræʃənəlaɪz/ vt racionalizar

rat race /'rætreɪs/ n lucha f incesante para triunfar

rattle /'rætl/ vi traquetear. ● vt (shake) agitar; (sl) desconcertar. ● n traqueteo m; (toy) sonajero m. ~ **off** (fig) decir de corrida

rattlesnake /'rætlsneɪk/ n serpiente f de cascabel

ratty /'rætɪ/ a (-ier, -iest) (sl) irritable

raucous /'rɔːkəs/ a estridente

ravage /'rævɪdʒ/ vt estragar. ~**s** /'rævɪdʒɪz/ npl estragos mpl

rave /reɪv/ vi delirar; (in anger) enfurecerse. ~ **about** entusiasmarse por

raven /'reɪvn/ n cuervo m. ● a (hair) negro

ravenous /'rævənəs/ a voraz; (person) hambriento. **be** ~ morirse de hambre

ravine /rə'viːn/ n barranco m

raving /'reɪvɪŋ/ a. ~ **mad** loco de atar. ~**s** npl divagaciones fpl

ravish /'rævɪʃ/ vt (rape) violar. ~**ing** a (enchanting) encantador

raw /rɔː/ a (-er, -est) crudo; (not processed) bruto; (wound) en carne viva; (inexperienced) inexperto; (weather) crudo. ~ **deal** n tratamiento m injusto, injusticia f. ~ **materials** npl materias fpl primas

ray /reɪ/ n rayo m

raze /reɪz/ vt arrasar

razor /'reɪzə(r)/ n navaja f de afeitar; (electric) maquinilla f de afeitar

Rd abbr (Road) C/, Calle f

re¹ /riː/ prep con referencia a. ● pref re...

re² /reɪ/ n (mus, second note of any musical scale) re m

reach /riːtʃ/ vt alcanzar; (extend) extender; (arrive at) llegar a; (achieve) lograr; (hand over) pasar, dar. ● vi extenderse. ● n alcance m; (of river) tramo m recto. **within** ~ **of** al alcance de; (close to) a corta distancia de

react /rɪ'ækt/ vi reaccionar. ~**ion** /rɪ'ækʃn/ n reacción f. ~**ionary** a & n reaccionario (m)

reactor /rɪ'æktə(r)/ n reactor m

read /riːd/ vt (pt **read** /red/) leer; (study) estudiar; (interpret) interpretar. ● vi leer; (instrument) indicar. ● n (fam) lectura f. ~ **out** vt leer en voz alta. ~**able** a interesante, agradable; (clear) legible. ~**er** /'riːdə(r)/ n lector m. ~**ership** n lectores m

readi|ly /'redɪlɪ/ adv (willingly) de buena gana; (easily) fácilmente. ~**ness** /'redɪnɪs/ n prontitud f. **in** ~**ness** preparado, listo

reading /'riːdɪŋ/ n lectura f

readjust /riːə'dʒʌst/ vt reajustar. ● vi readaptarse (**to** a)

ready /'redɪ/ a (-ier, -iest) listo, preparado; (quick) pronto. ~**-made** a confeccionado. ~ **money** n dinero m contante. ~**-reckoner** n baremo m. **get** ~ prepararse

real /rɪəl/ a verdadero. ● adv (Amer, fam) verdaderamente. ~ **estate** n bienes mpl raíces

realis|m /'rɪəlɪzəm/ n realismo m. ~**t** /'rɪəlɪst/ n realista m & f. ~**tic** /-'lɪstɪk/ a realista. ~**tically** /-'lɪstɪklɪ/ adv de manera realista

reality /rɪ'ælətɪ/ n realidad f

realiz|ation /rɪəlaɪ'zeɪʃn/ n comprensión f; (com) realización f. ~**e** /'rɪəlaɪz/ vt darse cuenta de; (fulfil, com) realizar

really /'rɪəlɪ/ adv verdaderamente

realm /relm/ n reino m

ream /ri:m/ n resma f

reap /ri:p/ vt segar; (fig) cosechar

re: ~**appear** /ri:ə'pɪə(r)/ vi reaparecer. ~**appraisal** /ri:ə'preɪzl/ n revaluación f

rear[1] /rɪə(r)/ n parte f de atrás. ● a posterior, trasero

rear[2] /rɪə(r)/ vt (bring up, breed) criar. ~ **one's head** levantar la cabeza. ● vi (horse) encabritarse. ~ **up** (horse) encabritarse

rear: ~**admiral** n contraalmirante m. ~**guard** /'rɪəgɑ:d/ n retaguardia f

re: ~**arm** /ri:'ɑ:m/ vt rearmar. ● vi rearmarse. ~**arrange** /ri:ə'reɪndʒ/ vt arreglar de otra manera

reason /'ri:zn/ n razón f, motivo m. **within** ~ dentro de lo razonable. ● vi razonar

reasonable /'ri:zənəbl/ a razonable

reasoning /'ri:znɪŋ/ n razonamiento m

reassur|ance /ri:ə'ʃʊərəns/ n promesa f tranquilizadora; (guarantee) garantía f. ~**e** /ri:ə'ʃʊə(r)/ vt tranquilizar

rebate /'ri:beɪt/ n reembolso m; (discount) rebaja f

rebel /'rebl/ n rebelde m & f. /rɪ'bel/ vi (pt **rebelled**) rebelarse. ~**lion** n rebelión f. ~**lious** a rebelde

rebound /rɪ'baʊnd/ vi rebotar; (fig) recaer. /'ri:baʊnd/ n rebote m. **on the** ~ (fig) por reacción

rebuff /rɪ'bʌf/ vt rechazar. ● n desaire m

rebuild /ri:'bɪld/ vt (pt **rebuilt**) reconstruir

rebuke /rɪ'bju:k/ vt reprender. ● n reprensión f

rebuttal /rɪ'bʌtl/ n refutación f

recall /rɪ'kɔ:l/ vt (call s.o. back) llamar; (remember) recordar. ● n llamada f

recant /rɪ'kænt/ vi retractarse

recap /'ri:kæp/ vt/i (pt **recapped**) (fam) resumir. ● n (fam) resumen m

recapitulat|e /ri:kə'pɪtʃʊleɪt/ vt/i resumir. ~**ion** /-'leɪʃn/ n resumen m

recapture /ri:'kæptʃə(r)/ vt recobrar; (recall) hacer revivir

reced|e /rɪ'si:d/ vi retroceder. ~**ing** a (forehead) huidizo

receipt /rɪ'si:t/ n recibo m. ~**s** npl (com) ingresos mpl

receive /rɪ'si:v/ vt recibir. ~**r** /-ə(r)/ n (of stolen goods) perista m & f; (of phone) auricular m

recent /'ri:snt/ a reciente. ~**ly** adv recientemente

receptacle /rɪ'septəkl/ n recipiente m

reception /rɪ'sepʃn/ n recepción f; (welcome) acogida f. ~**ist** n recepcionista m & f

receptive /rɪ'septɪv/ a receptivo

recess /rɪ'ses/ n hueco m; (holiday) vacaciones fpl; (fig) parte f recóndita

recession /rɪ'seʃn/ n recesión f

recharge /ri:'tʃɑ:dʒ/ vt cargar de nuevo, recargar

recipe /'resəpɪ/ n receta f

recipient /rɪ'sɪpɪənt/ n recipiente m & f; (of letter) destinatario m

reciprocal /rɪ'sɪprəkl/ a recíproco

reciprocate /rɪ'sɪprəkeɪt/ vt corresponder a

recital /rɪ'saɪtl/ n (mus) recital m

recite /rɪ'saɪt/ vt recitar; (list) enumerar

reckless /'reklɪs/ a imprudente. ~**ly** adv imprudentemente. ~**ness** n imprudencia f

reckon /'rekən/ vt/i calcular; (consider) considerar; (think) pensar. ~ **on** (rely) contar con. ~**ing** n cálculo m

reclaim /rɪ'kleɪm/ vt reclamar; recuperar (land)

reclin|e /rɪ'klaɪn/ vi recostarse. ~**ing** a acostado; (seat) reclinable

recluse /rɪ'klu:s/ n solitario m

recogni|tion /rekəg'nɪʃn/ n reconocimiento m. **beyond** ~**tion** irreconocible. ~**ze** /'rekəgnaɪz/ vt reconocer

recoil /rɪ'kɔɪl/ vi retroceder. ● n (of gun) culatazo m

recollect /rekə'lekt/ vt recordar. ~**ion** /-ʃn/ n recuerdo m

recommend /rekə'mend/ vt recomendar. ~**ation** /-'deɪʃn/ n recomendación f

recompense /'rekəmpens/ vt recompensar. ● n recompensa f

reconcil|e /'rekənsaɪl/ vt reconciliar (people); conciliar (facts). ~**e o.s.** resignarse (**to** a). ~**iation** /-sɪlɪ'eɪʃn/ n reconciliación f

recondition /ri:kən'dɪʃn/ vt reacondicionar, arreglar

reconnaissance /rɪ'kɒnɪsns/ n reconocimiento m

reconnoitre /rekə'nɔɪtə(r)/ vt (pres p -tring) (mil) reconocer. ● vi hacer un reconocimiento

re: ~**consider** /riːkən'sɪdə(r)/ vt volver a considerar. ~**construct** /riːkən'strʌkt/ vt reconstruir. ~**construction** /-ʃn/ n reconstrucción f

record /rɪ'kɔːd/ vt (in register) registrar; (in diary) apuntar; (mus) grabar. /'rekɔːd/ n (file) documentación f, expediente m; (mus) disco m; (sport) récord m. **off the** ~ en confianza. ~**er** /rɪ'kɔːdə(r)/ n registrador m; (mus) flauta f dulce. ~**ing** n grabación f. ~**player** n tocadiscos m invar

recount /rɪ'kaʊnt/ vt contar, relatar, referir

re-count /riː'kaʊnt/ vt recontar. /'riːkaʊnt/ n (pol) recuento m

recoup /rɪ'kuːp/ vt recuperar

recourse /rɪ'kɔːs/ n recurso m. **have** ~ **to** recurrir a

recover /rɪ'kʌvə(r)/ vt recuperar. ● vi reponerse. ~**y** n recuperación f

recreation /rekrɪ'eɪʃn/ n recreo m. ~**al** a de recreo

recrimination /rɪkrɪmɪ'neɪʃn/ n recriminación f

recruit /rɪ'kruːt/ n recluta m. ● vt reclutar. ~**ment** n reclutamiento m

rectang|le /'rektæŋgl/ n rectángulo m. ~**ular** /-'tæŋgjʊlə(r)/ a rectangular

rectif|ication /rektɪfɪ'keɪʃn/ n rectificación f. ~**y** /'rektɪfaɪ/ vt rectificar

rector /'rektə(r)/ n párroco m; (of college) rector m. ~**y** n rectoría f

recumbent /rɪ'kʌmbənt/ a recostado

recuperat|e /rɪ'kuːpəreɪt/ vt recuperar. ● vi reponerse. ~**ion** /-'reɪʃn/ n recuperación f

recur /rɪ'kɜː(r)/ vi (pt **recurred**) repetirse. ~**rence** /rɪ'kʌrns/ n repetición f. ~**rent** /rɪ'kʌrənt/ a repetido

recycle /riː'saɪkl/ vt reciclar

red /red/ a (redder, reddest) rojo. ● n rojo. **in the** ~ (account) en descubierto. ~**breast** /'redbrest/ n petirrojo m. ~**brick** /'redbrɪk/ a (univ) de reciente fundación. ~**den** /'redn/ vt enrojecer. ● vi enrojecerse. ~**dish** a rojizo

redecorate /riː'dekəreɪt/ vt pintar de nuevo

rede|em /rɪ'diːm/ vt redimir. ~**eming quality** n cualidad f compensadora. ~**mption** /-'dempʃn/ n redención f

redeploy /riːdɪ'plɔɪ/ vt disponer de otra manera; (mil) cambiar de frente

red: ~**handed** a en flagrante. ~ **herring** n (fig) pista f falsa. ~**hot** a al rojo; (news) de última hora

Red Indian /red'ɪndjən/ n piel m & f roja

redirect /riːdaɪ'rekt/ vt reexpedir

red: ~**letter day** n día m señalado, día m memorable. ~ **light** n luz f roja. ~**ness** n rojez f

redo /riː'duː/ vt (pt **redid**, pp **redone**) rehacer

redouble /rɪ'dʌbl/ vt redoblar

redress /rɪ'dres/ vt reparar. ● n reparación f

red tape /red'teɪp/ n (fig) papeleo m

reduc|e /rɪ'djuːs/ vt reducir. ● vi reducirse; (slim) adelgazar. ~**tion** /'dʌkʃn/ n reducción f

redundan|cy /rɪ'dʌndənsɪ/ n superfluidad f; (unemployment) desempleo m. ~**t** /rɪ'dʌndənt/ a superfluo. **be made** ~**t** perder su empleo

reed /riːd/ n caña f; (mus) lengüeta f

reef /riːf/ n arrecife m

reek /riːk/ n mal olor m. ● vi. ~ **(of)** apestar a

reel /riːl/ n carrete m. ● vi dar vueltas; (stagger) tambalearse. ● vt. ~ **off** (fig) enumerar

refectory /rɪ'fektərɪ/ n refectorio m

refer /rɪ'fɜː(r)/ vt (pt **referred**) remitir. ● vi referirse. ~ **to** referirse a; (consult) consultar

referee /refə'riː/ n árbitro m; (for job) referencia f. ● vi (pt **refereed**) arbitrar

reference /'refrəns/ n referencia f. ~ **book** n libro m de consulta. **in** ~ **to, with** ~ **to** en cuanto a; (com) respecto a

referendum /refə'rendəm/ n (pl -ums) referéndum m

refill /riː'fɪl/ vt rellenar. /'riːfɪl/ n recambio m

refine /rɪ'faɪn/ vt refinar. ~**d** a refinado. ~**ment** n refinamiento m; (tec) refinación f. ~**ry** /-ərɪ/ n refinería f

reflect /rɪ'flekt/ vt reflejar. ● vi reflejar; (think) reflexionar. ~ **upon** perjudicar. ~**ion** /-ʃn/ n reflexión f;

(*image*) reflejo *m*. ∼ive /rɪˈflektɪv/ *a* reflector; (*thoughtful*) pensativo. ∼or∼ reflector *m*

reflex /ˈriːfleks/ *a* & *n* reflejo (*m*)

reflexive /rɪˈfleksɪv/ *a* (*gram*) reflexivo

reform /rɪˈfɔːm/ *vt* reformar. ●*vi* reformarse. ●*n* reforma *f*. ∼er *n* reformador *m*

refract /rɪˈfrækt/ *vt* refractar

refrain¹ /rɪˈfreɪn/ *n* estribillo *m*

refrain² /rɪˈfreɪn/ *vi* abstenerse (from de)

refresh /rɪˈfreʃ/ *vt* refrescar. ∼er /rɪˈfreʃə(r)/ *a* (*course*) de repaso. ∼ing *a* refrescante. ∼ments *npl* (*food and drink*) refrigerio *m*

refrigerat|e /rɪˈfrɪdʒəreɪt/ *vt* refrigerar. ∼or *n* nevera *f*, refrigeradora *f* (*LAm*)

refuel /riːˈfjuːəl/ *vt/i* (*pt* refuelled) repostar

refuge /ˈrefjuːdʒ/ *n* refugio *m*. take ∼ refugiarse. ∼e /refjʊˈdʒiː/ *n* refugiado *m*

refund /rɪˈfʌnd/ *vt* reembolsar. /ˈriːfʌnd/ *n* reembolso *m*

refurbish /riːˈfɜːbɪʃ/ *vt* renovar

refusal /rɪˈfjuːzl/ *n* negativa *f*

refuse¹ /rɪˈfjuːz/ *vt* rehusar. ●*vi* negarse

refuse² /ˈrefjuːs/ *n* basura *f*

refute /rɪˈfjuːt/ *vt* refutar

regain /rɪˈgeɪn/ *vt* recobrar

regal /ˈriːgl/ *a* real

regale /rɪˈgeɪl/ *vt* festejar

regalia /rɪˈgeɪlɪə/ *npl* insignias *fpl*

regard /rɪˈgɑːd/ *vt* mirar; (*consider*) considerar. as ∼s en cuanto a. ●*n* mirada *f*; (*care*) atención *f*; (*esteem*) respeto *m*. ∼ing *prep* en cuanto a. ∼less /rɪˈgɑːdlɪs/ *adv* a pesar de todo. ∼less of sin tener en cuenta. ∼s *npl* saludos *mpl*. kind ∼s *npl* recuerdos *mpl*

regatta /rɪˈgætə/ *n* regata *f*

regency /ˈriːdʒənsɪ/ *n* regencia *f*

regenerate /rɪˈdʒenəreɪt/ *vt* regenerar

regent /ˈriːdʒənt/ *n* regente *m* & *f*

regime /reɪˈʒiːm/ *n* régimen *m*

regiment /ˈredʒɪmənt/ *n* regimiento *m*. ∼al /-ˈmentl/ *a* del regimiento. ∼ation /-enˈteɪʃn/ *n* reglamentación *f* rígida

region /ˈriːdʒən/ *n* región *f*. in the ∼ of alrededor de. ∼al *a* regional

register /ˈredʒɪstə(r)/ *n* registro *m*. ●*vt* registrar; matricular (*vehicle*); declarar (*birth*); certificar (*letter*); facturar (*luggage*); (*indicate*) indicar; (*express*) expresar. ●*vi* (*enrol*) inscribirse; (*fig*) producir impresión. ∼ office *n* registro *m* civil

registrar /redʒɪˈstrɑː(r)/ *n* secretario *m* del registro civil; (*univ*) secretario *m* general

registration /redʒɪˈstreɪʃn/ *n* registración *f*; (*in register*) inscripción *f*; (*of vehicle*) matrícula *f*

registry /ˈredʒɪstrɪ/ *n*. ∼ office *n* registro *m* civil

regression /rɪˈgreʃn/ *n* regresión *f*

regret /rɪˈgret/ *n* pesar *m*. ●*vt* (*pt* regretted) lamentar. I ∼ that siento (que). ∼fully *adv* con pesar. ∼table *a* lamentable. ∼tably *adv* lamentablemente

regular /ˈregjʊlə(r)/ *a* regular; (*usual*) habitual. ●*n* (*fam*) cliente *m* habitual. ∼ity /-ˈlærətɪ/ *n* regularidad *f*. ∼ly *adv* regularmente

regulat|e /ˈregjʊleɪt/ *vt* regular. ∼ion /-ˈleɪʃn/ *n* arreglo *m*; (*rule*) regla *f*

rehabilitat|e /riːhəˈbɪlɪteɪt/ *vt* rehabilitar. ∼ion /-ˈteɪʃn/ *n* rehabilitación *f*

rehash /riːˈhæʃ/ *vt* volver a presentar. /ˈriːhæʃ/ *n* refrito *m*

rehears|al /rɪˈhɜːsl/ *n* ensayo *m*. ∼e /rɪˈhɜːs/ *vt* ensayar

reign /reɪn/ *n* reinado *m*. ●*vi* reinar

reimburse /riːɪmˈbɜːs/ *vt* reembolsar

reins /reɪnz/ *npl* riendas *fpl*

reindeer /ˈreɪndɪə(r)/ *n invar* reno *m*

reinforce /riːɪnˈfɔːs/ *vt* reforzar. ∼ment *n* refuerzo *m*

reinstate /riːɪnˈsteɪt/ *vt* reintegrar

reiterate /riːˈɪtəreɪt/ *vt* reiterar

reject /rɪˈdʒekt/ *vt* rechazar. /ˈriːdʒekt/ *n* producto *m* defectuoso. ∼ion /ˈdʒekʃn/ *n* rechazamiento *m*, rechazo *m*

rejoic|e /rɪˈdʒɔɪs/ *vi* regocijarse. ∼ing *n* regocijo *m*

rejoin /rɪˈdʒɔɪn/ *vt* reunirse con; (*answer*) replicar. ∼der /rɪˈdʒɔɪndə(r)/ *n* réplica *f*

rejuvenate /rɪˈdʒuːvəneɪt/ *vt* rejuvenecer

rekindle /riːˈkɪndl/ *vt* reavivar

relapse /rɪ'læps/ n recaída f. ● vi recaer; (into crime) reincidir

relate /rɪ'leɪt/ vt contar; (connect) relacionar. ● vi relacionarse (**to** con). **~d** a emparentado; ⟨ideas etc⟩ relacionado

relation /rɪ'leɪʃn/ n relación f; (person) pariente m & f. **~ship** n relación f; (blood tie) parentesco m; (affair) relaciones fpl

relative /'relətɪv/ n pariente m & f. ● a relativo. **~ly** adv relativamente

relax /rɪ'læks/ vt relajar. ● vi relajarse. **~ation** /riːlæk'seɪʃn/ n relajación f; (rest) descanso m; (recreation) recreo m. **~ing** a relajante

relay /'riːleɪ/ n relevo m. ~ (**race**) n carrera f de relevos. /rɪ'leɪ/ vt retransmitir

release /rɪ'liːs/ vt soltar; poner en libertad ⟨prisoner⟩; lanzar ⟨bomb⟩; estrenar ⟨film⟩; (mec) desenganchar; publicar ⟨news⟩; emitir ⟨smoke⟩. ● n liberación f; (of film) estreno m; (record) disco m nuevo

relegate /'religeɪt/ vt relegar

relent /rɪ'lent/ vi ceder. **~less** a implacable; (continuous) incesante

relevan|ce /'reləvəns/ n pertinencia f. **~t** /'reləvənt/ a pertinente

reliab|ility /rɪlaɪə'bɪlətɪ/ n fiabilidad f. **~le** /rɪ'laɪəbl/ a seguro; ⟨person⟩ de fiar; (com) serio

relian|ce /rɪ'laɪəns/ n dependencia f; (trust) confianza f. **~t** a confiado

relic /'relɪk/ n reliquia f. **~s** npl restos mpl

relie|f /rɪ'liːf/ n alivio m; (assistance) socorro m; (outline) relieve m. **~ve** /rɪ'liːv/ vt aliviar; (take over from) relevar

religio|n /rɪ'lɪdʒən/ n religión f. **~us** /rɪ'lɪdʒəs/ a religioso

relinquish /rɪ'lɪŋkwɪʃ/ vt abandonar, renunciar

relish /'relɪʃ/ n gusto m; (culin) salsa f. ● vt saborear. **I don't ~ the idea** no me gusta la idea

relocate /riːləʊ'keɪt/ vt colocar de nuevo

reluctan|ce /rɪ'lʌktəns/ n desgana f. **~t** /rɪ'lʌktənt/ a mal dispuesto. be **~t to** no tener ganas de. **~tly** adv de mala gana

rely /rɪ'laɪ/ vi. ~ **on** contar con; (trust) fiarse de; (depend) depender

remain /rɪ'meɪn/ vi quedar. **~der** /rɪ'meɪndə(r)/ n resto m. **~s** npl restos mpl; (left-overs) sobras fpl

remand /rɪ'mɑːnd/ vt. ~ **in custody** mantener bajo custodia. ● n. **on ~** bajo custodia

remark /rɪ'mɑːk/ n observación f. ● vt observar. **~able** a notable

remarry /riː'mærɪ/ vi volver a casarse

remedial /rɪ'miːdɪəl/ a remediador

remedy /'remədɪ/ n remedio m. ● vt remediar

rememb|er /rɪ'membə(r)/ vt acordarse de. ● vi acordarse. **~rance** n recuerdo m

remind /rɪ'maɪnd/ vt recordar. **~er** n recordatorio m; (letter) notificación f

reminisce /remɪ'nɪs/ vi recordar el pasado. **~nces** npl recuerdos mpl. **~nt** /remɪ'nɪsnt/ a. be **~nt of** recordar

remiss /rɪ'mɪs/ a negligente

remission /rɪ'mɪʃn/ n remisión f; (of sentence) reducción f de condena

remit /rɪ'mɪt/ vt (pt **remitted**) perdonar; enviar ⟨money⟩. ● vi moderarse. **~tance** n remesa f

remnant /'remnənt/ n resto m; (of cloth) retazo m; (trace) vestigio m

remonstrate /'remənstreɪt/ vi protestar

remorse /rɪ'mɔːs/ n remordimiento m. **~ful** a lleno de remordimiento. **~less** a implacable

remote /rɪ'məʊt/ a remoto; (slight) leve; ⟨person⟩ distante. ~ **control** n mando m a distancia. **~ly** adv remotamente. **~ness** n lejanía f; (isolation) aislamiento m, alejamiento m; (fig) improbabilidad f

remov|able /rɪ'muːvəbl/ a movible; (detachable) de quita y pon, separable. **~al** n eliminación f; (from house) mudanza f. **~e** /rɪ'muːv/ vt quitar; (dismiss) despedir; (get rid of) eliminar; (do away with) suprimir

remunerat|e /rɪ'mjuːnəreɪt/ vt remunerar. **~ion** /-'reɪʃn/ n remuneración f. **~ive** a remunerador

Renaissance /rə'neɪsəns/ n Renacimiento m

rend /rend/ vt (pt **rent**) rasgar

render /'rendə(r)/ vt rendir; (com) presentar; (mus) interpretar; prestar ⟨help etc⟩. **~ing** n (mus) interpretación f

rendezvous /'rɒndɪvuː/ n (pl **-vous** /-vuːz/) cita f

renegade /'renɪgeɪd/ n renegado

renew /rɪ'nju:/ vt renovar; (*resume*) reanudar. ∼able a renovable. ∼al n renovación f

renounce /rɪ'naʊns/ vt renunciar a; (*disown*) repudiar

renovat|e /'renəveɪt/ vt renovar. ∼ion /-'veɪʃn/ n renovación f

renown /rɪ'naʊn/ n fama f. ∼ed a célebre

rent[1] /rent/ n alquiler m. ● vt alquilar

rent[2] /rent/ see rend

rental /rentl/ n alquiler m

renunciation /rɪnʌnsɪ'eɪʃn/ n renuncia f

reopen /ri:'əʊpən/ vt reabrir. ● vi reabrirse. ∼ing n reapertura f

reorganize /ri:'ɔ:gənaɪz/ vt reorganizar

rep[1] /rep/ n (com, fam) representante m & f

rep[2] /rep/ (theatre, fam) teatro m de repertorio

repair /rɪ'peə(r)/ vt reparar; remendar (clothes, shoes). ● n reparación f; (patch) remiendo m. in good ∼ en buen estado

repartee /repɑ:'ti:/ n ocurrencias fpl

repatriat|e /ri:'pætrɪeɪt/ vt repatriar. ∼ion /-'eɪʃn/ n repatriación f

repay /ri:'peɪ/ vt (pt repaid) reembolsar; pagar (debt); (reward) recompensar. ∼ment n reembolso m, pago m

repeal /rɪ'pi:l/ vt abrogar. ● n abrogación f

repeat /rɪ'pi:t/ vt repetir. ● vi repetir(se). ● n repetición f. ∼edly /rɪ'pi:tɪdlɪ/ adv repetidas veces

repel /rɪ'pel/ vt (pt repelled) repeler. ∼lent a repelente

repent /rɪ'pent/ vi arrepentirse. ∼ance n arrepentimiento m. ∼ant a arrepentido

repercussion /ri:pə'kʌʃn/ n repercusión f

reperto|ire /'repətwɑ:(r)/ n repertorio m. ∼ry /'repətrɪ/ n repertorio m. ∼ry (theatre) n teatro m de repertorio

repetit|ion /repɪ'tɪʃn/ n repetición f. ∼ious /-'tɪʃəs/ a, ∼ive /rɪ'petətɪv/ a que se repite; (dull) monótono

replace /rɪ'pleɪs/ vt reponer; (take the place of) sustituir. ∼ment n

sustitución f; (person) sustituto m. ∼ment part n recambio m

replay /'ri:pleɪ/ n (sport) repetición f del partido; (recording) repetición f inmediata

replenish /rɪ'plenɪʃ/ vt reponer; (refill) rellenar

replete /rɪ'pli:t/ a repleto

replica /'replɪkə/ n copia f

reply /rɪ'plaɪ/ vt/i contestar. ● n respuesta f

report /rɪ'pɔ:t/ vt anunciar; (denounce) denunciar. ● vi presentar un informe; (present o.s.) presentarse. ● n informe m; (schol) boletín m; (rumour) rumor m; (newspaper) reportaje m; (sound) estallido m. ∼age /repɔ:'tɑ:ʒ/ n reportaje m. ∼edly adv según se dice. ∼er /rɪ'pɔ:tə(r)/ n reportero m, informador m

repose /rɪ'pəʊz/ n reposo m

repository /rɪ'pɒzɪtrɪ/ n depósito m

repossess /ri:pə'zes/ vt recuperar

reprehen|d /reprɪ'hend/ vt reprender. ∼sible /-səbl/ a reprensible

represent /reprɪ'zent/ vt representar. ∼ation /-'teɪʃn/ n representación f. ∼ative /reprɪ'zentətɪv/ a representativo. ● n representante m & f

repress /rɪ'pres/ vt reprimir. ∼ion /-ʃn/ n represión f. ∼ive a represivo

reprieve /rɪ'pri:v/ n indulto m; (fig) respiro m. ● vt indultar; (fig) aliviar

reprimand /'reprɪmɑ:nd/ vt reprender. ● n reprensión f

reprint /'ri:prɪnt/ n reimpresión f; (offprint) tirada f aparte. /ri:'prɪnt/ vt reimprimir

reprisal /rɪ'praɪzl/ n represalia f

reproach /rɪ'prəʊtʃ/ vt reprochar. ● n reproche m. ∼ful a de reproche, reprobador. ∼fully adv con reproche

reprobate /'reprəbeɪt/ n malvado m; (relig) réprobo m

reproduc|e /ri:prə'dju:s/ vt reproducir. ● vi reproducirse. ∼tion /-'dʌkʃn/ n reproducción f. ∼tive /-'dʌktɪv/ a reproductor

reprove /rɪ'pru:v/ vt reprender

reptile /'reptaɪl/ n reptil m

republic /rɪ'pʌblɪk/ n república f. ∼an a & n republicano (m)

repudiate /rɪ'pju:dɪeɪt/ vt repudiar; (refuse to recognize) negarse a conocer

repugnan|ce /rɪ'pʌgnəns/ n repugnancia f. ~**t** /rɪ'pʌgnənt/ a repugnante

repuls|e /rɪ'pʌls/ vt rechazar, repulsar. ~**ion** /-ʃn/ n repulsión f. ~**ive** a repulsivo

reputable /'repjʊtəbl/ a acreditado, de confianza, honroso

reputation /repjʊ'teɪʃn/ n reputación f

repute /rɪ'pju:t/ n reputación f. ~**d** /-ɪd/ a supuesto. ~**dly** adv según se dice

request /rɪ'kwest/ n petición f. ●vt pedir. ~ **stop** n parada f discrecional

require /rɪ'kwaɪə(r)/ vt requerir; (need) necesitar; (demand) exigir. ~**d** a necesario. ~**ment** n requisito m

requisite /'rekwɪzɪt/ a necesario. ●n requisito m

requisition /rekwɪ'zɪʃn/ n requisición f. ●vt requisar

resale /'ri:seɪl/ n reventa f

rescind /rɪ'sɪnd/ vt rescindir

rescue /'reskju:/ vt salvar. ●n salvamento m. ~**r** /-ə(r)/ n salvador m

research /rɪ'sɜːtʃ/ n investigación f. ●vt investigar. ~**er** n investigador m

resembl|ance /rɪ'zembləns/ n parecido m. ~**e** /rɪ'zembl/ vt parecerse a

resent /rɪ'zent/ vt resentirse por. ~**ful** a resentido. ~**ment** n resentimiento m

reservation /rezə'veɪʃn/ n reserva f; (booking) reservación f

reserve /rɪ'zɜːv/ vt reservar. ●n reserva f; (in sports) suplente m & f. ~**d** a reservado

reservist /rɪ'zɜːvɪst/ n reservista m & f

reservoir /'rezəvwɑː(r)/ n embalse m; (tank) depósito m

reshape /ri:'ʃeɪp/ vt formar de nuevo, reorganizar

reshuffle /ri:'ʃʌfl/ vt (pol) reorganizar. ●n (pol) reorganización f

reside /rɪ'zaɪd/ vi residir

residen|ce /'rezɪdəns/ n residencia f. ~**ce permit** n permiso m de residencia. **be in** ~**ce** (doctor etc) interno. ~**t** /'rezɪdənt/ a & n residente (m & f). ~**tial** /rezɪ'denʃl/ a residencial

residue /'rezɪdjuː/ n residuo m

resign /rɪ'zaɪn/ vt/i dimitir. ~ **o.s. to** resignarse a. ~**ation** a. /rezɪg'neɪʃn/ n resignación f; (from job) dimisión f. ~**ed** a resignado

resilien|ce /rɪ'zɪlɪəns/ n elasticidad f; (of person) resistencia f. ~**t** /rɪ'zɪlɪənt/ a elástico; (person) resistente

resin /'rezɪn/ n resina f

resist /rɪ'zɪst/ vt resistir. ●vi resistirse. ~**ance** n resistencia f. ~**ant** a resistente

resolut|e /'rezəluːt/ a resuelto. ~**ion** /-'luːʃn/ n resolución f

resolve /rɪ'zɒlv/ vt resolver. ~ **to do** resolverse a hacer. ●n resolución f. ~**d** a resuelto

resonan|ce /'rezənəns/ n resonancia f. ~**t** /'rezənənt/ a resonante

resort /rɪ'zɔːt/ vi. ~ **to** recurrir a. ●n recurso m; (place) lugar m turístico. **in the last** ~ como último recurso

resound /rɪ'zaʊnd/ vi resonar. ~**ing** a resonante

resource /rɪ'sɔːs/ n recurso m. ~**ful** a ingenioso. ~**fulness** n ingeniosidad f

respect /rɪ'spekt/ n (esteem) respeto m; (aspect) respecto m. **with** ~ **to** con respecto a. ●vt respetar

respectab|ility /rɪspektə'bɪlətɪ/ n respetabilidad f. ~**le** /rɪ'spektəbl/ a respetable. ~**ly** adv respetablemente

respectful /rɪ'spektfl/ a respetuoso

respective /rɪ'spektɪv/ a respectivo. ~**ly** adv respectivamente

respiration /respə'reɪʃn/ n respiración f

respite /'respaɪt/ n respiro m, tregua f

resplendent /rɪ'splendənt/ a resplandeciente

respon|d /rɪ'spɒnd/ vi responder. ~**se** /rɪ'spɒns/ n respuesta f; (reaction) reacción f

responsib|ility /rɪspɒnsə'bɪlətɪ/ n responsabilidad f. ~**le** /rɪ'spɒnsəbl/ a responsable; (job) de responsabilidad. ~**ly** adv con formalidad

responsive /rɪ'spɒnsɪv/ a que reacciona bien. ~ **to** sensible a

rest[1] /rest/ vt descansar; (lean) apoyar; (place) poner, colocar. ●vi descansar; (lean) apoyarse. ●n descanso m; (mus) pausa f

rest[2] /rest/ n (remainder) resto m, lo demás; (people) los demás, los otros mpl. ●vi (remain) quedar

restaurant /'restərɒnt/ n restaurante m

restful /'restfl/ a sosegado

restitution /restɪ'tju:ʃn/ n restitución f

restive /'restɪv/ a inquieto

restless /'restlɪs/ a inquieto. ~ly adv inquietamente. ~ness n inquietud f

restor|ation /restə'reɪʃn/ n restauración f. ~e /rɪ'stɔ:(r)/ vt restablecer; restaurar ⟨building⟩; ⟨put back in position⟩ reponer; ⟨return⟩ devolver

restrain /rɪ'streɪn/ vt contener. ~ o.s. contenerse. ~ed a ⟨moderate⟩ moderado; ⟨in control of self⟩ comedido. ~t n restricción f; ⟨moderation⟩ moderación f

restrict /rɪ'strɪkt/ vt restringir. ~ion /-ʃn/ n restricción f. ~ive /rɪ'strɪktɪv/ a restrictivo

result /rɪ'zʌlt/ n resultado m. ● vi. ~ from resultar de. ~ in dar como resultado

resume /rɪ'zju:m/ vt reanudar. ● vi continuar

résumé /'rezjʊmeɪ/ n resumen m

resumption /rɪ'zʌmpʃn/ n continuación f

resurgence /rɪ'sɜ:dʒəns/ n resurgimiento m

resurrect /rezə'rekt/ vt resucitar. ~ion /-ʃn/ n resurrección f

resuscitat|e /rɪ'sʌsɪteɪt/ vt resucitar. ~ion /-'teɪʃn/ n resucitación f

retail /'ri:teɪl/ n venta f al por menor. ● a & adv al por menor. ● vt vender al por menor. ● vi venderse al por menor. ~er n minorista m & f

retain /rɪ'teɪn/ vt retener; ⟨keep⟩ conservar

retainer /rɪ'teɪnə(r)/ n ⟨fee⟩ anticipo m

retaliat|e /rɪ'tælɪeɪt/ vi desquitarse. ~ion /-'eɪʃn/ n represalias fpl

retarded /rɪ'tɑ:dɪd/ a retrasado

retentive /rɪ'tentɪv/ a ⟨memory⟩ bueno

rethink /ri:'θɪŋk/ vt (pt rethought) considerar de nuevo

reticen|ce /'retɪsns/ n reserva f. ~t /'retɪsnt/ a reservado, callado

retina /'retɪnə/ n retina f

retinue /'retɪnju:/ n séquito m

retir|e /rɪ'taɪə(r)/ vi ⟨from work⟩ jubilarse; ⟨withdraw⟩ retirarse; ⟨go to bed⟩ acostarse. ● vt jubilar. ~ed

a jubilado. ~ement n jubilación f. ~ing /rɪ'taɪərɪŋ/ a reservado

retort /rɪ'tɔ:t/ vt/i replicar. ● n réplica f

retrace /ri:'treɪs/ vt repasar. ~ one's steps volver sobre sus pasos

retract /rɪ'trækt/ vt retirar. ● vi retractarse

retrain /ri:'treɪn/ vt reciclar, reeducar

retreat /rɪ'tri:t/ vi retirarse. ● n retirada f; ⟨place⟩ refugio m

retrial /ri:'traɪəl/ n nuevo proceso m

retribution /retrɪ'bju:ʃn/ n justo m castigo

retriev|al /rɪ'tri:vl/ n recuperación f. ~e /rɪ'tri:v/ vt ⟨recover⟩ recuperar; ⟨save⟩ salvar; ⟨put right⟩ reparar. ~er n ⟨dog⟩ perro m cobrador

retrograde /'retrəgreɪd/ a retrógrado

retrospect /'retrəspekt/ n retrospección f. in ~ retrospectivamente. ~ive /-'spektɪv/ a retrospectivo

return /rɪ'tɜ:n/ vi volver; ⟨reappear⟩ reaparecer. ● vt devolver; ⟨com⟩ declarar; ⟨pol⟩ elegir. ● n vuelta f; ⟨com⟩ ganancia f; ⟨restitution⟩ devolución f. ~ of income n declaración f de ingresos. in ~ a cambio de. many happy ~s! ¡feliz cumpleaños! ~ing /rɪ'tɜ:nɪŋ/ a. ~ing officer n escrutador m. ~ match n partido m de desquite. ~ ticket n billete m de ida y vuelta. ~s npl ⟨com⟩ ingresos mpl

reunion /ri:'ju:nɪən/ n reunión f

reunite /ri:ju:'naɪt/ vt reunir

rev /rev/ n ⟨auto, fam⟩ revolución f. ● vt/i. ~ (up) ⟨pt revved⟩ ⟨auto, fam⟩ acelerar(se)

revamp /ri:'væmp/ vt renovar

reveal /rɪ'vi:l/ vt revelar. ~ing a revelador

revel /'revl/ vi (pt revelled) jaranear. ~ in deleitarse en. ~ry n juerga f

revelation /revə'leɪʃn/ n revelación f

revenge /rɪ'vendʒ/ n venganza f; ⟨sport⟩ desquite m. take ~ vengarse. ● vt vengar. ~ful a vindicativo, vengativo

revenue /'revənju:/ n ingresos mpl

reverberate /rɪ'vɜ:bəreɪt/ vi ⟨light⟩ reverberar; ⟨sound⟩ resonar

revere /rɪ'vɪə(r)/ vt venerar

reverence /'revərəns/ n reverencia f

reverend /'revərənd/ a reverendo

reverent /'revərənt/ a reverente

reverie /'revərɪ/ n ensueño m

revers /rɪ'vɪə/ n (pl revers /rɪ'vɪəz/) n solapa f

revers|al /rɪ'vɜ:sl/ n inversión f. **~e** /rɪ'vɜ:s/ a inverso. ● n contrario m; (back) revés m; (auto) marcha f atrás. ● vt invertir; anular (decision); (auto) dar marcha atrás a. ● vi (auto) dar marcha atrás

revert /rɪ'vɜ:t/ vi. **~ to** volver a

review /rɪ'vju:/ n repaso m; (mil) revista f; (of book, play, etc) crítica f. ● vt analizar (situation); reseñar (book, play, etc). **~er** n crítico m

revile /rɪ'vaɪl/ vt injuriar

revis|e /rɪ'vaɪz/ vt revisar; (schol) repasar. **~ion** /-ɪʒn/ n revisión f; (schol) repaso m

reviv|al /rɪ'vaɪvl/ n restablecimiento m; (of faith) despertar m; (of play) reestreno m. **~e** /rɪ'vaɪv/ vt restablecer; resucitar (person). ● vi restablecerse; (person) volver en sí

revoke /rɪ'vəʊk/ vt revocar

revolt /rɪ'vəʊlt/ vi sublevarse. ● vt dar asco a. ● n sublevación f

revolting /rɪ'vəʊltɪŋ/ a asqueroso

revolution /revə'lu:ʃn/ n revolución f. **~ary** a & n revolucionario (m). **~ize** vt revolucionar

revolve /rɪ'vɒlv/ vi girar

revolver /rɪ'vɒlvə(r)/ n revólver m

revolving /rɪ'vɒlvɪŋ/ a giratorio

revue /rɪ'vju:/ n revista f

revulsion /rɪ'vʌlʃn/ n asco m

reward /rɪ'wɔ:d/ n recompensa f. ● vt recompensar. **~ing** a remunerador; (worthwhile) que vale la pena

rewrite /ri:'raɪt/ vt (pt rewrote, pp rewritten) escribir de nuevo; (change) redactar de nuevo

rhapsody /'ræpsədɪ/ n rapsodia f

rhetoric /'retərɪk/ n retórica f. **~al** /rɪ'tɒrɪkl/ a retórico

rheumati|c /ru:'mætɪk/ a reumático. **~sm** /'ru:mətɪzəm/ n reumatismo m

rhinoceros /raɪ'nɒsərəs/ n (pl -oses) rinoceronte m

rhubarb /'ru:bɑ:b/ n ruibarbo m

rhyme /raɪm/ n rima f; (poem) poesía f. ● vt/i rimar

rhythm /'rɪðəm/ n ritmo m. **~ic(al)** /'rɪðmɪk(l)/ a rítmico

rib /rɪb/ n costilla f. —vt (pt ribbed) (fam) tomar el pelo a

ribald /'rɪbld/ a obsceno, verde

ribbon /'rɪbən/ n cinta f

rice /raɪs/ n arroz m. **~ pudding** n arroz con leche

rich /rɪtʃ/ a (-er, -est) rico. ● n ricos mpl. **~es** npl riquezas fpl. **~ly** adv ricamente. **~ness** n riqueza f

rickety /'rɪkətɪ/ a (shaky) cojo, desvencijado

ricochet /'rɪkəʃeɪ/ n rebote m. ● vi rebotar

rid /rɪd/ vt (pt rid, pres p ridding) librar (of de). **get ~ of** deshacerse de. **~dance** /'rɪdns/ n. **good ~ dance!** ¡qué alivio!

ridden /'rɪdn/ see **ride**. ● a (infested) infestado. **~ by** (oppressed) agobiado de

riddle[1] /'rɪdl/ n acertijo m

riddle[2] /'rɪdl/ vt acribillar. **be ~d with** estar lleno de

ride /raɪd/ vi (pt rode, pp ridden) (on horseback) montar; (go) ir (en bicicleta, a caballo etc). **take s.o. for a ~** (fam) engañarle a uno. ● vt montar a (horse); ir en (bicycle); recorrer (distance). ● n (on horse) cabalgata f; (in car) paseo m en coche. **~r** /-ə(r)/ n (on horse) jinete m; (cyclist) ciclista m & f; (in document) cláusula f adicional

ridge /rɪdʒ/ n línea f, arruga f; (of mountain) cresta f; (of roof) caballete m

ridicul|e /'rɪdɪkju:l/ n irrisión f. ● vt ridiculizar. **~ous** /rɪ'dɪkjʊləs/ a ridículo

riding /'raɪdɪŋ/ n equitación f

rife /raɪf/ a difundido. **~ with** lleno de

riff-raff /'rɪfræf/ n gentuza f

rifle[1] /'raɪfl/ n fusil m

rifle[2] /'raɪfl/ vt saquear

rifle-range /'raɪflreɪndʒ/ n campo m de tiro

rift /rɪft/ n grieta f; (fig) ruptura f

rig[1] /rɪg/ vt (pt rigged) aparejar. ● n (at sea) plataforma f de perforación. **~ up** vt improvisar

rig[2] /rɪg/ vt (pej) amañar

right /raɪt/ a (correct, fair) exacto, justo; (morally) bueno; (not left) derecho; (suitable) adecuado. ● n (entitlement) derecho m; (not left) derecha f; (not evil) bien m. **~ of way** n (auto) prioridad f. **be in the ~**

tener razón. **on the** ∼ a la derecha.
put ∼ rectificar. ● vt enderezar; (fig)
corregir. ● adv a la derecha; (directly) derecho; (completely) completamente; (well) bien. ∼ **away** adv
inmediatamente. ∼ **angle** n ángulo
m recto

righteous /'raɪtʃəs/ a recto; (cause)
justo

right: ∼**ful** /'raɪtfl/ a legítimo.
∼**fully** adv legítimamente. ∼**-hand**
man n brazo m derecho. ∼**ly** adv
justamente. ∼ **wing** a (pol) n de-
rechista

rigid /'rɪdʒɪd/ a rígido. ∼**ity**
/-'dʒɪdətɪ/ n rigidez f

rigmarole /'rɪgmərəʊl/ n galimatías
m invar

rig|orous /'rɪgərəs/ a riguroso.
∼**our** /'rɪgə(r)/ n rigor m

rig-out /'rɪgaʊt/ n (fam) atavío m

rile /raɪl/ vt (fam) irritar

rim /rɪm/ n borde m; (of wheel) llanta
f; (of glasses) montura f. ∼**med** a bor-
deado

rind /raɪnd/ n corteza f; (of fruit)
cáscara f

ring[1] /rɪŋ/ n (circle) círculo m; (circle
of metal etc) aro m; (on finger) anillo
m; (on finger with stone) sortija f;
(boxing) cuadrilátero m; (bullring)
ruedo m, redondel m, plaza f; (for circus) pista f. ● vt rodear

ring[2] /rɪŋ/ n (of bell) toque m; (tinkle)
tintineo m; (telephone call) llamada f.
● vt (pt rang, pp rung) hacer sonar;
(telephone) llamar por teléfono. ∼
the bell tocar el timbre. ● vi sonar.
∼ **back** vt/i volver a llamar. ∼ **off** vi
colgar. ∼ **up** vt llamar por teléfono

ring: ∼**leader** /'rɪŋliːdə(r)/ n cabecilla f. ∼ **road** n carretera f de
circunvalación

rink /rɪŋk/ n pista f

rinse /rɪns/ vt enjuagar. ● n aclarado
m; (of dishes) enjuague m; (for hair)
reflejo m

riot /'raɪət/ n disturbio m; (of colours)
profusión f. **run** ∼ desenfrenarse.
● vi amotinarse. ∼**er** n amotinador
m. ∼**ous** a tumultuoso

rip /rɪp/ vt (pt ripped) rasgar. ● vi
rasgarse. **let** ∼ (fig) soltar. ● n ras-
gadura f. ∼ **off** vt (sl) robar. ∼**-cord**
n (of parachute) cuerda f de abertura

ripe /raɪp/ a (-er, -est) maduro. ∼**n**
/'raɪpən/ vt/i madurar. ∼**ness** n
madurez f

rip-off /'rɪpɒf/ n (sl) timo m

ripple /'rɪpl/ n rizo m; (sound) murmullo m. ● vt rizar. ● vi rizarse

rise /raɪz/ vi (pt rose, pp risen)
levantarse; (rebel) sublevarse; (river)
crecer; (prices) subir. ● n subida f;
(land) altura f; (increase) aumento m;
(to power) ascenso m. **give** ∼ **to**
ocasionar. ∼**r** /-ə(r)/ n. **early** ∼**r** n
madrugador m

rising /'raɪzɪŋ/ n (revolt) sublevación
f. ● a (sun) naciente. ∼ **generation**
n nueva generación f

risk /rɪsk/ n riesgo m. ● vt arriesgar.
∼**y** a (-ier, -iest) arriesgado

risqué /'riːskeɪ/ a subido de color

rissole /'rɪsəʊl/ n croqueta f

rite /raɪt/ n rito m

ritual /'rɪtʃʊəl/ a & n ritual (m)

rival /'raɪvl/ a & n rival (m). ● vt (pt
rivalled) rivalizar con. ∼**ry** n rivalidad f

river /'rɪvə(r)/ n río m

rivet /'rɪvɪt/ n remache m. ● vt re-
machar. ∼**ing** a fascinante

Riviera /rɪvɪ'eərə/ n. **the (French)** ∼
la Costa f Azul. **the (Italian)** ∼ la
Riviera f (Italiana)

rivulet /'rɪvjʊlɪt/ n riachuelo m

road /rəʊd/ n (in town) calle f; (between towns) carretera f; (way) camino m. **on the** ∼ en camino. ∼**-hog**
n conductor m descortés. ∼**-house** n
albergue m. ∼**-map** n mapa m de carreteras. ∼**side** /'rəʊdsaɪd/ n borde
m de la carretera. ∼ **sign** n señal f de
tráfico. ∼**way** /'rəʊdweɪ/ n calzada
f. ∼**-works** npl obras fpl. ∼**-worthy**
/'rəʊdwɜːðɪ/ a (vehicle) seguro

roam /rəʊm/ vi vagar

roar /rɔː(r)/ n rugido m; (laughter)
carcajada f. ● vt/i rugir. ∼ **past**
(vehicles) pasar con estruendo. ∼
with laughter reírse a carcajadas.
∼**ing** /'rɔːrɪŋ/ a (trade etc) activo

roast /rəʊst/ vt asar; tostar (coffee).
● vi asarse; (person, coffee) tostarse.
● a & n asado (m). ∼ **beef** n rosbif m

rob /rɒb/ vt (pt robbed) robar;
asaltar (bank). ∼ **of** privar de. ∼**-**
ber n ladrón m; (of bank) atracador
m. ∼**bery** n robo m

robe /rəʊb/ n manto m; (univ etc)
toga f. **bath-**∼ n albornoz m

robin /'rɒbɪn/ n petirrojo m

robot /'rəʊbɒt/ n robot m, autómata
m

robust /rəʊ'bʌst/ a robusto

rock[1] /rɒk/ n roca f; (boulder) peñasco m; (sweet) caramelo m en forma de barra; (of Gibraltar) peñón m. **on the ~s** (drink) con hielo; (fig) arruinado. **be on the ~s** (marriage etc) andar mal

rock[2] /rɒk/ vt mecer; (shake) sacudir. ● vi mecerse; (shake) sacudirse. ● n (mus) música f rock

rock: **~-bottom** a (fam) bajísimo. **~ery** /'rɒkəri/ n cuadro m alpino, rocalla f

rocket /'rɒkɪt/ n cohete m

rock: **~ing-chair** n mecedora f. **~ing-horse** n caballo m de balancín. **~y** /'rɒkɪ/ a (-ier, -iest) rocoso; (fig, shaky) bamboleante

rod /rɒd/ n vara f; (for fishing) caña f; (metal) barra f

rode /rəʊd/ see **ride**

rodent /'rəʊdnt/ n roedor m

rodeo /rə'deɪəʊ/ n (pl -os) rodeo m

roe[1] /rəʊ/ n (fish eggs) hueva f

roe[2] /rəʊ/ n (pl **roe**, or **roes**) (deer) corzo m

rogue /rəʊg/ n pícaro m. **~ish** a picaresco

role /rəʊl/ n papel m

roll /rəʊl/ vt hacer rodar; (roll up) enrollar; (flatten lawn) allanar; aplanar (pastry). ● vi rodar; (ship) balancearse; (on floor) revolcarse. **be ~ing (in money)** (fam) nadar en (dinero). ● n rollo m; (of ship) balanceo m; (of drum) redoble m; (of thunder) retumbo m; (bread) panecillo m; (list) lista f. **~ over** vi (turn over) dar una vuelta. **~ up** vt enrollar; arremangar (sleeve). ● vi (fam) llegar. **~-call** n lista f

roller /'rəʊlə(r)/ n rodillo m; (wheel) rueda f; (for hair) rulo m, bigudí m. **~-coaster** n montaña f rusa. **~-skate** n patín m de ruedas

rollicking /'rɒlɪkɪŋ/ a alegre

rolling /'rəʊlɪŋ/ a ondulado. **~-pin** n rodillo m

Roman /'rəʊmən/ a & n romano (m). **~ Catholic** a & n católico (m) (romano)

romance /rəʊ'mæns/ n novela f romántica; (love) amor m; (affair) aventura f

Romania /rəʊ'meɪnɪə/ n Rumania f. **~n** a & n rumano (m)

romantic /rəʊ'mæntɪk/ a romántico. **~ism** n romanticismo m

Rome /rəʊm/ n Roma f

romp /rɒmp/ vi retozar. ● n retozo m

rompers /'rɒmpəz/ npl pelele m

roof /ru:f/ n techo m, tejado m; (of mouth) paladar m. ● vt techar. **~-garden** n jardín m en la azotea. **~-rack** n baca f. **~-top** n tejado m

rook[1] /rʊk/ n grajo m

rook[2] /rʊk/ (in chess) torre f

room /ru:m/ n cuarto m, habitación f; (bedroom) dormitorio m; (space) sitio m; (large hall) sala f. **~y** a espacioso; (clothes) holgado

roost /ru:st/ n percha f. ● vi descansar. **~er** n gallo m

root[1] /ru:t/ n raíz f. **take ~** echar raíces. ● vt hacer arraigar. ● vi echar raíces, arraigarse

root[2] /ru:t/ vt/i. **~ about** vi hurgar. **~ for** vi (Amer, sl) alentar. **~ out** vt extirpar

rootless /'ru:tlɪs/ a desarraigado

rope /rəʊp/ n cuerda f. **know the ~s** estar al corriente. ● vt atar. **~ in** vt agarrar

rosary /'rəʊzərɪ/ n (relig) rosario m

rose[1] /rəʊz/ n rosa f; (nozzle) roseta f

rose[2] /rəʊz/ see **rise**

rosé /'rəʊzeɪ/ n (vino m) rosado m

rosette /rəʊ'zet/ n escarapela f

roster /'rɒstə(r)/ n lista f

rostrum /'rɒstrəm/ n tribuna f

rosy /'rəʊzɪ/ a (-ier, -iest) rosado; (skin) sonrosado

rot /rɒt/ vt (pt **rotted**) pudrir. ● vi pudrirse. ● n putrefacción f; (sl) tonterías fpl

rota /'rəʊtə/ n lista f

rotary /'rəʊtərɪ/ a giratorio, rotativo

rotat|e /rəʊ'teɪt/ vt girar; (change round) alternar. ● vi girar; (change round) alternarse. **~ion** /-ʃn/ n rotación f

rote /rəʊt/ n. **by ~** maquinalmente, de memoria

rotten /'rɒtn/ a podrido; (fam) desagradable

rotund /rəʊ'tʌnd/ a redondo; (person) regordete

rouge /ru:ʒ/ n colorete m

rough /rʌf/ a (-er, -est) áspero; (person) tosco; (bad) malo; (ground) accidentado; (violent) brutal; (approximate) aproximado; (diamond) bruto. ● adv duro. **~ copy** n, **~ draft** n borrador m. ● n (ruffian) matón m. ● vt. **~ it** vivir sin comodidades. **~ out** vt esbozar

roughage /'rʌfɪdʒ/ n alimento m indigesto, afrecho m; (for animals) forraje m

rough: ~-and-ready a improvisado. ~-and-tumble n riña f. ~ly adv toscamente; (more or less) más o menos. ~ness n aspereza f; (lack of manners) incultura f; (crudeness) tosquedad f

roulette /ru:'let/ n ruleta f

round /raʊnd/ a (-er, -est) redondo. ● n círculo m; (slice) tajada f; (of visits, drinks) ronda f; (of competition) vuelta f; (boxing) asalto m. ● prep alrededor de. ● adv alrededor. ~ **about** (approximately) aproximadamente. **come** ~ **to**, **go** ~ **to** (a friend etc) pasar por casa de. ● vt redondear; doblar ⟨corner⟩. ~ **off** vt terminar. ~ **up** vt reunir; redondear ⟨price⟩

roundabout /'raʊndəbaʊt/ n tiovivo m; (for traffic) glorieta f. ● a indirecto

rounders /'raʊndəz/ n juego m parecido al béisbol

round: ~ly adv (bluntly) francamente. ~ **trip** n viaje m de ida y vuelta. ~-**up** n reunión f; (of suspects) redada f

rous|e /raʊz/ vt despertar. ~ing a excitante

rout /raʊt/ n derrota f. ● vt derrotar

route /ru:t/ n ruta f; (naut, aviat) rumbo m; (of bus) línea f

routine /ru:'ti:n/ n rutina f. ● a rutinario

rov|e /rəʊv/ vt/i vagar (por). ~ing a errante

row[1] /rəʊ/ n fila f

row[2] /rəʊ/ n (in boat) paseo m en bote (de remos). ● vi remar

row[3] /raʊ/ n (noise, fam) ruido m; (quarrel) pelea f. ● vi (fam) pelearse

rowdy /'raʊdɪ/ a (-ier, -iest) n ruidoso

rowing /'rəʊɪŋ/ n remo m. ~-**boat** n bote m de remos

royal /'rɔɪəl/ a real. ~**ist** a & n monárquico (m). ~ly adv magníficamente. ~ty /'rɔɪəltɪ/ n familia f real; (payment) derechos mpl de autor

rub /rʌb/ vt (pt rubbed) frotar. ~ **in** insistir en algo. ● n frotamiento m. ~ **off on s.o.** vi pegársele a uno. ~ **out** vt borrar

rubber /'rʌbə(r)/ n goma f. ~ **band** n goma f (elástica). ~ **stamp** n sello m de goma. ~-**stamp** vt (fig) aprobar maquinalmente. ~y a parecido al caucho

rubbish /'rʌbɪʃ/ n basura f; (junk) trastos mpl; (fig) tonterías fpl. ~y a sin valor

rubble /'rʌbl/ n escombros; (small) cascajo m

ruby /'ru:bɪ/ n rubí m

rucksack /'rʌksæk/ n mochila f

rudder /'rʌdə(r)/ n timón m

ruddy /'rʌdɪ/ a (-ier, -iest) rubicundo; (sl) maldito

rude /ru:d/ a (-er, -est) descortés, mal educado; (improper) indecente; (brusque) brusco. ~ly adv con descortesía. ~ness n descortesía f

rudiment /'ru:dɪmənt/ n rudimento m. ~ary /-'mentrɪ/ a rudimentario

rueful /'ru:fl/ a triste

ruffian /'rʌfɪən/ n rufián m

ruffle /'rʌfl/ vt despeinar ⟨hair⟩; arrugar ⟨clothes⟩. ● n (frill) volante m, fruncido m

rug /rʌg/ n tapete m; (blanket) manta f

Rugby /'rʌgbɪ/ n. ~ (**football**) n rugby m

rugged /'rʌgɪd/ a desigual; (landscape) accidentado; (fig) duro

ruin /'ru:ɪn/ n ruina f. ● vt arruinar. ~**ous** a ruinoso

rule /ru:l/ n regla f; (custom) costumbre f; (pol) dominio m. **as a** ~ por regla general. ● vt gobernar; (master) dominar; (jurid) decretar; (decide) decidir. ~ **out** vt descartar. ~**d paper** n papel m rayado

ruler /'ru:lə(r)/ n (sovereign) soberano m; (leader) gobernante m & f; (measure) regla f

ruling /'ru:lɪŋ/ a ⟨class⟩ dirigente. ● n decisión f

rum /rʌm/ n ron m

rumble /'rʌmbl/ vi retumbar; ⟨stomach⟩ hacer ruidos. ● n retumbo m; (of stomach) ruido m

ruminant /'ru:mɪnənt/ a & n rumiante (m)

rummage /'rʌmɪdʒ/ vi hurgar

rumour /'ru:mə(r)/ n rumor m. ● vt. **it is** ~**ed that** se dice que

rump /rʌmp/ n (of horse) grupa f; (of fowl) rabadilla f. ~ **steak** n filete m

rumpus /'rʌmpəs/ n (fam) jaleo m

run /rʌn/ *vi* (*pt* **ran**, *pp* **run**, *pres p* **running**) correr; (*flow*) fluir; (*pass*) pasar; (*function*) funcionar; (*melt*) derretirse; (*bus etc*) circular; (*play*) representarse (continuadmente); (*colours*) correrse; (*in election*) presentarse. ● *vt* tener (*house*); (*control*) dirigir; correr (*risk*); (*drive*) conducir; (*pass*) pasar; (*present*) presentar; forzar (*blockade*). ● *n* corrida *f*, carrera *f*; (*journey*) viaje *m*; (*outing*) paseo *m*, excursión *f*; (*distance travelled*) recorrido *m*; (*ladder*) carrera *f*; (*ski*) pista *f*; (*series*) serie *f*. **at a ~** corriendo. **have the ~ of** tener a su disposición. **in the long ~** a la larga. **on the ~** de fuga. **~ across** *vt* toparse con (*friend*). **~ away** *vi* escaparse. **~ down** *vi* bajar corriendo; (*clock*) quedarse sin cuerda. ● *vt* (*auto*) atropellar; (*belittle*) denigrar. **~ in** *vt* rodar (*vehicle*). ● *vi* entrar corriendo. **~ into** *vt* toparse con (*friend*); (*hit*) chocar con. **~ off** *vt* tirar (*copies etc*). **~ out** *vi* salir corriendo; (*liquid*) salirse; (*fig*) agotarse. **~ out of** quedar sin. **~ over** *vt* (*auto*) atropellar. **~ through** *vt* traspasar; (*revise*) repasar. **~ up** *vt* hacerse con (*bill*). ● *vi* subir corriendo. **~ up against** tropezar con (*difficulties*). **~away** /'rʌnəweɪ/ *a* fugitivo; (*success*) decisivo; (*inflation*) galopante. ● *n* fugitivo *m*. **~ down** *a* (*person*) agotado. **~down** *n* informe *m* detallado

rung¹ /rʌŋ/ *n* (*of ladder*) peldaño *m*

rung² /rʌŋ/ *see* **ring**

run: **~ner** /'rʌnə(r)/ *n* corredor *m*; (*on sledge*) patín *m*. **~ner bean** *n* judía *f* escarlata. **~ner-up** *n* subcampeón *m*, segundo *m*. **~ning** /'rʌnɪŋ/ *n* (*race*) carrera *f*. **be in the ~ning** tener posibilidades de ganar. ● *a* en marcha; (*water*) corriente; (*commentary*) en directo. **four times ~ning** cuatro veces seguidas. **~ny** /'rʌnɪ/ *a* líquido; (*nose*) que moquea. **~-of-the-mill** *a* ordinario. **~-up** *n* período *m* que precede. **~way** /'rʌnweɪ/ *n* pista *f*

rupture /'rʌptʃə(r)/ *n* ruptura *f*; (*med*) hernia *f*. ● *vt/i* quebrarse

rural /'rʊərəl/ *a* rural

ruse /ru:z/ *n* ardid *m*

rush¹ /rʌʃ/ *n* (*haste*) prisa *f*; (*crush*) bullicio *m*. ● *vi* precipitarse. ● *vt* apresurar; (*mil*) asaltar

rush² /rʌʃ/ *n* (*plant*) junco *m*

rush-hour /'rʌʃaʊə(r)/ *n* hora *f* punta

rusk /rʌsk/ *n* galleta *f*, tostada *f*

russet /'rʌsɪt/ *a* rojizo. ● *n* (*apple*) manzana *f* rojiza

Russia /'rʌʃə/ *n* Rusia *f*. **~n** *a* & *n* ruso (*m*)

rust /rʌst/ *n* orín *m*. ● *vt* oxidar. ● *vi* oxidarse

rustic /'rʌstɪk/ *a* rústico

rustle /'rʌsl/ *vt* hacer susurrar; (*Amer*) robar. **~ up** (*fam*) preparar. ● *vi* susurrar

rust: **~-proof** *a* inoxidable. **~y** (**-ier**, **-iest**) oxidado

rut /rʌt/ *n* surco *m*. **in a ~** en la rutina de siempre

ruthless /'ru:θlɪs/ *a* despiadado. **~ness** *n* crueldad *f*

rye /raɪ/ *n* centeno *m*

S

S *abbr* (*south*) sur *m*

sabbath /'sæbəθ/ *n* día *m* de descanso; (*Christian*) domingo *m*; (*Jewish*) sábado *m*

sabbatical /sə'bætɪkl/ *a* sabático

sabot|age /'sæbətɑ:ʒ/ *n* sabotaje *m*. ● *vt* sabotear. **~eur** /-'tɜ:(r)/ *n* saboteador *m*

saccharin /'sækərɪn/ *n* sacarina *f*

sachet /'sæʃeɪ/ *n* bolsita *f*

sack¹ /sæk/ *n* saco *m*. **get the ~** (*fam*) ser despedido. ● *vt* (*fam*) despedir. **~ing** *n* arpillera *f*; (*fam*) despido *m*

sack² /sæk/ *vt* (*plunder*) saquear

sacrament /'sækrəmənt/ *n* sacramento *m*

sacred /'seɪkrɪd/ *a* sagrado

sacrifice /'sækrɪfaɪs/ *n* sacrificio *m*. ● *vt* sacrificar

sacrileg|e /'sækrɪlɪdʒ/ *n* sacrilegio *m*. **~ious** /-'lɪdʒəs/ *a* sacrílego

sacrosanct /'sækrəʊsæŋkt/ *a* sacrosanto

sad /sæd/ *a* (**sadder**, **saddest**) triste. **~den** /'sædn/ *vt* entristecer

saddle /'sædl/ *n* silla *f*. **be in the ~** (*fig*) tener las riendas. ● *vt* ensillar (*horse*). **~ s.o. with** (*fig*) cargar a uno con. **~-bag** *n* alforja *f*

sad: ~**ly** *adv* tristemente; (*fig*) desgraciadamente.~**ness** *n* tristeza *f*

sadism /'seɪdɪzəm/ *n* sadismo *m*. ~**t** /'seɪdɪst/ *n* sádico *m*. ~**tic** /sə'dɪstɪk/ *a* sádico

safari /sə'fɑːrɪ/ *n* safari *m*

safe /seɪf/ *a* (**-er**, **-est**) seguro; (*out of danger*) salvo; (*cautious*) prudente. ~ **and sound** salvo y salvo. ● *n* caja *f* fuerte. ~ **deposit** *n* caja *f* de seguridad. ~**guard** /'seɪfgɑːd/ *n* salvaguardia *f*. ● *vt* salvaguardar. ~**ly** *adv* sin peligro; (*in safe place*) en lugar seguro. ~**ty** /'seɪftɪ/ *n* seguridad *f*. ~**ty belt** *n* cinturón *m* de seguridad. ~**ty-pin** *n* imperdible *m*. ~**ty-valve** *n* válvula *f* de seguridad

saffron /'sæfrən/ *n* azafrán *m*

sag /sæg/ *vi* (*pt* sagged) hundirse; (*give*) aflojarse

saga /'sɑːgə/ *n* saga *f*

sage¹ /seɪdʒ/ *n* (*wise person*) sabio *m*. ● *a* sabio

sage² /seɪdʒ/ *n* (*herb*) salvia *f*

sagging /'sægɪŋ/ *a* hundido; (*fig*) decaído

Sagittarius /sædʒɪ'teərɪəs/ *n* (*astr*) Sagitario *m*

sago /'seɪgəʊ/ *n* sagú *m*

said /sed/ *see* say

sail /seɪl/ *n* vela *f*; (*trip*) paseo *m* (en barco). ● *vi* navegar; (*leave*) partir; (*sport*) practicar la vela; (*fig*) deslizarse. ● *vt* manejar ⟨*boat*⟩. ~**ing** *n* (*sport*) vela *f*. ~**ing-boat** *n*, ~**ing-ship** *n* barco *m* de vela. ~**or** /'seɪlə(r)/ *n* marinero *m*

saint /seɪnt, *before name* sənt/ *n* santo *m*. ~**ly** *a* santo

sake /seɪk/ *n*. **for the** ~ **of** por, por el amor de

salacious /sə'leɪʃəs/ *a* salaz

salad /'sæləd/ *n* ensalada *f*. ~ **bowl** *n* ensaladera *f*. ~ **cream** *n* mayonesa *f*. ~**dressing** *n* aliño *m*

salary /'sælərɪd/ *a* asalariado. ~**y** /'sælərɪ/ *n* sueldo *m*

sale /seɪl/ *n* venta *f*; (*at reduced prices*) liquidación *f*. **for** ~ (*sign*) se vende. **on** ~ en venta. ~**able** /'seɪləbl/ *a* vendible. ~**sman** /'seɪlzmən/ *n* (*pl* -**men**) vendedor *m*; (*in shop*) dependiente *m*; (*traveller*) viajante *m*. ~**swoman** *n* (*pl* -**women**) vendedora *f*; (*in shop*) dependienta *f*

salient /'seɪlɪənt/ *a* saliente, destacado

saliva /sə'laɪvə/ *n* saliva *f*

sallow /'sæləʊ/ *a* (**-er**, **-est**) amarillento

salmon /'sæmən/ *n invar* salmón *m*. ~ **trout** *n* trucha *f* salmonada

salon /'sælɒn/ *n* salón *m*

saloon /sə'luːn/ *n* (*on ship*) salón *m*; (*Amer, bar*) bar *m*; (*auto*) turismo *m*

salt /sɔːlt/ *n* sal *f*. ● *a* salado. ● *vt* salar. ~**cellar** *n* salero *m*. ~**y** *a* salado

salutary /'sæljʊtrɪ/ *a* saludable

salute /sə'luːt/ *n* saludo *m*. ● *vt* saludar. ● *vi* hacer un saludo

salvage /'sælvɪdʒ/ *n* salvamento *m*; (*goods*) objetos *mpl* salvados. ● *vt* salvar

salvation /sæl'veɪʃn/ *n* salvación *f*

salve /sælv/ *n* ungüento *m*

salver /'sælvə(r)/ *n* bandeja *f*

salvo /'sælvəʊ/ *n* (*pl* -**os**) salva *f*

same /seɪm/ *a* igual (**as** que); (*before noun*) mismo (**as** que). **at the** ~ **time** al mismo tiempo. ● *pron*. **the** ~ el mismo, la misma, los mismos, las mismas. **do the** ~ **as** hacer como. ● *adv*. **the** ~ de la misma manera. **all the** ~ de todas formas

sample /'sɑːmpl/ *n* muestra *f*. ● *vt* probar ⟨*food*⟩

sanatorium /sænə'tɔːrɪəm/ *n* (*pl* -**ums**) sanatorio *m*

sanctify /'sæŋktɪfaɪ/ *vt* santificar

sanctimonious /sæŋktɪ'məʊnɪəs/ *a* beato

sanction /'sæŋkʃn/ *n* sanción *f*. ● *vt* sancionar

sanctity /'sæŋktətɪ/ *n* santidad *f*

sanctuary /'sæŋktʃʊərɪ/ *n* (*relig*) santuario *m*; (*for wildlife*) reserva *f*; (*refuge*) asilo *m*

sand /sænd/ *n* arena *f*. ● *vt* enarenar. ~**s** *npl* (*beach*) playa *f*

sandal /'sændl/ *n* sandalia *f*

sand: ~**castle** *n* castillo *m* de arena. ~**paper** /'sændpeɪpə(r)/ *n* papel *m* de lija. ● *vt* lijar. ~**storm** /'sændstɔːm/ *n* tempestad *f* de arena

sandwich /'sænwɪdʒ/ *n* bocadillo *m*, sandwich *m*. ● *vt*. ~**ed between** intercalado

sandy /'sændɪ/ *a* arenoso

sane /seɪn/ *a* (**-er**, **-est**) (*person*) cuerdo; (*judgement*, *policy*) razonable. ~**ly** *adv* sensatamente

sang /sæŋ/ *see* sing

sanitary /'sænɪtrɪ/ *a* higiénico; (*system etc*) sanitario. ~ **towel** *n*, ~

napkin n (*Amer*) compresa f (higiénica)

sanitation /sænɪ'teɪʃn/ n higiene f; (*drainage*) sistema m sanitario

sanity /'sænɪtɪ/ n cordura f; (*fig*) sensatez f

sank /sæŋk/ *see* **sink**

Santa Claus /'sæntəklɔ:z/ n Papá m Noel

sap /sæp/ n (*in plants*) savia f. ● *vt* (*pt* sapped) agotar

sapling /'sæplɪŋ/ n árbol m joven

sapphire /'sæfaɪə(r)/ n zafiro m

sarcas|m /'sɑ:kæzəm/ n sarcasmo m. ~**tic** /-'kæstɪk/ a sarcástico

sardine /sɑ:'di:n/ n sardina f

Sardinia /sɑ:'dɪnɪə/ n Cerdeña f. ~**n** a & n sardo m

sardonic /sɑ:'dɒnɪk/ a sardónico

sash /sæʃ/ n (*over shoulder*) banda f; (*round waist*) fajín m. ~**-window** n ventana f de guillotina

sat /sæt/ *see* **sit**

satanic /sə'tænɪk/ a satánico

satchel /'sætʃl/ n cartera f

satellite /'sætəlaɪt/ n & a satélite (m)

satiate /'seɪʃɪeɪt/ *vt* saciar

satin /'sætɪn/ n raso m. ● a de raso; (*like satin*) satinado

satir|e /'sætaɪə(r)/ n sátira f. ~**ical** /sə'tɪrɪkl/ a satírico. ~**ist** /'sætərɪst/ n satírico m. ~**ize** /'sætəraɪz/ *vt* satirizar

satisfaction /sætɪs'fækʃn/ n satisfacción f

satisfactor|ily /sætɪs'fæktərɪlɪ/ *adv* satisfactoriamente. ~**y** /sætɪs 'fæktərɪ/ a satisfactorio

satisfy /'sætɪsfaɪ/ *vt* satisfacer; (*convince*) convencer. ~**ing** a satisfactorio

satsuma /sæt'su:mə/ n mandarina f

saturat|e /'sætʃəreɪt/ *vt* saturar, empapar. ~**ed** a saturado, empapado. ~**ion** /-'reɪʃn/ n saturación f

Saturday /'sætədeɪ/ n sábado m

sauce /sɔ:s/ n salsa f; (*cheek*) descaro m. ~**pan** /'sɔ:spən/ n cazo m

saucer /'sɔ:sə(r)/ n platillo m

saucy /'sɔ:sɪ/ a (**-ier, -iest**) descarado

Saudi Arabia /saʊdɪə'reɪbɪə/ n Arabia f Saudí

sauna /'sɔ:nə/ n sauna f

saunter /'sɔ:ntə(r)/ *vi* deambular, pasearse

sausage /'sɒsɪdʒ/ n salchicha f

savage /'sævɪdʒ/ a salvaje; (*fierce*) feroz; (*furious, fam*) rabioso. ● n salvaje m & f. ● *vt* atacar. ~**ry** n ferocidad f

sav|e /seɪv/ *vt* salvar; ahorrar (*money, time*); (*prevent*) evitar. ● n (*football*) parada f. ● *prep* salvo, con excepción de. ~**er** n ahorrador m. ~**ing** n ahorro m. ~**ings** npl ahorros mpl

saviour /'seɪvɪə(r)/ n salvador m

savour /'seɪvə(r)/ n sabor m. ● *vt* saborear. ~**y** a (*appetizing*) sabroso; (*not sweet*) no dulce. ● n aperitivo m (no dulce)

saw¹ /sɔ:/ *see* **see**¹

saw² /sɔ:/ n sierra f. ● *vt* (*pt* sawed, *pp* sawn) serrar. ~**dust** /'sɔ:dʌst/ n serrín m. ~**n** /sɔ:n/ *see* **saw**¹

saxophone /'sæksəfəʊn/ n saxófono m

say /seɪ/ *vt/i* (*pt* said /sed/) decir; rezar (*prayer*). **I** ~**!** ¡no me digas! ● n. **have a** ~ expresar una opinión; (*in decision*) tener voz en capítulo. **have no** ~ no tener ni voz ni voto. ~**ing** /'seɪɪŋ/ n refrán m

scab /skæb/ n costra f; (*blackleg, fam*) esquirol m

scaffold /'skæfəʊld/ n (*gallows*) cadalso m, patíbulo m. ~**ing** /'skæfəldɪŋ/ n (*for workmen*) andamio m

scald /skɔ:ld/ *vt* escaldar; calentar (*milk etc*). ● n escaldadura f

scale¹ /skeɪl/ n escala f

scale² /skeɪl/ n (*of fish*) escama f

scale³ /skeɪl/ *vt* (*climb*) escalar. ~ **down** *vt* reducir (proporcionalmente)

scales /skeɪlz/ npl (*for weighing*) balanza f, peso m

scallop /'skɒləp/ n venera f; (*on dress*) festón m

scalp /skælp/ n cuero m cabelludo. ● *vt* quitar el cuero cabelludo a

scalpel /'skælpəl/ n escalpelo m

scamp /skæmp/ n bribón m

scamper /'skæmpə(r)/ *vi*. ~ **away** marcharse corriendo

scampi /'skæmpɪ/ npl gambas fpl grandes

scan /skæn/ *vt* (*pt* scanned) escudriñar; (*quickly*) echar un vistazo a; (*radar*) explorar. ● *vi* (*poetry*) estar bien medido

scandal /'skændl/ n escándalo m; (*gossip*) chismorreo m. ~**ize**

/'skændəlaɪz/ *vt* escandalizar. ∼ous
a escandaloso

Scandinavia /skændɪ'neɪvɪə/ *n*
Escandinavia *f*. ∼n *a* & *n* escandinavo (*m*)

scant /skænt/ *a* escaso. ∼ily *adv*
insuficientemente. ∼y /'skæntɪ/ *a*
(**-ier, -iest**) escaso

scapegoat /'skeɪpɡəʊt/ *n* cabeza *f* de
turco

scar /skɑː(r)/ *n* cicatriz *f*. ● *vt* (*pt*
scarred) dejar una cicatriz en. ● *vi*
cicatrizarse

scarc|e /skeəs/ *a* (**-er, -est**) escaso.
make o.s. ∼**e** (*fam*) mantenerse
lejos. ∼**ely** /'skeəslɪ/ *adv* apenas.
∼**ity** *n* escasez *f*

scare /skeə(r)/ *vt* asustar. **be** ∼**d**
tener miedo. ● *n* susto *m*. ∼**crow**
/'skeəkrəʊ/ *n* espantapájaros *m invar*.
∼**monger** /'skeəmʌŋɡə(r)/ *n*
alarmista *m* & *f*

scarf /skɑːf/ *n* (*pl* **scarves**) bufanda *f*;
(*over head*) pañuelo *m*

scarlet /'skɑːlət/ *a* escarlata *f*. ∼
fever *n* escarlatina *f*

scary /'skeərɪ/ *a* (**-ier, -iest**) que da
miedo

scathing /'skeɪðɪŋ/ *a* mordaz

scatter /'skætə(r)/ *vt* (*throw*) esparcir; (*disperse*) dispersar. ● *vi* dispersarse. ∼**brained** *a* atolondrado.
∼**ed** *a* disperso; (*occasional*) esporádico

scatty /'skætɪ/ *a* (**-ier, -iest**) (*sl*)
atolondrado

scavenge /'skævɪndʒ/ *vi* buscar (en
la basura). ∼**r** /-ə(r)/ *n* (*vagrant*) persona *f* que busca objetos en la basura

scenario /sɪ'nɑːrɪəʊ/ *n* (*pl* **-os**)
argumento *m*; (*of film*) guión *m*

scen|e /siːn/ *n* escena *f*; (*sight*) vista
f; (*fuss*) lío *m*. **behind the** ∼**es** entre
bastidores. ∼**ery** /'siːnərɪ/ *n* paisaje *m*; (*in theatre*) decorado *m*. ∼**ic**
/'siːnɪk/ *a* pintoresco

scent /sent/ *n* olor *m*; (*perfume*) perfume *m*; (*trail*) pista *f*. ● *vt* presentir;
(*make fragrant*) perfumar

sceptic /'skeptɪk/ *n* escéptico *m*. ∼**al**
a escéptico. ∼**ism** /-sɪzəm/ *n* escepticismo *m*

sceptre /'septə(r)/ *n* cetro *m*

schedule /'ʃedjuːl, 'skedjuːl/ *n* programa *f*; (*timetable*) horario *m*. **behind** ∼ con retraso. **on** ∼ sin
retraso. ● *vt* proyectar. ∼**d flight** *n*
vuelo *m* regular

scheme /skiːm/ *n* proyecto *m*; (*plot*)
intriga *f*. ● *vi* hacer proyectos; (*pej*)
intrigar. ∼**r** *n* intrigante *m* & *f*

schism /'sɪzəm/ *n* cisma *m*

schizophrenic /skɪtsə'frenɪk/ *a* & *n*
esquizofrénico (*m*)

scholar /'skɒlə(r)/ *n* erudito *m*. ∼**ly**
a erudito. ∼**ship** *n* erudición *f*;
(*grant*) beca *f*

scholastic /skə'læstɪk/ *a* escolar

school /skuːl/ *n* escuela *f*; (*of univ*)
facultad *f*. *a* (*age, holidays, year*)
escolar. ● *vt* enseñar; (*discipline*) disciplinar. ∼**boy** /'skuːlbɔɪ/ *n* colegial
m. ∼**girl** /-ɡɜːl/ *n* colegiala *f*. ∼**ing**
n instrucción *f*. ∼**master** /'skuːlmɑː
stə(r)/ *n* (*primary*) maestro *m*;
(*secondary*) profesor *m*. ∼**-mistress**
n (*primary*) maestra *f*; (*secondary*)
profesora *f*. ∼**-teacher** *n* (*primary*)
maestro *m*; (*secondary*) profesor *m*

schooner /'skuːnə(r)/ *n* goleta *f*;
(*glass*) vaso *m* grande

sciatica /saɪ'ætɪkə/ *n* ciática *f*

scien|ce /'saɪəns/ *n* ciencia *f*. ∼**ce
fiction** *n* ciencia *f* ficción.
∼**tific** /-'tɪfɪk/ *a* científico. ∼**tist**
/'saɪəntɪst/ *n* científico *m*

scintillate /'sɪntɪleɪt/ *vi* centellear

scissors /'sɪsəz/ *npl* tijeras *fpl*

sclerosis /sklə'rəʊsɪs/ *n* esclerosis *f*

scoff /skɒf/ *vt* (*sl*) zamparse. ● *vi*. ∼
at mofarse de

scold /skəʊld/ *vt* regañar. ∼**ing** *n*
regaño *m*

scone /skɒn/ *n* (*tipo m de*) bollo *m*

scoop /skuːp/ *n* paleta *f*; (*news*) noticia *f* exclusiva. ● *vt*. ∼ **out** excavar.
∼ **up** recoger

scoot /skuːt/ *vi* (*fam*) largarse corriendo. ∼**er** /'skuːtə(r)/ *n* escúter
m; (*for child*) patinete *m*

scope /skəʊp/ *n* alcance *m*;
(*opportunity*) oportunidad *f*

scorch /skɔːtʃ/ *vt* chamuscar. ∼**er** *n*
(*fam*) día *m* de mucho calor. ∼**ing** *a*
(*fam*) de mucho calor

score /skɔː(r)/ *n* tanteo *m*; (*mus*)
partitura *f*; (*twenty*) veintena *f*;
(*reason*) motivo *m*. **on that** ∼ en
cuanto a eso. ● *vt* marcar; (*slash*)
rayar; (*mus*) instrumentar; conseguir
(*success*). ● *vi* marcar un tanto; (*keep
score*) tantear. ∼ **over s.o.** aventajar
a. ∼**r** /-ə(r)/ *n* tanteador *m*

scorn /skɔːn/ *n* desdén *m*. ● *vt*
desdeñar. ∼**ful** *a* desdeñoso. ∼**fully**
adv desdeñosamente

Scorpio /'skɔːpɪəʊ/ n (astr) Escorpión m

scorpion /'skɔːpɪən/ n escorpión m

Scot /skɒt/ n escocés m. ~**ch** /skɒtʃ/ a escocés. ● n güisqui m

scotch /skɒtʃ/ vt frustrar; (suppress) suprimir

scot-free /skɒt'friː/ a impune; (gratis) sin pagar

Scot: ~**land** /'skɒtlənd/ n Escocia f. ~**s** a escocés. ~**sman** n escocés m. ~**swoman** n escocesa f. ~**tish** a escocés

scoundrel /'skaʊndrəl/ n canalla f

scour /skaʊə(r)/ vt estregar; (search) registrar. ~**er** n estropajo m

scourge /skɜːdʒ/ n azote m

scout /skaʊt/ n explorador m. Boy S~ explorador m. ● vi. ~ (for) buscar

scowl /skaʊl/ n ceño m. ● vi fruncir el entrecejo

scraggy /'skrægɪ/ a (-ier, -iest) descarnado

scram /skræm/ vi (sl) largarse

scramble /'skræmbl/ vi (clamber) gatear. ~ **for** pelearse para obtener. ● vt revolver (eggs). ● n (difficult climb) subida f difícil; (struggle) lucha f

scrap /skræp/ n pedacito m; (fight, fam) pelea f. ● vt (pt scrapped) desechar. ~**book** n álbum m de recortes. ~**s** npl sobras fpl

scrape /skreɪp/ n raspadura f; (fig) apuro m. ● vt raspar; (graze) arañar; (rub) frotar. ● vi. ~ **through** lograr pasar; aprobar por los pelos (exam). ~ **together** reunir. ~**r** /-ə(r)/ n raspador m

scrap: ~ **heap** n montón m de deshechos. ~-**iron** n chatarra f

scrappy /'skræpɪ/ a fragmentario, pobre, de mala calidad

scratch /skrætʃ/ vt rayar; (with nail etc) arañar; rascar (itch). ● vi arañar. ● n raya f; (from nail etc) arañazo m. **start from** ~ empezar sin nada, empezar desde el principio. **up to** ~ al nivel requerido

scrawl /skrɔːl/ n garrapato m. ● vt/i garrapatear

scrawny /'skrɔːnɪ/ a (-ier, -iest) descarnado

scream /skriːm/ vt/i gritar. ● n grito m

screech /skriːtʃ/ vi chirriar; (brakes etc) chirriar. ● n grito m; (of brakes etc) chirrido m

screen /skriːn/ n pantalla f; (folding) biombo m. ● vt (hide) ocultar; (protect) proteger; proyectar (film); seleccionar (candidates)

screw /skruː/ n tornillo m. ● vt atornillar. ~**driver** /'skruːdraɪvə(r)/ n destornillador m. ~ **up** atornillar; entornar (eyes); torcer (face); (ruin, sl) arruinar. ~**y** /'skruːɪ/ a (-ier, -iest) (sl) chiflado

scribble /'skrɪbl/ vt/i garrapatear. ● n garrapato m

scribe /skraɪb/ n copista m & f

script /skrɪpt/ n escritura f; (of film etc) guión m

Scriptures /'skrɪptʃəz/ npl Sagradas Escrituras fpl

script-writer /'skrɪptraɪtə(r)/ n guionista m & f

scroll /skrəʊl/ n rollo m (de pergamino)

scrounge /skraʊndʒ/ vt/i obtener de gorra; (steal) birlar. ~**r** /-ə(r)/ n gorrón m

scrub /skrʌb/ n (land) maleza f; (clean) fregado m. ● vt/i (pt scrubbed) fregar

scruff /skrʌf/ n. **the** ~ **of the neck** el cogote m

scruffy /'skrʌfɪ/ a (-ier, -iest) desaliñado

scrum /skrʌm/ n, **scrummage** /'skrʌmɪdʒ/ n (Rugby) melée f

scrup|**le** /'skruːpl/ n escrúpulo m. ~**ulous** /'skruːpjʊləs/ a escrupuloso. ~**ulously** adv escrupulosamente

scrutin|**ize** /'skruːtɪnaɪz/ vt escudriñar. ~**y** /'skruːtɪnɪ/ n examen m minucioso

scuff /skʌf/ vt arañar (shoes)

scuffle /'skʌfl/ n pelea f

scullery /'skʌlərɪ/ n trascocina f

sculpt /skʌlpt/ vt/i esculpir. ~**or** n escultor m. ~**ure** /-tʃə(r)/ n escultura f. ● vt/i esculpir

scum /skʌm/ n espuma f; (people, pej) escoria f

scurf /skɜːf/ n caspa f

scurrilous /'skʌrɪləs/ a grosero

scurry /'skʌrɪ/ vi correr

scurvy /'skɜːvɪ/ n escorbuto m

scuttle[1] /'skʌtl/ n cubo m del carbón

scuttle[2] /'skʌtl/ vt barrenar (ship)

scuttle[3] /'skʌtl/ vi. ~ **away** correr, irse de prisa

scythe /saɪð/ n guadaña f

SE abbr (south-east) sudeste m

sea /si:/ n mar m. **at** ～ en el mar; (fig) confuso. **by** ～ por mar. ～**board** /'si:bɔːd/ n litoral m. ～**farer** /'si:feərə(r)/ n marinero m. ～**food** /'si:fuːd/ n mariscos mpl. ～**gull** /'si:gʌl/ n gaviota f. ～**horse** n caballito m de mar, hipocampo m

seal[^1] /si:l/ n sello m. ● vt sellar. ～ **off** acordonar ⟨area⟩

seal[^2] /si:l/ (animal) foca f

sea level /'si:levl/ n nivel m del mar

sealing-wax /'si:lɪŋwæks/ n lacre m

sea lion /'si:laɪən/ n león m marino

seam /si:m/ n costura f; (of coal) veta f

seaman /'si:mən/ n (pl **-men**) marinero m

seamy /'si:mɪ/ a. **the** ～ **side** n el lado m sórdido, el revés m

seance /'seɪɑːns/ n sesión f de espiritismo

sea: ～**plane** /'si:pleɪn/ n hidroavión f. ～**port** /'si:pɔːt/ n puerto m de mar

search /sɜːtʃ/ vt registrar; (examine) examinar. ● vi buscar. ● n (for sth) búsqueda f; (of sth) registro m. **in** ～ **of** en busca de. ～ **for** buscar. ～**ing** a penetrante. ～**party** n equipo m de salvamento. ～**light** /'sɜːtʃlaɪt/ n reflector m

sea: ～**scape** /'si:skeɪp/ n marina f. ～**shore** n orilla f del mar. ～**sick** /'si:sɪk/ a mareado. **be** ～**sick** marearse. ～**side** /'si:saɪd/ n playa f

season /'si:zn/ n estación f; (period) temporada f. ● vt (culin) sazonar; secar ⟨wood⟩. ～**able** a propio de la estación. ～**al** a estacional. ～**ed** /'si:znd/ a (fig) experto. ～**ing** n condimento m. ～**ticket** n billete m de abono

seat /si:t/ n asiento m; (place) lugar m; (of trousers) fondillos mpl; (bottom) trasero m. **take a** ～ sentarse. ● vt sentar; (have seats for) tener asientos para. ～**belt** n cinturón m de seguridad

sea: ～**urchin** n erizo m de mar. ～**weed** /'si:wiːd/ n alga f. ～**worthy** /'si:wɜːðɪ/ a en estado de navegar

secateurs /'sekətɜːz/ npl tijeras fpl de podar

sece|**de** /sɪ'si:d/ vi separarse. ～**ssion** /-eʃn/ n secesión f

seclu|**de** /sɪ'klu:d/ vt aislar. ～**ded** a aislado. ～**sion** /-ʒn/ n aislamiento m

second[^1] /'sekənd/ a & n segundo (m). **on** ～ **thoughts** pensándolo bien.

● adv (in race etc) en segundo lugar. ● vt apoyar. ～**s** npl (goods) artículos mpl de segunda calidad; (more food, fam) otra porción f

second[^2] /sɪ'kɒnd/ vt (transfer) trasladar temporalmente

secondary /'sekəndrɪ/ a secundario. ～ **school** n instituto m

second: ～**best** a segundo. ～**class** a de segunda clase. ～**hand** a de segunda mano. ～**ly** adv en segundo lugar. ～**rate** a mediocre

secre|**cy** /'si:krəsɪ/ n secreto m. ～**t** /'si:krɪt/ a & n secreto (m). **in** ～**t** en secreto

secretar|**ial** /sekrə'teərɪəl/ a de secretario. ～**iat** /sekrə'teərɪət/ n secretaría f. ～**y** /'sekrətrɪ/ n secretario m. **S**～**y of State** ministro m; (Amer) Ministro m de Asuntos Exteriores

secrete /sɪ'kriːt/ vt (med) secretar. ～**ion** /-ʃn/ n secreción f

secretive /'si:krɪtɪv/ a reservado

secretly /'si:krɪtlɪ/ adv en secreto

sect /sekt/ n secta f. ～**arian** /-'teərɪən/ a sectario

section /'sekʃn/ n sección f; (part) parte f

sector /'sektə(r)/ n sector m

secular /'sekjʊlə(r)/ a seglar

secur|**e** /sɪ'kjʊə(r)/ a seguro; (fixed) fijo. ● vt asegurar; (obtain) obtener. ～**ely** adv seguramente. ～**ity** /sɪ'kjʊərətɪ/ n seguridad f; (for loan) garantía f, fianza f

sedate /sɪ'deɪt/ a sosegado

sedat|**ion** /sɪ'deɪʃn/ n sedación f. ～**ive** /'sedətɪv/ a & n sedante (m)

sedentary /'sedəntrɪ/ a sedentario

sediment /'sedɪmənt/ n sedimento m

seduc|**e** /sɪ'dju:s/ vt seducir. ～**er** /-ə(r)/ n seductor m. ～**tion** /sɪ'dʌkʃn/ n seducción f. ～**tive** /-tɪv/ a seductor

see[^1] /si:/ ● vt (pt **saw**, pp **seen**) ver; (understand) comprender; (notice) notar; (escort) acompañar. ～**ing that** visto que. ～ **you later!** ¡hasta luego! ● vi ver; (understand) comprender. ～ **about** ocuparse de. ～ **off** despedirse de. ～ **through** llevar a cabo; descubrir el juego de ⟨person⟩. ～ **to** ocuparse de

see[^2] /si:/ n diócesis f

seed /si:d/ n semilla f; (fig) germen m; (tennis) preseleccionado m. ～**ling**

n plantón *m*. **go to** ~ granar; (*fig*) echarse a perder. ~**y** /'si:dɪ/ *a* (**-ier, -iest**) sórdido

seek /si:k/ *vt* (*pt* **sought**) buscar. ~ **out** buscar

seem /si:m/ *vi* parecer. ~**ingly** *adv* aparentemente

seemly /'si:mlɪ/ *a* (**-ier, -iest**) correcto

seen /si:n/ *see* **see**¹

seep /si:p/ *vi* filtrarse. ~**age** *n* filtración *f*

see-saw /'si:sɔ:/ *n* balancín *m*

seethe /si:ð/ *vi* (*fig*) hervir. **be seething with anger** estar furioso

see-through /'si:θru:/ *a* transparente

segment /'segmənt/ *n* segmento *m*; (*of orange*) gajo *m*

segregat|e /'segrɪgeɪt/ *vt* segregar. ~**ion** /-'geɪʃn/ *n* segregación *f*

seiz|e /si:z/ *vt* agarrar; (*jurid*) incautarse de. ~**e on** *vi* valerse de. ~**e up** *vi* (*tec*) agarrotarse. ~**ure** /'si:ʒə(r)/ *n* incautación *f*, (*med*) ataque *m*

seldom /'seldəm/ *adv* raramente

select /sɪ'lekt/ *vt* escoger; (*sport*) seleccionar. ● *a* selecto; (*exclusive*) exclusivo. ~**ion** /-ʃn/ *n* selección *f*. ~**ive** *a* selectivo

self /self/ *n* (*pl* **selves**) sí mismo. ~**addressed** *a* con su propia dirección. ~**assurance** *n* confianza *f* en sí mismo. ~**assured** *a* seguro de sí mismo. ~**catering** *a* con facilidades para cocinar. ~**centred** *a* egocéntrico. ~**confidence** *n* confianza *f* en sí mismo. ~**confident** *a* seguro de sí mismo. ~**conscious** *a* cohibido. ~**contained** *a* independiente. ~**control** *n* dominio *m* de sí mismo. ~**defence** *n* defensa *f* propia. ~**denial** *n* abnegación *f*. ~**employed** *a* que trabaja por cuenta propia. ~**esteem** *n* amor *m* propio. ~**evident** *a* evidente. ~**government** *n* autonomía *f*. ~**important** *a* presumido. ~**indulgent** *a* inmoderado. ~**interest** *n* interés *m* propio. ~**ish** /'selfɪʃ/ *a* egoísta. ~**ishness** *n* egoísmo *m*. ~**less** /'selflɪs/ *a* desinteresado. ~**made** *a* rico por su propio esfuerzo. ~**opinionated** *a* intransigente; (*arrogant*) engreído. ~**pity** *n* compasión *f* de sí mismo. ~**portrait** *n* autorretrato *m*. ~**possessed** *a* dueño de sí mismo. ~**reliant** *a* independiente. ~**respect** *n*

amor *m* propio. ~**righteous** *a* santurrón. ~**sacrifice** *n* abnegación *f*. ~**satisfied** *a* satisfecho de sí mismo. ~**seeking** *a* egoísta. ~**service** *a* & *n* autoservicio (*m*). ~**styled** *a* sedicente, llamado. ~**sufficient** *a* independiente. ~**willed** *a* terco

sell /sel/ *vt* (*pt* **sold**) vender. **be sold on** (*fam*) entusiasmarse por. **be sold out** estar agotado. ● *vi* venderse. ~ **by date** *n* fecha *f* de caducidad. ~ **off** *vt* liquidar. ~ **up** *vt* vender todo. ~**er** *n* vendedor *m*

Sellotape /'seləteɪp/ *n* (*P*) (papel *m*) celo *m*, cinta *f* adhesiva

sell-out /'selaʊt/ *n* (*betrayal, fam*) traición *f*

semantic /sɪ'mæntɪk/ *a* semántico. ~**s** *n* semántica *f*

semaphore /'seməfɔ:(r)/ *n* semáforo *m*

semblance /'sembləns/ *n* apariencia *f*

semen /'si:mən/ *n* semen *m*

semester /sɪ'mestə(r)/ *n* (*Amer*) semestre *m*

semi... /'semɪ/ *pref* semi...

semi|breve /'semɪbri:v/ *n* semibreve *f*, redonda *f*. ~**circle** /'semɪs3:kl/ *n* semicírculo *m*. ~**circular** /-'s3:kjʊlə(r)/ *a* semicircular. ~**colon** /semɪ'kəʊlən/ *n* punto *m* y coma. ~**detached** /semɪdɪ'tætʃt/ *a* (*house*) adosado. ~**final** /semɪ'faɪnl/ *n* semifinal *f*

seminar /'semɪnɑ:(r)/ *n* seminario *m*

seminary /'semɪnərɪ/ *n* (*college*) seminario *m*

semiquaver /'semɪkweɪvə(r)/ *n* (*mus*) semicorchea *f*

Semit|e /'si:maɪt/ *n* semita *m* & *f*. ~**ic** /sɪ'mɪtɪk/ *a* semítico

semolina /semə'li:nə/ *n* sémola *f*

senat|e /'senɪt/ *n* senado *m*. ~**or** /-ətə(r)/ *n* senador *m*

send /send/ *vt/i* (*pt* **sent**) enviar. ~ **away** despedir. ~ **away for** pedir (por correo). ~ **for** enviar a buscar. ~ **off for** pedir (por correo). ~ **up** (*fam*) parodiar. ~**er** *n* remitente *m*. ~**off** *n* despedida *f*

senil|e /'si:naɪl/ *a* senil. ~**ity** /sɪ'nɪlətɪ/ *n* senilidad *f*

senior /'si:nɪə(r)/ *a* mayor; (*in rank*) superior; (*partner etc*) principal. ● *n* mayor *m* & *f*. ~ **citizen** *n* jubilado *m*. ~**ity** /-'ɒrɪtɪ/ *n* antigüedad *f*

sensation /sen'seɪʃn/ *n* sensación *f*. ∼al *a* sensacional

sense /sens/ *n* sentido *m*; (*common sense*) juicio *m*; (*feeling*) sensación *f*. **make** ∼ *vt* tener sentido. **make** ∼ **of** comprender. ∼**less** *a* insensato; (*med*) sin sentido

sensibilities /sensɪ'bɪlətiz/ *npl* susceptibilidad *f*. ∼**ibility** /sensɪ'bɪlətɪ/ *n* sensibilidad *f*

sensible /'sensəbl/ *a* sensato; (*clothing*) práctico

sensitiv|e /'sensɪtɪv/ *a* sensible; (*touchy*) susceptible. ∼**ity** /-'tɪvətɪ/ *n* sensibilidad *f*

sensory /'sensərɪ/ *a* sensorio

sensual /'senʃʊəl/ *a* sensual. ∼**ity** /-'ælətɪ/ *n* sensualidad *f*

sensuous /'senʃʊəs/ *a* sensual

sent /sent/ *see* **send**

sentence /'sentəns/ *n* frase *f*; (*jurid*) sentencia *f*; (*punishment*) condena *f*. ● *vt*. ∼ **to** condenar a

sentiment /'sentɪmənt/ *n* sentimiento *m*; (*opinion*) opinión *f*. ∼**al** /sentɪ'mentl/ *a* sentimental. ∼**ality** /-'tælətɪ/ *n* sentimentalismo *m*

sentry /'sentrɪ/ *n* centinela *f*

separable /'sepərəbl/ *a* separable

separate[1] /'sepərət/ *a* separado; (*independent*) independiente. ∼**ly** *adv* por separado. ∼**s** *npl* coordinados *mpl*

separat|e[2] /'sepəreɪt/ *vt* separar. ● *vi* separarse. ∼**ion** /-'reɪʃn/ *n* separación *f*. ∼**ist** /'sepərətɪst/ *n* separatista *m* & *f*

September /sep'tembə(r)/ *n* se(p)-tiembre *m*

septic /'septɪk/ *a* séptico. ∼ **tank** *n* fosa *f* séptica

sequel /'si:kwəl/ *n* continuación *f*; (*consequence*) consecuencia *f*

sequence /'si:kwəns/ *n* sucesión *f*; (*of film*) secuencia *f*

sequin /'si:kwɪn/ *n* lentejuela *f*

serenade /serə'neɪd/ *n* serenata *f*. ● *vt* dar serenata a

seren|e /sɪ'ri:n/ *a* sereno. ∼**ity** /-'enətɪ/ *n* serenidad *f*

sergeant /'sɑ:dʒənt/ *n* sargento *m*

serial /'sɪərɪəl/ *n* serial *m*. ● *a* de serie. ∼**ize** *vt* publicar por entregas

series /'sɪərɪz/ *n* serie *f*

serious /'sɪərɪəs/ *a* serio. ∼**ly** *adv* seriamente; (*ill*) gravemente. **take** ∼**ly** tomar en serio. ∼**ness** *n* seriedad *f*

sermon /'sɜ:mən/ *n* sermón *m*

serpent /'sɜ:pənt/ *n* serpiente *f*

serrated /sɪ'reɪtɪd/ *a* serrado

serum /'sɪərəm/ *n* (*pl* -**a**) suero *m*

servant /'sɜ:vənt/ *n* criado *m*; (*fig*) servidor *m*

serve /sɜ:v/ *vt* servir; (*in the army etc*) prestar servicio; cumplir ⟨*sentence*⟩. ∼ **as** servir de. ∼ **its purpose** servir para el caso. **it** ∼**s you right** ¡bien te lo mereces! ¡te está bien merecido! ● *vi* servir. ● *n* (*in tennis*) saque *m*

service /'sɜ:vɪs/ *n* servicio *m*; (*maintenance*) revisión *f*. **of** ∼ **to** útil a. ● *vt* revisar ⟨*car etc*⟩. ∼**able** /'sɜ:vɪsəbl/ *a* práctico; (*durable*) duradero. ∼ **charge** *n* servicio *m*. ∼**man** /'sɜ:vɪsmæn/ *n* (*pl* -**men**) militar *m*. ∼**s** *npl* (*mil*) fuerzas *fpl* armadas. ∼ **station** *n* estación *f* de servicio

serviette /sɜ:vɪ'et/ *n* servilleta *f*

servile /'sɜ:vaɪl/ *a* servil

session /'seʃn/ *n* sesión *f*; (*univ*) curso *m*

set /set/ *vt* (*pt* **set**, *pres p* **setting**) poner; poner en hora ⟨*clock etc*⟩; fijar ⟨*limit etc*⟩; (*typ*) componer. ∼ **fire to** pegar fuego a. ∼ **free** *vt* poner en libertad. ● *vi* ⟨*sun*⟩ ponerse; ⟨*jelly*⟩ cuajarse. ● *n* serie *f*; (*of cutlery etc*) juego *m*; (*tennis*) set *m*; (*TV, radio*) aparato *m*; (*of hair*) marcado *m*; (*in theatre*) decorado *m*; (*of people*) círculo *m*. ● *a* fijo. **be** ∼ **on** estar resuelto a. ∼ **about** *vi* empezar a. ∼ **back** *vt* (*delay*) retardar; (*cost, sl*) costar. ∼ **off** *vi* salir. ● *vt* (*make start*) poner en marcha; hacer estallar ⟨*bomb*⟩. ∼ **out** *vi* (*declare*) declarar; (*leave*) salir. ∼ **sail** salir. ∼ **the table** poner la mesa. ∼ **up** *vt* establecer. ∼**back** *n* revés *m*. ∼ **square** *n* escuadra *f* de dibujar

settee /se'ti:/ *n* sofá *m*

setting /'setɪŋ/ *n* (*of sun*) puesta *f*; (*of jewel*) engaste *m*; (*in theatre*) escenario *m*; (*typ*) composición *f*. ∼-**lotion** *n* fijador *m*

settle /'setl/ *vt* (*arrange*) arreglar; (*pay*) pagar; fijar ⟨*date*⟩; calmar ⟨*nerves*⟩. ● *vi* (*come to rest*) posarse; (*live*) instalarse. ∼ **down** calmarse; (*become orderly*) sentar la cabeza. ∼ **for** aceptar. ∼ **up** ajustar cuentas. ∼**ment** /'setlmənt/ *n* establecimiento *m*; (*agreement*) acuerdo *m*;

(com) liquidación *f*; *(place)* colonia *f*. ~r /-ə(r)/ *n* colonizador *m*

set ~-to *n* pelea *f*. ~-up *n* *(fam)* sistema *m*

seven /'sevn/ *a & n* siete *(m)*. ~teen /sevn'ti:n/ *a & n* diecisiete *(m)*. ~teenth *a & n* decimoséptimo *(m)*. ~th *a & n* séptimo *(m)*. ~tieth *a & n* setenta *(m)*, septuagésimo *(m)*. ~ty /'sevntɪ/ *a & n* setenta *(m)*

sever /'sevə(r)/ *vt* cortar; *(fig)* romper

several /'sevrəl/ *a & pron* varios

severance /'sevərəns/ *n* *(breaking off)* ruptura *f*

sever|e /sɪ'vɪə(r)/ *a* (-er, -est) severo; *(violent)* violento; *(serious)* grave; *(weather)* riguroso. ~ely *adv* severamente; *(seriously)* gravemente. ~ity /-'verətɪ/ *n* severidad *f*; *(violence)* violencia *f*; *(seriousness)* gravedad *f*

sew /səʊ/ *vt/i* *(pt* sewed, *pp* sewn, *or* sewed) coser

sew|age /'su:ɪdʒ/ *n* aguas *fpl* residuales. ~er /'su:ə(r)/ *n* cloaca *f*

sewing /'səʊɪŋ/ *n* costura *f*. ~ machine *n* máquina *f* de coser

sewn /səʊn/ *see* **sew**

sex /seks/ *n* sexo *m*. have ~ tener relaciones sexuales. • *a* sexual. ~ist /'seksɪst/ *a & n* sexista *(m & f)*

sextet /seks'tet/ *n* sexteto *m*

sexual /'seksʊəl/ *a* sexual. ~ intercourse *n* relaciones *fpl* sexuales. ~ity /-'ælətɪ/ *n* sexualidad *f*

sexy /'seksɪ/ *a* (-ier, -iest) excitante, sexy, provocativo

shabb|ily /'ʃæbɪlɪ/ *adv* pobremente; *(act)* mezquinamente. ~iness *n* pobreza *f*; *(meanness)* mezquindad *f*. ~y /'ʃæbɪ/ *a* (-ier, -iest) *(clothes)* gastado; *(person)* pobremente vestido; *(mean)* mezquino

shack /ʃæk/ *n* choza *f*

shackles /'ʃæklz/ *npl* grillos *mpl*, grilletes *mpl*

shade /ʃeɪd/ *n* sombra *f*; *(of colour)* matiz *m*; *(for lamp)* pantalla *f*. a ~ better un poquito mejor. • *vt* dar sombra a

shadow /'ʃædəʊ/ *n* sombra *f*. S~ Cabinet *n* gobierno *m* en la sombra. • *vt* *(follow)* seguir. ~y *a* *(fig)* vago

shady /'ʃeɪdɪ/ *a* (-ier, -iest) sombreado; *(fig)* dudoso

shaft /ʃɑ:ft/ *n* *(of arrow)* astil *m*; *(mec)* eje *m*; *(of light)* rayo *m*; *(of lift, mine)* pozo *m*

shaggy /'ʃægɪ/ *a* (-ier, -iest) peludo

shak|e /ʃeɪk/ *vt* *(pt* shook, *pp* shaken) sacudir; agitar *(bottle)*; *(shock)* desconcertar. ~e hands with estrechar la mano a. • *vi* temblar. ~e off *vt* deshacerse de. • *n* sacudida *f*. ~e-up *n* reorganización *f*. ~y /'ʃeɪkɪ/ *a* (-ier, -iest) tembloroso; *(table etc)* inestable; *(unreliable)* incierto

shall /ʃæl/ *v aux* *(first person in future tense)*. I ~ go iré. we ~ see veremos

shallot /ʃə'lɒt/ *n* chalote *m*

shallow /'ʃæləʊ/ *a* (-er, -est) poco profundo; *(fig)* superficial

sham /ʃæm/ *n* farsa *f*; *(person)* impostor *m*. • *a* falso; *(affected)* fingido. • *vt* *(pt* shammed) fingir

shambles /'ʃæmblz/ *npl* *(mess, fam)* desorden *m* total

shame /ʃeɪm/ *n* vergüenza *f*. what a ~! ¡qué lástima! • *vt* avergonzar. ~faced /'ʃeɪmfeɪst/ *a* avergonzado. ~ful *a* vergonzoso. ~fully *adv* vergonzosamente. ~less *a* desvergonzado

shampoo /ʃæm'pu:/ *n* champú *m*. • *vt* lavar

shamrock /'ʃæmrɒk/ *n* trébol *m*

shandy /'ʃændɪ/ *n* cerveza *f* con gaseosa, clara *f*

shan't /ʃɑ:nt/ = **shall not**

shanty /'ʃæntɪ/ *n* chabola *f*. ~ town *n* chabolas *fpl*

shape /ʃeɪp/ *n* forma *f*. • *vt* formar; determinar *(future)*. • *vi* formarse. ~ up prometer. ~less *a* informe. ~ly /'ʃeɪplɪ/ *a* (-ier, -iest) bien proporcionado

share /ʃeə(r)/ *n* porción *f*; *(com)* acción *f*. go ~s compartir. • *vt* compartir; *(divide)* dividir. • *vi* participar. ~ in participar en. ~holder /'ʃeəhəʊldə(r)/ *n* accionista *m & f*. ~-out *n* reparto *m*

shark /ʃɑ:k/ *n* tiburón *m*; *(fig)* estafador *m*

sharp /ʃɑ:p/ *a* (-er, -est) *(knife etc)* afilado; *(pin etc)* puntiagudo; *(pain, sound)* agudo; *(taste)* acre; *(sudden, harsh)* brusco; *(well defined)* marcado; *(dishonest)* poco escrupuloso; *(clever)* listo. • *adv* en punto. at seven o'clock ~ a las siete en punto. • *n* *(mus)* sostenido *m*. ~en /'ʃɑ:pn/ *vt* afilar; sacar punta a *(pencil)*.

∼ener n (mec) afilador m; (for pencils) sacapuntas m invar. **∼ly** adv bruscamente

shatter /'ʃætə(r)/ vt hacer añicos; (upset) perturbar. ● vi hacerse añicos. **∼ed** a (exhausted) agotado

shav|e /ʃeɪv/ vt afeitar. ● vi afeitarse. ● n afeitado m. **have a ∼e** afeitarse. **∼en** a (face) afeitado; (head) rapado. **∼er** n maquinilla f (de afeitar). **∼ing-brush** n brocha f de afeitar. **∼ing-cream** n crema f de afeitar

shawl /ʃɔ:l/ n chal m

she /ʃi:/ pron ella. ● n hembra f

sheaf /ʃi:f/ n (pl sheaves) gavilla f

shear /ʃɪə(r)/ vt (pp shorn, or sheared) esquilar. **∼s** /ʃɪəz/ npl tijeras fpl grandes

sheath /ʃi:θ/ n (pl -s /ʃi:ðz/) vaina f; (contraceptive) condón m. **∼e** /ʃi:ð/ vt envainar

shed[1] /ʃed/ n cobertizo m

shed[2] /ʃed/ vt (pt shed, pres p shedding) perder; derramar (tears); despojarse de (clothes). **∼ light on** aclarar

sheen /ʃi:n/ n lustre m

sheep /ʃi:p/ n invar oveja f. **∼-dog** n perro m pastor. **∼ish** /'ʃi:pɪʃ/ a vergonzoso. **∼ishly** adv tímidamente. **∼skin** /'ʃi:pskɪn/ n piel f de carnero, zamarra f

sheer /ʃɪə(r)/ a puro; (steep) perpendicular; (fabric) muy fino. ● adv a pico

sheet /ʃi:t/ n sábana f; (of paper) hoja f; (of glass) lámina f; (of ice) capa f

sheikh /ʃeɪk/ n jeque m

shelf /ʃelf/ n (pl shelves) estante m. **be on the ∼** quedarse para vestir santos

shell /ʃel/ n concha f; (of egg) cáscara f; (of building) casco m; (explosive) proyectil m. ● vt desgranar (peas etc); (mil) bombardear. **∼fish** /'ʃelfɪʃ/ n invar (crustacean) crustáceo m; (mollusc) marisco m

shelter /'ʃeltə(r)/ n refugio m, abrigo m. ● vt abrigar; (protect) proteger; (give lodging to) dar asilo a. ● vi abrigarse. **∼ed** a (spot) abrigado; (life etc) protegido

shelv|e /ʃelv/ vt (fig) dar carpetazo a. **∼ing** /'ʃelvɪŋ/ n estantería f

shepherd /'ʃepəd/ n pastor m. ● vt guiar. **∼ess** /-'des/ n pastora f. **∼'s pie** n carne f picada con puré de patatas

sherbet /'ʃɜ:bət/ n (Amer, water-ice) sorbete m

sheriff /'ʃerɪf/ n alguacil m, sheriff m

sherry /'ʃerɪ/ n (vino m de) jerez m

shield /ʃi:ld/ n escudo m. ● vt proteger

shift /ʃɪft/ vt cambiar; cambiar de sitio (furniture etc); echar (blame etc). ● n cambio m; (work) turno m; (workers) tanda f. **make ∼** arreglárselas. **∼less** /'ʃɪftlɪs/ a holgazán

shifty /'ʃɪftɪ/ a (-ier, -iest) taimado

shilling /'ʃɪlɪŋ/ n chelín m

shilly-shally /'ʃɪlɪʃælɪ/ vi titubear

shimmer /'ʃɪmə(r)/ vi rielar, relucir. ● n luz f trémula

shin /ʃɪn/ n espinilla f

shine /ʃaɪn/ vi (pt shone) brillar. ● vt sacar brillo a. **∼ on** dirigir (torch). ● n brillo m

shingle /'ʃɪŋgl/ n (pebbles) guijarros mpl

shingles /'ʃɪŋglz/ npl (med) herpes mpl & fpl

shiny /'ʃaɪnɪ/ a (-ier, -iest) brillante

ship /ʃɪp/ n buque m, barco m. ● vt (pt shipped) transportar; (send) enviar; (load) embarcar. **∼building** /'ʃɪpbɪldɪŋ/ n construcción f naval. **∼ment** n envío m. **∼per** n expedidor m. **∼ping** n envío m; (ships) barcos mpl. **∼shape** /'ʃɪpʃeɪp/ adv & a en buen orden, en regla. **∼wreck** /'ʃɪprek/ n naufragio m. **∼wrecked** a naufragado. **be ∼wrecked** naufragar. **∼yard** /'ʃɪpjɑ:d/ n astillero m

shirk /ʃɜ:k/ vt esquivar. **∼er** n gandul m

shirt /ʃɜ:t/ n camisa f. **in ∼-sleeves** en mangas de camisa. **∼y** /'ʃɜ:tɪ/ a (sl) enfadado

shiver /'ʃɪvə(r)/ vi temblar. ● n escalofrío m

shoal /ʃəʊl/ n banco m

shock /ʃɒk/ n sacudida f; (fig) susto m; (elec) descarga f; (med) choque m. ● vt escandalizar. **∼ing** a escandaloso; (fam) espantoso. **∼ingly** adv terriblemente

shod /ʃɒd/ see **shoe**

shodd|ily /'ʃɒdɪlɪ/ adv mal. **∼y** /'ʃɒdɪ/ a (-ier, -iest) mal hecho, de pacotilla

shoe /ʃu:/ n zapato m; (of horse) herradura f. ● vt (pt shod, pres p shoeing) herrar (horse). **be well shod** estar bien calzado. **∼horn** /'ʃu:hɔ:n/

n calzador *m*. **~-lace** *n* cordón *m* de zapato. **~-maker** /'ʃuːmeɪkə(r)/ *n* zapatero *m*. **~-polish** *n* betún *m*. **~-string** *n*. **on a ~-string** con poco dinero. **~-tree** *n* horma *f*

shone /ʃɒn/ *see* **shine**

shoo /ʃuː/ *vt* ahuyentar

shook /ʃʊk/ *see* **shake**

shoot /ʃuːt/ *vt* (*pt* **shot**) disparar; rodar ⟨film⟩. ● *vi* ⟨hunt⟩ cazar. ● *n* (*bot*) retoño *m*; ⟨hunt⟩ cacería *f*. **~ down** *vt* derribar. **~ out** *vi* ⟨rush⟩ salir disparado. **~ up** ⟨prices⟩ subir de repente; ⟨grow⟩ crecer. **~ing-range** *n* campo *m* de tiro

shop /ʃɒp/ *n* tienda *f*; ⟨work-shop⟩ taller *m*. **talk ~** hablar de su trabajo. ● *vi* (*pt* **shopping**) hacer compras. **~ around** buscar el mejor precio. **go ~ping** ir de compras. **~ assistant** *n* dependiente *m*. **~keeper** /'ʃɒpkiːpə(r)/ *n* tendero *m*. **~-lifter** *n* ratero *m* (de tiendas). **~-lifting** *n* ratería *f* (de tiendas). **~per** *n* comprador *m*. **~ping** /'ʃɒpɪŋ/ *n* compras *fpl*. **~ping bag** *n* bolsa *f* de la compra. **~ping centre** *n* centro *m* comercial. **~ steward** *n* enlace *m* sindical. **~ window** *n* escaparate *m*

shore /ʃɔː(r)/ *n* orilla *f*

shorn /ʃɔːn/ *see* **shear**

short /ʃɔːt/ *a* (**-er**, **-est**) corto; ⟨not lasting⟩ breve; ⟨person⟩ bajo; ⟨curt⟩ brusco. **a ~ time ago** hace poco. **be ~ of** necesitar. **Mick is ~ for Michael** Mick es el diminutivo de Michael. ● *adv* ⟨stop⟩ en seco. **~ of doing** a menos que no hagamos. ● *n*. **in ~** en resumen. **~age** /'ʃɔːtɪdʒ/ *n* escasez *f*. **~bread** /'ʃɔːtbred/ *n* galleta *f* de mantequilla. **~-change** *vt* estafar, engañar. **~ circuit** *n* cortocircuito *m*. **~-coming** /'ʃɔːtkʌmɪŋ/ *n* deficiencia *f*. **~ cut** *n* atajo *m*. **~en** /'ʃɔːtn/ *vt* acortar. **~hand** /'ʃɔːthænd/ *n* taquigrafía *f*. **~hand typist** *n* taquimecanógrafo *m*, taquimeca *f* (*fam*). **~-lived** *a* efímero. **~ly** /'ʃɔːtlɪ/ *adv* dentro de poco. **~s** *npl* pantalón *m* corto. **~-sighted** *a* miope. **~-tempered** *a* de mal genio

shot /ʃɒt/ *see* **shoot**. ● *n* tiro *m*; ⟨person⟩ tirador *m*; ⟨photo⟩ foto *f*; ⟨injection⟩ inyección *f*. **~ like a ~** como una bala; ⟨willingly⟩ de buena gana. **~-gun** *n* escopeta *f*

should /ʃʊd, ʃəd/ *v aux*. **I ~ go** debería ir. **I ~ have seen him** debiera haberlo visto. **I ~ like** me gustaría. **if he ~ come** si viniese

shoulder /'ʃəʊldə(r)/ *n* hombro *m*. ● *vt* cargar con ⟨responsibility⟩; llevar a hombros ⟨burden⟩. **~-blade** *n* omóplato *m*. **~-strap** *n* correa *f* del hombro; ⟨of bra etc⟩ tirante *m*

shout /ʃaʊt/ *n* grito *m*. ● *vt/i* gritar. **~ at s.o.** gritarle a uno. **~ down** *vt* hacer callar a gritos

shove /ʃʌv/ *n* empujón *m*. ● *vt* empujar; ⟨put, fam⟩ poner. ● *vi* empujar. **~ off** *vi* (*fam*) largarse

shovel /'ʃʌvl/ *n* pala *f*. ● *vt* (*pt* **shovelled**) mover con la pala

show /ʃəʊ/ *vt* (*pt* **showed**, *pp* **shown**) mostrar; ⟨put on display⟩ exponer; poner ⟨film⟩. ● *vi* ⟨be visible⟩ verse. ● *n* demostración *f*; ⟨exhibition⟩ exposición *f*; ⟨ostentation⟩ pompa *f*; ⟨in theatre⟩ espectáculo *m*; ⟨in cinema⟩ sesión *f*. **on ~** expuesto. **~ off** *vt* lucir; ⟨pej⟩ ostentar. **~ up** *vi* destacar; ⟨be present⟩ presentarse. ● *vt* ⟨unmask⟩ desenmascarar. **~-case** *n* vitrina *f*. **~-down** *n* confrontación *f*

shower /'ʃaʊə(r)/ *n* chaparrón *m*; ⟨of blows etc⟩ lluvia *f*; ⟨for washing⟩ ducha *f*. **have a ~** ducharse. ● *vi* ducharse. ● *vt*. **~ with** colmar de. **~proof** /'ʃaʊəpruːf/ *a* impermeable. **~y** *a* lluvioso

show: **~-jumping** *n* concurso *m* hípico. **~manship** /'ʃəʊmənʃɪp/ *n* teatralidad *f*, arte *f* de presentar espectáculos

shown /ʃəʊn/ *see* **show**

show: **~-off** *n* fanfarrón *m*. **~-place** *n* lugar *m* de interés turístico. **~-room** /'ʃəʊruːm/ *n* sala *f* de exposición *f*

showy /'ʃəʊɪ/ *a* (**-ier**, **-iest**) llamativo; ⟨person⟩ ostentoso

shrank /ʃræŋk/ *see* **shrink**

shrapnel /'ʃræpnəl/ *n* metralla *f*

shred /ʃred/ *n* pedazo *m*; ⟨fig⟩ pizca *f*. ● *vt* (*pt* **shredded**) hacer tiras; ⟨culin⟩ cortar en tiras. **~der** *n* desfibradora *f*, trituradora *f*

shrew /ʃruː/ *n* musaraña *f*; ⟨woman⟩ arpía *f*

shrewd /ʃruːd/ *a* (**-er**, **-est**) astuto. **~ness** *n* astucia *f*

shriek /ʃriːk/ *n* chillido *m*. ● *vt/i* chillar

shrift /ʃrɪft/ n. give s.o. short ∼ despachar a uno con brusquedad

shrill /ʃrɪl/ a agudo

shrimp /ʃrɪmp/ n camarón m

shrine /ʃraɪn/ n (place) lugar m santo; (tomb) sepulcro m

shrink /ʃrɪŋk/ vt (pt shrank, pp shrunk) encoger. ● vi encogerse; (draw back) retirarse; (lessen) disminuir. ∼age n encogimiento m

shrivel /ʃrɪvl/ vi (pt shrivelled) (dry up) secarse; (become wrinkled) arrugarse

shroud /ʃraʊd/ n sudario m; (fig) velo m. ● vt (veil) velar

Shrove /ʃraʊv/ n. ∼ Tuesday n martes m de carnaval

shrub /ʃrʌb/ n arbusto m

shrug /ʃrʌg/ vt (pt shrugged) encoger de hombros. ● n encogimiento m de hombros

shrunk /ʃrʌŋk/ see shrink

shrunken /ʃrʌnkən/ a encogido

shudder /ˈʃʌdə(r)/ vi estremecerse. ● n estremecimiento m

shuffle /ˈʃʌfl/ vi arrastrar los pies. ● vt barajar ⟨cards⟩. ● n arrastramiento m de los pies; (of cards) barajadura f

shun /ʃʌn/ vt (pt shunned) evitar

shunt /ʃʌnt/ vt apartar, desviar

shush /ʃʊʃ/ int ¡chitón!

shut /ʃʌt/ vt (pt shut, pres p shutting) cerrar. ● vi cerrarse. ∼ down cerrar. ∼ up vt cerrar; (fam) hacer callar. ● vi callarse. ∼-down n cierre m. ∼ter /ˈʃʌtə(r)/ n contraventana f; (photo) obturador m

shuttle /ˈʃʌtl/ n lanzadera f; (train) tren m de enlace. ● vt transportar. ● vi ir y venir. ∼-cock /ˈʃʌtlkɒk/ n volante m. ∼ service n servicio m de enlace

shy /ʃaɪ/ a (-er, -est) tímido. ● vi (pt shied) asustarse. ∼ away from huir. ∼ness n timidez f

Siamese /saɪəˈmiːz/ a siamés

sibling /ˈsɪblɪŋ/ n hermano m, hermana f

Sicil|ian /sɪˈsɪljən/ a & n siciliano (m). ∼y /ˈsɪsɪlɪ/ n Sicilia f

sick /sɪk/ a enfermo; (humour) negro; (fed up, fam) harto. be ∼ (vomit) vomitar. be ∼ of (fig) estar harto de. feel ∼ sentir náuseas. ∼en /ˈsɪkən/ vt dar asco. ● vi caer enfermo. be ∼ening for incubar

sickle /ˈsɪkl/ n hoz f

sick: ∼ly /ˈsɪklɪ/ a (-ier, -iest) enfermizo; (taste, smell etc) nauseabundo. ∼ness /ˈsɪknɪs/ n enfermedad f. ∼-room n cuarto m del enfermo

side /saɪd/ n lado m; (of river) orilla f; (of hill) ladera f; (team) equipo m; (fig) parte f. ∼ by ∼ uno al lado del otro. on the ∼ (sideline) como actividad secundaria; (secretly) a escondidas. ● a lateral. ● vi. ∼ with tomar el partido de. ∼board /ˈsaɪdbɔːd/ n aparador m. ∼boards npl, ∼burns npl (sl) patillas fpl. ∼car n sidecar m. ∼effect n efecto m secundario. ∼light /ˈsaɪdlaɪt/ n luz f de posición. ∼line /ˈsaɪdlaɪn/ n actividad f secundaria. ∼long /-lɒŋ/ a & adv de soslayo. ∼road n calle f secundaria. ∼-saddle n silla f de mujer. ride ∼-saddle adv a mujeriegas. ∼-show n atracción f secundaria. ∼-step vt evitar. ∼-track vt desviar del asunto. ∼walk /ˈsaɪdwɔːk/ n (Amer) acera f, vereda f (LAm). ∼ways /ˈsaɪdweɪz/ a & adv de lado. ∼-whiskers npl patillas fpl

siding /ˈsaɪdɪŋ/ n apartadero m

sidle /ˈsaɪdl/ vi avanzar furtivamente. ∼ up to acercarse furtivamente

siege /siːdʒ/ n sitio m, cerco m

siesta /sɪˈestə/ n siesta f

sieve /sɪv/ n cernedor m. ● vt cerner

sift /sɪft/ vt cerner. ● vi. ∼ through examinar

sigh /saɪ/ n suspiro. ● vi suspirar

sight /saɪt/ n vista f; (spectacle) espectáculo m; (on gun) mira f. at (first) ∼ a primera vista. catch ∼ of vislumbrar. lose ∼ of perder de vista. on ∼ a primera vista. within ∼ of (near) cerca de. ● vt ver, divisar. ∼-seeing /ˈsaɪtsiːɪŋ/ n visita f turística. ∼seer /-ə(r)/ n turista m & f

sign /saɪn/ n señal f. ● vt firmar. ∼ on, ∼ up vt inscribir. ● vi inscribirse

signal /ˈsɪgnəl/ n señal f. ● vt (pt signalled) comunicar; hacer señas a ⟨person⟩. ∼-box n casilla f del guardavía. ∼man /ˈsɪgnəlmən/ n (pl -men) guardavía f

signatory /ˈsɪgnətrɪ/ n firmante m & f

signature /ˈsɪgnətʃə(r)/ n firma f. ∼ tune n sintonía f

signet-ring /ˈsɪgnɪtrɪŋ/ *n* anillo *m* de sello

significan|ce /sɪgˈnɪfɪkəns/ *n* significado *m*. ~t /sɪgˈnɪfɪkənt/ *a* significativo; (*important*) importante. ~tly *adv* significativamente

signify /ˈsɪgnɪfaɪ/ *vt* significar. ● *vi* (*matter*) importar, tener importancia

signpost /ˈsaɪnpəʊst/ *n* poste *m* indicador

silen|ce /ˈsaɪləns/ *n* silencio *m*. ● *vt* hacer callar. ~cer /-ə(r)/ *n* silenciador *m*. ~t /ˈsaɪlənt/ *a* silencioso; (*film*) mudo. ~tly *adv* silenciosamente

silhouette /sɪluːˈet/ *n* silueta *f*. ● *vt*. be ~d perfilarse, destacarse (**against** contra)

silicon /ˈsɪlɪkən/ *n* silicio *m*. ~ **chip** *n* pastilla *f* de silicio

silk /sɪlk/ *n* seda *f*. ~**en** *a*, ~**y** *a* (*of silk*) de seda; (*like silk*) sedoso. ~**worm** *n* gusano *m* de seda

sill /sɪl/ *n* antepecho *m*; (*of window*) alféizar *m*; (*of door*) umbral *m*

silly /ˈsɪlɪ/ *a* (-ier, -iest) tonto. ● *n*. ~**billy** (*fam*) tonto *m*

silo /ˈsaɪləʊ/ *n* (*pl* -os) silo *m*

silt /sɪlt/ *n* sedimento *m*

silver /ˈsɪlvə(r)/ *n* plata *f*. ● *a* de plata. ~ **plated** *a* bañado en plata, plateado. ~**side** /ˈsɪlvəsaɪd/ *n* (*culin*) contra *f*. ~**smith** /ˈsɪlvəsmɪθ/ *n* platero *m*. ~**ware** /ˈsɪlvəweə(r)/ *n* plata *f*. ~ **wedding** *n* bodas *fpl* de plata. ~**y** *a* plateado; (*sound*) argentino

simil|ar /ˈsɪmɪlə(r)/ *a* parecido. ~**ar- ity** /-ˈlærətɪ/ *n* parecido *m*. ~**arly** *adv* de igual manera

simile /ˈsɪmɪlɪ/ *n* símil *m*

simmer /ˈsɪmə(r)/ *vt/i* hervir a fuego lento; (*fig*) hervir. ~ **down** calmarse

simpl|e /ˈsɪmpl/ *a* (-er, -est) sencillo; (*person*) ingenuo. ~**e-minded** *a* ingenuo. ~**eton** /ˈsɪmpltən/ *n* simplón *m*. ~**icity** /-ˈplɪsɪtɪ/ *n* sencillez *f*. ~**i- fication** /-ɪˈkeɪʃn/ *n* simplificación *f*. ~**ify** /ˈsɪmplɪfaɪ/ *vt* simplificar. ~**y** *adv* sencillamente; (*absolutely*) absolutamente

simulat|e /ˈsɪmjʊleɪt/ *vt* simular. ~**ion** /-ˈleɪʃn/ *n* simulación *f*

simultaneous /sɪmlˈteɪnɪəs/ *a* simultáneo. ~**ly** *adv* simultáneamente

sin /sɪn/ *n* pecado *m*. ● *vi* (*pt* sinned) pecar

since /sɪns/ *prep* desde. ● *adv* desde entonces. ● *conj* desde que; (*because*) ya que

sincer|e /sɪnˈsɪə(r)/ *a* sincero. ~**ely** *adv* sinceramente. ~**ity** /-ˈserətɪ/ *n* sinceridad *f*

sinew /ˈsɪnjuː/ *n* tendón *m*. ~**s** *npl* músculos *mpl*

sinful /ˈsɪnfl/ *a* pecaminoso; (*shock- ing*) escandaloso

sing /sɪŋ/ *vt/i* (*pt* sang, *pp* sung) cantar

singe /sɪndʒ/ *vt* (*pres p* singeing) chamuscar

singer /ˈsɪŋə(r)/ *n* cantante *m* & *f*

singl|e /ˈsɪŋgl/ *a* único; (*not double*) sencillo; (*unmarried*) soltero; ⟨bed, room⟩ individual. ● *n* (*tennis*) juego *m* individual; (*ticket*) billete *m* sencillo. ● *vt*. ~**e out** escoger; (*dis- tinguish*) distinguir. ~**e-handed** *a* & *adv* sin ayuda. ~**e-minded** *a* resuelto

singlet /ˈsɪŋglɪt/ *n* camiseta *f*

singly /ˈsɪŋglɪ/ *adv* uno a uno

singsong /ˈsɪŋsɒŋ/ *a* monótono. ● *n*. have a ~ cantar juntos

singular /ˈsɪŋgjʊlə(r)/ *n* singular *f*. ● *a* singular; (*uncommon*) raro; ⟨noun⟩ en singular. ~**ly** *adv* sin- gularmente

sinister /ˈsɪnɪstə(r)/ *a* siniestro

sink /sɪŋk/ *vt* (*pt* sank, *pp* sunk) hundir; perforar ⟨well⟩; invertir ⟨money⟩. ● *vi* hundirse; ⟨patient⟩ debilitarse. ● *n* fregadero *m*. ~ **in** *vi* penetrar

sinner /ˈsɪnə(r)/ *n* pecador *m*

sinuous /ˈsɪnjʊəs/ *a* sinuoso

sinus /ˈsaɪnəs/ *n* (*pl* -uses) seno *m*

sip /sɪp/ *n* sorbo *m*. ● *vt* (*pt* sipped) sorber

siphon /ˈsaɪfən/ *n* sifón *m*. *vt*. ~ **out** sacar con sifón

sir /sɜː(r)/ *n* señor *m*. S~ *n* (*title*) sir *m*

siren /ˈsaɪərən/ *n* sirena *f*

sirloin /ˈsɜːlɔɪn/ *n* solomillo *m*, lomo *m* bajo

sirocco /sɪˈrɒkəʊ/ *n* siroco *m*

sissy /ˈsɪsɪ/ *n* hombre *m* afeminado, marica *m*, mariquita *m*; (*coward*) gallina *m* & *f*

sister /ˈsɪstə(r)/ *n* hermana *f*; (*nurse*) enfermera *f* jefe. S~ **Mary** Sor María. ~**-in-law** *n* (*pl* ~**s-in-law**) cuñada f. ~ly a de hermana; (like sister) como hermana

sit /sɪt/ vt (pt **sat**, pres p **sitting**) sentar. ● vi sentarse; (committee etc) reunirse. **be ~ting** estar sentado. ~ **back** vi (fig) relajarse. ~ **down** vi sentarse. ~ **for** vi presentarse a (exam); posar para (portrait). ~ **up** vi enderezarse; (stay awake) velar. ~**in** n ocupación f

site /saɪt/ n sitio m. **building ~** n solar m. ● vt situar

sit: ~**ting** n sesión f; (in restaurant) turno m. ~**ting-room** n cuarto m de estar

situat|e /'sɪtjʊeɪt/ vt situar. ~**ed** a situado. ~**ion** /-'eɪʃn/ n situación f; (job) puesto m

six /sɪks/ a & n seis (m). ~**teen** /sɪk'stiːn/ a & n dieciséis (m). ~**teenth** a & n decimosexto (m). ~**th** a & n sexto (m). ~**tieth** a & n sesenta (m), sexagésimo (m). ~**ty** /'sɪkstɪ/ a & n sesenta (m)

size /saɪz/ n tamaño m; (of clothes) talla f; (of shoes) número m; (extent) magnitud f. ● vt. ~ **up** (fam) juzgar. ~**able** a bastante grande

sizzle /'sɪzl/ vi crepitar

skate[1] /skeɪt/ n patín m. ● vi patinar. ~**board** /skeɪtbɔːd/ n monopatín m. ~**r** n patinador m

skate[2] /skeɪt/ n invar (fish) raya f

skating /'skeɪtɪŋ/ n patinaje m. ~ **rink** n pista f de patinaje

skein /skeɪn/ n madeja f

skelet|al /'skelɪtl/ a esquelético. ~**on** /'skelɪtn/ n esqueleto m. ~**on staff** n personal m reducido

sketch /sketʃ/ n esbozo m; (drawing) dibujo m; (in theatre) pieza f corta y divertida. ● vt esbozar. ● vi dibujar. ~**y** /'sketʃɪ/ a (-**ier**, -**iest**) incompleto

skew /skjuː/ n. **on the ~** a sesgado

skewer /'skjuːə(r)/ n broqueta f

ski /skiː/ n (pl **skis**) esquí m. ● vi (pt **skied**, pres p **skiing**) esquiar. **go ~ing** ir a esquiar

skid /skɪd/ vi (pt **skidded**) patinar. ● n patinazo m

ski: ~**er** n esquiador m. ~**ing** n esquí m

skilful /'skɪlfl/ a diestro

ski-lift /'skiːlɪft/ n telesquí m

skill /skɪl/ n destreza f, habilidad f. ~**ed** a hábil; (worker) cualificado

skim /skɪm/ vt (pt **skimmed**) espumar; desnatar (milk); (glide

over) rozar. ~ **over** vt rasar. ~ **through** vi hojear

skimp /skɪmp/ vt escatimar. ~**y** /'skɪmpɪ/ a (-**ier**, -**iest**) insuficiente; (skirt, dress) corto

skin /skɪn/ n piel f. ● vt (pt **skinned**) despellejar; pelar (fruit). ~**deep** a superficial. ~**diving** n natación f submarina. ~**flint** /'skɪnflɪnt/ n tacaño m. ~**ny** /'skɪnɪ/ a (-**ier**, -**iest**) flaco

skint /skɪnt/ a (sl) sin una perra

skip[1] /skɪp/ vi (pt **skipped**) vi saltar; (with rope) saltar a la comba. ● vt saltarse. ● n salto m

skip[2] /skɪp/ n (container) cuba f

skipper /'skɪpə(r)/ n capitán m

skipping-rope /'skɪpɪŋrəʊp/ n comba f

skirmish /'skɜːmɪʃ/ n escaramuza f

skirt /skɜːt/ n falda f. ● vt rodear; (go round) ladear

skirting-board /'skɜːtɪŋbɔːd/ n rodapié m, zócalo m

skit /skɪt/ n pieza f satírica

skittish /'skɪtɪʃ/ a juguetón; (horse) nervioso

skittle /'skɪtl/ n bolo m

skive /skaɪv/ vi (sl) gandulear

skivvy /'skɪvɪ/ n (fam) criada f

skulk /skʌlk/ vi avanzar furtivamente; (hide) esconderse

skull /skʌl/ n cráneo m; (remains) calavera f. ~**cap** n casquete m

skunk /skʌŋk/ n mofeta f; (person) canalla f

sky /skaɪ/ n cielo m. ~**blue** a & n azul (m) celeste. ~**jack** /'skaɪdʒæk/ vt secuestrar. ~**jacker** n secuestrador m. ~**light** /'skaɪlaɪt/ n tragaluz m. ~**scraper** /'skaɪskreɪpə(r)/ n rascacielos m invar

slab /slæb/ n bloque m; (of stone) losa f; (of chocolate) tableta f

slack /slæk/ a (-**er**, -**est**) flojo; (person) negligente; (period) de poca actividad. ● n (of rope) parte f floja. ● vt aflojar. ● vi aflojarse; (person) descansar. ~**en** /'slækən/ vt aflojar. ● vi aflojarse; (person) descansar. ~**en** (**off**) vt aflojar. ~ **off** (fam) aflojar

slacks /slæks/ npl pantalones mpl

slag /slæg/ n escoria f

slain /sleɪn/ see **slay**

slake /sleɪk/ vt apagar

slam /slæm/ vt (pt **slammed**) golpear; (throw) arrojar; (criticize, sl) criticar. ~ **the door** dar un portazo. ● vi cerrarse de golpe. ● n golpe m; (of door) portazo m

slander /'slɑːndə(r)/ n calumnia f. ● vt difamar. ~**ous** a calumnioso

slang /slæŋ/ n jerga f, argot m. ~**y** a vulgar

slant /slɑːnt/ vt inclinar; presentar con parcialidad ⟨news⟩. ● n inclinación f; (point of view) punto m de vista

slap /slæp/ vt (pt **slapped**) abofetear; (on the back) dar una palmada; (put) arrojar. ● n bofetada f; (on back) palmada f. ● adv de lleno. ~**dash** /'slæpdæʃ/ a descuidado. ~**happy** a (fam) despreocupado; (dazed, fam) aturdido. ~**stick** /'slæpstɪk/ n payasada f. ~**up** a (sl) de primera categoría

slash /slæʃ/ vt acuchillar; (fig) reducir radicalmente. ● n cuchillada f

slat /slæt/ n tablilla f

slate /sleɪt/ n pizarra f. ● vt (fam) criticar

slaughter /'slɔːtə(r)/ vt masacrar; matar ⟨animal⟩. ● n carnicería f; (of animals) matanza f. ~**house** /'slɔːtəhaʊs/ n matadero m

Slav /slɑːv/ a & n eslavo (m)

slav|e /sleɪv/ n esclavo m. ● vi trabajar como un negro. ~**e-driver** /-əri/ n esclavitud f. ~**ish** /'sleɪvɪʃ/ a servil

Slavonic /slə'vɒnɪk/ a eslavo

slay /sleɪ/ vt (pt **slew**, pp **slain**) matar

sleazy /'sliːzɪ/ a (-ier, -iest) (fam) sórdido

sledge /sledʒ/ n trineo m. ~**hammer** n almádena f

sleek /sliːk/ a (-er, -est) liso, brillante; (elegant) elegante

sleep /sliːp/ n sueño m. **go to** ~ dormirse. ● vi (pt **slept**) dormir. ● vt poder alojar. ~**er** n durmiente m & f; (on track) traviesa f; (berth) cochecama m. ~**ily** adv soñolientamente. ~**ing-bag** n saco m de dormir. ~**ing-pill** n somnífero m. ~**less** a insomne. ~**lessness** n insomnio m. ~**walker** n sonámbulo m. ~**y** /'sliːpɪ/ a (-ier, -iest) soñoliento. **be** ~**y** tener sueño

sleet /sliːt/ n aguanieve f. ● vi caer aguanieve

sleeve /sliːv/ n manga f; (for record) funda f. **up one's** ~ en reserva. ~**less** a sin mangas

sleigh /sleɪ/ n trineo m

sleight /slaɪt/ n. ~ **of hand** prestidigitación f

slender /'slendə(r)/ a delgado; (fig) escaso

slept /slept/ see **sleep**

sleuth /sluːθ/ n investigador m

slew[1] /sluː/ see **slay**

slew[2] /sluː/ vi (turn) girar

slice /slaɪs/ n lonja f; (of bread) rebanada f; (of sth round) rodaja f; (implement) paleta f. ● vt cortar; rebanar ⟨bread⟩

slick /slɪk/ a liso; (cunning) astuto. ● n. (oil)-~ capa f de aceite

slid|e /slaɪd/ vt (pt **slid**) deslizar. ● vi resbalar. ~**e over** pasar por alto de. ● n resbalón m; (in playground) tobogán m; (for hair) pasador m; (photo) diapositiva f; (fig, fall) baja f. ~**e-rule** n regla f de cálculo. ~**ing** a corredizo. ~**ing scale** n escala f móvil

slight /slaɪt/ a (-er, -est) ligero; (slender) delgado. ● vt ofender. ● n desaire m. ~**est** a mínimo. **not in the** ~**est** en absoluto. ~**ly** adv un poco

slim /slɪm/ a (slimmer, slimmest) delgado. ● vi (pt **slimmed**) adelgazar

slime /slaɪm/ n légamo m, lodo m, fango m

slimness /'slɪmnɪs/ n delgadez f

slimy /'slaɪmɪ/ a legamoso, fangoso, viscoso; (fig) rastrero

sling /slɪŋ/ n honda f; (toy) tirador m; (med) cabestrillo m. ● vt (pt **slung**) lanzar

slip /slɪp/ vt (pt **slipped**) deslizar. ~ **s.o.'s mind** olvidársele a uno. ● vi deslizarse. ● n resbalón m; (mistake) error m; (petticoat) combinación f; (paper) trozo m. ~ **of the tongue** lapsus m linguae. **give the** ~ **to** zafarse de, dar esquinazo a. ~ **away** vi escabullirse. ~ **into** vi ponerse ⟨clothes⟩. ~ **up** vi (fam) equivocarse

slipper /'slɪpə(r)/ n zapatilla f

slippery /'slɪpərɪ/ a resbaladizo

slip: ~**-road** n rampa f de acceso. ~**shod** /'slɪpʃɒd/ a descuidado. ~**up** n (fam) error m

slit /slɪt/ n raja f; (cut) corte m. ● vt (pt **slit**, pres p **slitting**) rajar; (cut) cortar

slither /'slɪðə(r)/ vi deslizarse

sliver /'slɪvə(r)/ n trocito m; (splinter) astilla f

slobber /'slɒbə(r)/ vi babear

slog /slɒg/ vt (pt slogged) golpear.
● vi trabajar como un negro. ● n golpetazo m; (hard work) trabajo m penoso

slogan /'sləʊgən/ n eslogan m

slop /slɒp/ vt (pt slopped) derramar.
● vi derramarse. ~s npl (fam) agua f sucia

slop|e /sləʊp/ vi inclinarse. ● vt inclinar. ● n declive m, pendiente m. ~ing a inclinado

sloppy /'slɒpɪ/ a (-ier, -iest) (wet) mojado; (food) líquido; (work) descuidado; (person) desaliñado; (fig) sentimental

slosh /slɒʃ/ vi (fam) chapotear. ● vt (hit, sl) pegar

slot /slɒt/ n ranura f. ● vt (pt slotted) encajar

sloth /sləʊθ/ n pereza f

slot-machine /'slɒtməʃiːn/ n distribuidor m automático; (for gambling) máquina f tragaperras

slouch /slaʊtʃ/ vi andar cargado de espaldas; (in chair) repanchigarse

Slovak /'sləʊvæk/ a & n eslovaco (m). ~ia /sləʊ'vækɪə/ n Eslovaquia f

sloven|liness /'slʌvnlɪnɪs/ n despreocupación f. ~y /'slʌvnlɪ/ a descuidado

slow /sləʊ/ a (-er, -est) lento. be ~ (clock) estar atrasado. in ~ motion a cámara lenta. ● adv despacio. ● vt retardar. ● vi ir más despacio. ~ down, ~ up vt retardar. ● vi ir más despacio. ~coach /'sləʊkəʊtʃ/ n tardón m. ~ly adv despacio. ~ness n lentitud f

sludge /slʌdʒ/ n fango m; (sediment) sedimento m

slug /slʌg/ n babosa f; (bullet) posta f. ~gish /'slʌgɪʃ/ a lento

sluice /sluːs/ n (gate) compuerta f; (channel) canal m

slum /slʌm/ n tugurio m

slumber /'slʌmbə(r)/ n sueño m. ● vi dormir

slump /slʌmp/ n baja f repentina; (in business) depresión f. ● vi bajar repentinamente; (flop down) dejarse caer pesadamente; (collapse) desplomarse

slung /slʌŋ/ see sling

slur /slɜː(r)/ vt/i (pt slurred) articular mal. ● n dicción f defectuosa; (discredit) calumnia f

slush /slʌʃ/ n nieve f medio derretida; (fig) sentimentalismo m. ~

fund n fondos mpl secretos para fines deshonestos. ~y a (road) cubierto de nieve medio derretida

slut /slʌt/ n mujer f desaseada

sly /slaɪ/ a (slyer, slyest) (crafty) astuto; (secretive) furtivo. ● n. on the ~ a escondidas. ~ly adv astutamente

smack¹ /smæk/ n golpe m; (on face) bofetada f. ● adv (fam) de lleno. ● vt pegar

smack² /smæk/ vi. ~ of saber a; (fig) oler a

small /smɔːl/ a (-er, -est) pequeño.
● n. the ~ of the back la región f lumbar. ~ ads npl anuncios mpl por palabras. ~ change n cambio m. ~holding /'smɔːlhəʊldɪŋ/ n parcela f. ~pox /'smɔːlpɒks/ n viruela f. ~ talk n charla f. ~time a (fam) de poca monta

smarmy /'smɑːmɪ/ a (-ier, -iest) (fam) zalamero

smart /smɑːt/ a (-er, -est) elegante; (clever) inteligente; (brisk) rápido.
● vi escocer. ~en /'smɑːtn/ vt arreglar. ● vi arreglarse. ~en up vi arreglarse. ~ly adv elegantemente; (quickly) rápidamente. ~ness n elegancia f

smash /smæʃ/ vt romper; (into little pieces) hacer pedazos; batir (record).
● vi romperse; (collide) chocar (into con). ● n (noise) estruendo m; (collision) choque m; (com) quiebra f. ~ing /'smæʃɪŋ/ a (fam) estupendo

smattering /'smætərɪŋ/ n conocimientos mpl superficiales

smear /smɪə(r)/ vt untar (with de); (stain) manchar (with de); (fig) difamar. ● n mancha f; (med) frotis m

smell /smel/ n olor m; (sense) olfato m. ● vt/i (pt smelt) oler. ~y a maloliente

smelt¹ /smelt/ see smell

smelt² /smelt/ vt fundir

smile /smaɪl/ n sonrisa f. ● vi sonreír(se)

smirk /smɜːk/ n sonrisa f afectada

smite /smaɪt/ vt (pt smote, pp smitten) golpear

smith /smɪθ/ n herrero m

smithereens /ˌsmɪðə'riːnz/ npl añicos mpl. smash to ~ hacer añicos

smitten /'smɪtn/ see smite. ● a encaprichado (with por)

smock /smɒk/ n blusa f, bata f

smog /smɒg/ n niebla f con humo

smok|e /sməʊk/ n humo m. ● vt/i fumar. **∼eless** a sin humo. **∼er** /-ə(r)/ n fumador m. **∼e-screen** n cortina f de humo. **∼y** a ⟨room⟩ lleno de humo

smooth /smuːð/ a (-er, -est) liso; ⟨sound, movement⟩ suave; ⟨sea⟩ tranquilo; ⟨manners⟩ zalamero. ● vt alisar; (fig) allanar. **∼ly** adv suavemente

smote /sməʊt/ see **smite**

smother /'smʌðə(r)/ vt sofocar; ⟨cover⟩ cubrir

smoulder /'sməʊldə(r)/ vi arder sin llama; (fig) arder

smudge /smʌdʒ/ n borrón m, mancha f. ● vt tiznar. ● vi tiznarse

smug /smʌg/ a (**smugger**, **smuggest**) satisfecho de sí mismo

smuggl|e /'smʌgl/ vt pasar de contrabando. **∼er** n contrabandista m & f. **∼ing** n contrabando m

smug: **∼ly** adv con suficiencia. **∼ness** n suficiencia f

smut /smʌt/ n tizne m; (mark) tiznajo m. **∼ty** a (-ier, -iest) tiznado; (fig) obsceno

snack /snæk/ n tentempié m. **∼-bar** n cafetería f

snag /snæg/ n problema m; (in cloth) rasgón m

snail /sneɪl/ n caracol m. **∼'s pace** n paso m de tortuga

snake /sneɪk/ n serpiente f

snap /snæp/ vt (pt **snapped**) (break) romper; castañetear ⟨fingers⟩. ● vi romperse; ⟨dog⟩ intentar morder; ⟨say⟩ contestar bruscamente; ⟨whip⟩ chasquear. **∼ at** ⟨dog⟩ intentar morder; ⟨say⟩ contestar bruscamente. ● n chasquido m; (photo) foto f. ● a instantáneo. **∼ up** vt agarrar. **∼py** /'snæpɪ/ a (-ier, -iest) (fam) rápido. **make it ∼py!** (fam) ¡date prisa! **∼shot** /'snæpʃɒt/ n foto f

snare /sneə(r)/ n trampa f

snarl /snɑːl/ vi gruñir. ● n gruñido m

snatch /snætʃ/ vt agarrar; (steal) robar. ● n arrebatamiento m; (short part) trocito m; (theft) robo m

sneak /sniːk/ ● n soplón m. ● vi. **∼ in** entrar furtivamente. **∼ out** salir furtivamente

sneakers /'sniːkəz/ npl zapatillas fpl de lona

sneak|ing /'sniːkɪŋ/ a furtivo. **∼y** a furtivo

sneer /snɪə(r)/ n sonrisa f de desprecio. ● vi sonreír con desprecio. **∼ at** hablar con desprecio a

sneeze /sniːz/ n estornudo m. ● vi estornudar

snide /snaɪd/ a (fam) despreciativo

sniff /snɪf/ vt oler. ● vi aspirar por la nariz. ● n aspiración f

snigger /'snɪgə(r)/ n risa f disimulada. ● vi reír disimuladamente

snip /snɪp/ vt (pt **snipped**) tijeretear. ● n tijeretada f; (bargain, sl) ganga f

snipe /snaɪp/ vi disparar desde un escondite. **∼r** /-ə(r)/ n tirador m emboscado, francotirador m

snippet /'snɪpɪt/ n retazo m

snivel /'snɪvl/ vi (pt **snivelled**) lloriquear. **∼ling** a llorón

snob /snɒb/ n esnob m. **∼bery** n esnobismo m. **∼bish** a esnob

snooker /'snuːkə(r)/ n billar m

snoop /snuːp/ vi (fam) curiosear

snooty /'snuːtɪ/ a (fam) desdeñoso

snooze /snuːz/ n sueñecito m. ● vi echarse un sueñecito

snore /snɔː(r)/ n ronquido m. ● vi roncar

snorkel /'snɔːkl/ n tubo m respiratorio

snort /snɔːt/ n bufido m. ● vi bufar

snout /snaʊt/ n hocico m

snow /snəʊ/ n nieve f. ● vi nevar. **be ∼ed under with** estar inundado por. **∼ball** /'snəʊbɔːl/ n bola f de nieve. **∼drift** n nieve amontonada. **∼drop** /'snəʊdrɒp/ n campanilla f de invierno. **∼fall** /'snəʊfɔːl/ n nevada f. **∼flake** /'snəʊfleɪk/ n copo m de nieve. **∼man** /'snəʊmæn/ n (pl -men) muñeco m de nieve. **∼plough** n quitanieves m invar. **∼storm** /'snəʊstɔːm/ n nevasca f. **∼y** a ⟨place⟩ de nieves abundantes; ⟨weather⟩ con nevadas seguidas

snub /snʌb/ vt (pt **snubbed**) desairar. ● n desaire m. **∼-nosed** /'snʌbnəʊzd/ a chato

snuff /snʌf/ n rapé m. ● vt despabilar ⟨candle⟩. **∼ out** apagar ⟨candle⟩

snuffle /'snʌfl/ vi respirar ruidosamente

snug /snʌg/ a (**snugger**, **snuggest**) cómodo; (tight) ajustado

snuggle /'snʌgl/ vi acomodarse

so /səʊ/ adv (before a or adv) tan; (thus) así. ● conj así que. **∼ am I** yo

tambien. ~ **as to** para. ~ **far** *adv*
(*time*) hasta ahora; (*place*) hasta
aquí. ~ **as I know** que yo sepa.
~ **long!** (*fam*) ¡hasta luego! ~ **much**
tanto. ~ **that** *conj* para que. **and** ~
forth, and ~ **on** y así sucesivamente. **if** ~ si es así. **I think** ~ creo
que sí. **or** ~ más o menos

soak /səʊk/ *vt* remojar. ● *vi*
remojarse. ~ **in** penetrar. ~ **up**
absorber. ~**ing** *a* empapado. ● *n*
remojón *m*

so-and-so /'səʊənsəʊ/ *n* fulano *m*

soap /səʊp/ *n* jabón *m*. ● *vt* enjabonar. ~ **powder** *n* jabón en polvo.
~**y** *a* jabonoso

soar /sɔː(r)/ *vi* elevarse; (*price etc*)
ponerse por las nubes

sob /sɒb/ *n* sollozo *m*. ● *vi* (*pt*
sobbed) sollozar

sober /'səʊbə(r)/ *a* sobrio; (*colour*)
discreto

so-called /'səʊkɔːld/ *a* llamado,
supuesto

soccer /'sɒkə(r)/ *n* (*fam*) fútbol *m*

sociable /'səʊʃəbl/ *a* sociable

social /'səʊʃl/ *a* social; (*sociable*)
sociable. ● *n* reunión *f*. ~**ism** /-zəm/
n socialismo *m*. ~**ist** /'səʊʃəlɪst/ *a* &
n socialista *m* & *f*. ~**ize** /'səʊʃəlaɪz/
vt socializar. ~**ly** *adv* socialmente. ~
worker *n* asistente *m* social

society /sə'saɪətɪ/ *n* sociedad *f*

sociolog|ical /səʊsɪə'lɒdʒɪkl/ *a*
sociológico. ~**ist** *n* sociólogo *m*. ~**y**
/səʊsɪ'ɒlədʒɪ/ *n* sociología *f*

sock[1] /sɒk/ *n* calcetín *m*

sock[2] /sɒk/ *vt* (*sl*) pegar

socket /'sɒkɪt/ *n* hueco *m*; (*of eye*)
cuenca *f*; (*wall plug*) enchufe *m*; (*for
bulb*) portalámparas *m invar*, cas-
quillo *m*

soda /'səʊdə/ *n* sosa *f*; (*water*) soda *f*.
~**water** *n* soda *f*

sodden /'sɒdn/ *a* empapado

sodium /'səʊdɪəm/ *n* sodio *m*

sofa /'səʊfə/ *n* sofá *m*

soft /sɒft/ *a* (**-er, -est**) blando;
(*sound, colour*) suave; (*gentle*) dulce,
tierno; (*silly*) estúpido. ~ **drink** *n*
bebida *f* no alcohólica. ~ **spot** *n*
debilidad *f*. ~**en** /'sɒfn/ *vt* ablandar;
(*fig*) suavizar. ● *vi* ablandarse; (*fig*)
suavizarse. ~**ly** *adv* dulcemente.
~**ness** *n* blandura *f*; (*fig*) dulzura *f*.
~**ware** /'sɒftweə(r)/ *n* programa-
ción *f*, software *m*

soggy /'sɒgɪ/ *a* (**-ier, -iest**) empapado

soh /səʊ/ *n* (*mus, fifth note of any
musical scale*) sol *m*

soil[1] /sɔɪl/ *n* suelo *m*

soil[2] /sɔɪl/ *vt* ensuciar. ● *vi* ensu-
ciarse

solace /'sɒləs/ *n* consuelo *m*

solar /'səʊlə(r)/ *a* solar. ~**ium**
/sə'leərɪəm/ *n* (*pl* **-a**) solario *m*

sold /səʊld/ *see* **sell**

solder /'sɒldə(r)/ *n* soldadura *f*. ● *vt*
soldar

soldier /'səʊldʒə(r)/ *n* soldado *m*.
● *vi*. ~ **on** (*fam*) perseverar

sole[1] /səʊl/ *n* (*of foot*) planta *f*; (*of
shoe*) suela *f*

sole[2] /səʊl/ (*fish*) lenguado *m*

sole[3] /səʊl/ *a* único, solo. ~**ly** *adv*
únicamente

solemn /'sɒləm/ *a* solemne. ~**ity**
/sə'lemnətɪ/ *n* solemnidad *f*. ~**ly** *adv*
solemnemente

solicit /sə'lɪsɪt/ *vt* solicitar. ● *vi*
importunar

solicitor /sə'lɪsɪtə(r)/ *n* abogado *m*;
(*notary*) notario *m*

solicitous /sə'lɪsɪtəs/ *a* solícito

solid /'sɒlɪd/ *a* sólido; (*gold etc*)
macizo; (*unanimous*) unánime;
(*meal*) sustancioso. ● *n* sólido *m*.
~**arity** /sɒlɪ'dærətɪ/ *n* solidaridad *f*.
~**ify** /sə'lɪdɪfaɪ/ *vt* solidificar. ● *vi*
solidificarse. ~**ity** /sə'lɪdətɪ/ *n*
solidez *f*. ~**ly** *adv* sólidamente. ~**s**
npl alimentos *mpl* sólidos

soliloquy /sə'lɪləkwɪ/ *n* soliloquio *m*

solitaire /sɒlɪ'teə(r)/ *n* solitario *m*

solitary /'sɒlɪtrɪ/ *a* solitario

solitude /'sɒlɪtjuːd/ *n* soledad *f*

solo /'səʊləʊ/ *n* (*pl* **-os**) (*mus*) solo *m*.
~**ist** *n* solista *m* & *f*

solstice /'sɒlstɪs/ *n* solsticio *m*

soluble /'sɒljʊbl/ *a* soluble

solution /sə'luːʃn/ *n* solución *f*

solvable *a* soluble

solve /sɒlv/ *vt* resolver

solvent /'sɒlvənt/ *a* & *n* solvente (*m*)

sombre /'sɒmbə(r)/ *a* sombrío

some /sʌm/ *a* alguno; (*a little*) un
poco de. ~ **day** algún día. ~ **two
hours** unas dos horas. **will you have**
~ **wine?** ¿quieres vino? ● *pron* algunos; (*a little*) un poco. ~ **of us** algunos de nosotros. **I want** ~ quiero
un poco. ● *adv* (*approximately*) unos.
~**body** /'sʌmbədɪ/ *pron* alguien. ● *n*
personaje *m*. ~**how** /'sʌmhaʊ/ *adv*
de algún modo. ~**how or other** de

una manera u otra. **~one**
/'sʌmwʌn/ *pron* alguien. ● *n* personaje *m*

somersault /'sʌməsɔ:lt/ *n* salto *m*
mortal. ● *vi* dar un salto mortal

some: **~thing** /'sʌmθɪŋ/ *pron* algo
m. **~thing like** algo como; (*approximately*) cerca de. **~time**
/'sʌmtaɪm/ *a* ex. ● *adv* algún día; (*in past*) durante. **~time last summer**
a (durante) el verano pasado. **~times** /'sʌmtaɪmz/ *adv* de vez en
cuando, a veces. **~what** /'sʌmwɒt/
adv algo, un poco. **~where** /'sʌmweə(r)/ *adv* en alguna parte

son /sʌn/ *n* hijo *m*

sonata /sə'nɑːtə/ *n* sonata *f*

song /sɒŋ/ *n* canción *f*. **sell for a ~**
vender muy barato. **~-book** *n* cancionero *m*

sonic /'sɒnɪk/ *a* sónico

son-in-law /'sʌnɪnlɔː/ *n* (*pl* **sons-in-law**) yerno *m*

sonnet /'sɒnɪt/ *n* soneto *m*

sonny /'sʌnɪ/ *n* (*fam*) hijo *m*

soon /suːn/ *adv* (**-er, -est**) pronto; (*in a short time*) dentro de poco; (*early*) temprano. **~ after** poco después.
~er or later tarde o temprano. **as ~ as** en cuanto; **as ~ as possible** lo
antes posible. **I would ~er not go**
prefiero no ir

soot /sʊt/ *n* hollín *m*

soothe /suːð/ *vt* calmar. **~ing** *a*
calmante

sooty /'sʊtɪ/ *a* cubierto de hollín

sophisticated /sə'fɪstɪkeɪtɪd/ *a*
sofisticado; (*complex*) complejo

soporific /sɒpə'rɪfɪk/ *a* soporífero

sopping /'sɒpɪŋ/ *a*. **~ (wet)** empapado

soppy /'sɒpɪ/ *a* (**-ier, -iest**) (*fam*)
sentimental; (*silly, fam*) tonto

soprano /sə'prɑːnəʊ/ *n* (*pl* **-os**)
(*voice*) soprano *m*; (*singer*) soprano *f*

sorcerer /'sɔːsərə(r)/ *n* hechicero *m*

sordid /'sɔːdɪd/ *a* sórdido

sore /'sɔː(r)/ *a* (**-er, -est**) que duele,
dolorido; (*distressed*) penoso; (*vexed*)
enojado. ● *n* llaga *f*. **~ly** /'sɔːlɪ/ *adv*
gravemente. **~ throat** *n* dolor *m* de
garganta. **I've got a ~ throat** me
duele la garganta

sorrow /'sɒrəʊ/ *n* pena *f*, tristeza *f*.
~ful *a* triste

sorry /'sɒrɪ/ *a* (**-ier, -ier**) arrepentido;
(*wretched*) lamentable; (*sad*) triste.
be ~ sentirlo; (*repent*) arrepentirse.

be ~ for s.o. (*pity*) compadecerse de
uno. **~!** ¡perdón!, ¡perdone!

sort /sɔːt/ *n* clase *f*; (*person, fam*) tipo
m. **be out of ~s** estar indispuesto;
(*irritable*) estar de mal humor. ● *vt*
clasificar. **~ out** (*choose*) escoger;
(*separate*) separar; resolver (*problem*)

so-so /'səʊsəʊ/ *a & adv* regular

soufflé /'suːfleɪ/ *n* suflé *m*

sought /sɔːt/ *see* **seek**

soul /səʊl/ *n* alma *f*. **~ful** /'səʊlfl/ *a*
sentimental

sound¹ /saʊnd/ *n* sonido *m*; ruido *m*.
● *vt* sonar; (*test*) sondar. ● *vi* sonar;
(*seem*) parecer (**as if** que)

sound² /saʊnd/ *a* (**-er, -est**) sano; (*argument etc*) lógico; (*secure*) seguro. **~**
asleep profundamente dormido

sound³ /saʊnd/ (*strait*) estrecho *m*

sound barrier /'saʊndbærɪə(r)/ *n*
barrera *f* del sonido

soundly /'saʊndlɪ/ *adv* sólidamente;
(*asleep*) profundamente

sound: **~-proof** *a* insonorizado. **~-
track** *n* banda *f* sonora

soup /suːp/ *n* sopa *f*. **in the ~** (*sl*) en
apuros

sour /'saʊə(r)/ *a* (**-er, -est**) agrio;
(*cream, milk*) cortado. ● *vt* agriar.
● *vi* agriarse

source /sɔːs/ *n* fuente *f*

south /saʊθ/ *n* sur *m*. ● *a* del sur.
● *adv* hacia el sur. **S~ Africa** *n*
Africa *f* del Sur. **S~ America** *n*
América *f* del Sur, Sudamérica *f*.
S~ American *a & n* sudamericano
(*m*). **~-east** *n* sudeste *m*. **~erly**
/'sʌðəlɪ/ *a* sur; (*wind*) del sur. **~ern**
/'sʌðən/ *a* del sur, meridional. **~er-
ner** *n* meridional *m*. **~ward** *a* sur;
● *adv* hacia el sur. **~wards** *adv*
hacia el sur. **~-west** *n* sudoeste *m*

souvenir /suːvə'nɪə(r)/ *n* recuerdo *m*

sovereign /'sɒvrɪn/ *n & a* soberano
(*m*). **~ty** *n* soberanía *f*

Soviet /'səʊvɪət/ *a* (*history*) soviético. **the ~ Union** *n* la Unión *f* Soviética

sow¹ /səʊ/ *vt* (*pt* **sowed**, *pp* **sowed**
or **sown**) sembrar

sow² /saʊ/ *n* cerda *f*

soya /'sɔɪə/ *n*. **~ bean** *n* soja *f*

spa /spɑː/ *n* balneario *m*

space /speɪs/ *n* espacio *m*; (*room*)
sitio *m*; (*period*) período *m*. ● *a*
(*research etc*) espacial. ● *vt* espaciar.
~ out espaciar. **~craft** /'speɪs-

krɑːft/ n, ∼ship n nave f espacial. ∼suit n traje m espacial
spacious /'speɪʃəs/ a espacioso
spade /speɪd/ n pala f. ∼s npl (cards) picos mpl, picas fpl; (in Spanish pack) espadas fpl. ∼work /'speɪdwɜː k/ n trabajo m preparatorio
spaghetti /spə'getɪ/ n espaguetis mpl
Spain /speɪn/ n España f
span¹ /spæn/ n (of arch) luz f; (of time) espacio m; (of wings) envergadura f. ● vt (pt spanned) extenderse sobre
span² /spæn/ see spick
Spaniard /'spænjəd/ n español m
spaniel /'spænjəl/ n perro m de aguas
Spanish /'spænɪʃ/ a & n español (m)
spank /spæŋk/ vt dar un azote a. ∼ing n azote m
spanner /'spænə(r)/ n llave f
spar /spɑː(r)/ vi (pt sparred) entrenarse en el boxeo; (argue) disputar
spare /speə(r)/ vt salvar; (do without) prescindir de; (afford to give) dar; (use with restraint) escatimar. ● a de reserva; (surplus) sobrante; (person) enjuto; (meal etc) frugal. ∼ (part) n repuesto m. ∼ time n tiempo m libre. ∼ tyre n neumático m de repuesto
sparing /'speərɪŋ/ a frugal. ∼ly adv frugalmente
spark /spɑːk/ n chispa f. ● vt. ∼ off (initiate) provocar. ∼ing-plug n (auto) bujía f
sparkle /'spɑːkl/ vi centellear. ● n centelleo m. ∼ing a centelleante; (wine) espumoso
sparrow /'spærəʊ/ n gorrión m
sparse /spɑːs/ a escaso; (population) poco denso. ∼ly adv escasamente
spartan /'spɑːtn/ a espartano
spasm /'spæzəm/ n espasmo m; (of cough) acceso m. ∼odic /spæz'-mɒdɪk/ a espasmódico
spastic /'spæstɪk/ n víctima f de parálisis cerebral
spat /spæt/ see spit¹
spate /speɪt/ n avalancha f
spatial /'speɪʃl/ a espacial
spatter /'spætə(r)/ vt salpicar (with de)
spatula /'spætjʊlə/ n espátula f
spawn /spɔːn/ n hueva f. ● vt engendrar. ● vi desovar
speak /spiːk/ vt/i (pt spoke, pp spoken) hablar. ∼ for vi hablar en

nombre de. ∼ up vi hablar más fuerte. ∼er /'spiːkə(r)/ n (in public) orador m; (loudspeaker) altavoz m. be a Spanish ∼er hablar español
spear /spɪə(r)/ n lanza f. ∼head /'spɪəhed/ n punta f de lanza. ● vt (lead) encabezar. ∼mint /'spɪəmɪnt/ n menta f verde
spec /spek/ n. on ∼ (fam) por si acaso
special /'speʃl/ a especial. ∼ist /'speʃəlɪst/ n especialista m & f. ∼ity /-ɪ'ælətɪ/ n especialidad f. ∼ization /-'zeɪʃn/ n especialización f. ∼ize /'speʃəlaɪz/ vi especializarse. ∼ized a especializado. ∼ty n especialidad f. ∼ly adv especialmente
species /'spiːʃiːz/ n especie f
specific /spə'sɪfɪk/ a específico. ∼ically adv específicamente. ∼ication /-ɪ'keɪʃn/ n especificación f; (details) descripción f. ∼y /'spesɪfaɪ/ vt especificar
specimen /'spesɪmɪn/ n muestra f
speck /spek/ n manchita f; (particle) partícula f
speckled /'spekld/ a moteado
specs /speks/ npl (fam) gafas fpl, anteojos mpl (LAm)
spectacle /'spektəkl/ n espectáculo m. ∼les npl gafas fpl, anteojos mpl (LAm). ∼ular /spek'tækjʊlə(r)/ a espectacular
spectator /spek'teɪtə(r)/ n espectador m
spectre /'spektə(r)/ n espectro m
spectrum /'spektrəm/ n (pl -tra) espectro m; (of ideas) gama f
speculate /'spekjʊleɪt/ vi especular. ∼ion /-'leɪʃn/ n especulación f. ∼ive /-lətɪv/ a especulativo. ∼or n especulador m
sped /sped/ see speed
speech /spiːtʃ/ n (faculty) habla f; (address) discurso m. ∼less a mudo
speed /spiːd/ n velocidad f; (rapidity) rapidez f; (haste) prisa f. ● vi (pt sped) apresurarse. (pt speeded) (drive too fast) ir a una velocidad excesiva. ∼ up vt acelerar. ● vi acelerarse. ∼boat /'spiːdbəʊt/ n lancha f motora. ∼ily adv rápidamente. ∼ing n exceso m de velocidad. ∼ometer /spiːd'ɒmɪtə(r)/ n velocímetro m. ∼way /'spiːdweɪ/ n pista f; (Amer) autopista f. ∼y /'spiː dɪ/ a (-ier, -iest) rápido
spell¹ /spel/ n (magic) hechizo m

spell² /spel/ vt/i (pt spelled or spelt) escribir; (mean) significar. ∼ out vt deletrear; (fig) explicar. ∼ing n ortografía f

spell³ /spel/ (period) período m

spellbound /'spelbaʊnd/ a hechizado

spelt /spelt/ see spell²

spend /spend/ vt (pt spent) gastar; pasar ⟨time etc⟩; dedicar ⟨care etc⟩. ● vi gastar dinero. ∼thrift /'spendθrɪft/ n derrochador m

spent /spent/ see spend

sperm /spɜːm/ n (pl sperms or sperm) esperma f

spew /spju:/ vt/i vomitar

spher|e /sfɪə(r)/ n esfera f. ∼ical /'sferɪkl/ a esférico

sphinx /sfɪŋks/ n esfinge f

spice /spaɪs/ n especia f; (fig) sabor m

spick /spɪk/ a. ∼ and span impecable

spicy /'spaɪsɪ/ a picante

spider /'spaɪdə(r)/ n araña f

spik|e /spaɪk/ n (of metal etc) punta f. ∼y a puntiagudo; ⟨person⟩ quisquilloso

spill /spɪl/ vt (pt spilled or spilt) derramar. ● vi derramarse. ∼ over desbordarse

spin /spɪn/ vt (pt spun, pres p spinning) hacer girar; hilar ⟨wool etc⟩. ● vi girar. ● n vuelta f; (short drive) paseo m

spinach /'spɪnɪdʒ/ n espinacas fpl

spinal /'spaɪnl/ a espinal. ∼ cord n médula f espinal

spindl|e /'spɪndl/ n (for spinning) huso m. ∼y a larguirucho

spin-drier /spɪn'draɪə(r)/ n secador m centrífugo

spine /spaɪn/ n columna f vertebral; (of book) lomo m. ∼less a (fig) sin carácter

spinning /'spɪnɪŋ/ n hilado m. ∼top n trompa f, peonza f. ∼wheel n rueca f

spin-off /'spɪnɒf/ n beneficio m incidental; (by-product) subproducto m

spinster /'spɪnstə(r)/ n soltera f; (old maid, fam) solterona f

spiral /'spaɪərəl/ a espiral, helicoidal. ● n hélice f. ● vi (pt spiralled) moverse en espiral. ∼ staircase n escalera f de caracol

spire /'spaɪə(r)/ n (archit) aguja f

spirit /'spɪrɪt/ n espíritu m; (boldness) valor m. in low ∼s abatido. ● vt. ∼ away hacer desaparecer. ∼ed /'spɪrɪtɪd/ a animado, fogoso. ∼-lamp n lamparilla f de alcohol. ∼-level n nivel m de aire. ∼s npl (drinks) bebidas fpl alcohólicas

spiritual /'spɪrɪtjʊəl/ a espiritual. ● n canción f religiosa de los negros. ∼ualism /-zəm/ n espiritismo m. ∼ualist /'spɪrtjʊəlɪst/ n espiritista m & f

spit¹ /spɪt/ vt (pt spat or spit, pres p spitting) escupir. ● vi escupir; (rain) lloviznar. ● n esputo m; (spittle) saliva f

spit² /spɪt/ (for roasting) asador m

spite /spaɪt/ n rencor m. in ∼ of a pesar de. ● vt fastidiar. ∼ful a rencoroso. ∼fully adv con rencor

spitting image /spɪtɪŋ'ɪmɪdʒ/ n vivo retrato m

spittle /'spɪtl/ n saliva f

splash /splæʃ/ vt salpicar. ● vi esparcirse; ⟨person⟩ chapotear. ● n salpicadura f; (sound) chapoteo m; (of colour) mancha f; (drop, fam) gota f. ∼ about vi chapotear. ∼ down vi (spacecraft) amerizar

spleen /spli:n/ n bazo m; (fig) esplín m

splendid /'splendɪd/ a espléndido

splendour /'splendə(r)/ n esplendor m

splint /splɪnt/ n tablilla f

splinter /'splɪntə(r)/ n astilla f. ● vi astillarse. ∼ group n grupo m disidente

split /splɪt/ vt (pt split, pres p splitting) hender, rajar; (tear) rajar; (divide) dividir; (share) repartir. ∼ one's sides caerse de risa. ● vi partirse; (divide) dividirse. ∼ on s.o. (sl) traicionar. ● n hendidura f; (tear) desgarrón m; (quarrel) ruptura f; (pol) escisión f. ∼ up vi separarse. ∼ second n fracción f de segundo

splurge /splɜːdʒ/ vi (fam) derrochar

splutter /'splʌtə(r)/ vi chisporrotear; ⟨person⟩ farfullar. ● n chisporroteo m; (speech) farfulla f

spoil /spɔɪl/ vt (pt spoilt or spoiled) estropear, echar a perder; (ruin) arruinar; (indulge) mimar. ● n botín m. ∼s npl botín m. ∼-sport n aguafiestas m invar

spoke¹ /spəʊk/ see speak

spoke² /spəʊk/ n (of wheel) radio m

spoken /'spəʊkən/ *see* **speak**

spokesman /'spəʊksmən/ *n* (*pl* **-men**) portavoz *m*

spong|e /spʌndʒ/ *n* esponja *f*. ● *vt* limpiar con una esponja. ● *vi*. **~e on** vivir a costa de. **~e-cake** *n* bizcocho *m*. **~er** /-ə(r)/ *n* gorrón *m*. **~y** *a* esponjoso

sponsor /'spɒnsə(r)/ *n* patrocinador *m*; (*surety*) garante *m*. ● *vt* patrocinar. **~ship** *n* patrocinio *m*

spontane|ity /spɒntə'neɪtɪ/ *n* espontaneidad *f*. **~ous** /-'spɒn'teɪnjəs/ *a* espontáneo. **~ously** *adv* espontáneamente

spoof /spu:f/ *n* (*sl*) parodia *f*

spooky /'spu:kɪ/ *a* (**-ier, -iest**) (*fam*) escalofriante

spool /spu:l/ *n* carrete *m*; (*of sewing-machine*) canilla *f*

spoon /spu:n/ *n* cuchara *f*. **~-fed** *a* (*fig*) mimado. **~-feed** *vt* (*pt* **-fed**) dar de comer con cuchara. **~ful** *n* (*pl* **-fuls**) cucharada *f*

sporadic /spə'rædɪk/ *a* esporádico

sport /spɔ:t/ *n* deporte *m*; (*amusement*) pasatiempo *m*; (*person*, *fam*) persona *f* alegre, buen chico *m*, buena chica *f*. **be a good ~** ser buen perdedor. ● *vt* lucir. **~ing** *a* deportivo. **~ing chance** *n* probabilidad *f* de éxito. **~s car** *n* coche *m* deportivo. **~s coat** *n* chaqueta *f* de sport. **~s-man** /'spɔ:tsmən/ *n*, (*pl* **-men**), **~s-woman** /'spɔ:tswʊmən/ *n* (*pl* **-women**) deportista *m & f*

spot /spɒt/ *n* mancha *f*; (*pimple*) grano *m*; (*place*) lugar *m*; (*in pattern*) punto *m*; (*drop*) gota *f*; (*a little*, *fam*) poquito *m*. **in a ~** (*fam*) en un apuro. **on the ~** en el lugar; (*without delay*) en el acto. ● *vt* (*pt* **spotted**) manchar; (*notice*, *fam*) observar, ver. **~ check** *n* control *m* hecho al azar. **~less** *a* inmaculado. **~light** /'spɒtlaɪt/ *n* reflector *m*. **~ted** *a* moteado; (*cloth*) a puntos. **~ty** *a* (**-ier, -iest**) manchado; (*skin*) con granos

spouse /spaʊz/ *n* cónyuge *m & f*

spout /spaʊt/ *n* pico *m*; (*jet*) chorro *m*. **up the ~** (*ruined*, *sl*) perdido. ● *vi* chorrear

sprain /spreɪn/ *vt* torcer. ● *n* torcedura *f*

sprang /spræŋ/ *see* **spring**

sprat /spræt/ *n* espadín *m*

sprawl /sprɔ:l/ *vi* ⟨*person*⟩ repanchigarse; ⟨*city etc*⟩ extenderse

spray /spreɪ/ *n* (*of flowers*) ramo *m*; (*water*) rociada *f*; (*from sea*) espuma *f*; (*device*) pulverizador *m*. ● *vt* rociar. **~-gun** *n* pistola *f* pulverizadora

spread /spred/ *vt* (*pt* **spread**) (*stretch*, *extend*) extender; untar ⟨*jam etc*⟩; difundir ⟨*idea*, *news*⟩. ● *vi* extenderse; ⟨*disease*⟩ propagarse; ⟨*idea*, *news*⟩ difundirse. ● *n* extensión *f*; (*paste*) pasta *f*; (*of disease*) propagación *f*; (*feast*, *fam*) comilona *f*. **~-eagled** *a* con los brazos y piernas extendidos

spree /spri:/ *n*. **go on a ~** (*have fun*, *fam*) ir de juerga

sprig /sprɪg/ *n* ramito *m*

sprightly /'spraɪtlɪ/ *a* (**-ier, -iest**) vivo

spring /sprɪŋ/ *n* (*season*) primavera *f*; (*device*) muelle *m*; (*elasticity*) elasticidad *f*; (*water*) manantial *m*. ● *a* de primavera. ● *vt* (*pt* **sprang**, *pp* **sprung**) hacer inesperadamente. ● *vi* saltar; (*issue*) brotar. **~ from** *vi* provenir de. **~ up** *vi* surgir. **~-board** *n* trampolín *m*. **~time** *n* primavera *f*. **~y** *a* (**-ier, -iest**) elástico

sprinkl|e /'sprɪŋkl/ *vt* salpicar; (*with liquid*) rociar. ● *n* salpicadura *f*; (*of liquid*) rociada *f*. **~ed with** salpicado de. **~er** /-ə(r)/ *n* regadera *f*. **~ing** /'sprɪŋklɪŋ/ *n* (*fig*, *amount*) poco *m*

sprint /sprɪnt/ *n* carrera *f*. ● *vi* correr. **~er** *n* corredor *m*

sprite /spraɪt/ *n* duende *m*, hada *f*

sprout /spraʊt/ *vi* brotar. ● *n* brote *m*. (**Brussels**) **~s** *npl* coles *fpl* de Bruselas

spruce /spru:s/ *a* elegante

sprung /sprʌŋ/ *see* **spring**. ● *a* de muelles

spry /spraɪ/ *a* (**spryer, spryest**) vivo

spud /spʌd/ *n* (*sl*) patata *f*, papa *f* (*LAm*)

spun /spʌn/ *see* **spin**

spur /spɜ:(r)/ *n* espuela *f*; (*stimulus*) estímulo *m*. **on the ~ of the moment** impulsivamente. ● *vt* (*pt* **spurred**). **~ (on)** espolear; (*fig*) estimular

spurious /'spjʊərɪəs/ *a* falso. **~ly** *adv* falsamente

spurn /spɜ:n/ *vt* despreciar; (*reject*) rechazar

spurt /spɜːt/ *vi* chorrear; (*make sudden effort*) hacer un esfuerzo repentino. ● *n* chorro *m*; (*effort*) esfuerzo *m* repentino

spy /spaɪ/ *n* espía *m & f*. ● *vt* divisar. ● *vi* espiar. ~ **out** *vt* reconocer. ~**ing** *n* espionaje *m*

squabble /'skwɒbl/ *n* riña *f*. ● *vi* reñir

squad /skwɒd/ *n* (*mil*) pelotón *m*; (*of police*) brigada *f*; (*sport*) equipo *m*

squadron /'skwɒdrən/ *n* (*mil*) escuadrón *m*; (*naut, aviat*) escuadrilla *f*

squalid /'skwɒlɪd/ *a* asqueroso; (*wretched*) miserable

squall /skwɔːl/ *n* turbión *m*. ● *vi* chillar. ~**y** *a* borrascoso

squalor /'skwɒlə(r)/ *n* miseria *f*

squander /'skwɒndə(r)/ *vt* derrochar

square /skweə(r)/ *n* cuadrado *m*; (*open space in town*) plaza *f*; (*for drawing*) escuadra *f*. ● *a* cuadrado; (*not owing*) sin deudas, iguales; (*honest*) honrado; (*meal*) satisfactorio; (*old-fashioned, sl*) chapado a la antigua. **all** ~ iguales. ● *vt* (*settle*) arreglar; (*math*) cuadrar. ● *vi* (*agree*) cuadrar. ~ **up to** enfrentarse con. ~**ly** *adv* directamente

squash /skwɒʃ/ *vt* aplastar; (*suppress*) suprimir. ● *n* apiñamiento *m*; (*drink*) zumo *m*; (*sport*) squash *m*. ~**y** *a* blando

squat /skwɒt/ *vi* (*pt* **squatted**) ponerse en cuclillas; (*occupy illegally*) ocupar sin derecho. ● *n* casa *f* ocupada sin derecho. ● *a* (*dumpy*) achaparrado. ~**ter** /-ə(r)/ *n* ocupante *m & f* ilegal

squawk /skwɔːk/ *n* graznido *m*. ● *vi* graznar

squeak /skwiːk/ *n* chillido *m*; (*of door etc*) chirrido *m*. ● *vi* chillar; (*door etc*) chirriar. ~**y** *a* chirriador

squeal /skwiːl/ *n* chillido *m*. ● *vi* chillar. ~ **on** (*inform on, sl*) denunciar

squeamish /'skwiːmɪʃ/ *a* delicado; (*scrupulous*) escrupuloso. **be** ~ **about snakes** tener horror a las serpientes

squeeze /skwiːz/ *vt* apretar; exprimir (*lemon etc*); (*extort*) extorsionar (**from** de). ● *vi* (*force one's way*) abrirse paso. ● *n* estrujón *m*; (*of hand*) apretón *m*. **credit** ~ *n* restricción *f* de crédito

squelch /skweltʃ/ *vi* chapotear. ● *n* chapoteo *m*

squib /skwɪb/ *n* (*firework*) buscapiés *m invar*

squid /skwɪd/ *n* calamar *m*

squiggle /'skwɪgl/ *n* garabato *m*

squint /skwɪnt/ *vi* ser bizco; (*look sideways*) mirar de soslayo. ● *n* estrabismo *m*

squire /'skwaɪə(r)/ *n* terrateniente *m*

squirm /skwɜːm/ *vi* retorcerse

squirrel /'skwɪrəl/ *n* ardilla *f*

squirt /skwɜːt/ *vt* arrojar a chorros. ● *vi* salir a chorros. ● *n* chorro *m*

St *abbr* (*saint*) /sənt/ S, San(to); (*street*) C/, Calle *f*

stab /stæb/ *vt* (*pt* **stabbed**) apuñalar. ● *n* puñalada *f*; (*pain*) punzada *f*; (*attempt, fam*) tentativa *f*

stabili|ty /stə'bɪlətɪ/ *n* estabilidad *f*. ~**ze** /'steɪbɪlaɪz/ *vt* estabilizar. ~**zer** /-ə(r)/ *n* estabilizador *m*

stable[1] /'steɪbl/ *a* (**-er, -est**) estable

stable[2] /'steɪbl/ *n* cuadra *f*. ● *vt* poner en una cuadra. ~**boy** *n* mozo *m* de cuadra

stack /stæk/ *n* montón *m*. ● *vt* amontonar

stadium /'steɪdɪəm/ *n* estadio *m*

staff /stɑːf/ *n* (*stick*) palo *m*; (*employees*) personal *m*; (*mil*) estado *m* mayor; (*in school*) profesorado *m*. ● *vt* proveer de personal

stag /stæg/ *n* ciervo *m*. ~**-party** *n* reunión *f* de hombres, fiesta *f* de despedida de soltero

stage /steɪdʒ/ *n* (*in theatre*) escena *f*; (*phase*) etapa *f*; (*platform*) plataforma *f*. **go on the** ~ hacerse actor. ● *vt* representar; (*arrange*) organizar. ~**-coach** *n* (*hist*) diligencia *f*. ~ **fright** *n* miedo *m* al público. ~**-manager** *n* director *m* de escena. ~ **whisper** *n* aparte *m*

stagger /'stægə(r)/ *vi* tambalearse. ● *vt* asombrar; escalonar (*holidays etc*). ● *n* tambaleo *m*. ~**ing** *a* asombroso

stagna|nt /'stægnənt/ *a* estancado. ~**te** /stæg'neɪt/ *vi* estancarse. ~**tion** /-ʃn/ *n* estancamiento *m*

staid /steɪd/ *a* serio, formal

stain /steɪn/ *vt* manchar; (*colour*) teñir. ● *n* mancha *f*; (*liquid*) tinte *m*. ~**ed glass window** *n* vidriera *f* de colores. ~**less** /'steɪnlɪs/ *a* inmaculado. ~**less steel** *n* acero *m* inoxidable. ∿ **remover** n quitamanchas m invar

stair /steə(r)/ n escalón m. ∿s npl escalera f. **flight of** ∿s tramo m de escalera. ∿**case** /'steəkeɪs/ n, ∿ **way** n escalera f

stake /steɪk/ n estaca f; (for execution) hoguera f; (wager) apuesta f; (com) intereses mpl. **at** ∿ en juego. ●vt estacar; (wager) apostar. ∿ **a claim** reclamar

stalactite /'stæləktaɪt/ n estalactita f

stalagmite /'stæləgmaɪt/ n estalagmita f

stale /steɪl/ a (-er, -est) no fresco; (bread) duro; (smell) viciado; (news) viejo; (uninteresting) gastado. ∿**mate** /'steɪlmeɪt/ n (chess) ahogado m; (deadlock) punto m muerto

stalk¹ /stɔːk/ n tallo m

stalk² /stɔːk/ vi andar majestuosamente. ●vt seguir; (animal) acechar

stall¹ /stɔːl/ n (stable) cuadra f; (in stable) casilla f; (in theatre) butaca f; (in market) puesto m; (kiosk) quiosco m

stall² /stɔːl/ vt parar (engine). ●vi (engine) pararse; (fig) andar con rodeos

stallion /'stæljən/ n semental m

stalwart /'stɔːlwət/ n partidario m leal

stamina /'stæmɪnə/ n resistencia f

stammer /'stæmə(r)/ vi tartamudear. ●n tartamudeo m

stamp /stæmp/ vt (with feet) patear; (press) estampar; poner un sello en (envelope); (with rubber stamp) sellar; (fig) señalar. ●vi patear. ●n sello m; (with foot) patada f; (mark) marca f, señal f. ∿ **out** (fig) acabar con

stampede /stæm'piːd/ n desbandada f; (fam) pánico m. ●vi huir en desorden

stance /stɑːns/ n postura f

stand /stænd/ vi (pt stood) estar de pie; (rise) ponerse de pie; (be) encontrarse; (stay firm) permanecer; (pol) presentarse como candidato (for en). ∿ **to reason** ser lógico. ●vt (endure) soportar; (place) poner; (offer) ofrecer. ∿ **a chance** tener una posibilidad. ∿ **one's ground** mantenerse firme. **I'll** ∿ **you a drink** te invito a una copa. ●n posición f, postura f; (mil) resistencia f; (for lamp

etc) pie m, sostén m; (at market) puesto m; (booth) quiosco m; (sport) tribuna f. ∿ **around** no hacer nada. ∿ **back** retroceder. ∿ **by** vi estar preparado. ●vt (support) apoyar. ∿ **down** vi retirarse. ∿ **for** vt representar. ∿ **in for** suplir a. ∿ **out** destacarse. ∿ **up** vi ponerse de pie. ∿ **up for** defender. ∿ **up to** vt resistir a

standard /'stændəd/ n norma f; (level) nivel m; (flag) estandarte m. ●a normal, corriente. ∿**ize** vt uniformar. ∿ **lamp** n lámpara f de pie. ∿s npl valores mpl

stand ∿**-by** n (person) reserva f; (at airport) lista f de espera. ∿**in** n suplente m & f. ∿**ing** /'stændɪŋ/ a de pie; (upright) derecho. ●n posición f; (duration) duración f. ∿**offish** a (fam) frío. ∿**point** /'stændpɔɪnt/ n punto m de vista. ∿**still** /'stændstɪl/ n. **at a** ∿**still** parado. **come to a** ∿**still** pararse

stank /stæŋk/ see stink

staple¹ /'steɪpl/ a principal

staple² /'steɪpl/ n grapa f. ●vt sujetar con una grapa. ∿**r** /-ə(r)/ n grapadora f

star /stɑː/ n (incl cinema, theatre) estrella f; (asterisk) asterisco m. ●vi (pt starred) ser el protagonista

starboard /'stɑːbəd/ n estribor m

starch /stɑːtʃ/ n almidón m; (in food) fécula f. ●vt almidonar. ∿**y** a almidonado; (food) feculento; (fig) formal

stardom /'stɑːdəm/ n estrellato m

stare /steə(r)/ n mirada f fija. ●vi. ∿ **at** mirar fijamente

starfish /'stɑːfɪʃ/ n estrella f de mar

stark /stɑːk/ a (-er, -est) rígido; (utter) completo. ●adv completamente

starlight /'stɑːlaɪt/ n luz f de las estrellas

starling /'stɑːlɪŋ/ n estornino m

starry /'stɑːrɪ/ a estrellado. ∿**-eyed** a (fam) ingenuo, idealista

start /stɑːt/ vt empezar; poner en marcha (machine); (cause) provocar. ●vi empezar; (jump) sobresaltarse; (leave) partir; (car etc) arrancar. ●n principio m; (leaving) salida f; (sport) ventaja f; (jump) susto m. ∿**er** n (sport) participante m & f; (auto) motor m de arranque; (culin) primer plato m. ∿**ing-point** n punto m de partida

startle /'stɑːtl/ vt asustar

starv|ation /stɑːˈveɪʃn/ n hambre f. **~e** /stɑːv/ vt hacer morir de hambre; (deprive) privar. ● vi morir de hambre

stash /stæʃ/ vt (sl) esconder

state /steɪt/ n estado m; (grand style) pompa f. **S~** n Estado m. **be in a ~** estar agitado. ● vt declarar; expresar (views); (fix) fijar. ● a del Estado; (schol) público; (with ceremony) de gala. **~less** a sin patria

stately /'steɪtlɪ/ a (-ier, -iest) majestuoso

statement /'steɪtmənt/ n declaración f; (account) informe m. **bank ~** n estado m de cuenta

stateroom /'steɪtruːm/ n (on ship) camarote m

statesman /'steɪtsmən/ n (pl -men) estadista m

static /'stætɪk/ a inmóvil. **~s** n estática f; (radio, TV) parásitos mpl atmosféricos, interferencias fpl

station /'steɪʃn/ n estación f; (status) posición f social. ● vt colocar; (mil) estacionar

stationary /'steɪʃənərɪ/ a estacionario

stationer /'steɪʃənə(r)/ n papelero m. **~'s** (shop) n papelería f. **~y** n artículos mpl de escritorio

station-wagon /'steɪʃnwægən/ n furgoneta f

statistic /stəˈtɪstɪk/ n estadística f. **~al** /stəˈtɪstɪkl/ a estadístico. **~s** /stəˈtɪstɪks/ n (science) estadística f

statue /'stætʃuː/ n estatua f. **~sque** /-ʊˈesk/ a escultural. **~tte** /-ʊˈet/ n figurilla f

stature /'stætʃə(r)/ n talla f, estatura f

status /'steɪtəs/ n posición f social; (prestige) categoría f; (jurid) estado m

statut|e /'stætʃuːt/ n estatuto m. **~ory** /-ʊtrɪ/ a estatutario

staunch /stɔːnʃ/ a (-er, -est) leal. **~ly** adv lealmente

stave /steɪv/ n (mus) pentagrama m. ● vt. **~ off** evitar

stay /steɪ/ n soporte m, sostén m; (of time) estancia f; (jurid) suspensión f. ● vi quedar; (spend time) detenerse; (reside) alojarse. ● vt matar (hunger). **~ the course** terminar. **~ in** quedar en casa. **~ put** mantenerse firme. **~**

up no acostarse. **~ing-power** n resistencia f

stays /steɪz/ npl (old use) corsé m

stead /sted/ n. **in s.o.'s ~** en lugar de uno. **stand s.o. in good ~** ser útil a uno

steadfast /'stedfɑːst/ a firme

stead|ily /'stedɪlɪ/ adv firmemente; (regularly) regularmente. **~y** /'stedɪ/ a (-ier, -iest) firme; (regular) regular; (dependable) serio

steak /steɪk/ n filete m

steal /stiːl/ vt (pt stole, pp stolen) robar. **~ the show** llevarse los aplausos. **~ in** vi entrar a hurtadillas. **~ out** vi salir a hurtadillas

stealth /stelθ/ n. **by ~** sigilosamente. **~y** a sigiloso

steam /stiːm/ n vapor m; (energy) energía f. ● vt (cook) cocer al vapor; empañar (window). ● vi echar vapor. **~ ahead** (fam) hacer progresos. **~ up** vi (glass) empañar. **~-engine** n máquina f de vapor. **~er** /'stiːmə(r)/ n (ship) barco m de vapor. **~-roller** /'stiːmrəʊlə(r)/ n apisonadora f. **~y** a húmedo

steel /stiːl/ n acero m. ● vt. **~ o.s.** fortalecerse. **~ industry** n industria f siderúrgica. **~ wool** n estropajo m de acero. **~y** a acerado; (fig) duro, inflexible

steep /stiːp/ a (-er, -est) escarpado; (price) (fam) exorbitante. ● vt (soak) remojar. **~ed in** (fig) empapado de

steeple /'stiːpl/ n aguja f, campanario m. **~chase** /'stiːpltʃeɪs/ n carrera f de obstáculos

steep: **~ly** adv de modo empinado. **~ness** n lo escarpado

steer /stɪə(r)/ vt guiar; gobernar (ship). ● vi (in ship) gobernar. **~ clear of** evitar. **~ing** n (auto) dirección f. **~ing-wheel** n volante m

stem /stem/ n tallo m; (of glass) pie m; (of word) raíz f; (of ship) roda f. ● vt (pt stemmed) detener. ● vi. **~ from** provenir de

stench /stentʃ/ n hedor m

stencil /'stensl/ n plantilla f; (for typing) cliché m. ● vt (pt stencilled) estarcir

stenographer /steˈnɒgrəfə(r)/ n (Amer) estenógrafo m

step /step/ vi (pt stepped) ir. **~ down** retirarse. **~ in** entrar; (fig) intervenir. **~ up** vt aumentar. ● n paso *m*; (*surface*) escalón *m*; (*fig*) medida *f*. **in** ~ (*fig*) de acuerdo con. **out of** ~ (*fig*) en desacuerdo con. ~**brother** /'stepbrʌðə(r)/ *n* hermanastro *m*. ~**daughter** *n* hijastra *f*. ~**father** *n* padrastro *m*. ~**ladder** *n* escalera *f* de tijeras. ~**mother** *n* madrastra *f*. ~**ping-stone** /'step-ɪŋstəʊn/ *n* pasadera *f*; (*fig*) escalón *m*. ~**sister** *n* hermanastra *f*. ~**son** *n* hijastro *m*.

stereo /'steriəʊ/ *n* (*pl* -**os**) cadena *f* estereofónica. ● *a* estereofónico. ~**phonic** /steriəʊ'fɒnɪk/ *a* estereofónico. ~**type** /'steriəʊtaɪp/ *n* estereotipo *m*. ~**typed** *a* estereotipado

sterile /'steraɪl/ *a* estéril. ~**ity** /stə'rɪlətɪ/ *n* esterilidad *f*. ~**ization** /-'zeɪʃn/ *n* esterilización *f*. ~**ize** /'sterɪlaɪz/ *vt* esterilizar

sterling /'stɜːlɪŋ/ *n* libras *fpl* esterlinas. ● *a* (*pound*) esterlina; (*fig*) excelente. ~ **silver** *n* plata *f* de ley

stern[1] /stɜːn/ *n* (*of boat*) popa *f*

stern[2] /stɜːn/ *a* (-**er**, -**est**) severo. ~**ly** *adv* severamente

stethoscope /'steθəskəʊp/ *n* estetoscopio *m*

stew /stjuː/ *vt/i* guisar. ● *n* guisado *m*. **in a** ~ (*fam*) en un apuro

steward /stjʊəd/ *n* administrador *m*; (*on ship, aircraft*) camarero *m*. ~**ess** /-'des/ *n* camarera *f*; (*on aircraft*) azafata *f*

stick /stɪk/ *n* palo *m*; (*for walking*) bastón *m*; (*of celery etc*) tallo *m*. ● *vt* (*pt* **stuck**) (*glue*) pegar; (*put, fam*) poner; (*thrust*) clavar; (*endure, sl*) soportar. ● *vi* pegarse; (*remain, fam*) quedarse; (*jam*) bloquearse. ~ **at** (*fam*) perseverar en. ~ **out** sobresalir; (*catch the eye, fam*) resaltar. ~ **to** aferrarse a; cumplir (*promise*). ~ **up for** (*fam*) defender. ~**er** /'stɪkə(r)/ *n* pegatina *f*. ~**ing-plaster** *n* esparadrapo *m*. ~**-in-the-mud** *n* persona *f* chapada a la antigua

stickler /'stɪklə(r)/ *n*. **be a** ~ **for** insistir en

sticky /'stɪkɪ/ *a* (-**ier**, -**iest**) pegajoso; (*label*) engomado; (*sl*) difícil

stiff /stɪf/ *a* (-**er**, -**est**) rígido; (*difficult*) difícil; (*manner*) estirado; (*drink*) fuerte; (*price*) subido; (*joint*) tieso; (*muscle*) con agujetas. ~**en** /'stɪfn/ *vt* poner tieso. ~**ly** *adv* rígidamente. ~ **neck** *n* tortícolis *f*. ~**ness** *n* rigidez *f*

stifl|**e** /'staɪfl/ *vt* sofocar. ~**ing** *a* sofocante

stigma /'stɪgmə/ *n* (*pl* -**as**) estigma *m*. (*pl* **stigmata** /'stɪgmətə/) (*relig*) estigma *m*. ~**tize** *vt* estigmatizar

stile /staɪl/ *n* portillo *m* con escalones

stiletto /stɪ'letəʊ/ *n* (*pl* -**os**) estilete *m*. ~ **heels** *npl* tacones *mpl* aguja

still[1] /stɪl/ *a* (*inmóvil*); (*peaceful*) tranquilo; (*drink*) sin gas. ● *n* silencio *m*. ● *adv* todavía; (*nevertheless*) sin embargo

still[2] /stɪl/ *n* (*apparatus*) alambique *m*

still: ~**born** *a* nacido muerto. ~ **life** *n* (*pl* -**s**) bodegón *m*. ~**ness** *n* tranquilidad *f*

stilted /'stɪltɪd/ *a* artificial

stilts /stɪlts/ *npl* zancos *mpl*

stimul|**ant** /'stɪmjʊlənt/ *n* estimulante *m*. ~**ate** /'stɪmjʊleɪt/ *vt* estimular. ~**ation** /-'leɪʃn/ *n* estímulo *m*. ~**us** /'stɪmjʊləs/ *n* (*pl* -**li** /-laɪ/) estímulo *m*

sting /stɪŋ/ *n* picadura *f*; (*organ*) aguijón *m*. ● *vt/i* (*pt* **stung**) picar

sting|**iness** /'stɪndʒɪnɪs/ *n* tacañería *f*. ~**y** /'stɪndʒɪ/ *a* (-**ier**, -**iest**) tacaño

stink /stɪŋk/ *n* hedor *m*. ● *vi* (*pt* **stank** *or* **stunk**, *pp* **stunk**) oler mal. ● *vt*. ~ **out** apestar (*room*); ahuyentar (*person*). ~**er** /-ə(r)/ *n* (*sl*) problema *m* difícil; (*person*) mal bicho *m*

stint /stɪnt/ *n* (*work*) trabajo *m*. ● *vi*. ~ **on** escatimar

stipple /'stɪpl/ *vt* puntear

stipulat|**e** /'stɪpjʊleɪt/ *vt/i* estipular. ~**ion** /-'leɪʃn/ *n* estipulación *f*

stir /stɜː(r)/ *vt* (*pt* **stirred**) remover, agitar; (*mix*) mezclar; (*stimulate*) estimular. ● *vi* moverse. ● *n* agitación *f*; (*commotion*) conmoción *f*

stirrup /'stɪrəp/ *n* estribo *m*

stitch /stɪtʃ/ *n* (*in sewing*) puntada *f*; (*in knitting*) punto *m*; (*pain*) dolor *m* de costado; (*med*) punto *m* de sutura. **be in** ~**es** (*fam*) desternillarse de risa. ● *vt* coser

stoat /stəʊt/ *n* armiño *m*

stock /stɒk/ *n* (*com, supplies*) existencias *fpl*; (*com, variety*) surtido *m*; (*livestock*) ganado *m*; (*lineage*) linaje *m*; (*finance*) acciones *fpl*; (*culin*) caldo *m*; (*plant*) alhelí *m*. **out of** ~ agotado. **take** ~ (*fig*) evaluar. ● *a* corriente; (*fig*) trillado. ● *vt* abastecer

(with de). ● *vi.* ~ **up** abastecerse
(with de). ~-**broker** /'stɒkbrəʊkə(r)/ *n*
corredor *m* de bolsa. S~ **Exchange** *n*
bolsa *f.* **well-~ed** *a* bien provisto

stocking /'stɒkɪŋ/ *n* media *f*

stock: ~-**in-trade** /'stɒkɪntreɪd/ *n*
existencias *fpl.* ~**ist** /'stɒkɪst/ *n* distribuidor *m.* ~**pile** /'stɒkpaɪl/ *n* reservas *fpl.* ● *vt* acumular. ~-**still** *a*
inmóvil. ~-**taking** *n* (com) inventario *m*

stocky /'stɒkɪ/ *a* (-**ier, -iest**) achaparrado

stodg|e /stɒdʒ/ *n* (fam) comida *f*
pesada. ~**y** *a* pesado

stoic /'stəʊɪk/ *n* estoico. ~**al** *a*
estoico. ~**ally** *adv* estoicamente.
~**ism** /-sɪzəm/ *n* estoicismo *m*

stoke /stəʊk/ *vt* alimentar. ~**r**
/'stəʊkə(r)/ *n* fogonero *m*

stole[1] /stəʊl/ *see* **steal**

stole[2] /stəʊl/ *n* estola *f*

stolen /'stəʊlən/ *see* **steal**

stolid /'stɒlɪd/ *a* impasible. ~**ly** *adv*
impasiblemente

stomach /'stʌmək/ *n* estómago *m.*
● *vt* soportar. ~-**ache** *n* dolor *m* de
estómago

ston|e /stəʊn/ *n* piedra *f*; (med)
cálculo *m*; (in fruit) hueso *m*; (weight,
pl **stone**) peso *m* de 14 libras (= 6,
348 kg). ● *a* de piedra. ● *vt* apedrear;
deshuesar ⟨fruit⟩. ~**e-deaf** *a* sordo
como una tapia. ~**emason** /'stəʊn-
meɪsn/ *n* albañil *m.* ~**ework**
/'stəʊnwɜːk/ *n* cantería *f.* ~**y** *a*
pedregoso; (like stone) pétreo

stood /stʊd/ *see* **stand**

stooge /stuːdʒ/ *n* (in theatre)
compañero *m*; (underling) lacayo *m*

stool /stuːl/ *n* taburete *m*

stoop /stuːp/ *vi* inclinarse; (fig)
rebajarse. ● *n.* **have a** ~ ser cargado
de espaldas

stop /stɒp/ *vt* (pt **stopped**) parar;
(cease) terminar; tapar ⟨a leak etc⟩;
(prevent) impedir; (interrupt) interrumpir. ● *vi* pararse; (stay, fam)
quedarse. ● *n* (in bus etc) parada *f*;
(gram) punto *m*; (mec) tope *m*. ~
dead *vi* pararse en seco. ~**cock**
/'stɒpkɒk/ *n* llave *f* de paso. ~**gap**
/'stɒpgæp/ *n* remedio *m* provisional.
~**(-over)** *n* escala *f.* ~**page**
/'stɒpɪdʒ/ *n* parada *f*; (of work) paro
m; (interruption) interrupción *f.*
~**per** /'stɒpə(r)/ *n* tapón *m.* ~**press**
n noticias *fpl* de última hora. ~ **light**

n luz *f* de freno. ~-**watch** *n* cronómetro *m*

storage /'stɔːrɪdʒ/ *n* almacena-
miento *m.* ~ **heater** *n* acumulador
m. **in cold** ~ almacenaje *m* frigorífico

store /stɔː(r)/ *n* provisión *f*; (shop,
depot) almacén *m*; (fig) reserva *f.* **in**
~ en reserva. **set** ~ **by** dar importancia a. ● *vt* (for future) poner en
reserva; (in warehouse) almacenar.
~ **up** *vt* acumular

storeroom /'stɔːruːm/ *n* despensa *f*

storey /'stɔːrɪ/ *n* (pl -**eys**) piso *m*

stork /stɔːk/ *n* cigüeña *f*

storm /stɔːm/ *n* tempestad *f*; (mil)
asalto *m.* ● *vi* rabiar. ● *vt* (mil) a-
saltar. ~**y** *a* tempestuoso

story /'stɔːrɪ/ *n* historia *f*; (in newspaper) artículo *m*; (fam) mentira *f*,
cuento *m.* ~-**teller** *n* cuentista *m & f*

stout /staʊt/ *a* (-**er, -est**) (fat) gordo;
(brave) valiente. ● *n* cerveza *f* negra.
~**ness** *n* corpulencia *f*

stove /stəʊv/ *n* estufa *f*

stow /stəʊ/ *vt* guardar; (hide)
esconder. ● *vi.* ~ **away** viajar
de polizón. ~**away** /'stəʊəweɪ/ *n*
polizón *m*

straddle /'strædl/ *vt* estar a horcajadas

straggl|e /'strægl/ *vi* rezagarse. ~**y**
a desordenado

straight /streɪt/ *a* (-**er, -est**) derecho,
recto; (tidy) en orden; (frank) franco;
⟨drink⟩ solo, puro; ⟨hair⟩ lacio. ● *adv*
derecho; (direct) directamente;
(without delay) inmediatamente. ~
on todo recto. ~ **out** sin vacilar. **go**
~ enmendarse. ● *n* recta *f.* ~ **away**
inmediatamente. ~**en** /'streɪtn/ *vt*
enderezar. ● *vi* enderezarse. ~
forward /streɪt'fɔːwəd/ *a* franco;
(easy) sencillo. ~**forwardly** *adv*
francamente. ~**ness** *n* rectitud *f*

strain[1] /streɪn/ *n* (tension) tensión *f*;
(injury) torcedura *f.* ● *vt* estirar;
(tire) cansar; (injure) torcer; (sieve)
colar

strain[2] /streɪn/ *n* (lineage) linaje *m*;
(streak) tendencia *f*

strained /streɪnd/ *a* forzado; ⟨rela-
tions⟩ tirante

strainer /-ə(r)/ *n* colador *m*

strains /streɪnz/ *npl* (mus) acordes
mpl

strait /streɪt/ *n* estrecho *m.* ~-**jacket**
n camisa *f* de fuerza. ~-**laced** *a* remilgado, gazmoño. ~**s** *npl* apuro *m*

strand /strænd/ n (*thread*) hebra *f*;
(*sand*) playa *f*. ● vi (*ship*) varar. be
~ed quedarse sin recursos

strange /streɪndʒ/ a (**-er**, **-est**)
extraño, raro; (*not known*) desconocido; (*unaccustomed*) nuevo. ~ly
adv extrañamente. ~ness n extra-
ñeza *f*. ~r /'streɪndʒə(r)/ n desconocido *m*

strang||le /'stræŋgl/ vt estrangular;
(*fig*) ahogar. ~lehold /'stræŋgl-
hǝʊld/ n (*fig*) dominio *m* completo.
~ler /-ǝ(r)/ n estrangulador *m*. ~ul-
ation /stræŋgjʊ'leɪʃn/ n estrangulación *f*

strap /stræp/ n correa *f*; (*of garment*)
tirante *m*. ● vt (*pt* **strapped**) atar con
correa; (*flog*) azotar

strapping /'stræpɪŋ/ a robusto

strata /'strɑːtǝ/ *see* **stratum**

strat||agem /'strætǝdʒǝm/ n es-
tratagema *f*. ~egic /strǝ'tiːdʒɪk/ a
estratégico. ~egically adv estratégicamente. ~egist n estratega *m* & *f*.
~egy /'strætǝdʒɪ/ n estrategia *f*

stratum /'strɑːtǝm/ n (*pl* **strata**) estrato *m*

straw /strɔː/ n paja *f*. the last ~ el
colmo

strawberry /'strɔːbǝrɪ/ n fresa *f*

stray /streɪ/ vi vagar; (*deviate*)
desviarse (**from** de). ● a (*animal*)
extraviado, callejero; (*isolated*) aislado. ● n animal *m* extraviado,
animal *m* callejero

streak /striːk/ n raya *f*; (*of madness*)
vena *f*. ● vt rayar. ● vi moverse como
un rayo. ~y a (**-ier**, **-iest**) rayado;
(*bacon*) entreverado

stream /striːm/ n arroyo *m*; (*current*) corriente *f*; (*of people*) desfile *m*;
(*schol*) grupo *m*. ● vi correr. ~ out vi
(*people*) salir en tropel

streamer /'striːmǝ(r)/ n (*paper*)
serpentina *f*; (*flag*) gallardete *m*

streamline /'striːmlaɪn/ vt dar línea
aerodinámica a; (*simplify*) simpli-
ficar. ~d a aerodinámica

street /striːt/ n calle *f*. ~car /'striː-
tkɑː/ n (*Amer*) tranvía *m*. ~ lamp n
farol *m*. ~ map n, ~ plan n plano *m*

strength /streŋθ/ n fuerza *f*; (*of wall
etc*) solidez *f*. on the ~ of a base de.
~en /'streŋθn/ vt reforzar

strenuous /'strenjʊǝs/ a enérgico;
(*arduous*) arduo; (*tiring*) fatigoso.
~ly adv enérgicamente

stress /stres/ n énfasis *f*; (*gram*)
acento *m*; (*mec, med, tension*) tensión
f. ● vt insistir en

stretch /stretʃ/ vt estirar; (*extend*)
extender; (*exaggerate*) forzar. ~ a
point hacer una excepción. ● vi
estirarse; (*extend*) extenderse. ● n
estirón *m*; (*period*) período *m*; (*of
road*) tramo *m*. at a ~ seguido; (*in
one go*) de un tirón. ~er /'stretʃǝ(r)/
n camilla *f*

strew /struː/ vt (*pt* **strewed**, *pp*
strewn *or* **strewed**) esparcir; (*cover*)
cubrir

stricken /'strɪkǝn/ a. ~ with afec-
tado de

strict /strɪkt/ a (**-er**, **-est**) severo;
(*precise*) estricto, preciso. ~ly adv
estrictamente. ~ly speaking en
rigor

stricture /'strɪktʃǝ(r)/ n crítica *f*;
(*constriction*) constricción *f*

stride /straɪd/ vi (*pt* **strode**, *pp* **strid-
den**) andar a zancadas. ● n zancada
f. take sth in one's ~ hacer algo con
facilidad, tomarse las cosas con calma

strident /'straɪdnt/ a estridente

strife /straɪf/ n conflicto *m*

strike /straɪk/ vt (*pt* **struck**) golpear;
encender (*match*); encontrar (*gold
etc*); (*clock*) dar. ● vi golpear; (*go on
strike*) declararse en huelga; (*be on
strike*) estar en huelga; (*attack*) atacar; (*clock*) dar la hora. ● n (*of workers*) huelga *f*; (*attack*) ataque *m*; (*find*)
descubrimiento *m*. on ~ en huelga.
~ off, ~ out tachar. ~ up a friend-
ship trabar amistad. ~r /'straɪkǝ(r)/
n huelguista *m* & *f*

striking /'straɪkɪŋ/ a impresionante

string /strɪŋ/ n cuerda *f*; (*of lies,
pearls*) sarta *f*. pull ~s tocar todos
los resortes. ● vt (*pt* **strung**) (*thread*)
ensartar. ~ along (*fam*) engañar. ~
out extender(se). ~ed a (*mus*) de
cuerda

stringen||cy /'strɪndʒǝnsɪ/ n rigor *m*.
~t /'strɪndʒǝnt/ a riguroso

stringy /'strɪŋɪ/ a fibroso

strip /strɪp/ vt (*pt* **stripped**) desnudar; (*tear away, deprive*) quitar;
desmontar (*machine*). ● vi desnudarse. ● n tira *f*. ~ cartoon n historieta *f*

stripe /straɪp/ n raya *f*; (*mil*) galón *m*.
~d a a rayas, rayado

strip / $\sim$ light n tubo m fluorescente. $\sim$per /-ə(r)/ n artista m & f de striptease. $\sim$-tease n número m del desnudo, striptease m

strive /straıv/ vi (pt strove, pp striven). $\sim$ to esforzarse por

strode /strəud/ see stride

stroke /strəuk/ n golpe m; (in swimming) brazada f; (med) apoplejía f; (of pen etc) rasgo m; (of clock) campanada f; (caress) caricia f. ● vt acariciar

stroll /strəul/ vi pasearse. ● n paseo m

strong /strɒŋ/ a (-er, -est) fuerte. $\sim$box n caja f fuerte. $\sim$hold /'strɒŋhəuld/ n fortaleza f; (fig) baluarte m. $\sim$ language n palabras fpl fuertes, palabras fpl subidas de tono. $\sim$ly adv (greatly) fuertemente; (with energy) enérgicamente; (deeply) profundamente. $\sim$ measures npl medidas fpl enérgicas. $\sim$-minded a resuelto. $\sim$room n cámara f acorazada

stroppy /'strɒpı/ a (sl) irascible

strove /strəuv/ see strive

struck /strʌk/ see strike. $\sim$ on (sl) entusiasta de

structur|al /'strʌktʃərəl/ a estructural. $\sim$e /'strʌktʃə(r)/ n estructura f

struggle /'strʌgl/ vi luchar. $\sim$ to one's feet levantarse con dificultad. ● n lucha f

strum /strʌm/ vt/i (pt strummed) rasguear

strung /strʌŋ/ see string. ● a. $\sim$ up (tense) nervioso

strut /strʌt/ n puntal m; (walk) pavoneo m. ● vi (pt strutted) pavonearse

stub /stʌb/ n cabo m; (counterfoil) talón m; (of cigarette) colilla f; (of tree) tocón m. ● vt (pt stubbed). $\sim$ out apagar

stubble /'stʌbl/ n rastrojo m; (beard) barba f de varios días

stubborn /'stʌbən/ a terco. $\sim$ly adv tercamente. $\sim$ness n terquedad f

stubby /'stʌbı/ a (-ier, -iest) achaparrado

stucco /'stʌkəu/ n (pl -oes) estuco m

stuck /stʌk/ see stick. ● a (jammed) bloqueado; (in difficulties) en un apuro. $\sim$ on (sl) encantado con. $\sim$up (sl) presumido

stud[1] /stʌd/ n tachón m; (for collar) botón m. ● vt (pt studded) tachonar. $\sim$ded with sembrado de

stud[2] /stʌd/ n (of horses) caballeriza f

student /'stju:dənt/ n estudiante m & f

studied /'stʌdıd/ a deliberado

studio /'stju:dıəu/ n (pl -os) estudio m. $\sim$ couch n sofá m cama. $\sim$ flat n estudio m de artista

studious /'stju:dıəs/ a estudioso; (studied) deliberado. $\sim$ly adv estudiosamente; (carefully) cuidadosamente

study /'stʌdı/ n estudio m; (office) despacho m. ● vt/i estudiar

stuff /stʌf/ n materia f, sustancia f; (sl) cosas fpl. ● vt rellenar; disecar (animal); (cram) atiborrar; (block up) tapar; (put) meter de prisa. $\sim$ing n relleno m

stuffy /'stʌfı/ a (-ier, -iest) mal ventilado; (old-fashioned) chapado a la antigua

stumbl|e /'stʌmbl/ vi tropezar. $\sim$e across, $\sim$e on tropezar con. ● n tropezón m. $\sim$ing-block n tropiezo m, impedimento m

stump /stʌmp/ n cabo m; (of limb) muñón m; (of tree) tocón m. $\sim$ed /stʌmpt/ a (fam) perplejo. $\sim$y /'stʌmpı/ a (-ier, -iest) achaparrado

stun /stʌn/ vt (pt stunned) aturdir; (bewilder) pasmar. $\sim$ning a (fabulous, fam) estupendo

stung /stʌŋ/ see sting

stunk /stʌŋk/ see stink

stunt[1] /stʌnt/ n (fam) truco m publicitario

stunt[2] /stʌnt/ vt impedir el desarrollo de. $\sim$ed a enano

stupefy /'stju:pıfaı/ vt dejar estupefacto

stupendous /stju:'pendəs/ a estupendo. $\sim$ly adv estupendamente

stupid /'stju:pıd/ a estúpido. $\sim$ity /-'pıdətı/ n estupidez f. $\sim$ly adv estúpidamente

stupor /'stju:pə(r)/ n estupor m

sturd|iness /'stɜ:dınıs/ n robustez f. $\sim$y /'stɜ:dı/ a (-ier, -iest) robusto

sturgeon /'stɜ:dʒən/ n (pl sturgeon) esturión m

stutter /'stʌtə(r)/ vi tartamudear. ● n tartamudeo m

sty[1] /staı/ n (pl sties) pocilga f

sty[2] /staı/ n (pl sties) (med) orzuelo m

styl|e /staɪl/ n estilo m; (fashion) moda f. **in ~** con todo lujo. • vt diseñar. **~ish** /'staɪlɪʃ/ a elegante. **~ishly** adv elegantemente. **~ist** /'staɪlɪst/ n estilista m & f. **hair ~ist** n peluquero m. **~ized** /'staɪlaɪzd/ a estilizado

stylus /'staɪləs/ n (pl **-uses**) aguja f (de tocadiscos)

suave /swɑːv/ a (pej) zalamero

sub... /sʌb/ pref sub...

subaquatic /sʌbə'kwætɪk/ a subacuático

subconscious /sʌb'kɒnʃəs/ a & n subconsciente (m). **~ly** adv de modo subconsciente

subcontinent /sʌb'kɒntɪnənt/ n subcontinente m

subcontract /sʌbkən'trækt/ vt subcontratar. **~or** /-ə(r)/ n subcontratista m & f

subdivide /sʌbdɪ'vaɪd/ vt subdividir

subdue /səb'djuː/ vt dominar (feelings); sojuzgar (country). **~d** a (depressed) abatido; (light) suave

subhuman /sʌb'hjuːmən/ a infrahumano

subject /'sʌbdʒɪkt/ a sometido. **~ to** sujeto a. • n súbdito m; (theme) asunto m; (schol) asignatura f; (gram) sujeto m; (of painting, play, book etc) tema m. /səb'dʒekt/ vt sojuzgar; (submit) someter. **~ion** /-ʃn/ n sometimiento m

subjective /səb'dʒektɪv/ a subjetivo. **~ly** adv subjetivamente

subjugate /'sʌbdʒʊgeɪt/ vt subyugar

subjunctive /səb'dʒʌŋktɪv/ a & n subjuntivo (m)

sublet /sʌb'let/ vt (pt **sublet**, pres p **subletting**) subarrendar

sublimat|e /'sʌblɪmeɪt/ vt sublimar. **~ion** /-'meɪʃn/ n sublimación f

sublime /sə'blaɪm/ a sublime. **~ly** adv sublimemente

submarine /sʌbmə'riːn/ n submarino m

submerge /səb'mɜːdʒ/ vt sumergir. • vi sumergirse

submi|ssion /səb'mɪʃn/ n sumisión f. **~ssive** /-sɪv/ a sumiso. **~t** /səb'mɪt/ vt (pt **submitted**) someter. • vi someterse

subordinat|e /sə'bɔːdɪnət/ a & n subordinado (m). /sə'bɔːdɪneɪt/ vt subordinar. **~ion** /-'neɪʃn/ n subordinación f

subscri|be /səb'skraɪb/ vi suscribir. **~be to** suscribir (fund); (agree) estar de acuerdo con; abonarse a (newspaper). **~ber** /-ə(r)/ n abonado m. **~ption** /-rɪpʃn/ n suscripción f

subsequent /'sʌbsɪkwənt/ a subsiguiente. **~ly** adv posteriormente

subservient /səb'sɜːvjənt/ a servil

subside /səb'saɪd/ vi (land) hundirse; (flood) bajar; (storm, wind) amainar. **~nce** n hundimiento m

subsidiary /səb'sɪdɪərɪ/ a subsidiario. • n (com) sucursal m

subsid|ize /'sʌbsɪdaɪz/ vt subvencionar. **~y** /'sʌbsədɪ/ n subvención f

subsist /səb'sɪst/ vi subsistir. **~ence** n subsistencia f

subsoil /'sʌbsɔɪl/ n subsuelo m

subsonic /sʌb'sɒnɪk/ a subsónico

substance /'sʌbstəns/ n substancia f

substandard /sʌb'stændəd/ a inferior

substantial /səb'stænʃl/ a sólido; (meal) substancial; (considerable) considerable. **~ly** adv considerablemente

substantiate /səb'stænʃɪeɪt/ vt justificar

substitut|e /'sʌbstɪtjuːt/ n substituto m. • vt/i substituir. **~ion** /-'tjuːʃn/ n substitución f

subterfuge /'sʌbtəfjuːdʒ/ n subterfugio m

subterranean /sʌbtə'reɪnjən/ a subterráneo

subtitle /'sʌbtaɪtl/ n subtítulo m

subtle /'sʌtl/ a (-er, -est) sutil. **~ty** n sutileza f

subtract /səb'trækt/ vt restar. **~ion** /-ʃn/ n resta f

suburb /'sʌbɜːb/ n barrio m. **the ~s** las afueras fpl. **~an** /sə'bɜːbən/ a suburbano. **~ia** /sə'bɜːbɪə/ n las afueras fpl

subvention /səb'venʃn/ n subvención f

subver|sion /səb'vɜːʃn/ n subversión f. **~sive** /səb'vɜːsɪv/ a subversivo. **~t** /səb'vɜːt/ vt subvertir

subway /'sʌbweɪ/ n paso m subterráneo; (Amer) metro m

succeed /sək'siːd/ vi tener éxito. • vt suceder a. **~ in doing** lograr hacer. **~ing** a sucesivo

success /sək'ses/ n éxito m. **~ful** a que tiene éxito; (chosen) elegido

succession /sək'seʃn/ n sucesión f. **in ~** sucesivamente, seguidos

successive /sək'sesɪv/ a sucesivo. **~ly** adv sucesivamente

successor /sək'sesə(r)/ n sucesor m

succinct /sək'sɪŋkt/ a sucinto

succour /'sʌkə(r)/ vt socorrer. ● n socorro m

succulent /'sʌkjʊlənt/ a suculento

succumb /sə'kʌm/ vi sucumbir

such /sʌtʃ/ a tal. ● pron los que, las que; (so much) tanto. **and ~** y tal. ● adv tan. **~ a big house** una casa tan grande. **~ and ~** tal o cual. **~ as it is** tal como es. **~ like a** (fam) semejante, de ese tipo

suck /sʌk/ vt chupar; sorber (liquid). **~ up** absorber. **~ up to** (sl) dar coba a. **~er** /'sʌkə(r)/ n (plant) chupón m; (person, fam) primo m

suckle /sʌkl/ vt amamantar

suction /'sʌkʃn/ n succión f

sudden /'sʌdn/ a repentino. **all of a ~** de repente. **~ly** adv de repente. **~ness** n lo repentino

suds /sʌdz/ npl espuma f (de jabón)

sue /su:/ vt (pres p suing) demandar (for por)

suede /sweɪd/ n ante m

suet /'su:ɪt/ n sebo m

suffer /'sʌfə(r)/ vt sufrir; (tolerate) tolerar. ● vi sufrir. **~ance** /'sʌfərəns/ n. **on ~ance** por tolerancia. **~ing** n sufrimiento m

suffice /sə'faɪs/ vi bastar. **~iency** /sə'fɪʃənsɪ/ n suficiencia f. **~ient** /sə'fɪʃnt/ a suficiente; (enough) bastante. **~iently** adv suficientemente, bastante

suffix /'sʌfɪks/ n (pl -ixes) sufijo m

suffocat|e /'sʌfəkeɪt/ vt ahogar. ● vi ahogarse. **~ion** /-'keɪʃn/ n asfixia f

sugar /'ʃʊgə(r)/ n azúcar m & f. ● vt azucarar. **~bowl** n azucarero m. **lump** n terrón m de azúcar. **~y** a azucarado

suggest /sə'dʒest/ vt sugerir. **~ible** /sə'dʒestɪbl/ a sugestionable. **~ion** /-tʃən/ n sugerencia f; (trace) traza f. **~ive** /sə'dʒestɪv/ a sugestivo. **be ~ive of** evocar, recordar. **~ively** adv sugestivamente

suicid|al /su:ɪ'saɪdl/ a suicida. **~e** /'su:ɪsaɪd/ n suicidio m; (person) suicida m & f. **commit ~e** suicidarse

suit /su:t/ n traje m; (woman's) traje m de chaqueta; (cards) palo m; (jurid)

pleito m. ● vt convenir; (clothes) sentar bien a; (adapt) adaptar. **be ~ed for** ser apto para. **~ability** n conveniencia f. **~able** a adecuado. **~ably** adv convenientemente. **~case** /'su:tkeɪs/ n maleta f, valija f (LAm)

suite /swi:t/ n (of furniture) juego m; (of rooms) apartamento m; (retinue) séquito m

suitor /'su:tə(r)/ n pretendiente m

sulk /sʌlk/ vi enfurruñarse. **~s** npl enfurruñamiento m. **~y** a enfurruñado

sullen /'sʌlən/ a resentido. **~ly** adv con resentimiento

sully /'sʌlɪ/ vt manchar

sulphur /'sʌlfə(r)/ n azufre m. **~ic** /-'fjʊərɪk/ a sulfúrico. **~ic acid** n ácido m sulfúrico

sultan /'sʌltən/ n sultán m

sultana /sʌl'tɑ:nə/ n pasa f gorrona

sultry /'sʌltrɪ/ a (-ier, -iest) (weather) bochornoso; (fig) sensual

sum /sʌm/ n suma f. ● vt (pt summed). **~ up** resumir (situation); (assess) evaluar

summar|ily /'sʌmərɪlɪ/ adv sumariamente. **~ize** vt resumir. **~y** /'sʌmərɪ/ a sumario. n resumen m

summer /'sʌmə(r)/ n verano m. **~house** n glorieta f, cenador m. **~time** n verano m. **~ time** n hora f de verano. **~y** a veraniego

summit /'sʌmɪt/ n cumbre f. **~ conference** n conferencia f cumbre

summon /'sʌmən/ vt llamar; convocar (meeting, s.o. to meeting); (jurid) citar. **~ up** armarse de. **~s** /'sʌmənz/ n llamada f; (jurid) citación f. ● vt citar

sump /sʌmp/ n (mec) cárter m

sumptuous /'sʌmptjʊəs/ a suntuoso. **~ly** adv suntuosamente

sun /sʌn/ n sol m. ● vt (pt sunned). **o.s.** tomar el sol. **~bathe** /'sʌnbeɪð/ vi tomar el sol. **~beam** /sʌnbi:m/ n rayo m de sol. **~burn** /'sʌnbɜ:n/ n quemadura f de sol. **~burnt** a quemado por el sol

sundae /'sʌndeɪ/ n helado m con frutas y nueces

Sunday /'sʌndeɪ/ n domingo m. **~ school** n catequesis f

sun: ~dial /'sʌndaɪəl/ n reloj m de sol. **~down** /'sʌndaʊn/ n puesta f del sol

sundry /'sʌndrɪ/ a diversos. **all and ~** todo el mundo. **sundries** npl artículos mpl diversos

sunflower /'sʌnflaʊə(r)/ n girasol m
sung /sʌŋ/ see **sing**
sun-glasses /'sʌnglɑːsɪz/ npl gafas fpl de sol
sunk /sʌŋk/ see **sink**. ~en /'sʌŋkən/ ● a hundido
sunlight /'sʌnlaɪt/ n luz f del sol
sunny /'sʌnɪ/ a (-ier, -iest) ⟨day⟩ de sol; ⟨place⟩ soleado. **it is** ~ hace sol
sun: ~rise /'sʌnraɪz/ n amanecer m, salida f del sol. ~roof n techo m corredizo. ~set /'sʌnset/ n puesta f del sol. ~shade /'sʌnʃeɪd/ n quitasol m, sombrilla f; (awning) toldo m m. ~shine /'sʌnʃaɪn/ n sol m. ~spot /'sʌnspɒt/ n mancha f solar. ~stroke /'sʌnstrəʊk/ n insolación f. ~tan n bronceado m. ~tanned a bronceado. ~tan lotion n bronceador m
sup /sʌp/ vt (pt supped) sorber
super /'suːpə(r)/ a (fam) estupendo
superannuation /suːpərænjʊ'eɪʃn/ n jubilación f
superb /suː'pɜːb/ a espléndido. ~ly adv espléndidamente
supercilious /suːpə'sɪlɪəs/ a desdeñoso
superficial /suːpə'fɪʃl/ a superficial. ~ity /-ɪ'ælətɪ/ n superficialidad f. ~ly adv superficialmente
superfluous /suː'pɜːflʊəs/ a superfluo
superhuman /suːpə'hjuːmən/ a sobrehumano
superimpose /suːpərɪm'pəʊz/ vt sobreponer
superintend /suːpərɪn'tend/ vt vigilar. ~ence n dirección f. ~ent n director m; (of police) comisario m
superior /suː'pɪərɪə(r)/ a & n superior (m). ~ity /-'ɒrətɪ/ n superioridad f
superlative /suː'pɜːlətɪv/ a & n superlativo (m)
superman /'suːpəmæn/ n (pl -men) superhombre m
supermarket /'suːpəmɑːkɪt/ n supermercado m
supernatural /suːpə'nætʃrəl/ a sobrenatural
superpower /'suːpəpaʊə(r)/ n superpotencia f
supersede /suːpə'siːd/ vt reemplazar, suplantar
supersonic /suːpə'sɒnɪk/ a supersónico
superstition /suːpə'stɪʃn/ n superstición f. ~us a supersticioso

superstructure /'suːpəstrʌktʃə(r)/ n superestructura f
supertanker /'suːpətæŋkə(r)/ n petrolero m gigante
supervene /suːpə'viːn/ vi sobrevenir
supervis|e /'suːpəvaɪz/ vt supervisar. ~ion /-'vɪʒn/ n supervisión f. ~or /-zə(r)/ n supervisor m. ~ory a de supervisión
supper /'sʌpə(r)/ n cena f
supplant /sə'plɑːnt/ vt suplantar
supple /sʌpl/ a flexible. ~ness n flexibilidad f
supplement /'sʌplɪmənt/ n suplemento m. ● vt completar; (increase) aumentar. ~ary /-'mentərɪ/ a suplementario
suppl|ier /sə'plaɪə(r)/ n suministrador m; (com) proveedor m. ~y /sə'plaɪ/ vt proveer; (feed) alimentar; satisfacer ⟨a need⟩. ~y with abastecer de. ● n provisión f, suministro m. ~y and demand oferta f y demanda
support /sə'pɔːt/ vt sostener; (endure) soportar, aguantar; (fig) apoyar. ● n apoyo m; (tec) soporte m. ~er /-ə(r)/ n soporte m; (sport) seguidor m, hincha m & f. ~ive a alentador
suppos|e /sə'pəʊz/ vt suponer; (think) creer. **be** ~ed to deber. **not be** ~ed to (fam) no tener permiso para, no tener derecho a. ~edly adv según cabe suponer; (before adjective) presuntamente. ~ition /sʌpə'zɪʃn/ n suposición f
suppository /sə'pɒzɪtərɪ/ n supositorio m
suppress /sə'pres/ vt suprimir. ~ion n supresión f. ~or /-ə(r)/ n supresor m
suprem|acy /suː'preməsɪ/ n supremacía f. ~e /suː'priːm/ a supremo
surcharge /'sɜːtʃɑːdʒ/ n sobreprecio m; (tax) recargo m
sure /ʃʊə(r)/ a (-er, -est) seguro, cierto. **make** ~ asegurarse. ● adv (Amer, fam) ¡claro! ~ **enough** efectivamente. ~-footed a de pie firme. ~ly adv seguramente
surety /'ʃʊərətɪ/ n garantía f
surf /sɜːf/ n oleaje m; (foam) espuma f
surface /'sɜːfɪs/ n superficie f. ● a superficial, de la superficie. ● vt (smoothe) alisar; (cover) recubrir (with de). ● vi salir a la superficie;

(*emerge*) emerger. ∼ **mail** *n* por vía marítima

surfboard /'sɜːfbɔːd/ *n* tabla *f* de surf

surfeit /'sɜːfɪt/ *n* exceso *m*

surfing /'sɜːfɪŋ/ *n*, **surf-riding** /'sɜːfraɪdɪŋ/ *n* surf *m*

surge /sɜːdʒ/ *vi* (*crowd*) moverse en tropel; (*waves*) encresparse. ● *n* oleada *f*; (*elec*) sobretensión *f*

surgeon /'sɜːdʒən/ *n* cirujano *m*

surgery /'sɜːdʒərɪ/ *n* cirugía *f*; (*consulting room*) consultorio *m*; (*consulting hours*) horas *fpl* de consulta

surgical /'sɜːdʒɪkl/ *a* quirúrgico

surl|iness /'sɜːlɪnɪs/ *n* aspereza *f*. ∼**y** /'sɜːlɪ/ *a* (-**ier**, -**iest**) áspero

surmise /sə'maɪz/ *vt* conjeturar

surmount /sə'maʊnt/ *vt* superar

surname /'sɜːneɪm/ *n* apellido *m*

surpass /sə'pɑːs/ *vt* sobrepasar, exceder

surplus /'sɜːpləs/ *a & n* excedente (*m*)

surpris|e /sə'praɪz/ *n* sorpresa *f*. ● *vt* sorprender. ∼**ing** *a* sorprendente. ∼**ingly** *adv* asombrosamente

surrealis|m /sə'rɪəlɪzəm/ *n* surrealismo *m*. ∼**t** *n* surrealista *m & f*

surrender /sə'rendə(r)/ *vt* entregar. ● *vi* entregarse. ● *n* entrega *f*; (*mil*) rendición *f*

surreptitious /sʌrəp'tɪʃəs/ *a* clandestino

surrogate /'sʌrəgət/ *n* substituto *m*

surround /sə'raʊnd/ *vt* rodear; (*mil*) cercar. ● *n* borde *m*. ∼**ing** *a* circundante. ∼**ings** *npl* alrededores *mpl*

surveillance /sɜː'veɪləns/ *n* vigilancia *f*

survey /'sɜːveɪ/ *n* inspección *f*; (*report*) informe *m*; (*general view*) vista *f* de conjunto. /sə'veɪ/ *vt* examinar, inspeccionar; (*inquire into*) hacer una encuesta de. ∼**or** *n* topógrafo *m*, agrimensor *m*

surviv|al /sə'vaɪvl/ *n* supervivencia *f*. ∼**e** /-aɪv/ *vt/i* sobrevivir. ∼**or** /-ə(r)/ *n* superviviente *m & f*

susceptib|ility /səseptə'bɪlətɪ/ *n* susceptibilidad *f*. ∼**le** /sə'septəbl/ *a* susceptible. ∼**le to** propenso a

suspect /sə'spekt/ *vt* sospechar. /'sʌspekt/ *a & n* sospechoso (*m*)

suspend /sə'spend/ *vt* suspender. ∼**er** /səs'pendə(r)/ *n* liga *f*. ∼**er belt** *n* liguero *m*. ∼**ers** *npl* (*Amer*) tirantes *mpl*

suspense /sə'spens/ *n* incertidumbre *f*; (*in film etc*) suspense *m*

suspension /sə'spenʃn/ *n* suspensión *f*. ∼ **bridge** *n* puente *m* colgante

suspicion /sə'spɪʃn/ *n* sospecha *f*; (*trace*) pizca *f*

suspicious /sə'spɪʃəs/ *a* desconfiado; (*causing suspicion*) sospechoso

sustain /sə'steɪn/ *vt* sostener; (*suffer*) sufrir

sustenance /'sʌstɪnəns/ *n* sustento *m*

svelte /svelt/ *a* esbelto

SW *abbr* (*south-west*) sudoeste *m*

swab /swɒb/ *n* (*med*) tapón *m*

swagger /'swægə(r)/ *vi* pavonearse

swallow /'swɒləʊ/ *vt/i* tragar. ● *n* trago *m*. ∼ **up** tragar; consumir (*savings etc*)

swallow /'swɒləʊ/ *n* (*bird*) golondrina *f*

swam /swæm/ *see* **swim**

swamp /swɒmp/ *n* pantano *m*. ● *vt* inundar; (*with work*) agobiar. ∼**y** *a* pantanoso

swan /swɒn/ *n* cisne *m*

swank /swæŋk/ *n* (*fam*) ostentación *f*. ● *vi* (*fam*) fanfarronear

swap /swɒp/ *vt/i* (*pt* **swapped**) (*fam*) (inter)cambiar. ● *n* (*fam*) (inter) cambio *m*

swarm /swɔːm/ *n* enjambre *m*. ● *vi* (*bees*) enjambrar; (*fig*) hormiguear

swarthy /'swɔːðɪ/ *a* (-**ier**, -**iest**) moreno

swastika /'swɒstɪkə/ *n* cruz *f* gamada

swat /swɒt/ *vt* (*pt* **swatted**) aplastar

sway /sweɪ/ *vi* balancearse. ● *vt* (*influence*) influir en. ● *n* balanceo *m*; (*rule*) imperio *m*

swear /sweə(r)/ *vt/i* (*pt* **swore**, *pp* **sworn**) jurar. ∼ **by** (*fam*) creer ciegamente en. ∼**word** *n* palabrota *f*

sweat /swet/ *n* sudor *m*. ● *vi* sudar

sweat|er /'swetə(r)/ *n* jersey *m*. ∼**shirt** *n* sudadera *f*

swede /swiːd/ *n* naba *f*

Swede /swiːd/ *n* sueco *m*

Sweden /'swiːdn/ *n* Suecia *f*

Swedish /'swiːdɪʃ/ *a & n* sueco (*m*)

sweep /swiːp/ *vt* (*pt* **swept**) barrer; deshollinar (*chimney*). ∼ **the board** ganar todo. ● *vi* barrer; (*road*) extenderse; (*go majestically*) moverse majestuosamente. ● *n* barrido *m*;

(curve) curva *f*; *(movement)* movimiento *m*; *(person)* deshollinador *m*. ~ **away** *vt* barrer. ~**ing** *a* *(gesture)* amplio; *(changes etc)* radical; *(statement)* demasiado general. ~**stake** /'swiːpsteɪk/ *n* lotería *f*

sweet /swiːt/ *a* (**-er**, **-est**) dulce; *(fragrant)* fragante; *(pleasant)* agradable. **have a ~ tooth** ser dulcero. ● *n* caramelo *m*; *(dish)* postre *m*. ~**bread** /'swiːtbred/ *n* lechecillas *fpl*. ~**en** /'swiːtn/ *vt* endulzar. ~ **ener** /-ə(r)/ *n* dulcificante *m*. ~**heart** /'swiːthɑːt/ *n* amor *m*. ~**ly** *adv* dulcemente. ~**ness** *n* dulzura *f*. ~ **pea** *n* guisante *m* de olor

swell /swel/ *vt* (*pt* **swelled**, *pp* **swollen** or **swelled**) hinchar; *(increase)* aumentar. ● *vi* hincharse; *(increase)* aumentarse; *(river)* crecer. ● *a* *(fam)* estupendo. *n* *(of sea)* oleaje *m*. ~**ing** *n* hinchazón *m*

swelter /'sweltə(r)/ *vi* sofocarse de calor

swept /swept/ *see* **sweep**

swerve /swɜːv/ *vi* desviarse

swift /swɪft/ *a* (**-er**, **-est**) rápido. ● *n* *(bird)* vencejo *m*. ~**ly** *adv* rápidamente. ~**ness** *n* rapidez *f*

swig /swɪg/ *vt* (*pt* **swigged**) *(fam)* beber a grandes tragos. ● *n* *(fam)* trago *m*

swill /swɪl/ *vt* enjuagar; *(drink)* beber a grandes tragos. ● *n* *(food for pigs)* bazofia *f*

swim /swɪm/ *vi* (*pt* **swam**, *pp* **swum**) nadar; *(room, head)* dar vueltas. ● *n* baño *m*. ~**mer** *n* nadador *m*. ~**ming-bath** *n* piscina *f*. ~**mingly** /'swɪmɪŋlɪ/ *adv* a las mil maravillas. ~**ming-pool** *n* piscina *f*. ~**ming-trunks** *npl* bañador *m*. ~**suit** *n* traje *m* de baño

swindle /'swɪndl/ *vt* estafar. ● *n* estafa *f*. ~**r** /-ə(r)/ *n* estafador *m*

swine /swaɪn/ *npl* cerdos *mpl*. ● *n* *(pl* **swine)** *(person, fam)* canalla *m*

swing /swɪŋ/ *vt* (*pt* **swung**) balancear. ● *vi* oscilar; *(person)* balancearse; *(turn round)* girar. ● *n* balanceo *m*, vaivén *m*; *(seat)* columpio *m*; *(mus)* ritmo *m*. **in full** ~ en plena actividad. ~ **bridge** *n* puente *m* giratorio

swingeing /'swɪndʒɪŋ/ *a* enorme

swipe /swaɪp/ *vt* golpear; *(snatch, sl)* birlar. ● *n* *(fam)* golpe *m*

swirl /swɜːl/ *vi* arremolinarse. ● *n* remolino *m*

swish /swɪʃ/ *vt* silbar. ● *a* *(fam)* elegante

Swiss /swɪs/ *a* & *n* suizo (*m*). ~ **roll** *n* bizcocho *m* enrollado

switch /swɪtʃ/ *n* *(elec)* interruptor *m*; *(change)* cambio *m*. ● *vt* cambiar; *(deviate)* desviar. ~ **off** *(elec)* desconectar; apagar *(light)*. ~ **on** *(light)* encender; arrancar *(engine)*. ~**back** /'swɪtʃbæk/ *n* montaña *f* rusa. ~**board** /'swɪtʃbɔːd/ *n* centralita *f*

Switzerland /'swɪtsələnd/ *n* Suiza *f*

swivel /'swɪvl/ ● *vi* (*pt* **swivelled**) girar

swollen /'swəʊlən/ *see* **swell**. ● *a* hinchado

swoon /swuːn/ *vi* desmayarse

swoop /swuːp/ *vi* *(bird)* calarse; *(plane)* bajar en picado. ● *n* calada *f*; *(by police)* redada *f*

sword /sɔːd/ *n* espada *f*. ~**fish** /'sɔːdfɪʃ/ *n* pez *m* espada

swore /swɔː(r)/ *see* **swear**

sworn /swɔːn/ *see* **swear**. ● *a* *(enemy)* jurado; *(friend)* leal

swot /swɒt/ *vt/i* (*pt* **swotted**) *(schol, sl)* empollar. ● *n* *(schol, sl)* empollón *m*

swum /swʌm/ *see* **swim**

swung /swʌŋ/ *see* **swing**

sycamore /'sɪkəmɔː(r)/ *n* plátano *m* falso

syllable /'sɪləbl/ *n* sílaba *f*

syllabus /'sɪləbəs/ *n* (*pl* **-buses**) programa *m* (de estudios)

symbol /'sɪmbl/ *n* símbolo *m*. ~ **ic(al)** /-'bɒlɪk(l)/ *a* simbólico. ~**ism** *n* simbolismo *m*. ~**ize** *vt* simbolizar

symmetr|ical /sɪ'metrɪkl/ *a* simétrico. ~**y** /'sɪmətrɪ/ *n* simetría *f*

sympath|etic /sɪmpə'θetɪk/ *a* comprensivo; *(showing pity)* compasivo. ~**ize** /-aɪz/ *vi* comprender; *(pity)* compadecerse (**with** de). ~**izer** *n* *(pol)* simpatizante *m* & *f*. ~**y** /'sɪmpəθɪ/ *n* comprensión *f*; *(pity)* compasión *f*; *(condolences)* pésame *m*. **be in** ~**y with** estar de acuerdo con

symphon|ic /sɪm'fɒnɪk/ *a* sinfónico. ~**y** /'sɪmfənɪ/ *n* sinfonía *f*

symposium /sɪm'pəʊzɪəm/ *n* (*pl* **-ia**) simposio *m*

symptom /'sɪmptəm/ *n* síntoma *m*. ~**atic** /-'mætɪk/ *a* sintomático

synagogue /'sɪnəgɒg/ *n* sinagoga *f*

synchroniz|ation /sɪŋkrənaɪˈzeɪʃn/ n sincronización f. **~e** /ˈsɪŋkrənaɪz/ vt sincronizar

syncopat|e /ˈsɪŋkəpeɪt/ vt sincopar. **~ion** /-ˈpeɪʃn/ n síncopa f

syndicate /ˈsɪndɪkət/ n sindicato m

syndrome /ˈsɪndrəʊm/ n síndrome m

synod /ˈsɪnəd/ n sínodo m

synonym /ˈsɪnənɪm/ n sinónimo m. **~ous** /-ˈnɒnɪməs/ a sinónimo

synopsis /sɪˈnɒpsɪs/ n (pl **-opses** /-siːz/) sinopsis f, resumen m

syntax /ˈsɪntæks/ n sintaxis f invar

synthesi|s /ˈsɪnθəsɪs/ n (pl **-theses** /-siːz/) síntesis f. **~ze** vt sintetizar

synthetic /sɪnˈθetɪk/ a sintético

syphilis /ˈsɪfɪlɪs/ n sífilis f

Syria /ˈsɪrɪə/ n Siria f. **~n** a & n sirio (m)

syringe /ˈsɪrɪndʒ/ n jeringa f. ● vt jeringar

syrup /ˈsɪrəp/ n jarabe m, almíbar m; (treacle) melaza f. **~y** a almibarado

system /ˈsɪstəm/ n sistema m; (body) organismo m; (order) método m. **~atic** /-əˈmætɪk/ a sistemático. **~atically** /-əˈmætɪklɪ/ adv sistemáticamente. **~s analyst** n analista m & f de sistemas

T

tab /tæb/ n (flap) lengüeta f; (label) etiqueta f. **keep ~s on** (fam) vigilar

tabby /ˈtæbɪ/ n gato m atigrado

tabernacle /ˈtæbənækl/ n tabernáculo m

table /ˈteɪbl/ n mesa f; (list) tabla f. **~ of contents** índice m. ● vt presentar; (postpone) aplazar. **~cloth** n mantel m. **~-mat** n salvamanteles m invar. **~spoon** /ˈteɪblspuːn/ n cucharón m, cuchara f sopera. **~spoonful** n (pl **-fuls**) cucharada f

tablet /ˈtæblɪt/ n (of stone) lápida f; (pill) tableta f; (of soap etc) pastilla f

table tennis /ˈteɪbltenɪs/ n tenis m de mesa, ping-pong m

tabloid /ˈtæblɔɪd/ n tabloide m

taboo /təˈbuː/ a & n tabú (m)

tabulator /ˈtæbjʊleɪtə(r)/ n tabulador m

tacit /ˈtæsɪt/ a tácito

taciturn /ˈtæsɪtɜːn/ a taciturno

tack /tæk/ n tachuela f; (stitch) hilván m; (naut) virada f; (fig) línea f

de conducta. ● vt sujetar con tachuelas; (sew) hilvanar. **~ on** añadir. ● vi virar

tackle /ˈtækl/ n (equipment) equipo m; (football) placaje m. ● vt abordar (problem etc); (in rugby) hacer un placaje a

tacky /ˈtækɪ/ a pegajoso; (in poor taste) vulgar, de pacotilla

tact /tækt/ n tacto m. **~ful** a discreto. **~fully** adv discretamente

tactic|al /ˈtæktɪkl/ a táctico. **~s** /ˈtæktɪks/ npl táctica f

tactile /ˈtæktaɪl/ a táctil

tact: ~less a indiscreto. **~lessly** adv indiscretamente

tadpole /ˈtædpəʊl/ n renacuajo m

tag /tæg/ n (on shoe-lace) herrete m; (label) etiqueta f. ● vt (pt **tagged**) poner etiqueta a; (trail) seguir. ● vi. **~ along** (fam) seguir

tail /teɪl/ n cola f. **~s** npl (tailcoat) frac m; (of coin) cruz f. ● vt (sl) seguir. ● vi. **~ off** disminuir. **~-end** n extremo m final, cola f

tailor /ˈteɪlə(r)/ n sastre m. ● vt confeccionar. **~-made** a hecho a la medida. **~-made for** (fig) hecho para

tailplane /ˈteɪlpleɪn/ n plano m de cola

taint /teɪnt/ n mancha f. ● vt contaminar

take /teɪk/ vt (pt **took**, pp **taken**) tomar, coger (not LAm), agarrar (esp LAm); (contain) contener; (capture) capturar; (endure) aguantar; (require) requerir; tomar (bath); dar (walk); (carry) llevar; (accompany) acompañar; presentar para (exam); sacar (photo); ganar (prize). **~ advantage of** aprovechar. **~ after** parecerse a. **~ away** quitar. **~ back** retirar (statement etc). **~ in** achicar (garment); (understand) comprender; (deceive) engañar. **~ off** quitarse (clothes); (mimic) imitar; (aviat) despegar. **~ o.s. off** marcharse. **~ on** (undertake) emprender; contratar (employee). **~ out** (remove) sacar. **~ over** tomar posesión de; (assume control) tomar el poder. **~ part** participar. **~ place** tener lugar. **~ sides** tomar partido. **~ to** dedicarse a; (like) tomar simpatía a (person); (like) aficionarse a (thing). **~ up** dedicarse a (hobby); (occupy) ocupar; (resume) reanudar. **~ up with** trabar amistad

con. be ~n ill ponerse enfermo. ● n
presa f; (photo, cinema, TV) toma f
takings /'teikiŋz/ npl ingresos mpl
take: ~-**off** n despegue m. ~-**over** n
toma f de posesión.
talcum /'tælkəm/ n. ~ **powder** n
(polvos mpl de) talco (m)
tale /teil/ n cuento m
talent /'tælənt/ n talento m. ~**ed** a
talentoso
talisman /'tælizmən/ n talismán m
talk /tɔ:k/ vt/i hablar. ~ **about**
hablar de. ~ **over** discutir. ● n conversación f; (lecture) conferencia f.
small ~ charla f. ~**ative** a hablador.
~**er** n hablador m; (chatterbox)
parlanchín m. ~**ing-to** n represión
f
tall /tɔ:l/ a (-er, -est) alto. ~ **story** n
(fam) historia f inverosímil. **that's a**
~ **order** n (fam) eso es pedir mucho
tallboy /'tɔ:lbɔi/ n cómoda f alta
tally /'tæli/ n tarja f; (total) total m.
● vi corresponder (**with** a)
talon /'tælən/ n garra f
tambourine /tæmbə'ri:n/ n pandereta f
tame /teim/ a (-er, -est) ⟨animal⟩
doméstico; ⟨person⟩ dócil; (dull) insípido. ● vt domesticar; domar ⟨wild
animal⟩. ~**ly** adv dócilmente. ~**r**
/-ə(r)/ n domador m
tamper /'tæmpə(r)/ vi. ~ **with**
manosear; (alter) alterar, falsificar
tampon /'tæmpən/ n tampón m
tan /tæn/ vt (pt tanned) curtir
⟨hide⟩; ⟨sun⟩ broncear. ● vi ponerse
moreno. ● n bronceado m. ● a (colour) de color canela
tandem /'tændəm/ n tándem m
tang /tæŋ/ n sabor m fuerte; (smell)
olor m fuerte
tangent /'tændʒənt/ n tangente f
tangerine /tændʒə'ri:n/ n mandarina f
tangibl|e /'tændʒəbl/ a tangible. ~**y**
adv perceptiblemente
tangle /'tæŋgl/ vt enredar. ● vi
enredarse. ● n enredo m
tango /'tæŋgəʊ/ n (pl -os) tango m
tank /tæŋk/ n depósito m; (mil)
tanque m
tankard /'tæŋkəd/ n jarra f, bock m
tanker /'tæŋkə(r)/ n petrolero m;
(truck) camión m cisterna
tantaliz|e /'tæntəlaiz/ vt ator-
mentar. ~**ing** a atormentador;
(tempting) tentador

tantamount /'tæntəmaunt/ a. ~ **to**
equivalente a
tantrum /'tæntrəm/ n rabieta f
tap¹ /tæp/ n grifo m. **on** ~ disponible. ● vt explotar ⟨resources⟩;
interceptar ⟨phone⟩
tap² /tæp/ n (knock) golpe m ligero.
● vt (pt **tapped**) golpear ligeramente. ~-**dance** n zapateado m
tape /teip/ n cinta f. ● vt atar con
cinta; (record) grabar. **have sth** ~**d**
(sl) comprender perfectamente. ~-
measure n cinta f métrica
taper /'teipə(r)/ n bujía f. ● vt ahu-
sar. ● vi ahusarse. ~ **off** disminuir
tape: ~ **recorder** n magnetófon m,
magnetófono m. ~ **recording** n
grabación f
tapestry /'tæpistri/ n tapicería f;
(product) tapiz m
tapioca /tæpi'əʊkə/ n tapioca f
tar /tɑ:(r)/ n alquitrán m. ● vt (pt
tarred) alquitranar
tard|ily /'tɑ:dili/ adv lentamente;
(late) tardíamente. ~**y** /'tɑ:di/ a
(-ier, -iest) (slow) lento; (late) tardío
target /'tɑ:git/ n blanco m; (fig) objetivo m
tariff /'tærif/ n tarifa f
tarmac /'tɑ:mæk/ n pista f de aterrizaje. **T**~n (P) macadán m
tarnish /'tɑ:niʃ/ vt deslustrar. ● vi
deslustrarse
tarpaulin /tɑ:'pɔ:lin/ n alquitranado
m
tarragon /'tærəgən/ n estragón m
tart¹ /tɑ:t/ n pastel m; (individual)
pastelillo m
tart² /tɑ:t/ n (sl, woman) prostituta f,
fulana f (fam). ● vt. ~ **o.s. up** (fam)
engalanarse
tart³ /tɑ:t/ a (-er, -est) ácido; (fig)
áspero
tartan /'tɑ:tn/ n tartán m, tela f
escocesa
tartar /'tɑ:tə(r)/ n tártaro m. ~
sauce n salsa f tártara
task /tɑ:sk/ n tarea f. **take to** ~
reprender. ~ **force** n destacamiento
m especial
tassel /'tæsl/ n borla f
taste /teist/ n sabor m, gusto m;
(small quantity) poquito m. ● vt probar. ● vi. ~**e** of saber a. ~**eful** a de
buen gusto. ~**eless** a soso; (fig) de
mal gusto. ~**y** a (-ier, -iest) sabroso
tat /tæt/ see **tit**²

tatter|ed /'tætəd/ a hecho jirones. **~s** /'tætəz/ npl andrajos mpl

tattle /'tætl/ vi charlar. ● n charla f

tattoo¹ /tə'tu:/ (mil) espectáculo m militar

tattoo² /tə'tu:/ vt tatuar. ● n tatuaje m

tatty /'tætɪ/ a (-ier, -iest) gastado, en mal estado

taught /tɔ:t/ see **teach**

taunt /tɔ:nt/ vt mofarse de. ~ **s.o. with sth** echar algo en cara a uno. ● n mofa f

Taurus /'tɔ:rəs/ n (astr) Tauro m

taut /tɔ:t/ a tenso

tavern /'tævən/ n taberna f

tawdry /'tɔ:drɪ/ a (-ier, -iest) charro

tawny /'tɔ:nɪ/ a bronceado

tax /tæks/ n impuesto m. ● vt imponer contribuciones a (person); gravar con un impuesto (thing); (fig) poner a prueba. ~**able** a imponible. ~**ation** /-'seɪʃn/ n impuestos mpl. ~**-collector** n recaudador m de contribuciones. ~**-free** a libre de impuestos

taxi /'tæksɪ/ n (pl -is) taxi m. ● vi (pt taxied, pres p taxiing) (aircraft) rodar por la pista. ~ **rank** n parada f de taxis

taxpayer /'tækspeɪə(r)/ n contribuyente m & f

te /ti:/ n (mus, seventh note of any musical scale) si m

tea /ti:/ n té m. ~**-bag** n bolsita f de té. ~**-break** n descanso m para el té

teach /ti:tʃ/ vt/i (pt taught) enseñar. ~**er** n profesor m; (primary) maestro m. ~**-in** n seminario m. ~**ing** n enseñanza f. ● a docente. ~**ing staff** n profesorado m

teacup /'ti:kʌp/ n taza f de té

teak /ti:k/ n teca f

tea-leaf /'ti:li:f/ n hoja f de té

team /ti:m/ n equipo m; (of horses) tiro m. ● vi. ~ **up** unirse. ~**-work** n trabajo m en equipo

teapot /'ti:pɒt/ n tetera f

tear¹ /teə(r)/ vt (pt tore, pp torn) rasgar. ● vi rasgarse; (run) precipitarse. ● n rasgón m. ~ **apart** desgarrar. ~ **o.s. away** desgararse

tear² /tɪə(r)/ n lágrima f. **in ~s** llorando

tearaway /'teərəweɪ/ n gamberro m

tear /tɪə(r)/: ~**ful** a lloroso. ~**-gas** n gas m lacrimógeno

tease /ti:z/ vt tomar el pelo a; cardar (cloth etc). ● n guasón m. ~**r** /-ə(r)/ n (fam) problema m difícil

tea: ~**-set** n juego m de té. ~**spoon** /'ti:spu:n/ n cucharilla f. ~**spoonful** n (pl -fuls) (amount) cucharadita f

teat /ti:t/ n (of animal) teta f; (for bottle) tetilla f

tea-towel /'ti:taʊəl/ n paño m de cocina

technical /'teknɪkl/ a técnico. ~**ity** n /-'kælətɪ/ n detalle m técnico. ~**ly** adv técnicamente

technician /tek'nɪʃn/ n técnico m

technique /tek'ni:k/ n técnica f

technolog|ist /tek'nɒlədʒɪst/ n tecnólogo m. ~**y** /tek'nɒlədʒɪ/ n tecnología f

teddy bear /'tedɪbeə(r)/ n osito m de felpa, osito m de peluche

tedious /'ti:dɪəs/ a pesado. ~**ly** adv pesadamente

tedium /'ti:dɪəm/ n aburrimiento m

tee /ti:/ n (golf) tee m

teem /ti:m/ vi abundar; (rain) llover a cántaros

teen|age /'ti:neɪdʒ/ a adolescente; (for teenagers) para jóvenes. ~**ager** /-ə(r)/ n adolescente m & f, joven m & f. ~**s** /ti:nz/ npl. **the ~s** la adolescencia f

teeny /'ti:nɪ/ a (-ier, -iest) (fam) chiquito

teeter /'ti:tə(r)/ vi balancearse

teeth /ti:θ/ see **tooth**. ~**e** /ti:ð/ vi echar los dientes. ~**ing troubles** npl (fig) dificultades fpl iniciales

teetotaller /ti:'təʊtələ(r)/ n abstemio m

telecommunications /telɪkəmju:nɪ'keɪʃnz/ npl telecomunicaciones fpl

telegram /'telɪgræm/ n telegrama m

telegraph /'telɪgrɑːf/ n telégrafo m. ● vt telegrafiar. ~**ic** /-'græfɪk/ a telegráfico

telepath|ic /telɪ'pæθɪk/ a telepático. ~**y** /tɪ'lepəθɪ/ n telepatía f

telephon|e /'telɪfəʊn/ n teléfono m. ● vt llamar por teléfono. ~**e booth** n cabina f telefónica. ~**e directory** n guía f telefónica. ~**e exchange** n central f telefónica. ~**ic** /-'fɒnɪk/ a telefónico. ~**ist** /tɪ'lefənɪst/ n telefonista m & f

telephoto /telɪ'fəʊtəʊ/ a. ~ **lens** n teleobjetivo m

teleprinter /'telɪprɪntə(r)/ n teleimpresor m

telescop|e /'telɪskəʊp/ n telescopio m. ~**ic** /-'kɒpɪk/ a telescópico

televis|e /'telɪvaɪz/ vt televisar. ~**ion** /'telɪvɪʒn/ n televisión f. ~**ion set** n televisor m

telex /'teleks/ n télex m. ● vt enviar por télex

tell /tel/ vt (pt **told**) decir; contar ‹story›; (distinguish) distinguir. ● vi (produce an effect) tener efecto; (know) saber. ~ **off** vt reprender. ~**er** /'telə(r)/ n (in bank) cajero m

telling /'telɪŋ/ a eficaz

tell-tale /'telteɪl/ n soplón m. ● a revelador

telly /'telɪ/ n (fam) televisión f, tele f (fam)

temerity /tɪ'merətɪ/ n temeridad f

temp /temp/ n (fam) empleado m temporal

temper /'tempə(r)/ n (disposition) disposición f; (mood) humor m; (fit of anger) cólera f; (of metal) temple m. **be in a** ~ estar de mal humor. **keep one's** ~ contenerse. **lose one's** ~ enfadarse, perder la paciencia. ● vt templar ‹metal›

temperament /'temprəmənt/ n temperamento m. ~**al** /-'mentl/ a caprichoso

temperance /'tempərəns/ n moderación f

temperate /'tempərət/ a moderado; ‹climate› templado

temperature /'temprɪtʃə(r)/ n temperatura f. **have a** ~ tener fiebre

tempest /'tempɪst/ n tempestad f. ~**uous** /-'pestjʊəs/ a tempestuoso

temple¹ /'templ/ n templo m

temple² /'templ/ (anat) sien f

tempo /'tempəʊ/ n (pl **-os** or **tempi**) ritmo m

temporar|ily /'tempərərəlɪ/ adv temporalmente. ~**y** /'tempərɪ/ a temporal, provisional

tempt /tempt/ vt tentar. ~ **s.o. to** inducir a uno a. ~**ation** /-'teɪʃn/ n tentación f. ~**ing** a tentador

ten /ten/ a & n diez (m)

tenable /'tenəbl/ a sostenible

tenaci|ous /tɪ'neɪʃəs/ a tenaz. ~**ty** /-'æsətɪ/ n tenacidad f

tenan|cy /'tenənsɪ/ n alquiler m. ~**t** /'tenənt/ n inquilino m

tend¹ /tend/ vi. ~ **to** tener tendencia a

tend² /tend/ vt cuidar

tendency /'tendənsɪ/ n tendencia f

tender¹ /'tendə(r)/ a tierno; (painful) dolorido

tender² /'tendə(r)/ n (com) oferta f. **legal** ~ n curso m legal. ● vt ofrecer, presentar

tender: ~ly adv tiernamente. ~**ness** n ternura f

tendon /'tendən/ n tendón m

tenement /'tenəmənt/ n vivienda f

tenet /'tenɪt/ n principio m

tenfold /'tenfəʊld/ a diez veces mayor, décuplo. ● adv diez veces

tenner /'tenə(r)/ n (fam) billete m de diez libras

tennis /'tenɪs/ n tenis m

tenor /'tenə(r)/ n tenor m

tens|e /tens/ a (**-er**, **-est**) tieso; (fig) tenso. ● n (gram) tiempo m. ● vi. ~ **up** tensarse. ~**eness** n, ~**ion** /'tenʃn/ n tensión f

tent /tent/ n tienda f, carpa f (LAm)

tentacle /'tentəkl/ n tentáculo m

tentative /'tentətɪv/ a provisional; (hesitant) indeciso. ~**ly** adv provisionalmente; (timidly) tímidamente

tenterhooks /'tentəhʊks/ npl. **on** ~ en ascuas

tenth /tenθ/ a & n décimo (m)

tenuous /'tenjʊəs/ a tenue

tenure /'tenjʊə(r)/ n posesión f

tepid /'tepɪd/ a tibio

term /tɜːm/ n (of time) período m; (schol) trimestre m; (word etc) término m. ● vt llamar. ~**s** npl condiciones fpl; (com) precio m. **on bad** ~**s** en malas relaciones. **on good** ~**s** en buenas relaciones

terminal /'tɜːmɪnl/ a terminal, final. ● n (rail) estación f terminal; (elec) borne m. (air) ~ n término m, terminal m

terminat|e /'tɜːmɪneɪt/ vt terminar. ● vi terminarse. ~**tion** /-'neɪʃn/ n terminación f

terminology /tɜːmɪ'nɒlədʒɪ/ n terminología f

terrace /'terəs/ n terraza f; (houses) hilera f de casas. **the** ~**s** npl (sport) las gradas fpl

terrain /tə'reɪn/ n terreno m

terrestrial /tɪ'restrɪəl/ a terrestre

terribl|e /'terəbl/ a terrible. ~**y** adv terriblemente

terrier /'terɪə(r)/ n terrier m

terrific /tə'rɪfɪk/ a (excellent, fam) estupendo; (huge, fam) enorme. ~ally adv (fam) terriblemente; (very well) muy bien

terrify /'terɪfaɪ/ vt aterrorizar. ~ing a espantoso

territor|ial /terɪ'tɔ:rɪəl/ a territorial. ~y /'terɪtrɪ/ n territorio m

terror /'terə(r)/ n terror m. ~ism /-zəm/ n terrorismo m. ~ist /'terərɪst/ n terrorista m & f. ~ize /'terəraɪz/ vt aterrorizar

terse /tɜ:s/ a conciso; (abrupt) brusco

test /test/ n prueba f; (exam) examen m. ● vt probar; (examine) examinar

testament /'testəmənt/ n testamento m. New T~ Nuevo Testamento. Old T~ Antiguo Testamento

testicle /'testɪkl/ n testículo m

testify /'testɪfaɪ/ vt atestiguar. ● vi declarar

testimon|ial /testɪ'məʊnɪəl/ n certificado m; (of character) recomendación f. ~y /'testɪmənɪ/ n testimonio m

test: ~ **match** n partido m internacional. ~**tube** n tubo m de ensayo, probeta f

testy /'testɪ/ a irritable

tetanus /'tetənəs/ n tétanos m invar

tetchy /'tetʃɪ/ a irritable

tether /'teðə(r)/ vt atar. ● n. be at the end of one's ~ no poder más

text /tekst/ n texto m. ~**book** n libro m de texto

textile /'tekstaɪl/ a & n textil (m)

texture /'tekstʃə(r)/ n textura f

Thai /taɪ/ a & n tailandés (m). ~**land** n Tailandia f

Thames /temz/ n Támesis m

than /ðæn, ðən/ conj que; (with numbers) de

thank /θæŋk/ vt dar las gracias a, agradecer. ~ **you** gracias. ~**ful** /'θæŋkfl/ a agradecido. ~**fully** adv con gratitud; (happily) afortunadamente. ~**less** /'θæŋklɪs/ a ingrato. ~**s** npl gracias fpl. ~**s!** (fam) ¡gracias! ~**s to** gracias a

that /ðæt, ðət/ a (pl those) ese, aquel, esa, aquella. ● pron (pl those) ése, aquél, ésa, aquélla. ~ **is** es decir. ~'**s it!** ¡eso es! ~ **is why** por eso. is ~ **you?** ¿eres tú? like ~ así. ● adv tan. ● rel pron que; (with prep) el que, la que, el cual, la cual. ● conj que

thatch /θætʃ/ n techo m de paja. ~**ed** a con techo de paja

thaw /θɔ:/ vt deshelar. ● vi deshelarse; (snow) derretirse. ● n deshielo m

the /ðə, ði:/ def art el, la, los, las. at ~ al, a la, a los, a las. from ~ del, de la, de los, de las. to ~ al, a la, a los, a las. ● adv. all ~ better tanto mejor

theatr|e /'θɪətə(r)/ n teatro m. ~**ical** /-'ætrɪkl/ a teatral

theft /θeft/ n hurto m

their /ðeə(r)/ a sus, sus

theirs /ðeəz/ poss pron (el) suyo, (la) suya, (los) suyos, (las) suyas

them /ðem, ðəm/ pron (accusative) los, las; (dative) les; (after prep) ellos, ellas

theme /θi:m/ n tema m. ~ **song** n motivo m principal

themselves /ðəm'selvz/ pron ellos mismos, ellas mismas; (reflexive) se; (after prep) sí mismos, sí mismas

then /ðen/ adv entonces; (next) luego, después. **by** ~ para entonces. **now and** ~ de vez en cuando. **since** ~ desde entonces. ● a de entonces

theolog|ian /θɪə'ləʊdʒən/ n teólogo m. ~**y** /θɪ'ɒlədʒɪ/ n teología f

theorem /'θɪərəm/ n teorema m

theor|etical /θɪə'retɪkl/ a teórico. ~**y** /'θɪərɪ/ n teoría f

therap|eutic /θerə'pju:tɪk/ a terapéutico. ~**ist** n terapeuta m & f. ~**y** /'θerəpɪ/ n terapia f

there /ðeə(r)/ adv ahí, allí. ~ **are** hay. ~ **he is** ahí está. ~ **is** hay. ~ **it is** ahí está. **down** ~ ahí abajo. **up** ~ ahí arriba. ● int ¡vaya! ~, ~! ¡ya, ya! ~**abouts** adv por ahí. ~**after** adv después. ~**by** adv por eso. ~**fore** /'ðeəfɔ:(r)/ adv por lo tanto.

thermal /'θɜ:ml/ a termal

thermometer /θə'mɒmɪtə(r)/ n termómetro m

thermonuclear /θɜ:məʊ'nju:klɪə(r)/ a termonuclear

Thermos /'θɜ:məs/ n (P) termo m

thermostat /'θɜ:məstæt/ n termostato m

thesaurus /θɪ'sɔ:rəs/ n (pl -ri /-raɪ/) diccionario m de sinónimos

these /ði:z/ a estos, estas. ● pron éstos, éstas

thesis /'θi:sɪs/ n (pl theses /-si:z/) tesis f

they /ðeɪ/ pron ellos, ellas. ~ **say that** se dice que thick /θɪk/ a (-er, -est) espeso; (dense) denso; (stupid, fam) torpe; (close, fam) íntimo. ●adv espesamente, densamente. ●n. in the ~ of en medio de. ~en /'θɪkən/ vt espesar. ●vi espesarse

thicket/'θɪkɪt/ n matorral m

thick: ~ly adv espesamente, densamente. ~ness n espesor m

thickset /θɪk'set/ a fornido

thick-skinned /θɪk'skɪnd/ a insensible

thief/θi:f/ n (pl thieves) ladrón m

thievǀe /θi:v/ vt/i robar. ~ing a ladrón

thigh /θaɪ/ n muslo m

thimble/'θɪmbl/ n dedal m

thin /θɪn/ a (thinner, thinnest) delgado; (person) flaco; (weak) débil; (fine) fino; (sparse) escaso. ●adv ligeramente. ●vt (pt thinned) adelgazar; (dilute) diluir. ~ out hacer menos denso. ●vi adelgazarse; (diminish) disminuir

thing /θɪŋ/ n cosa f. for one ~ en primer lugar. just the ~ exactamente lo que se necesita. poor ~! ¡pobrecito! ~s npl (belongings) efectos mpl; (clothing) ropa f

think /θɪŋk/ vt (pt thought) pensar, creer. ●vi pensar (about, o en); (carefully) reflexionar; (imagine) imaginarse. ~ better of it cambiar de idea. I ~ so creo que si. ~ over vt pensar bien. ~ up vt idear, inventar. ~er n pensador m. ~-tank n grupo m de expertos

thin: ~ly adv ligeramente. ~ness n delgadez f; (of person) flaqueza f

third /θɜ:d/ a tercero. ●n tercio m, tercera parte f. ~-rate a muy inferior. T~ World n Tercer Mundo m

thirst /θɜ:st/ n sed f. ~y a sediento. be ~y tener sed

thirteen /θɜ:'ti:n/ a & n trece (m). ~tha & n decimotercero (m)

thirtǀieth /'θɜ:tɪəθ/ a & n trigésimo (m). ~y/'θɜ:tɪ/ a & n treinta (m)

this /ðɪs/ a (pl these) este, esta. ~ one éste, ésta. ●pron (pl these) éste, ésta, esto. like ~ así

thistle /'θɪsl/ n cardo m

thong /θɒŋ/ n correa f

thorn /θɔ:n/ n espina f. ~y a espinoso

thorough /'θʌrə/ a completo; (deep) profundo; (cleaning etc) a fondo; (person) concienzudo

thoroughbred /'θʌrəbred/ a de pura sangre

thoroughfare /'θʌrəfeə(r)/ n calle f. no ~ prohibido el paso

thoroughly /'θʌrəlɪ/ adv completamente

those /ðəʊz/ a esos, aquellos, esas, aquellas. ●pron ésos, aquéllos, ésas, aquéllas

though /ðəʊ/ conj aunque. ●adv sin embargo. as ~ como si

thought /θɔ:t/ see think. ●n pensamiento m; (idea) idea f. ~ful /'θɔ:tfl/ a pensativo; (considerate) atento. ~fully adv pensativamente; (considerately) atentamente. ~less /'θɔ:tlɪs/ a irreflexivo; (inconsiderate) desconsiderado

thousand /'θaʊznd/ a & n mil (m). ~tha & n milésimo (m)

thrash /θræʃ/ vt azotar; (defeat) derrotar. ~ out discutir a fondo

thread /θred/ n hilo m; (of screw) rosca f. ●vt ensartar. ~ one's way abrirse paso. ~bare /'θredbeə(r)/ a raído

threat /θret/ n amenaza f. ~en /'θretn/ vt/i amenazar. ~ening a amenazador. ~eningly adv de modo amenazador

three /θri:/ a & n tres (m). ~fold a triple. ●adv tres veces. ~some /'θri:səm/ n conjunto m de tres personas

thresh /θreʃ/ vt trillar

threshold /'θreʃhəʊld/ n umbral m

threw /θru:/ see throw

thrift /θrɪft/ n economía f, ahorro m. ~y a frugal

thrill /θrɪl/ n emoción f. ●vt emocionar. ●vi emocionarse; (quiver) estremecerse. be ~ed with estar encantado de. ~er /'θrɪlə(r)/ n (book) libro m de suspense; (film) película f de suspense. ~ing a emocionante

thrivǀe /θraɪv/ vi prosperar. ~ing a próspero

throat /θrəʊt/ n garganta f. have a sore ~ dolerle la garganta

throb /θrɒb/ vi (pt throbbed) palpitar; (with pain) dar puntadas; (fig) vibrar. ●n palpitación f; (pain) puntada f; (fig) vibración f. ~bing a (pain) punzante

throes /θrəʊz/ npl. in the ~ of en medio de

thrombosis /θrɒm'bəʊsɪs/ n thrombosis f

throne /θrəʊn/ n trono m

throng /θrɒŋ/ n multitud f

throttle /'θrɒtl/ n (auto) acelerador m. ● vt ahogar

through /θru:/ prep por, a través de; (during) durante; (by means of) por medio de; (thanks to) gracias a. ● adv de parte a parte, de un lado a otro; (entirely) completamente; (to the end) hasta el final. be ~ (finished) haber terminado. ● a (train etc) directo

throughout /θru:'aʊt/ prep por todo; (time) en todo. ● adv en todas partes; (all the time) todo el tiempo

throve /θrəʊv/ see thrive

throw /θrəʊ/ vt (pt threw, pp thrown) arrojar; (baffle etc) desconcertar. ~ a party (fam) dar una fiesta. ● n tiro m; (of dice) lance m. ~ away vt tirar. ~ over vt abandonar. ~ up vi (vomit) vomitar. ~-away a desechable

thrush /θrʌʃ/ n tordo m

thrust /θrʌst/ vt (pt thrust) empujar; (push in) meter. ● n empuje m. ~ (up)on imponer a

thud /θʌd/ n ruido m sordo

thug /θʌg/ n bruto m

thumb /θʌm/ n pulgar m. under the ~ of dominado por. ● vt hojear (book). ~ a lift hacer autostop. ~-index n uñeros mpl

thump /θʌmp/ vt golpear. ● vi (heart) latir fuertemente. ● n porrazo m; (noise) ruido m sordo

thunder /'θʌndə(r)/ n trueno m. ● vi tronar. ~ past pasar con estruendo. ~bolt /'θʌndəbəʊlt/ n rayo m. ~clap /'θʌndəklæp/ n trueno m. ~storm /'θʌndəstɔ:m/ n tronada f. ~y a con truenos

Thursday /'θɜ:zdeɪ/ n jueves m

thus /ðʌs/ adv así

thwart /θwɔ:t/ vt frustrar

thyme /taɪm/ n tomillo m

thyroid /'θaɪrɔɪd/ n tiroides m invar

tiara /tɪ'ɑ:rə/ n diadema f

tic /tɪk/ n tic m

tick[1] /tɪk/ n tictac m; (mark) señal f, marca f; (instant, fam) momentito m. ● vi hacer tictac. ● vt. ~ (off) marcar. ~ off vt (sl) reprender. ~ over vi (of engine) marchar en vacío

tick[2] /tɪk/ n (insect) garrapata f

tick[3] /tɪk/ n. on ~ (fam) a crédito

ticket /'tɪkɪt/ n billete m, boleto m (LAm); (label) etiqueta f; (fine) multa f. ~-collector n revisor m. ~-office n taquilla f

tickle /'tɪkl/ vt hacer cosquillas a; (amuse) divertir. ● n cosquilleo m. ~ish /'tɪklɪʃ/ a cosquilloso; (problem) delicado. be ~ish tener cosquillas

tidal /'taɪdl/ a de marea. ~ wave n maremoto m

tiddly-winks /'tɪdlɪwɪŋks/ n juego m de pulgas

tide /taɪd/ n marea f; (of events) curso m. ● vt. ~ over ayudar a salir de un apuro

tidings /'taɪdɪŋz/ npl noticias fpl

tid|ily /'taɪdɪlɪ/ adv en orden; (well) bien. ~iness n orden m. ~y /'taɪdɪ/ a (-ier, -iest) ordenado; (amount, fam) considerable. ● vt/i. ~y (up) ordenar. ~y o.s. up arreglarse

tie /taɪ/ vt (pres p tying) atar; hacer (a knot); (link) vincular. ● vi (sport) empatar. ● n atadura f; (necktie) corbata f; (link) lazo m; (sport) empate m. ~ in with relacionar con. ~ up atar; (com) inmovilizar. be ~d up (busy) estar ocupado

tier /tɪə(r)/ n fila f; (in stadium etc) grada f; (of cake) piso m

tie-up /'taɪʌp/ n enlace m

tiff /tɪf/ n riña f

tiger /'taɪgə(r)/ n tigre m

tight /taɪt/ a (-er, -est) (clothes) ceñido; (taut) tieso; (control etc) riguroso; (knot, nut) apretado; (drunk, fam) borracho. ● adv bien; (shut) herméticamente. ~ corner n (fig) apuro m. ~en /'taɪtn/ vt apretar. ● vi apretarse. ~-fisted a tacaño. ~ly adv bien; (shut) herméticamente. ~ness n estrechez f. ~rope /'taɪtrəʊp/ n cuerda f floja. ~s /taɪts/ npl leotardos mpl

tile /taɪl/ n (decorative) azulejo m; (on roof) teja f; (on floor) baldosa f. ● vt azulejar; tejar (roof); embaldosar (floor)

till[1] /tɪl/ prep hasta. ● conj hasta que

till[2] /tɪl/ n caja f

till[3] /tɪl/ vt cultivar

tilt /tɪlt/ vt inclinar. ● vi inclinarse. ● n inclinación f. at full ~ a toda velocidad

timber /'tɪmbə(r)/ n madera f (de construcción); (trees) árboles mpl

time /taɪm/ *n* tiempo *m*; (*moment*) momento *m*; (*occasion*) ocasión *f*; (*by clock*) hora *f*; (*epoch*) época *f*; (*rhythm*) compás *m*. ~ **off** tiempo libre. at ~s a veces. behind the ~s anticuado. **behind** ~ atrasado. **for the** ~ being por ahora. **from** ~ **to** ~ de vez en cuando. **have a good** ~ divertirse, pasarlo bien. **in a year's** ~ dentro de un año. **in no** ~ en un abrir y cerrar de ojos. **in** ~ a tiempo; (*eventually*) con el tiempo. **on** ~ a la hora, puntual. ● *vt* elegir el momento; cronometrar (*race*). ~ **bomb** *n* bomba *f* de tiempo. ~**-honoured** *a* consagrado. ~**-lag** *n* intervalo *m*

timeless /'taɪmlɪs/ *a* eterno

timely /'taɪmlɪ/ *a* oportuno

timer /'taɪmə(r)/ *n* cronómetro *m*; (*culin*) avisador *m*; (*with sand*) reloj *m* de arena; (*elec*) interruptor *m* de reloj

timetable /'taɪmteɪbl/ *n* horario *m*

time zone /'taɪmzəʊn/ *n* huso *m* horario

timid /'tɪmɪd/ *a* tímido; (*fearful*) miedoso. ~**ly** *adv* tímidamente

timing /'taɪmɪŋ/ *n* medida *f* del tiempo; (*moment*) momento *m*; (*sport*) cronometraje *m*

timorous /'tɪmərəs/ *a* tímido; (*fearful*) miedoso. ~**ly** *adv* tímidamente

tin /tɪn/ *n* estaño *m*; (*container*) lata *f*. ~ **foil** *n* papel *m* de estaño. ~ (*pt* tinned) conservar en lata, enlatar

tinge /tɪndʒ/ *vt* teñir (with de); (*fig*) matizar (with de). ● *n* matiz *m*

tingle /'tɪŋgl/ *vi* sentir hormigueo; (*with excitement*) estremecerse

tinker /'tɪŋkə(r)/ *n* hojalatero *m*. ● *vi*. ~ (**with**) jugar con; (*repair*) arreglar

tinkle /'tɪŋkl/ *n* retintín *m*; (*phone call, fam*) llamada *f*

tin ~**ned** *a* en lata. ~**ny** *a* metálico. ~**-opener** *n* abrelatas *m invar*. ~ **plate** *n* hojalata *f*

tinpot /'tɪnpɒt/ *a* (*pej*) inferior

tinsel /'tɪnsl/ *n* oropel *m*

tint /tɪnt/ *n* matiz *m*

tiny /'taɪnɪ/ *a* (-ier, -iest) diminuto

tip¹ /tɪp/ *n* punta *f*

tip² /tɪp/ *vt* (*pt* tipped) (*tilt*) inclinar; (*overturn*) volcar; (*pour*) verter ● *vi* inclinarse; (*overturn*) volcarse. ● *n̄* (*for rubbish*) vertedero *m*. ~ **out** verter

tip³ /tɪp/ *vt* (*reward*) dar una propina a. ~ **off** advertir. ● *n* (*reward*) propina *f*; (*advice*) consejo *m*

tip-off /'tɪpɒf/ *n* advertencia *f*

tipped /'tɪpt/ *a* (*cigarette*) con filtro

tipple /'tɪpl/ *vi* beborrotear. ● *n* bebida *f* alcohólica. **have a** ~ tomar una copa

tipsy /'tɪpsɪ/ *a* achispado

tiptoe /'tɪptəʊ/ *n*. **on** ~ de puntillas

tiptop /'tɪptɒp/ *a* (*fam*) de primera

tirade /taɪ'reɪd/ *n* diatriba *f*

tire /'taɪə(r)/ *vt* cansar. ● *vi* cansarse. ~**d** /'taɪəd/ *a* cansado. ~**d of** harto de. ~**d out** agotado. ~**less** *a* incansable

tiresome /'taɪəsəm/ *a* (*annoying*) fastidioso; (*boring*) pesado

tiring /'taɪərɪŋ/ *a* cansado

tissue /'tɪʃuː/ *n* tisú *m*; (*handkerchief*) pañuelo *m* de papel. ~**paper** *n* papel *m* de seda

tit¹ /tɪt/ *n* (*bird*) paro *m*

tit² /tɪt/ *n*. ~ **for tat** golpe por golpe

titbit /'tɪtbɪt/ *n* golosina *f*

titillate /'tɪtɪleɪt/ *vt* excitar

title /'taɪtl/ *n* título *m*. ~**d** *a* con título nobiliario. ~**deed** *n* título *m* de propiedad. ~**role** *n* papel *m* principal

tittle-tattle /'tɪtltætl/ *n* cháchara *f*

titular /'tɪtjʊlə(r)/ *a* nominal

tizzy /'tɪzɪ/ *n* (*sl*). **get in a** ~ ponerse nervioso

to /tuː, tə/ *prep* a; (*towards*) hacia; (*in order to*) para; (*according to*) según; (*as far as*) hasta; (*with times*) menos; (*of*) de. **give it** ~ **me** dámelo. **I don't want** ~ no quiero. **twenty** ~ **seven** (*by clock*) las siete menos veinte. ● *adv*. **push** ~, **pull** ~ cerrar. ~ **and fro** *adv* de aquí para allá

toad /təʊd/ *n* sapo *m*

toadstool /'təʊdstuːl/ *n* seta *f* venenosa

toast /təʊst/ *n* pan *m* tostado, tostada *f*; (*drink*) brindis *m*. **drink a** ~ **to** brindar por. ● *vt* brindar por. ~**er** *n* tostador *m* de pan

tobacco /tə'bækəʊ/ *n* tabaco *m*. ~**nist** *n* estanquero *m*. ~**nist's shop** *n* estanco *m*

to-be /tə'biː/ *a* futuro

toboggan /tə'bɒgən/ *n* tobogán *m*

today /tə'deɪ/ *n & adv* hoy (*m*). ~ **week** dentro de una semana

toddler /'tɒdlə(r)/ *n* niño *m* que empieza a andar

toddy /'tɒdɪ/ n ponche m

to-do /tə'du:/ n lío m

toe /təʊ/ n dedo m del pie; (of shoe) punta f. **big** ∼ dedo m gordo (del pie). **on one's** ∼**s** (fig) alerta. • vt. ∼ **the line** conformarse. ∼**-hold** n punto m de apoyo

toff /tɒf/ n (sl) petimetre m

toffee /'tɒfɪ/ n caramelo m

together /tə'geðə(r)/ adv junto, juntos; (at same time) a la vez. ∼ **with** junto con. ∼**ness** n compañerismo m

toil /tɔɪl/ vi afanarse. • n trabajo m

toilet /'tɔɪlɪt/ n servicio m, retrete m; (grooming) arreglo m, tocado m. ∼**paper** n papel m higiénico. ∼**ries** /'tɔɪlɪtrɪz/ npl artículos mpl de tocador. ∼ **water** n agua f de Colonia

token /'təʊkən/ n señal f; (voucher) vale m; (coin) ficha f. • a simbólico

told /təʊld/ see **tell**. • a. **all** ∼ con todo

tolerab|le /'tɒlərəbl/ a tolerable; (not bad) regular. ∼**y** adv pasablemente

toleran|ce /'tɒlərəns/ n tolerancia f. ∼**t** /'tɒlərənt/ a tolerante. ∼**tly** adv con tolerancia

tolerate /'tɒləreɪt/ vt tolerar

toll[1] /təʊl/ n peaje m. **death** ∼ número m de muertos. **take a heavy** ∼ dejar muchas víctimas

toll[2] /təʊl/ vi doblar, tocar a muerto

tom /tɒm/ n gato m (macho)

tomato /tə'mɑːtəʊ/ n (pl ∼**oes**) tomate m

tomb /tu:m/ n tumba f, sepulcro m

tomboy /'tɒmbɔɪ/ n marimacho m

tombstone /'tu:mstəʊn/ n lápida f sepulcral

tom-cat /'tɒmkæt/ n gato m (macho)

tome /təʊm/ n librote m

tomfoolery /tɒm'fu:lərɪ/ n payasadas fpl, tonterías fpl

tomorrow /tə'mɒrəʊ/ n & adv mañana (f). **see you** ∼! ¡hasta mañana!

ton /tʌn/ n tonelada f (= 1,016 kg). ∼**s of** (fam) montones de. **metric** ∼ tonelada f (métrica) (= 1,000 kg)

tone /təʊn/ n tono m. • vt. ∼ **down** atenuar. ∼ **up** tonificar (muscles). • vi. ∼ **in** armonizar. ∼**-deaf** a que no tiene buen oído

tongs /tɒŋz/ npl tenazas fpl; (for hair, sugar) tenacillas fpl

tongue /tʌŋ/ n lengua f. ∼ **in cheek** adv irónicamente. ∼**-tied** a mudo.

tonic /'tɒnɪk/ a tónico. • n (tonic water) tónica f; (med, fig) tónico m. ∼ **water** n tónica f

tonight /tə'naɪt/ adv & n esta noche (f); (evening) esta tarde (f)

tonne /tʌn/ n tonelada f (métrica)

tonsil /'tɒnsl/ n amígdala f. ∼**itis** /-'laɪtɪs/ n amigdalitis f

too /tu:/ adv demasiado; (also) también. ∼ **many** a demasiados. ∼ **much** a & adv demasiado

took /tʊk/ see **take**

tool /tu:l/ n herramienta f. ∼**-bag** n bolsa f de herramientas

toot /tu:t/ n bocinazo m. • vi tocar la bocina

tooth /tu:θ/ n (pl **teeth**) diente m; (molar) muela f. ∼**ache** /'tu:θeɪk/ n dolor m de muelas. ∼**brush** /'tu:θbrʌʃ/ n cepillo m de dientes. ∼**comb** /'tu:θkəʊm/ n peine m de púa fina. ∼**less** a desdentado, sin dientes. ∼**paste** /'tu:θpeɪst/ n pasta f dentífrica. ∼**pick** /'tu:θpɪk/ n palillo m de dientes

top[1] /tɒp/ n cima f; (upper part) parte f de arriba; (upper surface) superficie f; (lid, of bottle) tapa f; (of list) cabeza f. **from** ∼ **to bottom** de arriba abajo. **on** ∼ **(of)** encima de; (besides) además. • a más alto; (in rank) superior, principal; (maximum) máximo. ∼ **floor** n último piso m. • vt (pt **topped**) cubrir; (exceed) exceder. ∼ **up** vt llenar

top[2] /tɒp/ n (toy) trompa f, peonza f

top[3] ∼ **hat** n chistera f. ∼**-heavy** a más pesado arriba que abajo

topic /'tɒpɪk/ n tema m. ∼**al** /'tɒpɪkl/ a de actualidad

top[4] ∼**less** /'tɒplɪs/ a (bather) con los senos desnudos. ∼**most** /'tɒpməʊst/ a (el) más alto. ∼**-notch** a (fam) excelente

topography /tə'pɒgrəfɪ/ n topografía f

topple /'tɒpl/ vi derribar; (overturn) volcar

top secret /tɒp'si:krɪt/ a sumamente secreto

topsy-turvy /tɒpsɪ'tɜ:vɪ/ adv & a patas arriba

torch /tɔ:tʃ/ n lámpara f de bolsillo; (flaming) antorcha f

tore /tɔ:(r)/ see **tear**

toreador /'tɒrɪədɔ:(r)/ n torero m

torment /'tɔːment/ n tormento m. /tɔːˈment/ vt atormentar

torn /tɔːn/ see **tear**

tornado /tɔːˈneɪdəʊ/ n (pl -oes) tornado m

torpedo /tɔːˈpiːdəʊ/ n (pl -oes) torpedo m. ● vt torpedear

torpor /'tɔːpə(r)/ n apatía f

torrent /'tɒrənt/ n torrente m. ~ial /təˈrenʃl/ a torrencial

torrid /'tɒrɪd/ a tórrido

torso /'tɔːsəʊ/ n (pl -os) torso m

tortoise /'tɔːtəs/ n tortuga f. ~shell n carey m

tortuous /'tɔːtjʊəs/ a tortuoso

torture /'tɔːtʃə(r)/ n tortura f, tormento m. ● vt atormentar. ~r /-ə(r)/ n atormentador m, verdugo m

Tory /'tɔːrɪ/ a & n (fam) conservador (m)

toss /tɒs/ vt echar; (shake) sacudir. ● vi agitarse. ~ and turn (in bed) revolverse. ~ up echar a cara o cruz

tot[1] /tɒt/ n nene m; (of liquor, fam) trago m

tot[2] /tɒt/ vt (pt totted). ~ up (fam) sumar

total /'təʊtl/ a & n total (m). ● vt (pt totalled) sumar

totalitarian /təʊtælɪˈteərɪən/ a totalitario

total: ~ity /təʊˈtælətɪ/ n totalidad f. ~ly adv totalmente

totter /'tɒtə(r)/ vi tambalearse. ~y a inseguro

touch /tʌtʃ/ vt tocar; (reach) alcanzar; (move) conmover. ● vi tocarse. ● n toque m; (sense) tacto m; (contact) contacto m; (trace) pizca f. **get in** ~ **with** ponerse en contacto con. ~ **down** ⟨aircraft⟩ aterrizar. ~ **off** disparar ⟨gun⟩; (fig) desencadenar. ~ **on** tratar levemente. ~ **up** retocar. ~-**and-go** a incierto, dudoso

touching /'tʌtʃɪŋ/ a conmovedor

touchstone /'tʌtʃstəʊn/ n (fig) piedra f de toque

touchy /'tʌtʃɪ/ a quisquilloso

tough /tʌf/ a (-er, -est) duro; (strong) fuerte, resistente. ~**en** /'tʌfn/ vt endurecer. ~**ness** n dureza f; (strength) resistencia f

toupee /'tuːpeɪ/ n postizo m, tupé m

tour /tʊə(r)/ n viaje m; (visit) visita f; (excursion) excursión f; (by team etc) gira f. ● vt recorrer; (visit) visitar

tourism /'tʊərɪzəm/ n turismo m. ~t /'tʊərɪst/ n turista m & f. ● a turístico. ~t **office** n oficina f de turismo

tournament /'tɔːnəmənt/ n torneo m

tousle /'taʊzl/ vt despeinar

tout /taʊt/ vi. ~ (for) solicitar. ● n solicitador m

tow /təʊ/ vt remolcar. ● n remolque m. **on** ~ a remolque. **with his family in** ~ (fam) acompañado por su familia

toward(s) /təˈwɔːd(z)/ prep hacia

towel /'taʊəl/ n toalla f. ~**ling** n (fabric) toalla f

tower /'taʊə(r)/ n torre f. ● vi. ~ **above** dominar. ~**block** n edificio m alto. ~**ing** a altísimo; (rage) violento

town /taʊn/ n ciudad f, pueblo m. **go to** ~ (fam) no escatimar dinero. ~ **hall** n ayuntamiento m. ~ **planning** n urbanismo m

tow-path /'təʊpɑːθ/ n camino m de sirga

toxic /'tɒksɪk/ a tóxico. ~n /'tɒksɪn/ n toxina f

toy /tɔɪ/ n juguete m. ● vi. ~ **with** jugar con ⟨object⟩; acariciar ⟨idea⟩. ~**shop** n juguetería f

trace /treɪs/ n huella f; (small amount) pizca f. ● vt seguir la pista de; (draw) dibujar; (with tracingpaper) calcar; (track down) encontrar. ~**ing** /'treɪsɪŋ/ n calco m. ~**ing-paper** n papel m de calcar

track /træk/ n huella f; (path) sendero m; (sport) pista f; (of rocket etc) trayectoria f; (rail) vía f. **keep** ~ **of** vigilar. **make** ~s (sl) marcharse. ● vt seguir la pista de. ~ **down** vt localizar. ~ **suit** n traje m de deporte, chandal m

tract[1] /trækt/ n (land) extensión f; (anat) aparato m

tract[2] /trækt/ n (pamphlet) opúsculo m

traction /'trækʃn/ n tracción f

tractor /'træktə(r)/ n tractor m

trade /treɪd/ n comercio m; (occupation) oficio m; (exchange) cambio m; (industry) industria f. ● vt cambiar. ● vi comerciar. ~ **in** (give in part-exchange) dar como parte del pago. ~ **on** aprovecharse de. ~ **mark** n marca f registrada. ~**r** /-ə(r)/ n comerciante m & f. ~**sman** /'treɪdzmən/ n (pl -men) (shopkeeper) tendero m. ~ **union** n sindicato m. ~ **unionist** n sindicalista m & f. ~ **wind** n viento m alisio

trading /'treɪdɪŋ/ n comercio m. ~ **estate** n zona f industrial

tradition /trə'dɪʃn/ n tradición f. ~al a tradicional. ~alist n tradicionalista m & f. ~ally adv tradicionalmente

traffic /'træfɪk/ n tráfico m. ● vi (pt **trafficked**) comerciar (in en). ~**lights** npl semáforo m. ~ **warden** n guardia m, controlador m de tráfico

trag|edy /'trædʒɪdɪ/ n tragedia f. ~**ic** /'trædʒɪk/ a trágico. ~**ically** adv trágicamente

trail /treɪl/ vi arrastrarse; (lag) rezagarse. ● vt (track) seguir la pista de. ● n estela f; (track) pista f. (path) sendero m. ~**er** /'treɪlə(r)/ n remolque m; (film) avance m

train /treɪn/ n tren m; (of dress) cola f; (series) sucesión f; (retinue) séquito m. ● vt adiestrar; (sport) entrenar; educar (child); guiar (plant); domar (animal). ● vi adiestrarse; (sport) entrenarse. ~**ed** a (skilled) cualificado; (doctor) diplomado. ~**ee** n aprendiz m. ~**er** n (sport) entrenador m; (of animals) domador m. ~**ers** mpl zapatillas fpl de deporte. ~**ing** n instrucción f; (sport) entrenamiento m

traipse /treɪps/ vi (fam) vagar

trait /treɪ/ n característica f, rasgo m

traitor /'treɪtə(r)/ n traidor m

tram /træm/ n tranvía m

tramp /træmp/ vt recorrer a pie. ● vi andar con pasos pesados. ● n (vagrant) vagabundo m; (sound) ruido m de pasos; (hike) paseo m largo

trample /'træmpl/ vt/i pisotear. ~ (**on**) pisotear

trampoline /'træmpəli:n/ n trampolín m

trance /trɑ:ns/ n trance m

tranquil /'træŋkwɪl/ a tranquilo. ~**lity** /-'kwɪlətɪ/ n tranquilidad f

tranquillize /'træŋkwɪlaɪz/ vt tranquilizar. ~**r** /-ə(r)/ n tranquilizante m

transact /træn'zækt/ vt negociar. ~**ion** /-ʃn/ n transacción f

transatlantic /trænzət'læntɪk/ a transatlántico

transcend /træn'send/ vt exceder. ~**ent** a sobresaliente

transcendental /trænsen'dentl/ a trascendental

transcribe /træns'kraɪb/ vt transcribir; grabar (recorded sound)

transcript /'trænskrɪpt/ n copia f. ~**ion** /-ɪpʃn/ n transcripción f

transfer /træns'fɜ:(r)/ vt (pt **transferred**) trasladar; calcar (drawing). ● vi trasladarse. ~ **the charges** (on telephone) llamar a cobro revertido. /'trænsfɜ:(r)/ n traslado m; (paper) calcomanía f. ~**able** a transferible

transfigur|ation /trænsfɪgjʊ'reɪʃn/ n transfiguración f. ~**e** /'træns 'fɪɡə(r)/ vt transfigurar

transfix /træns'fɪks/ vt traspasar; (fig) paralizar

transform /træns'fɔ:m/ vt transformar. ~**ation** /-ə'meɪʃn/ n transformación f. ~**er** /-ə(r)/ n transformador m

transfusion /træns'fju:ʒn/ n transfusión f

transgress /træns'gres/ vt traspasar, infringir. ~**ion** /-ʃn/ n transgresión f; (sin) pecado m

transient /'trænzɪənt/ a pasajero

transistor /træn'zɪstə(r)/ n transistor m

transit /'trænsɪt/ n tránsito m

transition /træn'zɪʒn/ n transición f

transitive /'trænsɪtɪv/ a transitivo

transitory /'trænsɪtrɪ/ a transitorio

translat|e /trænz'leɪt/ vt traducir. ~**ion** /-ʃn/ n traducción f. ~**or** /-ə(r)/ n traductor m

translucen|ce /trænz'lu:sns/ n traslucidez f. ~**t** /trænz'lu:snt/ a traslúcido

transmission /træns'mɪʃn/ n transmisión f

transmit /trænz'mɪt/ vt (pt **transmitted**) transmitir. ~**ter** /-ə(r)/ n transmisor m; (TV, radio) emisora f

transparen|cy /træns'pærənsɪ/ n transparencia f; (photo) diapositiva f. ~**t** /træns'pærənt/ a transparente

transpire /træn'spaɪə(r)/ vi transpirar; (happen, fam) suceder, revelarse

transplant /træns'plɑ:nt/ vt trasplantar. /'trænsplɑ:nt/ n trasplante m

transport /træn'spɔ:t/ vt transportar. /'trænspɔ:t/ n transporte m. ~**ation** /-'teɪʃn/ n transporte m

transpos|e /træn'spəʊz/ vt transponer; (mus) transportar. ~**ition** /-pə'zɪʃn/ n transposición f; (mus) transporte m

transverse /'trænzvɜːs/ a transverso

transvestite /trænz'vestaɪt/ n travestido m

trap /træp/ n trampa f. ● vt (pt **trapped**) atrapar; (jam) atascar; (cut off) bloquear. ~**door** /'træpdɔː(r)/ n trampa f; (in theatre) escotillón m

trapeze /trə'piːz/ n trapecio m

trappings /'træpɪŋz/ npl (fig) atavíos mpl

trash /træʃ/ n pacotilla f; (refuse) basura f; (nonsense) tonterías fpl. ~**can** n (Amer) cubo m de la basura. ~y a de baja calidad

trauma /'trɔːmə/ n trauma m. ~**tic** /-'mætɪk/ a traumático

travel /'trævl/ vi (pt **travelled**) viajar. ● vt recorrer. ● n viajar m. ~**ler** /-ə(r)/ n viajero m. ~**ler's cheque** n cheque m de viaje. ~**ling** n viajar m

traverse /'trævɜːs/ vt atravesar, recorrer

travesty /'trævɪstɪ/ n parodia f

trawler /'trɔːlə(r)/ n pesquero m de arrastre

tray /treɪ/ n bandeja f

treacher|ous a traidor; (deceptive) engañoso. ~**ously** adv traidoramente. ~y /'tretʃərɪ/ n traición f

treacle /'triːkl/ n melaza f

tread /tred/ vi (pt **trod**, pp **trodden**) andar. ● on pisar. ● vt pisar. ● n (step) paso m; (of tyre) banda f de rodadura. ~**le** /'tredl/ n pedal m. ~**mill** /'tredmɪl/ n rueda f de molino; (fig) rutina f

treason /'triːzn/ n traición f

treasure /'treʒə(r)/ n tesoro m. ● vt apreciar mucho; (store) guardar

treasur|er /'treʒərə(r)/ n tesorero m. ~y /'treʒərɪ/ n tesorería f. the T~y n el Ministerio m de Hacienda

treat /triːt/ vt tratar; (consider) considerar. ~ s.o. invitar a uno. ● n placer m; (present) regalo m

treatise /'triːtɪz/ n tratado m

treatment /'triːtmənt/ n tratamiento m

treaty /'triːtɪ/ n tratado m

treble /'trebl/ a triple; (clef) de sol; (voice) de tiple. ● vt triplicar. ● vi triplicarse. ● n tiple m & f

tree /triː/ n árbol m

trek /trek/ n viaje m arduo, caminata f. ● vi (pt **trekked**) hacer un viaje arduo

trellis /'trelɪs/ n enrejado m

tremble /'trembl/ vi temblar

tremendous /trɪ'mendəs/ a tremendo; (huge, fam) enorme. ~**ly** adv tremendamente

tremor /'tremə(r)/ n temblor m

tremulous /'tremjʊləs/ a tembloroso

trench /trentʃ/ n foso m, zanja f; (mil) trinchera f. ~ **coat** n trinchera f

trend /trend/ n tendencia f; (fashion) moda f. ~**-setter** n persona f que lanza la moda. ~y a (-ier, -iest) (fam) a la última

trepidation /trepɪ'deɪʃn/ n inquietud f

trespass /'trespəs/ vi. ~ on entrar sin derecho; (fig) abusar de. ~**er** /-ə(r)/ n intruso m

tress /tres/ n trenza f

trestle /'tresl/ n caballete m. ~**table** n mesa f de caballete

trews /truːz/ npl pantalón m

trial /'traɪəl/ n prueba f; (jurid) proceso m; (ordeal) prueba f dura. ~ **and error** tanteo m. **be on** ~ estar a prueba; (jurid) ser procesado

triang|le /'traɪæŋgl/ n triángulo m. ~**ular** /-'æŋgjʊlə(r)/ a triangular

trib|al /'traɪbl/ a tribal. ~**e** /traɪb/ n tribu f

tribulation /trɪbjʊ'leɪʃn/ n tribulación f

tribunal /traɪ'bjuːnl/ n tribunal m

tributary /'trɪbjʊtrɪ/ n (stream) afluente m

tribute /'trɪbjuːt/ n tributo m. **pay** ~ **to** rendir homenaje a

trice /traɪs/ n. **in a** ~ en un abrir y cerrar de ojos

trick /trɪk/ n trampa f; engaño m; (joke) broma f; (at cards) baza f; (habit) manía f. **do the** ~ servir. **play a** ~ **on** gastar una broma a. ● vt engañar. ~**ery** /'trɪkərɪ/ n engaño m

trickle /'trɪkl/ vi gotear. ~ **in** (fig) entrar poco a poco. ~ **out** (fig) salir poco a poco

trickster /'trɪkstə(r)/ n estafador m

tricky /'trɪkɪ/ a delicado, difícil

tricolour /'trɪkələ(r)/ n bandera f tricolor

tricycle /'traɪsɪkl/ n triciclo m

trident /'traɪdənt/ n tridente m

tried /traɪd/ see **try**

trifl|e /'traɪfl/ n bagatela f; (culin) bizcocho m con natillas, jalea, frutas y nata. ● vi. ~e with jugar con. ~ing a insignificante

trigger /'trɪgə(r)/ n (of gun) gatillo m. ● vt. ~ (off) desencadenar

trigonometry /trɪgə'nɒmɪtrɪ/ n trigonometría f

trilby /'trɪlbɪ/ n sombrero m de fieltro

trilogy /'trɪlədʒɪ/ n trilogía f

trim /trɪm/ a (trimmer, trimmest) arreglado. ● vt (pt trimmed) cortar; recortar ⟨hair etc⟩; ⟨adorn⟩ adornar. ● n ⟨cut⟩ recorte m; ⟨decoration⟩ adorno m; ⟨state⟩ estado m. in ~ en buen estado; ⟨fit⟩ en forma. ~ming n adorno m. ~mings npl recortes mpl; ⟨decorations⟩ adornos mpl; ⟨culin⟩ guarnición f

trinity /'trɪnɪtɪ/ n trinidad f. the T~ la Trinidad

trinket /'trɪŋkɪt/ n chuchería f

trio /'triːəʊ/ n (pl -os) trío m

trip /trɪp/ vt (pt tripped) hacer tropezar. ● vi tropezar; ⟨go lightly⟩ andar con paso ligero. ● n ⟨journey⟩ viaje m; ⟨outing⟩ excursión f; ⟨stumble⟩ traspié m. ~ up vi tropezar. ● vt hacer tropezar

tripe /traɪp/ n callos mpl; ⟨nonsense, sl⟩ tonterías fpl

triple /'trɪpl/ a triple. ● vt triplicar. ● vi triplicarse. ~ts /'trɪplɪts/ npl trillizos mpl

triplicate /'trɪplɪkət/ a triplicado. in ~ por triplicado

tripod /'traɪpɒd/ n trípode m

tripper /'trɪpə(r)/ n (on day trip etc) excursionista m & f

triptych /'trɪptɪk/ n tríptico m

trite /traɪt/ a trillado

triumph /'traɪʌmf/ n triunfo m. ● vi triunfar (over sobre). ~al /-'ʌmfl/ a triunfal. ~ant /-'ʌmfnt/ a triunfante

trivial /'trɪvɪəl/ a insignificante. ~ity /-'ælətɪ/ n insignificancia f

trod, trodden /trɒd, trɒdn/ see tread

trolley /'trɒlɪ/ n (pl -eys) carretón m. tea ~ n mesita f de ruedas. ~bus n trolebús m

trombone /trɒm'bəʊn/ n trombón m

troop /truːp/ n grupo m. ● vi. ~ in entrar en tropel. ~ out salir en tropel. ● vt. ~ing the colour saludo m a la bandera. ~er n soldado m de caballería. ~s npl ⟨mil⟩ tropas fpl

trophy /'trəʊfɪ/ n trofeo m

tropic /'trɒpɪk/ n trópico m. ~al a tropical. ~s npl trópicos mpl

trot /trɒt/ n trote m. on the ~ ⟨fam⟩ seguidos. ● vi (pt trotted) trotar. ~ out ⟨produce, sl⟩ producir

trotter /'trɒtə(r)/ n ⟨culin⟩ pie m de cerdo

trouble /'trʌbl/ n problema m; ⟨awkward situation⟩ apuro m; ⟨inconvenience⟩ molestia f; ⟨conflict⟩ conflicto m; ⟨med⟩ enfermedad f; ⟨mec⟩ avería f. be in ~ estar en un apuro. make ~ armar un lío. take ~ tomarse la molestia. ● vt ⟨bother⟩ molestar; ⟨worry⟩ preocupar. ● vi molestarse; ⟨worry⟩ preocuparse. be ~d about preocuparse por. ~maker n alborotador m. ~some a molesto

trough /trɒf/ n ⟨for drinking⟩ abrevadero m; ⟨for feeding⟩ pesebre m; ⟨of wave⟩ seno m; ⟨atmospheric⟩ mínimo m de presión

trounce /traʊns/ vt ⟨defeat⟩ derrotar; ⟨thrash⟩ pegar

troupe /truːp/ n compañía f

trousers /'traʊzəz/ npl pantalón m; pantalones mpl

trousseau /'truːsəʊ/ n (pl -s /-əʊz/) ajuar m

trout /traʊt/ n (pl trout) trucha f

trowel /'traʊəl/ n ⟨garden⟩ desplantador m; ⟨for mortar⟩ paleta f

truant /'truːənt/ n. play ~ hacer novillos

truce /truːs/ n tregua f

truck[1] /trʌk/ n carro m; ⟨rail⟩ vagón m; ⟨lorry⟩ camión m

truck[2] /trʌk/ n ⟨dealings⟩ trato m

truculent /'trʌkjʊlənt/ a agresivo

trudge /trʌdʒ/ vi andar penosamente. ● n caminata f penosa

true /truː/ a (-er, -est) verdadero; ⟨loyal⟩ leal; ⟨genuine⟩ auténtico; ⟨accurate⟩ exacto. come ~ realizarse

truffle /'trʌfl/ n trufa f; ⟨chocolate⟩ trufa f de chocolate

truism /'truːɪzəm/ n perogrullada f

truly /'truːlɪ/ adv verdaderamente; ⟨sincerely⟩ sinceramente; ⟨faithfully⟩ fielmente. yours ~ ⟨in letters⟩ le saluda atentamente

trump /trʌmp/ n ⟨cards⟩ triunfo m. ● vt fallar. ~ up inventar

trumpet /'trʌmpɪt/ n trompeta f. ~er /-ə(r)/ n trompetero m, trompeta m & f

truncated /trʌŋ'keɪtɪd/ a truncado

truncheon /'trʌntʃən/ n porra f

trundle /'trʌndl/ vt hacer rodar. ● vi rodar

trunk /trʌŋk/ n tronco m; (box) baúl m; (of elephant) trompa f. ~-call n conferencia f. ~-road n carretera f (nacional). ~s npl bañador m

truss /trʌs/ n (med) braguero m. ~ up vt (culin) espetar

trust /trʌst/ n confianza f; (association) trust m. on ~ a ojos cerrados; (com) al fiado. ● vi confiar. ~ to confiar en. ● vt confiar en; (hope) esperar. ~ed a leal

trustee /trʌs'ti:/ n administrador m

trust: ~ful a confiado. ~fully adv confiadamente. ~worthy a, ~y a digno de confianza

truth /tru:θ/ n (pl -s /tru:ðz/) verdad f. ~ful a veraz; (true) verídico. ~fully adv sinceramente

try /traɪ/ vt (pt tried) probar; (be a strain on) poner a prueba; (jurid) procesar. ~ on vt probarse (garment). ~ out vt probar. ● vi probar. ~ for vi intentar conseguir. ● n tentativa f, prueba f; (rugby) ensayo m. ~ing a difícil; (annoying) molesto. ~-out n prueba f

tryst /trɪst/ n cita f

T-shirt /'ti:ʃɜ:t/ n camiseta f

tub /tʌb/ n tina f; (bath, fam) baño m

tuba /'tju:bə/ n tuba f

tubby /'tʌbɪ/ a (-ier, -iest) rechoncho

tube /tju:b/ n tubo m; (rail, fam) metro m. inner ~ n cámara f de aire

tuber /'tju:bə(r)/ n tubérculo m

tuberculosis /tju:bɜ:kjʊ'ləʊsɪs/ n tuberculosis f

tub|ing /'tju:bɪŋ/ n tubería f, tubos mpl. ~ular a tubular

tuck /tʌk/ n pliegue m. ● vt plegar; (put) meter; (put away) remeter; (hide) esconder. ~ in vt arropar (child). ● vi. ~ in(to) (eat, sl) comer con buen apetito. ~-shop n confitería f

Tuesday /'tju:zdeɪ/ n martes m

tuft /tʌft/ n (of hair) mechón m; (of feathers) penacho m; (of grass) manojo m

tug /tʌg/ vt (pt tugged) tirar de; (tow) remolcar. ● vi tirar fuerte. ● n tirón m; (naut) remolcador m. ~-of-war n lucha f de la cuerda; (fig) tira m y afloja

tuition /tju:'ɪʃn/ n enseñanza f

tulip /'tju:lɪp/ n tulipán m

tumble /'tʌmbl/ vi caerse. ~ to (fam) comprender. ● n caída f

tumbledown /'tʌmbldaʊn/ a ruinoso

tumble-drier /tʌmbl'draɪə(r)/ n secadora f (eléctrica con aire de salida)

tumbler /'tʌmblə(r)/ n (glass) vaso m

tummy /'tʌmɪ/ n (fam) estómago m

tumour /'tju:mə(r)/ n tumor m

tumult /'tju:mʌlt/ n tumulto m. ~uous /-'mʌltjʊəs/ a tumultuoso

tuna /'tju:nə/ n (pl tuna) atún m

tune /tju:n/ n aire m. be in ~ estar afinado. be out of ~ estar desafinado. ● vt afinar; sintonizar (radio, TV); (mec) poner a punto. ● vi. ~ in (to) (radio, TV) sintonizarse. ~ up afinar. ~ful a melodioso. ~r /-ə(r)/ n afinador m; (radio, TV) sintonizador m

tunic /'tju:nɪk/ n túnica f

tuning-fork /'tju:nɪŋfɔ:k/ n diapasón m

Tunisia /tju:'nɪzɪə/ n Túnez m. ~n a & n tunecino (m)

tunnel /'tʌnl/ n túnel m. ● vi (pt tunnelled) construir un túnel en

turban /'tɜ:bən/ n turbante m

turbid /'tɜ:bɪd/ a túrbido

turbine /'tɜ:baɪn/ n turbina f

turbo-jet /'tɜ:bəʊdʒet/ n turborreactor m

turbot /'tɜ:bət/ n rodaballo m

turbulen|ce /'tɜ:bjʊləns/ n turbulencia f. ~t /'tɜ:bjʊlənt/ a turbulento

tureen /tjʊ'ri:n/ n sopera f

turf /tɜ:f/ n (pl turfs or turves) césped m; (segment) tepe m. the ~ n las carreras fpl de caballos. ● vt. ~ out (sl) echar

turgid /'tɜ:dʒɪd/ a (language) pomposo

Turk /tɜ:k/ n turco m

turkey /'tɜ:kɪ/ n (pl -eys) pavo m

Turk|ey /'tɜ:kɪ/ f Turquía f. T~ish a & n turco (m)

turmoil /'tɜ:mɔɪl/ n confusión f

turn /tɜ:n/ vt hacer girar, dar vueltas a; volver (direction, page, etc); cumplir (age); dar (hour); doblar (corner); (change) cambiar; (deflect) desviar. ~ the tables volver las tornas. ● vi girar, dar vueltas; (become) hacerse; (change) cambiar. ● n vuelta f; (in road) curva f; (change) cambio *m*; (*sequence*) turno *m*; (*of mind*) disposición *f*; (*in theatre*) número *m*; (*fright*) susto *m*; (*of illness, fam*) ataque *m*. **bad ~** mala jugada *f*. **good ~** favor *m*. **in ~** a su vez. **out of ~** fuera de lugar. **to a ~** (*culin*) en su punto. **~ against** *vt* volverse en contra de. **~ down** *vt* (*fold*) doblar; (*reduce*)bajar;(*reject*)rechazar. **~ in** *vt* entregar. **~** (*go to bed, fam*) acostarse. **~ off** *vt* cerrar 〈*tap*〉; apagar 〈*light, TV, etc*〉. • *vi* desviarse. **~ on** *vt* 〈*tap*〉; encender 〈*light etc*〉; (*attack*)atacar; (*attract, fam*) excitar. **~ out** *vt* expulsar; apagar 〈*light etc*〉; (*produce*) producir; (*empty*) vaciar. • *vi* (*result*) resultar. **~ round** *vi* dar la vuelta. **~ up** *vi* aparecer. • *vt* (*find*) encontrar; levantar 〈*collar*〉; poner más fuerte 〈*gas*〉. **~ed-up** *a* 〈*nose*〉 respingona. **~ing** /'tɜːnɪŋ/ *n* vuelta *f*; (*road*) bocacalle *f*. **~ing-point** *n* punto *m* decisivo.

turnip /'tɜːnɪp/ *n* nabo *m*

turn: **~-out** *n* (*of people*) concurrencia *f*; (*of goods*) producción *f*. **~over** /'tɜːnəʊvə(r)/ *n* (*culin*) empanada *f*; (*com*) volumen *m* de negocios; (*of staff*) rotación *f*. **~pike** /'tɜːnpaɪk/ *n* (*Amer*) autopista *f* de peaje. **~stile** /'tɜːnstaɪl/ *n* torniquete *m*. **~table** /'tɜːnteɪbl/ *n* plataforma *f* giratoria; (*on record-player*) plato *m* giratorio. **~-up** *n* (*of trousers*) vuelta *f*

turpentine /'tɜːpəntaɪn/ *n* trementina *f*

turquoise /'tɜːkwɔɪz/ *a & n* turquesa (*f*)

turret /'tʌrɪt/ *n* torrecilla *f*; (*mil*) torreta *f*

turtle /'tɜːtl/ *n* tortuga *f* de mar. **~neck** *n* cuello *m* alto

tusk /tʌsk/ *n* colmillo *m*

tussle /'tʌsl/ *vi* pelearse. • *n* pelea *f*

tussock /'tʌsək/ *n* montecillo *m* de hierbas

tutor /'tjuːtə(r)/ *n* preceptor *m*; (*univ*) director *m* de estudios, profesor *m*. **~ial** /tjuːˈtɔːrɪəl/ *n* clase *f* particular

tuxedo /tʌkˈsiːdəʊ/ *n* (*pl* -**os**) (*Amer*) esmoquin *m*

TV /tiːˈviː/ *n* televisión *f*

twaddle /'twɒdl/ *n* tonterías *fpl*

twang /twæŋ/ *n* tañido *m*; (*in voice*) gangueo *m*. • *vt* hacer vibrar. • *vi* vibrar

tweed /twiːd/ *n* tela *f* gruesa de lana

tweet /twiːt/ *n* piada *f*. • *vi* piar

tweezers /'twiːzəz/ *npl* pinzas *fpl*

twelfth /twelfθ/ *a & n* duodécimo (*m*). **~ve** /twelv/ *a & n* doce (*m*)

twentieth /'twentɪəθ/ *a & n* vigésimo (*m*). **~y** /'twentɪ/ *a & n* veinte (*m*)

twerp /twɜːp/ *n* (*sl*) imbécil *m*

twice /twaɪs/ *adv* dos veces

twiddle /'twɪdl/ *vt* hacer girar. **~ one's thumbs** (*fig*) no tener nada que hacer. **~ with** jugar con

twig[1] /twɪg/ *n* ramita *f*

twig[2] /twɪg/ *vt/i* (*pt* **twigged**) (*fam*) comprender

twilight /'twaɪlaɪt/ *n* crepúsculo *m*

twin /twɪn/ *a & n* gemelo (*m*)

twine /twaɪn/ *n* bramante *m*. • *vt* torcer. • *vi* enroscarse

twinge /twɪndʒ/ *n* punzada *f*; (*fig*) remordimiento *m* (de conciencia)

twinkle /'twɪŋkl/ *vi* centellear. • *n* centelleo *m*

twirl /twɜːl/ *vt* dar vueltas a. • *vi* dar vueltas. • *n* vuelta *f*

twist /twɪst/ *vt* torcer; (*roll*) enrollar; (*distort*) deformar. • *vi* torcerse; (*coil*) enroscarse; (*road*) serpentear. • *n* torsión *f*; (*curve*) vuelta *f*; (*of character*) peculiaridad *f*

twit[1] /twɪt/ *n* (*sl*) imbécil *m*

twit[2] /twɪt/ *vt* (*pt* **twitted**) tomar el pelo a

twitch /twɪtʃ/ *vt* crispar. • *vi* crisparse. • *n* tic *m*; (*jerk*) tirón *m*

twitter /'twɪtə(r)/ *vi* gorjear. • *n* gorjeo *m*

two /tuː/ *a & n* dos (*m*). **in ~ minds** indeciso. **~-faced** *a* falso, insincero. **~-piece** (**suit**) *n* traje *m* (de dos piezas). **~some** /'tuːsəm/ *n* pareja *f*. **~-way** *a* 〈*traffic*〉 de doble sentido

tycoon /taɪˈkuːn/ *n* magnate *m*

tying /'taɪɪŋ/ *see* **tie**

type /taɪp/ *n* tipo *m*. • *vt/i* escribir a máquina. **~cast** *a* 〈*actor*〉 encasillado. **~script** /'taɪpskrɪpt/ *n* texto *m* escrito a máquina. **~writer** /'taɪpraɪtə(r)/ *n* máquina *f* de escribir. **~written** /-ɪtn/ *a* escrito a máquina, mecanografiado

typhoid /'taɪfɔɪd/ *n*. **~** (**fever**) fiebre *f* tifoidea

typhoon /taɪˈfuːn/ *n* tifón *m*

typical /'tɪpɪkl/ *a* típico. **~ly** *adv* típicamente

typify /'tɪpɪfaɪ/ *vt* tipificar

typi|ng /'taɪpɪŋ/ n mecanografía f.
~**st** n mecanógrafo m

typography /taɪ'pɒgrəfi/ n tipografía f

tyran|nical /tɪ'rænɪkl/ a tiránico.
~**ny** /'tɪrənɪ/ n tiranía f. ~**t** /'taɪrərənt/ n tirano m

tyre /'taɪə(r)/ n neumático m, llanta f (Amer)

U

ubiquitous /ju:'bɪkwɪtəs/ a omnipresente, ubicuo

udder /'ʌdə(r)/ n ubre f

UFO /'ju:fəʊ/ abbr (unidentified flying object) OVNI m, objeto m volante no identificado

ugl|iness /ʌglɪnɪs/ n fealdad f. ~**y** /'ʌglɪ/ a (-ier, -iest) feo

UK /ju:'keɪ/ abbr (United Kingdom) Reino m Unido

ulcer /'ʌlsə(r)/ n úlcera f. ~**ous** a ulceroso

ulterior /ʌl'tɪərɪə(r)/ a ulterior. ~ motive n segunda intención f

ultimate /'ʌltɪmət/ a último; (definitive) definitivo; (fundamental) fundamental. ~**ly** adv al final; (basically) en el fondo

ultimatum /ʌltɪ'meɪtəm/ n (pl -ums) ultimátum m invar

ultra... /'ʌltrə/ pref ultra...

ultramarine /ʌltrəmə'ri:n/ n azul m marino

ultrasonic /ʌltrə'sɒnɪk/ a ultrasónico

ultraviolet /ʌltrə'vaɪələt/ a ultravioleta a invar

umbilical /ʌm'bɪlɪkl/ a umbilical. ~ cord n cordón m umbilical

umbrage /'ʌmbrɪdʒ/ n resentimiento m. take ~ ofenderse (at por)

umbrella /ʌm'brelə/ n paraguas m invar

umpire /'ʌmpaɪə(r)/ n árbitro m.
● vt arbitrar

umpteen /'ʌmpti:n/ a (sl) muchísimos. ~**th** a (sl) enésimo

UN /ju:'en/ abbr (United Nations) ONU f, Organización f de las Naciones Unidas

un... /ʌn/ pref in..., des..., no, poco, sin

unabated /ʌnə'beɪtɪd/ a no disminuido

unable /ʌn'eɪbl/ a incapaz (to de). be ~ to no poder

unabridged /ʌnə'brɪdʒd/ a íntegro

unacceptable /ʌnək'septəbl/ a inaceptable

unaccountabl|e /ʌnə'kaʊntəbl/ a inexplicable. ~**y** adv inexplicablemente

unaccustomed /ʌnə'kʌstəmd/ a insólito. be ~ to a no estar acostumbrado a

unadopted /ʌnə'dɒptɪd/ a (of road) privado

unadulterated /ʌnə'dʌltəreɪtɪd/ a puro

unaffected /ʌnə'fektɪd/ a sin afectación, natural

unaided /ʌn'eɪdɪd/ a sin ayuda

unalloyed /ʌnə'lɔɪd/ a puro

unanimous /ju:'nænɪməs/ a unánime. ~**ly** adv unánimemente

unannounced /ʌnə'naʊnst/ a sin previo aviso; (unexpected) inesperado

unarmed /ʌn'ɑ:md/ a desarmado

unassuming /ʌnə'sju:mɪŋ/ a modesto, sin pretensiones

unattached /ʌnə'tætʃt/ a suelto; (unmarried) soltero

unattended /ʌnə'tendɪd/ a sin vigilar

unattractive /ʌnə'træktɪv/ a poco atractivo

unavoidabl|e /ʌnə'vɔɪdəbl/ a inevitable. ~**y** adv inevitablemente

unaware /ʌnə'weə(r)/ a ignorante (of de). be ~ of ignorar. ~**s** /-eəz/ adv desprevenido

unbalanced /ʌn'bælənst/ a desequilibrado

unbearabl|e /ʌn'beərəbl/ a inaguantable. ~**y** adv inaguantablemente

unbeat|able /ʌn'bi:təbl/ a insuperable. ~**en** a no vencido

unbeknown /ʌnbɪ'nəʊn/ a desconocido. ~ to me (fam) sin saberlo yo

unbelievable /ʌnbɪ'li:vəbl/ a increíble

unbend /ʌn'bend/ vt (pt unbent) enderezar. ● vi (relax) relajarse. ~**ing** a inflexible

unbiased /ʌn'baɪəst/ a imparcial

unbidden /ʌn'bɪdn/ a espontáneo; (without invitation) sin ser invitado

unblock /ʌn'blɒk/ vt desatascar

unbolt /ʌn'bəʊlt/ vt desatrancar

unborn /ʌnˈbɔːn/ a no nacido todavía

unbounded /ʌnˈbaʊndɪd/ a ilimitado

unbreakable /ʌnˈbreɪkəbl/ a irrompible

unbridled /ʌnˈbraɪdld/ a desenfrenado

unbroken /ʌnˈbrəʊkən/ a (intact) intacto; (continuous) continuo

unburden /ʌnˈbɜːdn/ vt. ~ o.s. desahogarse

unbutton /ʌnˈbʌtn/ vt desabotonar, desabrochar

uncalled-for /ʌnˈkɔːldfɔː(r)/ a fuera de lugar; (unjustified) injustificado

uncanny /ʌnˈkænɪ/ a (-ier, -iest) misterioso

unceasing /ʌnˈsiːsɪŋ/ a incesante

unceremonious /ʌnserɪˈməʊnɪəs/ a informal; (abrupt) brusco

uncertain /ʌnˈsɜːtn/ a incierto; (changeable) variable. be ~ whether no saber exactamente si. ~ty n incertidumbre f

unchanged /ʌnˈtʃeɪndʒd/ a igual. ~ing a inmutable

uncharitable /ʌnˈtʃærɪtəbl/ a severo

uncivilized /ʌnˈsɪvɪlaɪzd/ a incivilizado

uncle /ˈʌŋkl/ n tío m

unclean /ʌnˈkliːn/ a sucio

unclear /ʌnˈklɪə(r)/ a poco claro

uncomfortable /ʌnˈkʌmfətəbl/ a incómodo; (unpleasant) desagradable. feel ~ no estar a gusto

uncommon /ʌnˈkɒmən/ a raro. ~ly adv extraordinariamente

uncompromising /ʌnˈkɒmprəmaɪzɪŋ/ a intransigente

unconcerned /ʌnkənˈsɜːnd/ a indiferente

unconditional /ʌnkənˈdɪʃənl/ a incondicional. ~ly adv incondicionalmente

unconscious /ʌnˈkɒnʃəs/ a inconsciente; (med) sin sentido. ~ly adv inconscientemente

unconventional /ʌnkənˈvenʃənl/ a poco convencional

uncooperative /ʌnkəʊˈɒpərətɪv/ a poco servicial

uncork /ʌnˈkɔːk/ vt descorchar, destapar

uncouth /ʌnˈkuːθ/ a grosero

uncover /ʌnˈkʌvə(r)/ vt descubrir

unctuous /ˈʌŋktjʊəs/ a untuoso; (fig) empalagoso

undecided /ʌndɪˈsaɪdɪd/ a indeciso

undeniable /ʌndɪˈnaɪəbl/ a innegable. ~y adv indiscutiblemente

under /ˈʌndə(r)/ prep debajo de; (less than) menos de; (in the course of) bajo, en. ● adv debajo, abajo. ~ age a menor de edad. ~ way adv en curso; (on the way) en marcha

under... pref sub...

undercarriage /ˈʌndəkærɪdʒ/ n (aviat) tren m de aterrizaje

underclothes /ˈʌndəkləʊðz/ npl ropa f interior

undercoat /ˈʌndəkəʊt/ n (of paint) primera mano f

undercover /ʌndəˈkʌvə(r)/ a secreto

undercurrent /ˈʌndəkʌrənt/ n corriente f submarina; (fig) tendencia f oculta

undercut /ˈʌndəkʌt/ vt (pt undercut) (com) vender más barato que

underdeveloped /ʌndədɪˈveləpt/ a subdesarrollado

underdog /ˈʌndədɒg/ n perdedor m. the ~s npl los de abajo

underdone /ʌndəˈdʌn/ a (meat) poco hecho

underestimate /ʌndərˈestɪmeɪt/ vt subestimar

underfed /ʌndəˈfed/ a desnutrido

underfoot /ʌndəˈfʊt/ adv bajo los pies

undergo /ˈʌndəgəʊ/ vt (pt -went, pp -gone) sufrir

undergraduate /ʌndəˈgrædjʊət/ n estudiante m & f universitario (no licenciado)

underground /ʌndəˈgraʊnd/ adv bajo tierra; (in secret) clandestinamente. /ˈʌndəgraʊnd/ a subterráneo; (secret) clandestino. ● n metro m

undergrowth /ˈʌndəgrəʊθ/ n maleza f

underhand /ˈʌndəhænd/ a (secret) clandestino; (deceptive) fraudulento

underlie /ʌndəˈlaɪ/ vt (pt -lay, pp -lain, pres p -lying) estar debajo de; (fig) estar a la base de

underline /ʌndəˈlaɪn/ vt subrayar

underling /ˈʌndəlɪŋ/ n subalterno m

underlying /ʌndəˈlaɪŋ/ a fundamental

undermine /ʌndəˈmaɪn/ vt socavar

underneath /ʌndəˈniːθ/ *prep* debajo de. ● *adv* por debajo

underpaid /ʌndəˈpeɪd/ *a* mal pagado

underpants /ˈʌndəpænts/ *npl* calzoncillos *mpl*

underpass /ˈʌndəpaːs/ *n* paso *m* subterráneo

underprivileged /ʌndəˈprɪvɪlɪdʒd/ *a* desvalido

underrate /ʌndəˈreɪt/ *vt* subestimar

undersell /ʌndəˈsel/ *vt* (*pt* -sold) vender más barato que

undersigned /ˈʌndəsaɪnd/ *a* abajo firmante

undersized /ʌndəˈsaɪzd/ *a* pequeño

understand /ʌndəˈstænd/ *vt/i* (*pt* -stood) entender, comprender. ∼able *a* comprensible. ∼ing /ʌndəˈstændɪŋ/ *a* comprensivo. ● *n* comprensión *f*; (*agreement*) acuerdo *m*

understatement /ʌndəˈsteɪtmənt/ *n* subestimación *f*

understudy /ˈʌndəstʌdɪ/ *n* sobresaliente *m* & *f* (en el teatro)

undertake /ʌndəˈteɪk/ *vt* (*pt* -took, *pp* -taken) emprender; (*assume responsibility*) encargarse de

undertaker /ˈʌndəteɪkə(r)/ *n* empresario *m* de pompas fúnebres

undertaking /ʌndəˈteɪkɪŋ/ *n* empresa *f*; (*promise*) promesa *f*

undertone /ˈʌndətəʊn/ *n*. in an ∼ en voz baja

undertow /ˈʌndətəʊ/ *n* resaca *f*

undervalue /ʌndəˈvæljuː/ *vt* subvalorar

underwater /ʌndəˈwɔːtə(r)/ *a* submarino. ● *adv* bajo el agua

underwear /ˈʌndəweə(r)/ *n* ropa *f* interior

underweight /ˈʌndəweɪt/ *a* de peso insuficiente. be ∼ estar flaco

underwent /ʌndəˈwent/ *see* **undergo**

underworld /ˈʌndəwɜːld/ *n* (*criminals*) hampa *f*

underwrite /ʌndəˈraɪt/ *vt* (*pt* -wrote, *pp* -written) (*com*) asegurar. ∼r /-ə(r)/ *n* asegurador *m*

undeserved /ʌndɪˈzɜːvd/ *a* inmerecido

undesirable /ʌndɪˈzaɪərəbl/ *a* indeseable

undeveloped /ʌndɪˈveləpt/ *a* sin desarrollar

undies /ˈʌndɪz/ *npl* (*fam*) ropa *f* interior

undignified /ʌnˈdɪɡnɪfaɪd/ *a* indecoroso

undisputed /ʌndɪsˈpjuːtɪd/ *a* incontestable

undistinguished /ʌndɪsˈtɪŋgwɪʃt/ *a* mediocre

undo /ʌnˈduː/ *vt* (*pt* -did, *pp* -done) deshacer; (*ruin*) arruinar; reparar (*wrong*). leave ∼ne dejar sin hacer

undoubted /ʌnˈdaʊtɪd/ *a* indudable. ∼ly *adv* indudablemente

undress /ʌnˈdres/ *vt* desnudar. ● *vi* desnudarse

undue /ʌnˈdjuː/ *a* excesivo

undulat|e /ˈʌndjʊleɪt/ *vi* ondular. ∼ion /-ˈleɪʃn/ *n* ondulación *f*

unduly /ʌnˈdjuːlɪ/ *adv* excesivamente

undying /ʌnˈdaɪɪŋ/ *a* eterno

unearth /ʌnˈɜːθ/ *vt* desenterrar

unearthly /ʌnˈɜːθlɪ/ *a* sobrenatural; (*impossible, fam*) absurdo. ∼ hour *n* hora intempestiva

uneas|ily /ʌnˈiːzɪlɪ/ *adv* inquietamente. ∼y /ʌnˈiːzɪ/ *a* incómodo; (*worrying*) inquieto

uneconomic /ʌniːkəˈnɒmɪk/ *a* poco rentable

uneducated /ʌnˈedjʊkeɪtɪd/ *a* inculto

unemploy|ed /ʌnɪmˈplɔɪd/ *a* parado, desempleado; (*not in use*) inutilizado. ∼ment *n* paro *m*, desempleo *m*

unending /ʌnˈendɪŋ/ *a* interminable, sin fin

unequal /ʌnˈiːkwəl/ *a* desigual

unequivocal /ʌnɪˈkwɪvəkl/ *a* inequívoco

unerring /ʌnˈɜːrɪŋ/ *a* infalible

unethical /ʌnˈeθɪkl/ *a* sin ética, inmoral

uneven /ʌnˈiːvn/ *a* desigual

unexceptional /ʌnɪkˈsepʃənl/ *a* corriente

unexpected /ʌnɪkˈspektɪd/ *a* inesperado

unfailing /ʌnˈfeɪlɪŋ/ *a* inagotable; (*constant*) constante; (*loyal*) leal

unfair /ʌnˈfeə(r)/ *a* injusto. ∼ly *adv* injustamente. ∼ness *n* injusticia *f*

unfaithful /ʌnˈfeɪθfl/ *a* infiel. ∼ness *n* infidelidad *f*

unfamiliar /ʌnfəˈmɪlɪə(r)/ *a* desconocido. be ∼ with desconocer unfasten /ʌnˈfɑːsn/ vt desabrochar ‹clothes›; (untie) desatar

unfavourable /ʌnˈfeɪvərəbl/ a desfavorable

unfeeling /ʌnˈfiːlɪŋ/ a insensible

unfit /ʌnˈfɪt/ a inadecuado, no apto; (unwell) en mal estado físico; (incapable) incapaz

unflinching /ʌnˈflɪntʃɪŋ/ a resuelto

unfold /ʌnˈfəʊld/ vt desdoblar; (fig) revelar. ● vi ‹view etc› extenderse

unforeseen /ʌnfɔːˈsiːn/ a imprevisto

unforgettable /ʌnfəˈgetəbl/ a inolvidable

unforgivable /ʌnfəˈgɪvəbl/ a imperdonable

unfortunate /ʌnˈfɔːtʃənət/ a desgraciado; (regrettable) lamentable. ~ly adv desgraciadamente

unfounded /ʌnˈfaʊndɪd/ a infundado

unfriendly /ʌnˈfrendlɪ/ a poco amistoso, frío

unfurl /ʌnˈfɜːl/ vt desplegar

ungainly /ʌnˈgeɪmlɪ/ a desgarbado

ungodly /ʌnˈgɒdlɪ/ a impío. ~ hour n (fam) hora f intempestiva

ungrateful /ʌnˈgreɪtfl/ a desagradecido

unguarded /ʌnˈgɑːdɪd/ a indefenso; (incautious) imprudente, incauto

unhapp|ily /ʌnˈhæpɪlɪ/ adv infelizmente; (unfortunately) desgraciadamente. ~iness n tristeza f. ~y /ʌnˈhæpɪ/ a (-ier, -iest) infeliz, triste; (unsuitable) inoportuno. ~y with insatisfecho de ‹plans etc›

unharmed /ʌnˈhɑːmd/ a ileso, sano y salvo

unhealthy /ʌnˈhelθɪ/ a (-ier, -iest) enfermizo; (insanitary) malsano

unhinge /ʌnˈhɪndʒ/ vt desquiciar

unholy /ʌnˈhəʊlɪ/ a (-ier, -iest) impío; (terrible, fam) terrible

unhook /ʌnˈhʊk/ vt desenganchar

unhoped /ʌnˈhəʊpt/ a. ~ for inesperado

unhurt /ʌnˈhɜːt/ a ileso

unicorn /ˈjuːnɪkɔːn/ n unicornio m

unification /juːnɪfɪˈkeɪʃn/ n unificación f

uniform /ˈjuːnɪfɔːm/ a & n uniforme (m). ~ity /-ˈfɔːmətɪ/ n uniformidad f. ~ly adv uniformemente

unify /ˈjuːnɪfaɪ/ vt unificar

unilateral /juːnɪˈlætərəl/ a unilateral

unimaginable /ʌnɪˈmædʒɪnəbl/ a inconcebible

unimpeachable /ʌnɪmˈpiːtʃəbl/ a irreprensible

unimportant /ʌnɪmˈpɔːtnt/ a insignificante

uninhabited /ʌnɪnˈhæbɪtɪd/ a inhabitado; (abandoned) despoblado

unintentional /ʌnɪnˈtenʃənl/ a involuntario

union /ˈjuːnjən/ n unión f; (trade union) sindicato m. ~ist m & f sindicalista m & f. U~ Jack n bandera f del Reino Unido

unique /juːˈniːk/ a único. ~ly adv extraordinariamente

unisex /ˈjuːnɪseks/ a unisex(o)

unison /ˈjuːnɪsn/ n. in ~ al unísono

unit /ˈjuːnɪt/ n unidad f; (of furniture etc) elemento m

unite /juːˈnaɪt/ vt unir. ● vi unirse. U~d Kingdom (UK) n Reino m Unido. U~d Nations (UN) n Organización f de las Naciones Unidas (ONU). U~d States (of America) (USA) n Estados mpl Unidos (de América) (EE.UU.)

unity /ˈjuːnɪtɪ/ n unidad f; (fig) acuerdo m

univers|al /juːnɪˈvɜːsl/ a universal. ~e /ˈjuːnɪvɜːs/ n universo m

university /juːnɪˈvɜːsətɪ/ n universidad f. ● a universitario

unjust /ʌnˈdʒʌst/ a injusto

unkempt /ʌnˈkempt/ a desaseado

unkind /ʌnˈkaɪnd/ a poco amable; (cruel) cruel. ~ly adv poco amablemente. ~ness n falta f de amabilidad; (cruelty) crueldad f

unknown /ʌnˈnəʊn/ a desconocido

unlawful /ʌnˈlɔːfl/ a ilegal

unleash /ʌnˈliːʃ/ vt soltar; (fig) desencadenar

unless /ʌnˈles, ənˈles/ conj a menos que, a no ser que

unlike /ʌnˈlaɪk/ a diferente; (not typical) impropio de. ● prep a diferencia de. ~lihood n improbabilidad f. ~ly /ʌnˈlaɪklɪ/ a improbable

unlimited /ʌnˈlɪmɪtɪd/ a ilimitado

unload /ʌnˈləʊd/ vt descargar

unlock /ʌnˈlɒk/ vt abrir (con llave)

unluck|ily /ʌnˈlʌkɪlɪ/ adv desgraciadamente. ~y /ʌnˈlʌkɪ/ a (-ier, -iest) desgraciado; ‹number› de mala suerte

unmanly /ʌnˈmænlɪ/ a poco viril

unmanned /ʌnˈmænd/ a no tripulado

unmarried /ʌnˈmærɪd/ a soltero. ~ mother n madre f soltera

unmask /ʌnˈmɑːsk/ vt desenmascarar. ● vi quitarse la máscara

unmentionable /ʌnˈmenʃənəbl/ a a que no se debe aludir

unmistakable /ʌnmɪˈsteɪkəbl/ a inconfundible. ~y adv claramente

unmitigated /ʌnˈmɪtɪɡeɪtɪd/ a (absolute) absoluto

unmoved /ʌnˈmuːvd/ a (fig) indiferente (by a), insensible (by a)

unnatural /ʌnˈnætʃərəl/ a no natural; (not normal) anormal

unnecessarily /ʌnˈnesəsərɪlɪ/ adv innecesariamente. ~y /ʌnˈnesəsərɪ/ a innecesario

unnerve /ʌnˈnɜːv/ vt desconcertar

unnoticed /ʌnˈnəʊtɪst/ a inadvertido

unobtainable /ʌnəbˈteɪnəbl/ a inasequible; (fig) inalcanzable

unobtrusive /ʌnəbˈtruːsɪv/ a discreto

unofficial /ʌnəˈfɪʃl/ a no oficial. ~ly adv extraoficialmente

unpack /ʌnˈpæk/ vt desempaquetar (parcel); deshacer (suitcase). ● vi deshacer la maleta

unpalatable /ʌnˈpælətəbl/ a desagradable

unparalleled /ʌnˈpærəleld/ a sin par

unpick /ʌnˈpɪk/ vt descoser

unpleasant /ʌnˈpleznt/ a desagradable. ~ness n lo desagradable

unplug /ʌnˈplʌɡ/ vt (elec) desenchufar

unpopular /ʌnˈpɒpjʊlə(r)/ a impopular

unprecedented /ʌnˈpresɪdentɪd/ a sin precedente

unpredictable /ʌnprɪˈdɪktəbl/ a imprevisible

unpremeditated /ʌnprɪˈmedɪteɪtɪd/ a impremeditado

unprepared /ʌnprɪˈpeəd/ a no preparado; (unready) desprevenido

unprepossessing /ʌnpriːpəˈzesɪŋ/ a poco atractivo

unpretentious /ʌnprɪˈtenʃəs/ a sin pretensiones, modesto

unprincipled /ʌnˈprɪnsɪpld/ a sin principios

unprofessional /ʌnprəˈfeʃənəl/ a contrario a la ética profesional

unpublished /ʌnˈpʌblɪʃt/ a inédito

unqualified /ʌnˈkwɒlɪfaɪd/ a sin título; (fig) absoluto

unquestionable /ʌnˈkwestʃənəbl/ a indiscutible. ~y adv indiscutiblemente

unquote /ʌnˈkwəʊt/ vi cerrar comillas

unravel /ʌnˈrævl/ vt (pt unravelled) desenredar; deshacer (knitting etc). ● vi desenredarse

unreal /ʌnˈrɪəl/ a irreal. ~istic a poco realista

unreasonable /ʌnˈriːzənəbl/ a irrazonable

unrecognizable /ʌnrekəɡˈnaɪzəbl/ a irreconocible

unrelated /ʌnrɪˈleɪtɪd/ a (facts) inconexo, sin relación; (people) no emparentado

unreliable /ʌnrɪˈlaɪəbl/ a (person) poco formal; (machine) poco fiable

unrelieved /ʌnrɪˈliːvd/ a no aliviado

unremitting /ʌnrɪˈmɪtɪŋ/ a incesante

unrepentant /ʌnrɪˈpentənt/ a impenitente

unrequited /ʌnrɪˈkwaɪtɪd/ a no correspondido

unreservedly /ʌnrɪˈzɜːvɪdlɪ/ adv sin reserva

unrest /ʌnˈrest/ n inquietud f; (pol) agitación f

unrivalled /ʌnˈraɪvld/ a sin par

unroll /ʌnˈrəʊl/ vt desenrollar. ● vi desenrollarse

unruffled /ʌnˈrʌfld/ (person) imperturbable

unruly /ʌnˈruːlɪ/ a indisciplinado

unsafe /ʌnˈseɪf/ a peligroso; (person) en peligro

unsaid /ʌnˈsed/ a sin decir

unsatisfactory /ʌnsætɪsˈfæktərɪ/ a insatisfactorio

unsavoury /ʌnˈseɪvərɪ/ a desagradable

unscathed /ʌnˈskeɪðd/ a ileso

unscramble /ʌnˈskræmbl/ vt descifrar

unscrew /ʌnˈskruː/ vt destornillar

unscrupulous /ʌnˈskruːpjʊləs/ a sin escrúpulos

unseat /ʌnˈsiːt/ vt (pol) quitar el escaño a

unseemly /ʌnˈsiːmlɪ/ a indecoroso

unseen /ʌnˈsiːn/ a inadvertido. ● n (translation) traducción f a primera vista

unselfish /ʌnˈselfɪʃ/ *a* desinteresado

unsettle /ʌnˈsetl/ *vt* perturbar. ~**d** *a* perturbado; *(weather)* variable; *(bill)* por pagar

unshakeable /ʌnˈʃeɪkəbl/ *a* firme

unshaven /ʌnˈʃeɪvn/ *a* sin afeitar

unsightly /ʌnˈsaɪtlɪ/ *a* feo

unskilled /ʌnˈskɪld/ *a* inexperto. ~ **worker** *n* obrero *m* no cualificado

unsociable /ʌnˈsəʊʃəbl/ *a* insociable

unsolicited /ʌnsəˈlɪsɪtɪd/ *a* no solicitado

unsophisticated /ʌnsəˈfɪstɪkeɪtɪd/ *a* sencillo

unsound /ʌnˈsaʊnd/ *a* defectuoso, erróneo. **of ~ mind** demente

unsparing /ʌnˈspeərɪŋ/ *a* pródigo; *(cruel)* cruel

unspeakable /ʌnˈspiːkəbl/ *a* indecible

unspecified /ʌnˈspesɪfaɪd/ *a* no especificado

unstable /ʌnˈsteɪbl/ *a* inestable

unsteady /ʌnˈstedɪ/ *a* inestable; *(hand)* poco firme; *(step)* inseguro

unstinted /ʌnˈstɪntɪd/ *a* abundante

unstuck /ʌnˈstʌk/ *a* suelto. **come ~** despegarse; *(fail, fam)* fracasar

unstudied /ʌnˈstʌdɪd/ *a* natural

unsuccessful /ʌnsəkˈsesfʊl/ *a* fracasado. **be ~** no tener éxito, fracasar

unsuitable /ʌnˈsuːtəbl/ *a* inadecuado; *(inconvenient)* inconveniente

unsure /ʌnˈʃʊə(r)/ *a* inseguro

unsuspecting /ʌnsəˈspektɪŋ/ *a* confiado

unthinkable /ʌnˈθɪŋkəbl/ *a* inconcebible

untid|ily /ʌnˈtaɪdɪlɪ/ *adv* desordenadamente. ~**iness** *n* desorden *m*. ~**y** /ʌnˈtaɪdɪ/ *a* (**-ier**, **-iest**) desordenado; *(person)* desaseado

untie /ʌnˈtaɪ/ *vt* desatar

until /ənˈtɪl, ʌnˈtɪl/ *prep* hasta. ● *conj* hasta que

untimely /ʌnˈtaɪmlɪ/ *a* inoportuno; *(premature)* prematuro

untiring /ʌnˈtaɪərɪŋ/ *a* incansable

untold /ʌnˈtəʊld/ *a* incalculable

untoward /ʌntəˈwɔːd/ *a* (*inconvenient*) inconveniente

untried /ʌnˈtraɪd/ *a* no probado

untrue /ʌnˈtruː/ *a* falso

unused /ʌnˈjuːzd/ *a* nuevo. /ʌnˈjuːst/ *a*. ~ **to** no acostumbrado a

unusual /ʌnˈjuːʒʊəl/ *a* insólito; *(exceptional)* excepcional. ~**ly** *adv* excepcionalmente

unutterable /ʌnˈʌtərəbl/ *a* indecible

unveil /ʌnˈveɪl/ *vt* descubrir; *(disclose)* revelar

unwanted /ʌnˈwɒntɪd/ *a* superfluo; *(child)* no deseado

unwarranted /ʌnˈwɒrəntɪd/ *a* injustificada

unwelcome /ʌnˈwelkəm/ *a* desagradable; *(guest)* inoportuno

unwell /ʌnˈwel/ *a* indispuesto

unwieldy /ʌnˈwiːldɪ/ *a* difícil de manejar

unwilling /ʌnˈwɪlɪŋ/ *a* no dispuesto. **be ~** no querer. ~**ly** *adv* de mala gana

unwind /ʌnˈwaɪnd/ *vt* (*pt* **unwound**) desenvolver. ● *vi* desenvolverse; *(relax, fam)* relajarse

unwise /ʌnˈwaɪz/ *a* imprudente

unwitting /ʌnˈwɪtɪŋ/ *a* inconsciente; *(involuntary)* involuntario. ~**ly** *adv* involuntariamente

unworthy /ʌnˈwɜːðɪ/ *a* indigno

unwrap /ʌnˈræp/ *vt* (*pt* **unwrapped**) desenvolver, deshacer

unwritten /ʌnˈrɪtn/ *a* no escrito; *(agreement)* tácito

up /ʌp/ *adv* arriba; *(upwards)* hacia arriba; *(higher)* más arriba; *(out of bed)* levantado; *(finished)* terminado. ~ **here** aquí arriba. ~ **in** *(fam)* versado en, fuerte en. ~ **there** allí arriba. ~ **to** hasta. **be one ~ on** llevar la ventaja a. **be ~ against** enfrentarse con. **be ~ to** tramar *(plot)*; *(one's turn)* tocar a; a la altura de *(task)*; *(reach)* llegar a. **come ~** subir. **feel ~ to it** sentirse capaz. **go ~** subir. **it's ~ to you** depende de tí. **what is ~?** ¿qué pasa? ● *prep* arriba; *(on top of)* en lo alto de. ● *vt* (*pt* **upped**) aumentar. ● *n*. ~**s and downs** *npl* altibajos *mpl*

upbraid /ʌpˈbreɪd/ *vt* reprender

upbringing /ˈʌpbrɪŋɪŋ/ *n* educación *f*

update /ʌpˈdeɪt/ *vt* poner al día

upgrade /ʌpˈgreɪd/ *vt* ascender *(person)*; mejorar *(equipment)*

upheaval /ʌpˈhiːvl/ *n* trastorno *m*

uphill /ˈʌphɪl/ *a* ascendente; *(fig)* arduo. ● *adv* /ʌpˈhɪl/ cuesta arriba. **go ~** subir

uphold /ʌpˈhəʊld/ vt (pt **upheld**) sostener

upholster /ʌpˈhəʊlstə(r)/ vt tapizar. ~**er** /-rə(r)/ n tapicero m. ~**y** n tapicería f

upkeep /ˈʌpkiːp/ n mantenimiento m

up-market /ʌpˈmɑːkɪt/ a superior

upon /əˈpɒn/ prep en; (on top of) encima de. once ~ **a time** érase una vez

upper /ˈʌpə(r)/ a superior. ~ **class** n clases fpl altas. ~ **hand** n dominio m, ventaja f. ~**most** a (el) más alto. ● n (of shoe) pala f

uppish /ˈʌpɪʃ/ a engreído

upright /ˈʌpraɪt/ a derecho; (piano) vertical. ● n montante m

uprising /ˈʌpraɪzɪŋ/ n sublevación f

uproar /ˈʌprɔː(r)/ n tumulto m. ~**ious** /-ˈrɔːrɪəs/ a tumultuoso

uproot /ʌpˈruːt/ vt desarraigar

upset /ʌpˈset/ vt (pt **upset**, presp up-setting) trastornar; desbaratar (plan etc); (distress) alterar. /ˈʌpset/ n trastorno m

upshot /ˈʌpʃɒt/ n resultado m

upside-down /ʌpsaɪdˈdaʊn/ adv al revés; (in disorder) patas arriba. **turn** ~ volver

upstairs /ʌpˈsteəz/ adv arriba. /ˈʌpsteəz/ a de arriba

upstart /ˈʌpstɑːt/ n arribista m & f

upstream /ˈʌpstriːm/ adv río arriba; (against the current) contra la corriente

upsurge /ˈʌpsɜːdʒ/ n aumento m; (of anger etc) arrebato m

uptake /ˈʌpteɪk/ n. **quick on the** ~ muy listo

uptight /ˈʌptaɪt/ a (fam) nervioso

up-to-date /ʌptəˈdeɪt/ a al día; (news) de última hora; (modern) moderno

upturn /ˈʌptɜːn/ n aumento m; (improvement) mejora f

upward /ˈʌpwəd/ a ascendente. ● adv hacia arriba. ~**s** adv hacia arriba

uranium /jʊˈreɪnɪəm/ n uranio m

urban /ˈɜːbən/ a urbano

urbane /ˈɜːbeɪn/ a cortés

urbanize /ˈɜːbənaɪz/ vt urbanizar

urchin /ˈɜːtʃɪn/ n pilluelo m

urge /ɜːdʒ/ vt incitar, animar. ● n impulso m. ~ **on** animar

urgen|cy /ˈɜːdʒənsɪ/ n urgencia f. ~**t** /ˈɜːdʒənt/ a urgente. ~**tly** adv urgentemente

urin|ate /ˈjʊərɪneɪt/ vi orinar. ~**e** /ˈjʊərɪn/ n orina f

urn /ɜːn/ n urna f

Uruguay /ˈjʊərəɡwaɪ/ n el Uruguay m. ~**an** a & n uruguayo (m)

us /ʌs, əs/ pron nos; (after prep) nosotros, nosotras

US(A) /juːesˈeɪ/ abbr (United States (of America)) EE.UU., Estados mpl Unidos

usage /ˈjuːzɪdʒ/ n uso m

use /juːz/ vt emplear. ~ /juːs/ n uso m, empleo m. **be of** ~ servir. **it is no** ~ es inútil, no sirve para nada. **make ~ of** servirse de. ~ **up** agotar, consumir. ~**d** /juːzd/ a (clothes) gastado. /juːst/ pt. **he** ~**d to say** decía, solía decir. ● a. ~**d to** acostumbrado a. ~**ful** /ˈjuːsfl/ a útil. ~**fully** adv útilmente. ~**less** a inútil; (person) incompetente. ~**r** /-zə(r)/ n usuario m

usher /ˈʌʃə(r)/ n ujier m; (in theatre etc) acomodador m. ● vt. ~ **in** hacer entrar. ~**ette** n acomodadora f

USSR abbr (history) (Union of Soviet Socialist Republics) URSS

usual /ˈjuːʒʊəl/ a usual, corriente; (habitual) acostumbrado, habitual. **as** ~ como de costumbre, como siempre. ~**ly** adv normalmente. **he** ~**ly wakes up early** suele despertarse temprano

usurer /ˈjuːʒərə(r)/ n usurero m

usurp /jʊˈzɜːp/ vt usurpar. ~**er** /-ə(r)/ n usurpador m

usury /ˈjuːʒərɪ/ n usura f

utensil /juːˈtensl/ n utensilio m

uterus /ˈjuːtərəs/ n útero m

utilitarian /juːtɪlɪˈteərɪən/ a utilitario

utility /juːˈtɪlətɪ/ n utilidad f. **public** ~ n servicio m público. ● a utilitario

utilize /ˈjuːtɪlaɪz/ vt utilizar

utmost /ˈʌtməʊst/ a extremo. ● n. **one's** ~ todo lo posible

utter[1] /ˈʌtə(r)/ a completo

utter[2] /ˈʌtə(r)/ vt (speak) pronunciar; dar (sigh); emitir (sound). ~**ance** n expresión f

utterly /ˈʌtəlɪ/ adv totalmente

U-turn /ˈjuːtɜːn/ n vuelta f

V

vacan|cy /ˈveɪkənsɪ/ n (job) vacante f; (room) habitación f libre. ~**t** a (empty) vacío; (look) vago vacate /və'keɪt/ vt dejar

vacation /və'keɪʃn/ n (Amer) vacaciones fpl

vaccin|ate /'væksmeɪt/ vt vacunar. ~ation /-'neɪʃn/ n vacunación f. ~e /'væksi:n/ n vacuna f

vacuum /'vækjʊəm/ n (pl -cuums or -cua) vacío m. ~ cleaner n aspiradora f. ~ flask n termo m

vagabond /'vægəbɒnd/ n vagabundo m

vagary /'veɪgərɪ/ n capricho m

vagina /və'dʒaɪnə/ n vagina f

vagrant /'veɪgrənt/ n vagabundo m

vague /veɪg/ a (-er, -est) vago; (outline) indistinto. be ~ about no precisar. ~ly adv vagamente

vain /veɪn/ a (-er, -est) vanidoso; (useless) vano, inútil. in ~ en vano. ~ly adv vanamente

valance /'væləns/ n cenefa f

vale /veɪl/ n valle m

valentine /'væləntaɪn/ n (card) tarjeta f del día de San Valentín

valet /'vælɪt, 'væleɪ/ n ayuda m de cámara

valiant /'vælɪənt/ a valeroso

valid /'vælɪd/ a válido; (ticket) valedero. ~ate vt dar validez a; (confirm) convalidar. ~ity /-'ɪdətɪ/ n validez f

valley /'vælɪ/ n (pl -eys) valle m

valour /'vælə(r)/ n valor m

valuable /'væljʊəbl/ a valioso. ~s npl objetos mpl de valor

valuation /'væljʊ'eɪʃn/ n valoración f

value /'vælju:/ n valor m; (usefulness) utilidad f. face ~ n valor m nominal; (fig) significado m literal. ● vt valorar; (cherish) apreciar. ~ added tax (VAT) n impuesto m sobre el valor añadido (IVA). ~d a (appreciated) apreciado, estimado. ~r /-ə(r)/ n tasador m

valve /vælv/ n válvula f

vampire /'væmpaɪə(r)/ n vampiro m

van /væn/ n furgoneta f; (rail) furgón m

vandal /'vændl/ n vándalo m. ~ism /-əlɪzəm/ n vandalismo m. ~ize vt destruir

vane /veɪn/ n (weathercock) veleta f; (naut, aviat) paleta f

vanguard /'vængɑ:d/ n vanguardia f

vanilla /və'nɪlə/ n vainilla f

vanish /'vænɪʃ/ vi desaparecer

vanity /'vænɪtɪ/ n vanidad f. ~ case n neceser m

vantage /'vɑ:ntɪdʒ/ n ventaja f. ~ point n posición f ventajosa

vapour /'veɪpə(r)/ n vapor m

variable /'veərɪəbl/ a variable

varian|ce /'veərɪəns/ n. at ~ce en desacuerdo. ~t /'veərɪənt/ a diferente. ● n variante m

variation /'veərɪ'eɪʃn/ n variación f

varicoloured /'veərɪkʌləd/ a multicolor

varied /'veərɪd/ a variado

varicose /'værɪkəʊs/ a varicoso. ~ veins npl varices fpl

variety /və'raɪətɪ/ n variedad f. ~ show n espectáculo m de variedades

various /'veərɪəs/ a diverso. ~ly adv diversamente

varnish /'vɑ:nɪʃ/ n barniz m; (for nails) esmalte m. ● vt barnizar

vary /'veərɪ/ vt/i variar. ~ing a diverso

vase /vɑ:z, Amer veɪs/ n jarrón m

vasectomy /və'sektəmɪ/ n vasectomía f

vast /vɑ:st/ a vasto, enorme. ~ly adv enormemente. ~ness n inmensidad f

vat /væt/ n tina f

VAT /vi:er'ti:/ abbr (value added tax) IVA m, impuesto m sobre el valor añadido

vault /vɔ:lt/ n (roof) bóveda f; (in bank) cámara f acorazada; (tomb) cripta f; (cellar) sótano m; (jump) salto m. ● vt/i saltar

vaunt /vɔ:nt/ vt jactarse de

veal /vi:l/ n ternera f

veer /vɪə(r)/ vi cambiar de dirección; (naut) virar

vegetable /'vedʒɪtəbl/ a vegetal. ● n legumbre m; (greens) verduras fpl

vegetarian /vedʒɪ'teərɪən/ a & n vegetariano (m)

vegetate /'vedʒɪteɪt/ vi vegetar

vegetation /vedʒɪ'teɪʃn/ n vegetación f

vehemen|ce /'vi:əməns/ n vehemencia f. ~t /'vi:əmənt/ a vehemente. ~tly adv con vehemencia

vehicle /'vi:ɪkl/ n vehículo m

veil /veɪl/ n velo m. take the ~ hacerse monja. ● vt velar

vein /veɪn/ n vena f; (mood) humor m. ~ed a veteado

velocity /vɪ'lɒsɪtɪ/ n velocidad f

velvet /'velvɪt/ n terciopelo m. ~y a aterciopelado

venal /'vi:nl/ *a* venal. **~ity** /-'næləti/ *n* venalidad *f*

vendetta /ven'detə/ *n* enemistad *f* prolongada

vending-machine /'vendɪŋ məʃi:n/ *n* distribuidor *m* automático

vendor /'vendə(r)/ *n* vendedor *m*

veneer /və'nɪə(r)/ *n* chapa *f*; (*fig*) barniz *m*, apariencia *f*

venerable /'venərəbl/ *a* venerable

venereal /və'nɪərɪəl/ *a* venéreo

Venetian /və'ni:ʃn/ *a* & *n* veneciano (*m*). **v~ blind** *n* persiana *f* veneciana

vengeance /'vendʒəns/ *n* venganza *f*. **with a ~** (*fig*) con creces

venison /'venɪzn/ *n* carne *f* de venado

venom /'venəm/ *n* veneno *m*. **~ous** *a* venenoso

vent /vent/ *n* abertura *f*; (*for air*) respiradero *m*. **give ~ to** dar salida a. ● *vt* hacer un agujero en; (*fig*) desahogar

ventilat|e /'ventɪleɪt/ *vt* ventilar. **~ion** /-'leɪʃn/ *n* ventilación *f*. **~or** /-ə(r)/ *n* ventilador *m*

ventriloquist /ven'trɪləkwɪst/ *n* ventrílocuo *m*

venture /'ventʃə(r)/ *n* empresa *f* (arriesgada). **at a ~** a la ventura. ● *vt* arriesgar. ● *vi* atreverse

venue /'venju:/ *n* lugar *m* (de reunión)

veranda /və'rændə/ *n* terraza *f*

verb /vɜ:b/ *n* verbo *m*

verbal /'vɜ:bl/ *a* verbal. **~ly** *adv* verbalmente

verbatim /vɜ:'beɪtɪm/ *adv* palabra por palabra, al pie de la letra

verbose /vɜ:'bəʊs/ *a* prolijo

verdant /'vɜ:dənt/ *a* verde

verdict /'vɜ:dɪkt/ *n* veredicto *m*; (*opinion*) opinión *f*

verge /vɜ:dʒ/ *n* borde *m*. ● *vt*. **~ on** acercarse a

verger /'vɜ:dʒə(r)/ *n* sacristán *m*

verif|ication /verɪfɪ'keɪʃn/ *n* verificación *f*. **~y** /'verɪfaɪ/ *vt* verificar

veritable /'verɪtəbl/ *a* verdadero

vermicelli /vɜ:mɪ'tʃelɪ/ *n* fideos *mpl*

vermin /'vɜ:mɪn/ *n* sabandijas *fpl*

vermouth /'vɜ:məθ/ *n* vermut *m*

vernacular /və'nækjʊlə(r)/ *n* lengua *f*; (*regional*) dialecto *m*

versatil|e /'vɜ:sətaɪl/ *a* versátil. **~ity** /-'tɪləti/ *n* versatilidad *f*

verse /vɜ:s/ *n* estrofa *f*; (*poetry*) poesías *fpl*; (*of Bible*) versículo *m*

versed /vɜ:st/ *a*. **~ in** versado en

version /'vɜ:ʃn/ *n* versión *f*

versus /'vɜ:səs/ *prep* contra

vertebra /'vɜ:tɪbrə/ *n* (*pl* **-brae** /-bri:/) vértebra *f*

vertical /'vɜ:tɪkl/ *a* & *n* vertical (*f*). **~ly** *adv* verticalmente

vertigo /'vɜ:tɪgəʊ/ *n* vértigo *m*

verve /vɜ:v/ *n* entusiasmo *m*, vigor *m*

very /'verɪ/ *adv* muy. **~ much** muchísimo. **~ well** muy bien. **the ~ first** el primero de todos. ● *a* mismo. **the ~ thing** exactamente lo que hace falta

vespers /'vespəz/ *npl* vísperas *fpl*

vessel /'vesl/ *n* (*receptacle*) recipiente *m*; (*ship*) buque *m*; (*anat*) vaso *m*

vest /vest/ *n* camiseta *f*; (*Amer*) chaleco *m*. ● *vt* conferir. **~ed interest** *n* interés *m* personal; (*jurid*) derecho *m* adquirido

vestige /'vestɪdʒ/ *n* vestigio *m*

vestment /'vestmənt/ *n* vestidura *f*

vestry /'vestrɪ/ *n* sacristía *f*

vet /vet/ *n* (*fam*) veterinario *m*. ● *vt* (*pt* **vetted**) examinar

veteran /'vetərən/ *n* veterano *m*

veterinary /'vetərɪnərɪ/ *a* veterinario. **~ surgeon** *n* veterinario *m*

veto /'vi:təʊ/ *n* (*pl* **-oes**) veto *m*. ● *vt* poner el veto a

vex /veks/ *vt* fastidiar. **~ation** /-'seɪʃn/ *n* fastidio *m*. **~ed question** *n* cuestión *f* controvertida. **~ing** *a* fastidioso

via /'vaɪə/ *prep* por, por vía de

viab|ility /vaɪə'bɪləti/ *n* viabilidad *f*. **~le** /'vaɪəbl/ *a* viable

viaduct /'vaɪədʌkt/ *n* viaducto *m*

vibrant /'vaɪbrənt/ *a* vibrante

vibrat|e /vaɪ'breɪt/ *vt/i* vibrar. **~ion** /-ʃn/ *n* vibración *f*

vicar /'vɪkə(r)/ *n* párroco *m*. **~age** /-rɪdʒ/ *n* casa *f* del párroco

vicarious /vɪ'keərɪəs/ *a* indirecto

vice[1] /vaɪs/ *n* vicio *m*

vice[2] /vaɪs/ *n* (*tec*) torno *m* de banco

vice... /vaɪs/ *pref* vice...

vice versa /vaɪsɪ'vɜ:sə/ *adv* viceversa

vicinity /vɪ'sɪnɪtɪ/ *n* vecindad *f*. **in the ~ of** cerca de

vicious /'vɪʃəs/ *a* (*spiteful*) malicioso; (*violent*) atroz. **~ circle** *n* círculo *m* vicioso. **~ly** *adv* cruelmente

vicissitudes /vɪˈsɪsɪtjuːdz/ *npl* vicisitudes *fpl*

victim /ˈvɪktɪm/ *n* víctima *f*. ~**ization** /-aɪˈzeɪʃn/ *n* persecución *f*. ~**ize** *vt* victimizar

victor /ˈvɪktə(r)/ *n* vencedor *m*

Victorian /vɪkˈtɔːrɪən/ *a* victoriano

victor|ious /vɪkˈtɔːrɪəs/ *a* victorioso. ~**y** /ˈvɪktərɪ/ *n* victoria *f*

video /ˈvɪdɪəʊ/ *a* video. ● *n (fam)* magnetoscopio *m*. ~ **recorder** *n* magnetoscopio *m*. ~**tape** *n* videocassette *f*

vie /vaɪ/ *vi (pres p* **vying)** rivalizar

view /vjuː/ *n* vista *f*; *(mental survey)* visión *f* de conjunto; *(opinion)* opinión *f*. **in my** ~ a mi juicio. **in** ~ **of** en vista de. **on** ~ expuesto. **with a** ~ **to** con miras a. ● *vt* ver; *(visit)* visitar; *(consider)* considerar. ~**er** /-ə(r)/ *n* espectador *m*; *(TV)* televidente *m & f*. ~**finder** /ˈvjuːfaɪndə(r)/ *n* visor *m*. ~**point** /ˈvjuːpɔɪnt/ *n* punto *m* de vista

vigil /ˈvɪdʒɪl/ *n* vigilia *f*. ~**ance** *n* vigilancia *f*. ~**ant** *a* vigilante. **keep** ~ velar

vigo|rous /ˈvɪɡərəs/ *a* vigoroso. ~**ur** /ˈvɪɡə(r)/ *n* vigor *m*

vile /vaɪl/ *a (base)* vil; *(bad)* horrible; *(weather, temper)* de perros

vilif|ication /vɪlɪfɪˈkeɪʃn/ *n* difamación *f*. ~**y** /ˈvɪlɪfaɪ/ *vt* difamar

village /ˈvɪlɪdʒ/ *n* aldea *f*. ~**r** /-ə(r)/ *n* aldeano *m*

villain /ˈvɪlən/ *n* malvado *m*; *(in story etc)* malo *m*. ~**ous** *a* infame. ~**y** *n* infamia *f*

vim /vɪm/ *n (fam)* energía *f*

vinaigrette /vɪnɪˈɡret/ *n*. ~ **sauce** *n* vinagreta *f*

vindicat|e /ˈvɪndɪkeɪt/ *vt* vindicar. ~**ion** /-ˈkeɪʃn/ *n* vindicación *f*

vindictive /vɪnˈdɪktɪv/ *a* vengativo. ~**ness** *n* carácter *m* vengativo

vine /vaɪn/ *n* vid *f*

vinegar /ˈvɪnɪɡə(r)/ *n* vinagre *m*. ~**y** *a (person)* avinagrado

vineyard /ˈvɪnjəd/ *n* viña *f*

vintage /ˈvɪntɪdʒ/ *n (year)* cosecha *f*. ● *a (wine)* añejo; *(car)* de época

vinyl /ˈvaɪnɪl/ *n* vinilo *m*

viola /vɪˈəʊlə/ *n* viola *f*

violat|e /ˈvaɪəleɪt/ *vt* violar. ~**ion** /-ˈleɪʃn/ *n* violación *f*

violen|ce /ˈvaɪələns/ *n* violencia *f*. ~**t** /ˈvaɪələnt/ *a* violento. ~**tly** *adv* violentamente

violet /ˈvaɪələt/ *a & n* violeta (*f*)

violin /ˈvaɪəlɪn/ *n* violín *m*. ~**ist** *n* violinista *m & f*

VIP /viːaɪˈpiː/ *abbr (very important person)* personaje *m*

viper /ˈvaɪpə(r)/ *n* víbora *f*

virgin /ˈvɜːdʒɪn/ *a & n* virgen (*f*). ~**al** *a* virginal. ~**ity** /vəˈdʒɪnətɪ/ *n* virginidad *f*

Virgo /ˈvɜːɡəʊ/ *n (astr)* Virgo *f*

viril|e /ˈvɪraɪl/ *a* viril. ~**ity** /-ˈrɪlətɪ/ *n* virilidad *f*

virtual /ˈvɜːtʃʊəl/ *a* verdadero. **a** ~ **failure** prácticamente un fracaso. ~**ly** *adv* prácticamente

virtue /ˈvɜːtʃuː/ *n* virtud *f*. **by** ~ **of**, **in** ~ **of** en virtud de

virtuoso /vɜːtjʊˈəʊzəʊ/ *n (pl* -**si** /-ziː/) virtuoso *m*

virtuous /ˈvɜːtʃʊəs/ *a* virtuoso

virulent /ˈvɪrʊlənt/ *a* virulento

virus /ˈvaɪərəs/ *n (pl* -**uses)** virus *m*

visa /ˈviːzə/ *n* visado *m*, visa *f (LAm)*

vis-a-vis /viːzɑːˈviː/ *adv* frente a frente. ● *prep* respecto a; *(opposite)* enfrente de

viscount /ˈvaɪkaʊnt/ *n* vizconde *m*. ~**ess** *n* vizcondesa *f*

viscous /ˈvɪskəs/ *a* viscoso

visib|ility /vɪzɪˈbɪlətɪ/ *n* visibilidad *f*. ~**le** /ˈvɪzɪbl/ *a* visible. ~**ly** *adv* visiblemente

vision /ˈvɪʒn/ *n* visión *f*; *(sight)* vista *f*. ~**ary** /ˈvɪʒənərɪ/ *a & n* visionario (*m*)

visit /ˈvɪzɪt/ *vt* visitar; hacer una visita a *(person)*. ● *vi* hacer visitas. ● *n* visita *f*. ~**or** *n* visitante *m & f*; *(guest)* visita *f*; *(in hotel)* cliente *m & f*

visor /ˈvaɪzə(r)/ *n* visera *f*

vista /ˈvɪstə/ *n* perspectiva *f*

visual /ˈvɪʒʊəl/ *a* visual. ~**ize** /ˈvɪʒʊəlaɪz/ *vt* imaginar(se); *(foresee)* prever. ~**ly** *adv* visualmente

vital /ˈvaɪtl/ *a* vital; *(essential)* esencial

vitality /vaɪˈtælətɪ/ *n* vitalidad *f*

vital: ~**ly** /ˈvaɪtəlɪ/ *adv* extremadamente. ~**s** *npl* órganos *mpl* vitales. ~ **statistics** *npl (fam)* medidas *fpl*

vitamin /ˈvɪtəmɪn/ *n* vitamina *f*

vitiate /ˈvɪʃɪeɪt/ *vt* viciar

vitreous /ˈvɪtrɪəs/ *a* vítreo

vituperat|e /vɪˈtjuːpəreɪt/ *vt* vituperar. ~**ion** /-ˈreɪʃn/ *n* vituperación *f*

vivaci|ous /vɪ'veɪʃəs/ a animado, vivo. **∼ously** adv animadamente. **∼ty** /-'væsətɪ/ n viveza f

vivid /'vɪvɪd/ a vivo. **∼ly** adv intensamente; (describe) gráficamente. **∼ness** n viveza f

vivisection /vɪvɪ'sekʃn/ n vivisección f

vixen /'vɪksn/ n zorra f

vocabulary /və'kæbjʊlərɪ/ n vocabulario m

vocal /'vəʊkl/ a vocal; (fig) franco. **∼ist** n cantante m & f

vocation /vəʊ'keɪʃn/ n vocación f. **∼al** a profesional

vocifer|ate /və'sɪfəreɪt/ vt/i vociferar. **∼ous** a vociferador

vogue /vəʊg/ n boga f. **in ∼** de moda

voice /vɔɪs/ n voz f. ● vt expresar

void /vɔɪd/ a vacío; (not valid) nulo. **∼ of** desprovisto de. ● n vacío m. ● vt anular

volatile /'vɒlətaɪl/ a volátil; (person) voluble

volcan|ic /vɒl'kænɪk/ a volcánico. **∼o** /vɒl'keɪnəʊ/ n (pl -oes) volcán m

volition /və'lɪʃn/ n. **of one's own ∼** de su propia voluntad

volley /'vɒlɪ/ n (pl -eys) (of blows) lluvia f; (of gunfire) descarga f cerrada

volt /vəʊlt/ n voltio m. **∼age** n voltaje m

voluble /'vɒljʊbl/ a locuaz

volume /'vɒljuːm/ n volumen m; (book) tomo m

voluminous /və'ljuːmɪnəs/ a voluminoso

voluntar|ily /'vɒləntərəlɪ/ adv voluntariamente. **∼y** /'vɒləntərɪ/ a voluntario

volunteer /vɒlən'tɪə(r)/ n voluntario m. ● vt ofrecer. ● vi ofrecerse voluntariamente; (mil) alistarse como voluntario

voluptuous /və'lʌptjʊəs/ a voluptuoso

vomit /'vɒmɪt/ vt/i vomitar. ● n vómito m

voracious /və'reɪʃəs/ a voraz

vot|e /vəʊt/ n voto m; (right) derecho m de votar. ● vi votar. **∼er** /-ə(r)/ n votante m & f. **∼ing** n votación f

vouch /vaʊtʃ/ vi. **∼ for** garantizar

voucher /'vaʊtʃə(r)/ n vale m

vow /vaʊ/ n voto m. ● vi jurar

vowel /'vaʊəl/ n vocal f

voyage /'vɔɪɪdʒ/ n viaje m (en barco)

vulgar /'vʌlgə(r)/ a vulgar. **∼ity** /-'gærətɪ/ n vulgaridad f. **∼ize** vt vulgarizar

vulnerab|ility /vʌlnərə'bɪlətɪ/ n vulnerabilidad f. **∼le** /'vʌlnərəbl/ a vulnerable

vulture /'vʌltʃə(r)/ n buitre m

vying /'vaɪɪŋ/ see vie

W

wad /wɒd/ n (pad) tapón m; (bundle) lío m; (of notes) fajo m; (of cotton wool etc) bolita f

wadding /'wɒdɪŋ/ n relleno m

waddle /'wɒdl/ vi contonearse

wade /weɪd/ vt vadear. ● vi. **∼ through** abrirse paso entre; leer con dificultad (book)

wafer /'weɪfə(r)/ n barquillo m; (relig) hostia f

waffle¹ /'wɒfl/ n (fam) palabrería f. ● vi (fam) divagar

waffle² /'wɒfl/ n (culin) gofre m

waft /wɒft/ vt llevar por el aire. ● vi flotar

wag /wæg/ vt (pt wagged) menear. ● vi menearse

wage /weɪdʒ/ n. **∼s** npl salario m. ● vt. **∼ war** hacer la guerra. **∼r** /'weɪdʒə(r)/ n apuesta f. ● vt apostar

waggle /'wægl/ vt menear. ● vi menearse

wagon /'wægən/ n carro m; (rail) vagón m. **be on the ∼** (sl) no beber

waif /weɪf/ n niño m abandonado

wail /weɪl/ vi lamentarse. ● n lamento m

wainscot /'weɪnskət/ n revestimiento m, zócalo m

waist /weɪst/ n cintura f. **∼band** n cinturón m

waistcoat /'weɪstkəʊt/ n chaleco m

waistline /'weɪstlaɪn/ n cintura f

wait /weɪt/ vt/i esperar; (at table) servir. **∼ for** esperar. **∼ on** servir. ● n espera f. **lie in ∼** acechar

waiter /'weɪtə(r)/ n camarero m

wait: ∼ing-list n lista f de espera. **∼ing-room** n sala f de espera

waitress /'weɪtrɪs/ n camarera f

waive /weɪv/ vt renunciar a

wake¹ /weɪk/ vt (pt woke, pp woken) despertar. ● vi despertarse. ● n velatorio m. **∼ up** vt despertar. ● vi despertarse

wake² /weɪk/ n (naut) estela f. **in the ~ of** como resultado de, tras

waken /'weɪkən/ vt despertar. ● vi despertarse

wakeful /'weɪkfl/ a insomne

Wales /weɪlz/ n País m de Gales

walk /wɔːk/ vi andar; (not ride) ir a pie; (stroll) pasearse. **~ out** salir; ⟨workers⟩ declararse en huelga. **~ out on** abandonar. ● vt andar por ⟨streets⟩; llevar de paseo ⟨dog⟩. ● n paseo m; (gait) modo m de andar; (path) sendero m. **~ of life** clase f social. **~about** /'wɔːkəbaʊt/ n (of royalty) encuentro m con el público. **~er** /-ə(r)/ n paseante m & f

walkie-talkie /wɔːkɪ'tɔːkɪ/ n transmisor-receptor m portátil

walking /'wɔːkɪŋ/ n paseo m. **~ stick** n bastón m

Walkman /'wɔːkmən/ n (P) estereo m personal, Walkman m (P), magnetófono m de bolsillo

walk: **~out** n huelga f. **~over** n victoria f fácil

wall /wɔːl/ n (interior) pared f; (exterior) muro m; (in garden) tapia f; (of city) muralla f. **go to the ~** fracasar. **up the ~** (fam) loco. ● vt amurallar ⟨city⟩

wallet /'wɒlɪt/ n cartera f, billetera f (LAm)

wallflower /'wɔːlflaʊə(r)/ n alhelí m

wallop /'wɒləp/ vt (pt walloped) (sl) golpear con fuerza. ● n (sl) golpe m fuerte

wallow /'wɒləʊ/ vi revolcarse

wallpaper /'wɔːlpeɪpə(r)/ n papel m pintado

walnut /'wɔːlnʌt/ n nuez f; (tree) nogal m

walrus /'wɔːlrəs/ n morsa f

waltz /wɔːls/ n vals m. ● vi valsar

wan /wɒn/ a pálido

wand /wɒnd/ n varita f

wander /'wɒndə(r)/ vi vagar; (stroll) pasearse; (digress) divagar; ⟨road, river⟩ serpentear. ● n paseo m. **~er** /-ə(r)/ n vagabundo m. **~lust** /'wɒndəlʌst/ n pasión f por los viajes

wane /weɪn/ vi menguar. ● n. **on the ~** disminuyendo

wangle /'wæŋgl/ vt (sl) agenciarse

want /wɒnt/ vt querer; (need) necesitar; (require) exigir. ● vi. **~ for** carecer de. ● n necesidad f; (lack) falta f; (desire) deseo m. **~ed** a ⟨criminal⟩ buscado. **~ing** a (lacking) falto de. **be ~ing** carecer de

wanton /'wɒntən/ a (licentious) lascivo; (motiveless) sin motivo

war /wɔː(r)/ n guerra f. **at ~** en guerra

warble /'wɔːbl/ vt cantar trinando. ● vi gorjear. ● n gorjeo m. **~r** /-ə(r)/ n curruca f

ward /wɔːd/ n (in hospital) sala f; (of town) barrio m; (child) pupilo m. ● vt. **~ off** parar

warden /'wɔːdn/ n guarda m

warder /'wɔːdə(r)/ n carcelero m

wardrobe /'wɔːdrəʊb/ n armario m; (clothes) vestuario m

warehouse /'weəhaʊs/ n almacén m

wares /weəz/ npl mercancías fpl

war: **~fare** /wɔː'feə(r)/ n guerra f. **~head** /wɔː'hed/ n cabeza f explosiva

warily /'weərɪlɪ/ adv cautelosamente

warlike /'wɔːlaɪk/ a belicoso

warm /wɔːm/ a (-er, -est) caliente; (hearty) caluroso. **be ~** ⟨person⟩ tener calor. **it is ~** hace calor. ● vt. **~ (up)** calentar; recalentar ⟨food⟩; (fig) animar. ● vi. **~ (up)** calentarse; (fig) animarse. **~ to** tomar simpatía a ⟨person⟩; ir entusiasmándose por ⟨idea etc⟩. **~-blooded** a de sangre caliente. **~-hearted** a simpático. **~ly** adv (heartily) calurosamente

warmonger /'wɔːmʌŋgə(r)/ n belicista m & f

warmth /wɔːmθ/ n calor m

warn /wɔːn/ vt avisar, advertir. **~ing** n advertencia f; (notice) aviso m. **~ off** (advise against) aconsejar en contra de; (forbid) impedir

warp /wɔːp/ vt deformar; (fig) pervertir. ● vi deformarse

warpath /'wɔːpɑːθ/ n. **be on the ~** buscar camorra

warrant /'wɒrənt/ n autorización f; (for arrest) orden f. ● vt justificar. **~officer** n suboficial m

warranty /'wɒrəntɪ/ n garantía f

warring /'wɔːrɪŋ/ a en guerra

warrior /'wɒrɪə(r)/ n guerrero m

warship /'wɔːʃɪp/ n buque m de guerra

wart /wɔːt/ n verruga f

wartime /'wɔːtaɪm/ n tiempo m de guerra

wary /'weərɪ/ a (-ier, -iest) cauteloso

was /wɒz, wəz/ see **be**

wash /wɒʃ/ vt lavar; (flow over) bañar. ● vi lavarse. ● n lavado m;

(dirty clothes) ropa *f* sucia; *(wet clothes)* colada *f*; *(of ship)* estela *f*. **have a ~** lavarse. **~ out** *vt* enjuagar; *(fig)* cancelar. **~ up** *vi* fregar los platos. **~able** *a* lavable. **~-basin** *n* lavabo *m*. **~ed-out** *a (pale)* pálido; *(tired)* rendido. **~er** /'wɒʃə(r)/ *n* arandela *f*; *(washing-machine)* lavadora *f*. **~ing** /'wɒʃɪŋ/ *n* lavado *m*; *(dirty clothes)* ropa *f* sucia; *(wet clothes)* colada *f*. **~ing-machine** *n* lavadora *f*. **~ing-powder** *n* jabón *m* en polvo. **~ing-up** *n* fregado *m*; *(dirty plates etc)* platos *mpl* para fregar. **~-out** *n (sl)* desastre *m*. **~-room** *n (Amer)* servicios *mpl*. **~-stand** *n* lavabo *m*. **~-tub** *n* tina *f* de lavar

wasp /wɒsp/ *n* avispa *f*

wastage /'weɪstɪdʒ/ *n* desperdicios *mpl*

waste /weɪst/ ● *a* de desecho; *(land)* yermo. ● *n* derroche *m*; *(rubbish)* desperdicio *m*; *(of time)* pérdida *f*. ● *vt* derrochar; *(not use)* desperdiciar; *(time)*. ● *vi*. **~ away** consumirse. **~-disposal unit** *n* trituradora *f* de basuras. **~ful** *a* dispendioso; *(person)* derrochador. **~-paper basket** *n* papelera *f*. **~s** *npl* tierras *fpl* baldías

watch /wɒtʃ/ *vt* mirar; *(keep an eye on)* vigilar; *(take heed)* tener cuidado con; ver *(TV)*. ● *vi* mirar; *(keep an eye on)* vigilar. ● *n* vigilancia *f*; *(period of duty)* guardia *f*; *(timepiece)* reloj *m*. **on the ~** alerta. **~ out** *vi* tener cuidado. **~-dog** *n* perro *m* guardián; *(fig)* guardián *m*. **~ful** *a* vigilante. **~maker** /'wɒtʃmeɪkə(r)/ *n* relojero *m*. **~man** /'wɒtʃmən/ *n (pl* **-men)** vigilante *m*. **~-tower** *n* atalaya *f*. **~word** /'wɒtʃwɜːd/ *n* santo *m* y seña

water /'wɔːtə(r)/ *n* agua *f*. **by ~** *(of travel)* por mar. **in hot ~** *(fam)* en un apuro. ● *vt* regar *(plants etc)*; *(dilute)* aguar, diluir. ● *vi (eyes)* llorar. **make s.o.'s mouth ~** hacérsele la boca agua. **~ down** *vt* diluir; *(fig)* suavizar. **~-closet** *n* wáter *m*. **~-colour** *n* acuarela *f*. **~-course** /'wɔːtəkɔːs/ *n* arroyo *m*; *(artificial)* canal *m*. **~cress** /'wɔːtəkres/ *n* berro *m*. **~fall** /'wɔːtəfɔːl/ *n* cascada *f*. **~-ice** *n* sorbete *m*. **~ing-can** /'wɔːtərɪŋkæn/ *n* regadera *f*. **~-lily** *n* nenúfar *m*. **~-line** *n* línea *f* de flotación. **~logged** /'wɔːtəlɒgd/ *a* saturado de agua, empapado. **~ main** *n* cañería *f* principal. **~ melon** *n* sandía *f*. **~-mill** *n*

molino *m* de agua. **~ polo** *n* polo *m* acuático. **~power** *n* energía *f* hidráulica. **~proof** /'wɔːtəpruːf/ *a* & *n* impermeable *(m)*; *(watch)* sumergible. **~shed** /'wɔːtʃed/ *n* punto *m* decisivo. **~-skiing** *n* esquí *m* acuático. **~-softener** *n* ablandador *m* de agua. **~tight** /'wɔːtətaɪt/ *a* hermético, estanco; *(fig)* irrecusable. **~way** *n* canal *m* navegable. **~-wheel** *n* rueda *f* hidráulica. **~-wings** *npl* flotadores *mpl*. **~works** /'wɔːtəwɜːks/ *n* sistema *m* de abastecimiento de agua. **~y** /'wɔːtəri/ *a* acuoso; *(colour)* pálido; *(eyes)* lloroso

watt /wɒt/ *n* vatio *m*

wave /weɪv/ *n* onda *f*; *(of hand)* señal *f*; *(fig)* oleada *f*. ● *vt* agitar; ondular *(hair)*. ● *vi (signal)* hacer señales con la mano; *(flag)* flotar. **~band** /'weɪvbænd/ *n* banda *f* de ondas. **~length** /'weɪvleŋθ/ *n* longitud *f* de onda

waver /'weɪvə(r)/ *vi* vacilar

wavy /'weɪvɪ/ *a* **(-ier, -iest)** ondulado

wax[1] /wæks/ *n* cera *f*. ● *vt* encerar

wax[2] /wæks/ *vi (moon)* crecer

wax: **~en** *a* céreo. **~work** /'wækswɜːk/ *n* figura *f* de cera. **~y** *a* céreo

way /weɪ/ *n* camino *m*; *(distance)* distancia *f*; *(manner)* manera *f*, modo *m*; *(direction)* dirección *f*; *(means)* medio *m*; *(habit)* costumbre *f*. **be in the ~** estorbar. **by the ~** a propósito. **by ~ of** a título de. **either ~** de cualquier modo. **in a ~** en cierta manera. **in some ~s** en ciertos modos. **lead the ~** mostrar el camino. **make ~** dejar paso a. **on the ~** en camino. **out of the ~** remoto; *(extraordinary)* fuera de lo común. **that ~** por allí. **this ~** por aquí. **under ~** en curso. **~bill** *n* hoja *f* de ruta. **~farer** /'weɪfeərə(r)/ *n* viajero *m*. **~in** *n* entrada *f*

way: **~out** *n* salida *f*. **~-out** *a* ultramoderno, original. **~s** *npl* costumbres *fpl*. **~side** /'weɪsaɪd/ *n* borde *m* del camino

wayward /'weɪwəd/ *a* caprichoso

we /wiː/ *pron* nosotros, nosotras

weak /wiːk/ *a* **(-er, -est)** débil; *(liquid)* aguado, acuoso; *(fig)* flojo.

~en vt debilitar. **~kneed** a irresoluto. **~ling** /'wi:klɪŋ/ n persona f débil. **~ly** adv débilmente. ● a enfermizo. **~ness** n debilidad f

weal /wi:l/ n verdugón m

wealth /welθ/ n riqueza f. **~y** a (**-ier, -iest**) rico

wean /wi:n/ vt destetar

weapon /'wepən/ n arma f

wear /weə(r)/ vt (pt **wore**, pp **worn**) llevar; (put on) ponerse; tener (expression etc); (damage) desgastar. ● vi desgastarse; (last) durar. ● n uso m; (damage) desgaste m; (clothing) ropa f. **~ down** vt desgastar; agotar (opposition etc). **~ off** vi desaparecer. **~ on** vi (time) pasar. **~ out** vt desgastar; (tire) agotar. **~able** a que se puede llevar. **~ and tear** desgaste m

wear|ily /'wɪərɪlɪ/ adv cansadamente. **~iness** n cansancio m. **~isome** /'wɪərɪsəm/ a cansado. **~y** /'wɪərɪ/ a (**-ier, -iest**) cansado. ● vt cansar. ● vi cansarse. **~y of** cansarse de

weasel /'wi:zl/ n comadreja f

weather /'weðə(r)/ n tiempo m. **under the ~** (fam) indispuesto. ● a meteorológico. ● vt curar (wood); (survive) superar. **~beaten** a curtido. **~cock** /'weðəkɒk/ n, **~vane** n veleta f

weave /wi:v/ vt (pt **wove**, pp **woven**) tejer; entretejer (story etc); entrelazar (flowers etc). **~ one's way** abrirse paso. ● n tejido m. **~r** /-ə(r)/ n tejedor m

web /web/ n tela f; (of spider) telaraña f; (on foot) membrana f. **~bing** n cincha f

wed /wed/ vt (pt **wedded**) casarse con; (priest etc) casar. ● vi casarse. **~ded to** (fig) unido a

wedding /'wedɪŋ/ n boda f. **~cake** n pastel m de boda. **~ring** n anillo m de boda

wedge /wedʒ/ n cuña f; (space filler) calce m. ● vt acuñar; (push) apretar

wedlock /'wedlɒk/ n matrimonio m

Wednesday /'wenzdeɪ/ n miércoles m

wee /wi:/ a (fam) pequeñito

weed /wi:d/ n mala hierba f. ● vt desherbar. **~killer** n herbicida m. **~out** eliminar. **~y** a (person) débil

week /wi:k/ n semana f. **~day** /'wi:kdeɪ/ n día m laborable. **~end** n fin m de semana. **~ly** /'wi:klɪ/ a

semanal. ● n semanario m. ● adv semanalmente

weep /wi:p/ vi (pt **wept**) llorar. **~ing willow** n sauce m llorón

weevil /'wi:vɪl/ n gorgojo m

weigh /weɪ/ vt/i pesar. **~ anchor** levar anclas. **~ down** vt (fig) oprimir. **~ up** vt pesar; (fig) considerar

weight /weɪt/ n peso m. **~less** a ingrávido. **~lessness** n ingravidez f. **~lifting** n halterofilia f, levantamiento m de pesos. **~y** a (**-ier, -iest**) pesado; (influential) influyente

weir /wɪə(r)/ n presa f

weird /wɪəd/ a (**-er, -est**) misterioso; (bizarre) extraño

welcome /'welkəm/ a bienvenido. **~ to do** libre de hacer. **you're ~e!** (after thank you) ¡de nada! ● n bienvenida f; (reception) acogida f. ● vt dar la bienvenida a; (appreciate) alegrarse de

welcoming /'welkəmɪŋ/ a acogedor

weld /weld/ vt soldar. ● n soldadura f. **~er** n soldador m

welfare /'welfeə(r)/ n bienestar m; (aid) asistencia f social. **W~ State** n estado m benefactor. **~ work** n asistencia f social

well[1] /wel/ adv (**better, best**) bien. **~ done!** ¡bravo! **as ~** también. **as ~ as** tanto... como. **be ~** estar bien. **do ~** (succeed) tener éxito. **very ~** muy bien. ● a bien. ● int bueno; (surprise) ¡vaya! **~ I never!** ¡no me digas!

well[2] /wel/ n pozo m; (of staircase) caja f

well: **~appointed** a bien equipado. **~behaved** a bien educado. **~being** n bienestar m. **~bred** a bien educado. **~disposed** a benévolo. **~groomed** a bien aseado. **~heeled** a (fam) rico

wellington /'welɪŋtən/ n bota f de agua

well: **~knit** a robusto. **~known** a conocido. **~meaning** a, **~meant** a bienintencionado. **~ off** a acomodado. **~read** a culto. **~spoken** a bienhablado. **~to-do** a rico. **~wisher** n bienqueriente m & f

Welsh /welʃ/ a & n galés (m). **~rabbit** n pan m tostado con queso

welsh /welʃ/ vi. **~ on** no cumplir con

wench /wentʃ/ n (old use) muchacha f

wend /wend/ vt. ~ one's way encaminarse

went/went/ *see* go

wept/wept/ *see* weep

were/wɜ:(r), wə(r)/ *see* be

west/west/ n oeste m. the ~ el Occidente m. ●a del oeste. ●adv hacia el oeste, al oeste. go ~ (sl) morir. W~ Germany n Alemania f Occidental. ~erly a del oeste. ~erna occidental. ●n (film) película f del Oeste. ~erner /-ənə(r)/ n occidental m & f. W~ Indian a & n antillano (m). W~ Indies npl Antillas fpl. ~ward a, ~ward(s) adv hacia el oeste

wet/wet/ a (wetter, wettest) mojado; (rainy) lluvioso, de lluvia; (person, sl) soso. ~ paint recién pintado. get ~ mojarse. ●vt (pt wetted) mojar, humedecer. ~ blanket n aguafiestas m & f invar. ~ suit n traje m de buzo

whack /wæk/ vt (fam) golpear. ●n (fam) golpe m. ~ed /wækt/ a (fam) agotado. ~ing a (huge, sl) enorme. ●n paliza f

whale /weɪl/ n ballena f. a ~ of a (fam) maravilloso, enorme

wham /wæm/ int ¡zas!

wharf /wɔ:f/ n (pl wharves or wharfs) muelle m

what /wɒt/ a el que, la que, lo que, los que, las que; (in questions & exclamations) qué. ●pron lo que; (interrogative) qué. ~ about going? ¿si fuésemos? ~ about me? ¿y yo? ~ for? ¿para qué? ~ if? ¿y si? ~ is it? ¿qué es? ~ you need lo que te haga falta. ●int ¡cómo! ~ a fool! ¡qué tonto!

whatever/wɒt'evə(r)/ a cualquiera. ●pron (todo) lo que, cualquier cosa que

whatnot /'wɒtnɒt/ n chisme m

whatsoever /wɒtsəʊ'evə(r)/ a & pron = whatever

wheat /wi:t/ n trigo m. ~en a de trigo

wheedle /'wi:dl/ vt engatusar

wheel /wi:l/ n rueda f. at the ~ al volante. steering-~ n volante m. ●vt empujar ‹bicycle etc›. ●vi girar. ~ round girar. ~barrow /'wi:lbærəʊ/ n carretilla f. ~chair /'wi:ltʃeə(r)/ n silla f de ruedas

wheeze /wi:z/ vi resollar. ●n resuello m

when /wen/ adv cuándo. ●conj cuando

whence/wens/ adv de dónde

whenever/wen'evə(r)/ adv en cualquier momento; (every time that) cada vez que

where /weə(r)/ adv & conj donde; (interrogative) dónde. ~ are you going? ¿adónde vas? ~ are you from? ¿de dónde eres?

whereabouts /'weərəbaʊts/ adv dónde. ●n paradero m

whereas /weər'æz/ conj por cuanto; (in contrast) mientras (que)

whereby/weə'baɪ/ adv por lo cual

whereupon /weərə'pɒn/ adv después de lo cual

wherever /weər'evə(r)/ adv (in whatever place) dónde (diablos). ●conj dondequiera que

whet /wet/ vt (pt whetted) afilar; (fig) aguzar

whether /'weðə(r)/ conj si. ~ you like it or not que te guste o no te guste. I don't know ~ she will like it no sé si le gustará

which /wɪtʃ/ a (in questions) qué. ~ one cuál. ~ one of you cuál de vosotros. ●pron (in questions) cuál; (relative) que; (object) el cual, la cual, lo cual, los cuales, las cuales

whichever /wɪtʃ'evə(r)/ a cualquier. ●pron cualquiera que, el que, la que

whiff /wɪf/ n soplo m; (of smoke) bocanada f; (smell) olorcillo m

while /waɪl/ n rato m. ●conj mientras; (although) aunque. ~vt. ~ away pasar ‹time›

whilst/waɪlst/ conj = while

whim/wɪm/ n capricho m

whimper /'wɪmpə(r)/ vi lloriquear. ●n lloriqueo m

whimsical /'wɪmzɪkl/ a caprichoso; (odd) extraño

whine /waɪn/ vi gimotear. ●n gimoteo m

whip /wɪp/ n látigo m; (pol) oficial m disciplinario. ●vt (pt whipped) azotar; (culin) batir; (seize) agarrar. ~cord n tralla f. ~ped cream n nata f batida. ~ping-boy /'wɪpɪŋbɔɪ/ n cabeza f de turco. ~round n colecta f. ~ up (incite) estimular

whirl /wɜ:l/ vt hacer girar rápidamente. ●vi girar rápidamente; (swirl) arremolinarse. ●n giro m;

(*swirl*) remolino *m*. ~pool /'wɜ:l-pu:l/ *n* remolino *m*. ~wind /'wɜ:l-wɪnd/ *n* torbellino *m*

whirr /wɜ:(r)/ *n* zumbido *m*. ● *vi* zumbar

whisk /wɪsk/ *vt* (*culin*) batir. ● *n* (*culin*) batidor *m*. ~ away llevarse

whisker /'wɪskə(r)/ *n* pelo *m*. ~s *npl* (*of man*) patillas *fpl*; (*of cat etc*) bigotes *mpl*

whisky /'wɪskɪ/ *n* güisqui *m*

whisper /'wɪspə(r)/ *vt* decir en voz baja. ● *vi* cuchichear; (*leaves etc*) susurrar. ● *n* cuchicheo *m*; (*of leaves*) susurro *m*; (*rumour*) rumor *m*

whistle /'wɪsl/ *n* silbido *m*; (*instrument*) silbato *m*. ● *vi* silbar. ~-stop *n* (*pol*) breve parada *f* (en gira electoral)

white /waɪt/ *a* (*-er*, *-est*) blanco. go ~ ponerse pálido. ● *n* blanco; (*of egg*) clara *f*. ~bait /'waɪtbeɪt/ *n* (*pl* ~bait) chanquetes *mpl*. ~ coffee *n* café *m* con leche. ~-collar worker *n* empleado *m* de oficina. ~ elephant *n* objeto *m* inútil y costoso

Whitehall /'waɪthɔ:l/ *n* el gobierno *m* británico

white: ~ horses *n* cabrillas *fpl*. ~-hot *a* (*metal*) candente. ~ lie *n* mentirijilla *f*. ~n *vt/i* blanquear. ~ness *n* blancura *f*. W~ Paper *n* libro *m* blanco. ~wash /'waɪtwɒʃ/ *n* jalbegue *m*; (*fig*) encubrimiento *m*. ● *vt* enjalbegar; (*fig*) encubrir

whiting /'waɪtɪŋ/ *n* (*pl* whiting) (*fish*) pescadilla *f*

whitlow /'wɪtləʊ/ *n* panadizo *m*

Whitsun /'wɪtsn/ *n* Pentecostés *m*

whittle /'wɪtl/ *vt*. ~ (down) tallar; (*fig*) reducir

whiz /wɪz/ *vi* (*pt* whizzed) silbar; (*rush*) ir a gran velocidad. ~ past pasar como un rayo. ~-kid *n* (*fam*) joven *m* prometedor, promesa *f*

who /hu:/ *pron* que, quien; (*interrogative*) quién; (*particular person*) el que, la que, los que, las que

whodunit /hu:'dʌnɪt/ *n* (*fam*) novela *f* policíaca

whoever /hu:'evə(r)/ *pron* quienquiera que; (*interrogative*) quién (diablos)

whole /həʊl/ *a* entero; (*not broken*) intacto. ● *n* todo *m*, conjunto *m*; (*total*) total *m*. as a ~ en conjunto. on the ~ por regla general. ~-hearted *a* sincero. ~meal *a* integral

wholesale /'həʊlseɪl/ *n* venta *f* al por mayor. ● *a* & *adv* al por mayor. ~r /-ə(r)/ *n* comerciante *m* & *f* al por mayor

wholesome /'həʊlsəm/ *a* saludable

wholly /'həʊlɪ/ *adv* completamente

whom /hu:m/ *pron* que, a quien; (*interrogative*) a quién

whooping cough /'hu:pɪŋkɒf/ *n* tos *f* ferina

whore /hɔ:(r)/ *n* puta *f*

whose /hu:z/ *pron* de quién. ● *a* de quién; (*relative*) cuyo

why /waɪ/ *adv* por qué. ● *int* ¡toma!

wick /wɪk/ *n* mecha *f*

wicked /'wɪkɪd/ *a* malo; (*mischievous*) travieso (*very bad*, *fam*) malísimo. ~ness *n* maldad *f*

wicker /'wɪkə(r)/ *n* mimbre *m* & *f*. ● *a* de mimbre. ~work *n* artículos *mpl* de mimbre

wicket /'wɪkɪt/ *n* (*cricket*) rastrillo *m*

wide /waɪd/ *a* (*-er*, *-est*) ancho; (*fully opened*) de par en par; (*far from target*) lejano; (*knowledge etc*) amplio. ● *adv* lejos. far and ~ por todas partes. ~ awake *a* completamente despierto; (*fig*) despabilado. ~ly *adv* extensamente; (*believed*) generalmente; (*different*) muy. ~n *vt* ensanchar

widespread /'waɪdspred/ *a* extendido; (*fig*) difundido

widow /'wɪdəʊ/ *n* viuda *f*. ~ed *a* viudo. ~er *n* viudo *m*. ~hood *n* viudez *f*

width /wɪdθ/ *n* anchura *f*. in ~ de ancho

wield /wi:ld/ *vt* manejar; ejercer (*power*)

wife /waɪf/ *n* (*pl* wives) mujer *f*, esposa *f*

wig /wɪg/ *n* peluca *f*

wiggle /'wɪgl/ *vt* menear. ● *vi* menearse

wild /waɪld/ *a* (*-er*, *-est*) salvaje; (*enraged*) furioso; (*idea*) extravagante; (*with joy*) loco; (*random*) al azar. ● *adv* en estado salvaje. run ~ crecer en estado salvaje. ~s *npl* regiones *fpl* salvajes

wildcat /'waɪldkæt/ *a*. ~ strike *n* huelga *f* salvaje

wilderness /'wɪldənɪs/ *n* desierto *m*

wild: ~fire /'waɪldfaɪ(r)/ *n*. spread like ~fire correr como un reguero de pólvora. ~-goose chase *n* empresa *f* inútil. ~life /'waɪldlaɪf/ *n* fauna f. **~ly** adv violentamente; (fig) locamente

wilful /'wɪlfʊl/ a intencionado; (self-willed) terco. **~ly** adv intencionadamente; (obstinately) obstinadamente

will¹ /wɪl/ v aux. **~ you have some wine?** ¿quieres vino? **he ~ be** será. **you ~ be back soon, won't you?** volverás pronto, ¿no?

will² /wɪl/ n voluntad f; (document) testamento m

willing /'wɪlɪŋ/ a complaciente. **~ to** dispuesto a. **~ly** adv de buena gana. **~ness** n buena voluntad f

willow /'wɪləʊ/ n sauce m

will-power /'wɪlpaʊə(r)/ n fuerza f de voluntad

willy-nilly /wɪlɪ'nɪlɪ/ adv quieras que no

wilt /wɪlt/ vi marchitarse

wily /'waɪlɪ/ a (-ier, -iest) astuto

win /wɪn/ vt (pt won, pres p winning) ganar; (achieve, obtain) conseguir. ● vi ganar. ● n victoria f. **~ back** vi reconquistar. **~ over** vt convencer

wince /wɪns/ vi hacer una mueca de dolor. **without wincing** sin pestañear. ● n mueca f de dolor

winch /wɪntʃ/ n cabrestante m. ● vt levantar con el cabrestante

wind¹ /wɪnd/ n viento m; (in stomach) flatulencia f. **get the ~ up** (sl) asustarse. **get ~ of** enterarse de. **in the ~** en el aire. ● vt dejar sin aliento.

wind² /waɪnd/ vt (pt wound) (wrap around) enrollar; dar cuerda a (clock etc). ● vi (road etc) serpentear. **~ up** vt dar cuerda a (watch, clock); (provoke) agitar, poner nervioso; (fig) terminar, concluir

wind /wɪnd/: **~bag** n charlatán m. **~-cheater** n cazadora f

winder /'waɪndə(r)/ n devanador m; (of clock, watch) llave f

windfall /'wɪndfɔːl/ n fruta f caída; (fig) suerte f inesperada

winding /'waɪndɪŋ/ a tortuoso

wind instrument /'wɪndɪnstrəmənt/ n instrumento m de viento

windmill /'wɪndmɪl/ n molino m (de viento)

window /'wɪndəʊ/ n ventana f; (in shop) escaparate m; (of vehicle, booking-office) ventanilla f. **~-box** n

jardinera f. **~-dresser** n escaparatista m & f. **~-shop** vi mirar los escaparates

windpipe /'wɪndpaɪp/ n tráquea f

windscreen /'wɪndskriːn/ n, **windshield** n (Amer) parabrisas m invar. **~ wiper** n limpiaparabrisas m invar

wind /wɪnd/: **~-swept** a barrido por el viento. **~y** a (-ier, -iest) ventoso, de mucho viento. **it is ~y** hace viento

wine /waɪn/ n vino m. **~-cellar** n bodega f. **~glass** n copa f. **~-grower** n vinicultor m. **~-growing** n vinicultura f. ● a vinícola. **~ list** n lista f de vinos. **~-tasting** n cata f de vinos

wing /wɪŋ/ n ala f; (auto) aleta f. **under one's ~** bajo la protección de uno. **~ed** a alado. **~er** n -ə(r)/ n (sport) ala m & f. **~s** npl (in theatre) bastidores mpl

wink /wɪŋk/ vi guiñar el ojo; (light etc) centellear. ● n guiño m. **not to sleep a ~** no pegar ojo

winkle /'wɪŋkl/ n bígaro m

win: **~ner** /-ə(r)/ n ganador m. **~ning-post** n poste m de llegada. **~ning smile** n sonrisa f encantadora. **~nings** npl ganancias fpl

winsome /'wɪnsəm/ a atractivo

wint|er /'wɪntə(r)/ n invierno m. ● vi invernar. **~ry** a invernal

wipe /waɪp/ vt limpiar; (dry) secar. ● n limpión m. **give sth a ~** limpiar algo. **~ out** (cancel) cancelar; (destroy) destruir; (obliterate) borrar. **~ up** limpiar; (dry) secar

wire /'waɪə(r)/ n alambre m; (elec) cable m; (telegram, fam) telegrama m

wireless /'waɪəlɪs/ n radio f

wire netting /waɪə'netɪŋ/ n alambrera f, tela f metálica

wiring n instalación f eléctrica

wiry /'waɪərɪ/ a (-ier, -iest) (person) delgado

wisdom /'wɪzdəm/ n sabiduría f. **~ tooth** n muela f del juicio

wise /waɪz/ a (-er, -est) sabio; (sensible) prudente. **~crack** /'waɪzkræk/ n (fam) salida f. **~ly** adv sabiamente; (sensibly) prudentemente

wish /wɪʃ/ n deseo m; (greeting) saludo m. **with best ~es** (in letters) un fuerte abrazo. ● vt desear. **~ on** (fam) encajar a. **~ s.o. well** desear buena suerte a uno. **~bone** n espoleta f (de las aves). **~ful** a deseoso. **~ful thinking** n ilusiones fpl

wishy-washy /ˈwɪʃɪwɒʃɪ/ a soso; ⟨person⟩ sin convicciones, falto de entereza

wisp /wɪsp/ n manojito m; (of smoke) voluta f; (of hair) mechón m

wisteria /wɪsˈtɪərɪə/ n glicina f

wistful /ˈwɪstfl/ a melancólico

wit /wɪt/ n gracia f; (person) persona f chistosa; (intelligence) ingenio m. **be at one's ~s' end** no saber qué hacer. **live by one's ~s** vivir de expedientes, vivir del cuento

witch /wɪtʃ/ n bruja f. **~craft** n brujería f. **~doctor** n hechicero m

with /wɪð/ prep con; (cause, having) de. **be ~ it** (fam) estar al día, estar al tanto. **the man ~ the beard** el hombre de la barba

withdraw /wɪðˈdrɔː/ vt (pt withdrew, pp withdrawn) retirar. ● vi apartarse. **~al** n retirada f. **~n** a (person) introvertido

wither /ˈwɪðə(r)/ vi marchitarse. ● vt (fig) fulminar

withhold /wɪðˈhəʊld/ vt (pt withheld) retener; (conceal) ocultar (from a)

within /wɪðˈɪn/ prep dentro de. ● adv dentro. **~ sight** a la vista

without /wɪðˈaʊt/ prep sin

withstand /wɪðˈstænd/ vt (pt withstood) resistir a

witness /ˈwɪtnɪs/ n testigo m; (proof) testimonio m. ● vt presenciar; firmar como testigo ⟨document⟩. **~box** n tribuna f de los testigos

witticism /ˈwɪtɪsɪzəm/ n ocurrencia f

wittingly /ˈwɪtɪŋlɪ/ adv a sabiendas

witty /ˈwɪtɪ/ a (-ier, -iest) gracioso

wives /waɪvz/ see **wife**

wizard /ˈwɪzəd/ n hechicero m. **~ry** n hechicería f

wizened /ˈwɪznd/ a arrugado

wobbl|e /ˈwɒbl/ vi tambalearse; ⟨voice, jelly, hand⟩ temblar; ⟨chair etc⟩ balancearse. **~y** a ⟨chair etc⟩ cojo

woe /wəʊ/ n aflicción f. **~ful** a triste. **~begone** /ˈwəʊbɪgɒn/ a desconsolado

woke, woken /wəʊk, ˈwəʊkən/ see **wake**[1]

wolf /wʊlf/ n (pl **wolves**) lobo m. **cry ~** gritar al lobo. ● vt zamparse. **~ whistle** n silbido m de admiración

woman /ˈwʊmən/ n (pl **women**) mujer f. **single ~** soltera f. **~ize**

/ˈwʊmənaɪz/ vi ser mujeriego. **~ly** a femenino

womb /wuːm/ n matriz f

women /ˈwɪmɪn/ npl see **woman**. **~folk** /ˈwɪmɪnfəʊk/ npl mujeres fpl. **~'s lib** n movimiento m de liberación de la mujer

won /wʌn/ see **win**

wonder /ˈwʌndə(r)/ n maravilla f; (bewilderment) asombro m. **no ~** no es de extrañarse (that que). ● vi admirarse; (reflect) preguntarse

wonderful /ˈwʌndəfl/ a maravilloso. **~ly** adv maravillosamente

won't /wəʊnt/ = **will not**

woo /wuː/ vt cortejar

wood /wʊd/ n madera f; (for burning) leña f; (area) bosque m; (in bowls) bola f. **out of the ~** (fig) fuera de peligro. **~cutter** /ˈwʊdkʌtə(r)/ n leñador m. **~ed** a poblado de árboles, boscoso. **~en** a de madera. **~land** n bosque m

woodlouse /ˈwʊdlaʊs/ n (pl **-lice**) cochinilla f

woodpecker /ˈwʊdpekə(r)/ n pájaro m carpintero

woodwind /ˈwʊdwɪnd/ n instrumentos mpl de viento de madera

woodwork /ˈwʊdwɜːk/ n carpintería f; (in room etc) maderaje m

woodworm /ˈwʊdwɜːm/ n carcoma f

woody /ˈwʊdɪ/ a leñoso

wool /wʊl/ n lana f. **pull the ~ over s.o.'s eyes** engañar a uno. **~len** a de lana. **~lens** npl ropa f de lana. **~ly** a (-ier, -iest) de lana; (fig) confuso. ● n jersey m

word /wɜːd/ n palabra f; (news) noticia f. **by ~ of mouth** de palabra. **have ~s with** reñir con. **in one ~** en una palabra. **in other ~s** es decir. ● vt expresar. **~ing** n expresión f, términos mpl. **~-perfect** a. **be ~-perfect** saber de memoria. **~ processor** n procesador m de textos. **~y** a prolijo

wore /wɔː(r)/ see **wear**

work /wɜːk/ n trabajo m; (arts) obra f. ● vt hacer trabajar; manejar ⟨machine⟩. ● vi trabajar; ⟨machine etc⟩ funcionar; ⟨student⟩ estudiar; ⟨drug etc⟩ tener efecto; (be successful) tener éxito. **~ in** introducir(se). **~ off** desahogar. **~ out** vt resolver; (calculate) calcular; elaborar ⟨plan⟩. ● vi (succeed) salir bien; (sport) entrenarse. ~ up vt desarrollar. • vi excitarse. ~able /'wɜ:kəbl/ a (project) factible. ~aholic /wɜ:kə'hɒlɪk/ n trabajador m obsesivo. ~ed up a agitado. ~er /'wɜ:kə(r)/ n trabajador m; (manual) obrero m

workhouse /'wɜ:khaʊs/ n asilo m de pobres

work ~ing /'wɜ:kɪŋ/ a (day) laborable; (clothes etc) de trabajo. • n (mec) funcionamiento m. in ~ing order en estado de funcionamiento. ~ing class n clase f obrera. ~ing-class a de la clase obrera. ~man /'wɜ:kmən/ n (pl -men) obrero m. ~manlike /'wɜ:kmənlaɪk/ a concienzudo. ~manship n destreza f. ~s npl (building) fábrica f; (mec) mecanismo m. ~shop /'wɜ:kʃɒp/ n taller m. ~to-rule n huelga f de celo

world /wɜ:ld/ n mundo m. a ~ of enorme. out of this ~ maravilloso. • a mundial. ~ly a mundano. ~wide a universal

worm /wɜ:m/ n lombriz f; (grub) gusano m. • vi. ~ one's way insinuarse. ~eaten a carcomido

worn /wɔ:n/ see wear. • a gastado. ~out a gastado; (person) rendido

worr|ied /'wʌrɪd/ a preocupado. ~ier /-ə(r)/ n aprensivo m. ~y /'wʌrɪ/ vt preocupar; (annoy) molestar. • vi preocuparse. • n preocupación f. ~ying a inquietante

worse /wɜ:s/ a peor. • adv peor; (more) más. • n lo peor. ~n vt/i empeorar

worship /'wɜ:ʃɪp/ n culto m; (title) señor, su señoría. • vt (pt worshipped) adorar

worst /wɜ:st/ a (el) peor. • adv peor. • n lo peor. get the ~ of it llevar la peor parte

worsted /'wʊstɪd/ n estambre m

worth /wɜ:θ/ n valor m. • a. be ~ valer. it is ~ trying vale la pena probarlo. it was ~ my while (me) valió la pena. ~less a sin valor. ~while /'wɜ:θwaɪl/ a que vale la pena

worthy /'wɜ:ðɪ/ a meritorio; (respectable) respetable; (laudable) loable

would /wʊd/ v aux. ~ you come here please? ¿quieres venir aquí? ~ you go? ¿irías tú? he ~ come if he could vendría si pudiese. I ~ come every day (used to) venía todos los

días. I ~ do it lo haría yo. ~be a supuesto

wound[^1] /wu:nd/ n herida f. • vt herir

wound[^2] /waʊnd/ see wind[^2]

wove, woven /wəʊv, 'wəʊvn/ see weave

wow /waʊ/ int ¡caramba!

wrangle /'ræŋgl/ vi reñir. • n riña f

wrap /ræp/ vt (pt wrapped) envolver. be ~ped up in (fig) estar absorto en. • n bata f; (shawl) chal m. ~per /-ə(r)/ n, ~ping n envoltura f

wrath /rɒθ/ n ira f. ~ful a iracundo

wreath /ri:θ/ n (pl -ths /-ðz/) guirnalda f; (for funeral) corona f

wreck /rek/ n ruina f; (sinking) naufragio m; (remains of ship) buque m naufragado. be a nervous ~ tener los nervios destrozados. • vt hacer naufragar; (fig) arruinar. ~age n restos mpl; (of building) escombros mpl

wren /ren/ n troglodito m

wrench /rentʃ/ vt arrancar; (twist) torcer. • n arranque m; (tool) llave f inglesa

wrest /rest/ vt arrancar (from a)

wrestl|e /'resl/ vi luchar. ~er /-ə(r)/ n luchador m. ~ing n lucha f

wretch /retʃ/ n desgraciado m; (rascal) tunante m & f. ~ed a miserable; (weather) horrible, de perros; (dog etc) maldito

wriggle /'rɪgl/ vi culebrear. ~ out of escaparse de. ~ through deslizarse por. • n serpenteo m

wring /rɪŋ/ vt (pt wrung) retorcer. ~ out of (obtain from) arrancar. ~ing wet empapado

wrinkle /'rɪŋkl/ n arruga f. • vt arrugar. • vi arrugarse

wrist /rɪst/ n muñeca f. ~watch n reloj m de pulsera

writ /rɪt/ n decreto m judicial

write /raɪt/ vt/i (pt wrote, pp written, pres p writing) escribir. ~ down vt anotar. ~ off vt cancelar; (fig) dar por perdido. ~ up vt hacer un reportaje de; (keep up to date) poner al día. ~off n pérdida f total. ~r /-ə(r)/ n escritor m; (author) autor m. ~up n reportaje m; (review) crítica f

writhe /raɪð/ vi retorcerse

writing /'raɪtɪŋ/ n escribir m; (handwriting) letra f. in ~ por escrito. ~s

npl obras *fpl*. ~**-paper** *n* papel *m* de escribir
written /'rɪtn/ *see* write
wrong /rɒŋ/ *a* incorrecto; *(not just)* injusto; *(mistaken)* equivocado. **be** ~ no tener razón; *(be mistaken)* equivocarse. ● *adv* mal. **go** ~ equivocarse; *(plan)* salir mal; *(car etc)* estropearse. ● *n* injusticia *f*; *(evil)* mal *m*. **in the** ~ equivocado. ● *vt* ser injusto con. ~**ful** *a* injusto. ~**ly** *adv* mal; *(unfairly)* injustamente
wrote /rəʊt/ *see* write
wrought /rɔ:t/ *a*. ~ **iron** *n* hierro *m* forjado
wrung /rʌŋ/ *see* wring
wry /raɪ/ *a* (**wryer, wryest**) torcido; *(smile)* forzado. ~ **face** *n* mueca *f*

X

xenophobia /zenə'fəʊbɪə/ *n* xenofobia *f*
Xerox /'zɪərɒks/ *n* (P) fotocopiadora *f*. **xerox** *n* fotocopia *f*
Xmas /'krɪsməs/ *n abbr* (*Christmas*) Navidad *f*, Navidades *fpl*
X-ray /'eksreɪ/ *n* radiografía *f*. ~**s** *npl* rayos *mpl* X. ● *vt* radiografiar
xylophone /'zaɪləfəʊn/ *n* xilófono *m*

Y

yacht /jɒt/ *n* yate *m*. ~**ing** *n* navegación *f* a vela
yam /jæm/ *n* ñame *m*, batata *f*
yank /jæŋk/ *vt* (*fam*) arrancar violentamente
Yankee /'jæŋkɪ/ *n* (*fam*) yanqui *m* & *f*
yap /jæp/ *vi* (*pt* **yapped**) *(dog)* ladrar
yard¹ /jɑ:d/ *n* (*measurement*) yarda *f* (= 0.9144 metre)
yard² /jɑ:d/ *n* patio *m*; *(Amer, garden)* jardín *m*
yardage /'jɑ:dɪdʒ/ *n* metraje *m*
yardstick /'jɑ:dstɪk/ *n* (*fig*) criterio *m*
yarn /jɑ:n/ *n* hilo *m*; *(tale, fam)* cuento *m*
yashmak /'jæʃmæk/ *n* velo *m*
yawn /jɔ:n/ *vi* bostezar. ● *n* bostezo *m*
year /jɪə(r)/ *n* año *m*. **be three** ~**s old** tener tres años. ~**-book** *n*

anuario *m*. ~**ling** /'jɜ:lɪŋ/ *n* primal *m*. ~**ly** *a* anual. ● *adv* anualmente
yearn /'jɜ:n/ *vi*. ~ **for** anhelar. ~**ing** *n* ansia *f*
yeast /ji:st/ *n* levadura *f*
yell /jel/ *vi* gritar. ● *n* grito *m*
yellow /'jeləʊ/ *a* & *n* amarillo (*m*). ~**ish** *a* amarillento
yelp /jelp/ *n* gañido *m*. ● *vi* gañir
yen /jen/ *n* muchas ganas *fpl*
yeoman /'jəʊmən/ *n* (*pl* **-men**) Y~ **of the Guard** alabardero *m* de la Casa Real
yes /jes/ *adv* & *n* sí (*m*)
yesterday /'jestədeɪ/ *adv* & *n* ayer (*m*). **the day before** ~ anteayer *m*
yet /jet/ *adv* todavía, aún; *(already)* ya. **as** ~ hasta ahora. ● *conj* sin embargo
yew /ju:/ *n* tejo *m*
Yiddish /'jɪdɪʃ/ *n* judeoalemán *m*
yield /ji:ld/ *vt* producir. ● *vi* ceder. ● *n* producción *f*; *(com)* rendimiento *m*
yoga /'jəʊgə/ *n* yoga *m*
yoghurt /'jɒgət/ *n* yogur *m*
yoke /jəʊk/ *n* yugo *m*; *(of garment)* canesú *m*
yokel /'jəʊkl/ *n* patán *m*, palurdo *m*
yolk /jəʊk/ *n* yema *f* (de huevo)
yonder /'jɒndə(r)/ *adv* a lo lejos
you /ju:/ *pron (familiar form)* tú, vos (*Arg*), (*pl*) vosotros, vosotras, ustedes (*LAm*); (*polite form*) usted, (*pl*) ustedes; (*familiar, object*) te, (*pl*) os, les (*LAm*); (*polite, object*) le, la, (*pl*) les; (*familiar, after prep*) ti, (*pl*) vosotros, vosotras, ustedes (*LAm*); (*polite, after prep*) usted, (*pl*) ustedes. **with** ~ (*familiar*) contigo, (*pl*) con vosotros, con vosotras, con ustedes (*LAm*); (*polite*) con usted, (*pl*) con ustedes; (*polite reflexive*) consigo. **I know** ~ te conozco, le conozco a usted. **you can't smoke here** aquí no se puede fumar
young /jʌŋ/ *a* (**-er, -est**) joven. ~ **lady** *n* señorita *f*. ~ **man** *n* joven *m*. **her** ~ **man** *(boyfriend)* su novio *m*. **the** ~ *npl* los jóvenes *mpl*; *(of animals)* la cría *f*. ~**ster** /'jʌŋstə(r)/ *n* joven *m*
your /jɔ:(r)/ *a (familiar)* tu, (*pl*) vuestro; *(polite)* su
yours /jɔ:z/ *poss pron* (el) tuyo, (*pl*) (el) vuestro, el de ustedes (*LAm*);

(polite) el suyo. **a book of** ∼s un libro tuyo, un libro suyo. **Y**∼**s faithfully, Y**∼**s sincerely** le saluda atentamente

yourself /jɔːˈself/ *pron (pl* **yourselves***) (familiar, subject)* tú mismo, tú misma, *(pl)* vosotros mismos, vosotras mismas, ustedes mismos *(LAm)*; *(polite, subject)* usted mismo, usted misma, *(pl)* ustedes mismas, ustedes mismas; *(familiar, object)* te, *(pl)* os, se *(LAm)*; *(polite, object)* se; *(familiar, after prep)* ti, *(pl)* vosotros, vosotras, ustedes *(LAm)*; *(polite, after prep)* sí

youth /juːθ/ *n (pl* **youths** /juːðz/*)* juventud *f*; *(boy)* joven *m*; *(young people)* jóvenes *mpl.* ∼**ful** *a* joven, juvenil. ∼**hostel** *n* albergue *m* para jóvenes

yowl /jaʊl/ *vi* aullar. ● *n* aullido *m*

Yugoslav /ˈjuːɡəslɑːv/ *a* & *n* yugoslavo *(m).* ∼**ia** /-ˈslɑːvɪə/ *n* Yugoslavia *f*

yule /juːl/ *n*, **yule-tide** /ˈjuːltaɪd/ *n (old use)* Navidades *fpl*

Z

zany /ˈzeɪnɪ/ *a* (**-ier,-iest**) estrafalario

zeal /ziːl/ *n* celo *m*

zealot /ˈzelət/ *n* fanático *m*

zealous /ˈzeləs/ *a* entusiasta. ∼**ly** /ˈzeləslɪ/ *adv* con entusiasmo

zebra /ˈzebrə/ *n* cebra *f.* ∼ **crossing** *n* paso *m* de cebra

zenith /ˈzenɪθ/ *n* cenit *m*

zero /ˈzɪərəʊ/ *n (pl* **-os***)* cero *m*

zest /zest/ *n* gusto *m*; *(peel)* cáscara *f*

zigzag /ˈzɪɡzæɡ/ *n* zigzag *m.* ● *vi (pt* **zigzagged***)* zigzaguear

zinc /zɪŋk/ *n* cinc *m*

Zionis|m /ˈzaɪənɪzəm/ *n* sionismo *m.* ∼**t** *n* sionista *m* & *f*

zip /zɪp/ *n* cremallera *f.* ● *vt.* ∼ **(up)** cerrar (la cremallera)

Zip code /ˈzɪpkəʊd/ *n (Amer)* código *m* postal

zip fastener /zɪpˈfɑːsnə(r)/ *n* cremallera *f*

zircon /ˈzɜːkən/ *n* circón *m*

zither /ˈzɪðə(r)/ *n* citara *f*

zodiac /ˈzəʊdɪæk/ *n* zodiaco *m*

zombie /ˈzɒmbɪ/ *n (fam)* autómata *m* & *f*

zone /zəʊn/ *n* zona *f*

zoo /zuː/ *n (fam)* zoo *m*, jardín *m* zoológico. ∼**logical** /zəʊəˈlɒdʒɪkl/ *a* zoológico

zoolog|ist /zəʊˈɒlədʒɪst/ *n* zoólogo *m.* ∼**y** /zəʊˈɒlədʒɪ/ *n* zoología *f*

zoom /zuːm/ *vi* ir a gran velocidad. ∼ **in** *(photo)* acercarse rápidamente. ∼ **past** pasar zumbando. ∼ **lens** *n* zoom *m*

Zulu /ˈzuːluː/ *n* zulú *m* & *f*

Numbers · Números

zero	0	cero
one (first)	1	uno (primero)
two (second)	2	dos (segundo)
three (third)	3	tres (tercero)
four (fourth)	4	cuatro (cuarto)
five (fifth)	5	cinco (quinto)
six (sixth)	6	seis (sexto)
seven (seventh)	7	siete (séptimo)
eight (eighth)	8	ocho (octavo)
nine (ninth)	9	nueve (noveno)
ten (tenth)	10	diez (décimo)
eleven (eleventh)	11	once (undécimo)
twelve (twelfth)	12	doce (duodécimo)
thirteen (thirteenth)	13	trece (decimotercero)
fourteen (fourteenth)	14	catorce (decimocuarto)
fifteen (fifteenth)	15	quince (decimoquinto)
sixteen (sixteenth)	16	dieciséis (decimosexto)
seventeen (seventeenth)	17	diecisiete (decimoséptimo)
eighteen (eighteenth)	18	dieciocho (decimoctavo)
nineteen (nineteenth)	19	diecinueve (decimonoveno)
twenty (twentieth)	20	veinte (vigésimo)
twenty-one (twenty-first)	21	veintiuno (vigésimo primero)
twenty-two (twenty-second)	22	veintidós (vigésimo segundo)
twenty-three (twenty-third)	23	veintitrés (vigésimo tercero)
twenty-four (twenty-fourth)	24	veinticuatro (vigésimo cuarto)
twenty-five (twenty-fifth)	25	veinticinco (vigésimo quinto)
twenty-six (twenty-sixth)	26	veintiséis (vigésimo sexto)
thirty (thirtieth)	30	treinta (trigésimo)
thirty-one (thirty-first)	31	treinta y uno (trigésimo primero)
forty (fortieth)	40	cuarenta (cuadragésimo)
fifty (fiftieth)	50	cincuenta (quincuagésimo)
sixty (sixtieth)	60	sesenta (sexagésimo)
seventy (seventieth)	70	setenta (septuagésimo)
eighty (eightieth)	80	ochenta (octogésimo)

English	Number	Español
ninety (ninetieth)	90	noventa (nonagésimo)
a/one hundred (hundredth)	100	cien (centésimo)
a/one hundred and one (hundred and first)	101	ciento uno (centésimo primero)
two hundred (two hundredth)	200	doscientos (ducentésimo)
three hundred (three hundredth)	300	trescientos (tricentésimo)
four hundred (four hundredth)	400	cuatrocientos (cuadringentésimo)
five hundred (five hundredth)	500	quinientos (quingentésimo)
six hundred (six hundredth)	600	seiscientos (sexcentésimo)
seven hundred (seven hundredth)	700	setecientos (septingentésimo)
eight hundred (eight hundredth)	800	ochocientos (octingentésimo)
nine hundred (nine hundredth)	900	novecientos (noningentésimo)
a/one thousand (thousandth)	1000	mil (milésimo)
two thousand (two thousandth)	2000	dos mil (dos milésimo)
a/one million (millionth)	1,000,000	un millón (millonésimo)

Spanish Verbs · Verbos españoles

Regular verbs:

in -ar (*e.g.* comprar)
Present; compr|o, ~as, ~a, ~amos, ~áis, ~an
Future: comprar|é, ~ás, ~á, ~emos, ~éis, ~án
Imperfect: compr|aba, ~abas, ~aba, ~ábamos, ~abais, ~aban
Preterite: compr|é, ~aste, ~ó, ~amos, ~asteis, ~aron
Present subjunctive: compr|e, ~es, ~e, ~emos, ~éis, ~en
Imperfect subjunctive: compr|ara, ~aras, ~ara, ~áramos, ~arais, ~aran
compr|ase, ~ases, ~ase, ~ásemos, ~aseis, ~asen
Conditional: comprar|ía, ~ías, ~ía, ~íamos, ~íais, ~ían
Present participle: comprando
Past participle: comprado
Imperative: compra, comprad

in -er (*e.g.* beber)
Present: beb|o, ~es, ~e, ~emos, ~éis, ~en
Future: beber|é, ~ás, ~á, ~emos, ~éis, ~án
Imperfect: beb|ía, ~ías, ~ía, ~íamos, ~íais, ~ían
Preterite: beb|í, ~iste, ~ió, ~imos, ~isteis, ~ieron
Present subjunctive: beb|a, ~as, ~a, ~amos, ~áis, ~an
Imperfect subjunctive: beb|iera, ~ieras, ~iera, ~iéramos, ~ierais, ~ieran
beb|iese, ~ieses, ~iese, ~iésemos, ~ieseis, ~iesen
Conditional: beber|ía, ~ías, ~ía, ~íamos, ~íais, ~ían
Present participle: bebiendo
Past participle: bebido
Imperative: bebe, bebed

in -ir (*e.g.* vivir)
Present: viv|o, ~es, ~e, ~imos, ~ís, ~en
Future: vivir|é, ~ás, ~á, ~emos, ~éis, ~án
Imperfect: viv|ía, ~ías, ~ía, ~íamos, ~íais, ~ían
Preterite: viv|í, ~iste, ~ió, ~imos, ~isteis, ~ieron

Present subjunctive: viv|a, ~as, ~a, ~amos, ~áis, ~an
Imperfect subjunctive: viv|iera, ~ieras, ~iera, ~iéramos, ~ierais, ~ieran
viv|iese, ~ieses, ~iese, ~iésemos, ~ieseis, ~iesen
Conditional: vivir|ía, ~ías, ~ía, ~íamos, ~íais, ~ían
Present participle: viviendo
Past participle: vivido
Imperative: vive, vivid

Irregular verbs:

[1] cerrar
Present: cierro, cierras, cierra, cerramos, cerráis, cierran
Present subjunctive: cierre, cierres, cierre, cerremos, cerréis, cierren
Imperative: cierra, cerrad

[2] contar, mover
Present: cuento, cuentas, cuenta, contamos, contáis, cuentan
muevo, mueves, mueve, movemos, movéis, mueven
Present subjunctive: cuente, cuentes, cuente, contemos, contéis, cuenten
mueva, muevas, mueva, movamos, mováis, muevan
Imperative: cuenta, contad
mueve, moved

[3] jugar
Present: juego, juegas, juega, jugamos, jugáis, juegan
Preterite: jug|ué, jugaste, jugó, jugamos, jugasteis, jugaron
Present subjunctive: juegue, juegues, juegue, juguemos, juguéis, jueguen

[4] sentir
Present: siento, sientes, siente, sentimos, sentís, sienten
Preterite: sentí, sentiste, sintió, sentimos, sentisteis, sintieron
Present subjunctive: sienta, sientas, sienta, sintamos, sintáis, sientan
Imperfect subjunctive: sint|iera, ~ieras, ~iera, ~iéramos, ~ierais, ~ieran

sint|iese, ~ieses, ~iese,
~iésemos, ~ieseis, ~iesen
Present participle: sintiendo
Imperative: siente, sentid

[5] **pedir**
Present: pido, pides, pide, pedimos,
pedís, piden
Preterite: pedí, pediste, pidió,
pedimos, pedisteis, pidieron
Present subjunctive: pid|a, ~as, ~a,
~amos, ~áis, ~an
Imperfect subjunctive: pid|iera,
~ieras, ~iera, ~iéramos,
~ierais, ~ieran
pid|iese, ~ieses, ~iese,
~iésemos, ~ieseis, ~iesen
Present participle: pidiendo
Imperative: pide, pedid

[6] **dormir**
Present: duermo, duermes, duerme,
dormimos, dormís, duermen
Preterite: dormí, dormiste, durmió,
dormimos, dormisteis, durmieron
Present subjunctive: duerma,
duermas, duerma, durmamos,
durmáis, duerman
Imperfect subjunctive: durm|iera,
~ieras, ~iera, ~iéramos,
~ierais, ~ieran
durm|iese, ~ieses, ~iese,
~iésemos, ~ieseis, ~iesen
Present participle: durmiendo
Imperative: duerme, dormid

[7] **dedicar**
Preterite: dediqué, dedicaste, dedicó,
dedicamos, dedicasteis, dedicaron
Present subjunctive: dediqu|e, ~es,
~e, ~emos, ~éis, ~en

[8] **delinquir**
Present: delinco, delinques, delinque,
delinquimos, delinquís, delinquen
Present subjunctive: delinc|a, ~as,
~a, ~amos, ~áis, ~an

[9] **vencer, esparcir**
Present: venzo, vences, vence,
vencemos, vencéis, vencen
esparzo, esparces, esparce,
esparcimos, esparcís, esparcen
Present subjunctive: venz|a, ~as, ~a,
~amos, ~áis, ~an
esparz|a, ~as, ~a, ~amos, ~áis,
~an

[10] **rechazar**
Preterite: rechacé, rechazaste,
rechazó, rechazamos, rechazasteis,
rechazaron
Present subjunctive: rechac|e, ~es,
~e, ~emos, ~éis, ~en

[11] **conocer, lucir**
Present: conozco, conoces, conoce,
conocemos, conocéis, conocen
luzco, luces, luce, lucimos, lucís,
lucen
Present subjunctive: conozc|a, ~as,
~a, ~amos, ~áis, ~an
luzc|a, ~as, ~a, ~amos, ~áis,
~an

[12] **pagar**
Preterite: pagué, pagaste, pagó,
pagamos, pagasteis, pagaron
Present subjunctive: pagu|e, ~es, ~e,
~emos, ~éis, ~en

[13] **distinguir**
Present: distingo, distingues,
distingue, distinguimos,
distinguís, distinguen
Present subjunctive: disting|a, ~as,
~a, ~amos, ~áis, ~an

[14] **acoger, afligir**
Present: acojo, acoges, acoge,
acogemos, acogéis, acogen
aflijo, afliges, aflige, afligimos,
afligís, afligen
Present subjunctive: acoj|a, ~as, ~a,
~amos, ~áis, ~an
aflij|a, ~as, ~a, ~amos, ~áis,
~an

[15] **averiguar**
Preterite: averigüé, averiguaste,
averiguó, averiguamos,
averiguasteis, averiguaron
Present subjunctive: averigü|e, ~es,
~e, ~emos, ~éis, ~en

[16] **agorar**
Present: agüero, agüeras, agüera,
agoramos, agoráis, agüeran
Present subjunctive: agüere, agüeres,
agüere, agoremos, agoréis, agüeren
Imperative: agüera, agorad

[17] **huir**
Present: huyo, huyes, huye, huimos,
huís, huyen

Preterite: huí, huiste, huyó, huimos,
  huisteis, huyeron
Present: huy|a, ~as, ~a,
  ~amos, ~áis, ~an
Imperfect subjunctive: huy|era,
  ~eras, ~era, ~éramos, ~erais,
  ~eran
huy|ese, ~eses, ~ese, ~ésemos,
  ~eseis, ~esen
Present participle: huyendo
Imperative: huye, huid

[18] creer
Preterite: creí, creíste, creyó,
  creímos, creísteis, creyeron
Imperfect subjunctive: crey|era,
  ~eras, ~era, ~éramos, ~erais,
  ~eran
crey|ese, ~eses, ~ese, ~ésemos,
  ~eseis, ~esen
Present participle: creyendo
Past participle: creído

[19] argüir
Present: arguyo, arguyes, arguye,
  argüimos, argüís, arguyen
Preterite: argüí, argüiste, arguyó,
  argüimos, argüisteis, arguyeron
Present subjunctive: arguy|a, ~as,
  ~a, ~amos, ~áis, ~an
Imperfect subjunctive: arguy|era,
  ~eras, ~era, ~éramos, ~erais,
  ~eran
arguy|ese, ~eses, ~ese,
  ~ésemos, ~eseis, ~esen
Present participle: arguyendo
Imperative: arguye, argüid

[20] vaciar
Present: vacío, vacías, vacía,
  vaciamos, vaciáis, vacían
Present subjunctive: vacíe, vacíes,
  vacíe, vaciemos, vaciéis, vacíen
Imperative: vacía, vaciad

[21] acentuar
Present: acentúo, acentúas, acentúa,
  acentuamos, acentuáis, acentúan
Present subjunctive: acentúe,
  acentúes, acentúe, acentuemos,
  acentuéis, acentúen
Imperative: acentúa, acentuad

[22] atañer, engullir
Preterite: atañ|í, ~iste, ~ó, ~imos,
  ~isteis, ~eron
engull|í ~iste, ~ó, ~imos,
  ~isteis, ~eron

Imperfect subjunctive: atañ|era,
  ~eras, ~era, ~éramos, ~erais,
  ~eran
atañ|ese, ~eses, ~ese, ~ésemos,
  ~eseis, ~esen
engull|era, ~eras, ~era,
  ~éramos, ~erais, ~eran
engull|ese, ~eses, ~ese,
  ~ésemos, ~eseis, ~esen
Present participle: atañendo
  engullendo

[23] aislar, aullar
Present: aíslo, aíslas, aísla, aislamos,
  aisláis, aíslan
aúllo, aúllas, aúlla, aullamos,
  aulláis, aúllan
Present subjunctive: aísle, aísles,
  aísle, aislemos, aisléis, aíslen
aúlle, aúlles, aúlle, aullemos,
  aulléis, aúllen
Imperative: aísla, aislad
  aúlla, aullad

[24] abolir, garantir
Present: abolimos, abolís
  garantimos, garantís
Present subjunctive: not used
Imperative: abolid
  garantid

[25] andar
Preterite: anduv|e, ~iste, ~o,
  ~imos, ~isteis, ~ieron
Imperfect subjunctive: anduv|iera,
  ~ieras, ~iera, ~iéramos,
  ~ierais, ~ieran
anduv|iese, ~ieses, ~iese,
  ~iésemos, ~ieseis, ~iesen

[26] dar
Present: doy, das, da, damos, dais, dan
Preterite: di, diste, dio, dimos, disteis,
  dieron
Present subjunctive: dé, des, dé,
  demos, deis, den
Imperfect subjunctive: diera, dieras,
  diera, diéramos, dierais, dieran
diese, dieses, diese, diésemos,
  dieseis, diesen

[27] estar
Present: estoy, estás, está, estamos,
  estáis, están
Preterite: estuv|e, ~iste, ~o, ~imos,
  ~isteis, ~ieron
Present subjunctive: esté, estés, esté,
  estemos, estéis, estén

Imperfect subjunctive: estuv|iera,
～ieras, ～iera, ～iéramos,
～ierais, ～ieran
estuv|iese, ～ieses, ～iese,
～iésemos, ～ieseis, ～iesen
Imperative: está, estad

[28] **caber**
Present: quepo, cabes, cabe, cabemos,
cabéis, caben
Future: cabr|é, ～ás, ～á, ～emos,
～éis, ～án
Preterite: cup|e, ～iste, ～o, ～imos,
～isteis, ～ieron
Present subjunctive: quep|a, ～as, ～a,
～amos, ～áis, ～an
Imperfect subjunctive: cup|iera,
～ieras, ～iera, ～iéramos,
～ierais, ～ieran
cup|iese, ～ieses, ～iese,
～iésemos, ～ieseis, ～iesen
Conditional: cabr|ía, ～ías, ～ía,
～íamos, ～íais, ～ían

[29] **caer**
Present: caigo, caes, cae, caemos,
caéis, caen
Preterite: caí, caiste, cayó, caímos,
caisteis, cayeron
Present subjunctive: caig|a, ～as, ～a,
～amos, ～áis, ～an
Imperfect subjunctive: cay|era,
～eras, ～era, ～éramos, ～erais,
～eran
cay|ese, ～eses, ～ese, ～ésemos,
～eseis, ～esen
Present participle: cayendo
Past participle: caído

[30] **haber**
Present: he, has, ha, hemos, habéis,
han
Future: habr|é ～ás, ～á, ～emos,
～éis, ～án
Preterite: hub|e, ～iste, ～o, ～imos,
～isteis, ～ieron
Present subjunctive: hay|a, ～as, ～a,
～amos, ～áis, ～an
Imperfect subjunctive: hub|iera,
～ieras, ～iera, ～iéramos,
～ierais, ～ieran
hub|iese, ～ieses, ～iese,
～iésemos, ～ieseis, ～iesen
Conditional: habr|ía, ～ías, ～ía,
～íamos, ～íais, ～ían

[31] **hacer**
Present: hago, haces, hace, hacemos,
hacéis, hacen
Future: har|é, ～ás, ～á, ～emos,
～éis, ～án
Preterite: hice, hiciste, hizo, hicimos,
hicisteis, hicieron
Present subjunctive: hag|a, ～as, ～a,
～amos, ～áis, ～an
Imperfect subjunctive: hic|iera,
～ieras, ～iera, ～iéramos,
～ierais, ～ieran
hic|iese, ～ieses, ～iese,
～iésemos, ～ieseis, ～iesen
Conditional: har|ía, ～ías, ～ía,
～íamos, ～íais, ～ían
Past participle: hecho
Imperative: haz, haced

[32] **placer**
Preterite: plació/plugo
Present subjunctive: plazca
Imperfect subjunctive:
placiera/pluguiera
placiese/pluguiese

[33] **poder**
Present: puedo, puedes, puede,
podemos, podéis, pueden
Future: podr|é, ～ás, ～á, ～emos,
～éis, ～án
Preterite: pud|e, ～iste, ～o, ～imos,
～isteis, ～ieron
Present subjunctive: pueda, puedas,
pueda, podamos, podáis, puedan
Imperfect subjunctive: pud|iera,
～ieras, ～iera, ～iéramos,
～ierais, ～ieran
pud|iese, ～ieses, ～iese,
～iésemos, ～ieseis, ～iesen
Conditional: podr|ía, ～ías, ～ía,
～íamos, ～íais, ～ían
Past participle: pudiendo

[34] **poner**
Present: pongo, pones, pone,
ponemos, ponéis, ponen
Future: pondr|é, ～ás, ～á, ～emos,
～éis, ～án
Preterite: pus|e, ～iste, ～o, ～imos,
～isteis, ～ieron
Present subjunctive: pong|a, ～as, ～a,
～amos, ～áis, ～an
Imperfect subjunctive: pus|iera,
～ieras, ～iera, ～iéramos,
～ierais, ～ieran
pus|iese, ～ieses, ～iese,
～iésemos, ～ieseis, ～iesen

Conditional: pondr|ía, ~ías, ~ía,
~íamos, ~íais, ~ían
Past participle: puesto
Imperative: pon, poned

[35] querer
Present: quiero, quieres, quiere,
queremos, queréis, quieren
Future: querr|é, ~ás, ~á, ~emos,
~éis, ~án
Preterite: quis|e, ~iste, ~o, ~imos,
~isteis, ~ieron
Present subjunctive: quiera, quieras,
quiera, queramos, queráis, quieran
Imperfect subjunctive: quis|iera,
~ieras, ~iera, ~iéramos,
~ierais, ~ieran
quis|iese, ~ieses, ~iese,
~iésemos, ~ieseis, ~iesen
Conditional: querr|ía, ~ías, ~ía,
~íamos, ~íais, ~ían
Imperative: quiere, quered

[36] raer
Present: raigo/rayo, raes, rae,
raemos, raéis, raen
Preterite: raí, raíste, rayó, raímos,
raísteis, rayeron
Present subjunctive: raig|a, ~as, ~a,
~amos, ~áis, ~an
ray|a, ~as, ~a, ~amos, ~áis,
~an
Imperfect subjunctive: ray|era,
~eras, ~era, ~éramos, ~erais,
~eran
ray|ese, ~eses, ~ese, ~ésemos,
~eseis, ~esen
Present participle: rayendo
Past participle: raído

[37] roer
Present: roo/roigo/royo, roes, roe,
roemos, roéis, roen
Preterite: roí, roíste, royó, roímos,
roísteis, royeron
Present subjunctive: roa/roiga/roya,
roas, roa, roamos, roáis, roan
Imperfect subjunctive: roy|era,
~eras, ~era, ~éramos, ~erais,
~eran
roy|ese, ~eses, ~ese, ~ésemos,
~eseis, ~esen
Present participle: royendo
Past participle: roído

[38] saber
Present: sé, sabes, sabe, sabemos,
sabéis, saben

Future: sabr|é, ~ás, ~á, ~emos,
~éis, ~án
Preterite: sup|e, ~iste, ~o, ~imos,
~isteis, ~ieron
Present subjunctive: sep|a, ~as, ~a,
~amos, ~áis, ~an
Imperfect subjunctive: sup|iera,
~ieras, ~iera, ~iéramos,
~ierais, ~ieran
sup|iese, ~ieses, ~iese,
~iésemos, ~ieseis, ~iesen
Conditional: sabr|ía, ~ías, ~ía,
~íamos, ~íais, ~ían

[39] ser
Present: soy, eres, es, somos, sois, son
Imperfect: era, eras, era, éramos,
erais, eran
Preterite: fui, fuiste, fue, fuimos,
fuisteis, fueron
Present subjunctive: se|a, ~as, ~a,
~amos, ~áis, ~an
Imperfect subjunctive: fu|era, ~eras,
~era, ~éramos, ~erais, ~eran
fu|ese, ~eses, ~ese, ~ésemos,
~eseis, ~esen
Imperative: sé, sed

[40] tener
Present: tengo, tienes, tiene, tenemos,
tenéis, tienen
Future: tendr|é, ~ás, ~á, ~emos,
~éis, ~án
Preterite: tuv|e, ~iste, ~o, ~imos,
~isteis, ~ieron
Present subjunctive: teng|a, ~as, ~a,
~amos, ~áis, ~an
Imperfect subjunctive: tuv|iera,
~ieras, ~iera, ~iéramos,
~ierais, ~ieran
tuv|iese, ~ieses, ~iese,
~iésemos, ~ieseis, ~iesen
Conditional: tendr|ía, ~ías, ~ía,
~íamos, ~íais, ~ían
Imperative: ten, tened

[41] traer
Present: traigo, traes, trae, traemos,
traéis, traen
Preterite: traj|e, ~iste, ~o, ~imos,
~isteis, ~eron
Present subjunctive: traig|a, ~as, ~a,
~amos, ~áis, ~an
Imperfect subjunctive: traj|era,
~eras, ~era, ~éramos, ~erais,
~eran

traj|ese, ~eses, ~ese, ~ésemos,
~eseis, ~esen
Present participle: trayendo
Past participle: traído

[42] **valer**
Present: valgo, vales, vale, valemos,
valéis, valen
Future: vald|ré, ~ás, ~á, ~emos,
~éis, ~án
Present subjunctive: valg|a, ~as, ~a,
~amos ~áis, ~an
Conditional: vald|ría, ~ías, ~ía,
~íamos, ~íais, ~ían
Imperative: val/vale, valed

[43] **ver**
Present: veo, ves, ve, vemos, veis, ven
Imperfect: ve|ía, ~ías, ~ía, ~íamos,
~íais, ~ían
Preterite: vi, viste, vio, vimos, visteis,
vieron
Present subjunctive: ve|a, ~as, ~a,
~amos, ~áis, ~an
Past participle: visto

[44] **yacer**
Present: yazco/yazgo/yago, yaces,
yace, yacemos, yacéis, yacen
Present subjunctive:
yazca/yazga/yaga, yazcas,
yazca, yazcamos, yazcáis, yazcan
Imperative: yace/yaz, yaced

[45] **asir**
Present: asgo, ases, ase, asimos, asís,
asen
Present subjunctive: asg|a, ~as, ~a,
~amos, ~áis, ~an

[46] **decir**
Present: digo, dices, dice, decimos,
decís, dicen
Future: dir|é, ~ás, ~á, ~emos,
~éis, ~án
Preterite: dij|e, ~iste, ~o, ~imos,
~isteis, ~eron
Present subjunctive: dig|a, ~as, ~a,
~amos, ~áis, ~an
Imperfect subjunctive: dij|era, ~eras,
~era, ~éramos, ~erais, ~eran
dij|ese, ~eses, ~ese, ~ésemos,
~eseis, ~esen
Conditional: dir|ía, ~ías, ~ía,
~íamos, ~íais, ~ían
Present participle: dicho

Imperative: di, decid

[47] **reducir**
Present: reduzco, reduces, reduce,
reducimos, reducís, reducen
Preterite: reduj|e, ~iste, ~o, ~imos,
~isteis, ~eron
Present subjunctive: reduzc|a, ~as,
~a, ~amos, ~áis, ~an
Imperfect subjunctive: reduj|era,
~eras, ~era, ~éramos, ~erais,
~eran
reduj|ese, ~eses, ~ese,
~eseis, ~esen

[48] **erguir**
Present: irgo, irgues, irgue, erguimos,
erguís, irguen
yergo, yergues, yergue, erguimos,
erguís, yerguen
Preterite: erguí, erguiste, irguió,
erguimos, erguisteis, irguieron
Present subjunctive: irg|a, ~as, ~a,
~amos, ~áis, ~an
yerg|a, ~as, ~a, ~amos, ~áis,
~an
Imperfect subjunctive: irgu|iera,
~ieras, ~iera, ~iéramos,
~ierais, ~ieran
irgu|iese, ~ieses, ~iese,
~iésemos, ~ieseis, ~iesen
Present participle: irguiendo
Imperative: irgue/yergue, erguid

[49] **ir**
Present: voy, vas, va, vamos, vais, van
Imperfect: iba, ibas, iba, íbamos,
ibais, iban
Preterite: fui, fuiste, fue, fuimos,
fuisteis, fueron
Present subjunctive: vay|a, ~as, ~a,
~amos, ~áis, ~an
Imperfect subjunctive: fu|era, ~eras,
~era, ~éramos, ~erais, ~eran
fu|ese, ~eses, ~ese, ~ésemos,
~eseis, ~esen
Present participle: yendo
Imperative: ve, id

[50] **oír**
Present: oigo, oyes, oye, oímos, oís,
oyen
Preterite: oí, oíste, oyó, oímos, oísteis,
oyeron
Present subjunctive: oig|a, ~as, ~a,
~amos, ~áis, ~an

Imperfect subjunctive: oy|era, ~**eras,**
~**era,** ~**éramos,** ~**erais,** ~**eran**
oy|ese, ~**eses,** ~**ese,** ~**ésemos,**
~**eseis,** ~**esen**
Present participle: oyendo
Past participle: oído
Imperative: oye, oíd

[51] **reír**
Present: río, ríes, ríe, reímos, reís,
ríen
Preterite: reí, reíste, rió, reímos,
reísteis, rieron
Present subjunctive: ría, rías, ría,
riamos, riáis, rían
Present participle: riendo
Past participle: reído
Imperative: ríe, reíd

[52] **salir**
Present: salgo, sales, sale, salimos,
salís, salen
Future: saldr|é, ~**ás,** ~**á,** ~**emos,**
~**éis,** ~**án**

Present subjunctive: salg|a, ~**as,** ~**a,**
~**amos,** ~**áis,** ~**an**
Conditional: saldr|ía, ~**ías,** ~**ía,**
~**íamos,** ~**íais,** ~**ían**
Imperative: sal, salid

[53] **venir**
Present: vengo, vienes, viene,
venimos, venís, vienen
Future: vendr|é, ~**ás,** ~**á,** ~**emos,**
~**éis,** ~**án**
Preterite: vin|e, ~**iste,** ~**o,** ~**imos,**
~**isteis,** ~**ieron**
Present subjunctive: veng|a, ~**as,** ~**a,**
~**amos,** ~**áis,** ~**an**
Imperfect subjunctive: vin|iera,
~**ieras,** ~**iera,** ~**iéramos,**
~**ierais,** ~**ieran**
vin|iese, ~**ieses,** ~**iese,**
~**iésemos,** ~**ieseis,** ~**iesen**
Conditional: vendr|ía, ~**ías,** ~**ía,**
~**íamos,** ~**íais,** ~**ían**
Present participle: viniendo
Imperative: ven, venid

Verbos Irregulares Ingleses

Infinitivo	Pretérito	Participio pasado
arise	arose	arisen
awake	awoke	awoken
be	was	been
bear	bore	borne
beat	beat	beaten
become	became	become
befall	befell	befallen
beget	begot	begotten
begin	began	begun
behold	beheld	beheld
bend	bent	bent
beset	beset	beset
bet	bet, betted	bet, betted
bid	bade, bid	bidden, bid
bind	bound	bound
bite	bit	bitten
bleed	bled	bled
blow	blew	blown
break	broke	broken
breed	bred	bred
bring	brought	brought
broadcast	broadcast(ed)	broadcast
build	built	built
burn	burnt, burned	burnt, burned
burst	burst	burst
buy	bought	bought
cast	cast	cast
catch	caught	caught
choose	chose	chosen
cleave	clove, cleft, cleaved	cloven, cleft, cleaved
cling	clung	clung
clothe	clothed, clad	clothed, clad
come	came	come
cost	cost	cost
creep	crept	crept
crow	crowed, crew	crowed
cut	cut	cut
deal	dealt	dealt
dig	dug	dug
do	did	done
draw	drew	drawn
dream	dreamt, dreamed	dreamt, dreamed
drink	drank	drunk
drive	drove	driven
dwell	dwelt	dwelt
eat	ate	eaten
fall	fell	fallen
feed	fed	fed
feel	felt	felt
fight	fought	fought
find	found	found

Infinitivo	*Pretérito*	*Participio pasado*
flee	fled	fled
fling	flung	flung
fly	flew	flown
forbear	forbore	forborne
forbid	forbad(e)	forbidden
forecast	forecast(ed)	forecast(ed)
foresee	foresaw	foreseen
foretell	foretold	foretold
forget	forgot	forgotten
forgive	forgave	forgiven
forsake	forsook	forsaken
freeze	froze	frozen
gainsay	gainsaid	gainsaid
get	got	got, gotten
give	gave	given
go	went	gone
grind	ground	ground
grow	grew	grown
hang	hung, hanged	hung, hanged
have	had	had
hear	heard	heard
hew	hewed	hewn, hewed
hide	hid	hidden
hit	hit	hit
hold	held	held
hurt	hurt	hurt
inlay	inlaid	inlaid
keep	kept	kept
kneel	knelt	knelt
knit	knitted, knit	knitted, knit
know	knew	known
lay	laid	laid
lead	led	led
lean	leaned, leant	leaned, leant
leap	leaped, leapt	leaped, leapt
learn	learned, learnt	learned, learnt
leave	left	left
lend	lent	lent
let	let	let
lie	lay	lain
light	lit, lighted	lit, lighted
lose	lost	lost
make	made	made
mean	meant	meant
meet	met	met
mislay	mislaid	mislaid
mislead	misled	misled
misspell	misspelt	misspelt
mistake	mistook	mistaken
misunderstand	misunderstood	misunderstood
mow	mowed	mown
outbid	outbid	outbid
outdo	outdid	outdone
outgrow	outgrew	outgrown
overcome	overcame	overcome

Infinitivo	Pretérito	Participio pasado
overdo	overdid	overdone
overhang	overhung	overhung
overhear	overheard	overheard
override	overrode	overridden
overrun	overran	overrun
oversee	oversaw	overseen
overshoot	overshot	overshot
oversleep	overslept	overslept
overtake	overtook	overtaken
overthrow	overthrew	overthrown
partake	partook	partaken
pay	paid	paid
prove	proved	proved, proven
put	put	put
quit	quitted, quit	quitted, quit
read /ri:d/	read /red/	read /red/
rebuild	rebuilt	rebuilt
redo	redid	redone
rend	rent	rent
repay	repaid	repaid
rewrite	rewrote	rewritten
rid	rid	rid
ride	rode	ridden
ring	rang	rung
rise	rose	risen
run	ran	run
saw	sawed	sawn, sawed
say	said	said
see	saw	seen
seek	sought	sought
sell	sold	sold
send	sent	sent
set	set	set
sew	sewed	sewn, sewed
shake	shook	shaken
shear	sheared	shorn, sheared
shed	shed	shed
shine	shone	shone
shoe	shod	shod
shoot	shot	shot
show	showed	shown, showed
shrink	shrank	shrunk
shut	shut	shut
sing	sang	sung
sink	sank	sunk
sit	sat	sat
slay	slew	slain
sleep	slept	slept
slide	slid	slid
sling	slung	slung
slit	slit	slit
smell	smelt, smelled	smelt, smelled
smite	smote	smitten
sow	sowed	sown, sowed
speak	spoke	spoken

Infinitivo	*Pretérito*	*Participio pasado*
speed	speeded, sped	speeded, sped
spell	spelt, spelled	spelt, spelled
spend	spent	spent
spill	spilled, spilt	spilled, spilt
spin	spun	spun
spit	spat	spat
split	split	split
spoil	spoilt, spoiled	spoilt, spoiled
spread	spread	spread
spring	sprang	sprung
stand	stood	stood
steal	stole	stolen
stick	stuck	stuck
sting	stung	stung
stink	stank, stunk	stunk
strew	strewed	strewn, strewed
stride	strode	stridden
strike	struck	struck
string	strung	strung
strive	strove	striven
swear	swore	sworn
sweep	swept	swept
swell	swelled	swollen, swelled
swim	swam	swum
swing	swung	swung
take	took	taken
teach	taught	taught
tear	tore	torn
tell	told	told
think	thought	thought
thrive	thrived, throve	thrived, thriven
throw	threw	thrown
thrust	thrust	thrust
tread	trod	trodden, trod
unbend	unbent	unbent
undergo	underwent	undergone
understand	understood	understood
undertake	undertook	undertaken
undo	undid	undone
upset	upset	upset
wake	woke, waked	woken, waked
waylay	waylaid	waylaid
wear	wore	worn
weave	wove	woven
weep	wept	wept
win	won	won
wind	wound	wound
withdraw	withdrew	withdrawn
withhold	withheld	withheld
withstand	withstood	withstood
wring	wrung	wrung
write	wrote	written